W9-AOK-585

Economics

RALPH T. BYRNS
GERALD W. STONE

Both of Metropolitan State College
and The University of Colorado at Denver

Third Edition

Scott, Foresman and Company
Glenview, Illinois   London, England

Library of Congress Cataloging-in-Publication Data

Byrns, Ralph T.
  Economics.

  Includes bibliographical references and index.
  1. Economics.   I. Stone, Gerald W.   II. Title.
HB171.5.B99   1986   330   86–21897
ISBN 0–673–16675–9

Cover and part opening photos by Peter Bosy.

1 2 3 4 5 6 – VHJ – 91 90 89 88 87 86

TO THE INSTRUCTOR

Economists have many reasons to rejoice. In an era of declining college enrollments, the demand for economics courses continues to rise. Economic issues absorb an increasing share of national attention. Just as the demand for plumbers would soar if much of the world's plumbing failed, the economic difficulties of the recent past seem to have made our profession reasonably prosperous.

Yet, at the same time, there are reasons for concern. Most Americans understand economics only dimly, if at all. Many students have difficulty connecting the material from their economics courses with the real-world bombardment of economic issues in the media, and textbook analyses of current events too often seem abstract and irrelevant.

This third edition of *Economics* should guide your students around these pitfalls. Our major objective is to ensure that students learn the fundamental principles that provide unique insights into how the world works. Just as one task of any good actor is to keep the audience from yawning, our major goal cannot be realized if students find the material so difficult, theoretical, or dull that they will not read it—an all too common failing. Consequently, far more than most texts, this book applies economic theory to a rich variety of everyday experiences, historical occurrences, and recent headlines. These intuitively appealing examples help students internalize economic reasoning and apply it to new situations.

Special Features of This Text

This book is comprehensive and contains introductory discussions of the concepts that underpin economics. Our text is organized conventionally so that you should find it unnecessary to radically alter your principles syllabus. Each part of *Economics, Third Edition* opens with a broad introduction indicating how sequential chapters are related, and each chapter begins with a list of Key Terms and an overview of the topics it covers. Numerous other pedagogical aids run through the text:

1. Key terms are set in **bold type** when introduced, major concepts are *italicized,* and

    economic laws: *are set off from the rest of the text.*

2. Analytical graphs are rendered simply, to efficiently convey economic concepts, and attractively, to pique students' interest. Standardized notation in graphs and equations aids student comprehension. Descriptive and historical data are illustrated in a modern style that parallels the graphical techniques used when data are presented by the media—whether in local newspapers, publications such as *Time* or *Business Week,* or TV news broadcasts.

3. Liberal doses of boxed Focuses (e.g., the underground economy, corporate raiders, the 1986 tax reform) and Biographies give students a contemporary and historical introduction to economics.

4. Each chapter concludes with a comprehensive Chapter Review, several Questions for Thought and Discussion, and, where appropriate, problem sets (e.g., on multipliers, elasticity).

5. Immediately following a number of chapters are related Legal Cases that apply economic analysis to real-life situations.

6. Optional Materials covering selected analytical concepts (e.g., graphing, the mathematics of multipliers, indifference curves, and isoquants) are appended to some chapters for instructors who wish to enrich their courses by covering these topics.

7. An extensive Glossary and thorough Indexes at the end of the book provide handy references.

Printed Supplements

Our *Economics* package provides a *broader* spectrum of teaching supplements than is available for any other text:

1. *Great Ideas for Teaching Economics* now includes roughly 400 analogies, anecdotes, exercises, and general teaching tips contributed by instructors from across the country.

2. Our *Student Guide for Learning Economics* uses a variety of techniques to facilitate student mastery of economic concepts. Each chapter includes matching problems, true-false questions, fill-in reviews, and multiple-choice questions; most have problem sets and specialized exercises as well. Answers are keyed to the text, and step-by-step solutions to challenging problem sets are provided.

3. The *Instructor's Manual for Teaching Economics* contains chapter outlines, suggestions for lectures, references to related *Great Ideas,* suggested answers to end-of-chapter questions, and analyses of the legal cases that conclude some chapters.

4. Our *Test Bank for Economics* now includes 70 multiple-choice, 20 true-false, and 10 matching ques-

tions for each chapter in the text. Computerized versions of this 3,700-question *Test Bank* are available for microcomputers.

5. Our *Hyperinflation* sampler contains brief histories and actual samples of hyperinflation currency and stamps from such twentieth-century episodes of hyperinflation as Germany in the early 1920s and Hungary in the 1940s.

6. 100 four-color overhead *Transparencies* of selected important figures and tables from the text are provided.

Software Supplements

1. *Macrosim II,* a microcomputer-based simulation, allows students to manipulate policy instruments (e.g., government spending, tax rates, and the money supply) in attempts to stabilize economic activity and stimulate growth. Macrosim has been revised in two directions:
   a. The *Instructor's Edition, Create,* allows instructors to easily tailor simulations to reflect virtually any macroeconomic view of how the world works.
   b. The new *Student Edition* uses building blocks, starting with a very simple Keynesian model, so that the simulation can be used step-by-step throughout the macro course. The *Student Edition* contains *Macrosim II* and a 120-page booklet.

2. The new *Raiders* is a microeconomic simulation that students can begin to use by the second week of class. Available shrinkwrapped with a short paperback, this simulation sequentially tests students' mastery of simple demand and supply analysis, elasticity calculations, production and cost, and, ultimately, their ability to maximize profits in a series of progressively more complex product and resource markets. Students who successfully solve this simulation will understand virtually all fundamental microeconomic principles.

3. The *Diploma* classroom management system consists of four computer programs that operate on IBM, Apple IIc and IIe, and compatible microcomputers:
   a. *Exam* provides question creation and editing features for use in developing, maintaining, and altering test banks. Unlimited questions can be accommodated in each format: multiple-choice, true-false, matching, and short answer/essay. The 3,700 questions in our *Test Bank* are provided on diskettes for this program.
   b. *Gradebook* simplifies grade management. It automatically tracks running averages for both students and tests and can display letter grades, percentage averages, GPA, or points earned.
   c. *Proctor* allows students to take tests generated by *Exam* at a computer. While testing, students can browse, skip hard questions, alter answers, and review responses as if the test were being taken on paper. Automatic grading is featured. Our *Guides* software provides drills that use *Proctor* to cover 16 core economic concepts in ways that students will find hard to forget.

d. *Calendar* is a free-form scheduling tool that allows instructors to enter several events or messages for any particular day. A transfer feature automatically recycles recurring events without retyping. Messages can be easily entered, edited, saved, displayed, or printed. Our *Dates* software integrates over 300 important economic events into the *Calendar* program.

Any principles text is always in process. Suggestions that aid us in making the next edition of *Economics* or its supplements clearer, more topical, or more complete will be deeply appreciated and gratefully acknowledged. Please send your comments to us, c/o Scott, Foresman and Company, 1900 East Lake Avenue, Glenview, Illinois, 60025.

Key Changes in the Third Edition

This third edition of *Economics* has been revised to incorporate recent studies and current data. It has also been made smoother pedagogically in terms of organization and flow. The results of this revision are visible on every page.

These changes are far too numerous for an overall listing. However, some of the highlights of this revision are the following.

Introduction (Chapters 1–5)

The introductory section has been streamlined from six to five chapters for a quicker transition to the main part of the text.

The appendix on graphical techniques in economics has been moved to follow Chapter 1.

An especially timely issue concerning law and economics is our review of the crisis in liability insurance, newly added to Chapter 5.

Macroeconomics

As in previous editions, Aggregate Supply and Aggregate Demand are introduced in the first macroeconomics chapter, but this framework is integrated more thoroughly throughout the macro section.

This edition contains the same traditional organization regarding Keynesian and monetarist economics, yet more has been added on supply-side economics and rational expectations.

Timely issues have been analyzed in depth, such as the Gramm-Rudman tax bill, structural versus cyclical deficits, industrial policy, and international variations in the velocity of money.

The growing importance of international economics has been treated throughout, as well as focused at the end of the text. Topics covered include the new protectionism; the international debt crisis; the Mexican debt crisis and the problem of capital flight; and exchange rate volatility and the "dance of the dollar."

Microeconomics

The antitrust chapter has been thoroughly revised to include new guidelines on antitrust, more on the Herfindahl-Hirschman index and its application by the Reagan Justice Department, more on contestable markets, and the new merger movement (the urge to merge) as well as deconglomeration (the urge to purge).

There is a new chapter on public choice.

The income distribution chapter contains the latest studies on welfare, the Murray criticisms of current welfare policy, the issue of "voluntary" poverty, and new wealth distribution data (as well as income distribution data).

There is more on the changing composition and importance of labor unions, and more on labor market clearing.

The government finance chapter has been expanded to consider the changing face of tax reform.

The oligopoly and monopolistic competition chapter has been recast in the light of changing market concentrations and international competition.

Acknowledgements

Suggestions from numerous economists and students have done much to shape and improve this revision of *Economics*. A number of people who reviewed earlier editions of this book offered comments that were not implemented until this edition. Among those who contributed suggestions and useful comments for the first edition of our *Economics* teaching package were:

J. Gregory Ballentine
University of Florida
David Black
University of Delaware
Bruce Bolnick
Northeastern University
Steven T. Call
Metropolitan State College and the University of Colorado at Denver
E. Ray Canterbery
Florida State University

Randall Eberts
University of Oregon
John Elliott
University of Southern California
James Esmay
California State University, Northridge
Gary Gigliotti
Rutgers University
Robert F. Hebert
Auburn University
Thomas Ireland
University of Missouri, St. Louis
Jonathan Jones
Catholic University
Sol Kauffler
Los Angeles Pierce College
Tom Koplin
University of Oregon
Jerry Langin-Hooper
Rutgers University
Rodney Mabry
Clemson University
Hugh Macaulay
Clemson University
Michael Maloney
Clemson University
Michael McElroy
North Carolina State University
Stephen Mehay
Naval Postgraduate School
William Nelson
Indiana University Northwest
Ronald G. Reddall
Alan Hancock College
Eugene Swann
University of California, Berkeley
Victor Tabbush
University of California, Los Angeles
Holley Ulbrich
Clemson University
Don Wells
University of Arizona

Help on the second edition and its supplements was provided by:

Scott Aguais
Wellesley College
Dennis Appleyard
University of North Carolina, Chapel Hill
David Black
University of Delaware
Michael Brand
University of Texas, El Paso
T. Mack Brown
Brownstone Research Group
William Brown
Rollins College
John Cochran
Metropolitan State College
David Colander
Middlebury College
Frank Curtis
Ferris State College
Phil Duriez
University of Texas, El Paso

Mark Gertler
University of Wisconsin, Madison

Will Harris
University of Delaware

Dilmus James
University of Texas, El Paso

Robert Johnson
University of San Diego

Hugh Macaulay
Clemson University

Ronald Moses
University of Illinois, Chicago Campus

Dennis Olson
Ferris State College

James O'Neill
University of Delaware

Tom Rogers
Southern Methodist University

Mason Russell
Bentley College

Edward Sattler
Bradley University

Michael Shelby
Boston University

Frank Vorhies
Economics Institute, Boulder

Michael Watts
Purdue University

Leonard White
University of Arkansas

Allan Wilkens
University of Wisconsin, Madison

Joseph Ziegler
University of Arkansas

Robert B. Harris
Indiana University-Purdue University, Indianapolis

Stan Herren
University of Mississippi

Guss Herring
Brookhaven College

Jack High
George Mason University

Janos Horvath
Butler University

Monte Juillerat
Indiana University-Purdue University, Indianapolis

Stephen E. Lile
Western Kentucky College

Kenneth Long
New River Community College

Tony Loviscek
Indiana University-Purdue University, Fort Wayne

Denise Markovich
University of North Dakota

Drew E. Mattson
Anoka Ramsey Community College

Tommy C. Meadows
Austin Peay State University

G. W. Parker
Mississippi State University

Tom Porebski
Triton College

Tom Rogers
Southern Methodist University

George A. Spiva
University of Tennessee, Knoxville

Bruce Stecker
North Hennepin Community College

James L. Swofford
University of South Alabama

Claude A. Talley
Victoria College

C. Richard Waits
Texas Christian University

Michael Watts
Purdue University

Arthur L. Welsh
Indiana University, Bloomington

Rich Wobbekind
University of Colorado, Boulder

A few ideas from reviewers for this edition could not be implemented because of onrushing deadlines and so must await the next revision. Most, however, are reflected in these pages or in our supplements. We are deeply grateful for the many useful insights and suggestions for our texts and supplements provided by:

Jack E. Adams
University of Arkansas, Little Rock

Dale Bails
Memphis State University

Andy H. Barnett
Auburn University

Donna M. Bialek
Indiana University-Purdue University, Fort Wayne

Jeffrey A. Buser
Murray State University

Lou Cain
Loyola University

John Cochran
Metropolitan State College

Clinton Daniels
Western Wyoming College

Gary M. Galles
Pepperdine University

Patricia Garland
Northeast Louisiana University

Joseph R. Guerin
Saint Joseph's University

Capable and accommodating editors at Scott, Foresman have made working on this revision an unanticipated pleasure. Jim Sitlington, Editorial Vice-President, and George Lobell, Economics Editor, have graciously paved the way for many of our innovations. Special and heartfelt thanks are due Bruce Kaplan, our developmental editor, and Cathy Wacaser, our project editor. Their deft touches and professionalism have improved every chapter of this book. We have Debbie Costello to thank for a superb design, and Precision Graphics for our distinctive artwork.

Finally, we dedicate this book to Jennifer, Matthew, Melissa, Rachel, Sheila, and Trish, for their support and for patiently sharing in the opportunity costs incurred in this third revision.

TO THE STUDENT

A 1980 survey of almost 1,600 people in leadership positions all over the country generated the following list of the ten biggest problems facing the United States: *1. inflation, *2. energy development, *3. energy conservation, 4. national defense, *5. government growth and spending, 6. avoiding war, *7. industrial productivity and innovation, *8. unemployment, 9. containing the Soviet Union, and *10. restructuring the tax system.[1]

The seven problems marked with asterisks involve economics directly. The others—national defense, avoiding war, and containing the Soviet Union—indirectly involve economic trade-offs. The economic turmoil of the early 1980s has borne out that all of these are major national problems. But how does economics directly affect your life?

The basic economic problem confronting you, if you are typical, is that you would like to buy far more things than you can afford. Tuition and books probably absorb much of the income you would like to devote to clothes, cars, and entertainment. This means that you must make decisions about what you will or won't buy. In a similar way, all societies must choose between alternatives. How individuals and societies choose and the effects of their choices are the focal points of economics.

Economics can be as fascinating as any subject you have ever studied and, if you work diligently, it will seem very natural and logical. While some economic issues are complex, the methods of analysis you will learn in this book will enable you to answer many questions in a systematic fashion. When you complete this course, you may join one prominent economist, Robert Solow, in asking, "Why do I so often want to cry at what public figures, the press, and television commentators say about economic affairs?" Unfortunately, it can be frustrating to understand economic reasoning. Many people do not.

How to Study Economics

There are students who pull passing grades in some courses by merely skimming reading assignments on nights before exams. Superficial cramming is un-

likely to work very well in an economics course because understanding economics requires time and reflection. Economics is much more than the rote memorization of a few facts, definitions, and glib generalizations. It is very important for you to keep up in this course. Here is one systematic study strategy that many students have found successful in economics and have adapted for other classes.

First, be sure that you understand simple algebra and how to read graphs. The algebra used in this book is elementary, and it should prove no problem if you have learned the material from a basic course. Economics relies heavily on graphical techniques. Don't let this frighten you. There is a brief review of graphical analysis at the end of Chapter 1. If you will take the time to learn how graphs work, you will save yourself the agony of trying to memorize each graph—a formidable task. Proceed to Chapter 2 only after you have reduced your anxiety a bit about how to interpret graphs. As you become more familiar with how graphs work, you may be surprised to find yourself mentally graphing many noneconomic relationships, and even more amazed to find this process enjoyable.

Second, turn off the TV or stereo and sit in a hard chair, preferably in a cool (but not cold) room. Don't get too comfortable. Then, stop and think about the material as you read. Many students spend hours highlighting important points for later study, for which they somehow never find time. Too often this busy work substitutes for thinking about the material. Try to skim a chapter; then go back and really focus on five or six pages. Don't touch a pen or pencil except to make margin notes cross-referencing related materials you already know.

After you have finished a healthy dose of serious study, close the text and summarize the important points in what you have read with a half page of notes. If you cannot briefly summarize what you have just read, put your pen down and reread the material. You did not really digest the central ideas the first time. Don't be surprised if some concepts require several readings.

Third, be alert for graphs and tables that summarize some sections of the book. Read through the Chapter Reviews as you finish each chapter, and outline good, but brief, answers to the Questions for Thought and Discussion.

1. *U.S. News & World Report,* 14 April 1980. p. 39.

Fourth, obtain a copy of our *Student Guide for Learning Economics* and work through the material that parallels each chapter of the text. You will comprehend economic reasoning better, and it will be easier to apply economic analysis to the world around you.

Finally, be alert to everyday applications of economics. The news media constantly report economic events, and you may find this side of the news comprehensible for the first time. When this happens, you will be among the few who truly understand economic news. Try to use the economics you learn in this class to interpret your day-to-day behavior and that of your friends and relatives. This will provide new insights into how people function and how the world works.

We know that we have just given you a tall order, but if you will conscientiously follow these suggestions, we can guarantee you an enjoyable and enlightening course.

Careers in Economics

Many students are pleasantly surprised by how interesting economics is, but they wonder whether this discipline is really practical. "Could I get a good job with a bachelor's degree in economics?" is a question often asked of economics professors. We are not promising anything, but professional economists are employed in most large businesses, government agencies, and nonprofit organizations.

The broad training received by economics majors generates job opportunities for new graduates in such areas as public administration, operations analysis, sales, real estate and property appraisals, investment and financial analysis, insurance, production management, economic forecasting, or as management trainees and interns. What you might do as an economist would depend on your specific areas of study, your minor, and how far you continued your training.

Many economists devote most of their time to teaching because effective personal, business, and political decision making increasingly requires economic literacy. Quite a few also find that there are substantial and remunerative demands by business and government for their services as consultants or researchers. Lately, MBAs just joining the labor force are receiving the highest pay in finance-related positions. Finance is an applied branch of economics.

Business

Business is increasingly aware that applied economics may be useful in solving business problems and in the development of workable strategy and policy. Roughly one-third of all economists are employed by business firms and trade associations. Most of the medium-to-large firms in manufacturing, transportation, energy, communications, banking, insurance, retailing, utilities, investment, finance, and mining employ one or more economists. Many have large staffs of economists. In 1984, the median annual income of business economists was above $45,000, with entry salaries exceeding $20,000. While most business economists have advanced degrees, there are opportunities for bright, hard-working people with bachelor's degrees in economics. Business economists with only bachelor's degrees averaged more than $34,000 in 1984.

Government and Nonprofit Organizations

One economist in five works for the government or for a nonprofit corporation or foundation. Economists are employed in virtually all facets of federal, state, and local governments. For example, eight prominent economists have each served in six different cabinet-level posts in the administrations of Presidents Carter and Reagan. There are opportunities in government for people with backgrounds in economics ranging from the bachelor's level through postdoctoral training.

Teaching

Roughly 45 percent of all economists are teacher/researchers. Most of these are employed by colleges and universities, and have advanced degrees. At the university level, there are ample opportunities and rewards for economic research and consulting. The average annual income of academic economists in 1984 was above $35,000.

Many states have recently made economics a requirement for a high-school diploma. People who are highly motivated to teach economics, but not to endure extended graduate training, are finding a growing demand for their services as teachers in secondary schools.

We hope that you find this text helpful as you study economics. Students who have used earlier versions of this book were responsible for many changes. We are grateful for their many valuable suggestions and insights. If you have comments or suggestions, we would like to hear about them. Write us in care of Scott, Foresman and Company, 1900 East Lake Avenue, Glenview, Illinois, 60025.

Ralph T. Byrns
Gerald W. Stone

CONTENTS

PART 2 Measuring Economic Performance 98

PART 3 # Keynesian Macroeconomics

CHAPTER 8 ## Macroeconomics Before Keynes

CHAPTER 9   Aggregate Expenditures: Consumption, Investment, Government, and Foreign Spending   161

CHAPTER 10   Equilibrium Level of Output, Employment, and Income   181

CHAPTER 11   Fiscal Policy: Government Taxing and Spending   199

■ PART 4   Money, Monetary Theory, and Monetary Policy   222

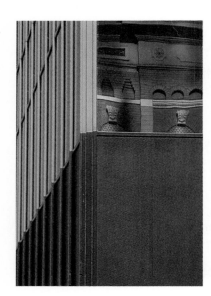

CHAPTER 12   Money and Its Creation   224

CHAPTER 13   The Federal Reserve System and Financial Institutions   242

CHAPTER 14 Monetary Theory

CHAPTER 19　Economic Growth and Development　365

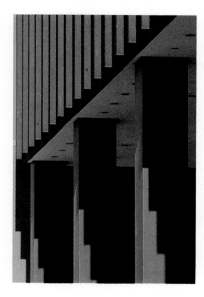

CHAPTER 24   Monopoly   480

CHAPTER 25   Imperfect Competition: Oligopoly and Monopolistic Competition   500

PART 8 Markets for Productive Resources 560

PART 9 The Microeconomics of Government Policy

620

CHAPTER 37   Capitalism and Its Alternatives   733

ECONOMICS

PART 1 Foundations of Economics

Most people have only a fuzzy idea of what economics is—that it addresses aspects of business and money in some fashion—but for many, the distinctions between economics, accounting, and finance are quite blurred. Just as putting a jigsaw puzzle together is easier if you first build its border by connecting all the straight-edged pieces, this first part of the book introduces a number of concepts that provide a framework for understanding economics. We then apply these concepts to a variety of problem areas so that when you finish this book, you will have a relatively complete picture of the world of economics.

In Chapter 1, we discuss how economists use scientific methods to investigate the way the world works and the division of economics into *positive* (scientific) versus *normative* (prescriptive) components. We also distinguish *macroeconomics*, which addresses national economic issues, from *microeconomics*, which examines the choices made by individual decision makers. The question of whether we can count on people behaving as humanitarians or selfishly is raised, and some implications of the answer are explored. How *scarcity* arises and makes decisions necessary is another area considered, leading to the concepts of *opportunity cost* and *economic efficiency*.

This provides a background for our first formal economic model, the production-possibilities frontier, introduced in Chapter 2. There, too, we examine various mechanisms used to answer the basic economic questions arising from scarcity. How our attempts to resolve the problem of scarcity affect economic growth and social well-being is interpreted using the production-possibilities frontier model.

A discussion of the foundations of capitalism leads us into Chapter 3, where *supply and demand* are introduced. Supply and demand analysis provides significant insights into how prices and outputs are determined in a market system; it also allows us to interpret a surprisingly wide range of human behavior. In Chapter 4, we apply supply and demand to a variety of public policy topics, ranging from agriculture to wage and price controls. Part One concludes with Chapter 5, which describes the roles played in a market economy by government and such private institutions as households and business firms.

CHAPTER 1 An Introduction to Economics

positive vs. normative
   economics
macroeconomics vs.
   microeconomics
scarcity
production and
   resources

labor and wages
land and rent
capital and interest
investment and
   financial capital

entrepreneurship and
   profit
opportunity cost
economic efficiency
comparative
   advantage

At least half the news these days seems directed at such questions as: What can Washington do to stop inflation and reduce unemployment? Why is gold down and the dollar up? Why does big business at times seem out of control? Should the government raise taxes or cut its spending, or both, to cure massive federal budget deficits? Why do the rich seem to get richer while most middle-class people seem caught on a treadmill—going to and from work but never really getting ahead? And why are some people seemingly denied opportunities to share in the "American Dream"? All these problems and many more are just part of the puzzle we face as we try to accomplish the ultimate economic goal—providing high standards of living for people everywhere.

History books are filled with stories of politicians who lost power at least in part because they failed to solve a variety of economic problems. Presidents Ford and Carter might have won their reelection bids had the economic outlooks of 1976 and 1980 seemed brighter. President Reagan's popularity also fell with

each downturn in the national economy, but he won reelection when the economy prospered during 1984.

Let's stop for a moment before you get the impression that economic problems are only relevant for decision making by business leaders and politicians. More of your personal life than you might suspect is touched by economic problems. Will you continue college? What are the benefits? . . . the costs? What will you take as a major field of study? Where will you live and work? Should you marry? If so, when? Should you have children? If so, how many? How will you spend your limited income? The decisions you make about these and other economic choices will shape the course of your life.

Even though economic decisions loom large in everyday life, you may know very little about economics as a field of study. You have probably heard words such as *economical, profitable, Gross National Product, inflation, unemployment, capitalism, socialism, supply and demand, price,* and *cost* bandied about for most of your life. Right now, you may be skeptical about the usefulness of the *theories, hypotheses, models,* and *graphs* that economists use to explain the way the world works. These ideas and many more are interwoven in the fabric of economics.

Some economic concepts may seem overly abstract at first glance, but as you proceed through this text you will find that many are simply precise descriptions of everyday events. In this chapter, we set the foundations for your study by looking at some bedrock economic concepts. First, we describe the ground covered by economics. Then we address the basic economic problem—scarcity—and discuss the key economic concepts of opportunity costs and economic efficiency. These building blocks enable us to examine the reasons people specialize in certain forms of production and exchange their outputs for goods produced by others.

The Nature of Economics

Economics is what economists do.

—*Jacob Viner*

The best-known definition of **economics** suggests that it is "the study of the ways that individuals and societies allocate their limited resources to try to satisfy their unlimited wants."[1] Although more helpful than Jacob Viner's circular definition (above), this definition still only hints at the full scope of the discipline. Economic reasoning involves studying and weighing alternatives. Economics is concerned with the choices we make and the consequences of these choices for ourselves and others. In fact, the central focus of economics is on choices and decision making.

Economic analysis conventionally has been concerned with how individuals' choices are coordinated to determine what a society will produce, which production techniques will be used, and to whom the final products will be distributed. Every society must resolve these problems in some fashion because resources are scarce and human wants are relatively unlimited—points that we will deal with in detail in a moment. Should government decide what goods we produce and who gets to enjoy them? Should brute force or tradition prevail? What role, if any, should the marketplace play?

Areas traditionally within the sphere of economists include consumer choice, business decision making, inflation, taxes, unemployment, international trade, and economic growth and development. More recently, economic analysis has been applied to other areas, ranging from marriage and the family to explanations for criminal behavior and war; from aspects of our political and legal systems to questions about environmental quality, education, and discrimination.

You might correctly infer that no short description of economics can cover all the varied concerns of economists.[2] One famous economist, John Maynard Keynes, summarized economics as: ". . . a method rather than a doctrine, an apparatus of the mind, a technique of thinking which helps its possessor to draw correct conclusions."

Economics borrows freely from the works of psychologists, sociologists, anthropologists, legal scholars, ecologists, biologists, political scientists, and philosophers, all of whom offer alternatives to the economic way of thinking about how the world works. We believe that when you have finished this book you will join us in the view that economic reasoning offers unique and valuable insights into the ways we interact with one another in our everyday activities—producing, consuming, voting, and striving for the good life.

Common Sense and Theory

Everything should be made as simple as possible, but not more so.

—*Albert Einstein*

We often hear disparaging remarks made about **theory** relative to **common sense.** Some people argue that theories are impractical and that most theorists barely cope in the "real world," finding it difficult to tie their shoes or to walk and chew gum simultaneously. These critics view common sense as practical for everyday life.

---

1. Adapted from Lionel C. Robbins, *An Essay on the Nature and Significance of Economic Science* (London: Macmillian, 1935).

2. Evidence of the diversity of economics is that only half of all academic Economics Departments are in Schools of Business, with most of the rest being housed with Social Sciences or Liberal Arts.

How can we judge whether a bit of common sense or theory is good or bad? Good common sense or good theory is reasonably accurate in describing how things work. Bad common sense or bad theory is not in accord with how the world works. In other words, we judge both theory and common sense by how accurate they are!

The saying "That's the exception that proves the rule" is wrong. Exceptions do not prove rules—they disprove them. For example, prior to Columbus's voyages, conventional European wisdom viewed our world as flat. It is difficult to discern Earth's roundness from casual observation. Just look out your window. Although slightly irregular, it basically looks flat. The flat Earth theory was gradually replaced by a better theory in the minds of most people when ships began to sail around the world, but there are still people who would call you crazy if you told them that Earth is a sphere. (The British Flat Earth Society still meets regularly.)

A social commentator once observed that nothing is less common than common sense. How can we get more of it? Common sense is nothing more than a collection of old theories that has been tested over a long period and found more or less useful. As old theories are disproved, they are replaced by better theories. Common sense progresses, but some becomes obsolete because new knowledge is only slowly absorbed. To see how this happens, we need to know how theories are developed and how new theories may become tomorrow's common sense.

The process of theorizing consists of initially collecting some facts that seem related to something we want to understand. Of course, we cannot collect all the facts simply because some things cannot be seen, smelled, tasted, touched, or heard. For example, sophisticated equipment is required to discern microwaves or radar, and subatomic particles cannot be viewed directly with even the most advanced technology available. Moreover, we cannot concentrate on everything that can be sensed. Our senses are selective. (If you live near the tracks, after a while you don't hear the trains.) Finally, gathering all potentially helpful data is prohibitively expensive, so we deal with incomplete information.

Once we have some information about things that seem relevant to whatever needs to be explained, we try to figure out how these facts are related. That is, we develop a theory. Then we test this theory to see how well it predicts what happens in similar situations. If our new theory does a better job of explaining how the world works than existing theories do, we replace the old ones with the new. As a new theory is repeatedly tested and found reliable, it becomes part of our common sense—until even better theories are developed.

Models are representations of theories. The terms *model* and *theory* are interchangeable for most purposes. Some models are graphical, such as the blueprints drawn when an architect designs a house or the highway maps you consult on your vacation. Some are physical, such as a watch, which models the passage of time. Others exist as mental images or mathematical equations. Many people are surprised to learn that their heads are filled with models. For example, most single people who ultimately plan to marry have in their minds general models of what their prospective spouses will be like (general appearance, intelligence, sense of humor, etc.).[3]

Many theories are criticized as too complicated. In fact, most scientists subscribe to an idea called **Occam's Razor,** which suggests that the simplest *workable* theories are also the most useful and best. For example, Earth was once thought a fixed point about which the rest of the universe spun. Incredibly complex equations were developed to trace movements of then observable planets and stars. Modern astronomy resulted from applying Occam's Razor to explain cosmic activity more simply—all the universe is in motion, and Earth revolves around the sun, not vice versa.

A good model may be so simple that it is unrealistic except for its intended use. Certainly a simple model is usually less costly than a complex one. For example, you can look at intricately detailed metal or plastic models if you want to see how an airplane looks, but if you want to understand aerodynamics, you will do better buying a cheap balsa glider and tossing it into the air. Watches come in tuning-fork, quartz-crystal, atomic, 21-jewel, and other varieties. Which is best? If all you care about is knowing what time it is, the best is the one that most simply, accurately, and reliably (and cheaply?) reflects the passage of time.

3. These examples are drawn from articles by Donald Elliott, Joe Garwood, Regan Whitworth, and Salvatore Schiavo-Campo in Ralph Byrns and Gerald Stone, ed., *Great Ideas for Teaching Economics,* 3d ed. (Glenview, Illinois: Scott, Foresman & Company, 1987).

To summarize, a good theory or model as simply as possible predicts how the real world works. Common sense evolves as exceptions to old theories compel acceptance of better theories after they have been tested extensively and appear reliable.

Positive Versus Normative Economics

If you took all of the economists in the country and laid them end to end, they'd never reach a conclusion.
—*George Bernard Shaw*

Shaw's famous line echoes a popular but erroneous view that economists seldom agree on anything. In fact, 90 percent of economists would probably accept 90 percent of the fundamental theory presented in this book (with only nit-picking differences about which 90 percent to accept). Why is there such a disparity between the fact of widespread agreement and the common perception of disagreement? Part of the answer is that economists may disagree sharply about how even a widely accepted theory applies to a particular situation. The differences among economists about how theory should be translated into policy receive tremendous publicity, while broad areas of agreement are ignored by the media. (If you were a reporter, would you concentrate on agreement or controversy?)

Even if economists agree, politicians may reject sound advice based on economic theory. For example, most economists favor free international trade, but Congress often erects tariff barriers in response to pressure from voters whose jobs are threatened by imports. Another misleading source of apparent discord arises when economists in government feel compelled to agree publicly with the politicians who appoint them, while most other economists offer advice that the politicians find unacceptable.

Economists agree most about **positive economics,** which involves scientific predictions about economic relationships. Ideally, positive economics is value free and addresses *what is,* while **normative economics** is based on value judgments and addresses *what should be.* Economists disagree most when value judgments are central to resolving an economic problem. For example, economists may differ sharply about the normative question of whether the government should ever take a life, even for the crime of murder, but most economists would agree that quicker, stiffer, and surer penalties deter crime, which is a value-free prediction drawn from positive economics.

Normative issues frequently turn on questions of **equity** (fairness) and generate arguments among economists and the public alike. Policy is inherently more normative than theory. An example of policy's inherently normative nature is contained in such statements as "We should redistribute wealth from the rich to the poor." This implies a value judgment that the benefits to the poor would outweigh the harm done to the rich. There is little reason to suppose that an economist's value judgments about equity are inherently superior to those of other people, but economic reasoning can offer unique insights into how effective alternative policies might be at achieving specific normative goals.

Questions of normative economics are seldom settled by looking at evidence because value judgments generally involve faith and argument, not scientific proof. Disputes about positive economics ultimately can be settled by scientific evidence, but people often differ about economic policy because it inescapably hinges on normative issues. Nevertheless, if economists try to find the policies that are most consistent with goals set by voters or policymakers, then their quest is positive in nature. For example, if minimizing unemployment is a national goal, then developing policies to accomplish this goal involves positive economics. We can evaluate policies by how well they accomplish our goals, but positive economics cannot determine whether any goal is good or bad.

Even economists who share common values may disagree because some areas of positive economics remain unsettled. For example, virtually everyone favors price-level stability and high employment, but economists may disagree about the proper cure for general economic instability. Some disputes remain unresolved for generations because of difficulty in finding the right evidence and then digesting and accurately interpreting it in changing circumstances.

Macroeconomics and Microeconomics

There are several ways to subdivide economics, but the most common is into macroeconomics and microeconomics. The prefixes *macro-* and *micro-* come from Greek words that mean "large" and "small," respectively. Thus, macroeconomics is concerned with the economics of the entire society, while microeconomics focuses on the behavior of the individual household, firm, or a specific industry. By analogy, the tools of macroeconomics are telescopes, while those of microeconomics are microscopes. Differences between macroeconomics and microeconomics are, however, more of degree than kind.

Macroeconomics **Macroeconomics** is the study of large, economy-wide *aggregate* variables such as indicators of total economic activity. Thus, macroeconomic analysis is concerned with our banking and monetary systems and how our Gross National Product (GNP), unemployment, inflation, and economic growth are determined. Macroeconomic policymaking considers such things as the effects of changing taxes and government spending, or growth in the money supply.

Commonly agreed-upon normative goals of macroeconomic policy include:

1. *High employment.* People suffer when many workers cannot find jobs and many manufacturing plants and much machinery sit idle.
2. *Price level stability.* If, on the average, prices rise or fall rapidly, people may become confused about how much their wages will buy, or whether to invest in the future or consume now.
3. *Economic growth.* People want to enjoy higher standards of living this year than last and most hope that their children will be even more prosperous than they are.
4. *Economic security.* People want to retain their jobs and the good things they have acquired. Security may be threatened by changes in what society wants (the birth of the auto put buggy-whip braiders out of work) or by such possibilities as nuclear war.

Microeconomics **Microeconomics** scrutinizes the components of an economy and is concerned with individual decision making; the allocation of resources; and how prices, production, and the distribution of income are determined. Thus, microeconomics focuses upon the interactions of individual households, firms, and specific government agencies.

Microeconomic policymaking considers the effects of taxes and government regulations on the structures of prices, agricultural and manufacturing outputs, the numbers of firms in an industry, and the distribution of income. Our ability to achieve the macroeconomic goals previously discussed is also highly dependent on microeconomic policy. Beyond ensuring that microeconomic policies are compatible with macroeconomic goals, there are three major normative goals for microeconomic policy. The first is generally accepted; the second and third depend on more controversial value judgments:

1. *Efficiency.* An inefficient economy wastes resources and fails to provide the highest possible standard of living for consumers.
2. *Equity.* Equity is another word for fairness. If disparities between the "haves" and "have nots" are enormous, a few may enjoy great luxury while most people live in misery.
3. *Freedom.* By freedom, we mean that the range of choices available to people should be as wide and deep as possible. As with equity, however, more freedom for some people may mean less for others. For example, you may be limited in how wildly you can swing your arms if my nose is in the way.

These three goals are inconsistent at times. For example, more efficiency may create inequity in the minds of many people. It might be efficient to grant a patent to the developer of a cure for cancer if the potential profit would stimulate research to cure the disease. But once a cure was discovered, it might seem unfair not to treat those unable to afford the patented treatment. Alternatively, if one person (a stickup artist) disrupts another's production (operating a gas station), there is a trade-off between freedom and efficiency. Such trade-offs are the reason that societies everywhere adopt a "rule of law" to govern people's relationships. Acceptably balancing freedom, efficiency, and equity is among society's major challenges.[4]

Prior to the Great Depression, most economists concentrated on microeconomics, believing that macroeconomics entailed merely adding together microeconomic variables and then tacking on an analysis of changes in the money supply to account for changes in the price level. The Depression forced us to realize that the actions of one decision maker may yield a far different result than if all decision

---

4. Equity is inescapably normative and a bit nebulous. As you read this book, you will often notice conflicts between efficiency and equity. We cannot avoid issues of equity, but focus on efficiency because it is easier to analyze with economic reasoning. Arthur Okun's *Efficiency vs. Equity: The Big Tradeoff* (Washington, D.C.: Brookings, 1973), discusses these conflicts in an interesting manner.

makers take the same action at once. For example, one person in the bleachers may see a football game better by standing up, but when others also stand up (as they will) this advantage is lost.

Early economists' failures to spend much time analyzing macroeconomic phenomena may have contributed to the boom-bust cycles that culminated in the Great Depression of the 1930s. That prolonged catastrophe forced us to pay more attention to macroeconomic policy. Indeed, it is now clear that reaching our microeconomic goals depends on achieving our macroeconomic goals, and that understanding both macroeconomics and microeconomics is essential for an accurate perception of how any economy operates.

You now know a bit about differences between macroeconomics and microeconomics, and between positive and normative approaches to economics. This leads us to the root cause of all economic reasoning—the fundamental problem of scarcity.

 ## Scarcity

Try to imagine a world in which all our needs and wants were instantly and perfectly fulfilled. Economics and economists would be unnecessary because no one would be forced to make any decisions. This imaginary world might be very boring, however; most of us thrive on overcoming a bit of adversity. The rest of this chapter provides an overview of the economic challenges confronted by people everywhere.

The hard reality is that productive resources, and hence, production, are limited. Moreover, human wants are virtually unlimited. Combining these facts yields **scarcity.** Scarcity is the basic economic problem facing all societies.

A *good* (anything that adds to human happiness) is scarce if the amounts people desire are greater than the amounts freely available. People generally are individually or collectively (through taxes) willing to pay a positive price for scarce goods—banana splits, public parks, or an apartment are obvious examples, but services such as haircuts or police protection are also goods because they add to our happiness. Garbage, an economic *bad* (something that detracts from happiness), is not scarce. Most of us are dismayed when trash accumulates. Thus, garbage collection is a scarce good.

The few desirable things that are not scarce are called *free goods.* For example, you can have all the seawater you want at zero cost (if you are on the beach), or freely breathe all the air your lungs will hold (accepting the current pollution level), or look at a sunset all you like (if you truly have nothing else to do).

Circumstances make goods either free or scarce. Drinking water is nearly free when you camp next to a clean mountain stream, but is extremely scarce if you are lost in the desert. Even air is scarce for scuba divers, astronauts, and people with flat tires. The fact that few of the things people enjoy are free is reflected in the cliche that "there ain't no such thing as a free lunch *(TANSTAAFL)."* Our insatiable desires for goods are one dimension of scarcity; resource limitations are the other.

 ## Production and Resources

Production occurs when we use knowledge or technology to apply energy to materials in order to make the materials more valuable.[5] Houses and yo-yos are obviously produced goods, but services also entail production. For example, pouring yourself a cup of coffee is productive—the coffee is more valuable in your cup than it was in the coffee pot. All **productive resources** (or *factors of production*) are limited, and are conventionally categorized as labor, land, capital, and entrepreneurship. These resources provide the knowledge, energy, or materials that make production possible.

Labor   **Labor** refers to the physical and mental talents people make available to produce goods and services. Labor resources typically are measured by the time available for work during a given period. Payments for labor services are called **wages.**

Land   **Land** includes all natural resources, such as unimproved land, minerals, water, air, climate, forests, and wildlife. Payments per time period for the use of land are called **land rent.**

---

5. Technology is the "recipe" used to combine resources so that production occurs. The technology used to grow roses is a simple example. If you know that roses need sunlight and moisture, you find a sunny spot and then apply energy (labor) to a shovel (capital) to dig a hole in the earth (land). Insert a rose bush, add fertilizer, dirt, and water (materials), and, with luck, roses will soon bloom.

Capital   **Capital** refers to improvements made to natural resources, such as buildings, machinery, and utility lines. Economic capital increases our capacity to produce other goods and services.

Investment refers to new capital produced each year. Some of our existing stock of capital wears out *(depreciates)* each year. The total amount of investment each year is called *gross investment*. Subtracting depreciation leaves *net investment,* which is the growth or decline in our capital stock. Suppose business buys $120 billion in new equipment, machinery, and other capital goods, but existing capital depreciates by $20 billion. The capital stock grows by $100 billion, and society's net investment for the year is $100 billion.

Financial capital refers to currency, money in a bank account, or other paper assets (like stocks or bonds) that ultimately permit claims on raw resources or finished products. Thus, financial capital may be a paper claim on economic capital. Many people think that economic capital is the same as financial capital, but the two are very different concepts. Capital is physical; financial capital is normally a document of some sort. The deed to a house is financial capital; the house itself is economic capital. The term *capital* in this text will normally refer to economic capital. Payments for both types of capital services are called **interest.**

Entrepreneurship   **Entrepreneurs** are people who combine labor, natural resources, and capital to produce goods and services and who incur risk in their quest for profits. After paying wages, rent, and interest for the use of other resources, entrepreneurs keep any money left over from the sales of the goods and services. The entrepreneur's **profit** is a reward for bearing business risks, organizing productive activities, and introducing innovations that improve our enjoyment of life.

It is hard to overstate the risk of loss when entrepreneurs develop new products or begin serving new markets. More than half of all new companies fail in their first 2 years. Texas Instruments, Coleco, and Atari are only three of numerous ventures that lost fortunes trying to develop small computers and software in the mid-1980s. Only prospects of profit can overcome fears of loss. (Note that providers of capital receive interest rather than profit; all profit goes to entrepreneurs.)

Resource constraints are one of two important dimensions of scarcity. The other dimension of scarcity stems from our unlimited capacities to enjoy goods and services.

Rational Self-Interest

An economist is a man with an irrational passion for dispassionate rationality.

—*John Maurice Clark*

We might be able to imagine consuming all the water, steak, or even automobiles that we would ever want if these items were costless. Even though our desires for some goods might be met completely, it is difficult to imagine being so satisfied that we could think of nothing that would add to our happiness. The Hindu concept of *nirvana* refers to a blissful state of complete satisfaction or freedom from further want. But *nirvana* is achieved only at death. You might conclude that you will always want more goods, services, and pleasures for as long as you live.

Most economic theory follows the lead of Adam Smith, the father of economics, by assuming that people act purposefully and rationally to maximize their satisfactions, given their limited information, resources, and budgets. This characterization of *homo sapiens* as *homo economicus* (not to be confused with home economists) views all human behavior as self-interested. Why Smith, an eighteenth-century philosopher, advocated this approach is addressed in Focus 1.

Humanitarian or charitable acts are not viewed as exceptions to self-interested behavior: Philanthropists and Good Samaritans act charitably because it makes them feel better. People pick up litter or establish orphanages because they enjoy doing so or seek the public reputation and self-esteem derived from these activities. Most economic theory ignores charitable activities in order to make its analysis simple. You may object to models that view all behavior as attempts by people to maximize their pleasure and minimize their pain, but theories based on individual "happiness maximization" or "wealth maximization" are better at predicting economic activity than models that assume people are selfless or humanitarian.

In fact, the behaviors of so-called selfish people and so-called altruists often will be identical. For

FOCUS 1

Is Self-Interest Immoral or Unavoidable?

Suppose that you heard on this morning's TV news that an earthquake had swallowed China and its billion people. Then, 15 minutes later, you sliced off your little finger while buttering your toast. Which event would cause you the most dismay? In his first book, *Theory of Moral Sentiments* (1759), Adam Smith, the father of economics, suggested that the loss of a little finger would keep the average European from sleeping that night, ". . . but, provided he never saw them, he will snore with the most profound security over the loss of millions of his brethren, and the destruction of that immense multitude seems plainly an object less interesting to him than this paltry misfortune of his own."

Smith illustrated the power of self-interest with this example, and argued that disasters to others elicit sympathy only to the extent that you can imagine yourself in similar straits. Suppose that the calamity in China would be prevented if you inserted your little finger into a crack in the space/time continuum of our universe, but that you would lose your finger in the process. Would you?

Smith thought that most of us would, not out of love for humanity, but rather because of ". . . love of what is honourable and noble, of the grandeur, and dignity, and superiority of our own characters." That is, you probably would not be able to live with yourself if you failed to give up your finger. But

our individual senses of morality yield a spectrum of willingness to sacrifice for others. Would you give up your life for the lives of a billion anonymous Chinese? This question is much more difficult for anyone but a saint to answer automatically.

Self-interest tends to limit, but not eliminate, charitable acts. Viewing human behavior as self-interested also leads to a different perspective on why people sometimes sacrifice for others. You will encounter more of Adam Smith's thoughts in this book, and will learn how self-interested behavior, far from being appalling, may automatically resolve many major economic problems.

---

example, if the price of fruit falls relative to other goods, both the selfish person and the altruist may buy more—the selfish person to personally devour the fruit and the altruist to distribute it to needy children. This raises the question of what we mean when we say *price* or *cost*. The answer is less obvious than you might think.

Forgone Alternatives: Opportunity Costs

How much does anything cost? Most people think of costs as the amounts of money that must be paid to produce or acquire goods. For many purposes, money is a reasonable measure of economic prices or costs. More generally, however, when economists say price, they mean **opportunity price** or **cost. Opportunity cost** is the value of the best alternative

surrendered when a choice is made. The fact of scarcity forces us to choose; the best alternative to the choice we make is the opportunity cost of our decision. Because opportunity cost measures the value of the most desirable forgone alternative, it is also called *alternative cost.*

To show how broad the concept of opportunity cost is, consider the romantic example of a lovers' triangle. Suppose that Hortense and Wilhelmina both love Alphonse. Alphonse reciprocates fully; resigned to the indifference of Eudora, his true heartthrob, he loves both Hortense and Wilhelmina. Unfortunately, Hortense is a jealous type who threatens to find "someone new" if Alphonse does not quit seeing Wilhelmina. While soap opera fans might commiserate with Alphonse's dilemma, economists view this situation as very similar to that faced by the middle-class family that would really like lobster but can afford either small steaks or big hamburgers, but not

"You can't assign a value to human life" is a cliché frequently voiced in debates about public policies. In reality, however, people constantly and unavoidably assign prices to their own lives and those of others. Some of this is obvious, but some is quite subtle. Here are a few of the countless ways that life is priced.

1. Choosing more dangerous over less dangerous activities. For example, every time you ride in a car without using a seat belt, you (perhaps subconsciously) weigh the inconvenience of buckling up against the increased probability of death or injury. In so doing, you implicitly assign prices to your life and body parts. And parents assign prices for their children when they fail to buckle up their kids. Smoking cigarettes, sky diving, hitch hiking, swimming, or even taking a walk all involve risks that assign prices to life.

2. After adjusting for the training required and the pleasantness of working conditions, higher wages are paid for riskier jobs.

3. High prospective medical bills cause some people to forgo treatment that would prolong their lives, or the lives of seriously ill relatives.

4. The lives of millions of starving children in famine-plagued countries could be saved for only a few dollars each.

5. Every major war has been fought with draftees, whose lives are implicitly priced by political leaders and military strategists.

6. We could reduce the incidence of murder and traffic fatalities by surer and swifter law enforcement, but choose not to because expanding our police forces, the judicial system, and prisons seems too costly.

7. The fees of paid killers range from $200 to $500,000.

both. The real cost to Alphonse of a continued relationship with Hortense is giving up a relationship with Wilhelmina, and vice versa.

Have you ever estimated the cost of your college education? There is far more to it than just summing up your tuition fees and book receipts. How about the value of your time? Instead of studying and attending class, you could be holding a full-time job (or maybe two). You may be giving up a nice car, a comfortable apartment, fancy food, and snazzy clothing. These forgone alternatives are the true costs of your education. But suppose you quit school. Then the true costs of your nice car, apartment, food, and clothing would be the sacrificed enjoyment of learning and campus life, and the higher future income and consumption your degree may have made possible.

Opportunity costs, so crucial for rational decision making, are also unavoidable. Even if we try to ignore them at times, the alternatives we sacrifice when we make choices are still very real costs to us, and failing to consider opportunity is often disastrous. People sometimes refer to something as "priceless", implying that its value is so high that trying to specify opportunity cost is a futile exercise. This is generally an exaggeration, as Focus 2 indicates.

Many people feel trapped because they fail to recognize their alternatives: suicidal teenagers who lose "the only one I'll ever love;" workers who lose their jobs when plants shut down; high-roller entrepreneurs who go bankrupt when market conditions change. Several alternatives are available in almost any situation. The choices you make are ideally the best and most efficient of those available.

Economic Efficiency

Different people may mean very different things when they use the word *efficiency*. For example, engineers or physicists call a system efficient if it minimizes the amount of energy lost in accomplishing some task. Environmentalists may talk about efficiency as the absence of waste in an ecological system. The concept of economic efficiency is a bit different.

Economic efficiency for society as a whole is achieved when we produce the combination of outputs with the highest attainable total value, given our limited resources. Alone, this definition suggests few guidelines for achieving economic efficiency. Breaking economic efficiency down into **production (technical) efficiency** and **consumption efficiency** yields clearer insights for policy.

Production Efficiency

Production will be technically efficient when:

1. the opportunity cost of a given value of output is minimized, or
2. the value of output produced from given resources is maximized, or
3. the value of output produced for a given cost is maximized.

If you think about these requirements for production efficiency for a few moments, you will recognize that if any of these conditions is attained, the other two are also achieved automatically. All three are specified to make it easier to recognize inefficient situations.

Production is economically inefficient whenever production costs are unnecessarily high or if more output could be produced without raising costs or using more resources. For example, the saying that "Too many cooks spoil the pot" implies that too much company in the kitchen causes economic inefficiency. Presumably, more good quality food could be produced at lower cost using fewer resources if some of the cook's helpers left.

Consumption Efficiency

Allocative efficiency in consumers' purchasing patterns requires that they:

1. maximize the satisfaction attainable from their budgets, or
2. minimize the outlays required to obtain goods that yield a given amount of satisfaction.

This means that if you could be happier if you changed the goods you now buy for a given cash outlay, you are currently an inefficient consumer. Moreover, you could reduce your total spending and achieve the same satisfaction that you attained when your purchasing pattern was inefficient.

Most people try to act in ways that are efficient for them. Here is an everyday example. You can buy cola in either returnable bottles or no-return containers. The money you pay per ounce of cola is reduced if you return bottles "for deposit" instead of buying throwaway cans or bottles. This does not necessarily mean that you should buy cola only in returnable bottles. Returning bottles is inconvenient and takes time. You will buy cola in throwaways if the value of the time and inconvenience of returning bottles exceeds the monetary savings you might realize by returning bottles to the store.

Economic efficiency for the entire society requires that the purchasing patterns of all consumers be efficient and that all outputs be produced in a technically efficient manner. Whenever opportunity costs are at their minimums for all forms of consumption and production, then every drop of potential net benefits is squeezed from the resources available.

The gains from the bargains people make represent movements towards greater economic efficiency. People expect to gain when they voluntarily transact with each other, or else they will not bother. For example, you will not give me an apple for my orange unless you value the orange more than the apple, and vice versa. Thus, a trade of your apple for my orange raises your satisfaction from a given outlay because you now have a subjectively (to you) more valuable orange. I gain by the exchange in a similar fashion. Thus, economic efficiency is enhanced through trade, and a failure to trade when such gains are possible is inefficient. In fact, if only *one* of us would gain by a trade but no other party would be harmed, failure to trade is inefficient. This leads to some general rules describing an economy-wide state of economic efficiency.

Economic efficiency for the entire economy has been achieved when any further change in the production or distribution of goods would harm at least one person. This implies that resources are allocated so that they produce the most valuable combination of outputs possible. Alternatively, economic inefficiency exists if production could be changed or goods could be exchanged so that no one lost and at least one person gained. Thus, whenever we can show potential but unrealized gains to someone entailing losses to none, the current situation is inefficient. A few moments spent thinking about the concepts in Focus 3 will aid you in distinguishing efficient from inefficient situations.

FOCUS 3

Economic Inefficiency

The original situation is economically inefficient whenever:

1. the opportunity cost of a given amount of production is above the minimum possible value.
2. less than the maximum possible output is produced, given the resources available.
3. less than the maximum possible output is produced for a given cost.
4. consumers could enjoy more satisfaction by changing their purchasing patterns, given their budgets.
5. consumers could change their purchasing patterns and spend less income while still enjoying a given satisfaction level.
6. someone could gain while no one else loses if we alter the current situation in some feasible fashion.

 ## Comparative Advantage

Imagine how low your standard of living would be if your family had to be totally self-sufficient—no convenience foods, no ready-made clothing, no utilities or machines. You could consume only what you produced yourself, and life would be "nasty, brutish, and short." Specialized production and exchange yield tremendous advantages: the gains to Floridians and Iowans from trading Florida oranges for Iowa wheat are fairly obvious examples, but similar gains can be realized whether we trade with Americans or foreigners.

Specialization occurs when different people produce different things.[6] It allows individuals to produce more and, through exchange, to consume more. But how should people specialize? Specialization generates the largest gains when you concentrate on doing that which you can do at the lowest cost relative to other people; areas of relative efficiency are known as **comparative advantages.** Bra-

zilians can grow coffee more easily than they can make fur coats, while Alaskans find it difficult to grow coffee but relatively easy to make fur coats, so an exchange of Alaskan fur for Brazilian coffee will definitely yield gains to both trading parties. In this case, Alaskans have a comparative advantage in fur production; the Brazilians, in coffee production.

What if Alaskans had an *absolute advantage* in everything; that is, could do virtually every task faster and easier than Brazilians? You might think that Brazilians could gain from exchange, but that Alaskans would lose if Brazilians gained. This happens to be incorrect. Both can gain. Suppose, for example, that a lawyer whose fees run $100 an hour can type twice as fast as her secretary, whose wage is $10 an hour. She will gain by hiring the secretary to do her typing; her time is worth more in the courtroom, even though she has absolute advantages in both typing and legal work.

The critical point is that efficiency requires all resources to be used where they are relatively the most productive. Table 1 shows how both parties to a trade can gain as long as their opportunity costs are not identical. In this case, Alaskans and Brazilians each specialize in their areas of comparative advantage—fur coats and coffee, respectively. If we assume that 1 fur coat trades for, say, 1 pound of coffee, then Alaskans can consume an extra 4 pounds of coffee

---

6. Specialization involves producing different products and should not be confused with the *division of labor,* which entails dividing the work associated with producing a given good. The division of labor allows such gains to occur as when one person on an assembly line puts a bumper on a car, another works on the engine, a third installs headlights, and so on.

TABLE 1 *Opportunity Costs and Efficiency*

Before Specialization	Hours Worked	Production and Consumption
Alaskan	4	5 fur coats
	4	*1 pound of coffee*
Brazilian	4	*1 fur coat*
	4	5 pounds of coffee

After Specialization	Hours Worked	Production	Consumption
Alaskan	8	10 fur coats	5 fur coats
			5 pounds of coffee
Brazilian	8	10 pounds of coffee	*5 fur coats*
			5 pounds of coffee

daily while Brazilians can consume an additional 4 fur coats.

Notice that the Alaskans' opportunity cost of producing 1 pound of coffee is 5 fur coats before trade, while the Brazilians' opportunity cost of 1 pound of coffee is only ⅕ of a fur coat. Thus, opportunity cost guides us to comparative advantage: Nations and individuals gain when they produce goods with relatively low opportunity costs and then exchange their products for goods that others can produce at lower opportunity cost. Specialization and exchange can raise the standards of living of all potential trading partners by enormous amounts.

Among the bedrock concepts we have explored in this chapter is scarcity and how it makes decisions and opportunity costs unavoidable. We have also discussed economic efficiency, a concept that permits us to evaluate economic circumstances. You will encounter these "building block" concepts repeatedly when we investigate more advanced topics in the coming chapters. In the next chapter, we develop a device called the *production-possibilities frontier* to illustrate how scarcity limits the choices available to a society, and we examine some of the mechanisms that people use in their attempts to cope with scarcity.

CHAPTER REVIEW: KEY POINTS

1. *Economics* is concerned with the choices we make and their consequences. It has been described as the study of the ways that individuals and societies allocate their limited resources to satisfy relatively unlimited wants.

2. *Common sense* is theory that has been tested over a long period of time and found to be useful. In general, good theory accurately predicts how the real world operates. *Occam's Razor* suggests that the simplest workable theories are the most useful or "best."

3. *Positive economics* is scientifically testable and involves value-free descriptions of economic relationships, dealing with "what is." *Normative economics* involves value judgments about economic relationships and addresses "what should be." Normative theory can be neither scientifically verified nor proven false.

4. *Macroeconomics* is concerned with aggregate (the total levels of) economic phenomena, including such items as Gross National Product, unemployment, and inflation.

5. *Microeconomics* concentrates on individual decision making, resource allocation, and how prices and output are determined.

6. *Scarcity* occurs because our relatively unlimited wants cannot be completely met from the limited resources available. A good is scarce if people cannot freely get all they want, so that the good commands a positive price.

7. *Productive resources* (factors of production) include:

    a. *Labor.* Productive efforts made available by human beings. Payments for labor services are called *wages.*

    b. *Land.* All natural resources such as land, minerals, water, air. Payments for land are called *land rents.*

    c. *Capital.* Improvements that increase the productive potential of other resources. Payments for the use of capital are called *interest.* When economists refer to capital, they mean *physical* capital rather than *financial capital,* which consists of paper claims to goods or resources.

    d. *Entrepreneurship.* The organizing, innovating, and risk-taking function that combines other factors to produce goods. Providers of this resource receive *profits.*

8. *Production* occurs when knowledge or technology is used to apply energy to materials to make them more valuable.

9. The *opportunity costs* (also known as alternative costs) of the consumption choices you make are measured by the subjective values of alternatives you sacrifice.

10. *Economic efficiency* occurs when a given amount of resources produces the most valuable combination of outputs possible. *Production (technical) efficiency* is obtained when a given output is produced at the lowest possible cost. Another way of looking at efficiency is that it occurs when the opportunity cost of obtaining some specific amount of a good is at its lowest. *Consumption efficiency* requires consumers to adjust their purchasing patterns to maximize their satisfactions from given budgets.

11. The concept of *comparative advantage* is a guide to efficient specialization: You should specialize in producing things where your opportunity costs are lowest and trade your production for things other people can produce at lower opportunity cost.

QUESTIONS FOR THOUGHT AND DISCUSSION

1. Some critics of the market system claim that people are not intrinsically self-interested, but are taught to be "selfish" by our society's stress on competition. According to these critics, if we encouraged cooperation as much as we now reward competitive behavior, children would be far less selfish when they became adults. Are people naturally selfish? If you agree with these critics, can you think of ways to restructure typical child-rearing practices and our education system to discourage selfish behavior and to foster cooperation among future generations? Whether you agree or disagree that selfishness is a learned behavior, would the world be better off if people acted in less self-interested ways? Why, or why not?

2. Modern sociobiologists contend that the basic human motivation is to perpetuate one's gene pool, and offer numerous examples of behavior that appear to conflict with the economist's *homo economicus* assumption: Parents sacrifice their lives for their children, or invest in their kids' college educations so that the next generation will enjoy richer lives. On the other hand, people adopt other people's biological children and some childless people voluntarily have themselves sterilized or join religious orders that require sexual abstinence. To what extent might perpetuation of one's gene pool conflict with self-interested behavior? Which of these assumptions do you think will be more accurate in predicting human behavior?

3. Do you agree with the adage that "You can't get rich working for someone else"? In what senses must successful entrepreneurs serve others to enrich themselves? Can wage earners achieve high levels of wealth without investing? How might you test the correctness of your answers to these questions?

4. It is almost impossible to conceive of goods that are truly free. Some alternative is nearly always forgone. Why are none of the following goods "free"?
   a. A mother's love.
   b. An all-expense-paid trip to Paris, won on a TV game show.
   c. Free popcorn at a theater.
   d. A free school lunch program for poor children.
   e. Leftovers dug from a fancy restaurant's garbage by a bum.

5. Does everything have a price? Can you think of anything you would not do regardless of price? Remember: prices and money are not synonyms; the price may be nonmonetary.

6. Henry Hazlitt, author of *Economics in One Easy Lesson,* claims that "economics is haunted by more fallacies than any other study known to man." He offers the following anecdote to prove his point:

> A young hoodlum, say, heaves a brick through the window of a baker's shop. The shopkeeper runs out furious, but the boy is gone. A crowd gathers, and begins to stare with quiet satisfaction at the gaping hole in the window and the shattered glass over the bread and pies. After a while the crowd feels the need for philosophic reflection. And several of its members are almost certain to remind each other or the baker that, after all, the misfortune has its bright side. It will make business for some glazier. As they begin to think of this they elaborate upon it. How much does a new plate glass window cost? A hundred dollars? That will be quite a sum. After all, if windows were never broken, what would happen to the glass business? Then, of course, the thing is endless. The glazier will have a hundred dollars more to spend with other merchants, and these in turn will have a hundred dollars more to spend with still other merchants, and so *ad infinitum*. The smashed window will go on providing money and employment in ever-widening circles. The logical conclusion from all this would be, if the crowd drew it, the little hoodlum who threw the brick, far from being a public menace, was a public benefactor.

Eliminating the moral question of criminal activity, is the little hoodlum a public benefactor from an economic point of view?

7. Why do people commonly let water run onto sidewalks and into the street when they are watering their lawns? Is this wasted water a sign of inefficiency?

8. In what kinds of goods do Americans enjoy comparative advantages over production by foreigners? How is this related to the relative abundance of resources here in the United States compared to abroad?

Does the sight of an equation, figure, or graph strike fear in your heart? Do you still have nightmares about the geometry class you nearly flunked? You may be among the many intelligent and otherwise well-educated people whose palms sweat when they are confronted with elementary mathematical analysis. The biggest problem you have to overcome is "math/graph-phobia."

Try to cast aside your apprehensions and spend an hour or so studying this section. Working through the parallel exercises in our *Student Guide for Learning Economics* should also help tremendously. This will make it much easier to follow the economic analysis in this course, and may help you in other areas of study.

With the approach of the twenty-first century, mathematics and computer programming vie as useful second languages. Your reaction may be that well written or properly spoken English is enough for your purposes. The major advantages of mathematical expression reside in its precision and efficiency in relating certain concepts that cannot be expressed easily in words. Graphs and mathematics can simplify many discussions. For example, try to describe in simple English how much you would be paid if you worked 42½ hours in a week at an hourly rate of $4.00 per hour, with time and a half for anything in excess of 40 hours. Isn't

$$(40 \times \$4) + (2.5 \times \$4 \times 1.5)$$
$$= (\$160) + (\$15.00) = \$175.00$$

much easier?

Most economic relationships can be described in any of four ways: with English, graphs, tables, or equations. We try to use more than one technique each time we treat an important concept. However, you need to be able to deal with all four if you want to understand economic reasoning fully. Graphs are visual aids that make analysis easier. In this section, we will show you how to read, interpret, and use simple graphs. Concentrating on the graphical analysis as you proceed through the first few chapters will yield proficiency and confidence in your ability to understand graphical techniques.

Graphical Analysis

Even to students . . . who possess the mathematical tools to handle a more formal approach, there is just no substitute for the [economic] intuition that one acquires with lots of curve bending.

—*James P. Quirk (1976)*

Graphs are snapshots of information. They can be used descriptively, as in maps and charts, or analytically, to gain insights into theory. The most commonly used descriptive graphs are maps. Almost all city, street, and state road maps use systems of coordinates as guides to locations. These coordinates are then indexed. If you are reading a California map and trying to locate Fresno, you could look up Fresno on the map index. The coordinates provided, *G-9,* guide you to Fresno by directing you to a certain part of the map. Looking at the sides of the map, coordinate *G* tells you how far north or south Fresno is. Glance at the top of the map, and coordinate *9* indicates Fresno's east/west orientation. Thus, *G-9* lets you know where to look for Fresno on the map. Aha!—Fresno! The coordinate systems of maps are called *Cartesian coordinates.*

Cartesian Coordinates

Economic graphs are also based on Cartesian coordinate systems. A thorough grasp of this graphing system will aid your understanding and enjoyment of such economic theory as supply and demand analysis.

The Cartesian coordinate system is constructed by drawing two lines (or *axes*) perpendicular to each other. These axes, labeled *x* and *y,* are numbered and normally intersect at their respective zeros. The black lines in Figure 1 are axes for a standard set of Cartesian coordinates.

This coordinate system divides a "space" into four areas called *quadrants.* The quadrants are numbered I through IV, beginning from the northwest area and then moving in a counterclockwise direction. A point

FIGURE 1 *Cartesian Coordinates*

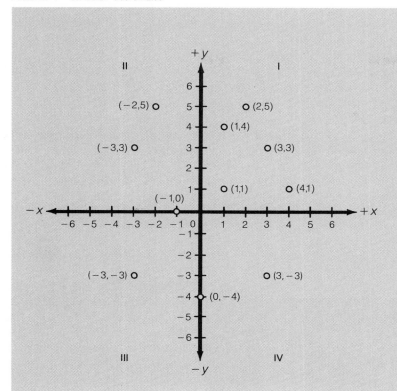

The coordinate system is divided into four areas called *quadrants*; starting from the northeast, they are numbered in a counterclockwise fashion. A point is located numerically by an ordered pair, denoted (*x,y*). Various ordered pairs are located on the graph. The *x* value represents a rightward movement from the vertical axis if the number is positive, and vice versa. The second coordinate (*y*) value is the vertical distance from the horizontal axis (upward movement if *y* is positive and downward if *y* is negative).

in any one of the quadrants is located numerically by an *ordered pair,* denoted (*x,y*). The first coordinate or number, *x,* directs rightward movement if *x* is positive, or leftward movement if *x* is negative. The second coordinate, *y,* governs upward movement if *y* is positive, or downward movement if *y* is negative. Thus Quadrant I contains pairs for which both *x* and *y* are positive, Quadrant II shows pairs for which *x* is negative and *y* is positive, Quadrant III shows situations where both *x* and *y* are negative, and Quadrant IV depicts positive values of *x* paired with negative values of *y.*

The following points are placed on the coordinate system in Figure 1: (1,1), (1,4), (3,3), (4,1), (2,5), (−2,5), (−3,3), (−1,0), (−3,−3), (0,−4), and (3,−3). Be sure that you know how to locate these coordinates graphically before proceeding. Remember, each set of numbers in parentheses gives two pieces of information; left-right for the value of *x;* then up-down for the value of *y.* Even though economists

consider multidimensional problems, this technique allows us to deal with very complex issues by considering only two dimensions of a problem at a time.

Most economic analysis uses only the first, or positive, quadrant (Quadrant I). Negative values of many economic variables do not make sense; examples of such nonsense include negative prices or negative unemployment rates.

Descriptive Graphs

Economists and other users of business and social data (such as anthropologists or people in the media) have devised some ingenious methods for depicting relationships among numerous variables. The introduction of computer-generated graphics has enhanced their ability to present these data in new and interesting ways. Perhaps you have noticed that you are seeing more and more graphs on the network news, in your local newspaper, and in news magazines, and that these graphs are not simple lines on grids. All of us are being asked to develop a certain amount of sophistication about graphs to keep pace with these changes. It will be easier for you to read and understand these graphs if you keep a few basic points in mind, and perhaps the most important of these is that the same set of data can be presented in a number of different ways. The following discussion will show you what we mean.

Let's begin by examining Figure 2. In this advertisement, Macron uses a set of vertical bars to indicate increased sales of their software over the period 1983–87. Is this figure based on a Cartesian coordinate system? The answer is yes, and Figure 3 shows why.

The bars in the Macron advertisement show sales in recent years. Cartesian coordinates for these data are also shown in Panels B and C of Figure 3. Sales are on the vertical axis and are graphed against years on the horizontal axis. Panels B and C are called *bar graphs* because they use bars to represent sales in each year.

Line graphs are shown in Panels D and E. Rather than using a series of bars, the Cartesian points showing sales data over time are connected by a line. All five panels illustrate the same information. Only five data points are presented in the graphs in Panels A through E. Graphs can be used to present much more complex pictures of data, but reading them is easy if you concentrate on what the graph shows.

FIGURE 2 *An Example of How Economic Data Can Be Graphically Depicted in an Advertisement*

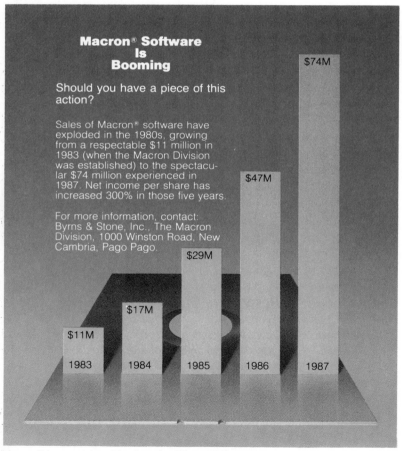

Macron® Software Is Booming

Should you have a piece of this action?

Sales of Macron® software have exploded in the 1980s, growing from a respectable $11 million in 1983 (when the Macron Division was established) to the spectacular $74 million experienced in 1987. Net income per share has increased 300% in those five years.

For more information, contact: Byrns & Stone, Inc., The Macron Division, 1000 Winston Road, New Cambria, Pago Pago.

$74M
$47M
$29M
$17M
$11M
1983 1984 1985 1986 1987

Macron® is a registered trademark of Byrns & Stone, Inc.

FIGURE 3 *Different Ways the Same Data Can Be Depicted*

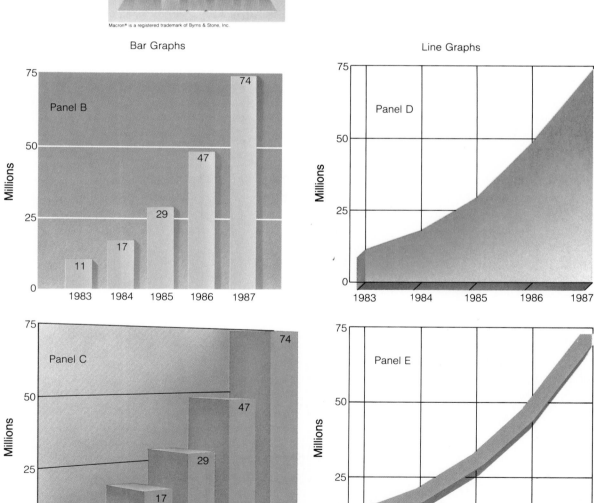

Panel A

The sales data shown in the Macron® advertisement are converted directly into the bar graphs, and then into the line graphs, using the Cartesian coordinate system.

Bar Graphs

Line Graphs

Measuring the Slope of a Line

Many important economic concepts hinge on how much one variable changes in response to changes in another. Graphically, such relationships are equivalent to the *slope* of the line depicting the association between the two variables. Typically, two variables will be positively or negatively related to each other. That is, higher values of *x* will be associated either with higher values of *y* (a *positive relation*) or with lower values of *y* (a *negative relation*).

For example, Figure 4 depicts possible relationships for students with good, typical, and poor study habits between hours spent studying (*x*) and grade point average (*y*). Generally, the more you study, the higher your grade point average. Thus, the relationship is positive. But how much will you have to study to raise your grade point one full grade? The answer is found by determining the slope of the grade point average/study hours line. You may have heard slope described as "rise over run" (rise/run). In this case,

the grade is the rise, measured by the vertical axis; study hours is the run, measured along the horizontal axis. Thus, if you have typical study habits and study each subject for 30 hours a semester, your grade point average will be a 2.0, or C. If you increase your study time to 45 hours per subject, your average will rise to 3.0, or B. Fifteen extra hours of study per subject will raise your grade point average by one full point if the middle line in Figure 4 corresponds to the relationship between your average and the hours you study.

The *slope of a line* is defined as the ratio of the vertical change (*rise*) to the horizontal change (*run*) as we move along a line from left to right. In the case of average study habits, the slope is $\frac{1}{15}$. Notice that the slope of each line reflects the efficiency of each individual's study time. For the student with good study habits, only 7.5 hours of study are necessary to raise the average grade by one point. The person with poor habits, however, must study an additional 30 hours to achieve the same results. Thus, the slopes

FIGURE 4 *Hypothetical Relationship Between Hours Spent Studying and Cumulative Grade Point Average*

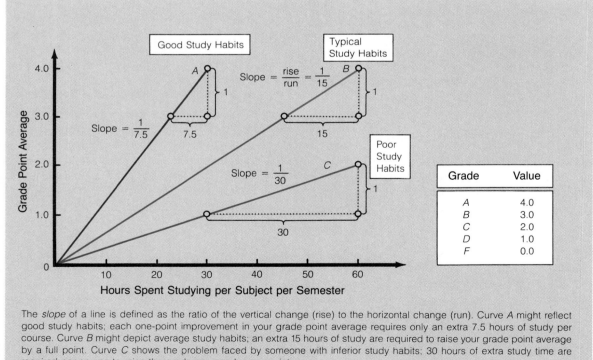

The *slope* of a line is defined as the ratio of the vertical change (rise) to the horizontal change (run). Curve *A* might reflect good study habits; each one-point improvement in your grade point average requires only an extra 7.5 hours of study per course. Curve *B* might depict average study habits; an extra 15 hours of study are required to raise your grade point average by a full point. Curve *C* shows the problem faced by someone with inferior study habits; 30 hours of extra study time are required per course to raise the grade average by one point.

FIGURE 5 *Hypothetical Relationship Between Hours of Partying and Grade Point Average*

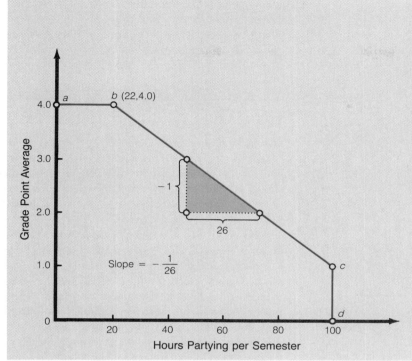

The slope of a line can be negative, zero, or infinite. Between points *a* and *b* the slope is zero, indicating that a little partying will not affect grades. Between points *b* and *c* the slope is −1/26, suggesting that each additonal 26 hours of partying will reduce your grade point average by one point. Between points *c* and *d*, the slope is infinite, which means that a small change in partying may result in a one point or more decline in your grade point average.

showing these relationships are ⅐₅ and ⅟₃₀, respectively.

The slope of a line can also be negative. Extensive partying almost invariably results in lower grades. This typically negative relationship is reflected in Figure 5. As the graph suggests, you can party for up to 22 hours with negligible harm to your grade point average (point *b*). After that, for every 26 hours you party, your grade point average falls by one grade point until point *c* is reached (1.0 grade point average and 100 hours of partying). Once you party beyond 100 hours, your grades drop to 0.0, or failing. Thus, between points *a* and *b*, the slope of the curve is zero (change in partying has no effect on grades or, alternatively, the two variables are unrelated). The slope of the line is −¹⁄₂₆ between 22 and 100 hours of party time (between points *b* and *c*). This means that for every 26 hours partied, your grade average falls by one full grade point. The slope is infinite if you party 100 hours (between points *c* and *d*). Any small change (as little as 5 seconds) may result in a full point increase or decrease in your grade point average.

Intercepts

Much economic analysis is most easily understood if we assume that the relationship studied is *linear,* which means that a graph of the relationship has a constant slope. The only information we need beyond slope to specify a linear relationship completely is the *intercept,* which is the value of the *y* variable when the *x* variable has a value of zero.

For example, Figure 6 shows a hypothetical relationship between lumber yields from a forest and the amount of annual maintenance per acre to clear debris (reducing fire hazards) and control diseases of trees. Even with zero maintenance ($x = 0$) we will be able to harvest some lumber (the *y* intercept = 10,000). As the level of maintenance increases, the harvest rate rises. Specifically, for every extra hour of maintenance per acre, annual lumber yields from the forest rise by 2,000 board feet. This slope (2,000) is constant (given the linear relationship) until the ability to harvest lumber peaks when 45 hours of annual maintenance are devoted to each acre of forest.

FIGURE 6 *Forest Maintenance and Lumber Production (Hypothetical Data)*

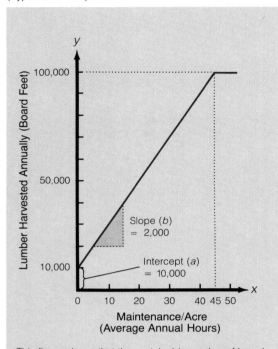

This figure shows that the sustainable number of board feet of lumber that can be harvested from a forest annually is 10,000 board feet, if no one works to maintain the forest. As the number of hours rises that forestry experts devote to each acre of forest, the forest's yield rises by 2,000 board feet/hour.

In general, linear relationships can be written algebraically as: $y = a + bx$, where y and x are the variables being considered, b is the slope of their relationship, and a is the intercept term. For this forestry example, $a = 10,000$, $b = 2,000$, and the equation is: $y = 10,000 + 2,000x$, where,

y = annual yield of lumber in board feet,
10,000 = the intercept (the value of y, which is board feet of lumber annually, when x, maintenance, is zero), and
x = hours of maintenance per acre, annually.

To find the harvest rate for each maintenance level, just plug in the value of x, multiply it by 2,000, and add 10,000.

To ensure that you understand how the intercept and slope of a line are influenced by how variables interact, you should construct graphs of $y = a + bx$ where you select values of a and b as if you were blindly drawing them out of a hat.

The Misuse of Graphs

Darrell Huff and Irving Geis wrote a popular book called *How to Lie with Statistics*. They also show how you can be misled by cleverly drawn graphs. You should be alert for several pitfalls when graphs are used to illustrate, support, or prove an analytical point.

First, make sure the time period selected for the graph is typical for the point made by the analysis. For example, during the 1960s, mutual funds and stocks were sold on the basis of booming performance in the previous decade. It seemed that the prices of stocks and shares of mutual funds could only rise. Unfortunately, mutual funds were losers during the 1970s—they did not even come close to their average performance in the 1950s and 1960s.

Second, be aware that the appearance of a graph depends on the choice of measurement units. One distortion caused by using different units on the axes is illustrated in Figure 7. Curve *A* appears to have a greater slope than curve *B*, but both curves accurately portray the same data, so this is impossible. The vertical axes are measured on different scales, accounting for the illusion that they have different slopes.

Finally, the data used should be tightly linked to the analysis. Thus, comparing standards of living between countries cannot be done by simply looking at countries' total production or income; for example, India is much bigger but far less prosperous than Kuwait. Income per person or family is a much closer measure.

As you read through the remainder of this book, you will be confronted with numerous graphs, both analytical and descriptive. We hope this section has helped ease your mind and that you will find our graphs helpful to your understanding of economics. The adage that one picture is worth a thousand words is often especially true in economics.

FIGURE 7 *Consumer Prices, 1967–85*

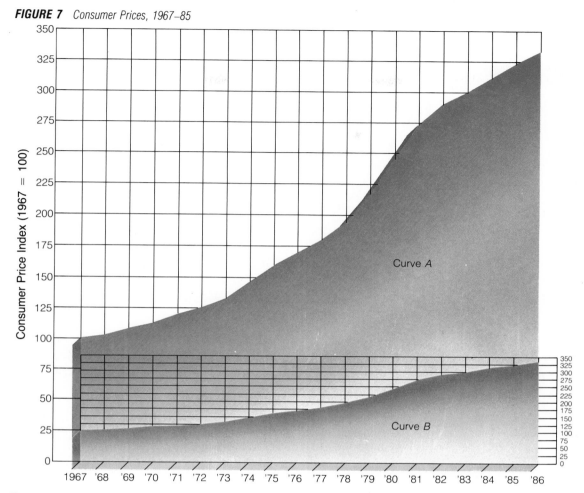

The unit of measurement on the axes can make the line appear steeper (have a greater slope), even though the slope remains constant. Both curves *A* and *B* have the same slope; the units of measurement on the vertical axes have been expanded in curve *A*.

Source: Bureau of Labor Statistics.

CHAPTER 2 Resolving the Problem of Scarcity

What? How? Who? When?	*brute force*	*property rights*
	queuing	*laissez-faire*
production-possibilities frontier (PPF)	*random selection*	*socialism*
	tradition	*central planning*
law of diminishing returns	*capitalism and markets*	

Your exploration into economics was launched in the preceding chapter. Now we will examine broad types of choices made necessary by the basic economic problem—scarcity—and survey some mechanisms used to choose among the alternatives available. What will be produced? How will it be produced? Who will get to consume our production? Shall we use brute force, tradition, government, the market system, or some other mechanism to answer these questions? How do capitalism and socialism differ in resolving such issues? These and related questions are our concern in this chapter.

Basic Economic Questions

Scarcity confronts every society with four **basic economic questions:**

1. **What** economic goods will be produced?
2. **How** will resources be used in production?
3. **Who** will get to consume economic goods?
4. **When** will resources or goods be used?

What?

A society can select only one from the innumerable combinations of goods that could be produced during a particular period, given its resources and the state of technology. How much of each good would we like? Shall we choose more guns and less butter? More health care and less housing? If production is technically efficient, more of any good means less of another. Ideally, the combination of goods a society chooses will be the one most in accord with its consumers' wants.

How?

A variety of technologies and resources can be used to produce most goods. For example, excavating for a swimming pool can be done in 1 day with 1 bulldozer and 1 operator, or by 30 people with shovels in 1 week, or in 1 month by 300 people wielding teaspoons. Cotton, oranges, and most other agricultural products can be harvested by hand or by machine. Shirts can be carefully cut out and sewn at home or mass-produced in a factory. Choosing the most efficient technology and combination of resources for every form of production enables a society to reach the combination of goods most compatible with the allocatively efficient choices of consumers. When this occurs, there is economic efficiency throughout the society.

Who?

Even if we efficiently produce what consumers want, we still need to address to whom income and wealth will be distributed because these distributions determine, in turn, how large individuals' budgets are and whose preferences matter. Every society is faced with hard questions about equity that inevitably arise when it decides for whom to produce. Should the desires of the rich and powerful count more than those of the poor?

When?

Perishables such as ice-cream cones or newspapers must be used shortly after production or they quickly lose value, but durable goods such as stained glass windows or canned coffee can be stored for years. Similarly, some productive resources are perishable, while others last for centuries. For example, 8 hours of labor are lost forever each day that a worker is unemployed, but a vein of copper ore or a barrel of oil can be stored indefinitely.

Production Possibilities

You have a limited budget. Can you afford a flight in a hot air balloon if you already spent all your income each week? Of course, but only by buying less of something else. If you only have $10 to spend, you cannot see a movie, buy a record, fill your gas tank, eat lunch at Burger King, and still get your flat tire fixed. Something has to give! Just as your budget constrains your purchases, scarcity forces society as a whole to make choices about the goods we produce and consume. We represent the limits to what a society can produce by devices called production-possibilities frontiers.

Production-Possibilities Frontiers

A **production-possibilities frontier (PPF)** is among the simplest models of an economy and relies on three critical assumption:[1]

1. The amounts of the various factors of production (land, labor, capital, and entrepreneurship) are fixed. However, these resources can be allocated among different types of production.
2. Technology is assumed constant. (Technology includes such things as the state of knowledge about production and the qualities of available resources.)
3. All scarce resources are fully and efficiently employed.

Suppose you live in Ruritania: a mythical empire ruled by the dictator Atilla, who has appointed himself president-for-life and minister of production. He believes that "balanced" production requires all industries to use the same proportional mixes of capital, land, and labor. There are 1,000 units of each of these productive resources in Ruritania.

Some production possibilities for the Ruritanian economy are detailed in Table 1, located in Figure 1. Points *a, b, c, d,* and *e* in the figure designate five of the many possible combinations of armaments and bread that can be produced during a given period when resources are used in the same fixed proportions in both industries. (For simplicity, we will assume that only two goods are produced.) As factors of production are shifted from armaments to bread, weaponry output falls and bread output rises. When all resources are used to produce guns, no bread is produced, and vice versa.

Alternatives *a* through *e* are only five of the many feasible combinations. Atilla can choose any point on the production-possibilities frontier *(PPF)* graphed when combinations *a* through *e* are connected by a smooth line. The point Atilla chooses will depend on whether he wants Ruritanians to be better fed and less well defended, or vice versa. Would he ever choose a point such as *x?* Not likely, because at point *x* many resources would be either idle or used in wasteful ways. Atilla could eliminate the underemployment of resources and improve efficiency by

---

1. If you are concerned because you think that these assumptions are unrealistic, remember (from Chapter 1) that a model need be no more realistic than is necessary for the purpose at hand.

FIGURE 1 *Production-Possibilities Frontier*

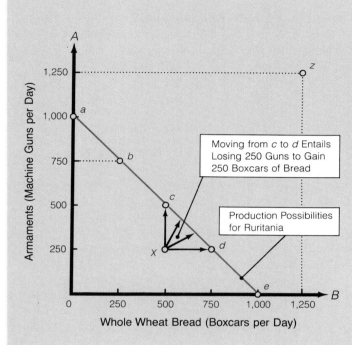

This straight-line *PPF* reflects the availability of resources (1,000 units each of capital, land, and labor) and the crude technology used (Atilla's "balanced" production formula). If production of both arms and bread is exactly proportional to the amounts of resources used and a maximum of 1,000 boxcars of bread (or 1,000 guns) can be produced daily, then total production when all resources are employed will equal 1,000 total units of bread plus weapons. Each gun produced costs 1 boxcar of bread, and vice versa.

TABLE 1 *Production-Possibilities Schedule*

Production Alternative	Arms (Machine Guns per Day)	Bread (Box Cars per Day)
a	1,000	0
b	750	250
c	500	500
d	250	750
e	0	1,000

moving from point *x* to a point between *c* and *d* and produce more of both goods.

Producing 1,250 units of each commodity at point *z* is clearly preferable to all points on the existing frontier. Resources cannot be stretched to attain point *z*, however, in part because of Atilla's neurotic fixation on a "balanced" production technology. Remember that an economy operating on its production-possibilities frontier is producing efficiently, given the technology available.

What does bread cost in our example? If Ruritanians move from point *c* in Figure 1 to production possibility *d*, they gain 250 boxcars of bread but lose 250 machine guns per period; the cost of each extra boxcar of bread is one machine gun. The guns that must be sacrificed for extra bread are the opportunity costs (in guns) of producing and consuming more bread, and vice versa.

Diminishing Returns and Increasing Opportunity Costs

You may have heard the phrase "diminishing returns." Here is a very general statement.

The **law of diminishing returns:** *As any activity is extended, it eventually becomes increasingly difficult to pursue the activity further.*[2]

For example, the faster you drive, the harder it is to gain another 10 miles per hour and your car's gas mileage drops. Diminishing returns are encountered in physics, biology, and a host of other areas outside of economics. Within economics, this concept has wide and varied applications: Expanding a given form of production eventually becomes ever more difficult. Increasing your total satisfaction from any good ultimately also becomes more difficult the more of the good you have already consumed. Would your enjoyment from eating 5 candy bars per week quadruple if you ate 20?

One corollary of the law of diminishing returns is that raising any form of production eventually entails **increasing opportunity costs.** This means that repeatedly increasing production by some set proportion ultimately requires more than proportional

---

2. The occurrence of a law of diminishing *marginal* returns in production is only an example of the broader tendency described here.

increases in resources and costs. For example, the more you study, the better your grades tend to be. It requires more effort to earn a C than a D. But raising your grade from a B to an A normally requires far more extra work than moving from a D to a C. Thus, there are increasing costs to raising your grade point average. Let's see how this concept applies to the production-possibilities frontier.

Atilla's "balanced" production formula required all types of production to use the same proportional mix of capital, land, and labor. This is a very primitive technology. Suppose Atilla now appoints you minister of production. You might reason that, relative to armaments, efficient bread production requires more land and labor and less capital, while armaments production should use capital relatively more intensively. This new knowledge is a technological breakthrough! After experimenting with different mixes of resources until you discover the appropriate technology, you will find that increasing costs are encountered as production of either good is expanded. This yields production-possibilities curves that are concave (bowed away) from the origin. Here is why.

Ruritania's production-possibilities frontier for bread and arms under this new technology is detailed in Figure 2 and Table 2, located in the figure. When bread production is raised from zero to 100 boxcars daily, machine gun output falls only from 1,000 units to 995 daily (from point *a* to point *b*). Why do the first 100 boxcars of bread cost only 5 machine guns? Because the resources first shifted into food production will be those relatively best suited for bread and least suited for arms. Far more land than capital will be transferred to bread production. But as bread output is continually increased, the resources shifted are decreasingly suited for bread production relative to the production of armaments, and the cost of extra bread rises. Thus, moving from point *f* to point *g* results in an extra 100 boxcars of bread per day, but costs 66 machine guns, while moving from point *i* to point *j* also yields 100 extra boxcars of bread, but the cost is higher: 164 machine guns.

When bread output is finally expanded from 900 boxcars to 1,000 boxcars daily (point *j* to point *k*), the last resources shifted from armaments production are very productive for machine guns but ill-suited

FIGURE 2 *Production Possibilities and Increasing Costs*

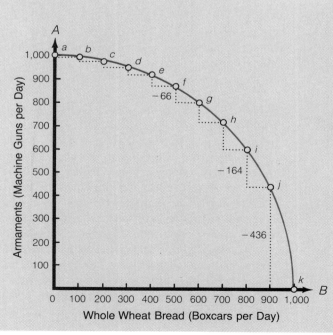

If the resources available (1,000 units each of capital, land, and labor) are used in the combinations that best fit the various forms of production, the *PPF* will be concave from the origin. In this example, arms are capital intensive (use more capital relative to land), and bread is land intensive. The differences in the appropriate mixes of capital/labor/land causes a society to encounter diminishing returns (increasing costs) as more and more boxcars of bread (or arms) are produced.

TABLE 2 *Production Possibilities and Increasing Costs*

(1)	(2) Average Daily Production	(3)	(4) Average Opportunity Costs (Average Machine Guns Sacrificed per
Point	Arms	Bread	Extra Boxcar of Bread)
a	1,000	0	—
b	995	100	0.05
c	980	200	0.15
d	954	300	0.26
e	917	400	0.37
f	866	500	0.51
g	800	600	0.66
h	714	700	0.86
i	600	800	1.14
j	436	900	1.64
k	0	1,000	4.36

for producing food. Thus, 436 machine guns are sacrificed for the last 100 boxcars of bread. Less and less land is available for shifting, so more and more capital moves into agriculture. The ever increasing cost of extra bread in terms of forgone machine guns, as shown in Column 4 of Table 2, is depicted in Figure 3. You will learn in the next chapter that Figure 3 illustrates the typical shape of a society's long-run supply curve for bread.

To summarize, note that three important concepts are illustrated in the production-possibilities model: scarcity, opportunity costs, and choice. Our desires for "more" are boundless, but resources are scarce, so only limited quantities of goods can be produced. Scarcity forces every society to choose among competing goods. And finally, the most valued alternative sacrificed to obtain another unit of a given good is its opportunity cost. Opportunity costs eventually rise if the production of any good is repeatedly expanded.

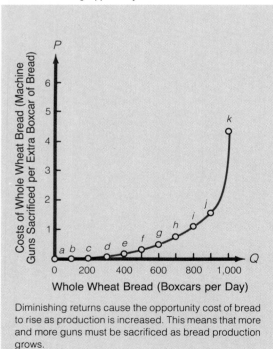

FIGURE 3 *Rising Opportunity Cost of Bread*

Diminishing returns cause the opportunity cost of bread to rise as production is increased. This means that more and more guns must be sacrificed as bread production grows.

Economic Growth

Using resources more efficiently is one way that **economic growth** occurs, but growth in an efficient economy requires either that more resources become available or that technology advances. An outward shift of a production-possibilities frontier reflects growth because more of both goods can be produced, as shown in Panel A of Figure 4.

Investment in new capital is one source of economic growth. Opening up new land is another possibility, but there is little unexplored land on Earth and settling other planets remains in the realm of science fiction. Expanding the labor force is yet another way to stimulate economic growth. Labor resources can grow in two ways: increases in the number of workers, or improvements in their quality and productivity. Economic growth also occurs if more people become entrepreneurs willing to risk implementing new technologies.

Technological advances occur when given quantities of resources become capable of greater production. Suppose that technology improves only in the clothing industry. It may seem surprising that more of *both* food and clothing can be produced, as illustrated in Panel B of Figure 4, but this breakthrough means that fewer resources are required to produce a given amount of textiles. Resources will be freed for food production. Although point *a* in Panel B remains stationary, most of the curve shifts to the right, reflecting not only an increase in the potential output of clothing but also increased possibilities for the production of food.

Choices Between the Present and Future

We confront choices between consumer goods and military goods, among various commodities, and between work and leisure. The basic question *When?* means we also must choose between consuming now and consuming later. Low levels of investment may severely restrict the goods available in the future if a society produces mostly perishable consumer goods but builds very few manufacturing plants and little new machinery. A society can produce investment goods only to the extent that it forgoes potential current consumption.

FIGURE 4 *Production Possibilities and Growth*

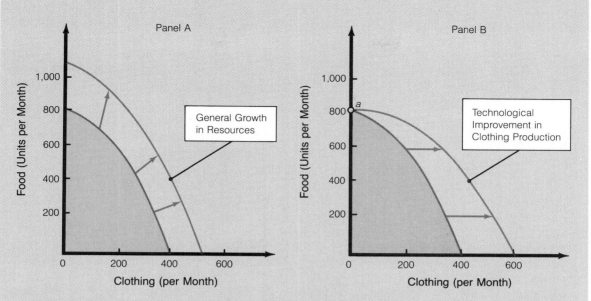

Growth in an economy can be generated through a general increase in resources (Panel A) or through technological improvement (Panel B). The entire *PPF* clearly expands when available resources increase. Note that technological improvement, even if only in one commodity, expands production opportunities for both commodities because technological advances make resources available for other uses.

National income that is not consumed, making resources available for new capital investments, is called **saving.** Rapid investment directly augments productive capacity and updates technology, and it often boosts labor productivity and generates new products as side benefits. On the other hand, society's productive capacity declines if investment is less than depreciation. Stagnation inevitably follows if worn-out capital is not replaced. In such cases, the production-possibilities frontier shrinks towards the origin.

Thus, the choice we make between current consumption and saving (to allow investment) determines our future prosperity, as shown in Figure 5. Panel A indicates some possible choices between consuming and investing in 1988, with point *a* reflecting greater consumption than point *b*, point *b* more consumption than point *c*, and so on. Curves *PPF*ₐ through *PPF*ₑ in Panel B show the production possibilities in 1998 that result from 1988 choices of

a, b, c, d, and *e,* respectively. In sum, more rapid growth in an efficient economy is stimulated by higher investment, which requires more saving (less consumption).

This analysis partially explains why, on average, U.S. economic growth since 1970 has been so anemic compared to that in some other countries. Americans have typically saved only about 5–6 percent of their income since 1970, while various nationalities of Europeans saved 8–16 percent of their incomes. During this same period, the Japanese saved over 20 percent of their income, facilitating substantial new investment in capital goods. The result is that numerous antiquated American industries now try to compete with foreign firms that use newer machinery and more advanced technology. For example, our automobile industry has faltered recently in competition with prosperous Japanese carmakers, who rely much more on industrial robots in their assembly lines.

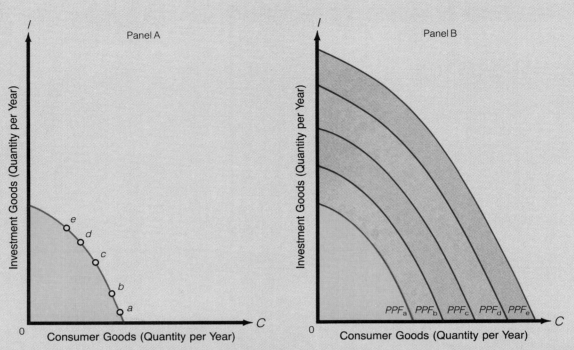

Society must make choices between present and future consumption. If, in 1988, this society selects a mix of production that emphasizes consumer goods (point *a* in Panel A) rather than investment (capital) goods (point *e* in Panel A), the 1998 *PPF* will be relatively smaller. Choice *a* in Panel A yields only enough investment to replace the capital that has depreciated, so PPF_a is the same in both panels. Moving from point *a* to point *b* in Panel A causes capital to grow somewhat, so that in Panel B more of both consumption and investment are possible along PPF_b than on PPF_a. Moving to point *c* in Panel A enables still greater growth yielding PPF_c in Panel B. And so on.

Many of President Reagan's policies were intended to stimulate investment and growth. A 25 percent cut in tax rates phased in during 1981–83 was directed largely at business firms and upper-income individuals. The president and his advisors were optimistic that investment tax credits and other tax breaks would stimulate investment and strong economic growth. Brisk growth of our national income that began early in 1984 was hailed as evidence that these policies had finally rescued the economy from a severe recession that had plagued the early 1980s.

However, high interest rates and record $100+ billion deficits in the federal budget caused many observers to question the wisdom of simultaneous tax cuts and vigorous attempts by the Reagan administration to expand military spending. The debacle of the early 1980s is an example of the recurring dilemma every society faces when it makes choices between "guns" and "butter."

★ Unemployment, Inflation, and National Defense

Wars unavoidably alter economic activity. Some interesting comparisons between the World War II and Vietnam War eras can be illuminated by production-possibilities analysis. At the onset of World War II, the United States was only sluggishly recovering from its deepest depression ever. Unemployment had fallen from its 25 percent peak in 1933 to roughly 15–16 percent by 1939. In reasonably prosperous times, the unemployment rate averages 4–6 percent. Thus, many idle resources were available for production when the United States entered World War II. This initial situation is represented by point *a* in Figure 6.

Some consumer goods (butter) and a few military goods (guns) were being produced, but high unemployment signalled that the economy operated well inside its production-possibilities frontier. When hostilities erupted, mobilizing these idle resources enabled military production to grow rapidly without cutting back on outputs of consumer goods. In fact, consumption actually rose in the early 1940s. This drive towards full employment is graphed as a movement from point *a* to point *b*.

The production-possibilities frontier also grew rapidly in the early war years as new technologies were introduced, patriotism spurred worker productivity, and women flocked into the work force to support the defense effort. The economy moved from point *b* to point *c* in Figure 6 as the production-

possibilities frontier expanded. Then, when the war ended, the United States experienced a transition phase as the economy retooled from military hardware to consumer goods, gradually approaching point *d*.

The World War II era contrasts sharply with what happened during the Vietnam War. The economy was close to full employment in the mid-1960s, with a jobless rate of around 4 percent. This is represented by point *a* in Figure 7. President Johnson strove for "more guns and more butter", attempting to increase military involvement in Vietnam while simultaneously expanding domestic programs (e.g., the "War Against Poverty"). His goals required a movement to point *b* in Figure 7, but unfortunately, such movements are impossible. The economy experienced moderate growth, moving, say, to point *c* by 1969, but at least part of the persistent double-digit inflation suffered during the 1970s was a hangover from pressures exerted on the U.S. economy by the Vietnam conflict.

FIGURE 6 *Production-Possibilities Analysis of World War II*

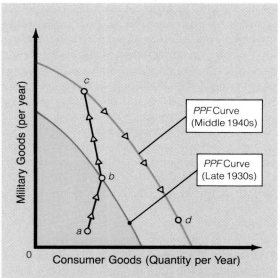

When hostilities erupted in World War II, the economy suffered from considerable excess capacity and was operating well inside the *PPF* at point *a*. The military buildup drew on these idle resources as the economy moved from *a* to *b*. During the war years, the *PPF* expanded because of technological advances, enhanced patriotism that increased worker productivity, and the influx of women into the labor force. As the war ended, the society reallocated resources from military to consumer goods (from point *c* to point *d*).

FIGURE 7 *Production-Possibilities During the Vietnam War*

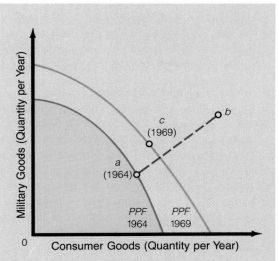

At the beginning of the Vietnam War the economy was roughly at full employment (point *a*). By trying to expand both the Indochina conflict and domestic programs, the government attempted to reach point *b*. However, this was unattainable. Actually, the economy experienced moderate growth, and we achieved point *c*. The result of attempting the unattainable contributed to the inflationary pressures of the early 1970s.

Production-possibilities frontiers depict the menu available to a society, given its resources and technology. Just as every family has a limited budget, a *PPF* represents society's limited budget. Neither nature nor human industry can provide everything that everyone wants, so the alternatives chosen automatically eliminate other options. One way to gain insights into problems posed by scarcity and the need to choose is to examine various mechanisms used to resolve the competition among people for scarce goods.

⅄ Allocative Mechanisms

Some of the **allocative mechanisms** used to deal with scarcity yield less satisfactory solutions than others. The mechanisms discussed in this section are all used in some situations, and in all countries. This is why all societies have *mixed* economic systems. Although different allocative mechanisms channel competition in different ways, no mechanism eliminates competition because people everywhere try to "beat the system", competing to attain their own interests. Each mechanism works well in certain circumstances, but at other times their consequences can be tragic.

The Market System

The **market system** is the principal device used in the United States to address economic problems. Private buyers and sellers trade money for resources or goods in our market economy, which some people call the *free enterprise system*. Much of this book describes how markets allocate resources and distribute income and production. Before we examine how markets resolve economic issues, however, we will look at some nonmarket methods of choosing.

Brute Force

Brute force is one way to decide who gets what, when, from whom, and how. You could be threatened with loss of life, limb, or loved ones if you refused to hand over your goods to a neighborhood bully. You may think that brute force sounds like a fine system for people who are inclined to be thugs—but the film *The Godfather* provides a good example of how violence begets unending cycles of violence. And consider how much waste occurs when goods are allocated through brute force and how little productive activity is likely.

Queuing

Queuing (lining up) is another way of deciding who gets what. The first-come, first-served principle operates for staking mining claims or making purchases at bookstores and ice-cream parlors. However, if waiting in a queue were the dominant means of allocating resources and goods, so much time would be spent standing in line that little production would occur—and you would be forced to be very selective about which long waiting line you chose. Should production then be oriented towards the goods that have the longest queues? It's hard to say, because what people want may change quickly. There are few buyers for winter coats in July.

Random Selection

Random selection is yet another way to allocate goods and services. All economic questions could be decided by such random means as throwing dice, drawing straws, or other games based on pure luck. Once again, little production is likely. If your job were randomly assigned, without regard to your talents, you probably would not be a very motivated worker and the advantages of specialization would be lost as well. Many of us would be round pegs in square holes. Young men are now required to register with the Selective Service. Is a lottery to determine who will serve in the Army fair? Is a draft efficient? Would you want all college educations, new cars, or food to be distributed by lottery?

Tradition

Tradition may also be used to resolve the basic production and distribution questions. Feudal European monarchies and the caste system in India operated largely on this basis. In our society, women and minority members have often been pushed into low-paying jobs because tradition has limited their access to better positions. Most of us reject the notion that only senators' children should become senators, or that garbage collectors' kids necessarily should haul tomorrow's trash. Too many resources and far too much human talent are wasted when tradition alone rules.

Government

Government is the major alternative to the marketplace when fundamental economic issues must be resolved—but how should government decide? Even if we unanimously agreed that a democratic government should make all economic decisions, we would still confront the questions of who should be given what and how to produce the things to be distributed. Among the criteria that government might use to distribute production are equal shares and need.

Equal Shares

An egalitarian approach entitling everyone to equal shares might seem a fair way to distribute goods and services, but equal amounts of food may be more than can be eaten by a person weighing 100 pounds, yet a starvation diet for a 250-pound all-pro linebacker. Should we all be issued equal paychecks and identical housing and clothing? Moreover, egalitarianism offers few incentives for production. Why should an American farm family work hard to produce wheat if its share is only 1/240 millionth of the farm's production?

Another difficulty arises because government decision makers are as self-interested as the rest of us. If you had the right to decide what is equal or fair, you would probably give yourself and your relatives and friends every benefit of any doubt. Quite often an egalitarian policy may deteriorate to the state of George Orwell's *Animal Farm:* "All animals are equal, but some animals are more equal than others."

Need

An alternative is for government to distribute goods in accord with need. Unfortunately, it is extremely difficult for anyone to judge someone else's needs. Moreover, distribution according to need is costly and likely to be inaccurate. It might cause people to exaggerate their needs. Here is one horrifying example. Beggars in underdeveloped countries sometimes cripple their children so that the children will appear more pathetic to compassionate strangers.

A less brutal example is a 1950s TV game show called "Queen for a Day." Contestants told heartbreaking tales of children needing operations, un-employed husbands, and foreclosed mortgages. The woman who drew the loudest applause from the audience was crowned "Queen for a Day" and awarded a washer and dryer or a trip to Las Vegas. If you had been a contestant, would you have stretched the truth a bit? If all goods were distributed on a needs basis, the officials making distribution decisions might become calloused to the plights of the truly unfortunate. Do you think even well-intentioned decision makers might become especially sensitive to their own material needs?

Still another difficulty is that distribution according to need causes special interest groups to spend time and effort lobbying to make decision makers aware of their special needs. What better way to make your needs known than through cash contributions to campaign funds? The potential for graft and corruption is enormous—few politicians can be expected to be Good Samaritans. Finally, only minimal production is likely. How many people would exert themselves to produce things only for redistribution to the "needy"?

Production and Consumption Choices

If government dictated production and consumption in detail, we could count on policymakers' preferences being reflected but should not be surprised if there were only two sizes of everything—too big and too little. Even if government decision makers try to mirror the varied desires of millions of consumers, they face an almost unsolvable dilemma. Here is an example to show why even a democratic government is always in a quandary.

Suppose that Xavier, Yolanda, and Zelda are elected to specify our national priorities for the coming years and that each perfectly reflects the sentiments of one third of the populace. Their rankings of national priorities are shown in the blue rectangles shown in Table 3. If you study this table for a moment, you will conclude that no matter which priorities are finally chosen, at least one-third of all citizens will have their first choice placed last and their last choice ranked first. This example illustrates why it may be impossible for democratic decisions to be consistent with voter preferences.[3]

---

3. A similar example has been offered by Nobel Laureate Kenneth Arrow to illustrate a theorem proving the impossibility of democratic choices being consistent with voter preferences.

TABLE 3 *Choices About National Priorities Versus Choices about Meals*

	Decision Makers		
	Xavier	**Yolanda**	**Zelda**
First Choice	Stronger National Defense	Cleaner Environment	Controlling Inflation
	Ham	Roast Beef	Turkey
Second Choice	Cleaner Environment	Controlling Inflation	Stronger National Defense
	Roast Beef	Turkey	Ham
Third Choice	Controlling Inflation	Stronger National Defense	Cleaner Environment
	Turkey	Ham	Roast Beef

Now consider the green rectangles in Table 3, which show the committee members' preferences for main courses at a Thanksgiving meal. It might seem that similarly irreconcilable differences exist. In this case, however, we can leave the decisions up to the individuals and their families. Each family can have its first choice because decisions about what to eat can be made individually rather than by democratic vote. The point is that decision making by government is inherently crude relative to the fine-tuning made possible through individual choice in a marketplace.

You can probably identify situations in which each of the allocative mechanisms just discussed seems to work well. However, most economic decisions in the United States are made through markets in which prices and productivity are major factors in determining what is produced and who gets it. One important exception is the family, whose decisions are based on varying degrees of command, tradition, and communal sharing, whether equally, by need, or based on some other criterion. The second most important mechanism for decision making in our society is government. In many countries, government is the dominant economic decision maker.

✕ Economic Systems

Although all societies must address the basic economic questions, each has considerable leeway in how it answers *What? How? Who?* and *When?* Brute force, tradition, queuing, and other allocative mechanisms all play roles in every society. Economic systems are conventionally classified, however, by who makes decisions and who owns which resources. These questions are critical in determining the importance of government relative to the market system.

Who Decides?

Some economies rely heavily on **decentralized decision making.** This is generally true in the United States. The bulk of decisions regarding what to produce, how to produce, and who shall get the production are determined by the individual actions of numerous consumers and producers. The other extreme is **centralized decision making,** where most important decisions are made by the government. Elaborate plans for output (production quotas) and distribution to consumers are drawn up and enforced. This type of organization, called a **command economy,** is epitomized by the Soviet Union.

Who Owns?

Economic systems can also be broken down by whether their pattern of ownership is private or public. The means of production are owned primarily by individual citizens in capitalistic nations. In socialist countries, most productive resources are owned by the state, acting as collective trustee for its citizens.

TABLE 4 *Economic Decision Making*

	Decision Making	
	Decentralized	**Centralized**
Private Ownership	**Capitalism** United States Canada Western Europe Australia	**Wartime Capitalism or Fascism** Japan (Tojo) Germany (Hitler) Italy (Mussolini)
Public Ownership	**Decentralized Socialism** Yugoslavia Romania Czechoslovakia (before 1968) China (Deng Xiaoping)	**Communism** USSR East Germany (today) Czechoslovakia (after 1968) China (Mao Tse-tung)

However, whether resources are privately or publicly owned is not rigidly determined by whether decisions are made in centralized or decentralized fashion. Table 4 summarizes the four basic types of economic systems and lists some countries where each system has dominated.

In the early 1960's, the Soviet Union began an erratic drive to rely less on centralized decision making. China began decentralizing decisions early in the 1980s. Coupled with increasing government controls over economic activity in the United States during the past six decades, it appears that "we" are becoming somewhat more like "them" and "they" are becoming somewhat more like "us." Only the future can reveal whether this trend will continue, although staunch old Soviet bureaucrats and some American politicians try to accentuate our differences. The suppression of the Solidarity union in Poland is one symptom of the Soviet bloc's move back towards greater centralization, while President Reagan has been among the American leaders calling for greater reliance on decentralized capitalism.

Foundations of Capitalism

Capitalism is not like it used to be, and never was.
—Anonymous

Capitalism and its ideological foundations are only a few centuries old, although its roots go back to the dawn of history when primitive people first began staking claims to territory. The hallmarks of "pure" **capitalism** are the institution of private property and laissez-faire policies by government.

Private Property Rights It is common to refer to something as being "owned" by someone. You probably own textbooks, sports equipment, perhaps a car, and so on. Exactly what does your ownership mean? Generally it means that you have certain rights to use these things in certain ways. **Fee-simple property rights** are the broadest of **private property rights,** and include rights to: (*a*) use a good as you choose as long as no one else's rights are violated; (*b*) trade or give these rights to other people; and (*c*) deny use of the good to others.

Most property rights are much more limited than this, however. For example, you cannot shoot people or dogs for trespassing on your land, or burn rubbish in smog-filled cities. You cannot use leaded gas in most new cars. You cannot raise pigs in New York City (or Des Moines, Iowa, for that matter). You cannot abuse your children, burn your house for the insurance money . . . the list goes on and on. The point is that most property rights are circumscribed.

How does a person acquire rights to property? John Locke, a seventeenth-century English philosopher, offered the labor theory of value to justify natural property rights. The *labor theory of value* assumes that all value is created by human labor. According to Locke, mixing your labor with "gifts of nature" makes land and the crops it produces valuable. Thus, he viewed improvements to natural resources as the ethical cornerstones of original property rights, which could then be legally transferred to others.

This view of labor as the basis for property rights raises several moral and practical problems, however. If you are the first to pour a pint of blood into the sea, should the oceans and all their riches be yours? Should those who encounter "gifts of nature" have property rights on a first-come, first-served basis? And what about rules for transferring property? Who should have property rights to things produced by employees? . . . by slaves? Should you own a piece of land, not because of anything you have done, but because you inherited it from your parents who inherited it from their parents who bought it from the family who cleared the land? What if the family who cleared it murdered the previous owner? Should property rights be a matter of convention, so that property rights become ever stronger over time, regardless of whether a transfer of property long ago was legal or illicit? Difficulties posed by these and similar questions for Locke's "natural rights" theory suggest that we need a more practical view of the foundations of property rights.

Property rights might be based on brute force. Whatever is yours is yours only if you have the muscle to enforce your claims. This system would be both violent and brutal. Moreover, many resources would be devoted to aggressively protecting your rights and trying to take from others. Because of this inefficiency, we surrender to government the right to be violent, giving it a near-monopoly on the use of force. Most legal scholars would argue that your property rights are determined by law—what the law says is yours is yours; neither more nor less. Society can be viewed as specifying sets of rights by law and then redefining rights through changes in statutes or legal opinions.

Most of us think of property rights only with respect to tangible goods. Property rights and most legal rights, however, are almost synonymous to many economists. For example, traffic laws define how we may use our cars; zoning ordinances, how we may use our land and buildings; and criminal laws, how we must treat our neighbors. We place ourselves in legal jeopardy if we abuse any of them. You do not have the right to slander your neighbor, litter, or shout "FIRE" in a crowded theater. All laws establish boundaries governing our uses both of our own and our neighbors' property. Laws can be viewed as setting the framework of property rights within which we deal with others, where the concept of property rights is defined very broadly. Naturally, changes in rights occur whenever there are changes in laws. And just as laws create property rights, they

can take them away. For example, before 1974, you could go 70 miles an hour on most freeways. After 1974, your rights were restricted to 55 miles an hour. Some legal rights of drivers were withdrawn.

Thus, the major role of government in a capitalist economy is to establish a system of laws prescribing rules that govern who owns what and how ownership rights can be transferred. The property rights government creates it can also change—tariffs, entitlement programs, and similar laws help determine who gets what. Beyond this, pure capitalism requires very little of government except reasonable consistency. Frequent legal changes, even those that seem trivial, may create uncertainty and discourage production and investment.

The major challenger of capitalism is **socialism,** which holds that productive resources should not be privately owned, but instead should be owned jointly by all people in society. The differences between capitalism and socialism also tend to be very pronounced when we try to specify appropriate roles for government.

Laissez-Faire Policies

That government is best which governs least.
—*Thomas Jefferson*

Feudal monarchs ruled by "divine right," claiming they were chosen by God to lead their countries. Even so, their policies often failed. Vexed by the economic plight of seventeenth-century France, Louis XIV's finance minister asked for advice from a leading industrialist. Without hesitation, the manufacturer responded, *"Laissez-nous faire,"* roughly, "Leave us alone." **Laissez-faire** has ever since been a rallying cry for those who believe that the market system works best with only minimal government.

But what specific roles should government play? Nearly everyone recognizes needs for national defense and police protection. In the economic sphere, a laissez-faire government only specifies property rights and enforces contracts. Under pure capitalism, private individuals own virtually all resources and decide their uses. Market prices determine the range of choices available to us, given our budgets, which are in turn determined by the resources we individually own. Most socialist economies replace the marketplace with government coordination, or **central planning.**

Private property and laissez-faire policies distinguish capitalism from alternative economic systems. Ideological battles between advocates of capitalism and socialism have raged for centuries. Capitalism's defenders cite numerous virtues of the price system, but the two most important are freedom and efficiency. Capitalism, it is argued, allows individuals the greatest possible freedom because it requires only minimal government. A tradition predating the American Revolution views all "Big Brother" governments as enemies of freedom.

All societies have elements of both capitalism and socialism, so people everywhere live in **mixed economies.** Thus, in the Soviet economy, almost all fruits, vegetables, and meats are produced for capitalistic *kolkhoz* markets. These private markets tend to be efficient relative to other aspects of the Soviet economy. In the United States, socialism appears in the form of government-provided education, highways, and medical care for the aged or poor.

Many aspects of American government represent political attempts to achieve what some people perceive as greater equity. Where efficiency is our major goal, we tend to rely on the marketplace. The efficiency of capitalism depends on how well it meets consumer wants, given the resources available. In the next chapter, we examine the forces of supply and demand, which are the devices determining *What? How? Who?* and *When?* in a market system.

CHAPTER REVIEW: KEY POINTS

1. Every economic system must answer four *basic economic questions:* (*a*) *What* economic goods will be produced? (*b*) *How* will productive resources be used? (*c*) *Who* will get the production? (*d*) *When* will production and consumption occur?

2. A *production-possibilities frontier (PPF)* shows the maximum combinations of goods that an economy can produce. The *PPF* curve assumes that (*a*) resources are fixed, (*b*) technology is constant, and (*c*) all scarce resources are fully and efficiently employed.

3. Opportunity costs are the values of outputs if resources were switched to their best alternative uses. Opportunity costs are not constant because resources are not equally suited for all types of production. Increasing a particular form of production invariably leads to *diminishing returns* and increasing opportunity costs, so the production-possibilities curve is concave (bowed away) from its origin.

4. *Economic growth* occurs when there are advances in technology or when the amounts of resources available for production increase. Economic growth can be shown as an outward shift of the production-possibilities curve; more of all goods can be produced.

5. When technology advances for one good in a production-possibilities model, most of the curve will shift outward and to the right; fewer resources are needed to produce that good and thus are available for producing other goods.

6. The choices a society makes between consumption and investment goods affect its future production-possibilities curve. Lower saving and investment restricts economic growth and *PPF* expansion.

7. Alternative *allocative mechanisms* include: (*a*) the *market system,* (*b*) *brute force,* (*c*) *queuing,* (*d*) *random selection,* (*e*) *tradition,* and (*f*) *government.*

8. Many different economic systems are used in attempts to resolve the problem of scarcity. They can be classified by who makes the decisions (*centralized* or *decentralized*) and who owns the resources (*public* versus *private*).

9. Property is privately owned under pure *capitalism* and government follows *laissez-faire* (hands off) policies. Thus, decisions are decentralized and rely on individual choices in a market system. Under *socialism,* government acts as a trustee over the nonhuman resources jointly owned by all citizens, with many socialist economies also relying heavily on centralized production and distribution decisions.

QUESTIONS FOR THOUGHT AND DISCUSSION

1. What is the mix of allocative mechanisms used within most American families to decide which family members get what, given limited family income? How are different mechanisms used for different kinds of decisions?

2. One way to illustrate that an economic arrangement is inefficient is to show how, through some rearrangement, some people could gain with no one else losing. Use this approach to evaluate the following situations:

   a. *Brute force.* The Soviet Union and the United States each devote valuable resources to national defense because each side fears attack by the other.

   b. *Queuing.* A $100-per-hour lawyer is at the end of a 2-hour waiting line to renew driving licenses, and a vacationing college student is at the front of the line.

   c. *Random selection.* A rock star who makes $10+ million annually is drafted, while an unemployed 18-year-old high-school drop-out who would be willing to join the Army for a $9,000 salary is not drafted and does not enlist because the pay is only $7,000 annually.

   d. *Tradition.* Quota systems once limited the numbers of women, Jews, blacks, and Hispanic Americans admitted to medical school.

   e. *Government.* Procurement procedures sometimes require that imported goods be used to fulfill government contracts only if American-made goods are not available.

3. Use the concept of the opportunity cost of time to explain why our welfare system involves long queues for those who seek food stamps, housing allowances, or aid for dependent children.

4. Suppose that government could perfectly control the rate of interest, the rate of inflation, the level of taxes, and the relative levels of wages and prices. How could the government foster economic growth through low consumer spending and more saving and investment via each of these tools?

5. Evaluate the following argument: Grades and athletic medals should be allocated through a market system. The buyers would be the people who value such awards the most, so this would be more efficient than awarding according to merit. For example, if a C student could buy an A from a more diligent student, both could gain from the exchange without harming anyone else in the process.

CHAPTER 3 — Demand and Supply

supply and demand	*principle of diminishing marginal utility*	*equilibrium price and quantity*
absolute vs. relative prices	*demand curves and supply curves*	*market equilibrium*
demand prices vs. supply prices	*normal and inferior goods*	*surpluses and shortages*
laws of demand and supply	*substitutes vs. complementary goods*	
income and substitution effects		

Supply and demand analysis is as basic to an economist's toolbox as saws and hammers are to a carpenter's. Models of supply and demand yield profound insights into why prices are what they are, and why prices or sales of goods move in particular directions. Your objective in this chapter is a tall order that requires only a short sentence: Learn how demand and supply interact in markets to determine prices and outputs. We first discuss markets and prices a bit, then look at some fundamentals of demand and supply, and finally, show how these two concepts are linked in markets. After you have worked through this chapter and the next, you should be able to use supply and demand to interpret output and price changes in markets for oil, gold, food, home computers, air fares, and many other goods.

✈ Markets and Prices

Markets enable buyers and sellers to transact business, and range from commodity exchanges where millions of bushels of grain change hands in thousands of daily transactions to markets where one huge contract may require years to complete (construction projects). Markets range from geographically limited (children's lemonade stands) to global (international markets for petroleum engineers). Some deal in a single type of good (brickyards), while others offer thousands of products (shopping centers). Every market is somewhat unique, but all share certain characteristics: (*a*) buyers who demand goods or the resources that produce them and (*b*) suppliers who will make products or resources available if the price is right.

It is important to distinguish the relative price of a good from its monetary or **absolute price.** Whether we use francs, pesos, inflated dimes, or solid gold dollars to measure absolute prices is largely irrelevant for the market decisions of buyers and sellers. The **relative prices** of goods or resources are their prices in terms of one another, and so reflect opportunity costs and guide our market decisions. How many sundaes must you sacrifice for a new record album? For a ski vacation to Aspen?

You can compute relative prices by dividing the absolute prices of goods by one another. If hot fudge sundaes are $1, while records are $7 and all-expense-paid ski vacations are $280, then a record costs 7 sundaes and a vacation costs 280 sundaes or 40 records. (7/1 = 7; 280/1 = 280; 280/7 = 40. To test your understanding, compute the relative prices of sundaes and records in terms of vacations.)

Suppose there were a one-time-only, fixed proportional increase in all absolute prices. Relative prices would not change, nor would the decisions of rational people. A mental experiment should prove our point: What would you do if your income and the prices of all your assets and liabilities, as well as the prices of all goods and resources, increased once and for all by half? Answer: You would handle 50 percent more dollars, but otherwise your behavior should not change. Reflect on this for a moment. *Conclusion:* Relative prices are important for *micro*economic decisions; absolute prices are not important for most decisions about the goods we buy in the marketplace or the resources we supply.

We do need to qualify this result somewhat because inflationary changes in absolute prices are unimportant only if relative prices and the distribution of income remain unchanged. Unfortunately, inflation always disrupts both of these, distorting economic activity and creating uncertainty, and so it is a major concern for *macro*economic policymakers. In the following discussion, however, our references are to relative, not absolute, prices.

✗ Demand

Economists view your buying a good as casting a vote with money. "Dollar votes" are signals that guide business decisions about how to profitably satisfy consumer wants. Items with the highest prices relative to their production costs earn the greatest profits. Firms compete to provide these items so that the needs consumers perceive as most pressing tend to receive top priority.

You may wonder whether our "needs" can be met with available resources. A real problem arises if we focus on what many view as "necessities." Most suburbanites find a car a "necessity," and many of us go through withdrawal symptoms when deprived of television for only a day or two. And in a wealthy society like ours, even much of the food we eat is recreational and unnecessary.

What is truly needed for survival? Two thousand or so calories daily, some vitamins and minerals, and shelter and sufficient clothing to prevent sunstroke or frostbite. What do absolute necessities cost? Well, you can get by on soybean curd and vitamin pills, a shack made of discarded cardboard, and a few clothes from Goodwill Industries. Life could be sustained for $1,000 a year, although most of us would view anyone trying to live on that little as still needy.

Economists concentrate on consumer demands because "needs" is a very normative and ambiguous concept. **Demands** are the quantities of various goods that people are willing and able to buy during some period, given the choices available to them. Consider a typical consumption choice.

Many of us attend concerts, listen to tapes or records, and watch television. These different forms of entertainment have varying prices, with the price of viewing TV being approximately $0, and rock concert tickets ranging from $6 to $100 apiece. (For now, we will ignore pay TV and the value of your time.) If we rank these activities from the cheapest to the most expensive, you probably spend the most time watching TV and the least going to concerts, with listening to a stereo falling somewhere in between. Even though different people choose different combinations, this example suggests that there is a negative relationship between the price of a good and the quantity that consumers purchase.

Consumer decisions are based on two sets of relative prices—market prices and demand prices. **Market prices** are the prices sellers charge for goods whether we buy or not; **demand prices** are the relative values that individuals *subjectively* place on having a bit more or less of a good. You buy chewing gum or pizzas only when they are subjectively worth more to you than their market prices.

Our budgets help determine whether or not our demand prices are aligned with market prices. Rolls-Royces are worth their market price to those who buy them. The demand prices at which many of us would purchase a new Rolls-Royce are far below the market price. Thus, Rolls-Royces are not subjectively "worth the price" to us, given our budgets, and we drive cheaper cars, if we drive at all.

The Law of Demand and Substitution

The basic principle of the theory of consumer choice is the law of demand.

> The **law of demand:** *All else assumed equal, consumers purchase more of a good during a given time interval the lower its opportunity cost* (relative price), *and vice versa.*[1]

This relationship occurs primarily because as the relative price of a good falls, you will find it advantageous to substitute it for others where possible. Conversely, when a good becomes more expensive, you find substitutes for it. This is known as the **substitution effect** of a change in relative prices.

Most goods have many possible uses. Substituting a good into more uses the lower its price is advantageous. For example, caviar is now a delicacy, but if its price fell to $0.50 per pound, it might replace bologna on sandwiches for children's school lunches. If it were free, we might use caviar for dog food, hog slop, or fertilizer. If diamonds were as cheap as gravel, we would use them as a base material for highways. On the other hand, if gasoline cost $10 a gallon, cities would be more compact and we would rely far more on bicycles, walking, or public transit; few people would waste gasoline on meandering pleasure trips or hit-and-run shopping. If peanut butter were $50 per pound, gourmets might consider it a delicacy to be savored on fancy crackers at posh parties. The critical point is that people substitute for goods that become relatively more costly and find wider uses for goods that become cheaper.

---

1. Note that all influences on consumption of the good other than price are held constant! Throughout economic analysis, this "all else assumed equal" methodology is used so that we can examine, one at a time, the variables that affect human behavior. The Latin term *ceteris paribus* is used by many economists to refer to the idea that "all other influences" on some *dependent* variable are held constant while examining the effect of changing a single *independent* variable. Thus, the law of demand deals with the independent influence of price on the quantity demanded (the dependent variable), *ceteris paribus.*

Focus 1 indicates how people's uses of water change as its price varies.

Substitution occurs for several reasons, including a facet of the law of diminishing returns known as the **principle of diminishing marginal utility** (satisfaction): *The more you have of any good relative to others, the less you desire and are willing to pay for additional units of that good.* For example, it is unlikely that you would value a ninth chocolate chip ice-cream cone as much as the first you ate on a given day. The same principle holds true for hair transplants, rides in hot air balloons, or any other good.

A second reason that purchases of a good rise when its price falls is that the purchasing power of your limited income increases, and you can buy more of the good while maintaining or even increasing your other purchases. This is known as the **income effect** of a price change, but it is far less important than the substitution effect.

The Demand Curve

The negative relationship between the price of any good and the quantity consumed asserted by the law of demand generates a negatively sloped **demand curve** that, all else assumed equal, depicts *the maximum quantities of a good that given individuals will purchase at various prices during a given period.* An alternative perspective yielding different insights but identical demand curves views them as showing the maximum price that people are willing to pay for an additional unit of a good, given their current consumption.

Figure 2 uses Arlene's demand for paperback novels to illustrate the law of demand; lower market prices make her willing and able to buy more books. When novels are $3.75 apiece, Arlene purchases 10 annually; at $1.75 each, she buys 30. But if the price rises to $4.75, she purchases none, possibly watching more TV or renewing her public library card instead.

Suppose that Arlene currently buys 14 books at $3.30 apiece. Her demand price (the subjectively determined maximum she would pay) for a fifteenth book is $3.25 (point *a.*) Figure 2 also includes Arlene's demand schedule. A **demand schedule** is a table listing the maximum quantities of a good that will be purchased by a consumer at various prices during some period, and summarizes points on a demand curve.

Substitution and the Uses of Water as its Price Changes

The extent of substitution when prices change depends on the options available. If a good has close relatives (cotton and wool are examples), we may switch from one product to another with little inconvenience as their relative prices change. In other situations, substitution is difficult and entails a loss of efficiency or quality (replacing light bulbs with candles, for instance). In extreme cases, adjusting to higher prices may require that we simply do without.

Figure 1 shows how our uses of water might be influenced by different prices. If water were incredibly scarce and costly because you were stranded in the desert, you might sip only a little to avoid feeling parched and trust your camel to make it to the next oasis without a drink. Once there, the subjective value of water decreases and you would find ever broader uses for water—brushing your teeth, washing, and so on. You will see water flowing down streets when people water their lawns only when the price of water is incredibly low.

FIGURE 1 *How the Use of Water Typically Expands as the Price Falls*

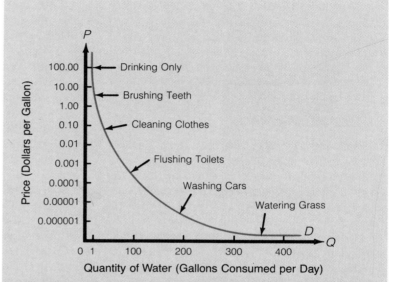

When water is quite scarce and costly, people will use it sparingly, confining its uses to those most necessary. As the price falls, more and more uses are considered economical.

Market Demand Curves

Individual demand curves are interesting from a theoretical standpoint, but market demand curves are far more important both practically and for most analytical purposes. How are these curves related? Market demand is simply the sum of all individual demands.

Figure 3 depicts the demand curves of Arlene and Bert, and the market demand curve if they alone bought paperbacks. Below each demand curve is a corresponding demand schedule. *Horizontal summation* of the individual demand curves of all potential buyers yields a **market demand curve.** This means that we sum the quantities per period that individuals buy at each price. At a price of $3.75,

FIGURE 2 *An Individual's Demand Curve for Paperback Books*

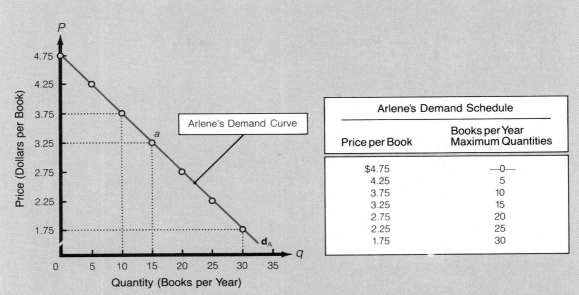

Arlene's Demand Schedule	
Price per Book	Books per Year Maximum Quantities
$4.75	—0—
4.25	5
3.75	10
3.25	15
2.75	20
2.25	25
1.75	30

Arlene's demand for paperback books can be shown as a demand curve or schedule. Demand reflects the willingness of an individual to purchase various quantities of a commodity at various prices. The demand curve is negatively sloped, reflecting the *law of demand*—at lower prices individuals will purchase larger quantities of a particular product. In this instance, more paperback books will be purchased at lower prices per book.

Arlene buys 10 paperbacks annually while Bert buys none. Thus, at $3.75, the quantity demanded in this market is 10 books (10 + 0). At $2.25, Arlene purchases 25 books and Bert buys 15, so the quantity demanded is 40 (25 + 15), and so on.

This seems a simple procedure, but estimating actual market demand curves requires sophisticated statistical techniques that lie beyond the scope of this book. Many professional economists spend much of their time estimating market demands for particular goods.

Other Influences on Demand

Demand curves reflect relationships between the prices and quantities of goods bought during a given period, but prices alone do not determine our purchases. Other influences generally fall into one of six categories: (*a*) tastes and preferences; (*b*) income;

(*c*) prices of related goods; (*d*) numbers of buyers; (*e*) expectations about future prices, incomes, and availability; and (*f*) government taxes, subsidies, and regulations.

Tastes and Preferences People's preferences for goods vary because of styling, quality, personal idiosyncracies, or status characteristics (whether or not our friends or neighbors have them). Cars, clothes, music, and numerous other products are subject to consumers' whims. "Knockoffs" of the latest fashions and the numerous clones of hit TV shows and *Cabbage Patch Kids* are evidence that business reacts quickly to changes in consumer tastes. If everyone abandoned rock-and-roll for country music, how long do you think it would take for top-40 disk jockeys to cultivate drawls and twangs while announcing the songs of Ricky Scaggs and Dolly Parton?

Demands obviously depend on consumer tastes and preferences, but measuring these precisely is

FIGURE 3 *Individual and Market Demand Curves for Paperbacks*

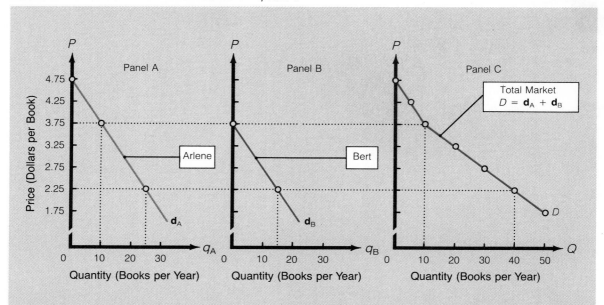

Demand Schedule Arlene		+	Demand Schedule Bert		=	Demand Schedule Total Market	
Price	Quantity (q_A)		Price	Quantity (q_B)		Price	Quantity (Q)
$4.75	—0—		$4.75	—0—		$4.75	—0—
4.25	5		4.25	—0—		4.25	5
3.75	10		3.75	—0—		3.75	10
3.25	15		3.25	5		3.25	20
2.75	20		2.75	10		2.75	30
2.25	25		2.25	15		2.25	40
1.75	30		1.75	20		1.75	50

The market demand curve can be derived from a series of individual demands by horizontally summing the individual demand curves. That is, for each price, we add the quantities that each individual will purchase. At a price of $2.25, Arlene is willing to purchase 25 books, while Bert demands 15 books. Thus the quantity demanded in the market at a price of $2.25 is 40 books. To obtain market demand, this process is followed for each price.

almost as impossible as predicting the next fad. You should, however, be able to evaluate whether a given change in preferences will raise or lower demand. For example, if the 1988 Olympics popularized judo as a way for people to stay in shape, what would happen to the demand for gym mats and judo lessons?

Income and Its Distribution   Income also influences consumer demands. As your income rises, your demands for higher quality goods will tend to rise markedly. Products for which demand is positively related to income are called **normal goods.** Vacations, live entertainment, and most other products and services are normal goods. Normal goods include such luxuries as fur coats, jewelry, and limousines. Demands for luxuries are especially responsive to changes in income.

On the other hand, when a poor family's income rises, its demands for such **inferior goods** as lye soap and pinto beans falls. Clunker cars and peanut butter sandwiches may be inferior goods. When students graduate and get "real" jobs, their incomes jump and their consumption of these inferior goods typically falls. All else equal, it follows that income redistribution alters the structure of demands: Taking from the rich to provide welfare for the poor causes declines in demands for both inferior goods and luxuries, whereas rising inequality stimulates the demands for both.

Prices of Related Goods

The price of a good is important, but prices of related products also influence demand. Most goods are at least mild *substitutes* for one another. For example, if golf balls climbed to $5 each, you would golf less frequently, but your consumption of such **substitute goods** as tennis balls and racquets might rise. This would be especially true for duffers who drop at least one golf ball in every water hazard. When coffee prices soared in the 1970s, sales of tea bags also zoomed. Like tennis and golf, tea and coffee are *close* substitutes. Other examples include chicken and pizza; phone calls and letters; Datsun 300Zs and Porsches; or hot tubs, Jacuzzis, and saunas.

Cars, tires, and gasoline are examples of **complementary goods;** they are consumed together. Other sets of *complements* are tuition and textbooks; steak and A-1 sauce; computers and diskettes; or left shoes and right shoes. As the prices of complementary goods rise, the demand for the good in question falls, and vice versa.

Numbers and Ages of Buyers

Population growth raises the number of potential buyers and, hence, market demands for most products. The age structure of the consuming public is also a factor. Expanding average life spans have increased the demands for retirement communities and related products such as medical services. Demands for baby products slumped when birth rates fell in the 1960s, but producers of diapers and formula recovered somewhat when many "baby boomers" belatedly began their families.

Expectations about Prices, Incomes, or Availability

Consumers who expect shortages or sharp price hikes in the coming weeks or months may rush out and buy storable products now, thus boosting current demands. Buying sprees were widespread at the onset of the Korean War. Americans had been subjected to shortages, rising prices, and rationing during World War II, and many expected similar problems during the Korean War. Sugar, flour, appliances, tires, and autos were among the many goods people tried to stockpile because of wartime memories. This created shortages and drove up prices. Today, many consumers react to news that a killing frost threatens Florida's citrus crop by hoarding frozen orange juice concentrate.

Buying binges may also occur if people expect their income to rise substantially in the near future. You might buy a car on credit after accepting a job but before you have even received your first paycheck. Many people fall deeply in debt because they spend income before they make it.

Expectations about government actions also reshape buying patterns. A Food and Drug Administration proposal to ban saccharine in 1977 because it was suspected as a cause of cancer resulted in shoppers stripping grocers' shelves. These consumers worried more about the health hazards of "fat attacks" than about greater risks from cancer.

Taxes and Subsidies

Until now, we have focused on ways that the behavior of private individuals causes shifts in demand. But taxes, subsidies, and regulations may also strongly influence demand. From the buyer's perspective, demand is a relationship between the quantity bought and the price *paid.* Sellers, on the other hand, view demand as the relationship between the quantity sold and the price *received.* These approaches normally yield the same results, but taxes or subsidies can drive a wedge between the demand price that buyers are willing to pay and the price the seller receives. Figure 4 illustrates this.

Suppose the government imposes a tax of $1 per paperback novel. Buyers perceive no change in their willingness to purchase, so they view their demand for paperback books as being stable at D_0. They are still willing to buy 200 million books annually at a demand price of $3.75. However, publishers view demand as having declined to D_2 because the after-

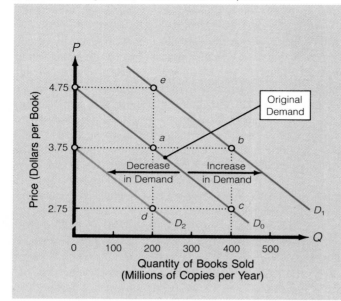

FIGURE 4 *Changes in the Market Demand for Paperback Books*

A change in demand means a shift in the demand curve. A shift to the right (D_0 to D_1) represents an increase in demand, while a shift to the left (D_0 to D_2) is a decrease in demand. These shifts result from changes in factors other than the product price itself.

tax prices they receive are reduced by $1 for each novel sold. They would receive only $2.75 per book if they priced books so that 200 million were bought.

Now suppose the government offered a $1 per book subsidy to encourage national literacy. Buyers would view their demand curves as remaining at D_0, but from the vantage points of publishers, demand would rise to D_1. They would receive $1 more per paperback at every level of output. Regulation may either dampen demand, as it does for narcotics and other illicit activities, or bolster demand, as the effect of compulsory education on the demand for grade school textbooks demonstrates.

To summarize, the demand for a good increases if: (*a*) consumer tastes and preferences change so that people are more inclined to buy it; (*b*) consumer incomes rise (*fall*) in the case of a normal (*inferior*) good; (*c*) the price of a substitute (*complementary*) good rises (*falls*); (*d*) the number of consumers increases; (*e*) consumers anticipate higher prices or incomes, or expect shortages of the good; or (*f*) favorable regulation is adopted, or taxes are reduced, or government subsidizes the good. Decreases in demand would result if the changes were reversed for these influences on demand.

Changes in Demand

A demand curve shows the negative relationship between the price and quantity of a good demanded during a given interval, holding all other influences constant. But what happens if influences on demand other than the price of the good change?

Tastes and preferences may be reshaped by a firm's marketing strategy. Publishers often mail novels to reviewers gratis, hoping to promote a bestseller. When male beer drinkers worried about their weight but viewed light beers as tasteless and unmacho, one brewer's advertising featured retired jocks debating whether the beer was "less filling" or "tastes great." And the suds flowed and flowed.

Another marketing technique is to tie products to each other. Producers of kids' lunch boxes, underwear, and toys regularly mirror the latest crazes, from *Masters of the Universe* to *Transformers*. Firms commonly link new films and books in their advertising, trying to boost both book and box-office receipts. Figure 4 shows how increased promotion can shift a demand curve to the right (from D_0 to D_1) so that more books are demanded at every price.

If paperbacks are normal goods, demand will increase if income rises. Beginning on D_0 in Figure 4, boosts in income cause consumers to purchase more paperbacks at every price, moving demand to D_1. On the other hand, a drop in income normally causes demand to fall (a shift of the demand curve toward the origin—from D_0 to D_2). Naturally, such effects are reversed if novels are inferior goods.

Now consider changes in the availability or prices of related products. The advent of cable TV, for example, broadens the range of available programs, and some readers might become TV addicts, shrinking the demand for books (again in Figure 4, from D_0 to D_2). Or if libraries began offering home delivery or if ticket prices for movies fell, substitution could cause consumer demands for books to fall. Take a moment to think of examples of how demand would shift if there were changes in the number of buyers or in consumers' expectations.

Thus, *a change in demand means a shift in the demand curve.* Declines in demand cause shifts to the left, while rightward shifts show increases in demand. These shifts result from changes in: tastes and preferences, incomes, related prices, numbers of consumers, expectations, or government policies. Although consumers may perceive no changes in their demands with the imposition of taxes or subsidies, sellers will. Demand increases when consumers become willing to purchase more of a good at every price, or to pay a higher demand price for a given quantity of the good, and vice versa. These relationships are summarized in Figure 5.

Changes in Quantity Demanded Versus Changes in Demand

Distinguishing between **changes in demand** and **changes in quantities demanded** is crucial. Changes in the quantities of a good demanded are *movements along a given demand curve* and are

FIGURE 5 *Factors Causing Shifts in Demand*

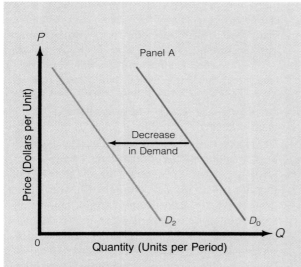

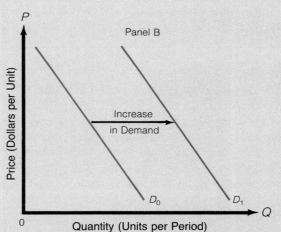

A decrease in demand results when

1. a negative change in tastes or preferences occurs.
2. (a) income declines, for normal goods.
   (b) income rises, for inferior goods.
3. the price of a complement increases.
4. the price of a substitute decreases.
5. the number of buyers decreases.
6. income or price expectations decrease.
7. expected surpluses or expectations of greater product availability occur.
8. the government reduces subsidies or increases taxes.

An increase in demand results when

1. a positive change in tastes or preferences occurs.
2. (a) income increases, for normal goods.
   (b) income declines, for inferior goods.
3. the price of a complement decreases.
4. the price of a substitute increases.
5. the number of buyers increases.
6. income or price expectations increase.
7. expected shortages or expectations of decreased product availability occur.
8. the government increases subsidies or reduces taxes.

caused by one thing and one thing only—a change in its price. Changes in demand, on the other hand, involve *shifts* of demand curves.

A review of these differences using Figure 4 will help you avoid errors on this point. Suppose 200 million books are currently sold annually at a price of $3.75. How might sales be raised to 400 million paperbacks? One way is for the demand curve to grow from D_0 to D_1, so that 400 million would be bought at $3.75 (point *b*). Alternatively, 400 million copies would be sold annually if the price were cut to $2.75 (point *c*). Increased income is only one of many ways to increase *demand* (to point *b*), while simply reducing price yields an equivalent increase, but in *quantity demanded* (point *c*).

Similar differences apply to decreases in demand versus a decrease in quantity demanded. A shift in the entire demand curve in Figure 4 from D_0 to D_2 represents a decrease in demand. Given demand curve D_0, an increase in price from $2.75 (point *c*) to $3.75 (point *a*) reduces the quantity demanded from 400 to 200 million books. Knowing the differences between changes in demand and changes in the quantity demanded will spare you a lot of grief in the coming chapters.

Supply

You cannot learn much about prices and the amounts of goods traded from demand curves alone; you need supply curves as well. **Supply** refers to the outputs that sellers provide under various conditions during a given period. One critical condition is that producers must expect to gain by selling their outputs or else they will refuse to incur production costs. This section focuses on several influences on firms' decisions to produce and sell.

The Law of Supply

Producers' decisions about the amounts of output to sell hinge on the law of supply.

> The **law of supply**: *All else assumed equal, higher prices induce greater production and sales of output; firms provide less during a given period at lower prices.*

One reason is that higher prices provide greater production incentives. More importantly, attempts to expand output cause diminishing returns and increasing costs to be encountered, and only higher prices can maintain the incentives that lead suppliers to produce and sell their goods.

The Supply Curve

Just as the law of demand yields *negatively sloped* demand curves, the law of supply generates *positively sloped* supply curves. A **supply curve** shows *the maximum amounts of a good that firms are willing to furnish during a given time period at various prices*. A different perspective views the same supply curve as showing the minimum prices that will induce specific quantities supplied.

The positive slopes of supply curves reflect eventual increases in costs per unit when output grows because firms: (*a*) ultimately encounter diminishing returns; (*b*) may be forced to pay current workers overtime wages for extra hours; or (*c*) successfully attract more labor or other resources only by paying more for them. Working closer to capacity also causes more scheduling errors and equipment breakdowns. Such problems raise costs when firms increase output.

A typical supply curve and schedule are shown in Figure 6. Dell will produce and sell 40 million paperbacks annually at $4.25, but only 10 million books if the price falls to $2.75. A **supply price** is the minimum price that will induce a seller to increase production beyond its current level. For example, if Dell were selling 9 million books annually at a price of $2.70, the market price would have to grow to Dell's supply price of $2.75 (point *a*) before production would be expanded to 10 million books annually.

Paralleling demands, market supplies are more interesting than individual supplies. And just as market demands are the horizontal summation of individual demands, computing **market supply curves** requires *horizontally* summing individual firms' supply curves, as shown in Figure 7, which assumes the paperback market to contain only two firms, Dell and Bantam. At a $2.75 price, Dell will produce and sell 10 million books, and Bantam, 15 million, making the annual quantity supplied 25 million books, and so on. The law of supply asserts that quantities supplied per period are positively related to prices; as the price of a good rises, the quantity supplied grows.

FIGURE 6 *Supply Curve of Paperback Books for Dell Publishing Co., Inc.*

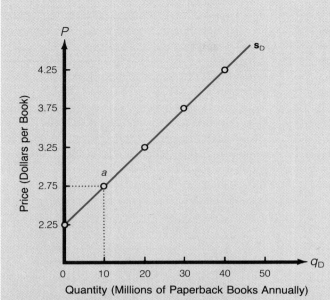

The supply curve and schedule represent the maximum amounts of a commodity firms are willing to produce and sell during a given period at different prices. The supply curve depicted reflects the *law of supply*—at higher prices, more of the commodity will be offered to the market.

Supply Schedule Dell Publishing Co. Inc.	
Price	Quantity (Millions)
$4.25	40
3.75	30
3.25	20
2.75	10
2.25	—0—

Other Influences on Supply

Just as there are a number of influences on demand, a number of influences other than the price of the good affect market supply. Thus, a supply curve shows the positive relationship between price and quantity supplied per period, holding constant: (*a*) production technology; (*b*) resource costs; (*c*) prices of other producible goods; (*d*) expectations; (*e*) the number of sellers (producers) in the market; and (*f*) taxes, subsidies, and government regulations. Changes in any of these influences can shift the short-run supply curve.

Changes in Supply

Shifts in the supply curve outward and to the right show increases in supply, while movements upward and to the left reflect decreases in supply, as shown in Figure 8. Along S_0, the original supply curve, 50 million paperbacks are supplied at $3.25 per book. If supply grows to S_1, 80 million books are supplied at the same price. If supply falls to S_2, only 30 million books will be offered at $3.25 each. Thus, an increase in supply means that more of the good is offered for sale at every market price; the supply prices required to induce various levels of output fall. On the other hand, decreases in supply cause supply prices (the minimum required per unit to induce extra production) to rise.

Caution: Supply curve movements may seem confusing because the shift from S_0 to S_1 is vertically downward even though supply is increasing. You should always think of horizontal movements *away* from the price axis as increases, and shifts *towards* the price axis as decreases. This rule also works for shifts of demand curves. Parallels between our development of supply and earlier discussions of demand may correctly have led you to expect that shifts in supply result from changes in one or more of the influences on supply.

Production Technology Technology is a broad term applied to the environment within which resources are transformed into outputs, and it is a major determinant of production costs. It includes such influences on production as the state of knowledge and such natural phenomena as physical laws (e.g., gravity) and weather.

Costs fall and supply grows when technology advances. Consider the revolution in markets for calculators and computers. Desktop calculators were $400 to $600 in the 1960s. New technology enabled cheap microchip processors to displace heavy mechanical calculators from the market, and computer capacity that once occupied huge rooms can now be carried in a briefcase. Supplies jumped dramatically and prices fell so that $10 hand-held calculators are now common, and home computers that are more powerful than most business computers of a few years ago are available for $200 and up.

There are occasions when technology regresses, however. Two examples of negative technological changes should shed light on how broad this term is: plagues of locusts or drought might cause agricultural production to plummet, or a nuclear war could blast production technology back to the Stone Age. Technology is very difficult to quantify, but you should be prepared to predict whether a given technological change will boost or inhibit supply.

FIGURE 7 *Individual Firm and Market Supply Curves for Paperback Books*

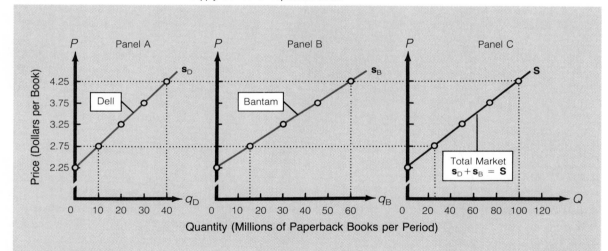

Supply Schedule Dell		+	Supply Schedule Bantam		=	Supply Schedule Total Market (Dell + Bantam)	
Price	Quantity (q_D) (Millions)		Price	Quantity (q_B) (Millions)		Price	Quantity (Q) (Millions)
$4.25	40		$4.25	60		$4.25	100
3.75	30		3.75	45		3.75	75
3.25	20		3.25	30		3.25	50
2.75	10		2.75	15		2.75	25
2.25	—0—		2.25	—0—		2.25	—0—

To obtain market supply, the supplies of 60 million individual producers are added horizontally. For example, at $4.25 per paperback, Dell will furnish 40 million and Bantam 60 million books. Thus, quantity supplied to the market at $4.25 per paperback is 100 million books. The same procedure is followed for all possible prices to obtain the market supply curve.

FIGURE 8   *Changes in the Supply of Paperback Books*

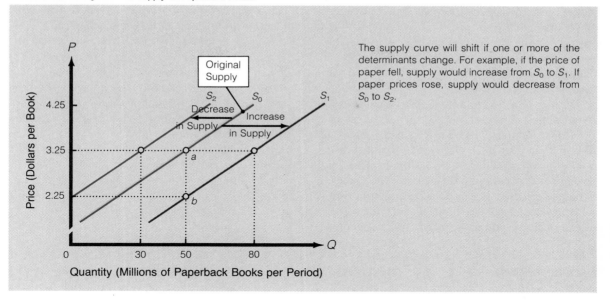

The supply curve will shift if one or more of the determinants change. For example, if the price of paper fell, supply would increase from S_0 to S_1. If paper prices rose, supply would decrease from S_0 to S_2.

Resource Costs   As resource costs rise, supply declines. Higher wages, rents, or interest rates raise production costs and squeeze business profits. Higher prices for raw or semifinished materials do the same. For example, higher prices for coal raise steel companies' costs. Firms have reduced incentives to produce, causing supply to shrink. Conversely, falling resource prices cause supply to increase. Thus, lower fertilizer prices cause agricultural production to expand.

Prices of Other Goods   Most firms have options to produce a variety of goods, so changes in the prices of potential products can influence the supply of the current good. Increases in the price of a good increase the quantity supplied of that good, but decrease the resources available to supply other products. Shirtmakers, for example, might substitute into sewing parachutes if skydiving became more popular and profits from making parachutes grew. The supply of shirts would fall. If the price of corn rose, soybean farmers might plant some of their acreage in corn, thus reducing the supply of soybeans. These are examples of goods that are *substitutes in production*. On the other hand, where one product is a by-product of another (beef and leather), an increase in the price of one often yields an increased supply of the other because they are *joint products*; production of one is complementary for production of the other.

Expectations of Producers   If a firm expects its output prices to rise in the near future, it may react by increasing production now. Then, because this producer would like larger inventories to sell when prices rise, it may temporarily cut back supplies if its product is easily stored.

These reductions occur regularly in agriculture as farmers attempt to time their sales to obtain the highest prices. For example, ranchers increased breeding but withheld cattle from the market in 1978, temporarily lowering the supply. This reduction in beef shipped to market actually raised 1978 prices, but prices fell by 1980 when these extra cattle were finally marketed. Short-term withholding of products from the market triggers higher prices that, in the longer term, generate larger supplies. Thus, the longer term effect of expectations of rising prices is that supplies of durable goods grow when swollen inventories are sold.

Firms may adjust very differently, however, if building up inventories is impossible. For example, if newspaper publishers thought that booming market conditions would soon justify a higher price, they could not store the news but would probably increase supply immediately, partially to justify expanding their capacity to print newspapers and partially to hook more customers into reading the publisher's paper each day.

Other expectations may influence production and sales as well. For example, a steel company may reduce current supplies and try to expand production and inventories if it foresees union workers going on strike. This will enable the firm to serve some of its customers during the strike. Generalizing about the effects of expectations on supply, however, is somewhat difficult because they vary with the form of expectations and the nature of products and technology.

Number of Sellers As the number of sellers in a particular market increases, the supply also increases (shifts to the right). The reason is straightforward: More producers generate more output.

Taxes, Subsidies, and Government Regulation Government policies affect supply as much as they influence demand. From the sellers' vantage point, supply is the relation between the prices *received* per unit and the numbers of units produced and sold. Buyers perceive supply as the relationship between the quantities available and the prices *paid*. Again, taxes or subsidies cause these prices to differ. In Figure 8, a subsidy to buyers of $1 per book yields no change in the original supply curve (S_0) from the perspective of sellers. But buyers would perceive an increase in supply from S_0 to S_1, which is the same as a price cut of $1 for every quantity purchased. For example, 50 million paperbacks could now be sold for a $2.25 retail price (point *b*).

The taxes and subsidies we have considered are elementary examples of the differences that government policies cause between sellers' and buyers' supply curves. These differences result from numerous taxes, subsidies, and regulatory policies. Regulations either increase or decrease supplies, depending on their effects on production costs. For example, regulations to control pollution often drive up costs and reduce supplies.

In sum, supply decisions are influenced by numerous factors other than the price of the product.

Specifically, the supply of any good will increase (the curve will shift to the right) if: (*a*) costs decline because resource prices fall or technology improves; (*b*) substitute goods that firms can produce decline in price, or the price of a by-product increases; (*c*) the number of suppliers increases. Expectations of higher prices normally cause lower supplies in the short term and higher supplies in a longer term if products can be inventoried, but generate uncertain results for less durable goods. Subsidies tend to expand supply from buyers' perspectives, while taxes tend to shrink supply.

Changes in Quantity Supplied Versus Changes in Supply

A **change in supply** occurs only when the supply curve shifts. A **change in the quantity supplied** (a movement along the curve) is caused by only one thing—a change in the price of the good in question. Again, the distinction is not trivial. Consider a change in the quantity supplied caused by a change in the market price. The supply curve stays constant because it is defined by the entire relationship between price and quantity. A change in supply (caused by a change in a nonprice determinant) shifts the supply curve because this price/quantity relationship is altered. Figure 9 summarizes the things that shift supply curves.

Demands, Supplies, and Time

Consumers demand certain amounts of shrimp dinners, surf boards, or bottles of perfume weekly, larger amounts monthly, and still larger amounts annually. A Pizza Hut that on average sells 827 pizzas per day is probably much more profitable than one selling 827 weekly. These examples illustrate that both demand and supply are *flows;* consumer purchases or sales by firms mean little unless time intervals are specified. But this is not the only important way that time influences demands and supplies.

One interesting effect time has on demands is that as longer time intervals are considered, the quantity demanded becomes more sensitive to any changes in

FIGURE 9 *Factors Causing Shifts in Supply*

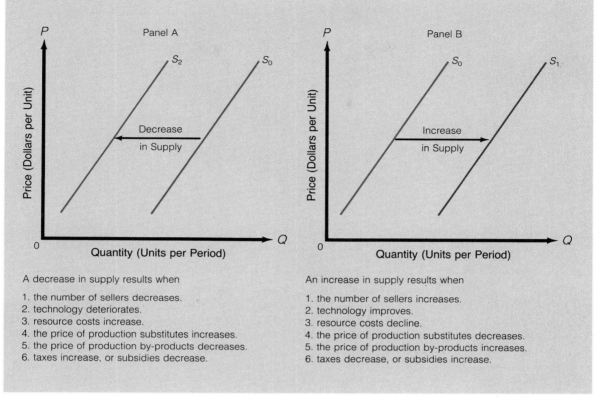

A decrease in supply results when

1. the number of sellers decreases.
2. technology deteriorates.
3. resource costs increase.
4. the price of production substitutes increases.
5. the price of production by-products decreases.
6. taxes increase, or subsidies decrease.

An increase in supply results when

1. the number of sellers increases.
2. technology improves.
3. resource costs decline.
4. the price of production substitutes decreases.
5. the price of production by-products increases.
6. taxes decrease, or subsidies increase.

price. For example, an increase in the price of gasoline will not cause much reduction in the amount of gasoline bought in the *very short run* (say, a week or two), and a slightly greater reduction in gasoline bought in the *short run* (say, 6 months to a year). People will gradually modify their habitual driving patterns to save some gasoline and thus, will demand a little less. However, in the *longer run* (say, 2–5 years), big gasoline price hikes cause people to buy smaller cars, get tune-ups more regularly, or to rely more on mass transit. They may even relocate to be closer to work, shopping, and so on. The longer the adjustment period, the more consumers will reduce gas consumption in response to any given price increase.

Another interesting aspect of the influence of time on demand is that some goods require substantial time for consumption. Time limits your enjoyment of your favorite food. (Your stomach does not have

unlimited capacity.) You can only wear one hat at a time. Vacations are expensive not only because of the money you spend but also because of the income you sacrifice by not working. Airline tickets typically have higher monetary prices than touring by car, but the time saved by air travel makes it increasingly popular.

Just as time spans affect demand, they also affect supply. Production is time consuming, and longer periods obviously enable firms to make more of a good available. Less obviously, supplies become increasingly sensitive to price changes as time elapses. For example, if broccoli prices rise, vegetable growers can do little to raise production in a short period, say a month or so. However, a year or so enables a farmer to acquire more seed, plow and fertilize more ground, and put more acreage into production. Figure 10 summarizes these effects of time on supply and demand.

FIGURE 10 *Demands, Supplies, and Time*

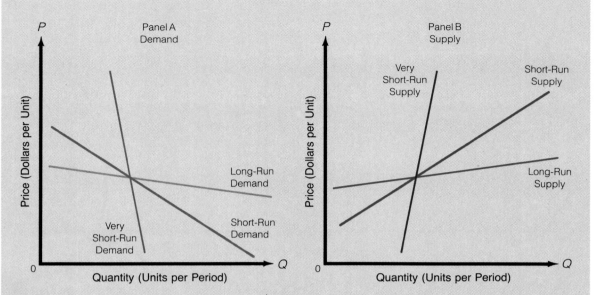

The longer the time interval considered, the more sensitive will be the quantity demanded or quantity supplied to any changes in the price of the product. The more time consumers have to make adjustments to increased prices, the less they will demand. Similarly, the longer business has to adjust supplies, the more sensitive supplies are to price changes.

⭐ Market Equilibrium

It's easy to train economists. Just teach a parrot to say "Supply and demand."

—*Thomas Carlyle*

Supply and demand go together like diapers and babies or the top and bottom blades of a pair of scissors; each is incomplete without the other. Supply and demand jointly determine prices and quantities so that markets achieve *equilibrium,* a term meaning that all forces for change are in balance.

Buyers and sellers use prices as signals to communicate their wants, and then exchange money for goods or resources, or vice versa. You accept or reject thousands of offers during every trip to a shopping center or perusal of the newspaper. Because prices efficiently transmit an incredible amount of information, economists often call our market economy the *price system.*

Suppose that every potential buyer and seller of a good submitted demand and supply schedules to an auctioneer, who then calculated the price at which the quantities demanded and supplied were equal. All buyers' demand price (the maximum they are willing to pay) equal all sellers' supply price (the minimum they will accept per unit for a given amount), and the market *clears.* This means that the amounts buyers will purchase exactly equal the amounts producers are willing to sell, a solution called the **equilibrium price and quantity.** Let's examine the sense in which this is an equilibrium.

Figure 11 summarizes the market supplies and demands for paperbacks. (Note that there are more readers and publishers than in our earlier examples.) After studying the supply and demand schedules, our auctioneer ascertains that at $3.25 per book, the quantities demanded and supplied both equal 300 million books annually. Sellers will provide exactly as many paperbacks as readers will purchase at this price, so the market clears.

But what if the auctioneer set a price of $3.75 per book, or $2.75 per book? First, let us deal with the problem of a price set above equilibrium. A **surplus** is the excess of the quantity supplied over quantity demanded when the price is above equilibrium. At a price of $3.75 per book, publishers would print 400 million books annually, but readers would only buy 200 million books. This yields a surplus of 200 million paperbacks in Figure 11, which would wind up as surplus inventories in the hands of publishers.

Most firms would cut production as their inventories grew, and some might cut prices, hoping to unload surplus paperbacks on bargain hunters and readers willing to buy more at sale prices. Other firms with unwanted inventories would join in the price war. Prices would fall until all surplus inventories were depleted. As prices fell, some businesses might stop producing temporarily; others might leave the industry permanently.

Just how much the quantity supplied would decline is shown in the table accompanying Figure 11. When the price falls to $3.25 per book, consumers will buy 300 million books annually, and publishers

will supply 300 million books—the quantity demanded equals the quantity supplied. The market-clearing price is $3.25 per book. At this **market equilibrium,** any pressures for price or quantity changes are exactly counterbalanced by opposite pressures.

When the quantity of a good supplied is less than the quantity demanded, there is a **shortage** of the product. This occurs when the market price is below equilibrium, and it is basically the opposite of a surplus. At $2.75 per book, readers demand 400 million books, but publishers only provide 200 million. There is a shortage of 200 million books annually, as depicted in Figure 11. Publishers will respond to bookless customers who clamor for the limited quantities available. They will try to satisfy these unhappy customers by raising the price until the market clears, so that books are readily available for the people who are the most desperate to buy them.

FIGURE 11 *Equilibrium in the Paperback Book Market*

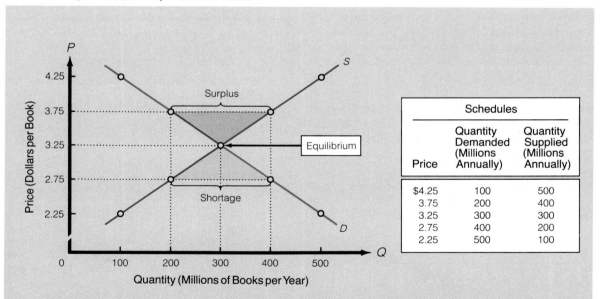

Schedules		
Price	Quantity Demanded (Millions Annually)	Quantity Supplied (Millions Annually)
$4.25	100	500
3.75	200	400
3.25	300	300
2.75	400	200
2.25	500	100

At a price of $3.75 per paperback, there is a surplus of 200 million books annually. (The *surplus* is the horizontal distance between the demand and supply curves when the price is *above* $3.25.) At a price of $2.75, there is a shortage of 200 million books annually. (The *shortage* is the horizontal distance between the demand and the supply curves when the price is *below* $3.25.) When the price is $3.25, quantity demanded is equal to quantity supplied, and the market is in equilibrium.

Achieving equilibrium is not instantaneous. Firms experiment with the prices of their products in a process resembling an auction. Inventories vanishing from store shelves are signals that prices may be too low. Retailers will order more goods and may tend to raise prices on future deliveries from manufacturers. If orders to manufacturers grow rapidly, prices tend to rise at the wholesale level as well. This process quickly eliminates most shortages.

When shortages appear in a market, people refer to it as a "tight market," or a "sellers' market." Suppliers have no difficulty selling all they produce, so quality may decline somewhat at the same time that sellers raise prices. Many sellers also exercise some favoritism in deciding which customers to serve during shortages.

When prices are above equilibrium, surpluses create "buyers' markets" and force sellers to consider price cuts. This is especially painful if production costs seem immune to downward pressures even though sales drop and inventories swell. (Most workers stubbornly resist wage cuts.) In many cases, firms can shrink inventories and cut costs only by laying workers off and drastically reducing production. The price system ultimately forces prices down if there are continuing surpluses. Idle auto workers and record losses by Ford, GM, and Chrysler during 1979–83 are testimony that this process may be long and traumatic.

Price hikes eliminate shortages fairly rapidly, and price cuts eventually cure surpluses, but these automatic market adjustments may be uncomfortable for many buyers and sellers. These self-corrections are what Adam Smith described as the *invisible hand* of the marketplace. Long-term shortages or surpluses are, almost without exception, consequences of governmental price controls. We will discuss price controls and other applications of supply and demand in the next chapter.

Transaction Costs

The major differences between market prices and opportunity costs occur because of transaction costs. We often refer to "the price" of a good as if each good had only one price at a given time. But gas prices differ between service stations, and stores commonly charge different prices for what seem to be the same groceries. How can this be reconciled with economic models that arrive at a single price? The answer lies in transaction costs.

Transaction costs are the costs associated with gathering *information* about prices and availability, and *mobility,* or transporting goods and people between markets. The value of the time you take reading newspaper ads and driving to a store to take advantage of a bargain is one form of transaction costs. Gasoline used and wear and tear on your car in gathering information and locating goods are also transaction costs. Would you drive 50 miles to save $5 by going from store to store, or would you simply go to a department store or shopping mall?

If transaction costs were zero, sellers would always sell at the highest possible price, while buyers would only pay the lowest possible price. Therefore, the highest and lowest possible prices would have to be identical and only one price could exist for identical goods. Thus, transaction costs, of which the value of time is an important component, account for ranges in the monetary prices of any single good. It may sometimes be that paying a higher monetary price is efficient if the transaction cost of acquiring the good at the lower monetary price is high.

Supplies and Demands Are Independent

While specific demands and supplies jointly determine prices and quantities, it is important to realize that they are normally independent of each other, at least in the short run. Many people have difficulty with the idea that demands and supplies are independent. It would seem that demand depends on availability—or that supply depends on demand. The following examples show that supplies and demands are normally independent in the short run.

1. Suppose that nonreusable "teleporter buttons" could instantly transport you anywhere you chose. Your demand price to go on the first (most valuable) tour would be quite high, but it would decline steadily for subsequent journeys. Using teleporter buttons for little shopping trips would be economical only if these buttons were very inexpensive. By asking how many buttons you would buy at various prices, we can construct your demand curve for such devices—even though there is no supply.

2. Would you have made more mud pies when you were a kid if your parents had bought them for a penny apiece? At two cents each, might you have

hired some of your playmates to help you? If mud pies were worth $1 each today, might you be a mud pie entrepreneur? Our point is that a supply curve can be constructed for mud pies even if there is no demand for them.

3. You might be willing to pay a little to hear some professors' lectures, even if you did not receive college credit for gathering the pearls of wisdom they offer. However, some professors like to talk even more than you like to listen. Such a set of demand and supply curves is illustrated in Figure 12. It is fortunate for both you and your professors that your demands for their lectures are supplemented by contributions from taxpayers, alumni, and possibly your parents because only later and upon mature reflection will you realize just how valuable those lectures really were!

We hope these examples convince you that specific supplies and demands are largely independent of each other, and that they are relevant for markets only when they intersect. Markets establish whether the interests of buyers from the demand side are compatible with the interests of sellers from the supply side, and then coordinate decisions where mutually beneficial exchange is possible. Keep this in mind as you study the applications of supply and demand in the next chapter.

FIGURE 12   *The Demand and Supply of a Professor's Lectures*

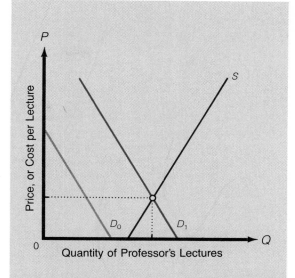

This figure depicts the supply of a professor's lectures and student demand for them (D_0). Without supplementing their demand through lower tuition or other contributions (D_1), this professor would have to lecture for free . . . and, at times, to an empty room (S and D_0 do not intersect at any positive price and quantity.)

CHAPTER REVIEW: KEY POINTS

1. A *market* is a social institution that enables buyers and sellers to strike bargains and transact. *Absolute* (monetary) *prices* are far less important for consumer or business decisions than *relative prices*, of which consumers' *demand* (subjective) *prices* and *market prices* must be in accord before people will purchase goods.

2. *The law of demand*. People buy less of a good per period at high prices than at low prices. *Demand curves* slope downward and to the right, and show the quantities demanded at various prices for a good. Changes in market prices cause changes in quantity demanded.

3. Consumers buy more of a product per period only at lower prices because consuming the additional units typically does not yield as much satisfaction as consuming previous units; *diminishing marginal utility* causes demand prices to fall as consumption rises. In addition, a lower price for one product means that the purchasing power of a given income rises (the *income effect*). Most importantly, the cheaper good will be used more ways as it is substituted for higher priced goods (the *substitution effect*).

4. In addition to the price of a good, demand depends on: (*a*) tastes and preferences; (*b*) income and its distribution; (*c*) prices of related goods; (*d*) numbers and ages of buyers; (*e*) expectations about prices, income, and availability; and (*f*) taxes, subsidies, and regulations. Changes in nonprice variables that influence demand cause shifts in demand curves. Taxes and subsidies shift demand curves from the perspectives of sellers, who are concerned with the price *received* when a good is sold, while buyers focus on the price *paid*. Taxes or subsidies make these two prices differ.

5. *The law of supply*. Higher prices cause sellers to make more of a good available per period. The *supply curve* shows the positive relationship between the price of a good and the quantity supplied. Supply curves generally slope upward and to the right because: (*a*) diminishing returns cause opportunity costs to increase; (*b*) to expand output, firms must bid resources away from competing producers or use other methods (such as overtime) that increase cost; and (*c*) profit incentives are greater at higher prices.

6. In addition to the price paid to producers of a good, supply depends on: (*a*) the number of sellers; (*b*) technology; (*c*) resource costs; (*d*) prices of other producible goods; (*e*) producers' expectations; and (*f*) specific taxes, subsidies, and governmental regulations. Changes in prices cause *changes in quantities supplied*, while changes in other influences on production or sales of goods cause shifts in supply curves that are termed *changes in supply*.

7. When markets operate without government intervention, prices tend to move towards market *equilibrium* so that quantity supplied equals quantity demanded. At this point, the demand price equals the supply price.

8. When the market price of a good is below the intersection of the supply and demand curves, there will be *shortages* and pressures for increases in price. If price is above the intersection of the supply and demand curves, there will be *surpluses* and pressures for reduction in price.

9. *Transaction costs* arise because information and mobility are costly. This allows the price of a good to vary between markets.

10. Supply and demand are largely independent in the short run.

QUESTIONS FOR THOUGHT AND DISCUSSION

Use scratch paper to draw graphs illustrating the changes in supply or demand described in questions 1–7. If only one curve shifts, assume that the other is stationary.

1. What happens in the market for bananas if the FDA announces research results suggesting that eating 5 pounds of bananas monthly raises IQ scores by an average of 10 points? What would happen in the markets for apples or other fruit?

2. What happens to the demand for college professors in the short run if government raises its funding of graduate school educations? What happens to the supply of college professors over a longer time span? What will happen to their wages during the adjustment periods?

3. What happens if new "miracle" seeds allow grain to be grown in shorter periods and colder climates? If the world population mushrooms because starvation ceases to be so widespread?

4. What happens in the U.S. clothing market if freer trade with the People's Republic of China expands our imports of textiles? If after two years import tariffs and quotas are imposed?

5. Around the middle of every January, the annual crop of mink furs is put on the auction block. How will the following affect the supplies and demands for mink pelts?

   a. More fur-bearing animals are classified as endangered species.

   b. The price of mink food rises.

   c. Extraordinarily mild winters for 5 years are followed by a long period of severe blizzards.

   d. A massive, worldwide (1929-type) depression occurs.

   e. Higher income tax rates and a new wealth tax are imposed, and the added revenues are used to raise welfare payments.

6. If oil prices suddenly fell after rising rapidly for several years, what might happen to the:

   a. demand for small cars?

   b. demand for luxury sedans?

   c. demand for air travel?

   d. supply of records?

   e. supply of synthetic fabrics?

   f. demand for wool and cotton?

   Hint: Records and synthetic fabrics are made from petroleum products.

7. Use supply and demand curves to show why the monetary price of color TVs declined consistently over the past 25 years in spite of inflation that more than tripled the absolute prices of other goods.

8. Is the law of demand refuted if snobs are willing to buy more mink coats only at high prices, or if some people buy more high-priced aspirin than low-priced aspirin? Discuss.

9. Imports of oil rose during the 1970s even though prices skyrocketed over the decade. Is this an exception to the law of demand? Why or why not?

10. Is the assertion that "Everyone always buys everything at the lowest possible price" correct? Have you ever paid more than you had to for any good, after allowing for transaction costs? Discuss.

1.

encrease in demand
increase in price
increase in QTY Applied

5. a.) ↑ D
       ↑ P
       ↑ QTY Supp

   b.) ↓ Supply of mink

   c.) ↓ D — ↑ D

   d.) ↓ D

   e.) ↓ D

8.

6. a. ↓ D
   b. ↑ D
   c. ↑ D
   D. ↑ ØS
   E. ↑ S
   F. ↓ D

CHAPTER 4

Markets and Equilibrium

invisible hand	*speculators*	*black market*
middlemen	*price controls*	*price floor*
arbitrage	*price ceiling*	

Every individual endeavors to employ his capital so that its produce may be of greatest value. He generally neither intends to promote the public interest, nor knows how much he is promoting it. He intends only his own security, only his own gain. And he is in this led [as if] by an **invisible hand** *to promote an end which was not part of his intention. By pursuing his own interest he frequently promotes that of society more effectually than when he really intends to promote it.*
—Adam Smith
WEALTH OF NATIONS (1776)

Prices sometimes move slowly and unevenly towards equilibrium. If information were perfect and mobility instantaneous and costless, prices would be driven to their equilibrium values like arrows shot at a bullseye by an expert archer. Instead, prices may resemble apples at an apple bobbing contest—moving up, down, and sideways before finally reaching equilibrium. In this chapter, we explore the ways prices and outputs move when supplies and demands fluctuate and then apply supply and demand analysis to specific social problems.

The Search For Equilibrium

Some markets are not very stable because consumers can be fickle, forever changing their minds. Changes in income, expectations, taxes, or the prices of related goods also constantly shift the demands for some goods. On the supply side, the business environment is in constant flux: resource prices vary and technology advances, altering costs and consequently, supplies. Changes in taxes and regulations, producer expectations, or the prices of alternative products also shift supply curves.

Let's examine in a general way how changes in supplies and demands affect prices and quantities. (You should get pencil and paper and duplicate the graphing we do in this section.) We will use the wheat market to explore how Adam Smith's "invisible hand" accommodates changes in both supply and demand.

Adam Smith (1723–90)

Modern economics is by no means the product of a single mind, but probably no one is more deserving of the title "Father of Economics" than Adam Smith. Smith was a Scottish philosopher of international fame even before he published *An Inquiry into the Nature and Causes of the Wealth of Nations* in 1776. This enduring work attracted widespread attention and helped establish economics as a field of study apart from moral philosophy.

Smith, a lifelong bachelor, described himself to a friend as "a beau in nothing but my books." Shortly before his death he burned sixteen large volumes of unpublished manuscripts, but his published remains are literary classics. Smith's *Wealth of Nations* covered the spectrum of the then current knowledge of economics and was the starting point for virtually every major economic treatise until 1850.

This work provided: (*a*) an impressive collection of economic data gleaned from Smith's wide reading of history and his keen insights into human affairs; (*b*) an ambitious attempt to detail the nature of economic processes in an individualistic society; and (*c*) a radical critique of existing society and government. Smith strongly dissented from the interventionist policies prevalent in the eighteenth century, advocating their replacement by laissez-faire policies in most economic matters.

Laissez-faire ideas were a sharp departure from *mercantilism*, the conventional wisdom of his era. Among other policies, mercantilist doctrines supported (*a*) imperialism in an era when European powers competed to colonize the rest of the world, and (*b*) restrictions on imports because it was erroneously thought that a country grew powerful by exporting goods in exchange for gold. Smith thought such policies were balderdash, arguing that the real "wealth of nations" consisted of the goods available for its people, and not shiny metal.

A major point of his argument is that economic freedom is an efficient way to organize an economy. The model of the marketplace was the centerpiece of Smith's economic inquiry. Decisions freely made by buyers and sellers are coordinated in the marketplace by what he called *the invisible hand* of competition. Competition harmonizes the driving force of self-interest with the public interest, yielding increases in real national wealth.

The freshest idea in Smith's argument is that the public interest is not served best by those who intend (or pretend) to promote it through government regulation, but rather by those who actively seek their own gain in disregard of the public interest. Economic competition compels self-interested merchants to serve consumers' interests better if the merchants are to increase their sales and gain advantage over rival sellers. Monopoly, on the other hand, is destructive of the public interest because it restricts output and forces prices up.

Government restricted competition and created monopolies in Smith's day; hence, he called for a minimal economic role for government. Were Smith alive today, he would undoubtedly oppose the anticompetitive laws and regulations that pervade modern industrial societies.

Changes in Supply

Suppose that the initial supply and demand for American wheat are S_0 and D_0, respectively, in Figure 1. Equilibrium at point *a* occurs when Q_0 bushels of wheat sell at a price of P_0. Suppose that extraordinarily fine weather yields a bumper crop, so that supply grows from S_0 to S_1 in Panel A. The market now clears at point *b*; price declines from P_0 to P_1, and equilibrium quantity rises from Q_0 to Q_1. We conclude that increases in supplies put downward pressures on prices and increase the quantities sold.

FIGURE 1 *The Effects of Increases and Decreases of Supply (American Wheat Market)*

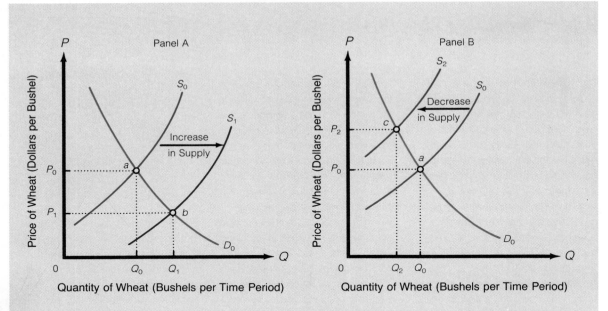

Panel A illustrates that increases in supply put downward pressures on prices. When supply increases from S_0 to S_1, prices fall to P_1 and quantities sold rise from Q_0 to Q_1 (equilibrium point *a* to point *b*). The opposite is true when supply declines as depicted in Panel B. Supply declines from S_0 to S_2, causing prices to rise and quantity sold to fall (from point *a* to point *c*).

Now consider what happens if higher seed or fuel prices raise the costs of farming wheat. Starting at the original equilibrium point *a*, now shown in Panel B of Figure 1, supply declines from S_0 to S_2. The equilibrium price rises from P_0 to P_2 at point *c*, while equilibrium quantity falls from Q_0 to Q_2. Thus, decreases in supply exert upward pressures on prices and decrease the quantities traded.

We have held demand constant while shifting supply. We will now hold supply constant and review how shifts of demand curves affect equilibrium prices and quantities.

 ## Changes in Demand

The original demand D_0 and supply S_0 from Figure 1 are duplicated in Figure 2. Assume that gasahol production from grain is stimulated by rising oil costs. Demand for wheat would rise to, say, D_1 in Panel A. Equilibrium price will rise to P_1, and quantity to Q_1 (point *b*). Here we see that increases in demand yield upward pressures on both prices and quantities.

Suppose that new dietary findings recommend replacement of wheat bread by soybran loaf, causing the demand for American wheat to fall from D_0 to D_2 in Panel B of Figure 2. The equilibrium price and quantity both fall (point *c*). Thus, decreases in demand exert downward pressures on both prices and quantities.

Earlier we distinguished a change in demand from a change in the quantity demanded, and changes in supply from changes in the quantity supplied: Changes in demand (*or supply*) refer to *shifts* of the curve, while changes in the quantity demanded (*or supplied*) refer to movements *along* a curve. Review Figures 1 and 2. If you compare equilibrium positions in Figure 1, you will notice that changes in the quantities demanded result from changes in supply. It would be wrong to say that demand changed; it was supply that shifted. Similarly, Figure 2 shows that changes in quantities supplied are caused by changes in demand. Demand shifted; supply did *not* change. This is why it is important to keep your terminology straight in this area.

FIGURE 2 *The Effects of Increases and Decreases in Demand (American Wheat Market)*

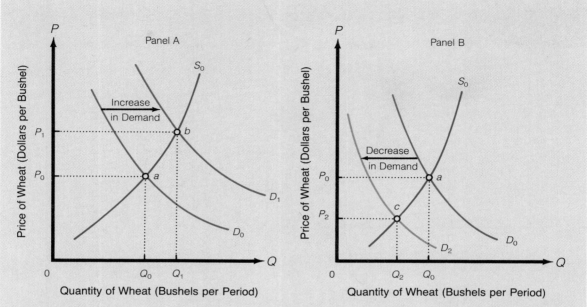

Increases in demand put upward pressures on price. In Panel A, when demand increases from D_0 to D_1, equilibrium price rises to P_1 and equilibrium quantity sold rises as well. As Panel B illustrates, declines in demand (from D_0 to D_2) cause prices to fall (from P_0 to P_2) and equilibrium quantity to decline from Q_0 to Q_2.

If you are still with us, congratulations. If not, please review the preceding material before reading on because now we are going to shift supply and demand curves simultaneously.

Shifts in Supply and Demand

Numerous forces for change are constantly at work in most markets. Technology may advance during periods when consumer preferences are also changing or resource costs are rising. We need to fit each change into our supply/demand framework to determine the net changes in equilibrium price and quantity. As you will see, the net impact on equilibrium price or quantity depends on the relative magnitudes of shifts in supplies and demands.

The wheat market is now diagrammed in Figure 3, allowing us to examine the effects of shifting the supply and demand curves in the same direction. Demand and supply are originally at D_0 and S_0, respectively, with equilibrium price at P_0 and equilibrium output at Q_0 (point a). Assume that the Soviet Union

begins buying more U.S. wheat in a year when we experience a bumper crop. These events increase *both* demand and supply in Figure 3. Unfortunately, this information by itself leaves us unsure whether the price at the new equilibrium (point b) is higher or lower than P_0, but equilibrium quantity (now Q_1) is definitely higher than its old value of Q_0. The lesson here is that when both demand and supply grow, quantity increases but price changes are unknowable without more information.

As you may have guessed, whether the new price of wheat will be above or below P_0 depends on the relative magnitudes of the two shifts. For example, if the Soviet Union's new demand were relatively large and drove market demand to D_2, equilibrium price would rise (point c). Symmetric results occur if both demand and supply decrease, say, from D_1 and S_1 to D_0 and S_0: quantity falls, but price changes cannot be predicted without more information.

What happens if supplies and demands move in opposite directions? The wheat market is again initially in equilibrium at point a in Figure 4. If popu-

FIGURE 3 *The Effects of Increases in Both Supply and Demand (American Wheat Market)*

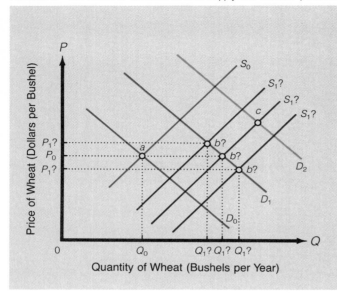

When both supply and demand increase, equilibrium quantity traded will always rise, but the change in price will depend upon the relative magnitudes of the two shifts. When both supply and demand decline, quantity will always fall, and again the price change is uncertain, being dependent upon the relative magnitudes of the two shifts.

lation growth raises demand to D_1 while drought causes supply to drop to S_1, the new equilibrium is at point *b*. Price increases to P_1, but we need more information to be sure whether quantity increases, decreases, or remains constant. In this case, quantity changes depend on the relative magnitudes of the shifts. Thus, if demand rises while supply falls, the price rises but we cannot predict quantity changes without more information.

Similar results occur if demand falls and supply rises. Thus, declines in demand and increases in supply cause prices to fall, but predicting quantity changes requires more data. Figure 5 summarizes these effects of supply and demand changes on prices and quantities.

Price volatility may plague a market economy. If prices are high and profit opportunities abound, existing firms will expand and new firms will enter the market, boosting supply and driving the high price down. Low prices and low profits, on the other hand, cause some firms to exit an industry, while the survivors cut back on output and reduce their hiring. This pushes low prices up. When there are long lags between planning for production and selling output, prices and outputs may swing wildly before they finally settle at equilibrium.

Suppose, for example, that wheat prices rose sharply after a drought wiped out most of a crop. The high price relative to cost could cause wheat farmers to overproduce in the next year, driving the price down. Discouraged by this low price, farmers might cut production back too much in the third year, causing the price to again rise far above production costs. And so on. Similarly cyclical price swings have been observed for engineering wages (it takes four years to get an engineering degree) and in other markets in which training and/or production take a long time.

Middlemen and Speculators

People search for bargains only to the extent that they expect the benefits from shopping (price reductions) to exceed the transaction costs they expect to incur. We live in an uncertain world and constantly make decisions based on incomplete or inaccurate information. Acquiring better market information is a costly process, as is moving goods or resources between markets. Firms popularly known as **middlemen** specialize in reducing uncertainty and cutting the transaction costs of conveying goods from

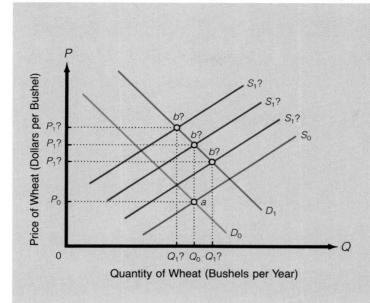

FIGURE 4 *The Effects of an Increase in Demand and a Decrease in Supply (American Wheat Market)*

When demand and supply curves move in opposite directions, the price change is predictable, but the quantity adjustment is not. When demand increases and supply falls, price will rise, but the change in equilibrium quantity depends on the nature of the two shifts. When demand declines and supply increases, prices will fall, but again the change in quantity is uncertain without further information.

the original producers to final users, often transforming the good so that it is more compatible with the ultimate users' demands. Surprisingly, price swings are moderated by the activities of speculators, who are special types of middlemen.

Speculators and middlemen are standard targets when some people try to identify the villains who cause inflation, or shortages, or a host of other economic maladies. Middlemen and speculators actually absorb risk and help move prices towards equilibrium. This process reduces transaction costs and aids in getting goods to those who desire them most while boosting the incomes of the original suppliers. In fact, middlemen reduce the opportunity costs of goods to consumers, and speculators reduce both the volatility of prices and the net costs of products.

✴ *Middlemen*

Have you ever paid more than you had to for anything you bought from a retailer or other middleman? If you behave rationally, the answer must be NO! You might object that, say, buying apples from a grocery store costs more than buying them from an apple grower. But if you bought from a store, it must

have charged less than if you had bought the apples directly from the orchard, after considering all information costs, travel, and time entailed in going to the orchard. Otherwise, you would have bought directly from the apple grower.

Similarly, the monetary prices you pay at convenience stores are higher than at supermarkets. However, after we adjust for greater accessibility because of the longer hours typical of convenience stores and the frequent extended waits in checkout lanes at supermarkets, the customers of convenience stores must be paying less, or they would buy elsewhere. No matter how hard you think about it, we doubt that you can come up with a single example where you have paid more than the lowest price possible for any good, once you account for all transaction costs.

✴ *Arbitrage*

Profit is ensured if you can buy low and sell high. **Arbitrage** is the process of buying at a lower price in one market and selling at a higher price in another, where the arbitrager knows both prices and the price differential exceeds transaction costs. For example, if gold is priced at $328 per ounce in London while the New York price is $337 per ounce, an arbitrager can make $9 per ounce (mi-

FIGURE 5 *Summary of Price and Quantity Responses to Changing Demands and Supplies*

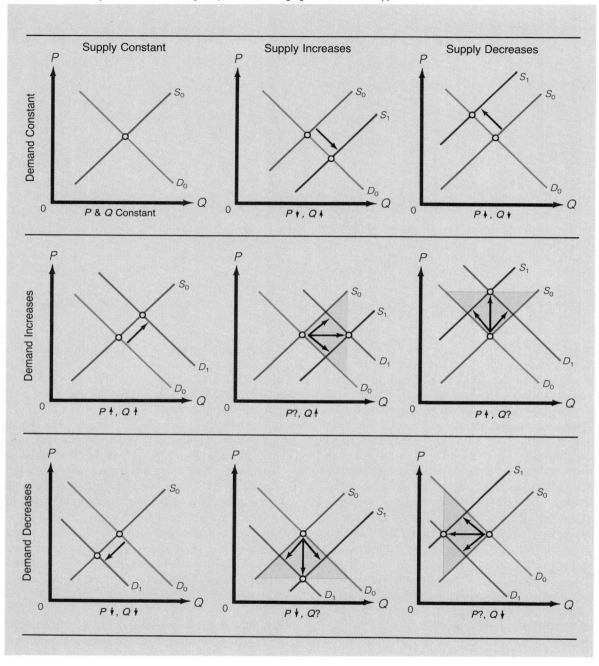

nus transaction costs) by buying in London and selling in New York.

Traders constantly seek opportunities to arbitrage because profits can be made without risk. When middlemen buy in the market with the lower price, demand is increased, which drives up the price. When they sell in the market with the higher price, the greater supply pushes the price down. Thus, arbitrage reduces transaction costs and forces relative prices toward equality in all markets. This middleman activity promotes economic efficiency by linking markets that are spread geographically, so that goods are moved from areas where they have a relatively low value to markets where the goods are more highly valued.

✱ Speculators

Speculators derive income by buying something at a low price and storing it in the hope of selling it *later* at a higher price. Thus, speculators buy things if they think prices are going to rise and sell them if they expect prices to fall. Speculation is unlike arbitrage because this time delay makes speculation risky. Speculators can make fortunes if they predict correctly; if they are wrong too often they go broke and cease being speculators.

If speculators believe that prices will soon rise, then they expect demands to grow faster than supplies. They respond by buying now, increasing the *current* demand and price, so that they can sell later at a higher price. Do they cause prices to be higher later? NO! If speculators are more often right than wrong, they sell when prices are high and add to the supply at that time. Thus, successful speculation shifts the consumption of a good from a period in which it would have a relatively low value into a period when its value to consumers is higher. Correct speculation reduces price peaks and boosts depressed prices, so successful speculators reduce price swings and, by absorbing some risks to others of doing business, raise the net incomes of the ultimate suppliers. Overall, costs fall because speculators absorb risks and the prices consumers pay are lower and more predictable.

Markets and Public Policy

The level of the sea is not more surely kept than is the equilibrium of value in society by supply and demand; and artifice or legislation punishes itself by reactions, gluts, and bankruptcies.
—*Ralph Waldo Emerson*

A laissez-faire economic system cannot allocate all goods and resources or distribute income to everyone's satisfaction. In our mixed economy, the list of regulations and governmentally provided goods and services seems endless: from police and fire protection to dog leash laws and financial regulations; from national defense to education and interstate high-

ways; and on and on. In this section, we examine some effects of policies that alter market solutions. Taxes, one way government activity is financed, can have a major effect on market prices and quantities.

Taxes and Subsidies

Taxing a good drives a *wedge* between the price paid by buyers and the price received by sellers. The initial equilibrium in Figure 6 is at point *e* without taxes, and 16 million video cassettes are sold monthly at a price of $7 each. Suppose that a $2 tax per cassette is imposed. The market demand curve from sellers' perspectives shifts vertically downwards by $2 to D_2, while the supply of cassettes falls from the vantage points of buyers to S_2. (Although this supply curve "rises" vertically by $2 at each quantity, recall that shifts towards the price axis reflect declines in both supply and demand curves.)

At the new equilibrium, the quantities supplied and demanded must be equal, but the demand price and the supply price differ by the $2 tax. One easy way to identify this new equilibrium is to slide a $2 tax wedge in from the left of the original curves (D_0 and S_0) until the vertical distance between them (*ac*) just equals the tax. Thus, at the new equilibrium, buyers pay $8 for each of 12 million video cassettes per month, while, net of the $2 tax, suppliers receive $6 per cassette.

The intersection of taxed supplies and demands helps to identify the proportions of the tax borne by buyers and sellers, respectively. In this simple case, each side bears $1 of the tax, but different slopes of the supply and demand curves will yield different proportional burdens. (Vary the slopes of these curves on graph paper to prove this assertion for yourself.) Note that the tax reduces incentives to produce video cassettes, and incentives to buy them as well. This may create inefficiency and is one reason economists refer to tax wedges as creating disincentive effects.

Subsidies are the flip side of taxes. If a $2 subsidy were placed on video cassettes, a subsidy wedge can be slid between the original supply and demand curves from the right of the original equilibrium, so that the vertical distance (*bd*) between them reflects this subsidy. This bolsters demand to D_1 from sellers' perspectives, while raising supply to S_1 in the views of buyers. The buyer's (demand) price falls to $6, while the seller's (supply) price rises to $8.

FIGURE 6   *The Effects of Taxes or Subsidies on Equilibrium*

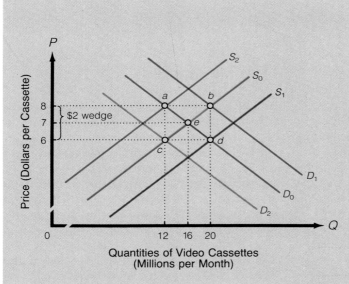

Taxes and subsidies are normally shared by buyers and sellers. A $2 tax shrinks demand from the seller's perspective (from D_0 to D_2), but does not affect demand from the consumer's perspective. Rather, the consumer perceives supply as shrinking from S_0 to S_2 because of the $2 tax, while the sellers view their supply as unchanged. On the other hand, a $2 subsidy expands supply from S_0 to S_1 from the perspective of consumers, but does not change demand in the view of buyers. Sellers, however, view demand as growing from D_0 to D_1, but perceive no changes in their supplies. In this example, the tax burden (or the benefits from subsidies) are split evenly between buyers and sellers, but the tax or subsidy may be quite unevenly split in other situations. The actual split depends on the relative slopes of these curves, as you can discover by drawing your own examples.

You might think that the enhanced incentives to produce and buy cassettes reflect an efficient strategy. There is a problem, however, because more scarce resources must be diverted from other goods into producing video cassettes, and the other goods not produced are normally more socially valuable than these extra cassettes. If markets are competitive, supply reflects production costs and demand reflects the values consumers place on goods. Taxes or subsidies distort the price signals that lead to efficient exchanges.

Some regulations inefficiently raise costs. If production costs rise by more than the benefits of a regulation, this is another example of an inefficient wedge between buyers and sellers. Let's see how specific laws and regulations may cause inefficiency.

★Price Controls

You can't repeal the Laws of Supply and Demand.
—Anonymous

Influences on supplies and demands change continuously, so we might expect relative prices to bounce around like ping-pong balls. We all want low prices for the things we buy and high prices for the things we sell. Whenever prices rise or fall, some people gain while others lose. Consequently, a lot of people are angered by volatile prices. There is not much that any individual can do alone to directly control market forces. However, acting through government, special interest groups often attempt to establish **price controls.**

Price Ceilings   A *maximum* legal price is termed a **price ceiling.** Price ceilings keep monetary prices from rising but not average opportunity costs. Unfortunately, they also often cause shortages. Shortages needlessly absorb resources because when the price mechanism does not operate, other, less efficient mechanisms will be used to allocate goods. Severe shortages were the major result when President Nixon imposed a wage and price freeze in August 1971. This price freeze initially covered virtually all markets in the United States, although controls were phased out and then largely abandoned by 1976.

Suppose that a price ceiling of $1 per gallon is set in the market for gasoline depicted in Figure 7. The quantity of gasoline demanded will be 75 million gallons daily, but the quantity supplied will be only 30 million gallons. There will be an *excess demand* (or shortage) of 45 million gallons. Who will get gasoline? People who bribe service station attendants, or who are able to persuade government to give them priority access, or those who wait through long lines. Even people who waited 2–4 hours in gasoline queues in 1974–75 often went without because the pumps ran dry.

But price ceilings keep prices down, don't they? Unfortunately, the answer is NO! The people who most value the 30 million gallons of gas available daily tend to get it. They are willing to pay at least $2 per gallon for gasoline; that is, an extra dollar per gallon in waiting time, lobbying efforts, bribery, or as a black market premium. (A **black market** is an illegal market where price controls are ignored.) Had the price ceiling not been imposed, the price of a gallon of gasoline would have been around $1.25. Although the monetary price of gasoline is held at $1 per gallon, this price ceiling raises its opportunity cost to $2 per gallon to the average customer.

Ceilings do not hold costs down; they raise them. When ceilings are effective, there will be shortages so that opportunity costs—including money prices, time wasted in lines, and illegal side payments—unnecessarily exceed free-market prices. Only pump prices are controlled; real costs to average consumers are not.

Price Floors A *minimum* legal price is termed a **price floor.** Price floors are most prevalent in labor markets (minimum wage laws) and agriculture, where the government commonly attempts to stabilize or raise farm incomes by maintaining the prices of farm commodities above their equilibrium values. Figure 8 depicts the consequence of price floors, or "parity" prices, in the cotton market.

The equilibrium price and quantity are $0.60 per pound and 4 million bales of cotton annually (point *e*). At a price floor of $0.75 per pound, the quantity supplied is 5 million bales annually, but the quantity demanded is only 3 million bales. There is an *excess supply* (surplus) of 2 million bales annually. The government can ensure the $0.75 price by buying and storing these excess supplies. (Over the years, government warehouses have been filled to their bursting points with gluts of surplus wheat, peanuts, soybeans, corn, beet sugar, and cotton.) Alternatively, the government can pay cotton farmers not to produce or forbid a certain amount of planting. (It has done both.)

In any case, these price floors are quite inefficient. In our example, consumers view the 5-millionth bale as worth only $0.45 per pound, even though this last bale produced costs $0.75 per pound to grow and

FIGURE 7 *Governmentally Induced Shortages in the Gasoline Market*

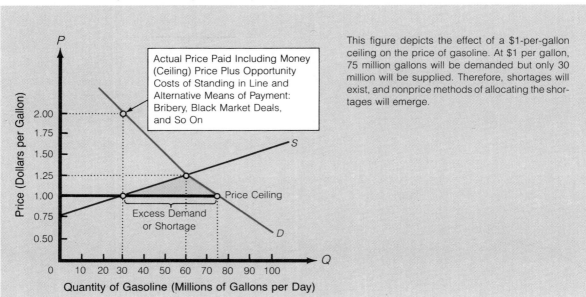

This figure depicts the effect of a $1-per-gallon ceiling on the price of gasoline. At $1 per gallon, 75 million gallons will be demanded but only 30 million will be supplied. Therefore, shortages will exist, and nonprice methods of allocating the shortages will emerge.

harvest. Worse than that, people do not get to use the surplus 2 million bales society buys from farmers. Hardly a bargain.

Price ceilings cause shortages and do not hold down the real prices paid by most consumers. Transaction costs during shortages are sometimes outrageous, so the opportunity costs associated with acquiring goods are actually raised by price ceilings. On the other hand, price floors cause surpluses. Production costs of the surplus goods are far greater than their values to consumers.

If price controls are typically counterproductive, why are they so common? In some cases, price ceilings are enacted because the voting public clamors for them, mistakenly perceiving controls as a solution for inflation. Most of the time, however, controls are the result of political pressures from special interest groups.

The beneficiaries of controls are at times obvious: Price floors in agriculture have existed for three generations because of bloc voting by farmers. Even price supports have not prevented recurring crises in agriculture, however, as the widespread foreclosures of family farms during 1981–86 attest. Advances in technology have made it possible for ever smaller numbers of farmers to feed our growing population. Price supports have merely slowed the inevitable flow of people from agriculture into other work.

In other instances, however, the beneficiaries of price controls are far less obvious. For example, minimum wage laws establish wage floors that create surpluses of labor. These surplus workers, most of whom are young or unskilled, wind up being unemployed. Why have labor unions long sought high minimum wage laws even though union workers invariably receive wages far above these wage floors? Misguided humanitarianism may play a role, but another reason is that wage floors limit the ability of unskilled workers to compete with skilled union workers. For example, if two unskilled workers willing to work for $3.00 hourly apiece can do the job of a $6.50-per-hour skilled worker, a $3.35 minimum wage eliminates their ability to compete.

Society as a whole loses from price controls. The winners tend to be special interest groups who lobby for controlled prices, and even their gains are eroded by lobbying costs and related inefficiencies. One lesson from price controls is that government policies may distort supply and demand, yielding unintended and undesirable side effects.

FIGURE 8 *Surpluses in the Cotton Market*

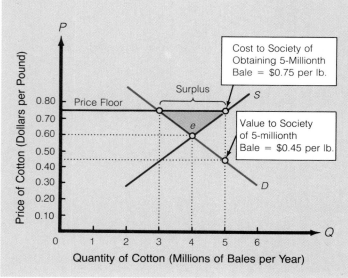

Price floors generate surpluses, as this figure illustrates. If the government maintains the price of cotton at $0.75 per pound, quantity supplied exceeds that demanded by 2 million bales. The surplus ends up in the hands of the government, which is forced to buy it up to maintain the price at $0.75. Furthermore, the cost to society to produce the 5-millionth bale is far greater than its value. As a result, such policies tend to waste scarce resources.

Market forces often thwart policies that, on the surface, seem compatible with certain social goals. Some people are outraged when human desires and actions are viewed from an economic perspective. The following analyses suggest that economic reasoning may lead to more humane policies for issues ranging from illicit drugs to adoption than policies based on good intentions or "gut feelings."

Heroin Addiction

Drug addiction, once thought confined to the nation's ghettos, has become much more widespread in the past 20 years. Standard approaches to the drug problem have emphasized punishing users somewhat, but pushers much more harshly. This reduces demands for drugs but shrinks their supplies much more. The result is that the prices of illicit drugs are far greater than free-market prices would be, causing addiction to pose more problems for the rest of society.

Suppose that S_0 and D_0 in Figure 9 represent the demand and supply of heroin if it were legal. The price of heroin, P_0, would probably fall somewhere between the prices of aspirin and penicillin because its production is not overly complicated nor are presently legal narcotics very expensive. (Some estimates suggest that completely legalized and untaxed marijuana would sell for about $8 a bale—roughly the price of prime hay.)

Penalizing heroin users reduces demand to D_1 while the stiffer punishment of dealers reduces supply to S_1, boosting the price to P_1. This high price permits successful pushers to drive luxury cars and live in plush houses, but many users are pushed into prostitution, mugging, and other street crimes. Thus, higher crime rates are among the social costs of policies that reduce the supply of heroin more than the demand for it.

One alternative to this approach is complete legalization. The few who advocate letting the heroin market be determined strictly by demand and supply argue that heroin would be so cheap that few addicts would feel driven to commit crimes against others. Instead, they would spend a lot of time nodding off, bothering people no more than derelict alcoholics. Most people, however, are unwilling to allow others to waste away their lives in such a fashion.

FIGURE 9 *The Heroin Market*

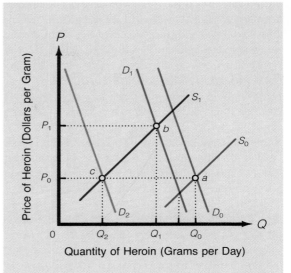

Prosecuting pushers reduces supply more than demand, but the resulting hike in price from P_0 to P_1 makes selling heroin very profitable. Severe prosecutions of addicts might reduce demand to D_2, eliminating much of this profit. Alternatively, giving heroin to addicts through government clinics might dry up the supply of illegal heroin.

What policies will reduce heroin usage below Q_0 (the free-market amount in Figure 9) without stimulating addicts to commit crimes? One option is to punish users far more than suppliers. This would reduce demand to, say, D_2 in Figure 9, yielding a low price for heroin and reduced addiction (Q_2). Most people, however, are reluctant to impose life sentences or the death penalty to punish drug users, especially when minors or experimenters are involved.

Paradoxically, allowing clinics to give heroin freely to proven addicts while maintaining stiff penalties against pushers may be a workable solution if we as a society want to suppress both addiction and the crime that accompanies this expensive habit. Such a policy would leave suppliers with only experimenters as potential customers and might, over time, reduce the illicit demand for heroin even below D_2. Pushers would be more vulnerable to undercover police work because they would not know their customers, and the illegal supply of heroin should dry up. A similar approach has been followed in England for over two decades and appears to work reasonably well. It does not, however, cure those who are addicted, which causes some people to view it as a failure.

The Market for Adoptable Children

You can buy or sell pedigreed puppies—indeed, some of the prices paid for show quality pets seem stupendous to poor mortals who are content with "Heinz 57" mongrels. Why can't you purchase children if you want them and either can't have them through normal reproduction or choose not to?

Are Children Investment or Consumption Goods?

In the past, children were often treated as investments or cheap labor, especially in rural areas. Many parents instilled in their children a sense that duty dictated caring for their elders in their declining years. Today, most wanted children, whether adopted by or born to their parents, are viewed as sources of joy rather than income. Although every child is an individual possessing individual rights, we can gain insight into the adoption issue by recognizing that, because they add to their parents' happiness, children fall under the definition of consumer goods.

The Current System of Adoption

Every year a number of children are abandoned, orphaned, or otherwise made available for adoption. Laws governing adoption were fairly lax during the Depression and the post-World War II baby boom, when orphans and foundlings typically outnumbered the families seeking to adopt. In recent years, the supply of children available for adoption has fallen because of widespread birth control, legalized abortion, and a reduction in the stigma assigned to unwed mothers who keep their children. Demand, however, has grown rapidly over this period, in part because of increases in the incidence of sterility and in the higher age at which people now typically marry. As is the case of most lasting shortages, the current baby shortage is a predictable consequence of government policy.

Figure 10 shows the supply and demand for adoptable children in the absence of government controls. Some children will be available for adoption without compensation to the relinquishing par-

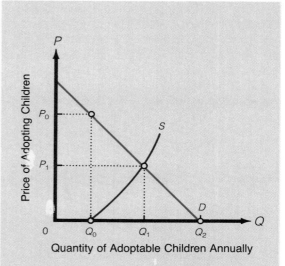

FIGURE 10 *The Demand and Supply of Adoptable Children*

Children are sources of joy, and so can be viewed as economic goods. Higher rewards for surrendering children to adoption yield greater numbers available for adoption. Lower prices charged adopting families would result in a greater number of adoptions. Thus, demands and supplies in this market conform to the laws of supply and demand.

ents; the quantity of these children is Q_0 in Figure 10. The supply curve is positively sloped because, as the price paid for children is increased, some women may decide not to have abortions and others who would otherwise keep their unexpected or unwanted children may relinquish them for a price. At sufficiently high prices, babymaking might become a cottage industry. The price paid for a child need not be monetary; in current legal markets, the biological parents may consider payment of medical costs by adoptive parents or assurances about a reasonably bright future for the child to be adequate payment. In a black market exchange, of course, cold cash changes hands.

The demand curve in Figure 10 slopes downward because people find substitutes as prices rise; you may know people who view their pets as surrogate children. Other families may just give up their quest for an adoptive child or postpone kids until they can afford them. At the legally permissible explicit price of zero, there will be Q_0 children available for adoption and Q_2 children demanded, leaving a shortage of at least $Q_2 - Q_0$. Does this mean that under the current adoption system Q_0 children are adopted, or that the economic costs to adopting parents is zero? The answer to both questions is no.

Social concern about the well-being of foster and adopted children has generated a large bureaucracy to oversee their care. Applicants for adoption are carefully screened, and extensive efforts are made to match the characteristics of children and adoptive parents. Many questions are asked about finances, attitudes about sex, religion, race, discipline, etc. Common grounds for rejecting applicants may seem capricious: obesity, atheism, radical politics, or the desire for a career by the female member of an applying couple are all frequently cited as supporting rejection. Even when all barriers are hurdled, the process of becoming an "approved home" may take years because there are few incentives for social workers to act quickly or efficiently. Indeed, persistently jumping through the hoops of this process is viewed as a way for potential adoptive parents to demonstrate their commitment to adopting a child.

Unfortunately, approval does not guarantee that a family will be able to adopt. Each infant or child also undergoes screening procedures; relinquished children and prospective adoptive parents alike must wait for a "match." Infants are seldom placed in an adoptive home at ages of less than three months; six months is reasonably common. Older children or those with severe handicaps remain "hard to place," but the adoption shortage has become so acute that such previously hard-to-place children as those who are racially mixed or mildly handicapped are relatively easily placed. Even so, adoption agencies fail to find homes for many of the children who are available for adoption (Q_0 in Figure 10) when a zero price is paid to the relinquishing parents.

Is the economic cost of these adoptions zero? Far from it. Long queuing periods for both prospective parents and adoptable children entail substantial costs. Successful adoptive families typically are willing to pay a demand price of at least P_0 for the children available for adoption at Q_0. The parents who most desire children pay this price by courting the social workers to prove their commitment to adoption. Prospective adoptive parents, however, are legally forbidden to pay an explicit monetary price

greater than zero for a child. The result? Gray and black markets for infants flourish, with high prices being paid to doctors and lawyers who are willing to flirt with prosecution by acting as baby brokers.

Black market babies have been sold for as much as $60,000 apiece. We should note, however, that the economic cost per current legal adoption is probably not far from the average of $25,000 or so that children bring on black or gray markets. More than $36,000 in tax revenues were spent per legal adoption in 1981, and the costs of extended periods of waiting that confront both adoptive parents and children must be considered.

A Market Solution Many childless couples place values on children that are higher than the (re)production costs to some natural parents. (Evidence of this include the highly publicized option of surrogate motherhood by artificial insemination.) The demand prices for children are higher than the supply prices up to Q_1 adoptable children in Figure 10. Allowing the market to resolve the allocation of adoptable children would cause children who were not especially valued by their natural parents (those whose supply prices range from zero to P_1) to be sold to people who would value them more (those whose demand prices equal or exceed P_1). Presumably, the people who would value these children more would also care for them better and love them more.

Drawbacks of the Market Solution One counterargument against reliance on the market is that only the rich would be able to adopt. Under the current system, however, adoption agencies typically disqualify the childless poor because these agencies do weigh income heavily when approving homes. The poor might find adoption easier under a free-market system. In the absence of other evidence, willingness to pay is a reasonable measure of how much someone values something.

Another objection to the market solution is that explicit prices provide incentives for kidnapping for the market. Birth certificates and footprinting would provide only partial protection against determined thieves, and using tatoos (as some people do for valuable pets) is not a socially acceptable solution. It is also possible that a "baby" industry might emerge. This would be morally repugnant to many people. Still another problem is that some people might buy children for unacceptable reasons: child prostitution, for example. Of course, child protection laws apply to all homes, whether natural or adoptive. Current kiddie-porn stars are often exploited by their natural parents.

Although a market for adoption would have many shortcomings, proposals to change current policy in any area should not be evaluated against perfection, but rather against the current system, warts and all. At the very least, the current system might be modified so that market forces are allowed to play a role wherever this would benefit adoptees, adopters, and relinquishing parents.

Are there simple solutions to such problems as heroin addiction and baby shortages? Should supply and demand be allowed to operate without tight government controls? The answer probably depends on the conditions of the particular market. We hope, however, that these overviews of the heroin and adoption markets convince you that market forces cannot be ignored when structuring social policies, even in areas that are closely tied to people's views of morality.

You have now had an overview of supply and demand in action. It is time to address how effectively, equitably, and efficiently market mechanisms answer the questions of *What? How? Who?* and *When?*

☆ The Market in Operation

Our analysis of the price system relies on two critical assumptions:

1. *individuals are self-interested* and try to maximize their personal satisfaction through the goods they consume. If goods add less to your satisfaction (valued in terms of money) than they cost, you will not buy them. Consumer willingness to buy underpins the demands for goods.

2. *firms attempt to maximize profits.* They do this by selling goods to consumers who are willing to pay for them. The drive for profit underpins the supply side of the market.

Thus, the price system answers the *What?* question by producing the things consumers demand.

Two things limit a firm's ability to take advantage of consumers. First, competition among sellers keeps prices from straying much above costs for very long because high profits attract new firms, increasing supply so that prices and profits fall. Second, suppliers strive to be efficient because any firm that cuts costs or introduces a successful technology temporarily reaps higher profits. Before long, any firm not using the new technology will be trying to sell outdated products, or its costs will exceed its competitors' prices and it will fail. Competition among producers ensures that price is approximately equal to the opportunity cost (sacrifice to society) entailed in production. Thus, a competitive market system answers the *How?* question by using the least costly method of production.

How are products distributed among consumers? The answer to this *Who?* question is relatively simple. Consumers who hold "dollar votes" and are willing to pay market prices purchase and consume products. Those who do not own many resources cannot buy a lot of goods. It is this distributional side that is most vigorously attacked by critics of the market system. The question of *When?* is automatically answered by the cumulative answers a society gives over time to the questions of *What? How?* and *Who?*

Many people perceive the price system as impersonal and inequitable. However, the market offers some major compensating advantages. Decisions are decentralized; no government agency tells you what you must (or cannot) buy or produce. Moreover, markets tend to be efficient. Consumers usually pay prices for goods that roughly reflect the minimal costs of producing these goods.

As you proceed through this book, you will constantly encounter the supply and demand analysis presented in this and the previous chapter. No tool of economics is more important. Material in the next chapter discusses the institutions within which supply and demand operate in a market economy.

CHAPTER REVIEW: KEY POINTS

1. Increases in supplies or decreases in demands tend to reduce prices. Decreases in supplies or increases in demands tend to increase prices. Increases in either supplies or demands tend to increase quantities. Decreases in either supplies or demands tend to decrease quantities. If both supply and demand shift, the effects on price and quantity may be either reinforcing or at least partially offsetting. (If these points make little sense to you, you need to review this important material.)

2. Government can set prices at values other than equilibrium price, but *price ceilings* or *price floors* do not "freeze" opportunity costs; instead, these *price controls* create economic inefficiency and either shortages or surpluses, respectively.

3. Prices do not always quickly adjust to their equilibrium values. At times, they swing up and down as they slowly approach the intersections of demands and supplies.

4. Speculators and middlemen play important roles in many markets. *Middlemen* are successful only if they reduce the transactions costs associated with getting products from the ultimate producers to the ultimate consumers. *Speculators* aid in movements towards equilibrium because they try to buy when prices are below equilibrium (increasing demand) and sell when prices are above equilibrium (increasing supply). This dampens swings in prices and reduces the costs and risks of doing business with others.

5. *Arbitrage* involves buying in a market where the price is low and selling in a market where the price is higher. If this price spread is greater than the transaction cost, arbitrage is profitable without risk. *Competition* for opportunities to arbitrage prevents these profits from being very large and facilitates efficiency by ensuring that price spreads between markets are minimal.

QUESTIONS FOR THOUGHT AND DISCUSSION

1. Draw supply and demand graphs for the relevant markets to show the impact of the following changes on prices and quantities. Be as explicit as possible about the market adjustment mechanisms.

a. There is a major technological breakthrough in producing natural gas from coal. What happens in the market for natural gas? The market for coal?

b. What happens to the world market for coffee if coffee blight destroys three quarters of the crop in Brazil? The market for tea?

c. Gasoline prices soar. What happens in the markets for big cars? Bicycles? Tune-up shops? Rapid transit systems?

d. The economy goes sour. What happens to the market for economists?

e. Tomorrow afternoon AT&T announces that oil has been discovered under every telephone pole. What happens to the market for AT&T stock? How rapidly would this occur? Do you think you could get rich buying AT&T stock the next day? (The answer is NO!) Who would get rich from this discovery?

f. A legal maximum price for denim jeans is set at $1 per pair. What happens to quantity? To quality? To opportunity cost? Is the government doing denim jean wearers any favor?

g. A "miracle seed" for corn is developed. Analyze the markets for corn and wheat.

h. The birthrate suddenly increases enormously. What would happen in the market for baby furniture? The market for babysitters? The market for nightclub entertainment or movies? Are the answers to these questions different in the short run and long run? How?

i. In 1989, the government announces a major renewal of space exploration. In 1997, this program is discontinued. What will happen to the market for aeronautical engineers in 1989–90? Between 1990 and 1997? In 1997–98?

j. There is a radical overhaul and simplification of the income tax system. What happens to the market for accountants? Lawyers? Erasers?

k. The minimum legal wage is raised from $3.35 per hour to $5.00 per hour. What happens in labor markets for teenagers and other unskilled workers?

2. Ticket scalpers provide consumers with various services. The latecomer can avoid standing in line for tickets and can wait until the last moment before deciding to attend. Should these services be free? What can promoters of any event do to prevent scalping? Do they really want to prevent scalping? See if you can devise graphs to explain this form of speculation.

3. Senator Ernest Hollings (D–South Carolina), in advocating wage-price controls, has asserted that "most people would prefer shortages to higher prices." Do you think this is true? Why or why not? Do you think advocates of wage-price freezes understand that shortages arise from controls?

4. Casual surveys of our students at the beginning of each semester reveal an amused but overwhelming support for a proposal to raise the legal minimum wages of college graduates to $50,000 per year. (They assumed our proposal was facetious.) After covering this chapter, student support for this idea evaporated. How might such a minimum wage law be harmful to most new college graduates?

5. Pharmaceutical companies have recently developed and tested drugs that reverse the influence of alcohol on the brain within a half hour. These pills enable drivers to sober up before driving home, and also tend to reduce the severity of hangovers. In the past few years, many states have imposed stiff mandatory penalties for drunk driving convictions. How do you think these two separate events will interact to influence alcohol consumption?

6. In 1979, President Carter imposed quotas limiting the oil that could be imported, using the argument that ". . . we import inflation every time we import another barrel of expensive oil into this country." Do import quotas (on such things as oil, clothes, or cars) drive prices up, or will prices be held down as President Carter suggested?

7. Laws forbid or severely limit free-market transactions in atomic bombs, adoptable babies, murder-for-hire, sex, marijuana, surrogate motherhood, pornography, and a host of other forms of production. At the same time, minimal education and inoculations against communicable diseases are compulsory. Which of these or other illegal or mandatory goods do you think could be allocated more efficiently and equitably through the market system? Are there goods that are now bought and sold freely that you believe the government should control tightly? What are they? Why?

CHAPTER 5 Economic Institutions: Households, Firms, and Government

<table>
<tr>
<td>circular flow
services
durable and
    nondurable goods
plants, firms, and
    industries</td>
<td>horizontal and vertical
    integration
conglomerates
sole proprietorship
partnerships
corporations</td>
<td>monopoly power
externalities and public
    goods
business cycles</td>
</tr>
</table>

Supplies and demands do not operate in a vacuum but, rather, within an institutional framework. This chapter provides an overview of the major institutions that shape economic behavior: households, firms, and government. A market system pivots on the decisions of households and business firms, which together are called the *private sector*. Government, or the *public sector,* takes a back seat only to the marketplace in its importance as an allocative mechanism in our mixed economy. To set the stage for an examination of public and private relationships, we will use a simple model of the private economy.

Circular Flows of Resources, Goods, and Income

Households are centers for consumption and ultimately own both the wealth and the resources that are supplied to business firms in exchange for income. They are also the firms' ultimate customers, as shown in the **circular flow** diagram in Figure 1. In this model of a purely private economy, households demand food, shelter, and a host of other goods, and own all resources used for production. Households supply labor services, land, capital, and

FIGURE 1 *The Circular Flow of Income, Resources, and Goods*

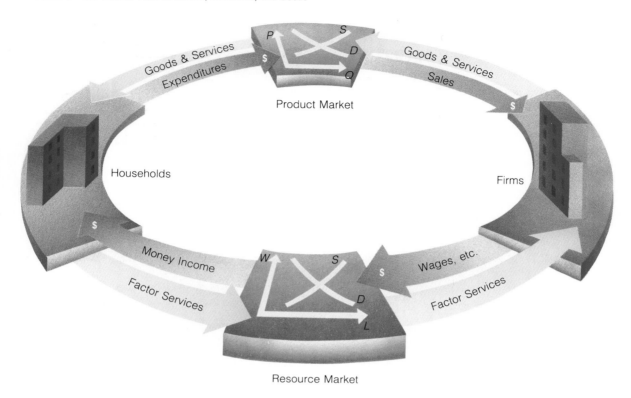

The circular flow of income is a simple model depicting a private economy. Firms provide goods and services to households and receive dollars for these products. Households in turn provide factors of production to business in exchange for money income, which is used to purchase goods and services from business.

entrepreneurial skills to firms, and then spend their incomes for consumer goods.

In turn, firms use sales revenues to pay for the resources that households provide. Firms interpret prices and profits as signals about consumer demands, and use the wage rates paid for specific labor skills, rental rates for land, or rates of return on capital to signal households about the resources demanded for production.

It is important to remember that firms are not the final owners of resources, nor do they truly own products. Businesses and all the assets they use are owned by individuals. Thus, firms ultimately do not reap profits; they only relay profits to their owners. Nor can firms bear tax burdens; only their owners,

customers, or resource suppliers actually pay taxes. It is common to speak of a firm profiting, changing prices, or introducing a new product, but regularly remind yourself that firms are merely conduits for individual decisions and economic behavior. Activities that matter affect people, not business firms per se.

Households

Households is a catchall term that covers richly diverse forms of income and consumption. By 1985, 240 million Americans were spread among more than 85 million households. Sociologists perceive

TABLE 1 *Functional Distribution of Income, 1929–85*

Year	Total Income	Percentage of Total Income				
		Compensation of Employees	Proprietors' Income	Net Rents	Corporate Profits	Interest
1929	84.8	60.3	17.6	5.8	10.8	5.5
1933	39.9	73.9	14.5	5.5	−4.3	10.3
1940	79.7	65.4	16.2	3.4	10.9	4.1
1950	236.2	65.5	16.3	3.0	14.3	1.0
1960	412.0	71.6	11.4	3.3	11.3	2.4
1970	798.4	76.3	8.2	2.3	8.5	4.7
1980	2,117.1	75.5	5.7	3.1	8.6	8.9
1985	3,228.0	73.9	7.4	0.6	9.6	8.7

Source: *Economic Report of the President,* 1986.

constant upheavals in modern family structures, but changes in the basic economic roles of households occur only at a snail's pace.

Sources of Household Income

Circular flow diagrams indicate that households are the ultimate receivers of income. Table 1 shows that rent, interest, and profit provide less than one-fourth of total income to households. The rest of all income from supplying resources is from *wages*—which include salaries, commissions, fringe benefits, and so on. The major asset of most households is the labor provided by family members.

A century ago, most families relied on income from agriculture. Today, over half of all labor is in white-collar occupations—a category that includes doctors, lawyers, teachers, managers, and sales and clerical workers. Blue-collar work (assembly lines and construction are examples) and, especially, farming have receded as major forms of employment.

The most dramatic change in labor markets over the past few decades has been the surge of women into the labor force. In the 1950s, only one woman in three worked outside the home; more than half hold jobs today, and 44 percent of all workers are women. This rise in the proportion of women in the labor force is charted in Figure 2. Even more remarkable is the threefold increase in working mothers with small children.

Several theories have been advanced to explain these changes. A revolution of rising expectations about living standards propelled many women into the work force who might have been housewives in an earlier era. Also, changing laws and attitudes about women's work roles opened doors to careers that were previously closed. The flight from the worst types of household drudgery was facilitated by such innovations as washers and dryers, microwave ovens, and permanent-press clothing. Options to postpone children and curb their family's size have been made available by cheap and effective birth control, also increasing women's labor force participation rates.

These changes have not occurred in a vacuum. Figure 2 reveals that the labor force participation rates of men fell slightly over this same period, partially because more young men are going to college, while mature men have typically been retiring at earlier ages.

Household Uses of Income

Household income is totally exhausted by *consumer spending, saving,* and *taxes.* Consumer spending absorbs about 70 percent of national income, and can be used for the services and durable or nondurable goods sold by private firms. **Services** include medical care, haircuts, education, and so on, and account for a growing share of total spending. Furniture, appliances, cars, and other **durable goods** normally last more than a year. **Nondurable goods** tend to be used up quickly and include such things as food, clothes, and gasoline.

FIGURE 2 *Men and Women in the Labor Force*

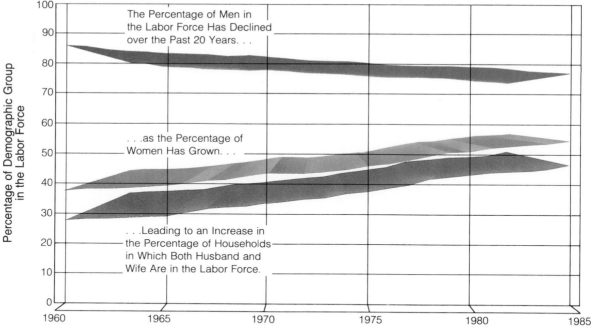

Source: Bureau of Labor Statistics, Bulletin 2096, updated.

Spending on food as a proportion of income has fallen over time, reflecting advances in agricultural technology and decreases in the relative prices of food. Five out of six Americans lived and worked on farms in 1800, but fewer than one in thirty now depends primarily on agriculture for income. This small group feeds all of us and many foreigners as well, but predicted worldwide droughts may soon enlarge the role of food in typical family budgets. The share of income spent on housing fell after the Depression, but recently rose as average home prices climbed past the $100,000 mark.

Consumption expenditures have fallen from 83 percent of income in 1929 to roughly 70 percent today. Over the same interval, net taxes rose from about 12 percent to nearly 25 percent of income. This reflects growing demands for government services over the past half century, although budget cuts in the 1980s may reverse this trend.

Saving has fluctuated a bit over the past half century or so, but has averaged roughly 5 percent of income. Families save only if their incomes exceed the spending required for what they view as necessities. In fact, the bulk of personal saving in our society is done by families with annual incomes exceeding $60,000. Figure 3 shows uses of total income by typical modern households.

We have now looked at the roles of households as resource suppliers to business firms and as customers for the final products of business. This leads to the roles played by the business sector.

The Business Sector

The business of America is business.
—*Calvin Coolidge*

Over 75 percent of employment and 80 percent of U.S. production flows from the business sector, with most of the rest being accounted for by government. Although business dominates the economic landscape, many people take it for granted. In this section, you should gain an understanding of what firms do and how they interact with households and government.

FIGURE 3 *The Composition of Personal Consumer Expenditures, 1985*

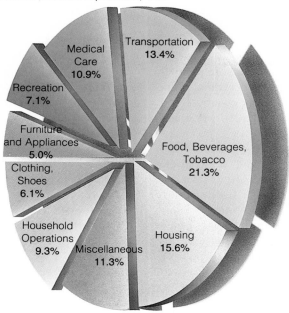

Source: U.S. Department of Commerce.

Plants, Firms, and Industries

Your favorite pro football team, IBM, and the local phone company are all business **firms.** Firms operate one or more **plants,** which refer to the facilities clumped together at a specific location. Plants may be used for manufacturing, processing, fabrication, assembly, or sales. Firms that operate more than one plant are called *multiplant* firms; if they provide a number of products, they are *multiproduct* or diversified firms. Giant multiproduct firms are termed **conglomerates.**

An **industry** is composed of all firms competing in a given product market; for example, tobacco, chemicals, or clothing. **Horizontally integrated** firms operate at a number of locations, each doing essentially the same thing. For example, General Motors produces the same cars in plants in Michigan and Ohio, and McDonald's "golden arches" grace the scenery from Berlin to Singapore. It might seem easy to identify the firms that make up an industry, but consider motor vehicles. Are Lincolns and Chevettes really close substitutes? Should imported cars be included? Vans? Trucks? Is it reasonable to lump all these products into a single industry?

Another problem in defining the boundaries of an industry is that conglomerates are often major producers in several industries. Even nonconglomerates may operate at different production levels within an industry; these firms are called **vertically integrated.** Most steel producers are examples of vertical integration. They operate mines, smelting plants, mills for producing rolled steel, and fabrication plants. Conglomerates, in contrast, operate plants in several different industries. For example, Gulf and Western produces movies, publishes books, and is also involved in electronics and mining. In fact, most large corporations are so diversified that they are conglomerates.

Legal Forms of Business

Businesses are operated as sole proprietorships, partnerships, or corporations. Over three-fourths of all U.S. firms are sole proprietorships, but they account for less than one-third of all profits. At the other extreme, only one firm in seven is incorporated, but corporations generate over 60 percent of total profits in the United States. The message seems to be that a first step towards success is to incorporate. Then why do over 10 million sole proprietorships exist? The answer comes from an examination of the strengths and weaknesses of each type of business organization.

Sole Proprietorships

Establishing a **sole proprietorship** requires little more than declaring, "I am in business for myself." You are your own boss, and your profits depend on your skill, hard work, and luck. The major advantages to sole proprietorships are that such firms are (*a*) easy to organize, (*b*) simple to control, (*c*) quite flexible, and (*d*) relatively free from government regulation.

There are, however, some major disadvantages. The firm's size is limited by the proprietor's initial wealth and credit standing and by the profits of the business as time unfolds. Capital accumulation for expansion is difficult. Proprietors normally perform most management functions, and such firms lack permanence because they cannot outlive their owners. The greatest disadvantage, however, is a proprietor's *unlimited liability*. Nearly all a proprietor owns, including possessions unrelated to the business, may be sold to pay a firm's debts if it fails or is held liable for a huge judgment in a lawsuit. Much more is at risk than the owner's investment, although insurance can protect proprietors from some legal hazards.

Partnerships

Partnerships are extensions of proprietorships; two or more people combine their resources to form a business, hoping to overcome some financial and managerial disadvantages faced by a sole proprietor. Partnerships are easy to establish, relatively simple to control, allow some specialized management, and are subject to relatively few regulations. Pooled resources in a partnership may make capital accumulation easier than for sole proprietorships.

However, partners continue to face unlimited personal liability for the firm's debts, and dishonest, incompetent, or accident-prone partners can cost you all your assets. Shared ownership also often creates discord over a firm's policies. Other drawbacks are that resources for growth tend to remain quite limited, and partnerships automatically dissolve upon the withdrawal or death of any partner.

Corporations

Corporations are organizations sanctioned by state laws and are considered *legal persons* separate and distinct from their owners. Incorporating a firm requires submitting a *charter* to a state government outlining the business operations intended and specifying how the firm would be financed and governed. Once formed, numerous special taxes and regulations hinder corporate operations.

Then why do people incorporate a business? One major reason is that corporations excel at raising financial capital because they can sell **common stocks** (ownership shares in a corporation) and **bonds** (corporate IOUs). Combined with undistributed profits, these funds may permit acquisition of vast amounts of economic (physical) capital. This is primarily due to a second corporate advantage: the *limited liability* of stockholders, which means that owners of a corporation cannot lose more than they have paid for stock. Their other assets are not directly jeopardized if the corporation fails.

Other advantages include the stability and potential permanence of corporations. A stockholder's death does not require an end to a corporation. A final advantage is that large corporations are able to employ highly specialized management. In fact, large corporations are often controlled by their top managers because stock is so widely spread that individual stockholders have very little influence on business policies. This is a gain for corporate managers, but can be a disadvantage for the stockholders who own the corporation.

Other negative aspects of incorporation are special corporate taxes and regulations. The divorce of ownership from managerial control opens up opportunities for fraud, so strict accounting and reporting requirements govern corporate life and add to business costs. Because corporations are viewed as fruitful sources of tax revenue, corporate profits are subject to double taxation. This *double taxation* occurs because corporations pay taxes on their incomes and then, when some aftertax income is distributed to stockholders as dividends, they are taxed again at the individual's personal income tax rate. Table 2 summarizes the attributes of the three major forms of business organization.

Although proprietorships, partnerships, and corporations dominate private production, other types of organizations exist. *Producer cooperatives* share the profits from marketing such things as handicrafts or agricultural goods. *Consumer cooperatives* share savings achieved through large-scale buying. *Non-profit corporations* operate hospitals, charities, pri-

TABLE 2 Summary of Legal Forms of Business Organization

Form of Business	Advantages	Disadvantages
Sole Proprietorship	1. Easy to organize. 2. Simple to control. 3. Freedom of operation. 4. Not subject to much government regulation.	1. Difficult to acquire funds (capital) for expansion. 2. Firm lacks permanence. 3. Unlimited liability. 4. Owner must perform all management functions.
Partnership	1. Easy to organize. 2. Greater specialization of management is possible. 3. Securing financial resources easier than in sole proprietorship (pooling of funds). 4. Subject to limited regulation.	1. Division of ownership may lead to disagreements. 2. Death or withdrawal of one partner automatically ends the organization. 3. Subject to unlimited liability. 4. Financial resources are typically quite limited.
Corporation	1. Capability of raising large amounts of capital through sale of stocks and bonds. 2. Limited liability of stockholders. 3. Stability and permanence: is a legal entity (person) all its own. 4. Employment of specialized management personnel.	1. Subject to considerable government regulation. 2. Taxes and organizing costs for corporations are heavy burdens. 3. Double taxation of corporate income and dividends. 4. Separation of ownership and control.

vate schools, and such community services as educational TV. *Closely held corporations* and *limited partnerships* are legal devices to obtain certain tax advantages and limited liability for family-owned businesses or partnerships. Still other minor forms of business organization abound, varying in their particulars according to the state laws that govern them.

Corporate Goals and Control

Some firms fail while others prosper. The market system rewards those who serve the consumer and society, while competitive pressures force inefficient firms to adapt or exit the market. Many firms vie for the patronage of consumers in competitive markets. Will society derive the same benefits if a few firms dominate a market? Most people think not.

Criticisms of Corporate America   Economist John Kenneth Galbraith and consumer advocate Ralph Nader achieved fame by attacking economic theories that stress competitive markets and the goal of profit

maximization. In one of his many books, *The New Industrial State,* Galbraith argued that giant corporations:

1. dominate economic activity because small competitive firms cannot afford the modern technologies required for efficient production.

2. are controlled by corporate managers who seek maximum power and pay for themselves instead of maximum profits for stockholders.

3. tend to corrupt government policies to help consolidate managerial power and achieve managers' goals rather than the public interest.

4. use extensive advertising to avoid meaningful competition.

What evidence supports Galbraith's claims? First, corporations do account for $5 out of $6 of U.S. business revenues, and control a large share of our national resources. The top 2,000 manufacturing corporations have assets exceeding $10 million each, and the largest 200 control roughly 60 percent of all manufacturing assets. There is also an erratic long-term trend towards even greater concentration in the ownership of total manufacturing assets. According to Galbraith, our only hope for a just society is for modern corporate managers to become more *socially responsible,* but he is pessimistic about the prospects for such changes of heart.

Ralph Nader agrees with many of Galbraith's points, but with a different focus. He believes that giant corporations are too profit-oriented and has lobbied long and hard for laws and regulations to limit corporate discretion about pricing, pollution, product safety, and a long list of other areas.

Are Corporate Giants Immune from Market Pressures?

Much of modern economic life seems far removed from competitive models of the economy. Indeed, some corporate giants dwarf the govern-ments of even sizable countries, as Figure 4 indicates. There is, however, evidence that markets serve con-sumers reasonably well and that size alone does not insulate huge firms from competitive pressures. Gi-ants compete with giants.

Such once dominant retailers as Sears, Montgom-ery Ward, and J. C. Penney have lost ground to firms like K-Mart, Corvette, Venture, and Target, while Woolco and other giants have collapsed. In the late 1950s, Ford Motor Company lost millions of dollars when it launched the ill-fated Edsel. It more than recouped these losses when it developed the Mus-tang, a car that passed the test of the marketplace. A shaky economy and competition from foreign auto-

FIGURE 4 *Thirty of the Largest Organizations in the World, by Annual Receipts or Expenditures, Billions of Dollars, 1984–85*

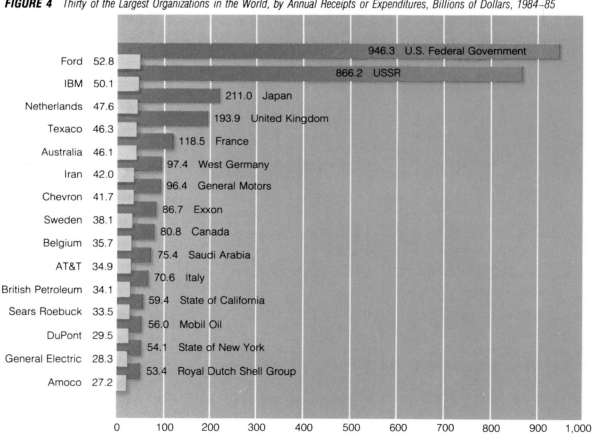

The 30 largest organizations are not all governments. Nearly half, in fact, are private organizations—oil companies being the most numerous. *Note:* Some giants may not be represented because reasonable estimates are not available.

Source: CIA, *The World Factbook 1985; Fortune,* April 28, 1986; United Nations, *Statistical Yearbook,* 1985; and *Information Please Almanac,* 1985.

TABLE 3 Turnover among the Top 10 and Top 50 U.S. Corporations, 1969–85

Dates	Entered the Top 10		Left the Top 10	
1969–74	Standard Oil of California		Chrysler	
1974–79	AMOCO (Standard Oil of Indiana)		International Telephone and Telegraph	
1979–85	American Telephone and Telegraph E.I. du Pont de Nemours		Gulf Oil AMOCO (Standard Oil of Indiana)	

Dates	Entered the Top 50		Left the Top 50	
1969–74	Esmark Union Oil of California Amerada Hess Xerox	Beatrice Foods Greyhound Borden R.J. Reynolds Ashland Oil	General Telephone and Telegraph Swift McDonnell Douglas General Dynamics	Litton Industries Armour Singer General Foods Rapid American
1974–79	General Foods Phillip Morris Cities Service	Marathon Oil Standard Oil of Ohio	Greyhound Borden Lockheed	W.R. Grace Firestone
1979–85	McDonnell Douglas Lockheed Allied Signal Pepsi Co. Coca Cola	Minnesota Mining and Manufacturing General Dynamics W.R. Grace Coastal	Monsanto Cities Service Marathon Oil Bethlehem Steel RCA	Caterpillar International Harvester Conoco Gulf Oil

Source: *Fortune,* "The Fortune 500: The Largest U.S. Industrial Corporations," May 1970, May 1975, May 1980, and April 1986.

makers imposed billions of dollars in losses on U.S. automakers in the late 1970s, and Chrysler teetered on the brink of bankruptcy. Automakers recovered only when they marketed more fuel efficient and reliable cars. And where are last century's giant railroads? Most disappeared or were absorbed into Amtrak, a government-subsidized money loser.

Interindustry competition has become increasingly important. Xerox once had a near monopoly on copying equipment, but now competes with IBM and a host of Japanese firms. IBM had a stranglehold on computers in the 1960s, but is now besieged with competition from Apple, Radio Shack, Control Data, Wang, NCR, DEC, Xerox, Compaq, AT&T, and hundreds of small electronics firms.

Giants often emerge from nowhere when entrepreneurs perceive a void in the marketplace. A 17-year-old and a 22-year-old launched Apple Computers in a home garage in 1978 for under $500, creating a billion-dollar firm within 4 years after they built the first low-cost personal computer. It is hard to overstate how risky business can be. A boom in personal computer sales and software in the early 1980s made overnight millionaires of hundreds of young workaholics in the "Silicon Valley", an area just south of San Francisco. Gluts on the market quickly appeared, however, and numerous computer firms of all sizes collapsed during 1984–86.

Another type of adjustment occurs when huge firms headed by inefficient top managers are targeted for "hostile" takeovers by such highly publicized "corporate raiders" as T. Boone Pickens, Carl Icahn, and Ted Turner. The absorbed companies generally grow more profitable when new managers direct these firms toward areas more compatible with consumer demands. This often involves shutting down the unprofitable subsidiaries of overly diversified conglomerates, or selling them if more specialized management can run them better.

There are almost innumerable examples of dynamic competition. Some companies that have, relatively, lost or gained a lot during the past few years are listed in Table 3, which indicates how the corporate pecking order can change over time.

The key point is that high profits attract aggressive competition, both foreign and domestic, so that consumers' needs are met in a reasonably efficient fashion. Many people are still unhappy with the outcomes of the marketplace, however, and increasingly have turned to government to resolve economic problems. The distribution of income as determined in the market is widely perceived as unfair. And what about national defense, or such problems as pollution and persistent unemployment? These are among the areas in which government plays an active role in our society.

The Role of Government

Government directly provides some goods, and indirectly channels resources and the production and consumption of other goods via taxes and regulations. As we approach the twenty-first century, our society is much more regulated and taxed than in earlier times when government economic policies were restricted by a more laissez-faire philosophy. Federal, state, and local governments now directly allocate roughly one-fifth of national production; another 15 percent is redistributed through transfer payments, with two-thirds of all transfers being made by the federal government. *Transfer payments* include welfare expenditures, loans to farmers and students, interest on the national debt, and similar outlays. Figure 5 provides some measures of the size and recent growth of total government activity.

Many people see government action as necessary whenever markets apparently fail to respond to our desires for equity, efficiency, full employment, stable prices, and prosperous growth. Widely accepted economic goals for government in a market economy are to:

1. provide a stable legal environment for business activity;
2. promote and maintain competitive markets;
3. allocate resources in order to meet public wants efficiently;
4. facilitate equity through redistributions of income; and,
5. ensure full employment, a stable price level, and a growing standard of living.

Although macroeconomic and microeconomic policies are unavoidably interdependent, goals 1–4 tend to be microeconomic concerns, while goal 5 is the focus of macroeconomic policymaking.

Providing a Stable Legal Environment

A reasonably certain legal environment helps to prevent chaos. If ownership rights or the rules of business were uncertain, could an economy still function? Private property rights or contracts, if they existed, would be enforced only through brute force or individual persuasion. Primitive trading would occur, but complex financial transactions would be impossible.

The government sets rules establishing legal relationships between parties, regulates public utilities and other important industries, establishes standard weights and measures, sets monetary standards, insures bank deposits, and engages in other activities to protect public confidence and health.

Promoting Competition

Competition allows us to enjoy the benefits of efficient private markets. Profits signal that consumers want more than current levels of particular products; losses signal that too much is being offered. New technologies that create better and cheaper products force older firms to adapt or perish. This is why hand-cranked autos don't clog our highways and motor-driven calculators don't clutter our desks.

Monopoly lies at the opposite end of the spectrum of market structures from competition, and occurs when a single firm dominates a market. **Monopoly power** exists whenever individual firms significantly influence the supply and price of a good, and may be present even when several firms share a market. In competitive markets, buyers and sellers are so small that, alone, none can noticeably affect total output or prices. A firm possessing monopoly power increases profits by restricting output and setting higher prices. This yields inefficiency because equilibrium monopoly prices exceed the opportunity costs of additional production.

The basic approach to controlling monopoly power in the United States has been through antitrust laws and regulation. Antitrust laws are attempts to curb unfair business practices and prevent huge firms from absorbing all their competitors. Where competition is impractical, regulation is used to limit the abuse of monopoly power.

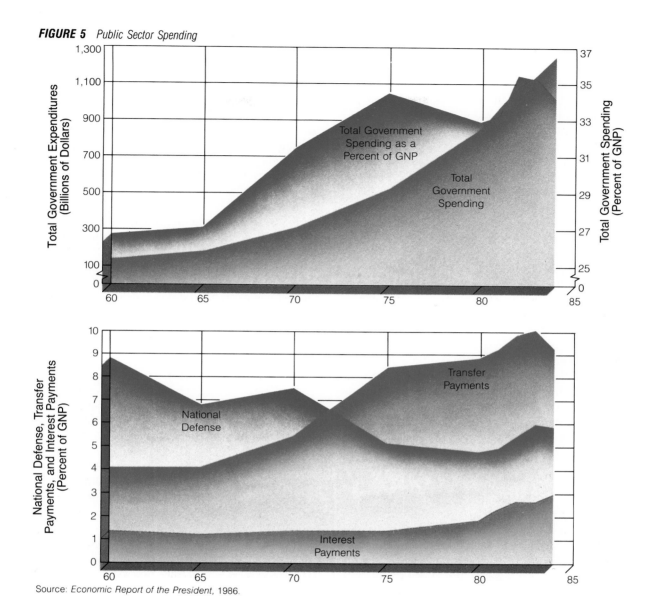

FIGURE 5 *Public Sector Spending*

Source: *Economic Report of the President,* 1986.

Providing for Public Wants

What happens if the price signals from consumers are distorted, or firms are unable to market a desired good profitably? Even if firms operate in a stable and competitive environment, certain market failures may still seem to justify government action. Externalities, of which pollution is one form, can warp price signals so that our demands are not accurately reflected. A second difficulty, called the public goods problem, results when shared consumption is possi-

ble but people cannot be denied access to the benefits of a good. National defense is an example.

Externalities **Externalities** occur when some benefits or costs of an activity spill over to parties not directly involved in the activity. For example, when farmers spray their crops, some pesticide may eventually wash into nearby lakes or streams. If the pesticide is absorbed by microorganisms and works its way up the ecological chain, your fishing or health may deteriorate so that you partially bear the cost of the use of chemical sprays. Most human activities generate externalities, some trivial and some of major concern. Cooking creates heat and smoke, every car emits noxious fumes, loud stereos annoy your neighbors, and so on. All forms of pollution—chemical, air, noise, and litter—are *negative externalities.*

Producers whose activities generate negative externalities tend to ignore costs imposed on others, and the prices they charge reflect only their private costs. Pollution-generating goods consequently tend to be overproduced and underpriced. The government uses various regulations to control different pollutants because absolutely prohibiting pollution would probably eliminate all production.

Inefficiency may also occur when *positive externalities* spill over from an activity. Immunization against contagious diseases is one such activity. You are less likely to suffer from the flu if you are inoculated, and we who are your neighbors are less likely to catch it as well. But you tend to ignore our benefits when you decide whether or not to be immunized, and so are less likely to get a flu shot than is socially optimal. Thus, private market decisions result in underproduction and overpricing of goods that generate positive externalities because the value to society exceeds the demand price individuals willingly pay when they are uncompensated for external benefits.

Public Goods   **Public goods** are both *nonrival,* meaning that everyone can consume such goods simultaneously, and *nonexclusive,* meaning that denying people access to such goods is prohibitively expensive. Most goods are *private goods,* however; they are *rival* and *exclusive.* If you eat a corn chip laden with guacamole, no one else can enjoy that particular morsel; food and other private goods are rival. But we need not compete with each other to use public goods once they are produced because our uses of public goods do not involve rivalry.

This may sound impossible, but consider police protection. Each violent criminal taken off the street makes us all safer. Other public goods include weather reports, cancer research, democratic government, and national defense. Once the armed forces are maintained and ready, every person in the United States consumes defense services simultaneously, and we all receive this protection whether we pay (through taxes) or not, and whether we want it or not!

Public goods cannot be privately and profitably marketed to efficiently service our collective demands for them. A few people might contribute funds for a nonrival good from which exclusion was impossible, but not in amounts sufficient for efficient provision. There is little incentive to reveal your demands for space exploration, spraying against mosquitos, landscaping along a public highway, or maintaining courts and prisons if you will be taxed accordingly. Why not be a "free rider"? Private firms could not adequately market such services, so government provides a variety of public goods and forces us to pay for them through taxes.

Note, however, that public provision does not require public production. For example, NASA space probes use equipment built by private firms. Alan Shepard, the first American astronaut in space, reported that the last thought that flashed through his mind before his rocket was launched was that it was made of millions of parts, ". . . all built by the lowest bidder."

Income Redistribution

The market mechanism seems impersonal and yields distributions of income and wealth that many people view as inequitable. Goods are channeled to those who own valuable resources, whether they "need" them or not. Most people are distressed by the suffering of those who live in abject poverty and, if they are modestly prosperous, will donate some money to help the unfortunate poor or the starving children of the world. But private charity is inadequate to fulfill society's collective desire for equity because "curing poverty" is a public good—I may not donate if your charitable contribution makes me more comfortable when thinking about the poor. This leads to such government programs as welfare and disaster relief.

Stabilizing Income, Prices, and Employment

A market economy may not have strong natural mechanisms that consistently yield full employment without inflation. In fact, wide swings in economic activity, called **business cycles,** may be a natural tendency in a market economy. During business cycles, employment and inflation fluctuate, dislocating workers, firms, and consumers, and generally disrupting our social institutions.

Shortly after World War II, Congress stated some general goals in the Employment Act of 1946:

> The Congress hereby declares that it is the continuing policy and responsibility of the federal government to . . . promote maximum employment, production, and purchasing power.

The major tools government uses to try to achieve these macroeconomic goals include variations in taxes, government spending, and the supply of money.

The Scope of Government

Now that you know some reasons for government action in a market economy, we will briefly survey the extent of the public sector. Total government spending on goods and services now tops $700 billion annually, or roughly 20 percent of our national production. When we include transfer payments (so-

cial security, welfare, and other income payments that are not tied to production), government outlays exceed one-third of all spending.

Figure 6 breaks down government spending by its major functions. Nearly half of the 1970 federal budget was devoted to national defense; today that figure is less than one-third. During the 1970s, outlays on such domestic programs as income security, health, education, natural resources, environmental protection, and energy policy more than absorbed the funds freed by reductions in national defense. The Reagan administration's budgets beginning in 1982 and projected through 1988 may have signaled a reversal of this trend, with renewed emphasis on defense and attempts to slash the growth of welfare and other domestic programs. The "Star Wars" proposal alone is expected to cost over $1 trillion during the next 20 years; this is more than it would cost to replace all existing U.S. schools, streets, and highways.

FIGURE 6 *Revenue Sources and Expenditure Patterns for Federal, State, and Local Governments, 1985*

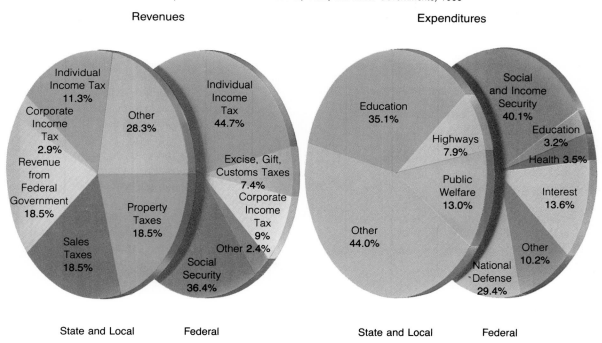

The federal government relies almost exclusively on income and payroll taxes for revenues. State and local governments, on the other hand, get the bulk of their revenues from property and sales taxes, from user fees, and from the federal government through grants-in-aid. Federal expenditures are focused on those activities that are national in scope (national defense and social security), while state and local expenditures are for services that affect people within limited geographical areas.

Source: *Economic Report of the President,* 1986.

Federal expenditures tend to focus on activities that have national implications. State and local government spending is directed at services that affect people within limited geographical areas. In contrast to federal outlays, the composition of state and local spending has changed little since the early 1960s, although there has been a relative reduction in highway spending and a rising proportion of outlays for welfare.

Figure 6 also shows that different levels of government rely on different taxes as revenue sources. State and local governments generate roughly two-thirds of their revenues from three major sources: (*a*) grants from the federal government, (*b*) property taxes, and (*c*) sales taxes. On the other hand, almost 60 percent of federal revenues come from taxes on individual or corporation incomes. When we include the second largest source of federal revenues, social security taxes (which are based solely on wage incomes), the figure is over 90 percent. Thus, less than 10 percent of total federal tax revenues are based directly on sources other than income.

You may have heard our income tax system referred to as *progressive* which means that the rich pay a greater percentage of their income as taxes than do the poor. There are three basic ways that taxes can be related to income:

1. *progressive.* A tax is progressive if the percentage tax rate rises as income rises: higher incomes are taxed proportionally higher than lower incomes.
2. *proportional.* Taxes collected are a fixed percentage of income. The "flat rate" tax proposal would institute a proportional tax.
3. *regressive.* A tax is regressive when the percentage of income paid as taxes declines as income rises.

Even after allowing for gaping tax loopholes, our federal income tax is a progressive tax: people with higher incomes tend to pay greater percentages of their incomes as taxes. Social Security taxes totalling roughly 14 percent of the first $50,000 of an individual's wages are collected, and the tax is roughly proportional in the range $0–$50,000 of wage income. Fixed-rate sales taxes may be regressive because low-income individuals tend to spend larger proportions of their income than high-income families.

Taxing and spending are only two of the tools that government uses to mold economic activity. Laws and regulations also have very powerful economic effects. Several studies have concluded that compliance with regulation absorbs 5–15 percent of our national income.

In Chapter 2 we described some allocative mechanisms people use to resolve economic questions. If the effects of people's choices were perfectly foreseeable and if everyone could costlessly acquire all the information bearing on every decision, the most useful mechanisms would be obvious. Information is costly and the future, sadly, is uncertain. Information for decision making is sought only as long as the benefits expected from acquiring a bit more information exceed the costs. Beyond that point, we rationally choose to be ignorant. Thus, private decision making is flawed because we are unavoidably somewhat *rationally ignorant* when we choose, and cannot know what the future holds. One question is whether, in an environment in which everyone, including policymakers, is somewhat ignorant and uncertain, government can make better decisions for us than we could make for ourselves.

An inequitable distribution of income is one perceived flaw of a market system, and markets tend to be inefficient when firms exercise monopoly power or when property rights are unenforceable or are not clearly specified. At the macroeconomic level, persistent high unemployment, erratic swings of the price level, or sluggish growth may also signal inefficiency.

Much of the rest of this book addresses the operation of a market economy and government policies intended to correct for market failures. This chapter has provided a discussion of the institutions within which the market system operates.

CHAPTER REVIEW: KEY POINTS

1. Households are both consumers of goods and providers of labor and other resources to business. Interactions between business and households are illustrated in *circular flow* models.

2. All household income is spent, saved, or taxed. Three major trends are discernible in U.S. household spending patterns during the past half century: (*a*) consumption expenditures as a percentage of personal income have declined from 90 percent to 80 percent; (*b*) taxes have increased from roughly 3 percent to nearly 14 percent of income; (*c*) saving has been roughly stable as a percentage of income.

3. Wages and salaries make up approximately three quarters of the income of typical families. During the last two decades, women's rates of participation in the labor force have risen markedly, while those of men have fallen slightly. The proportion of families in which both husband and wife are employed has also been climbing.

4. Six businesses out of seven are either *sole proprietorships* or *partnerships,* but *corporations* account for more than 80 percent of all goods and services sold and receive roughly two-thirds of all profits in the United States. Compared to corporations, however, sole proprietorships and partnerships are easily formed and less subject to government regulation. The major advantages of corporations are the limited liabilities of stockholders and better access to financial capital markets.

5. An erratic trend towards increased concentration of economic power in America has continued for more than a century—well over half of all manufacturing assets are held by the 200 largest corporations in the United States.

6. Corporate goals of making profits are under attack by people who believe "the new industrial state" is much too powerful, both politically and economically. These critics argue that big business should be "socially responsible."

7. Though much of modern economic life is concentrated in the hands of those who control giant corporations, changing market shares and the growth of various imports are evidence that the processes of competition are still reasonably vigorous.

8. Where the price system is incapable of providing certain goods or fails to provide the socially optimal levels, *government* steps in to supplement the private sector in five major ways. It attempts to: (*a*) provide a legal, social, and business environment for stable growth; (*b*) promote and maintain competitive markets; (*c*) redistribute income and wealth equitably; (*d*) alter the allocation of resources in an efficient manner where *public goods* or *externalities* are present; and (*e*) stabilize income, employment, and prices.

9. If negative externalities (costs) exist, the private market will provide too much of the product and the market price will be too low because full production costs are not being charged to consumers. If positive externalities (benefits) exist, too little of the product will be produced by the private market and the market price will be too high, requiring a government subsidy or government production or provision of the commodity.

10. Once public goods are produced, it is extremely costly to exclude people from their use, and everybody can consume the goods simultaneously. The free market will not adequately provide public goods because of the "free rider" problem.

11. Total spending on goods and services by all three levels of government exceeds 20 percent of GNP. State and local governments spend the bulk of their revenues on services that primarily benefit people in their local communities and rely heavily on the property and sales taxes as sources of revenue. Federal spending is generally aimed at national activities. Over 90 percent of federal revenue comes from individual and corporate income taxes plus social security and other employment taxes.

QUESTIONS FOR THOUGHT AND DISCUSSION

1. A record breaking 12 million women entered the labor force during the 1970s. Experts estimate that as many as 17 million more have found employment during the 1980s. And these women are spending more of their lives working. For example, in 1970, the average 20-year-old woman could expect to spend 21.3 years in paid employment compared with 37.3 years for an average 20-year-old

man. By 1983, the average number of working years rose to 27 for typical women and declined to 36.6 for men. During this same period, the earnings gap between men and women narrowed slightly, and the percentage of families with two earners had jumped by over 14 percent. How have these changes affected the following areas of our economy?

   a. Consumer spending.
   b. Unemployment rates.
   c. Unemployment as a measure of economic hardship.
   d. Productivity growth. (Some commentators argue that the slow growth in productivity of the 1970s was due to large numbers of relatively unskilled women entering the labor market, lowering the overall increase in productivity.)
   e. Population growth rates.
   f. The demand for such products as:
      (1) day-care centers.
      (2) clothes.
      (3) automobiles.
      (4) central city property.
      (5) restaurants.

2. Suppose you were the chief executive officer of a major corporation. Would your primary goal be to maximize profits for stockholders or to maximize your own subjective income via a high salary, friendly subordinates, plush offices, private airplanes, and other "perqs"? What does your answer suggest about the compatibility of maximum corporate profits and the separation of ownership from control? What does this imply for economic efficiency?

3. Should United States corporations that do business in several states or internationally be chartered by state governments, or by the federal government?

4. Since World War II, government transfer payments as percentages of national income have grown sharply, and federal spending on goods and services have fallen relative to state and local spending. What might be some explanations for these changes in patterns of government outlays?

5. Suppose you wanted a measure to estimate the importance of government in the economy over time. Would you use government spending on goods and services alone relative to national income, or would you include transfer payments? Can you think of any way to quantify increases in regu-

lation by government? Are there other dimensions of government activity that should be measured? If so, which ones, and how?

6. One possible way to affect the distribution of wealth in this country is to impose a 100 percent inheritance tax. Do you feel that such an action would produce a substantial change in how wealth is distributed? What loopholes would need to be closed to make the law effective? Might some parents invest huge amounts in their children's education as a consequence of such laws? How could such a loophole be closed? Would productive capital leave the country? Insofar as there is an American aristocracy based on inherited wealth (the Vanderbilts, Harrimans, Rockefellers, among others), this action might replace that aristocracy with a meritocracy. Would such a change be beneficial?

7. Inherent in all policies adopted by political decision makers are some characteristics of public goods. Explain the sense in which the policies themselves are public goods (or public bads).

8. Can you think of ways to induce people to reveal their preferences for certain public goods so that they will not be free riders? Try this for such things as schools, highways, and national defense.

9. "Small firms are less able to comply with stringent government regulations than are large corporations, so regulatory growth has the undesirable effect of strangling competition in our economy." Your reaction?

10. Corporations have traditionally been private institutions that generate profits, create jobs, and accumulate capital—pursuits that Milton Friedman, Nobel Prize winner in economics, thinks they should continue to concentrate upon to promote economic efficiency. Friedman feels that corporate operations should ignore the "social responsibility" that critics of corporate policies would foist upon them because he sees the job of promoting social goals as belonging to government, not corporate management. These critics, however, want to make corporations accountable to the American public. How might corporations be forced to develop social "consciences"? Would profits and share prices be lower? Who would bear the burden of the changes critics have advocated? Would society benefit? What are the arguments for and against these proposals to make corporations quasi-public institutions?

The Crisis in Liability Coverage

When a burglar sues for injuries incurred while trying to break into a California high school, you know that something is wrong with the law. And when the school's insurance company pays him more than a quarter of a million dollars rather than risk going to court, you know something is really wrong.

—*Tomas Sowell*

Awards for damages in liability cases are soaring. Legal actions conform to the law of supply; the number of suits filed have also mushroomed. In some cases, huge awards have pushed firms into bankruptcy (the Johns-Mansville asbestos suits). In other cases, soaring insurance rates have forced firms to shut down (General Motor Lines of Roanoke, Virginia) or some business operations to cease (the number of doctors willing to deliver babies is plummeting).

A more typical response to the skyrocketing liability awards and insurance premiums charted in Figure 7 has been for firms to boost prices to cover these higher costs. Price hikes are consistent with current legal standards that impose strict liability for damages caused by products on their manufacturers. These standards are based on the notion that

firms can more easily bear the burdens of product failure than can people whose lives may be shattered. Jury awards are designed to compensate victims as well as money can. This notion seems reasonable, but there is much debate about how far it should go. To what extent should individuals be held responsible for the ways they use products?

One day two neighbors decided that it would be easier to use their lawn mower to trim their common hedge than to use hand clippers. After starting the engine, they grabbed and lifted opposite edges of the mower's base and tried to "mow" the top of the hedge as if it were a lawn. Result? Sixteen fingers were lost. Their successful suit for damages was based on defective product theory—the firm was negligent because this use for mowers should have been anticipated and the lawn mower should have been designed (with handles?) to prevent injuries.

Should bars be held liable for the subsequent actions of drunk patrons? Should trampoline makers be forced to compensate amateur gymnasts who are injured? Should people who misuse products bear responsibility for their actions? Should pharmaceutical companies be liable if the harmful side effects of a drug are unknown until 20 years after the medicine is administered? These are the types of questions that are being dealt with in courts every day.

Business and the insurance industry claim that strict liability standards and excessive awards bolster incentives for lawsuits and result in a "get rich quick mentality." Strict liability is now being applied in areas that previously required a showing of negligence. Further, suits

FIGURE 7 *The Liability Crunch*

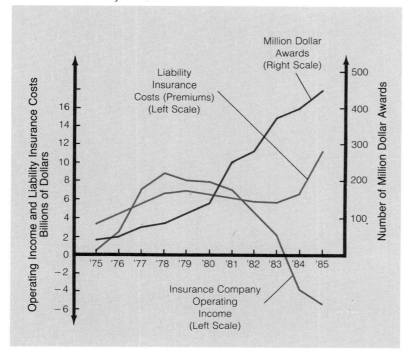

Source: "Business Struggling to Adapt as Insurance Crisis Spreads," *The Wall Street Journal*, January 21, 1986, p. 33.

are encouraged by the doctrine of joint and several liability, whereby any wealthy codefendant (a "deep pocket") who is only partially at fault is liable for the entire award. For example, plaintiffs who are injured by uninsured drivers may contend that automakers are liable because design defects contributed to their accidents. Juries often sympathize with injured parties, and then award exorbitant sums from the accused deep pockets. These factors have driven up insurance and legal costs in areas such as medical malpractice and corporate officer liability.

Critics of business and the insurance industry argue that higher awards merely reflect inflation, that lawsuits per capita have risen very little, and that insurance companies are attempting to feather their nests by boosting their rates. High investment yields in the 1970s caused insurance companies to compete for investment dollars by reducing premiums. Critics charge that mismanagement has driven down investment yields, and that insurance firms are unfairly trying to recover these profits through rate gouging. (If this is so, why are insurance firms simply refusing to renew many insurance policies?)

Whatever the reasons for the problem, firms are struggling to adapt. Ten thousand physicians in Los Angeles now subscribe to a computer service that identifies patients who are likely to file malpractice lawsuits. Many firms now go "naked" (self-insure) or carry significantly reduced coverage. In some industries where liability coverage is unavailable, the industry has formed its own mutual insurance company to ensure coverage. Many firms have dropped risky products or services, and have joined the growing effort to change liability laws across the land.

In 1986, California voters passed Proposition 51 to limit joint and several liability rules. Other states are adopting similar laws. Under the new rules, firms are liable for punitive damages or pain and suffering that they personally caused. Congress is currently considering similar restrictions nationwide. These changes may reflect a recognition that society cannot guarantee perfect safety and a happy outcome for everyone in every situation. We may be moving into an era in which people absorb more risk and are more responsible for their own health and well-being.

MACROECONOMICS

PART 2 Measuring Economic Performance

The major macroeconomic goals of all societies are achieving high employment, price-level stability, and economic growth. Achieving all three goals simultaneously is difficult, but not impossible. For example, raising employment rates appears to cause inflation to rise, at least temporarily, while attempting to cure inflationary pressures can push hordes of workers into unemployment lines. To discuss these goals, formulate policy, and evaluate the actions of policymakers, we must have reasonably accurate estimates and definitions of employment, inflation, Gross National Product, and other important economic aggregates.

In Chapter 6, we investigate how unemployment and inflation are measured, the shortcomings of these measurement techniques, and the problem policymakers face when using unemployment and inflation as guides to economic policy. We also lay the groundwork for understanding the causes and cures of unemployment and inflation.

One possible cure for excessive rates of both unemployment and inflation is economic growth. Economists attempt to measure economic growth and stagnation by tracing changes over time in the levels of our national income and output. This is the focus of Chapter 7. Once you understand the concepts we present in Part Two, you will be ready to begin analyzing macroeconomic theory and policy in greater depth. Over the last two decades, as we attempted to cure inflation, the economy suffered alternating bouts of high inflation and high unemployment. This experience illustrates the major challenge facing policymakers—maintaining steady economic growth.

CHAPTER 6

Unemployment and Inflation

unemployment	index number	real-income cost of
labor force	Consumer Price Index	inflation
costs of unemployment	(CPI)	social costs of inflation
benefits from	Producer Price Index	discomfort (misery)
unemployment	(PPI)	index
inflation vs. deflation	GNP Deflator	

Unemployment and inflation, the major macroeconomic problems of the post-World War II era, have been addressed almost endlessly by politicians, pundits, and editorial writers. Why are so many people concerned about these issues? To answer this question, we must examine what we mean by these terms, how each is measured, and their costs and benefits. (Surprisingly, there are *some* benefits from both.) Only then can we address the questions of how to reduce the level of unemployment and dampen the inflationary pressures that built up over the past quarter century.

Aggregate Demand and Aggregate Supply

The demand and supply analysis from Chapter 4 provides a broad framework useful in explaining not only movements of the prices and quantities of individual goods, but also the movements of broad aggregates such as the price level and national income. The foundations of the macroeconomic Aggregate Demand and Aggregate Supply curves (shown in Figures 1 and 2) differ somewhat from the microeconomic bases of demands and supplies for particular goods.

As the aggregate price level falls, the value of your wealth may increase. Assets such as stocks, bonds, cash, and checking account balances will now buy more; hence, the Aggregate Demand curve slopes downward. The positive slope of the Aggregate Supply curve reflects the fact that as prices rise, cost increases often lag. Delayed cost increases cause rising profits which encourage firms to produce more. Detailed derivations of these curves are complex, but for now, examining shifts in these Aggregate Demand and Supply curves provides some immediate insights into a number of problems faced by macroeconomic policymakers.

Prior to World War II, all American depressions and recessions were periods when output, employment, and the price level all declined. In Figure 1, note that if the Aggregate Demand curve falls from

FIGURE 1 *Inflationary Growth and Recession*

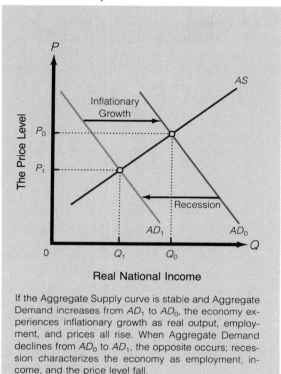

If the Aggregate Supply curve is stable and Aggregate Demand increases from AD_1 to AD_0, the economy experiences inflationary growth as real output, employment, and prices all rise. When Aggregate Demand declines from AD_0 to AD_1, the opposite occurs; recession characterizes the economy as employment, income, and the price level fall.

FIGURE 2 *Deflationary Growth and Stagflation*

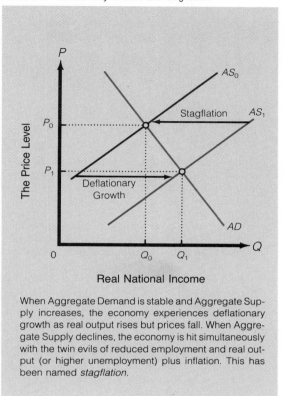

When Aggregate Demand is stable and Aggregate Supply increases, the economy experiences deflationary growth as real output rises but prices fall. When Aggregate Supply declines, the economy is hit simultaneously with the twin evils of reduced employment and real output (or higher unemployment) plus inflation. This has been named *stagflation*.

AD_0 to AD_1, the price level and the level of real national income (Q) both decline. Since employment is closely tied to the nation's output, employment also declines and unemployment rates tend to rise. Thus, one reasonable explanation for recessions or depressions is a decline in the Aggregate Demand for goods and services.

If Aggregate Demand rises from AD_1 to AD_0, both the price level and real output rise; employment also rises and, all else equal, unemployment falls. Thus, periods when inflation is accompanied by real economic growth and rising employment might be explained as periods when Aggregate Demand grows relative to Aggregate Supply. The 1960s were such a period of mild inflation and substantial economic growth.

The period from roughly 1870–95 was marked by substantial real economic growth, but marred by occasional minor financial crises. Over the same interval, the price level fell fairly consistently. What movements of Aggregate Demand and Supply are consistent with these changes in prices and outputs? In Figure 2, increases in Aggregate Supply from AS_0 to AS_1 yield a lower price level and a higher level of national income. Thus, growth in Aggregate Supply relative to Aggregate Demand allows both real national income and employment to rise while the price level falls.

During the 1970s, real output grew very slowly; on the average, unemployment rates rose, while the United States experienced its highest rates of fairly consistent inflation since Revolutionary War days. Although the economy as a whole grew, the growth in Aggregate Supply remained below that of Aggregate Demand; the shift from AS_1 to AS_0 in Figure 2 reflects this relative movement. Thus, declines (or slower growth rates) in Aggregate Supply relative to Aggregate Demand may account for our poor overall economic performance during the late 1970s and early 1980s. An extended discussion of the underpinnings of Aggregate Demand and Aggregate Supply is postponed until Part Five.

This Aggregate Demand and Supply framework allows us to illustrate the major goals of macroeconomic policy—full employment, price stability, and economic growth. However, before we discuss goals and policy options in detail, we need to examine how both unemployment and inflation are measured.

Unemployment

Friday begins like any other morning. The shrill beep-beep-beep of the alarm, the steam rising from the shower, the smell of brewing coffee. Driving to the office provides the usual irritations. Morning conferences and activities are the standard fare. Thoughts are focused on the upcoming weekend's activities.

At 2:00 p.m., the bomb is dropped. The plant manager calls a meeting to announce that the firm has lost a major contract. Layoffs will affect not only assembly-line workers this time but executives as well. Everything is prepared; two-weeks' severance pay and accrued vacation are included in the final check. There are firm handshakes accompanied by condolences and sincere wishes for the best of luck in future ventures. Then, out the door, carrying a cardboard box filled with personal effects. The trip home is a nightmare. "My skills are strong; there are competitors who need my expertise. But will they be willing to hire now? The newscasters have been talking recession lately. How will the mortgage be paid? Will I have to move to find work?" The happily anticipated weekend has disintegrated into pure gloom.

Every worker faces the possibility of unforeseen joblessness, and most have experienced it at one time or another. Earlier economic, psychological, and social hardships created by extended periods of unemployment led to the Employment Act of 1946. This act set *maintaining maximum employment* as one government goal. Evaluating its achievement of this goal usually begins with a look at the overall unemployment rate—a statistic you hear regularly on the nightly news. However, this single measure is only a crude guide to policy because there are numerous reasons for unemployment. Each form has different implications for government policies. Before examining the different types of unemployment, however, we must discover who the unemployed are.

The Concept of Unemployment

There are roughly 240 million Americans, of whom about half are in the labor force. Does this mean that roughly half of all Americans are unemployed?

Hardly. In fact, if you think that housewives are *not* working, a short stint on the "home front"—up to your elbows in dish suds, a screaming 2-year-old tugging at your leg, the phone and doorbell both ringing—will quickly change your mind. Adults can elect to be, or not be, members of the labor force. People can be classified as either "employed" or "unemployed" only if they choose to be in the labor force. Conceptually, **unemployment** occurs when people are able to work and would willingly accept the prevailing wage paid to someone with their skills but either cannot find or have not yet secured suitable employment.

Voluntary Versus Involuntary Unemployment

Unemployment can be viewed as either voluntary or involuntary. **Voluntary unemployment** occurs when people could find work very quickly but choose to look for what they view as better jobs in terms of pay, location, or working conditions. For example, you would be voluntarily unemployed if you turned down the night shift or a job that required a 50-mile round trip each work shift, choosing instead to look for 9-to-5 work or a position closer to your home.

Some people believe that almost all unemployment is voluntary: If you really want a job and are willing to work for "what you're worth," you can find work almost immediately. I am willing to hire you to paint my home, mow my lawn, or babysit as long as you accept a wage equal to what these activities are worth to me. My neighbor would do the same. Hence, if you are unemployed for more than a few hours, it *must* be voluntary.

The counterargument is that people should not be forced to accept just any job. If you are willing to work but there are no jobs presently available at an acceptable wage rate and suitable for a person with your training and skills, you are **involuntarily unemployed.** Human worth is involved, and people should have jobs that do not underemploy their skills. Moreover, this argument continues, there are simply times and places where business conditions are so bad that no jobs are available.

We will not try to tell you which of these positions is correct. It is impossible to measure willingness to work at prevailing wages with any precision, so any measure of involuntary unemployment is only an educated guess. In any event, published unemployment statistics are based on surveys of people 16 years of age or older and use criteria only loosely related to our conceptual definition of unemployment.

Measuring Unemployment

The United States Department of Labor uses the following definitions to classify people as employed, unemployed, and in or out of the labor force.

Employed persons include (*a*) all civilians who worked for pay any time during the week which includes the 12th day of the month or who worked unpaid for 15 hours or more in a family-operated enterprise and (*b*) those who were temporarily absent from their regular jobs because of illness, vacation, industrial dispute, or similar reasons. Members of the Armed Forces stationed in the United States are also included in the employed total. A person working at more than one job is counted only in the job at which he or she worked the greatest number of hours.

Unemployed persons are those who did not work during the survey week but were available for work except for temporary illness and who had looked for jobs within the preceding 4 weeks. Persons who did not look for work because they were on layoff or waiting to start new jobs within the next 30 days are also counted among the unemployed. The overall unemployment rate represents the number unemployed as a percent of the labor force, including the resident Armed Forces. The unemployment rate for all civilian workers represents the number unemployed as a percent of the civilian labor force.

The **labor force** consists of all employed or unemployed civilians plus members of the Armed Forces stationed in the United States. A labor force participation rate is the proportion of a specific population group that is in the labor force. The employment-population ratio is total employment as a percent of the population.[1]

Our major source of unemployment statistics in the United States is a monthly Department of Labor survey of about 60,000 households. The survey (provided in Focus 1) asks detailed questions to determine the labor force status of each adult family member. This large sample ensures that the statistics collected in the Department of Labor survey are rea-

sonably good. Among the reasons for inaccuracy are discouraged workers and dishonest nonworkers.

Flaws in Unemployment Statistics

Some people are so pessimistic about their job prospects that they do not look for work, although they would like jobs. These *discouraged workers* are not counted among the unemployed but should be, under the economic definition of unemployment. Thus, published statistics may understate true unemployment. Figure 3 shows that the discouraged worker syndrome is most pronounced during economic downturns, when many people perceive that job openings are few and far between.

On the other hand, unemployment statistics may be overstated because of the incentives embedded in our unemployment compensation system. Some people have no intention of taking a job, but report that they are available for work so that they can draw unemployment benefits.

The discouraged worker and dishonest nonworker syndromes each cause inaccuracy in unemployment statistics, but in opposite directions. Which effect is stronger is a source of continuing debate.

The Sources of Unemployment

There are five major types of unemployment: frictional, structural, seasonal, cyclical, and induced. These are related to the major forces generating unemployment. Each of these sources poses different problems for macroeconomic policy.

Frictional Unemployment   People enter or reenter the work force, are fired or permanently laid off, or voluntarily quit one position to look for another. Information about job openings and applicants is far from perfect, and mobility (e.g., relocating to get a job) is often quite costly. It takes time for workers to move between jobs and match their skills with the work requirements of business. Finding job openings, interviewing, processing applications, and making hiring decisions all absorb resources. All these activities involve transaction costs, which give rise to *frictional unemployment,* an unavoidable by-product of normal economic activity.

There is considerable **turnover** (the term given to workers changing jobs) among both the employed and unemployed. For example, employment in 1985 averaged more than 100 million persons per month,

---

1. United States Department of Labor. *Monthly Labor Review,* numerous issues.

Determining Who Is Unemployed

The unemployment rate is not only a function of how the term is defined but how the Department of Labor questionnaire is administered as well. The interview questions are designed to elicit the most accurate picture of each person's labor force activities. The survey asks one adult to report for all members of the household who are over age 16. The major questions that determine one's employment status are:

1. What was _____ doing most of last week—working, keeping house, going to school, or something else?

For everyone not working and not reported unable to work because of a physical or mental disability, the next question is:

2. Did _____ do any work at all last week, not counting work around the house?

For those who say no, the next question is:

3. Did _____ have a job or business from which _____ was temporarily absent or on layoff last week?

For those who say yes, the next question is:

4. Why was _____ absent from work last week?

If the response to this question indicates that the person is waiting for a new job to begin within 30 days or awaiting recall from layoff, he or she is counted as unemployed.

For those who are reported as having no job or business from which they were absent, the next question is:

5. Has _____ been looking for work during the last four weeks?

For those who say yes, the next question is:

6. What has _____ been doing during the last four weeks to find work?

If a specific activity, such as applying directly to an employer, placing or answering ads, registering with either a public or private employment agency, being on a union or professional roll, or checking with friends and relatives is mentioned, the following question is asked:

7. Is there any reason why _____ could not take a job last week?

If there is not a reason, except temporary illness, that the person could not take a job, he or she is considered to be not only looking but also available for work, and he or she is counted as unemployed.

---

but about 130 million different persons worked at some time during the year. While unemployment averaged around 9 million per month, nearly 35 million people experienced unemployment at some time during those 12 months.

Structural Unemployment Structural unemployment occurs when a worker's skills do not mesh with the requirements of virtually any job opening. Some individuals are unable to find work during even the best of times. Their unemployment may be of long duration for a variety of reasons.

First, people may be out of work because of structural change. For example, a significant technological innovation may make certain skills obsolete. Many typesetters found themselves jobless with the introduction of computerized typesetting equipment that does the same job at less cost and with far fewer labor requirements. Some economists have argued that blue-collar occupations in our primary industries are drying up, which means that we can expect higher than normal unemployment rates for blue-collar workers throughout the next decade.

Second, some people have acquired few, if any, job skills. Examples include many high-school dropouts, most ex-convicts, and some housewives who decide to work after their children leave the nest. Firms may find it unprofitable to hire and train workers if they expect their training costs to exceed the benefits to the firm. This is especially a problem if employees commonly find better jobs once trained.

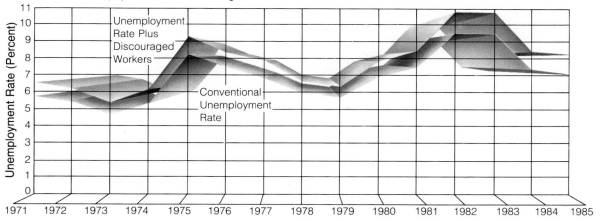

FIGURE 3 *The Unemployment Rate and Discouraged Workers*

Failure to include discouraged workers among the unemployed causes the measured unemployment to be understated. In a similar fashion, dishonest nonworkers may cause the measured unemployment rate to be overstated. Obtaining an accurate count of both discouraged workers and dishonest nonworkers is extremely difficult.

Source: U.S. Department of Labor, Bureau of Labor Statistics, *Handbook of Labor Statistics,* 1985, and Monthly Labor Review; U.S. Department of Commerce, *Statistical Abstract of the United States,* 1986; and *Economic Report of the President,* 1986.

3.) Seasonal Unemployment   Some activities are inherently seasonal. For example, from the demand side, weather often determines whether employment is available in the agriculture and construction industries. Department store Santa Clauses may only work a few weeks annually. Beach towns and ski resorts also experience seasonal fluctuations in employment. Seasonal influences emerge on the supply side as well, especially in teenage labor markets. Students' summer vacations are the major cause of seasonality in this market. Teenage unemployment rises in June and falls in September. These and many other published economic statistics are seasonally adjusted to make the figures comparable during the year.

4. Cyclical Unemployment   Unemployment resulting from a general business recession is called **cyclical unemployment** because it coincides with downturns in business cycles. As an economy gains momentum, employment and output increase. When output falls, employment and output do, too. During a recession, business expansions decline and there are widespread company closings and bankruptcies. These changes throw people out of work and

increase overall rates of unemployment. Figure 4 shows that there have been tremendous variations in rates of joblessness over the past century. Most of these swings reflect cyclical unemployment. Reducing this component of unemployment is a major focus of government fiscal and monetary policies.

Not all groups of workers are affected in the same way by a cyclical downturn. Table 1 shows unemployment rates for specific groups during selected periods of high and low employment. Cyclical swings are far less severe in the service sector of our economy than in construction and manufacturing. Professional and technical workers suffer only moderate unemployment compared to blue-collar, service, manufacturing, and construction workers.

5. Induced Unemployment   Finally, some unemployment is induced by certain government policies. The minimum-wage law, for example, limits employment opportunities for unskilled and inexperienced workers by overpricing their services. Unemployment compensation also provides an incentive for people who sincerely desire work to turn down some offers of employment in the hope that, if they keep looking,

FIGURE 4 *The Rate of Unemployment, 1900–85*

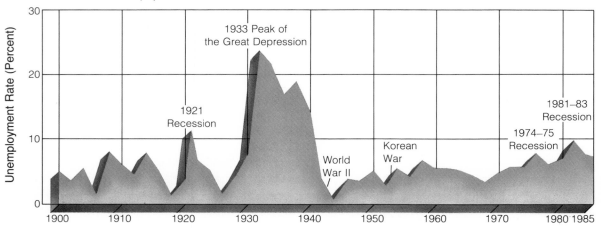

As this figure illustrates, the unemployment rate has varied considerably over time. Unemployment reached a peak in 1933 when almost one in four was out of work. Unemployment rates dropped to 1.2 percent, an all-time low, during World War II.

Source: 1900–28 derived from Stanley Lebergott, *Manpower in Economic Growth* (New York: McGraw-Hill Book Co., 1964); 1929–85 derived from the Bureau of Labor Statistics and *Economic Report of the President,* 1986.

they will find the perfect jobs. Laws requiring wages at the union scale on government contract work are another hindrance to full employment—they leave workers unemployed who would be willing to work for less on government contracts.

The Costs and Benefits of Unemployment

Unemployment imposes costs on all of us. Those out of work typically receive unemployment compensation, which reduces their individual burdens from lost wages, but spreads the cost across all workers and employers through unemployment compensation taxes. The aggregate costs of unemployment fall into two categories: lost income and social costs.

Losses in Aggregate Income

The **lost-income costs of unemployment** consist of the value of the output the unemployed individuals could have produced. These costs are not trivial. The recession of 1981–83 has been estimated to have cost nearly $600 billion in lost national income or almost 15 percent of potential annual Gross National Product at that time. Even if the unemployed are par-

tially buffered from losses of income by unemployment compensation, society as a whole suffers because production falls when the jobless rate soars.

Social Costs of Unemployment

The **social and psychic costs of unemployment** may be as tragic as the economic consequences. Table 1 shows that the burdens of unemployment and recessions are not spread equally. Dry statistics sometimes cloud our view of the people behind the numbers. Consider the memories of a woman who was a college student during the Great Depression:

> *When I attended Berkeley in 1936 so many of the kids had actually lost their fathers. They had wandered off in disgrace because they couldn't support their families. Other fathers had killed themselves, so the family could have the insurance. Families had totally broken down. Each father took it as his personal failure . . . so they killed themselves.*
>
> *It was still the Depression. There were kids who didn't have a place to sleep, huddling under bridges on the campus. I had a scholarship, but there were times when I didn't have food. The meals were often three candy bars.*[2]

---

2. Studs Terkel, *Working: People Talk About What They Do All Day & How They Feel About What They Do* (New York: Pantheon Books, Inc., 1974).

TABLE 1 *Percentage of Unemployment by Industry and Occupation (Selected Periods of High and Low Unemployment)*

	(1973) Peak Low Unemployment	(1975) Trough High Unemployment	(1981) Peak Low Unemployment	(1982) Trough High Unemployment
Total unemployment	4.9	8.5	7.6	9.8
Professional and technical	2.2	3.2	2.8	3.3
Government	2.7	4.1	4.7	4.9
Blue-collar	6.2	14.7	12.2	17.7
Manufacturing	4.4	10.9	8.3	12.3
Service	5.8	8.6	8.9	10.6
Construction	8.9	18.0	15.6	20.0

Source: U.S. Department of Labor, *Monthly Labor Review,* 1985.

Extended unemployment places tremendous psychological pressure on family structures. Families may plunge deeply into debt after exhausting most of their assets, irrevocably changing their children's futures. Plans for college educations can go up in smoke. Teenagers experience especially high unemployment rates, and some may acquire criminal records. Table 2 provides estimates of some human costs of unemployment. The shocks imposed by severe long-term unemployment are among the major reasons that the Employment Act of 1946 focused on promoting full employment.

In 1960, both spouses worked full time in only one quarter of all families; today, 50 percent have two earners. In 1984, in two-thirds of all households where the husband was unemployed, another family member held a full-time job. These changes in employment patterns, along with improved unemployment compensation benefits, have reduced the desperation associated with unemployment.

✗ Benefits from Unemployment

The bad press unemployment receives may make it hard to believe that there actually are benefits from some types of unemployment. These break down into allocative benefits and disciplinary benefits.

Allocative Benefits A primary benefit of unemployment is that it is easier for unemployed workers to search for new employment than it is for workers who are holding full-time jobs. At the same time, a pool of unemployed labor affords firms the opportunity to interview more potential employees than would be the case if jobless rates were zero. This process, whereby the unemployed search for work while employers search for suitable help, can be viewed as an investment in information. Thus, unemployment yields **allocative benefits** by permitting better match ups between workers and jobs; better information reduces transaction costs and improves our economy's overall efficiency.

Disciplinary Benefits We all know people who overestimate the worth of their own work and who consequently make demands for wages, vacations, coffee breaks, and other perquisites that far exceed the value of their contributions. There are also workers who do not pull their own weight. Some economists view the possibility of widespread layoffs as a curb to excessive demands for wages and fringe benefits. The threat of unemployment may also reduce "goldbricking" and may be a good work incentive for people who respond better to "sticks" than to "carrots." These are the **disciplinary benefits** to firms (and consumers) from having some slack in labor

TABLE 2 *Estimates of the Total Effects of a 1 Percent Change in Unemployment Rates Sustained Over a 6-Year Period on the Incidence of Social Trauma*

Measures of Social Trauma	Incidence of Death Related to a 1 Percent Increase in Unemployment (Based on 1980 Population)
Total mortality	41,088
Whites	
Males	13,769
Females	18,418
Nonwhites	
Males	4,266
Females	4,635
Cardiovascular mortality	22,547
Cirrhosis of liver mortality	1,025
Homicide	722
State mental hospital	
First admissions	4,709
Males	3,407
Females	1,302
State prison admissions	3,720

Source: M. Harvey Brenner, "Influence of the Social Environment on Psychopathology: The Historical Perspective," in *Stress and Mental Disorder*, ed., James E. Barrett (New York: Raven Press, 1979).
Note: Estimates represent updates to the 1980 population, as calculated by the authors.

markets. The workers affected naturally do not view pressures for greater work discipline as beneficial.

We have surveyed various aspects of the unemployment problem. Accurate measurement of unemployment is difficult, but it is essential as a guide to macroeconomic policy. The size of the various categories of unemployment help to determine which macro policies will be effective. Finally, keeping unemployment low is a major goal because high unemployment carries high social and economic costs. Now we are ready to take a look at the other great problem of macroeconomics—inflation.

Inflation

Whip inflation now.
> —*President Gerald Ford, 1975
> (Lost Reelection Bid in 1976)*

Inflation is Public Enemy #1.
> —*President Jimmy Carter, 1977
> (Lost Reelection Bid in 1980)*

Inflation is America's most pressing economic problem.
> —*President Ronald Reagan, 1981
> (Won Reelection bid in 1984)*

Beating inflation may be a bit like spanking a child—it hurts you more than it does the child. Politicians have railed against the evils of inflation ever since the Roman Emperor Diocletian tried to combat inflation with price controls. In the United States, the political battle against inflation has been on a front burner since World War II, but each passing decade has yielded ever greater average rates of price increases.

Some observers think that inflation, like the weather, is something that everyone talks about but that no one can do anything about. They cite failures to achieve political solutions to inflation as evidence that attempts to control it are futile. Most economists view these failures as proof that effective anti-inflationary policies are very costly, either politically —for those who have the power to enact such policies—or economically. The benefits from dampening inflationary trends in our economy may be less than the political costs or the costs in terms of potential damage to the economy. The Reagan Administration's policies reduced inflation but temporarily threw the economy into its most severe slump (1981–83) since the Great Depression. By 1986, unemployment rates had recovered, with only modest inflationary pressures, to the levels of the late 1970s. Before we deal with the costs and benefits of inflation, however, we need to specify what we mean by inflation and how it is measured; we also need to survey briefly some of its possible causes.

The Concept of Inflation

For macroeconomic analysis, we are concerned with changes in the level of *absolute* prices because these changes represent inflation or deflation. Most people view increases in any of the prices they pay for goods or services as inflationary. For the purposes of economic analysis, **inflation** occurs whenever there are increases in the average level of prices, while **deflation** occurs when prices fall on the average. An increase in the price of a single good is not necessarily inflationary. For example, an increase in the price of football tickets is not inflationary if it is offset by declines in the prices of, say, domestic wine or long-distance phone calls. Only when increases occur in the average overall price level do we actually have inflation.

However, not all economists accept this definition. Some argue that *one-shot* increases in the average price level should not be viewed as evidence of inflation. According to them, only continuous and prolonged increases in the price level should be termed inflationary. But even one-shot general price hikes take some time, so it is often hard to distinguish between *continuing* inflation and one-shot increases in average prices.

Price Index Numbers

If the prices of houses, straw hats, and candy bars rise while the prices of sweaters, juke boxes, and gasoline fall, how can we tell whether or not we have experienced inflation? Answering this question systematically requires that we deal with price indices.

Even the most casual readers of newspapers and magazines frequently encounter indices of one kind or another. An **index** is a summary of what happens over time to prices (inflation or deflation), productivity, labor market conditions, new construction, or some agglomeration of other items. Index numbers compress, sharpen, and simplify information. The

ability to understand and interpret these statistics is essential to understanding economic changes. We will begin with a discussion of index numbers and then proceed to the three major indices published as measures of inflation.

An index is a series of index numbers, calculated as:

$$\frac{\text{value of variable in current period}}{\text{value of variable in base period}} \times 100.$$

Suppose that you wanted to develop an index for job opportunities in your community. You might count the number of help wanted advertisements reported in your local newspaper each month. Then you would need to determine a base period against which all other periods will be compared. Suppose January 1987 was the base period, and 38,510 help wanted ads appeared in your newspaper over the month. During February 1988, you count 47,230 ads. The February 1988 index of job opportunities (as measured by the number of help wanted advertisements) would be:

$$\frac{47,230}{38,510} \times 100 = 122.6.$$

Looking at the index for February 1988, you can see that job opportunities in the community during February are estimated to be 122.6 percent of those available during January 1987, which indicates that job opportunities have grown 22.6 percent. Interpreting change is much simpler using index numbers than using the original (raw) numbers. Notice that the value of the index for the base period is 100 $[(38,510/38,510) \times 100 = 100]$.

As you developed track records for the job opening index, you might notice that the overall index tends to rise in November and December, reflecting Christmas employment, and to decrease in spring. This phenomenon is termed *seasonality* in the data, and it refers to those changes that regularly occur over the year. Most indices are seasonally adjusted to show comparable data over time.

With this discussion in mind, we will now examine the three principal measures of inflation: (*a*) the Consumer Price Index (*CPI*); (*b*) the Producer Price Index (*PPI*); and (*c*) the Gross National Product Deflator (GNP Deflator).

Measuring Consumer Prices (CPI)

The most widely known of the price indices computed by the Department of Labor is the **Consumer Price Index (*CPI*).** The *CPI* is a statistical measure of changes, over time, in the prices of the goods purchased by typical consumers. Revised in 1987, the *CPI* is based on buying patterns for over 80 percent of all households. The *CPI* measures changes in consumer purchasing power by tracking changes in what a sample "market basket" costs over time. This market basket includes most major expenditure categories, such as food, housing, apparel, and transportation.

Consumer expenditure surveys help keep the *CPI* up-to-date when consumer patterns change over the years. Each year the Bureau of Labor Statistics (BLS) samples thousands of households in over 1,000 marketing areas to determine typical spending patterns. The 1982–84 Consumer Expenditure Surveys provide information about the relative importance of different categories of goods. The information is used to weight various components of the *CPI*. For example, if typical families spend twice as much on electricity as on natural gas, the weight assigned to elec-tricity rates will be twice that of the weight for natural gas prices.

The prices of over 600 different products and services are sampled each month in nearly 100 different markets. These BLS samples focus on consumer products that make up the bulk of sales at the most popular stores. Table 3 summarizes the methods currently used by the Bureau of Labor Statistics to compile the *CPI*.

How the CPI is Used

The *CPI* is used to estimate changes in the purchasing power of money and as an escalator in contracts calling for future payments of money. Unfortunately, there are some inherent problems in using the *CPI* or, for that matter, with any other index used for diagnosing the economy and prescribing policy.

Moving from Nominal to Real Values   Most values of economic variables are presented in their current dollar, or nominal, values. The **nominal** (or *monetary*) **value** is the dollar amount you receive or pay. For example, suppose that your current income is $20,000 annually. How does the purchasing power of

TABLE 3   *Summary of the Procedures and Methods Used to Compute the* CPI

Item	Methods and Procedures
Title	1. Consumer Price Index for All Urban Consumers (*CPI*-U) 2. Consumer Price Index for Urban Wage Earners and Clerical Workers (Revised Series) (*CPI*-W)
Population covered	*CPI*-U—All urban residents, including salaried workers, self-employed workers, retirees, unemployed persons, and urban wage earners. *CPI*-W—Urban wage earner and clerical worker families and single individuals living alone. At least one family member must be employed for 37 weeks or more during the year in wage or clerical worker occupations.
Geographic coverage	278 urban areas selected to represent all urban places in the United States, including Alaska and Hawaii.
Sample of items priced	Consumer Expenditure Survey (1982–84) data classified into 68 expenditure classes covering roughly 650 goods.
Sample of stores	A sample of retail stores and other outlets was selected from the results of a Point-of-Purchase Survey covering about 23,000 families across the country.
Number of price quotations obtained	About 650,000 food prices per year. About 70,000 rent charges per year. About 350,000 quotations per year for items other than food, rent, and property taxes. About 28,000 property tax quotations per year.

TABLE 4 *Converting Nominal Income (Before Taxes) to Real Annual Income*

Year	Aggregate Monetary Income ($ Billions)	Population (Millions)	Per Capita Money Income (Dollars)	CPI (1967 = 100)	Real per Capita Income (Deflated)
1929	$ 84.9	121.8	$ 697	51.3	$1,359
1933	46.9	124.8	376	38.8	969
1940	77.8	132.6	587	42.0	1,398
1950	226.1	152.3	1,485	72.1	2,060
1960	399.7	180.7	2,212	88.7	2,494
1970	801.3	204.9	3,911	116.3	3,363
1980	2,160.0	222.3	9,717	246.8	3,937
1985	3,215.6	238.8	13,466	322.2	4,179

Sources: *Statistical Abstract*, 1986; *Economic Report of the President*, 1986.

that nominal income compare with your $10,000 family income of 10 years ago? Your real income (purchasing power) is your current income ($Y_{current}$) adjusted for inflation or deflation. Real income (Y_{real}) is computed using the following formula:

$$Y_{real} = \frac{Y_{current}}{CPI/100}.$$

If your family income was $10,000 in 1978, you could purchase a given amount of goods and services. Suppose that by 1988 your income had doubled to $20,000 but that over the same time period all prices in the economy doubled as well. Would you be any better or worse off? Since all prices doubled, it would take twice as much money in 1988 to buy the same goods and services that you purchased in 1978. Thus, your real income in 1988 would still be $10,000, with 1978 as the base year.

Using the formula above, the *CPI* for 1988 in terms of 1978 (the base year) would be 200 (prices are assumed to have doubled—remember, 100 is the index for the base year). Consequently, you compute real income for 1988 by dividing your income in 1988 by 1 percent of the *CPI* ($20,000/2.00 = $10,000). Table 4 illustrates this conversion process for per capita income during selected years since 1929.

Just as we have adjusted nominal income to account for changes in the price level, we can adjust other nominal variables to see how relative prices are changing. This process is called **deflating.** The general formula for deflating any variable is:

$$\text{real value} = \frac{\text{nominal variable in dollars}}{\text{price index/100}}.$$

For example, the price of a barrel of oil rose from roughly $3 in 1967 to around $29 in 1985. How large was the increase in real oil prices? The consumer price index (based on 1967 prices) rose to roughly 300. Therefore, the real 1985 cost of oil (in 1967 prices) was $29/3.00, or around $9.67 per barrel. This means that the relative price (real cost) of oil more than tripled in this 18-year period, while the nominal price rose nearly 10 times. You can use similar computations to deflate housing prices, wages, or any other nominal variables.

CPI *as an Income/Payment Escalator* Altogether, the payments received by nearly half of our population are directly tied to the *CPI.* For example, if a union wage contract has an escalator clause, wages and monetary fringe benefits rise by roughly the same percentage that the *CPI* increases. Escalator clauses providing insurance against losses in purchasing power due to inflation are included in collective bargaining contracts covering more than 8.5 million workers. Many pension plans, Social Security retirement benefits, and various welfare payments are also tied to the *CPI* in one way or another.

CPI *as an Economic Indicator* Inflation has been a critical economic problem since the middle 1960s. Attempts to reduce the double-digit inflation rates of the middle 1970s and early 1980s gained some success by 1983, but they led to unemployment rates exceeded only during the Great Depression. As inflation seemed to rise and become more persistent, Americans paid more attention to the Consumer Price Index.

The *CPI* is a major yardstick by which the success of economic policy is measured. Every president since George Washington has promised price stability. Presidents, congressional leaders, and other policymakers keep a close watch on movements in price indices for some indication of their success in keeping inflation under control.

Problems with the CPI Estimating changes in consumer prices poses major conceptual and statistical problems for the Bureau of Labor Statistics. How can the Bureau (*a*) keep the index current with respect to changing consumer patterns, (*b*) adjust for quality changes and new products in the marketplace, and (*c*) accurately adjust for changes in prices and costs of major consumer assets such as housing?

In 1986, the Bureau began conducting annual Consumer Expenditure Surveys to keep up with changing consumption patterns. The composition of area and item samples are now gradually updated over a period of years instead of once a decade, as was done in the past. However, constant consumption patterns are assumed in computing the *CPI* between revisions. Since the representative "market basket" is fixed, changes in typical consumer buying patterns may reduce the accuracy of the *CPI*. Because consumers tend to expand their purchases of goods where the prices rise most slowly and to cut back on items where prices rise most rapidly, this problem causes overstatement of growth in the *CPI*. For example, between 1972 and 1980, average energy prices rose 218 percent, but consumer expenditures on these products only rose by 140 percent. Annual surveys and phased updating help to eliminate the fixed market basket limitations of the *CPI*.

Changes in quality may also affect the accuracy of the *CPI*. Quality changes in products *should not* cause changes in the price index because the index ideally measures the cost to consumers of purchasing a *constant* "market basket." The *CPI* will overstate inflation if prices rise to reflect greater quality and this changing quality is ignored. Suppose, for example, that the movies of 1989 are much better than the movies of 1988. If ticket prices rise only because better production quality costs more money, then the *CPI* might still show inflation because of these hikes. Ideally, a dollar measure would be obtained because consumers value the improvement in the quality of products; these values would then be deducted from the increase in price. Similarly, deteriorating quality may result in an under-statement of inflation. Inflation occurs even though money prices stay constant, as when, say, the tastiness of restaurant meals declines because soy beans are substituted for ground beef in hamburgers. Direct measurements of the values consumers place on quality changes are unobtainable, however, so the Bureau is forced to use an indirect method of estimating the costs of quality changes. When figures are available, the cost differences between the old and the new feature are treated as approximations of the real values of quality changes. There are many problems with this approach. For example, does the cost of installing pollution control equipment on cars represent an increase in the quality of an automobile? Maybe what we are actually buying is cleaner air.

Another problem of measuring inflation is that some asset owners gain from higher prices. Thus, if inflationary pressures cause both wages and housing prices to rise, this does not mean that current home owners who have fixed mortgage payments pay more for housing services. In fact, after deflating for inflation, "real" mortgage payments fall. For this reason, in 1981 the Bureau of Labor Statistics changed the way the *CPI* measures housing costs. Previously, the Bureau measured the costs to acquire a house (its price as reflected in the monthly payment) rather than the price of "housing services" consumed. As a result, when mortgage interest rates rose or fell, significantly altering monthly payments, the *CPI* reflected these changes as if all families bought new houses each month. The new approach of the BLS is to estimate rental values to represent the cost of shelter. These changes permit the *CPI* to more truly reflect inflation for established American households. Despite these problems, the *CPI* is a reasonable estimate of changes in consumer prices.

Other Price Indices

The *CPI* only tracks changes in the prices consumers pay. Other prices are important as well.

Producer Price Index (PPI) The **Producer Price Index (*PPI*)** measures average price changes for over 2,800 primary products. The *PPI* is a general purpose index for nonretail markets; it covers such intermediate goods as flour, steel, rubber, computers, and office supplies. Most of the prices used to compute this index are the wholesale selling prices of representative producers. However, some prices come from specialized markets such as commodity exchanges. The prices used for imported products (for example, coffee beans) are the prices paid by the original importer (for example, Folgers).

The GNP Implicit Deflator   Adjusting Gross National Product (total output in the economy) for price changes is done with an index called the **GNP Deflator.** (We deal with GNP accounting in the next chapter.) The GNP Deflator is based on components drawn from other price indices—primarily the *CPI* and *PPI*. For example, each component of consumer spending is adjusted using the appropriate data from the Consumer Price Index. Business expenditures for such items as capital equipment or raw materials are deflated using the appropriate parts of the Producer Price Index. Components of other indices are used to deflate the prices of items not included in the *CPI* or the *PPI*, such as government services, construction, and agricultural production.

The History of U.S. Inflation

Only a shrinking minority of Americans can remember when the price level fell. Because prices fell by an average of one-third between 1929 and 1933 while wages dropped by roughly one-fourth, wages after adjustment for deflation actually *rose*. It sounds as though workers gained during this period. Remember, however, that 1929 was the year the Great Depression began. By 1933, the unemployment rate was roughly 25 percent, and average working-class families were not doing well. There have been other periods when we experienced deflation, as you can see in Figure 5. For example, prices fell on average by roughly 40 percent between 1870 and 1895.

Before we got used to continually creeping inflation in the 1970s, an annual inflation rate of 4 percent seemed outrageous. Nevertheless, Americans became accustomed to annual inflation rates ranging

FIGURE 5   *Inflation Since 1860*

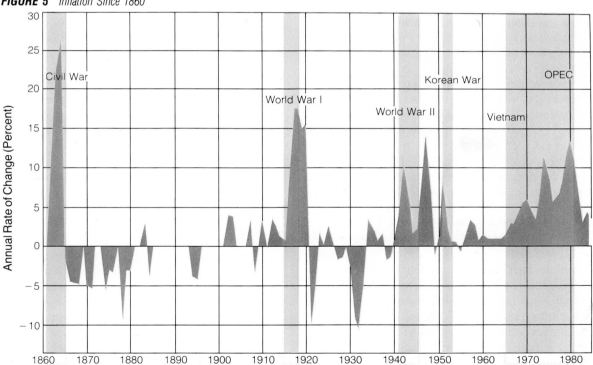

This figure highlights the various inflationary periods experienced by the United States since 1860. The majority of these periods have occurred during extended military hostilities; however, although the 1970s and early 1980s were relatively peaceful, the price level crept up briskly.

Source: U.S. Department of Labor, Bureau of Labor Statistics.

from 6 percent to 14 percent during the 1970s. Today, most of us view 2–4 percent inflation as price-level stability. To some extent, what you are accustomed to determines what you consider moderate or excessive inflation. Many South Americans perceive inflation rates of 40–50 percent as no big deal. Rates of inflation in some of these countries ranged as high as 400–800 percent annually at times during the period 1950–85.

Types of Inflation

One way to categorize inflation is by how rapidly prices rise on average. Other distinctions try to pinpoint the *causes* of inflation. Both approaches are examined in this section.

Creeping Versus Galloping Inflation

The average level of prices may rise for a number of reasons and at different rates over time. When prices rise consistently but at fairly low rates, an economy is said to have a case of **creeping inflation.** Most Americans view double-digit inflation as almost unbearable. However, most economists would follow the lead of Phillip Cagan, a specialist in the study of inflation, in defining inflation as **galloping** only when average prices rise by 50 percent or more *per month.* Galloping inflation is also known as **hyperinflation.**

At times, some countries have experienced average rates of price increases that can only be described as astronomical. In 1919, it took only 9 German marks to buy an American dollar. A kilogram of bread cost less than 1 mark. By the end of 1923, an incredible 4.2 trillion German marks were worth only 1 dollar. Between the beginning of World War I and 1923, average prices in Germany increased 1,422,900 million percent. A stack of 5 million mark notes an inch thick was needed to buy 1 egg. As remarkable as these numbers seem, even more rapid inflation has occurred. Hungary experienced an annual inflation rate of 3.81 octillion (381 followed by 27 zeros!) percent between 1945 and 1946. Figure 6 graphically depicts these and other twentieth-century episodes of hyperinflation.

Interestingly, studies by Phillip Cagan indicate that a monetary system still works reasonably well as long as inflation stays below 50 percent monthly. This is only one indication of the strength and resilience of market-based economies. Creeping inflation clearly poses fewer problems for macroeconomic policymakers than does the galloping variety. If inflation "gallops" too rapidly, market systems falter and then collapse because people quit accepting monetary payments. *Barter* takes over when people no longer trust money: goods and resources are only traded for other goods or resources.

Now that we have seen the difference between creeping and galloping inflation, let us go on to look at the causes of inflation.

Demand-Side Inflation

Whenever a given price increases, we know that either *(a)* demand has increased or *(b)* supply has decreased. Demand-side inflation occurs if Aggregate Demand grows and the economy is near full employment output (Q_0). As illustrated in Figure 7, when Aggregate Demand increases from AD_0 to AD_1, the price level rises from P_0 to P_1. Continued increases in Aggregate Demand will simply be reflected in a higher rate of inflation.

If the average price level rises due to increased demands, the economy experiences **demand-side,** or *demand-pull,* **inflation.** Economists are nearly unanimous in believing that inflation results whenever our demands for goods and services grow faster than our capacity to produce them. Indeed, a substantial minority of economists insist that this is the only realistic explanation for inflation. Excessive demands ripple through a fully employed economy when the supply of money is expanded too rapidly or government spends far more than it collects in taxes.

Supply-Side Inflation

Most economists agree that some inflation may originate with disturbances to the supply side of the economy. Creeping inflations in many industrialized Western style economies during the 1960s and 1970s were commonly diagnosed as, at least partially, originating with shocks from the supply side. Figure 8 illustrates a supply-side "shock" as a shift in Aggregate Supply from AS_0 to AS_1. Skyrocketing energy costs, worldwide crop failures, growing monopoly power, and disputes between labor unions and management are only a few of the culprits that some peo-

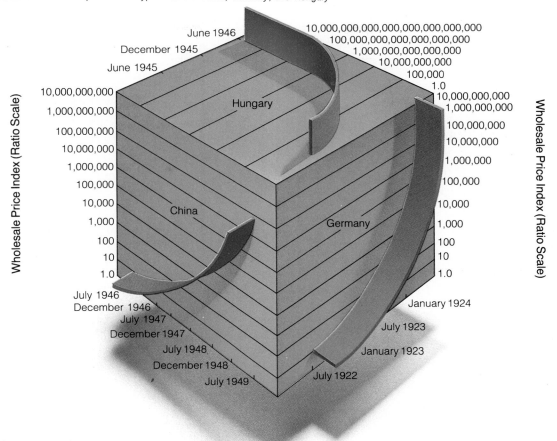

FIGURE 6 *Selected Episodes of Hyperinflation: China, Germany, and Hungary*

Source: For China: Shun-Hsin Chou, *The Chinese Inflation 1937–1949* (New York: Columbia University Press, 1963), p. 261; for Germany: Fritz K. Ringer, *The German Inflation of 1923* (New York: Oxford University Press, 1969), p. 79; for Hungary: B. Nogaro, "Hungary's Monetary Crises," *The American Economic Review*, XXXVIII (1948), pp. 526–42.

ple identify as causal factors. As Aggregate Supply shrinks, the price level increases and aggregate output falls. Supply-side shocks can be grouped into the broad categories of cost-push, administered-price, composition-shift, and expectational explanations for inflation.

Cost-Push Inflation You may have heard people blame inflation on large hikes in union wages. This is one example of a **cost-push** theory of inflation. Powerful unions presumably demand wage increases not warranted by increased worker productivity. Increased labor costs are then passed forward to con-

sumers as "pushed up" prices. This explanation points to unions as the villains causing inflation. Blaming unions is especially popular among anti-union politicians and some business leaders. Other cost-push theories point to rising prices for oil used in manufacturing processes or to increases in the prices of imported goods, foods, fibers, ores, or other raw materials.

Administered-Price Inflation Some economists borrow the mechanics of the union-based, cost-push inflation explanation, but turn the theory inside out. According to the **administered-price** theory of in-

FIGURE 7 *Demand-Side Inflation*

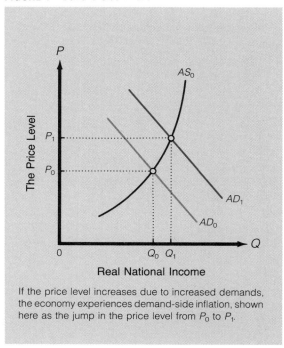

If the price level increases due to increased demands, the economy experiences demand-side inflation, shown here as the jump in the price level from P_0 to P_1.

FIGURE 8 *Supply-Side Inflation*

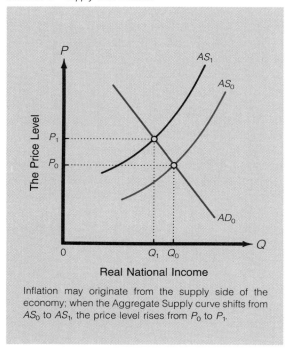

Inflation may originate from the supply side of the economy; when the Aggregate Supply curve shifts from AS_0 to AS_1, the price level rises from P_0 to P_1.

flation, firms possessing monopoly power may be hesitant to raise prices because they fear adverse publicity, antitrust actions, or similar threats to their domination of a market. They use increases in wages or the costs of other resources as excuses to raise prices, generally by more than can be justified by the higher costs. Hence, huge firms do not resist excessive wage demands. This pattern, it is argued, tends to perpetuate inflationary momentum in an economy.

Composition-Shift Inflation The foundation of **composition-shift** inflation theory is the assumption that prices rise more easily than they fall. Thus, if demands increase in one sector of the economy, prices rise. But if there are offsetting decreases in demands in other sectors, prices do *not* fall, at least in the short run. Instead, as sales shrink, firms reduce output and lay workers off. As the composition of demands and supplies changes, there will be pressures for inflation. Growing sectors will typically experience increases in prices, while declining sectors suffer from stagnation and unemployment rather than long-term price cuts.

Expectational Inflation Widespread expectations of inflation may cause **expectational** inflation because our forecasts about the economy are at least partially self-fulfilling—we create our own future realities by what we anticipate. Thus, if most of us expect inflation, producers will try to increase production while cutting back on current sales to build their inventories. Why sell now when, if firms just wait a bit, prices will be higher? The reduction of current sales is accomplished by immediately raising prices and temporarily lowering supplies.

At the same time, if buyers expect inflation, they will try to accumulate their own inventories of durable goods. This bolsters their current demands as they attempt to avoid the higher prices expected later. Thus, inflationary expectations quickly cause price hikes because such expectations lead to reduced supplies and increased demands. These adjustments explain why inflation may develop incredible momentum. Inflation causes expectations of inflation, which stimulates more inflation, and so forth. You may have heard people refer to the "wage-price inflationary spiral" or to the "vicious circle of inflation." Expectations of inflation are important in explaining why inflation is so difficult to suppress.

These are only some of the possible explanations of inflation. They are not mutually exclusive; many inflations are caused or intensified by combinations of these forces. An accurate portrait of any given episode of inflation normally requires that we consider forces from both the supply side and the demand side. For example, all European hyperinflations following World Wars I and II were triggered by political turmoil and supply-side disturbances, which were followed by incredibly rapid growths of these countries' money supplies. When the money supply grows faster than real output, there is inflationary pressure from the demand side. When we explore these sources of inflation in detail in Chapters 11 through 17, you will learn why inflation cannot be sustained for very long without expansions of the money supply.

Inflation's Costs and Benefits

You now have some ideas about how various price indices are calculated and compiled and about various types of inflation. We need to examine some of the effects of inflation. You may be surprised to learn that it brings both gains and losses and that there are people with vested interests in rising prices.

Losses from Inflation

There are two major sources for losses arising from inflation. First, inflation may cause reductions in our capacity to produce or losses of efficiency in production and distribution. In either case, there will be declines in standards of living. These are the **real-income costs of inflation.** Second, inflation creates fractures in the implicit and explicit agreements that bind people together. These are the **social costs of inflation.**

Unanticipated inflation is generally far more harmful than inflation that people have learned to expect. If you accurately forecast the rate of inflation, you can buffer yourself against its real-income costs. For example, you can invest in commodities that are "hedges" against inflation. If most people accurately anticipate inflation, the social costs of inflation are minimal.

Real-Income Costs of Inflation

How might inflation cause declines in our real incomes?

Repricing (Menu) Costs One of the real costs of inflation is that resources that could have been used productively elsewhere must be used to reprice goods. Some repricing occurs because relative prices change even when the price level is stable. During an inflationary period, however, it is not unusual to find that most items in your grocery cart have been marked up since they were first put on the shelf. Menus in restaurants and airline and bus ticket schedules must be reprinted with higher prices. Gas pumps, as well as candy and cold drink machines must be adjusted to accept different denominations of coins. Where prices are regulated by government (for example, utility rates or transportation fares), considerable time and effort may be expended in redesigning rate schedules. All these expenses of repricing are collectively known as the **repricing (menu) costs of inflation.**

Distortions Costs Another and even more important cost arises from the fact that inflation may cause savers and investors to feel increased uncertainty. Saving and investing reflect our faith in the future. The incentive to save may be dampened by the uncertainty caused by inflation.

Reduced incentives to save coupled with widespread uncertainty may cause rates of capital accumulation to fall, and the growth of our national productive capacity may decline. Funds that would normally flow into new capital may be diverted into real estate or inventories, so that growth and technological advances sputter well below the levels needed for a healthy economy. Business firms may also mark up their prices to compensate for the increased risks they perceive. If so, the quantity of goods and services available over the long run may be reduced because of inflation.

Some economists argue that distortions in relative prices that occur because prices rise at different rates during inflationary episodes are another major cost of inflation. These price distortions cause inefficient decisions about production and consumption. For example, in the early 1980s, many people signed enormous obligations for mortgages that required monthly payments that they could not afford. By

1985–86, there was an epidemic of bankruptcies and foreclosures. These people would have waited to buy homes were it not for their fear that "if we don't buy now, housing prices will rise by so much that we won't ever be able to afford one." This is only one way that inflation warps efficient decision making. These sorts of responses are known collectively as **distortions costs.**

Social Costs of Inflation

When markets are out of equilibrium and prices are unstable, there is far more strife than normal between buyers (who want low prices maintained) and sellers (who want prices raised to reflect rising production costs). Conflicts among consumers, producers, and regulatory agencies are accentuated during inflationary episodes. Ignoring menu and distortions costs for a moment, inflation is roughly what mathematicians call a *zero sum game*. For every loser during inflation (someone who must pay more for a given good), there is a winner (someone who receives a greater price for the things he or she sells). The somewhat arbitrary redistributions of income caused by inflation are the major source of inflation's social cost. Even though losses to some are offset by gains to others, the process seems capricious and erodes the trust we have in each other.

You gain during inflation if the prices of the items you sell go up faster than the prices of the things you buy. Generally, inflation is most advantageous to you the more accurately you anticipate it. And, since the gains from inflation going to one party almost exactly offset the losses to some other party, the biggest losers are normally those who do not correctly anticipate inflation. Some people lose when their incomes do not keep pace with the average prices of the products they purchase. Why all the furor over inflation if the gains and losses are roughly in balance? There are several reasons. One is that most of the gains from recent inflation went to people who sell petroleum—and many of them are foreigners.

A fundamental problem is that inflation is blamed for many unfavorable circumstances that would have arisen because of shifts in *uninflated* demands and supplies. Most of us feel that increases in our paychecks are much-deserved rewards for hard work. Have you ever considered that your raise is an increase in the price of your services and that it can be seen as inflation by purchasers of the services or the goods you produce? If your neighbor's pay rises faster than your own, supply and demand may be at work, not inflation.

Even recognizing that our income may have risen, we find that the value of money we have saved has declined because of inflation. A past irritant was that the progressivity of our tax system permitted inflation to bump all of us into higher tax brackets, a process called **bracket creep.** Congress, with pressure from the Reagan Administration, indexed tax rates to inflation beginning in 1985, virtually eliminating bracket creep. But the prices of physical assets such as land and housing often increase more rapidly than the rate of inflation. Home owners gain during inflation; first-time home buyers lose.

One important group that gains from inflation is borrowers. Home owners with huge mortgages are prime examples. Repaying loans gets easier and easier if both incomes and the price level rise. Of course, the gains to borrowers are almost exactly offset by losses in the real wealth of lenders. Government, business firms, farmers, and young families are often net debtor/borrowers, and they may gain from unexpected inflation. Established households and mature people looking forward to retirement are generally savers and lose from inflation. (The ultimate lender is the person with bank deposits, not the banker.) Another major problem with inflation is that this redistributional effect of rewarding borrowing and penalizing saving provides substantial incentives for the use of credit. It is probably undesirable for most of us to become even more debt ridden than we already are.

Still another consideration is that some people live on fixed incomes—their pensions or wage contracts are not adjusted for changes in the cost of living. The increasing prevalence of contracts containing escalator clauses illustrates how people adjust to inflation over time. Even so, there are people whose incomes are at least partially fixed; those living on life insurance annuities or who long ago contracted for long-term fixed-dollar payments to take care of their old age are examples. Many senior citizens are harmed by inflation to the extent that some portions of their incomes are fixed.

The government also tends to gain from inflation because it is a major debtor, and because bracket creep formerly bumped people into higher tax brackets. Holders of U.S. bonds and taxpayers are the losers in this exchange of wealth.

FIGURE 9 *Effects on Real Income of a 2 Percent Increase in the Inflation Rate*

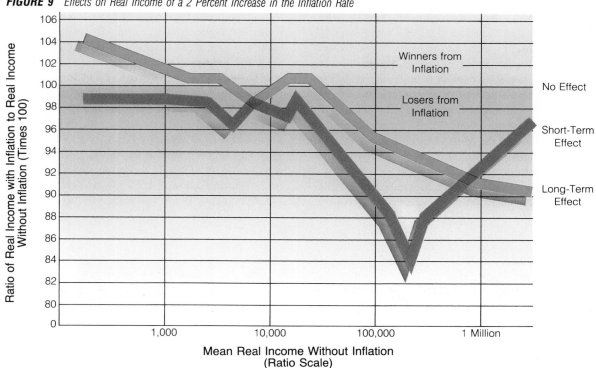

Mean real income is a measure of accrued comprehensive income that adds to census income such items as income in kind (e.g. employer-paid fringe benefits and government in-kind transfers), appreciation in home values, and all taxes (federal, state, and local). When these adjustments are made, the results of inflation are striking—by and large, inflation hurts higher income families more than lower income ones. Low-income families and the elderly are groups commonly identified as losers to inflation; however, Social Security, food stamps, and certain other government transfer programs are explicitly indexed to the Consumer Price Index, reducing the impact of inflation on the poor.

Source: Joseph J. Minarik, "Who Wins, Who Loses from Inflation," *The Brookings Bulletin,* 15, 1 (1980): 6.

These income redistributions caused by inflation are commonly seen as unfair and capricious. However, many of the social ills attributed to inflation are actually the results of other forces. You may have seen television programming indicating that low-income people suffer the most from inflation. This common charge is not in accord with most studies of this problem. The difficulties faced by the poor result from poverty, not inflation per se. The results of one study are presented in Figure 9. In this study by Joseph Minarik, census data on income were the basis of a conclusion that the sustained but moderate inflation of the 1970s harmed people at the top proportionally far more than it did people at the lower end of the income spectrum.

The income redistribution aspects of inflation generally do not affect the real level of national production, which Adam Smith (in 1776) rightly termed the *wealth of nations.* Rather, the redistributive properties of inflation are part of the larger problem of achieving and maintaining an equitable distribution of our real national income.

Benefits of Inflation

There are times when the effect of inflation on capital accumulation and economic growth may actually be positive. If managers believe that equipment will cost more in the future than at present, firms may increase their rates of investment in capital equipment, thereby increasing the real supplies of goods available for purchase. Such planning may backfire, however; some investment decisions made because of inflationary expectations may prove premature and disastrous for the investors.

Another possible benefit from inflation is that needed changes in relative prices may be accomplished more easily if there is a little inflationary pressure in the economy. This is especially true if price reductions are resisted more vigorously than price increases. For example, in the 1970s the demand for professors fell due to declines in enrollment, but the supply of professors increased. Market pressures for reduction in the real wages of college

professors were accommodated fairly easily by allowing the purchasing power of professional salaries to decline because of inflation. This process would have been far more traumatic if colleges had been forced to negotiate lower money wages for faculty, which might have been necessary had the price level been stable.

A third possible (but dubious) benefit from inflation is that it may ease expanding government spending relative to private purchases of goods and services. If the alternative is increased reliance on an inequitable or inefficient tax system, inflation may be preferred by political leaders—spending can increase without paying for it directly via taxes. For

FIGURE 10 *The Discomfort (Misery) Index (Under Post-World War II Presidents)*

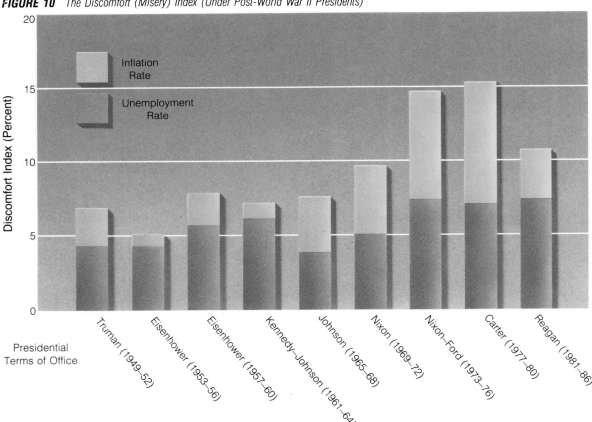

The discomfort index is the sum of the inflation rate and the unemployment rate. After being relatively stable during the 1950s and 1960s, the index grew from the early 1970s until the mid 1980s. Combining the twin evils of inflation and unemployment is a simple way to illustrate the state of the economy.

Source: *Economic Report of the President*, 1986.

example, inflationary pressures were allowed to build during World War II. If taxes had been raised sufficiently to finance the war in a noninflationary way, there might have been severe disincentives for production. Of course, many people would argue that under normal circumstances, inflationary growth of government is a cost, not a benefit, of inflation. This issue will be treated in more detail in Chapters 11 and 17.

The Discomfort Index

Arthur Okun, chairman of President Lyndon Johnson's Council of Economic Advisors, developed an economic discomfort index as a method of illustrating the general state of the economy. The economic **discomfort index** equals the inflation rate plus the overall unemployment rate.

In 1976, Jimmy Carter renamed this the **misery index** and used it to brand President Ford's eco-nomic policies as failures. Ronald Reagan then resurrected the misery index to condemn the economic performance of President Carter's Administration. The political campaigns of 1984 saw continued publicity for this index.

The index for 4-year presidential terms (averaged to smooth fluctuations) since 1950 is presented in Figure 10. The index showed remarkable stability during the 1950s and 1960s but took a big leap upward during the 1970s and early 1980s. By 1985, however, the discomfort index had returned to levels accepted as normal before 1970.

Macroeconomic goals focus on attaining the goals of full employment, price stability, and economic growth. Implementing appropriate policies requires relatively accurate measures of unemployment and inflation. You should keep the various costs and benefits of unemployment and inflation in mind, as well as data limitations, as you study the material in the next few chapters.

CHAPTER REVIEW: KEY POINTS

1. The major macroeconomic goals are full employment, price stability, and economic growth.

2. People who choose to be in the *labor force* are *unemployed* if they are able to work and are willing to accept prevailing wage rates for people with their skills, but cannot find work or have not yet secured suitable employment.

3. Unemployed people who are so discouraged about job prospects that they do not look for work are not counted in unemployment statistics. Some people who are not truly out of work indicate that they are in order to draw unemployment compensation. Thus, unemployment statistics may either understate the true unemployment rate because of *discouraged workers* or overstate it because of *dishonest nonworkers*.

4. Unemployment originates in five different ways: *(a)* frictional, *(b)* structural, *(c)* seasonal, *(d)* cyclical, and *(e)* induced. *Frictional unemployment* is a natural by-product of normal entry and exit from the labor market, voluntary job changes, or layoffs or firings. *Structural unemployment* results from mismatches between workers and jobs because of changes in the skill requirements of job openings or the failure of individuals to obtain marketable skills. *Seasonal unemployment* is a result of the annually recurring influences of weather, vacations, and the like on labor markets. *Cyclical unemployment* results from downturns in the overall levels of economic activity (recessions). *Induced unemployment* is caused by some government policies that reduce job openings or the incentives to work.

5. The *costs of unemployment* are both *economic* and *social*. The entire economy suffers from the lost output the unemployed individuals could have produced. These individual losses are cushioned through such programs as unemployment compensation. Individuals and their families suffer socially and psychologically when they are unemployed for long periods of time.

6. Unemployment is not distributed equally across all groups in the economy. Workers in manufacturing and construction are hit harder by cyclical unemployment during recessions than employees in most other lines of work.

7. *Index numbers* are used to make relative comparisons of particular variables over time. The *Consumer Price Index* (CPI) measures the changes in the prices of a given bundle of consumer goods over time. The *CPI* is based on typical consumer patterns for approximately 80 percent of the urban population.

8. The *CPI* has become an important factor in labor contracts and is used extensively as an escalator clause (cost-of-living adjustment). It is also an economic indicator and is used to convert nominal values to real values. *Deflating* nominal variables means dividing their monetary values by (1 percent of) a price index.

9. Among the major difficulties in computing the *CPI* are the problems inherent in adjusting the index for: (*a*) new products, (*b*) changes in the qualities of existing products, (*c*) changes in the composition of consumer expenditures, and (*d*) already owned consumer durables such as housing.

10. The *Producer Price Index* (PPI) measures the changes in the prices of goods in other than retail markets. The *GNP Implicit Deflator* is used to adjust the GNP for changes in prices. It is composed of relevant portions of the *CPI* and the *PPI,* plus some additional prices covered by neither.

11. Relative prices and economic decision making are distorted by *inflation,* and incentives to save are depressed. Capital accumulation may or may not be hampered by inflation, depending on business expectations and the availability of funds for investment. These are the *distortions costs of inflation.* Inflation causes resources that could be used productively elsewhere to be used for repricing. These are the *repricing (menu) costs of inflation.*

12. There are *social costs of inflation* because people feel increased uncertainty during inflationary periods. People living on fixed incomes are hurt by inflation. However, many of today's transfer payments and wage contracts have escalator clauses that adjust payments for changes in price levels. Borrowers tend to gain from unexpected inflation, while the ultimate lender loses. As incomes increase from inflation, meeting a fixed mortgage payment becomes easier, so heavily mortgaged home owners tend to gain.

13. The *discomfort (misery) index* equals the sum of the inflation rate and the unemployment rate. It averaged 6–7 percent during the 1950s and 1960s. During the late 1970s and early 1980s, the index ranged from 13 to more than 20 percent. By 1986, economic growth had pushed the index down to nearly 10 percent.

QUESTIONS FOR THOUGHT AND DISCUSSION

1. In October of 1982, the Reagan Administration faced political embarrassment: The unemployment rate had soared into the double-digit range (10.1 percent) for the first time since the 1930s. In that same month, the White House resurrected a proposal, advanced by numerous politicians in the past—to base unemployment rates on the total (civilian plus military) labor force instead of on the civilian labor force alone. Our military force is between 2 and 3 million people. What effect would this change have on published unemployment rates? Why have several incumbent presidents advocated this change?

2. Some critics believe that unemployment statistics tremendously underestimate unemployment because so many potential workers have become discouraged. Other critics suggest that the published unemployment rate "measures with considerable lack of reliability the number of people in the labor force of this country who, if the pay were right and the hours were right, might be available for a little work once in a while." Which of these positions do you think is correct?

3. Changes in the Consumer Price Index are the most frequently quoted measures of inflation. However, the way the index is computed often has perverse consequences for public policy. For example, the index includes property, sales, and Social Security taxes, but not income taxes. If elected officials wanted to lower taxes and "cut" inflation at the same time, which tax rates would they prefer to cut? Does this method make any sense, or would we simply be the victims of a political con?

4. The *CPI* traditionally used fixed consumer budgets (expenditure categories) that were updated every few years. However, when the price of one commodity rises relative to another, consumers do not wait to change their buying habits or patterns. What kinds of adjustments will consumers make? Did the *CPI* consequently overstate or understate the true inflation rate? What was the effect of this over- or understatement on contracts containing cost-of-living adjustments? Could this inaccuracy fuel the fires of inflation? How was the *CPI* altered to remedy such problems? Do you think implementing these changes was very costly?

5. Table 5 lists aggregate personal income in current dollars for selected years since 1929 and the *CPI* for the same years.
   a. Compute real personal income in 1972 dollars for each year.
   b. How much did real income increase between 1929 and 1985?
   c. Convert the *CPI* to a base year of 1985 = 100. Adjust current dollar personal income to 1985 dollars.
   d. What percent did prices fall between 1929–33?
   e. If between 1986 and 1987 nominal personal income is forecasted to grow 7 percent and the inflation rate is expected to be 4 percent, how much will real personal income grow?

TABLE 5 *Personal Income (Billions of Dollars)*

Year	Current Dollars	1972 Dollars	CPI (1972 = 100)
1929	$ 85.0	$ 229.5	37.0
1933	47.0	169.6	27.7
1960	402.3	489.7	82.2
1972	810.3	810.3	100.0
1980	2,165.2	1,021.6	212.0
1985	3,294.2	1,319.3	249.7

	CHAPTER 7	Gross National Product (GNP)

Gross National Product (GNP)	government purchases (G)	Net National Product (NNP)
personal consumption expenditures (C)	net exports (X − M)	Personal Income (PI)
Gross Private Domestic Investment (GPDI)	National Income (NI) depreciation/capital consumption allowance	Disposable Personal Income (DPI) Measure of Economic Welfare (MEW)

Statisticians commonly are regarded as even duller people than economists, and sometimes they deserve the reputation.

—John Lewis and Robert Turner

Feature articles in news magazines regularly discuss the latest figures for unemployment, inflation, and Gross National Product. You now know a bit about unemployment and inflation, but what is Gross National Product (GNP)? When the Commerce Department unveils its estimates of GNP, Wall Street gurus and economic analysts pore over these figures the way fortune-tellers read tea leaves or tarot cards for signals about the future. How accurate are the available data? Do you feel better if GNP rose last month? This chapter provides an understanding of what GNP estimates represent and suggests some of the problems with GNP accounting.

Gross National Product (GNP)

Gross National Product (GNP) is the total market value of all production during some specified period, usually one year. There are other definitions of GNP, but each has errors and omissions. For example, some describe GNP as the total market value of all final goods and services produced annually. This is an acceptable definition only if the many intermediate commodities produced and held as inventories at the end of the accounting year are viewed as final goods. We will return to this point a bit later.

GNP as an Economic Indicator

Why should you care about measuring Gross National Product? A major purpose for measuring it is to provide regular and continuing gauges of total economic activity that are comparable over time. When production drops, we know that many people are laid off and have difficulty finding jobs. Forecasting future levels of GNP aids government policymakers in determining when to take corrective policy actions, and measurements of GNP allow us to assess the success or failure of specific policies.

The level of economic performance is also important to managers who must constantly review their business plans. Measures and forecasts of GNP assist in planning employment, production, sales, and investment in new plants and equipment.

GNP and Economic Well-Being

Gross National Product has a second major function. It provides us with a crude yardstick for measuring national well-being. Employment and income are related to aggregate production, so our individual incomes and spending tend to rise or fall with aggregate economic activity. A rough measure of well-being is obtained if we divide real GNP by the population. Per capita GNP can be used to estimate how well off the average American is now compared with previous periods or with average people in other countries. Measures such as per capita GNP are also used to compare growth rates among various countries.

There are some inconsistencies in the uses of GNP as a measure of total production *and* as a measure of economic well-being. Some numbers that should be included in GNP if we are measuring economic welfare cause inaccuracies when we measure production, and vice versa. For example, if we produce more atomic weapons because the Soviet Union is doing so, are we better off than people in countries with lower per capita GNP who do not have to engage in extensive defense spending? Most of the choices made have favored accurate measurement of production. This is why we include such things as business investments, inventory accumulation, and exports in the GNP calculation.

Measuring GNP

There are two conceptually different ways of measuring Gross National Product: (*a*) the expenditure approach and (*b*) the income approach. Neither is perfect. Figure 1 illustrates the income and expenditure

approaches with a version of the circular flow diagram you studied earlier. This shows that everything *bought* (expenditures) is *sold* by someone who receives income from the sale. As you read about these approaches, keep in mind that each approach only approximates true economic GNP. Most data used to measure GNP are initially recorded for accounting purposes and are only roughly suitable for economic analysis. Naturally, there are many different categories of both income and expenditures. The proportions making up some important categories of income and expenditure are shown in Figure 2.

The Expenditure Approach

The **expenditure approach** to calculating Gross National Product leads us to the final users of our output. All goods produced in our economy are purchased by either: (*a*) consumers, (*b*) business investors, (*c*) government, or (*d*) foreigners. Figure 2 illustrates this division of the national pie into consumption (*C*), investment (*I*), government purchases (*G*), and net exports—exports − imports (*X* − *M*). Naturally, foreigners also provide goods that we may consume, invest, or use for governmentally provided goods and services. We will clarify why foreign buyers are shown as having such a small share of our GNP after examining the expenditure of domestic purchasers in more detail.

Personal Consumption Expenditures (C)   Personal consumption expenditures (*C*) are the values of all commodities and services that households and individuals purchase. Consumption includes spending for *nondurable* goods (food and clothing), *durable* goods (appliances, cars, televisions), and *services* (such as medical care, legal assistance, automobile repairs). This category is familiar because personal consumption is something we all engage in every day.

Business Spending on Capital Goods (I)   The technical term given to business spending in the GNP accounts is **Gross Private Domestic Investment, or GPDI.** Remember that *investment,* as economists use the term, refers to acquisition of physical capital rather than to the flows of money that we term *financial investment.* The word *gross* means that all purchases of *new* buildings, equipment, and the like are included. It does not matter whether or not invest-

FIGURE 1   The Circular Flow and National Income Accounting

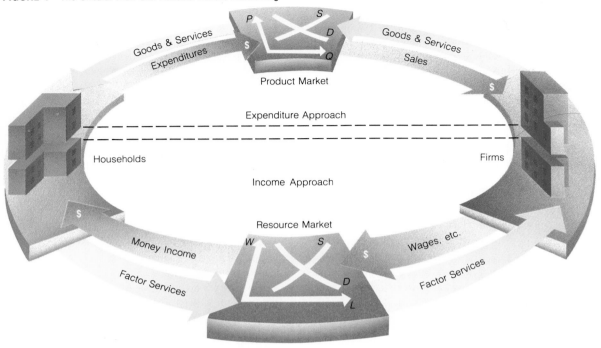

The two major approaches to GNP accounting are illustrated in this figure using the circular flow of income model. In this simple model, all goods are traded in the product market, and total expenditures equal the total value of output. Similarly, income is paid to factors of production, and summing all of these payments will provide an estimate of GNP. Note that all expenditures on goods and services must necessarily equal all of the payments to factors to produce the output. That is, what is bought must have been sold. (*Note:* Clockwise arrows show money flow; counterclockwise arrows show flow of goods and resources.)

ment is intended to replace obsolete or worn-out capital. *Private* means that government investment is not counted in this category. *Domestic* means that the new capital is put to use in the United States. We exclude foreign investments by American firms, but we do count investments by foreign companies in the United States as part of GPDI.

The three major components of investment spending are: (*a*) all final purchases of new capital equipment (like machinery and tools), (*b*) all new construction, and (*c*) changes in inventories. The first of these items, capital equipment, enhances the productive capacities of firms and quite naturally fits the category of investment. But what about purchases of stocks and bonds? These are *financial* rather than *economic* investments. Financial investment may facilitate expenditures on economic capital, but buying and selling securities merely transfers the ownership

from sellers of stock to buyers; this does not directly enhance our productive capability. For this reason, transactions in financial instruments are not economic investments.

In our GNP accounts, all new construction is considered investment. New production facilities, rental housing, and office space seem to fit the definition of investment, but what about construction of residential dwellings? Why not treat this as consumer spending? One reason is that residential housing can be purchased for rental purposes. In addition, the useful life of residential housing is quite long in comparison with most consumer goods. Consequently, housing is regarded as a capital good, and newly constructed housing is included in investment. The rental value of owner-occupied housing is considered consumption because housing produces the service of providing shelter year after year.

FIGURE 2 *Expenditure and Income Approach to GNP*

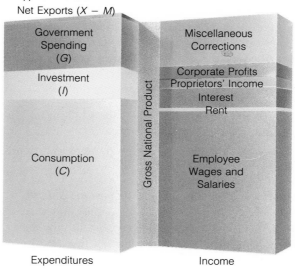

Net Exports (X − M)

Government
Spending
(G)

Investment
(I)

Consumption
(C)

Gross National Product

Miscellaneous
Corrections

Corporate Profits
Proprietors' Income
Interest
Rent

Employee
Wages and
Salaries

Expenditures   Income

Gross National Product can be estimated using either the expenditure approach or the income approach. As this figure illustrates, the sum of factor incomes approximately equals the totality of spending in the economy.

Increases in inventories are considered investments as well. Decreases in inventories are **disinvestments.** Inventories include: (*a*) raw materials or intermediate goods that firms buy for use as productive inputs, and (*b*) finished goods held in stock to rapidly meet the demands of customers. Your customers would soon become the customers of other firms if they constantly had difficulty getting prompt delivery.

Adjustments for inventory changes are needed since we use sales data to estimate production. If we excluded increases in inventories from GNP, total production would be understated. Goods held as inventories should be counted in GNP in the year produced rather than the year sold. Since inventories vary from year to year, changes in inventories must be estimated to consistently measure total production and keep our national income accounts correct. Increases in inventories *add to* investment, and decreases *reduce* investment.

Government Purchases (G)

Individuals consume commodities and services both privately and through government. When the government provides goods, it may buy them in finished form from private firms. Alternatively, it may buy resources or

intermediate products and use them to produce the goods it provides. Government employees provide labor, the most important resource government buys. **Governmental purchases of goods and services (G)** are then provided at zero or minimal prices to the people who use them. Because these items are seldom traded in regular markets, we do not know their value with any precision. Hence, all government goods are entered into the GNP accounts at the prices government pays for them. This means that, for GNP accounting purposes, government is assumed to add nothing to the value of the labor and other resources it uses.

An important point to remember is that transfer payments are excluded from government purchases. Transfer payments (welfare payments, Social Security, and others) are simply shifts in income from one set of households to another set and are not connected with production.

Net Exports (X − M)

Net exports are defined as exports (*X*) minus imports (*M*). **Exports** are goods manufactured in this country and purchased by foreigners. We obviously need to include exports in GNP as a measure of the value of all production in a year. But what about imports? **Imports** are produced in foreign countries and consumed or invested in the United States. Do imports reflect American production? The answer is clearly no. A Subaru purchased in the United States is part of Japanese production (and adds to Japanese consumption when the owners of the resources that produce the car spend their pay). When Americans buy a Japanese auto, this expenditure must be subtracted from U.S. consumption or it will appear that the car was produced in the United States. Similarly, if an American investor buys Swedish machinery, the purchase appears in the U.S. investment category and should be subtracted. Thus, imports are subtracted from exports to arrive at the net effect of foreign trade on GNP in our economy.

To summarize briefly: Using the expenditure approach, Gross National Product is the sum of consumer spending (C), business investment (I), government spending for goods and services (G), and net exports ($X - M$):

$$C + I + G + (X - M) = \text{GNP}.$$

These expenditure categories are shown in Table 1. Measurements of GNP by these categories were developed by Nobel Prize-winning economist Simon Kuznets (see his Biography).

The Income Approach

The second approach to measuring GNP is the **income approach.** By adding together all the payments to the factors of production—wages and salaries, rents, interest, and profits—we obtain what is called National Income (NI).

The Components of National Income (NI) Conceptually, **National Income (NI)** is the sum of all incomes—wages, interest, rent, and profit—received by the owners of the various resources (labor, capital, land, and entrepreneurship). In fact, however, National Income is measured as the sum of five slightly different categories: (a) wages and salaries, (b) noncorporate proprietors' income, (c) corporate profits before taxes, (d) rental income, and (e) interest. Table 2 presents accounting data showing the proportions and trends in these income payments for selected years.

Wages and Salaries This accounting category includes not only **wages and salaries** paid to employees, but also the monetary values of fringe benefits, tips, bonuses, stock option plans, paid vacations, and the employers' contributions to Social Security. As you can see from Table 2, wages and salaries constitute by far the largest single category in National Income. Throughout this century, wages and salaries have increased as a percentage of National Income, growing from less than half in 1900 to roughly three-fourths today.

Proprietors' Income Entrepreneurial profits are typically separated by National Income accountants into two distinct categories: proprietors' net income and corporate profits. **Proprietors' incomes** are the incomes received by sole proprietorships, partnerships, professional associations, and (unincorporated) farms. Included in farm income is an estimate of the value of food grown and consumed on farms—although it is not marketed, this clearly represents production.

TABLE 1 *Components of Gross National Product: Expenditure Approach (1985 Billions of Dollars)*

Component	$ Billions
Personal consumption expenditures (C)	$2,581.9
Gross private domestic investment (I)	670.4
Government purchases of goods and services (G)	814.6
Net exports of goods and services ($X - M$)	−74.4
Gross National Product (GNP)	$3,992.5

Source: *Economic Report of the President*, 1986.

Simon Kuznets (1901–85)

Russian-born but American-educated, Simon Kuznets received his Ph.D. in Economics at Columbia University in 1926 and began an association with the National Bureau of Economic Research that lasted for a half century. Kuznets first developed and then refined the concepts and measurement procedures used in national income accounting.

When Kuznets began trying to measure economic aggregates, empirical knowledge of many aspects of economic life was either crude or nonexistent. Although the concept of national income could be traced to François Quesnay, an eighteenth-century Frenchman, methods for estimating national income and product remained in a primitive state.

Kuznets changed all that by pioneering modern estimation techniques that sum expenditures by different classes of purchases over different classes of goods. Thus, he is responsible for providing the statistical foundations for modern studies of the relationships among income, consumption, and investment, and well deserves the title, "Father of GNP."

Without Kuznets's work it would have been impossible to use quantitative methods to evaluate the Keynesian revolution in economic thought. This realization prompted one modern economist to declare that "we live in the age of Keynes and Kuznets." For his monumental achievements in empirical economics, Kuznets was awarded the Nobel Prize in economics in 1971.

Perhaps because of his almost single-handed construction of the national income accounts, Kuznets was keenly aware of the deficiencies of GNP as a measure of economic well-being.

Because GNP ignores working conditions (for example, stress and strain) and most nonmarket activities, Kuznets has continually cautioned against reliance on national income data as the only indicators of economic performance. Nevertheless, GNP is generally accepted today by economists, businesspeople, and politicians as a crude barometer of the state of the economy.

Much of this income category represents wages, interest, or rent that proprietors would have earned if they had not been operating these firms personally. Dividing this category according to purely economic concepts (to distinguish opportunity costs) is not possible, however, given the limitations of the accounting data available. Thus, here we will follow accounting conventions and label it as *profit*.

Over the last several decades, income accruing to proprietors has been a declining percentage of National Income, falling from 17.5 percent in 1929 to less than 8 percent today. Part of the reason for the decline in proprietors' incomes and the growth in wages and salaries is that many people whose families once owned small farms have sold these farms and moved to urban areas where they could realize greater incomes through wages and salaries.

Corporate Profits   Corporations use their **profits** in three ways. First, they *may* pay corporate income taxes. Second, they *can* pay dividends to stockholders from what is left after taxes. Finally, remaining profits *can* be kept in the firm to help finance expansion, to be used as working capital, or for other purposes. Economists call the corporate profits kept within the firm *undistributed corporate profits;* to accountants they are *retained earnings.*

Much of the accounting category called *corporate profit* actually represents interest that stockholders could have made had they bought bonds instead of stock. Again, because the data are difficult to divide, it is conventional to lump this figure in with corporate profits.

Since proprietors' income has been falling as a percentage of National Income, you might expect

TABLE 2 *National Income: Income Approach to GNP (Selected Years 1929–85)*

Category	1929 Billions $	%	1933 Billions $	%	1960 Billions $	%	1980 Billions $	%	1985 Billions $	%
Wages and salaries	51.1	58.9	29.5	73.1	294.2	71.0	1,598.6	75.5	2,372.7	73.8
Proprietor's income	15.2	17.5	5.9	14.6	46.2	11.2	116.3	5.5	242.4	7.5
Corporate profits	10.5	12.0	−1.2	−3.0	49.9	12.0	181.6	8.6	299.0	9.3
Rental income	5.4	6.2	2.0	5.1	15.8	3.8	32.9	1.5	14.0	.5
Interest	4.7	5.4	4.1	10.2	8.4	2.0	187.7	8.9	287.7	8.9
National income	86.8	100.0	40.3	100.0	414.1	100.0	2,117.1	100.0	3,215.8	100.0

Source: *U.S. Department of Commerce.*
Note: Rounding may cause each total to be slightly different from the sum of each column.

that the share accruing to corporate profit would be rising. However, a glance at Table 2 reveals that corporate profits as a percentage of National Income have been falling somewhat. What accounts for the increase in wages and salaries and the erratic declines in both corporate and proprietors' entrepreneurial profits? The explanation lies partially in the fact that government outlays as a percentage of total output have risen markedly in the last half century. Since the bulk of governmentally provided services requires substantial labor, wages and salaries have been growing steadily.

Rental Income **Rental income** is derived from leasing various resources. Accounting rents are usually associated with the leasing of real property (such as land, houses, offices), but can be obtained from renting any asset. Determining what part conforms to the economic definition of rent is impossible, so again we use the accounting classification. As you can see in Table 2, rental income is the smallest category in our National Income accounts.

Interest **Interest,** like rental income, is rather self-explanatory. Accountants include the payments made for the use of borrowed capital (usually, financial capital). These payments are made to or by banks, or to holders of bonds. In the 1970s, rising interest rates caused interest income to be the most rapidly growing component of National Income. Inexplicably, national income accounting conventions treat interest paid to holders of government bonds as a transfer payment and exclude it from the interest component of National Income.

Reconciling GNP and NI

Gross Private Domestic Investment (GPDI) overstates the growth of the nation's stock of capital. The decline in value of capital because of wear and tear or obsolescence must be considered. Accountants refer to these declines in value as **depreciation.** Accounting estimates of depreciation reflect rapid write-offs because of advantageous tax treatment. To economists, accounting depreciation is known as the **capital consumption allowance.**

Subtracting the capital consumption allowance from Gross Private Domestic Investment yields **Net Private Domestic Investment,** which is an estimate of the growth of the nation's capital stock over the year. All else equal, depreciation reduces the wealth and income of capital owners. Consequently, one step in reconciling GNP and NI requires subtracting the capital consumption allowance from GNP, which yields **Net National Product,** or **NNP.**

Conceptually, Net National Product is an estimate of how much we could consume in a given year and still have the same amount of capital available for production at the beginning of the next year. This means that Net National Product is the net value of goods and services produced in the economy *after* we have adjusted for the depreciation of some of our productive capacity during the year. Failing to consider depreciation would cause overstatement of the net value of our production. In a sense, depreciation represents a "death rate of capital" that must be subtracted from the "birth rate of capital" (GPDI) to arrive at net capital formation.

There is one more adjustment to our Gross National Product before it equals National Income. The amounts you pay for products and the amounts received by businesses are not equal. There is the matter of sales and excise taxes to consider. These are called **indirect business taxes,** and they drive wedges between what consumers or investors spend and the amounts received by sellers. For example, sales and excise taxes must be subtracted from the buyer's payment for a new car before we arrive at the amount that auto workers or manufacturers will receive as income. Consequently, indirect business taxes must be subtracted from Net National Product. We will obtain National Income only after these and other miscellaneous adjustments and allowances have been made. Table 3 shows the adjustments necessary to reconcile GNP and NI.

The Value-Added Technique What are the mechanics for computing GNP? Government statisticians could wait for all households to file their income tax returns. Calculating GNP would then be accomplished by summing all declared incomes and adding the figures for indirect business taxes and depreciation. However, this strategy depends crucially on people's honesty. Worse yet, revised figures would only be available in May or June, which would make them five or six months old since the income tax returns due on April 15 are only for the preceding year. For these reasons and more, National Income is calculated primarily as a double check on GNP figures.

An alternative is to collect all sales figures for a year. Since most businesses are subject to sales and income taxes and to other government controls requiring extensive reporting, sales figures are available on a regular and continuing basis. But what then? If we just total the sales figures, there will be a lot of *double counting*. For example, if U.S. Steel's sales are added to General Motor's sales, we count steel production twice—once when it is sold to GM, and then again when GM sells the steel in the form of, say, Chevettes to the final customers.

For this reason, National Income statisticians use the **value-added technique.** A firm's purchases of intermediate goods from other firms are subtracted from its sales, yielding only the value of the production done within the firm, or the **value added.** Summing the values added from all firms in the economy generates reasonably accurate GNP figures, after adjusting for such things as changes in inventories, the imputed (estimated) rental values of owner-occupied housing, and the imputed values of food grown and consumed on the farm.

TABLE 3 *Reconciling the Income and Expenditure Approaches to GNP (1985 Billions of Dollars)*

Expenditure Approach	$ Billions
Gross National Product (GNP)	$3,992.5
minus: Capital consumption allowance (depreciation)	−438.2
equals: Net National Product (NNP)	$3,554.3
minus: Indirect Business Taxes (IBT) and misc.	−338.8
equals: National Income (NI)	$3,215.7
Income Approach	**$ Billions**
Wages and salaries	$2,372.7
plus: Proprietor's income (business, professional, farm)	242.4
plus: Corporate profits before taxes	299.0
plus: Rental income	14.0
plus: Interest	287.5
equals: National Income (NI)	$3,215.6

Source: U.S. Department of Commerce, 1986

FIGURE 3 *Value Added: The Woodcarving Example*

Your Receipt from
Sale of Wood: $20

Value Added by You: $20

Artist's Receipts
from Sale of Woodcarving: $100

Value Added by Artist: $80

Store Receipts
from Final Sale of Artwork: $150

Value Added by Retailer: $50

Total Consumer Expenditure = $150   Total Value Added (Total New Income) = $150

The value-added technique is used to provide reasonable estimates of GNP. Summing together all sales figures for all firms would result in "double counting" because most firms buy intermediate goods. Adding together the value added by each firm (sales minus purchases of intermediate products) results in total final expenditures or GNP. Note that the sum of the values added is equal to the value of the final commodity.

Consider the following example. While wandering in the forest one weekend, you find an interesting piece of weathered wood. You backpack it home and show it to an artist friend. Your friend indicates a desire to carve a figure from the piece of wood and offers you $20 for it. When you accept, GNP has increased by $20. Your friend carves the wood and sells the finished sculpture to a gift shop for $100. The gift shop then sells the carving to a customer for $150.

Has GNP increased by $270 ($20 + $100 + $150)? The answer is no. If we were to sum all these transactions, your original sale of the wood for $20 would be counted three times—in the original sale, in the sale to the shop, and then in the final sale to the customer. During the first two sales, the piece of wood is an **intermediate good**—something used in the production of another good. The sale to the customer is the final sale, and the carving sold by the shop is the **final good.**

The value-added approach sums the value added at each stage of production. In the example of the wood carving, $20 in value was added by you in finding and selling the piece of wood to your friend, who generated $80 in value added by sculpting the wood. Then the store created a value added of $50 by putting the carving in the hands of the ultimate buyer. This example is diagrammed in Figure 3.

From GNP Accounts to Disposable Personal Income_____

The models we use to explain how national income is determined largely ignore the differences among GNP, National Income (NI), Net National Product (NNP), Personal Income (PI), and Disposable Personal Income (DPI). GNP can be distilled into categories that reflect household income before taxes (PI) and the actual income households have left to spend after taxes (DPI). In this section, we will note how these categories differ.

From GNP to NNP to NI

We already know that capital consumption allowances (depreciation) must be subtracted from GNP to compute Net National Product (NNP). NNP may be thought of as the total value of goods and services available for individual and governmental consumption and net investment. Subtracting indirect business taxes from our NNP yields the total income earned by the suppliers of productive resources, which is known as National Income (NI). A few more adjustments are needed, however, before arriving at the amount that households can actually spend—their Disposable Personal Income (DPI). The following section explains how we arrive at Personal Income (PI) as an intermediate step.

From NI to Personal Income (PI)

National Income includes wages, interest, rents, proprietors' incomes, and corporate profits. Business firms often act as tax collection points for government; in fact, some households never see parts of the income attributed to them. For example, corporate taxes must be paid before stockholders have any claims on corporate incomes, which means that these taxes must be subtracted from National Income. Dividends to stockholders are parts of their Personal Income, but undistributed corporate profits must also be subtracted from National Income. Also, business firms are legally obligated to match employees' Social Security taxes. The National Income accounts then subtract both employer and employee contributions to Social Security from National Income on this journey towards Personal Income.

In addition to these incomes that are earned but not received by households, there are two forms of household incomes that are *received* but *not earned*.

A growing proportion of our National Income is composed of government transfer payments (e.g., welfare payments). Many business firms also engage in charitable activities. Funds transferred through either government or business to private individuals must be added to National Income. At this point, we have finally arrived at the total amount of money income received by households, known as **Personal Income,** or **PI** (see Figure 4).

From PI to Disposable Personal Income (DPI)

You might think that Personal Income is the amount available for personal consumption and saving. However, direct taxes on individuals must be paid out of your Personal Income. Thus, federal, state, and local income taxes must be subtracted. In Figure 4, we have arrived at the income households can consume or save as they choose—their **Disposable Personal Income (DPI).** Table 4 provides a detailed breakdown and summary of GNP for selected years.

Some Limitations of GNP Accounting_____

How well do Gross National Product and the other measures of National Income measure economic performance? Although the National Income accounts are fine for some purposes, they suffer from certain limitations. These limitations fall into three categories: (*a*) accuracy, (*b*) inclusion of only "legal" market transactions, and (*c*) measurement of government output. Among the most ardent critics of the accuracy of GNP data was the late Oskar Morgenstern (see his Biography on page 136).

Accuracy of GNP Figures

There is a tendency toward specious accuracy, a pretense that things have been counted more precisely than they can be—e.g., the U.S. Army published enemy casualties for the Korean war to $1/1000$ of 1 percent, at a time when our own losses were not well known even to the thousands of men! The classic case is, of course, that of the story in which a man, asked about the age of a river, states that it is 3,000,021 years old. Asked how he could give such accurate information, the answer was that twenty-one years ago the river's age was given as three million years. There is a fair amount of this in economic (and other social) statistics.
　　　　　　　　　　—Oskar Morgenstern
　　　　　　　　　　(*"Qui Numerare Incipit Errare Incipit"*)

FIGURE 4 *Various Measures of the Income of the Nation, 1985*

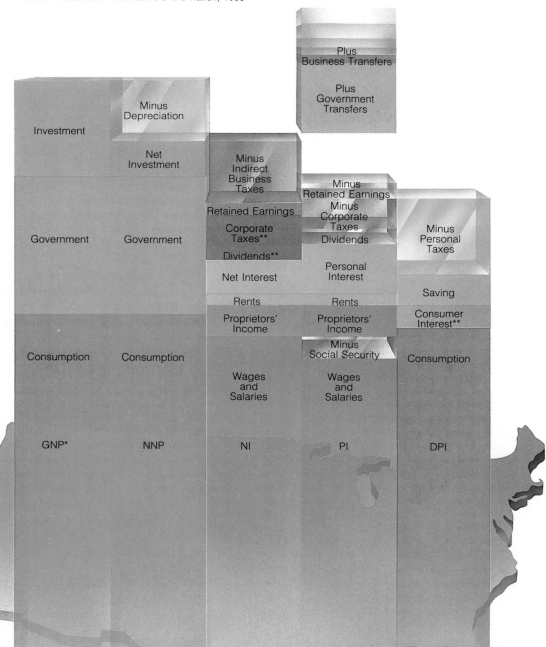

This figure illustrates how the various measures of aggregate economic activity are related. For example, NNP is equal to GNP minus the capital consumption allowance; disposable personal income is personal income minus taxes, and so on.
Notes:
  *Includes net exports in the total.
 **Includes inventory and capital consumption adjustments.
***Includes transfers to foreigners.

Source: U.S. Department of Commerce.

Just how accurate must GNP accounts be to be useful to economic planners, business forecasters, and others concerned with the health of our economy? There is reason to believe that there are biases in the data. For example, many people systematically understate the incomes they report on their tax forms. Statisticians commonly assume that errors of measurement are offsetting, but anyone who thinks that this is so for income is extremely naive.

Another problem is that many of our social accounts are reported to the exact dollar. For example, per capita personal income for California in 1980 was reported as $6,114. Numbers like these are disclosed each month by various data-gathering agencies and firms. Would it be just as useful (and less misleading) to know that personal income in California in 1980 was something over $6,000? Social and economic statistics need be no more accurate than their use dictates. Further, social scientists should not report results from studying these numbers in a fashion that creates a false sense of precision.

Exclusion of Nonmarket Transactions

Since GNP is defined as the total value of all production during a year, it should include all products. Our system of national accounts focuses on market transactions because dollar sales figures are reasonably available. However, not all productive activity goes through the marketplace. Some nonmarket transactions are included in GNP because estimates of their values are available (e.g., estimated rents for owner-occupied housing and estimates of the value of food produced and consumed on farms). However, the values of housewives' services are excluded from GNP because of the difficulty of generating even crude estimates. This leads to the ludicrous situation where a maid hired to clean your home causes GNP to rise, while the same work done by a family member does not enter our GNP accounts. The same is true of homemade haircuts, mowing your own lawn rather than hiring your neighbor's kid, and many other nonmarket activities.

TABLE 4 *Gross National Product and Related Data (Billions of Dollars)*

	1929	1950	1985
Gross National Product (GNP)	$103.1	$284.8	$3,992.5
minus: Capital consumption allowance (depreciation)	−7.9	−18.3	−438.2
equals: Net National Product (NNP)	$ 95.2	$266.5	$3,554.3
minus: Indirect business taxes	−3.4	−14.1	−338.7
equals: National Income (NI)	$ 86.8	$241.1	$3,215.6
minus: Corporate profits with inventory evaluation adjustment	−10.5	−37.7	−299.0
Contributions for social insurance	−.2	−6.9	−354.9
Net interest	−4.7	−3.0	−287.7
plus: Government transfer payments	0.9	14.3	465.2
Personal interest income	2.5	7.2	456.5
Dividends	5.8	8.8	78.9
Business transfer payments	0.6	0.8	19.3
equals: Personal Income (PI)	$ 85.9	$227.6	$3,294.2
minus: Personal taxes	−2.6	−20.7	−493.1
equals: Disposable Personal Income (DPI)	$ 83.3	$206.9	$2,801.1
minus: Consumer interest and personal transfer payments to foreigners	−1.9	−2.8	−89.5
Consumption expenditures	−77.2	−191.0	−2,581.9
equals: Personal saving	$ 4.2	$ 13.1	$ 129.7

Source: U.S. Department of Commerce.
Note: Totals may not add due to rounding.

Oskar Morgenstern (1902–77)

Simon Kuznets conscientiously warned of the incompleteness of National Income data, but Oskar Morgenstern went a step further, persistently criticizing the accuracy of economic reporting. He was convinced that the results of statistical analyses are no better than the raw material in which they are based and believed that the maxim "Garbage In, Garbage Out (GIGO)" applied to GNP accounting.

Many economists have striven for the reasonably precise empirical validations of theory that are possible in some of the physical sciences. Morgenstern argued that there are several reasons why data problems in the social sciences are essentially different from data problems in the physical sciences. Incentives often exist for collectors of aggregate data to fabricate statistics and for those who give the data to report incorrect figures.

"Disguised" or inaccurate data may be reported to avoid or evade taxes, to throw competitors off the track, or to guard trade secrets. Estimates of many highly aggregated variables, moreover, are little better than guesses because they require data for parts of the economy about which there is little precise and reliable information. For example, should old machinery that has been idle for years be considered when we estimate *capacity utilization rates?* Growth of the underground economy compounds problems of this type.

Accuracy is extremely important in the gathering of national income data, according to Morgenstern, because errors that creep into the data at different levels of collection have a way of compounding. He asserted that "national income is a total of composites which differ in reliability from sector to sector and year to year, and hence the error of the composite is a complex amalgam of errors in the parts whose magnitude is not easily determined." In a speech in 1975, Morgenstern argued that the data errors that enter calculations of GNP *are larger than the fluctuations of GNP that most economists consider significant.* If Morgenstern was correct, this seriously undermines the reliance usually placed on GNP as a predictor of booms and recessions.

Morgenstern was born in Silesia, Germany. The son of a small businessman, he came to America after the Nazi invasion of Vienna.

It is also true that the government is generally unable to estimate accurately the values of unrecorded economic activities (such as barter transactions) and excludes them as well as all illegal activities (see Focus 1). Should legalization of gambling or marijuana lead to an increase in measured GNP figures even if there were no changes in people's behavior? Under the current accounting system, it would. Such problems mean that comparisons of GNP over time or among countries must be tempered by recognition that GNP accounts are affected by the relative importance of nonmarket to market transactions, by the frequency of barter, and by differences in laws and regulations.

In addition to these difficulties, some items seem to be misclassified. For example, individual investment in education is treated as personal consumption spending. Football games, parties, many other collegiate social activities, and a number of frivolous courses *are* consumption activities. However, the time and effort you spend studying will increase your future productivity and should be considered investment, not consumption. (Should the deterioration of your body as you age be considered "depreciation"?) Government investments in research and development, transportation, flood control, and so on are treated in similar fashion. These investments are reported as government spending rather than as investment. Classification in this way tends to understate the extent to which present consumption is diverted to activities that tend to enhance our future productivity, output, growth, and well-being.

Measuring Government Output

Measuring the value of government output poses special problems. Since most government services are not directly charged to their users, statisticians confront considerable difficulty in valuing the output of government. Consequently, government statisticians use the next best estimate—the cost of the inputs (primarily, governmental workers) used to produce the output.

The many problems with GNP accounting cause some critics to assert that the GNP and NI figures are worthless. It may be that parts of our measures of GNP and some of its relatives are a bit like the following example. Imagine that all the members of your class are transported back in time to around 1803. Each is assigned, by President Thomas Jefferson, the task of traveling to various parts of North America and then returning to Washington, D.C. with estimates of the distances between certain points. To standardize measurements, everyone is to pace the distances. People pacing the distance to Philadelphia, New York, or Boston would cross-check each other, making estimates of these short distances fairly accurate. However, some people would differ in the length of their strides, some people would just wander in circles, and others might guess at the distance while they rode on horses or in wagons. Still others might not even go to faraway distances but would fill in travel vouchers as though they had. The mishmash of distance estimates turned in to President Jefferson might be a lot like parts of GNP accounting—far from precise, but still better than no data at all.

GNP and Social Welfare

GNP accounts were created to measure economic performance. These accounts may be abused when they are used to make comparisons about the well-being of citizens in various countries. This is especially true if the relative size of barter or the underground economy varies much among countries.

When our government reports that per capita GNP rose by 1 percent last month, this need not imply that your personal quality of life improved by 1 percent. There may be some correlation between the growth of GNP and the increase in your income, but the relationship is far from perfect.

Differences Between GNP and Well-Being

If you decided to take a year off to see the world, GNP in the United States would surely fall, assuming that your present activities add to GNP. You might gain subjectively from this decision, but the GNP accounts would not reflect that your desires for added travel and leisure were met. One of the most important recent changes in our economy that reflects an improvement in the quality of life is the increased leisure time that most of us enjoy. The GNP accounts neglect the value of leisure.

Furthermore, the accounting system fails to deduct for many negative aspects of economic growth, particularly environmental degradation. While greater outlays on packaging for products add to GNP output figures, the accounting process fails to deduct the accompanying destruction of national forests. GNP does include the costs of removing litter and of increased medical care caused by pollution or auto accidents, but do injurious wrecks increase our welfare? Are we better off if a disastrous leak from a nuclear reactor necessitates a billion-dollar cleanup? Some people argue that we need an index that measures economic well-being rather than economic production.

A Measure of Economic Welfare (MEW)

Work in this direction has been done by William Nordhaus and James Tobin. They attempted to adjust GNP to account for some of the deficiencies we have described. They call their statistic the **Measure of Economic Welfare,** or **MEW.** GNP is adjusted by deducting these items that do not contribute to economic welfare and adding items that do but that are not now counted in GNP.

The major noncontributing items that are deducted from GNP are (*a*) household expenditures that do not add to a better life—for example, expenditures for commuting, police protection, and

FOCUS 1

The Underground Economy

We all know people who cheat on their taxes by understating their income. The waiter who reports only half of his tips, the plumber who gives customers a break if they pay cash, and the gambler who keeps no records are all part of the growing "underground economy." Estimates of its size range from a conservative 3 percent to an astounding 20 percent of GNP, which means that our official 1985 GNP of $4 trillion could have been as high as $5 trillion if everyone had reported all their income. Moreover, it means that the U.S. Treasury may be cheated out of as much as $250 billion in taxes annually by participants in this underground. Figure 5 presents one set of estimates of the size of the underground economy.

Although researchers disagree on the size of the subterranean economy, all agree that it is growing roughly twice as fast as GNP. Why is this happening? One part of the answer is that economic growth and inflation have driven many Americans into higher and higher tax brackets, so there is more incentive to cheat.

Another aspect of this problem is the falling probability of an Internal Revenue Service audit. About 3 percent of all tax returns were audited in the late 1960s; today, the proportion is around 1.5 percent. Finally, the Vietnam era and Watergate made tax protesters respectable in the eyes of some.

Cataloguing all the ways that people have discovered to cheat on their taxes would generate a book as thick as a New York City telephone directory. Legitimate business people may not report cash income or may overstate their tax deductions and, thus, understate their incomes. If you falsely claim that new drapes in your home are a business expense, you are involved in the underground economy.

Barter is perfectly legitimate but is a major avenue for tax evasion. When a dentist trades a root canal for brickwork on a backyard fireplace, both the dentist and the bricklayer should report as income the value of what they received.

Nearly 70 percent of the underground economy consists of income that, if reported, would be legitimate; 30 percent or so of the income flowing through untaxed channels is derived from criminal activities. Bank robbers, shoplifters, drug dealers, prostitutes, and loan sharks understandably try to minimize their contact with the Internal Revenue Service.

FIGURE 5   *Sources of Underground Income, 1985*

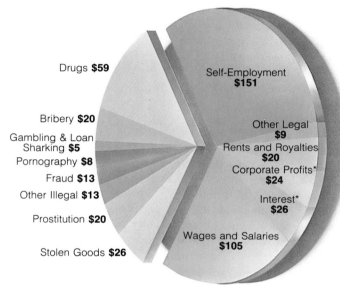

Unreported Income from Illegal Sources (Billions of Dollars)

Unreported Income from Legal Sources (Billions of Dollars)

Drugs **$59**

Bribery **$20**

Gambling & Loan Sharking **$5**

Pornography **$8**

Fraud **$13**

Other Illegal **$13**

Prostitution **$20**

Stolen Goods **$26**

Self-Employment **$151**

Other Legal **$9**

Rents and Royalties **$20**

Corporate Profits* **$24**

Interest* **$26**

Wages and Salaries **$105**

*Partly included in recorded GNP accounts

Total Illegal **$163** billion   Total Legal **$332** billion

Total Legal and Illegal **$495** billion

Source: Carl R. Simon and Ann D. Witte, *Beating the System: The Underground Economy* (Boston, Mass.: Auburn House Publishing Co., 1981); updated by authors.

It is obvious that the failure of the Treasury to collect taxes is important because those of us who scrupulously pay our taxes suffer from higher tax rates. And what are the implications of the underground economy for economic statistics and public policy? For one thing, the slowdown of GNP growth during the 1970s may have been overstated to the extent that unreported income grew in importance nationally. In January 1986, the Department of Commerce improved its adjustments to the GNP accounts to try to account for misreporting on tax returns. These methods resulted in adjustments totaling nearly $200 billion for 1985.

Another consideration is that unemployment statistics may be overstated (or labor force participation understated) if underground activity is not taken into account. Still another is that, if poor people participate in cash or barter transactions proportionally more than do high-income individuals, the degree of income inequality and the need for welfare programs may be overstated; conversely, if high-dollar, white-collar crime is rampant, income may be even less evenly distributed than we think. The list of reasons for the importance of accounting for underground transactions could be extended considerably.

We can wish that compliance with tax laws was more widespread among Americans but, at the same time, we can be grateful that we do not suffer from the underreporting that appears common in parts of Europe. As Figure 6 shows, the underground economy is estimated to run as high as one-third of Italian GNP.

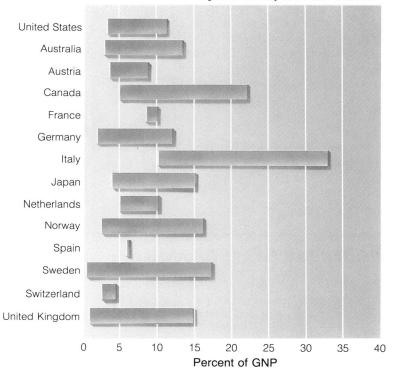

FIGURE 6 *Estimates of the Size of the Underground Economy in Selected Countries*

Percent of GNP

Source: U.S. Department of Commerce, Bureau of Economic Analysis; Carol S. Carson, "The Underground Economy: An Introduction," *Survey of Current Business,* May 1984, p. 33.

Note: The estimates are from many sources; when a range is shown, the high and low estimates for a country may bracket one or more estimates. Both among countries and for a particular country, the estimates vary in the scope of the underground economy measured, the methodology used, and the time period covered.

national defense and (*b*) losses associated with pollution, urban congestion, and so on. The major additions are estimates for: (*a*) the value of goods and services that do not pass through the market and (*b*) increased leisure.

The MEW estimates done by Nordhaus and Tobin suggest that our welfare has grown more slowly than has GNP. One important question we must answer is: How much growth in GNP might we be willing to sacrifice to improve our quality of life (as measured by MEW growth)?

Construction of the MEW accounts still leaves many questions unanswered. For example, if water prices rose because of drought, should we rejoice because the value of water consumed as measured by our water bill has risen?

Despite the many difficulties associated with accurately measuring GNP and its related subcomponents, GNP remains the best measure of aggregate economic activity available today. In the discussions of macroeconomic theory and policy that follow, we will use GNP (both real and nominal) and the rates of unemployment and inflation to judge present and past policymaking. While making these evaluations, however, you should keep in mind the limitations described in this chapter.

CHAPTER REVIEW: KEY POINTS

1. *GNP* is the *total market value* of a nation's annual production. GNP measures estimate the economic performance of an economy and are important for government policy and business decisions.
2. The *expenditures approach* to GNP sums *consumer spending* (*C*), business investment spending (*I*), *government purchases* (*G*), and *net exports* (*X* − *M*):

    $$GNP = C + I + G + (X - M).$$

3. *Gross Private Domestic Investment (GPDI)* is the economic term for business spending. To arrive at net investment, we need to subtract depreciation from GPDI.
4. Government purchases (*G*) do not include *transfer* (welfare) *payments,* which are treated as flows of income from some households to others.
5. The *income approach* to GNP sums wages, interest, rent, and profits. We use the figures available, which are (*a*) wages and salaries, (*b*) proprietors' income, (*c*) corporate profits, (*d*) rental income, and (*e*) interest. The sum of these figures is *National Income (NI).* Addition of *indirect business taxes,* which is not anyone's income, yields *Net National Product (NNP).*

The *capital consumption allowance (depreciation)* is the difference between GNP and NNP.
6. The *value-added approach* to GNP sums the sales of all firms and subtracts their purchases of intermediate products, which are goods bought by one firm from another for further processing. Failure to exclude purchases of intermediate goods from GNP figures would result in substantial *double counting* of production.
7. GNP figures should be used cautiously in any discussions of economic welfare. One problem is that they may be systematically biased and are often presented in an artificially precise fashion. Another problem is that they ignore most nonmarket production (for example, housewives' services, do-it-yourself projects, and the like). GNP accounts include as production many *disproducts* (for instance, pollution abatement equipment is added to GNP, while environmental decay is not subtracted).
8. A *Measure of (Net) Economic Welfare (MEW),* which attempts to correct for some of these flaws in GNP accounts, shows much less rapid growth than does GNP.

QUESTIONS FOR THOUGHT AND DISCUSSION

1. National Income accounting values government services at the costs of the inputs used to produce the services. Why does the government value its output in this manner? Do you feel that this understates or overstates the value of government services? How would you measure the value of government services?

2. Should the purchase of education be viewed as consumption or investment expenditure? Why? What would happen to the National Income accounts if purchases of education, medical care, and dental care were counted as investment and not consumption?

3. Why is NNP a more appropriate measure of true economic productivity than GNP? As they are currently constructed, which do you think is the best measure of economic welfare on a per capita basis: (*a*) GNP, (*b*) NNP, (*c*) NI, (*d*) PI, (*e*) DPI, or (*f*) consumption? What makes the category you selected preferable to each of the others?

4. What would be the effect on GNP accounting if marijuana, prostitution, and gambling were legalized nationwide? What do you think would happen to economic well-being? Why?

5. Suppose a car dealer sells a new car in September 1987 for $10,400, but allows a trade-in of $3,000 for a car that turns out to be a clunker. After $600 worth of repairs, the clunker is sold for $2,900. The new car cost the dealer $9,000. How will each phase of these transactions affect the GNP accounts? What were the values added at each step?

6. Suppose one-fourth of all young female workers take a maternity leave and then, after their child is born, decide to stay home permanently. What will happen to our GNP accounts? As we defined GNP conceptually, what happens to actual GNP relative to measured GNP? Measured GNP relative to economic welfare?

7. The government has gone to great lengths to compile and distribute measurements of aggregate economic activity. Some economists would say, "This information is not all that useful, and collecting it is just a method to employ a sizeable portion of the federal bureaucracy." Your reaction?

8. You own a company that has annual sales of $500,000. The value added of your company's production (your addition to GNP) is estimated to be $250,000. Is your company making a profit of $250,000? If not, how is the difference between your firm's sales and your firm's addition to GNP explained?

9. If you start your own business and use $23,000 of your savings to buy used equipment from a dealer, is the $23,000 considered economic investment? Will any part of the $23,000 add to GNP? Explain.

10. What is the effect of arson on estimates of GNP? What should it be?

11. Suppose that all home owners in America decided to move into their next-door neighbor's house and pay that neighbor rent. What would happen to GNP? Would your answer be the same if GNP estimates did not include an estimate of the rental value of owner-occupied housing? How would it differ?

12. Using the data in the table below, calculate the following:
   a. Gross National Product.
   b. Net National Product.
   c. Personal saving.

Gross Private Domestic Investment	666.1
Exports	363.2
Personal Tax Payments	498.2
State and Local Purchases of Goods and Services	467.7
Capital Consumption Allowance	441.4
Imports	451.0
Personal Consumption Expenditures	2,606.1
Federal Government Purchases of Goods and Services	364.8
Personal Income	3,298.5

PART 3 Keynesian Macroeconomics

Isaac Newton's theories of gravity and mechanics suggest that the laws of nature provide for natural harmony and stability throughout the universe. Adam Smith extended Newton's view into the realm of economics by appealing to the idea that an "invisible hand" governs the marketplace. Smith's theory of markets led to *laissez-faire* policy prescriptions—government should maintain a "hands-off" policy with business.

The Wealth of Nations was published by Smith in 1776, also the year of the American Declaration of Independence. The political climate and Smith's theories combined to substantially shape an early American economy that was relatively unfettered by government. In Chapter 8, we review the macroeconomic implications of several early theories, including Smith's "invisible hand" approach, to help you understand why classical economic theory concludes that market economies naturally and quickly gravitate to full employment.

This free market perspective dominated American economic policy with few exceptions from roughly 1790 until 1930. Economies throughout Western Europe and North America developed beyond their agricultural roots during this period, however, becoming largely industrialized. Economic theories adapted very slowly to these changes. The frequent booms and busts that occurred did little to shake economists' faith in laissez-faire policies until the 1930s, when a worldwide depression launched the *Keynesian Revolution* in economic theory. Keynesian theory is the centerpiece of Chapters 9 and 10 and is blended with Keynesian policy in Chapter 11. This Keynesian approach to macroeconomics suggests that the government budget (taxing and spending) must be manipulated for a market economy to be macroeconomically stable. We will look at the opposing view once again in Part Four, which revisits the classical perspective in which money plays an important role. Part Five combines Keynesian and classical analytics in a more sophisticated model of the economy that explains movements of both unemployment and inflation and provides the background necessary to understand modern macroeconomic problems.

CHAPTER 8

Macroeconomics Before Keynes

business cycle	Marxian "capitalistic	wage and price
recession and	crises"	flexibility
depression	classical theory	the Keynesian
long-wave theory of	Say's Law	Revolution
business cycle		

Booms and busts have plagued economic activity since the onset of industrialization, sporadically ejecting many workers from their jobs, pushing many businesses into bankruptcy, and leaving many politicians out in the cold. Most early macroeconomic theories were developed to explain these business cycles and financial panics, and then gradually evolved into a general theory of aggregate economic activity.

We begin this chapter with an overview of how business cycles are measured and with an examination of early theories of business cycles, which range from a "sunspot" theory to the Marxist approach. Our attention then turns to a historical overview of business cycles in the United States. Finally, we explore how the classical theory of markets dismissed the possibility of severe or protracted business cycles. This theory set the stage for the Keynesian analysis, which will be discussed in the next few chapters. The Keynesian revolution in economic theory occurred in the 1930s, but even today, major macroeconomic debates rage between modern Keynesians and those who have resurrected the classical tradition.

Measuring Business Cycles

The **business cycle** consists of alternating periods of expansion and contraction in economic activity. Although "boom–bust" patterns have been a persistent feature of economic history, not all economists believe cycles are inevitable. In the early 1960s, many economists viewed the business cycle as obsolete. Although extensive studies of business cycle activity in both Western capitalist and socialist countries indicate that severe business cycles leading to deep depressions may be obsolete, smaller recessions and minor economic disruptions continue to nag societies everywhere.

A Typical Business Cycle Pattern

Business cycles are typically divided into two major alternating stages—a period of economic expansion and a period of economic contraction. Economists have found it useful to further divide the cycle into four distinct phases: (*a*) **peak,** (*b*) **contraction,** (*c*) **trough,** and (*d*) **expansion.** These phases are illustrated in the insert of Figure 1. Some prefer the terms

FIGURE 1 *Business Activity, 1900–85*

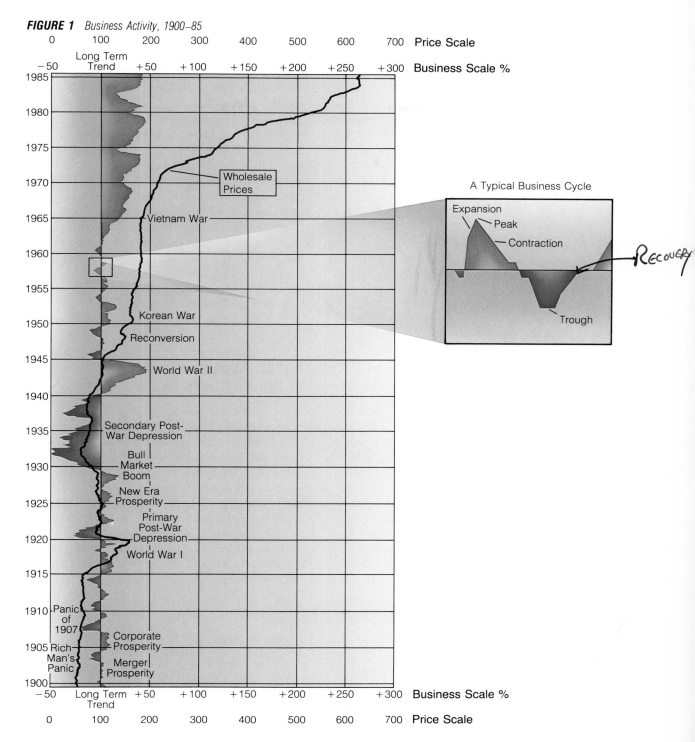

The business cycle is classified into four distinct phases: the peak (*boom*), contraction (*recession*), trough (*depression*), and expansion (*recovery*). As this figure illustrates, the business cycle is quite irregular and varies considerably in intensity.

Source: AmeriTrust Company (Cleveland, Ohio), *American Business Activity from 1790 to Today*, 57th edition, January 1986.

boom, recession, depression, and *recovery,* respectively, to describe cyclical activity. These sets of terms are used interchangeably in the remainder of this book.

Figure 1's insert depicts a relatively smooth cycle. As you can see, however, fluctuations are seldom this regular. Expansion phases range in length from as little as 10 months to as long as 105 months, while each contraction phase may range anywhere from 7 to 65 months in length. Notice that long contractions may be associated with short expansions, or vice versa.

NBER Classification System

The *National Bureau of Economic Research (NBER)* was founded in the 1920s by one of America's first students of the business cycle, Wesley C. Mitchell. Since that time, the NBER has devoted much of its resources to studies of business fluctuations. Business cycles are dated and analyzed using over 5,000 series of economic data, many of which have been collected on a monthly basis since the early 1920s. Among the many important data series are unemployment rates, the Dow-Jones stock market index, new capital orders, rates of inventory accumulation, and new car sales. Troughs of the cycle occur when most of the measures of business activity are at their low points; peaks are dated when the bulk of these economic variables are at their high points. As a general practice, the turning points used to date peaks and troughs are not official until the next peak or trough is reached and designated. For example, the latest trough, tentatively dated as November 1982,

will not become official until after the peak of the 1983–? expansion is reached.

Today, the Bureau of Economic Analysis of the Department of Commerce follows the NBER's system and classifies time-series data by timing and economic process. *Timing* considers a series' historical performance at reference cycle peaks and troughs. Data series that show consistent relationships with the overall level of economic activity are called business cycle indicators. **Leading indicators** are series that reach their respective highs and lows before the cyclic peak and trough. **Coincident indicators** move almost simultaneously with aggregate economic activity. Finally, **lagging indicators** reach their respective highs and lows after the economy has peaked or troughed. Table 1 provides some examples of the three types of indicators. The relationships between these leading, coincident, and lagging indicators are shown in Figure 2.

Social Aspects of the Business Cycle

The excesses of booms and the repressive influences of **depressions** leave indelible stamps on our social structure. The plans of individuals are often altered so severely that the effects are felt for several generations. Business cycles strongly affect general mental and physical health and can lead to divorce, suicide, alcoholism, prostitution, illegitimacy, and crime. Some analysts focus too much on declines in production due to recessions and ignore the costs of increased social problems.

TABLE 1 *Selected Leading, Lagging, and Coincident Indicators*

Leading	Coincident	Lagging
Average workweek for production workers	Real Personal Income less transfers	Average duration of unemployment
Index of net business formation	Index of industrial production	Labor cost per unit of production
New building permits (housing)	Employees on nonagricultural payrolls	Average prime rate charged by banks
Index of stock prices (500 common)	Manufacturing and trade sales	Commercial and industrial loans

Source: *Business Conditions Digest,* June 1986.

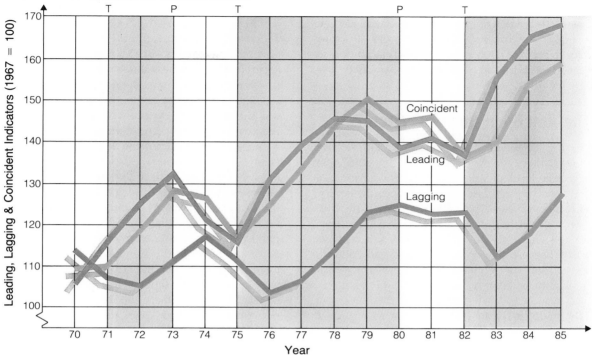

FIGURE 2 Leading, Lagging, and Coincident Indicators

Leading indicators turn up or down ahead of the economy. Coincident indicators parallel the economy's movements. Lagging indicators follow the movements of the economy.

Source: *Business Conditions Digest*, June 1986.

Various studies show that marriages and divorces both are positively related to swings in the economy. When times are hard, both marriages and divorces tend to be postponed. Demands for these two "luxuries" seem to be highly sensitive to income. Changes in marital status tend to be "purchased" when incomes are secure. Would you be more or less likely to marry if you expected to lose your job? Would families with dependent children be as apt to divorce during hard times?

Interestingly, both suicide and illegitimate birth rates rise when the economy heads into a **recession.** At the peak of the Great Depression, suicide rates were 60–70 percent above their normal levels. High suicide rates during the trough of a business cycle probably reflect the despair associated with severe losses of income and forced idleness. One study indicates that roughly 240 additional males aged 20 to 60 commit suicide with each 1 percent hike in the unemployment rate. Heart attacks and

other stress-related diseases also become more common.

Mental illness becomes more prevalent when despair about unemployment gives way to depression. Mental hospitals admit more patients and jails begin to fill when the economy falls into a slump. Crime in general tends to be inversely related to the business cycle. Crime rates typically abate as prosperity becomes the order of the day. Crime increases with the onset of a recession, especially property crime. More individuals may slide into illegal activities when legitimate income-earning opportunities shrink.

These ugly consequences of the economic cycle prompt policymakers to search for ways to steady the economy. If prosperity were perpetual, with only modest swings around a sustained upward trend, the major social effects of business cycle downturns presumably would be dampened. In the depths of the Great Depression, policymakers developed systems of relief for the individuals hit hardest by recessions and depressions. These systems included our Social Security and unemployment compensation programs. Today, downturns in business cycles do considerably less harm to family and social structures than in the past. However, the social maladies associated with business cycles have not vanished.

The American Business Cycle

There is extended discussion in this and the next nine chapters of how the economy functions at the aggregate level and of ways the federal government and monetary authorities might reduce the severity of business cycles. This section highlights the business cycles of the last six decades to help prepare you for this material. Our discussion begins with the 1920s because the events of that decade and the 1930s significantly changed the ways many of us think about capitalism.

The Prosperity of the 1920s

By any yardstick, the 1920s were a period of growth and prosperity. A minor dip in business activity followed World War I, and then the United States enjoyed a boom that lasted until 1929. This sustained prosperity can be attributed to (*a*) rapid expansions of technology and productive capacity; (*b*) development and wide distribution of such new and important products as radios, autos, and telephones; (*c*) the electrification of industry and most homes; (*d*) significantly enhanced labor productivity; and (*e*) a wave of optimism prevailing throughout this decade.

Increased auto production stimulated oil production and subsidiary industries such as tire manufacturing and service stations. In addition, the electrification of the country caused the demand for both business capital equipment and consumer goods to skyrocket. Combine these two ingredients and you get unprecedented growth. Add rapidly improving technology and productivity and you have growth without inflation because growth in Aggregate Supply keeps pace with growing Aggregate Demand. The prosperity of the majority of urbanized Americans unfortunately bypassed most rural areas, however, because agricultural prices were falling. Against this background, it is easy to see why the severity of the recession in the early Thirties caught most people by surprise.

The Devastating Depression of the 1930s

The year 1929 began with widespread expectations of another boom year. By October, however, it was apparent that a business slump was under way. Most forecasters predicted a moderate recession followed by another period of prosperity. Almost everyone was shocked when the economy collapsed, not to recover fully until the eve of World War II.

Statistical evidence of the severity of the Great Depression is provided in Table 2. Real disposable income fell by more than 26 percent, while unemployment rates soared from 3.2 percent in 1929 to nearly 25 percent in 1933. One person was looking for work for every three people employed. Skimpy public welfare and unemployment compensation programs imposed the burden of most economic assistance on private charities. Donations to these were sparse because times were harsh. Income evaporated in families where the heads of households became unemployed. Even though consumption spending fell sharply, years of accumulated savings were eroded. Investment was insignificant.

Families commonly stopped paying rent and waited to be evicted. They would then move to another dwelling, or live with friends or relatives for as long as possible. Landlords were caught in the middle because meeting their mortgage obligations required rental payments. When they failed to pay their mortgages, their buildings were sold, often for less than the mortgage due. Landlords' own homes might then be sold to make up the deficit, leaving them out in the street, trapped in the same cycle that had ensnared their tenants earlier.

It was as if a large segment of the population had stepped through doors into the distant past. Entire families spent their days as hunter-gatherers, prowling streets and garbage dumps looking for scraps of food and clothing with which to keep warm and alive.

The War and Postwar Years: The 1940s and 1950s

Massive government spending associated with financing World War II snapped the economy out of the Depression in the early 1940s. The economy falteringly began to recover after the trough of 1933, but unemployment still stood at almost 15 percent in 1940. The war effort quickly moved the economy to

TABLE 2 *The Severity of the Great Depression*

Measure	1929 High	1933 Low	Percentage Change
GNP (billions, 1972 dollars)	$314.6	$215.6	−31.5%
Gross private domestic investment (billions, 1972 dollars)	55.9	8.4	−85.0
Disposable income (billions, 1972 dollars)	229.8	169.7	−26.2
Total new construction (billions, current dollars)	10.8	2.9	−73.1
Unemployment rate (percentage)	3.2%	24.9%	+678.1
Producer prices (1926 = 100)	$ 98.0	$ 59.8	−40.0
Consumer prices (1967 = 100)	51.3	38.8	−24.4
Stock prices (1935–39 = 100)	238.0	36.0	−84.9

Sources: *Economic Report of the President,* 1986; and R. A. Gordon, *Economic Instability and Growth: The American Record* (New York: Harper & Row, 1974), p. 47.

full employment and brought a new age of prosperity, as well as knowledge and experience in dealing with recessions. John Maynard Keynes wrote *The General Theory of Employment, Interest, and Money* during 1935; its publication in 1936 has reshaped economic thought. The magnitude of government spending during World War II seemed to confirm this theory of how to pull an economy out of a depression.

The economy experienced four complete business cycles between World War II and 1960. None of these were as severe as the Great Depression for several reasons:

1. The massive bank failures of the 1930s caused several banking reforms to be implemented that now buffer the banking community against another collapse. These include the deposit insurance program (FDIC) and a strengthened role for the Federal Reserve System.

2. The Depression imposed hardships on so many families that lawmakers enacted numerous assistance programs and other "automatic stabilizers." For example, unemployment compensation programs tend to halt declines in disposable income to families where an individual has lost a job. This buoys consumer spending and strengthens a stagnant economy. Conversely, when the economy is booming, few are unemployed and the funds paid out from such programs are reduced.

3. Government spending grew during World War II and permanently became a larger part of Gross National Product. These relatively stable expenditures may help prevent fluctuations in our economy. Furthermore, governments throughout

the world became committed to maintaining full employment. After World War II, the federal government was legally obligated by the Employment Act of 1946 to follow policies directed at maintaining maximum employment.

Although there are other reasons why recent business downturns have been less severe than the Great Depression, these are the main forces dampening cyclical slumps.

Inflation was a serious problem during the war years, and the government imposed rationing and price controls to divert the bulk of production to the war effort. After World War II, many consumers had amassed substantial savings because they could buy little during the war—most consumer goods were either tightly rationed or not produced at all. This pent-up demand resulted in a serious round of inflation after the war ended when price controls were lifted. The price level jumped about 10 percent in 1946. Consumers had done without for years and would not be denied. Favorite targets of this consumption binge were automobiles and appliances because the plants where these products were made had been devoted entirely to war goods during the war years.

The decade of the 1950s was a period of modest growth, with occasional mild doses of creeping inflation. The most notable economic event that occurred in those years was a short-term jump in the inflation rate at the beginning of the Korean conflict. Many consumers, remembering the problems associated with rationing and price controls during World War

II, attempted to stockpile commodities that they expected to be rationed. This panic buying caused prices for numerous goods to soar temporarily. Over the rest of the decade the price level was relatively stable, rising at an average rate of only 1–2 percent annually.

The Prosperous 1960s and the Stagnant 1970s

John F. Kennedy really introduced the country to the policy uses of economic theory. For the first time, expansionary policies were proposed when the economy was not in the depths of a depression. The Johnson Administration used tax cuts in 1964 and 1965 in attempts to drive the economy to full employment. The experiment worked, and the nation heralded a new era of prosperity and growth under the guiding hand of Washington's resident economists. A minor trade-off between unemployment and inflation seemed to exist; all that was left for policymakers was to choose a combination of the two that the country could endure.

Escalation of the Vietnam War pushed the economy further toward full employment, but in the end it overheated our economic engine. President Johnson's decision to send more troops to Indochina without concurrent increases in taxes to finance the war effort heightened inflationary pressures that lasted into the 1970s. These demand-induced inflationary forces caused President Nixon to introduce peacetime wage and price controls on August 15, 1971.

The middle 1970s saw our first brush with serious supply-side inflation. Increases in the prices of food, energy, and other raw materials, coupled with lagging productivity, set off a round of both high inflation and high unemployment during 1974–76. Attempts by the Carter Administration to solve the unemployment problem of the late 1970s generated double-digit inflation.

The Rough Riding 1980s

The Reagan Administration's attempts to reduce inflation and high interest rates resulted in the most severe slump since the 1930s, with double-digit unemployment in 1982. Reagan's "supply-side" tax policies, enacted in 1981, began to bear fruit as the level of economic growth improved in 1984. By the mid-1980s, inflation and unemployment were both relatively low, but federal government deficits had mushroomed. Today, curing these deficits appears as impossible as curing the Depression seemed in 1933.

Early Business Cycle Theories

Since the dawn of commercial transactions, scholars have attempted to explain why the level of economic activity suffers periodic fluctuations. There are substantial strategic advantages in knowing when the next rise or decline in business activity is going to take place. Fortunes have been made by those who have accurately foreseen the future of the economy. (Perhaps you thought fortune-tellers were used only for romantic forecasts.)

In the past, economists were limited to impressionistic theorizing about changing levels of economic activity. Today's methods are more precise. First, intricate models are used to forecast each sector of the economy. Then, a simultaneous forecast of the macroeconomy is made using modern computers and statistical techniques. Some early theories of business cycles may appear ludicrous from the vantage point of modern knowledge of business activity.

Sunspot Theory

Many early theories of business cycles focused upon events external to the economy, partly because **external force theories** do not require elaborate macroeconomic models. One early external force theory, known as the **sunspot theory,** was developed in 1875 by a prominent economist, W. Stanley Jevons. He hypothesized that variations in sunspots cause fluctuations in economic activity. Sunspots are storms on the sun's surface caused by violent nuclear explosions. Jevons reasoned that sunspots affect weather and, hence, agricultural yields. Since economies of his time were heavily dependent upon agriculture, sunspots supposedly caused swings in agriculture that reverberated throughout the economy. (If we ever become heavily dependent upon solar energy, a new sunspot theory may be developed.)

Other early theorists also concentrated on swings in agriculture as a source of business instability.

Many analysts watched weather cycles to predict general business conditions. Today, weather is still watched closely because agriculture remains important throughout the international economy.

Psychological Theories

Psychological theories of the business cycle take many forms. All seem to focus on how human herd instincts result in prolonged periods of optimism or pessimism. These theories recognize that people are swayed by both psychological and economic influences. Psychological theories of business cycles explain the momentum of booms or busts initiated by real changes in such things as agricultural yields, the profitability of investments, or natural resource availability.

Once some "real" disturbance occurs, there will be secondary "shock waves" caused by the reactions of households and businesses. These shock waves are the psychological part of the cycle. Household and business decisions are often based on educated guesses (much as you sometimes answer multiple-choice questions on exams) because information is relatively imperfect and expensive. Most business managers operate from the same information bases, which include government and market research data. There is a general reluctance to go it alone. It is not surprising, therefore, that many firms often move in the same direction.

Business cycles are created when the majority of firms develop similar new expectations about economic expansion or contraction and act accordingly. Waves of pessimism or optimism, once set off, seem to have a life of their own. Economic recoveries commence when business becomes optimistic and begins to expand production. This requires that more workers be hired, which tends to bolster household optimism and spending, creating more employment, and so on. A wave of pessimism can operate in just the opposite way. (With psychology involved, is there any wonder at the term *depression*?)

Although psychological theories illustrate why a recovery or downturn is a cumulative process, they do not help us predict swings in economic activity. For this reason, economists have devoted most of their research to discovering more fundamental causes of ups and downs in business cycles.

Population Dynamic Theories

Two hundred years ago, Adam Smith, Thomas Malthus, and their colleagues pondered the long-term economic effects on the course of human history of such things as wars, plagues, famines, natural disasters, and the opening of new territory. They were convinced that increases in the supplies of natural resources normally generate decreases in infant mortality and increases in longevity. From this assumption, they developed early long-run business cycle theories based on the adjustments of populations to the congeniality of their habitat and to the states of international conflict.

According to the **population dynamics approach,** the birthrate is almost unalterable because of biological urges, but survival rates depend on the state of prosperity. When circumstances change in ways that are favorable to production, the resulting booms cause population explosions; death rates fall for infants and mature individuals alike. As human congestion increases and population presses against available resources, conflicts over the use of resources result in declines in population and, hence, economic activity. Naturally, the adjustments to unfavorable changes follow the reverse pattern. Booms and then busts in economic activity, according to this line of reasoning, should alternate across generations.

These early economists understandably failed to anticipate technological advances and birth control programs; so their speculations apply more to primitive economies than to today's industrial giants. Indeed, even today one of the first results of growth in less developed countries is commonly a population explosion.

Innovations

In 1911, Joseph Schumpeter developed a **long-wave theory of the business cycle** suggesting that economic development in capitalistic systems is propelled by innovations (see his Biography). **Innovations,** according to Schumpeter, include: (*a*) introduction of a new good or new quality in a familiar product, (*b*) technological advances, (*c*) opening of new markets, (*d*) discovery of new sources of raw materials, and (*e*) major reorganizations of industries.

J. A. Schumpeter (1883–1950)

As a young man, Joseph Schumpeter had three ambitions in life: to be the world's greatest economist, greatest lover, and greatest horseman. He joked that he had achieved two of the three, confessing in his wry way that he never was much of an equestrian. The issue of his ambitions aside, Schumpeter was unquestionably a man of extraordinary energy and accomplishment. Widely versed in economics, mathematics, statistics, history, and social philosophy, he was far more than a scholarly observer of the world of affairs. At one time or another he was a lawyer, banker, teacher, and public official, serving a stint as finance minister in his native Austria. Two books on economics, both published before he was 30 years old, are still highly regarded. In 1932, he became a professor of economics at Harvard University, where he taught until his death 18 years later.

Schumpeter's writings contain concepts of the whole economic process: equilibrium, business cycles, and the survival prospects of capitalism. Schumpeter viewed competition as a learning process and an ordering force. Somewhat paradoxically, he considered business cycles essential to economic progress. Cycles occur because equilibrium is destroyed by innovations, but since innovations improve the economic conditions of society, this destruction of equilibrium is "creative."

Schumpeter considered certain institutional features essential to the continued vitality of an economy. First, there must be broad scope for the operation of innovators (Schumpeter's *entrepreneurs*). Second, it must be possible for new entrepreneurs to break into the system. This second condition requires well-developed credit markets that allow entrepreneurs to capture income streams and use them in production even before actually contributing anything to national income.

Schumpeter distinguished three types of business cycles, naming the cycles for earlier pioneers in business cycle theory. The length of each depends on the kind of disturbance that causes it. The shortest (*Kitchin*) cycle is associated with inventory changes and usually lasts about 3 years. An intermediate (*Juglar*) cycle depends on fairly small innovations, such as microwave ovens or electronic calculators, and runs its course in 8–11 years. The long (*Kondratieff*) cycle lasts 40–60 years and is caused by sweeping innovations such as electrification or jet flight.

Significant innovations generate **spin-offs**—imitations of the original innovation, other new inventions and products, and the development of new industries. For example, the space program generated such advances as microelectronic circuitry and Teflon. Economic activity expands as an economy adapts to a major innovation. After a long period of expansion, an economy peaks: entrepreneurs quit innovating because markets for closely related innovations become saturated. The market economy will not sustain further emulation of technology or increases in supplies. At this point, retrenchment occurs. Businesses reevaluate their roles, and the economy slumps while industry awaits another great wave of innovation. The long-wave process begins anew

when another major innovation appears. Of course, less significant innovations might explain shorter cycles.

Schumpeter used railroads as an example of a major innovation.[1] In a similar fashion, the advent of

---

1. He noted: "Expenditures on, and the opening of, a new line has some immediate effects on business in general, on competing means of transport, and on the relative position of centers of production. It requires more time to bring into use the opportunities of production newly created by the railroad and to annihilate others. And it takes still longer for population to shift, cities to decay, and, generally, the new face of the country to take a shape that is adapted to the environment as altered by railroadization." Joseph A. Schumpeter, *Business Cycles: A Theoretical, Historical, and Statistical Analysis of the Capitalist Process* (New York: McGraw-Hill Book Company, Inc., 1939).

automobiles and airplanes were significant influences on economic development in the United States. A major recent innovation, the computer, has enabled some industries to develop and grow to sizes that had been impossible due to the inefficiencies associated with large-scale information processing. An important innovative spin-off is the development of miniaturization using microchips. These chips have allowed hand-held calculators and minicomputers to do today what only a few years ago required rooms full of calculating equipment. And perhaps the most underrated innovation of our time is the supermarket. Supermarkets reduce transaction costs for an incredible variety of products and provide outlets for specialized firms that would have been denied shelf space in an old-fashioned general store.

Kondratieff Long Waves

Another theory of long waves in economic activity was developed in the 1920s by the Russian economist Nikolai Dmietrievich Kondratieff. After studying data on numerous economic aggregates over the period 1780–1920, he identified two complete long waves (40–60 years each) and the beginning of a third. Kondratieff hypothesized that the world economy would boom and then plummet every 40–60 years. The third wave began its decline in the early 1920s, culminating in the "Crash of '29." Kondratieff's theory suggests that a serious worldwide depression will begin during the 1980s or 1990s. However, studies of long cycles have found no convincing evidence that **Kondratieff long waves** are anything but a statistical accident, so most economists are skeptical about prophecies that the world economy will collapse in the near future. Nevertheless, believers predict that the fourth Kondratieff wave should begin in the next few years and that it will reach a trough around the year 2000 (see Figure 3). Some observers felt the 1982 recession was the beginning of this decline, but a strong recovery has since weakened their case.

Marxian "Capitalistic Crises"

Contrary to common perceptions of Karl Marx, he was in awe of the economic growth wrought by capitalism. In the *Communist Manifesto* (1848), he marveled that

> . . . *capitalism has created more massive and more colossal forces than have all preceding generations together.* . . . *It has accomplished wonders far surpassing Egyptian pyramids, Roman aqueducts, and Gothic cathedrals; it has conducted expeditions that put in the shade all former migrations of nations and crusades.*

Marx declared himself the enemy of the market system as pitting man against man, with the rich and powerful exploiting workers.[2] Describing his views as scientific socialism, he predicted that capitalism would move spasmodically through expansions and contractions, with each peak higher than its predecessor and each successive crash deeper than the last. Ultimately, the working class would overthrow its exploiters, the spark of a communist takeover igniting during the deep abyss of a depression.

The driving forces behind Marxian business cycles are ever greater concentrations of wealth and power in the hands of capitalists. Briefly, periods of rapid investment and growth are assumed to result in increasingly unfair distributions of income. Impoverished workers do not have the money to buy the goods they have produced, resulting in overproduction (or underconsumption). Because capitalists lack markets, capitalism plunges into depressions or imperialistic wars. Then wars, the openings of new markets, or the discoveries of new sources of raw materials result in an upswing. The next downswing then emerges, and so on. Marx's views of these **capitalistic crises** are treated more completely in later chapters.

Most early business cycle theories use broad brush strokes to paint impressionistic portraits of an economy in motion. The most important early theory is known as *classical theory,* and it dominated economic reasoning from the middle of the eighteenth century until the Great Depression of the 1930s. Studying classical theory will enable you to tie together some of the strands of analysis that explain how the world works.

Classical Theory

Not the creation of any single economist, **classical theory** is a conglomerate of theories arising over the past two centuries from systematic study of how markets operate and why business cycles occur. Even

---

2. One of the oldest jokes floating around communist countries is that, "Under capitalism, man exploits man. Under socialism, it's vice versa."

FIGURE 3 *The Kondratieff Wave*

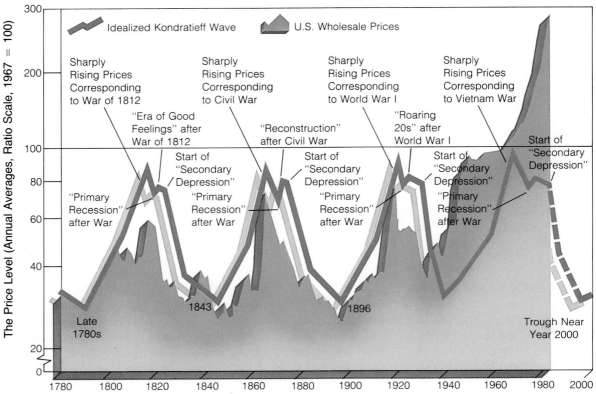

Source: Adapted and updated from *New York Times* graphic, October 17, 1982. (Based on data from *Media General Financial Weekly*, 1974.)

today, the development and extension of classical economic reasoning continues. In fact, many economists view the reemergence of classical analysis as the central force advancing the frontiers of modern economic knowledge.

While not a theory of business cycles per se, classical economic reasoning does suggest that aggregate supplies and demands will adjust to dampen and then defeat any pressures for substantial or long-term unemployment or economic inefficiency. Thus, classical macroeconomics shows how the negative effects of the business cycle are automatically overcome.

Classical economics offers mechanisms that are very similar to the stabilizing biological processes called *homeostases*. Here is an example of one biological homeostasis: you break into a sweat if your temperature rises above 98.6° F. Your body cools as

your perspiration evaporates. Conversely, a low temperature causes shivering and your teeth to chatter. The resulting friction in your muscle tissues generates heat, raising your temperature towards 98.6°. Just as homeostasis automatically moves your body toward health, classical economics suggests that an idea known as Say's Law will ensure full employment and economic health if combined with flexible prices, wages, and interest rates.

Say's Law

Say's Law is named after the nineteenth-century French economist Jean Baptiste Say. Say felt that the very act of production created an equivalent amount of demand. Simply stated:

> **Say's Law** *asserts that supply creates its own demand.*

He based his law on the argument that people do not work for the sake of working. They only work to obtain wage income to spend on other products they desire. People produce (*supply*) roller skates or biscuits only so that they can buy (*demand*) cars or fur coats. Similarly, investors do not seek income per se. Rather, they seek what their income will buy. Thus, the act of producing requires that resources be hired and paid, which in turn leads to the resource owners' incomes being spent on other products.

Say conceded that there might be an occasional glut of some product. However, he reasoned that surpluses or excess supplies in some markets must be offset by shortages or excess demands in other markets. This means that economywide gluts of most goods are impossible. Surpluses and shortages in specific markets are remedied over the long run because prices fall and production declines if there are surpluses, and prices and production both rise if there are shortages.

Flexible Interest Rates and Underconsumption

Some economists have challenged Say's Law, pointing out that people do not generally spend all of their earnings, and that saving might result in a deficiency of Aggregate Demand. If consumers do not spend all of their incomes, firms may find inventories rising, resulting in reductions in employment as businesses adjust to insufficient demand. Classical economists respond that all saving by consumers is invested by business. Early classical reasoning argued that consumers save only so they can consume more in the future. In a monetary economy, saving is translated into funds available for loans. Stocks and bonds are financial investments representing saving. According to classical reasoning, interest is a payment necessary to encourage consumers to forego present consumption. Higher interest rates paid by borrowers encourage more saving. Thus the amount of saving supplied is positively related to the interest rate, as shown in Figure 4.

The other side of the saving/investment market is business demands for loans for capital investments. Lower rates of interest encourage greater amounts of investment. This occurs because businesses rank their potential investment opportunities from those with the highest expected rates of return, after adjusting for risk, to those with the lowest. Individual companies then attempt to borrow funds to invest in

those activities for which the rate of return is greater than the interest they must pay. Thus, saving is positively related to interest rates, while investment is negatively related to interest rates, as shown in Figure 4.

Flexible interest rates tend to equalize the quantities of saving and investment. If interest rates were below i_e in Figure 4, there would be pressure for interest rates to rise as business firms sought more financial capital for investment than savers willingly provided. Conversely, the savers who were unable to loan funds at current interest rates would bid interest rates down if interest rates exceeded i_e. It follows that interest rates adjust to changes in the demands and supplies of loanable funds available for capital investment; this balances aggregate saving with investment. Any deficiency in consumption demand caused by saving is exactly matched in equilibrium by business demands for financial capital for investment purposes.

FIGURE 4 *The Classical Capital Market*

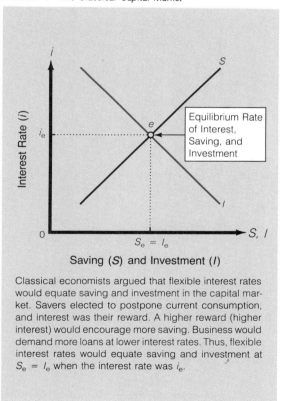

Classical economists argued that flexible interest rates would equate saving and investment in the capital market. Savers elected to postpone current consumption, and interest was their reward. A higher reward (higher interest) would encourage more saving. Business would demand more loans at lower interest rates. Thus, flexible interest rates would equate saving and investment at $S_e = I_e$ when the interest rate was i_e.

Flexible Wages and Prices

Classical economists went a step further, suggesting that even if the capital market failed to achieve equilibrium, **flexible wages and prices** would keep the economy at full employment. Wages and prices are like readings on an automatic thermostat. If savings exceeds investment, Aggregate Supply will exceed Aggregate Demand. This deficiency of demand yields downward pressures on prices as business accumulates unwanted inventories, resulting in layoffs and causing temporary surpluses in labor markets. If wages and prices fall, the quantities of goods and labor demanded will rise, restoring the economy to full employment. On the other hand, excess demands would cause the thermostat of price adjustments to generate wage hikes and price increases.

FIGURE 5 *Unemployment: The Classical View*

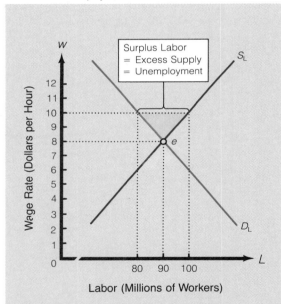

Labor (Millions of Workers)

Unemployment occurs, according to classical reasoning, primarily because wages are too high. The economy will self-correct for this problem when workers bid wages down to get jobs. This is what has happened at point *e*. The 90 million people who are willing to work have found employment at an hourly wage of $8. This fails to occur only if unions or legal minimum wages prevent wages from falling. Without legal wage floors, most who are unemployed must be so voluntarily. They could cure their own unemployment by accepting lower pay.

Notice that much of classical economics just applies supply-and-demand analysis to macroeconomics.

Suppose that the average wage rate is $10 per hour, as shown in Figure 5. One hundred million people are willing to work at $10 per hour, but businesses are only willing to hire 80 million people. In this example there will be 20 million unemployed. But will this unemployment persist? Classical reasoning answers no to this question, arguing that when this labor surplus causes average wages to drop to $8 per hour, the 90 million people willing to work at such a wage will be employed. What about the other 10 million? They would drop out of the labor force because they lack willingness to work at an $8 hourly wage.

Thus, flexible wages and prices provide another safety valve for the economy. Which brings us back to our discussion of voluntary and involuntary unemployment from Chapter 6. In the eyes of the classical economist, anyone who is unemployed for very long in a pure market economy is *voluntarily* unemployed. This means that continually unemployed people offer their labor only at higher than equilibrium wages. If people are willing to work at sufficiently low wages, there will always be jobs. Anyone unemployed might simply be exercising a preference for unemployment over working for the going wage or a bit less. In large measure, classical economists use intuition and logic to define away the problem of involuntary unemployment.

Classical Theory and the Price Level

Extended periods of involuntary unemployment are impossible according to classical reasoning. Inflation and declining price levels remain as major potential macroeconomic problems. Classical economists believed that Aggregate Demand is closely tied to the amounts of money available for people to spend. (We will delve into exactly why this is so in Chapters 12–14.)

Say's Law, coupled with flexible interest rates, prices, and wages would, according to classical theory, keep workers in the economy fully employed. Essentially, classical reasoning views the Aggregate Supply curve as vertical at full employment. Figure 6 illustrates this concept, assuming an initial equilibrium level of national output of Q_f at point *a* with an initial price level of P_0.

Suppose something causes Aggregate Demand to fall from AD_0 to AD_1. For example, this would result if saving increased and caused consumption to fall (the underconsumption problem discussed above) or if the money supply declined. Initial excess supplies would result in layoffs, reduced output, and increased inventories (point *b*). Eventually, according to classical economics, the economy would move to point *c* as prices and wages fell, restoring full employment. If the opposite pressures occur (Aggregate Demand increases to AD_2), the economy would expand along a path like *ade*, restoring full employment (Q_f) with a higher price level P_2. Thus, there might be short-run deviations from full employment, but the economy would self-correct rapidly with no need for government intervention. All this is consistent with the laissez-faire political atmosphere of earlier times.

Classical analysis teaches that the price level will be directly related to aggregate spending, which in turn depends strictly on the supply of money. Thus, the key to solving price level instability is to have a stable money supply. Modern day classical economists who believe most fervently in laissez-faire government policies advocate a gold standard. They believe that the supply of gold is inherently stable, so that policies requiring that all money be backed 100 percent by gold would prevent rapid changes in the value of gold-based money, preventing significant inflation or deflation.

In summary, classical economics depends on Say's Law and flexible interest rates, prices, and wages to ensure full employment. This theory suggests that a stable price level depends only on a stable money supply so that aggregate spending is stable. Many classical economists believe the gold standard would guarantee a stable money supply.

The Great Depression: Classical Theory at Bay

Prior to the Great Depression, classical economists were smug in their belief that a capitalistic laissez-faire economy would automatically gravitate towards full employment. The (short-run?) decline of classical macroeconomics commenced on October 24, 1929, when the New York Stock Exchange experienced the greatest sell-off in its history. Dana Thomas recalled that day, known since as "Black Friday," with the following story:

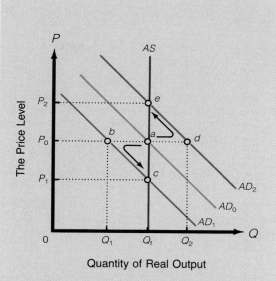

FIGURE 6 *Aggregate Supply and Classical Theory*

Quantity of Real Output

Unexpected expansions of Aggregate Demand (from AD_0 to AD_2) result in a temporary boom (movement of the economy along a path like *ade*). Unexpected contractions of Aggregate Demand (from AD_0 to AD_1) would cause the economy to suffer a temporary recession (movement along a path like *abc*).

The newspapers recounted the plight of a jury that before the crash had been sworn in for the trial of a former State Banking Superintendent indicted on charges of bribery. Several jurors had heavy commitments in the stock market. They were under strict orders from the judge not to read newspapers or engage in any conversation with outsiders. Nevertheless, news of the debacle in Wall Street had leaked into them and they pleaded with court attendants to let them contact their brokers to find out how they stood. But there was nothing that could be done. One juror, while he sat in a sweat listening to courtroom testimony, lost $80,000.[3]

In the four years between 1929 and 1933, the ranks of the unemployed grew from about 3 percent to around 25 percent of the labor force. While the unemployment roles swelled, investment spending collapsed even though the interest rate dropped to around 1.5

---

3. Dana L. Thomas, *The Plungers and the Peacocks* (New York: G. P. Putnam's Sons, 1967), p. 211.

percent. Many people were willing to work for almost nothing; but for some, the classical economists' promise of employment opportunities seemed a mirage. The September 1932 issue of *Fortune* noted:

> *Dull mornings last winter the sheriff of Miami, Florida, used to fill a truck with homeless men and run them up to the county line. Where the sheriff of Fort Lauderdale used to meet them and load them into a second truck and run them up to his county line. Where the sheriff of Saint Lucie's would meet them and load them into a third truck and run them up to his county line. Where the sheriff of Brevard County would not meet them. And whence they would trickle back down the roads to Miami. To repeat.*

It seems very insensitive to accept the classical economic reasoning that the individuals described in the *Fortune* article were "voluntarily unemployed." They were willing to work for considerably less than the prevailing wages of the time, but were unable to find jobs.

A Prelude to Modern Macroeconomic Theory

The persistence of 15 to 25 percent unemployment rates worldwide throughout the 1930s led John Maynard Keynes to scrutinize the traditional assumptions about the economy and precipitated the **Keynesian**

Revolution. He maintained that the capitalistic system, for several reasons, may not quickly and automatically rebound from a depression and reestablish full employment. In the next three chapters, we examine the macroeconomic model developed by Keynes and his followers during the Great Depression. The knowledge gained in studying this model will aid you in analyzing current macroeconomic problems that confront policymakers and analysts. As you can see in Figure 7, the growth rate of GNP appears to have become more stable since 1950. A large part of this reduced instability over the last few decades must be attributed to the work of John M. Keynes.

Keynes's writings are a starting point for modern business cycle theory. The paradox for classical theory presented by the Great Depression set the stage for the development of a theory to explain involuntary unemployment. Classical economics, which assumed mechanisms of flexible interest rates, wages, and prices, had apparently broken down. We begin with a very simple Keynesian model. As you might suspect, Keynes's original model has been refined and integrated with classical reasoning into a more complete theory. This more sophisticated amalgam of Keynesian and classical models is developed further in Chapters 15–18. But first, you will need to master the simple Keynesian macroeconomic model.

FIGURE 7 *Changes in the Growth Rate of Real GNP, 1910–85*

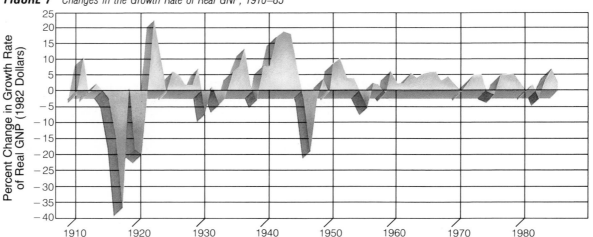

Our Gross National Product has grown at a 2–3 percent average rate over the past century, but was quite erratic prior to 1950. Negative growth has occurred at times since then, but the overall upward trend has been smoother over the past 35 years or so.

Source: *Business Conditions Digest,* January 1986.

CHAPTER REVIEW: KEY POINTS

1. *Business cycles* consist of alternating periods of expansion and contraction in economic activity. For a short period during the early 1960s, many economists felt that the business cycle was obsolete because government could fine-tune the economy with monetary and fiscal policy. This optimistic point of view is no longer widely held.

2. The business cycle is typically broken down into four phases: (*a*) *peak* (boom), (*b*) *contraction* (recession or downturn), (*c*) *trough* (depression), and (*d*) *expansion* (recovery or upturn). Business cycles are measured from peak to peak and have averaged roughly 4 years, although some have been as short as 18 months, while others have lasted a decade.

3. Business cycles are dated and analyzed by the *National Bureau of Economic Research (NBER)*. Reference dates are established by a detailed examination of data from past cycles.

4. NBER has examined thousands of individual data series and classified those that seem systematically related to cycles into three groups: (*a*) *leading indicators* reach their respective highs and lows before the general cycle peak and trough; (*b*) *coincident indicators* tend to turn roughly with the general business cycle; and (*c*) *lagging indicators* reach their respective peaks and troughs after the general business cycle.

5. Business cycles affect personal incomes but also leave their mark on people and families in many other ways. Such things as mental and physical health problems, marriage tensions, divorces, suicides, alcoholism, prostitution, illegitimacy, and both personal and property crime are closely related to changes in business conditions. Marriages and divorces alike tend to be positively related to the business cycle. Mental disorders and some physical diseases, suicides, crimes, and illegitimate births appear to be inversely related to changing business conditions. That is, they all rise when the economy turns down. Declines in income and the negative social effects of business slumps together have prompted policymakers to look for ways to keep the economy on a steady path.

6. The 1920s were a period of widespread prosperity caused primarily by the rapid growth of the automobile industry and the spread of other technological innovations such as radio, electricity, and the telephone. A wave of optimism lasted through much of the period.

7. The Great Depression of the 1930s was the most severe in American history. At the trough, nearly one quarter of the labor force was unemployed and real disposable personal income had dropped by more than 26 percent. Many were left homeless and hungry. The devastation of the Depression led to new economic theories and to numerous reforms in banking and social welfare programs.

8. World War II rapidly lifted the country out of the Depression. Massive government spending to fight the war brought unemployment down from 15 percent in 1940 to less than 3 percent during 1944–45. Inflation became a major problem after World War II as the federal government focused its policies on achieving full employment.

9. The 1960s were prosperous, based largely on the government's perceived ability to "fine-tune" the economy using the latest techniques of macroeconomic policy. President Johnson's decision to expand both domestic programs and the Vietnam conflict generally overheated the economy in the late 1960s and early 1970s. In 1971, wage and price controls were used by President Nixon to slow the rate of inflation. In the middle 1970s, the economy was battered with large doses of both unemployment and inflation—a combination generally called stagflation. The economy remained sluggish, with substantial amounts of both unemployment and inflation lingering into the early 1980s. Attempts by the Reagan Administration to reduce both inflation and interest rates resulted in high unemployment in 1982, but a sustained recovery brought unemployment back down by the mid-1980s.

10. Many early business cycle theories were *external force theories,* focusing on events outside of the economic system. The *sunspot theory* and various other external force theories were based on changing weather conditions and wars as sources of instability.

11. *Psychological theories* of the business cycle use people's herd instincts to explain the effects of extended periods of optimism or pessimism. These theories may partially account for the cumulative nature of business cycle downturns or recoveries, but provide little insight into the reasons for turning points.

12. *N. D. Kondratieff* suggested that long waves of economic activity (40–60 years) underlie the minor reverberations that occur roughly every four to eight years. This *long-wave theory* has not been especially convincing to economists, being widely viewed as a statistical coincidence.

13. *Joseph Schumpeter* developed a business cycle theory around major innovations that may partially

explain major long-term business fluctuations. He cited the developments of railroads, automobiles, and similar innovations as generating significant investment leading to tremendous economic growth for a period of time.

14. *Classical theory* is not a business cycle theory per se, but a systematic examination of how the economy operates. Classical theory is a conglomeration of the thoughts of many economic thinkers dating back to Adam Smith.

15. Classical economists based their theory on *Say's Law: Supply creates its own demand.* Coupled with assumptions that wages, prices, and interest rates are all perfectly flexible, Say's Law drives the economy towards full employment. All unemployment is considered voluntary—simply a refusal to work at the equilibrium wage. The protracted unemployment of the early 1930s diluted acceptance of classical theory and led to the development of the radically different Keynesian theory.

QUESTIONS FOR THOUGHT AND DISCUSSION

1. The word "recession" replaced "depression," which was called "panic" a century ago. Why do you think the terms for economic downturns change over time?

2. Most people alive today had not been born before the Great Depression of the 1930s. Those who remember the Depression have a different perception of the effect of the business cycle on economic well-being than those whose memories span only the 1950s, 1960s, 1970s, or 1980s. How do you think the perception of economic cycles differs between generations?

3. Some people are convinced economic catastrophe is just around the corner, while others are optimistic about the economic trends in the United States. Do you think economic cycles are inevitable? Of the theories of business cycles presented in this chapter, which do you find most believable?

4. Are the classical writers correct in asserting that all unemployment is voluntary? Can you conceive of circumstances under which people willing to work for the wages paid other people with similar skills and experience would be involuntarily employed?

5. Productivity grew very slowly, if at all, through the 1970s. Can you think of a number of reasons why labor productivity grew comparatively slowly during this period?

6. Use Aggregate Demand and Aggregate Supply curves to show the circumstances under which lower unemployment means higher inflation, and vice versa; the circumstances when unemployment and inflation would rise or fall together.

CHAPTER 9 Aggregate Expenditures: Consumption, Investment, Government, and Foreign Spending

Aggregate Expenditures (AE)	*average propensity to consume (**apc**)*	*autonomous investment* (I_a)
fundamental psychological law of consumption	*average propensity to save (**aps**)*	*autonomous government purchases* (G_a)
dissaving	*marginal propensity to consume (**mpc**)*	*autonomous net exports* ($X_a - M_a$)
autonomous consumption (C_a)	*marginal propensity to save (**mps**)*	
induced consumption		

Before the Great Depression, macroeconomic theory was primarily concerned with expanding our ability to produce. Say's Law states that *supply creates its own demand,* so the central goals of classical macroeconomics were (*a*) expanding the Aggregate Supply of goods and services, and (*b*) preventing Aggregate Demand from growing so rapidly that inflation reared its ugly head.

Classical macroeconomics failed to explain or provide solutions for the deepening depression. Classical economists were befuddled at the severity and persistence of the Depression and stressed long-term solutions. The absence of a short-term solution provided a challenge to the economics profession.

The first major economist to challenge this classical emphasis on supply was John Maynard Keynes.

Keynes's *The General Theory of Employment, Interest, and Money* (1936) turned Say's Law upside down. Keynesian theory assumes that "demand creates its own supply."

Keynesian Focus on Aggregate Spending

Keynes's major macroeconomic concern was ensuring that overall demand is adequate for full employment of all resources (see his Biography). Keynes and his early followers demoted expansion of productive capacity and maintenance of price level stability as goals to be pursued only *after* the economy achieved full employment.

John Maynard Keynes (1883–1946)

Bernard Baruch once put an end to an economist's badgering with the question, "If you're so smart, why aren't you rich?" John Maynard Keynes would not have been daunted by such a question. A keen observer of economic and human affairs, Keynes amassed a private fortune by speculating in commodities, foreign currencies, and stock market securities. He was equally successful in the social, political, and academic arenas. Keynes married a world famous Russian ballerina and was a gay and shining light in the illustrious Bloomsbury group, England's foremost intellectual set. He served as a treasury official and major representative of the British government during important negotiations following both World Wars. Nevertheless, he will be remembered longest as a leading figure in economics. Only the works of Smith and Marx rival Keynesian theories and policies in their impact on economic thought and practice in the twentieth century.

Much of modern macroeconomics is derived from Keynes's 1936 treatise, *The General Theory of Employment, Interest, and Money*—his reaction to contradictions between classical economic theory and the worldwide Great Depression. This work challenged the conventional view that *aggregate equilibrium* is synonymous with *full employment*. Keynes was concerned about persistent and high unemployment throughout market-oriented economies, and he reconstructed economic theory to explain this phenomenon. He concluded that, far from being inconsistent with aggregate equilibrium, unemployment might be a consequence of it.

In brief, Keynes argued that a capitalist economy might experience high unemployment as a permanent situation unless some external force were used to reduce it. For practical and political reasons, he thought that this external force must come from government and should take the form of large expenditures on public works projects capable of mobilizing idle manpower. Therefore, Keynes turned away from the long tradition of laissez-faire economic thought, which held that any government intervention in the economy is misguided and harmful.

There is generally a long lag between ideas and actions. In the United States in the early 1960s, the Kennedy Administration ushered in our major experiments with Keynesian economic policies. Keynesianism cut across party lines and continued to dominate economic policy until the election of Ronald Reagan. Two decades of activist Keynesian economic policies in this country have yielded mixed results. Because the spectre of deep depression largely gave way to persistent inflation in the 1960s and 1970s, Keynesian economics has been under fire from many quarters. President Reagan's "supply-side" economic policies represented an attempt to turn back the Keynesian clock in favor of classical economic remedies.

Keynes argued that, although classical theory is basically correct for a fully employed economy, Aggregate Demand alone determines the levels of output and employment when an economy is in the midst of a depression. Keynes's reasons for ignoring the price level and focusing only on the quantity dimensions of our overall demand can be seen in Figure 1, which shows real GNP and the price level during the Great Depression.

Real output began to grow after the Great Depression bottomed out in 1933. This recovery of real output occurred when Aggregate Demand grew without stimulating major increases in the price level. Real output grew over 60 percent during the seven years after the Depression reached its trough, while the price level rose less than 12 percent. Keynes argued that when an economy has considerable excess capacity, increases in Aggregate Demand are matched by rising output; production and income stretch to accommodate any growth in demand without generating significant upward price pressures. The Keynesian model is essentially a *depression* model. To some degree, its widespread acceptance in non-depression times stems from the fact that its major policy prescriptions (increased spending) are relatively easy for politicians to implement. In this and the next two chapters, we will use a step-by-step method to develop the Keynesian model.

In Chapters 10 and 11, we will look in more detail at the interactions of Aggregate Expenditures and national output, and we will explore macroeconomic adjustments that move an economy to an overall equilibrium. Learning the determinants of Aggregate Expenditures is a necessary first step; it will be the focus of our attention for the remainder of this chapter.

Keynesian Aggregate Expenditures

Certain terminologies have become conventional in macroeconomics, largely following Keynes's lead. **Aggregate Expenditures (*AE*)** applies to the total value of spending on domestically produced goods during a given year. An **Aggregate Expenditure curve** is the relationship between the total value of spending and national income. Since spending generally rises when income increases, there is a positive relationship between Aggregate Expenditures and income.

Components of Aggregate Spending

In Chapter 7, you learned that Gross National Product (GNP) consists of consumer goods (*C*), capital investment (*I*), government purchases of goods and services (*G*), and net exports (*X − M*). These are useful categories for examining the total level of Aggregate Expenditures. A quick glance at Figure 2 shows that consumption absorbs almost two-thirds of GNP, with investment and government spending comprising most of the rest. Exports are part of Aggregate Expenditures, while imports add to the goods and services available; hence, imports contribute to Aggregate Supply. By convention, only the net influence of foreign trade is considered.

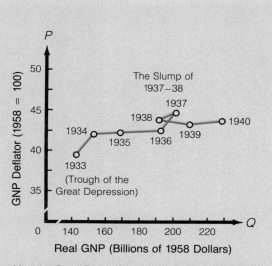

FIGURE 1 *Real GNP and the Price Level During the Great Depression*

After the Great Depression reached bottom in 1933, output began to grow. The economy increased its real annual output by roughly $100 billion between 1933 and 1940 without a signficant increase in the price level. For this and other reasons, Keynes argued that Aggregate Demand alone determined the level of real output in a severely depressed economy. Source: U.S. Department of Commerce.

Consumption and Saving

What factors determine total consumer spending? You may be able to identify other things that influence your own family's spending, but the single most important factor is probably your family's current income. In *The General Theory of Employment, Interest, and Money* (1936), John Maynard Keynes observed:

> *The fundamental psychological law, upon which we are entitled to depend with great confidence both* a priori *from our knowledge of human nature and from the detailed facts of experience is that men are disposed, as a rule and on the average, to increase their consumption as their income increases, but not by as much as the increase in their income.* (p. 96)

This insight, which seems simple by today's standards, reflected a tremendous change in the thrust of economic reasoning. Classical economists had rec-

FIGURE 2 *Components of Gross National Product*

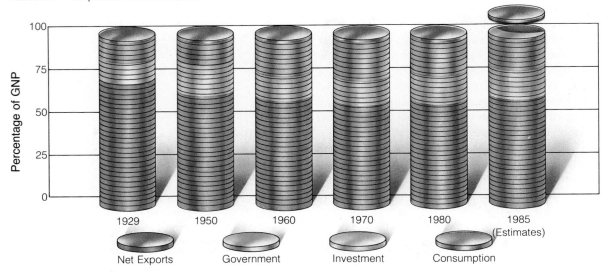

The four major components of GNP, from the vantage point of Aggregate Demand, are consumption, investment, net exports, and government spending. Consumer spending is rather stable at roughly two thirds of the total. Investment and government spending constitute the bulk of the remainder. Net exports are a relatively minor proportion of the total.

Source: *Economic Report of the President,* 1986.

ognized earlier that consumer spending is influenced by income. They believed, however, that national income automatically moves to a full employment level. Their focus on supply considerations caused the division of a given full employment level of income into consumption and saving to seem far more important than the relation between consumption and income. They viewed this division as determined primarily by the rate of interest.

Consumption and Saving Schedules

Classical theory emphasizes that interest is a reward for saving. Higher interest rates foster higher saving and lower consumption out of a given income. As you will see in the following chapters, Keynes's **fundamental psychological law of consumption** is just a hint of the totally different orientation of Keynesian analysis. Figure 3 provides some evidence in support of Keynes's observation.

The 45° line in Figure 3 represents the points we would map if consumption were exactly equal to disposable income. (Any variable plotted against an equal variable is a 45° line.) If the consumption

points for all years were located on this reference line, then consumption would always equal disposable income. The 45° line may be labeled $Y_d = C + S$, because what you consume and save absorbs your disposable income. Notice that during World War II, saving was relatively high, while during the Great Depression, typical households sometimes consumed more than they earned in income. Spending more than one's income is called **dissaving,** and it occurs when one borrows or dips into past savings. Aggregate consumption and saving absorb relatively stable shares of aggregate disposable income over time. Saving has averaged roughly 7 percent of disposable income, except during World War II and the Great Depression. Consumption is one of the most stable components of Aggregate Expenditures.

What are the potential uses of your after-tax (disposable) income? Anything not consumed is, by definition, saved ($S = Y_d - C$). Consumption occurs when goods are exhausted in attempts to satisfy our human wants. Many durable goods provide services and satisfaction over a number of years. Ideally, only the declines in value of these goods should be counted as consumption during the relevant year.

FIGURE 3 *Income and Consumption in the United States, 1929–85*

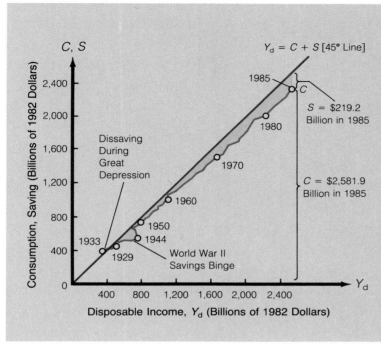

Keynes stressed the relationship between income and saving or consumption. The 45° line represents income plotted against itself. Since disposable income is either consumed or saved, the 45° line is labelled $Y_d = C + S$. The darkened area represents saving (or dissaving). During the Great Depression, saving was negative (dissaving), while during World War II, saving was over 20 percent of disposable income.

Source: *Economic Report of the President,* 1986.

For example, if you buy a new house, you are making an investment; the amount of consumption is the rental value of the house while you enjoy the services of shelter during the years you occupy it. Similarly, only about 10 percent of a television set with an expected life of 10 years is used up in any single year. (Unfortunately, our GNP accounting system does not divide consumer durables, other than housing, into their consumption and investment components.)

Saving is not necessarily the amount of money you put in a financial institution during some income period. An economic definition of **saving** is the change in your total wealth over some period of time. Thus, the amount your wealth changes is the amount of your unconsumed income. Your wealth is the **stock of savings** accumulated out of past saving periods. Figure 3 provides a picture of how aggregate consumption varies with aggregate disposable income. But how do individual families allocate their incomes? Figure 4 shows how typical urban families allocate their gross (before-tax) income. Consumption falls into five main categories: food, housing,

transportation, clothing, and medical expenses. Lower income families often find that they must spend everything and then some on bare necessities. Lower income dissaving consists of extensive use of credit or depleting sparse wealth to stay afloat. As gross incomes increase, ever higher proportions of income are allocated to taxes, transportation and housing services, and various luxuries. Since Figure 4 is based on the family's gross income, the figure also shows taxes. [We ignored taxes in Figure 3 because we considered only disposable (after-tax) income, Y_d.] As a result, the 45° reference line in Figure 4 can be described as $Y = C + S + T$.

Autonomous and Induced Consumption and Saving

Keynes's fundamental psychological law suggests that consumption is directly related to income. As income increases, so does a family's planned consumption—but not by as much as income. However, even if their incomes are zero, people still must

FIGURE 4 *The Components of Consumption Expenditures at Different Levels of Income, 1980–81*

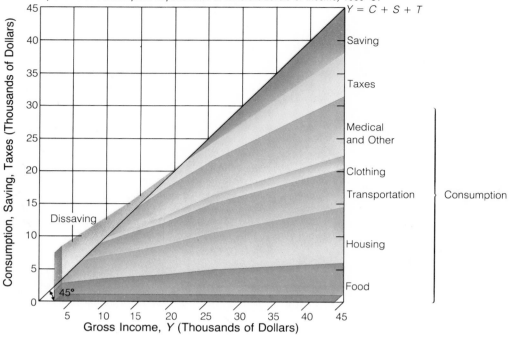

This figure presents some general estimates of how urban families allocate their gross family income. Consumption has five main components: food, housing, transportation, clothing, and medical expenses. At lower income levels, families tend to spend more than they earn. They dissave. Since the figure depicts gross family income, which includes taxes, the 45° line is labeled $Y = C + S + T$.

Source: U.S. Department of Labor, Bureau of Labor Statistics, *Consumer Expenditure Survey: Interview Survey, 1980–81*, April 1985.

TABLE 1 *Representative Annual Consumption and Savings Schedules*

(1) Annual Disposable Income	(2) Annual Planned Consumption	(3) Annual Planned Saving (1) − (2)	(4) Average Propensity to Consume (2)/(1)	(5) Average Propensity to Save (3)/(1)	(6) Marginal Propensity to Consume (Δ2)/(Δ1)	(7) Marginal Propensity to Save (Δ3)/(Δ1)
0	$ 1,600	−$1,600	—	—	—	—
$ 2,000	3,200	−1,200	1.60	−.60	.80	.20
4,000	4,800	−800	1.20	−.20	.80	.20
6,000	6,400	−400	1.07	−.07	.80	.20
8,000	8,000	0	1.00	0	.80	.20
10,000	9,600	400	.96	.04	.80	.20
12,000	11,200	800	.93	.07	.80	.20

consume in order to live. This component of consumption is independent of income and is called **autonomous consumption (C_a).** People finance autonomous consumption by spending their accumulated savings or by borrowing.

The more income people have, the more they will plan to spend on consumer goods, as indicated in Figure 4. That part of consumption that occurs because you have income to spend is called **induced consumption.** Thus, planned consumption is composed of both autonomous and induced elements.

Consider the hypothetical data in columns 1, 2, and 3 of Table 1. At low levels of disposable income, planned consumption exceeds income; there is planned dissaving. At zero income, autonomous consumption requires dissaving that equals spending, which in this case is $1,600. Thus, autonomous saving is negative $1,600. Notice that in Table 1, dissaving occurs at all income levels below $8,000. When income is exactly $8,000, planned consumption equals $8,000 and planned saving is zero. This is sometimes referred to as the break-even point. When income exceeds $8,000, plans for positive saving result.

The data from Table 1 have been used to construct Figure 5. In Panel A, the vertical distance between the 45° reference line (in blue) and the consumption line (red) is saving or dissaving. Panel B plots the amount of planned saving associated with the levels of planned consumption from Panel A. For example, when disposable income is $12,000, saving is $800.

Average Propensities to Consume and Save

Keynes's fundamental psychological law suggested that consumption increases as income increases, but by less than the increase in income. We would now

FIGURE 5 *Consumption and Savings Schedules*

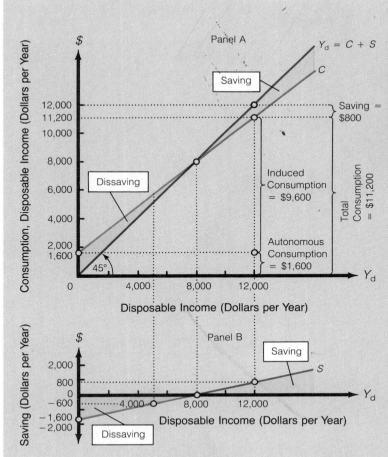

This figure graphically depicts the consumption (*C*) and saving (*S*) schedules from Table 1. Consumption (column 2) is plotted against disposable income (column 1) in Panel A. Again, the 45° line represents $Y_d = C + S$. When disposable income is $8,000, saving is zero and is plotted on the horizontal axis in Panel B. At income levels below $8,000, dissaving occurs, and this is reflected by the red shading in both panels. Above $8,000, saving occurs and is represented by the blue shading in both panels.

like to determine the proportion of spending—both on average and at the margin—as income rises.

You have seen that disposable income can be either consumed or saved. That is, however, not the end of our analysis. We need to develop these relationships a little further by examining both the average and marginal propensities to consume and save.

The **average propensity to consume (apc)** is defined as:

$$apc = \frac{\text{consumption}}{\text{disposable income}} = \frac{C}{Y_d}.$$

This is simply the fraction of disposable income consumed. For example, if you spend 80 percent of your income, your **apc** = 0.8. In Table 1, the average propensity to consume is (*a*) greater than 1 at incomes below $8,000, (*b*) exactly 1 when income is $8,000, and (*c*) less than 1 when income exceeds $8,000.

In a similar fashion, the **average propensity to save (aps)** is defined as:

$$aps = \frac{\text{saving}}{\text{disposable income}} = \frac{S}{Y_d}.$$

The **aps** is the fraction of disposable income that is saved. Like the **apc,** it varies with the level of income. Since $C + S = Y$, we can divide both sides of this equation by Y and find that:

$$\frac{C}{Y} + \frac{S}{Y} = \frac{Y}{Y} = 1,$$

so the **apc** + **aps** = 1. This means that the **aps** = 1 − **apc.** Thus, if you spend 80 percent of your income (**apc** = 0.8), it follows that you save 20 percent (**aps** = 0.2). The **apc** for the economy has varied only slightly over time, averaging approximately 93 percent. The **aps** has averaged roughly 6–7 percent of disposable income.

Marginal Propensities to Consume and Save

While the average propensities to consume and save tell us what fractions of total income will be spent and saved, they do not tell us how an *additional* dollar of disposable income will be divided between consumption and saving. It is easier for governmental macroeconomic policymakers to influence how much *extra* disposable income you have or do not

have than it is to control directly your total income. This is why it is important for policymakers to know what you will do with a bit more or less income.

The **marginal propensity to consume (mpc)** is a measure of the change in planned consumption associated with a small change in disposable income. Throughout this book, we will use Δ (the Greek letter delta) to represent a change in a variable. The **mpc** is defined by the following formula:

$$mpc = \frac{\text{change in planned consumption}}{\text{change in disposable income}}$$
$$= \frac{\Delta C}{\Delta Y_d}.$$

The marginal propensity to consume in the example in Table 1 is 0.8. For every dollar increase (*decrease*) in disposable income, consumption increases (*decreases*) by $0.80. For example, when disposable income rises from $8,000 to $10,000 (by $2,000), planned consumption rises from $8,000 to $9,600 (by $1,600). Thus, the marginal propensity to consume is:

$$\frac{\$1,600}{\$2,000} = 0.8.$$

A geometric treatment of the **mpc** is illustrated in Panel A of Figure 6. In the graphical section of the Introduction to this book, slope is defined as rise over run. The change in planned consumption is measured by the vertical increase (rise) on the graph of consumption and is labeled ΔC. The change in disposable income is measured along the horizontal axis (run) and is labeled ΔY_d. Thus, the slope of the consumption function is $\Delta C/\Delta Y_d$, which equals the **mpc.**

The other half of this analysis is the **marginal propensity to save (mps)**—the change in planned saving associated with a change in disposable income. In conformity with the marginal propensity to consume (**mpc**), the marginal propensity to save (**mps**) is defined as:

$$mps = \frac{\text{change in planned saving}}{\text{change in disposable income}}$$
$$= \frac{\Delta S}{\Delta Y_d}.$$

For example, in Table 1, as disposable income increases from $8,000 to $10,000, planned saving increases by $400 and the **mps** equals 400/2,000, or 0.2. You may already see that the sum of the **mpc** and

FIGURE 6 *Marginal Propensity to Consume (**mpc**) and Marginal Propensity to Save (**mps**)*

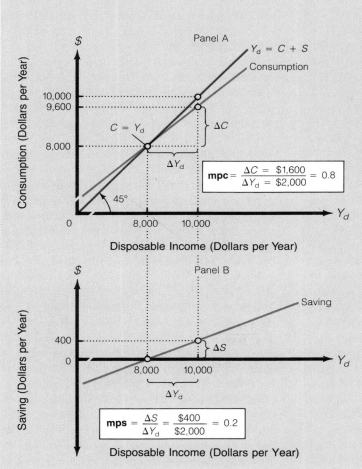

This figure depicts the **mpc** and the **mps** and is based on the data in Table 1. The **mpc** is defined as the change in planned consumption associated with a change in disposable income, and it equals the slope of the consumption schedule. If, for example, disposable income increases from $8,000 to $10,000, planned consumption rises from $8,000 to $9,600. Thus, the **mpc** equals $1,600/$2,000, or 0.8. Similarly, in Panel B, when disposable income increases from $8,000 to $10,000, planned saving increases by $400, and the **mps** equals 0.2 ($400/$2,000).

the **mps** is equal to 1. We know that $C + S = Y_d$. Furthermore, we know that any change in disposable income (ΔY_d) must result in changes in planned consumption (ΔC) or changes in planned saving (ΔS). Thus:

$$\Delta C + \Delta S = \Delta Y_d.$$

Dividing both sides of this equation by ΔY_d yields

$$\frac{\Delta C}{\Delta Y_d} + \frac{\Delta S}{\Delta Y_d} = \frac{\Delta Y_d}{\Delta Y_d} = 1,$$

so **mpc** + **mps** = 1. Thus, any change in your disposable income is divided between changes in

planned consumption and planned saving. A graphic representation of the **mps** is shown in Panel B of Figure 6.

The consumption function in Figure 6 portrays Aggregate Expenditures by consumers for goods and services. The major determinant of this demand is Aggregate Disposable Income (Y_d). There are also several other determinants (discussed in the next section) of consumption. These other variables determine the level of autonomous consumption. When they change, the entire consumption/income relationship is shifted up or down. These shift variables tend to change fairly slowly, however, so the relationship between consumption and disposable income has been fairly stable over time.

Other Determinants of Consumption and Savings

There are five major determinants of consumption and saving other than current income. They are (*a*) wealth and expectations about lifetime income, (*b*) average size and age composition of households, (*c*) stocks of consumer goods on hand, (*d*) household balance sheets, and (*e*) consumer expectations about the prices and availability of products. These influences, in concert with customary standards of living and habitual purchasing patterns, determine the amount of autonomous spending. Current disposable income alone determines the amount of induced consumption in the simple Keynesian model we are developing here.

Wealth and Lifetime Income

Suppose a computer science major and a philosophy major will each graduate from the same college this year. All else equal, who is more likely to buy a new car before graduating? The computer science major is, in all likelihood, because of the expectation of higher income upon graduation. Now consider the relative spending patterns of a wealthy retired tycoon and a retired postal employee. Even if the retired tycoon has a bad year on the stock market and received only Social Security checks equal to the postal employee's pension, the tycoon is still likely, by a huge margin, to be the bigger spender. These examples suggest that wealthy people or those who expect high income in the near future typically will consume more than other people who have identical current incomes.

Household Size and Age Composition

Young families beginning to acquire many standard consumer durable goods (washer, dryer, refrigerator, automobile, house, and so on) generally have higher consumption demands than older families who have already purchased these commodities. The latter often have only replacement demands for these items as their existing household goods break down or become obsolete. It is also true that bigger families generally have greater average propensities to consume than smaller families. (That should come as no surprise.) Thus, an economy full of young or large families will have higher average propensities to consume and lower rates of saving than will an economy comprised of older or smaller families.

Stocks of Goods on Hand

At the end of World War II, the American people tried to relieve their pent-up demands. During the war, there were shortages of a wide variety of consumer goods; many were rationed or did not exist at all. At the end of hostilities, consumers had enormous "wish lists" of items they wanted to purchase, and they went on spending binges. When consumers have been on lengthy buying sprees recently, large stocks of new durable goods alleviate the necessity to purchase more.

Household Balance Sheet

A household that is fairly secure financially will be more willing to spend out of current income. If a family is heavily in debt, it tends not to incur additional debt. All else being equal, as the level of household debt increases, consumers postpone further consumption so they can pay off existing debt. Conversely, declines in indebtedness may result in splurges of consumer spending.

Consumer Expectations

If a wave of inflationary expectations hits consumers, either of two things may occur: (*a*) they may buy now to avoid high prices in the future or (*b*) their confidence may be shaken, causing them to buy less.

Consumer debt may soar if people try to buy now to buffer themselves against future inflation, or their confidence may be dampened and their use of credit may fall. In the late 1970s, many young people bought houses because real estate prices were skyrocketing. They were afraid they would not be able to buy homes if they waited. Of course, this panic buying stimulated housing prices to rise even faster. If consumers expect shortages of a specific product in the near future, they tend to empty the shelves immediately. In 1974, there was talk in the media of a "toilet paper shortage." Consumers responded by stripping the stocks from supermarket store shelves. The source of the rumor was traced to a joke by Johnny Carson on the "Tonight Show." When people expect widespread shortages, they buy and hoard almost anything that can be stored.

Consumption and Aggregate Expenditures

Consumption spending is the major component of total spending, representing nearly two-thirds of Aggregate Expenditures. Three other components must be added to consumption to reach Aggregate Expenditures: investment, government spending, and net exports. We turn now to a discussion of investment and its determinants. Then we briefly consider government spending (a more detailed discussion is left to Chapter 11), and take a quick look at the foreign component of Aggregate Expenditures.

Investment

In Chapter 7, you learned that Gross Private Domestic investment (GPDI) is an important component of GNP. If we subtract capital depreciation from GPDI, the result is net investment; Net National Product (NNP) is GNP adjusted for depreciation. We have indicated that consumption is the most stable component of GNP and Aggregate Expenditures. Investment is the most volatile (least stable) segment of GNP and aggregate spending. Investment's instability may be the root cause of most business cycles.

Types of Investment

People commonly talk about investing in stocks or bonds or existing real estate. Remember that these are what economists call **financial investments** and that purchases of new output that can be used in the future to produce other goods and services are called **economic** or **capital investments.** Most investment entails purchases of capital goods (machinery, equipment, tools, and the like). Some financial investments facilitate economic investments (for instance, purchases of newly issued stocks or bonds, which are just forms of saving); others do not (speculative purchases of land are an example).

You may recall from our discussion in Chapter 7 that there are three major categories of economic investment: (*a*) new structures, which include such things as office buildings, manufacturing facilities, warehouses, hotels, retail stores, and private homes; (*b*) new machinery and equipment, including tools and office equipment and furnishings; and (*c*) inventory accumulation. The composition of investment is illustrated in Figure 7.

You may already know that construction of residential and office buildings, manufacturing facilities, and such are extremely cyclical. Business investment in new machinery and equipment is also very sensitive to the ups and downs in economic activity. How-

ever, the most volatile component of investment is inventory accumulation (see Figure 8). One important reason for this volatility in inventories is that business firms only have partial control over inventory accumulation or shrinkage. Customers frequently fail to buy according to business forecasts.

Business firms maintain inventories because they cannot predict their sales accurately on a week-to-week, month-to-month, or even year-to-year basis. If they knew exactly when (or if) sales were going to occur, their merchandise could arrive for sale simultaneously with their customers and inventories would be miniscule or unnecessary. Firms (sometimes intuitively) forecast their sales and calculate the amounts of inventories they would like to maintain. If sales are below the levels forecasted, inventories grow and businesses unintentionally invest in new inventories. If sales are unexpectedly high, inventories dwindle and there is unintentional disinvestment.

Unexpected changes in inventories are signals to businesses either to increase or decrease purchases from their suppliers. In the next chapter, you will see how inventory adjustments are used to bring aggregate spending and production into balance.

The reasons people consume are fairly obvious—they are trying to maximize their individual satisfactions. Why people invest, and under what circumstances, is less obvious.

Expected Returns from Investment

A simple explanation for firms' investments in new capital goods is that they expect to profit by them. If the stream of income is expected to be greater than the opportunity costs of a given investment, the investment will be made. The annual percentage by which assets will grow if the profits from an investment are continually reinvested is known as the **rate of return** on investment. This rate is quite similar to a percentage interest rate. We will discuss factors that influence the expected returns from investment before delving into some of the intricacies of the costs of investment.

Expectations about the Business Environment
New capital goods are expected to generate extra output which, if sold, means additional revenues for the firm. Confidence that there will be demand for new production is necessary before businesses will

FIGURE 7 *The Composition of Gross Private Domestic Investment*

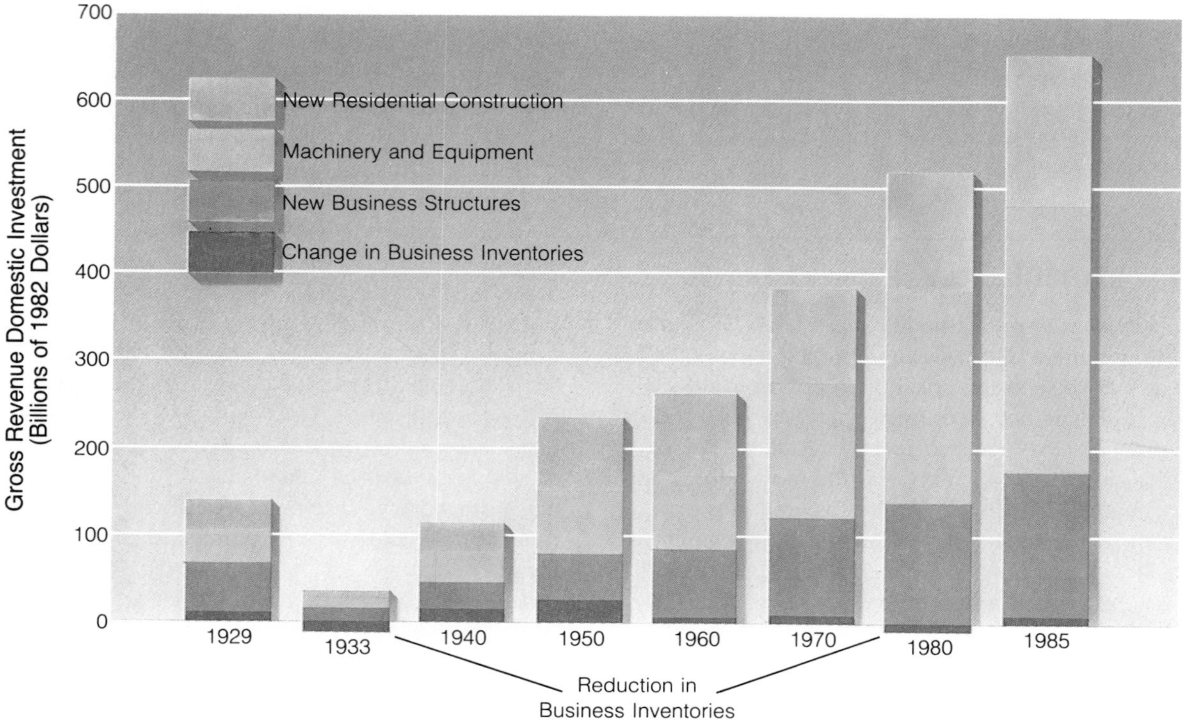

This figure details the composition of investment spending, the least stable component of GNP.

Source: *Economic Report of the President,* 1986.

make new investments. When consumer spending is expected to grow and existing capital is already pressed to capacity, the stream of new investment will be very high. Conversely, if consumer demands are expected to be weak, or if there is substantial excess capacity in existing production facilities, businesses will not invest very much.

One major difficulty for business investors is the long lag that is common between placing orders for new investment goods and actually achieving the greater capacity made possible by these investments. It takes time to acquire the appropriate building, environmental, or other permits to construct new buildings or to produce new equipment. Another lag arises between production from the new capital goods and the final sale of the output. These lags make it necessary to forecast consumer demand far into the future. The risks involved in long-range projections make firms leery of many investments.

Difficulties in predicting swings in a firm's sales and economic activity are only one source of risk for investors. Expected changes in government policies may either encourage or inhibit investment. For example, when the New Jersey government was expected to legalize gambling, there was a flurry of investment in Atlantic City as people readied casinos and "tourist traps." Similarly, huge defense budgets result in excessive investment by defense contractors. On the other hand, if policies restricting foreign trade are expected to be adopted, firms that export or import products might indefinitely postpone plans for investment.

Technological Innovations The federal government and many companies are extensively involved in research and development (R & D). Methods are developed to produce new or better products, or less costly ways of turning out existing products are

FIGURE 8 *Changes in Business Inventories (1982 Dollars)*

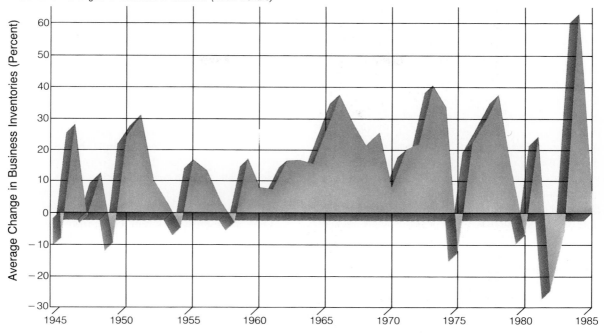

Inventory changes are by far the most volatile component of investment, which, in turn, is the most erratic part of GNP. Inventories decline sharply when business sales unexpectedly boom or when business firms become very pessimistic in forecasting future sales. Inventories mushroom when business anticipates sharp increases in sales or when customers unexpectedly quit buying.

Source: *Economic Report of the President,* 1986.

found. New technologies tend to occur erratically and in waves. Consequently, investment to implement technological breakthroughs is clustered over time. Some economists attribute much of the volatility in investment to this clustering. For example, the space program catapulted refinement of the computer, gave birth to solid-state electronics, and generated a host of other technological innovations.

Stocks of Capital Relative to Total Production   Just

as the amounts of consumer durables possessed by households relative to their incomes affect levels of consumption, the stock of physical capital relative to GNP influences the level of investment. If near-peak levels of economic activity press against capital capacity, there will be strong incentives for new capital investment. On the other hand, if economic activity fades so that substantial amounts of capital are idle, purchases of new capital will decline.

The Equilibrium Rate of Investment

Firms will buy machinery, construct buildings, or attempt to increase inventories whenever they expect the gross returns on these investments to exceed the total opportunity costs of acquiring them. Let us see how the interactions of expectations and costs determine the level of investment.

Diminishing Returns to Investment   Suppose that

most economic forecasts point up, reflecting substantial business optimism. Many potential investors probably know of a few investments that could be expected to generate healthy rates of return (r) of, say 30–40 percent—a new hamburger franchise, an apartment complex, or a plant to manufacture solar cells might be examples. Once these investments were made, only less profitable investments would be available—a fried chicken outlet, a duplex, or a new laundromat might be expected to yield annual rates of return of 20–30 percent. Once these investments were made, still less profitable investments would be the only options available—a hot dog franchise, renovation of a seedy motel, or a used book store might be anticipated to return 10–20 percent on investment. We are now at rock bottom—a greasy spoon franchise or a shovel-sharpening shop might generate near-zero rates of return, plus or minus 10 percent. By now you should get the idea. For a given mood among investors, the higher the level of investment in the economy, the lower the expected rate of return on additional investment. Changes in business expectations shift the investment demand schedule. Expected rate of return schedules when investors are optimistic and when they are pessimistic are shown in Figure 9.

Costs of Investment The costs of new capital equipment or buildings are important considerations for business investment. All else equal, rate of return schedules like those shown in Figure 9 increase (shift rightward) when capital prices fall and decrease (move to the left) when capital costs rise. The demand for new capital tends to rise during prosperity, causing increases in the prices of capital goods and choking off short-term surges in investment. Conversely, pessimism among investors during periods of economic stress reduces the demand for new capital goods. Capital suppliers accumulate what they view as excessive inventories. As they liquidate parts of their inventories, the costs of new equipment decline, slightly dampening downturns in investment.

Taxes on investment income are another important cost consideration. For example, higher corporate income taxes cause the (after-tax) rate of return curve to fall. Investment tax credits, on the other hand, may increase the demand for investment goods.

One of the most important costs, from investors' perspectives, is the interest rate. When the interest rate rises, investors' opportunity costs rise. If investors have money, they might make loans instead of buying investment goods. If most investors borrow to invest, then a hike in the interest rate makes investment less attractive. Interest rates (i) and rates of return (r) are both expressed as annual percentages, making it possible to put both on the vertical axis of Figure 10. Changes in interest rates involve move-

FIGURE 9 *The Negative Relationship Between Expected Rates of Return and the Level of Investment*

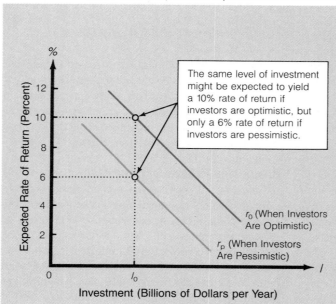

The same level of investment might be expected to yield a 10% rate of return if investors are optimistic, but only a 6% rate of return if investors are pessimistic.

For any given level of business optimism, a negative relationship exists between the quantity of investment and the rate of return. The most profitable investments will be made first, and, as more projects are undertaken, those with lower profit opportunities (lower rates of return) will be included. Furthermore, as the level of optimism or pessimism changes, the entire curve (relationship) will shift—for example, from r_0, the expected rate of return when investors are optimistic, to r_p, the rate of return when they are pessimistic.

FIGURE 10 *How Changes in Interest Rates and Expected Rates of Return Cause Changes in Investment*

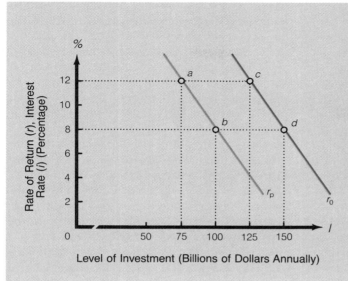

One important cost of investment is interest rates. If investors do not have money, they must borrow and the level of interest, combined with the expected rate of return schedule, will determine the level of investment. If investors have money, they can make loans. Thus, the interest rate represents the opportunity cost of investing a given amount of capital. If the expected rate of return curve is r_p and interest rates fall from 12 percent to 8 percent, investment rises from $75 billion to $100 billion. Similarly, if interest rates are stable at 8 percent and the expected return schedule shifts from r_p to r_0, investment rises from $100 billion to $150 billion.

ments *along* rate of return curves. Any other changes generate shifts in these curves.

Ignoring risk for simplicity's sake, investment will occur as long as the expected rate of return is at least as great as the interest rate. Here is an example that explains why. If you can borrow money at 11 percent interest and expect an 11.5 percent rate of return from some investment, you probably will make the investment. If not, then someone else will go after this profit. It is just like trading 11 cents for 11.5 cents. How many times will you go for a deal like this? If you can do it infinitely, you will become infinitely rich. Any investment expected to yield a rate of return greater than the interest rate will be profitable and will be undertaken. Those yielding returns lower than interest rates will not be profitable and will not be made. This is why investment will move to $100 billion in Figure 10 if the interest rate is 8 percent and the expected rate of return is reflected in curve r_p.

In summary, the expected rate of return schedule increases when GNP rises and investors become optimistic or when the prices of capital decline. Expected rates of return and investment are reduced by pessimistic economic forecasts or increases in capital prices. For a given expected rate of return, high interest rates discourage investment (this is a

movement along a rate of return curve) while falling interest rates foster investment and economic growth. Interest rate changes induce movements along a rate of return curve.

Our inability to perfectly predict the future leads to unexpected changes in inventories. When these are coupled with the effects of herdlike changes in investors' expectations and wide swings in interest rates, no wonder investment is the most volatile component of GNP. The example in Figure 10 suggests that investment would grow from $75 billion annually (point *a*) to $100 billion annually (point *b*) if investors were somewhat pessimistic about future economic conditions (along the r_p curve) and the interest rate fell from 12 to 8 percent.

A similar decline in interest rates will cause investment to rise from $125 billion annually to $150 billion annually if investors are more optimistic (along the r_0 curve from point *c* to point *d*). For every interest rate, shifts from optimistic to pessimistic outlooks (shifts in the curves), or vice versa, mean decreases or increases in investment of $50 billion annually. Thus, in this example, swings in investors' moods and interest rates may mean that investment is doubled or halved. The real-world volatility of investment is probably attributable to changes both in expectations and in interest rates.

Investment and Aggregate Expenditures

We know that investment is affected by the level of national income because the state of the economy is a major influence on investors' expectations. A booming economy raises business profits and gives corporations greater opportunities to retain earnings for investment purposes. Figure 11 shows the level of **autonomous investment (I_0)** to be determined by expected rates of return and the market rate of interest. The figure also shows how this externally determined level of investment affects Aggregate Expenditures.

In Panel A, autonomous investment of $100 billion results when interest rates are 8 percent. In Panel B, the $100 billion of autonomous investment is added to the consumption curve to obtain the private sector Aggregate Expenditures curve ($AE = C + I_a$).

Optimism joined with low interest rates creates high levels of autonomous investment. Pessimism or high interest rates cause autonomous investment to be very low. In fact, Keynesians believe that pessimism may so overwhelm even very low interest rates that investment will be trivial.

Government Purchases_____

Some government purchases are similar to private investment in that they yield benefits over time. Highways, flood control projects, and education are examples. Other purchases result in an immediate exhaustion of resources and so are like private consumption. Police and fire protection, school lunch programs, and Medicare payments are examples. Both consumption and investment types of government purchases involve direct demands for additional output and so are parts of Aggregate Expenditures. However, some government outlays do not directly affect spending. For example, cash transfer payments are only translated into Aggregate Expenditures when the recipients spend these funds on consumer goods. Thus, these outlays are not considered to be part of government purchases.

The percentage of GNP absorbed by government purchases has grown substantially, although erratically, over the past two centuries. This growth has been greatest at the onset of wars. The Civil War, World Wars I and II, the Korean conflict, and the Vietnam War were high points of governmental demands. Following these high levels of wartime spending, government purchases have tended to fall—but not to prewar levels.

One possible explanation for the upward trend of government spending is that rising standards of living make people willing, through their votes, to devote ever larger percentages of their income to publicly provided goods such as education, public parks, or highways. Nevertheless, while government purchases seem to be related to income, they are even more affected by the state of international relations. For these reasons and, more importantly, to keep our analysis of Aggregate Expenditures simple, we will assume that government purchases are independent of income. We call these **autonomous government purchases (G_a).**

The Foreign Sector_____

Exports (X) reflect foreign demands for American goods. Thus, they add to Aggregate Expenditures. Imports (M) are goods produced by foreigners but available for use by American consumers, investors, or government. In fact, the accounting categories of consumption, investment, and government spending include goods produced abroad. These imported goods are a part of Aggregate Supply. In a sense, however, they represent *negative* Aggregate Expenditures on domestically produced goods because, presumably, domestic production would be purchased were it not for these imports. This is one reason cries for protection from foreign competition are loudest when an industry is in a downturn. The pleas from the clothing and steel industries in 1981–86 are examples.

It is conventional to look only at the net effect of the foreign sector on Aggregate Expenditures, so that $AE = C + I + G + (X - M)$. The level of our national income undoubtedly influences our imports. When times are prosperous domestically, we import more Toyotas and Mercedes-Benz automobiles and more Minolta and Nikon cameras; our vacations and booming industrial production require more foreign oil. On the other hand, our exports depend primarily on economic conditions abroad, which may be in the doldrums even if the American economy is prosperous. However, international economic interdependence is captured accurately in the saying that "When

FIGURE 11 *Aggregate Expenditures for the Private Sector (Households + Businesses)*

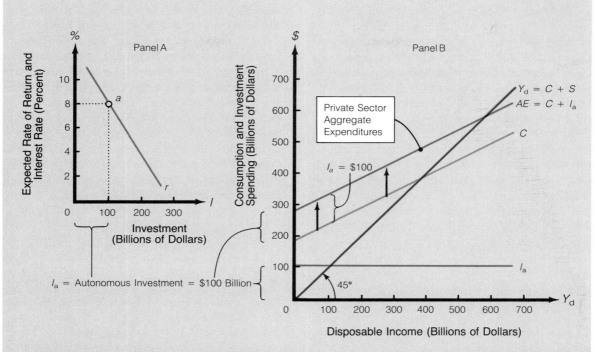

In Panel A, the level of investment is determined by the intersection of the rate of return (r) curve and the level of interest rates (i). This capital-market-determined level of investment (I_a = $100 billion) is then included on the Aggregate Expenditure (AE) curve in Panel B. If the interest rate is 8 percent, autonomous investment (I_a) will be $100 billion (point a, Panel A). Adding this level of investment to the consumption line (C) in Panel B results in the Aggregate Expenditure curve labeled AE = $C + I_a$. Notice that the Aggregate Expenditure curve is equal to consumption plus investment ($AE = C + I_a$) when the economy consists only of households and businesses. Finally, note that the 45° reference line is equal to $Y_d = C + S$.

America sneezes, the rest of the world catches a cold."

Although the foreign sector is vital for the strength and health of our economy, its net effect on Aggregate Expenditures is relatively small. Exports and imports each *average* around 10 percent of GNP, so net exports ($X - M$) are usually plus or minus roughly two percent of aggregate spending. Sophisticated Keynesian models take interdependencies between nations into account explicitly. For the purposes of the simple Keynesian model of Aggregate Expenditures we are building here, however, we will treat net exports as being independent of income, as **autonomous net exports ($X_a - M_a$).**

Aggregate Expenditures

Some of our national product is consumed in the same year it is produced (C), some is invested (I_a), some is bought by foreigners ($X_a - M_a$), and the rest is purchased by government (G_a). In the simple Keynesian model used in the next two chapters, we assume that income is the major influence on consumption, while private investment, net exports, and government spending are not affected by income. Aggregate Expenditures (AE) is the sum of all autonomous demands [$C_a + I_a + G_a + (X_a - M_a)$], plus consumption induced by having positive levels of income. Induced consumption = **mpc**(Y) in a simple linear model, so

$$AE = C_a + mpc(Y) + I_a + G_a + (X_a - M_a).$$

Suppose we assume that: (*a*) autonomous investment (I_a) is $100 billion, (*b*) autonomous net exports ($X_a - M_a$) is $25 billion, (*c*) autonomous government purchases (G_a) is $150 billion, (*d*) autonomous consumption (C_a) is $175 billion, and (*e*) the marginal propensity to consume (**mpc**) is 0.5. Figure 12 depicts the resulting relationship between national income (Y) and Aggregate Expenditures. The autonomous components of Aggregate Expenditures total to $450 billion, which corresponds to point *a* in Figure 12. [$C_a + I_a + G_a + (X_a - M_a)$ = $450 billion.] We

still must consider induced consumption, which equals the **mpc** times income, or 0.5Y. Thus, total Aggregate Expenditures rises by one-half of any increase in income as income rises and vice versa.

Note that all of these categories of spending are summed vertically to arrive at Aggregate Expenditures. Moreover, note that this Keynesian depression model assumes that the price level is fixed. In the next chapter, we will explore the way that equilibrium in National Income and product is determined by Aggregate Expenditures. After you have been thoroughly exposed to this Keynesian income determination model, we will introduce you to a slightly different model of Aggregate Demand and Supply which incorporates price level flexibility.

FIGURE 12 *Aggregate Expenditures for the Entire Economy (Private + Public + Foreign Sectors)*

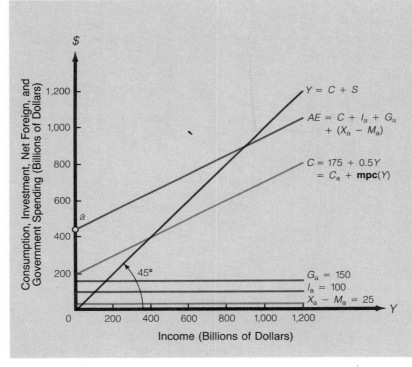

The Aggregate Expenditures curve (AE) is the sum of consumption (C), investment (I), government (G), and net foreign spending ($X - M$). All four are summed vertically to obtain the Aggregate Expenditures curve (AE).

CHAPTER REVIEW: KEY POINTS

1. Keynesian analysis focuses on the Aggregate Demand (spending) side of the economy. The economy during and right after the Great Depression had considerable excess productive capacity. During the slow recovery which lasted from 1933 to 1940, real output in the economy expanded by more than 60 percent with only slight increases in the price level. Keynesian economics ignores Aggregate Supply and price level changes and is primarily concerned with maintaining overall demand (spending) consistent with full employment.

2. *Aggregate Expenditures (AE)* is the total spending on domestically produced goods and services during any given year. Aggregate Expenditures has four components: (*a*) personal consumption expenditures, (*b*) gross private domestic investment, (*c*) government purchases of goods and services, and (*d*) net exports of goods and services.

3. The single most important determinant of consumer spending is disposable income through its influence on *induced consumption*. Consumer spending is related directly to disposable income and is a stable component of Aggregate Expenditures. Other important determinants of consumption and saving include: (*a*) wealth and expectations of future income, (*b*) the average size and age composition of typical households, (*c*) the stocks of consumer goods on hand, (*d*) the level of household assets and debts, (*e*) consumer expectations regarding prices and availability of products. These determine the level of *autonomous consumption* (C_a).

4. The *average propensity to consume (apc)* is the proportion of total disposable income that is consumed (C/Y_d). The *average propensity to save (aps)* is the fraction of total disposable income that is saved (S/Y_d). In addition, **apc** + **aps** = 1. Both the average propensity to consume and the average propensity to save have been relatively constant over time, at roughly 93 percent and 7 percent, respectively.

5. The *marginal propensity to consume (mpc)* is the change in planned consumption associated with a given small change in disposable income; it tells us how much of an additional dollar of income will be consumed. The *marginal propensity to save (mps)* is how much of an additional dollar in income will be saved. Furthermore, **mpc** + **mps** = 1.

6. Capital investment refers to purchases of new output that can be used in the future to produce other goods and services. There are three major components of investment: (*a*) new business and residential structures, (*b*) machinery and equipment, and (*c*) inventory accumulation.

7. The primary factors determining the quantity of investment are (*a*) expected returns from investment, (*b*) expectations about the business environment, (*c*) rates of technological change and innovation, (*d*) the level of existing stocks of business capital relative to total production, and (*e*) the costs of investment, including the interest rate. In simple Keynesian models, investment is treated as *autonomous investment (I_a).*

8. While government spending is probably influenced by changes in income, it is even more strongly affected by the state of international relations and domestic politics. Thus government spending as a component of Aggregate Expenditures is also treated as autonomous.

9. Exports and imports are reasonably balanced, so net exports ($X - M$) make a comparatively small contribution to Aggregate Expenditures. The foreign sector is, however, very important to the strength and vitality of our economy by providing markets for our producion and imported goods that would be more costly if produced domestically. Simple Keynesian models treat net exports as autonomous.

QUESTIONS FOR THOUGHT AND DISCUSSION

1. Saving was negative for the economy as a whole during part of the Great Depression of the 1930s. How did this occur? What were the long-term effects of this negative rate of saving?

2. People have no difficulty in rapidly raising their consumption to accommodate any increases in their incomes, but adjusting to sharp declines in income tends to be a slow and painful process. What implications does this have for swings in consumption over the business cycle?

3. Do you think people's consumption depends most on their current income or on their expectations of income over the future? What does this imply about the stability of Keynes's *consumption function?* Why?

4. How might the psychological theory of the business cycle (described in Chapter 8) account for huge swings in investment over the cycle?

5. We are treating investment, government spending, and net exports as autonomous. To what extent do you think each of these spending categories is influenced by the level of national income? Why are we treating them as autonomous here if they are all influenced by income in fairly consistent ways?

6. Given the following relationship, construct a graph showing the Aggregate Expenditures curve.

   Consumption = $500 + 0.6 (Income)
   Autonomous government spending = $400
   Autonomous investment spending = $200

Autonomous exports = $300
Autonomous imports = $200

Plot the new Aggregate Expenditures curve if the consumption relationship changes to consumption = $800 + .75 (Income).

7. Using the values for Disposable Income and Planned Consumption listed below, complete the table.

Disposable Income	Planned Consumption	Planned Savings	aps	mpc	mps
$ 0	$ 500	——	——	——	——
500	800	——	——	——	——
1,000	1,100	——	——	——	——
1,500	1,400	——	——	——	——
2,000	1,700	——	——	——	——
2,500	2,000	——	——	——	——

CHAPTER 10 Equilibrium Level of Output, Employment, and Income

disequilibrium	*multiplier effect*	*GNP gap*
saving equals	*autonomous spending*	*recessionary gap*
investment (S = I)	*multiplier*	*inflationary gap*
injections	*paradox of thrift*	
withdrawals	*potential GNP*	

The market forces of supply and demand yield an equilibrium when, at the current price, the quantity demanded of a specific good just equals the quantity supplied. All forces are in balance, so there are no net pressures for prices, outputs, or purchases to change. The concept of macroeconomic equilibrium is similar. However, John Maynard Keynes and his followers have sharply different perceptions of exactly what constitutes equilibrium than do Keynes's classical predecessors and today's adherents of classical positions.

Classical macroeconomics, introduced in Chapter 8, takes a long-run view and suggests that the economy will hover around full employment if the market system is allowed to adjust to any shocks. Keynes responded that "in the long run, we are all dead." He viewed the pressures classical writers cited for driving market economies to full employment as weak or nonexistent. Keynes compared the continuous

changes that occur in an economy to waves in the ocean—waiting for the long-run classical equilibrium is like waiting for the ocean to become flat. Consequently, Keynes focused on short-run problems and demonstrated how the economy might be stuck in a short-run equilibrium with substantial idle capital and unemployed labor.

In Chapter 9, we explored how purchases by consumers, business investors, government, and foreigners are summed to form Aggregate Expenditures. This is called a *Keynesian cross diagram*. In this chapter, the analysis is extended to illustrate Keynes's view that macroeconomic equilibrium might occur at less than full employment. For now, we will focus exclusively on the activities of the private sector. In Chapter 11, government spending and taxes are brought into the picture so that we can scrutinize what policymakers might do to correct for excessive inflation or unemployment.

The Aggregate Expenditures Approach to Equilibrium

We will assume initially that there are no taxes, depreciation, transfer payments, government expenditures, or undistributed corporate profits. This simplification blurs distinctions among GNP, NNP, and disposable income and permits us to use the term *income* (Y) to refer to all three.

Labor is required to produce the output, which, if sold, translates production into National Income and maintains employment and income. If output is not salable at prices that cover costs, some workers will lose their jobs and incomes. Thus, when we say that National Income is rising or falling, employment will also be rising or falling. Normally, increases in employment mean declines in unemployment, and vice versa; thus, increases in National Income or product tend to cause unemployment to fall, while drops in National Income imply that unemployment rates rise. The interactions of Aggregate Expenditures and National Output yield a macroeconomic equilibrium.

National Output

Table 1 presents hypothetical data for levels of income, employment, and output. An examination of how these data are related will illustrate how the aggregate economy approaches equilibrium. Column 1 shows the levels of employment required to produce the levels of National Output listed in column 2. The National Output schedule (column 2) indicates the output that producers are willing to offer at current prices if they are confident that it will be sold. You might think of the National Output schedule as reflecting a Keynesian Aggregate Supply curve because firms willingly produce whatever is demanded. For example, business firms are willing to employ 85 million workers and produce $2,750 billion in output and income *only* if they expect to be able to sell the output for $2,750 billion. Remember, *demand creates its own supply* in Keynesian analysis.

In Figure 1, the National Output schedule is graphed as a 45° line from the origin. We do this because in Keynesian analysis, Aggregate Supply (output) is passive; it adjusts to Aggregate Demand (expenditures). The economy is in equilibrium only when Aggregate Output and Income, measured on the horizontal axis, are just equal to Aggregate Expenditures, measured on the vertical axis. This occurs when the Aggregate Expenditures curve intersects the 45° line. (Any variable plotted against an equal variable is a 45° line.) Following convention, we use Y, on the horizontal axis, to denote real National Income when it is measured against Aggregate Expenditures, which is measured on the vertical axis.

TABLE 1 *Levels of Income, Employment, and Output (Billions of Dollars)*

(1) Employment (Millions of Workers)	(2) National Output & Income	(3) Planned Consumption	(4) Planned Savings	(5) Planned Investment	(6) Unplanned Inventory Changes	(7) Aggregate Expenditures (AE) (Columns 3 + 5)	
70	$2,000	$2,100	$−100	$100	$−200	$2,200	Tendency for income to increase
75	2,250	2,300	−50	100	−150	2,400	
80	2,500	2,500	0	100	−100	2,600	
85	2,750	2,700	50	100	−50	2,800	
90	3,000	2,900	100	100	0	3,000	Equilibrium
95	3,250	3,100	150	100	+50	3,200	Tendency for income to decrease
100	3,500	3,300	200	100	+100	3,400	
105	3,750	3,500	250	100	+150	3,600	

FIGURE 1 *Consumption, Investment, and Income*

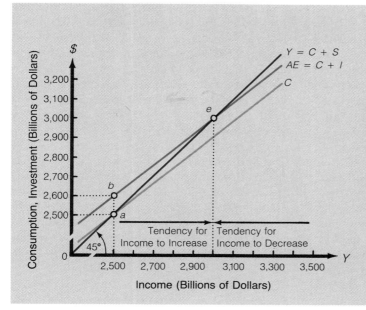

Equilibrium income (point *e*) is found where National Output is just equal to Aggregate Expenditures. Whenever the system is not in equilibrium, pressures will exist to move the economy to an equilibrium income level of $3,000 billion. If National Output is $2,500 billion, Aggregate Expenditures will equal $2,600 billion. This excess Aggregate Demand generates expansionary pressures in the form of declining inventories moving the economy upward to point *e*. When income exceeds $3,000 billion, pressures mount to move the economy back to equilibrium. Note: This figure is based on the data in Table 1.

Aggregate Expenditures

You learned in the last chapter that the Aggregate Expenditures schedule is the sum of consumer spending, investment, government purchases, and net foreign spending. Since the government and foreign sectors are being ignored in this basic model to simplify our analysis, column 7 in Table 1 represents Aggregate Expenditures (*AE*), which is the sum of planned consumption (column 3) and planned investment (column 5). Aggregate Expenditures (*AE* = *C* + *I*) represents the planned level of spending for each level of output and income.

Keynesian Equilibrium

There is **disequilibrium** whenever Aggregate Spending differs from Aggregate Income and Output. What forces push the economy back into equilibrium? Classical economics and many contemporary theories based on classical reasoning suggest that *supply creates its own demand*. This means that Aggregate Spending automatically rises to accommodate the full employment level of output. Keynesians disagree and argue that *demand creates its own sup-*

ply—that supply passively adjusts to demand. In this context, *spending* and *demand* are synonymous. We will now explore the nature of Keynesian adjustment processes—in situations of disequilibrium, National Output adjusts to the level of Aggregate Spending.

Eight possible levels of National Output and Aggregate Expenditures are listed in Table 1. At what level of income and output will the economy be in equilibrium? Consider for a moment an employment level of 75 million with National Output equal to $2,250 billion. Aggregate Expenditures equal $2,400 billion and so exceed the $2,250 billion National Output. What adjustments will yield an equilibrium such that National Output equals Aggregate Spending?

In this situation, most firms will be unable to maintain sufficient inventories to meet the demands of customers. Not enough output is produced to meet the demands of other businesses and consumers. When firms see inventories shrink below desired levels, they respond by expanding employment and output. This causes income to grow. Suppose employment in the economy increases from 75 to 80 million. Even at employment of 80 million workers, the problem remains—Aggregate Expenditures (now $2,600 billion) still exceed National Output (now $2,500 billion). Employment, output, and income will continue to climb until 90 million people are working. Aggregate Expenditures and National Output both equal $3,000 billion at this employment level. Any further pressures to expand output are countered by offsetting pressures to contract output because firms are able to maintain the inventories needed to meet their customer's demands.

The pressures to move the economy toward equilibrium can also be seen in Figure 1. For example, if National Output is only $2,500 billion (point *a*), the level of planned Aggregate Expenditures is $2,600 billion (point *b*). The excess Aggregate Spending ($100 billion = *b* − *a*) causes inventories to shrink and generates expansionary pressures that push the economy rightward from both *a* and *b* up the 45° reference line (National Output) to equilibrium at point *e* ($3,000 billion).

What happens if the level of National Output exceeds planned *AE*? Suppose that most firms were overly optimistic in forecasting consumer and investor demands and produced $3,750 billion worth of goods and services. Firms would find their inventories of unsold goods swelling. Business firms cannot precisely regulate their inventories because customers may buy either more or less than firms expect. In this case, firms would reduce inventories and output by cutting back production, necessitating layoffs of employees. As the equilibrium level of output fell to point *e* in Figure 1, business inventories would shrink to the planned levels. This economy settles at an equilibrium income of $3,000 billion.

Both Table 1 and Figure 1 indicate that National Income will expand when output is less than $3,000 billion because spending exceeds production. When income or output exceed $3,000 billion, income falls because production exceeds spending. Only when National Output is *exactly* $3,000 billion are all economic decision makers content to continue operating at existing levels of production, consumption, and investment. All forces are balanced, and there are no net pressures for the economy to shrink or grow from this short-run equilibrium.

Price Versus Quantity Adjustments

In Chapter 3, we suggested that price adjustments are part of the cure for disparities between the quantities of individual goods demanded and supplied. Price rises in individual markets if quantity demanded exceeds quantity supplied; if quantity supplied exceeds quantity demanded, price falls. You may wonder why such price adjustments are absent in this example. The reason is that Keynesian analysis assumes that only **quantity adjustments** occur in situations of high unemployment and excess capacity. The price level does not change because the simple Keynesian depression model assumes that capacity poses no problem. Expanding production in an economy where many workers are idle will not require higher wage or price incentives. Classical analysis presumes severe capacity constraints because the economy is thought to hover close to full employment. Hence, a classical model would use **price-level adjustments** to solve the problem we have laid out here. Since we are focusing on the Keynesian model in this part of the book, we will ignore price movements for now, but they will be treated in detail in Chapters 14–18.

Keynesian Saving = Investment Approach to Equilibrium Income

Closer scrutiny of Table 1 and Figure 1 reveals that equilibrium is achieved only when the planned levels of saving and investment are equal. Investigating the relationships between investment and saving provides another view of the way the levels of National Income and Output are determined.

Planned Saving and Investment

Take a look at columns 4 and 5 in Table 1, which are graphed in Figure 2. In our simple Keynesian model, business plans to invest $100 billion regardless of the level of income, while consumers' plans to save are tied to income. Suppose income were $3,500 billion. Consumers would try to save $200 billion (point *f* in Figure 2), but investment plans are for only $100 billion (point *g* in Figure 2). What will be the result?

Saving is the act of not consuming. Because income saved is money not spent, saving is a **withdrawal** of funds from the system. This withdrawal means that firms will accumulate unwanted inventories because output exceeds sales. (This discussion parallels our previous description of adjustments to excess supply.) Firms will find total consumer and business spending (*C* + *I*) *insufficient* to clear new output from the market. Production and employment will be reduced because firms do not desire

FIGURE 2 *Saving and Investment Approach*

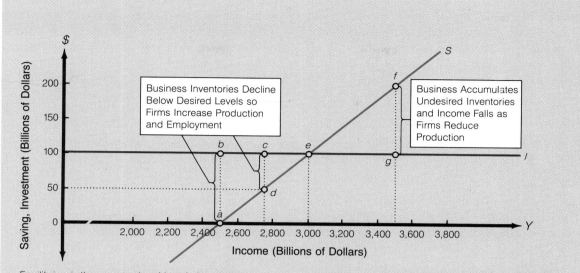

Equilibrium in the economy is achieved when desired saving and desired investment are equal. If income falls below equilibrium (point *e* = $3,000 billion), business inventories decline below desired levels. Firms will increase production and employment to bring inventories back to desired levels. When income is above equilibrium, business accumulates undesired inventories and, consequently, cuts production to bring inventories back into line. Only at equilibrium are desired saving and desired investment equal. Note: Points *a*, *b*, and *e* correspond to points *a*, *b*, and *e* in Figure 1. This figure is also based on the data in Table 1.

these investments in inventory. Income falls as the economy moves back from points *f* and *g* toward equilibrium at point *e*, where planned saving and planned investment are equal. Planned and realized saving and investment are all equated and income stops falling as the economy approaches equilibrium.

This adjustment process works in the opposite direction when National Output and Income are below the equilibrium level of $3,000 billion. For example, when National Output is $2,750 billion, consumers desire to save $50 billion and consume $2,700 billion, while business plans to invest $100 billion; Aggregate Expenditures (*C* + *I*) are $2,800 billion. The $50 billion shortfall of goods required to satisfy the demands of consumers and investors causes existing inventories to shrink. Firms unintentionally disinvest in inventories, which shrink by $50 billion in each period. Business will adjust by increasing production to raise the level of inventories back to desired levels. Output and income increase to $3,000 billion (from *c* and *d* to point *e* in Figure 2) before planned inventories can be maintained; planned saving and investment are equal at

$100 billion. Thus, equilibrium requires that **planned saving equals planned investment (S = I).**

Equilibrium: Planned Saving, Realized Saving, and Investment Are All Equal

As you can see, inventories play an important role in the movement from disequilibrium to equilibrium. Unintended inventory changes ensure that actual saving and investment are equal at all times. Firms use inventory changes as barometers. If inventories drop, there is an unintended disinvestment in inventories and firms boost their production. If inventories unexpectedly rise, firms view this unplanned investment as a signal to cut production and employment. Thus, changes in inventories resolve any differences between planned saving and planned investment.

Fluctuating inventories provide signals to raise or lower output so that planned saving equals planned investment. But there are other mechanisms that aid in equilibration. Sometimes consumers are unable to purchase all the goods they demand and waiting lines and shortages appear. These queues and shortages signal business to expand existing production facilities or, perhaps, to raise prices.

Since Keynesian models generally assume excess production capacity, equilibrium takes the form of changes in quantities—real National Income and employment adjust to eliminate disparities between Aggregate Spending and National Output. Classical reasoning assumes full employment so that all adjustments take the form of wage and price changes. The differing economic conditions that generate quantity adjustments instead of price adjustments are treated toward the end of this chapter.

In sum, only when planned investment exactly equals planned saving will the economy stay in equilibrium. Sales by business will just be sufficient to maintain equilibrium output, and there will be no net tendency for the economy to move away from this equilibrium.

The Multiplier Effect

Look back at Figure 1. You can see that if there were no investment in our simple example, Aggregate Expenditures would consist only of consumption (C), and equilibrium income would be $2,500 billion (point a). However, when an autonomous **injection** of investment of $100 billion is introduced, its effect is multiplied so that equilibrium income increases to $3,000 billion (point e). The total change in income is five times the initial increase in spending! You may wonder why such a small injection of investment ($100 billion) is so powerful that it results in a major expansion of equilibrium income ($500 billion). The answer rests in a concept called the **multiplier effect:** one person's spending becomes someone else's income, and some of the second person's income is subsequently spent, becoming the income of a third person, and so on. But when does this multiple spending–income–spending cycle stop? And at what level of income? Answers to these questions require a bit of arithmetic.

The **autonomous spending multiplier** is the total change in income generated divided by the change in autonomous spending that triggered the spending–income–spending sequence. When the new autonomous spending is investment, this ratio is:

$$\Delta Y / \Delta I.$$

Based on the example described in Table 1 and Figures 1 and 2, the marginal propensity to consume (**mpc**) is 0.8. Suppose we begin with zero investment. According to Table 1, equilibrium income will be $2,500 billion because only at that level do planned saving and planned investment both equal zero.

TABLE 2 A Tabular Example of the Multiplier

Round	Increases in Expenditures (Billions of Dollars)	Increases in Saving (Billions of Dollars)
Initial Increase	$100	
Round 2	80	$ 20
Round 3	64	16
Round 4	51	13
Round 5	41	10
Round 6	33	8
Round 7	26	7
Round 8	21	5
Round 9	17	4
Round 10	13	3
Sum of First 10 Rounds	$446	$ 86
Sum of All Other Rounds	54	14
Total Increase in Spending (Income)	$500	
Total Increase in Saving		$100

Note: Data in the table are from Table 1. The **mpc** is 0.8 and the **mps** is 0.2. Figures after Round 3 are rounded off to the nearest dollar.

Now suppose that firms decide to invest $100 billion on new capital goods. Workers and owners of firms producing capital goods receive increases of $100 billion in their incomes. How will the workers and owners of firms who produce capital goods respond? Their **mpc** is 0.8 in their roles as consumers, so these producers can be expected to spend $80 billion of this new income on consumer goods and save $20 billion. When they spend the $80 billion, this second round of spending adds $80 billion to Aggregate Expenditures; National Output must increase by $80 billion, which becomes new income to the firms providing these consumer goods and to their employees. In turn, they will spend 80 percent of the $80 billion, or $64 billion, and so on throughout the system.

This round-by-round spending is illustrated in Table 2 and Figure 3. The cumulative effect of an autonomous investment injection of $100 billion is also illustrated in Figure 4, which is based on the data introduced in Table 1. As we noted earlier, the **mpc** is 0.8, so the **mps** is 0.2 and the multiplier for our example is 5. It is no coincidence that the multiplier is the reciprocal of the **mps**: $1/\text{mps} = 1/.2 = 5$. In fact, any change in injections (for example, either autonomous consumption or investment) divided by the marginal propensity to save yields the total multiplied effect on National Output and Income.

In our highly simplified model, the only withdrawal is saving, so the multiplier is $1/\text{mps}$. (A higher **mps** means a greater rate of withdrawal and a smaller multiplier.) Alternatively, the multiplier is the change in income divided by the change in injections; so:

$$\Delta Y/\Delta I = 1/\text{mps}.$$

Since the **mps** + **mpc** = 1, the **mps** = 1 − **mpc** and the multiplier may also be written as $1/(1 - \text{mpc})$. If we consider withdrawals other than saving:

autonomous spending multiplier	= 1/withdrawal fraction per spending round
	= 1/(1 − fraction respent),

and

total changes in income	= amount of injection × multiplier.

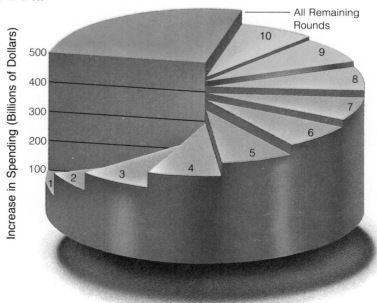

FIGURE 3 *The Multiplier Effect*

The round-by-round cumulative spending effect is illustrated in this figure. An additional $100 billion in spending in Round 1 is multiplied throughout the economy and results in a total increase in income of $500 billion when the **mpc** = 0.8. Each increase in spending in each round, when multiplied by the **mpc**, is the increase in spending for the subsequent round. When this infinite series is cumulated, aggregate income grows by $500 billion from an initial new injection of $100 billion.

FIGURE 4 *The Total Effect of the Multiplier*

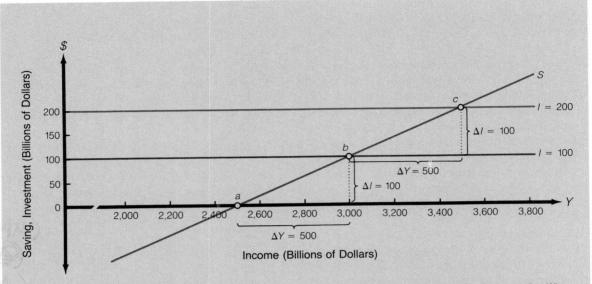

The effect on total income from a spending injection is equal to the injection times the autonomous spending multiplier. When the **mpc** = 0.8, this multiplier is 5. Therefore, an increase in investment (an injection) of $100 billion results in a total increase in income of $500 billion. This simple multiplier is $\Delta Y/\Delta I = 1/\text{mps} = 1/(1 - \text{mpc})$.

A mathematical derivation of this autonomous spending multiplier is provided in the optional material at the end of this chapter.

Our highly simplified model may seem to suggest that the multiplier effect will be quite large. Historically, the marginal propensity to save is about 7 percent, which suggests a multiplier of between 14 and 15. However, the linkages between spending rounds are much looser in the real world than in this model. More sophisticated models consider other withdrawals of funds from the American spending–income–spending sequence. Withdrawals include taxes (roughly 30 percent) and other "leakages" such as imports—a case where the funds we spend go into the hands of foreign suppliers. Moreover, the full multiplier effect is felt only after all spending rounds have been completed. Realistically, only the first four or five rounds of spending will be completed in the year in which an injection occurs. For all these reasons and more, prudent statistical estimates of the value of the autonomous spending multiplier place its maximum effective value at around 2. The Depression is a prime case of the multiplier at work.

The Great Depression: The Multiplier in Action

Brother, can you spare a dime?
—A Hit Song During the Depression

No one in the United States in the early 1930s escaped the effects of the Great Depression. The labor force was roughly at full employment in 1929; unemployment was only 3.2 percent. By 1933, unemployment had soared to 25 percent—one worker was unemployed for every three at work. Soup kitchens were opened to ease widespread hunger and malnourishment. Windows along Wall Street became diving boards for those who saw defenestration as a cure for bankruptcy. Widespread failures threatened to make U.S. banks fall like a line of dominoes. Unfortunately for the people of that era, programs such as unemployment compensation and Social Security were not available to provide temporary replacement incomes. Economically, these were the hardest times this country has ever experienced.

Figure 5 uses the Keynesian framework we have discussed to describe the first four years of the Great

FIGURE 5 *Saving, Investment, and Income During the Great Depression*

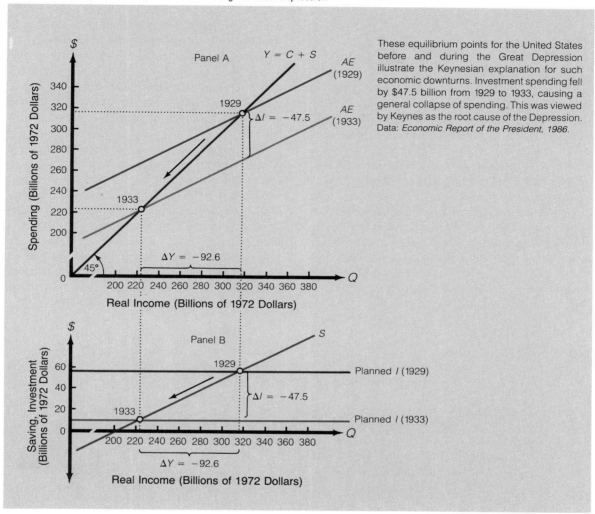

These equilibrium points for the United States before and during the Great Depression illustrate the Keynesian explanation for such economic downturns. Investment spending fell by $47.5 billion from 1929 to 1933, causing a general collapse of spending. This was viewed by Keynes as the root cause of the Depression. Data: *Economic Report of the President, 1986.*

Depression (1929–33). While this fairly accurate perspective of the Great Depression seems rather simple by today's standards, it was not understood at all during the early 1930s.

The actual data for the four components of Aggregate Expenditures (*C, I, G, X − M*) show that changes in net foreign spending and government purchases were quite small and largely offset each other during this period. The huge decline in Gross Private Domestic Investment (*I* in Figure 5) between 1929 and 1933 can be viewed as the root cause of most of the collapse in Aggregate Spending. During this period, investment fell from $55.9 billion to only $8.4 billion,

and "induced consumption" plummeted almost $45 billion. This $47.5 billion decline in investment spending was accompanied by a $92.6 billion drop in income (from $314.7 billion in 1929 to $222.1 billion in 1933). The multiplier is the change in income divided by the change in injections, which in this case is roughly $\Delta Y / \Delta I$; so applying our highly simplified model to these data suggests a multiplier during this period of 1.95 ($-92.6/-47.5 = 1.95$).

In future chapters, we detail the effects that government monetary and fiscal policies have on the economy. Could such a collapse occur again? Most economists think not. What policies do you think the government might have taken to prevent this collapse or at least to cushion its effects? In Chapters 11–18, we examine the tools government can use to combat both recessions and inflations.

The Paradox of Thrift

What happens if we as a society try to save more? The classical analysis in Chapter 8 suggests that saving facilitates investment and economic growth. Keynesian analysis, however, points to a potential problem known as the **paradox of thrift.** Most of us consider thrift a virtue. Ben Franklin's adage, "A penny saved is a penny earned," haunts many of our psyches when we shop, and we think we might be better off if we saved more. The term *paradox* correctly reflects, however, Keynesians' belief that Ben's adage is inappropriate for the general economy. Keynesian analysis indicates that if we *all* try to save more, we may *all* wind up worse off and actually save less.

Showing how the desire to save more may result in a decline in actual saving requires a slight, but temporary, change in the assumptions used to build our simple Keynesian model. We have assumed that investment is autonomous, or unaffected by income. A more realistic assumption is that as income rises, firms become increasingly optimistic about the profit prospects for new investment. Hence, for the moment we will assume that investment rises as income rises.

The paradox of thrift is illustrated in Figure 6, which shows households initially saving, and firms initially investing, $100 billion. National Income is $600 billion, with equilibrium at point *a* on curves S_0 and *I*. Suppose consumers decide to save more (consume less) at each level of income, causing the saving curve to rise from S_0 to S_1. The average propensity to save (**aps**) rises, but note that the marginal propensity to save (**mps**) is constant at 20 percent. With the increased desire to save, people want to set aside

FIGURE 6 The Paradox of Thrift

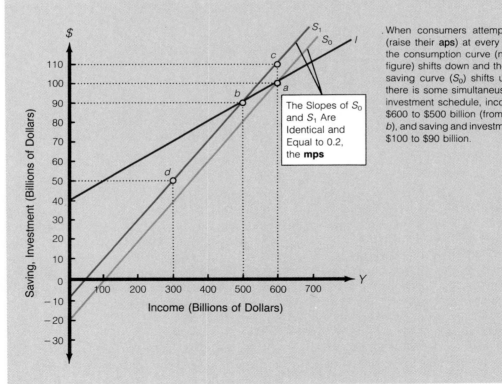

When consumers attempt to save more (raise their **aps**) at every level of income, the consumption curve (not shown in this figure) shifts down and the corresponding saving curve (S_0) shifts up to S_1. Unless there is some simultaneus increase in the investment schedule, income will fall from $600 to $500 billion (from point *a* to point *b*), and saving and investment both fall from $100 to $90 billion.

$110 billion (point c) if total National Income is $600 billion, and $50 billion (point d) if National Income is $300 billion. What happens as the economy adjusts to this increased desire to save?

First, consumers will reduce their consumption in attempts to save more. Firms will counter the resultant declines in sales and rising inventories with cutbacks in production, employment, and investment. As employment falls, so does income. Does this sound familiar? The economy moves from the original equilibrium income and output of $600 billion (point a), to a new equilibrium position at $500 billion (point b). Notice that saving actually declines by $10 billion, to a level of $90 billion. Why? Because actual saving and investment and planned saving and investment all must be equal in equilibrium; at point b, consumers want to save $90 billion because income is $500 billion and investors want to invest $90 billion at this new lower level of income. But observe that consumption has fallen from $500 billion ($600 − 100$) to $410 billion ($500 − 90$). Thus, this Keynesian model suggests that increased desires to save may lead to cuts in actual consumption, investment, saving, and income—and to a declining standard of living. This line of reasoning certainly poses a paradox for those of us who think that more saving is always good for the economy.

Unfortunately, increased saving may be a typical household response at the worst possible time, when the economy begins slipping into a recession. If families fear that breadwinners will lose their jobs, they may begin saving a little more each payday, trying to build nest eggs to cover expenses should income cease. If growing numbers of households adopt this strategy, they increase the likelihood of a recession and compound the task of government policymakers who are trying to restore the economy to full employment.

The paradox of saving may prove no problem if the economy is close to full employment. Classical reasoning reveals that increased desires to save may cause interest rates to fall, which may result in increases in investment and, thus, may yield the dividend of bolstering economic growth. President Reagan and his advisors were relying on classical economics when, in 1981, they launched "supply-side" economic policies intended to stimulate saving and investment and to reduce inflation. Shortly thereafter, the economy tumbled headlong into its deepest recession since the 1930s, but inflation subsided

and interest rates began to fall. Between 1980 and 1985, Gross Private Saving as a percent of National Income remained roughly constant at around 22 percent. Although these "supply-side" policies may have helped to reduce inflation and interest rates and to promote economic growth, they were credited (along with free-spending politicians) with causing enormous budget deficits. In Chapter 19, we will explore how successful policies that raise saving enhance economic growth.

The Investment Accelerator

The multiplier process relies on the fact that any increase in autonomous spending creates income, which generates further consumer spending, creating more income, and so on. The pressure to generate new income because rising consumption also causes new capital investment is known as the **investment accelerator.** (More sophisticated Keynesian models than any we consider in depth in this book describe interaction between aggregate output and investment by interweaving investment accelerators with the multiplier process.) New autonomous spending causes investment to accelerate, so that Aggregate Expenditures are both *multiplied* by induced consumption and *accelerated* by induced investment. The effects on equilibrium income of this interaction of the multiplier and accelerator are summarized in Figure 7.

Potential Versus Equilibrium Income

We now turn to the most important conclusion of Keynesian analysis. Keynes was the first internationally prominent mainstream economist to argue that the mechanisms that push a market economy towards full employment may be very *weak*. Keynesian analysis was an important challenge to the classical economists of the 1930s, most of whom believed that flexible wages and prices automatically restores the economy to full employment. The Great Depression taught us that mechanisms that automatically stabilize capitalistic economies sometimes operate very slowly at best. Unemployment increased sharply between 1929 and 1933, and the economy showed few signs of automatic recovery prior to World War II.

FIGURE 7 Integrating an Investment Accelerator into a Keynesian System

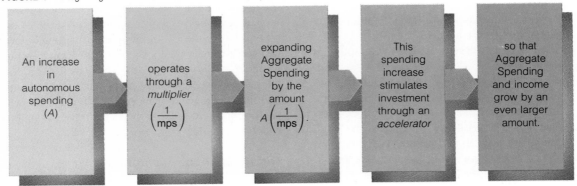

Investment is stimulated by a change in autonomous spending (A) through the accelerator principle. This change in autonomous spending magnifies Aggregate Expenditures even more than is suggested by the multiplier process, but it also makes Aggregate Spending highly volatile.

FIGURE 8 Actual and Potential GNP, 1960–85

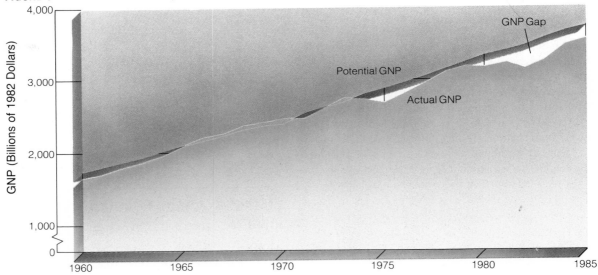

Potential GNP is an estimate of what the economy could produce if all factors of production were fully employed. As this figure illustrates, the economy operated in excess of potential GNP during the latter half of the 1960s. However, the economy consistently operated below potential during the decade of the 1970s.

Source: *Economic Report of the President*, 1986, and Frank de Leeuw and Thomas M. Holloway, "Cyclical Adjustment of the Federal Budget and the Federal Debt," *Survey of Current Business*, December 1983.

Potential GNP

Potential GNP is an estimate of what the economy could produce at high rates of utilization of our available resources, especially full employment of labor.

Thus, *potential GNP* and *full employment GNP* (or income) basically refer to the same thing. Estimates of potential GNP reflect trends in productivity, the size and composition of the labor force, and other influences on our capacity to produce. Estimates of potential GNP for 1960–85 are illustrated in Figure 8, which also shows the difference between potential and actual GNP; this is termed the **GNP gap.**

The GNP Gap

In the simple Keynesian model described by Table 1 and graphed in Figure 9, equilibrium income is $3,000 billion along expenditure curve AE_0. Suppose that potential GNP at full employment is $3,250 billion, so that a *GNP gap* exists of $250 billion. Would market pressures quickly move the economy above its original equilibrium of $3,000 billion? Keynesians believe the answer is no. How might the economy be manipulated to fill this $250-billion GNP gap and achieve equilibrium income and output of $3,250 billion? The Keynesian answer is to increase Aggregate Spending from AE_0 to AE_1. How much of an increase in autonomous spending is required? Given that the

multiplier in our example is 5, an increase in autonomous investment spending of $50 billion will result in increases in Aggregate Spending and output of $250 billion, filling the GNP gap and moving the economy to full employment.

The Recessionary Gap

This deficiency in autonomous spending is referred to as the recessionary gap. The **recessionary gap** measures the amount by which *autonomous spending* falls short of that needed to bring equilibrium income to full employment. Notice that the recessionary gap is measured along the vertical axis in Figure 9. This means that the gap is defined by any shortfall in autonomous spending and *not* by the amount by which equilibrium income falls short of full employment income (measured along the horizontal axis). This shortfall is the GNP gap and equals

FIGURE 9 *Inflationary and Recessionary Gaps*

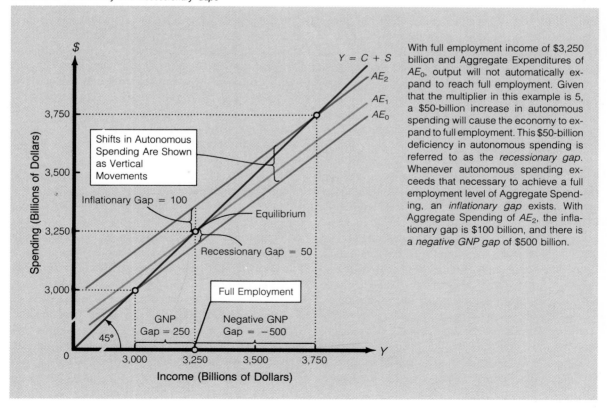

With full employment income of $3,250 billion and Aggregate Expenditures of AE_0, output will not automatically expand to reach full employment. Given that the multiplier in this example is 5, a $50-billion increase in autonomous spending will cause the economy to expand to full employment. This $50-billion deficiency in autonomous spending is referred to as the *recessionary gap*. Whenever autonomous spending exceeds that necessary to achieve a full employment level of Aggregate Spending, an *inflationary gap* exists. With Aggregate Spending of AE_2, the inflationary gap is $100 billion, and there is a *negative GNP gap* of $500 billion.

the recessionary gap times the autonomous spending multiplier:

GNP gap = recessionary gap × multiplier.

The Inflationary Gap

An inflationary gap is the reverse of the recessionary gap. An **inflationary gap** is the amount by which autonomous spending exceeds that needed to achieve full employment equilibrium. Graphically, it is the vertical distance between AE_1 and AE_2 shown in Figure 9. The inflationary gap is $100 billion if Aggregate Spending is AE_2. Since the economy can only produce $3,250 billion in output, this additional demand will result in upward pressures on prices when potential buyers compete for this limited real output.

Keynesian Equilibrium and the Price Level

National Income (Y) is a monetary value and can be thought of as the product of the price level (P) and the level of real output (Q). Thus, $Y = PQ$. In our example, real income and output (Q) cannot exceed the $3,250-billion full employment level. The $100-billion inflationary gap is expanded through the multiplier, which equals 5, so that equilibrium monetary income (Y) equals $3,750 billion. Thus:

$3,750 billion $= P \times$ $3,250 billion,

which means that the equilibrium price level must rise to 3,750/3,250, or roughly 1.154. (A price index would rise from 100 to 115+.) Thus, this $100-billion inflationary gap will cause the price level to rise a bit more than 15 percent. Preventing this inflationary adjustment to excessive Aggregate Spending entails cutting the autonomous spending of either consumers, investors, government, or foreigners. Some methods government might use to reduce these inflationary pressures are presented in the next chapter.

Keynesian analysis largely focuses on achieving full employment if the economy is operating below its potential; it generally ignores the inflation that might emerge if Aggregate Demand is excessive.

However, the price level is sensitive to total spending by both consumers and investors, and vice versa. Let us see why.

Simple Keynesian theory views production decisions as being based strictly on expected sales; prices are assumed fixed. This is implicit in the idea that "demand creates its own supply." Consequently, the Aggregate Supply curve compatible with Keynesian analysis of a recession is horizontal until a full employment level of output is reached. Then, just like the Aggregate Supply curve of classical analysis (discussed in Chapter 8), this Aggregate Supply curve becomes vertical, as shown in Figure 10. Once the economy reaches full employment, expanding spending further would result in pure price increases.

If Aggregate Demand is AD_0 in Figure 10, equilibrium output will be Q_0 at a price level of P_0 (point a). There is substantial excess capacity and unemployment in this equilibrium, and the GNP gap $= Q_f - Q_0$. The Keynesian prescription is to increase Aggregate Spending so that Aggregate Demand increases to AD_1, and the economy achieves full employment with price-level stability at point b. The growth in output from Q_0 to Q_f to fill the GNP gap can be accomplished by increases in autonomous spending equal to the recessionary gap described earlier. If Aggregate Spending increases more than the difference between Q_f and Q_0 and Aggregate Demand shifts to AD_2, the economy will suffer inflation as prices rise to P_2 from P_0 (point c). The vertical distance $P_2 - P_0$ reflects inflation caused by excessive autonomous spending, in accord with the inflationary gap we described above.

The central topic in the next chapter is how government fiscal policy (spending and taxing) can be used to eliminate inflationary or recessionary gaps so that GNP moves to a noninflationary full employment level. A word of caution is in order. You have acquired considerable insight into the workings of our economy by studying the model developed in this chapter. When Keynes wrote *The General Theory of Employment, Interest, and Money* in 1936, he was primarily concerned with filling a huge recessionary gap and suggested massive government spending as the best way to increase Aggregate Expenditures sufficiently to pull an economy out of a depression. Policies to shrink inflationary or recessionary gaps require accurate estimates of the sizes of these gaps and then timely and appropriate actions to achieve full employment with price-level stability. This is actually an incredibly difficult task, obscured by the crude oversimplification of our model. However, this analysis will help you to understand and formu-

late solutions to problems that we encounter in the next chapter. The model presented there is slightly more complex, making it possible for us to consider a broader range of stabilization problems and policies.

FIGURE 10 *Relationship Between Output and Price Level in Simple Keynesian Analysis*

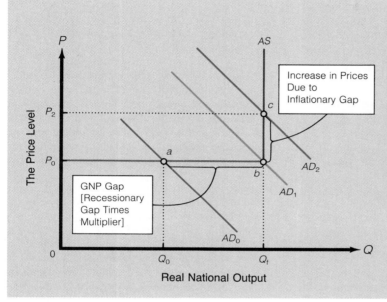

Simple Keynesian theory operates as though "demand creates its own supply" since prices are assumed fixed. As a result, the Aggregate Supply curve is horizontal until full employment is reached. If Aggregate Demand is AD_0, the GNP gap is $Q_f - Q_0$, which is equal to the recessionary gap times the multiplier. Once full employment is reached (Q_f), the Aggregate Supply curve (AS) becomes vertical. Thus, if Aggregate Demand rises from AD_1 to AD_2, the price level will rise from P_0 to P_2 due to excessive autonomous spending and the inflationary gap just described.

CHAPTER REVIEW: KEY POINTS

1. Keynesian theory suggests that erratic changes in *business investment spending* (especially changes that occur in inventories) play a major role in causing fluctuations in aggregate income and employment.

2. Equilibrium income and employment occur at the output level at which *Aggregate Spending equals National Output;* firms desire to produce and sell exactly the amounts consumers and investors want to purchase. Any deviation from equilibrium income sets forces in motion to drive the economy toward equilibrium.

3. When *planned saving equals planned investment* (S = I), the economy will be in *equilibrium.* Actual saving and investment are equal at all times because inventory adjustments and similar mechanisms ensure this balance.

4. When *autonomous spending* in the economy increases by $1, income rises by an amount equal to the *autonomous spending multiplier* times the original $1. The multiplier exists because the original $1 in new spending becomes $1 in new income, parts of which are then spent by successive consumers and businesses. The simple autonomous spending multiplier equals:

$$\Delta Y/\Delta A = 1/\mathbf{mps} = 1/(1 - \mathbf{mpc}),$$

where *A* represents some form of autonomous spending. More generally, the multiplier equals 1/(withdrawal fraction per spending round).

5. Investment spending dropped precipitously during the 1929–33 period. The effect of this decline was to reduce equilibrium income sharply, and it may have been a principal cause of the Great Depression.

6. The *paradox of thrift* appears to be an important challenge to our conventional wisdom. If more consumers decide to increase their saving, the result might be declining income, consumption, and saving.

7. *Potential GNP* is an estimate of the output the economy could produce at full employment. The *GNP gap* is the difference between potential and actual GNP.

8. The *recessionary gap* is the amount by which autonomous spending falls short of that necessary to achieve a full employment level of income; it is measured on the vertical axis. An *inflationary gap* is the amount that autonomous spending exceeds what is necessary for a full employment equilibrium and is a measure of upward pressure on the price level.

9. Keynes felt that in a depression, increases in output with no increase in the price level could be stimulated by raising demand. Simple Keynesian theory suggests that the Aggregate Supply curve is horizontal up to the point of full employment. Once full employment and the economy's capacity to produce are reached, the economy follows classical reasoning. The Aggregate Supply curve becomes vertical because higher prices cannot generate extra production. When the economy is at full employment, any increase in Aggregate Demand simply bids up prices and results in inflation.

QUESTIONS FOR THOUGHT AND DISCUSSION

1. What are the similarities and the differences between equilibrium for Aggregate Expenditure and National Output curves and equilibrium for Aggregate Demand and Supply when the price level is a consideration? How do these macroeconomic equilibria compare with the equilibria in markets for individual goods and services?

2. In the simple Keynesian model presented in this chapter, the only forms of injection considered are autonomous investment and the only withdrawal is saving. What are other possible injections? Other withdrawals? How might exports and imports be incorporated to make this model a more complete picture of the way the world really works?

3. Do you think prices will fall in response to declines in Aggregate Demand, as classical economists suggest? Or will quantities decline, as Keynesians believe? What bearing does your answer have for designing policies to combat inflationary pressures? If the economy has considerable excess capacity, will expanding Aggregate Expenditures cause output to grow, or will the price level simply rise?

4. What are the alternatives available to a retailer whose inventories are growing because sales are not as large as planned? Will the alternative retailers typically select be important in determining National Income? How? How will the strategies chosen by retailers with excess inventories vary over the business cycle? Why is this important?

5. One simple way to calculate an autonomous spending multiplier is to invert (turn upside-down) the fraction representing the **mps.** For example, if **mps** = ⅙, this multiplier equals 6. Compute the **mps** and the autonomous spending multiplier for the following values of the **mpc:** ½, ⅗, ⅔, ¾, ⅘, ⅚, 6/7, ⅞, 8/9, and 9/10.

6. Answer the following questions using the consumption relationship described in the following table.

National Output and Income	Planned Consumption
$ 0	$1,000
1,000	1,800
2,000	2,600
3,000	3,400
4,000	4,200
5,000	5,000
6,000	5,800
7,000	6,600

a. If autonomous investment is $200, what is equilibrium income?

b. Assume that full employment income is $4,000. What is the GNP gap equal to? What is the inflationary gap equal to?

c. How much is the autonomous spending multiplier?

d. If extreme pessimism fell over the economy and investment spending fell to −$600, what would the equilibrium income be? What would the recessionary gap equal?

OPTIONAL MATERIAL: THE MATHEMATICS OF THE KEYNESIAN AUTONOMOUS SPENDING MULTIPLIER

A more rigorous treatment of our hypothetical model will help you to understand why income changes by some multiple of any change in autonomous spending. How large will be the total change in income (ΔY) from a given change in, say autonomous investment spending (ΔI)? This ratio ($\Delta Y/\Delta I$) is known as the **autonomous spending multiplier.** First, we have assumed that consumption will be related to income and that changes in income will cause consumption to change by a value equal to the **mpc** times the change in income. Since we know that:

$$Y = C + I \qquad \text{Equation 1}$$

(output is either consumed or invested at equilibrium), then:

$$\Delta Y = \Delta C + \Delta I \qquad \text{Equation 2}$$

(changes in output reflect changes in consumption and/or investment), where the delta (Δ) refers to change. Thus, ΔC is read "change in consumption." However, as we indicated above, consumption spending is related to income by the **mpc,** or:

$$\Delta C = \textbf{mpc} \times \Delta Y \qquad \text{Equation 3}$$

(this is the change in induced consumption). The change in consumption is equal to the change in income times the proportion you intend to spend. To simplify the notation, let $b = \textbf{mpc}$. Substituting $b\Delta Y$ (from Equation 3) for ΔC (in Equation 2), we have:

$$\Delta Y = b\Delta Y + \Delta I. \qquad \text{Equation 4}$$

Now we have a rather simple problem of solving Equation 4 for ΔY. This is done by subtracting $b\Delta Y$ from each side of the equation, which results in:

$$\Delta Y - b\Delta Y = \Delta I. \qquad \text{Equation 5}$$

Factoring the ΔY terms on the left-hand side of the equation leaves:

$$\Delta Y(1 - b) = \Delta I, \qquad \text{Equation 6}$$

and dividing both sides by $(1 - b)$ yields:

$$\Delta Y = \Delta I \frac{1}{(1 - b)}. \qquad \text{Equation 7}$$

The term $1/(1 - b)$ is also known as the **autonomous spending multiplier.** If the marginal propensity to consume is 0.8, the autonomous spending multiplier will be 5 because $[1/(1 - 0.8) = 1/0.2 = 5]$. Observe what happens to multipliers as **mpc**s rise and **mps**s fall. Since the sum of the **mpc** and the

mps is equal to 1 and **mps** = $1 -$ **mpc,** another way to write the autonomous spending multiplier is $1/$**mps.** In fact, the following are all equivalent ways to write the autonomous spending multiplier:

$$\frac{\Delta Y}{\Delta I} = \frac{1}{1 - b} = \frac{1}{1 - \textbf{mpc}}$$

$$= \frac{1}{\textbf{mps}}. \qquad \text{Equation 8}$$

We have used investment as the example of autonomous spending that, when increased, results in increases in income via the multiplier. Mathematically identical effects occur if autonomous consumption, government spending, or exports are increased. Naturally, reversed multiplier effects follow cuts in autonomous spending. The various multipliers that are appropriate for government purchases and taxes are treated in the optional material following Chapter 11.

CHAPTER 11 Fiscal Policy: Government Taxing and Spending

Keynesians believe that government spending and tax policies can play a major role in stabilizing Aggregate Expenditures (*AE*) so that households do not suffer extreme year-to-year swings in their incomes and economic well-being. Many Keynesians favor active fiscal policy to "fine-tune" Aggregate Expenditures, smothering cyclical fluctuations in output, income, and employment.

Classical economics has been reborn as "supply-side" economics—the idea that government macroeconomic policies shape the business environment and can set the stage for growth in Aggregate Supply (*AS*). Supply-siders advocate permanent low tax rates and low government spending, asserting that these will stimulate private work effort and that high saving rates will facilitate private investment in new capital goods. Supply-side economics emphasizes that government spending may force reductions in private investment and consumption and that higher tax rates may prove to be such disincentives to work

effort and investment that incomes will fall and total tax revenues may actually decrease. In this chapter we will examine both approaches to fiscal policy.

Fiscal Policy: Some Definitions

Fiscal policy is the use of government spending and tax policies to stimulate or contract economic activity. If federal outlays and tax revenues are equal, the government is operating a **balanced budget.** When the government's outlays of funds are greater than tax revenues, government is running a **budgetary deficit.** If tax revenues exceed outlays, we have a **budgetary surplus.** Many Americans believe the government must eventually balance its budget or face national bankruptcy. Both the wisdom of balancing the federal budget and the prospect of eventual bankruptcy are addressed in this chapter.

The spending and taxing policies of the federal government can be lumped into two broad categories: discretionary and nondiscretionary. **Discretionary fiscal policy** involves deliberate legislative changes in government spending or taxes to alter Aggregate Demand (*AD*) and stabilize the economy. **Nondiscretionary fiscal policies** create automatic changes in spending and taxes—legislative changes are not required as economic conditions change.

Discretionary Fiscal Policy

Discretionary fiscal policies occur when the federal government legislates changes in its taxes or outlays to alter Aggregate Spending. We must now expand the model built in Chapter 10 so that the Keynesian view of the effects of fiscal policy on Aggregate Expenditures can be considered. This task is most easily done in stages. To keep the analysis simple, we will initially assume: (*a*) that government spending (*G*) is autonomous and affects neither the consumption nor the investment schedules; (*b*) that invest-

ment (*I*) is also autonomous—a constant level that is independent of income; and (*c*) that taxes (*T*) are also autonomous—at a constant level not affected by income. After you become more comfortable with our expanded Keynesian model, we will examine the consequences of relaxing these restrictive assumptions.

Government Spending and Equilibrium

The data outlined in Table 1 and diagrammed in Figure 1 extend the simple numerical model developed in the preceding chapter. Equilibrium spending and income without the government sector equal $3,000 billion (point *a* in Figure 1). But if the full employment level of income is $3,250 billion, there is a GNP gap of $250 billion. Because Keynesian analysis presumes that any forces pushing the economy toward full employment are weak, there is a recessionary gap of $50 billion that will not be remedied quickly through private actions. Note that $50 billion in new autonomous spending will close the $250 billion GNP gap because the multiplier is 5. The economy

TABLE 1 *Curing a Recessionary Gap with the Keynesian Remedy of Government Spending (Billions of Dollars)*

	Private Sector Only							Addition of Government Sector		
(1) Employment (Millions)	(2) National Output	(3) C	(4) S	(5) I	(6) Aggregate Expenditures Without Government (*AE_0*)	(7) Pressures on Income & Output	(8) G	(9) Aggregate Expenditures with Government (*AE_1*)	(10) Pressures on Income & Output
70	2,000	2,100	−100	100	2,200	Tendency for income to increase	50	2,250	Tendency for income to increase
75	2,250	2,300	−50	100	2,400		50	2,450	
80	2,500	2,500	0	100	2,600		50	2,650	
85	2,750	2,700	50	100	2,800		50	2,850	
90	3,000	2,900	100	100	3,000	Equilibrium	50	3,050	
95	3,250	3,100	150	100	3,200		50	3,250	Full employment equilibrium
100	3,500	3,300	200	100	3,400	Tendency for income to decrease	50	3,450	Tendency for income to decrease
105	3,750	3,500	250	100	3,600		50	3,650	

FIGURE 1 *Hypothetical Model of Equilibrium Income*

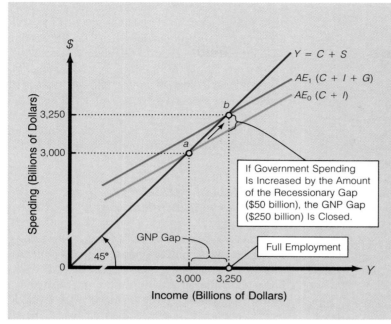

This figure graphically depicts the data in Table 1. Equilibrium without government spending is $3,000 billion (point *a*) and a GNP gap of $250 billion exists. The economy can be brought to full employment by adding $50 billion to government spending. This increases Aggregate Spending from AE_0 ($C + I$) to AE_1 ($C + I + G$). The $50 billion in government spending is subject to the multiplier just like private autonomous spending. Thus, the $50 billion times the multiplier (5 in this example) closes the GNP gap and moves the economy to full employment.

would achieve its potential GNP if this recessionary gap were somehow closed.

One way for the government to fill this recessionary gap so that full employment will be reached is for the government to add $50 billion to autonomous spending (column 8 in Table 1). Aggregate Expenditures shift from AE_0 to AE_1 in Figure 1, and equilibrium moves from point *a* to point *b* as government spending rises from zero to $50 billion.

Notice that autonomous government spending and autonomous private spending are subject to the multiplier in the same way. Although the multiplier was originally described in terms of investment ($\Delta Y/\Delta I$ = **autonomous spending multiplier**), all injections and withdrawals from the economy are subject to the multiplier principle. Government spending is simply another form of injection, so it should not be surprising that, dollar for dollar, it is as powerful as investment spending in increasing Aggregate Expenditures. For example, a new government contract places new income in the hands of government contractors and their employees. Some of their new income is saved, but most will be spent. This spending in turn becomes new income for

those from whom they buy and is then spent or saved. And so on.[1]

The effect of an increase in government purchases on equilibrium income can be described in a manner parallel to the planned-savings-equal-investment approach outlined in the previous chapter. Saving and taxes are both forms of withdrawals, while investment and government purchases are both forms of injections. *Planned injections must equal planned withdrawals at equilibrium.*[2] In Figure 2, we have diagrammed the planned-injections-equal-planned-withdrawals approach, which parallels the savings-equals-investment approach we developed

---

1. You may wonder how the government can spend more without raising taxes. One possibility is for the government to borrow the money by selling Treasury bonds. Alternatively, the budget deficit can be financed by printing more money. The ability to print money certainly distinguishes the federal government from the rest of us. (We address the specific mechanisms used by the Federal Reserve System (FED) in Chapter 13. The FED is the arm of government empowered to print and regulate money. The process of printing money to cover a deficit is a bit more complex than we suggest here.)

2. Algebraically, since $C + I + G = C + S + T = Y$ in equilibrium, then $I + G = S + T$ is an equilibrium condition.

FIGURE 2 *Injections-Equals-Withdrawals Approach to Equilibrium National Income (I + G = S + T)*

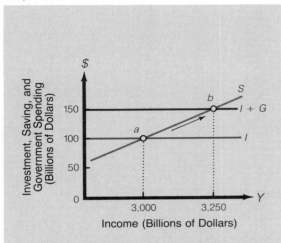

Income (Billions of Dollars)

This figure examines the effect of an increase in government spending on equilibrium income using the injection-equals-withdrawals approach. Without government, the private economy will reach equilibrium at $3,000 billion (point *a*). Introducing $50 billion in government spending into the system increases income by $250 billion, so the economy moves to equilibrium at $3,250 (point *b*). Total injections (*I* + *G*) are $150 billion and are equal to total withdrawals (*S* + *T*) at the new equilibrium. Note that in this example, since *T* = 0, *S* = *I* + *G*.

when only private spending was considered. Households would save $150 billion if the income level were $3,250 billion. With the introduction of $50 billion in new government spending into the system, total injections (*I* + *G*) are $150 billion. Planned saving ($100 billion in planned withdrawals) at the initial equilibrium of $3,000 billion is less than planned investment and government spending ($150 billion in planned injections), so output will rise until injections and withdrawals are equal. Equilibrium is reached only when output has risen to $3,250 billion.

The Effects of Taxation on Equilibrium Income

Now that we know how increased government spending affects equilibrium, we can move another step closer to reality by introducing taxes (*T*) into our model. The **autonomous tax multiplier** can be expressed much like the autonomous expenditures multiplier. It is defined as $\Delta Y/\Delta T$, which means that it is a ratio expressing the proportional change in income caused by a given change in autonomous taxes. Taxes, like saving, are withdrawals from spending in the economy. Therefore, when taxes rise, spending and income fall; thus, the autonomous tax multiplier is a *negative* number.

TABLE 2 *Curing an Inflationary Gap with Taxes*

(1) Employment (Millions)	(2) National Output & Income (Y)	(3) C	(4) S	(5) I	(6) Spending Without Taxes (C + I)	(7) T	(8) Y_d	(9) C_t	(10) S_t	(11) Aggregate Spending ($C_t + I$)	(12) Net Pressure on Output
90	3,000	3,150	−150	100	3,250	250	2,750	2,950	−200	3,050	Tendency for income to rise
95	3,250	3,350	−100	100	3,450	250	3,000	3,150	−150	3,250	0
100	3,500	3,550	−50	100	3,650	250	3,250	3,350	−100	3,450	Tendency for income to fall
105	3,750	3,750	0	100	3,850	250	3,500	3,550	−50	3,650	
110	4,000	3,950	50	100	4,050	250	3,750	3,750	0	3,850	
115	4250*	4,150	100	100	4,250*	250	4,000	3,950	50	4,050	
120	4,500	4,350	150	100	4,450	250	4,250	4,150	100	4,250	

*Note: Equilibrium without taxes equals 4,250 (Y = C + I = 4,150 + 100 = 4,250).

FIGURE 3 *Eliminating Inflationary Pressure with Taxes (Injections-Equals-Withdrawals Approach)*

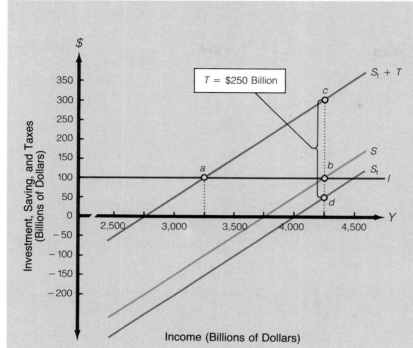

This figure introduces taxes into the simple Keynesian model but ignores government spending in the interest of simplicity. The model assumes that taxes affect only spending behavior, not productive effort. Taxes reduce saving by the **mps** times autonomous taxes, or 0.2 ($250 billion), for a total reduction of $50 billion in autonomous saving. However, total net withdrawals increase by $200 billion at each income level: $\Delta S + \Delta T = -\$50$ billion + $250 billion. Thus, through the multiplier process, income is reduced from $4,250 billion to $3,250 billion, so inflationary pressure is diminished by tax withdrawals. The tax multiplier $\Delta Y / \Delta T$ is -4 in this case ($-\$1,000$ billion/$250 billion = -4).

Suppose that an inflationary psychology is rampant so that consumers are spending their incomes roughly as soon as they receive them. The data in columns 1–6 of Table 2 reflect the assumption of expected inflation by showing planned consumption (column 3) at $250 billion higher for each income level than was the case for Table 1. As a result, planned saving (column 4) is $250 billion lower at each income than in Table 1.

Without any government involvement, equilibrium income (where column 2 equals column 6) is $4,250 billion; so Aggregate Spending is $1,000 billion too high for a fully employed economy with price-level stability. This occurs only with $3,250 billion in output. There is a negative GNP gap of $1,000 billion ($3,250 billion − $4,250 billion). Given the autonomous spending multiplier of 5 (**mpc** = 0.8), this GNP gap implies an inflationary gap of $200 billion in this situation, which means that autonomous spending is $200 billion too high. Alternatively, autonomous saving is $200 billion too low (distance *bc*

in Figure 3). This model contains no government spending, and so increasing withdrawals by raising taxes is the government's only available option to reduce Aggregate Expenditures.

Suppose autonomous taxes of $250 billion are now imposed (column 7). What will be the effect of this $250 billion in autonomous taxes on Aggregate Spending? Consumers base decisions about spending on disposable income (Y_d) instead of aggregate income (Y) because households alone ultimately bear all tax burdens. Subtracting taxes (column 7) from National Income (column 2) yields disposable income ($Y - T = Y_d$), shown as column 8 in Table 2. Notice that the relationship between disposable income and consumption is identical to the relationship between income and consumption from Table 1 when we ignored taxes.

How much of this $250 billion in taxes will come from consumption and how much from saving? With an **mpc** of 80 percent and an **mps** of 20 percent (0.8 and 0.2, respectively), consumption initially will be reduced 0.8 times the $250 billion in taxes, for a total of $200 billion. This shifts the consumption component of the Aggregate Expenditures schedule down by $200 billion for all levels of gross (before-tax) income. Similarly, the saving schedule is decreased by $50 billion at all income levels.

The impact of these new taxes is illustrated in Figure 3. The new saving curve S_t (savings after taxes are imposed) is drawn below the original saving curve S because it is exactly $50 billion lower (measured on the vertical scale). (Remember, a reduction in saving is shown as a shift of the saving curve to the right because consumers will now save less at each income level.) Let's look at this using the injections-equal-withdrawals approach.

Withdrawals in the form of saving (after taxes) are now shown as S_t. Taxes of $250 billion are withdrawn from the economy as well. Consequently, total withdrawals now equal S_t plus T. This combined withdrawal function is labeled $S_t + T$ in Figure 3 and is exactly $250 billion above S_t (distance cd in Figure 3); thus, it is $200 billion above the original S curve for each income$_{level}$.

On the other side of the ledger, injections into the economy are still only $100 billion in business investment. Equilibrium results where total leakages (another term for withdrawals) equal total injections, which means that $S_t + T = I$ (point a in Figure 3). Equilibrium National Income (determined now by Aggregate Spending of $C_t + I$, where C_t represents consumption after taxes have been collected) falls from $4,250 billion to $3,250 billion. The autonomous tax multiplier ($\Delta Y/\Delta T_a$) equals $-\$1,000/\$250$, so it is -4 in this case. This example shows that in equilibrium, inflationary expectations cause saving to be $-\$150$ billion; therefore, taxes (withdrawals) of $250 billion will offset investment injections ($100 billion) and dissaving ($150 billion) to keep this economy at full employment without inflation.

The Tax Multiplier

In our example, the marginal propensity to consume is 0.8, and the autonomous spending multiplier ($\Delta Y/\Delta A$) equals 5. Our calculations indicate that the autonomous tax multiplier ($\Delta Y/\Delta T_a$) equals -4 in this case. Notice the relationship: one minus the autonomous spending multiplier equals the tax multiplier [$1 - (1/\textbf{mps}) = \Delta Y/\Delta T$; $1 - 5 = -4$]. The general form of this simple tax multiplier

is $-\textbf{mpc}/\textbf{mps}$.[3] The *autonomous tax multiplier* is the negative value of one less than the spending multiplier. An example of why this is so is shown in Table 3.

Table 3 traces the effects on spending of $100-billion increases in government purchases and taxes, both individually and together, through a few rounds of transactions, assuming that the $\textbf{mpc} = 0.8$. In column 1, 80 percent of each extra dollar of income is spent and becomes someone else's income. Thus, a new injection of $100 billion in government spending (Round 1) means that $80 billion in consumer spending is induced in the second round. The people whose incomes rise by this $80 billion then spend $64 billion, which becomes other people's extra income. And so on. The autonomous spending multiplier is 5, indicated at the end of column 1.

The effect that new autonomous taxes of $100 billion have on spending and income is shown in column 2 of Table 3. Note that in Round 1, the imposition of this tax does not affect the gross (before-tax) incomes of taxpayers. The $100-billion tax hike may be viewed by taxpayers as a cut in disposable income, but it does not initially reduce production or National Income. It is only when this decline in disposable income is translated into lower spending that National Income is reduced. Thus, new government purchases have an initial effect on Aggregate Spending; in Round 1, new taxes do not. This is why the tax multiplier is the negative value of one less than the spending multiplier.

The Balanced-Budget Multiplier

You may have noticed something startling in Table 3. Expanding both government spending (column 1) and autonomous taxes (column 2) by $100 billion causes equilibrium income to rise, on balance, by exactly $100 billion (end of column 3). The reasoning is actually straightforward: The spending multiplier ($1/\textbf{mps}$) plus the tax multiplier ($-\textbf{mpc}/\textbf{mps}$) equals ($1 - \textbf{mpc})/\textbf{mps}$. Since $\textbf{mps} + \textbf{mpc} = 1$, then $1 - \textbf{mpc} = \textbf{mps}$, and the ratio ($1 - \textbf{mpc})/\textbf{mps}$ must equal 1.

---

3. We know that $\textbf{mpc} + \textbf{mps} = 1$. Substitute this into part of $1 - (1/\textbf{mps})$, and we get $1 - [(\textbf{mpc} + \textbf{mps})/\textbf{mps}]$. Factoring, we have $1 - (\textbf{mpc}/\textbf{mps}) - (\textbf{mps}/\textbf{mps})$, which simplifies to $1 - (\textbf{mpc}/\textbf{mps}) - 1$, which equals ($-\textbf{mpc}/\textbf{mps}$). This is the value of the autonomous tax multiplier.

TABLE 3 Round-by-Round Effects of $100 Billion Increases in Spending, Taxing, and the Balanced Budget (in Billions of Dollars)

Effect	(1) $100 Billion Extra Government Purchases	+	(2) $100 Billion Extra Autonomous Taxation	=	(3) $100 Billion Extra Taxing and Purchases
Round 1: Initial effect of change on income	$100		0		$100
Round 2: induced spending	80		$ −80		0
Round 3: induced spending	64		−64		0
Round 4 through all subsequent rounds	256		−256		0
TOTAL CHANGE	$500		$−400		$100
MULTIPLIER (**mpc** = 0.8)	5		−4		1

Note: Each $1 increase in government purchases creates $1 in new income in Round 1, but each $1 in new taxes does not influence first-round income. In Round 2, each $1 in new government purchases has caused the person whose income was increased to spend $0.80, but this is offset by the reduced spending of $0.80 caused by each $1 in new taxes. Moreover, the effects of the new spending and taxing offset each other in all subsequent rounds. Thus, only Round 1 spending has any net effect on income, and the balanced-budget multiplier equals one.

This bit of algebra suggests that the **balanced-budget multiplier** in a simple Keynesian model is exactly one. The conclusion is that equal increases (*decreases*) in government spending and taxes will increase (*decrease*) equilibrium National Income by an identical amount. Studying Table 3 should help you discern the fiscal mechanisms at work when either spending or taxing is changed. The autonomous spending and tax multipliers and the balanced-budget multiplier are described in more detail in the optional material at the end of this chapter.

Let us summarize the fiscal policies Keynesians prescribe to remedy specific economic ills. Inflationary pressures can be reduced through tax hikes or cuts in government purchases, or both. Both tax increases and government spending cuts will drive the government budget towards surplus (or reduce deficits) during inflationary periods. If excessive unemployment is the major problem, then tax cuts or increases in governmental purchases will temporarily move the budget into a deficit (or reduce a surplus) and cause expansions of output, income, and employment.

This analysis suggests that budgetary deficits are the right medicine to cure a recession and that budgetary surpluses are a remedy when the economy suffers from inflation. Most political decision makers enjoy granting the tax cuts and new government spending projects that are appropriate to combat recession because such measures are popular with voters. However, the tax increases and slashed budgets needed to fight inflation are unpopular with the public and, consequently, are anathema to many political leaders. Explicit political actions to create surpluses during inflation, fortunately, are not always necessary. There are certain features of our tax system and some government spending programs that automatically push budgets towards surpluses during inflationary periods and into deficits during economic downturns.

Nondiscretionary Fiscal Policy

Discretionary variations in spending and taxes require congressional action. Fortunately, they are not the only fiscal instruments available to move us toward full employment and price-level stability. There are several built-in mechanisms called **automatic stabilizers** that Keynesians regard as dampeners of swings in Aggregate Spending and economic activity. Until now, we have assumed that both government spending and taxes were unrelated to income. This is, of course, unrealistic. The fact that both taxes and government outlays are sensitive to changes in National Income lends an automatic resilience to the economy. Let us see how.

FIGURE 4 *Unemployment, Corporate Profits, and Federal Government Surplus or Deficit*

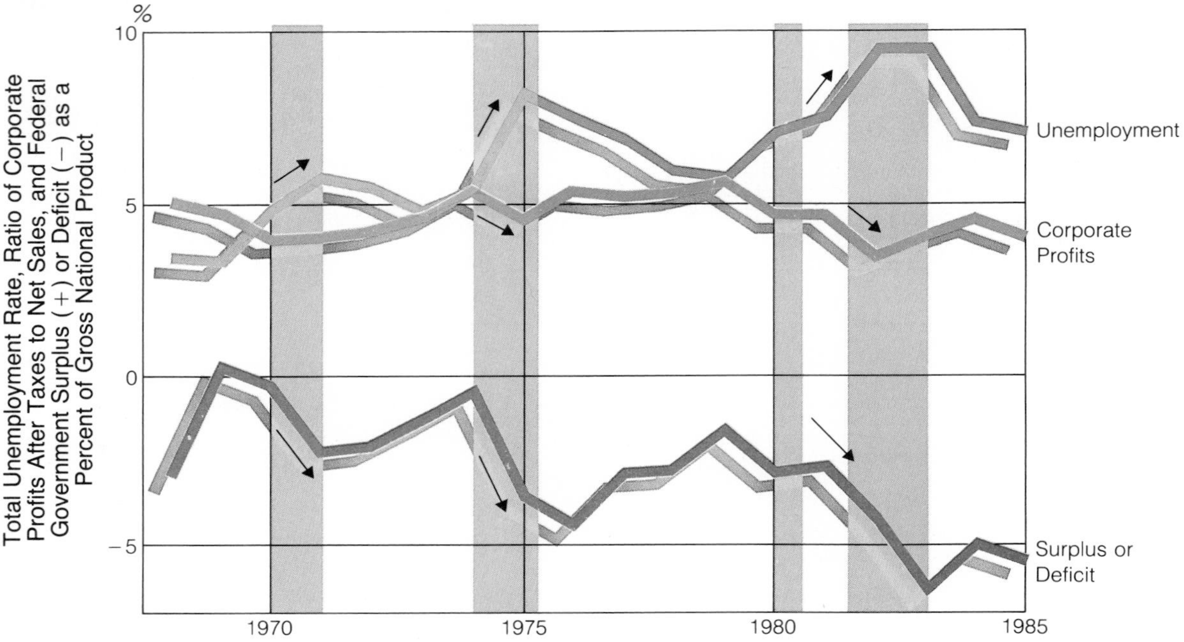

This figure illustrates the effect of automatic tax adjustments when unemployment increases or the economy enters a recession. A downturn in economic activity causes unemployment to rise, which causes personal income and corporate profits to decline (or their rates of growth to decline). Our progressive tax structure then causes tax revenues to decline more than proportionally. This, coupled with the expansion of government transfer payments, results in rising budget deficits. In this figure, recessions are shaded.

Source: *Economic Report of the President,* 1986.

Automatic Tax Adjustments

Personal and corporate income taxes are both very closely related to income. In prosperous times when National Income is rising, federal revenues from progressive corporate and personal income taxes rise as well, and more than proportionally. Corporate profits are the most sensitive of all incomes to swings in economic activity. A 10 percent decline in National Income may totally wipe out corporate profits, while a 10 percent increase may cause profits to double or even triple, as illustrated in Figure 4. Thus, tax revenues from corporate profits are highly cyclical.

Our progressive personal income tax structure is the main reason why tax collections rise or fall proportionally faster than does income. This process acts as an automatic stabilizer during inflationary episodes because as income rises, tax collections rise even faster and the overall rate of withdrawal from

the economy increases. The rate of increase in nominal income is slowed as withdrawals rise. This effect is partially offset today because Congress indexed personal income tax *rates* to inflation beginning in 1985. Just the opposite occurs when the economy enters a recession. Tax revenues tumble even faster than gross income falls, swelling the deficits as shown in Figure 4. Deficits tend to grow as the economy enters a recession and shrink or (rarely) become surpluses when the economy turns up.

Automatic Changes in Spending

Transfer payments rise during recessions and bolster Aggregate Spending by keeping consumption up because disposable income does not fall as fast as gross income does. More people are eligible for welfare payments when times are hard. People retire earlier during recessions and later during booms. Consequently, Social Security payments buffer the economy against both downturns and inflationary expansion. Unemployment compensation is another built-in stabilizer because workers' incomes do not drop to zero when they are laid off. Consumption by unemployed workers' families would plummet during widespread layoffs without unemployment compensation, and economic downturns would be worse than they are. The Great Depression would probably have been far less severe had our modern automatic stabilizers been in effect.

Falling tax collections and rising transfer payments during downturns help consumers maintain their previous levels of consumption. The easier it is for households to maintain consumption, the less will be the momentum of any decline in gross income. Just how powerful are the automatic stabilizers in our economy? Although they are insufficient to completely offset strong pressures for a recession, they do tend to slow abrupt changes in the economy and give policymakers more time to formulate discretionary policy. Some studies suggest that declines in income during recent recessions would have been from one-third to one-half more severe in the absence of automatic stabilizers. Unfortunately, automatic stabilizers may be a mixed blessing.

Fiscal Drag

When the economy is booming and potential income is growing rapidly, our built-in stabilizers may retard actual economic growth, a problem Keynesians refer to as **fiscal drag.** Fiscal drag occurs with any increase in GNP.

Suppose that the economy is at full employment and the government is running a balanced budget. Since our economy is a growing one, income can be expected to increase. With no changes in government spending or tax rates, higher National Income stimulates rising tax revenues; a budget surplus may even emerge and grow. This ballooning surplus hinders growth in disposable income and, hence, in Aggregate Expenditures—withdrawals grow but injections do not. The lag in Aggregate Spending may retard economic growth. Cuts in tax rates or increased government spending may unshackle the economy and let it grow. Both of these approaches are politically popular, so Keynesian policies to counter potential recessions pass through Congress quickly.

You often may have wondered why government spending and deficits seem to grow each year. One reason may be the desire of dedicated politicians to overcome the effects of fiscal drag. Further, it is not difficult for Congress or any president to find worthy projects. Most of us can think of areas where we would like to see the government spend more money or where we would like to cut taxes.

The Full Employment Budget

To this point, we have treated government surpluses or deficits as inconsequential in themselves, having importance only to the extent that they stimulate or dampen Aggregate Spending. However, the suggestion that the federal budget be balanced annually receives a lot of popular support and has been proposed as a constitutional amendment. Imbedded in the appealing notion of balancing the budget are some serious pitfalls. A surplus or deficit in the federal budget may be more a symptom of economic distress than a result of intentional fiscal policy. As we just discussed, automatic stabilizers in our economy cause tax revenues to fall and government spending to rise during economic downturns, resulting in mounting budgetary deficits. Conversely, when the economy mushrooms into unsustainable and inflationary growth, budgetary surpluses may emerge as tax revenues surge and government welfare spending drops.

Does the Actual Budget Reflect the Thrust of Policy?

If the economy slides into a recession, should taxes be raised and government spending cut to balance the budget? If inflation looms, should we cut taxes or raise spending to balance the budget? The government deficit or surplus is affected by the level of GNP as well as by discretionary fiscal policy, so we cannot judge the appropriateness of policy merely by seeing whether we have an actual budget deficit or surplus.

Economists who were perplexed by this problem developed the concept of the **full employment budget.** The question addressed is, "If our economy was approximately at full employment, what would be the amount of budgetary surplus or deficit, given current tax structures and government spending programs?" If the economy is well below full employment, answering this question entails adding the extra tax revenues that would be collected if the economy moved to full employment and then subtracting the current outlays on unemployment benefits and other transfers caused by cyclical unemployment.

Government transfer payments can be treated as *negative* taxes (*negative* because the government pays people), which decline in importance as National Income rises. Figure 5 illustrates various possible relationships between **net taxes** (tax revenues minus transfer payments) and government purchases under three alternative tax structures. Notice that the

FIGURE 5 *The Full Employment Budget*

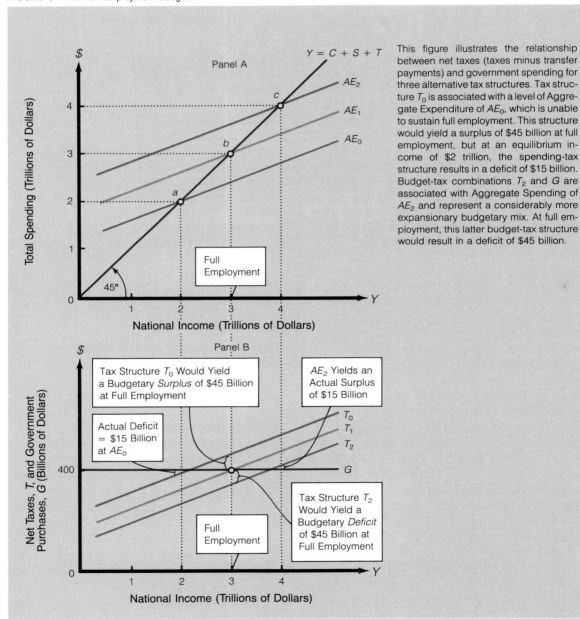

This figure illustrates the relationship between net taxes (taxes minus transfer payments) and government spending for three alternative tax structures. Tax structure T_0 is associated with a level of Aggregate Expenditure of AE_0, which is unable to sustain full employment. This structure would yield a surplus of $45 billion at full employment, but at an equilibrium income of $2 trillion, the spending-tax structure results in a deficit of $15 billion. Budget-tax combinations T_2 and G are associated with Aggregate Spending of AE_2 and represent a considerably more expansionary budgetary mix. At full employment, this latter budget-tax structure would result in a deficit of $45 billion.

tax functions are all positively sloped; net taxes rise as income rises. We will assume that the noninflationary full employment level of income is $3 trillion and that government purchases of goods and services (G) are independent of income.

Very high tax rates may be associated with a level of Aggregate Spending that is inadequate for full employment. This is the case with tax structure T_0 and Aggregate Expenditures AE_0, which together yield equilibrium at point a in the Panel A of Figure 5. Because tax rates are high, the *full employment* budget is in surplus to the tune of $45 billion; however, the actual budget at equilibrium ($2 trillion income) is $15 billion in deficit in this example.

Contrast this with the budgetary mix of G and tax structure T_2. Simultaneous inflationary pressures and budgetary surpluses coexist if Aggregate Spending is AE_2 and the tax schedule is T_2; there is equilibrium at point c, and a realized budgetary surplus of $15 billion. This budget combination yields a deficit of $45 billion at full employment (ignoring inflationary pressure). The full employment budget is in deficit and is considerably more expansionary than that represented by G and T_0. Finally, a budget combination that will result in a full employment balanced budget is represented by the tax schedule T_1, which yields Aggregate Expenditures AE_1. Deficits result below full employment, while surpluses are generated above full employment.

Suppose Aggregate Spending is excessive because tax rates are quite low. If the Aggregate Expenditure curve is AE_2 and the tax curve is T_2, there is a substantial budget surplus. If we follow a rule of perpetually balancing the budget, we would cut taxes and raise spending. This is a bad policy, certain to accelerate any inflationary tendencies. Fiscal policy of either raising tax rates or cutting spending can cure this inflation by temporarily creating a budget surplus.

During inflation, however, many voters react harshly to any proposal that "the cost of government, in addition to other prices, should be raised." On the other hand, the beneficiaries of public programs, including those whose livelihoods depend on government contracts, vigorously fight slashes in budgets because they perceive inflation as shrinking their real income. In fact, political opposition to spending cuts or tax hikes is now so intense that we need not worry about the simultaneous occurrence of actual surpluses and inflation.

The reverse situation is a budget structure yielding a full employment surplus but an actual budget deficit because tax rates are so high that the economy is stuck well below full employment; fiscal drag is quite powerful. Some analysts have suggested that the sluggish American economy of the late 1950s and the early 1980s suffered from this malady.

The critical point to be made by this section is that huge deficits do not imply a very expansionary tilt to fiscal policy, nor are large surpluses evidence of contractionary policies. Deficits may arise because high tax rates produce a sick economy. Congress can only set tax *rates;* it cannot dictate the resulting tax *revenues.*

Structural and Cyclical Deficits

This concept of a full employment budget can help us split the actual budget deficit into two distinct components that reflect different reasons for it. The **structural deficit** results directly from the mix of tax and spending decisions that Congress and the president enact. A structural deficit (a synonym for a full employment deficit) is the deficit that would have resulted if the economy were at full employment, given existing tax and spending structures. A **cyclical deficit** occurs when there is excessive slack in our economy. As economic conditions deteriorate, the cyclical (and actual) budget deficit worsens, and vice versa.

The composition of the actual budget deficit is illustrated in Figure 6. Suppose that government spending and net taxes are G_0 and T_0, respectively, and that the economy is currently at a full employment equilibrium real income of $1,500 billion. Thus, the structural deficit is $100 billion ($300 − $200 billion, distance ab in Figure 6). If the economy went into a slump without any change in federal policy and real output fell to $1,400 billion, the deficit would increase to $150 billion (distance cd). Of this, $100 billion would be structural (distance ed) and $50 billion would be cyclical (distance ce). Similarly, if the economy moved to $1,600 billion, the resulting deficit would be $50 billion less than the structural deficit of $100 billion because the growing economy produced added tax revenues of $50 billion. Given the existing tax and spending structure, a balanced budget would require an equilibrium income of $1,700 billion. Finally, if Congress enacted a reduction in the tax rates (illustrated by a shift in the Net

FIGURE 6 *The Structural Deficit and the Cyclical Deficit*

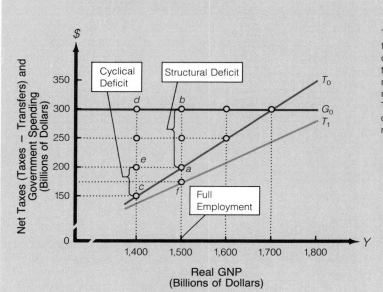

The actual budget deficit can be split into two components, a structural and cyclical component. The structural deficit is the deficit that would exist at full employment given the existing mix of government spending and tax rate structures. The cyclical deficit is due to economic circumstances that prevent full employment.

Tax curve from T_0 to T_1), the structural deficit would grow to $125 billion (distance *fb*). Recent estimates place the structural deficit at nearly two-thirds of the actual deficit and growing.[4]

In summary, the actual deficit is determined by the fiscal policy mix of the federal government and the state of the economy. Expansionary fiscal policy creates structural deficits, and depressed economic conditions create cyclical deficits.[5]

Fiscal Policy and Supply-Side Economics

Keynesian analysis recognizes the possibility that high tax rates may stifle an economy because they reduce disposable income and spending. Classical economics, under the modern name of **supply-side economics**, points to another way high tax rates may be harmful.

The Laffer Curve

There is a danger that very high tax rates may result in severe disincentives against work effort and private investment, causing actual GNP and tax revenues to fall. This idea has been traced back to a financial advisor to an Egyptian pharaoh. Arthur Laffer, a prominent supply-sider, explained this concept to a journalist after dinner at a restaurant in Washington, D.C.—illustrating his point which is now known as the Laffer curve.

The basic idea behind the **Laffer curve** is that very low tax rates might be increased to generate increases in tax revenues, but eventually a heavily tax-burdened population will decide that the extra effort necessary to generate extra income is not worth it. If Uncle Sam's bite is too fierce, many taxpayers will choose leisure over additional work and will consume immediately from income instead of saving and investing. Some may also divert more of

4. William Beeman, Jacob Dreyer, and Paul Van de Water, "Dimensions of the Deficit Problem," in Phillip Cagan (ed.), *Essays in Contemporary Economic Problems, 1985: The Economy in Deficit* (Washington, D.C.: American Enterprise Institute, 1985).

5. The rising structural deficit of the 1970s and 1980s was not totally independent of changing economic conditions. Beeman et al. suggest that the reduced rate of productivity growth in the last two decades has added to rising structural deficits.

their activities into the underground economy. A modified Laffer curve is shown in Figure 7.

Supply-siders argue that high tax rates erode incentives to work and to invest, so that the income shrinks as tax rates climb. This means that given tax revenues might be generated by both a high tax rate and a low one. In the example diagrammed in Figure 7, marginal tax rates (the percentage taxes paid on small amounts of extra income) that average either 15 percent or 75 percent yield tax revenues of $100 billion, while a marginal tax rate that averages X percent yields $200 billion to the tax collector. Any increase in marginal tax rates over X percent actually causes tax collections to fall.

What will people do if high marginal income tax rates reduce the advantages of working and of saving to invest? Like classical economists, many supply-side economists see little difference between saving and investing. Keynes argued that, in a modern monetary economy, savers and investors are very distinct groups with very different motives. Savers seek security, while investors bear risks and seek profits. As a result, savings may not necessarily be invested.

Potential workers may respond to high tax rates by engaging in many more nonmarket activities, such as do-it-yourself projects. Potential savers and investors will realize less interest income and profit if marginal tax rates are high; therefore, they will consume more currently, forgoing future consumption. Evidence of this sort of behavior was provided when wealthy people in Britain went on shopping sprees in the 1970s, buying fur coats and Rolls-Royces. It was not worthwhile to invest because of high inflation and high British tax rates on investment incomes. The British economy stagnated while areas of London where high society gathered abounded with conspicuous consumption of luxury goods.

Some economists believe the United States has been in the outer region of the Laffer curve and advocate reductions in taxes to eliminate major impediments to work effort and investment. They believe reduced tax rates will simultaneously stimulate economic growth and generate higher tax revenues. This idea picked up a lot of converts in the past decade, including Ronald Reagan. Congress enacted a 5 percent tax cut in 1981, an additional 10 percent cut in 1982, and another 10 percent cut in 1983. Between 1980 and 1985, federal revenues rose over 30 percent, but government outlays grew by nearly

FIGURE 7 The Laffer Curve

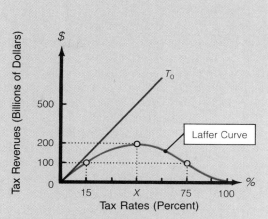

If the tax base were unaffected by the tax rate, tax revenues would be exactly proportional to tax rates and could be graphed as a straight line, such as T_0. Declines in the tax base that result when people legally avoid taxed behavior or illegally evade taxes cause the base to erode, so that tax revenues actually reach a peak and then decline.

twice that amount, resulting in record budget deficits. This occurred partly because tax revenues were held down by a depressed economy and partly because Congress and the Reagan Administration were unwilling to reduce the growth in federal spending.[6]

Before we move on, notice that Keynesians have no difficulty in believing the general form of the Laffer curve, but dispute the reasons for this problem. Supply-siders blame declines in tax revenues as tax rates rise on reduced incentives to supply goods and services. Keynesians perceive high tax rates and fiscal drag as smothering Aggregate Spending. Admitting that high tax rates also inhibit supply incentives, Keynesians still perceive most macroeconomic problems as originating from the demand side, while supply-siders see high tax rate disincentives as more powerful on the supply side.

---

6. In *The Triumph of Politics: Why the Reagan Revolution Failed* (New York: Harper & Row, 1986), former Budget Director David Stockman documents political reluctance to slash any government spending programs. Even politicians who constantly attack "big government" appear to fear the backlash from voters whose pet programs are cut.

Government Purchases and Transfer Payments: The Supply Side

Keynesians view government purchases as direct sources of Aggregate Spending and transfer payments as quickly translated by recipients into new consumer spending. Supply-siders perceive this concentration on demand as shortsighted and worry about the incentive effects of government programs. Their reasoning goes like this: Modern government provides school lunch programs, public parks and highways, medical care for the poor and the aged, subsidized housing and transportation, and a host of other goods. There is less incentive to sacrifice our time by working and less net gain from investing if the government guarantees us a reasonably comfortable life by providing many of its necessities.

Transfer payments are viewed as a problem for two reasons. First, those who are taxed lose the incentive to work and invest. Second, those who receive transfer payments also suffer from disincentives to work or save. (Would you work as hard if you were forced to give your neighbors 20 percent of your income? Would your neighbors?) According to some supply-side advocates, *extensive* government purchases and transfer payments trap low-income individuals in a rut from which escape is almost impossible; they are discouraged from work effort and from trying to improve their economic status.

In conclusion, **supply-side fiscal policy** focuses on the long run and views massive government spending as embodying disincentives that dampen Aggregate Supply; Keynesians focus on curing short-run problems and see activist fiscal policy as being needed to augment Aggregate Demand. Specific differences between these schools of thought are summarized in Table 4. Now we will review a little of the history of fiscal policy.

TABLE 4 *The Effects of Fiscal Policy*

Policy Change	Keynesian (Short-Run) View of Effect	Classical Supply-Sider (Long-Run) View of Effect
Tax policy Increase *(decrease)* tax revenues	Reduces *(increases)* Aggregate Spending via a tax multiplier because consumers have less *(more)* disposable income.	Reduces *(raises)* Aggregate Supply because workers and investors have fewer *(more)* incentives to produce.
Raise *(lower)* tax rates	Generates more *(less)* revenue for government unless fiscal drag smothers Aggregate Spending, in which case, higher *(lower)* tax rates may generate less *(more)* revenues. If an economy is in a recession, higher tax rates may also worsen the state of the economy and actually reduce tax revenues because high taxes dampen consumer spending.	Reduces *(raises)* Aggregate Supply because of incentive effects. Disincentives from very high tax rates may cut Aggregate Supply so much that tax revenues fall, a possibility shown in the upper region of a Laffer curve.
Government purchases Raise *(lower)*	Raises *(lowers)* Aggregate Spending and income both directly and through a multiplier effect. (Demand creates its own supply.)	Reduces (expands) Aggregate Supply because people have fewer *(more)* incentives to produce and generate income if the government does more *(less)* for them. (Supply creates its own demand.)
Transfer payments Raise *(lower)*	Increases *(reduces)* Aggregate Spending and income by the multiplier process. Transfer payments can be thought of as negative taxes, to which the tax multiplier **(−mpc/mps)** can be applied.	Reduces *(raises)* the incentives of both transfer (tax) payers and transfer receivers, so Aggregate Supply is diminished *(raised)*.

FIGURE 8 *The Tax Increase of 1932*

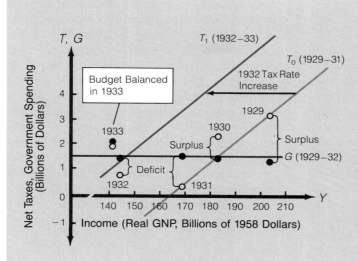

This figure uses Keynesian analysis to examine the effects of tax increases in 1932. Actual government purchases and net taxes (taxes minus transfers) are traced graphically from 1929 to 1933. A modest deficit in 1931 persuaded Congress and President Hoover to increase tax rates in 1932 in an attempt to balance the budget. Unfortunately, the result was a shift in the net tax function to the left and a reduction in equilibrium income. It was small comfort that by 1933 (the trough of the Depression), the budget was balanced. While other factors were at work during the Great Depression, this tax increase certainly worsened the problem. *Note*: ● denotes government purchases of goods and services; ○ denotes taxes minus transfer payments. Source: *Economic Report of the President*, 1986.

Fiscal Policy in Action

For almost half a century, changes in tax rates and spending by government have been viewed by Keynesians as cures for macroeconomic problems. The conventional wisdom before the Keynesian Revolution was that taxation and spending should be adjusted to balance the actual budget at all times. Then the economy would automatically adjust to a noninflationary full employment equilibrium. A problem with putting this idea into practice is that higher tax rates may yield lower tax revenues, and vice versa, because of the influence of tax rates on our major tax base—income. Failure to understand this led President Hoover and the Congress to raise tax rates in 1932, exacerbating the economic collapse of 1929–33. The success of expansionary fiscal policy in the mid-1960s also hinged on this relationship between tax rates and tax revenues.

The Tax Increase of 1932

Keynesians and modern "supply-siders" argue that a fetish for balancing the budget was one reason why the economy, following what should have been a minor recession in 1929, continued tumbling downwards until 1933. Their explanation for the intensity

and duration of the Great Depression is that President Hoover and the Congress reacted to a minor recession-caused deficit (like the $15 billion for AE_0 and T_0 in Figure 5 on page 208) by raising tax rates. This caused National Income and tax revenues to fall further, which resulted in still higher tax rates in attempts to balance the budget, and so on.

Figure 8 presents the actual relationships between expenditures and net tax revenues (after subtracting transfers) to real Gross National Product for 1929–33. We have superimposed curves showing government spending and taxes before and after the tax rate increase of 1932. This tax increase was designed to generate roughly one-third more revenue in fiscal 1932 than in 1931. Policymakers failed to realize that higher tax rates could force GNP down. Keynesians interpret Figure 8 as evidence that the massive withdrawal of funds arising from these higher tax rates led to much of the severity of the Great Depression. Some modern supply-siders see this as proof that, even in the 1930s, high tax rates strangled Aggregate Supply.

The Tax Cut of 1964–65

Keynesians recommend tax rate cuts or increased government purchases when a recession causes even a slight cyclical budget deficit. In the example illustrated in Figure 5, cutting tax rates from T_0 to T_1 raises Aggregate Spending to AE_1, tax revenues increase to $400 billion at an income level of $3 trillion, and the federal budget is balanced. Notice that tax collections actually increase in response to cuts in tax rates.

The idea that cutting tax rates might stimulate Aggregate Spending so that both National Income and tax revenues would rise first gained wide acceptance in the early 1960s. President Kennedy's Council of Economic Advisors perceived the 1950s as a period of slow economic growth and stagnation caused by high tax rates that created severe fiscal drag. They argued that substantial reductions in tax rates would stimulate substantial growth, reduce unemployment and poverty, and generate higher tax revenues. In 1964, a massive tax cut engineered by President Kennedy and enacted during the Johnson Administration supported these predictions. These tax cuts were sold politically largely based on Keynesian (demand-side) reasoning, although Arthur Laffer has pointed out that supply-side arguments were also used.

The 1964–65 tax cuts were broad-based reductions in income tax rates. Personal income tax rates were reduced from brackets of 18–91 percent to 14–70 percent. Corporate taxes for corporate incomes over $25,000 were cut from 52 to 48 percent. The results of this experiment with broad-based cuts in tax rates are shown in Figure 9. The economy, and hence, the tax base, expanded so rapidly that the 1964 deficit actually gave way to a small surplus in

1965. Supply-siders naturally interpret the success of these policies as evidence that the economy was on the wrong side of the Laffer curve and that growth was stimulated as Aggregate Supply grew.

These examples have shown that putting fiscal policy to work is more complex than our simple theory suggests. Whether changes in tax rates will reduce budget deficits often depends on the state of the economy and the level of tax rates themselves. Tax rate reductions may stimulate economic growth but, in the short run, revenues may not grow sufficiently. This can result in soaring budget deficits, as President Reagan discovered in the early 1980s. The Kennedy round of tax cuts suggests that if the economy is poised for growth, tax cuts may simultaneously stimulate growth and reduce deficits.

Functional Finance Versus Balanced Budgets

In the past, the success of fiscal policy has typically been measured by low rates of unemployment and inflation. Recently, however, the budget deficit has taken a front row seat. Should the federal budget be balanced continuously or only over the business cycle? Or is the question of balancing the budget irrelevant? Each of these positions finds some adherents among politicians, economists, and the public at large.

FIGURE 9 *The 1964–65 Tax Cut*

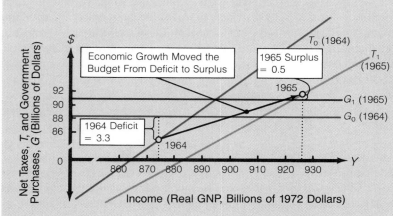

In 1964–65, tax rates were cut substantially, shifting the net tax schedule from T_0 to T_1. Income, employment, and tax revenues rose, converting a deficit in 1964 into a small surplus in 1965. Source: *Economic Report of the President,* 1986.

Balancing Budgets Annually

Most of those who advocate continually balancing the budget do so for political reasons because they favor a minimal role for government. Their view is that an amendment to our Constitution requiring a balanced budget would force Congress to limit its spending. Regardless of whether or not you agree that government should be limited, however, you should recognize that a balanced-budget amendment does open up some dangerous possibilities.

We might find ourselves confronted with Herbert Hoover's dilemma if we ever adopt a rule about balancing the budget every year. If National Income began falling, tax revenues would fall. At the same time, rising unemployment would mandate higher outlays for unemployment compensation and other public assistance programs. How might we balance the budget in the face of potential massive deficits? Raising tax rates would result in substantial declines in both Aggregate Supply and Aggregate Spending and might cause tax revenues to fall. Attempts to slash government spending might even cause National income to fall so much that tax revenues would fall even more than the spending reduction, worsening any deficit. Very few economists are convinced that fiscal policy has absolutely no effect on National Income, and even fewer are advocates of rigidly balanced budgets.

Balanced Budgets Over the Business Cycle

A more sophisticated view recognizes the problems for economic stability posed by an annually balanced budget. This proposal is to balance the budget *over the business cycle.* Its advocates realize that we should not raise taxes or cut spending to cover cyclical deficits caused by recessions, or liquidate inflation-caused surpluses through tax cuts or hikes in spending. This group contends that cyclical deficits should be offset by surpluses collected during periods of prosperity. Thus, over a complete business cycle, there would be no growth in the level of the amount of national debt issued by the U.S. Treasury.

A major problem with this approach is that we have no assurance that periods of prosperity will be long enough or strong enough to permit the generation of surpluses sufficient to offset deficits, especially if periods of recession tend to be either extended or especially severe. Our economy might equilibrate around a lower average level of income than might otherwise be sustainable.

Functional Finance

Most Keynesian economists are adherents of "activist" fiscal policies. They argue that we need to balance the economy at a full employment level and that the effect on the national debt of balancing or not balancing the budget is irrelevant. In this view, injections (investment plus government spending) need to be set so that, at a high rate of capacity utilization, they equal withdrawals (saving plus taxes). The mix that works best should be used; taxes and government spending never need to balance precisely.

This **functional finance** approach emphasizes that taxation is only one way to finance government spending. How best to pay for government spending depends on which policies are least costly under existing economic conditions. Taxation to cover new government spending is the least expansionary of all alternatives and is most appropriate when the economy is close to full employment. If the Treasury covers a deficit through borrowing, the people who buy government bonds may reduce their spending somewhat. This is still a more expansionary method for financing government outlays than is taxation. (In Chapter 15, we will explore an even more expansionary possibility—printing money to cover a deficit.)

The Ability to Control Government Spending

After his first inauguration, President Reagan found that substantially reducing the federal budget was an overwhelming task. Doing so quickly seemed virtually impossible. **Relatively uncontrollable outlays** are those which can neither be increased nor decreased by presidential decisions without a change in existing federal laws or those which are beyond administrative control. (Examples would be benefit payments that beneficiaries are entitled to by law or contractual agreements and other existing binding commitments.) Many enormous items in the federal budget are continuing programs that Congress is legally obligated to fund. For example, Social Security payments are guaranteed by law to recipi-

FIGURE 10 *Controllability of Budget Outlays (Percent of Outlays)*

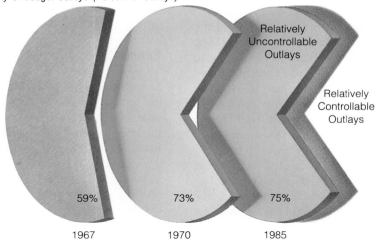

Relatively
Uncontrollable
Outlays

Relatively
Controllable
Outlays

59%   73%   75%

1967   1970   1985

Many public spending programs are virtually uncontrollable. Programs such as Social Security, Medicare, long-term transportation, defense, and public works projects are examples. These uncontrollable programs are largely exempt from discretionary fiscal policy. As this figure illustrates, the proportion of the budget that is relatively uncontrollable is growing and is estimated at more than three quarters of the current budget. For those policymakers bent on reducing the federal budget, the choice of areas to make cuts is becoming more circumscribed each year.

Source: The Conference Board, "Federal Budget," *Economic Road Maps;* and U.S. Department of Commerce, *Statistical Abstract of the United States,* 1986.

ents, commitments for Medicare funding were made by the Congress years ago, and contracts for some transportation or defense systems take years to complete. Moreover, the government's legal obligations to provide public assistance, to operate the Post Office, to regulate pollution and industrial safety—the list seems to go on forever—are long-term commitments that simply cannot be abandoned during short periods of time.

Suppose that we view all defense spending as capable of being cut and try to identify all civilian programs over which any single Congress has budgetary control. Estimates by the Conference Board, a research organization, indicate that roughly one-fourth of all government outlays were relatively easy to control by Congress in fiscal year 1985. Moreover, as Figure 10 shows, the ability of Congress to easily control its spending has declined since the 1960s. In 1967, roughly 60 percent of all outlays were relatively uncontrollable, compared to 75 percent today.

In 1985, Congress adopted an extraordinary measure in an attempt to control soaring deficits: the Gramm-Rudman-Hollings Deficit Reduction Act set specific deficit reduction targets. If these targets were not met, "across-the-board" cuts in spending were

mandated. However, many parts of the budget were excluded from the across-the-board cuts, including many in the categories the Conference Board had labeled relatively uncontrollable. It would appear that despite the threat of Gramm-Rudman, many areas of federal spending are still relatively uncontrollable. Cold comfort, indeed, for those who would like to reduce the size of government!

The Budget Deficits of the 1980s

The American economy followed a rocky path through the 1970s, with budget deficits at new record levels almost each year. (Our most recent budget surplus was experienced in fiscal year 1968–69.) By the late 1970s, discomfort with the growth of federal spending had reached epidemic levels. Congress and Ronald Reagan tried numerous measures to reduce the impact of government in the economy. It proved, however, far harder for Congress to restrain spending growth than revenue growth. The result has been persistent $200 billion deficits, with high levels forecasted into the early 1990s.

Budget Deficits and the Reagan Administration

Many observers blamed Keynesian fiscal policies for the rising deficits, inflation, and unemployment of the 1970s and saw classical (supply-side) economics as the remedy. President Reagan sought, and the Congress passed, a 25 percent tax cut in 1981, phased in over three years. At the same time, eligibility for transfer payments was tightened, and nonmilitary government spending was slowed sharply. Advocates of these policies hoped to stimulate Aggregate Supply so much that inflation and unemployment would fall quickly. They also hoped that tax revenues would be so responsive to economic growth that persistent budget deficits would abate.

The short-term effects of this supply-side approach, shown in Figure 11, were below the optimistic predictions that had accompanied the adoption of supply-side policies. Monetary policy sharply reduced inflation in 1981–83 and as a result, unemployment rose and the economy didn't recover until 1983. Federal budget deficits hovered around the $200 billion mark, and forecasts for continued high deficits provided the pressure needed to pass the Gramm-Rudman Act in 1985. As Figure 11 illustrates, the 1981–83 tax rate reductions appeared to have shifted the net tax function downward and to the right, increasing the structural deficit. By 1986, solid economic growth, low inflation, and falling interest rates reduced budget deficit estimates, making the initial Gramm-Rudman cuts less severe.

The Gramm-Rudman-Hollings Balanced-Budget Law

Our national debt topped $2 trillion in 1986, and the first cuts mandated by the Gramm-Rudman Deficit Reduction Act kicked in. Critics of Gramm-Rudman charged that it makes federal spending a captive of some deficit target instead of making the deficit the result of congressionally determined spending.

Gramm-Rudman limited the fiscal year 1986 deficit to be no more than $171.9 billion and the 1987 deficit to only $144 billion. In the four fiscal years after 1987, the targeted federal deficit is reduced

FIGURE 11 *The 1981–84 Tax Cuts and the Structural Deficit*

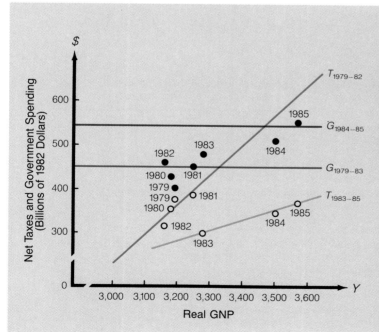

President Reagan sought and received tax rate reductions between 1981 and 1983 that appear to have increased the structural deficit. Increased government spending coupled with a flatter net tax function ($T_{1983-85}$), has resulted in swelling deficits. *Note*: ● denotes government purchases of goods and services; ○ denotes taxes minus transfer payments.

Source: *Economic Report of the President, 1986.*

by $36 billion until it is zero in 1991. The law sets up specific processes to enable agreement between Congress and the administration on a deficit-reduction package. If Congress and the president are unable to reach an agreement, there are automatic selective spending cuts.

Half of these spending cuts come from defense spending and the other half from domestic social programs. Several large components of federal spending, however, are legally exempted from any reductions, including Social Security, food stamps, some long-term defense contracts, and, of course, interest payments on the national debt. Limits were also placed on the automatic reductions in selected health programs such as Medicare.

Required spending cuts are to be based on deficit projections provided jointly by the Congressional Budget Office (CBO) and the Office of Management and Budget (OMB). Their joint projection is then submitted to the Comptroller General, who is the head of the Congressional General Accounting Office (GAO). Next, the GAO issues a report to the president specifying the cuts necessary to meet the deficit goal. Spending cuts then take effect the next fiscal year, which provides Congress and the president time to reach a compromise. The budget processes and timetable outlined in the Gramm-Rudman Act are detailed in Table 5.

Critics of Gramm-Rudman argue that the official estimates of the deficit should be adjusted downward to reflect the impact of inflation on the national debt. Robert Eisner has calculated that, with a $2 trillion national debt and an inflation rate of 4 percent, the value of the debt to those who own it falls approximately $75 billion a year.[7] He argues that the deficit reported should be reduced annually by roughly that amount. Eisner also points out that much of the deficit is the result of capital spending, not spending on current services. He believes this is an outdated accounting practice, long abandoned by business, and it causes overstatement of the real deficit.

Other critics contend that reducing the deficit too rapidly could lead us into a disastrous recession, putting further pressures on the deficit that may require further spending cuts and so on. Herbert Hoover attempted to balance the budget in 1932, plunging the economy further into the Depression. Others argue that a balanced budget is unduly restrictive, suggesting a compromise that would limit the deficit so that it could not grow faster than GNP.

---

7. Robert Eisner and Paul J. Pieper, "A New View of the Federal Debt and Budget Deficits," *American Economic Review*, March 1984, pp. 11–29, and testimony before the Joint Economic Committee of Congress on January 16, 1986.

TABLE 5 *The Gramm-Rudman Budget Process (1987–91)*

The Gramm-Rudman Act established budgeting deadlines that overlap with the traditional Congressional budget process.

First Monday after	
January 3	President submits budget for next fiscal year (begins October 1). Cost-of-living increases are deferred until it is determined that automatic spending cuts are unnecessary.
April 15	Congress completes action on the budget resolution for the next fiscal year.
June 15	Congress reconciles appropriations with targets set by the budget resolution.
June 30	The House finishes the annual appropriations bills for the next fiscal year. (There is no deadline for action by the Senate.)
August 20	The Congressional Budget Office (CBO) and the Office of Management and Budget (OMB) submit the joint deficit estimate to the Government Accounting Office (GAO).
August 25	If the deficit ceiling is exceeded, the GAO issues a report to the president detailing the automatic spending cuts necessary to comply with the law.
September 1	President issues automatic spending cut order.
October 1	Fiscal year begins. Automatic spending cuts take effect unless Congress and the president have reached an alternative budget that meets the Gramm-Rudman deficit target.
October 5	The OMB and CBO issue their final deficit projection to the GAO.
October 10	The GAO revised report is sent to the president.
October 15	The president issues the final order for automatic spending cuts.

Source: *Facts on File*, February 5, 1986.

For several reasons, all of the hoopla surrounding Gramm-Rudman may be wasted effort. First, within hours after Gramm-Rudman became law, it was challenged in the courts. In February of 1986, a federal district court ruled that the automatic spending cut process (especially the role of the Comptroller General—see Table 5) was an unconstitutional delegation of executive power. The Gramm-Rudman Act, however, contains a fallback provision because Congress anticipated this constitutional challenge. Congress is required to pass a binding budget resolution and submit it to the president. If the Supreme Court affirms the lower court's ruling, this might ". . . take the guts out of the law," as one lawmaker observed.

Second, falling interest rates, collapsing oil prices, lower inflation rates, and sharp reductions in the international value of the dollar all brighten our prospects for economic prosperity. If these conditions continue to prevail, budget deficit projections may fall, making any cuts far more palatable to Congress.

This chapter has examined government spending and tax policies from both Keynesian and supply-side perspectives. We have seen that the structure of government spending and taxation play an important role for achieving economic growth and price stability. Our next task is to examine the macroeconomic role of monetary policy.

CHAPTER REVIEW: KEY POINTS

1. *Keynesian fiscal policy* is the use of federal spending and tax policies to stimulate or contract Aggregate Spending and economic activity to offset cyclical fluctuations. *Classical (supply-side) fiscal policies* rely on low tax rates and minimal government spending to allow Aggregate Supply to grow.

2. *Discretionary fiscal policy* consists of deliberate changes in federal government spending and taxation for stabilization purposes. *Nondiscretionary fiscal policy* refers to automatic stablizers (changes in spending and taxation that occur without congressional action) as economic conditions change, and often even before the need for Keynesian changes in discretionary policy is recognized.

3. Increases in government spending increase Aggregate Expenditures and National Income through the multiplier process in the same way as do changes in investment or autonomous consumer spending.

4. Changes in *net tax revenues* affect Aggregate Spending differently than do changes in government spending. Changes in net taxes directly affect disposable income and, therefore, saving. These effects are transmitted into spending through the *autonomous tax multiplier ($\Delta Y/\Delta T$)*. The tax multiplier is negative, and is weaker than the *autonomous spending multiplier ($\Delta Y/\Delta A$)*.

5. The *balanced-budget multiplier* equals one, suggesting that equal increases (*decreases*) in government spending and taxes will increase (*decrease*) Aggregate Spending and equilibrium income by an equal amount. This result follows from the fact that the autonomous tax multiplier ($-$**mpc/mps**) is one minus the autonomous spending multiplier.

6. *Automatic stabilizers* tend to cushion the economy. When income falls, automatic stabilizers keep the level of disposable income from falling as rapidly as income. Our progressive income tax causes tax collections to fall proportionally faster when income is falling and to increase proportionally faster when income is rising.

7. These built-in stabilizers can become a problem. When potential income is rising, automatic stabilizers brake the economy and slow the rate of growth. This problem is referred to as *fiscal drag*.

8. The *full employment budget* is the amount of surplus or deficit that would be generated at full employment with the existing tax and expenditure structure. The full employment budget is a way of estimating the expansionary or contractionary influence of any tax and expenditure mix.

9. The *Laffer curve* indicates that high tax rates may impose such large disincentives to productive effort that Aggregate Supply and tax revenues are both restricted.

10. Annually balancing the budget might result in incorrect fiscal actions to combat either inflation or recession. Some have suggested balancing the budget over the business cycle. This would entail running deficits during recessions and surpluses over the boom. Unfortunately, business cycles are not symmetric, and the budget may not be easy to balance over the cycle without hampering prosperity. Others believe that the size of the public debt is unimportant. They have suggested that we ignore the problem of balancing the budget and focus on balancing the economy instead.

11. Some government spending is uncontrollable (roughly three quarters today). These programs are long-range or are committed by law each and every year. Reducing these expenditures is virtually impossible.

12. *Structural deficits* result directly from the mix of spending and tax policies enacted by Congress. The *cyclical deficit* is attributable to business conditions. As unemployment grows, the cyclical deficit grows, and vice versa.

QUESTIONS FOR THOUGHT AND DISCUSSION

1. Calculate the autonomous spending multiplier, the autonomous tax multiplier, and the balanced-budget multiplier for values of the **mpc** equal to ½, ⅗, ⅔, ¾, ⅘, ⅚, 6/7, ⅞, 8/9, and 9/10.

2. Professional football teams sometimes trade their future draft choices for veteran players. In what sense is this like government financing current purchases through deficits? What are the crucial differences, if any, between the two situations in terms of future production?

3. The Kemp-Roth bill cut federal income tax rates by 25 percent in stages over the three years following its enactment in 1981. What happened to budget deficits over this period? By roughly what percentage would National Income need to have grown in order to have generated more revenues than would have oc-

curred without the tax cut? Do you think it likely that National Income would ever grow at such a rate?

4. Explain the sense in which federal taxes determine how much each of us will help control inflation. If you could print money, would you ever try to remove any from circulation as long as there were trees and green ink? Why? Then why does the federal government bother to collect taxes?

5. What are the similarities and differences between taxes and savings? Are these differences important for the purposes of determing National Income? Why or why not?

6. Do you think cuts in tax rates stimulate Aggregate Supply more than Aggregate Spending? Why or why not? Why is the answer to this question important in explaining what will happen to the price level?

OPTIONAL MATERIAL: MORE MATHEMATICS OF KEYNESIAN MULTIPLIERS

In our simple model of fiscal policy and equilibrium income, equal increases in government spending or cuts in taxes will have different effects on National Income and employment. Let us briefly review the analysis of tax multipliers, balanced-budget multipliers, and autonomous government spending multipliers. Then you will have a better perspective when you try to understand what the president and Congress are trying to do the next time a policy change is under consideration. You may benefit from trying to graph some of the discussion that follows.

The Autonomous Spending and Tax Multipliers

A recessionary gap can be eliminated (or an inflationary gap might be created) by increased autonomous spending. This will occur irrespective of whether it

comes from increased government spending, increased investment, increased autonomous consumption, or more autonomous exports. The autonomous spending multiplier applies to all these forms of spending; they are perfect substitutes for one another in their impacts on equilibrium income. Alternatively, tax cuts can be used to expand the economy. The autonomous tax multiplier equals one minus the autonomous spending multiplier. To see why, we will look at it algebraically.

We know that income is the sum of consumption, investment, government spending, and net exports: $Y = C + I + G + (X - M)$. We assume that taxes (T), investment (I_a), government purchases (G_a), net exports ($X_a - M_a$), and part of consumption (C_a) are autonomous and that $b(Y - T_a)$ is induced consumption (b equals the marginal propensity to consume from disposable income). Then:

$$Y = C_a + b(Y - T_a) + I_a + G_a + (X_a - M_a).$$

We define total autonomous spending as $A = C_a + I_a + G_a + (X_a - M_a)$. This leaves $Y = A + b(Y - T_a)$ or $Y = A + bY - bT_a$. Subtracting bY from both sides leaves $Y - bY = A - bT_a$. Simplifying by factoring Y out of the left side yields $Y(1 - b) = A - bT_a$. Dividing both sides by $1 - b$ gives the results we seek:

$$Y = A\left(\frac{1}{1 - b}\right) + T_a\left(\frac{-b}{1 - b}\right).$$

Translated into English, this equation means that aggregate income (Y) equals autonomous spending ($C_a + I_a + G_a + (X_a - M_a) = A$) times the autonomous spending multiplier [$1/(1 - b)$], plus the level of taxes (T_a) times the autonomous tax multiplier [$-b/(1 - b)$]. The autonomous tax multiplier [$-b/(1 - b)$] can be rewritten ($-\textbf{mpc}/\textbf{mps}$). Thus, if the spending multiplier is 5, the tax multiplier is -4; if the spending multiplier is 4, the tax multiplier is -3; and so on.

The Balanced-Budget Multiplier

All else equal, any changes in National Income can be traced to changes in autonomous spending or taxes:

$$\Delta Y = \Delta A\left(\frac{1}{1 - b}\right) + \Delta T\left(\frac{-b}{1 - b}\right).$$

If the **mpc** equals 0.8, the spending multiplier equals 5 and the tax multiplier equals -4. Thus:

$$\Delta Y = \Delta A(5) + \Delta T(-4).$$

If government spending and taxes each rise by $20 billion, total income also increases by $20 billion: $20 billion times 5 plus $20 billion times -4 equals $20 billion. We can generalize: Equal changes in autonomous government spending and taxes cause income to change in the same direction and by the same amount. The applicable multiplier is termed the *balanced-budget multiplier* and always equals one.

Why don't equal increases in government spending and taxes exactly offset each other? The change in income from such a policy results because the first-round effect of a $1 increase in government spend-

ing is to increase income by $1. The autonomous spending multiplier then applies. However, while the first-round effect of the $1 increase in taxes is to cut disposable income by $1, gross pretax income is not affected. Hence, the multiplied effect does not apply to income until the next round, when the taxpayers' spending falls by $1(0.8) = $0.80. This example suggests that if both government purchases and taxes are increased by $1, then, because the balanced-budget multiplier equals one, equilibrium income will rise by exactly $1. The balanced-budget multiplier equals one because it reflects the numerical sum of the autonomous spending and tax multipliers:

$$\frac{1}{1 - b} + \frac{-b}{1 - b} = \frac{1 - b}{1 - b} = 1.$$

Much more realistic assumptions than the ones used in this chapter are the bases for the econometric models used to forecast national economic activity. For example, investment, government purchases, and taxes are all assumed to be influenced by income. Even though these forecasting models are much more complex than those we have considered, the approaches are similar. Assumptions are made about the behavior of various economic agents; these assumptions generate predictions regarding National Income.

We know that these concepts of multipliers are difficult. We also know that students in principles of economics courses are often tested extensively over autonomous spending and taxing multipliers and equilibrium income. To be sure that you have mastered the material, compute all three types of multipliers when the marginal propensity to consume (**mpc**) is 0.8, 0.75, 2/3, 0.6, and 0.5. Try to compute National Income with these different values of multipliers when taxes equal $100 billion, government spending equals $200 billion, investment spending equals $150 billion, and autonomous consumption equals $400 billion. (Remember, *the balanced-budget multiplier equals 1 in all cases.*) Now, try other values for each of these autonomous components of Aggregate Spending. Work examples until you get these sorts of calculations down pat. Be sure you understand the meaning of these computations for determination of the equilibrium levels of National Income.

PART 4

Money, Monetary
Theory, and
Monetary Policy

Keynesians believe that income is the major determinant of spending. Classical economists typically join with modern monetarists in the view that the amount of money available is the major influence on Aggregate Expenditures. To understand the reasons for these areas of agreement and disagreement among Keynesians and classical economists, you need to know more about the monetary economy. What money is, what services it performs, and how money is created are the questions answered in Chapter 12. Then, Chapter 13 provides an overview of the Federal Reserve System and the tools it uses to regulate our financial system and to determine the money supply.

Chapter 14 looks at the demand for money and how the supply and demand for money jointly determine the price level, the rate of inflation, aggregate output, and the rate of interest. Chapter 15 examines how government is financed, how monetary and fiscal policy interact, and the Keynesian-Monetarist debate regarding the effectiveness of monetary versus fiscal policy.

To this point we have developed the Keynesian model of Aggregate Demand focusing primarily on fiscal policy—government spending and taxation. This part builds the monetarist model, focusing on the effects of money on Aggregate Demand. In Part Five, we integrate the two models and introduce a more formal model of Aggregate Supply. This synthesis provides a more sophisticated view of the economy and a more satisfactory perspective on recent macroeconomic problems.

CHAPTER 12 Money and Its Creation

barter	fiat money	reserves
money	seignorage	money creation
liquidity	M1, M2, M3	process
commodity money	fractional reserve banking	actual and potential money multiplier

The love of money as a possession—as distinguished from the love of money as a means to the enjoyment and realities of life—will be recognized for what it is, a somewhat disgusting morbidity, one of those semi-criminal, semi-pathological propensities which one hands over with a shudder to the specialists in mental disease. . . .

—*John Maynard Keynes*

Any list of inventions that shaped the development of civilization would include the wedge, the wheel—and *MONEY.* Suppose that a cultural anthropologist from Venus visited Earth. Scientific journals on Venus would report many curiosities, but one of the biggest puzzles for Venusians might be trying to understand why Earthlings work, invest, lie, cheat, steal, or commit murder for stones, beads, dirty pieces of paper, bits of metal, or bookkeeping entries in computers in buildings called "banks." It would probably take the Venusians a long time to understand the important roles played by money—unless they had a monetary system themselves. And, of course, they would.

Barter: Exchange Without Money

You may have heard some pundit predicting "a cashless society" in which all transactions will be executed via computer. But can you imagine a moneyless society? Our ancestors used some forms of money at least as early as the seventh century B.C., but we know that our earliest ancestors had no money. Anthropologists have recorded occasional cases of primitive tribes who lived without monetary systems before the encroachment of modern civilization. The 1976 discovery of the Tasadays in the Philippines is an example.

If you lived in a society without money, you would be limited to producing or stealing everything you used or engaging in **barter,** which means directly exchanging your goods for someone else's goods. One drawback of barter is that you must find someone who has what you want *and* who wants what you have before any exchange occurs. This requirement is called the **double coincidence of wants.** Even having a double coincidence of wants, however, might not be enough for trade to occur. For example, you might have a spare horse and want a loaf of bread, and a baker with a lot of bread might be in need of a horse. However, you still might not strike a bargain—making change without money is nearly impossible.

The costs of securing information about potentially profitable transactions are huge in a barter economy. Few transactions occur because exchange tends to be very costly. As a result, most people tend to be largely self-sufficient producers/consumers. This means that few of the advantages of specialization of labor will be realized, and it explains in part why standards of living tend to be very low in moneyless economies. Small wonder that money is often rated with the wheel as an invention crucial to the development of the modern world.

What Is Money?

I measure everything I do by the size of a silver dollar. If it don't come up to that standard then I know it's no good.
—*Thomas A. Edison*

What money is may seem obvious. However, if you were asked how much money you have, you might respond in a number of ways. You could count only the bills and coins in your purse or pocket. More likely, you would extend this to "money" you keep in checking accounts or savings accounts. You could include deposits at a savings and loan association or credit union or even the total value of any United States Savings Bonds or corporate stocks or bonds you might own. But why stop there? Most of your possessions are worth money. Your answer might include the values of all your assets—a car, a house, clothes, books, a Ping-Pong table, and whatever else you own. Just how much money do you have? The ambiguities in this question lie in a common failure to differentiate between wealth and money. Your **wealth** is the difference between the value of your assets and the value of your liabilities. In addition to being an asset itself, money has the unique characteristic of being the unit by which other assets or liabilities are measured.

Functions of Money

Economists have identified some functions that money performs in all but the most primitive societies. These functions provide a descriptive definition of money. **Money** is a:

1. medium of exchange.
2. measure of value or standard unit of account.
3. store of value.
4. standard of deferred payment.

Memorization of this list might help you a little on an examination, but money will be more understandable if you consider what each part of this description implies. You may even be able to anticipate the operational definitions of money used by modern monetary analysts.

Medium of Exchange

Money makes the world go around. . . .
—*Lyrics to the Song "Money, Money, Money" from* Cabaret, *a Hit Musical and Movie of the Late 1960s*

The most important service that money provides is that it is used to execute transactions. Money as a *medium of exchange* is also its most easily understood function. If you have assets for sale (for example, labor services), you normally expect to be paid in the form of cash or a check, although you may be willing to trade your assets for other assets. Also, when you want something, you generally expect to shell out cash or a check, although you may choose to use a credit card or take out a loan. **Credit** is simply an extension of money. The eminent economist Robert Clower has characterized monetary economies as societies in which "money is traded for goods, and goods are traded for money, but goods are not traded for goods."

We might qualify this statement by paraphrasing it: Goods are *seldom* traded for goods in a monetary economy. Even the barter organizations that have sprung up to avoid or evade taxes have bookkeeping "credits" that serve as a medium of exchange. Credits are really a form of money. A carpenter who gets credits for framing a house and trades them for a shar-pei puppy is using these credits as money.

Relative Prices in a Four-Good Economy

In our four-good economy, each good is priced in terms of every other good. Follow the horizontal "Apples" column across the table until you hit the vertical "Burritos" column. That fraction, P_b/P_a, represents the price of burritos in terms of apples. We might find, for example, that it takes 4 apples to buy 1 burrito. Thus, the price of 1 apple is ¼ burrito. Notice the fractions P_a/P_a, P_b/P_b, P_c/P_c, and P_d/P_d are shaded. These elements are items priced in terms of themselves (1 apple/1 apple = 1) and, thus, can be ignored. Moreover, each price in the area below the shaded diagonal is the reciprocal of a price above this diagonal. Thus, information is duplicated and these prices below this diagonal also can be ignored. The formula for determining the number of basic relative prices in an n-good economy (where n equals the number of goods) is:

$$[n(n-1)]/2,$$

where n can be any number. For our example, the formula becomes $[4(4-1)]/2 = 6$ prices.

Good Used to Price	Good to Be Priced			
	Apples	Burritos	Carrots	Doughnuts
Apples	$\dfrac{P_a}{P_a} = 1$	$\dfrac{P_b}{P_a}$	$\dfrac{P_c}{P_a}$	$\dfrac{P_d}{P_a}$
Burritos	$\dfrac{P_a}{P_b}$	$\dfrac{P_b}{P_b} = 1$	$\dfrac{P_c}{P_b}$	$\dfrac{P_d}{P_b}$
Carrots	$\dfrac{P_a}{P_c}$	$\dfrac{P_b}{P_c}$	$\dfrac{P_c}{P_c} = 1$	$\dfrac{P_d}{P_c}$
Doughnuts	$\dfrac{P_a}{P_d}$	$\dfrac{P_b}{P_d}$	$\dfrac{P_c}{P_d}$	$\dfrac{P_d}{P_d} = 1$

Measure of Value

Money is an elastic yardstick.

—Anonymous

Suppose that we did not have money as a common denominator by which to state the relative prices of goods. The values of bearskin rugs might be stated in terms of bath brushes or Butterfingers, which in turn might be stated in terms of shirts or shoelaces. Use of money as a *standard unit of account* substantially reduces the amount of information we need to make sound market decisions. Measuring the values of all goods in terms of all other goods would be tedious, involving enormous transaction costs, because the relative prices between goods increase faster than the number of goods considered.

For example, suppose apples (a) and burritos (b) are the only two goods in an economy. In this case, there is only one relative price to consider. If you know how many apples must be traded to get a burrito, you automatically know how many burritos must be traded for an apple. Introducing a third good, carrots (c), complicates things. You still need to know the rates of exchange between apples and burritos, but it is now also necessary to know the price of carrots in terms of both burritos and apples. There are three relative prices to worry about now: P_a/P_b, P_a/P_c, and P_b/P_c. Addition of a fourth good, doughnuts (d), means that there are six relative prices. Spend a moment studying Focus 1 so that you understand why the number of relative prices expands faster than does the number of goods exchanged.

The invention of money permitted people in 100-good economies to worry about only 100 prices instead of 4,950. Use of money as a unit of account permits a tremendous reduction in the information costs associated with exchange. Because acquiring information requires time and effort, using money increases the efficiency of the market system. Because exchange costs are reduced, more exchange occurs. And because monetary exchange makes greater specialization feasible, small groups can reduce reliance on self-production. Much greater production will occur as people specialize in producing things in which they have comparative advantage.

Store of Value

Money . . . lulls our disquietude.
—*John Maynard Keynes*

People hold money not only for the transactions they anticipate but also because money is normally a relatively risk-free way of holding wealth. The values of stocks, bonds, capital equipment, or real estate tend to be much more volatile than is the purchasing power of money in most economies. There is some risk, however, because money may lose its value during inflationary periods, but bonds do also.

Another way that risk enters the picture emerges from **diversification.** If you hold your wealth in a number of different forms, it is unlikely that the value of each will be influenced in the same ways by the same things. For example, if you own both a new-car dealership and a junkyard, a recession will kill new-car sales but your junkyard will do very well. In Chapter 6, you learned that the purchasing power of a dollar is $1/P$, where P is (1/100th of) the price level: if the price level doubles, the value of the dollar is cut in half. Since World War II, inflation has consistently pushed the price level up. Even so, the old admonition "Don't put all of your eggs in one basket" suggests that it would be wise for many people to include some money in their portfolios of assets.

Prior to the Depression-era writings of John Maynard Keynes, orthodox economists did not accept the idea that you would want money for other than reasonably immediate purchases. Since then, money has played an integral role in the development of modern "portfolio" theory, which is an important part of modern financial analysis in American business.

Standard of Deferred Payment

Money is a contract with parties unknown for the future delivery of pleasures undecided upon.
—*David Bazelon*
THE PAPER ECONOMY (1965)

Although using money as a *standard of deferred payment* is implicit in the other three functions of money, it is worth discussing to illustrate the relationship between time and money. Money is a link between the past, present, and future. Many contracts call for production that requires time for completion and that would not be done without a contract. Examples are military or construction contracts. Naturally, these contracts call for future payments of money. Other exchanges occur so continuously that it is more efficient if only one contract is used for many present and future transactions. Labor contracts are examples. Still other deals are negotiated for immediate delivery of a good or service with delayed payment for the buyer's convenience. For example, you may be borrowing money to finance your education. When you sign a credit contract, you agree to make later payment of the money you borrow—plus interest. All these contracts are measured in money.

Liquidity and Money

One important aspect of any asset is its **liquidity,** which depends on the cost of converting the asset into cash. Many people think that liquidity is defined only by the time required for the conversion; however, any asset can be converted into cash almost immediately. If you are willing to accept $10 for your stereo system, I will buy it right now. *Time required to sell* is one aspect of asset liquidity. *Certainty regarding price* is another important dimension of liquidity. Both time and certainty are inextricably tied together in transaction costs.

Liquidity is negatively related to the transaction costs incurred in purchase or sale of an asset. A reasonable way to rank assets in terms of liquidity is to estimate the percentage you would lose if you had to sell them almost immediately. A house is an example of a relatively illiquid asset. You must pay realtor fees, closing costs, a number of special finance charges, and various other transaction costs when you sell one house and buy another. On the other hand, savings accounts tend to be very liquid. You can go to your bank, close one savings account and open another, losing virtually no interest or principal in the process—just your time.

Wampum

You probably learned in a history course that the Manhattan Indians sold their island to the Dutch in the seventeenth century for $24 worth of beads, hatchets, knives, and firewater. History books generally give the impression that the Dutch took advantage of the unsophisticated Indians in this deal, although some estimates suggest that, at 6 percent interest, the $24 could now repurchase Manhattan.

Suppose that you were offered a box containing ten thousand $100 bills in exchange for everything you own (that's $1 million). You would probably count yourself very fortunate to be able to walk away from your house, car, stereo, and clothes with all that green stuff, even though you would be temporarily naked. However, if seventeenth-century Indians viewed the transaction, they would think you had been swindled.

The two situations are really very similar because the Indians used strings of beads (wampum) for money and thought themselves rich because they had received so much money for a pitiful little island. In effect, the Dutch were counterfeiters; the Indians could not have predicted that Europeans would "counterfeit" so much wampum that it soon would become almost worthless as anything other than ornamentation. In effect, the Indians experienced hyperinflation in wampum.

Types of Money

An incredible diversity of items has served as money at various times and places. However, all these monies can be classified as either commodity money or fiat money. The simplest differentiation between these types of money is that **commodity money** has substantial value apart from what it will buy, while **fiat money** is valuable only because of its use as money. Ultimately, our use of fiat money is based on faith—faith in its purchasing power, in its general acceptability, and in the stability of the government that issues it.

Commodity Monies

Rubber balls of various sizes were once used as money in the jungles of the Amazon. On the Pacific island of Yap, sculptured stones weighing as much as three tons served as money until after World War I. From the beginning of the sixteenth century until the end of the nineteenth, American Plains Indians had no money as such, but measured their wealth in horses. Throughout Europe, Africa, and the Americas, beads, stone spearheads, and arrowheads once were used as money. Focus 2 describes one well-known transaction from American History.

What caused these forms of money to fall into disuse? For any commodity to be widely accepted as money over a long period, several attributes are necessary:

1. durability.
2. divisibility.
3. homogeneity (uniformity or standardization).
4. portability (high value-to-weight and value-to-volume ratios).
5. relative stability of supply.
6. optimal scarcity.

These characteristics are reasonably self-explanatory. Ice cream will not do for money—it is not durable (it melts). Diamonds are insufficiently homogeneous—there are good diamonds, and then there are "diamonds" that some shifty-eyed rascal tries to sell you in a parking lot. Water and elephants are insufficiently portable, and elephants are indivisible. (If divided, they are not durable.) The supply of wheat is too volatile—if the supply of money (wheat) increased too rapidly, the value of money would plummet; if this supply shrank precipitously, a severe recession or depression might occur. Thus, the state of the economy would be too closely tied to good and bad wheat harvests, something that is often out of our control. **Optimal scarcity** means that any commodity used as money cannot be common. Sand, bricks, or two-by-fours are insufficiently scarce.

Historically, the only commodities that seem to combine most of the desirable characteristics for use as money are rare metals, especially gold and silver. Standardization was achieved by making small ingots or coins of these precious metals and stamping "face values" on them. The earliest known metal coins date back to Imperial Rome in the sixth century B.C. Governments soon discovered that the face values of coins had to exceed substantially the values of the metal in the coins; otherwise, small increases in the values of these metals would cause people to melt the coins down. The profits made by governments when they coin or print currencies whose face values exceed their commodity values is known as **seignorage.**

Some advocates of laissez-faire capitalism are vehement in their opposition to government discretion in printing money. These advocates often favor a return to the gold standard because the amount of money in circulation would then be controlled by the forces of supply and demand. These "gold bugs" are willing to accept the inefficiency of the costly process of producing money through mining and then burying this base for money in a place like Fort Knox in order to limit government control over the money supply.

When the world relied almost exclusively on gold and silver coins for money, kings and queens often found royal treasuries inadequate for the palaces, ornate finery, and large armies and navies they thought due them. One common solution was to try, through war, to secure foreign treasures. This solution was seldom successful. (War is a **negative-sum game,** which means that the total losses to all participants outweigh the gains to the "winners," if any.) An alternative for semi-impoverished (by their standards) heads of state was to **debase** the coinage so that profits from seignorage were increased. This means that the government mint melted down relatively pure gold and silver coins and "stretched" these precious metals by adding generous portions of nickel, copper, zinc, or lead before restamping coins. (You may have wondered where the people who put soybeans and sawdust into hamburgers got the idea.) Focus 3 explores one of the predictable consequences of **debasement.**

Paper money dates back to the Ming Dynasty in China, from 1368 to 1399 A. D. Until recently, many paper monies could have been classified as "pseudo-commodity" money because governments would convert the paper money into specified amounts of gold or silver on demand. The United States was the last country in the world to abandon the gold and silver standards; it was not until 1933 that this country went off the gold standard domestically. From 1933 until 1974, foreign bankers and governments could proffer $35 and get an ounce of gold from the United States Treasury, but it was illegal for American citizens to hold gold coins or ingots. However, American dollars were redeemable for silver until the late 1960s.

Fiat Money

Paper money and coined money are collectively called **currency.** Many of us still believe that American currency is "backed by the gold in Fort Knox." Take a dollar bill from your purse or wallet. You will see "Federal Reserve Note" above George Washington's picture, but nowhere will you find any statement about the worth of the bill in gold or silver. Now look at any of your "silver" coins. These coins are "sandwiches" of cupronickel (not silver) around copper—the face value of the coin is about 15–40 times the total value of the metal. What makes this paper and these bits of metal valuable if they are not "backed" by gold or silver? One hint lies just to the left of George's picture: THIS NOTE IS LEGAL TENDER FOR ALL DEBTS, PUBLIC AND PRIVATE. The government declares that the pieces of paper printed by the Federal Reserve System and the bits of metal issues by the United States Mint are money by fiat. (**Fiat** can be interpreted as: "Because we say so.")

Now that you know the secret that our money has no gold or silver backing, should your behavior change in any way? NO! Even if you are convinced that the government perpetrates fraud in issuing coins and bills, the fact that you can buy just about anything for which you have the money means that you will continue to try to get money in the same ways as previously. The real foundation for fiat money is the *faith* we have that it can be used to buy goods and services. In other words, our money is "backed" by Chevrolets, stereo systems, college educations, and also by government's ability and willingness to maintain money at a relatively stable value by controlling the money supply.

FOCUS 3

Gresham's Law

In the 1950s, it was very common to use silver coins minted 40–60 years earlier. What happened to all the gold and silver coins minted in the United States prior to 1964? Sir Thomas Gresham, a sixteenth-century financial adviser to Queen Elizabeth, may have had the answer. He observed that debased coins remained in circulation while relatively pure coins disappeared rapidly after debasement. This led him to state a famous economic doctrine that has stood the test of time: *"Bad money drives out good."* This idea is known as **Gresham's Law.** People will spend coins that contain far less valuable metal than their face values and hoard (save) coins that contain close to or more than the face values. This explains why almost all our current dimes, quarters, half dollars, and "silver" dollars are relatively recently minted cupro-nickel "sandwiches."

The major advantages of fiat money are (*a*) that its supply can be controlled fairly precisely by government; (*b*) that it is much less costly than commodity money, and, therefore, its use is comparatively efficient; and (*c*) that if monetary policymakers do a good job, fiat money possesses all of the characteristics required of a good commodity money.

The Supply of Money

You may be surprised to learn that the purchasing power of money and the cost of credit (interest rates) are determined by supply and demand in much the same manner that prices are determined for such goods as wheat, paperback novels, or fudge. In the remainder of this chapter, we will describe the assets that make up the United States money supply and examine the role of financial institutions in determining the money supply. This sets the stage for a look at how the demand and supply of money jointly determine the price level, the rate of inflation, and the rate of interest.

The functions of money discussed earlier in this chapter provide us with a descriptive definition: Money is a medium of exchange, a measure of value, a store of value, and a standard of deferred payment. This definition guides us into operational definitions of money. Be aware, however, that just as no measure of unemployment conforms precisely to the economic concept of unemployment, no measure of the money supply is in perfect accord with the concept of money.

Narrowly Defined Money (M1)

Currency (paper coins and bills) is probably the most easily identified component of the money supply because: (*a*) it may be used for virtually all transactions, (*b*) it is used to price goods and services, and (*c*) it is counted as an asset. The only other assets that perform all functions of money are demand deposits. **Demand deposits** are funds in checking accounts in commercial banks, savings and loans, or credit unions. These funds are legally required to be available to depositors *on demand*. Together, currency and demand deposits are the **narrowly defined money supply,** which is known as *M1*:

> *M1* = currency + demand deposits
> in financial institutions.

We do need to qualify this a bit. Only currency held by the nonbanking public is included in the money supply. We would be "double counting" if we included both the currency you deposit in your checking account and your demand deposits. We also ignore the deposits of the federal government since the government, via the Federal Reserve System, can print money at will. Moreover, since the federal government's spending is not constrained by the money it has in banks, inclusion of federal deposits would not aid in predicting Aggregate Expenditures using money supply data.

"But," you might object, "credit cards can be used to pay for just about everything. Aren't credit cards money? And how about my savings account?" Unfortunately, a credit card is simply an easy way to get into debt; a credit card is not a store of value, so credit cards are not money. Standard savings accounts are not money because spending funds from a savings account first requires converting your savings account "money" into currency or a demand deposit. Just try to pay for your next meal out by presenting your savings passbook to a waiter—you will be washing dishes in no time!

Federal laws formerly prohibited banks from paying interest on checking accounts. These laws began to be phased out in 1980. Now, savings and loan associations and credit unions also offer checking account services where deposit holders receive interest on some checking accounts. These changes in legal constraints effectively make these thrift institutions into banks and some of their deposits into checking accounts. In most of the discussion in the next few chapters, we include all banklike institutions when we say "banks" and consider all checkable accounts when we refer to "checks."

Currently, only checking accounts or currency are assets that represent mediums of exchange and are widely accepted as money. We admit that parking meters do not accept checks, that few taxi drivers are willing to change a $100 bill for a $3 fare, and that you cannot present 10 million loose pennies to a bank and expect them to settle a $100,000 mortgage. However, currency and checks are assets that can be used for most transactions much more easily than can other assets.

Near-Monies (M2 and M3)

Some economists do count certain highly liquid assets, such as savings accounts in commercial banks (*time deposits*), as parts of the money supply. The economists who use broader definitions of the money supply than $M1$ believe that people's spending levels are more predictable by monetary data if we include the liquid assets that are highly interchangeable with currency and demand deposits.

One such broader definition is **M2,** which currently adds noninstitutional money market funds and savings and small time deposits in commercial banks and thrift institutions to $M1$:

$$M2 = M1 + \text{time deposits}$$
$$= \text{currency} + \text{demand deposits}$$
$$+ \text{small time deposits.}$$

Other monetary theorists expand the definition of money to $M3$, which includes large time deposits and institutional money market mutual funds:

$$M3 = M2 + \text{institutional money}$$
$$\text{market mutual funds}$$
$$+ \text{large time deposits.}$$

Exactly which definition of the money supply is most useful will depend on the purpose for which we want to measure money. Throughout this book when we say *money,* we mean *currency plus any funds available by writing checks* ($M1$). Various measures of the money supply are shown in Figure 1.

All these measures of the money supply have grown substantially over the years, as have GNP and the cost of living (*CPI*). How should we interpret these positive correlations? Does monetary growth cause inflation? Does it cause GNP to grow, or does economic growth cause the money supply to expand? How does monetary growth affect the total output of goods, and vice versa? These questions are at the heart of a continuing controversy between monetarists and Keynesians, and they are examined in the next few chapters.

Banks and the Creation of Money

Where does money come from? We know that U.S. currency is printed by the Federal Reserve System (bills) or minted by the Treasury (coins). But demand deposits (checking accounts) are the largest component of our money supply. Currency is little more than convenience money (less than 30 percent of $M1$). How or where do demand deposits originate? To help you see how banks create money, we will look at the origins of modern fractional reserve banking. **Fractional reserve banking** refers to a system in which financial institutions can legally hold less than 100 percent of their deposits as currency in their vaults.

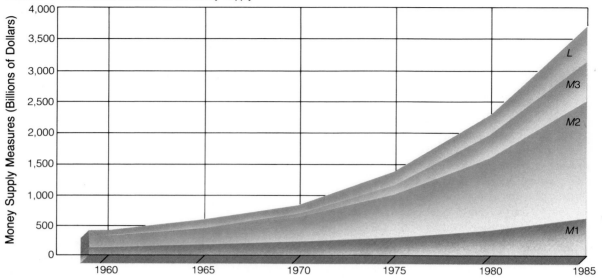

FIGURE 1 *The Various Measures of the Money Supply*

The money supply is composed of various aggregates, depending on how broadly you define it. *M*1 is the narrowest definition, while *L* is the most expansive.

Source: Economic Report of the President, 1986.

The Origin of Fractional Reserve Banking

Several centuries ago, almost all money was in the form of gold coins. Wealthy people found the quantities of gold they accumulated quite heavy. (Gold is only semiportable.) An even bigger disadvantage of gold is that it is difficult to discourage thieves from taking it; stolen gold pieces (or modern coins for that matter) are rarely identified. Looking around for safe places to store their gold, people in medieval Europe thought of goldsmiths. Goldsmiths made jewelry, gold statues, and other precious goods—they also generally had some excess space in their heavily guarded vaults.

Goldsmiths were generally willing to store other people's money for a small fee and issued receipts for the gold deposited with them. Buyers found it convenient to transact by exchanging these receipts instead of physically getting the gold, and sellers were happy to take these receipts because they knew they could redeem them for gold from the goldsmith whenever they wished. As you may have guessed, this was the beginning of checking accounts—the receipts issued by the goldsmiths were effectively demand deposits.

Goldsmiths observed that they stored nearly all of a community's coins and that the amounts of gold in their vaults did not fluctuate very much. When a buyer paid for a purchase with a gold receipt, the seller was typically content to leave the gold with the goldsmith. After all, the receipt could be used for purchases just like gold. One depositor's withdrawal was just another customer's deposit. The goldsmiths began lending some of the gold on deposit to borrowers who would pay interest. In fact, it was not even necessary to relinquish physical control of the gold—just like depositors, borrowers generally preferred a receipt to the actual gold. This was the origin of modern fractional reserve banking.

Money Creation: Demand Deposit Expansion

Because, on occasion, some people physically withdrew gold, the goldsmith was limited in the total amount of receipts he could write as loans. The amounts held in the vault to meet withdrawals of deposits became the goldsmith's **reserves.** Suppose a goldsmith observed that even though deposits and withdrawals were sporadic, the total amounts of gold in his vault did not vary more than 10 percent a year. How much might the goldsmith be able to loan from a given amount of gold deposits?

To keep the analysis simple, we assume that the goldsmith is a monopolist who has the only bank vault in the area. We will examine a multibank world in a few moments. Just to be on the safe side, the goldsmith prudently stops making loans when the value of receipts (demand deposits) issued is five times as large as the amount of gold on deposit. That is, the goldsmith keeps reserves equal to 20 percent of deposits. This is twice as much in reserve as the variations in current deposits (10 percent) that the goldsmith has observed, so this level is viewed as good insurance against a large number of people simultaneously wanting to withdraw gold. Furthermore, we assume the goldsmith already has substan-tial deposits and loans outstanding prior to the transactions we will be considering and views himself as "fully loaned up" (reserves equal 20 percent of earlier deposits).[1] Finally, we initially assume that no one actually withdraws any gold during the period we are considering; receipts for gold are perfectly acceptable as money.

Suppose Allen, a gold miner, deposits $1,000 worth of newly mined gold into Goldsmith's bank. This deposit and issuance of a receipt are written in the bank's "T-account" statement shown in Table 1. These T-accounts represent partial balance sheets for the bank. The left-hand and right-hand side entries must be equal, and they reflect only the changes in the bank's accounts following the new $1,000 deposit. The $1,000 recorded on the right side (credit) represents a liability or debt of the bank—Goldsmith owes Allen $1,000 on demand. The left side (debit) shows an increase of $1,000 in the bank's reserves, which is Goldsmith's new asset.

TABLE 1 *Initial Deposit of $1,000 in a New Account in Goldsmith's Bank*

Assets (Debits)	Liabilities (Credits)
+$1,000 Reserves (Gold) $200 Planned reserves (*RR*) $800 Excess reserves (*XR*)	+$1,000 (Demand Deposit–Allen)

When Bob, a local customer, wants to borrow money, Goldsmith is happy to accommodate him with as much as $800. How did we arrive at $800? Goldsmith calculates 20 percent times $1,000 equals $200, which is planned for reserves (*RR*). Actual reserves of $1,000 minus $200 in planned reserves equals $800 in excess reserves (*XR*) that are available for the loan. When Bob borrows the full $800, the bank deposits $800 to Bob's account, and the bank's accounts change as shown in the T-account of Table 2. When you borrow money from a bank, the stan-dard practice is to credit your account instead of giving you cash. The bank's assets are increased by an $800 IOU from Bob; its new liability is Bob's demand deposit for $800.

---

1. When we introduce the Federal Reserve System in the next chapter, you will learn that banks legally are required to keep certain proportions of deposits in reserves. The process of money creation is essentially the same analytically, regardless of whether banks plan to hold reserves in the interest of prudence or because the FED required them to do so.

TABLE 2 *First-Round Lending: Changes in Accounts in Goldsmith's Bank*

Assets (Debits)	Liabilities (Credits)
+$800 (IOU–Bob)	+$800 (Demand Deposit–Bob)

Suppose that Bob writes Carol a check for $800—he did intend to spend the money he borrowed. Table 3 shows the transaction from the bank's viewpoint. Bob's $800 demand deposit simply becomes Carol's demand deposit. In fact, since all deposits stay in the bank, we can ignore further transactions between the bank's customers. Such transactions are irrelevant for the bank's asset/liability position and for the amount of money in circulation. Notice that the $1,000 in gold reserves now "backs" $1,800 in demand deposit money. This may sound like a magician's trick, but it is the way banks operate.

TABLE 3 Transaction Between Customers of the Bank: Changes in Accounts in Goldsmith's Bank

Assets (Debits)	Liabilities (Credits)
(No change)	−$800 (Demand Deposit–Bob) +$800 (Demand Deposit–Carol)

When Deirdre wants to borrow money, Goldsmith can still lend up to $640 because actual reserves of $1,000 − [0.20 × ($1,000 + $800)] = $640 (excess reserves available to lend her). Alternatively, 80 percent of Carol's deposit (0.80 × $800) is $640. Her IOU and the loan that is deposited to Deirdre's account are shown in the T-account in Table 4.

TABLE 4 Second-Round Lending: Changes in Accounts in Goldsmith's Bank

Assets (Debits)	Liabilities (Credits)
+$640 (IOU–Deirdre)	+$640 (Demand Deposit–Deirdre)

When Ed comes in to borrow money, Goldsmith offers a loan of as much as $512 because $1,000 − [0.20 × ($1,000 + $800 + $640)] = $512. Again, 80 percent of Deirdre's $640 deposit is $512 and is available to loan. Table 5 depicts this loan and demand deposit (*DD*).

TABLE 5 Third-Round Lending: Changes in Accounts in Goldsmith's Bank

Assets (Debits)	Liabilities (Credits)
+$512 (IOU–Ed)	+$512 (Demand Deposit–Ed)

At this point, the $1,000 the bank holds as reserves supports $2,952 in demand deposits ($1,000 + $800 + $640 + $512). How much longer can this process continue? The bank can make more loans as long as 20 percent times all demand deposits is less than the $1,000 held in reserve. To spare you further agony, we have summarized all possible subsequent loans and demand deposits (*DD*) in Table 6.

TABLE 6 All Remaining Rounds: Changes in Accounts in Goldsmith's Bank

Assets (Debits)	Liabilities (Credits)
+$2,048 (IOU–All others)	+$2,048 (Demand Deposit–All others)

How did we know how large this entry would be? Well, we know the bank will continue to make loans until: $0.20(DD) = \$1,000$. If both sides of this equation are multiplied by five, we get: $DD = 5(\$1,000) = \$5,000$. The \$1,000 reserves held by the bank will support up to \$5,000 in *DD*, irrespective of whether these *DD*s are based on loans or not. In fact, the original \$1,000 in new money deposited by Allen has allowed the creation of an additional \$4,000 in demand deposits that has been generated as loans. All these transactions are summarized below in Table 7.

TABLE 7 *Summary of Transactions: Accounts in Goldsmith's Bank*

Entry (Assets) (Debits)	(Liabilities) (Credits)
1 +\$1,000 Reserves	+\$1,000 (Demand Deposit–Allen)
2 +800 (IOU–Bob)	+800 (Demand Deposit–Bob)
3 No change	−800 (Demand Deposit–Bob)
	+800 (Demand Deposit–Carol)
4 +640 (IOU–Deirdre)	+640 (Demand Deposit–Deirdre)
5 +512 (IOU–Ed)	+512 (Demand Deposit–Ed)
6 +2,048 (IOU–All others)	+2,048 (Demand Deposit–All others)
Total +\$5,000 (\$1,000 gold reserves) (\$4,000 IOUs)	+\$5,000 (Total new Demand Deposits)

It is not absolutely necessary for Goldsmith, as a monopoly banker, to go through all these lending rounds. After experimenting a bit, he would learn that Allen's \$1,000 deposit could be translated directly into a \$4,000 loan to Bob. We have gone through each step of this **loan-money creation process** because of its relevance for a multiple-bank financial system.

The Potential Money Multiplier (m$_p$)

You may have noticed that the multiplier by which the money supply is expanded (5) is the reciprocal of the percentage Goldsmith plans to use as reserves against demand deposits (1/5 or 0.20). The arithmetic works in a manner identical to that used to compute the autonomous spending multiplier. (This procedure was described in the optional material at the end of Chapter 10.) The autonomous spending multiplier is 1/**mps** (the marginal propensity to save), while the **potential money multiplier** is 1/**rr**, where **rr** is the reserve ratio or percentage of demand deposits (*DD*) held as reserves. If we denote total planned reserves as *RR*, the proof is simple:

Since rr (*DD*) = *RR*, then
$$DD = (1/rr) \times (RR).$$

The potential money multiplier ($\mathbf{m}_p = 1/\mathbf{rr}$) indicates the amount in demand deposits that can be generated from a new deposit of \$1 in a monopoly bank that is "fully loaned up" if people keep all their currency (gold, in our example) in the bank and no one keeps *any* cash on hand. Actually, banks are seldom fully loaned up, and most people do hold some currency as a convenience for small transactions.

The Actual Money Multiplier (m$_a$)

When banks hold reserves in excess of the planned (or legally required) amounts, these reserves are available for loans. These available funds, or **excess reserves (XR),** can be expressed as a proportion of the bank's total deposits:

XR/DD = xr.

Thus, the **actual money multiplier (m$_a$)** would be as high as 1/(**rr** + **xr**), but *only* if there are no other drains on the value of the money multiplier. In reality, people keep some of their money as cash, and firms hold some currency. These currency drains from the banking system are the major reason why the actual money multiplier never reaches its potential value. The Federal Reserve Bank of St. Louis estimates the historical average real money multiplier (which we label **m$_a$**) at 2.6.

It is possible to express this "real world" multiplier through a very complex formula that accounts for every form of withdrawal of cash from the banking system. The critical thing for you to remember is that the actual money multiplier (m_a) never reaches its potential value ($1/rr = m_p > m_a$) because of these and other drains of cash. The simplest algebraic expression of the actual multiplier (m_a) is:

$$m_a = MS/MB,$$

where MS is the money supply and MB is the gold, currency, or whatever else serves as reserves for banks. MB is known as the **monetary base,** or **high-powered money;** it is the base on which the money multiplier operates in the money creation process. In the United States, the "monetary base" now equals currency in the hands of the nonbanking public plus all bank reserves.

A Multibank Model

When there are many banks in a community, each bank expects most checks written by its customers to be deposited in the banks of the payees. Does this mean that the total amount of deposits in any single bank is likely to be highly volatile? Not really. Most banks find that even though their customers' individual accounts vary tremendously over the month, the average daily amount in a given account is fairly stable on a month-to-month basis over the year. This occurs because most people have reasonably stable patterns of income and spending and seldom let their accounts drop below some comfortable minimum value.

Flows of deposits among banks do not affect the total amounts of reserves in the banking system but will cause individual banks to hold slightly higher percentages of excess reserves (**xr**) than would be the case for a monopoly banker. This reduces the size of the real world money multiplier. Other than this, the process of money creation follows the pattern outlined in the preceding section, which assumed a monopoly bank.

Let us look at an example in which IBM sells a $1 million computer system to an oil firm in Venezuela. The payment is from a Venezuelan bank, and so represents new money to the American banking system. IBM deposits this $1 million in new money in the First National Bank, which enabled First National to create $800,000 by giving U.S. Steel a loan. The two entries in First National's accounts are shown in Table 8. U.S. Steel borrowed the money to buy smelting equipment; it writes a check for $800,000 to American Smelting. Unfortunately for First National, American Smelting banks with Pittsburgh National Bank. When Pittsburgh National takes American Smelting's deposit of U.S. Steel's check and demands $800,000 from First National, First National loses $800,000 in reserves and reduces U.S. Steel's account by $800,000. This is shown as entry 2b in Table 8. Notice that First National still has U.S. Steel's IOU for $800,000 plus $200,000 on reserve in the event that IBM wants to withdraw some money.

TABLE 8 *Transaction with Another Bank Account in First National Bank*

Entry (Assets)		(Liabilities)	
1	+$1,000,000 Reserves	+$1,000,000 (Demand Deposit–IBM)	
2a	+800,000 (IOU–U.S. Steel)	+800,000 (Demand Deposit–U.S. Steel)	
2b	−800,000 Reserves	−800,000 (Demand Deposit–U.S. Steel)	

Reserve Position after Transaction			
(Assets)		**(Liabilities)**	
	$ 200,000 Reserves	$1,000,000 (Demand Deposit–IBM)	
	800,000 Loan (IOU–U.S.Steel)		
Total	$1,000,000	$1,000,000 (Total Demand Deposits)	

When American Smelting deposits U.S. Steel's check and Pittsburgh National collects the check from First National, Pittsburgh's accounts change per entry 1 in Table 9. Pittsburgh can loan $640,000 to Security Life Insurance if it regards anything greater than 20 percent as excessive reserves, shown as entry 2. (First National had to turn down Security Life's loan application—they had no excess reserves to spare.) If Security Life writes a check to Xerox, which banks with New York's City Bank, Pittsburgh loses $640,000 in reserves and Security Life's account falls to its original balance (entry 3). However, Pittsburgh still has $160,000 in reserves plus Security Life's IOU for $640,000.

TABLE 9 *Second-Round Transactions Accounts in Pittsburgh National Bank*

Entry (Assets)		(Liabilities)
1	+$800,000 Reserves	+$800,000 (Demand Deposit–American Smelting)
2	+640,000 (IOU–Security Life)	+640,000 (Demand Deposit–Security Life)
3	−640,000 Reserves	−640,000 (Demand Deposit–Security Life)
Reserve Position after Transaction		
(Assets)		**(Liabilities)**
$160,000 Reserves (Cash)		$800,000 (Demand Deposits–American Smelting)
640,000 Loan (IOU–Security Life)		
Total $800,000		$800,000 (Total Demand Deposits)

City Bank's accounts now change as shown in entry 1 of Table 10. It can now lend Sony $512,000 (neither First National nor Pittsburgh has excess reserves available). When Sony takes the loan, City Bank makes entry 2 in their books. The multiple expansion process can be continued from customer to customer as reserves flow between banks until an additional total of $4,000,000 in newly created money in the form of demand deposits is generated through loans. The money creation process for an entire banking system parallels that for a single monopoly bank.

TABLE 10 *Third-Round Transactions Accounts in City Bank of New York*

Entry (Assets)		(Liabilities)
1	+$640,000 Reserves	+$640,000 (Demand Deposit–Xerox)
2	+512,000 (IOU–Sony)	+512,000 (Demand Deposit–Sony)
3	−512,000 Reserves	−512,000 (Demand Deposit–Sony)
Reserve Position after Transaction		
(Assets)		**(Liabilities)**
$118,000 Reserves (Cash)		$640,000 (Demand Deposit–Xerox)
512,000 Loan (IOU–Sony)		
Total $640,000		$640,000 (Total Demand Deposits)

Fixed Assets, Or: Why A Loan in Yap Is Hard to Roll Over

Yap, Micronesia—On this tiny South Pacific island, life is easy and the currency is hard.

Elsewhere, the world's troubled monetary system creaks along; floating exchange rates wreak havoc in currency markets, and devaluations are commonplace. But on Yap the currency is as solid as a rock. In fact, it *is* rock. Limestone to be precise.

For nearly 2,000 years the Yapese have used large stone wheels to pay for major purchases, such as land, canoes and permission to marry. Yap is a U.S. trust territory, and the dollar is used in grocery stores and gas stations. But reliance on stone money, like the island's ancient caste system and the traditional dress of loincloths and grass skirts, continues.

The people of Yap have been using stone money ever since a Yapese warrior named Anagumang first brought the huge stones over from limestone caverns on neighboring Palau, some 1,500 to 2,000 years ago. Inspired by the moon, he fashioned the stone into large circles. The rest is history.

Yapese lean the stone wheels against their houses or prop up rows of them in village "banks." Most of the stones are 2-1/2 to five feet in diameter, but some are as much as 12 feet across. Each has a hole in the center so it can be slipped onto the trunk of a fallen betel-nut tree and carried. It takes 20 men to lift some wheels.

By custom, the stones are worthless when broken. You never hear people on Yap musing about wanting a piece of the rock. Rather than risk a broken

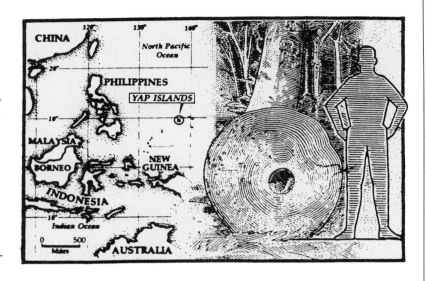

stone—or back—Yapese tend to leave the larger stones where they are and make a mental accounting that the ownership has been transferred—much as gold bars used in international transactions change hands without leaving the vault of the New York Federal Reserve Bank.

There are some decided advantages to using massive stones for money. They are immune to black market trading, for one thing, and they pose formidable obstacles to pickpockets. In addition, there aren't any sterile debates about how to stabilize the Yapese monetary system. With only about 6,600 stone wheels remaining on the island, the money-supply level stays put.

But stone money has its limits. Linus Ruuamau, the manager of one of the island's few retail stores, won't accept it for general merchandise. And Al Azuma, who manages the local Bank of Hawaii

branch, the only conventional financial institution here, isn't interested in limestone deposits. So the money, left uninvested, just gathers moss.

But stone money accords well with Yapese traditions. "There are a lot of instances here where you cannot use U.S. money," Mr. Gurtmag says. One is the settling of disputes. Unlike most money, stones sometimes *can* buy happiness, of a sort; if a Yapese wants to settle an argument, he brings his adversary stone money as a token. "The apology is accepted without question," Mr. Chodad says. "If you used dollars, there'd be an argument over whether it was enough."

You may have some nagging feelings that something is wrong because new money seems to have appeared out of thin air. If so, you are not alone in being a bit mystified by bankers' juggling acts. Focus 4 indicates that some outposts of civilization have had a hard time accepting any monetary system that is so abstract. Still, the fractional reserve process of money creation is very old and is widely accepted as compatible with sound banking practices.

You may be concerned that there is not enough money in bank vaults to meet withdrawals of deposits. Suppose IBM tries to withdraw its $1,000,000 from First National. Will this system fall like a house of cards? One part of the answer is that we have only covered the changes in bank accounts as $1,000,000 in new reserves was used to create an original demand deposit of $1,000,000 million and an additional $4,000,000 in demand deposits based on loans. The reserves backing other deposits in First National are available to cover IBM's withdrawal. Another option is that First National might sell U.S. Steel's $800,000 IOU to another bank. This is effectively what has happened if you have ever borrowed money from one lender for, say, a car, and then received a request that you pay a different lender. The paper IOU for your loan was sold (or *factored,* as it is known in banking circles).

The ''Money Destruction'' Process

The reverse of the money creation process is **money destruction.** There generally are adequate funds so that IBM can withdraw its $1,000,000 from First National because all banks hold substantial reserves. Suppose that IBM withdraws its $1,000,000 and keeps it in the corporate vault. First National will feel uncomfortably short of reserves, to the tune of $800,000. Remember, First National was holding $200,000 in reserves against the $1,000,000 deposit, so it loses $800,000 in reserves that backed other accounts ($1,000,000 − $200,000 = $800,000). When

U.S. Steel's $800,000 loan is due, First National will not renew the loan, nor will First National make new loans when U.S. Steel repays its loan. U.S. Steel's repayment must come from existing bank reserves. Ultimately, Pittsburgh National Bank will reduce outstanding loans by Security Life's $640,000, City Bank will reduce loans by Sony's $512,000, and so on. IBM's withdrawal of $1,000,000 from the reserves of the banking system will cause a $4,000,000 decline in demand deposit money, originally created by expansionary lending. IBM's $1,000,000 demand deposit will also be lost, so demand deposits will drop by a total of $5,000,000. However, IBM will have $1,000,000 in currency, which was not included in the money supply while it was held as bank reserves. Thus, there is a net $4,000,000 reduction in the money supply caused by IBM's decision to hoard $1,000,000 in its vault.

If individual banks hold 20 percent of all deposits in reserves, then there will be no problem unless they rapidly lose 20 percent or more of their deposits. Has this ever happened? Yes. Does this mean that such banks are insolvent? NO! When only a few banks are short of reserves, other financial institutions will buy (at a discount) the IOUs from the loans these banks have made. Alternatively, banks that are short of reserves might just borrow funds from institutions that have excess reserves available. Such borrowing has become common through a privately operated banking network called the **federal funds market.** These mechanisms normally enable banks that have inadequate reserves to replenish their reserves and honor all their demand deposit liabilities.

Unfortunately, there have been times when there were inadequate reserves in the financial system as a whole, and there were a lot more loans for sale than there were buyers. The "runs on banks" and financial panics that resulted finally caused the Congress to establish a "banker's bank" with the enactment of the Federal Reserve Act of 1913. In the next chapter, we will examine the powers of the Federal Reserve System.

CHAPTER REVIEW: KEY POINTS

1. *Barter* requires a *double coincidence of wants*—trade can only occur if each party has what the other wants and if divisibility poses no problems.

2. *Money* ensures this double coincidence of wants—the seller will accept money because of what it will buy, while the buyer is willing to exchange money (and, thus, all else it will buy) for the good or service in question.

3. Money facilitates specialization and exchange by decreasing transaction costs. The more sophisticated the financial system, the greater the level of production and consumption and the higher the standard of living.

4. Money is a *medium of exchange*. It is used for most transactions in monetary economies.

5. Money is a *measure of value*. Used as a standard unit of account, it is the common denominator for pricing goods and services.

6. Money is a *store of value*. It is among the most nominally secure of all assets people can use to hold their wealth.

7. Money is a *standard of deferred payment*. Serving as a link between the past, present, and future, it is used as a measure of *credit* to execute contracts calling for future payments.

8. *Liquidity* is negatively related to the transaction costs incurred in exchanges of assets. *Time, certainty regarding price,* and the *quality of information in a market* are all dimensions of liquidity. Assets are liquid if transaction costs are low, *illiquid* if transaction costs are high.

9. *Commodity monies* (precious metals, stones, or arrowheads) have values that are independent of what they will buy. *Fiat money* (paper currency) is valuable only because it is money; its use is based on *faith.*

10. The profit governments make from printing money or stamping coins is called *seignorage.*

11. According to *Gresham's Law,* "*Bad money drives out good.*"

12. The very narrowly defined money supply (*M1*) is the total of: (*a*) *currency* (coins and bills) in the hands of the nonbanking public, plus (*b*) *demand deposits* (checking accounts of private individuals, firms, and nonfederal government units in financial institutions).

13. Some highly liquid assets are viewed as near-monies and are included in broader definitions of the money supply (*M2* and *M3*) by monetary analysts who believe the spending of the public can be predicted better if these assets are included. Examples of such highly liquid assets include short-term *time deposits* (savings accounts) or *certificates of deposit (CDs).* The assets included in "money supplies" defined more broadly than *M1* are judgmental because these assets are not mediums of exchange.

14. Banks and some thrift institutions "create" money through loan-based expansions of demand deposits (checking account money). They make loans based on currency they hold as reserves, and these loans take the form of new demand deposit money.

15. Banks hold *reserves* that are far less than their deposit liabilities. The larger the proportion of deposits held as either excess or required reserves, the smaller are the money multiplier and resulting money supply, given some fixed total amount of reserves.

16. The *potential money multiplier* ($\mathbf{m}_p$) equals $1/\mathbf{rr}$, where $\mathbf{rr}$ is the banking system's planned or legally required reserves as a percentage of deposits. The *actual money multiplier* ($\mathbf{m}_a$) is much smaller because: (*a*) households and firms hold currency that could be used as a base for the money creation process were this currency held in bank vaults as reserves against deposits; and (*b*) banks hold excess reserves to meet withdrawals of deposits. The actual money multiplier equals *MS/MB*, where *MS* is the money supply and *MB* is the *monetary base*, or high-powered money.

QUESTIONS FOR THOUGHT AND DISCUSSION

1. Explain how the introduction of money permits society to better realize the advantages of specialization of labor. Would you expect to find a sophisticated division of labor in a barter economy? Explain why the standards of living tend to be very low in moneyless economies.

2. Explain what is meant by the phrase: "Money is a link between the past, present, and future." Can you explain how the use of money makes the economy operate more smoothly through time?

3. How would you define *money?* Do you feel that the degree of liquidity is important in determining what

things are money and what things are not? List the following items according to their degree of liquidity, from least liquid to most liquid: (*a*) dollar bill, (*b*) U.S. government bond, (*c*) house, (*d*) car, (*e*) pedigreed dog, (*f*) television set, (*g*) savings account, and (*h*) human skills.

4. The functions of money include (*a*) a medium of exchange, (*b*) a unit of account or measure of value, (*c*) a store of value, and (*d*) a standard of deferred payment. There are items that perform some, but not all, of these functions. Which functions do credit cards (Visa, MasterCard, Discovery) serve? Which are not served? How about time deposits? Gold or silver? Stocks and bonds?

5. What problems might confront people who live in different societies with different monetary systems and who wish to trade with one another? Would it be advantageous if the entire world used a common currency? What do you think are some of the reasons we do not have a world currency?

6. In 1933, Adolph Hitler decreed that the old German deutsche mark was worthless and could be exchanged at a fixed rate for new reichsmarks. The British redeemed their old currency in the late 1960s, replacing it with a "metric" style currency. What circumstances might make it appropriate to completely withdraw one currency from circulation and replace it with a new currency?

CHAPTER 13 # The Federal Reserve System and Financial Institutions

Federal Reserve System (FED)	*reserve-requirement ratio (**rr**)*	*discount rate (d)*
Board of Governors	*federal-funds market*	*margin requirements*
Federal Open-Market Committee (FOMC)	*open-market operations (OMO)*	*usury laws*
		credit rationing

Whoever controls the volume of money in any country is absolute master of all industry and commerce.
—*President James A. Garfield*

Financial institutions probably are more closely regulated than any other aspect of American business except, perhaps, secret weapons research and atomic energy. This is not surprising, given the potential for fraud and general abuse afforded the owners and managers of the institutions we trust with our money. The **Federal Reserve System (FED)** regulates commercial banks and is among the most powerful of government agencies in that its policies control the volume of money in circulation.[1] Paradoxically, the FED itself is among the least accountable and most independent agencies of government. During

hearings on the FED's policies, one senator compared getting an answer out of the chairman of the FED's Board of Governors to "nailing a chocolate cream pie to a wall."

Early Experiments with Central Banks

Most of the founders of this country feared concentration of either economic or political power. The persuasive skills of Alexander Hamilton were taxed to the limit to overcome his countrymen's resistance to the establishment of the United States' first central bank. The First Bank of the United States was founded shortly after the adoption of the Constitution and replaced a system in which the federal government, the various states, and many private banks all issued different currencies. The phrase "Not worth a continental" crept into our language due to the worthlessness of money issued by the Continen-

---

1. Jack Kemp, on being asked whether he would run for president in 1988, replied that he wanted to hold the most powerful position in the world: Chairman of the FED.

tal Congress before the Bank of the United States was established. The dollar became a sound currency only when this central bank honored government debts incurred from fighting the American Revolutionary War.

Although the Bank of the United States was privately owned and operated, it was also the government's bank because it (*a*) was the depository for tax revenues, (*b*) arranged for loans to and from the government for various projects, and (*c*) paid the government's obligations. The Bank's power generated tremendous opposition among Westerners and those with agricultural interests, who felt it served only the rich and the "Eastern Establishment." The death of Hamilton and ascendancy of his political rival, Thomas Jefferson, led to the abolition in 1811 of our first experiment with central banking.

The Second Bank of the United States was chartered in 1816 and operated with some success under the direction of Nicholas Biddle, a member of a prominent Philadelphia family. However, the Bank's foes triumphed when, in 1832, President Andrew Jackson vetoed the act to recharter it. In 1836, the original charter expired. Nicholas Biddle lost his power in a minor financial scandal, and the collapse of the Bank precipitated the financial crash of 1837. For the next 75 years, the American economy experienced substantial but erratic growth without a central bank.

The Federal Reserve System

The American economy prospered even though it suffered major financial crises roughly every 20 to 25 years from the time of the American Revolution through the Great Depression. These financial panics were usually followed by periods of stagnation or depression. A wave of bank failures in 1906–07 led to the passage of the Federal Reserve Act in 1913, which established a third central bank, the Federal Reserve System. One of the FED's major objectives is to act as a "lender of last resort." This means that the FED lends money to inherently sound banks so that they can survive financial panics.

The seven members of the **Board of Governors** of the Federal Reserve System are appointed to staggered 14-year terms of office because Congress feared the instability of a highly politicized central bank. Each president and Congress have limited

power over the Federal Reserve System because they appoint only one new member of the Board of Governors every other year. The majority of Board members traditionally have been bankers, causing some people to question how diligent they are as public "watchdogs" over the banking system. Recently, however, presidents have nominated increasing numbers of governors from the general public, including more than a few economists.

The FED (in concert with the Comptroller of the Currency, the Federal Deposit Insurance Corporation, and various state government agencies) is responsible for regulating banks. It audits the books of federally chartered banks to guard against fraud and to ensure compliance with a variety of regulations. Among its other services to the banking community, the FED processes checks drawn on one bank and cashed or deposited elsewhere. However, the most important macroeconomic role of the FED is conducting monetary policy. Before we examine monetary policymaking, it is helpful to know a bit more about the FED's structure.

Federal Reserve Bank Districts

There are 12 regional districts in the Federal Reserve System, each having a primary bank with one or more branch offices. Figure 1 depicts the locations of these primary and branch banks and outlines their boundaries. If you check the money you have in your billfold or purse, you will probably find that many of the bills have traveled far from their points of issue.

The Federal Reserve Banks and their branches do not serve the general public directly. They are "bankers' banks" that help member banks clear checks drawn on other banks, make loans to bankers, and otherwise facilitate efficiency in the financial sector of the economy. The FED operates under the fiction that it is a private organization "owned" by federally chartered private banks. However, the FED is an arm of the government created by an act of Congress. The FED's actions and decisions have the force of law, and any returns on investment greater than 6 percent annually must be paid to the U.S. Treasury.

Member Banks   Approximately 14,000 commercial banks are in operation in the United States, all of them privately owned and managed. Fewer than 5,000 of these are national banks chartered by the

FIGURE 1 Federal Reserve Branch Banks

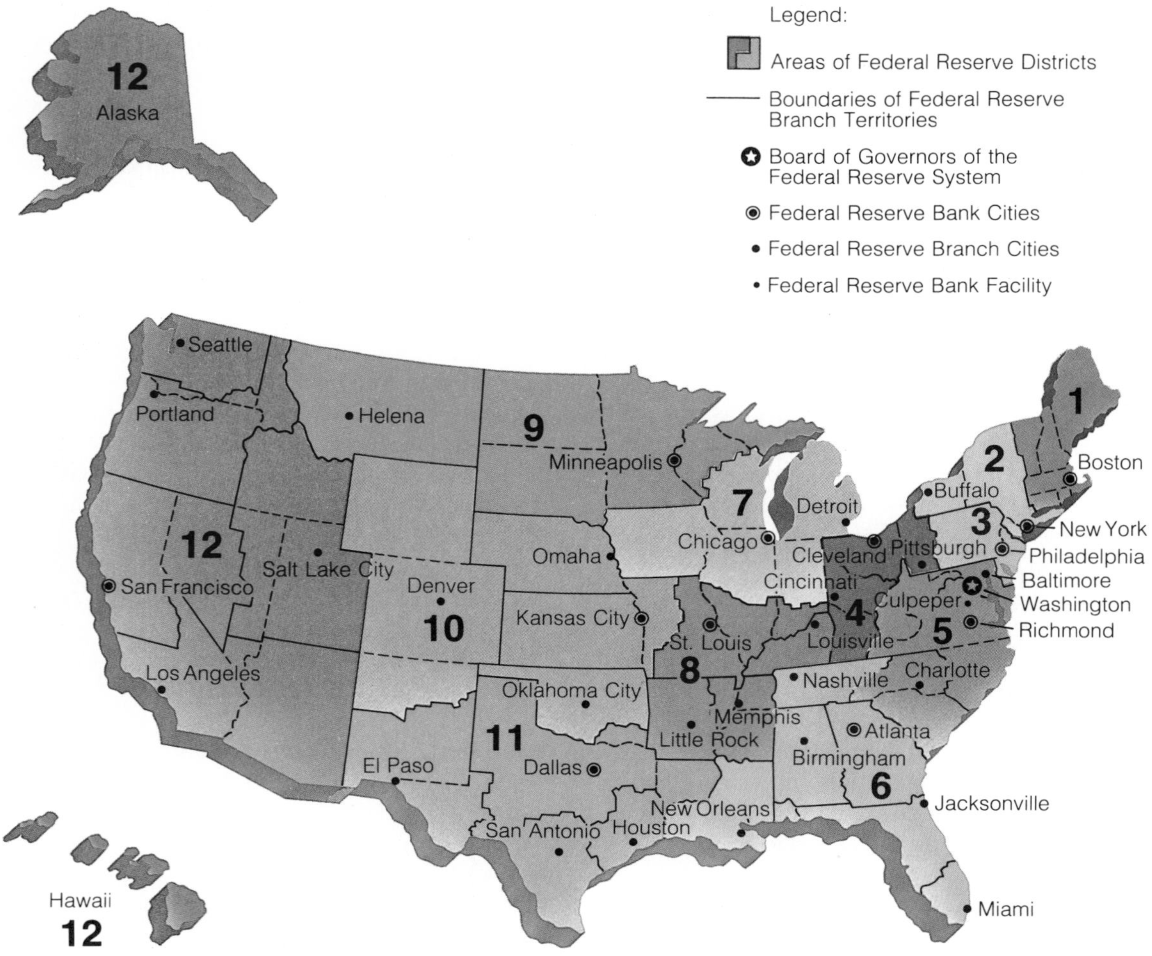

Legend:

▦ Areas of Federal Reserve Districts

— Boundaries of Federal Reserve Branch Territories

✪ Board of Governors of the Federal Reserve System

◉ Federal Reserve Bank Cities

• Federal Reserve Branch Cities

• Federal Reserve Bank Facility

The Federal Reserve System consists of 12 districts. Each district has a Federal Reserve Bank; some of the larger districts also have branch banks. This figure depicts the locations of these primary and branch banks and outlines their boundaries.

Source: Federal Reserve Bulletin.

Comptroller of the Currency. The remaining 9,000 or so are state banks chartered by state governments. **National banks** must be members of the Federal Reserve System; **state-chartered banks** have the option (upon approval) of becoming **member banks.** More than 70 percent of all deposits are in member banks, and the FED has set legal reserve requirements on all checkable deposits in *all* financial institutions since 1980. As a result, the Federal

Reserve System has considerable direct power over most of the financial system in the United States.

The Organization of the FED

The formal structure of the Federal Reserve System is shown in Figure 2. The chairman of the Board of Governors is supposedly only a "first among equals." Like the chief justice of the Supreme Court, he nom-

FIGURE 2 *The Formal Organization of the Federal Reserve System*

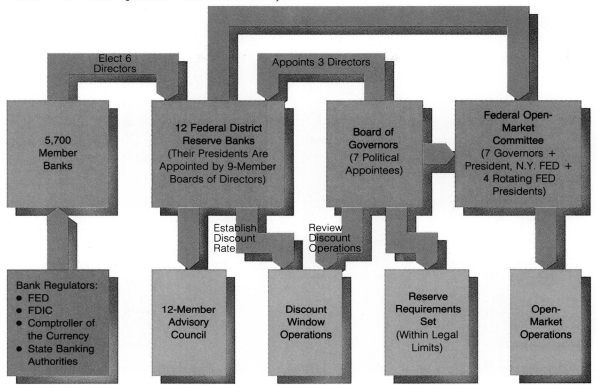

inally has only one vote in any decisions made. However, the chairman in fact has disproportionate power within the Board of Governors. Of course, the effectiveness of the chairman in controlling monetary policy depends on personality and on the dynamics of the relationships among the various governors.

Concerned that political shenanigans might distort financial regulatory and stabilization activities, Congress tried to shield the FED from political pressures by making it a pseudoprivate organization. As a "private" organization, the FED's member banks elect six of the nine directors of each District Bank; the remaining three are appointed by the Board of Governors. These directors appoint the presidents of their District Banks. While the presidents of the various banks are free to make speeches about policy, their jobs are primarily concerned with administration, not policymaking.

The real policymaking power of the FED is exercised through the **Federal Open-Market Committee (FOMC),** which is composed of all seven members of the Board of Governors plus the president of the New York District Bank. Four other District Bank presidents rotate on the committee. Through its conduct of monetary policy, the FOMC has enormous control over our entire financial system and the economy in general. Committee members' terms of office and votes give the real clout within the FOMC to the Board of Governors, especially the chairman. Figure 3 portrays the actual channels of power within the FED.

Economists are concerned with incentives. Should the FED maximize profits? Should monetary policymakers be subjected to political pressures in our democracy? Before we tackle these problems, let us see why the answers to these questions are important.

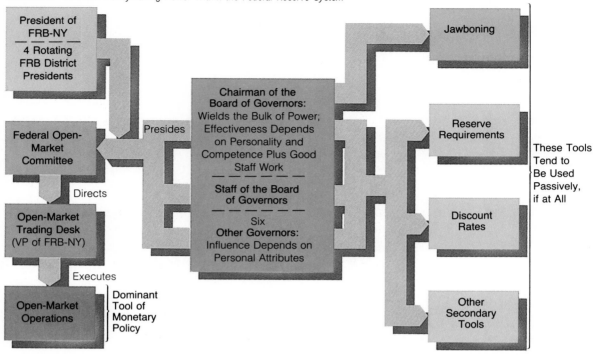

In many organizations, the real policymaking power does not follow the formal organization chart of the institution. The Federal Reserve System is no exception. This figure depicts the flow of real policymaking power within the FED.

The Tools of the FED

The Federal Reserve System uses three primary and several secondary tools to control the money supply and conditions in the financial sector. The FED's major tools are: (*a*) reserve requirements, (*b*) open-market operations, and (*c*) discounting operations. Secondary tools of the FED include controls over stock market credit and "jawboning"—all of which will be discussed in further detail.

The FED's Primary Tools

Reserve requirements and discounting operations are important, though generally passive, monetary policy instruments. Day in and day out, the FED actively uses open-market operations to implement its ever changing policies.

Reserve Requirements (rr) The Federal Reserve System sets a legal floor on the percentage of a bank's deposits that must be held in reserves. These reserves can be kept in banks' vaults or on deposit at Federal Reserve Banks (see Focus 1). Suppose the **reserve-requirement ratio (rr)** is 1/6 or 16.7 percent. For the actual money multiplier (m_a) to reach 6 and, thus, equal the potential money multiplier ($m_p = 1/rr = 1/.167 = 6$), banks need to be "fully loaned up" (no excess reserves), and no currency can be held outside the banking system. Only then are the actual (m_a) and potential ($m_p = 1/rr$) money multipliers equal.

Banks that want to stay in business never permit their reserves to sink to the legal minimum. If they did, they would be unable to meet any demands for withdrawals of deposits without being in trouble with the FED. Hence, banks hold excess reserves to accommodate any outflows of funds. The overall sys-

Is There Any "Real" Money in Banks?

If *real money* is interpreted as meaning bills and coins, the answer to the above question is "Not much." Banks keep enough currency on hand to meet their customers' demands for cash, and that is about it.

Since average banks have deposits of over $10 million, where do they store our money? You learned in Chapter 12 that in a fractional reserve banking system, banks only hold about 15–30 per-cent of deposits as reserves. However, a $10-million bank will not keep $1.5 to $3 million on hand in cash—keeping track of the inventory might be a problem, and there is no sense in tempting thieves. Consequently, banks keep most of their reserves on deposit with Federal Reserve Branch or District Banks.

Even these FED banks do not hold your bank's deposits in the form of cash. To do so would mean that literally tons of the green stuff would need to be warehoused. You have probably figured out that your bank account is simply a few electronic impulses stored in the bank's computer. The FED does the same thing with the reserves that banks keep on deposit at Branch or District Banks—it is all in the computer. Roughly two-thirds of the nation's money supply exists only in computers.

tem is usually able to operate with very few excess reserves, however, because banks lend and borrow money from each other daily through the privately operated **federal-funds market.**

The total amount of **legal reserves (LR)** held by a bank can be divided into **required reserves [RR = rr(DD)]** and **excess reserves (XR):**

$$legal\ reserves = required\ reserves \\ + excess\ reserves$$

$$LR = RR + XR.$$

It is important to emphasize that the reserves available to meet the FED's reserve requirements are called *legal reserves* and that they include *excess reserves,* which differentiate them from *required reserves.*

One way the Federal Reserve System can vary the money supply is through changes in the reserve-requirement ratio (**rr**). If the FED *raises* the reserve-requirement ratio, then $1/rr$ falls. The smaller potential money multiplier (**m_p**) means the total reserves in the banking system will support only smaller potential totals of loan-based demand deposits. Conversely, a *decrease* in the reserve-requirement ratio enables banks to increase the money supply through expansion of demand deposit-based loans. Banks will typically want to hold roughly the same percent-age of excess reserves against demand deposits no matter what happens to the reserve-requirement ratio because the percentage fluctuations of bank deposits depend on people's behavior rather than on Federal Reserve System reserve requirements. (You may need to review the section on monetary expansion in Chapter 12 if this is not clear.) Notice that the reserve-requirement ratio does not influence the total amount of reserves in the banking system. Instead, it affects the **m_p**. Naturally, whenever the **m_p** changes, the actual money multiplier (**m_a**) moves in the same direction.

The amounts of excess reserves held by banks will depend on: (*a*) the expected profitability of lending any excess reserves, and (*b*) the expected costs of acquiring reserves should borrowing be necessary to meet the FED's reserve requirements. In other words, the percentage of deposits held as excess reserves will be *negatively* related to the difference between the interest rates banks can charge borrowers and the interest rates banks themselves must pay to borrow reserves from other banks or the FED.

The reserve-requirement ratio (**rr**) is the FED's most powerful tool. Suppose that the **rr** was increased from 1/6 (16.7 percent) to 1/5 (20 percent)—a change of 3.3 percentage points. The potential money supply would fall by roughly 1/6 (**m_p** falls from 6 to 5). Curiously, this powerful tool is seldom used; reserve-requirement ratios have been changed only about two dozen times since the Great Depression. Why? The very power of changes in **rr** make it difficult to predict the magnitude of their effect.

An analogy may help you understand why. Imagine that you were scheduled for brain surgery. Would you want the surgeon to use the most powerful tool available—a chain saw? Or would you prefer that the surgery be done with more finesse, using a tool such as a scalpel? A second tool of the FED, open-market operations, is the best tool available for the conduct of monetary policy. It is the FED's scalpel.

Open-Market Operations (OMO)

The FED's most important implement, **open-market operations (OMO),** entails buying and selling securities issued by the U.S. Treasury and is used to increase or decrease the size of the monetary base. Recall from Chapter 12 that the monetary base (*MB*) is the total of currency held by the nonbanking public plus reserves held by banks:

$$MB = \text{currency} + \text{bank reserves.}$$

Hence, the monetary base is the foundation for our money supply because the money creation process depends on the amounts of reserves in the banking system.

The actions of the FED's Open-Market Committee (FOMC) directly change the monetary base. The monetary base is changed through *open-market* purchases or sales of U.S. Treasury securities. When the FOMC decides to increase the money supply by expanding the monetary base, the "open-market desk" buys Treasury bonds, primarily from commercial banks. (A significant amount of the "lending" done by banks is simply purchases of government securities.) If the FOMC sells bonds, the monetary base is reduced.

Banks are not the only buyers of bonds from the FED or sellers of bonds to the FED. Private individuals or firms can also be the FED's trading partners. The funds paid by the FED invariably are deposited in banks by private sellers, however, and so end up as bank reserves. Similarly, private buyers of bonds withdraw funds held in banks to pay for their purchases. Thus, the effects on total bank reserves and the money supply is the same regardless of with whom the FED deals.

When the FED buys bonds, bank reserves are increased and the banking system will increase loan-based demand deposits in accord with the money creation process discussed previously. You may wonder where the FED gets the money to buy the bonds. Answer: The FED can print new currency, or it can simply credit the reserve accounts of the private banks via computer at one of the Federal Reserve District Banks.

"T-account" entries for a typical expansionary open-market transaction are shown in Table 1. When the FOMC buys $1,000 in Treasury bonds from Bank A, the Federal Reserve Bank's liabilities are increased by $1,000 in reserves held for Bank A; its assets are debited by $1,000 in Treasury bonds. Bank A's assets change from $1,000 in Treasury bonds to $1,000 in

TABLE 1 *T-Account Changes for a Typical Open-Market Transaction*

Federal Reserve Bank	
Assets	**Liabilities**
+$1,000 Treasury bonds	+$1,000 Reserves held for Bank A

Member Bank A	
Assets	**Liabilities**
−$1,000 Treasury bonds +$1,000 Loanable reserves	No change

new reserves. Bank A views the sale of the bond to the FED in the same way that it would the payback of a loan by a private borrower. Note, however, that this "payoff" creates new reserves for the banking system as a whole, while payment of a private loan does not. These new reserves can then be loaned to private borrowers, creating new demand deposit money via the expansionary money multiplier process.

If the FED decides to reduce the money supply, it sells bonds to commercial banks. This sops up excess reserves and may even threaten to cut into banks' required reserves. As banks attempt to rebuild their reserves to desired levels, they turn down applications for new loans or renewals of old loans, and the amount of loan-based demand deposits falls. The "money destruction" process that results from FED sales of Treasury bonds is exactly the opposite of the money creation process. If the positive numbers in Table 1 were negative, and vice versa, it would illustrate a contractionary open-market operation.

You may wonder how the FED can persuade banks or private individuals to sell bonds when the FOMC conducts expansionary open-market operations. A bidding process is used; the sellers are those willing to offer desired amounts of bonds at the lowest prices. No matter how high the prices are, the FED buys the bonds. When the FED desires to withdraw reserves from the banking system to reduce the money supply, it sells some of the Treasury bonds in its portfolio. As Focus 2 illustrates, the FED takes the highest bids for bonds it sells, no matter how low the bids are.

Actually, the open-market desk of the FOMC both buys and sells bonds every business day.

1. If the FED buys more bonds than it sells, total bank reserves are increased and the money creation process leads to an expansion of the money supply.
2. When the FED sells more bonds than it buys, reserves are reduced and the money destruction process causes a contraction of the money supply.

Open-market operations ultimately affect the money supply *only* through changes in the amounts of reserves in the banking system, *not* through changes in the money multiplier. The maximum possible value of the multiplier (m_p) is determined by the reserve-requirement ratio (**rr**). The FED's discounting operations affect both the size of the monetary base (MB) and the value of the actual money multiplier (m_a).

Discounting Operations As we have said, the FED is a bankers' bank. When commercial banks have sufficient reserves to meet the FED's reserve requirements or want to increase their reserves, they can borrow money from the *discount windows* of the FED's District or Branch banks. The loans become a part of bank reserves and, hence, the monetary base. The interest rate the FED charges bankers is called the **discount rate (d).**

Most bank borrowing from the FED is to cover temporary deficiencies. The likelihood that banks will have deficient reserves, however, depends strongly on the discount rate. Whenever the discount rate (d) is substantially less than market interest rates (i), the monetary base grows; bankers will borrow from the FED with the intention of expanding their loans and demand deposits. They do so because the interest rate the bank pays is less than the interest rate it charges on loans. (It's a bit like trading nickels for dimes.) On the other hand, if the discount rate is substantially greater than the market rate of interest, it penalizes bankers who are forced to borrow from the FED because of unforeseen withdrawals of deposits. Consequently, banks try to avoid any need to borrow by holding greater excess reserves. Thus, the actual multiplier m_a shrinks as the difference between the discount rate and the market interest rate grows.

All else being equal,

1. When the FED raises the discount rate, banks will borrow less, reducing total reserves or limiting their increase. Banks will also lend less, so excess reserves in individual banks grow and the actual money multiplier and money supply decline.
2. When the FED decreases the discount rate, banks increase their borrowing from the FED and cut holdings of excess reserves; this results in increases in the actual money multiplier and money supply.

The FED's Secondary Tools

Although the reserve-requirement ratio, open-market operations, and the discount rate are the major mechanisms at the FED's disposal, there are some other devices in the FED's toolbox to help it control financial markets and economic activity:

1. The FED sets the margin requirements to control stock market credit (Regulations G, T, and U).
2. The FED "jawbones," which means it rages at people or institutions who do things it does not like.

FOCUS 2

The "Go-Around"

The time is early afternoon on a Wednesday in mid-June. The place is the trading room on the eighth floor of the Federal Reserve Bank of New York. The manager of the Open Market Account for Domestic Operations gathers with his trading room officers to reaffirm the judgment reached earlier to buy about $1¼ billion of Treasury bills. The banking system has a clear need for additional reserves to meet the increased public demand for currency and deposits expected as the end of the quarter and July 4 approach. The markets for bank reserves and Treasury securities are functioning normally with prices moving narrowly. After a brief discussion, the manager gives final approval to the planned operation.

The officer-in-charge at the FED's Trading Desk turns to the ten officers and securities traders who sit before telephone consoles linking them to three dozen primary dealers in U.S. government securities. "We're going to ask for offerings of all bills for regular delivery," she says. Each trader knows this means delivery and payment will take place the next day. Each picks up the vertical strips on which the offerings will be recorded for the four dealers he will call.

Bill, one of the group, presses a button on his telephone console, sounding a buzzer on the corresponding console of a government securities dealer.

"John," Bill says, "we are looking for offerings of bills for regular delivery."

John replies, "I'll be right back." He turns and yells, "The FED is in, asking for all bills for delivery tomorrow." Moments later information screens around the country and abroad flash the news. Salesmen begin ringing their customers to see if they have bills they want to offer. Meanwhile, John checks with the trading manager of his firm to see how aggressive he should be in pricing the firm's own securities.

Twenty minutes later John rings back. "Bill, I can offer you $15 million of bills maturing August 9 at 9.20 percent, $40 million September 13 bills at 9.42, $25 million of September 20's at 9.46 and another 25 at 9.44. I'll sell $75 million December 13's at 10.12 and another 100 at 10.09. I can offer $20 million of March 21's at 10.25 and 50 May 16's at 10.28. All for delivery tomorrow."

Bill reads back each of the offerings to double check, then says, "Can I have those firm?"

"Sure."

Within ten or fifteen minutes each trader has written the offerings obtained from his calls on preprinted strips. The officer-in-charge arrays the individual dealer strips on an inclined board placed atop a stand-up counter. A quick tally shows that dealers have offered $7.8 billion of bills for regular delivery—that is, on Thursday.

The officer and a colleague begin comparing rates across the different maturities, seeking those that are high in relation to adjoining issues. She circles any special bargains with a red pencil. With an eye on heavy existing holdings, she circles other propositions that offer yields on or above a yield curve she draws mentally through the more heavily offered issues. Her associate keeps a running total of the amounts being bought. When the desired volume has been circled and cross-checked, the individual strips are returned to the traders, who quickly ring up the dealers.

Bill says, "John, we'll take the $25 million of September 20's at 9.46, the 75 of December 13's at 10.12, and the 50 of May 16's at 10.28 for regular delivery. A total of $150 million. No, thanks, on the others."

Forty-five minutes after the initial entry, the follow-up calls have been completed. The Trading Desk has bought $1,304 million of Treasury bills. Only the paperwork remains. The traders write up tickets, which authorize the accounting section to instruct the Reserve Bank's Government Bond Department to receive and pay for the specific Treasury bills bought.

Source: Paul Meek, Open Market Operations *(New York: Federal Reserve Bank of New York), 1985. Reprinted by permission.*

Until 1980, the FED could also regulate credit to consumers and business firms during wars or crises. And before 1986, the FED determined the maximum interest rate that could be paid on bank deposits. Congress rescinded both of these powers during economic deregulation that began in the 1970s.

Margin Requirements   Many people believe that the Stock Market Crash of 1929 and the Great Depression were caused by overspeculation. People could buy stock in the 1920s with a down payment of as little as 10 percent. This practice is called *buying on margin;* the *margin* referred to is the percentage down payment required. Some investors used almost all their assets for down payments. Then, when stock prices fell, they were wiped out financially. In the aftermath of the Crash, the Federal Reserve System was granted power to determine **margin requirements,** which have hovered around 50 percent for the past three decades. Presumably, higher margin requirements reduce speculation and lower margin requirements cause increases in speculation.

There is, however, little evidence that margin requirements significantly influence the average level of stock prices. Indeed, a powerful economic theory suggests that even if low margin requirements cause some individuals to speculate, their behavior will be offset by adjustments on the parts of more prudent financial investors. Suppose that financial investors expected a 10 percent return on stocks but a 12 percent return on equally risky real estate. Funds would flow into real estate from the stock market. The stock market would fall a bit, and real estate prices would rise until the returns were equalized at, say, 11 percent. This is precisely the type of adjustment that would follow even minor overspeculation in stocks. When low margin requirements encourage speculation so that stock prices rise slightly, the expected returns (dividends, etc.) per dollar of financial investment in stocks decline. This result makes real estate or other investments comparatively more attractive to prudent investors, so money will flow from the stock market until expected returns on all investments are equated. Overspeculation in stocks due to low margin requirements is eliminated automatically.

Jawboning   Self-restraints on union wage increases or price increases by business are commonly advocated by presidents seeking to contain inflation. This is only one example of **jawboning,** which is oratory used by policymakers who want people or institutions to act against their individual interests (or to see their interests in a different light). The FED occasionally has tried to use jawboning to persuade banks either to expand or contract credit. Economists tend to be skeptical of the effectiveness of

appeals to public-spiritedness. However, because the FED's jawboning is backed up by the power to audit and otherwise harass banks, it may have some effect. A major problem is that the effects of jawboning are less predictable than those of virtually any other tool. Because the FED has learned this lesson, few recent chairmen of the Federal Reserve System have spent time exhorting banks to do something other than maximize their banks' profits.

Which Tools Are Used?

The Federal Reserve System strongly influences the money supply, but lacks precise and direct control. In Chapter 12, we identified the actual money multiplier (m_a) as the relationship between the money supply (MS) and the monetary base (MB):

$$m_a = MS/MB.$$

This equation implies that the money supply is the product of the money multiplier and the monetary base:

$$MS = m_a(MB).$$

The FED can use active changes in the discount rate, reserve-requirement ratios, or interest ceilings on deposits to try to manipulate the value of the actual money multiplier and, thus, change the money supply. Alternatively, it can use open-market operations (and, to a lesser extent, discount operations) to vary the monetary base in attempts to alter the money supply. Table 2 summarizes how tools of the FED affect the money supply by altering the behavior of banks and the public.

If the FED does not independently determine the money supply, then what other groups have some influence, and how? The FED directly, and with some precision, controls the monetary base through open-market operations. The nonbanking public can affect the money multiplier through its holding of cash. As private stores of cash increase, currency available for bank reserves is reduced; the actual money multiplier (and, hence, the money supply) is reduced because the money expansion process only applies to currency in bank vaults. Independently of FED policies, banks may unintentionally influence the actual money multiplier through variations in the percentage of total demand deposits held as excess reserves. The greater the excess reserves held by banks, the smaller will be the actual money multiplier and, hence, the money supply. If private activi-

TABLE 2 *FED Tools and Effects*

Tool Used	Potential Money Multiplier ($m_p = 1/rr$)	Excess Reserves Ratio ($xr = XR/DD$)	Actual Money Multiplier ($m_a = MS/MB$)	Monetary Base (MB)	Currency NBP[a]	Bank Reserves	Loans, Demand Deposits, and Money Supply (M1)
Reserve-requirement ratios (rr)							
Raise **rr**	Lower	No change	Lower	No change	No change	No change	Lower
Lower **rr**	Higher	No change	Higher	No change	No change	No change	Higher
Open-market operations (FMOC)							
Buys bonds	No change	No change	No change	Higher	Higher	Higher	Higher
Sells bonds	No change	No change	No change	Lower	Lower	Lower	Lower
Discounting operations							
Lower rate	No change	Lower	Higher	Higher	Higher	Higher	Higher
Raise rate	No change	Higher	Lower	Lower	Lower	Lower	Lower
Jawboning	No change	Ambiguous		No change	Ambiguous		
Stock market margin requirements	Lower margin requirements presumably cause more stock market speculation while higher margin requirements presumably discourage speculation. There is, however, little statistical support for this proposition and a powerful theory to refute the idea.						

[a]Note: Unless interest rates paid on deposits change, households and firms are assumed to keep stable proportions of their money holdings in the forms of cash and demand deposits, respectively.

ties can alter the actual money multiplier and thwart the desire of the FED to change the money supply, then which tools are most effective in accomplishing the FED's objectives?

Any versatile do-it-yourselfer accumulates a number of tools that rust because they are seldom, if ever, used. This analogy applies to changes in stock market margin requirements and jawboning, which are used only rarely. Interest ceilings paid on deposits have been phased out. Reserve-requirement ratios are seldom varied, and then only slightly. They are too powerful to be very useful.

Since roughly 1967, the discount rate has been "pegged" slightly above interest rates in the federal-funds market. This encourages banks to borrow from each other and discourages them from borrowing reserves from the FED. At times, the discount rate and market interest rates have been inconsistent because the FED historically viewed it as undignified to change the discount rate more than two or three

times a year to reflect changes in interest rates in the federal-funds market. Changes in the discount rate normally are not intended to affect the money supply directly because the FED would like the actual money multiplier to be stable. Thus, discount rate changes are used primarily to keep constant the percentage of deposits held as excess reserves.

Open-market operations are the best tool to control the money supply. It took a long time for the FED to understand this, but open-market operations are now normally the only discretionary tool used actively by the Federal Reserve System. Open-market operations directly alter the reserves in the banking system. In the long run, open-market operations have no effect on the money multiplier. Active use of changes in reserve-requirement ratios or the discount rate operate primarily through changes in the actual money multiplier. The results of policy-caused changes in the actual multiplier have been erratic and unsatisfactory when used.

Financial Institutions and Regulations

Among our more important financial institutions are commercial banks, savings and loan associations, credit unions, insurance companies, and the various stock exchanges. These institutions are simply very specialized businesses.

The Role of Financial Institutions

The most crucial economic function of financial institutions is *to make the savings of households whose incomes exceed their spending available to investors* or to other households that wish to spend more on consumer goods than their incomes allow. This process is called **financial intermediation.** Other important roles of financial institutions are: (*a*) to provide secure places for savers to keep their deposits, and (*b*) to facilitate flows and payments of funds. For example, most payments are made through checking accounts.

Households allocate their after-tax incomes between consumption and saving. If you do not intend to use your savings for a while, you should be willing to let other people use them if they pay you interest so that you ultimately receive more than they have borrowed. Financial institutions find borrowers who are willing to pay higher interest rates than must be paid to savers. Differences between the interest paid by borrowers and that paid to savers provide incomes to the owners of financial institutions. You can imagine the disruptions to the economy if all savers had to seek out their own investors or borrowers, and vice versa. Transaction costs would be enormous. Financial institutions improve the efficiency of the economic system by cutting transactions costs.

The Diversity of Financial Institutions

Different financial institutions use different methods to secure the savings of individuals, which then can be either loaned or invested directly. Since people have different ideas about the best way to save (or borrow) and firms differ in the types of debt they are willing to incur, it seems natural that various types of financial intermediaries have developed to meet these diverse needs. A second reason for the diversity of financial institutions is the mix of federal and state laws and regulation governing them. Many of these institutions, however, are growing less distinct because of major banking deregulations that began in 1980.

Commercial Banks "Full service" **commercial banks** provide more services to their customers than simple maintenance of checking and savings accounts. Most banks offer a variety of personal and commercial loan services, issue bank credit cards such as MasterCharge and Visa, and have trust departments available to administer wills and estates.

Thrift Institutions Savings and loan associations, mutual savings banks, and credit unions are all called **thrift institutions.** The major difference between thrift institutions and commercial banks *used to be* that commercial banks offered checking accounts while thrift institutions could not. However, a major revision of our banking laws in 1980 made it possible for thrift institutions to offer accounts that are almost identical to bank checking accounts.

Most of the loans made by savings and loan associations and mutual savings banks are used to finance housing. Membership in a credit union is normally limited to the employees of a particular firm or members of a particular labor union or profession, although in some rural areas a geographic boundary determines eligibility for membership. Unlike savings and loans, credit unions offer their members loans for consumer purchases other than housing.

Insurance Companies Many people will bet a small amount of money on the outcome of the flip of a coin. However, only a few high rollers are willing to bet thousands of dollars with no better than even odds of winning. Most of us want the probable outcome of risky activities to favor us substantially or we just don't want to play. This widespread characteristic, called **risk aversion,** provides insurance companies with opportunities for profit.

Since most of us are willing to pay money to avoid some of the financial consequences of taking risks, **insurance companies** can sell us a guarantee against risk for a fee that is large enough to cover their claims and operating costs and still permit a profit. No one can predict whose house will burn down next—yours or your neighbor's. Thus, all insurance policy buyers make small contributions toward a fund that can be used to compensate the person whose house goes up in flames.

Insurance companies can provide this service and expect to make profits as long as the fee (or the **premium**) is greater than the amount they might have to pay multiplied by the probability of payment. Vast amounts are paid to insurance companies as premiums for life, auto, and health insurance, or as contributions to pension funds, many of which are administered by insurance companies. These funds are made available for loans to business firms or are invested directly by the insurance companies.

Securities Markets   **Securities** include paper assets such as stocks and bonds. Brokers, through whom securities are bought and sold, also provide financial intermediation. A **bond** is simply an IOU issued by a corporation or government agency that pays interest to the lender. A **share of stock** is a claim to partial ownership of a corporation. Most corporations and government agencies do not solicit you directly for funds that you might be willing to lend or invest. Instead, they typically leave this specialized sort of solicitation to brokers, who communicate offers to buy or sell securities through stock exchanges. Although the New York Stock Exchange (also known as *Wall Street*) is the best known, there are a number of lesser and regional stock exchanges.

The Changing Natures of Financial Institutions

Table 3 summarizes the major roles played by various types of financial intermediaries, but you should be aware that the differences between these institutions is increasingly blurred, in large measure because of recent deregulation of the financial sector of our economy.

TABLE 3   *Financial Intermediaries*

| | Commercial Banks | Thrift Institutions | | Insurance Companies | Securities Markets |
		Savings and Loans Mutual Savings Banks	Credit Unions		

Primary sources of funds (liabilities)	Deposits
	  Checking accounts
	  Savings accounts
		Deposits
		  Shares (savings)
		  Checking accounts
		  Other
			Deposits
			  Shares
			  Checking
			    accounts
				Insurance
				  policies
					Sales of stocks and bonds are accomplished primarily through stockbrokers and investment bankers who charge brokerage fees for getting savers (purchasers) together with business firms that do the direct economic investment with the funds made available

Primary uses of funds (assets)	Business loans
	Consumer loans
	  Automobiles
	  Home
	    improvements
	  Furniture and
	    appliances
	  Education
	  Personal
		Home mortgages
		Home
		  improvements
			Consumer loans
			  autos, etc.
				Business loans
				Real estate
				Direct financial
				  investment	

Notes	Banks "create" money by crediting your account when they extend a loan to you	Major function is to finance housing (not business construction)	Focus on consumer loans for members only	Insurance company premiums exceed their expected payouts; people buy insurance because they are risk averse	

During the 1970s, international inflation, the dollar's decline from complete dominance in world money markets, and a host of other factors generated pressures for changes in the financial sector of our economy. Major deregulation occurred in 1980, but many reforms were phased in gradually. As inflation subsided in the 1980s, resulting in a strong dollar abroad, further pressures for deregulation abated. However, there still exist many regulations that promote inefficiency.

The FED's Independence Under Attack

The Great Depression of the 1930s caused a widespread loss of faith in monetary policy. The Keynesian Revolution, from 1936 into the late 1960s, convinced most economists that fiscal policy is the best way to stabilize the economy. Since the 1970s, however, monetary policy has made a strong comeback, and few economists today believe that "money doesn't matter."

The gradual reaffirmation of the importance of monetary policy began in the late 1950s. At that time, the FED's policy of slow monetary growth was widely attacked as hindering the economy from achieving its potential. In the early 1960s, William McChesney Martin, Jr., was the chairman of the Board of Governors. He was roundly condemned by Keynesians for following contractionary monetary policies that partially offset the expansionary fiscal policies adopted by the Kennedy and Johnson Administrations. The failure of a 1968 tax surcharge to slow inflation was blamed by some on too rapid monetary growth during 1968–69. In the 1970s, "stop-go" monetary policies were partially blamed for stagflation and the reemergence of the business cycle. Then, in the early 1980s under the chairmanship of Paul Volcker, the FED was blamed by many for following restrictive monetary policies that caused a severe slump in business activity. Most observers conceded, however, that these restrictive policies did much to reduce inflation and interest rates.

One consequence of the renewed recognition of the power of monetary policy is pressure for the FED to be "politically accountable." Many regulatory agencies are thought to be controlled by the industries they are supposed to oversee. The FED is often accused of being a captive of banking interests and of following monetary policies that benefit bankers without regard for the public interest. A recent proposed reform is that the four-year term of the chairman of the Board of Governors begin and end in the presidential election years. A new president could ensure that the chairman would conduct monetary policy compatible with "the people's choice." Opponents of this reform argue for close checks on presidential power over both monetary and fiscal policies.

Another proposal is intended to eliminate shocks to the economy arising from erratic and unexpected changes in monetary policy. A congressional resolution prescribes that the FED should limit monetary growth to a range of 2–6 percent annually and should announce its targets for growth well in advance so that businesses and financial institutions can adjust. (This proposal is closely related to the argument that rules, not discretion, should determine the course of demand-management policies. Reasons for monetary growth rules are described in more detail in Chapter 18.)

The FED has mounted a multifaceted defense of its independence and discretion over policy. The fear of politicization is a central issue. The FED argues that it should be free to follow what it perceives to be the best monetary policies possible, not policies based on political considerations.

What incentives do the governors of the FED have to follow policies most beneficial for the economic well-being of the American people? The banks that "invest" in the FED are limited to a 6 percent rate of return, and there are no strong political checks on FED governors. The FED responds that its officers and administrators are public-spirited people who simply want the satisfaction of knowing that they are doing the best job they can for the American public. This answer is not very satisfying to economists, who believe that the most powerful of human motivations is self-interest. However, subjecting the FED to political pressure is not an especially appealing alternative to relying on the FED management's interest in the public welfare. Will the role of the FED change? Should it? If so, how? Only time will tell.

The Purposes of Financial Regulations

The purpose of any financial system is to channel saving to its most productive uses. The major goals in regulating financial institutions are: (*a*) protection of savers, (*b*) stabilization of the economy, and (*c*) promotion of efficiency. The government traditionally has been willing to forgo some efficiency in the financial system in order to achieve other objectives.

Financial institutions are not lenders per se, but only act as intermediaries between savers and borrowers. In this context, **financial efficiency** means minimizing the costs of intermediation, or the bankers' "spread"—the differences between the costs of loans to borrowers and the interest incomes received by ultimate lenders. This is the financial equivalent of the principle that efficiency requires all services to be produced at the lowest possible opportunity cost. Unfortunately, protecting people's savings and ensuring economic stability are often in conflict with efficiency in financial intermediation. Recent trends in deregulation have allowed many financial institutions to become "money supermarkets" capable of providing virtually all financial services. There are, however, still some inefficient regulations governing many parts of our financial system.

Constraints on Interest Rates: A Critique

The economic distortions associated with price controls have long been recognized and are discussed in Chapters 4 and 17. Controls on interest rates are no exception to this principle.

Interest on Deposits
In the past, financial intermediaries were limited in their ability to compete for deposits through explicit interest payments. As a result, they paid "interest" in the form of "free" checking accounts and toaster ovens and radios. One Boston bank gave away "free" Rolls-Royces in 1979.

Under these circumstances the real rates of interest paid savers by competing institutions were difficult to assess, reducing the quality of information and, therefore, the level of competition among financial intermediaries. Flows of funds that destabilized the financial sector occurred whenever market rates of interest substantially exceeded the maximum interest legally payable on deposits.

Constraints on interest paid generated both inefficiency and instability. In addition, these controls seemed inequitable. Most low-income savers hold their savings in financial institutions, while high-income savers invest their funds directly in capital or in financial instruments (Treasury bonds, corporate stocks, and the like) where rates of return are not controlled. Laws that forced low-income savers to receive smaller rates of return than are received by high-income savers seem unfair to most of us. Recent declines in saving and capital accumulation are among the factors that caused policymakers to be concerned enough about these small savers to phase out these interest ceilings on deposits.

Usury Laws and Credit Rationing
Most states and several federal agencies impose ceilings, called **usury laws,** on the maximum interest rates that can be charged to borrowers. For example, agencies that guarantee home mortgages set maximum permissible interest rates for many home loans. Whenever market interest rates exceed these ceilings, funds are not available for mortgages. Usury laws and regulations undoubtedly account for more of the volatility of commercial and residential construction than does any other single factor. In addition, usury laws may cause interstate money (credit) flows.

When ceilings on interest rates apply, credit is rationed on some other basis—quite often **credit worthiness.** The extent of **credit rationing** varies considerably over the business cycle, and the bulk of the distortive impacts of the numerous "credit crunches" over the past three decades can be attributed directly to interest rate ceilings.

Another important reason to eliminate usury laws is that they are inequitable. People who are poor often cannot borrow at rates allowed by law because of lack of "credit worthiness," while wealthier borrowers pay lower interest rates because the competition for loanable funds is reduced when low-income borrowers are *rationed* out of the market. Loan applications from poor people who wish to borrow are rejected in favor of extending loans to people who are less risky. If usury ceilings were eliminated, flows of credit to poor people would grow, and the interest rates paid by those who are better off would rise a bit.

In this chapter, we have outlined the most heavily regulated industry in America. These regulations stem from the disasters of the Great Depression and a recognition that controlling monetary aggregates is necessary to control aggregate economic activity. The FED uses three main tools to alter the money supply: reserve requirements, open-market operations, and discounting operations. Monetary policy used to control inflation or avert a recession is the focal point of the next chapter.

CHAPTER REVIEW: KEY POINTS

1. Since fractional reserve banking makes it impossible for all banks to pay all demand deposits simultaneously, resolutions of monetary crises may require intervention by a *central bank*.

2. The value of the potential money multiplier (m_p) is the reciprocal of the *reserve-requirement ratio (1/rr)*. Excess reserves in the financial system and cash holdings by the public are drains on the potential multiplier. The actual multiplier (m_a) is the amount of currency and bank reserves issued by the Federal Reserve System (*MB*) divided into the money supply (*MS*): $m_a = MS/MB$.

3. The FED's most powerful but least used primary tool is its power to change reserve requirements (**rr**). Increases in **rr** reduce the money multiplier and money supply, and vice versa.

4. The most useful tool of the FED is *open-market operations* (*OMO*). After all adjustments, open-market operations affect the monetary base, not the money multiplier. When the FED sells government bonds, bank reserves are reduced and the money supply declines. FED purchases of bonds increase bank reserves and the money supply.

5. The *discount rate* (d) is the interest rate the FED charges member banks. When the discount rate is low relative to market interest rates, banks hold few excess reserves and will borrow funds from the FED. Consequently, the money supply increases. High discount rates relative to market interest rates cause banks to borrow less from the FED and provide incentives for larger holdings of excess reserves. The actual money multiplier and total bank reserves fall, and the money supply falls.

6. The FED's other tools include *margin requirements* to limit stock market credit and *jawboning*.

7. *Financial institutions* facilitate flows and payments of funds and provide secure places for savers' deposits. Their most important economic function is to channel funds from savers to financial investors and other borrowers through a process called *financial intermediation*.

8. *Usury laws* reduce the availability of credit to the poor. Interest ceilings on deposits hold down interest rates paid depositors, and cause higher interest rates to be charged to borrowers.

QUESTIONS FOR THOUGHT AND DISCUSSION

1. Until 1980, the reserve-requirement ratios for state-chartered banks were generally lower than for national banks. How might this partially explain the growth in state banks relative to national banks during the preceding 60 years? What effects would this have on the FED's ability to control the money supply? On pressures for the FED to reduce reserve requirement ratios for national banks? How might you test to see whether your answers to these questions are correct?

2. Banks have been forbidden to establish branches across state borders, and many states absolutely forbid branch banking. Bank "holding companies" have finessed those laws in some places, and there is now substantial political pressure to relax these laws. What potential gains and losses do you perceive from allowing nationwide branch banking?

3. Should opening a financial institution be more complicated than starting a business such as a florist? What special controls, if any, should the government exercise over financial institutions?

4. Since most bank deposits are insured for up to $100,000 by the Federal Deposit Insurance Corporation (FDIC), do reserve requirements add to the safety of depositors? If not, what is the purpose of requiring banks to hold reserves?

5. What effect will a million-dollar bank robbery have on the *M*1 money supply? (Remember that *M*1 is cash in the public's hands plus demand deposits.)

6. Would it matter if the FED eliminated the discount rate entirely and abolished bank borrowing from the Federal Reserve? One of the original roles played by discounting operations was averting panics touched off by the withdrawal of currency from banks in response to the fear of bank insolvency. Is this role still valid today? What benefits are derived from current discounting operations?

7. It is argued that the major function of reserve requirements is to preserve the liquidity and solvency of member banks and thus protect the public from bank failures. Critics of reserve requirements argue that these requirements are nothing more than an "interest free" loan to the government or a "tax on banking." What would be the effect on (a) solvency of banks, and (b) ability of the FED to control the money supply if reserve requirements were eliminated? Would banks still continue to hold reserves? Why or why not?

CHAPTER 14 Monetary Theory

Money is but a symbol of all that is worth having. Its possession in quantity can be a blessing to the virtuous individual, but a curse to masses afflicted by gluttony. Prudent coiners of a society's money gain for their country a stable prosperity, but profligate masters of money can visit ruin on their nation and all its neighbors.

—*Daniel Webster*

Money is important to each of us. You would be better off if the amount of money you have now were doubled. Just how important to our economic welfare is the total quantity of money in circulation? If everyone suddenly had twice as much money as they presently do, would you benefit? Would the average person?

Controversy raged over questions like these even before the conquistadors shipped enormous amounts of stolen gold from the "New World" to sixteenth-century Spain and created a wave of inflation throughout Europe. The Depression-era work of John Maynard Keynes rekindled the fires surrounding these issues. They are still far from being resolved.

The Demand for Money: A Preview

I have all the money I need for the rest of my life—provided I die by 4 o'clock this afternoon.

—*Henny Youngman*

You would probably say NO! if asked, "Do you have enough money?" As with the question "What is money?", the answer seems obvious. However, your behavior probably indicates that at times you have too much money, and so you spend it; at other times you try to acquire more money because you have too little. Ambiguity arises because people commonly use the word *money* as a synonym for *wealth*. They may also say *money* when they mean *income*. If asked if you had enough income or enough wealth, you could undoubtedly justify an answer of no. Money is not the same thing as income, nor is it identical to wealth—although it is related to both. Money is the device used to buy goods or resources and by which we measure our incomes, wealth, and the prices we pay.

Just as markets for commodities are in equilibrium only if the quantities supplied and demanded are equal at current prices, the quantity of money supplied must equal the quantity demanded to balance money markets. In this chapter, you will learn that money markets must be in equilibrium for equilibration of the level of national income, the price level, and the market rate of interest.

Most people spend in predictable patterns and receive money at regular intervals. When you spend money, you see the goods you buy as more desirable than the money they cost; relative to these goods, you have temporary surpluses of money. Over the same time periods, if you act to secure more money income by selling your time or your goods, or by saving more money out of your income, you must have temporary shortages of money relative to your time or these goods.

Motives for Holding Money

Our individual demands for money are a bit more complicated than this. It would be fruitless to break up our demand for cars into "vacation," "work," "commuter," or "shopping" motives. Economists, however, have found it useful to compartmentalize the reasons we hold money instead of investing in other assets or engaging in higher levels of consumption. We have already examined some of the functions money performs: money is a medium of exchange, a unit of account, a store of value, and a standard of deferred payment (from Chapter 12). One trivial way of explaining your demand for money is to say that you desire money for the functions it performs. You can gain more insights into the way money works by looking at three categories of motives for holding money.

Transactions Demands

Possibly the most important reason for holding money is because you plan to spend it. In fact, classical economic reasoning focuses almost exclusively on this motive. This intent is called the **transactions demand** for money. You can predict many if not most transactions fairly accurately. You know how much your monthly rent and car payment will be,

and roughly how much you will spend on utilities, gasoline, and meals. You probably also have a good idea about how much money you will receive in the near future.

Most workers receive their paychecks regularly—either daily, weekly, biweekly, or monthly. Students may receive money monthly or once or twice a semester. Predictable and regular transaction flows of money to and from an individual who is paid $2,000 monthly are reflected in the blue line in Figure 1. The vertical rise of the area shaded in red shows money-holding patterns for someone with an identical $2,000 monthly income, but who is paid $1,000 at the middle and again at the end of each month. Notice that this person's average holdings of money are much lower than for the individual paid monthly. We have shown more rapid declines in money holdings right after a payday than toward the end of the pay period. You are typical if you write a lot of checks right after you get paid, and then find yourself almost broke before you are paid again.

FIGURE 1 *Transactions Balances*

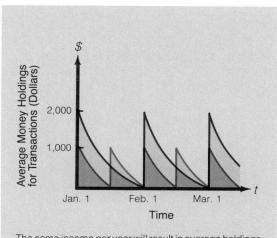

The same income per year will result in average holdings of money that are inversely related to the frequency of receipts of income. All else equal, a person paid twice a month will hold only half the average money balances held by someone paid once a month. Our spending patterns ensure that most of us will have far less money on hand at the end of a pay period than at the beginning because we use money to make transactions.

Precautionary Demands

Even if you hold enough money to cover your spending plans, you probably feel very uncomfortable if you have no extra money in reserve. There always seem to be little—and sometimes big—emergencies that require money. For example, you may have the hard luck of a flat tire or lost textbooks, or you may pleasantly discover that the "Blue Light Special" at a department store is a record you want. You hold precautionary balances to ensure that you will have money on hand to meet unexpected expenditures.

The major difference between the transactions and **precautionary demands** for money lies in the degree of predictability about future spending. However, both motives suggest that your average of money balances held will be positively related to your income—you probably hold more money now than when you were ten years old, and far less than you will hold when you put your student days behind you and find employment that pays well. Figure 2 stacks the precautionary demand for money on top of the transactions demand to show how the total of these two demands are related to income. One of Keynes's innovations in monetary theory is the idea of the precautionary motive. While earlier classical writers ignored this motive in their writings on money, they would have had little difficulty accepting this idea because, like transactions balances, precautionary balances of money are closely related to income.

Asset Demand

Keynes's major innovation in monetary theory is the concept of an **asset demand** for money, an idea that clashes with early classical theory. Early classical theory presumes that no one will hold money as an asset because they could earn interest on stocks or bonds if they made these financial investments instead. The desire to hold some of your assets or wealth in the form of money originates from: (*a*) any expectation that the prices of stocks or bonds will fall in the near future, (*b*) reluctance to hold only assets that tend to swing widely in value over time, or (*c*) a belief that transactions costs are higher than any expected return from investments in stocks or bonds.

Speculative Balances   Suppose that you have saved some of your income and plan to buy stocks, bonds, or real estate. If you expect the prices of these financial investments to fall in the near future, you will postpone their purchase until prices are down, holding money as an asset in the interim.

Bond Prices and Interest Rates   Rising interest rates cause bond prices to fall and lower interest rates mean higher bond prices. Suppose you were offered a chance to buy a government bond that offered the following terms:

> The bearer of this bond will be paid $100.00 on January 31 of each year, forever.

If it required a 10 percent return to persuade you to buy this bond, you would be willing to pay $1,000 for it because 10 percent times $1,000 equals $100, which is the annual payment. If you required a 20 percent return on your financial investment, the bond would be worth only $500 to you [0.20($500) = $100]. Thus, higher interest rates imply lower bond prices (20 percent > 10 percent, and $500 < $1,000). The general formula for the special bond of the type we have dealt with here (called a **perpetuity**) is:

$$\text{present value} = \frac{\text{annual payment}}{\text{interest rate}}.$$

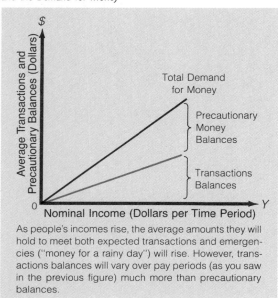

FIGURE 2 *Nominal Income, Precautionary Balances, and the Demand for Money*

As people's incomes rise, the average amounts they will hold to meet both expected transactions and emergencies ("money for a rainy day") will rise. However, transactions balances will vary over pay periods (as you saw in the previous figure) much more than precautionary balances.

FIGURE 3 *Typical Patterns of Money Holdings*

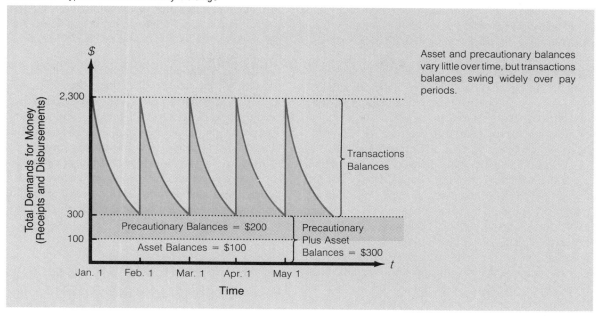

Asset and precautionary balances vary little over time, but transactions balances swing widely over pay periods.

Remember that higher interest rates mean lower bond prices, while falling interest rates drive bond prices up. If you and other potential bond buyers believe that interest rates will rise soon, you should speculate against bonds and hold money while you wait for bond prices to fall.

Risk Avoidance   Keynes emphasized the speculative aspect of the asset demand for money. Other economists have developed other reasons to explain why individuals may hold money as an asset. Assets that yield high average rates of return tend to be very risky. We tend to invest only if the assets we buy with money are expected to yield returns that compensate us for our reduced liquidity *and* the increased risk of loss. Some people are so risk averse that they hold (hoard) money because they view the rates of return on any other asset as too low to overcome the associated risks.

Transaction Costs   Money is the most liquid of all assets. If you have so little wealth that transaction costs overshadow any potential gains, you will hold money instead of investing. For example, if you have only $50 to invest and expect a $50 share of stock to generate a $5 profit, it is better to hold money if the stockbroker's fee is more than $5.

All these reasons for people to hold money as an asset lead to the conclusion that their money holdings will be negatively related to the interest rate.

Transactions demands are related to time, as suggested in Figure 1. However, there is no reason to believe that either precautionary or asset demands for money are systematically related to time. Although it is not possible to precisely isolate particular chunks of money into handy compartments, the transactions, precautionary, and asset motives are reasonable explanations for why most of us keep positive balances of money handy. Typical total money holdings for a person paid $2,000 once a month are depicted in Figure 3.

The Costs of Holding Money

As with other goods, the quantity of money demanded will depend on its opportunity cost. Since most things can be bought with money, it might seem difficult to specify the sacrifice associated with holdings of money. However, these sacrifices take the form of either interest forgone from income-earning assets not held (the Keynesian view) or forgone consumer goods and services (the classical view).

The Classical View The subjective value of a dollar in exchange for consumer goods from the vantage point of the typical consumer is roughly the reciprocal of the price level ($1/P$). This occurs because the greater the cost of living, the lower consumption sacrificed by holding a dollar. Each dollar will buy fewer goods. Thus, the higher the price level, the more dollars you need to hold for expected transactions. This relationship between the quantity of money demanded and the reciprocal of the price level is at the root of classical monetary theory.

However, the relationship between the cost of living and the quantity of money demanded is not quite this simple. Suppose that we have experienced inflation for a substantial period of time and that you expect inflation to continue. Fearing the decline in value of a dollar, you will want to *reduce* your dollar holdings and purchase more goods since those dollars buy more today than in the future given inflationary price increases. Consequently, there tends to be a *negative* relationship between the expected rate of inflation and the demand for money. We know that this is a bit sketchy at the moment, but these relationships are explored in more detail when we examine modern monetarism later in this chapter.

The Keynesian View The closest alternatives to money as an asset are stocks, bonds, or other liquid assets that pay interest. You receive no interest on your cash holdings and relatively low interest rates on your demand deposits. If interest rates are relatively high on nonmonetary assets, you are far more likely to hold your wealth in stocks or bonds than if interest rates are low; then money is a much more attractive asset. This contrasts sharply with the classical view that the major costs of holding money are the goods that might be enjoyed if the money were spent.

Classical Monetary Theory

Before Adam Smith cleared the air with his book *Wealth of Nations,* the economic policies of the monarchs who ruled Europe were grounded in **mercantilism,** a doctrine based on the failure to understand the difference between money and wealth. Gold and silver were thought to be real wealth, so England, Spain, Portugal, and other European countries engaged in colonial expansion to find gold or silver and fought numerous wars in the process. The losers

were invariably forced to pay the winners out of their national treasuries. Aztec gold and Incan silver poured into Spain. Various monarchs debased their currencies to finance wars in the Old World and colonization of the New World.

Whether debasement or foreign conquest was used to enrich the royal coffers, the amount of money in circulation grew. Numerous early economic thinkers noted that inflation seemed invariably to follow these increases in money supplies. These early versions of the **Quantity Theory of Money** were formalized around the beginning of the twentieth century by some British economists at Cambridge University and by Irving Fisher of Yale University. Fisher's analysis began with the Equation of Exchange.

The Equation of Exchange

Gross National Product has price level (P) and "real" output (Q) components; therefore, nominal GNP can be written as PQ. Just how is the supply of money (M) related to our GNP? One extremely important consideration is the average number of times that money changes hands annually for purchases of final output. For example, GNP in 1985 was roughly $4 trillion, while the money supply ($M1$) was about $620 billion (or $0.62 trillion)—the average dollar was used about seven times for purchases of output produced in 1985. This number, the average number of times a unit of money is used annually, is called the **income velocity (V)** of money, and is computed by dividing GNP by the money supply: $V \equiv PQ/M$. If we multiply both sides of $V \equiv PQ/M$ by M, the result is the **Equation of Exchange**:

$$M \times V \equiv P \times Q.$$

This equation is definitionally true, given our computation of velocity, and is interpreted: *The quantity of money times its velocity is equal to the price level times real output, which equals GNP.* Note that this equation suggests that the *velocity* of money is just as important as the *quantity* of money in circulation. A mathematically proximate corollary is that *the percentage change in the money supply **plus** the percentage change in velocity **equals** the percentage change in the price level **plus** the percentage change in real output:*

$$\frac{\Delta M}{M} + \frac{\Delta V}{V} = \frac{\Delta P}{P} + \frac{\Delta Q}{Q}.$$

Concentrate for a moment on the right-hand side of this equation. Does it make sense that if the price of, say, oranges rose by 1 percent and you cut your purchases of them by 2 percent, your spending on oranges would fall by 1 percent? Intuitively, the percentage change in price plus the percentage change in quantity equals the percentage change in spending. Now examine the equation once more. Suppose that real output grew by 3 percent, that velocity did not change, and that the money supply increased by 7 percent. Prices would increase by 4 percent (7 percent + 0 percent = 4 percent + 3 percent). Remembering these relationships will help you comprehend arguments between classical monetary theorists and their detractors.

The Crude Quantity Theory of Money

From certain assumptions about the variables in the Equation of Exchange ($M, V, P,$ and Q), classical economists (including Fisher) conclude that, in equilibrium, the price level (P) is exactly proportional to the money supply (M). Let us see how they arrived at this conclusion.

The Constancy of Velocity
Classical economic reasoning views the income velocity (V) of money as determined solely by institutional factors, such as the organizational structure and efficiency of banking and credit, and by people's habitual patterns of spending money after receiving income. Velocity is thought to be constant, at least in the short run, because changes tend to occur slowly in: (*a*) the technologies of financial institutions (the ways checks clear or loans are granted or repaid); and (*b*) in the inflows and outflows of individuals' money (frequencies of receipts of incomes and the habits that people have about spending their money). Thus, we see a central assumption of the classical quantity theory: $\Delta V/V = 0$. However, as Focus 1 reveals, this assumption may not always hold.

But why does classical economics view velocity (V) as unaffected by the price level (P), the real level of output (Q), or the money supply (M)? The answer lies in why people demand money. Classical macroeconomic models assume that people want to hold money only to consummate transactions and that people's spendings are fixed proportions of their incomes. Our previous discussion of the transactions motive is basically classical. Since national income is

approximately GNP (or $P \times Q$), then the demand for money M_d (a transactions demand) can be written:

$$M_\text{d} = kPQ,$$

where k is the constant proportion of income that would be held in monetary balances.[1] For example, if each family habitually held one-fifth of their average annual income of $10,000 in the form of money, then the average quantity of money each family would demand would be $M_\text{d} = 0.20(\$10,000) = \$2,000$. The quantity of money demanded in the entire economy would be $2,000 times the number of families.

The Constancy of Real Output
Classical theory also assumes that real output (Q) does not depend on the other variables ($M, V,$ and P) in the Equation of Exchange. Classical economists believe that the natural state of the economy is full employment, so real output is influenced solely by the state of technology and by the amounts of resources available. Full employment is ensured by Say's Law if prices, wages, and interest rates are perfectly flexible. Moreover, both the amounts of resources available and the state of technology are thought to change slowly, if at all, in the short run. Therefore, real output (Q) is assumed to be approximately constant and $\Delta Q/Q = 0$. This may seem like a very strong assertion, but the intuitive appeal of the argument that real output is independent of the quantity of money (M), its velocity (V), or the price level (P), is convincing to both classical monetary theorists and to the modern supply-side economists who have updated the classical tradition.

It seems reasonable to believe that the amount of paper currency or coins issued by the government has virtually no effect on the economy's productive capacity. Similarly, the velocity of money should not influence capacity. But what about the price level? After all, the law of supply suggests that the quantities of individual goods and services supplied will be

---

1. We know that the Equation of Exchange relates the supply of money to national income through velocity: $MV \equiv PQ$. Let us divide both sides by V:

$$M = PQ/V.$$

Since the quantities of money supplied and demanded must be equal in equilibrium ($M = M_\text{d}$), k must be equal to $1/V$, both k and V being constants. As a result, classical monetarists discerned a fixed relationship between k (the proportion of annual income people want to hold as money) and V (the velocity of money).

FOCUS 1

Velocity in the 1980s

The results postulated by monetarism and the Quantity Theory of Money depend heavily on the relative constancy of velocity. If velocity is constant, then a more rapid rate of monetary growth would mean higher inflation. But what happens if the public desires more money as the FED expands the money supply? Income velocity falls and the inflationary effects forecasted by monetarists may not be forthcoming.

Velocity fell substantially in most Western countries during the first half of the 1980s, as shown in Figure 4. The inflationary effects of increased monetary growth were partially offset by declining velocity. High real interest rates attracted saving into interest-bearing accounts, and these accounts now constitute a large fraction of all monetary aggregates. The deregulation of financial markets in the 1980s generated dozens of new instruments and virtually eliminated the boundaries between different types of financial institutions. Monetarists would argue that the early 1980s were unique and that once people have thoroughly adjusted to deregulation, velocity will regain its relative stability and the classical relationship between the rate of change of the money supply and inflation will resume.

FIGURE 4   *The Velocity of Money, 1980–85 (Selected Western Countries)*

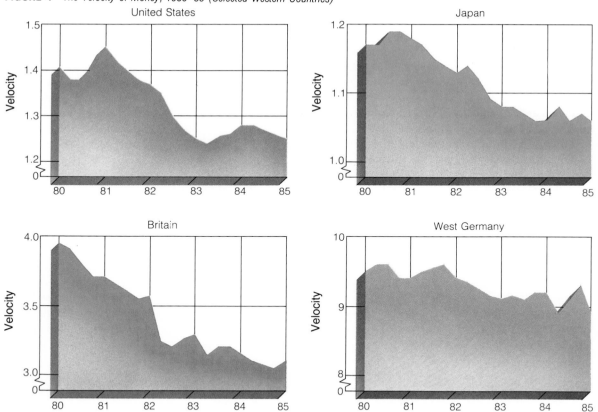

The velocity of money is nominal GNP divided by the money supply. The measure of the money supply used for the United States is *M*3; for Britain, £*M*3; for Japan, *M*2 + CDs; and for West Germany, Central Bank Money (CBM).

Source: *The Economist*, July 27, 1985, p. 63.

greater the higher the market prices are. Shouldn't the nation's output increase if the price level rises? Classical economists say NO! Here is why.

A Crude Monetary Theory of the Price Level

Suppose that your income and the values of all your assets exactly double. (That's the good news.) Suppose that the prices of everything you buy and all your debts also precisely double. (That's the bad news.) Should your behavior change in any way? Your intuition should suggest not. Using similar logic, classical economists conclude that neither real output nor any other aspect of "real" economic behavior is systematically affected by changes in the price level. Economic behavior is shaped by relative prices, not the absolute level of prices.

Recall that the percentage changes in the money supply and velocity roughly equal the percentage changes in the levels of prices and real output. If velocity is constant and output is stable at a full employment level in the short run, then $\Delta V/V$ and $\Delta Q/Q$ both equal zero. Classical economists are left with a relationship between the money supply (M) and the price level (P): *In equilibrium, the rate of inflation is exactly the same as the percentage rate of increase in the money supply* ($\Delta M/M = \Delta P/P$). Thus, any increase in the rate of growth of the money supply would not affect real output, just inflation.

The Classical View of Investment

Firms will buy machinery, construct buildings, or attempt to increase inventories whenever they expect the gross returns on these investments to exceed the total costs of acquiring them. Because classical economists assume relatively stable and predictable economies, they focus on the costs of acquiring investment goods; business investors' expectations of profits are assumed realized, and the costs of new capital goods are presumed stable.

Investment occurs as long as the expected rate of return on investment is greater than the interest rate. Since the prices of capital equipment are fairly stable, any changes in the costs of acquiring capital are primarily the result of changes in interest rates. [Investors are effectively trading dimes for dollars as long as the cost of borrowing (the interest rate) is less than the return from investments made possible by borrowing.] Naturally, business people will not make an investment unless they expect a return at least as

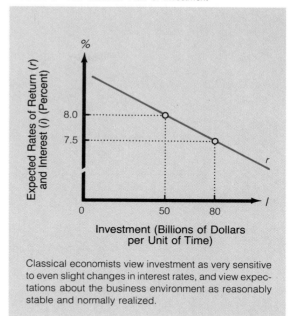

FIGURE 5 *The Classical View of Investment*

Classical economists view investment as very sensitive to even slight changes in interest rates, and view expectations about the business environment as reasonably stable and normally realized.

high as they would receive if they simply lent the money out at interest.

Classical writers believe that investment is very sensitive to the interest rate and that large swings in the level of investment occur because of minute changes in interest rates. The *expected rate of return* (r) curve in Figure 5 is relatively sensitive, or flat. In this example, a decline in interest of 1/2 percent (from 8 percent to 7.5 percent) will cause a 60 percent increase in investment $[(80 - 50)/50 = 30/50 = 0.60]$. Flexible interest rates and a highly sensitive investment (rate of return) schedule easily equate planned saving and investment, stabilizing the economy at full employment.

The Classical Monetary Transmission Mechanism

Many monetarists believe that the linkage between the money supply and national income is not only strong, but direct. This **classical monetary transmission mechanism** (how money enters the economy) is shown in Figure 6. Panel A reflects the effects of money on nominal income and Panel B translates these changes into effects on real output.

Initially, if the money supply is $2 trillion ($M_{s0}$), nominal income in Panel A will be $4 trillion (point a). Note that $\boldsymbol{MV = PQ,}$ and, thus, $M = kPQ$ where k

FIGURE 6 *The Classical Monetary Transmission Mechanism and the Price Level*

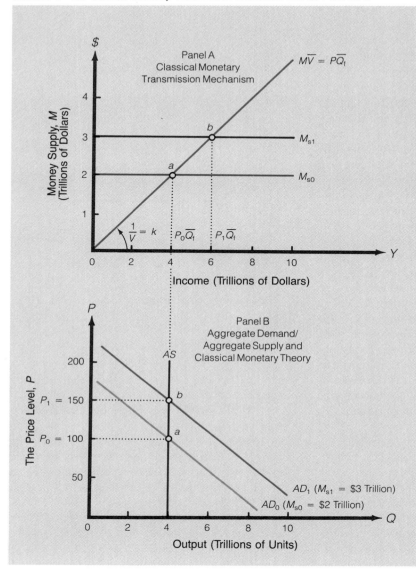

Expanding the money supply from M_{s0} ($2 trillion) to M_{s1} ($3 trillion) causes Aggregate Spending to grow in Panel A so that nominal income ($P \times Q$) rises from $4 trillion to $6 trillion. Output is assumed to be at a full employment level of 4 trillion units in Panel B, however, so all of this growth is absorbed by price increases. When Aggregate Demand rises from AD_0 to AD_1 in Panel B, the price level inflates from its base of 100 to a new level of 150.

$= 1/V$. Panel A of Figure 6 assumes that $V = 2$ and, thus, $k = 0.5$. This $4-trillion nominal income ($Y = P_0\overline{Q}_f$) is equal[2] in Panel B to 4 trillion units of real output (point *a*) at an average price level P_0 of 100 ($M\overline{V} = P\overline{Q} \rightarrow 2 \times 2 = 1 \times 4$). Increasing the money supply to $3 trillion ($M_{s1}$) increases nominal income to $6 trillion (point *b* in Panel A). Since output is

fixed at full employment ($\overline{Q}_f$) and velocity is constant at 2, the result from introducing this extra money into the economy is to push the price level to 150 (point *b* in Panel B where $M\overline{V} = P\overline{Q} \rightarrow 3 \times 2 = 1.5 \times 4$). Thus, in a classical world, monetary policy will have only price effects, not quantity effects.

Summary: The Crude Quantity Theory of Money
Summarizing the foundations of the early **Crude Quantity Theory of Money,** we know that the

---

2. Bars over variables indicate constancy.

Equation of Exchange is a truism because of the way velocity is computed: $MV = PQ$. It follows that:

$$\frac{\Delta M}{M} + \frac{\Delta V}{V} = \frac{\Delta P}{P} + \frac{\Delta Q}{Q}.$$

If velocity is assumed constant (written $\overline{V}$) and real output is fixed at a full employment level (written $\overline{Q_f}$), then $\Delta V/V = 0$, and $\Delta Q/Q = 0$. Moreover, $\Delta M/M = \Delta P/P$. Any changes in the money supply will be reflected in proportional changes in the price level. This is the major result of the Crude Quantity Theory of Money:

$$M\overline{V} = P\overline{Q_f}.$$

Another conclusion is that real output (or any other "real" economic behavior) is unaffected in the long run by either the money supply or the price level. Clearly, these early and subsequent versions of the Quantity Theory of Money are misnamed—they should be called *Monetary Theories of the Price Level*.

Classical theorists conclude by saying "Money is a veil." By this they mean that money, inflation, or deflation may temporarily disguise the real world; but in the long run, money affects only the price level, with virtually no effect on such real variables as production, employment, labor force participation, unemployment, or relative prices. Even though classical theorists were vociferous opponents of large expansions of the money supply because of fear that inflation temporarily distorts behavior, it is probably fair to say that classical monetary theory leads to the conclusion that in the long run, "money does not matter." It does not affect production, consumption, investment, or any other "real" economic behavior. When we deal graphically with the demand and supply of money in later sections, we will resurrect some of these classical propositions about money to see what they contribute to modern monetary theory.

Keynesian Monetary Theory

The brunt of Keynes's attack on the classical Quantity Theory of Money was directed at the assumptions that: (*a*) velocity is constant, and (*b*) full employment is the natural state of a market economy.

Early classical economists believed that money balances are held only for transactions purposes and that the transactions anyone engages in are roughly proportional to that individual's nominal income. Thus, planned money balances were assumed roughly proportional to nominal income. "Why," they asked, "would people want to hold money unless they intend to spend it? Virtually any other asset yields a positive rate of return—and money holdings do not. No one holds more money than they need for transactions. They hold income-earning assets instead of money whenever possible." Keynes responded by adding the precautionary and asset (speculative) motives to the transactions motive for holding money.

Remember that people adjust their money balances so that what they want, or demand, equals what they have. If you have more money than the quantity you demand, you spend or invest more, reducing your money balances. If you demand more money than you presently hold, you acquire more by cutting back on your spending out of income, liquidating some of your assets, or selling more of your time. Keynes emphasized financial investments (in stocks or bonds) as the major way to reduce one's money holdings.

The Asset Demand for Money

One major difference between the classical model and Keynes's model is that classical economists view the world as a reasonably certain place, while Keynesian reasoning emphasizes uncertainty and describes how our expectations about uncertain futures might affect the economy. Rising uncertainty is a major reason for growth of the asset demand for money.

Suppose you are working on an assembly line when the economy nose-dives. Many of your co-workers are laid off. You would probably increase your saving because you could be the next one to find a "pink slip" in your pay envelope. As your savings mount, assets in the form of money balances grow. What happens to the velocity of money? Velocity falls as saving increases. Why not invest these funds in a stock or bond that pays interest or some positive rate of return? You must be kidding! The economy is in a tailspin—a depression may be approaching rapidly. The crucial point here is that when people expect hard times, the velocity of money falls when people convert money from transactions balances to precautionary or asset balances. Conversely, money balances are increasingly held for transactions purposes when prosperity seems just around the corner. This causes velocity to rise.

Let us see what all this means within the context of the Equation of Exchange. Since the percentage changes in the money supply plus velocity are equal to the percentage changes in the price level plus the real level of output, a 5 percent decline in velocity (money supply assumed constant) will cause nominal GNP to fall by 5 percent. If prices do not fall fairly rapidly, output and employment will decline by about 5 percent. (One of the rules of economics is that *if circumstances change and prices do not adjust, quantities will.*) The economy may settle in equilibrium at less than full employment.

Keynes and his followers assumed that prices adjust slowly, especially on the down side, and that people's expectations are volatile. This implies that the velocity of money may vary considerably over time and that the real economy may adjust only very slowly, if at all, to these variations.

The Liquidity Trap

Classical economists viewed the interest rate as an incentive for saving—you are rewarded for postponing consumption. Keynes's rebuttal was that interest is a reward for sacrificing liquidity. According to Keynes, how much you save is determined by your income and will be affected very little by interest rates. However, interest rates are important in deciding the form your saving takes. You will hold money unless offered some incentive to hold a less liquid asset. Interest is such an inducement. Higher interest rates will induce you to relinquish money in order to hold larger amounts of illiquid assets.

As Keynes viewed the situation, very high interest rates cause people to hold very little, if any, money in asset balances—the demand for money consists almost exclusively of transactions and precautionary balances. But low interest rates result in large asset balances of money. Just as we horizontally sum individual demands for goods to arrive at market demands, we can sum transactions, precautionary, and asset demands for money to obtain the total demand for money.

The demand for money vis-à-vis the interest rate is shown in Figure 7. Note that at a very low interest rate, the demand curve for money becomes flat. This part of the demand curve for money is called the

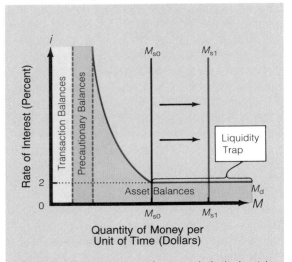

FIGURE 7 *Liquidity Preference and the Demand for Money*

The Keynesian total demand for money is the horizontal summation of transactions, precautionary, and asset demands for money. At very low interest rates, Keynesian theory predicts a *liquidity trap,* in which increases in the supply of money result in no extra spending and no declines in interest rates. In a liquidity trap, extra money is simply absorbed through hoarding into idle cash balances.

liquidity trap. It implies that if the money supply grew (say, from M_{s0} to M_{s1}), any extra money you received would not be spent, but hoarded; that is, absorbed into idle cash balances. Expansionary monetary policy would increase Aggregate Spending very little, if at all. Expectations about economic conditions might become so pessimistic that people would squirrel away every cent they could "for a rainy day," an instance of the liquidity trap. Alternatively, historically low interest rates might persuade nearly everyone that interest rates will rise, and soon. You would not want to hold bonds because rising interest rates would reduce bond prices and you would suffer a capital loss—you and many other investors would hold money while waiting for interest rates to rise and bond prices to fall.

Even though Keynes was writing during the Depression (1935), he suggested that no economy had ever been in a perfect liquidity trap. At the deepest part of the Great Depression, however, the interest rate hovered around 1.5 percent and we may have been in a "near"-liquidity trap. Severe depressions may cause near-liquidity traps because: (*a*) banks pile up huge excess reserves when nominal interest rates are very low because the returns from lending are small; (*b*) bankers fear that all loans are very risky, even those that normally would pose no problem of repayment; and (*c*) private individuals hoard their own funds, fearing that neither their job prospects nor investment opportunities are very bright.

Keynes differed from classical theory in his thinking about the demand for money, broadening the earlier perspective to consider precautionary and asset demands for money. Keynes believed that interest rates are determined solely by the demand and supply of money. His classical predecessors viewed interest rates as being determined in the market for capital goods. Thus, Keynesian and classical economists differ sharply in their perceptions of investment.

The Keynesian View of Investment

The capital stock in the United States consists of all the improvements to our natural resources that make them more productive than they are in their natural (raw) states—equipment, buildings, inventories, and so forth. Physical capital accumulated during any period is called **economic investment.** Classical and Keynesian theories differ about how variations in the money supply affect investment. Over the business cycle, investment (I) fluctuates proportionally more than either consumption (C) or government purchases (G). Inventory accumulation is especially unstable.

Keynes and his followers concentrated on the volatility of investors' moods: confidence about the future and expectations of large returns generate high levels of investment, while pessimism stifles investment. Both Keynesian and classical writers agree that higher rates of investment eventually lead to lower rates of return.

Keynesian analysis takes the position that the interest rate, which is the major opportunity cost of investment, is only one consideration in investment decisions and is not the overwhelming influence posited by classical economists. The Keynesian perspective is that changes in investors' expectations about future economic conditions are far more important in explaining changes in investment. Figure 8 shows why.

FIGURE 8 The Keynesian Explanation of Volatile Investment

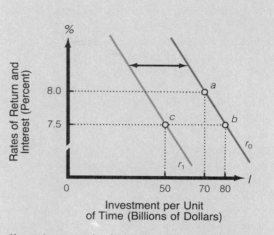

Keynesians perceive investment as only mildly influenced by interest rates but very sensitive to even minor changes in business perceptions of the future of the economy. Pessimism causes investment to plummet, while optimism causes sudden, and perhaps unsustainable, surges in investment.

Suppose that the initial investment curve is r_0 and that investment is $70 billion in equilibrium (point *a*) when the interest rate is 8 percent. Note that the rate of return curves are relatively "steep" in this Keynesian view of the world. A decline in interest to 7.5 percent moves the equilibrium from point *a* to point *b*, causing investment to increase only slightly, from $70 billion to $80 billion. Now suppose that investors become very skeptical about future economic conditions so that the expected rate of return schedule shifts leftward from r_0 to r_1. Equilibrium shifts from point *b* to point *c*, and investment falls sharply to $50 billion. If investors then begin to bubble over with optimism, the schedule shifts rightward, moving the equilibrium from *c* back to *b*, so that investment increases back to $80 billion. Keynesians argue that investment is not very responsive to small changes in interest rates but that investment demand shifts a great deal in response to changing expectations.

Summarizing, both Keynesian and classical economists agree that equilibrium investment requires the expected rate of return on investment to equal the rate of interest. However, Keynesians attribute cyclical swings of investment to changes in investors' expectations of future returns. They believe that changes in interest rates do not influence investment nearly as much as the unpredictable expectations of investors. Classical economists perceive investors' expectations about returns as quite stable and explain large variations in investment as responses to small changes in interest rates.

The Keynesian Monetary Transmission Mechanism

The demand and supply of money determine the nominal rate of interest in financial markets, as shown in Panel A of Figure 9. Keynesian theory suggests that during recessions, changes in the interest rate (Panel A) may cause small changes in the level of investment (Panel B) and thus, in national income (Panel C). However, the demand for money is thought to be fairly sensitive with respect to the interest rate, especially during economic downturns. Hence, interest rates may not decrease (*increase*) very much as the money supply is increased (*decreased*). Even if expansionary monetary policies do reduce interest rates a bit, Keynesians believe that investment is relatively insensitive to the interest rate, and so income is affected little, if at all, by monetary policies.

Keynesians argue that changes in the money supply do not affect consumer spending directly, but only indirectly through the

money → interest rate → investment → income

sequence. Even then, the effects of monetary policy are thought to be slight and erratic because the linkages are perceived to be weak. This view of the chain of events emanating from a change in the money supply is called the **Keynesian monetary transmission mechanism.** If the money supply is increased from $400 billion to $500 billion (a 20 percent increase) in Panel A of Figure 9, the interest rate falls from 8 percent to 7 percent and investment grows slightly from $100 billion to $110 billion (a 10 percent increase). Total output grows via the multiplier effect from $2 trillion to $2.02 trillion (only a 1 percent increase). This suggests that monetary policy will be weak compared to fiscal policy. The Keynesian view assumes that the economy is slack, and so the adjustment to monetary expansion is purely a quantity change; the price level is unaffected.

Keynesian Analyses of Depressions and Inflations

The differences between classical and Keynesian predictions are the greatest during depressions. Classical economists and modern supply-siders generally advocate laissez-faire policies because they believe that the natural long-run state of the economy is a full employment equilibrium. If pressed, however, classical economists would assert that expansionary monetary policies increase Aggregate Spending enough to rapidly boost the economy out of any depression if that depression had lasted a bit too long. Classical reasoning also suggests that restrictive monetary policies are the only lasting cure for inflation.

Most Keynesians agree that monetary restraint dampens inflationary pressures, but they disagree with the notion that monetary expansion will cure a depression. During a depression people are generally pessimistic and interest rates tend to plummet. Consequently, Keynesians suggest that expansionary monetary policies will not bring the economy out of a recession because any extra money people receive is seldom spent but is hoarded. This is another way of saying that *the velocity of money falls to offset expansions of the money supply.* Keynesians compare money to a string—you can pull on it to restrain inflation, but trying to push the economy out of the doldrums through expansionary monetary policy is like "pushing on a string." Expansionary monetary policy is viewed as stringlike both because banks may not lend out their reserves if their view of the economic horizon is pessimistic and because people may simply hoard rather than spend most of any extra money that comes their way.

Early Keynesians recommended massive government spending and tax cuts to cure recessions. They emphasized fiscal policy because of a widespread (though mistaken) belief that central banks throughout the world attempted to push their respective nations out of the Great Depression with highly expansionary monetary policies. Only long after the Depression did researchers discover that even though the U.S. monetary base rose slightly between 1929 and 1933, the money multiplier shrank and the money supply fell precipitously. Remember that good information is costly; the economic data of the time were awful.

FIGURE 9 *The Keynesian Transmission Mechanism: Money, Interest Rates, and National Income*

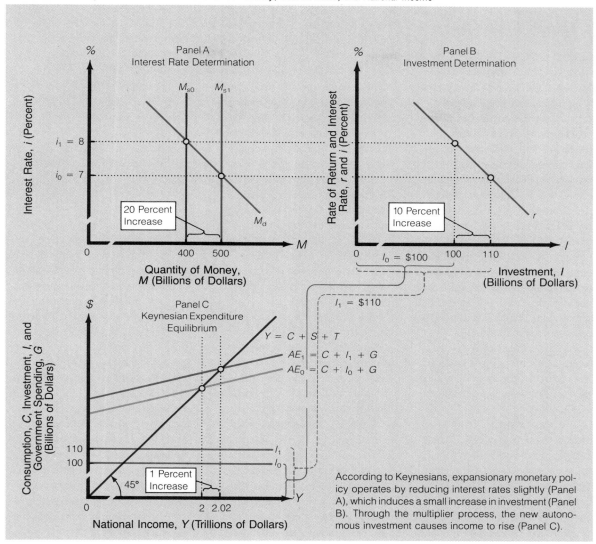

According to Keynesians, expansionary monetary policy operates by reducing interest rates slightly (Panel A), which induces a small increase in investment (Panel B). Through the multiplier process, the new autonomous investment causes income to rise (Panel C).

Modern Monetarism

The Keynesian Revolution soon stirred a counterrevolution by **modern monetarists,** who recognize some of the holes in classical monetary theory but reject the necessity for massive government intervention to stabilize the economy. Their counterattack, led by Milton Friedman, began with a reformulation of the demand for money. (See his Biography.)

The Demand for Money Revisited

Modern monetarists concede that money might be demanded for reasons other than anticipated transactions, but they see no reason to compartmentalize the demand for money as Keynesians have. Instead, they have identified certain variables that influence the amounts of money demanded. Milton Friedman has arrived at the most widely accepted formulation of the **New Quantity Theory of**

BIOGRAPHY

Milton Friedman (b. 1912)

Milton Friedman is one of the most publicly visible of modern economists. He has won the respect of both his followers and those economists who disagree strongly with his views. There are few significant honors in economics that have not come Friedman's way. He was elected president of the American Economic Association in 1967 and in 1976 received the Nobel Prize in economics. Looking very much like everyone's "favorite uncle," Friedman often disarms his adversaries with a wink and a gentle smile, but those who have argued with him find him a formidable debater. He is able to express complicated ideas in simple terms understandable by those untrained in formal economic theory. This makes him popular with the media and keeps Friedman in touch with a wide audience.

Friedman has been a vital force in attacking the orthodoxy of the "new" (Keynesian) economics. He has done this in a way that combines his argumentative talents with solid, empirical research and a desire not merely to tear down existing economic theory but to restructure it. The major thrust of Friedman's arguments has involved monetary theory, but, as with all master economists, his thoughts have touched many areas of economics. In the monetary field, Friedman has reconstructed and tested the Quantity Theory of

Money, reemphasized the importance and significance of monetary policy, questioned the Keynesian interpretation of the Great Depression, and developed his own prescriptions for preventing future economic catastrophe.

Friedman has also made major contributions in such areas as risk and insurance (answering why people will simultaneously gamble and buy insurance) and has developed a theory of consumption based on wealth, as opposed to the Keynesian view that consumption depends only on current income.

Along the way, he has attempted to restate the classical liberal philosophy of Adam Smith in terms pertinent to the modern era. (Friedman's admiration of Adam Smith is virtually unbounded—he has a necktie patterned with cameos of Smith that he wears during public appearances.) Friedman has offered many ideas about replacing the influence of government with market solutions. For example, he argues that government could eliminate public schools and give the parents of students vouchers (grants) so that all children could attend private schools tailored to their individual needs. He also argues that cash grants to poor people make more sense than such programs as food stamps because these grants would leave more choices in the hands of the poor as well as require fewer tax dollars.

Friedman's restatement of the Quantity Theory of Money is important because it made the theory statistically testable, something the old theory was not. His restatement is essentially a theory of the demand for money, whereas the original version was a theory of the price level. Friedman's analyses of the statistical evidence indicate that the demand for money is stable over the long run and conclude that large changes in the supply of money cause undesirable fluctuations in employment and in the price level. His disenchantment with fiscal policy is due in large measure to the fact that government deficits are most often financed by inflationary expansions of the supply of money and credit. Finally, Friedman has been critical of the performance of the Board of Governors of the Federal Reserve System because he sees the FED as either following the wrong policy (trying to control interest rates instead of the money supply) or yielding to political pressure rather than sound economic logic.

Money. Friedman differentiates between the nominal money people hold and their "real" money holdings. **"Real" money** means the purchasing power of the money a person holds. It can be computed by dividing the face values of money assets by the price level (M/P). As the price level rises, the face amount of money needed to buy a particular bundle of goods rises proportionally.

Variables Positively Related to Money Demand

According to Friedman, the variables (besides the price level) that will be *positively* related to the quantity of money demanded are: (*a*) people's total real wealth (including the value of their labor), (*b*) the interest rate, if any, paid on money holdings, and (*c*) the illiquidity of nonmonetary assets.

Wealth (or Permanent Income)   Classical economists (and Keynesians, to a lesser extent) relate the demand for money to current income. Friedman suggests that expected lifetime income better explains both a person's patterns of consumption and money holdings. Take two twenty-five-year-olds—one, a recent college graduate in accounting and the other, a manager of a convenience store. Each has a current annual income of $18,000. The consumption level of the young accountant is likely to be higher than that of the convenience store manager because of a greater possibility of borrowing money; thus, the accountant will hold more money for transactions purposes.

The Interest Rate on Money   You do not receive interest on cash you hold and only relatively low interest on your demand deposits. Banks do, however, offer free checking accounts and other incentives for depositors who maintain certain minimum balances in their accounts. Most people would probably hold larger money amounts in checking account balances if the interest rates paid to depositors were increased.

The Illiquidity of Nonmonetary Assets   Most college students are not poor, they are just broke. That is, they have highly marketable skills. Another way of saying this is that they have substantial wealth in the form of human capital but not many other assets. According to Friedman, if most of your assets are very illiquid, you will want higher money holdings than will people who have similar amounts of wealth but whose major assets tend to be more liquid. His reasoning is that some liquidity is desired to meet emergencies, and people with large amounts of human capital may not be able to liquidate their major

assets (themselves) very easily. Selling yourself into bondage or slavery is illegal, and marketing your skills takes time. Consequently, Friedman expects that you will probably hold more cash than similarly "wealthy" people who are not in college. (Our memory is that when we were students, we were flat broke most of the time.)

Variables Negatively Related to Money Demand

Friedman also identifies certain variables that he believes are *negatively* related to the real (purchasing power) amounts of money people will hold: (*a*) the interest rate on bonds, (*b*) the rate of return on physical capital, and (*c*) the expected rate of inflation.

Bond Interest Rates and Rates of Return on Investment   The major alternatives to holding money are spending it on consumer goods *or* buying stocks, bonds, or capital goods. While modern monetarists emphasize the value of consumption as the alternative cost of holding money ($1/P$), they also recognize either direct investment or purchases of stocks or bonds as possibilities. If such activities are your best alternatives to holding money, then the prices you pay for holding money are the interest (i) that could be received from a bond or the rate of return (r) you might expect from buying stocks or investing directly in physical capital.

While Friedman accepts a negative relationship between the interest rate or rate of return on capital and the quantity of money demanded, his studies conclude that the demand for money is comparatively insensitive to the interest rate. Any hint that a liquidity trap has ever existed is totally rejected.

The Expected Rate of Inflation   You may have heard that if you want to "get rich," you should "buy low and sell high." This advice implies that if you expect inflation, then you should get rid of your money while it has a high value and buy durable assets instead. During inflation, money becomes a hot potato because expectations of inflation cause people to reduce their holdings of money. The greater the expected inflation, the more rapid the velocity of money.

The Stability of the Demand for Money

While modern monetarists are willing to accept the idea that the demand for money is influenced by variables other than income, they contend that these are very stable relationships. Moreover, they believe that most variables that influence the demand for money are relatively constant because they are the outcomes of an inherently stable market system. Table 1 summarizes the variables that influence the demand for money. Monetarists believe that the bulk of any instability in a market economy arises because of erratic government policy—the Federal Reserve System is the main villain in their scenario. Before investigating in the next chapter why the FED is perceived as the culprit, we need to examine the modern monetarist monetary transmission mechanism.

The Modern Monetarist Monetary Transmission Mechansim

Modern monetarists, like their classical predecessors, believe that the linkage between the money supply and national income is strong and direct. Monetarists think that the demand for money is stable, so an expansion in the money supply is viewed as putting surpluses of money in the hands of both consumers and investors. Monetarists predict that consumers and investors will quickly spend these surpluses.

TABLE 1 *Variables Affecting the Nominal Demand for Money*

Positively
1. Income
2. Wealth
3. Cost of living (*CPI*)
4. Uncertainty about future income and expenses
5. Expected hikes in interest rates
6. Expected declines in the prices of bonds, stocks, or real estate

Negatively
1. Interest rate (*i*)
2. Rate of return on capital (*r*)
3. Expected inflation
4. Frequency of receipt of income

Classical economics emphasizes Aggregate Supply, believing that Aggregate Demand adjusts automatically and almost instantaneously when supply conditions change. (Supply creates its own demand.) Recognizing the importance of Aggregate Demand in the short run because the economy may falter occasionally, most monetarists believe that increases in the money supply will expand spending and rapidly drive a slumping economy toward full employment. Moreover, modern monetarists, much like classical theorists, perceive the market system as inherently stable and think that the economy will seldom deviate for long from full employment.

Modern monetarists consequently predict that, in the long run, increases in the money supply will be translated strictly into higher prices, even if monetary expansion occurs during a recession. Expansionary macroeconomic policies will, however, induce greater output quicker in the midst of a recession. In other words, the Aggregate Supply curve described by Keynesians may accurately represent a recessionary economy, but only in the very short run. This view of the world is portrayed in Figure 10.

Suppose the money supply is initially at $400 billion and the price level is 100. The economy is temporarily producing at point *a*, which is half a trillion units of real GNP below capacity, because full employment income is 4 trillion units. If the money supply and Aggregate Demand were held constant, then prices and wages would eventually fall so that a long-run equilibrium at point *b* would be achieved. Full employment would be realized when the price level fell to 80. If the money supply were expanded to $500 billion, Aggregate Demand would grow and full employment output of 4 trillion units would be realized more rapidly (point *c*). However, the price level is higher in this long-run equilibrium, being maintained at 100.

Most modern monetarists oppose active monetary policy to combat recessions. They view long-run adjustments as fairly rapid, believing instead that deflation will quickly restore an economy to full employment. An even greater concern is their fear that discretionary monetary policy might "overshoot," causing recession to move into inflation. This is shown in Figure 10 by the too rapid growth of Aggregate Demand when the money supply is increased to $600 billion. In this case, the consequence of policy to combat recession is a 20 percent increase in the price level (point *d*). According to this monetarist

FIGURE 10 *Modern Monetarist Views of the Short-Run and Long-Run Effects of Expansionary Monetary Policy*

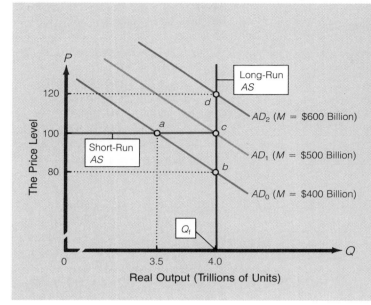

Modern monetarists recognize that variations in Aggregate Demand may entail short-term quantity adjustments so that recessions are possible. For example, movement from *c* to *a* would be a recessionary movement caused by falling Aggregate Demand. Monetarists perceive Aggregate Demand as proportional to the money supply but are extremely leery of short-term adjustments to the money supply as a means of correcting for recessions. In their view, the long-term effect of any increase in the money supply is a proportional movement of the price level, which raises the prospect of inflation.

line of thinking, overly aggressive monetary expansion can eliminate recession and unemployment more quickly than "do-nothing" policies, but only at the risk of sparking inflation.

Summary: Keynesian Versus Modern Monetary Theory

The monetary theories of classical economists, Keynesians, and modern monetarists are outlined in Table 2. The major differences in these schools of thought are found in (*a*) the nature of the demand for money, (*b*) the nature of the investment relationship, (*c*) the monetary transmission mechanism, and (*d*) assumptions about the velocity of money.

Assumptions about the creation of money and, thus, the effectiveness of monetary policy is a crucial difference between Keynesians and monetarists. Most monetarist models ignore the institutional mechanisms used to create money (for example, that the FED might buy government bonds from banks, thereby increasing excess reserves that are multiplied into new loan-based demand deposits). Remember, however, that the FED directly controls the monetary base, not the money supply. Monetarists

often simply assume that increases in the money supply become money in the hands of the consuming or investing public. A common monetarist analogy is that a helicopter dumps money into the economy. They then argue, not unreasonably, that if sufficient new money is given to the public, people will feel wealthier, quit worrying about "bad times," and spend it. This part of the monetarist scenario dispenses with theoretical difficulties like liquidity traps.

Modern Keynesians describe not only consumer or investor liquidity traps, but bank liquidity traps as well. Here is their story. Suppose that an economic downturn is under way and interest rates have plummeted. The FED buys government bonds from banks to counteract the recession. Will the banks' new excess reserves be translated into borrowing, increased demand deposits, and then spending? (This is necessary for the monetarist transmission mechanism to work.) Keynesians think not.

If you were a banker and the economy was depressed, would you want to reduce already low interest rates in order to attract new borrowers, many of whom look like dead beats? Would the small declines in interest that are feasible be sufficiently attractive to prudent borrowers to induce them to apply for new loans? Keynesians answer NO to both

TABLE 2 *Summary of the Important Differences Between Classical, Keynesian, and Modern Monetarist Monetary Theories*

	Classical	Keynesian	Modern Monetarist
Demand for money	For transaction purposes only	Money demanded for: Transactions Precautionary purposes Asset purposes Speculative Risk aversion Transaction costs	Money demand is *stable*, but influenced by: Wealth (or permanent income) Interest rates Liquidity of other assets Expected rate of inflation
Money and investment	Investment is related to interest rate and is very sensitive	Investment is related to interest rate but is insensitive; related primarily to business expectations	Investment is related to interest rate and is very sensitive
Monetary transmission mechanism	Direct: $MV \equiv PQ$ $\dfrac{\Delta M}{M} = \dfrac{\Delta P}{P}$ Velocity (V) is constant; output (Q) is fixed at full employment	Indirect: ΔM (money) $\rightarrow \Delta i$ (interest rates) $\rightarrow \Delta I$ (investment) $\rightarrow \Delta AE$ (expenditures) $\rightarrow \Delta Y$ (income) $\rightarrow \Delta Q$ (output) Money is transmitted through interest rates to investment to Aggregate Spending to income and output	Direct: $\Delta M \rightarrow \Delta C$ or $\rightarrow \Delta I$ $\rightarrow \Delta Y$ $\rightarrow \Delta P$ or ΔQ Money is transmitted directly through changing real balances that result directly in altering spending or investment; these changes then cause changes in income, output, or the price level
Velocity	Constant	Volatile	Relatively Stable

questions. They suggest that the banks will simply accumulate more and more vault cash if the FED tries to counter recessionary tendencies through open-market operations. This is just another aspect of the argument that money (and monetary policy) is a string that is useless for pushing the economy out of the doldrums.

We will look at the integration of monetary and fiscal policies and examine the effects of various methods of financing government activity on the economy in the next chapter. Then, in Chapters 16–18, we will examine several macroeconomic issues from the perspectives of both Keynesians and modern monetarists.

CHAPTER REVIEW: KEY POINTS

1. You increase your *spending* when you have "too much" money; your rate of *saving* increases when you have "too little" money.

2. People hold money for predictable spending (*transaction demands*) with a cushion for uncertain outlays or income receipts (*precautionary demands*). People also have *asset demands* for money because: (*a*) money is relatively risk free, (*b*) transaction costs associated with less liquid assets may exceed expected returns, or (*c*) people speculate by holding money when they believe that alternative assets (for instance, stocks, bonds, or real estate) are going to decline in price.

3. According to classical monetary theory, the sole rational motive for holding money is *to consummate transactions*.

4. Interest rates and bond prices are *inversely related*. Bond prices fall if interest rates rise, and vice versa.

5. The costs of holding nominal amounts of money are: (*a*) *the reciprocal of the price level* (1/*P*) if the choice is between saving money or buying consumer goods; or (*b*) *the interest rate*, if money is viewed as an asset substitutable for some highly liquid income-generating asset, say a bond. *Inflation* also imposes costs on holdings of money.

6. The *income velocity* (*V*) of money equals GNP (*PQ*) divided by the money supply (*M*).

7. The *Equation of Exchange*, a truism, is written $MV \equiv PQ$. Therefore, the percentage change in the money supply plus the percentage change in velocity roughly equals the percentage change in the price level plus the percentage change in real output:

$$\frac{\Delta M}{M} + \frac{\Delta V}{V} = \frac{\Delta P}{P} + \frac{\Delta Q}{Q}.$$

8. Classical economics assumes that *velocity* (*V*) and output (*Q*) are reasonably constant and independent of the money supply (*M*) and the price level (*P*). Classical economists believe that changes in the money supply result in proportional changes in the price level and expressed this belief in early versions of the *Quantity Theory of Money*. The Quantity Theory of Money is more accurately a *Monetary Theory of the Price Level*.

9. Keynes's attack on Quantity Theory disputes the assumptions: (*a*) that the natural state of the economy is full employment, (*b*) that the velocity of money is inherently stable, and (*c*) that the only rational motive for holding money is for transactions purposes.

10. Modern monetarists believe there is a direct linkage between the money supply and national income. Since the demand for money is relatively stable, increases in the supply of money put excess money balances in the hands of consumers and investors who in turn spend these money balances on goods and services. Growth in the supply of money may expand output in the short run, but modern monetarists conclude that in the long run, higher prices will result.

QUESTIONS FOR THOUGHT AND DISCUSSION

1. According to monetarists, expanding the money supply inevitably causes higher prices. In what ways do Keynesians disagree and why?

2. Do you think most people want to balance illiquid assets against highly liquid assets, such as money? Why? How does your line of reasoning lead to the demand for money? Does your answer suggest that the demand for money will be sensitive to interest rates? To the cost of living? How, and why or why not?

3. Describe the differences between Keynesian and monetarist monetary transmission mechanisms. Why are these differences important? In what way does Keynesian fiscal policy short-circuit the difficulties they perceive in transforming new money into new spending?

4. If the economy took a tailspin into a recession, would you expect any (short-run) liquidity trap to emerge more from the banking sector or from the behavior of the nonbanking public?

5. According to Keynesians, interest is a reward for sacrificing liquidity. Classical and modern monetarists describe interest as a reward for postponing consumption or as a return on investment. Which of these explanations seem most plausible to you? Is either approach totally false?

6. As people expect more inflation, they may begin treating money as a "hot potato"; average money holdings may fall, with the result that velocity increases. On the other hand, increased inflation may generate more uncertainty, which may cause people to *increase* their money holdings. People who anticipate higher inflation and want to accumulate a given real amount of saving before retirement, but who are leery of most financial investments, may try to build their holdings of money. On average, do you think the inflation of the past 20 years has caused real money balances per capita to rise or fall? How would you test this hypothesis? To what extent can inflation be considered a tax on money balances?

7. Do you think the evidence better supports the Keynesian view that velocity is erratic or the monetarist position that velocity is stable? What social or economic forces are you aware of that might explain trends and fluctuations in velocity?

8. In late 1979, the Federal Reserve announced that it would focus its attention primarily on rates of monetary growth instead of interest rates. While this action has often been urged by monetarists, the monetarist camp received the announcement with less than full enthusiasm. Many monetarists would like the FED to concentrate on the monetary base, citing statistical studies that have shown that a reasonably stable and predictable relationship between the base and GNP seems to exist. The FED does not yet seem ready to adopt such a simple approach.

What is necessary for the monetary base and money supply to be tightly linked? Is it possible for the FED to maintain money supply or monetary base growth rate goals in the face of political pressures if interest rates rise to levels that are perceived to be too high? Can both targets (money supply growth rates and reasonable interest rates) be controlled simultaneously? How? Numerous economists are skeptical because the FED has made similar announcements in the past, but policies did not change. What makes a monetary growth approach so hard for the FED to implement?

9. Keynesian theory suggests that the relevent substitutes for money are securities, while monetarists argue for a broader range of substitutes that include consumer and investment goods. How important is this difference in explaining the impact of money on economic activity? Why?

CHAPTER 15 Monetary and Fiscal Policy

government budgeting	creating monetary	rules versus discretion
taxation	base	fixed monetary growth
borrowing	confiscation and	rule
	regulation	national debt
	crowding-out	
	hypothesis	

The 1980s witnessed the largest budget deficits in history. During the first five years of the Reagan Administration, the national debt more than doubled, reaching over $2 trillion in 1986. By the end of Ronald Reagan's presidency, the total public debt probably will have tripled. Since the Federal Reserve Board is the federal government's banker and must pay the bills and finance this debt, the existence of this enormous debt clearly affects its monetary policy.

Until now, we have treated fiscal and monetary influences on Aggregate Demand independently. In Chapter 11, we examined the isolated effects of government spending and taxation. Chapters 13 and 14 looked at how the FED controls the supply of money and the impact of monetary policy on the economy. In this chapter, we will examine how budget deficits are financed; how monetary and fiscal policies interact; the nature, burdens, and benefits of the public debt; and under what circumstances monetary and fiscal policy each may be either powerful or ineffective.

Financing Government

Most economists agree that the impact of fiscal policy depends on how the government finances its spending. The FED is the government's banker and, with the Treasury, determines how deficits and surpluses are financed. This resolution is crucial in determining the levels of prices, interest rates, income, and output. We will examine these issues in detail.

Private Versus Public Finance

Many people draw an incorrect analogy between government finance and business or private household budgeting because they fail to understand the different financing constraints facing the private and the public sectors.

Private Budget Constraints The availability of funds limits the spending of households, proprietorships, and partnerships. Their funds are made available through: (*a*) sales of current assets, (*b*) current income (including gifts or inheritance), and (*c*) potential borrowing against current assets or expected future income.

Most corporate borrowing comes from issuing bonds. Bonds tend to be more salable than the promissory notes (IOUs) of households, proprietorships, or partnerships because large corporations are typically good credit risks. Corporations have one additional source of purchasing power available to neither households nor to noncorporate firms: they can sell shares of stock to finance spending. The ability to sell bonds and to offer ownership shares (stock) makes corporations more flexible and powerful than other firms in securing funds to cover operating expenses or new investments in plant and equipment.

Local Government Budget Constraints

States, counties, cities, school districts, and other local government units face slightly different constraints on their spending. Like proprietorships or partnerships, they can use the revenues from the sale of assets or the goods and services they provide to finance current spending. Like corporations, they may issue bonds to obtain purchasing power. But unlike corporations, government does not sell ownership shares. Another major difference between private and government organizations is that government can finance its spending through **taxation,** which gives government tremendous power to use resources as it wishes.

Government can also channel the allocation of resources through **regulation** or **confiscation.** For example, regulation now forces car owners to buy emission-controlling exhaust systems and compels firms to reduce their pollution levels. Through such regulations, the government buys a cleaner environment for all of us and makes us pay for it without explicit tax increases. You may think that direct confiscation is not used by governments in the United States. However, the right of eminent domain can be and is used by all levels of government to secure land for such things as highway rights-of-way or areas for dams or parks. When the government exercises **eminent domain,** those who are forced to surrender their property to government are typically paid a fair-market value. Although the military draft is not used at present, it is another example of government confiscating resources.

Federal Budget Constraints

A national government has one additional and important mechanism in its toolbox: it has the ability to print money to pay for the goods it provides and, thus, it **creates new monetary base.** (Recall that the monetary base equals currency plus the reserves in the banking system.) This means of financing spending is somewhat disguised in the United States because of the separate identities of the Federal Reserve System (FED) and the Department of the Treasury. In an accounting sense, the Treasury "borrows" the money from the FED, which actually creates new money.[1]

In summary, the government can secure resources to provide us with goods and services through (*a*) sales of its current assets or production; (*b*) **borrowing** from U.S. citizens, corporations, foreign citizens or governments, or commercial banks; (*c*) taxation; (*d*) confiscation; or (*e*) expansion of the monetary base (currency in circulation plus bank reserves).

Since confiscation is a relatively unimportant source of revenues for government, we might summarize **government budgeting** as:

$$G = T + \Delta B + \Delta MB, \text{ or}$$
$$G - T = \Delta B + \Delta MB,$$

where,

G = total governmental spending,
T = total governmental revenues from taxes, charges, and sales,
ΔB = change in the national debt,
ΔMB = change in the monetary base (currency in circulation plus bank reserves).

This means that if the federal government spends more than it collects ($G - T > 0$), it must either borrow ($\Delta B > 0$) and/or create (print) the monetary difference ($\Delta MB > 0$). If the government collects more than it spends ($G - T < 0$), it can either retire

---

1. Technically, the United States uses a roundabout method to finance a budget deficit by creating new monetary base. The Treasury first issues new bonds to cover its deficit. The FED then uses expansionary open-market operations (discussed in Chapter 13) to purchase these bonds. This expands bank reserves, which are then transformed into new money through the money multiplier process. Curiously, the bonds bought by the FED when it expands the monetary base are still considered, for accounting purposes, to be a part of our national debt. It makes no sense, however, to suggest that our national debt is enlarged because one government agency (Treasury) owes another (the FED). Thus, in what follows, we ignore Treasury bonds held by the FED when we count the national debt.

some of its outstanding debt ($\Delta B < 0$) and/or retire some of the money it has previously created ($\Delta MB < 0$). Budgetary deficits cause increases either in the national debt and/or in the money supply, while government surpluses make it possible to pay off some of the national debt and/or remove some money from circulation.

Borrowing money or selling current assets to secure purchasing power is common to both private and government decision makers. However, private citizens cannot legally tax, confiscate, or create (print) more monetary base. The money expansion process then applies to this increase in the monetary base, as described in Chapter 12. Critics of fiscal policy do not believe that the increase in government spending will expand Gross National Product very much because government purchases tend to replace or "crowd out" private spending. How government is financed strongly affects the impact of government purchases on GNP.

Crowding Out

What the government gives it must first take away.
—*John S. Coleman*

The idea that increases in government purchases inevitably cause reductions in private consumption or investment is known as the **crowding-out hypothesis.**[2] Keep in mind that the crowded-out activity may be less valuable than the goods government provides. Less leisure for workers, less purchasing power for consumers (caused by inflation or tax increases), or fewer profits for investors (because of higher interest rates)—each are ways government purchases may crowd out private individuals or firms. Crowding out and paying for government are closely related.

Government's Costs when Resources Are Idle

The alternatives lost by individuals as government acquires more resources are crucial in determining who really pays for government. Suppose that our economy is in a Keynesian recessionary equilibrium with considerable amounts of land, labor, and capital

---

2. Early versions of the crowding-out hypothesis focused only on how government deficits drive interest rates up and, consequently, reduce investment. Our treatment follows the more recent convention that crowding out encompasses all reductions in private activities caused when government programs grow.

unemployed. Government might increase total production by drafting (confiscating) the idle resources. Or, it could secure sufficient money to buy these resources through taxation, expansion of the monetary base, or borrowing. If these resources would have been completely unproductive in the absence of such government action, the opportunity costs of the increased output are zero; the additional government services would not cost anyone anything.

The production-possibilities frontier in Figure 1 allows us to examine an increase in government spending and the resulting induced consumption. If many resources are idle and the economy is initially at point *a*, raising government spending from G_0 to G_1 closes the recessionary gap in this idealized case. Consumption induced through the Keynesian multiplier process will drive total consumption from C_0 to

FIGURE 1 *The Costs of Additional Government: Crowding Out*

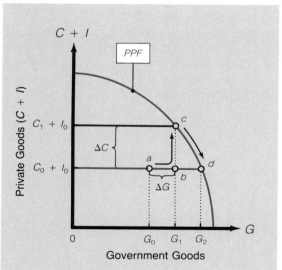

The general problem of government spending crowding out private activity is illustrated in this figure. Beginning from a point of considerable unemployment (*a*), government can increase spending from G_0 to G_1; new consumption equal to $C_1 - C_0$ will be induced through the multiplier. The opportunity costs of such increases are the value of the private uses to which the ΔG would have been put, including the leisure forgone by the newly employed. Once the economy has achieved full employment (point *c*), increased government spending to G_2 (point *d*) necessarily causes a reduction in private spending from C_1 to C_0.

C_1. This completes the closure of the GNP gap so that the path to full employment is $a \rightarrow b \rightarrow c$.

Have we discovered an exception to the *TANSTAAFL* rule that "There ain't no such thing as a free lunch"? Probably not. It is very unlikely that resources are ever totally without valuable uses "in the absence of government action." For example, idle labor produces leisure; most of us prefer no work to work with no pay. To induce idle labor to work, a noncoercive government must pay a wage that offsets the value of the leisure lost by the workers employed in producing the extra output; increases in employment come at the cost of forgone leisure.

Government might use simple confiscation to impose on the owners of idle resources the full cost of providing extra government goods; drafting unemployed labor for armies of conservation workers or highway repair crews would be examples. (Siberian salt mines developed under the Russian czars continue today under the Soviet regime.) If tax revenues are used to pay the owners of the newly employed resources, the burden falls largely on taxpayers. If government creates money to pay for these resources, then the increase in the incomes of the owners of previously idle resources may be partially offset by inflationary reductions in the purchasing power of other private citizens.

Suppose the government issues bonds to buy the resources used to produce extra government goods. The consequences are illustrated in Figure 2. Bond prices fall when additional Treasury bonds are issued, increasing the supply of bonds from S_0 to S_1 (in Panel A). The falling price of bonds causes interest rates to climb from i_0 to i_1 (from points a to b in Panel B). Successful borrowers pay higher interest rates, but some private investment may be crowded out. This dampens the net increase in Aggregate Spending, which rises only from AE_0 to AE_1—not to AE_2—in Panel C, as would occur without crowding out.

The short-run burden of paying for more government expenditures falls on borrowers and potential borrowers in this case. In the longer run, consumers will pay higher prices because of the constriction of investment and lower growth in our stock of capital. With less than full employment, the degree of crowding out depends on the interest sensitivity of demands by investors and consumers. Crowding out restricts the power of the Keynesian multiplier process to expand real income. When many resources are unemployed, however, the induced Keynesian increase in income can overwhelm any losses in purchasing power.

Government's Costs During Full Employment

Our discussion to this point has assumed that some resources were idle when government purchases were increased. Expansion of government spending is a standard Keynesian fiscal policy prescription whenever the economy is in a slump. Who pays for increases in government spending if the economy is fully employed? Either private consumption, investment, or exports must decline if there is efficient and full employment of all resources and government purchases are increased. Figure 1 shows that if the economy were initially fully employed at point c, increasing government purchases from G_1 to G_2 would move the economy to point d and decrease the sum of private consumption and investment from $C_1 + I_0$ to $C_0 + I_0$.

Government can bring about the necessary crowding out through confiscation, inflation, tax hikes, or through higher interest rates. Excessive reliance on any single mechanism may cause political turmoil and significantly reduce some resource owners' incentives to be productive; therefore, government commonly chooses a mix of these ways to cover new government spending.

For example, President Johnson realized that tax increases to pay for the War in Vietnam and the "War on Poverty" would encounter tremendous political resistance in the late 1960s. In spite of advice from his Council of Economic Advisors that tax increases were necessary to avoid inflationary pressures, President Johnson chose to run budgetary deficits. What choices were available? Because $G - T = \Delta B + \Delta MB$, the alternatives were either to borrow the money or print it.

The Treasury initially covered the deficits by issuing new bonds. A large proportion of the loanable funds available would have been absorbed if these bonds had been purchased solely by the public; interest rates would have soared, leaving little money available for private investment. The Federal Reserve Board elected to buy many of the new bonds issued by the Treasury. This expanded the monetary base and caused the money supply to rise dramatically, preventing the full brunt of financing the Vietnam War from falling exclusively on private investment.

FIGURE 2 *The Crowding-Out Effect: Investment*

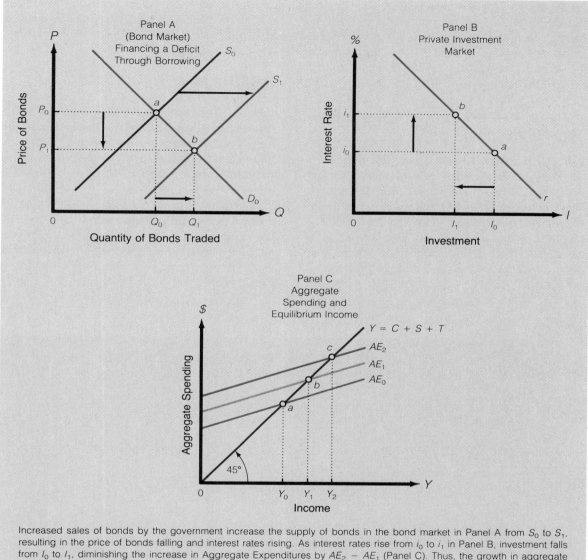

Increased sales of bonds by the government increase the supply of bonds in the bond market in Panel A from S_0 to S_1, resulting in the price of bonds falling and interest rates rising. As interest rates rise from i_0 to i_1 in Panel B, investment falls from I_0 to I_1, diminishing the increase in Aggregate Expenditures by $AE_2 - AE_1$ (Panel C). Thus, the growth in aggregate income is hindered because of crowding out.

Inflation caused prices and nominal income to swell so that total tax revenues increased. The overall result was that crowding out spread the costs of the War on Poverty and the Vietnam War across three groups: (*a*) investors, who paid higher interest rates; (*b*) consumers, who paid higher prices; and (*c*) taxpayers, who paid higher taxes. Through the Selective Service draft, confiscation of labor was also used to pay for the Vietnam War. This example correctly suggests that the mix of policies government uses to finance its spending has important implications for the distribution of income; each method of reducing private activity imposes burdens on different groups.

The government budget equation ($G = T + \Delta B + \Delta MB$) reveals that government deficits can be funded through expansionary open-market operations by the FED or by having the Treasury borrow via the issuance of new bonds. If the FED does not monetize the deficit by buying Treasury bonds, privately held national debt grows.

The Public Debt

You may have heard someone say that the United States teeters on the verge of bankruptcy. Figure 3 shows that, although the federal debt is enormous and growing, private debt is growing even faster. Growth in our national debt is often cited by prophets of doom as evidence that national economic insolvency is just around the corner. The doomsayers, fortunately, are wrong. They fail to

consider: (*a*) the previously discussed ability of government to tax and to create money to cover budget deficits or to pay off the national debt, and (*b*) the basic differences between internal and external debts.

External Versus Internal Debt

The major difference between private and public debt is that all private debt is held externally—the borrowers owe other people—whereas public debt is primarily held internally—we owe most of our **national debt** to Americans. That is, we owe it to ourselves. (Do you own any U.S. Savings Bonds?)

Borrowing from internal sources does not change the total current amount that may be spent. When the government issues new bonds, the purchasing power temporarily surrendered by American bond buyers just offsets the government's gain in purchas-

FIGURE 3 Public and Private Debt (Billions of Dollars)

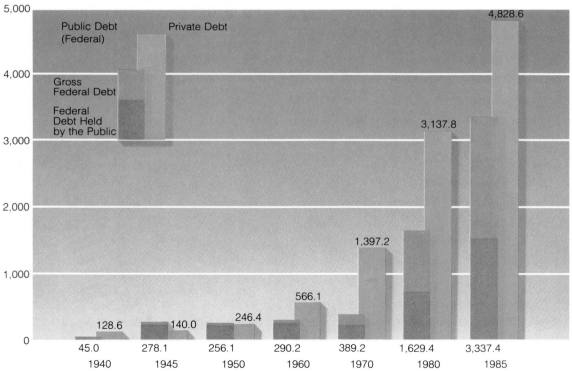

As this figure illustrates, private debt is considerably larger than federal debt. Both have grown dramatically since 1960, but private debt has grown much more rapidly.

Sources: U.S. Treasury, *Bulletin*, January 1983; *Federal Reserve Bulletin*, October 1985; and *Economic Report of the President*, 1986.

ing power. People in the United States as a whole neither gain nor lose immediately through such transactions, although the uses of these funds may affect future American purchasing power. If borrowed funds are used for a government investment in, say, a hydroelectric dam, then real future income may be increased because more and cheaper electricity may be available over the productive life of the facility. If the funds from government borrowing are used for police protection, welfare payments, or other current operating costs and if funds are diverted from private investments, then future purchasing power may be reduced. For example, if borrowed funds are used to finance a war, domestic capital formation may be reduced, lowering standards of living for future generations. However, just as borrowing funds internally does not change total current purchasing power, repayment of internally held debt does not affect total American purchasing power at the time of repayment. People who cash their bonds receive purchasing power exactly equal to the loss of purchasing power to the government sector.

When private households or firms borrow externally, they immediately gain the purchasing power that lenders temporarily sacrifice. Similarly, when the government sells bonds to foreign governments or investors, the United States as a whole temporarily gains purchasing power. Gains from external borrowing normally entail eventual repayment of purchasing power to the external sources of funds. If the borrowed funds were used for investment goods that were sufficiently productive to cover the principal borrowed plus interest charges, the borrowers still would be ahead after repayment. If, on the other hand, the loans were used to finance consumption, then repayment to the external lenders could entail net losses of purchasing power. This case requires curtailing future consumption because higher consumption is enjoyed today.

Figure 4 shows that, until recently, the national debt was declining as a proportion of Gross National Product. Beginning in 1982, rising deficits and relatively high interest rates have caused total public debt and interest payments—as a percentage of GNP—to grow. With the sharp decline in interest rates in 1986, this trend in rising interest costs will reverse as old debt is rolled over and new debt is financed at lower rates.

One aspect of federal debt that is often overlooked is that the FED acquires large chunks of our national debt when it buys bonds during expansionary open-market operations. Other government agencies (e.g., the Social Security Administration) also commonly buy bonds when they run temporary surpluses. Although accountants count these organizations' bond holdings as national debt, doing so is a lot like saying that your right pocket owes your left pocket money when you shift spare change from one pocket to another.

If taxes are raised to pay the interest on federal debt, incentives to work and invest may be diminished. In 1985, the interest cost of the national debt was more than $200 billion, or about 20 percent of all government outlays. This equaled over half of all expenditures by the federal government for everything but defense and Social Security. Furthermore, when the federal government finances a huge deficit by selling debt securities, interest rates climb, and considerable private borrowing for investment may be crowded out of financial markets as government spending replaces private investment. The exact effect will depend on the state of the economy and private saving rates. If the economy is especially sluggish, increased deficits may not crowd out investment. If saving rates rise, increased deficits may not raise interest rates. However, in general, increased deficits put upward pressure on interest rates. The end result is that future generations may inherit a smaller capital stock and, hence, reduced production possibilities—one real burden of the public debt.

The Burden of the National Debt On Future Generations

Is the burden of the national debt passed on to future generations? As we discussed previously, if newly incurred debt diverts funds from private investments to satisfy present consumption, then future generations will lose the income that might have been generated through the private investments. However, future generations do not lose because the current generation opts for more consumption and less investment out of today's income.

Future generations may bear increased tax payments to pay interest on the national debt. Of course, members of future generations also receive the interest payments as bondholders, so the burden nets out as long as the national debt is held internally—that is, as long as we owe it to ourselves. But what about the part of the national debt that is held externally?

FIGURE 4 *Federal Debt Held by the Public and Interest on the Debt as a Percentage of GNP*

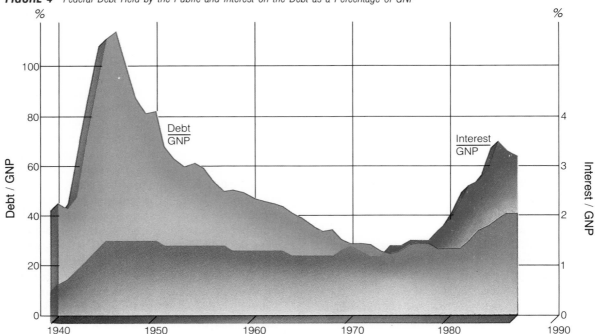

The public debt as a percentage of GNP was declining until relatively recently. Right after World War II, the public debt exceeded GNP; today, the ratio is nearly 40 percent. When greater public debt has been financed, interest rates have risen. New debt and old debt that was rolled over have had to be floated at these higher rates of interest. The result is that interest paid on public debt as a percentage of GNP rose during the early 1980s. Quite recently, however, interest rates have fallen, and as debt is refinanced, interest costs should fall both absolutely and as a percentage of GNP.

Source: *Economic Report of the President,* 1986.

Table 1 indicates that the proportion of the national debt held by foreigners has grown markedly in the past few years. Until the mid 1970s, foreign holdings of U.S. government debt were negligible. As real interest rates rose, foreigners bought greater quantities of our debt and simultaneously increased the value of the dollar. When foreigners buy U.S. bonds, we experience gains in purchasing power. It is possible that future generations of Americans will lose purchasing power when these bonds are redeemed, and that they will bear the burdens of paying the interest on externally held debt. However, this situation can only occur if foreigners decide to reduce their holdings of U.S. bonds. It is not obvious that they will, or that the national debt will ever be retired, or that it would be desirable for us to do so.

Must the National Debt Be Repaid?

What would happen if we retired the national debt? Would the government be ruined? Suppose government raised income taxes enormously to repay the outstanding debt. People who hold the existing public debt tend to be individuals in high-income categories, so they would be paying a lot of the higher taxes and then would receive the payments—a transfer to themselves. Alternatively, the value of all Treasury bonds could be taxed 100 percent. Good-bye national debt. (This is not a likely option.)

Actually, the government can and does perpetually **roll over** the debt. When any given issue comes due, the debt can be refinanced. (Most large corporations also roll over their debts—and most successful corporations go deeper and deeper into debt as time passes.) However, investors who buy government bonds must have confidence in the continued existence and taxing power of the government. Politically unstable countries find it difficult to borrow because investors fear that the current government may fall. New regimes commonly disavow the debt of overthrown governments, rendering it worthless. For example, owners of bonds issued by czarist Russia experienced this misfortune. As long as the government is stable and maintains good credit, however, the debt can be floated perpetually.

Some critics of national debt policies argue that if the government can issue debt without limits, it will continually spend more than is justified. These critics argue that Congress often treats the ability to issue debt like a "free lunch" and is unwilling to exercise appropriate fiscal restraint. Persistent increases in both government debt and spending tend to support this line of argument. It may be easier to increase the national debt (and the debt ceiling) than to say no to projects supported by powerful special interest groups.

Some Benefits of the Public Debt

Like most economic issues, the national debt has a benefit side. Stabilization policy depends heavily on the ability of the federal government to deficit spend and pay for this spending with bonds. Annually balancing the budget could prove disastrous during recessionary periods. President Herbert Hoover at-

TABLE 1 Percentage of the Public Debt Held by Foreigners

Year	Percentage of Public Debt Owned by Foreigners
1939	.5
1946	.8
1965	5.2
1970	5.3
1975	11.5
1978	17.5
1980	16.3
1985	15.7

Source: Board of Governors of the Federal Reserve System, *Federal Reserve Bulletin*, October 1985; and *Economic Report of the President*, 1986.

tempted to balance the budget by raising taxes when faced with rapidly growing deficits between 1929 and 1932. This policy accelerated the decline of our economy into its deepest depression ever. Additionally, the national debt provides a relatively risk-free asset (government bonds) for individuals who need that kind of protection for their financial capital. (Of course, there is the risk of inflation.) You should realize by now that manipulation of the public debt is an integral part of the most effective instrument of monetary policy—open-market operations. The FED buys bonds from banks when it wants to expand the money supply and sells bonds to restrict the money supply.

The government budget constraint ($G - T = \Delta B + \Delta MB$) makes it quite clear that fiscal and monetary policy are interrelated. This does not mean, however, that both are equally effective in moving the economy out of a recession or stopping an inflationary spiral. Economists are divided into two camps on the question of whether monetary or fiscal policy is more effective.

The Relative Potency of Monetary and Fiscal Policies

Classical economics and supply-side approaches lead to the conclusion that Aggregate Demand matters little, if at all, in the long run. Keynesians and monetarists alike, however, focus on Aggregate Demand. Modern monetarists and contemporary Keynesians clearly have different views on some things, but this should not cloud their common areas of agreement. Their differences lie in different views of how important monetary policy is relative to fiscal policy, and not that one alone matters to the total exclusion of the other.

The Ineffectiveness Argument

First, both Keynesians and monetarists believe that money matters, but differ as to *how much* money matters. Keynesians view monetary policy as very weak during a slump and suggest that monetary expansion will be ineffective in expanding spending or reducing interest rates. Figure 5 shows why. Keynesians view investment as relatively insensitive

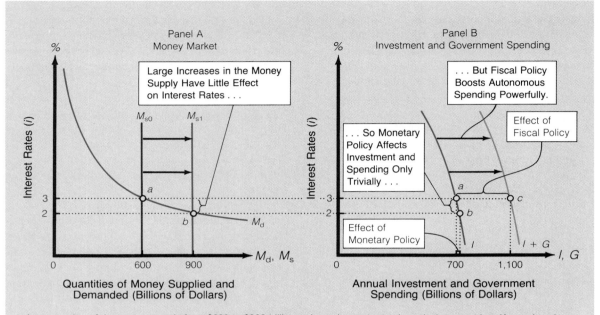

FIGURE 5 *Monetary Versus Fiscal Policy: The Keynesian View*

Panel A
Money Market

Large Increases in the Money Supply Have Little Effect on Interest Rates . . .

Panel B
Investment and Government Spending

. . . But Fiscal Policy Boosts Autonomous Spending Powerfully.

. . . So Monetary Policy Affects Investment and Spending Only Trivially . . .

Effect of Fiscal Policy

Effect of Monetary Policy

Quantities of Money Supplied and Demanded (Billions of Dollars)

Annual Investment and Government Spending (Billions of Dollars)

An expansion of the money supply from $600 to $900 billion reduces interest rates by only 1 percent in a Keynesian slump (Panel A). This small decline in interest rates only raises investment by $50 billion in Panel B because investment is insensitive to interest rates in the Keynesian view. Fiscal policy, on the other hand, is very effective in a Keynesian slump because it is, dollar for dollar, just as powerful as new investment in inducing further income through the multiplier process. New government spending of $400 billion ($c - a$) in Panel B expands autonomous spending far more powerfully than did the 50 percent monetary growth depicted in Panel A.

to interest rates, depending instead primarily upon business expectations. This suggests that slight declines in interest rates when the money supply grows (Panel A) will have little effect on investment and output, as shown in Panel B. Fiscal policy, on the other hand, is extremely powerful in a slump. The addition of government spending to investment in Panel B boosts autonomous spending and, through the multiplier process, massively raises national production and income.

Monetarists see the demand for money as relatively insensitive to interest rates but perceive investment as highly responsive to interest rates. Even a small increase in the money supply drives interest rates down sharply in the monetarist view (Panel A in Figure 6), which in turn strongly stimulates investment (Panel B). Monetarists also see expansionary monetary policy as bolstering consumer spending, both because extra money "burns holes" in people's

pockets and because reduced interest rates make buying on credit easier and cheaper. Thus, to the modern monetarist, monetary policy is very powerful.

Fiscal policy has only a negligible effect, according to monetarist reasoning, because new government spending does not raise injections ($I + G$) nearly as much as does even a small decline in interest rates. Moreover, monetarists object that government spending may "crowd out" investment. Careful study of Figures 5 and 6 will enable you to understand the fundamental reasons why Keynesians advocate fiscal policy to regulate Aggregate Spending, while monetarists prefer monetary policy.

Keynesians and modern monetarists agree that when an economy is at full employment, increasing Aggregate Demand results in a rising price level. When an economy is in a severe slump, both would agree that increases in Aggregate Demand will re-

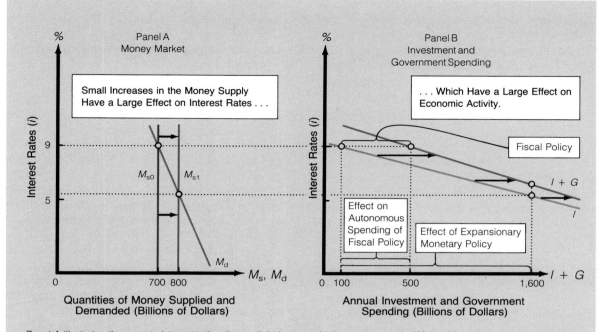

FIGURE 6 *Monetary Versus Fiscal Policy: The Monetarist View*

Panel A illustrates the monetarist contention that a slight increase in the money supply (M_{s0} to M_{s1}) will reduce interest rates dramatically (from 9 to 5.5 percent) because the demand for money (M_d) is relatively insensitive to interest rate changes. Marked declines in interest rates resulting from the extra $100 billion in money cause investment to soar by $1.5 trillion (in Panel B), stimulating autonomous spending far more than even a massive dose ($400 billion) of new government spending.

store full employment. They would, however, *disagree* on the appropriate method of increasing Aggregate Demand. Monetarists favor expansionary monetary policy to increase private consumption and investment, while Keynesians view that approach as ineffective because of widespread pessimism on the parts of workers, consumers, and business firms. Keynesians, therefore, favor expansionary fiscal policy.

We have examined the theoretical arguments that explain why Keynesians prefer fiscal policy and why monetarists prefer monetary policy to stabilize the economy. But just how convincing are these positions when applied to the art of policymaking? The next section examines the extent to which policy can be either Keynesian or monetarist and some of the problems inherent when policymakers exercise discretion in designing a mix of ways to spread the cost of government.

Rules Versus Discretionary Policies

Most modern monetarists believe that designing discretionary monetary and fiscal policies to buffer business cycles is an impossible task. They favor doing away with all **discretion** in policymaking and adopting stable and permanent monetary and fiscal **rules.** These critics believe that the market system is inherently stable and that severe swings in business activity inevitably follow ill-advised discretionary policies.

Suppose you are driving a high-powered car down a fairly straight highway that is banked slightly along the edges to keep you on the road. Unfortunately, someone has blackened the front and side windows—you cannot see where you are or what lies ahead. To make matters worse, your gas pedal sticks at times, the steering wheel is loose, and your brakes alternate between pure mush and grabbing so sharply that you skid. Luckily, you can vaguely see where you have been through a fogged-over rear-view mirror. What is your best strategy?

If you press the gas pedal too hard, you may go so fast that the curbs at the edge of the road will fail to keep you on course. If you try to steer, you may guide yourself over the side. Your best strategy will be to adjust the accelerator carefully to maintain a slow but steady speed and let the car steer itself away from the road's edges.

The economists who blame cyclical swings on improper monetary or fiscal policies perceive macroeconomic policymakers as being in our economy's "driver's seat." Attempts to fine-tune the economy through discretionary policies are viewed as the fumblings of people who barely deserve learners' permits playing with the controls of an Indianapolis 500 racer. There is a tendency to oversteer and to jump back and forth from the accelerator to the brake. The resulting stop-and-go economic pattern might resemble your path when you were learning to drive—and, unlike policymakers, you knew what you were passing and could see what lay ahead. We also hope that the steering, braking, and acceleration of the car you drove responded more precisely than the cumbersome tools available to monetary and fiscal policymakers.

Economists opposed to discretionary policymaking generally advocate the following rules:

1. Government spending should be set at the amounts of government goods and services that the public would demand if the economy were at full employment; no "make work" projects should be permitted.
2. Tax rates should then be structured so that the federal budget would be roughly in balance if the economy were at full employment.
3. Growth of the money supply should be limited to a fixed rate that is compatible with the historical average rate of growth of our potential Gross National Product (roughly 3 percent yearly).

Although monetarists perceive some problems emerging from improper spending and tax policies (Hoover's tax increase in 1930–32 and Johnson's simultaneous wars on poverty and in Vietnam), they cast central bankers (the FED) as the major villains in their explanations of cyclical chaos in market economies.

Improper Targets and the Natural Rate of Interest

Critics of active demand management policies also assert that macroeconomic policymakers often focus on unattainable goals.

Improper Targets   Attempts to achieve lower unemployment rates or interest rates than are consistent with people's individual decisions are viewed as ultimately self-defeating. Economists who favor rules over discretionary policies believe that policymakers will be frustrated if they attempt to maintain unemployment and interest rates below their "natural" values. The natural rate of unemployment hypothesis is discussed in Chapter 17. For now, we will examine the natural real rate of interest hypothesis and discover why the interest rate may not be the appropriate variable for monetary authorities to target.

The Natural "Real" Rate of Interest Hypothesis
Just as there are any number of wage rates or prices in the economy, there are also any number of interest rates. The interest rates paid by borrowers to lenders reflect, among other considerations, risk, length of time to maturity of the note or bond, the availability of credit, and legal constraints. For simplicity, we generally assume that there is only one interest rate for borrowing.

When people discuss "the" interest rate, they usually mean the average annual percentage monetary premium paid for the use of money. Economists refer to this percentage monetary premium as the **nominal rate of interest.** The **real rate of interest** is the annual percentage of purchasing power paid by a borrower to a lender for the use of money. Estimating the realized real rate of interest (r) is simple—the nominal interest (i) minus the percentage rate of inflation ($\dot{P}$) yields the percentage purchasing power premium, or real interest rate (r), paid over the life of a note, bond, or Certificate of Deposit (CD):

$$r = i - \dot{P} \quad \text{(real interest rate paid on a debt).}$$

For example, if the nominal interest rate is 12 percent and the price level increases by 15 percent, the real rate of interest is -3 percent and lenders lose 3 percent of purchasing power in each such year.

Workers bargain for higher nominal wages in order to protect their real wages when they anticipate inflation. Naturally, people whose incomes are based on interest will act similarly. The natural real rate of interest hypothesis suggests that borrowers and lenders adjust nominal interest to expected inflation $E(\dot{P})$, so that the nominal rate of interest charged for borrowing money reflects lenders' desires and borrowers' willingness to pay puchasing power premiums (desired real interest, r_d) for the use of money. Thus, when a note or bond is issued:

$$i = r_d + E(\dot{P}) \quad \text{(nominal cost of borrowing).}$$

If inflation is expected, lenders try to charge higher interest rates to ensure that they will not lose purchasing power; but why will borrowers be willing to pay such "high" interest rates? To understand this essential point, consider the housing market during the late 1970s, during which housing prices increased from 10 to 30 percent annually in some regions. Suppose that you expect housing prices in your area to increase by 15 percent annually. To keep it simple, we will assume that you can borrow money at a nominal interest rate of 10 percent. If you are able to repay the loan with dollars that have depreciated in value by 15 percent annually, this situation is similar to being paid 5 percent of the price of your house annually to live in your own home. Negative real rent sounds pretty good to most of us, which explains, in part, the 1970s boom in housing prices.

The **natural real interest rate hypothesis** suggests that the desired real rate of interest (r_d) reflects: (*a*) the real (purchasing power) premium necessary to induce savers to delay gratification—most people value having goods today more than having goods tomorrow; (*b*) the premiums necessary to induce people to hold their wealth in less liquid forms; and (*c*) the expected productivity of capital, which yields extra goods in the future. The real interest rate is the percentage of extra goods that can be enjoyed if consumption is delayed so that extra capital is available for production.

Keynes and Fisher Effects

According to the natural real interest rate hypothesis, monetary policymakers might temporarily reduce nominal interest rates through expansionary policy; but in the long run, overly expansionary policies will cause nominal interest rates to climb, not fall. Let us see why using Figure 7, which relates the supply and demand for loanable funds to nominal interest rates. The supply and demand for loanable funds is linked closely to the supply and demand for money we discussed in Chapters 13 and 14. Changes in real interest rates will cause these supplies and demands to shift.

Suppose that monetary policymakers view the nominal interest rate of 6 percent (given by the intersection of D_0 and S_0 at point *a*) as too high—they perceive it as an inhibitor to investment and spending. If they follow expansionary open-market operations, the supply of loanable funds initially expands to S_1 and the nominal interest rate falls to 4 percent (point *b*). This temporary decline in nominal interest rates caused by expansionary policies will result in even larger declines in real interest rates since natural rate theory predicts that inflation inevitably follows overly expansionary policies. We call such declines in interest rates following expansionary monetary policy the **Keynes effect.**

If expansionary policies cause the price level to rise by 4 percent annually, the real rate of interest is zero ($r = i - \dot{P} = 4$ percent $- 4$ percent $= 0$ percent). Borrowers eventually will increase their real demands for funds to, say, D_1 because borrowing seems so cheap since they repay these loans in depreciated dollars. Lenders will reduce supplies to S_2 because they have gained no real purchasing power at a real interest rate of zero. In the long run, the nominal interest rate will rise to 10 percent (point *c* in Figure 7) because of the **Fisher effect,** which is the name given to changes in nominal interest rates as borrowers and lenders compensate for expected inflation or deflation. Contractionary monetary policies tend to reduce the availability of credit in the short run; thus, in such cases the Keynes effect drives nominal interest rates up. After borrowers and lenders have learned to expect the deflationary pressures resulting from contractionary policies, however, the Fisher effect brings nominal interest rates down. Focus 1 provides an example of both Keynes and Fisher effects in recent years.

Overall, natural rate analysis suggests that discretionary macroeconomic policies are futile in the long run; they cannot permanently reduce real interest below its natural rate. The advocates of a **fixed monetary growth rule** believe that discretionary policies work temporarily only if people suffer from

FIGURE 7   *The Keynes and Fisher Effects in the Market for Real Loanable Funds*

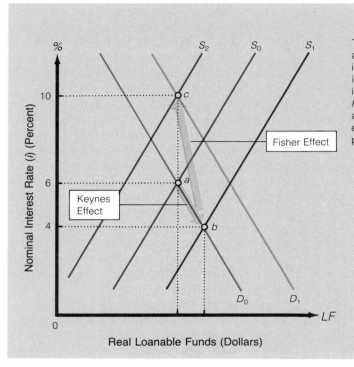

The *natural rate of real interest theory* suggests that an expansion of the money supply may temporarily increase the supply of loanable funds and drive nominal interest rates down via the *Keynes effect*; but if inflation results and comes to be expected, the *Fisher effect* may cause nominal interest rates to rise above the initial level. These effects operate in exactly opposite directions when contractionary policies are followed.

money illusion. Even temporary reductions of interest are harmful because they are achieved only by thwarting people's desires; everyone eventually compensates for having been fooled by policymakers.

The Culpability of the FED

Modern monetarists view the capitalist system as largely self-stabilizing and predictable; they perceive erratic government policies as the leading cause of business cycles. Monetarists believe that rapid inflation is explained by unwarranted growth of the money supply, which results in "too much money chasing too few goods." Alternatively, severe deflations, recessions, or depressions result when the money supply grows too slowly (or even falls), resulting in "too little money chasing too many goods."

Modern monetarists think it obvious that economic stability is the natural state of the market system. In their view, the velocity of money is very sta-

ble, so that severe economic instability occurs only when the money supply and the demand for money grow at different rates. How can government prevent macroeconomic convulsions? It can do so by simply holding the rate of growth of the money supply roughly in line with our (slow growing) capacity to produce; monetarists view income (or wealth) as the major determinant of the demand for money. Recall the Equation of Exchange, which underpins the Quantity Theory of Money: $MV = PQ$. If the money supply (M) grows at the same rate as our ability to produce (Q), and if velocity (V) is constant, then the price level (P) will be stable. Given that

$$\frac{\Delta M}{M} + \frac{\Delta V}{V} = \frac{\Delta P}{P} + \frac{\Delta Q}{Q}.$$

If $\Delta M/M = \Delta Q/Q$, and if $\Delta V/V = 0$, then $\Delta P/P = 0$.

This sounds fairly easy. Why has government not learned these simple monetary facts of life and followed policies to achieve a stable price level and facilitate smooth economic growth? The monetarist

FOCUS 1

Keynes and Fisher Effects in Action—1978–82

The Federal Reserve eased monetary policy in 1978, reducing real rates of interest (the Keynes effect). During most of 1978–80, real rates of interest were actually negative or nearly zero. By 1981, real and nominal interest rates began to soar as financial markets adjusted to higher expected inflation (the Fisher effect). Figure 8 illustrates the Keynes and Fisher effects as they occurred during 1978–82.

FIGURE 8   *The Keynes and Fisher Effects in Action*

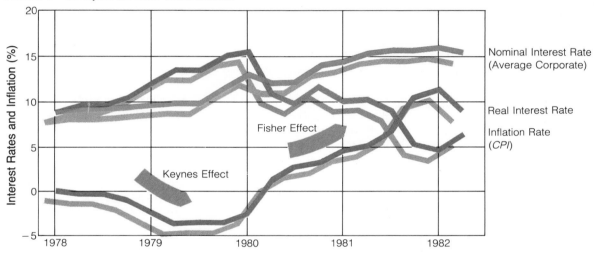

Expansionary monetary policies in 1978 drove real interest rates down via the Keynes effect as inflation exceeded nominal interest in 1979. Nominal interest rates rose to compensate for expected inflation in 1980–81, even though inflation was falling; this was the Fisher effect in action.
Sources: *Moody's Bond Record* and *Business Conditions Digest*.

answer to this question is that no one is able to predict precisely what will happen to our productive capacity in the near future. Moreover, instituting policies and having them take effect requires time. (We discuss time lag problems in Chapter 18.) Monetarists also believe that the Federal Reserve System is trying too hard to control the economy (see Focus 2). Finally, political considerations too often dominate sound monetary policymaking. The solution, according to many monetarists, is to follow a rule of expanding the money supply at a fixed annual rate in the 2–4 percent range: this is equal to the historical average growth of our productive capacity.

The Failure of Discretionary Fine-Tuning

Many economists view the Great Depression and the Kennedy years as evidence that government should use Keynesian engineering to keep the economy sta-

FOCUS 2

Monetary Targets and Stop-and-Go FED Policies: 1976–85

Abrupt changes in monetary policy can cause economic chaos. Monetary growth was erratic in the late 1970s and early 1980s. Indeed, many observers lay the full blame for a deep recession during 1981–83 at the FED's doorstep. Supply-side economists blame restrictive monetary policies for keeping the full effects of Reagan's tax cuts from taking effect in the early 1980s.

Uneven but growing inflation plagued the 1970s. Money supply growth accelerated, and monetarists believed it to be the root cause of this erosion of the dollar's purchasing power. Keynesians tended to point to other causes, such as the monstrous OPEC oil price hikes of 1974 and 1979–80.

Paul Volcker, Chairman of the FED, believed the monetarist prescription that lowering the growth rate of money was the key to curbing inflation. His policies to halt accelerating inflation were successful in 1980. Because the side effects (high unemployment and high real rates of interest) of the rapid cuts in monetary growth were politically unpalatable, monetary restrictiveness was loosened in late 1982 and early 1983.

Figure 9 shows that achieving a stable growth rate of 2–4 percent annually is a painful process when people are accustomed to more rapid monetary growth. The economy has followed a jerky path since World War II. The disruptions of the Vietnam War or other shocks to our economy may be partial explanations, but most monetarists believe that attempts to fine-tune the economy were doomed to failure.

Attempts at monetary fine-tuning are illustrated in Figure 9. In 1979, the FED announced it would target $M1$ and control its rate of growth. Since then, as the figure illustrates, monetary growth and GNP growth have been on a roller coaster—up for a few quarters and then down the next few. The FED announces targets in one period, then adjusts them later when economic conditions warrant it. Milton Friedman compares the FED to the farmer who used his barn door for target shooting. "A visitor was astounded to find that each of the numerous targets on the door has a bullet hole precisely in the center of the bull's-eye. He later discovered the secret of such remarkable accuracy. Unobserved, he saw the farmer first shoot at the door and then paint the target."[*] He contends that the FED "simply repaints the target" to cover its discretionary policymaking.

[*]*Milton Friedman, "The FED Hasn't Changed Its Ways,"* The Wall Street Journal, *August 20, 1985.*

FIGURE 9 *Rate of Change of M1 and GNP (Current Dollars, Quarterly Percentage Change)*

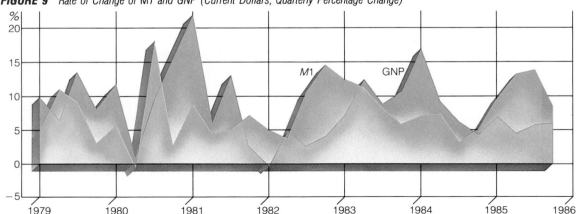

In 1979, the FED announced it would target and control the rate of growth of $M1$. Since then, both $M1$ and GNP have risen for a few quarters, then fallen the next few. Targeting $M1$ in the 1980s has proven so difficult for the FED that it recently broadened the targeted rate of growth for $M1$ to an annual rate anywhere between 3–8 percent.

Source: *Business Conditions Digest,* January 1986.

ble. Taxing and spending are the fiscal tools Keynesians recommend to stabilize our economy. Others argue that the FED can keep the economy on track by expanding or contracting the money supply as needed. Fiscal and monetary policies both have been frequently changed to try to fine-tune the economy so that Aggregate Demand and Aggregate Supply are balanced.

Tax rates were cut and the money supply was expanded to stimulate a previously sluggish economy during the early 1960s. Then, monetary restraint was applied in 1966 to curb mounting inflationary pressures. A temporary tax surcharge was imposed in 1969. The money supply grew rapidly in the early 1970s, screeched to a halt causing a short collapse in 1975–76, accelerated from 1977 to 1979, and then slowed sharply in the early 1980s. Cuts in tax rates from 1981 to 1983 were coupled with a monetary slowdown to yield mixed results.

Keynes believed that central banks tried to follow expansionary policies but failed to combat the Great Depression. This is, in part, why Keynes and his followers sought to replace passive monetary policy with active fiscal policy. Milton Friedman and other monetarists question the widely held belief that the Great Depression occurred despite highly expansionary monetary policies. Through their collection and review of the monetary data for the United States for the past century, they discovered that the money supply fell considerably just before and during the Depression. Their interpretation is that the Federal Reserve System caused the Depression because (perhaps unwittingly) it followed contractionary policies.

In fact, most monetarists believe that the business cycle is largely a consequence of erratic and improper monetary policy—when the money supply grows too slowly, economic downturns and stagnation soon follow; when the money supply mushrooms, increases in the price level are inevitable. These difficulties are the major reasons for monetarists' advocacy of stable monetary growth rates. The crucial differences between fiscal and monetary policies, according to the theories of Keynesians, monetarists, and classically oriented supply-siders, are summarized in Table 2.

TABLE 2 *Alternative Views of Monetary and Fiscal Policies*

Keynesians	Monetarists	Supply-Siders
1. Fiscal policy is very powerful.	1. Fiscal policy is relatively unimportant due to *crowding out*.	1. High tax rates and vast government spending both reduce the incentives for people to be productive.
2. Monetary policy is not very powerful or important during economic slumps.	2. Erratic monetary policy is the major cause of business cycles. Money is important at all times.	2. Erratic fiscal policy confuses investors and workers, reducing incentives for productivity. Erratic monetary policy diverts resources from production into hedges against inflation or deflation.
3. Monetary policy affects spending through changes in interest rates and investments.	3. Monetary policy affects spending in all markets simultaneously ($MV = PQ$).	3. Money is a veil.
4. Discretionary policies are necessary to offset the economy's inherent instability.	4. Smooth growth of the money supply is crucial. Rules should replace discretion in policy. Economy is inherently stable.	4. Steady monetary policy enhances the quality of information about economic decisions.
5. Velocity is erratic; it rises during inflation but falls sharply during recessions.	5. Velocity is relatively stable.	5. Velocity is stable if monetary policy is stable.
6. During deep depressions, fear causes velocity to plummet, resulting in *liquidity traps*.	6. Liquidity traps are highly implausible and have never actually occurred.	6. Liquidity traps are irrelevant to the real world.

You now know alternative views of how monetary and fiscal policy interact and effect spending, as well as the implications of these policies for such issues as the public debt and the crowding-out hypothesis. In the next part, we examine how changes in private sector activities and macroeconomic policies jointly influence Aggregate Supply and Aggregate Demand, and how shifts in Aggregate Demand and Supply dictate the movements of employment, unemployment, inflation, and economic growth.

CHAPTER REVIEW: KEY POINTS

1. The federal government can finance *public spending* by collecting taxes, printing money, selling government securities, or through confiscation.
2. The *crowding-out hypothesis* states that increases in government purchases inevitably cause some reductions in private consumption, investment, or leisure.
3. A major difference between private and public debt is that *private debt* is entirely owned by persons *external* to the issuing institution, while the bulk of *public debt* is *internal,* being owed to ourselves. Private debt has grown roughly three times faster than public debt since the early 1950s and is currently three times as large.
4. The *real burden of the national debt* stems from the federal government "crowding out" private investment as it drives interest rates up when competing with the private sector for loanable funds. As a result, future generations may inherit a smaller capital stock and a smaller production-possibilities frontier.
5. Among the major benefits of the public debt are its use as a *stabilization instrument* and as a *risk-free asset* for savers.
6. The difficulties confronting monetary and fiscal policymakers have caused many economists to favor putting the economy on "automatic pilot." The advocates of replacing *discretionary policy* with set *rules* would replace the Federal Open-Market Committee with a couple of reliable but unimaginative clerks who would increase the money supply by a fixed small (3 percent?) increase annually, and the federal budget would be set to balance at full employment.

QUESTIONS FOR THOUGHT AND DISCUSSION

1. Explain the sense in which federal taxes determine how much each of us will help control inflation. If you could print money, can you imagine a reason why you would ever try to remove any from circulation as long as there were trees and green ink? Why? Why does the federal government bother to collect taxes?
2. Government spending can be financed by taxation, borrowing, or by creating new money. Rank these from least expansionary to most expansionary and explain your ranking system.
3. What mechanisms cause the Federal Reserve System to experience pressure to expand the money supply when the Treasury runs a huge deficit? When the FED yields to this pressure, does this add or detract from the goal of achieving macroeconomic stability? Why?
4. Suppose a rule of 3 percent annual monetary growth were imposed. How long should policymakers doggedly follow such a policy if inflation soared to more than 20 percent or unemployment hovered around 15 percent?

5. Why do foreigners willingly hold Treasury bonds that represent so much of our national debt? Is it desirable from our vantage point for them to do so? What are the long-term consequences of these loans?

6. Paul Volcker, in testimony before Congress in 1986, noted that NOW and other interest-bearing demand deposit accounts, disinflation, and falling interest rates have (at least in the short run) altered the basic relationship between the rate of change in $M1$ and inflation. Accordingly, given the greater uncertainty associated with the relationship between $M1$ and economic activity, the FED decided to adopt a broader range for its $M1$ growth rate. Thus, if velocity continues to fall, $M1$ growth can be near the upper end of the target range, and vice versa. Does Volcker's testimony of a wider $M1$ range confirm Milton Friedman's argument that the FED simply adjusts its target to cover its discretionary policymaking? What would be the effect on the economy of a fixed (3 percent) rule for $M1$ growth if velocity is falling?

PART 5

Challenges to Macroeconomic Policymaking

You now have some ideas about how fiscal policy works (from Part Three) and how money affects economic activity (from Part Four).

The foundations of Aggregate Demand and Aggregate Supply curves are featured in Chapter 16. We use these curves to investigate some of the reasons for the prosperity of the 1960s, the "stagflation" of the erratic 1970s, and the economic crunch and disinflation of the early 1980s.

Stagflation, our major focus in Chapter 17, combines the difficulties of high rates of inflation and high rates of unemployment and is a problem of fairly recent vintage. We also discuss policies to deal with the *Phillips curve*, which suggests that there may be a trade-off between unemployment and inflation.

We hope that our earlier descriptions of monetary and fiscal policy have not convinced you that macroeconomic problems are easily solved. Some of the difficulties of tinkering with the economy are treated in Chapter 18: the problem of timing and lags in policymaking, and *rational expectations analysis*—a recent challenge to the conventional monetarist and Keynesian framework that suggests the public will adjust to discretionary monetary and fiscal policy in such a manner as to thwart its effectiveness.

This part of the book concludes with Chapter 19, where we examine the problems encountered in achieving long-run economic growth and development. It would be difficult to overestimate the hurdles confronted in countries plagued by inadequate natural resources, high rates of population growth, and insufficient capital as people attempt to improve their living standards.

CHAPTER 16 Aggregate Demands and Supplies

stagflation	demand-side	supply-side
Aggregate Demand	(demand-pull)	(cost-push) inflation
curve	inflation	disinflation
Aggregate Supply		
curve		

Neither the conventional monetarist approach nor the Keynesian Aggregate Expenditure approach offer much insight into why or how an economy might simultaneously experience high rates of inflation and unemployment. The major reason is that conventional Keynesian and monetarist models focus on variations in Aggregate Demand, while in the 1970s, much of economic disruption battered Aggregate Supply. Students of economics have been puzzled by the failure of demand-side models to explain the events of the past several years. Although most economists once tended to ignore shocks to the supply side of the economy, recent macroeconomic models have begun to address the macroeconomic problems posed by changes in Aggregate Supply.

High rates of unemployment and inflation occurred simultaneously for the first time in 1974–75, giving rise to the term **stagflation**—a contraction of stagnation and inflation. This malady unfortunately proved persistent. Inflation and unemployment remained well above historical norms for a full decade. Attempts to checkmate inflation in the double-digit range during 1979–81 had partially succeeded by 1982, but temporarily drove unemployment above

10 percent. By the mid 1980s, inflation had fallen to below 3 percent, while unemployment hovered between 7 and 8 percent.

Coupling double-digit inflation with high rates of unemployment (or double-digit unemployment with rapid hikes in price levels) was thought virtually impossible during the 1950s and 1960s. Policymakers familiar with Keynesian theory believed that very low unemployment rates might force the nation to suffer high rates of inflation, and vice versa; but faith in government's ability to fine-tune Aggregate Demand to produce continuous growth and a reasonably stable price level was commonplace. By the end of the 1970s, this belief in the government's ability to fine-tune the economy had all but disappeared. In the early 1980s, the Reagan Administration turned its attention to expanding Aggregate Supply.

The paths through time of macroeconomic variables such as employment, national output and income, inflation, and unemployment can be explained by relative shifts in Aggregate Demand and Aggregate Supply. We now turn to an examination of both the demand side and the supply sides of our economy.

Determinants of the Aggregate Demand Curve

Keynesian policy analysis is largely a prescription for achieving full employment if the economy is operating below its potential, but it generally ignores the inflation that might emerge if Aggregate Demand is excessive. On the other hand, total spending by both consumers and investors is sensitive to the price level, and vice versa. Let us see why.

The Aggregate Demand Curve

The demand curve for a specific good is negatively sloped because consumers substitute other goods for the good in question when its price rises, and vice versa. Rationalizing a negative slope for an **Aggregate Demand curve** for the entire economy is more difficult. If the general price level rises, toward what goods will consumers move (what will they substitute)? Why is an Aggregate Demand curve for the economy negatively sloped? Substitution is still important but shows up in a different guise when we consider the economy as a whole.

All else equal, higher domestic prices will reduce planned spending on American products because higher domestic prices:

1. Result in higher interest rates that reduce planned investment, Aggregate Expenditures, and ultimately, output.
2. Reduce the purchasing power of assets stated in terms of money, causing wealth to decline.
3. Cause American and foreign consumers to substitute goods produced elsewhere for American-made goods.
4. Cause investors to find foreign investment relatively more profitable than U.S. investment.

Let us examine each of these relationships briefly. You will see that each effect results in reduction of the Aggregate Expenditures schedule. For simplicity, we will temporarily assume that all domestic prices—including wages and rents—increase by the same proportion.

Interest Rate/Investment Adjustments
The major reason for the negative slope of the Aggregate Demand curve is the effect that higher prices have on the chain reaction from interest rates to investment to Aggregate Spending, and then to income and output. These adjustments closely parallel the Keynesian monetary transmission mechanism you examined earlier.

When prices rise, the real purchasing power of a fixed money supply (M/P) falls. Consider Figure 1. Raising the price level from P_0 to P_1 (Panel D) has the following effect in Panel A: The nominal money supply is assumed constant at M_{s0}; so the real supply of money shifts from M_{s0}/P_0 to M_{s0}/P_1. Equilibrium interest rates rise from i_0 (point a) to i_1 (point b). Rising interest rates result in equilibrium moving from point a to point b in Panel B; thus, planned investment falls from I_0 to I_1. This reduction in planned investment shifts the Aggregate Expenditures schedule in Panel C from AE_0 to AE_1, resulting in a reduction in real national income from Y_0 (point a) to Y_1 (point b). Finally, this reduced national income at higher prices means real output must fall from Q_0 (point a) to Q_1 (point b), as shown in Panel D. Duplicating this same process for every possible price level results in the negatively sloped Aggregate Demand curve illustrated in Panel D. The higher interest rates that result from higher prices squeeze both government spending at the local and state levels (especially that which is bond financed) and consumer credit, in addition to crowding out investment. Thus, higher interest rates reduce all these sources of Aggregate Spending.

The Wealth Effect
Another reason for the negative slope of the Aggregate Demand curve is termed the **wealth effect.** Most of us hold some of our wealth in such assets as cash or savings accounts. Changes in the price level alter the purchasing power of these assets and, hence, our wealth. As our wealth rises, we tend to spend more for both consumption and investment goods, and vice versa.

Suppose the price level fell sharply. To the extent that your wealth rises because of the increased purchasing power of your assets stated in monetary terms, you will be able to buy more goods and services and so you will spend more. Conversely, even if your monetary income keeps pace with the price level during an inflationary episode, you will lose to the extent that your wealth is stored as cash or in bank accounts and you will reduce your spending.

Another adjustment occurs because most of us want to maintain a fairly stable amount of liquid assets relative to our income. Thus, even if your income increases at the same rate that the price level rises, you may temporarily reduce the proportion of income devoted to consumption so that the purchas-

FIGURE 1 *Interest Rates, Investment, and the Negatively Sloped Aggregate Demand Curve*

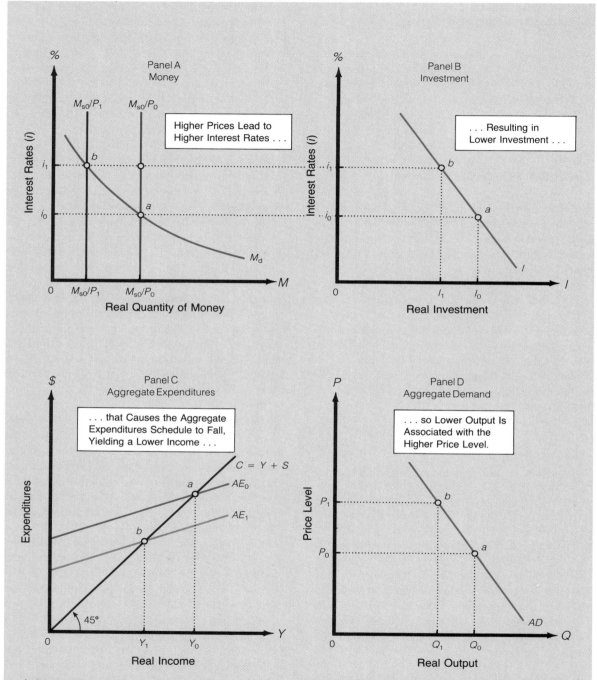

A rising price level, all else equal, reduces the real supply of money (Panel A), which increases interest rates, reducing investment (Panel B) and Aggregate Expenditures and income (Panel C). Reduced income at higher prices means real output has fallen (Panel D) Repeating this process for all possible price levels produces a negatively sloped Aggregate Demand curve.

ing power of your liquid assets is restored through a short-term higher rate of saving. Because consumption declines as the price level climbs due to the wealth effect, Aggregate Spending also falls in a manner similar to that described for interest rate/investment adjustments and shown in Figure 1.

Exports and Imports   We import goods when foreigners can produce them at lower costs than we can and export goods when American production costs are lower than those in other countries. (International trade is addressed in detail in a later chapter.) If the prices of American goods rise, you will buy more imported goods than previously because they will be relatively cheaper. At the same time, foreign consumers will reduce their purchases of now higher priced American goods. Thus, inflation causes imports to increase and exports to decrease, resulting in reduced Aggregate Expenditures and National Income and Output.

Foreign Investment   Increases in American prices generally are accompanied by increases in American costs of production. Investors will find that increased wages and higher costs for land and machinery in the United States make it profitable to reduce domestic investment and substitute foreign investment, which reinforces the decline in Aggregate Spending as the price level rises from P_0 to P_1 (shown in Figure 1).

To summarize, higher prices cause lower quantities of Aggregate Demand because: (*a*) rising prices result in higher interest rates that reduce investment and purchases of consumer durables; (*b*) rising prices reduce the real value of assets stated in monetary terms (the wealth effect); (*c*) imports grow and exports fall; and (*d*) domestic investment declines and foreign investment by American firms flourishes.

Shifts of Aggregate Demand   Movements of the Aggregate Demand curve are caused by changes in government monetary or fiscal policies or by changes in planned consumption, investment, or foreign spending. Any increases in planned Aggregate Expenditures (upward shifts in Keynesian cross diagrams) are paralleled by rightward shifts of the Aggregate Demand curve. These shifts originate in increases in government purchases or transfer payments, reductions in taxes, or more optimistic expectations by consumers and investors (see Figure 2).

Expansionary monetary policies such as open-market purchases of bonds or reductions in either reserve requirements or the discount rate have the same effect. Symmetrically, when the government pursues contractionary monetary or fiscal policies, the Aggregate Demand curve shifts to the left. This is shown as the movement from AD_0 to AD_1 in Panel A of Figure 2. The factors that will cause the Aggregate Demand curve to shift are summarized in the chart below Figure 2.

Determinants of the Aggregate Supply Curve

The general law of diminishing returns partially accounts for the upward slope of supply curves for individual firms and for market supply curves. Additional production eventually becomes ever more costly as the level of production grows. Moreover, higher prices embody greater incentives for firms to produce more output because of the enhanced opportunities for profits. Alternatively, higher prices elicit increases in production because producers' costs rise with output. Thus, firms may require higher prices to justify expanding their outputs. A similar logic applies for the economy as a whole.

The Aggregate Supply Curve

The availability of idle resources shrinks when higher employment presses against society's productive capacity. If Aggregate Demand grows, however, the resource costs of a firm tend to rise less rapidly than the prices it can charge. Thus, profit per unit of output grows during a business upturn. Business firms naturally respond by producing and selling more goods. For example, if demand expands for food and sundries from your local grocery store, the manager will order more goods and quickly mark up prices. Employees' wages and other costs will rise, but much less rapidly than prices, so that total profits swell. What happens if demand collapses? The prices the grocer charges will fall much faster than wages or other production costs. Profit per unit of output may even become negative. Declining profit margins cause firms to cut back drastically on their orders and to lay off a large number of workers.

Production costs per unit are much slower to adjust to changes in Aggregate Demand than are the

FIGURE 2 *Factors Causing Shifts in the Aggregate Demand Curve*

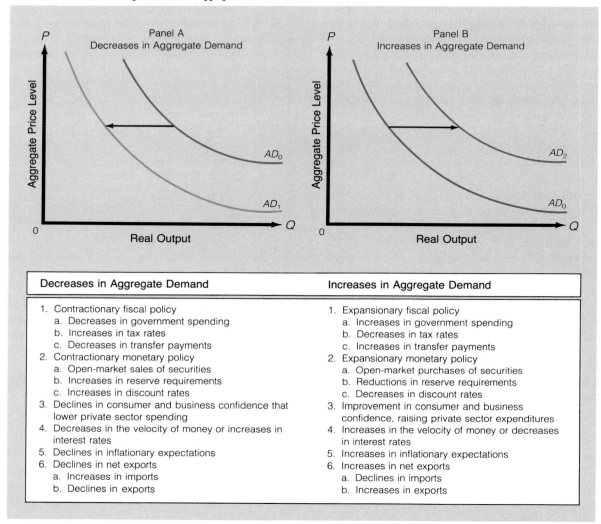

Decreases in Aggregate Demand	Increases in Aggregate Demand

1. Contractionary fiscal policy
  a. Decreases in government spending
  b. Increases in tax rates
  c. Decreases in transfer payments
2. Contractionary monetary policy
  a. Open-market sales of securities
  b. Increases in reserve requirements
  c. Increases in discount rates
3. Declines in consumer and business confidence that lower private sector spending
4. Decreases in the velocity of money or increases in interest rates
5. Declines in inflationary expectations
6. Declines in net exports
  a. Increases in imports
  b. Declines in exports
	1. Expansionary fiscal policy
	  a. Increases in government spending
	  b. Decreases in tax rates
	  c. Increases in transfer payments
	2. Expansionary monetary policy
	  a. Open-market purchases of securities
	  b. Reductions in reserve requirements
	  c. Decreases in discount rates
	3. Improvement in consumer and business confidence, raising private sector expenditures
	4. Increases in the velocity of money or decreases in interest rates
	5. Increases in inflationary expectations
	6. Increases in net exports
	  a. Declines in imports
	  b. Increases in exports

prices of output. This is the major reason why a short-run Aggregate Supply curve reflects a positive relationship between the price level and the real quantity of national output, as shown in Figure 3. Note that if much of our capacity is idle, as Keynes suggested, so that output is less than Q_0, output can increase in the short run without significant increases in the price level. But when the classical prediction of full employment is approached, even small increases in output above Q_1 necessitate huge increases in the price level. Between output levels Q_0 and Q_1, moderate

increases in output result in moderate increases in prices.

National Output and the Work Force

National output expands as increasing numbers of workers are employed productively. However, because of diminishing returns, at some point each additional worker adds less and less to total output. The labor market operates on the basis of supply and demand much like the other markets we have studied. Higher wages may induce greater effort, attract increasing numbers of people into the labor force, or cause unemployed workers to take jobs sooner without extended shopping for better jobs. Thus, unless the economy is extremely slack, labor's supply curve has a positive slope.

Increases in the total demand for labor generate pressure for higher levels of employment and output and for hikes in wages and prices as well. Conversely, declines in the economywide demand for labor result in pressure for lower employment, output, wages, and prices. There are, however, differences between short-run and long-run adjustments. Understanding Aggregate Supply requires an appreciation of these differences.

Labor Market Adjustments: The Short Run

Let us begin our discussion of short-run adjustments by reexamining the Keynesian depression model. In a severe depression like that of the 1930s, Keynes believed that business could fill any vacant positions at the going wage. Suppose that Aggregate Demand grew. There would be no need to increase wages to attract additional labor because so much of the labor force would be out of work. This portion of labor's supply curve is assumed to be flat because growing business demands for labor could be met at the prevailing market wage. Large quantities of idle capital also prevent diminishing returns from posing a problem. Thus, if the demand for labor grows during a depression, employment and output rise but wages and prices may not. Consequently, Keynesian analysis assumes a horizontal **Aggregate Supply curve** (see the Keynesian depression range in Figure 3). Remember that from Keynes's point of view, Say's Law was backwards and should have read "Demand creates its own supply."

Keynes's assumptions about depressed labor markets are drawn from the 1930s experience of an extended and severe depression. Labor's supply curve normally has a positive slope, reflecting the fact that higher wages induce additional workers into the labor force; rising wages also enable unemployed workers to more rapidly find jobs they perceive as suitable. As firms pay higher wages to attract additional employees, wages rise for all workers. This results in a moderate positive slope in the Aggregate Supply curve, shown as the intermediate range in Figure 3.

FIGURE 3 The Aggregate Supply Curve

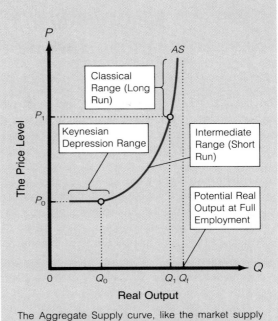

The Aggregate Supply curve, like the market supply curve, is positively sloped. This suggests that increases in National Output normally entail increases in the price level.

Workers recognize that increases in the price level will lower their real wages, but there is a time lag between a given inflationary reduction in real wages and labor's comprehension of this loss. Workers may temporarily be fooled by increases in money wages that are less than the increases in the price level so that more labor services may be offered even though real wages decline. Business firms hire more labor to produce more output if they can sell that output at higher prices. They do so because they perceive new profit opportunities from selling their products at higher prices and because real wages have declined. In the short run, workers fail to revise their expectations about changes in the price level and are fooled because they believe the original price level will prevail. Workers may suffer from inflation illusion in the very short run, but their misconceptions are not likely to persist forever.

Why John Smith, but Not General Motors, May Be Fooled by Inflation

There are at least a couple of reasons why workers may be more easily fooled by inflation than are the firms that employ them. First, firms devote more resources to forecasts of inflation than do individual workers. Second, a firm needs only to estimate how much extra revenue will be generated if extra workers are hired to know how much of a monetary wage (w) it can profitably af-

ford to pay. This calculation requires only estimates of the worker's physical productivity and a forecast of the price (P_i) at which the firm will be able to sell its own product.

Thus, the real wage paid a worker from the vantage point of the firm is w/P_i. Workers, on the other hand, must have forecasts of all the prices of all products they expect to buy (e.g., the

CPI) before they can estimate the purchasing power of their monetary wages. The real wage from the point of view of a typical worker equals w/CPI. Thus, firms may need less information about future prices (only P_i) to make profitable decisions than workers need (forecasts of most prices in the CPI) in order to make personally beneficial decisions.

Labor Market Adjustments: The Longer Run

Workers in the longer run will recognize price increases as reducing their real wages (W/P) and will react by reducing the real supply of labor. Suppose Aggregate Demand grows even though the economy is close to full employment. Higher money wages may temporarily lure more workers into the labor force if they assume that the price level will remain constant. Workers try to base decisions about their work loads on real wages, not on nominal money wages. People work for what their earnings will buy, not for the money itself. Once workers recognize that prices have risen, they will demand commensurate raises, resulting in a vertical long-run Aggregate Supply curve similar to the classical range shown in Figure 3.

This analysis represents the polar extreme from Keynesian analysis, being derived from the classical reasoning we have described previously. Classical economics assumes that workers react to changes in real wages almost instantly, keeping the economy close to full employment. At the very least, there can be no involuntary unemployment.

In reality, workers react imperfectly to changes in real earnings. Their reactions are imperfect because: (a) unions get locked into long-term contracts that often specify nominal wages over the lives of the agreements; (b) raises for many workers not covered

by collective bargaining contracts are adjusted only at scheduled intervals; and (c) changing jobs often entails considerable "search time" and lost income. These are only some of the many reasons why workers cannot instantly adjust their supplies of labor to changing inflationary expectations, as Focus 1 indicates.

Shifts In Aggregate Supply

Labor is just one of the resources used to produce goods; other resources will also shape the Aggregate Supply curve through their effects on productive capacity and costs. In addition, regulations and technology affect the relationships between resource inputs and production.

We begin our discussion of Aggregate Supply curve shifts with a quick review of the factors that affect individual market supply curves facing buyers, already detailed in Chapter 3. In addition to price, the major determinants are: (a) costs of resources, (b) production technology, (c) expectations, (d) regulations and taxes or subsidies to producers, (e) prices of other producible goods, and (f) number of producers in the market. Changes in influences other than its own price cause market supplies of a good to shift.

We are dealing with the Aggregate Supply curve for the economy, however, which encompasses all production and all producers. Substitutions between domestic production of different goods cancel each other out, so we can ignore the changes in the prices of other producible goods. We are left with changes in the quantities and costs of available resources, technology, expectations, and regulations and government policy as the four major shifters of the Aggregate Supply curve.

You may be getting tired of this curve bending, but we urge you to bear with us for a few more moments. You nearly have the tools necessary for understanding and formulating solutions to the greatest economic problem of the 1970s and early 1980s—solving the stagflation dilemma; disruptive shocks to Aggregate Supply are the ultimate explanation of stagflation.

Shocks Originating in the Labor Market
Labor supplies depend on individual preferences for income from labor versus personal enjoyment of leisure. As our economy has matured, there seem to be strong tendencies for shorter workweeks, more part-time employment, and for other forms of work sharing that allow people more leisure time. Increases in labor's preference for leisure over work cause the labor supply curve to shift to the left, reducing total labor supplies. This reduction in labor supply shifts Aggregate Supply to the left, as illustrated in Panel A of Figure 4 by the shift from AS_0 to AS_1. Alternatively, if more people chose to work or began working longer hours, Aggregate Supply might shift from AS_0 to AS_2 (shown in Panel B).

Work-leisure choices for many people are strongly influenced by taxes and social welfare policies. For example, if the federal government increases personal income tax rates, fewer people may work or those who do may work fewer hours. Increases in Social Security taxes accomplished by raising either the tax rate or the maximum amount of income covered will probably also shrink the supply of labor. These leftward shifts of the labor supply curve occur because higher taxes make earning additional income worth less. Workers base their work-leisure decisions on take-home pay, not gross wages.

Unemployment compensation or welfare payments also affect the supply of labor. If unemployment compensation payments are raised or extended for longer periods, more people will draw these benefits, and so the supply of labor will shrink. You may have heard stories like the one about the Michigan golf pro who works summers in Michigan and spends winters in Florida. Competition from other migratory Northern golf pros is so severe that he draws unemployment compensation in Florida each winter while he practices putting. This type of behavior occurs because people qualify for unemployment compensation payments unless they are offered and subsequently decline "comparable" positions.

Analysis of this type was at the heart of the 25 percent cut in tax rates phased in during 1981–83 and also was partially responsible for vigorous attempts to cut growth in government transfer payments and other social programs. The Reagan Administration hoped that revitalization of incentives to produce would raise Aggregate Supply more than these tax cuts raised Aggregate Demand so that substantial growth would defeat any emerging inflationary pressure.

A second type of labor market disturbance would occur if the power of unions grew and organized labor commanded higher wages; the Aggregate Supply curve would decline. Rising wages raise production costs and push prices upwards. A third source of disruption would be any increase in the inflation rate expected by labor. Inflationary expectations continuously shift the supply of labor curve leftward as workers try to protect the real purchasing power of their earnings. Naturally, decreases in inflationary expectations or in union power will shift the labor supply and Aggregate Supply curves toward the right.

Incomes Policies
Incomes policies might be used to reduce labor's inflationary expectations. The term *incomes policy* refers to a wide variety of measures designed to curb inflation without reducing Aggregate Demand. These methods include such practices as jawboning, wage-and-price guidelines, and wage-price controls. The most extreme of these is a **wage-price freeze** of the type imposed by President Nixon in 1971. It was hoped that this freeze would reduce the anticipated inflation rate to zero and stop continuous shrinkage of Aggregate Supply. Ideally, it might even increase the supplies of labor and output, shown as the shift of the Aggregate Supply curve from AS_0 to AS_2 in Figure 4.

Incomes policies, unfortunately, may have perverse effects on both inflationary expectations and Aggregate Supply. If workers and firms share a belief

FIGURE 4 *Factors Causing Shifts in the Aggregate Supply Curve*

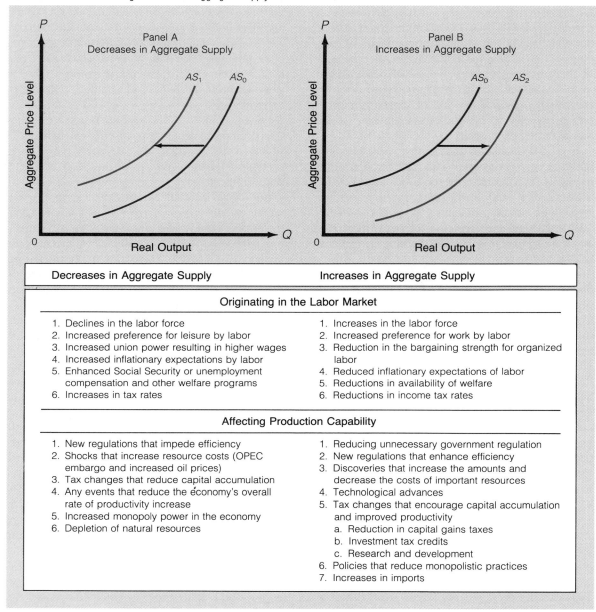

Decreases in Aggregate Supply	Increases in Aggregate Supply
Originating in the Labor Market	
1. Declines in the labor force	1. Increases in the labor force
2. Increased preference for leisure by labor	2. Increased preference for work by labor
3. Increased union power resulting in higher wages	3. Reduction in the bargaining strength for organized labor
4. Increased inflationary expectations by labor	4. Reduced inflationary expectations of labor
5. Enhanced Social Security or unemployment compensation and other welfare programs	5. Reductions in availability of welfare
6. Increases in tax rates	6. Reductions in income tax rates
Affecting Production Capability	
1. New regulations that impede efficiency	1. Reducing unnecessary government regulation
2. Shocks that increase resource costs (OPEC embargo and increased oil prices)	2. New regulations that enhance efficiency
3. Tax changes that reduce capital accumulation	3. Discoveries that increase the amounts and decrease the costs of important resources
4. Any events that reduce the economy's overall rate of productivity increase	4. Technological advances
5. Increased monopoly power in the economy	5. Tax changes that encourage capital accumulation and improved productivity
6. Depletion of natural resources	a. Reduction in capital gains taxes
	b. Investment tax credits
	c. Research and development
	6. Policies that reduce monopolistic practices
	7. Increases in imports

that prices will soar as soon as wage or price controls are lifted, they may withhold production from the market now in hopes of realizing higher wages or prices later. For example, suppose you have the following choices: (*a*) you could work during a period when wages are frozen and save money to cover your college expenses, or (*b*) you could borrow to go to college during a freeze and then repay the loan from money you earn after the lid is removed from wage hikes. You will be like a lot of other people if you delay offering your labor until after the freeze. There is also the problem that relative price adjustments are hampered by incomes policies; in the next chapter we will extend this discussion of how the resulting distortions in economic behavior retard Aggregate Supply.

Other Shocks Affecting Our Productive Capacity

Numerous factors other than labor determine our national productive capacity. Many people argue that massive growth of government regulation causes inefficiency. Some recent estimates suggest that between 5 and 10 percent of GNP is absorbed in complying with federal regulations.[1]

If new regulations smother the private business sector, the resulting inefficiency shifts the Aggregate Supply curve to the left (a movement from AS_0 to AS_1 in Figure 4). Elimination of burdensome federal regulation in turn shifts the Aggregate Supply curve rightward. For example, airline deregulation in 1978 resulted in sharp declines in fares and the introduction of several new airlines. On the other hand, new regulations that facilitate efficiency increase the Aggregate Supply curve. For example, the supplies of professional services were enhanced by Federal Trade Commission orders forbidding the American Medical Association and American Bar Association from setting medical or legal fees and banning these organizations from prohibiting advertising by doctors and lawyers.

Increases in the concentration of economic power also decrease Aggregate Supply. Firms with monopoly power extract high prices and profits by reducing their output. Consumers become, in a sense, more desperate for these products, so they pay higher prices. Growth in competition may occur for a number of reasons, including other firms' quests for a share of the profits of monopolists, major technological breakthroughs, more vigorous antitrust actions, or the invasion of a market by imports. Events that enhance competition cause Aggregate Supply to grow.

Government policies that reduce incentives to accumulate capital or to introduce new technologies hamper economic growth. If government policies impede investment and technological advances, the economy declines (or fails to grow as fast as it could), and the Aggregate Supply curve shifts to the left (or is held back). Government policy encouraging capital accumulation (for example, a reduction in capital gains taxation) or speeding the introduction of the latest production equipment (increases in investment tax credits) shift the Aggregate Supply curve to the right.

From the mid-1970s onward, drives to deregulate many sectors of our economy were directed at removing inefficiency and bolstering Aggregate Supply. Deregulation was a major feature of the Reagan Administration's supply-side policies. Supply-side policy also combined substantial cuts in corporate taxes with favorable tax treatments for savers and with investment tax credits and accelerated depreciation allowances in hopes that these policies would also expand Aggregate Supply. Politicians who favored these policies conceded that they would be most advantageous to upper income groups, but they argued that the benefits of expanding Aggregate Supply would accrue to workers and the poor as well. Opponents, fearing that the benefits to the rich would far outweigh those to the poor, labeled this "trickle-down" economics.

External shocks to the system that increase the cost of imports or resources cause Aggregate Supply to shrink. Drastic shocks to the U.S. economy in the energy area occurred when OPEC coalesced in 1973 and world oil prices quadrupled. The United States and other industrialized countries endured the pains of leftward shifts in their Aggregate Supply curves. Rightward shifts occur when new resources are discovered. For example, Great Britain and Mexico, respectively, were aided by Britain's North Sea oil finds and the discoveries of huge pools of Mexican oil during the late 1970s. The glut of oil on world markets and the relative instability of OPEC drove prices down; energy costs fell in the mid 1980s, giving our Aggregate Supply a boost to the right.

Factors causing shifts in Aggregate Supply are listed in the chart below Figure 4. Make sure that you understand why each factor moves Aggregate Supply as it does. Grasping this concept is essential to understanding stagflation.

Now that you have been exposed to the foundations of both the Aggregate Supply and Aggregate Demand curves, we can turn to the interesting problems of demand-side and supply-side inflation.

---

1. See Murray L. Weidenbaum and Robert DeFina, *The Rising Cost of Government Regulation* (St. Louis, Mo.: Center for the Study of American Business, 31 January 1977).

Supply-Side and Demand-Side Inflation

Equilibrium prices rise only if demands increase or supplies decrease. Inflation that originates on the *demand side* is referred to as **demand-pull inflation,** while *supply-side* inflation is commonly termed **cost-push inflation.**

You have probably heard some people complain, "If those #*%! . . . unions were less greedy and powerful, we would not suffer the inflation we have." Others blame all inflation on overly expansionary monetary policies. Still others chant that it is government deficits that cause inflation: "If the government would balance its budget, inflation would disappear." Then there are those who blame wars or foreigners for our problems. What have been the basic causes of inflation in the last few decades? We must explore the expected equilibrium paths during both supply-side and demand-side inflation to begin to answer this complex question. Then we can compare these results with our experience in the United States over the recent past.

Demand-Side Inflation

Growth in Aggregate Demand causes employment, output, income, and, perhaps, the price level to grow if the economy is well below full employment. End of the Keynesian story. But suppose the economy is in a noninflationary equilibrium at full employment, such as the equilibrium labeled point *a* in Figure 5: full employment or potential GNP equals Q_f, and the price level is P_0. "Full employment" includes an allowance for frictional unemployment caused by flows of workers between jobs and in and out of the work force. Workers' labor supplies reflect no expectations of inflation, which, along with other institutional characteristics and aggregate productive capacity, results in an Aggregate Supply curve of AS_0.

Now assume that Aggregate Demand increases from AD_0 to AD_1 because of an increase in government spending. As this occurs, the economy moves toward a new short-run equilibrium, point *b*. We have assumed that the economy started at full employment, but employment can exceed a full employment level if frictional unemployment falls and if business can be induced to employ the extra work-

FIGURE 5 *Demand-Side Inflation*

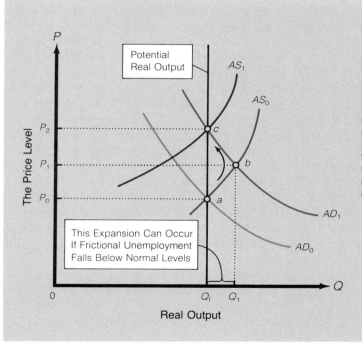

Frictional unemployment, a normal by-product of economic activity, is represented by the difference between Q_1, which assumes that everyone who wants to work is employed, and Q_f, which makes allowances for frictional unemployment. Frictional unemployment may artificially be reduced below normal levels ($Q_1 - Q_f$) if expansions of Aggregate Demand temporarily fool some frictionally unemployed workers into taking jobs that pay low real wages (movement from *a* to *b*). However, in the long run, workers will adjust their wage demands to reflect higher prices, and unemployment will rise back to normal levels (movement from *b* to *c*).

ers. If firms can pass the costs of hiring these workers forward to consumers, they will hire beyond the full employment point. The price level rises to P_1 with this swollen Aggregate Demand.

But what happens to the real wages of the workers? Money wages do not rise as quickly as prices rise, so real wages (W/P) fall. When labor eventually demands higher money wages to correct for this reduction in purchasing power, the Aggregate Supply curve shifts leftward toward AS_1. Along the equilibrium path between points b and c, labor finds that although it receives higher money wages, these wages are partially eroded by continuing increases in the price level. How long will this process continue? Labor repeatedly reacts to increases in prices by demanding higher wages until equilibrium at point c is reached. At this point, real wages have regained their original values and the economy is back to full employment with the aggregate price level equal to P_2, which is just equivalent to labor's expectations about the price level.

The price increases that occur when the Aggregate Demand curve increases (shifts to the right) are called demand-side or demand-pull inflation. Although prices continue to rise when labor adjusts its inflationary expectations and might be thought of as supply-side inflation, these adjustments are simply the second phase of a demand-side cycle because the original impetus for inflation came from increased demand. In effect, prices are pulled up by rising demand. The initial forces that set this inflationary spiral in motion are demand induced, and they result in rightward movements of the Aggregate Demand curve. Notice that as labor reacts to the inflationary spiral, the economy's equilibrium path runs from point a to b to c, following a *counterclockwise path*.

In the Keynesian discussion in Chapter 10, we indicated that inflationary pressures mount when there is an inflationary gap, such as that reflected by $Q_1 - Q_f$ in Figure 5. In a sense, this is a "negative" GNP gap. As you can see, there are natural pressures that reduce output down from *overfull employment*, toward full employment levels. Overfull employment occurs because frictional unemployment is artificially driven down by expansions of Aggregate Demand. These adjustments are not instantaneous. The economy depicted in Figure 5 first moves from a to point b. When workers eventually discover that

they have been fooled, declines in the labor supply return the system to full employment at point c—but at a higher price level. Note that we initially assumed a full employment economy, with allowances only for normal frictional unemployment. Remember also that if the economy is initially plagued by excess capacity, only the first phase of this cycle needs to occur—growing demand yields slightly higher prices and larger output.

Supply-Side Inflation

What happens if workers simply demand higher wages and their demands are not responses to inflation? This situation might occur if unions become stronger, if legislation making it easier to organize labor were enacted, or if hard bargaining by existing unions became the norm in key industries.

The effect of such actions by workers is illustrated in Figure 6. Their demands for higher wages will shift Aggregate Supply to the left. Suppose that the economy originally is in equilibrium at point d. As the Aggregate Supply curve shrinks from AS_0 to AS_1, equilibrium moves from point d to e. Business will demand less labor at the higher wages because these higher costs can only partially be passed on to consumers in the form of higher prices. Unless some-

FIGURE 6 *Supply-Side Inflation*

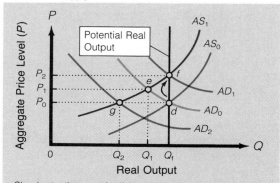

Shocks to the supply side cause prices to rise while output and employment fall (movement from point d to e). If policymakers follow expansionary policies to counter unemployment, prices will rise further (from point e to f). If, on the other hand, they fight inflation by reducing Aggregate Demand, the price level will remain at the P_0 level, but output and employment will shrink dramatically (from point d to g).

thing happens to change Aggregate Demand, less real output is demanded at the new price level P_1, and real output and employment are reduced to Q_1. For incumbent policymakers, this is the worst of all worlds; rising prices and unemployment and declining real incomes and output.

As the economy moves to point e, policymakers may become worried about the effect of recessions on voters. Policymakers may also perceive a duty to maintain full employment under the Employment Act of 1946 and the Full-Employment and Balanced Growth Act of 1978 (the Humphrey-Hawkins Act). The movement from point d to point e portrays an economy moving into a recession and political pressures will mount to launch expansionary monetary and fiscal policies.

An alternative to expanding Aggregate Demand would be to institute policies to restore Aggregate Supply from AS_1 to AS_0. This action seems ideal, generating greater employment and more real output at lower prices. If you consider what the government would have to do to accomplish this, you will see why the federal government has historically tended to be demand-management oriented. President Reagan and many supply-siders were repeatedly chagrined in the early 1980s to learn that policies to increase Aggregate Supply may take considerable time to become effective. Supply-side policies are aimed at increasing our productive capacity, a task not accomplished overnight. (You may benefit at this point by returning to Figure 4 on page 308 and reviewing the policies that shift the Aggregate Supply curve to the right.)

Increasing Aggregate Demand is a relatively simple and quick process; government cuts tax rates or increases its outlays for goods and services or transfer payments, or the FED increases monetary growth. Voters become very unsympathetic to the president's party when unemployment begins to soar. Many have attributed President Ford's election loss to Jimmy Carter in 1976 to the joint occurrence of double-digit inflation and mounting unemployment during 1974 and 1975. Carter faced similar problems and lost the 1980 election. Republican losses in the 1982 congressional elections were in part a response to the sharp recession of 1981–83. Many observers attributed the 1984 Reagan landslide to a solid economic recovery that began early in 1984 and continued into 1986.

In any event, government commonly responds to declines in Aggregate Supply by increasing Aggregate Demand, shown by a shift from AD_0 to AD_1 in Figure 6. With demand management, the economy will move along the equilibrium path described by the arrows from point e to f. Employment ultimately returns to a full employment level, but at a higher price level. Notice that the long-term equilibrium path for supply-side inflation is from point d to e to f, a *clockwise pattern*. (Remember, demand-side inflation follows a counterclockwise pattern.)

A few qualifications should be noted at this point. First, shifts in the Aggregate Supply curve from AS_0 to AS_1 originate in a multitude of ways, summarized previously under Figure 4. Second, the federal government need not increase government spending to shift the Aggregate Demand curve from AD_0 to AD_1. For example, monetary authorities might allow rapid growth of the money supply in attempts to push the economy out of a recession.

Inflation in the United States: Demand-Side or Supply-Side?[2]

We are now in a position to examine the inflationary experiences of the 1960s and 1970s. The previous sections suggest that demand-side inflations caused the economy to equilibrate in a counterclockwise fashion, while supply-side inflations cause the economy to follow a clockwise pattern.

The inflations of the 1960s and 1970s are graphed in Figure 7. The most significant difference between this and previous graphs is that we have altered the axes slightly to accommodate the data. The GNP deflator (described in Chapter 6) is still measured on the vertical axes, but each period starts out at a base of 100. We also have converted the horizontal axis to real GNP divided by potential GNP so that we adjust for growth in our productive capacity. Potential GNP grows because of technological advances, capital accumulation, growth of the labor force, and a host of other factors.

---

2. For an extended discussion of this issue, see Robert J. Gordon, *Macroeconomics*, 3rd ed. (Boston: Little Brown, 1984), especially Part III. Our discussion owes much to Gordon's pioneering efforts.

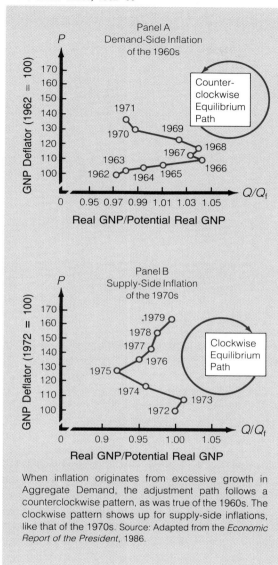

FIGURE 7 *Supply-Side and Demand-Side Inflations in the United States, 1962–80*

Panel A
Demand-Side Inflation
of the 1960s

Counter-clockwise Equilibrium Path

GNP Deflator (1962 = 100)

Real GNP/Potential Real GNP

Panel B
Supply-Side Inflation
of the 1970s

Clockwise Equilibrium Path

GNP Deflator (1972 = 100)

Real GNP/Potential Real GNP

When inflation originates from excessive growth in Aggregate Demand, the adjustment path follows a counterclockwise pattern, as was true of the 1960s. The clockwise pattern shows up for supply-side inflations, like that of the 1970s. Source: Adapted from the *Economic Report of the President*, 1986.

The demand-pull inflation of the 1960s resulted primarily from increased government spending for domestic programs, the space program, the escalation of the Vietnam conflict, the aftermath of the 1964 tax cut, and rising monetary growth. As you can see in Panel A, the equilibrium process followed a counterclockwise path.

Contrast the inflation of the 1960s with that of the middle 1970s, which may have been triggered by rising prices of oil and other imported goods. A second major external shock was a worldwide drought and agricultural shortage, leading to rising prices in the United States as substantial domestic farm production found its way into the world market. The Arab oil embargo and subsequent OPEC price increases contributed strongly to the inflationary pressures of this period. Many economists would include the 1971–73 price controls as a shock to the supply side. Panel B of Figure 7 shows that the system equilibrated in a clockwise fashion, although price controls disguised inflationary pressure during 1971–73. This figure indicates that inflation in the 1970s derived primarily from supply-side pressures.

Prosperity in the 1960s

The economy was just recovering from a recession when John F. Kennedy took the oath of office in 1961. President Kennedy used moderate doses of fiscal spending to support expansion and, in late 1962, suggested that tax rates be reduced to stimulate the economy and to reduce the government deficit as well. Appealing somewhat to "supply-side" arguments, he relied principally on Keynesian multiplier analysis. Together, these approaches suggest that cuts in tax rates might increase both Aggregate Demand and Aggregate Supply (and, hence, GNP and income) sufficiently that tax revenues would actually rise rather than fall.

The 1960s were an era of increasing fiscal stimulus unmarred by serious supply-side shocks. The path of the American economy from 1961 to 1970 is depicted in Panel A of Figure 8 and is based on the actual data for real GNP and the GNP deflator.[3] In terms of the model we have developed, this path appears to be the result of expansionary monetary and fiscal policies that accommodated the growth in potential GNP as the post-World War II baby boom began to enter the work force.

In Panel B, we have superimposed a set of curves representing Aggregate Demands and Supplies over the equilibrium path described in Panel A of Figure

---

3. This figure does not incorporate the adjustment of GNP by potential GNP, which was used to depict clockwise and counterclockwise patterns in Figure 7.

FIGURE 8 *Prosperity of the 1960s*

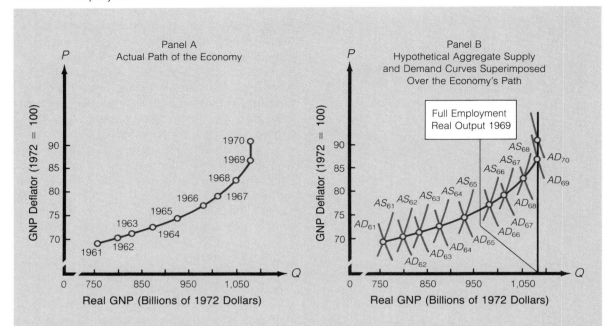

Aggregate Supply grew smoothly in the 1960s; Aggregate Demand grew even faster, but relatively smoothly as well, causing the price level to rise somewhat while unemployment rates fell a bit. Inflation was a minor but growing problem by the end of the decade. The Aggregate Supply and Aggregate Demand curves in Panel B are simply suggestive of the path of the economy; you should not infer from Panel B that the economy was perpetually in equilibrium because symptoms of disequilibrium did occur from time to time. Source: *Economic Report of the President*, 1986.

8. The smooth rightward shifts in Aggregate Supply (Panel B) reflect regularity in the growth of potential output (full employment real GNP) each year. The vertical portion of the curve represents potential GNP in 1969. This figure reveals that the slightly more rapid growth of Aggregate Demand than Aggregate Supply during 1960–69 did not precipitate substantial increases in prices. Generally, there is considerable excess productive capacity in the early stages of a recovery, which was the case between 1961 and 1964. As the economy recovered and approached full employment, further increases in demand brought forth ever greater increases in prices and smaller increases in output.

As the United States escalated its role in Vietnam and domestic spending accelerated, the economy experienced mild but increasing inflation. This can be seen in Panel A of Figure 8 by looking at the economy's path from 1966 to 1970. The events of 1969–70

are especially interesting. The economy reached full employment and there was a slight surplus in the government budget for fiscal year 1969. Still, government continued to increase spending.

By 1971, the rate of inflation had become a matter of widespread concern, compounded because real output grew very little. Federal tax receipts fell 6 percent short of budget outlays, the prelude to a series of then record-breaking deficits—deficits that seem small by today's standards. As workers began to realize that the purchasing power of their wages had declined, the shrinking supply phase of that demand-side cycle of inflation was activated. Rapid price increases unaccompanied by increases in real output between 1969 and 1970 prompted President Nixon to introduce a wage-price freeze in August 1971, even though the rate of inflation had begun to subside. The *CPI* grew at annual rates of 6.2 percent in 1969 and 5.2 percent in 1970, but inflation had fallen to 4.2 percent by the first half of 1971. As you will see, the freeze had only a temporary and artificial effect in holding down inflation, which seems to have been subsiding anyway.

Stagflation in the 1970s

As the demand-side inflation of the 1960s erupted in 1969 and lingered through 1970, President Nixon became worried that workers' inflationary expectations would provide momentum for further inflation and would reap economic havoc. Although he was attempting to wind down the Vietnam War, the war effort still absorbed considerable spending. The administration's fear of the political repercussions of tax increases resulted in federal deficits, which further fueled inflation.

Under pressure from Congress and the general public, President Nixon took an unusual step for an avowed conservative: on August 15, 1971, he announced a 90-day wage-price freeze. Less stringent

price controls were phased in when this freeze expired. As you can see in Panel A of Figure 9, these controls seemed partially effective in that nominal inflation abated during the 1971–73 period. In reality, inflationary pressures continued to build throughout the period, only being disguised by price controls. In fact, some people argue that the public anticipated substantial inflation when Nixon's temporary controls were scheduled to end; so controls may actually have increased our inflationary momentum.

The economy suffered substantial stagflation (high rates of both inflation and unemployment) for the first time ever as price controls were relaxed between 1973 and 1975. This "stagflationary" recession was, at that time, the most severe since the Great Depression of the 1930s. There were numerous reasons for the downturn, the bulk of which were supply shocks: the worldwide agricultural shortage, depreciation of the dollar relative to most foreign currencies (which caused import prices to soar), and

FIGURE 9 *Stagflation of the 1970s and Early 1980s*

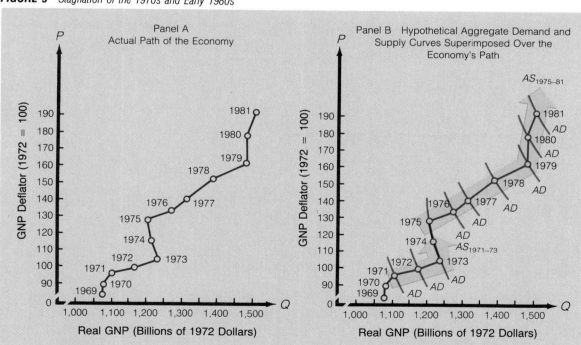

The economy suffered from stagflation during 1973–75 when the Aggregate Supply curve shifted to the left. The shift in the Aggregate Supply curve was due to: (*a*) rising oil prices, (*b*) agricultural shortages. (*c*) a 20 percent depreciation of the dollar raised import prices, and (*d*) rising inflationary expectations. Source: *Economic Report of the President*. 1986.

the Arab oil embargo, which was followed immediately by an OPEC decision to raise oil prices from $2.50 to more than $10.00 per barrel. The economy went into a tailspin, with inflation more than 12 percent and unemployment soaring above 9 percent of the labor force during 1975. In the period from 1975 to 1978, the economy followed a fairly steady recovery path. Inflation remained high but stayed below the double-digit range until 1979. Fiscal policy was aimed at continuing the economic recovery from supply shocks with the hope of avoiding a resurgence of inflation, although politicians spun a lot of rhetoric about balancing the budget.

In Panel B of Figure 9, we have superimposed the Aggregate Supply/Aggregate Demand model over the actual data from Panel A, showing only the most important changes. The period from 1971 to 1973 was characterized by shifts in Aggregate Demand that moved the economy up along the supply curve labeled $AS_{1971-73}$. The supply shocks of 1973–75 shrank Aggregate Supply, resulting in equilibration along the 1973–75 demand curves. The stagflation of the 1973–75 period might be traceable in part to the lifting of price controls. Both workers and businesses attempted to recoup their precontrol positions by boosting wages and prices. By late 1975, Aggregate

FIGURE 10 *Disinflation in the 1980s*

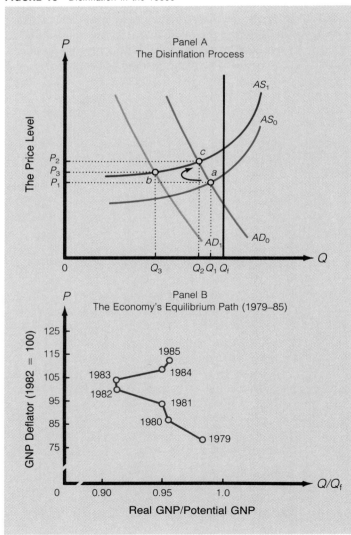

Panel A illustrates the disinflation process after a number of years of an inflationary spiral. Leftward shifts of the Aggregate Supply curve (due to rising inflationary expectations) are combined with reduced Aggregate Demand to produce a recession and quash inflation. Disinflation occurs between points *a* and *b*. Once the inflationary psychology is removed from the economy, rising Aggregate Demand allows growth without rising inflation. Panel B shows the actual equilibrium values for the economy during the first half of the 1980s.

Supply appears to have become relatively stable, and the economy resumed its equilibrating movement along the supply curve labeled $AS_{1975-81}$. Although the federal government used demand-management policies in trying to steer the economy to a smooth and steady recovery, policies to reduce unemployment toward the full employment level fostered the reemergence of inflationary pressures.

Disinflation in the 1980s

Inflation escalated throughout the 1970s, setting in motion restrictive monetary policies that pushed the economy into a severe slump beginning in 1981. But inflation continued at high rates. Interest rates skyrocketed in 1979 and again in 1981. Tighter monetary policies than had been followed in over a decade were principally responsible for inflation and interest rates both drifting down after 1982. One side effect, however, was that during 1983 unemployment rose to its highest rate since the Great Depression. Some economists in and out of the Reagan Administration claimed that the 1981–83 slump represented needed adjustments to overly expansionary policies of the past decade.

Panel A of Figure 10 uses our Aggregate Demand and Aggregate Supply framework to illustrate these general movements. Several years of expanding demand and high inflation had boosted inflationary expectations, causing the Aggregate Supply curve to shrink. This is shown as the shift from AS_0 to AS_1. To slow this inflationary spiral, the Federal Reserve Board tightened the screws during 1981–82, shifting Aggregate Demand from AD_0 to AD_1. This dampened inflationary expectations and, coupled with tax cuts that kicked in during 1982–83, helped to stabilize the Aggregate Supply curve at AS_1. The resumption of mildly expansionary fiscal and monetary policies late in 1983 allowed Aggregate Demand to drift back toward AD_0. The overall result was disinflation and falling real output between points a and b (1980–82), and then steady growth along AS_1 with significantly reduced inflation (1983–85).

The clockwise equilibration path is reflected in the actual equilibrium path for the economy illustrated in Panel B of Figure 10. The path of the economy between 1979 and 1985 indicates that Aggregate Supply continued to shrink and that tight monetary policies during this period decompressed inflation,

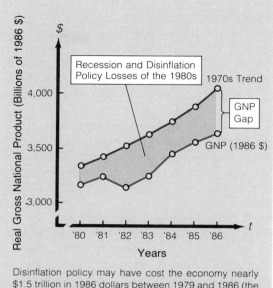

FIGURE 11 *The Losses in Real Output due to the 1981–82 Recession and Disinflation Policies*

Disinflation policy may have cost the economy nearly $1.5 trillion in 1986 dollars between 1979 and 1986 (the shaded area). Source: *Economic Report of the President,* 1986.

but only by precipitating a severe recession. The growth in the economy between 1983 and 1985 points to an economy moving to a more stable and flatter Aggregate Supply curve.

Decompressing inflation did not come cheaply, as Figure 11 shows. In the early 1980s, the economy slipped below its previous growth trend to a lower path. Through 1986, cumulative losses of real income in 1986 dollars were approximately $1.5 trillion, due in large part to policies designed to offset the accelerating inflation in the 1970s.

Disinflation—a significant reduction in the rate of inflation—has caused other problems for both business and consumers. Many people who had expected inflation to continue through the 1980s had invested heavily in real estate and other inflation "hedges." Inflation abated and they found themselves deeply in debt at high real rates of interest. When inflation faltered and failed to reduce the real value of future mortgage payments, many investors were clobbered by huge losses. Many houses and other assets that had cost $75,000 in 1975 had shot up to over $100,000 by 1980. Disinflation drove down asset prices that had swollen because of inflationary expectations, and simultaneously disrupted the declines in real mortgage payments that many had relied upon as a way of reducing their real debt in the future. Real estate foreclosures reached record highs by the mid-1980s. A similar outcome befell farmers and the rural banks that supported them. Farmers who had borrowed to purchase high-priced land faced bankruptcy as both farm incomes and land values plummeted.

Business had grown accustomed to using price increases as an elixir to heal many sins. When disinflation made it impossible to raise prices, firms were forced to find other ways to boost sales and profits. During disinflationary times, increased productivity and new products are more important to business success because prices cannot be increased. New products typically have a higher profit rate and improve a firm's market penetration efforts. Another solution to the problems posed by disinflation is to cut labor costs. Disinflation causes firms to bargain harder and workers, sensing reduced inflation, tend to be more receptive to lower wage increases.

Pressures to raise productivity during disinflation cause changes in firms' investment patterns. First, more investment is directed toward productivity-enhancing plant and equipment, and less is devoted to expanding capacity. Second, more investment is financed internally as firms attempt to limit their debt burdens. Finally, the acquisition binge that some firms undertake during inflationary periods is reversed when debt consolidation requires the selling off of subsidiaries.

You should now have some appreciation for how difficult it is to predict and then deal with stagflation. It is doubtful whether any demand-management policy can completely resolve the problems posed by supply-side disturbances. As we have seen, disinflation can be an extremely painful cure. The next chapter turns to a discussion of some other possible ways to overcome the problems posed by inflation and stagflation.

CHAPTER REVIEW: KEY POINTS

1. *Stagflation,* a contraction of the terms *stagnation* and *inflation,* is the simultaneous occurrence of high rates of both unemployment and inflation.

2. Decreases in the Aggregate Supply curve cause *supply-side inflation* and declines in real incomes and output. Excessive increases in the Aggregate Demand curve cause *demand-side inflation,* which initially is accompanied by increased incomes and output.

3. If the economy begins at full employment and is subjected to excessive Aggregate Demand, the first phase of the *demand-side cycle* results in rising prices, outputs, employment, and incomes. In the second phase, supply-side adjustments to the demand-originated disturbances cause prices to continue to rise, but total employment, production, and income fall. *Demand-side* inflation induces a *counterclockwise adjustment* path of inflation versus real output. If the economy starts at less than full employment, only the first phase necessarily occurs when Aggregate Demand is increased.

4. Supply-side inflation generates a *clockwise adjustment* pattern. During the first phase of a *supply-side*

(cost-push) *cycle,* prices increase while real output and incomes fall. If the government attempts to correct for the resulting inflationary recession by increasing Aggregate Demand, the second phase occurs—prices continue to rise, but real output and income rise as well.

5. Mild but increasing demand-side inflation accompanied the prosperity of the 1960s. From the mid-1970s into the early 1980s, stagflation took over with a vengeance. Whether this stagflation was the supply-adjustment phase of the earlier demand-pull cycle or originated solely from supply-related shocks cannot be established conclusively. However, given the force of the *supply shocks* already listed, it seems that even if the economy had been stable when they emerged, considerable supply-side inflation would have plagued the American economy from 1973 to 1980.

6. *Disinflation* is a significant reduction in the rate of inflation. Policies that reduce the rate of inflation often cause losses in real income before they bring the economy back to a relatively stable growth path.

QUESTIONS FOR THOUGHT AND DISCUSSION

1. If you were a fiscal policymaker, would you rather face the problem of a recession or inflation? Which set of fiscal policies would be most popular with voters? Now suppose you were confronted by stagflation—both recession and inflation. Should you fight inflation, fight unemployment, or do nothing? What course of action do you think politicians would follow? What are the long-term effects of such policies?

2. Do you think that fiscal and monetary policies differ in their effectiveness in dealing with high unemployment and high inflation, respectively? From a political perspective, against which is monetary policy most likely to be used? Fiscal policy? Does this seem appropriate?

3. How might wage-price controls increase Aggregate Supply or at least prevent it from falling? How might wage-price controls actually cause Aggregate Supply to fall? Do you think it more likely that incomes policy would cause increases or decreases in Aggregate Supply? If your answer is "It depends," on what does it depend?

4. How might certain social programs cause Aggregate Demand to rise and Aggregate Supply to decline? Do you think that growth of these programs is important in explaining why the economy has experienced high rates of both unemployment and inflation?

5. Suppose your friends asked how they might protect themselves from inflation. What advice would you give them? Suppose they then asked how to protect themselves from an economic slump. Would your advice to them be consistent with your previous suggestions? Can people buffer themselves from the risks of stagflation?

6. Paul Samuelson has argued that "democracies have a persistent inflationary bias." A look at inflation data since the Great Depression supports this statement. Why do you suppose this might be true? We know that disinflation involves costs. What would be some of the problems with deflation (an actual reduction in the price level)? What level of unemployment would you expect the economy to experience during deflation? What would this level depend upon?

CHAPTER 17 The Policymaker's Dilemma

Phillips curves
compositional shocks
natural rate theory
incomes policies
wage-price controls

voluntary wage-price
  guideposts/
  guidelines
Tax-Based Incomes
  Policies (TIP)
Market Anti-Inflation
  Plan (MAP)

jawboning
Humphrey-Hawkins Act
national industrial
  policy

Demand-side and supply-side inflation are the two dominant categories of general price hikes, but we need to recognize that any inflationary episode usually involves elements of both. *Stagflation* is the simultaneous occurrence of high rates of inflation and high rates of unemployment. Curing high unemployment by increasing Aggregate Demand may stimulate inflation. Similarly, reducing inflation may lead to rising unemployment. Political leaders face a policymaking dilemma because high rates of unemployment and inflation each create considerable economic stress and are unpopular with voters.

This chapter focuses on trade-offs between inflation and unemployment and explanations for why these trade-offs may worsen, resulting in stagflation. Our discussion centers on the relationship between equilibrium output and inflation. Aggregate output is positively related to employment and negatively related to unemployment. We use these relationships to explore the trade-off between unemployment and inflation. This analysis then provides the background for an examination of various proposals intended to reduce both inflation and unemployment.

Phillips Curves: Trade-Offs Between Inflation and Unemployment

We all, or nearly all, consent,
when wages rise by ten percent,
it leaves the choice before the nation
of unemployment or inflation.
                    —Kenneth Boulding (1967)

Increases in Aggregate Demand lead to increases in real output and employment as long as an economy has excess capacity. Ever greater upward pressures on prices and wages emerge as excess capacity disappears. Increases in output cannot be sustained in the long run once the economy reaches its productive capacity; further increases in Aggregate Demand only cause inflation. Our general Aggregate Demand/ Aggregate Supply framework in the previous chapter hinted at a possible inverse relationship between unemployment and inflation. This section explores this trade-off in much more detail.

FIGURE 1 *Phillips Curve for the 1960s (U.S. Data)*

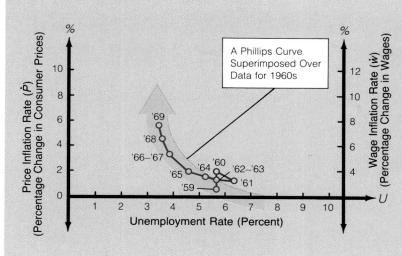

A Phillips Curve Superimposed Over Data for 1960s

Phillips curves indicate that if Aggregate Demand is high and rising steadily, there will be substantial inflation but little unemployment; consistently low Aggregate Demand will yield less inflation but greater problems of unemployment. Wages may rise faster than prices if productivity advances. We have assumed that productivity grew by 2 percent annually in calibrating the two vertical axes differently.
Source: *Economic Report of the President*, 1986.

More than three decades ago, A. W. Phillips compared plotted data for wage inflation and unemployment rates for the preceding century in Great Britain. Curves that seem to fit such data have become known as **Phillips curves.** Although Phillips's original work was concerned with wage inflation, subsequent work by other researchers suggests trade-offs between unemployment and price inflation.

Wage Increases, Productivity, and Inflation

There are fairly tight relationships between nominal wage inflation, price inflation, and productivity. This relationship can be expressed as:

$$\text{percentage } \Delta \text{ prices} = \text{percentage } \Delta \text{ wages} - \text{percentage } \Delta \text{ in productivity.}$$

For example, if workers are, on the average, able to produce 5 percent more this year than last, then wages can increase by 5 percent before firms encounter any pressure to raise prices to maintain profit margins. This relationship is illustrated in Figure 1. The rate of increase in productivity is assumed to be 2 percent per year and is reflected by shifting the scale for the rate of price inflation ($\dot{P}$) down by 2 percentage points relative to wage inflation. Thus, a 4 percent wage hike combined with a 2 percent pro-

ductivity increase only imposes pressures for prices to rise by 2 percent. However, if productivity increases for the economy are nil and workers successfully demand higher wages, the end result is likely to be considerable price inflation.

American Phillips Curves

Figure 1 shows a Phillips curve superimposed over U.S. data for the 1960s. Because Aggregate Supply was thought relatively stable, the Phillips curve was thought to be so, too; policymakers could regulate Aggregate Demand through monetary or fiscal policies to achieve the least harmful combination of unemployment and inflation. The dilemma seemed clear if high rates of inflation were associated with low levels of unemployment, and vice versa; the Phillips curve became a "menu" showing the trade-off available to policymakers who sought to minimize our economic woes.[1]

The Phillips curve depicted in Figure 1 was thought to be roughly reflective of a trade-off confronting American macroeconomic policymakers. If

---

1. Recall (from Chapter 6) that the misery index is the sum of the rates of unemployment and inflation. High interest rates, low rates of investment and productivity growth, and a variety of other difficulties are also sources of macroeconomic distress.

policymakers insisted on zero price inflation, American workers would suffer roughly 6–8 percent unemployment. Unemployment rates as low as 3–4 percent were thought feasible only with inflation rates of 4–6 percent. Policymakers would have preferred less of each but, according to Phillips curve analysis, this was just not in the macro "cards."

Shifts in Aggregate Demand and the Stable Phillips Curve

National output and income are closely related to the level of employment. In turn, there tends to be a close negative relationship between employment and unemployment. That is, higher employment generally means lower unemployment, and vice versa. However, changes in the size or composition of the labor force may obscure this relationship. For example, rapidly rising labor force participation rates may cause the unemployment rate to rise even if real output and employment are growing.

The Aggregate Supply curve indicates a positive relationship between the level of output and the price level, while a typical Phillips curve depicts an inverse correlation between unemployment and inflation. Thus, the Phillips curve for an economy roughly mirrors the Aggregate Supply curve, as shown in Figure 2. Points $a, b, \ldots g$ in Panel A roughly correspond to points $a, b, \ldots g$ in Panel B. Expanding Aggregate Demand from AD_a to AD_b in Panel A moves the economy from point a to point b in Panel B. Maintaining the economy at point b requires increasing Aggregate Demand by the same proportion in each subsequent period. Similarly, expanding Aggregate Demand from AD_a to AD_c moves the economy to point c in Panel B; staying at point c would require continuous similar expansions of Aggregate Demand. And so on, for points $d, e, f,$ and g.[2]

---

2. Readers familiar with differential equations will recognize this discussion as a description of moving from static analysis of price level changes to a more dynamic analysis of sustained inflation.

FIGURE 2 *Aggregate Supply and the Phillips Curve*

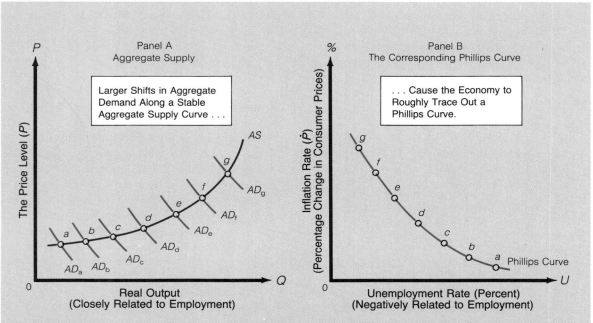

Ever larger sustained increases in Aggregate Demand in Panel A along a stable Aggregate Supply curve would trace out a series of equilibria like $a, b, \ldots g$ in Panel A as employment and output increased. The unemployment rate would fall during these movements, but prices would rise, tracing a pattern roughly like $a, b, \ldots g$ along the stable Phillips curve in Panel B.

FIGURE 3 *The Shifting Phillips Curve Relationship*

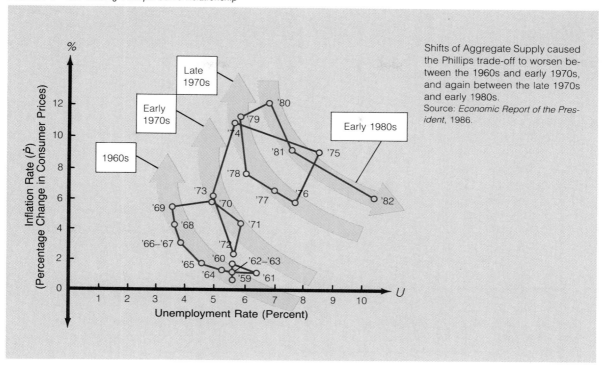

Shifts of Aggregate Supply caused the Phillips trade-off to worsen between the 1960s and early 1970s, and again between the late 1970s and early 1980s.
Source: *Economic Report of the President*, 1986.

The Stagflation of the Seventies: The Stable Phillips Curve at Bay?

The advent of the 1970s saw the trade-off between inflation and unemployment worsen. Ever greater sacrifices of inflation appeared necessary to keep unemployment rates in the 5–6 percent range. The worsening trade-off is illustrated in Figure 3. We have superimposed four Phillips curves over the data. What happened in the 1970s to cause the Phillips curve relationship to worsen?

Shifts in Aggregate Supply and Shifting Phillips Curves

Continually expanding the growth rate of Aggregate Demand while Aggregate Supply is relatively stable results in upward movements along a stable Phillips curve, as in Figure 2. The 1960s seemed to many economists to provide evidence that the Phillips curve was roughly stable, but bouts of stagflation in the 1970s and early 1980s betrayed the naivete of this view. Disruptions to Aggregate Supply apparently worsened the short-run trade-off between unemployment and inflation, as shown in Figure 4. Suppose that Aggregate Supply begins to shrink, declining from AS_0 to AS_1 to AS_2, and so on in Panel A. Output and employment fall while the price level rises (stagflation), which means that policymakers are presented with worse short-run options such as curves PC_0, PC_1, PC_2, and so on in Panel B. As Phillips curves move to the right, achieving a given level of unemployment requires acceptance of a higher rate of inflation.

Recent Keynesian and modern classical economic reasoning offer alternative explanations for the existence of Phillips curves. In the following section, we examine these alternative theories and, more importantly for economic policy, explore the different interpretations of why Phillips curves shifted so that the economy experienced stagflation during the 1970s and early 1980s.

FIGURE 4 *Shifting the Phillips Curve*

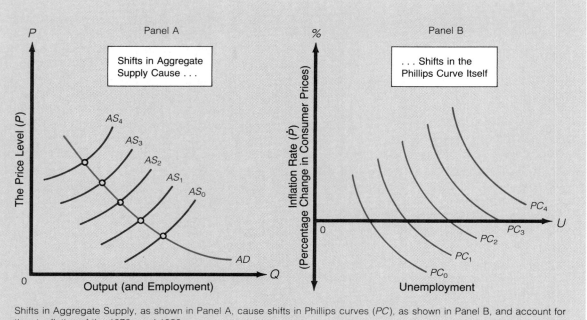

Shifts in Aggregate Supply, as shown in Panel A, cause shifts in Phillips curves (*PC*), as shown in Panel B, and account for the stagflation of the 1970s and 1980s.

Aggregate Equilibrium and the Rate of Inflation

Almost from its inception, the Phillips curve hypothesis has been in the eye of a stormy controversy about macroeconomic theory and policy. Keynesians view Phillips's discovery of a negative statistical relationship between unemployment and inflation as a reflection of a trade-off confronting policymakers. Economists of a classical persuasion, including modern monetarists, view the Phillips relationship as a very short-run artifact and argue that policymakers who attempt to trade inflation for lower unemployment will soon find that the Phillips curve is a mirage. These theorists perceive no permanent connection between unemployment and inflation. Their reasoning is based on the idea that money is a veil in the long run; nominal things, such as the price level, are determined by the money supply and will not be related to any aspect of real behavior, such as unemployment.

In this section, we explore the views of classically oriented economists and monetarists. Their theory proclaiming the transitoriness of the Phillips curve is widely known as **natural rate theory.** This theory states that the Aggregate Supply and Phillips curves shift persistently only because of changing inflationary expectations. Next, we will examine the Keynesian view of the Phillips curve trade-off. Modern Keynesians recognize that Aggregate Supply will decline if inflationary expectations build, but they also consider other disruptions as important to the explanation of recent stagflation and the apparent deterioration of the Phillips curve.

Wage Adjustments: The Natural Rate Approach

Would it be good if unemployment in the U.S. economy were always exactly zero? "Yes, of course" seems an easy answer. But keeping the unemployment rate at zero would require people who were unhappy with their jobs to stay in them until they found new ones—otherwise there would be unemployment. Moreover, there would be pressures on firms to hire immediately anyone who applied for work. And if you were not in the labor force and then decided to look for a job, you would be forced to take the first job offered—otherwise you would be unemployed. Zero unemployment is not as attractive a goal as it sounds.

Natural Rate Theory

Economists who adhere to natural rate theory believe that nearly all unemployment is voluntary, the sole exception being unskilled people who are unemployed because minimum-wage legislation prevents employers from hiring these workers at the low wages commensurate with their productivity. Natural rate theorists view all other unemployment as the result of friction—it takes people time to find what they regard as suitable employment, and while they are looking for work they are unemployed by choice. Individuals can presumably get jobs almost instantly if they are willing to take the wage they are worth to the first employer willing to hire them. Frictional unemployment can be viewed as a cost of investment in labor market information and mobility. The natural rate of frictional unemployment is currently estimated at between 5 and 7 percent.

Expansionary macroeconomic policy reduces frictional unemployment, according to natural rate theory, only because workers are fooled by unanticipated inflation into thinking that the higher wages offered by employers represent real increases in the purchasing power of their earnings. Anyone who is unemployed can get a seemingly "suitable" high-paying job quickly during expansionary periods, when the pool of frictionally unemployed workers is small. In the natural rate view, these artificial declines in frictional unemployment reflect cyclical overemployment that is a consequence of inadequate investment in labor market information. But why do employers offer higher wages when expansionary policies are followed? Expansionary policies cause business firms to forecast booming sales that will enable them to raise the prices of their products. After workers recognize that their wages do not buy as much as expected because prices are also rising, many will become dissatisfied and quit to look for more lucrative work.

The eventual result is that frictional unemployment will rise back to its "natural rate" when workers cease being fooled. The natural rate of unemployment is the rate that exists before expansionary policy is initiated; it is achieved when all economic transactors have accurate expectations about inflation. If expansionary policies are continued, workers will learn to expect inflation and will demand wages that increase continuously to compensate for inflation. This means that Aggregate Supply will decline continuously.

Wage Adjustments to Inflation

Consider Figure 5. A starting point for the natural rate explanation for Phillips curves is to assume that the economy is in equilibrium with no inflation at points a in both panels. The price index is 100 (point a in Panel A) and unemployment is at a level compatible with potential real output (point a in Panel B). The rate of inflation is initially zero, and the natural rate of unemployment, U_n, is somewhere between 5 and 7 percent. The shaded portions of Figure 5 represent output and unemployment below and above the natural rate, respectively.

Now assume that excessively expansionary monetary policy drives Aggregate Demand up to AD_1. Real output will rise to Q_1 (point b), but the adjustment process entails 6 percent inflation and the price level rises from 100 to 106. We suggested in the previous chapter that this equilibrium will not be maintained for long. Workers will find their real wages falling, precipitating attempts to catch up. As they do so, the Aggregate Supply curve shifts leftward to AS_1 and the economy moves toward point c in Panel A. If policymakers try to preserve real output at Q_1 and unemployment at U_1 by shifting Aggregate Demand to AD_2, this unleashes another inflationary round equal to roughly 6 percent as the economy moves to equilibrium at point d in Panel A. The equilibrium path for the economy is denoted by the arrow.

Notice that if policymakers want to maintain the unemployment rate at U_1, continual 6 percent inflation is required. The model to this point naively supposes that workers always expect inflation to be zero and only seek wage adjustments after the price level has increased. If workers begin to anticipate inflation, policymakers are confronted with additional problems.

FIGURE 5 *Equilibrium Output and the Rate of Inflation (Natural Rate Approach)*

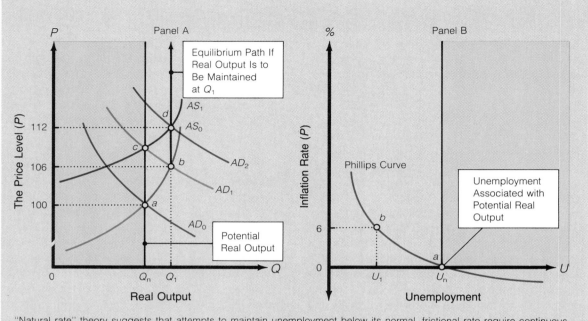

"Natural rate" theory suggests that attempts to maintain unemployment below its normal, frictional rate require continuous expansions of Aggregate Demand, raising the possibility of accelerating inflation.

The Long-Run Phillips Curve

This natural rate extension of classical reasoning suggests that Phillips curves do not present policymakers with stable frontiers along which inflation can be "traded off" against unemployment. Natural rate theory implies that each Phillips curve is associated with a particular expected rate of inflation. As workers foresee higher rates of inflation, the Phillips curve worsens by shifting outward. Panel A of Figure 6 illustrates how this occurs. Suppose that the economy is at point *a* initially; there is frictional unemployment equal to U_n, with zero inflation and zero inflation expected; $E(\dot{P})$ indicates the inflation rate that workers expect. What happens if policymakers view an unemployment rate of U_n as unacceptably high and follow expansionary policies? Increases in Aggregate Demand result in increased sales for business firms; therefore, they offer higher wages to attract new workers to accommodate the higher demands for their products. Frictionally unemployed workers will have little difficulty in finding what they perceive as good, high-paying jobs. Thus, expansionary policies push the economy along the $E(\dot{P}) = 0$ Phillips curve from point *a* toward point *b*.

The fly in this ointment is that increased demands for products enable firms to increase prices. As workers learn to expect 5 percent price hikes, the Phillips curve shifts rightward and the economy moves to point *c* at the old natural rate of unemployment U_n. This occurs because workers will demand wage increases of 10 percent, 5 percent to cover the past inflation plus 5 percent for expected inflation. But firms forecast only a 5 percent growth in the nominal demands for their products and will refuse to meet these demands for 10 percent wage increases. Frictional unemployment rises as workers hit the pavement looking for better jobs.

If policymakers again view unemployment (U_n) as unacceptably high, they might follow even more expansionary policies. If so, the economy initially will move from point *c* to *d*, but then ultimately to *e* as workers again cease being fooled. All the policymakers will have achieved for their efforts is 10 percent inflation, with no long-term reduction in unemployment. If policymakers were undaunted by their failures, they might even proceed to *f*. If they had learned their lessons, however, they would find mov-

FIGURE 6 *Natural Rate Theory and the Shifting Phillips Curve*

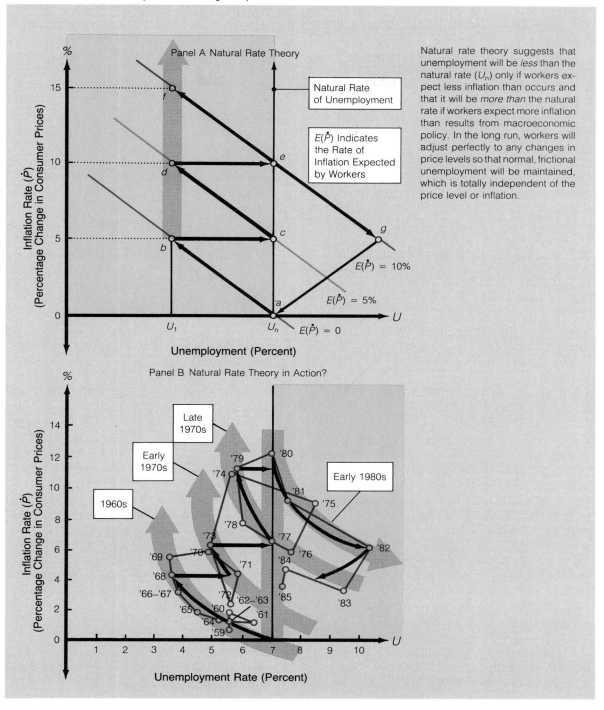

Natural rate theory suggests that unemployment will be *less* than the natural rate (U_n) only if workers expect less inflation than occurs and that it will be *more than* the natural rate if workers expect more inflation than results from macroeconomic policy. In the long run, workers will adjust perfectly to any changes in price levels so that normal, frictional unemployment will be maintained, which is totally independent of the price level or inflation.

ing directly and quickly back from *e* to *a* almost impossible. The economy will have a lot of inflationary momentum, and policymakers will find that a

recession to point *g* may be necessary to dampen inflationary expectations. Only after an extended bout with recession will the economy return to point *a*. These adjustments may explain why a severe recession occurred in 1981–83 when deflationary monetary policies brought inflation under control. Panel B of Figure 6 shows data for 1960–85, suggesting that natural rate theory explains the stagflation of the last two decades reasonably well.

Pure natural rate theorists view rising expectations of inflation as the only explanation for any worsening of the short-term relationship between inflation and unemployment. There is a family of short-run Phillips curves; each is transitory, depending on different expectations of inflation by labor. The unemployment rate will gravitate back to its natural rate in the long run. Thus, there is no long-run trade-off between inflation and unemployment. In Figure 6, the long-run Phillips "curve" is the vertical line represented by path *ace*. According to natural rate analysis, if policymakers attempt to maintain unemployment below the natural rate, the short-run Phillips curve trade-off worsens. Ever accelerating bouts of inflation (up the vertical arrow in Panel A) are inevitable until policymakers accept the futility of trying to hold unemployment below its natural rate.

Keynesian Phillips Curves: Sticky Wages and Prices

The major Keynesian explanation for the shape of the Phillips curve hinges on two key ideas: (*a*) shocks to demands and supplies continually bombard all economies and (*b*) wages and prices are assumed to be downwardly "sticky." That is, wages and prices tend to rise much more easily than they fall. At any moment in time the composition of demands—both private and public—is changing. These are shocks to the economy. As new products are developed or national priorities change, the demands for some products rise, while those for others fall.

When demand grows in any sector of our economy, output growth is limited in the short run by existing plant, equipment, and trained labor. As a result, adjustments to increases in demand usually take the forms of price increases and rising wages. In sectors where demand declines, much of the adjustment is through layoffs and cutbacks in production rather than through price reductions. Workers are reluctant to accept wage cuts, so firms find it easier to cut wage costs through reductions in employment.

Some temporary price cuts (e.g., automobile rebates) may be used to liquidate unwanted inventories, but these price cuts will be accompanied by reductions in output and rising unemployment.

Suppose that the level of Aggregate Demand is constant. As the composition of demand changes, prices in growing sectors rise faster than outputs, but prices fall slowly or not at all in sectors facing declining demands, while outputs plummet. The net result is an increase in the price level, higher unemployment, and less total output. Thus, compositional "shocks" to the economy cause temporary but recurring reductions in Aggregate Supply because of friction encountered in moving resources from declining to growing sectors. How this modern Keynesian analysis is consistent with the Phillips curve can be seen in Figure 7.

At our initial equilibriums at both points *a*, the price level is 100 and there is no inflation. Assume that Aggregate Demand remains constant at AD_0 but that the composition of demand changes. This causes Aggregate Supply to decline from AS_0 to AS_1 because of dislocations to labor and other resources. The economy moves to a new equilibrium at point *b*. Given the downward wage-price stickiness in declining markets, compositional changes cause the price level to rise. Again, if policymakers desire to maintain output at Q_f and unemployment at U_f, expansionary policies are necessary so that Aggregate Demand increases from AD_0 to AD_2. These expansionary policies will move the economy from point *b* to point *c* in both panels of Figure 7. Thus, adopting policies to maintain unemployment at U_f will result in an annual inflation rate of 3 percent if compositional changes of the same magnitudes and frequencies continually recur. This result suggests that there is a "natural" *inflationary bias* in our economy caused by continuous changes in the structure of economic activity. If policymakers choose to suppress this natural inflation, they might reduce Aggregate Demand to AD_1 (point *d* in Panel A), but unemployment would rise to U_1 in Panel B. Thus, policymakers can reduce either the unemployment or the inflation caused by compositional changes in economic activity, but not both. Lower inflation means higher unemployment, and vice versa.

Another Keynesian explanation for the Phillips curves—the structuralist approach—goes like this: As unemployment falls and full employment is approached, it becomes increasingly costly to produce

FIGURE 7 *Full Employment Output, Shocks, and the Rate of Inflation: The Modern Keynesian Approach*

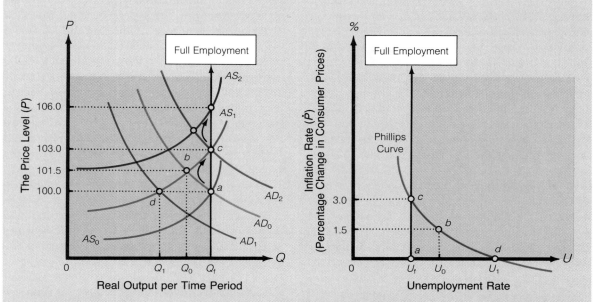

A modern Keynesian approach suggests that constant shocks to the supplies and demands in individual markets may create excessive unemployment that can only be overcome by expansionary policies that lend a natural bias for inflation to the economy. This theory is elaborated in James Tobin's article, "Inflation and Unemployment," *The American Economic Review*, 62, No. 1 (March 1972), pp. 1–18.

extra output. One reason is that as more and more businesses and industries operate nearer their capacities, their costs rise and are passed along to consumers as higher prices. Another reason costs rise as unemployment falls is the increasing competition among firms for the best workers. Even when unemployment is high, most of the best labor is employed. The majority of those remaining in the unemployed labor pool are, for the most part, nearly unemployable. These workers lack the skills necessary for jobs during hard times; the skills of many other workers may have depreciated during extended periods of joblessness. Employers begin "pirating" workers from other firms when unemployment rates are low by offering higher wages to secure qualified workers. This competition drives up costs, prices, and so on. The Keynesian structuralist and "shock" theories explain the existence of Phillips curves, but we need to probe a bit deeper to see how these approaches illuminate the rocky path of our economy over the past two decades.

A Modern Keynesian View of Stagflation

Natural rate theorists believe that mounting expectations of inflation sustained by overly expansionary macroeconomic policies are the only reason for leftward shifts of the Aggregate Supply curve and worsening Phillips curves. Modern Keynesians accept inflationary expectations as only one destabilizing influence on Phillips curves. Other causes can be classified under four broad headings: (*a*) external shocks, (*b*) disturbances to labor markets, (*c*) compositional changes in product markets, and (*d*) disruptions emerging in the public sector. Let us examine each, remembering that Aggregate Supply and the Phillips relationship can be shifted in either direction.

Shocks to the System   Any event that reduces Aggregate Supply (shifts it to the left) causes supply-side inflation and tends to worsen the trade-off between unemployment and inflation. During 1974–76 and again between 1979 and 1981, oil price increases and the subsequent impact on firms' energy costs caused shocks to our economy that reduced Aggregate Supply and eroded the short-run Phillips curve. This is shown in Figure 7. Wars, weather disturbances that reduce crop yields, or other natural disasters will have similar effects. On the other hand, discoveries of new resources, significant technological advances, prolonged periods of economic stability, or reductions in international tensions may improve the Phillips trade-off.

Labor Market Changes   Natural rate theory pivots on changing inflationary expectations to explain instability in the Phillips relationship. Incentive structures that encourage or discourage work effort also play roles. Unemployment compensation, Social Security, and other transfer programs all affect the labor-leisure choices of workers. For example, raising unemployment compensation payments will encourage greater unemployment and will intensify inflationary pressure. Unemployment compensation has been found to encourage temporary layoffs by firms because it eases the distress felt by firms' workers when slack demand causes reductions in production; it also appears to extend the average duration of unemployment. Social Security currently encourages early retirement. Increases in the sizes of payments under most welfare programs also worsen the trade-off between unemployment and inflation.

However, some recently implemented reforms are intended to reverse the negative effects of these programs. For example, welfare recipients who work can use subsidized day-care facilities for their children, the government now supports job training for the "hard core" unemployed, and the penalties exacted from Social Security recipients who earn income have been reduced. All these reforms may reduce the severity of the inflation/unemployment trade-off by increasing work effort and Aggregate Supply. Policies to enhance job mobility and improve matches between workers and available job openings also improve the Phillips trade-off, as will programs to reduce discrimination so that productivity becomes the primary criterion for employment.

Demographic changes also influence the relationships between inflation and unemployment. The World War II baby boom provided an expanding source of labor in the 1960s. However, because younger workers bounce from job to job and experience higher unemployment rates, the Phillips relationship worsened. As this group becomes older, the changing age structure of the population should reduce the severity of this trade-off. The rate of women's participation in the labor force increased markedly from the late 1950s onward—evidently faster than the economy was comfortably able to absorb them. Even though this influx of labor increased Aggregate Supply, it also seems to have worsened the inflation/unemployment relationship because women's unemployment rates are typically higher than those of males.

The ground rules for collective bargaining may also affect the Phillips curve. If the power of labor unions increases, enabling them to extract contracts with inflationary wage hikes, or if strike activities intensify, the trade-off between inflation and unemployment will deteriorate.

Product Market Composition Changes   As you saw earlier, continuous changes in the composition of demands for products, together with wage and price stickiness and a policy of trying to maintain full employment, provide one explanation for the shape and existence of Phillips curves. The menu of choices between unemployment and inflation worsens as these compositional changes occur more rapidly or as the external shocks to the system become stronger. If consumer tastes and preferences or investors' perceptions of the economic outlook change markedly, the composition of output may also change drastically. Of course, this trade-off is more favorable the slower or less extreme these changes are during a given interval.

Changes in laws governing foreign trade become more important as our economy becomes more internationally oriented. Hikes in tariffs or cuts in import quotas raise the prices of imported goods and can certainly worsen the dilemma posed by the Phillips curve. Competition is also reduced. Similarly, increases in domestic monopoly power and the resulting drives for greater profits will worsen the inflation/unemployment trade-off.

Public Sector Changes   Just as the amounts of disruption to the composition of private demands can shift the Phillips curve, so can changes in the composition of public sector demands for goods and services. Changes in tax structures, subsidies, and transfer payments will also influence the trade-off. Major revisions of such government regulations as those policed by the Occupational Safety and Health Administration (OSHA), minimum-wage laws, environmental protection regulations, leasing policies for mineral exploration on public lands, or changes in property rights structures may all shift the inflation/unemployment relationship. The direction of the shift depends on whether a particular regulatory change enhances or encumbers economic efficiency.

For modern Keynesians, a partial explanation for stagflation since the early 1970s goes something like this: Rising inflationary expectations and economic disruption associated with the Vietnam War caused the first shift in the Phillips curve in the early 1970s. The increase in world oil prices in 1974 caused the second shift. Even higher oil prices in 1979 and 1981, coupled with a worldwide crop shortage, caused the final shift of the Phillips curve in the early 1980s.

Supply-Side Policies

One way to improve the trade-off represented by the short-run Phillips curve is to expand Aggregate Supply. As we indicated previously, expanding Aggregate Supply yields a multitude of economic blessings—output, job opportunities, and employment all grow. This, in turn, reduces unemployment, dampens inflation, and raises standards of living. President Reagan's *supply-side* economic package was launched in 1981 amid much fanfare and glowing promises that prosperity was just around the corner. Among the cornerstones of his supply-side policies were: (*a*) cuts in the growth rates of domestic social programs, (*b*) cuts in individual and corporate income tax rates, (*c*) accelerated depreciation allowances, (*d*) investment tax credits, and (*e*) special tax incentives for savers.

Cuts in the Growth of Domestic Social Programs

Welfare programs were largely funded by private means prior to the Great Depression. Social Security, unemployment compensation, and a number of other transfer programs were launched to ease the misery common among the aged, unemployed, and poor in the 1930s. Then, in the mid-1960s, President Lyndon Johnson declared a *War on Poverty* to substantially raise Americans' minimum standard of living.

The result was an explosion of outlays that made transfer payments the most rapidly growing major component of the federal budget. Although the cause of equity may have been served in the minds of many observers, others felt that too many welfare recipients, capable of providing for themselves and their families, chose not to do so.

In later years, President Reagan and his budget advisors were convinced that more labor effort would be forthcoming if many people who relied on transfer payments had to provide for themselves. Their reasoning follows: If you must give me some of your income because I don't work and you do, neither of us is as likely to strive very much. Thus, cuts in transfer payments should increase Aggregate Supply because we will both work harder. Although President Reagan did not succeed in cutting transfer payments and other social programs in absolute dollar amounts, his administration was successful in substantially cutting the growth rate of social spending.

Cuts in Personal Income Tax Rates

Many key officials in the Reagan Administration believed strongly that work and investment incentives were severely hampered by high marginal tax rates—so much so that they felt the economy might be operating in the upper range of the Laffer curve (described in Chapter 11). By cutting personal income tax rates a total of 25 percent over three years, they expected to stimulate substantially greater effort from workers and more rapid investments, increasing Aggregate Supply. They also expected higher tax revenues. In addition, by reducing tax rates, the Reagan Administration expected money to be moved out of tax shelters and into more productive investments.

Cuts in Corporate Income Tax Rates

The corporate income tax rate was 46 percent from the 1960s until 1986. This meant that a corporate investment had to generate almost twice as much pretax profit as a noncorporate investment to yield the same rate of return from the vantage point of the individual investor. Some analysts point to this special tax penalty on corporate investments as a major cause for the low rates of investment in the United States compared to other industrialized nations. Among other problems, it appears that faltering growth in labor productivity may be attributable to our failure to accumulate sufficient new capital.

The Reagan Administration's attempts to reduce corporate tax rates were a part of a broader strategy to stimulate investment while simultaneously reducing what it saw as an unfair burden on the corporate sector of our economy. Economists from across the political spectrum are generally opposed to the corporate income tax, some for these reasons and others because they are convinced that the tax is forward-shifted, falling most heavily on the poor. As percentages of their incomes, the poor are most prone to buy the standardized products manufactured in the corporate sector. Thus, these economists consider corporate taxes to be hidden and regressive. The corporate income tax is politically popular, however, because most people see it as a tax on big business. Thus, a furor arose in the media when President Reagan raised the possibility of eliminating corporate income taxes. The idea was quickly abandoned. Corporate tax rates were reduced sharply, however, as part of a comprehensive tax reform package in 1986.

Incentives for Saving

Investment to facilitate capital accumulation cannot occur unless there is a corresponding amount of saving. Reagan's supply-side policies introduced special tax incentives in an attempt to persuade Americans to save more. Individual Retirement Accounts (IRAs) were one such program. Individuals were allowed to set aside up to $2,000 each year and could deduct this amount from their taxable income. Penalty-free withdrawal of principal and accumulated interest from an approved IRA plan was permitted only at age 59. These withdrawals would then be taxable, but the individuals would be paying at lower tax rates because they would be past their peak earning years. Moreover, they would have the advantage of postponing their tax payments. The interest you can draw always makes it better for you to delay paying a given dollar amount in taxes as long as possible. IRAs were only one of a number of programs intended as incentives for saving.

Another facet of the attempt to bolster saving was the attack on inflation spearheaded by the FED. With the encouragement of the Reagan Administration, the FED had begun reducing the rate of monetary growth in 1981. Unanticipated inflation rewards borrowers who pay back their debts in less valuable dol-

FIGURE 8   *Percentage Change in Real Federal Government Revenues (1982 Dollars)*

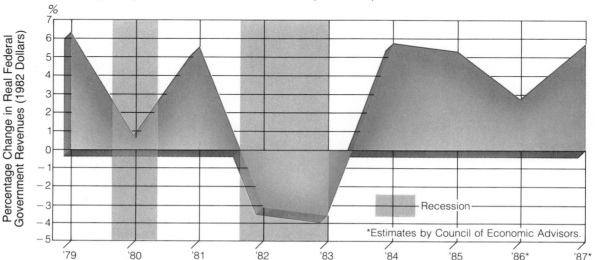

The added revenue expected from the growth dividend of President Reagan's supply-side tax cuts were totally squelched by a severe recession. Only recently have real federal revenues begun to grow.

Source: *Economic Report of the President,* 1986.

lars, but it penalizes savers because it erodes the purchasing power of their savings. Thus, the FED's policy of squelching growth in Aggregate Demand was seen as a necessary step along the path toward long-term growth of Aggregate Supply.

The overall thrust of supply-side economics was to offer positive incentives to middle- and upper-income workers and investors while reducing transfer payments so that welfare recipients would have less to lose by working. The administration's response to widespread charges that this approach was grossly inequitable was its belief that the long-term benefits of these policies to expand Aggregate Supply would accrue to the disadvantaged among us when the economy boomed; to them, the best antipoverty program is a strong and growing economy.

Although a strong economic recovery began in 1983, certain questions remained about why the desirable effects predicted from supply-side policies were so delayed. Part of the explanation is that the FED was pursuing anti-inflationary policies during 1980–83, the period when supply-side policies were instituted. In addition, government deficits skyrocketed when President Reagan's program of expanding defense spending absorbed most of the reduction in growth in transfer outlays. The recession of 1981–83 slowed the much anticipated surge in Aggregate Supply and thus did not swell tax revenues (see Figure 8). The combination of tight monetary policy and high deficits caused real interest rates to remain high until 1986. Thus, real investment was weak throughout the early 1980s but jumped substantially in 1985. If real interest rates continue to remain low, rising investment expenditures should enhance economic growth in the latter half of this decade. Let us now examine some other strategies in the battle against economic instability.

Using Intentional Recessions to Reduce Inflationary Pressures

Restraining Aggregate Demand can reduce inflationary pressures in the economy, but unemployment will probably rise. If inflation is caused by excessive demand, a mild recession may defuse inflationary pressure. Hair-raising depressions may emerge, however, if contractionary demand-management policies are used to combat severe supply-side inflation. If, as Figure 9 illustrates, Aggregate Supply is

FIGURE 9 Dampening Supply-Side Inflation with Contractionary Demand-Management Policies

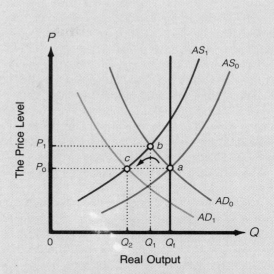

Dampening supply-side inflation with contractionary demand-management policies may diffuse inflationary pressures, but it is sure to generate a severe recession. If the Aggregate Supply curve shifts from AS_0 to AS_1, output falls to Q_1 but prices rise to P_1. If Aggregate Demand is reduced to AD_1, inflation is halted, but the economy suffers a serious recession.

shifting leftward from AS_0 to AS_1, equilibrium output will fall to Q_1. However, if contractionary demand-management policies are used to keep prices stable, a severe recession (or worse) will result as output falls to Q_2. Mild supply-side inflations already bear the seeds of recession.

Labor markets tighten and businesses scramble to fill their needs for labor as a boom caused by excessive demand proceeds. Wages begin to rise, putting a squeeze on profits. At the same time, prices are pushed up because many firms seem to set prices by applying fixed percentage mark-ups to their costs, a procedure known as **cost-plus**, or mark-up, **pricing.** Labor unions become more militant, strikes for higher pay or other benefits become more common, and labor productivity declines as increasing numbers of workers with lower skill levels find jobs during prosperity. Labor cost per unit of output rises as this occurs, generating further upward pressures on prices.

Recessions to Discipline Labor

Some analysts of the business cycle have suggested that following a long period of prosperity, a recession may be needed to dampen inflationary expectations and to "discipline labor." They assert that the labor force needs to be disciplined so that it will work harder and accept less. Only a sustained bout of unemployment will bring labor's expectations about wages, fringe benefits, and other working conditions into line with the real value of their production and business's desire for higher profits. This is a minority view, unpalatable to most economists and policymakers. However, the idea contains some kernels of truth.

Among the major benefits of recessions are the opportunities afforded firms to clear the shelves of "deadwood" and to increase worker productivity. Workers know that during recessions, finding other jobs is more difficult, and that they are likely to lose substantial disposable income if they quit their present jobs. Therefore, they work harder and complain less. The natural long-run result of a recession is that profits rise and owners and managers of firms are again happy. The recurrence of this process led one radical economist, David Gordon, to entitle an article, "Recession Is Capitalism as Usual."

Policymakers' Abhorrence of Recessions

Most policymakers dislike the prospect of plunging the economy into a recession to reduce inflationary pressure. High or rising unemployment creates political discontent and can lead to changes of the guard at the White House and in Congress, an unpleasant prospect in the minds of incumbent politicians. As we have seen, rising unemployment elicits pressures to restore full employment via resumption of expansionary policies that rekindle inflationary pressures. While radical economists such as David Gordon argue that recession is capitalism's way of restoring equilibrium in labor markets, such an approach is very unpopular in Washington, where it is pursued only reluctantly. However, the slumps of 1969–70, 1973–75, 1980, and 1981–83 all resulted, to some degree, from such policies.

The techniques that seem to be most favored by our government have been judicious use of either monetary and fiscal policies or what have been dubbed **incomes policies.** Incomes policies include such strategies as wage and price controls, wage and price guideposts or guidelines, and presidential jawboning.

Incomes Policies to Combat Inflation/Stagflation

Seven of the nine presidents following Herbert Hoover employed some form of *incomes policy.* President Truman dismantled wartime wage and price controls when World War II ended. For roughly five years, the economy was without explicit controls, but the onset of the Korean War prompted Truman to reinstate some curbs. Both sets of wartime restraints were mandatory, having the force of law. The Eisenhower era, from 1953 to 1961, was free of controls.

Guideposts were introduced under President Kennedy in 1962 and stiffened by President Johnson, who accompanied these efforts with considerable **jawboning.** These voluntary guideposts lost their bite as inflationary pressures mounted in the late 1960s when both domestic spending and outlays for the Vietnam conflict escalated. President Nixon instituted full-fledged price controls, beginning with a 90-day price freeze in August 1971. In 1979, President Carter resorted to jawboning (with threatened losses of government contracts) to make his "voluntary" wage and price guidelines more effective.

Incomes policies are designed to reduce inflationary pressures without actually changing government spending, taxing, or monetary policy. If successful, the Phillips curve would shift to the left, reducing the painful feasible combination of unemployment and inflation. A wage and price freeze is the most restrictive form of incomes policy, followed by wage and price controls, guidelines and guideposts, and finally, jawboning. Let us examine each a little more closely.

Mandatory Wage-Price Controls

Mandatory and wide-ranging **wage-price controls** normally have been associated only with war. However, President Nixon introduced Americans to peacetime controls with his announcement of a 90-day freeze on wages and prices in August of 1971. The freeze was followed by several phases that provided legal ceilings for increases in specific prices and wages.

These mandatory controls were intended to suppress inflationary pressures that had built up during the Vietnam War. Mandatory controls are legally enforceable price ceilings that carry penalties for noncompliance. Enforcement costs are high because the government is heavily involved in monitoring compliance by both business and labor. For example, in 1983, the government was still prosecuting violations of oil price ceilings, nearly a decade after the ceilings had been rescinded.

Voluntary Wage-Price Guideposts/Guidelines

Voluntary price guidelines and wage guideposts have traditionally been tied to rates of growth of labor productivity. The theory behind wage guideposts is that wages can increase by amounts equal to increases in productivity without forcing manufacturers to raise prices. Thus, if average wage increases equal only average increases in productivity, inflation (average price increases) can be held to zero. In the early years of the Kennedy Administration, the wage guideposts were set to allow for a small, but tolerable, amount of wage inflation.

On the price side, the same logic was used to set the guidelines. Prices were expected to be stable in industries with average growth in productivity. Industries experiencing more rapid than average rates of productivity increases were expected to lower their prices. Finally, in those industries where productivity growth was below the national average, permissible prices rose by the difference between productivity growth and the national average.

Tax-Based Incomes Policies (TIPs)

The general idea behind **Tax-Based Incomes Policies (TIPs)** is to use tax policies to restructure incentives so that decisions made by both business and labor will conform to certain politically determined wage-price guidelines. The basic theory behind TIP proposals is that higher prices are often the consequences of firms' decisions to allow wage hikes that exceed workers' average gains in productivity, these decisions contribute to general inflation. Most TIP proposals attempt to "internalize" these added inflationary costs through tax incentives that give tax breaks to workers and firms who hold the line on wage and price increases. These proposals also impose tax penalties on unions and firms who raise wages or prices more than a given baseline percentage. Either incentives or disincentives may work, just as you can induce a child to behave through either rewards or punishment.

Market-Based Incomes Policies

The **Market Anti-Inflation Plan (MAP)** proposes that the government auction off a certain number of licenses to raise prices more than some established guideline. These rights to raise prices could be resold, which would create a market price for these rights. Increases in inflationary pressures would raise the demand for licenses to inflate prices, driving the market prices for these rights even higher. Thus, the MAP approach makes it ever more costly for firms to raise prices as inflationary pressures mount, but it does permit flexibility in relative prices for those sectors of the economy in which pressures are the greatest.

Evaluation of Incomes Policies

Incomes policies, like many other government policies, have both friends and foes. Supporters of wage-price policies point principally to their impression that market shares in many important markets in the United States are so concentrated that pricing decisions made within these "monopolistic" industries are not in the public interest. Properly administered controls presumably will make the behavior of these firms more compatible with the interests of society. Monopolistic attempts to expand profits are thought to cause price hikes that translate into supply-side inflation. Where unions and industries have considerable control over the market, they may be able to increase prices unilaterally, adding to already existing inflationary pressures. Since many industries that exhibit these characteristics are primary products industries (steel, lumber, oil, among others), their price increases tend to be compounded as they ripple through the economy.

TIP and MAP proposals represent compromises between mandatory wage and price controls and voluntary decision making. The advantage to the TIP and MAP proposals in comparison to standard wage and price controls is that wages and prices can change to

FIGURE 10 *Inflation During the 1971–81 Wage-Price Controls/Guidelines*

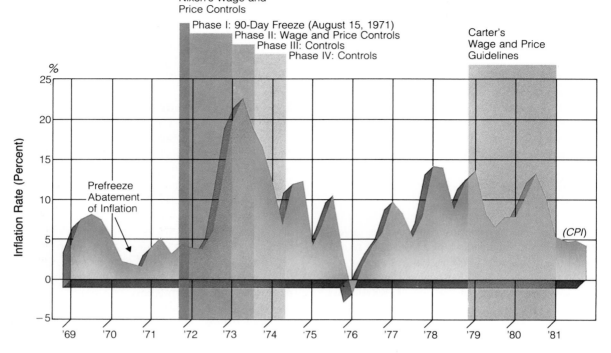

Inflation actually increased during President Nixon's four phases of wage and price controls, and intensified, erratically, throughout the 1970s.
Source: *Business Conditions Digest,* January 1986.

signal needed reallocations of resources and to alleviate shortages, even though there are penalties for noncompliance with guidelines. Proponents also argue that when the principal underlying cause of continuing inflation is the inflationary expectations of workers and businesses, controls can simultaneously reduce these expectations and reduce the basic rate of inflation.

Opponents cite the results of the 1971–74 wage and price controls as strong evidence that controls do not work. The evidence is diagrammed in Figure 10. The rate of inflation was actually declining just prior to President Nixon's announcement of a wage-price freeze. Throughout the freeze inflation was relatively constant, but during Phase II when wage and price increases were strictly controlled, the inflation rate began soaring. Inflation continued even after controls were lifted in 1973, and it took a severe

recession in 1975–76 to temporarily slow the inflationary spiral. As Figure 10 shows, President Carter's guidelines had little effect on inflation in the late 1970s.

Critics have pointed to this evidence to counter the view that controls reduce the inflationary expectations of workers and businesses. These opponents contend that controls actually create the worst kind of expectation—the expectation that when the controls are lifted, prices will rise more rapidly than before the restraints were instituted.

Further, critics maintain that artificial wage and price restraints warp market signals and lead to widespread shortages. Long-term controls breed corruption in government as bribery for the right to raise prices becomes common. Black markets emerge when people seek shortcuts around shortages. Distortions are greater the tighter controls are or the longer they are in effect. Price signals to reallocate production from less desired to more desired items get lost in the shuffle because they are masked by controls. These problems might be handled by granting exceptions to the controls, but each exception precipitates numerous applications for other exceptions. The monitoring process and the complexity of regulations have a tendency to escalate, and eventually the economy may suffer from terminal red tape.

Guideline or guidepost policies without any legal muscle rely on appeals to patriotism. The battle is already lost if unions and managements of vital industries do not respond to the call. Most presidents have recognized this fact and have coupled voluntary controls with moral suasion or jawboning. Business and labor leaders are invited to the White House for little chats about antitrust investigations, public admonition, or various forms of regulatory harassment. Such confrontations with business and labor seldom achieve more than surface compliance and public relations rhetoric. Firms commonly learn to announce even higher price hikes than they desire so that, when faced with political heat, they can roll back the prices a bit. In this way, business leaders and politicians can each claim victory.

Critics contend that TIPs require complex regulations that must be formulated and enforced. Under MAP, how many licenses to raise prices will be sold? How will the price or wage increase standard for MAP or TIPs be set? And how will this price or wage standard be translated into practice? These and other questions mean that administering any TIP or MAP plan will inevitably call for bureaucracy to deal with these problems. The MAP plan also requires that a market for inflation rights be established; establishing such a market would absorb resources.

The most important question about incomes policies is whether such schemes, without appropriately restrictive monetary and fiscal policies, would actually solve the inflationary dilemma. An incomes policy could be seen as a panacea by policymakers who might then feel free to follow expansionary monetary or fiscal policy if that suited their particular whims. Incomes policies are, at best, temporarily effective when expansionary monetary and fiscal policies are pursued; incomes policies will fail to hold the economy together for any longer than the very short run.

National Economic Planning

The basic guide to national economic policy from World War II until 1978 was the Employment Act of 1946, which established the Council of Economic Advisors and set full employment with price stability as national economic priorities. The **Humphrey-Hawkins Full Employment and Balanced Growth Act of 1978** augments the Employment Act of 1946 in several important ways. The Humphrey-Hawkins Act: (*a*) identifies several specific economic priorities and objectives; (*b*) directs the president to establish goals and objectives based on those priorities (Congress is to review these goals periodically); and (*c*) creates procedures to improve coordination and development of economic policy by the president, Congress, and the Federal Reserve System.

Section 206 of the act, which provides standby public employment powers to the president, ignites most of the controversy that surrounds this "economic planning act." The president must ensure, however, that no workers from private employment are drawn into public employment projects. Second, the jobs made available must be productive and in the lower range of skills and pay. Third, the administration must identify target areas of high unemployment and focus on the structurally unemployed—those whose skills are obsolete or absent.

Critics of the act assert that the lack of coordinated economic planning is not the major cause of our economic ills. In fact, they see government actions as the major problem—not the solution. They assert that misdirected federal programs have created disincentives to invest in the private sector; counterproductive tax and regulatory policies also hinder the efficiency of the marketplace that they consider vital to a healthy economy.

National Industrial Policy

Many interpreted the stagflation of the 1970s as evidence of profound structural changes in our economy. The U.S. economy appeared to move away from its traditional strength in basic industries (steel, autos, and manufacturing) toward expanding new service-oriented sectors. Productivity grew only about a third as fast as in previous decades, and real wages declined somewhat during the decade.

Some policymakers have called for a **national industrial policy** to counteract these changes. The concept of industrial policy or **reindustrialization** (which calls for a second industrial revolution) requires government support of targeted industries. Industrial policy offers a sophisticated rationale for certain pork barrel legislation and enjoys some support in Congress from both ends of the political spectrum. The fact that the specifics of an industrial policy are yet to be defined may account for some of its support.

The means used to target industries for supportive government policies and subsidies are extremely important to the success of any plan. Proponents of industrial policies argue that resources should be directed to industries where (a) productivity is the highest, (b) linkages to the rest of the economy are high, (c) future competitiveness is important, and (d) foreign governments target their resources. Proponents argue that shifting resources to high productivity industries will generate higher real national income and, thus, higher aggregate income per capita. Industries like steel, autos, or semiconductors that have extended linkages (or multipliers) to the rest of the economy would be targets for industrial policies, regardless of specific rates of productivity growth. This is seen as especially important where the federal tax code, OPEC, labor unions, or other factors are perceived as distorting efficient market operations.

Almost two centuries ago, Alexander Hamilton suggested that "infant industries" were appropriate for government support, Today, some proponents of industrial policies would limit their support to industries that would eventually be internationally competitive. Others suggest that the United States should fight fire with fire by targeting industries that other foreign governments support. They believe that this will enable U.S. industries to compete in international markets and reestablish a balance of international trade.

Opponents argue that reallocating workers into high productivity sectors may not increase national income. High productivity industries tend to be capital intensive; a given investment in these industries will employ fewer workers relative to less capital-intensive industries. As employment growth declines, unemployment will rise, putting downward pressure on real wages, and there will be overbuilding in capital-intensive industries.

Opponents further argue that the market will provide the right level of investment in those industries that have extended "linkages" to the rest of the economy. They contend that forecasting which industry may, at some time in the future, be internationally competitive is almost impossible. And finally, letting our industrial policy be dictated by that of foreign governments means that we would be ignoring market forces within our economy. Opponents stress that industrial policy will, for political reasons, be directed toward "troubled high wage, unionized, politically powerful traditional heavy industries" or emerging high-tech industries. Finally, market forces are often so powerful that industrial policies may be ineffective.

The idea of a national industrial policy is an offshoot of national economic planning, but on a smaller scale. A form of industrial policy has existed since the Great Depression. For example, in the 1950s we stimulated oil and mineral production with the depletion allowance; in the 1960s we underwrote the high-tech space program; in the 1970s we encouraged solar energy development using tax credits; and in the 1980s we returned to high tech with military spending on the Strategic Defense Initiative ("Star Wars") program.

What proponents of a national industrial policy want is a coherent set of long-run policies to promote economic growth and international competitiveness of U.S. industries. For example, Robert Reich has suggested a program to "create a dynamic economy" and speed the movement of capital into higher valued productivity.[3] His plan includes such proposals as: (a) use of employment vouchers for on-the-job training; (b) a human capital tax credit and community tax deduction for firms which retrain older workers and remain in their communities; (c) regional development banks to extend low-interest loans to targeted industries; (d) applied research centers where firms could join together with a regional university to fund research; (e) replacing the current income tax with a progressive consumption tax to encourage savings; and (f) a national

---

3. Robert B. Reich, "Industrial Policy", *The New Republic*, March 31, 1982, pp. 28–32.

industrial board to monitor all government programs that allocate capital in the economy.

For industrial policy to succeed, restructuring of industry (promoting high productivity industries) will require that employment opportunities are available in other sectors. Industrial policy without sound macroeconomic policy to promote full employment will be virtually worthless. Ironically, good macroeconomic policy to promote full employment may mitigate the need for a national industrial policy.

CHAPTER REVIEW: KEY POINTS

1. The *Phillips curve* depicts a trade-off for policymakers between unemployment and inflation. Lower unemployment rates presumably might be purchased through higher inflation, or vice versa; it is up to policymakers to choose the least harmful mix of evils. The Phillips curve appeared to be relatively stable through the 1960s, but it shifted sharply in the 1970s and early 1980s so that much higher rates of unemployment appeared necessary to dampen inflationary pressures. The reasons for the instability of the Phillips curve are the subject of a continuing debate within the economics profession.

2. The *natural rate theory* of the instability in the Phillips trade-off focuses on worker expectations of inflation. As labor begins to anticipate inflation, greater increases in wages are required for a given level of real output. Thus, accelerating inflation is required if policymakers desire to hold unemployment below its "natural rate," but even this policy will not work forever.

3. Modern Keynesian analysis suggests that several factors in addition to inflationary expectations can cause stagflation and instability in the Phillips curve. Unexpected shocks to the supply side, rapid compositional changes in demand or output, changes in labor institutions that generate disincentives for work, and changes in public regulatory policies are all capable of shifting the Phillips curve.

4. *Intentional recessions* can decompress accumulated inflationary pressures and inflationary expectations. However, recessions tend to be very hard on political incumbents (among others), so many politicians favor incomes policies of various sorts.

5. *Incomes policies* (mandatory wage-price freezes or controls, voluntary guidelines, or "jawboning") muzzle the effectiveness of the price system, creating shortages and widespread misallocations of resources.

6. *TIPS (Tax-Based Incomes Policies)* proposals use either positive or negative tax incentives to keep labor and management in rough compliance with a socially acceptable rate of inflation. You can raise your wages or prices, but if you do, you either pay a tax penalty or lose some tax advantages. *MAP (Market Anti-Inflation Plan)* would auction the rights to raise prices more than some guideline amount. Either TIPs or MAP allow price structures to change to prevent shortages and to signal needed reallocations of resources, but each raises the prospect of more bureaucratic red tape.

7. The *Humphrey-Hawkins Full Employment and Balanced Growth Act of 1978* makes government the "employer of last resort" and requires that the administration submit continuous five-year plans for achieving various macroeconomic objectives. It also encourages coordination of government macroeconomic policies.

8. *National industrial policy* involves government policies designed to support targeted industries. Proponents argue that a coherent industrial policy is needed to increase economic growth, enhance U.S. industrial competitiveness, and counteract industrial policies of foreign governments. Opponents maintain that free markets will provide the appropriate investment in various industries, and that an industrial policy will misallocate resources to politically powerful, heavily unionized industries.

QUESTIONS FOR THOUGHT AND DISCUSSION

1. When double-digit inflation erupted in the United States during the middle 1970s, many economists became advocates of *indexing;* putting cost-of-living adjustment (COLA) clauses into all contracts calling for future monetary payments. They argued that indexing wages and other incomes such as rents, pensions, and interest payments would help fight inflation and, more importantly, would offset its negative effects. The theory was that indexation would make it impossible for policymakers to use inflation to fool workers into reducing their voluntary frictional unemployment, eliminate arbitrary redistributions of income, and so on. If the federal government used contractionary monetary and fiscal policies to fight inflation, indexation of income shares would cause the rates of growth of resource costs to slow automatically, making the process relatively painless. In theory, indexing some or all sectors could help slow inflation or at least cushion its impact.

   Trace the effects of indexing if demand-side inflation is the problem. Some economists hold that indexing factor incomes may make controlling an inflationary spiral more difficult. How could this be true? How would supply-side shocks, such as OPEC oil price increases, work their way through an indexed economy? Through an economy without indexation? Would politicians have incentives to introduce inflationary or contractionary monetary and fiscal policies if all incomes were indexed? Why or why not?

2. If indexation is used for such retirement programs as Social Security, should pensions be adjusted using average changes in take-home salaries so that retirees share in the gains and losses of workers, or should cost-of-living adjustments be used to ensure pensioners a constant purchasing power income? What are the advantages and disadvantages of each approach?

3. Keynes argued during the Great Depression that the way to put unemployed workers back on payrolls and get machinery humming again was to increase the demand for goods and services by putting more money in people's pockets. His main argument concerned insufficient demand. If Aggregate Demand were increased, the economy would climb out of any recession or depression. Many economists believe that the Keynesian method for resolving the problems of recession may not produce the desired results in an era of stagflation. Why do most economists now believe that Keynesian demand management is effective only for problems like those of a depression era and that such management cannot remedy the multitude of problems facing the economy today?

4. The 1979 Annual Report of the Joint Economic Committee of Congress states that stagflation is the result of policies that have stimulated demand while retarding supply. In other words, our national economic policies have concentrated on the economics of demand while neglecting the economics of supply. Would you agree with this diagnosis? Which of the policies in effect during the 1960s and 1970s may have inhibited the growth of Aggregate Supply?

5. Policies that enhance competition and economic efficiency tend to reduce inflation, unemployment, or both. Can you think of changes from current American policies in the following areas that would move the Phillips curve leftward and down? Try to do at least three or four areas: (*a*) labor markets; (*b*) international trade; (*c*) transportation; (*d*) communications; (*e*) welfare; (*f*) housing; (*g*) government procurement; (*h*) big, highly concentrated industries; (*i*) education; and (*j*) finance. How or why would your policies be preferable to the current system?

University of Southern California v. *Cost of Living Council and Office of Emergency Preparedness (1972)*

Some government agency must develop and promulgate definitions, rules, and regulations whenever wage and price guidelines are imposed. These are invariably complex, and some groups are bound to be harmed in some manner. The University of Southern California found itself inadvertently in violation of the 1971 wage-price freeze. This case points out only some of the controversies that inevitably accompany incomes policies.

The University of Southern California (USC) seeks, among other things, a ruling that its prices for tickets to its 1971 football games were not in violation of the Phase I "price freeze" signed by the President on 15 August 1971.

The Presidential Executive Order decreed that for a period of ninety days prices were to be stabilized "at levels not greater than the highest of those pertaining to a substantial volume of actual transactions by each firm during the thirty-day period in which transactions did occur."

On 28 January 1971, USC established the prices of reserved seats for each of its home football games in 1971 at fifty cents above those charged during the 1970 football season. On 30 April 1971, USC distributed brochures that announced the 1971 football schedule and solicited the purchase of tickets for reserved seats, at the increased price on a season-ticket basis or for individual games. Before 16 July 1971 (the beginning of the thirty-day base period established by the executive order), USC had sold and received payment for about 125,000 tickets to the six home games on a season basis and several thousand additional tickets to individual games. During the thirty-day base period (16 July to 14 August), USC sold about 5,000 more tickets. Five of the six home games were played during the ninety-day "freeze" established by the executive order; the last game was played on 20 November 1971.

On 5 October 1971, the Cost of Living Council (CLC) notified USC that the price increase was in violation of the freeze and demanded that refunds of fifty cents per ticket be made.

The obvious purpose of the executive order was to stabilize prices as of 15 August 1971, and to prohibit sellers from increasing their prices beyond those charged prior to that date. There is no suggestion in the order that such controls would have a retroactive effect and require refunds of prices charged in transactions that preceded the executive order.

The CLC insists, however, that their demand does not involve retroactivity. They contend that the "transactions" affected by the order were not the sales of tickets but, instead, were the playing of the games. According to the CLC, inasmuch as there were no such "transactions" during the base period (16 July to 14 August 1971 inclusive), the 1971 prices could not exceed those of the 1970 football season, which was the "nearest preceding thirty-day period in which transactions did occur," required in the executive order.

The university asserts that a tackle on the USC Varsity would be surprised to hear that his performance in a game is in fulfillment of his employment to provide a service for the spectators as his customers or clients, comparable to services rendered by an electrician or a lawyer. The goal of a college football player is to represent his school as a member of the team and to help win games and perhaps a championship. The ticket holders are incidental; and the game presumably would be played with comparable motivation whether or not there were spectators in attendance. It is relevant to note that many intercollegiate athletic contests are held and earnestly fought virtually without paying spectators.

The university points out that purchasers of season tickets, rather than contracting for future services, are completing a transaction in which they give and receive value. They obtain the right to view the games from reserved seats, and their names are put on a preference list that accords them the availability of progressively better seats in successive seasons. In return, they pay the full purchase price without any right to a refund, and the games are played whether or not the ticket holders are present.

Questions

1. How would you decide the case? Why?

2. Do you feel the playing of a football game constitutes a service as suggested by the CLC? Why or why not? Does selling tickets constitute a service?

3. For this price-freeze regulation, what constitutes a "transaction"? Which is the most important for determining violations of the "freeze": transactions or services?

4. What are the practical problems in a case like this if you (the judge) decide for the council? If you decide for the University of Southern California?

5. What are some of the difficulties inherent in implementing wage and price controls that are illustrated by this case?

6. Do you think that problems like this are common when wage and price controls are imposed? If so, what is the likely effect on the size of the government bureaucracy assigned to monitor prices if controls remain in effect for a long period? On the number of cases brought to court?

7. Suppose that you were scheduled for a raise next week and I received one yesterday. What problems do you think would arise if a wage-price freeze were implemented tomorrow? If you are young and ambitious, how might you achieve a higher income despite a rigid wage freeze? (What does a wage freeze do to your incentive to switch jobs?)

8. What distortions would you expect if wages were frozen but prices were not? Vice Versa? If a freeze was imposed on industry, but not agriculture? Do uniform price controls make more or less sense than selective controls? Why?

9. What would happen if interest rates were frozen but the government continued to follow inflationary policies? How might this affect capital markets and economic growth?

CHAPTER 18

Limitations of Stabilization Policy

recognition lag	*political business*	*efficient markets*
administrative lag	*cycles*	*rational expectations*
impact lag	*new classical*	
financial insulation	*macroeconomics*	

Business today, and indeed America today, is much like the story of the late Supreme Court Justice Oliver Wendell Holmes who, at 88, found himself on a train and unable to find his ticket. When the conductor came around, Holmes was searching through all his pockets without success. Of course the conductor recognized the distinguished justice, so he said, "Don't worry, Mr. Holmes. You don't need a ticket. You'll probably find it when you get off the train, and I'm sure the Pennsylvania Railroad will trust you to mail it back later!" Holmes looked up at the conductor with some irritation and said: "My dear man, that is not the problem at all. The problem is not where my ticket is. The problem is where am I going?"

*—From the Back of a Box
of Celestial Seasonings' Red Zinger Tea*

The past few chapters may have convinced you that economic stabilization policy is a reasonably straightforward process: you first decide which goals to pursue in employment, price-level stability, and economic growth, and you then translate these goals into the appropriate mix of fiscal and monetary policies. You may have concluded that even though hard choices about macroeconomic goals must be made, fault for any failure to achieve reasonable macrosta-

bility can be laid at the doors of politicians and policymakers who are just "too dumb" to apply a few principles of economics.

There is growing acceptance of a view that political actions are more often the source of macroeconomic problems than the solution to these problems. Adam Smith's doubts about government are mirrored in modern monetarism, which has borrowed much from the *Austrian* school, a group of thinkers typified by Ludwig Von Mises and Friedrich Hayek. (See their Biography).

In this chapter, you will learn more about some of the problems that make it very difficult to properly design and implement discretionary countercyclical policies. Frankly, macroeconomic policymaking is as much an art as it is a science. Some common difficulties facing policymakers include problems of timing and imperfect information, imperfect monetary and fiscal policymaking institutions, and imperfect politicians who adopt specific policies to maximize their prospects for reelection. Finally, the reactions to policy by private individuals and firms may even eliminate the seemingly desirable effects of some

Ludwig Von Mises (1881–1973) and Friedrich A. Hayek (b. 1899)

Ludwig Von Mises was born in Austria and taught at the University of Vienna before migrating to America to escape Hitler's invasion. As a youth he was fond of tennis, but when someone remarked that he was not very good at it, he replied: "The fate of the ball does not interest me very much." What did interest him was human reasoning's potential.

Von Mises chose not to limit himself to a narrowly defined economics. He attempted, instead, to survey the whole range of human action.

Von Mises's system of thought focused on the supremacy of the individual as a purposeful decision maker, constantly adjusting price, production, and consumption in order to live better and enjoy maximum personal freedom. In a free marketplace, **economic calculation** provides prices and profits as signals that motivate business to adjust production to the demands of consumers. But in a government-directed economy, agencies have no economic measure comparable to profits by which their operations can be evaluated.

Von Mises also rejected the Keynesian idea that a nation can solve the problems of inflation and unemployment by *countercyclical* fiscal policy. Such an idea ignores the fact that politicians have a strong propensity to spend in good times as well as bad. Von Mises added the conviction that government economic managers are always fumbling in the dark because they cannot possibly know all the data needed to make "correct" macroeconomic adjustments.

He concluded that the likely outcome of *budget management* is inflation, followed by price controls, and, ultimately, stagnation.

Friedrich Hayek is one of Von Mises's many brilliant former students who later achieved prominence. This elder statesman of the Austrian school of economics became a Nobel Laureate in 1974. While Keynes advocated a very active role for government in controlling the economy, Hayek argues that the extension of government control is the enemy of freedom. He denounces a growing government role as "the road to serfdom."

Hayek decries constructivism more than anything else, calling it "the pretense of knowledge" and "the illusion of human omnipotence." **Constructivism** is the idea that enlightened leaders can remake society in the current fashionable image. Hayek believes that culture and civilization are not consequences of deliberate human design but are instead the products of the survival of society's successful groups. Hence, civilization depends on rules of behavior, not on goals. A couple of examples of constructivism in action follow. In the early 1980s Iran's theocratic dictator, the Ayatollah Khomeini wanted his people to be more zealous in following the precepts of Islam. His regime killed thousands in order to reconstruct society to his design. Hitler, too, was a constructivist, as was Stalin.

Hayek believes that Keynesianism is a much less virulent strain of the constructivism disease. Keynes's message is very seductive: Through simple manipulation of total spending, a government can control the twin problems of unemployment and unstable prices. Keynes's comforting message has not been lost on many politicians, who no longer consider themselves to be helpless before the convulsions of a business cycle nor limited in what they can deliver voters. Keynesian policy analysis looks like an instruction manual for running the economy as a well-oiled machine.

The trouble, says Hayek, is that the economy is an organism, not a machine. Individual behavior and economic interactions are so complex that they cannot be manipulated in the ways many modern macroeconomists suppose. In vain attempts to maintain very low unemployment, government may feel compelled to spend faster and faster, so that prices wind up rising faster and faster as well. This kind of artificial stimulant, says Hayek, distorts the price signals that indicate genuine scarcities in the marketplace when intervention is absent.

countercyclical measures. These problems severely limit discretionary policymaking and stand as arguments for following macropolicy rules.

Lags and Stabilization Policy

Stabilization policy suffers from fits and starts because of lags in recognition, administration, and impact. Suppose that discretionary monetary and fiscal policies are equally powerful and have equally harmful side effects. There is still a question of whether monetary or fiscal policy is preferable because of the different timing lags that characterize each.

Recognition Lags

Our perceptions of present economic conditions are clouded, and our predictions about the future emerge only from more or less educated guesswork. This problem is known as the **recognition lag** and affects monetary and fiscal policymakers equally. It takes time and effort to gather, compile, process, and interpret economic data so that we have some feel for any widespread changes in economic activity. Even then, the data may be sketchy, contradictory, or misleading. For example, until 1986, the Commerce Department published a "flash" estimate of GNP. While clearly a preliminary estimate (since it was available a week before the quarter ended), the estimate was dropped because, according to the Commerce Department, "the public was coming to regard it as a legitimate statistic." Of course, if 25 percent of the work force were laid off tomorrow, policymakers would know by next weekend that we (and they) were in deep trouble. However, economic change is seldom so apparent. Our economy moves sluggishly, making it difficult for policymakers to determine exactly how hard and in which direction they should be steering.

Administrative Lags

After a change in our economy has been identified, it still takes time to institute proper countercyclical policies, a problem known as the **administrative** (or *implementation*) **lag.** If recession seems to be on the horizon, monetary policymakers could print money and buy bonds (open-market operations), or they might lower the discount rate or reserve requirements. (You should remember these from Chapter 13.) The reverse of these measures would be appropriate if inflationary pressures were picking up steam. Changes in monetary policy can be implemented quickly by the Federal Reserve Board's Federal Open Market Committee. Consequently, administrative lags are not much of a problem for monetary policymaking.

Fiscal policymaking, however, does encounter substantial administrative lags because discretionary changes in taxation or government expenditures require legislative changes. A crisis may well be over by the time: (*a*) new laws are drafted, (*b*) congressional subcommittees have a chance to wrestle with the questions of whose taxes to cut or increase or whose pork-barrel legislation to pass or sacrifice, (*c*) both the House and Senate pass some compromise bill, (*d*) the president signs the bill, and finally (*e*) all of the legal challenges have cleared the courts. The entire legislative process often takes years, and what begins as the president's proposed budget may look entirely different when Congress finishes.

This long administrative lag for fiscal policy might suggest a strong preference for monetary policy, which exhibits only an insignificant administrative lag. However, some advocates of fiscal policy suggest that this lag could be finessed if the president were granted discretionary power to raise or lower tax rates within narrow limits—say, 10 percent. Alternatively, the president might be given the discretion to impound funds for certain public works projects to fight inflation or to authorize preselected projects if recession threatens. One major difficulty with this proposal is that Congress and the voters seem loath to give any president this much new power.

Impact Lags

The time it takes for any newly implemented policy to effect the economy is known as the **impact lag.** Our $4-trillion economy can develop a lot of momentum—changing the direction through fiscal and monetary policies might be compared to using a rowboat oar to steer an ocean liner against a strong tide.

Even after legislation is passed, changes in government purchases have long impact lags because it takes time for old government contracts to lapse or for new contracts to be awarded and then begun. However, the major fiscal policy tool for altering consumer spending via the multiplier process is the personal income tax system. Consumers quickly learn about personal tax cuts or increases because their paychecks almost immediately reflect changes in withholdings. People then rapidly translate tax cuts that increase their take-home pay into new cars, video cassette recorders, clothes, or more frequent chocolate chip ice-cream cones. While adjusting to tax increases may be painful, most consumers do so fairly rapidly because they must. The impact lag for fiscal policy may be long for changes in government purchases, but it is comparatively short when tax rates are changed.

In contrast, monetary policy may take a relatively long and variable time before affecting the economy. When expansionary open-market operations are used, excess reserves in banks increase. Bankers may "hoard" these funds during periods when their confidence is down, but the amounts of loanable funds available generally increase and interest rates drop. While consumers may view this as an inducement to buy more durable goods, a decline in interest rates does not generally have nearly as large or immediate an effect on consumer spending as does a healthy cut in tax rates.

Lowered interest rates will boost business investment, but investors may take some time to respond. Changes in productive capacity involve extensive deliberations in the major corporations that do the bulk of investment in our economy. Modern corporate planning is so complex that most investment decisions require heavy commitments of funds years before additional capacity comes on line. This extended investment process is countercyclical in itself since changes in economic activity may have little effect on these decisions in the short run. The impact

TABLE 1 *A Summary of Approximate Lags, Timing of Major Effects, and Uses of Selected Specific Fiscal and Monetary Policies*

Policy	Administrative Lag	Impact Lag	Major Effects: Short-Run Versus Long-Run	Major Use
Fiscal Policies				
Change in taxes	L*	S	LR	Private to public transfers, and vice versa
Change in investment tax credits	L	L	LR	Stimulate investment, capital formation, and economic growth
Change in government purchases	L	L	SR	Countercyclical fiscal policy, pork barrel, etc.
Change in regulations	S	S	LR	Increase regulation to curb abuses and "cutthroat" competition; reduce regulations to improve efficiency in the market
Change in composition of government purchases	L	S	LR	Change the distribution of government spending— guns versus butter
Monetary Policies				
Change in discount rate	S	L	SR	Encourage or discourage borrowing (signals to market)
Change in reserve requirements	S	L	LR	Change the potential money multiplier
Open-market operations	S	L	SR	Week-to-week control of the money supply and interest rates

*The recognition lag is equal for both types of policymaking. The letter L stands for a relatively long lag, while S means that the lag is relatively short. The major effects of policies occur roughly in the short run, SR (1–3 years), or they occur in the long run, LR (over 4 years).

FIGURE 1 The Business Cycle with Poorly Timed Policies

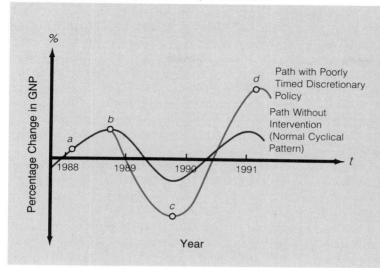

If monetarists are correct, minor fluctuations in economic activity are normal and self-correcting without any discretionary changes in monetary or fiscal policy. Fluctuations may pose problems for proper timing of macroeconomic policy because of lags in: (*a*) recognition, (*b*) administration, and (*c*) impact. It is even possible that self-correction in the economy may begin to occur before all these lags have elapsed.

of monetary expansion on consumption and investment spending is positive, but it may be both slow and erratic. While estimates of the effect of monetary policy on spending place the beginnings of the new spending at as soon as two or three months, the full effects of monetary expansion or contraction appear to take about seven years.

Discretionary monetary policy is like an automatic baseball pitching machine that randomly selects its pitches. The first pitch a batter faces may take five minutes to float over home plate belt high, while the second pitch whistles by low and outside. (If all pitches were identical, batters' problems would be over.) Just as the batter tires of waiting for the third pitch and starts across home plate for the dugout, the ball suddenly arrives.

This analogy suggests that a variable lag is just as dangerous as a long lag. Baseball pitchers vary their speed or placement on purpose to frustrate batters. The variable impact lags of monetary policy are unintentional, but they similarly frustrate discretionary monetary policymaking. Thus, although fiscal policy exhibits a longer administrative lag than monetary policy, this difference may be offset by the shorter and more certain impact lag of revisions in tax rates. Prolonged discussion of the need for "tax reform" or higher tax rates to eliminate ballooning deficits have, according to opponents of discretionary fiscal policy, introduced greater uncertainty for investment decisionmaking. And the long and variable impact lag of

monetary policy is a major shortcoming of discretionary policy in the eyes of proponents of monetary growth rules. Table 1 summarizes lags, effects, and major uses of several specific fiscal policies and the three main monetary policies. The table provides a glimpse of the complexity involved in choosing a policy mix.

Destabilizing Effects of Policy Lags

Critics of discretionary policies contend that recognition, administrative, and, especially, impact lags make it very difficult to actively fine-tune demand-management policies. Suppose that the economy is self-stabilizing but that it does have a natural cyclical pattern as shown in Figure 1. The story of the effect of these lags goes like this. Suppose the economy begins to heat up at the beginning of 1988. Policymakers recognize the emergency of inflationary pressures by the end of the first quarter of 1988 and implement contractionary policies by midyear. The braking effect of the engineered reduction in Aggregate Demand begins just as the economy would have begun to cool down by itself (point *b*). The effect of this seemingly correct policy is to cause a deeper recession than would have occurred normally in the latter half of 1989 (point *c*). Lags lead to a timing problem, making the cycle more severe. The recognition, administrative, and impact lags consume nine months before proper expansionary policy measures to counteract this recession are felt in the economy—again, just as self-correction mechanisms would have brought the economy out of the recession. Mistiming means that expansionary policies are too powerful and that the inflationary pressure of mid-1990 is accelerated (point *d*). And so on.

Figure 1 portrays the worsening of the business cycle by correct, but poorly timed, policies. This example suggests that active countercyclical policy may be self-defeating, actually making the business cycle worse than it would be in the absence of discretionary policy actions. For instance, you can stabilize "waves" in a water bed if you push down on a wave at just the right time and with just the right pressure, but if your timing or pressure is off, you may synchronize with the waves and amplify them substantially. In a similar fashion, mistimed or incorrect policies may cause minor economic fluctuations to become severe.

Overdosing or Undermedicating a Sick Economy

Inflationary and recessionary gaps indicate, respectively, the appropriate decreases or increases in autonomous spending needed to decompress inflationary pressure or to push the economy out of a recession by filling the GNP gap. Unfortunately, these gaps cannot be measured precisely because we never know the precise limits of our productive capacity, nor do we know in advance the exact sizes of autonomous spending or tax multipliers. As we'll see later in Focus 1, monetary policymakers are plagued with similar ignorance about capacity, and the values of either the money multiplier or velocity may vary. (Recall that velocity (V) helps us measure how a stock of money is translated into spending: $V \equiv PQ/M$.) Another problem for monetary authorities is that the growth rates of $M1$, $M2$ and $M3$ may vary substantially. Which of these should policymakers try to control? Of course, this is also a hurdle for establishing a monetary growth rule.

These difficulties make it nearly impossible for monetary and fiscal policymakers to know how much stimulus to inject or withdraw. At times, as with Franklin Roosevelt's first two administrations during the Great Depression (1933–39), discretionary policies may be "too little, too late." In the eyes of critics

who advocate putting the economy on automatic pilot, policymakers more commonly administer too much medicine. Lags in discretionary policies make it very easy to overdose the economy with stimulants so that recessions lead into periods of hyperactivity and inflation. The American economy began to exhibit these symptoms in 1968 under President Johnson. Alternatively, excessive doses of sedatives may cause an overstimulated economy to crash into a deep depression. Opponents of fine-tuning cite the economic nosedives of 1974–75 and 1981–83 as evidence of the harm done by abrupt reductions in monetary growth after extended periods of inflationary growth. In situations where occasional aspirin would cure our economic headaches, the FED may administer uppers and downers in a cyclical fashion. The result is that the economy follows a snakelike stop-go path, with demand-side inflationary cycles causing supply-side cycles, causing demand-side cycles, and so on, as shown in Figure 2.

Financial Insulation to Counter Monetary Policymaking

Some modern Keynesians, most notably Hyman Minsky, also refute the possibility that countercyclical monetary policy can be consistently effective. Their objection is based on a belief that technological changes in financial institutions are induced by *tight money* or *easy money* policies. Here is one example of the way the financial system adjusts to tight money policies and, in the process, reduces the power of the FED's monetary tools.

Suppose monetary authorities attempt to combat inflationary pressures through contractionary policies. Excess reserves throughout the banking system fall, and credit availability throughout the economy is diminished. Especially during periods of high interest rates, the profits of any single bank are enhanced if new ways are found to support more loans with a given total amount of reserves.

In the 1960s, bank officials found that they could conserve on reserves by pooling their excess reserves. If one bank needed funds temporarily to meet its reserve requirements, it would borrow some of the excess reserves of another bank at a lower interest rate than the FED charged at the discount window. The **Federal Funds Market** (the

FIGURE 2 *The Economy's Snakelike Path*

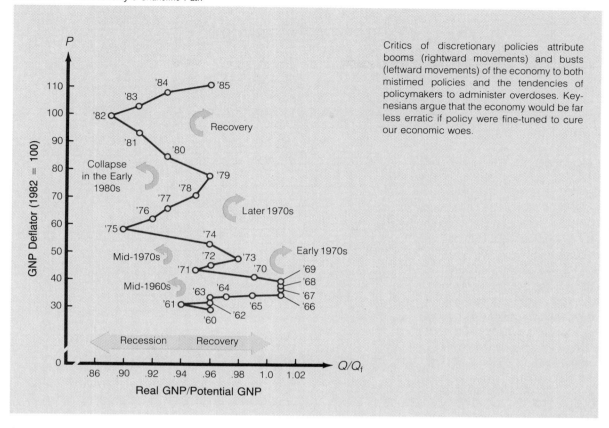

Critics of discretionary policies attribute booms (rightward movements) and busts (leftward movements) of the economy to both mistimed policies and the tendencies of policymakers to administer overdoses. Keynesians argue that the economy would be far less erratic if policy were fine-tuned to cure our economic woes.

Source: *Economic Report of the President,* 1986; Frank deLeeuw and Thomas M. Holloway, "Cyclical Adjustment of the Federal Budget and the Federal Debt," *Survey of Current Business,* December 1983. Updates by authors.

market for excess reserves) that grew out of this pooling effort is now available to bankers across the country. Because of this **financial insulation,** banks can literally lend or borrow millions of dollars for as little as one or two days at comparatively low interest rates.

Banks are not the only institutions that learn ways to shield themselves from tight credit conditions. Other financial intermediaries, major corporations, accountants, and stockbrokers, among others, have developed new techniques for minimizing money balances whenever a credit crunch hits. This is a "creative response" within the financial system. The net result of these discoveries of techniques to dampen the effects of contractionary policy is an increase in both velocity and the money multiplier

and a reduction of the power of the Federal Reserve System. As Focus 1 illustrates, the FED's tools do not work as well when banks take steps to insulate themselves from the effects of FED policies.

Discretionary monetary policy can be compared to a pesticide, with firms being a variety of insects. Just as initial doses of a new pesticide wipe out a lot of bugs, contractionary monetary policies may reduce the availability of credit, causing marginal firms to succumb. And just as the insects that survive repeated administration of the pesticide become immune to it after a few generations, the firms that have learned to adjust to credit crunches become immune to doses of contractionary monetary policies. Moreover, these surviving firms have a profitable advantage: many of their competitors will have collapsed

Money, Prices, and Financial Insulation

Figure 3 illustrates how financial institutions may adjust to counter monetary policy. The growth rates of *M*1 (lagged eight quarters), real GNP, and the GNP deflator are graphed. Both real GNP and the GNP deflator track *M*1 growth during the 1970s. Beginning in 1982, price changes and *M*1 growth uncharacteristically diverged while real GNP continued on track. Most recently, high rates of money growth have not translated into price increases because velocity has fallen. Many factors may account for velocity's decline including financial inventiveness, monetary deregulation, disinflation, and declining interest rates.* One fact stands out: basic departures from past relationships make implementing monetary policy much more difficult.

For a detailed discussion of these issues, see J. A. Cacy, "Recent M1 Growth and Its Implications," Economic Review, Federal Reserve Bank of Kansas City, December 1985, pp. 18– 23.

FIGURE 3 *Growth Rates of* M1 *(Lagged Eight Quarters), GNP Deflator, and Real GNP*

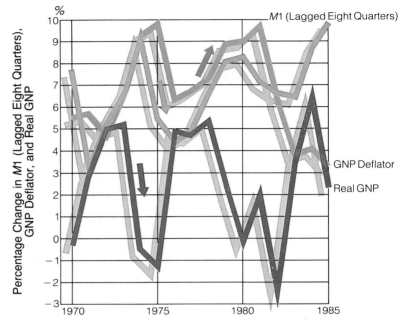

Real GNP and the GNP Deflator generally tracked the rate of growth in *M*1 until the 1980s. During the 1980s, the velocity of money has fallen due to financial inventiveness, monetary deregulation, disinflation, and declining interest rates.

Source: *Economic Report of the President,* 1986.

during periods of tight money. Thus, adjustments by financial institutions to FED policies further limit the power of discretionary policies.

Political Dimensions of Macropolicy

Every recovery is hailed by an incumbent president as the result of his own wise policies, while every recession is condemned by him as the result of the mistaken policies of his predecessor.

—*Gardner Ackley*

We have described how macropolicy should be conducted if policymakers, for all their limitations, were selfless people interested only in the economic welfare of the entire populace. You should never lose sight of the fundamental truth that monetary and fiscal policymakers are first and foremost either politicians or political appointees. The Keynesian and monetarist theories described in the last few chapters suggest that, in the short run, macropolicymakers can use expansionary policies to move us toward a full employment economy. Through contractionary policies, they can combat inflationary pressures. Are these policies affected by political goals? If so, how are they affected?

Are Business Cycles Politically Induced?

Macropolicy has occasionally been compared to alcohol. Alcohol can be medicinal; a little can loosen you up and allow you to have more fun. At least in the short run, expansionary policies stimulate employment, investment, and new sales for business firms. Everything looks rosy. But just as a pleasant buzz is often followed by a hangover, a binge of expansionary policies may be followed by a period of drying out. Unemployment and inflation soar, and business activity slumps.

The theory that political considerations may cause economic instability is reasonably straighforward. Incumbent politicians, worried about reelection, may hope for spillovers into the ballet box from the short-lived preelection upswings that follow tax cuts and a shot of new government spending. If monetary authorities are in cahoots with incumbents, they can help out with a chaser of expansionary monetary policy. Incumbents do well in elections during prosperity and are turned out of office in droves when the economy sours. After the election, inflationary problems emerging from politically motivated expansionary policies can be dealt with by a strong dose of tax increases, cuts in government pork-barrel projects, and monetary restraint. Thus, democracies may be plagued by **political business cycles.** Obviously, politicians who adopt policies to influence voting patterns hope that voters have short memories. Various studies do indicate that the success of incumbents seeking to retain their offices is closely related to how fast disposable income grows during the year immediately preceding elections.

With these strong incentives for politicians to pursue policies leading to boom years just prior to elections and then to slowdowns immediately after the voting, what does the record show? Table 2 shows that between 1952 and 1985, real disposable income in the United States typically grew at higher average rates during election years than during off-election years. The relationships are not perfect, but the growth rate in disposable income was generally highest during the years when there were presidential elections and lowest in the year before elections began.

TABLE 2 *Annual Percentage Change in Real Disposable Personal Income*

President(s)	Election Years	Off-Election Years
Eisenhower (1953–56)	2.7	1.0
Eisenhower (1957–60)	5.9	1.1
Kennedy/Johnson (1961–64)	4.1	4.2
Johnson (1965–68)	3.3	4.9
Nixon (1969–72)	4.1	4.0
Nixon/Ford (1973–76)	3.7	−.08
Carter (1977–80)	2.0	4.4
Reagan (1981–84)	3.1	.08
Reagan (1985–88)	7.3	1.6
Average	4.0	2.4

In Chapter 13, we dealt with the issue of the FED's independence. Recall the FED's contention that it can do a better job if it is independent from political pressures and processes. Figure 4, which relates monetary growth to presidential election years, shows that in the past two decades, monetary growth has generally been higher than average immediately before presidential elections.

The political business cycle is not unique to the United States. Among the more striking foreign examples is the case of Israel. There were six major elections during the period 1952–73. In every instance, the period immediately preceding an Israeli election was more prosperous than the period immediately after the election. After reviewing 1961–72 data for 90 elections in 27 countries, an American political scientist found that for 19 of the 27 countries, "real disposable income accelerated in 77 percent of election years compared with 46 percent of years without election."[1]

In 1943, Michael Kalecki, a Polish economist working in Britain, suggested that after World War II, commercial business cycles caused by business instability would be supplanted by political business cycles in modern democracies. The evidence seems to support his contention that when politicians have a working knowledge of fiscal and monetary tools, they try to use these tools for their own ends.

---

1. E. Tufte, *Political Control of the Economy* (Princeton, N.J.: Princeton University Press, 1978), p. 11.

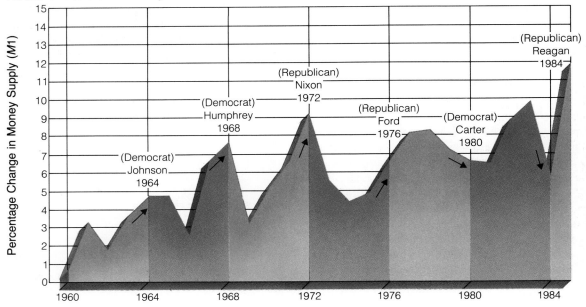

FIGURE 4 *Elections and Monetary Growth*

In the past two decades, monetary growth has generally been higher than average immediately before presidential elections.
Note: The incumbent party and its candidate are shown for election years.

Source: *Economic Report of the President,* 1986.

Has Keynesian Theory Induced Government Growth?

A final criticism of activist countercyclical policies is that as politicians use these tools, the government sector will grow larger relative to the private sector. Opponents of large government have lost most of their battles in the past 50 years; the economic role of government has expanded in most of the world's economies. Some of these critics have identified Keynesian theory as the culprit.

Keynesian fiscal policy originated amid attempts to end a massive worldwide depression associated with inadequate demand during the 1930s. The Keynesian prescription? Spend your way into prosperity; ignore budget deficits and fight unemployment by increasing government spending and cutting taxes. Although largely ignored, the Keynesian cure for inflation is a healthy budgetary surplus. In fact, we sustained more total deficits during the inflationary period from 1970 to 1976 than in the previous 200 years. (The deficits experienced by the Reagan Administration make even these previous record

deficits look trivial.) Many conservative politicians and economists continued into the 1960s to preach the old-time religion of cyclically balanced budgets, but the Keynesian approach gained increasing acceptance from 1936 into the 1970s. Critics of Keynesian policies have argued that government spending inevitably mushrooms once politicians learn that increases in governmentally provided goods and services need not be paid for by politically unpopular tax increases.

The immense deficits of the Reagan Administration produced the Gramm-Rudman Act, an attempt by Congress to force itself to "bite the bullet." Eliminating programs and cutting budgets has proved to be a difficult task for both the administration and Congress. Critics see large deficits, a $2-trillion national debt, Gramm-Rudman, and $1-trillion federal budget as evidence that Keynesian theory promotes the growth of government.

In the post-World War II period, government spending and transfer payments as percentages of GNP have grown substantially in most democratic countries. This growth may be the result of the respectability of Keynesian policies. Until recently, deficits were not viewed with much alarm, even during inflationary periods. To the extent that deficits cause inflation, inflation should be viewed as a hidden tax. However, if poorly informed voters blame government-generated inflation on unions or businesses, then politicians are encouraged to hand out "free lunches"—popular new government programs without unpopular tax increases. Many voters are very aware of the direct benefits of deficit-financed special-interest spending, but fail to recognize the inflation indirectly caused by such deficits.

During depressions, the deficits caused by higher government spending and lower taxes have beneficial effects—output and employment grow. But government grows as well. During inflationary periods, few government programs are cut, and proposals to raise taxes are political suicide. Few politicians are willing to be accused of "raising the price of government" by raising tax rates. The net result is that government grows during economic downturns but does not decline during inflationary periods, as proper fiscal policy would dictate. According to the critics of Keynesian policies, this occurs because the inflationary effects of high and rising government spending are disguised.

In summary, macroeconomic policies may be misused by politicians who cut taxes and increase government spending: (*a*) shortly before elections, anticipating a short-lived prosperity that will aid them in reelection; and (*b*) during economic slumps, without offsetting increases in taxes or cuts in government spending during prosperity or inflation. The former leads to political business cycles; the latter, to expansion of the government and declining reliance on the private acts of individual households and firms.

New Classical Macroeconomics___

You can fool some of the people all of the time, and all of the people some of the time, but you can't fool all of the people all of the time.
— *Abe Lincoln*

You can fool some of the people all of the time, and all of the people some of the time, and them's pretty good odds.
— *Motto of Brett Maverick, a Gambler/Con Man Played by James Garner in the TV Western "Maverick"*

The strongest of recent challenges to discretionary demand-management policies has been issued by economists who question whether either monetary or fiscal policies will work consistently, if at all. Much of their pessimism about active policy is based on assumptions drawn from classical theories about the operations of competitive markets and, thus, this analysis has become known as the **new classical macroeconomics.**

Competitive Markets

The theory of competitive markets is predicated on a number of assumptions. The most important of these for analyzing macroeconomic policy are:

1. All economic behavior is based on perfect information among market participants.
2. Transportation costs are zero, so all goods and resources can be moved freely and instantaneously between markets.
3. Buyers try to maximize their satisfactions; sellers, their profits; and workers, their net well-being.
4. All prices are perfectly flexible.

A logical consequence of these assumptions is that any profitmaking opportunities or opportunities for workers and consumers to increase their welfare will be exploited instantly. Thus, the economy will operate efficiently at all times.

The problem posed for demand-management policymaking is that fiscal and monetary policies based on Keynesian analysis only work if the economy is inefficiently operating inside its production-possibilities frontier. If the economy is efficient and at its capacity, then there can be no quantity adjustments to policy (changes in output and employment), only price adjustments (inflation or deflation). Equally critical is the fact that fiscal and monetary policies will have different effects in the short run than in the long run only if people are ignorant either about policies' thrusts or their long-run effects. We discussed in the previous section how expansionary or contractionary policies might have different effects in the short run than in the long run. Let us see why perfectly efficient competitive markets might cause long-run adjustments to occur instantly when demand-management policies are used.

Efficient Markets

Efficient markets theories suggest that discretionary policymakers try to fool people in the fashion of riverboat gamblers, but these policies do not work because Lincoln was a better observer of human nature than was the scriptwriter who contributed Maverick's famous line. In fact, these modern classically oriented theorists go beyond Lincoln, asserting that you can't fool all of the people *any* of the time.

Markets will operate efficiently if substantial information about profitable opportunities is widely available. The **efficient markets** theory is based on the idea that there are sufficient numbers of people in this world to ensure vigorous competition for any ideas or information that might prove profitable. Competition causes any predictable abnormal gain from an investment to be exploited almost instantly. Profits that might reasonably be expected from some activity will draw alert profit seekers like garbage trucks draw flies. Thus, easily anticipated economic profits will evaporate because of competition. When an attractive investment becomes public knowledge, the cost of investing will be bid up so that only normal returns can be realized. Only above normal profits that reasonable people would not anticipate remain as possibilities. Thus, extraordinarily high returns from an investment are largely a matter of luck.

Rational Expectations

A close relative of efficient markets theory is the theory of rational expectations. If people's expectations are formed rationally, they will learn to identify the variables that shape the circumstances affecting their lives. Thus, the theory of **rational expectations** suggests that after policymakers pursue either expansionary or contractionary policies a few times, people learn how to predict both the effects of changes in policies and the policies themselves. Consumers and investors then will behave in ways that prevent predictable policies from having the desired results. Accordingly, adherents of the rational expectations approach believe that policy goals cannot be achieved, even in the short run, unless the effects of demand-management policies come as complete surprises to the public. Rational expectations theorists believe that predictable policies cannot consistently fool the public. This is a modern extension of the idea that inflation illusion is never permanent.

Natural rate theory (discussed in previous chapters) is an important cornerstone for rational expectations theory. The concepts of natural rates of interest and unemployment are starting points in exploring the view that demand-management policy is impotent even in the short run.

Consider Figure 5. Suppose that a heavy short-run dose of expansionary monetary policy shifts Aggregate Demand from AD_0 to AD_1, causing prices and real output to rise to P_1 and Q_1, respectively (point *b*). This drives down unemployment rates and both nominal and real interest rates. When people eventually begin to anticipate inflation, then output, unemployment, and the real rate of interest return to their original values, while prices and nominal interest rates increase (point *c*). After this cycle occurs once or twice, most people learn to anticipate it and try to turn this ability to "predict the future" to their advantage.

Suppose that you are one of those who have observed this cycle and begin following the FED's policies closely. If increases in the prices of bonds and declines in interest rates invariably follow expansionary monetary policies within a few weeks, then you should make some money if you buy bonds the instant that monetary expansion begins. Since you will be holding bonds when interest rates fall, the increase in bond prices should profit you immensely. (Recall the inverse relationship between bond prices and interest rates.) As you and other "money watchers" try to put this strategy into practice, the demand for bonds, and hence, their prices, would begin to rise just as soon as expansionary monetary policies are adopted. The short-run lag between expansionary policies and the declining interest rate will collapse to zero—the adjustment becomes instantaneous. In Figure 5, as individuals anticipate the effects of policy, the economy will move directly from point *a* to point *c* and aggregate employment will not change.

This is not, however, the end of the story. In the long run, nominal interest rates presumably rise to reflect inflationary expectations. Therefore, you and all the other people who watch the FED's actions will want to sell all your bonds before interest rates increase. Because the short run is now extremely short, the time to sell bonds is the instant you discern an expansionary policy. Since you will only be one

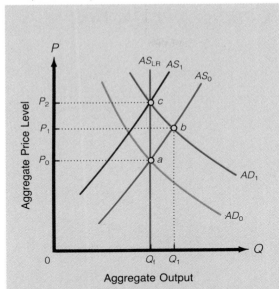

Expansionary monetary or fiscal policy shifts the Aggregate Demand curve from AD_0 to AD_1. As both output and the price level rise, people begin to anticipate inflation and take steps to counter the effects of inflation and federal policymaking. Simple natural rate theory would predict a path for the economy of $a \longrightarrow b \longrightarrow c$, while rational expectation theorists would expect the economy to move directly from $a \longrightarrow c$ as individuals instantly take countermeasures to expansionary policies.

among many unloading bonds when the money supply increases, the almost immediate result of an expansionary monetary policy will be to drive bond prices down and interest rates up in anticipation of inflation. But the story goes on.

If you expect inflation, you (and just about everyone else who is paying attention) will want to spend your money on goods and services while they are still cheap. (Remember, *buy low.*) If you manage a firm, you will immediately raise prices when monetary expansion begins; higher prices might help you build inventories that will be worth more money if you just wait a bit before you sell. Thus, inflationary policies will cause almost immediate increases in nominal demands for goods and reductions in their nominal supplies.

If you are unemployed, your inflationary expectations will adjust quickly to expansionary policies, and

you will be unwilling to accept a job at lower real wages. Therefore, unemployment will not fall below the natural rate as a consequence of expansionary policy. The end of this rational expectations story is that unless the government disguises its policies, an expansionary policy will almost instantly drive up the price level and nominal interest rates, with little or no effect on employment and output. A reversal of this story can be told for contractionary policies (see Focus 2).

Note that one essential difference between the simple natural rate theory and rational expectations theory is the speed with which accurate expectations are assumed to be realized. Simple natural rate analysis would predict a path like $a \rightarrow b \rightarrow c$ in Figure 5, while rational expectationists would expect a direct movement from point a to point c, with no temporary increases in output and employment.

Limitations of Rational Expectations Theory

Just how realistic is rational expectations theory? You and most of the population may ignore monetary and fiscal policies. However, there are a number of economic institutions that devote considerable resources to studying government policies in the hopes of predicting future economic activity so that they can get the jump on their competition or buffer themselves from hardship. Examples include banks, major corporations, unions, trade groups, and foreign governments. These groups do have substantial resources that can be shifted rapidly whenever the direction of policy appears likely to change. For example, price hikes are common adjustments whenever the imposition of wage and price controls seems imminent.

Other factors, however, may limit the potential impact of rational expectations adjustments. First, rational expectations analysis assumes that people are able to accurately forecast government policymaking when often it seems the government is unable to do this itself. Information about government policies is unavoidably expensive and imprecise. As a result, many people remain "rationally ignorant." Critics contend that, in the short run at least, government policy may push employment, prices, and interest rates away from their natural levels.

Rational Expectations and Hyperinflation

Several major economies have suffered bouts of hyperinflation—inflation of at least 50 percent per month. When this occurs, the monetary system generally collapses and barter takes over. Most contemporary analyses of inflationary spirals suggest that bringing inflation under control requires protracted high unemployment; presumably, the higher the rate of inflation, the more severe the adjustment process. Surprisingly, most hyperinflations have been brought under control with a minimum of increased unemployment and have occurred virtually overnight.

Figure 6 provides inflation data for major hyperinflations in Austria, Hungary, Poland, and Germany right after World War I. For each country, the abruptness of the halt in inflation was as spectacular as the rise itself. How did policymakers in these economies

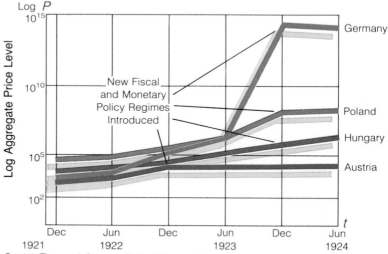

FIGURE 6 *The Ends of Four Major Hyperinflations*

Source: Thomas J. Sargent, *Rational Expectations and Inflation* (New York: Harper & Row, Publishers), 1986.

gain control of their monetary systems to end hyperinflation? The answer lies in examining the events preceding the hyperinflations and the actions taken that ended them. Paul Samuelson's observation (above) provides a clue to the

solution, but first let's examine the causes.

In commenting on inflationary finance, John Maynard Keynes noted:

It is common to speak as though, when a government pays its way by

Second, public policy may alter the composition of output. For example, the Reagan Administration increased defense spending in the 1980s, changing the composition of aggregate output. Similarly, expansionary monetary policy may reduce interest rates in the short run, resulting in rising investment which may alter the long-run production possibilities for the economy.

Finally, rational expectations theory presumes that wages and prices are perfectly flexible and adjust

instantaneously to market forces. Unions, long-term contracts, civil service rules, and other obstacles all keep wages and prices from adjusting immediately to changes in Aggregate Demand and Supply. The plans of private investors and households are subject to recognition, administrative, and impact lags much like those faced by public policymakers. For these reasons, critics of the new classical macroeconomics believe that short-run changes in the economy can be directed by appropriate policies.

*inflation, the people of the country avoid taxation. We have seen this is not so. What is raised by printing notes is just as much taken from the public as is beer-duty or an income-tax. What a government spends the public pays for. There is no such thing as an uncovered deficit. But in some countries it seems possible to please and content the public, for a time at least, by giving them, in return for the taxes they pay, finely engraved acknowledgments on water-marked paper. The income tax receipts, which we in England receive from the surveyor, we throw into the wastepaper basket; in Germany they call them bank-notes and put them into their pocketbooks; in France they are termed Rentes and are locked up in the family safe.**

After World War I, Austria, Germany, Hungary, and Poland all faced severe economic hardships and financed massive budget deficits by printing fiat money. In addition, all except Poland owed sizable war reparations. Their currencies depreciated at alarming rates

and inflation had a momentum that appeared unstoppable. However, in Thomas Sargent's view, ". . . inflation only *seems* to have a momentum of its own; it is actually the long-term government policy of persistently running large deficits and creating money at high rates that imparts the momentum to the inflation rate."**

One rational expectations perspective is that stopping inflation, especially hyperinflation, would require more than just temporary adjustments in monetary and fiscal policy. It would necessitate an alteration in the entire policy *regime*. Deficits and their financing must be altered in a *credible* way so that the public *believes* that the government is committed to eliminating the policy abuses that caused hyperinflation. These were essentially the measures that ended hyperinflation in all four countries.

First, all four countries created independent central banks and legally restrained them from issuing unsecured credit. Second, each country drastically altered its fiscal policy regime. All four governments committed to relatively

small deficits or balanced budgets and agreed to cover its debt strictly through bond financing. Finally, each country negotiated reduced or certain war reparations. Thus, by altering the "rules of the game", these governments literally stopped hyperinflation in its tracks.

A similar experience occurred recently in Argentina. Throughout the 1970s and early 1980s, inflation in Argentina rose until it exceeded 500 percent per year. In 1985, a new government instituted austerity measures, a new currency, and the will to stop hyperinflation. By early 1986, relative normalcy had returned to Argentina and it appears that policies that worked after World War I in Europe continue to work today.

---

*John Maynard Keynes, Monetary Reform *(New York: Harcourt Brace Jovanovich), 1924, pp. 68–69.*

**Thomas J. Sargent, Rational Expectations and Inflation, *(New York: Harper & Row, Publishers), 1986. This book has an excellent discussion of the ends of these four hyperinflations and examines the process of ending several modern inflationary spirals.*

A Brief Evaluation of Policy Rules Versus Discretion

This chapter focused on the shortcomings of discretionary policy. Advocates of stable macroeconomic policy rules continue to mount powerful and often persuasive arguments that discretionary policies do not work as intended. However, their assertions are at times contradictory. Can discretionary policies be perverse because of inefficiencies caused by lags,

incorrect doses, improper targets, or venal politicians, and simultaneously impotent because markets operate efficiently or because of rational expectations? In combination, these arguments are logically inconsistent.

Advocates of discretionary policies also offer persuasive arguments, many of which were presented in Chapters 9–15. At times, discretionary policies have performed as advertised. The economic boom following the 1964 tax cut is only one example of suc-

TABLE 3 *A Summary of Theories about Demand-Management Policies*

	Critical Assumptions	Discretionary Monetary Policy	Discretionary Fiscal Policy	Monetary Growth Rules
Classical (old-style pre-Keynesian)	Flexible wages, prices, and interest rates ensure full employment. *Supply creates its own demand.*	Only the price level is affected, and then in precise proportion to the money supply.	Irrelevant except to the extent that the size of government relative to the private sector is changed.	Might prevent price level declines in a growing economy, but largely irrelevant. Money is a veil, not affecting real variables.
Keynesian	Wages and prices are downwardly sticky but upwardly flexible. Interest rates will not fall below the level of interest of the liquidity trap. *Demand creates its own supply.*	Ineffectual in a liquidity trap. Only influences Aggregate Demand through any decreases in interest rates causing increases in autonomous investment, which expands demand through the multiplier process.	Immediately increases Aggregate Demand via the multiplier process.	Irrelevant except to the extent that the interest rate is affected, and hence investment and Aggregate Demand are also affected.
Post-Keynesian monetarists	Keynesian analysis may be correct for the very short run in its Aggregate Demand orientation, but classical assumptions are correct for the long run. Velocity and the demand for money are stable.	Nominal GNP will be proportional to the money supply. Discretionary policy causes business cycles. The Depression was a consequence of contractionary policies; inflation is the result of overly expansionary policies.	Affects the size of government relative to the private sector and may pose problems because of political pressures to print money to cover government deficits. Otherwise, irrelevant for macroeconomics, although crowding out may be a severe problem if government spending grows. Modern supply siders also argue that potential GNP is shrunk because of disincentives when tax rates are high.	Permits the private sector to anticipate policy and facilitates noninflationary growth without raising the possibility of contractionary policies causing severe recessions.
Natural rate theory	There are "natural" rates of frictional unemployment and natural real rates of interest. Differences between natural rates and actual rates occur only when people inaccurately forecast changes in price levels.	Unemployment and real interest rates will decline below their natural rates only if people are fooled by overly expansionary policies. This can happen only in the short run; in the long run, everyone catches on.		A monetary growth rule will eliminate swings in real output because of changes in policies. Prices will rise only slightly if economic growth falls below monetary growth, and prices will fall if economic growth exceeds monetary growth.
New classical macroeconomics	Markets are efficient. Rational expectations theory suggests that inflationary expectations will reflect predictable changes in policies quickly.	People will not be fooled by predictable policies, even in the short run, so expansionary policies will be immediately translated into higher prices and higher nominal interest rates.		

cessful discretionary policy. On the other hand, the abysmal policy failures during the 1970s are testimony to the folly of fighting supply-side disturbances with demand-management techniques.

Whether discretionary policies or rules work better depends in part on the circumstances and on the people who control policies. However, the central questions remain: (*a*) Is the economy inherently stable, or is the market system unstable? (*b*) Can changes in spending, taxes, and monetary policies lend greater stability to a market economy, or are erratic government policies major sources of business cycles and instability? These questions cannot be answered definitively at this point.

Just as generals are sometimes accused of always fighting the last war, economic policymakers in the 1970s used the demand-management tools that were developed to solve the demand-side problems of earlier decades. Table 3 encapsulates the various theories about demand-management policies and should help in organizing your thoughts about these issues.

The wave of supply-side problems that have plagued the world economy for the past two decades requires development of policy tools that address the supply side. The next chapter focuses on some aspects of the supply side that enhance economic growth and development.

CHAPTER REVIEW: KEY POINTS

1. Macroeconomic policymaking is at least as much art as it is a science. A multitude of problems preclude perfect analysis and policy.

2. A *recognition lag* occurs because it takes time to get even a modestly accurate picture of changes in the state of the economy. An *administrative* (implementation) *lag* exists because it takes a while to get the tax and monetary machinery in gear even when policymakers' plans are made. An *impact lag* confounds the proper timing of policy; the economy budges only stubbornly to the prods of the policymakers' tools. These lags, which may be long and variable, may cause discretionary policy to be more destabilizing than stabilizing.

3. Lack of precise knowledge about recessionary gaps, inflationary gaps, and GNP gaps, as well as uncertainty about multipliers and velocity, means that estimating the correct doses of monetary and fiscal medicine is extremely difficult.

4. Some modern Keynesians challenge the long-term effectiveness of monetary policy, arguing that adjustments in financial technologies will ultimately *insulate financial institutions* and make monetary tools inoperative.

5. Incumbents' prospects for return to office improve as per capita disposable income grows immediately prior to elections. There is some evidence that policymakers try to manipulate Aggregate Demand to enhance their positions in the eyes of voters, which induces *political business cycles*.

6. Some critics of Keynesian fiscal policies also suggest that the government grows relative to the private sector when policymakers increase spending and cut taxes during downturns. Policymakers neither cut spending nor restore taxes, however, during periods of prosperity or inflation.

7. The model of perfect competition, or *efficient markets*, suggests that even in the short run, macropolicy only works when the economy is operating inefficiently and that this does not occur.

8. The theory of *rational expectations* suggests that people eventually figure out how a given change in policy affects the economy and learn to predict how policymakers react to swings in economic activity. Thereafter, people will focus on what policymakers are doing and make adjustments that prevent the policies from accomplishing their objectives.

QUESTIONS FOR THOUGHT AND DISCUSSION

1. Suppose a rule of 3 percent annual monetary growth were imposed. How long should policymakers doggedly follow such a policy if inflation soared to more than 20 percent or unemployment hovered around 15 percent?

2. Evaluate the proposal of granting the president discretionary power to raise or lower taxes 10 percent in order to overcome the administration lag that plagues fiscal policy. If there are substantial differences between this proposal and the power the FED now has over the money supply, what are they? If such a presidential power were enacted, would the president or the FED have more discretionary power to control economic activity? Why?

3. If you were the president and were intent on having "four more years," what actions would you take to ensure a booming economic climate around election time? What might be the longer term consequences of your policies?

4. Some economists argue that the Smoot-Hawley Tariffs enacted in 1930 were a major cause of the collapse in the stock market and the resulting Great Depression. Rational expectations analysis suggests that the impact of future events will be rapidly capitalized into stock prices. One political sage recently suggested that the Gramm-Rudman Act pointed to a new fiscal policy regime, accounting for the stock market's record performance in 1985–86. What argument could you make that passage of Gramm-Rudman would be beneficial for the stock market? Are there other factors that might account for the stock market's sustained rise in 1985–86?

5. Interest rates skyrocketed in late 1979, with the prime rate exceeding 20 percent, but they then plummeted even more rapidly than they had risen. Interest rates then soared again in 1981 but dropped afterward. From today's perspective, which parts of these violent fluctuations represented the Keynes effect and which parts the Fisher effect? (See Optional Material.)

OPTIONAL MATERIAL: A NATURAL RATE EXPLANATION FOR UNEMPLOYMENT AND INTEREST RATE MOVEMENTS OVER AN INFLATIONARY CYCLE

In this section, we follow interest rates and unemployment through a typical demand-side inflationary episode. By tracing through this rather intricate example, you should gain considerable insight into the nature of a business cycle that occurs because of overly expansionary policies.

Suppose that the natural real rate of interest is 6 percent, that the natural rate of unemployment is 5 percent, and that stable prices have been experienced for quite some time. What will happen if policymakers are unhappy with this situation and pursue policies that cause Aggregate Demand to grow 4 percent faster than Aggregate Supply? In the next page

or two, we will graphically trace short-run and long-run adjustments to this expansionary policy.

Figure 7 shows that the values of both the nominal and real interest rates equal 6 percent during the initial period (Time 0 to Time 1). Nominal and real interest rates are equal because there is no inflation and none is expected. The unemployment rate is 5 percent because of the frictional, seasonal, and structural forces at work. At Time 1, suppose that the money supply begins to grow 4 percent faster than potential real output. Between Times 1 and 2, the supply of loanable funds increases and the nominal interest rate declines, say, from 6 to 4 percent because of the

FIGURE 7 *The Initial Effects of Overly Expansive Policies on Inflation, Unemployment, and Interest*

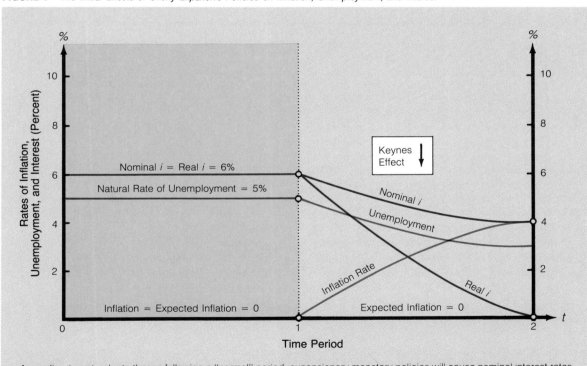

According to *natural rate theory,* following a "normal" period, expansionary monetary policies will cause nominal interest rates to fall because of the Keynes effect, the unemployment rate to fall because workers suffer from inflation illusion, and the real rate of interest to fall even faster than the nominal rate because inflation is not anticipated.

FIGURE 8 *Intermediate Effects of Overly Expansionary Policies on Inflation, Unemployment, and Interest*

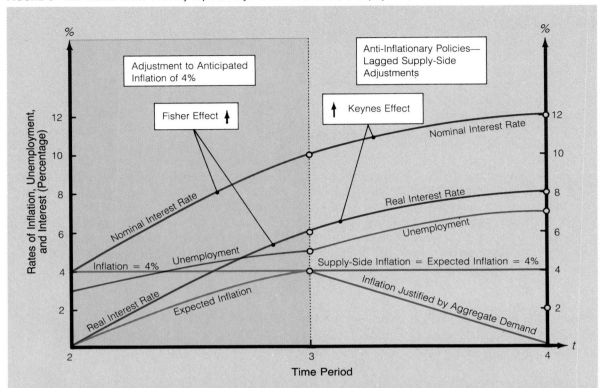

The Fisher effect causes both nominal and real interest rates to rise as borrowers and lenders learn to expect inflation; as workers adjust to inflation of 4 percent, unemployment also rises. If government then follows deflationary policies, the Keynes effect causes both nominal and real interest rates to rise because both borrowers and lenders expect more inflation than will occur. Similarly, unemployment will climb because workers will insist on pay increases that overcompensate for inflation.

Keynes effect. Simultaneously, spending and employment increase, and unemployment declines, say, from 5 to 3 percent. However, this excessive rate of monetary growth causes the price level to rise 4 percent; so real wages fall and real interest rates dip to zero percent.

Eventually people become accustomed to this overly expansionary policy. The paths of interest and unemployment rates as lenders, borrowers, and workers adjust to 4 percent inflation are shown on Figure 8 between Times 2 and 3. Unemployment rates rise to the "natural" 5 percent rate, the Fisher effect kicks the nominal interest rate up to 10 per-

cent, and the real interest rate climbs back to the "natural" 6 percent rate.

Suppose (naively?) that policymakers have quickly learned their lesson and decide to fight inflation. Beginning at Time 3, the rate of monetary expansion is reduced to the same rate as real growth of potential output. Unfortunately, this disinflation is contractionary because of people's inflationary expectations. In Chapter 17, we described the lagged supply adjustment phase of demand-side inflationary cycles. This phase kicks in during the period between Times 3 and 4, and prices continue to rise at 4 percent annually. This will be a period of stagflation because the

FIGURE 9 *Final Decompression from Overly Expansionary Policies*

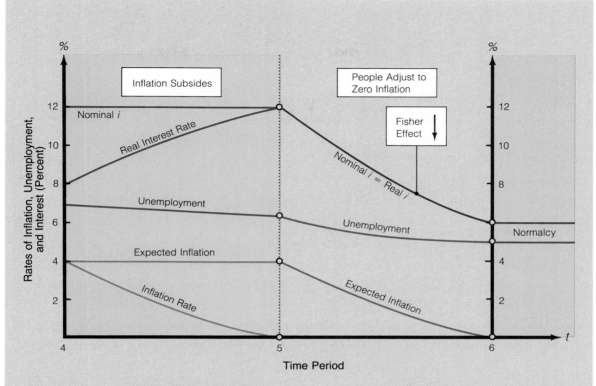

As inflation subsides, nominal interest rates initially remain high, while real interest rates climb. Then, as expectations of inflation gradually decline, the rate of unemployment slowly gravitates back to its natural rate, and the Fisher effect causes both nominal and real interest rates to fall to the natural rate.

reduced growth of spending will cause unemployment to exceed its natural rate, rising to, say, 7 percent. The Keynes effect of the *contractionary* policy will cause the nominal interest rate to jump to, say, 12 percent, while the real rate climbs to above normal at 8 percent.

Figure 9 portrays adjustments as inflation finally subsides during the period from Time 4 to Time 5. Unemployment rates begin to trickle back toward the natural rate, but the real rate of interest skyrockets to 12 percent. Neither lenders nor borrowers anticipated the abatement of inflation; thus, the nominal

rate continues at 12 percent ($r = i - P = 12$ percent $- 0$ percent $= 12$ percent). During the period from Time 5 to Time 6, people adjust to zero inflation, so the unemployment rate settles toward 5 percent and the Fisher effect causes drops in both nominal and real interest rates to 6 percent. Finally, at Time 6, all adjustments to expansionary and contractionary policies are complete, and the economy has stabilized to the natural state that existed before policymakers started tinkering. The various effects of this complete inflationary episode are summarized in Figure 10.

FIGURE 10 *Keynes and Fisher Effects (The Complete Cycle)*

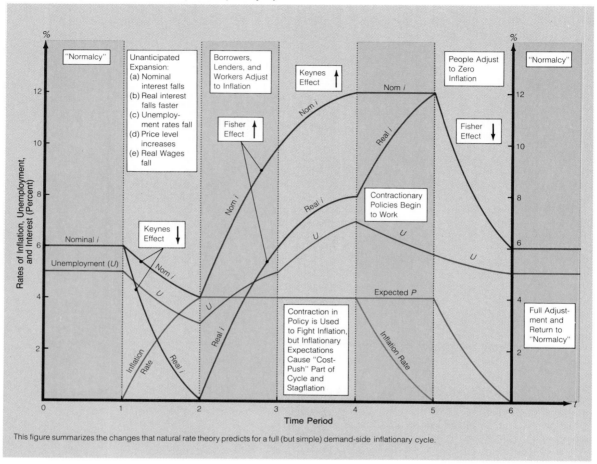

This figure summarizes the changes that natural rate theory predicts for a full (but simple) demand-side inflationary cycle.

CHAPTER 19 Economic Growth and Development

economic growth	population S curves	capital deepening
economic	capital accumulation	technological change
development	capital widening	trap of
Rule of 72		underdevelopment

Most Americans expect a higher standard of living than their parents or grandparents enjoyed. For almost two centuries, such progress has been common throughout much of the world. However, before the industrial revolution, each generation lived very much as had their immediate ancestors. Identifying the changes in the human condition that make rapid growth and development possible has been a challenge that has occupied economists and social philosophers for centuries.

One central macroeconomic goal is a healthy rate of economic growth. People in the United States have a stake in more vigorous international economic growth because growth is a mutually reinforcing process that links our economic fate with that of people in many countries. For example, when the United States recovers from a recession, the world economy often rebounds. Similarly, sluggish foreign economies can retard growth in our economy because of weak demands for our exports.

From the end of World War II into the 1960s, communist countries and countries that rely primarily on the market system competed intensely to see which would grow faster. Former Premier Khrushchev's oft-quoted prediction, "We will bury you,"

referred as much to economic rivalry between the United States and Soviet Union as to anything else. During this early episode of the Cold War, economic growth (at least our own) was regarded unambiguously as a good thing. More recently, mounting concern over the environment and recognition that the world's resources are finite have produced the Zero Population Growth (ZPG) and Zero Economic Growth (ZEG) movements. The most crucial questions seem to be "Why economic growth?" or "Economic growth for what?"

Economic Growth

Most of us applaud economic development that enriches the quality of our lives, but is all economic growth necessarily good? If a population explosion increased the size of the work force and caused growth in our GNP, it might simultaneously reduce our average standard of living. Do we want maximum income? Maximum income per capita? And what about pollution and other economic bads that often accompany economic growth?

Growth and the Rule of 72

Many people are bewildered by all the hoopla generated over whether the economy grows at rates of 2 percent, 3 percent, 4 percent, or whatever the small number happens to be. American policymakers and economists concern themselves with these small numbers because each 1 percent of growth represents extra production of more than $40-billion worth of 1986 output— hardly small change. Because continuous growth is compounded over the years, a 1 percent difference in the annual growth rate would mean a total difference of approximately $400 billion in production between 1987 and 1995.

Growth is a cumulative process analogous to compound interest. If you are paid 10 percent interest on $100 compounded annually, then at the end of the first year your $100 stake is worth $110. At the end of two years you have interest on both the principal plus the accumulated interest, so your original $100 is now $121: [1.10 × ($100 + $10) = $121]. And so on. Compounding calculations can be simplified by using the Rule of 72.

The **Rule of 72:** *A "rule of thumb" for the time required for any variable to double is calculated by dividing its percentage rate of growth into 72.*

The rule works because of the compounding characteristic of growth or decline. Thus, if the annual interest rate is 10 percent, financial investments will double in about 7.2 years, not 10 years. A country's population will double in 36 years if population growth is 2 percent annually, but it will require only 18 years to double at a 4 percent annual rate of increase.

Connections Between Growth and Development

What are the relationships between economic growth and economic development? As people emerge from the shelter of the womb and proceed through infancy, childhood, adolescence, and into adulthood, they grow in size. But there are both quantitative and qualitative differences between infants and adults. In a similar vein, as economies grow, it is important to ask if they are also maturing.

Growth refers to quantitative change. **Economic growth** occurs when more goods become available for consumption and investment. **Economic development** occurs over time when there are improvements in the quality of life, in the quality of goods available, or in the ways production is organized and carried out. Thus, economic growth has only a *quantitative* dimension, while economic development refers to the *qualitative* advances occurring in any economy. Both are needed to describe economic progress. Focus 1 discusses the Rule of 72, which is a handy technique for calculating economic growth and several other quantitative variables.

Aggregate Demand, Aggregate Supply, and Economic Growth

What causes increases in potential Gross National Product? Before we confront the problem of growth in real per capita income or GNP, we need to explore the circumstances and events that cause potential real income itself to grow. The macroeconomic theory covered in Chapters 9–18 suggests that increases in Aggregate Demand during economic slumps can boost GNP toward full employment levels of output. While management of Aggregate Demand through monetary and fiscal policies may cause GNP to increase, this is not what we mean here by economic growth. Management of Aggregate Demand is basically a short-term concept. Varying Aggregate Demand is similar to administering food and medicine to a malnourished child.

The area of economic growth and development focuses on increasing potential real GNP. Because this is a long-run concept, we need not be concerned with demand but with expanding the limits of Aggregate Supply. Just as the malnourished child whom we have fed and medicated may remain developmentally impaired, so, too, proper Aggregate Demand policies do not ensure that a disabled economy will exhibit healthy economic growth. For the purposes of this chapter, we will assume that monetary and fiscal policies are used to ensure that Aggregate Demand is adequate to accommodate economic growth, which is defined as any increases in productive capacity.

Potential Aggregate Supply depends on the state of technology and the qualities and quantities of resources available for productive activities during some time period. We know that not all labor is identical. The same is true of other resource categories: land, capital, and entrepreneurship.

How does growth in potential real GNP occur? Potential output rises through technological advances, increases in the amounts of land available, new discoveries of resources, capital accumulation, or through increases in the size or quality of the labor force. Although the land available to a given populace might be expanded by space exploration or imperialism, these strategies are so risky and expensive that, in the long run, they are more likely to fail than to succeed. However, growth may be stimulated by a more efficient use of existing land or land reclamation. New discoveries of resources are so sporadic that we cannot rely on them. This reduces the feasible sources of economic growth to: (*a*) increases in population and the labor force, (*b*) capital accumulation, or (*c*) technological advances. Let us examine aspects of each of these sources of growth.

Population and Labor Force Changes

Increased population per se may not result in economic growth. More people mean nothing for production unless the labor force grows, and the labor force drawn from a given population can either grow or decline. We will treat this relationship first and then describe the interactions between population and national income.

Population and the Work Force   Population growth expands the size of the potential work force. All else being equal, if the work force increases proportionally as population grows, per capita GNP will decline. Why? Additional labor reduces the capital and land per worker, so labor productivity and per capita GNP will decline. This is one more example of the law of diminishing returns rearing its ugly head.

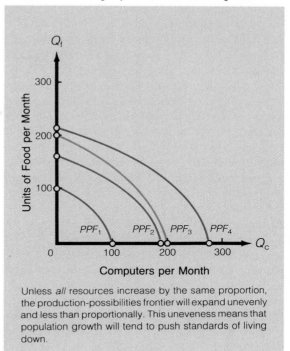

FIGURE 1   *Increasing Population and Diminishing Returns*

Unless *all* resources increase by the same proportion, the production-possibilities frontier will expand unevenly and less than proportionally. This unevenness means that population growth will tend to push standards of living down.

Consider Figure 1. Suppose that with 100 workers, 100 machines, and 1,000 acres of land we can produce 100 computers, 100 units of food, or any of the combinations on the production-possibilities frontier labeled PPF_1. We are assuming that the use of labor is relatively more intensive in computer production, while capital and land are most intensively used in the production of food. If all these resources were exactly doubled, we would expect potential output to double. Feasible outputs are shown as the combinations along the PPF_3, which is a radial expansion of (that is, it approximately parallels) PPF_1. Now suppose we held capital at 100 machines, land at 1,000 acres, and doubled labor alone to 200 workers. The production-possibilities frontier expands from PPF_1 to PPF_2; maximum food production only expands to 160 units and only 190 computers can be produced. The PPF does not expand to PPF_3 as labor doubled because we have not doubled land and capital inputs. Similarly, if labor were quadrupled to 400 units, diminishing returns would prevent the potential outputs of computers or food from also quadrupling. As we have constructed PPF_4 for 400 workers, 100 machines, and 1,000 acres of land, maximums of only 205 units of food or 275 computers can be produced per month.

In such a densely populated country as India, it is possible that the need for extra roads, schools, and housing would mean that per capita standards of living would fall even if the labor force grew at much faster rates than the population. However, in all but the most heavily populated countries, additional workers do add something to total production, so per capita GNP normally will rise when the ratio of the work force to a given population increases.

The labor force as a percentage of the population is known as the **labor force participation rate.** Labor force participation rates are also calculated for such subpopulations as working women between the ages of 25 and 35 as a percentage of all women between those ages. Just what determines labor force participation rates? Certainly social customs and mores play a role. For example, the "Protestant work ethic" and the resulting expectations about men's roles are probably responsible for the fact that roughly 80 percent of all American males between the ages of 25 and 55 are in the work force. Wage rates are also clearly important. High wage rates raise the cost of not working and encourage labor force participation.

Another important determinant of the work force relative to population is the rate of population growth. Variations in population growth rates may cause a society to have high proportions of young dependent members during one decade and large numbers of old dependent members five or six decades later. Of course, this is only one of many possibilities.

Suppose that birth rates have been declining for some time. Labor force participation rates will first rise as the number of children in the population falls and more women are free to enter the labor force if custom permits. Then the work force will gradually decline relative to population as smaller numbers of young people enter the work force and the number of retirements rises relative to population. Finally, labor force participation will stabilize. Can you outline some of the short- and long-term economic effects of the post-World War II "baby boom"? Couple the high birth rates of the late 1940s and 1950s with the recent declines in birth rates and the gradually lengthening life span in the United States. What will happen to the number of dependents per worker over time? What are the implications for our

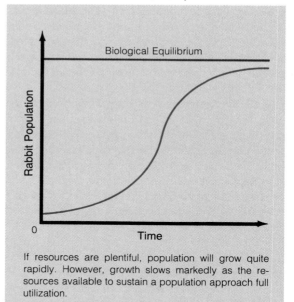

FIGURE 2 An S Curve for a Rabbit Population

If resources are plentiful, population will grow quite rapidly. However, growth slows markedly as the resources available to sustain a population approach full utilization.

Social Security system? For the health care industry? Other groups?

Subsistence and Population S Curves Biologists have developed a theory of animal populations that goes something like this. Beginning at Time 0 in Figure 2, we have given amounts of land, vegetation, water, and other requirements for life along with a very small number of rabbits. With a substantial amount of space and food available per pair of rabbits, the rabbit population grows at an increasing rate for some time. When this population ultimately becomes congested, however, there will be ever increasing competition for food and territory. A parallel population explosion among rabbit predators and the emergence of malnutrition will cause a gradual reduction in the growth of the rabbit population. Pressure for "survival of the fittest" will mount. Finally, many rabbits will fail to secure territory and the specter of starvation will loom. Even if rabbits continue to reproduce at the same rate as they previously did, a sufficient number of their young will die and the average life span of the population will decline so that an equilibrium population will be achieved. This sequence is called a **population S curve.**

Using similar reasoning, early economists concluded that human life would almost continuously be at only a subsistence level. Technological advances or an extended period of favorable weather for agriculture would simply result in higher wages, then population growth and, ultimately, the misery of an even larger number of people. In the oft-quoted words of the Reverend Thomas Malthus, written in 1798:

> I think I may fairly make two postulata. First, that food is necessary to the existence of man. Secondly, that the passion between the sexes is necessary, and will remain nearly in its present state.
>
> These two laws ever since we have had any knowledge of mankind, appear to have been fixed laws of our nature. . . .
>
> Assuming, then my postulata as granted, I say, that the power of population is indefinitely greater than the power in the earth to produce subsistence for man.
>
> Population, when unchecked, increases in a geometrical ratio. Subsistence only increases in an arithmetical ratio. A slight acquaintance with numbers will show the immensity of the first power in comparison of the second. . . .[1]

Reverend Malthus meant that food production might expand in a sequence like 1, 2, 3, 4, 5, 6, and so on. But if there were enough food, space, and other necessities, the human population would grow as follows: 1, 2, 4, 8, 16, 32, and so on (much like rabbits). However, population would be kept in check by starvation, disease, or war, to grow only at the same pace as food: 1, 2, 3, 4, ... This theory may draw a grim picture of a cruel world in which human population is naturally regulated, but such a fate seemed inevitable during Malthus's time.

A corollary of this theory is that the number of people in society will be constantly pressing on the means of physical subsistence. The theory provides for a number of checks that Malthus classified as either positive (things that increase deaths) or preventive (things that reduce births). Each possible check to increased population was seen as being derived from limited food supply; starvation constitutes the ultimate check in Malthus's theory. In this way, Malthus introduced the notion of a physiological "standard of living" that regulates population.

The second edition of Malthus's *Essay on the Principle of Population* (1st ed., 1798) also added the notion of a standard of living determined by habit—a notion designed to explain the empirical fact of Malthus's day that laboring classes in several countries were living at standards considerably above subsistence. Malthus's theory stressed the constancy of the standard of living, regardless of how it was determined. He felt that almost insurmountable difficulties block permanent improvement of the condition of the working classes. His theory states that changes in economic conditions ultimately yield no change in the average quality of life, only a decrease or increase of people living at this constant standard. This represented a departure from the more optimistic economic growth theory of Adam Smith. Malthus preached that only through sexual continence could we avoid his grim predictions, but he was so pessimistic about the prospects for worldwide chastity that, to him, a razor's edge existence for the bulk of humanity seemed inevitable.

Malthusian population theory, influential and popular throughout much of the nineteenth century, lost favor rapidly once scholars recognized that Malthus had underestimated the rate of technical change. The most pertinent technological advances include several efficient birth control techniques and machinery and knowledge that have allowed food supplies to grow rapidly during the past century. Modern critics of Malthus's theory point out that humans, unlike rabbits, possess the ability to innovate and alter the carrying capacity of their environment. Prophets of doom and eternal optimists share an inability to predict the direction technological advances will take. For example, someone in the late 1800s might have predicted that the United States would "never sustain 240 million people because there wouldn't be enough land to pasture each person's horse." Our imaginations tend to be limited to the here and now, prisoners of current technologies.

Nevertheless, since World War II the problems facing underdeveloped countries have reawakened interest in Malthus's ideas. Today, many emerging countries have the worst of both worlds: the high birth rates of a typical agrarian economy and the low death rates of a modern industrialized economy. Barring major changes in the near future, these countries may face the unsavory choice of limiting the sizes of families—in opposition to widespread social values and religious beliefs—or the Malthusian

---

1. Rev. Thomas Malthus, *Essay on the Principle of Population,* 1st ed. (London: 1798), privately published (Malthus's emphasis).

checks of famine and disease that stem from limited food supply. Small wonder that Thomas Carlyle, a historian who was a contemporary of Malthus, characterized economics as "the dismal science."

What is not clear today is whether overpopulation is the cause of underdevelopment or whether economic development is the cure for overpopulation. In the advanced economies of the world, children seem to be regarded as "inferior goods." That is, as per capita income increases in these countries, there is a tendency to substitute a higher standard of living and more leisure for more children, despite the fact that more children can be afforded at the higher income levels.

The belief that wages and incomes are at subsistence levels in equilibrium might seem naive to people in advanced and highly industrialized nations. However, the widespread misery and hardship experienced throughout much of Africa, Asia, and South America at least partially confirm long-term economic forecasts made more than 180 years ago by Malthus and some of his colleagues.

How have the people of Western Europe, Japan, and North America escaped this fate? Their production and incomes have grown faster than their populations, which in some advanced nations have recently seemed at a standstill. In fact, as Table 1 indicates, population in many developed countries tends to be relatively stable or even declining, while primitive and less developed nations continue to experience explosive population growth.

But why has population growth in highly developed economies not responded to the growth in national incomes, driving per capita income to subsistence levels? At least a partial answer to this question lies in the recent availability of low cost, effective birth control devices—a development that Malthus would have regarded as immoral. More critically, rapid technological advances and the accumulation of both physical and human capital have caused income in developed nations to grow more rapidly than population. Hence, although war has been all too common, we have not had to endure the plagues and starvation that Malthus and his followers viewed as some other natural checks on population.

Capital Formation: Savings, Investment, and the Capital Stock

Potential real output will grow with increases in the labor force, but per capita income will grow only when the quality and/or quantities of the resources we work with expands. Let us take a bird's-eye view at how the capital stock grows so that you can appreci-

TABLE 1 *Percentage Annual Population Growth for Selected Countries (Average Rates for 1970–85)*

Developed Countries		Less Developed Countries	
Country	**Percent**	**Country**	**Percent**
Austria	0.2	Algeria	3.0
Belgium	0.2	Bangladesh	2.7
Canada	1.1	Brazil	2.5
Czechoslovakia	0.4	China	1.5
France	0.5	Ecuador	2.9
East Germany	−0.2	Ghana	3.2
West Germany	0.0	Honduras	3.4
Italy	0.4	India	2.2
Japan	1.0	Iran	2.9
Norway	0.4	Jordan	3.7
Sweden	0.2	Mexico	2.7
U.S.A.	1.0	Pakistan	2.9
USSR	0.9	Uganda	2.7
		Zambia	3.2
Average	0.5		2.8

Source: U.S. Department of Commerce, Bureau of the Census, *Statistical Abstract of the United States, 1986.*

ate the difficulty of traveling this route to the good life.

Recall that investment is a major component of GNP and that both production and income (and, consequently, investment) are flow variables. How is the flow of investment translated into a newer and bigger capital stock (K)? Well, gross investment minus depreciation is net investment (I), which equals net **capital accumulation** during a given time period (t). That is:

$$\frac{\Delta K}{\Delta t} = I.$$

Omitting both government and the foreign sector for now, investment during any period will equal saving:

$$C + S = C + I.$$

Thus, $S = I$. This familiar equation reveals that rates of saving must be high to achieve the high levels of investment necessary for rapid capital formation. Figure 3 indicates that if we choose to consume much and invest little of our national income (point a on PPF_{1987}), economic growth will proceed slowly. On the other hand, if our society chooses to sacrifice substantial potential consumption (point b), we will be able to produce and consume at higher levels in the future because of the extra capital accumulation that lower current consumption permits.

Devoting certain portions of national output to the production of capital goods instead of consumer goods may be an individual choice or a collective choice through government. When the decision is left to individuals, there is **voluntary saving.** When governments follow policies that force consumption down to allow capital accumulation, we describe the process as **involuntary saving.**

Voluntary Saving

The act of saving can be viewed as a decision to delay consumption. Just what factors influence the choice between consuming now and postponing consumption so that we can enjoy more later? Although there are a number of considerations, two important influences on individuals' consumption/saving choices are the interest rates paid to savers and the level of income. A third significant influence may be the distribution of income.

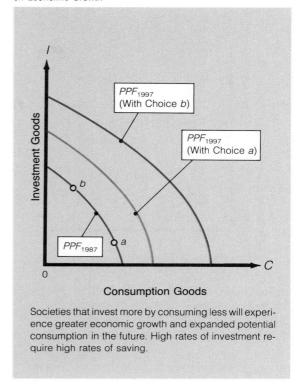

FIGURE 3 The Effects of Consumption/Savings Choices on Economic Growth

Societies that invest more by consuming less will experience greater economic growth and expanded potential consumption in the future. High rates of investment require high rates of saving.

Interest Rates The Keynesian Revolution ushered in a deemphasis on the importance of interest rates in determining rates of saving, suggesting that income is a major, and perhaps (in very simple Keynesian models) the sole determinant of the level of saving. There has been a recent resurgence in the classical belief that the interest rate paid savers is critical in determining the saving/investment decision. The argument runs along the following lines.

An increase in the interest rate received by savers (who are the ultimate lenders) raises the relative price of consumption today versus consumption tomorrow. Thus, higher interest rates cause people to postpone consumption. Increases in interest rates will also discourage people who are marginal borrowers and who would use their borrowings for consumer purchases. This means that the quantity of funds supplied to investors will grow as interest rates rise, facilitating investment.

FIGURE 4 Saving, Investment, and Interest Rates

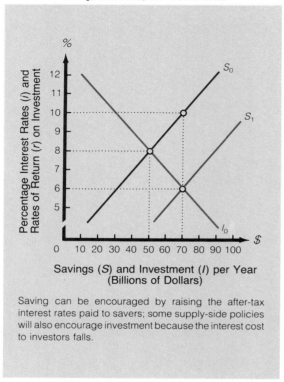

Savings (S) and Investment (I) per Year
(Billions of Dollars)

Saving can be encouraged by raising the after-tax interest rates paid to savers; some supply-side policies will also encourage investment because the interest cost to investors falls.

Must higher interest rates paid to savers discourage investment? Not necessarily. After-tax interest income is the concern of savers, and high after-tax rates of return are the goals of investors. A variety of government policies can be manipulated so that the net interest rates received by savers rise, while the interest costs of investors fall. For example, many of President Reagan's advisers believed that saving and investment in the United States had plummeted relative to national income throughout the 1970s. They felt that this was caused by the combination of very high tax rates on investment and interest incomes coupled with very low ceilings on the interest rates that could be paid to depositors by financial institutions. Exempting interest incomes from taxation through such devices as **Individual Retirement Accounts (IRAs)** might increase saving from S_0 to S_1 in Figure 4 if savers view an untaxed 6 percent interest rate (on S_1) as equal to a taxed interest rate of 10 percent (on S_0). In this example, savers had been

receiving and investors had been paying a taxable 8 percent interest rate on $50 billion. After interest is exempted from taxes, investors have $70 billion available to invest at an interest cost of 6 percent annually.

Other policies that would simultaneously increase after-tax interest payments to savers and after-tax rates of return to investors include rapid depreciation allowances and investment tax credits as well as a general reduction in marginal tax rates. Direct government subsidies to investors would also automatically reward savers as the demand for investment grew. A current proposal that would affect tax consumption rather than income would stimulate saving and facilitate investment; saving would be deducted from taxable income if this proposal were enacted.

This line of attack is increasingly popular. For example, after suffering a serious recession in 1985, Singapore's Economic Committee recommended a strong supply-side approach to revive Singapore's sagging economic growth rate. The proposals included: (*a*) sharply reduced corporate and personal income tax rates, (*b*) tax breaks for firms engaged in research and development, (*c*) reductions in compulsory pension fund payments (similar to our Social Security taxes), and (*d*) pressure on Singapore's government to stabilize laws and regulations and reduce the uncertainty encountered in business planning. These are only a few examples of the supply-side policies that many analysts see as the road to economic growth.

Income The Keynesian idea that income (*Y*) is a major determinant of saving (*S*) was developed in previous chapters. The relationship between the average propensity to save (*S/Y*) and income is important in understanding the problem of fostering economic growth in undeveloped, impoverished countries. If you are poor, the difficult alternatives facing you are to consume at low levels forever or to force yourself to reduce already low levels of consumption today so that you will be able to make investments that might pay off in the future. You may have faced a similar choice when you decided to invest in your education; you could be consuming more if you were not in school. The hardship encountered in this saving/consumption decision is far less of a burden for wealthy people or wealthy countries. Widespread poverty, on the other hand, inhibits saving and capital accumulation.

Inequality of Income   Impoverished countries tend to have much less equal distributions of income than do highly developed nations. One way to accumulate capital is to rely on high saving rates by the wealthy and to hope that current deprivation of the masses will be offset by higher incomes for future generations. This idea is called the **trickle-down theory.** The wealthy may not save in a manner that facilitates domestic growth, however; instead they might, for example, buy foreign stocks or bonds or consume imported luxury goods. Opponents of income redistribution programs commonly declare that saving and investment will fall if money is transferred from the rich to the poor. They suggest that recent declines in American saving relative to GNP are partially a consequence of our recent "War on Poverty" and other social programs.

Involuntary Saving

Governments do have some alternatives to voluntary saving if, for whatever reasons, they view voluntary saving and capital accumulation as inadequate for the rate of growth they desire. The trick is to force consumption down relative to total production so that the difference can be put into the production of new capital goods.

Central Planning and Confiscation   In a centrally planned economy such as the Soviet Union, the government sets wages and prices. Under the various five-year plans initiated in 1929 by Joseph Stalin and still used, wages have been held very low relative to individual production, and the prices of consumer goods have been set very high. People have no choice but to "save"; their consumption has been held far below their production. As a result of this forced saving, the Soviet Union experienced enormous industrial growth and rapidly attained the status of a world power. The costs of this growth were declines in already low standards of living.

Marxists apply the term **surplus values** to the differences between what people are paid and the average value of their total production. They contend that capitalists exploit workers by seizing surplus values. It is ironic, therefore, that among the most exploitative regimes ever have been Marxist governments. Even though Stalin was succeeded by Khrushchev, followed by Brezhnev, Andropov, Chernenko, and now Gorbachev—each seemingly more moderate than his predecessor—the Soviet Union has only gradually reduced its "expropriation" of surplus value to generate high rates of economic growth.

This sort of exploitation is just one way a government can confiscate resources to use them for capital accumulation and economic growth. Revolutionary "land reform" programs are another confiscation method: large estates are seized and allocated to peasants. Revolutionary governments also rely on direct confiscation of the factories or financial assets of deposed wealthy elites as sources for "social" capital accumulation.

The comparatively rapid evolutions of the Soviet Union and, more recently, China from "sleeping giants" to industrial powers have caught the attention of many leaders of underdeveloped countries. Some have tried to follow these examples, and their countries have suffered from the economic inefficiency that often characterizes central planning. There are, however, other ways to force higher saving in semidemocratic, market-oriented economies: inflation and taxation.

Inflation   A government can issue contracts for schools, highways, or industrial facilities and then pay the contractors with freshly printed money. If the economy is initially at full employment, the resultant inflation will crowd out private consumption. This has been a very popular form of forced saving in a number of countries, most notably Brazil. Throughout the 1950s, 1960s, and 1970s, Brazil experienced high rates of real economic growth despite high inflation.

Taxation   High rates of taxation may also be used to reduce private purchasing power and consumption and to increase rates of government investment. However, the Laffer curve described in Chapter 11 points to the danger that very high tax rates may result in severe disincentives for work effort and private investment, actually causing GNP to fall so much that tax revenues shrink.

Capital Widening and Capital Deepening

If the capital stock grows, but only at or below the percentage growth rate of the labor force, we use the term **capital widening.** Let us assume that the labor force is a fixed percentage of population. Capital widening (if population and capital grow at identical rates) will not even stabilize per capita GNP because the increased doses of capital and labor relative to land result in diminishing returns. Since land resources cannot grow, it is likely that even if the growth of the capital stock does keep pace with population, standards of living will fall.

Suppose that the capital stock grows faster than population. This is known as **capital deepening.** The cumulative effect of high rates of saving and investment (capital deepening) over an extended period is a higher ratio of capital to labor (the K/L ratio). This tends to raise labor productivity and yield higher levels of real per capita income. However, the fixity of land yields diminishing returns in the enhanced labor productivity that occurs as the capital stock grows. Thus, the higher a country's capital to labor ratio, the harder it is to use new capital formation as a source of additional economic growth.

Recently, the growth rates of the "four tigers"—South Korea, Taiwan, Hong Kong, and Singapore—have slowed down. Earlier double-digit real growth was based on the simple formula of producing labor intensive export products. However, as these economies grew, wage levels rose faster than productivity. As growth slowed in the early 1980s, policymakers in all four countries sought to expand their capital-labor ratios by encouraging investment in capital intensive and high-tech industries.

South Korea's and Singapore's solutions involved tax breaks, credits for private groups, government public works projects, and increased wage rates to discourage labor intensive investment. The results have been disappointing. Capital deepening has not produced growth rates that exceed those in Hong Kong and Taiwan, whose governments decided to do nothing to make one industry more attractive than another.

The preceding analysis suggests that even though rich countries with high capital-to-labor ratios may find it easier than poor countries to finance capital accumulation through saving, capital deepening is less likely to be effective in fostering growth in rich countries than in poor ones. It is crucial, however, that saving be channeled to the most productive form of investment—a task that unregulated financial markets seem to do much better than government planners. Nevertheless, many people who are concerned with American growth rates being lower than those experienced by the Russians, Chinese, Japanese, or Western Europeans predict that rates of GNP growth elsewhere in the world will slow down as other countries attain our levels of per capita GNP.

The rate of capital formation is generally considered to be important for economic growth. Decisions on investment and saving can be made voluntarily or governments can use various tactics to compel greater saving. For people to save voluntarily, interest rates must be attractive and income must be high enough to permit saving. Centrally planned economies are able to force consumption below production, thus creating forced savings. Several Far Eastern countries have recently discovered that as a country's capital-to-labor ratio grows, the generation of further growth through capital deepening faces diminishing returns.

Finally, critics of the traditional capital formation → economic development sequence point out that added capital may not help for several reasons. First, housing construction typically is a sizable chunk of total investment (over 25 percent in the U.S. in 1985). This spending, critics argue, might be better classified as spending on consumer durables. Second, considerable investment is often public investment for social/political reasons where the rate of return may be quite low. Third, investment that produces excess capacity and underutilization of plants and equipment is useless. The British steel industry spent huge sums on plant modernization in the 1970s. But their new plants have been underutilized and, therefore, have added little to national income. These critics argue that real long-term economic growth is the result of technological advances, changes in habits, and advances in education. We will now examine one widely accepted ingredient of growth—technological change.

Technological Advances

Given amounts of resources, if used efficiently, will produce specific levels of output over a stated time interval. Later, it may be possible to produce more output with the same resources. Is this magic? No. **Technological change** is the name we apply to the "black box" that permits us to produce more from a given resource bundle, or the same output with fewer resources. Subcategories of technological change include greater efficiency in market processes, improved knowledge about how to combine productive resources, the introduction of totally new production processes, improvements in the qualities of human and nonhuman resources, and new inventions and innovations. The idea of "progress" is inextricably bound up in the process of technological change.

Technological change can be viewed in two ways. In one sense it is embodied in new forms of capital; in another, technical changes or innovations encourage substantial investment and thus increase the capital stock. The emergence of money, electricity, automobiles, supermarkets, and computer chips are examples. Joseph Schumpeter (discussed in Chapter 8) saw major technological breakthroughs as avenues for increased profits for capitalists and as the major source of progress for society.

Technological change can be stimulated by research and development. Innovative entrepreneurs such as Thomas Edison, Alexander Graham Bell, and Henry Ford were responsible for much of the early technological progress in the United States. Governments can foster technological advances by either directly funding research and development projects or by offering tax incentives to innovators. Less developed countries may stimulate growth and progress by importing new technologies. Another possibility is to import capital goods from more advanced countries. A slightly different method of securing technology is followed by countries that send some of their most promising young people to more advanced countries to study at colleges and universities. This is one popular way to build the foundations for economic growth.

Social Foundations: The Infrastructure

The path to economic growth in some societies rests on rich lodes of natural resources. The world beats paths to the doors of oil-rich sheikdoms and mineral-rich feudal societies, strewing money left and right

that can be used as developmental "seed" money. Other primitive economies have tougher rows to hoe—they must build the foundations of economic development in a careful fashion. The path to economic maturity requires a well-organized financial system, efficient communication and transportation networks, and an educated and disciplined work force. All these institutions come under what is referred to as **social overhead capital** or **infrastructure.**

Any smooth-running economy needs a well-organized and sophisticated financial system. Without such a system, existing firms and industries must rely on internally generated funds (retained earnings) or on foreign sources to finance capital expansion. The same is true for other types of social overhead capital like communication and transportation networks. Methods for selling their products nationwide or worldwide are needed because most businesses exhibit some range of production over which the average costs of production fall as output increases. Well-developed communication and transport systems aid firms in exploiting these declining costs.

Finally, no country grows very rapidly or experiences industrialization without a capable labor force. This includes not only a well-educated population but a healthy one as well. Thus, a nation must set high priorities in the areas of health and education if its economy is to sustain a high level of growth. Edward S. Denison, an expert in this area, attributes almost 14 percent of the growth that occurred in the United States between 1929 and 1969 to improvements in education.

Economic Development and the Unfolding of History

Numerous historians and social philosophers have attempted to chart the progress of civilizations in broader terms than we have been discussing. Economic events often play central roles on the stage of history. Are there long-term patterns of growth and development common to the economic advances of all societies? Many observers believe that there are. Does growth ultimately bring stagnation? Most of us hope not, but some students of civilization believe it does.

Economic Development According to Marx

One of the most influential thinkers of the last century was Karl Marx, who suggested an unabated course of progress and development. (Some who are optimistic about the prospects for humankind hope he was wrong about many specific details.) Marx's prognosis was that every society goes through six major stages of history, culminating in an ideal state.

1. *Prehistory.* Prior to the dawn of civilization, humankind consisted largely of self-sufficient but nomadic hunters/scavengers/foragers. Gradually, these random groups evolved into

2. *Primitive culture.* During this period, extended families and tribes emerged. Agriculture began to bind small groups to specific territories, but activities like animal herding and hunting continued to be important. As claims to exclusive rights to territory grew in importance, some families were more successful than others in establishing their rights to land, resulting in a system known as

3. *Feudalism.* The offspring of successful warlords became wealthy landholders, who were titled but most of whom owed their ability to protect their turf to a sovereign or king. Kings typically extracted "protection" tributes from lesser royalty; however, the actual production on the manors held by the minor lords and barons was done by peasants, who owned no land and paid a share of their crops to the titled landowners. (Sharecropping continues to this day in many agricultural countries.) This chain of exploitation governed the social and economic behavior of all members of society from the highest born prince to the humblest peasant. Industrialization and the gradual evolution of shopkeepers into powerful merchants slowly eroded the powers of feudal royalty, although some of the merchants and feudal lords became industrial magnates during the transition to

4. *Capitalism.* The Industrial Revolution and growth in commerce were accompanied by movements from the countryside into towns and cities. Dispossessed peasants streamed into the cities. They generally owned no resources except their own labor because their incomes were held at subsistence levels. According to Marx, capitalists were able to accumulate enormous wealth during this period only through the expropriation of a surplus value, which equals the difference between the total value of production and the subsistence wages paid to workers. In Marxist jargon, all rents,

interest payments, and profits are surplus values. Marx predicted that ever growing disparities between the wealth of capitalists and the impoverishment of labor would generate class conflict and the triumph of a workers' revolution. The successful revolution would lead to a transition period called the

5. *Dictatorship of the proletariat.* During this period, all basic industries and productive resources would be *nationalized,* which means that revolutionary governments would seize them from the capitalist class and hold them in trust for the workers, or proletariat. Each worker would receive compensation only for his or her own production to ensure an absence of capitalistic exploitation. There would be a highly progressive income tax and a confiscatory inheritance tax. Gradually, all material wants would be satisfied, and the need for government would fade—leading to the ultimate state of

6. *Communism or socialism.* In this highest stage of economic development, basic human needs and wants would be met according to the Marxist principle, "From each according to his ability to produce, to each according to need." And everyone would live happily ever after.

Stages of Economic Growth

There have been many non-Marxist theories of the stages of economic development. Among the most noteworthy is one offered by Walt W. Rostow, who concerned himself with the stages of transition from a primitive economy to a fully developed and mature industrial economy. According to Rostow, growth and development to economic maturity proceed through the following stages:

1. *Traditional society.* This is essentially an agrarian society employing primitive technology.

2. *Preconditions for growth.* The traditional economy begins to change, with rapid increases in agricultural productivity. Growing agricultural surpluses free workers for industry and allow investment in capital goods. At this point, entrepreneurship begins to blossom.

3. *Take-off.* The saving rate grows during this period and permits rapid expansion of productive capacity.

4. *Drive to maturity.* Output and income from industrialization grow rapidly.

FIGURE 5 *The Trap of Underdevelopment*

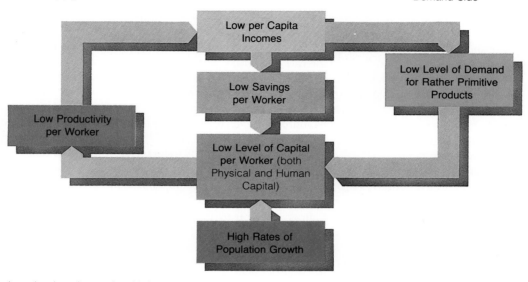

In many less developed countries, high rates of population growth lead to little physical or human capital per worker, which results in low productivity and income, which leads to low levels of saving and Aggregate Demand. This in turn leads to little capital per worker, and so on. Such a cycle makes it extremely difficult for primitive economies to escape the trap of underdevelopment and achieve economic growth.

Source: Ragnar Nurkse, *Problems of Capital Formation in Underdeveloped Countries* (New York: Oxford University Press, 1953); and adapted from Frances Steward, "Technology and Employment in LDC's," *Employment in Developing Nations: Report on a Ford Foundation Study*, ed. Edgar O. Edwards (New York: Columbia University Press, 1974), p. 92.

5. *High mass consumption.* During this stage, services become very important, and high levels of consumer goods are available for all members of society.

Since both Marxist and non-Marxist models are highly abstract, they do not provide less developed countries with adequate guides about starting and sustaining economic development. Many countries seem caught in a maze of problems that seem almost insurmountable.

The Problems of Developing Nations

Underdeveloped countries often seem caught in what has been called the **trap of underdevelopment.** For these countries, there appears to be no workable solutions to poverty and despair, with most families living on the razor's edge of subsistence. The trap of underdevelopment is illustrated in Figure 5.

The Trap of Underdevelopment

Less developed countries typically experience high rates of population growth that result in low per capita incomes. These meager incomes leave families so little extra that saving per worker is very low, resulting in low national capital-to-labor ratios. Further, low incomes require families to spend most of their earnings on rather primitive products. Finally, low saving rates and little capital per worker lead to scant productivity on the supply side. This again translates into poor wages and, thus, low per capita income. No matter where you begin in Figure 5, the story is the same. How do countries escape from this vicious circle of poverty?

Breaking the Bonds of Underdevelopment

We have seen that the major impediments to economic development include: (*a*) explosive population growth and lack of broad education and job skills, (*b*) very low levels of capital per worker, (*c*) low levels of technology, (*d*) various cultural impediments to business and commerce, (*e*) low levels of domestic natural resources, and (*f*) primitive and unstable political systems. How can countries suffering from a number of such barriers hope to break the bonds of underdevelopment?

Economic development does not happen overnight, but less developed countries (LDCs) can do several things to facilitate development. They can eliminate and streamline government impediments to business activity, encourage the adoption of modern agricultural technology, improve the country's infrastructure so that the labor force can use modern agricultural and industrial technologies efficiently, and institute policies to reduce population growth and increase saving.

This is a tall order for any country. Consider the task of reducing population growth. Providing free birth control programs is barely more successful than exhorting people to abstain from sex. Many people in underdeveloped lands view children as old-age insurance and measure their own success by how many of their children attain adulthood. New medical technology or any increases in national income are quickly translated into population growth. One example is the recent population explosion in Mexico following major discoveries of oil and other natural resources. Some countries consider population growth to be such a desperate problem that they have resorted to involuntary programs. Mrs. Gandhi's government in India lost power for a period in the 1970s when her oldest son, Sanjay, directed the army to grab men off the streets in rural areas and sterilize them. In 1981, China passed laws limiting rural couples to two children, while urban couples were prohibited from having more than one child. Press releases periodically reveal that thousands of infant girls have been killed by Chinese parents who want male children. This is further evidence that gov-

FIGURE 6 *Breaking the Bonds of Underdevelopment*

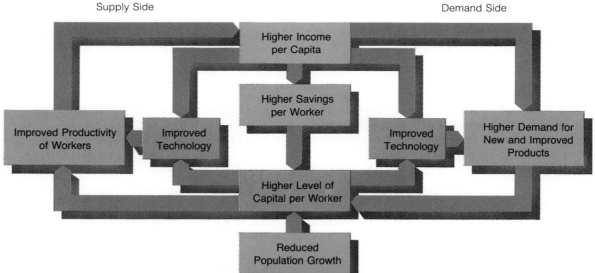

Facilitating advancement in developing nations may require reducing population growth, improving technology, and increasing the saving rate—all very difficult tasks.

Source: Adapted from Frances Steward, "Technology and Employment in LDC's," Edgar O. Edward, ed., *Employment in Developing Nations: Report on a Ford Foundation Study* (New York: Columbia University Press, 1974), p. 92.

FOCUS 2

Two Paths to Development in the Far East

The stage is set as two of Asia's most dynamic economies test competing development theories.* South Korea and Taiwan are taking strikingly different paths in their development strategies. Taiwan is the land of "mom and pop" enterprises, with nearly 60,000 registered trading companies where profit rules supreme. In South Korea, less than 7,000 trading companies and a few large corporations dominate commerce. Unlike Taiwan, the South Korean government is heavily involved in industrial policy and South Korean corporations focus more on building international markets.

Much of the differences in their approach to development stem from cultural differences between the Koreans and the Chinese of Taiwan. The Koreans are viewed as aggressive (or even reckless) spenders, while the Chinese are more conservative and cautious, with a

tendency to save. Korean companies are borrowing heavily to finance massive factories in capital-intensive industries like steel, appliances, automobiles, and semiconductors. Taiwan's focus is on development of high-tech research and development to suit specific market niches.

Per capita GNP in Taiwan is currently 50 percent greater than in Korea, and Taiwan runs a trade surplus while Korea still has a deficit. South Korean exchange reserves are low and its international debt is much larger than that of Taiwan. However, if Korea's large investment pays off in the future, these positions could be reversed.

The different development strategies represented by both Taiwan and Korea illustrate that there may be "more than

one way to skin a cat." Heavy government intervention and large corporate organizations in Korea are consistent with the Korean culture, which subordinates personal interest to national interests. The Chinese tend to be more entrepreneurial and want to "be their own boss", making development of large organizations more difficult and less efficient. The approach that will ultimately prove to be better is still unknown. What seems clear is that each country has chosen a route that best suits its people, and in the end, this may be more important than anything.

*Based on "South Korea and Taiwan: Two Strategies," *The Wall Street Journal*, May 1, 1986, p. 30.

ernment policies may have unforeseen and undesirable (or even tragic) side effects, and that devising policies to accomplish growth and development may be an overwhelming task.

The effect of adopting policies that succeed in breaking the bonds of underdevelopment is diagrammed in Figure 6. Reducing population growth, increasing capital per worker, and implementing improved technology produces self-reinforcing benefits. (Some alternative development strategies are discussed in Focus 2.) As per capita incomes rise, saving per worker and consumer demands for new and improved products also rise. As more capital per worker is acquired, worker productivity will rise, resulting in greater wages and income. The circle

begins again, this time for the better. It is generally very difficult, however, for any country to begin the development process on its own. Start-up capital often comes from foreign, more highly developed countries.

Is There Really a Trap of Underdevelopment?

The vicious circle of underdevelopment suggests that breaking the bonds of poverty requires domestic sacrifices supplemented by aid from abroad. Growth is a function of the rate of capital accumulation (investment) which in turn is a function of saving which is determined by income. Low levels of income prevent the saving necessary for sufficient investment to fuel economic growth.

Critics of the trap of underdevelopment thesis point out that it is refuted by the very existence of developed countries. These countries all started out poor with low levels of capital; if the vicious circle of poverty thesis were true, developed countries would not exist today.

For example, in the early 1800s Hong Kong was a barren rock; by 1900 it was a substantial port. Hong Kong has very little land and is probably the most densely populated country in the world. It has few natural resources and must import most of its raw materials. Today, Hong Kong is a major manufacturing, trading, and banking center. In fact, the Hong Kong experience is so successful that India is now considering turning the Andaman Islands located in the Bay of Bengal into a free port and huge export processing zone. Critics ask, "How can all of this be true if the trap of underdevelopment thesis is true?"

Critics of this thesis further argue that development is based on factors other than natural resources, capital accumulation, and reduced population growth. They argue that such factors as human aptitudes and attitudes, social and political institutions, external contacts, market opportunities, and natural resources (to a lesser extent) account for success in the development arena. Development is not just a matter of capital accumulation and saving; it is vitally related to individuals (entrepreneurs) being able to perceive opportunities and then to take advantage of them. Growth is, of course, conditioned by the opportunities offered by the environment—like natural resources and social institutions—but the pace and pattern of growth will depend on the quality of the entrepreneurial talent in the economy.

These critics point to countries such as Hong Kong, Taiwan, and Singapore as counterexamples to the traditional capital accumulation theory of growth and development. They emphasize the needs for free trade and unrestricted entrepreneurial activity as the springboards to economic growth. Only then will injections of foreign capital be helpful since, as P. T. Bauer has noted, "A society which cannot develop without external gifts is altogether unlikely to do so with them."

What Developed Countries Can Do to Aid Less Developed Nations

The case for foreign aid is regarded as axiomatic, so that either progress or lack of progress can be used to argue for more aid. Progress is evidence of success, and lack of progress is evidence that more must be done.
—*P. T. Bauer*

Many people perceive the most pressing needs of developing nations to be enormous injections of capital, introduction of new technology, and substantial education and job training programs. More developed nations are often in a good position to provide physical capital since many have an abundance and their investors are looking for profitable places to invest. Similarly, the educational systems of developed countries can train technically qualified people for developing industries. Moreover, industrialized countries can provide the technology needed to raise the productivity of workers in less developed countries.

The Role of International Credit

International capital flows permit countries with more attractive investment opportunities than their domestic savings can finance to obtain resources from countries with excess saving. Countries experiencing temporary economic problems might borrow from world capital markets rather than suffer sharp contractionary policies that restrict consumption and investment. Countries such as Hong Kong, Taiwan, Malaysia, and Israel, to name a few, have benefitted from foreign capital infusions. Since World War II, the United States has been a net supplier of capital to the rest of the world, primarily through direct investment by private firms in foreign countries. Before World War I, the United States financed domestic investments with loans from Great Britain and other European countries. In general, international capital flows move into countries with good growth and profit opportunities. (See Focus 3.)

New capital may also be provided in the form of foreign aid—either grants or loans. The United States provides billions of dollars in aid each year, administered through the Agency for International

The external debts of Latin America had mounted to roughly $380 billion by 1986. Many of these countries teetered on the brink of default during 1981–86, but nowhere was the crisis more severe than in Mexico. The Mexican government owed foreign bankers over $100 billion dollars. There was $1,250 of foreign debt for each of Mexico's 80 million citizens, and scheduled interest payments alone absorbed one-sixth of Mexico's national income.

The major problem is that ambitious development programs were financed with foreign debt during the 1970s. Mexico's oil reserves tripled between 1976 and 1982, making it a major oil exporter. The government expected rapid economic growth and went on a borrowing binge, expecting rising oil revenues to enable easy debt repayment. Mexican economic planners had assumed that world oil prices would be $60–$90 per barrel by 1985, but oil peaked at roughly $34 per barrel in 1981–82. By 1986, oil prices had fallen to the $10–$14 range, and Mexico's export earnings were only 10 percent of its forecasts.

The result was that Mexico was devastated by soaring inflation and unemployment. In common with most developing nations, Mexico's income distribution is traditionally very unequal; the few rich families are envied and resented by masses of destitute peasants and urban slum dwellers. An emerging middle class depended on the success of Mexico's development programs, but the state-controlled industries that devoured so much development money

have been plagued by red tape and massive corruption. Middle-class dreams were crushed by falling oil prices and the stagnation of government industries.

Mexico's problems were worsened by international adjustments to its plight. In 1982 alone, the number of pesos required to buy $1 rose from 22 to 150, increasing external (dollar-denominated) debt from the Mexican perspective by 700 percent. Fear of continuing declines in peso exchange rates (relative prices of currencies) caused middle-class and wealthy Mexicans to pour their financial assets into dollar deposits in U.S. banks. A dollar would buy 600 pesos by 1986. Between 1976 and 1985, roughly $53 billion in private financial capital left Mexico; even small banks in Texas border towns grew by as much as $1 billion in new deposits. This *capital flight* has been a huge obstacle to financing economic growth internally and has increased Mexico's dependence on foreign banks.

Debt repayment as originally scheduled would have required drastic measures, but the Partido Revolucionario Institucional (PRI), which has ruled Mexico for six decades, depends on a fragile coalition that limits it to conservative policy changes. An austerity program cost one-third of government workers their jobs but did little to cure the basic problem. Selling government industries to private firms might enable Mexico to staunch the flight of private capital and repay more of its debts, but opposition by the bureaucrats who run these industries probably makes this approach politically impossible.

Any quick solution to Mexico's problems would be destabilizing. These problems have been partially exported. Falling incomes and high unemployment rates have increased illegal immigration. The United States, however, has been attempting to tighten control over its border. This might close one safety valve that has helped keep Mexico's social and economic problems from erupting.

Even policies necessary to pay the interest on Mexico's external debt threaten to topple the government. Some analysts compare Mexico's debt to the burden of war reparations imposed on Germany following World War I. The German economy was crippled for over a decade and governments fell left and right. Recovery began only when Hitler's Nazis abandoned repayment of Germany's external debt.

Mexico may be forced to operate like a U.S. firm that has filed Chapter 11 bankruptcy—a procedure that allows continued operation and holds creditors at bay. Debt repayment by Mexico has been rescheduled to a slower rate. Further rescheduling is likely because there would be havoc in international banking circles if Mexico disavowed its debts. (Some analysts suggest that defaults on all shaky Latin American loans would leave 90 percent of the top 100 U.S. banks insolvent.) Final resolution of Mexico's problems will take decades and will require repeated renegotiation between U.S. lenders, our two governments, and international financial agencies.

Development (AID). Another source of funds for less developed countries is the World Bank, funded by highly developed member nations, which arranges loans of billions of dollars annually, principally for social overhead and infrastructure. This aid permits investments such as dams, education, communications, and transportation systems. Most investment flows between countries, however, are private and are channeled through multinational corporations. These companies must perceive substantial potential profits before they invest, and seek opportunities where there are abundant natural resources, a ready (and cheap) labor force, and a favorable political climate.

One problem that arises when development is financed by long-term loans from more mature economies is that regular payments must be made for a less developed country to maintain an acceptable credit rating. A worldwide recession such as the 1981–83 slump reveals how much financial juggling this can entail. Hundreds of billions of dollars in development loans were due for repayment to major American banks. These banks had primarily loaned out the deposits of OPEC countries, and many of the OPEC countries wanted to withdraw funds because of declining oil revenues. The worldwide recession, high nominal and real interest rates, the strengthening of the U.S. dollar, and the fall in the prices of many commodities exported by developing countries put incredible strains on debtor countries' ability to service their external debt. Some analysts warned that the entire international financial system teetered on the brink of collapse. However, refinancing (or rescheduling) of the debt payments, collapsing oil prices, and the sustained economic recovery of the mid-1980s have reduced the financial pressures on many developing nations that do not rely too much on oil revenues.

The world's industrialized nations are not totally philanthropic in contributing to the growth and development of less developed countries. Facing diminishing returns to more capital within their own borders, these countries seek outlets for their internally generated technological advances and capital growth, sources of raw materials and cheap labor, and markets for their finished products. Viewing our world as a self-enclosed "Spaceship Earth" emphasizes the international scope of our interdependencies. As the entire world matures economically, the disparities in living standards between countries will decrease. Many have argued that developed countries have a moral responsibility to aid less developed countries in their search for the good life. For whatever reason, most observers believe that the fortunes of the developed nations and their less developed neighbors are inextricably intertwined.

CHAPTER REVIEW: KEY POINTS

1. *Economic growth* refers to quantitative changes in the capacity to produce goods and services in a country. It occurs through expanding capital or labor resources or discovering new sources of raw materials or technologies. *Economic development* refers to improving the qualitative aspects of economic growth, including changes in the quality of life.

2. The *Rule of 72* is a rule of thumb for estimating how long it takes for a variable to double in value given some percentage growth rate: simply divide 72 by the growth rate. For example, if growth in GNP is occurring at 6 percent per year, GNP will double in approximately 12 years (72/6 = 12).

3. *Diminishing returns* because of the fixity of land cause output to grow more slowly, even if labor and capital increase in fixed proportions.

4. *Population S curves* are theories of the growth paths of populations as they approach their biological limits. Reverend Thomas Malthus and other nineteenth-century economists theorized that equilibrium is attained only when bare subsistence is common to all.

5. *Population growth* tends to slow as a country develops. The least developed countries of the world tend to have the highest rates of population growth.

6. *Capital formation* requires high saving rates. If *voluntary saving* is used to finance development, greater incomes, higher interest rates paid to savers, and (perhaps) less equal income distributions will lead to higher rates of investment. *Involuntary saving* may be used to free investment resources through confiscation, taxation, or inflation.

7. *Capital widening* occurs when the capital stock and labor force grow at the same rates. *Capital deepening* requires the capital stock to grow faster than the labor force.

8. *Technological advances* occur when the same amounts of resources acquire greater productive capacity.

9. Rapid development requires a strong *social infrastructure*—education, communications, transportation, and other networks that facilitate production.

QUESTIONS FOR THOUGHT AND DISCUSSION

1. The saving rate in the United States is currently about 5 percent of national income. This compares to rates of 20 percent in Japan, 15 percent in West Germany, and 13 percent in Great Britain. Why is saving so small in the United States? What effect does this low saving rate have on future economic growth in the United States? How might the federal government encourage greater voluntary saving? Involuntary saving? Are the two sets of policies compatible?

2. In spite of relatively low saving rates in the United States, we have enjoyed greater economic growth than many countries with higher rates of saving (e.g., England). What does this say about the importance of the structure of investment relative to its level?

3. Sylvia Porter has suggested eliminating all taxes on savings to combat stagflation and increase the real growth in our economy. She estimates that by eliminating all taxes on saving, the average saver's return would be increased by roughly 40 percent. This increased incentive to save would add $30–$40 billion in new savings each year. Would such a policy increase productivity? Long-term growth? The real earnings of workers? Reduce inflation? Reduce unemployment? How? How would the loss in tax revenue be made up? What would be the effect of this? Who would be the primary short-run beneficiaries of such a policy? Would different groups gain over the long run? Do you think such a policy is politically feasible? Why or why not?

4. If you were the leader of an impoverished and densely populated country, what policies might you adopt to foster economic growth and development? To what extent would you encourage private entrepreneurs and for which kinds of projects? What role should your government play in developing social infrastructure?

5. How do people in wealthy countries gain through foreign aid to impoverished countries? Do you think the costs to us exceed the benefits? Should foreign aid programs be shrunk or expanded? Why?

6. Why do many highly trained people from developing nations seek employment in advanced countries? Why are these highly educated people apparently more productive and highly paid in these advanced countries than in their home countries?

7. P. T. Bauer, a critic of foreign aid, has argued that "development depends on personal and social factors, not on handouts." He further asserts that "foreign aid means at most some capital is cheaper than if it had been raised independently at market rates." He then goes on to argue that this is different from saying that foreign aid is indispensable for progress. Do you agree with him? Why or why not?

8. Is foreign aid nothing more than a conscience-appeasing payment from rich to poor nations? Is there something wrong with developed countries seeking greater economic growth even if it means that the gap between rich and poor nations may grow wider? Would we in the United States accept greater unemployment for the long run if it meant a greater rate of growth for some developing countries? Are development questions really questions of income distribution on an international scale?

MICROECONOMICS

385

PART 6 Foundations of Microeconomics

Macroeconomic issues were the central concern of Parts Two to Five of this book. Our next task is to look at microeconomic theory and policy, which is the focus of Parts Six to Nine. We concentrate on the private decisions of households and business firms for the next six chapters, and will then introduce, in stages, the microeconomic role of government.

You may breathe a sigh of relief upon reading that the tools you learned in macroeconomics should aid you in mastering the concepts and issues you will study in the coming weeks. For example, you have seen that supply and demand are useful in analyzing problems ranging from the price of molasses to the quandary posed for policymakers by stagflation. Supply and demand analysis also provides important insights into microeconomic decision making. This part of the book allows you to explore in greater detail exactly why supply curves are positively sloped while demand curves are negatively sloped.

Two important tools are introduced in Chapter 20: marginalism and elasticity. *Marginal analysis* provides guideposts for efficient decision making and pressure for movements towards equilibrium; *elasticity* computations enable a more precise use of supply and demand analysis in predicting how market prices and quantities change as circumstances evolve. Then, in Chapter 21, we analyze consumer choice more fully and develop the underpinnings of consumer demand curves. Chapter 22 delves into the nature of production—how inputs are transformed into outputs and how technology shapes the production costs of a firm. You need to understand both of these foundations for firms' decisions in the next part of this book; firms decide which goods to produce and sell and what prices to charge by balancing consumer demands against production costs.

CHAPTER 20 Elasticity and Marginalism

price-elasticity of demand	unitary elasticity	legal incidence
midpoint bases	income-elasticity of demand	economic incidence
relatively elastic and inelastic	cross-elasticity of demand	total, average, and marginal
perfectly elastic and inelastic	price-elasticity of supply	law of equal marginal advantage

Firms that raise their prices know that less of their products will be sold because buyers' demand curves slope downwards. But how much less? Buyers who offer higher prices know that more will be available because supply curves are positively sloped. But how much more? This chapter introduces the concept of elasticity, a tool used to provide estimates that answer these and similar questions.

Elasticity can be a very useful guide to the consequences of decisions. Predictions about the costs and benefits of the alternatives available are necessary before people can make informed choices. What people do with information about costs and benefits is at the heart of marginal analysis, the second major topic of this chapter. Marginal analysis offers some operating rules for how members of households try to maximize their satisfaction and how business decision makers try to maximize the profits of their firms.

Elasticity

Suppose that you are the chief executive officer (CEO) of United Bullmoose Enterprises (UBE) and are concerned because profit seems below what you think possible. Your economic consultant assures you that the demand curves for all UBE products are negatively sloped, so that if you raise the price of plastic mooseheads (UBE's big novelty seller), annual sales will slip below the million you currently sell. Total production costs will fall, but will sales revenues rise? . . . fall? . . . remain constant?

Suppose each moosehead costs $10 to produce. It would be disastrous if you raised the price from $20 to $25 and lost half of your customers, but if only 50,000 out of UBE's million annual sales of mooseheads were lost, profits would rise by $4.25 million. (Why?) How should UBE deal with this dilemma? The problem you are wrestling with is the price-elasticity of the demand for mooseheads.

The general concept of *elasticity* provides a technique to estimate the response of one variable to changes in some other variable and has applications not only in economics, but throughout the behavioral sciences and in physics and engineering as well.

The Price-Elasticity of Demand

Price-elasticity of demand is a measure of the proportional decline *(increase)* in units purchased when price is increased *(cut)* by a given small proportion. If both changes are quite small, this roughly equals the percentage change in quantity divided by the percentage change in price. Price-elasticity can be written:

$$e_p = \frac{\text{change in } Q}{Q} \bigg/ \frac{\text{change in } P}{P} = \frac{\Delta Q}{Q} \bigg/ \frac{\Delta P}{P}$$

$$\cong \frac{\text{percentage change in } Q}{\text{percentage change in } P} = \frac{\%\Delta Q}{\%\Delta P}$$

Such calculations always yield negative numbers because if price is increased, quantity demanded falls, and vice versa. To simplify things, economists conventionally use the *absolute value* of price-elasticity, eliminating the need to deal with negative numbers.

The Problem of Bases   Suppose that the price of plastic mooseheads is dropped from $20 to $12, and annual sales surge from 1 million units to 5 million. The price-elasticity is 10 if we use the percentage formula:

$$e_p \cong \frac{\%\Delta Q}{\%\Delta P} = \frac{5 - 1}{1} \bigg/ \frac{12 - 20}{20} = \frac{400\%}{-40\%}$$
$$= -10. \quad (\text{Absolute value} = 10.)$$

Now watch what happens if we turn this example around. An increase in price from $12 to $20 per moosehead causes sales to dip from 5 million to 1 million units, and the percentage formula yields:

$$e_p \cong \frac{\%\Delta Q}{\%\Delta P} = \frac{1 - 5}{5} \bigg/ \frac{20 - 12}{12} = \frac{-80\%}{66.7\%}$$
$$= -1.2. \quad (\text{Absolute value} = 1.2.)$$

The disparity of the elasticity estimates in this example (10 if price is cut, 1.2 if price is raised) demonstrates that the percentage formula is inconsistent because it depends on whether prices rise or fall. We need to discuss this inconsistency before we provide a cure for it.

The basic problem results from the standard practice in mathematics courses of using the initial value as the base when computing percentage changes. Percentage changes computed in this way may create substantial ambiguity. For example, suppose that the annual profit of UBE's subsidiary, United Bullmoose Oil, jumps from $200 million to $1 billion. The media report the 400 percent increase and imply that UBE's profits are somehow responsible for inflation. The next year, profit drops to $150 million, and the media dutifully report an 85 percent decline. John Q. Public is likely to think that UBE is still way ahead because a 400 percent gain would seem to overpower an 85 percent decline, but it does not . . . $200M → $1.000M → $150M. Although UBE had one very good year, its profit is now less than it was initially.

Elasticity estimates computed by standard percentage changes may be only trivially inconsistent if prices and quantities change very little, but inconsistency poses major problems when prices or quantities change drastically. Such problems with percentages as normally computed have led economists to compute elasticity using as bases the *midpoints* of changes in prices and quantities:

$$e_p = \frac{Q_n - Q_o}{(Q_n + Q_o)/2} \bigg/ \frac{P_n - P_o}{(P_n + P_o)/2}.$$

The subscript o refers to the original price and quantity and the subscript n refers to the new price and quantity.[1] Naturally, the 2s in both denominators can be canceled out, but we will use them here to provide consistency.

Returning to our example of prices of $12 and $20 for plastic mooseheads generating sales of 5 million and 1 million units, respectively, we now get the

---

1. The formula for elasticity can be manipulated in ways that some students find easier to calculate. One example is:

$$e_p = \frac{\text{change in } Q}{\text{change in } P} \times \frac{\text{sum of } P}{\text{sum of } Q}.$$

same elasticity estimate, 2.67, regardless of whether the price is raised or lowered:

$$e_p = \frac{1 - 5}{(1 + 5)/2} \Big/ \frac{20 - 12}{(20 + 12)/2}$$

$$= \frac{-(4/3)}{8/16} = -2.67,$$

and

$$e_p = \frac{5 - 1}{(1 + 5)/2} \Big/ \frac{12 - 20}{(12 + 20)/2}$$

$$= \frac{4/3}{-(8/16)} = -2.67.$$

(Absolute value = 2.67.)

Thus, using **midpoint bases** to calculate price-elasticity clears up the ambiguity arising with percentage measurements.

Ranges of Elasticity Price-elasticity of demand is a measure of the relative responsiveness of quantity demanded to given price changes. If the *elasticity coefficient* (the absolute value of the ratio of proportional changes) is less than 1.0, then price changes are proportionally greater than the resulting quantity changes and demand is referred to as *inelastic*. Inelastically demanded goods include what people tend to consider "necessities"—the quantities you demand are somewhat immune to changes in price, and the share of your income absorbed by such items grows if prices rise, or fall if prices decline. For example, if the price of dog food doubled, would people put their pets on half rations? No. Many people view their pets, and consequently pet food, as necessities.

Curve D_0 in Figure 1 depicts a demand curve that is **relatively inelastic** at a price of $2. When price rises from $2 to $2.50, quantity demanded only falls from 100 to 98—not much of a change. Compare this to demand curve D_1 in the same figure, where a change in price from $2 to $2.50 results in quantity demanded falling from 100 to 40. Quantity demanded is very responsive to a change in price. Thus, D_1 depicts a product with a **relatively elastic** demand; the elasticity coefficient is greater than 1.0, and many consumers are willing to do without the good if the price rises to much over $2—a sign that the product may have numerous close substitutes.

Examples of goods that exhibit relatively elastic demand curves include Volkswagens, Carnation ice cream, McDonald's hamburgers, or Salem cigarettes. Note that total cigarette consumption is probably very unresponsive to price changes, while the de-

FIGURE 1 *Demand Curves with Different Elasticities*

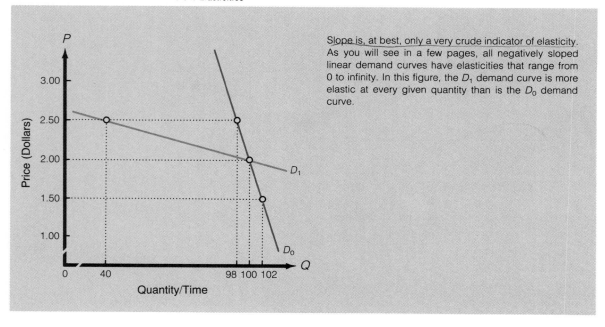

Slope is, at best, only a very crude indicator of elasticity. As you will see in a few pages, all negatively sloped linear demand curves have elasticities that range from 0 to infinity. In this figure, the D_1 demand curve is more elastic at every given quantity than is the D_0 demand curve.

mand for a particular brand is likely to be extremely sensitive to price changes because numerous substitutes are available.

Elasticity and Total Revenue

Price-elasticities of demand are guides to what will happen to *total revenue* (the dollar sales of firms) if prices change slightly. The total revenue of a firm equals the price charged times the quantity sold $(TR = P \times Q)$. For example, a hamburger stand will generate $1 million in total revenue if it sells a million burgers at $1 apiece. Naturally, firms' total revenues equal total spending by consumers. We will use two extreme cases to illustrate how total revenue and price-elasticity are related.

Firms producing outputs that have perfect substitutes in the eyes of buyers confront horizontal demand curves. Any attempt to raise the price even slightly above the market price causes all potential buyers to switch towards the substitutes. For example, one soybean farmer's product is the same as another's. Because even the largest soybean farmers produce only a small part of total world supplies, no single farm's output has a distinguishable impact on world soybean prices. This means that the soybean farmer represented in Figure 2 faces a horizontal demand curve, and any price above $10 per bushel will generate zero sales. At $10, the farmer can sell all the farm can produce, and so would never charge less than $10. Since price will not vary from $10 per bushel, the farm's total revenue will be exactly proportional to its output. For example, if the farm initially produces 1,000 bushels of soybeans annually and then expands output by 10 percent to 1,100 bushels, revenue also increases by 10 percent, rising from $10,000 to $11,000. These horizontal demand curves have price elasticities of infinity and are called **perfectly elastic** demands.[2]

The other extreme case would occur if a demand curve were vertical, as in Figure 3. The elasticity of a vertical demand curve is zero because quantity is unaffected by price changes; such curves are termed **perfectly inelastic.** If such cases existed, the firm's total revenue would be exactly proportional to the price charged.

---

2. Note for those who are mathematically adept: As the slope of the demand curve approaches zero, the elasticity of demand approaches infinity.

FIGURE 2 The Demand Curve that Confronts Individual Soybean Farmers (Perfectly Elastic Demand)

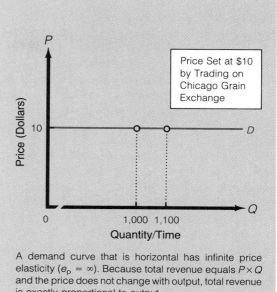

A demand curve that is horizontal has infinite price elasticity $(e_p = \infty)$. Because total revenue equals $P \times Q$ and the price does not change with output, total revenue is exactly proportional to output.

FIGURE 3 A Perfectly Inelastic Demand

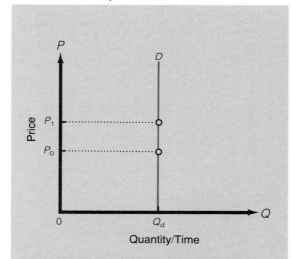

Vertical demand curves have price elasticity of zero $(e_p = 0)$. Although such perfectly inelastic demand curves are impossible, this figure shows that total revenue will be exactly proportional to price. This example is useful because it represents the opposite end of the spectrum from the perfectly elastic demand shown in the previous figure.

Perfectly inelastic demand curves are nonsensical; one is shown here only to aid you in understanding elasticity. Zero price-elasticity implies not only a total lack of substitutes for the good, but also that consumers could and would pay any price to receive a specific quantity of it. A profit-maximizing manager of a firm faced with a perfectly inelastic demand would charge an infinitely high price for the product. Any such good would be essential for life, but we could not afford it because our budgets are limited.

You might think that the prices of insulin for diabetics or dialysis for people with defective kidneys would not affect the quantities demanded by patients who needed them. The cruel facts are that if the prices of these medical necessities were raised, more diabetics would try to control their disease with diet therapy. If prices were raised sufficiently, poorer patients would die and the quantities of insulin or dialysis demanded would fall. Every year millions of people die because they cannot afford medical treatment.

An interesting case when demand curves are neither perfectly elastic nor perfectly inelastic occurs when the total amount of money spent on a product does not vary with the price charged. An example was provided by a farmer who observed that revenues from peach sales were about the same regardless of whether there was a bumper harvest or whether blight wiped out most of a peach crop. If a 1 percent decrease in the peach harvest causes the price of peaches to rise by 1 percent, total spending on peaches is virtually unchanged and the price-elasticity of demand equals one. Such demand curves have **unitary elasticity.** Examples of unitarily elastic demands occur when a person budgets a certain amount of money for, say, meat or magazines and will not deviate from that figure regardless of price. A representative unitary elastic demand curve is shown in Figure 4.

If the price-elasticity of demand for a product is greater than zero but less than one, the demand curve is *relatively inelastic*. Economists sometimes shorten this to *inelastic*. If the price elasticity is greater than one but less than infinity, the demand for the product is *relatively elastic,* or *elastic.*

Price-elasticities of demand are obviously important to firms because they indicate what will happen to sales revenues when prices are raised or lowered. Price-elasticities of demand are also important to

FIGURE 4 *A Demand Curve with Unitary Elasticity*

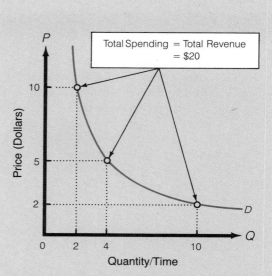

The total revenue ($P \times Q$) is unaffected by price or quantity if demand is unitarily elastic. Unitarily elastic demand curves ($e_p = 1$) are rectangular hyperbolas, which have the characteristic that all rectangles drawn from the curve to the axes have exactly the same geometric area ($P \times Q$). You will see more rectangular hyperbolas as we proceed further in economics.

consumers since they reflect how desperately buyers want particular goods and how the composition of consumer budgets will change as relative prices change. Table 1 summarizes how the firm's total revenue (and consumers' total spending) for a good changes as prices change.

Demand curves rarely have constant elasticities along the full range of possible prices and quantities, but Table 2 presents some estimates of the elasticities of demand for a number of products within the range of prices that you would roughly expect each to have. If you will spend a few moments studying this table, you will notice that the elasticities of demand tend to be larger:

1. the more substitutes there are for a good;
2. the more an item absorbs as a share of typical budgets; *the more elastic*
3. the less "necessary" (more of a "luxury") a particular good is; and
4. the longer the time interval considered.

TABLE 1 *Price Changes, Elasticities, and Total Revenues/Expenditures*

Price Elasticity of Demand	How Total Revenues Change	
	Price Increases	**Price Decreases**
Inelastic $0 < e < 1$	*TR* increases	*TR* decreases
Unitarily Elastic $e = 1$	No change in *TR*	No change in *TR*
Elastic $\infty > e > 1$	*TR* decreases	*TR* increases

TABLE 2 *Price-Elasticities of Demand for Selected Goods and Services*

Good or Service	Price-Elasticity of Demand
Marijuana	1.51
Automobiles	1.35
Beer	1.13
Housing	1.00
Alcohol	0.92
Hospital and physician services	0.05 to 0.15
Gasoline (transportation only)	
short run	0.1 to 0.3
long run	1.50
Electricity	
long-run residential	
and commercial usage	0.88
short-run residential	0.13

Sources: Marijuana—T. C. Misket and F. Vakil, "Some Estimates of Price and Expenditure Elasticities among UCLA Students," *Review of Economics and Statistics,* November 1972. Automobiles—Gregory C. Chow, *Demand for Automobiles in the United States* (Amsterdam: North-Holland Publishing Company, 1957). Beer—T. F. Hogarty and K. G. Elzinga, "The Demand for Beer," *The Review of Economics and Statistics,* May 1972. Housing—Richard F. Muth, "The Demand for Non-Farm Housing," *The Demand for Durable Goods,* Arnold C. Harberger, ed. (Chicago: University of Chicago Press, 1960). Alcohol—H. S. Houthakker and Lester D. Taylor, *Consumer Demand in the United States,* 2/e (Cambridge: Harvard University Press, 1970). Hospital and physician services—Joseph P. Newhouse and Charles E. Phelps, "New Estimates of Price and Income Elasticities of Medical Care Services," *The Role of Health Insurance in the Health Services Sector,* Richard N. Rosett, ed. (New York: National Bureau of Economic Research, 1976). Gasoline and electricity—J. M. Griffin, *Energy Conservation in the OECD, 1980–2000* (Cambridge, MA: Ballinger, 1979).

The number of substitutes available is by far the most important determinant of price-elasticity of demand. Rising prices drive consumers towards substitutes; falling prices are incentives to find more uses for a good. For example, the demand for Campbell's pork and beans is very price-elastic because slight price hikes will cause consumers to substitute other brands and slight price cuts will raise Campbell's sales at the expense of competing brands. On the other hand, the demand for local telephone services is relatively inelastic because few substitutes are available.

Another important determinant of price-elasticity is the period allowed for adjustments to price changes. Elasticity rises as longer intervals are considered because as time elapses, more substitutes become feasible. Elasticities are measured for a specified period for this reason. For example, Table 2 indicates that the demand for gasoline is relatively inelastic in the short run, but relatively elastic in the long run. Increases in gasoline prices eventually induce some people to buy smaller cars, get more frequent tune-ups, use mass transit, or relocate closer to their schools or jobs.

If a firm faces a demand curve with a price-elasticity of less than one, it will always find it profitable to raise the product's price since revenue will increase and, as output and units sold fall, total production costs will decline. (Profit must rise if revenue increases and total costs fall.) As the price is increased, growing numbers of consumers will buy substitutes for the good; those who cannot find substitutes ultimately will be forced to do without.

Elasticity Along a Demand Curve
We have indicated that price-elasticity varies along most demand curves. You might think that the linear demand curve in Panel A of Figure 5 would have a constant price-elasticity. Not so. The rectangle we have drawn at point a represents the highest revenue available with this demand curve. That is, $P \times Q$ is at its maximum possible value. Whether we raise or lower the price from $10, revenue falls, as shown in the table and in Panel B. This demand curve is price-elastic above point a because any price increase causes revenue to decline; e_p is greater than one. Symmetrically, price decreases from $10 cause revenue to fall, so below point a the demand curve is price inelastic; e_p is less than one. At point a, demand is unitarily elastic; e_p equals one.

The conclusion is that the price-elasticity of demand tends to rise as we charge higher and higher prices. Slope alone is not a good indicator of elasticity because the price and quantity bases used to compute proportions change continuously. In fact, other than vertical or horizontal demand curves, every linear demand curve has elasticities that range from zero to infinity. Refer back to Figure 1 for a moment and note that both D_0 and D_1, if extended, would have elasticities ranging from 0 to infinity, even though D_1 is more elastic than D_0 for each possible shared price or quantity. Slope is only a crude indicator of elasticity and may mislead you about the elasticity of a given curve.

Other Elasticities

Later in this chapter, we will examine how price-elasticity of demand interacts with price-elasticity of supply to determine such things as who bears the burdens of specific types of taxes. Before we address such questions, however, we will look at other important types of elasticities.

Income-Elasticity of Demand
Rich people do not just buy more goods; the things they buy also differ from the purchases of poor people. The **income-elasticity of demand** for a good measures the proportional change in the amount demanded resulting from a given small proportional change in income. For simplicity, you might think of income-elasticity as the ratio of percentage changes in the amount of a good demanded relative to income. However, for reasons that parallel the rationale for midpoint-based computations of price-elasticities, we actually compute income-elasticity as:

$$e_y = \frac{Q_n - Q_o}{(Q_n + Q_o)/2} \Big/ \frac{Y_n - Y_o}{(Y_n + Y_o)/2}.$$

Again, subscript n refers to new values while subscript o represents old values, and both 2s could be dropped from the denominators without affecting this calculation.

Such goods as scuba lessons or limousines are *income-elastic* because each 1 percent rise in income causes the amounts sold to rise by more than 1 percent. If income increases by 1 percent and the amount of a good demanded rises somewhat, but by less than 1 percent, demand is *income-inelastic*. As long as increases in income stimulate more purchases of a good, it is a *normal good*.[3] Income-elasticity is negative and goods are *inferior goods* if purchases of a good decline as income rises. Lard, pinto beans, and used tires are examples.

Why are these numbers important for, among other things, business decision making? As the CEO of United Bullmoose Enterprises, would you want to know the implications of a recession for plastic moosehead sales? For oil and gasoline? For used auto part sales from your United Bullmoose Junkyards subsidiary? Of course! Would the manager of your travel trailer subsidiary be optimistic about sales prospects if an economic boom were predicted, and downcast if a recession hit? Clearly yes, if the demand for trailers is income-elastic. Estimates of the income-elasticities of demand for particular goods help firms

---

3. Sometimes data for the prices or quantities of goods are not available, but sales data ($P \times Q$) are. In such cases, economists approximate income elasticities by:

$$\frac{\text{percent change in expenditures}}{\text{percent change in income}}.$$

If the result exceeds (*is less than*) one, demand is presumed to be income elastic (*inelastic*).

FIGURE 5 *Varying Price Elasticities along a Linear Demand Curve*

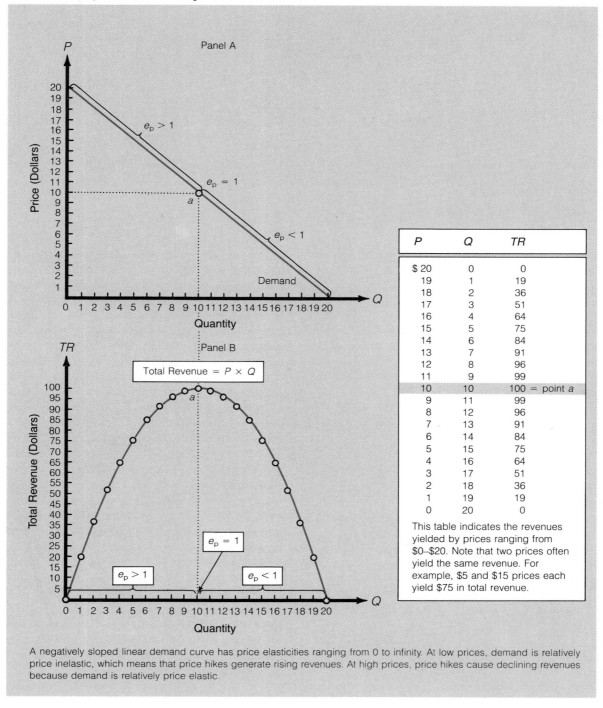

P	Q	TR
$ 20	0	0
19	1	19
18	2	36
17	3	51
16	4	64
15	5	75
14	6	84
13	7	91
12	8	96
11	9	99
10	10	100 = point *a*
9	11	99
8	12	96
7	13	91
6	14	84
5	15	75
4	16	64
3	17	51
2	18	36
1	19	19
0	20	0

This table indicates the revenues yielded by prices ranging from $0–$20. Note that two prices often yield the same revenue. For example, $5 and $15 prices each yield $75 in total revenue.

A negatively sloped linear demand curve has price elasticities ranging from 0 to infinity. At low prices, demand is relatively price inelastic, which means that price hikes generate rising revenues. At high prices, price hikes cause declining revenues because demand is relatively price elastic.

forecast sales and plan production, employment, and investment. Income-elasticities of demand for some broad product categories are displayed in Table 3.

Cross-Elasticity of Demand Another important measure of consumer behavior is the **cross-elasticity of demand,** which estimates the proportional

TABLE 3 Income-Elasticities of Demand for Selected Goods and Services

Good or Service	Income-Elasticity of Demand
Automobiles	3.00
Housing	1.15
Beer	0.93
Charitable donations	0.70
Hospital and physician services	0.09

Sources: Automobiles—Gregory C. Chow, *Demand for Automobiles in the United States* (Amsterdam: North-Holland Publishing Company, 1957). Housing—Richard F. Muth, *Cities and Housing: The Spatial Pattern of Urban Residential Land Use* (Chicago: The University of Chicago Press, 1969). Beer—T. F. Hogarty and K. G. Elzinga, "The Demand for Beer," *Review of Economics and Statistics,* May 1972. Charitable donations—M. Feldstein and A. Taylor, "The Income Tax and Charitable Contributions," *Econometrica,* November 1976. Hospital and physician services—Joseph P. Newhouse and Charles E. Phelps, "New Estimates of Price and Income Elasticities of Medical Care Service," in *The Role of Health Insurance in the Health Services Sector,* Richard N. Rosett, ed. (New York: National Bureau of Economic Research, 1976).

changes in units sold when the prices of related goods are changed slightly. Formally, cross-elasticity can be calculated as:

$$e_{xy} = \frac{Q_{xn} - Q_{xo}}{(Q_{xn} + Q_{xo})/2} \Bigg/ \frac{P_{yn} - P_{yo}}{(P_{yn} + P_{yo})/2},$$

where Q_{xo} (old) and Q_{xn} (new) are the quantities of good x bought before and after price changes for good y (P_{yo} and P_{yn}, respectively). Again, the 2s could be dropped from the equation.

FIGURE 6 Elastic Supply Curves

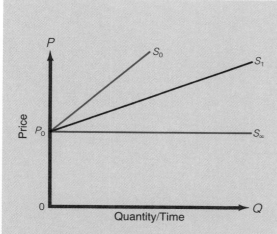

Supply curves that intersect the price axis are relatively elastic ($e_s > 1$). A horizontal supply curve is perfectly price elastic ($e_s = \infty$). In such cases, total revenue or expenditures ($P \times Q$) will be exactly proportional to the quantity demanded.

Consider the sales of American cars (Brand X) after U.S. import restrictions in the early 1980s drove up the prices of Japanese cars (Brand Y). All else constant, we would expect American car sales to grow when imported cars became higher priced. Thus, we would expect a positive relationship between the prices of imported cars and the quantities of American cars sold domestically; the price cross-elasticity of demand (e_{xy}) should be positive. When price cross-elasticities of demand are *positive,* the items in question are *substitute goods.* Other sets of substitutes are artificial turf and natural grass, golf clubs and tennis racquets and vans and travel trailers. In fact, broad competition for consumers' dollars causes most goods to be at least weak substitutes for each other.

When the price cross-elasticity of demand is *negative,* the goods in question are **complementary goods.** For example, as the price of hand-held calculators has declined, the demand for alkaline batteries has jumped markedly. Other examples of complementary goods include ham and eggs, cameras and film, suits and ties, and pretzels and beer.

The Price-Elasticity of Supply The **price-elasticity of supply** measures suppliers' responses to price changes. This elasticity formula is the same as for computing demand price-elasticity:

$$e_s = \frac{Q_n - Q_o}{(Q_n + Q_o)/2} \Bigg/ \frac{P_n - P_o}{(P_n + P_o)/2}.$$

This elasticity is typically positive because supply curves slope up.

If extending the supply curve of a good would result in an intersection with the vertical (price) axis, the amount of the good supplied is highly responsive to its price. In such cases as S_0 and S_1 in Figure 6, the elasticity of supply exceeds one and the supply curve is described as *relatively elastic*. If a supply curve is horizontal, such as S_∞ in Figure 6, then the elasticity of supply is infinity and the supply is *perfectly price-elastic*. Buyers can demand any amounts of these goods without affecting the price at all. Examples of goods having perfectly elastic supplies include such things as a family's groceries—no matter how many cans of tuna your family personally consumes, your purchases will not affect the price you pay. Thus, the supply of tuna to you is perfectly elastic even though the market supply of tuna is positively sloped. Similarly, a single baker who buys flour in bulk is faced with a perfectly elastic supply of flour. In these and similar cases, individual demands determine the amounts people buy, but not the prices they pay.

If extending the supply curve would result in intersection with the quantity axis, the amount of a good supplied is comparatively unresponsive to its price. Supply curves such as S_1 and S_2 in Figure 7 are examples of *relatively inelastic supplies*. In the extreme situation where the quantity supplied is totally unresponsive to price, the supply curve is vertical (S_0 in Figure 7) and the elasticity of supply is zero ($e_s = 0$). Examples of these *perfectly inelastic supplies* include land (the fixed amount available is unaffected by price) and other highly specialized items or resources—Rembrandt paintings, Stradivarius violins, and the comedy of Eddie Murphy are each unique. When supplies are fixed, demand alone determines a good's price or person's wage, but the quantity exchanged is not related to the price paid.

You may have noticed that perfectly inelastic supplies look just like perfectly inelastic demands, and that perfectly elastic demands and supplies also appear to be identical. How about *unitarily elastic* supply curves ($e_s = 1$)? Do they resemble unitarily elastic demand curves? Not at all. For e_s to equal one, the quantity supplied must change in fixed proportion with price. All supply curves that are straight lines through the origin have this characteristic, as shown in Figure 8.

FIGURE 7 *Inelastic Supply Curves*

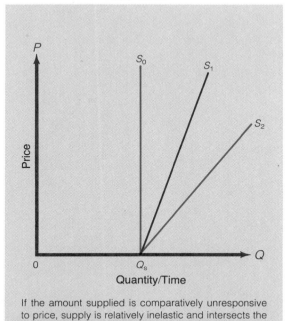

If the amount supplied is comparatively unresponsive to price, supply is relatively inelastic and intersects the quantity axis. A vertical supply curve is perfectly price inelastic ($e_s = 0$). Although rare, such supplies do exist. Land sites are an example. In such cases, total spending (revenue) is exactly proportional to price.

FIGURE 8 *Examples of Supply Curves where Elasticity of Supply Equals One*

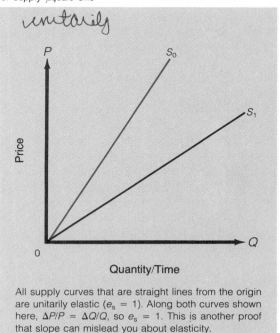

All supply curves that are straight lines from the origin are unitarily elastic ($e_s = 1$). Along both curves shown here, $\Delta P/P = \Delta Q/Q$, so $e_s = 1$. This is another proof that slope can mislead you about elasticity.

We can summarize the concept of elasticity: Elasticity measures the proportional response of one variable with respect to another. If X influences Y, then the elasticity of Y with respect to X equals:

$$\frac{\Delta Y}{Y} \bigg/ \frac{\Delta X}{X}.$$

Elasticity, as a summary measure of responsiveness, is used in many other ways. For example, measures of elasticity have been developed to address the following problems:

1. If wage rates increase relative to the costs of capital, then firms will find it profitable to substitute some capital for labor. How much substitution occurs as resource prices change?

2. People's expectations of inflation are related to prior inflation. How does past inflation influence how much inflation people expect?

Being able to specify how elasticity would be calculated for these examples is unimportant at this point, but it is important for you to realize that the concept of elasticity may be useful whenever variables are systematically related.

Elasticity and the Burdens of Taxation

One of the most pressing issues facing the U.S. is tax reform. The phrase *tax reform* is just empty rhetoric unless we know who bears the burden of various taxes. Elasticity plays a major role in answering the question of who bears the tax burden.

Tax Incidence

The **legal incidence** of a tax falls on the individual or firm responsible for writing the check for taxes to government. The **economic incidence** of taxation (or *tax burden*) falls on the person who suffers reduced purchasing power because of the tax. Tax burdens are often avoided by the party bearing the legal incidence through *tax-shifting*. If the tax is passed on to the consumer in the form of higher prices, we say the tax is *forward-shifted*. Taxes are *backward-shifted* if the tax burden is transferred to workers in the form of lower take-home wages, or to other resource suppliers in the form of lower factor payments. Considering extreme elasticities allows us to develop some general principles.

Inelastic Supply: Land Taxes

They ain't makin' any more of the stuff.
　　　　　　　　　　—An Unknown Land Promoter

The supply of land is perfectly inelastic. The rental price paid for land reflects the demand for land, and demanders do not care whether the rent is kept by the landlord or split between the owner and his Uncle Sam. Figure 9 illustrates the effects of taxes on the demand and supply of land. The annual rental value of the land is $100 per acre when demand is D_0 and supply is S_0. (If landowners do not rent their land out, we might treat them as their own tenants; the opportunity cost of not renting is $100 per acre per year.)

Suppose that a 50 percent tax on land rents were imposed. If landlords tried to recoup the $50-per-acre tax by raising rents to above $100, there would be a surplus of rentable land. As landlords with vacant land tried to attract renters, the gross rental price of land will fall back to $100. The owners cannot avoid the $50 tax burden per acre by selling because any buyer would base the value of land on

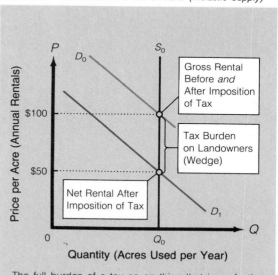

FIGURE 9　*The Burden of a Tax on Land (Inelastic Supply)*

The full burden of a tax on anything that is perfectly inelastically supplied is borne by the current owner or seller. Attempts to forward-shift such taxes cause excess supplies and downward pressures on prices.

the $50 net rent per acre it yields, not the initial $100. Thus, land prices would be halved because of the 50 percent land rent tax; landowners bear both the legal and the economic incidence of the land tax because the supply of land is perfectly inelastic.[4]

Inelastic Demand

The demand for common table salt is among the least price-elastic of all regular household purchases. Recognizing the inelasticity of this demand, the early Romans enacted a tax on salt in order to ensure that the tax burden fell on the consumer. Let us see why you as a consumer would bear nearly the full burden of a salt tax. Suppose that your annual demand for salt is shown in Figure 10. Because spending on salt absorbs so little of your budget and because of an absence of substitutes, even a 300 or 400 percent increase in the price probably would not noticeably affect the amount you use on your eggs or the rest of your food. You will consume roughly four pounds of salt annually, whether salt is free, costs $0.30 a pound, $1 a pound, or whatever.

Initially, competition among salt producers permits you to buy almost any amount you would like without affecting the market price of $0.30 a pound. If a tax of $0.20 a pound were imposed, suppliers could easily forward-shift the tax by raising the price to $0.50 a pound, at which there is neither an excess supply nor excess demand. The conclusion is that if demand is perfectly inelastic, the consumer will bear the full burden of any taxes.

We stated earlier that demands are never perfectly inelastic. This salt example is intended only to show that if demand were very inelastic, the burden of a tax will fall primarily on the consumer. Would people reduce the salt in their diets if it rose to $100 per pound? Of course. Would salt be used on snowy roads or icy sidewalks at such prices? Of course not.

Elasticities of demand reflect buyers' desperation for goods because of the availability or lack of substitutes. Similarly, supply curves mirror the urgency of sellers' needs for customers because of the availability or the lack of good options for their resources.

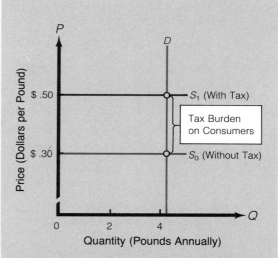

FIGURE 10 The Burden of a Tax on Salt (Inelastic Demand)

If demand were ever perfectly inelastic (and it cannot be), the full burden of the tax would be borne by the consumer.

The more desperate buyers or sellers are, the less elastic their respective demands or supplies and the more difficult it is for them to alter their behavior to avoid a tax. This makes it easier to stick them with the burdens of taxes.

Our analyses of land and salt show why governments are fond of taxes on inelastically demanded goods (tobacco) or inelastically supplied resources: it maximizes government revenue. The story is a bit different when elastic demands or supplies are taxed.

Elastic Demand

You and most other people do not care whether the paper clips you use are produced domestically or imported; imported paper clips and domestic paper clips are perfect substitutes. Suppose, therefore, that the demand for imported paper clips is perfectly elastic at the current market price.

If a Bornean paper clip producer is somewhat dependent on the American market, this firm's supply curve slopes upward, as in Figure 11; before any tariff, the Bornean producer sells 121 million paper

---

4. An issue addressed later in this book is the "single tax movement," whose advocates like the idea that landowners fully bear any tax on land.

FIGURE 11 *The Burden of a Tax on Imported Paper Clips (Elastic Demand)*

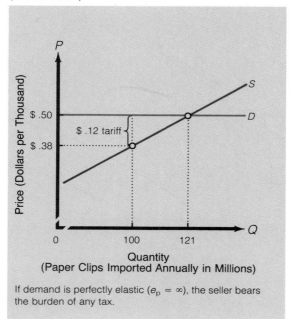

If demand is perfectly elastic ($e_p = \infty$), the seller bears the burden of any tax.

FIGURE 12 *The Burden of a Tax on Aluminum (Elastic Supply)*

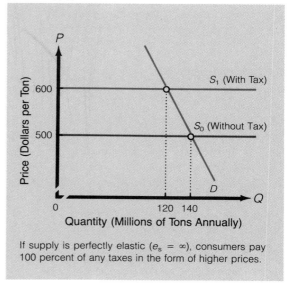

If supply is perfectly elastic ($e_s = \infty$), consumers pay 100 percent of any taxes in the form of higher prices.

clips per year in the United States at a price of $0.50 per thousand. If our government imposes a tariff of $0.12 per thousand on imported paper clips, the Borneans cannot forward-shift this tax to consumers in the form of higher prices.

At any price greater than $0.50 per thousand, Americans who have been using Bornean paper clips will completely switch over to American-made paper clips. The Borneans must absorb this tariff and will wind up with a net price received of $0.38 per thousand. In this case, the tax is completely backward-shifted to the Bornean factory's resource suppliers. Their wages, profits, rents, or receipts of interest will suffer. Whenever demand for a product is perfectly elastic, suppliers will bear the full burden of any taxes.

Elastic Supply

The supply curve of the aluminum industry has been estimated to be roughly perfectly elastic because average production costs are constant, no matter how much or how little aluminum is produced. Many materials are substitutes for aluminum in some uses, but none are close substitutes in all uses. Thus, Fig-

ure 12 shows a perfectly elastic supply of aluminum and a less elastic demand for it.

Without taxation, 140 million tons of aluminum will be sold annually for $500 a ton. Suppose that a tax of $100 a ton were levied on aluminum producers. They would be unable to cover production costs unless they received at least $600 per ton from consumers, who would cut back purchases to 120 million tons annually at this higher price. (As an exercise, compute the price-elasticity of demand.) Notice that at $600 a ton, there are neither excess supplies nor excess demands. Production and consumption are both 120 million tons annually. The conclusion is that taxes will be 100 percent forward-shifted if supplies are perfectly elastic.

Summary: Taxes and Elasticity   Taxes will be 100 percent forward-shifted (borne by consumers) if either *(a)* demand is perfectly inelastic (salt) or *(b)* supply is perfectly elastic (aluminum). Taxes will be backward-shifted completely (borne by suppliers) if either *(a)* supply is perfectly inelastic (land), or *(b)* demand is perfectly elastic (paper clips). You may believe that these extreme cases of elasticities seldom occur in the "real world." Three chapters hence, you will learn that competition makes perfectly elastic supplies and demands reasonably common.

Although the great majority of products have demands and supplies that are neither perfectly inelastic nor perfectly elastic, our results do suggest a workable general principle: The greater the elasticity of demand relative to the elasticity of supply, the greater the backward-shifting of any tax burden. The smaller the ratio *(elasticity of demand)/(elasticity of supply)*, the greater the forward-shifting of the tax burden.

You will encounter numerous applications of elasticity in the coming chapters. A tool that is even more pervasive is marginal analysis. Indeed, the "economic way of thinking" is almost synonymous with "thinking at the margin."

Totals, Averages, and Marginals

All decision making is at the margin.

—*Unknown*

Rational decision making is an **incremental** or **marginal** process. For example, you generally do not decide whether you are going to have three brownies before you begin eating dessert; instead, your hunger after finishing your first determines whether you will eat another, and then, having finished your second, whether you will have a third. Similarly, most firm managers decide whether to expand or contract their operations a bit *(marginally)* rather than whether to close their doors or hire 10,000 workers. *Marginalism* exists in most everyday activities. A journey of 1,000 miles begins with a single step. And then another. And yet another.

In microeconomics you will constantly encounter relationships between **total, average,** and *incremental* (or *marginal*) units. You probably know what total and average mean, but marginal may be a mystery. Just as the margin of a piece of paper refers to its boundaries, margin refers to "the edge", or the last few bits one way or another of some thing. If you pass an exam *marginally,* this means that you are close to failing. A *marginal* firm teeters on the brink of bankruptcy.[5]

---

5. Several of these examples are drawn from "The Relevance of Marginal Analysis", by Michael Behr, in *Great Ideas for Teaching Economics,* 3/e, edited by R. T. Byrns and G. W. Stone (Glenview, Illinois: Scott, Foresman & Co., 1987).

Economists often refer to the marginal unit of some thing as the *last* or *extra* unit, and at times students think that this requires the marginal unit to be identifiable as a particular unit. This is not generally the case. For example, if there are 30 students in your class, who is the thirtieth? If any one of you had not enrolled, or if any of you drops the course, there would only be 29 students in the class. Thus, each of you is the thirtieth (marginal) student. (Does that make you uneasy?) Similarly, there is no way to ascertain which is the sixth (marginal) slice out of a cherry pie until the other five are eaten. Nor can we identify a particular individual as the last (marginal) soldier in an army of 3 million, or the marginal worker employed by General Motors. In a sense, every unit of any grouping is the marginal unit. Keep this in mind in the next few chapters and you will avoid a lot of confusion and grief.

Most marginals in economics refer to the ratios of the changes in one thing in response to small changes in another. For example, the *marginal utility* of a brownie is the extra satisfaction derived from the consumption of an extra piece, and the *marginal physical product of labor* refers to the extra output generated by the last worker added to a production process.

The two rules governing how marginals influence totals or averages are:

1. If the marginal unit is positive *(negative),* the total will rise *(fall).* If the marginal unit equals zero, the total is unaffected.
2. If the marginal exceeds *(is less than)* an average, the average rises *(falls).* The average is unchanged if marginal equals average.

For example, an obese dieter does not lose 100+ pounds instantly but, rather, incrementally—a pound at a time. If, in the next few (marginal) days, the dieter eats only a little lean meat and fresh vegetables (generating *negative* marginal pounds), total weight will drop a bit. Cheating with some hot fudge sundaes will yield *positive* marginal pounds and a jump in total weight. Similarly, if your next few (marginal) grades are above your average, your GPA will rise, but it will fall if your marginal grades are below your previous average.

Geometry and Marginal Units

This section builds on the graphical analysis provided at the beginning of this book. Most functions used in economic analysis involve curved lines. Re-

FIGURE 13 Relationships Between Total, Average, and Marginal Profit

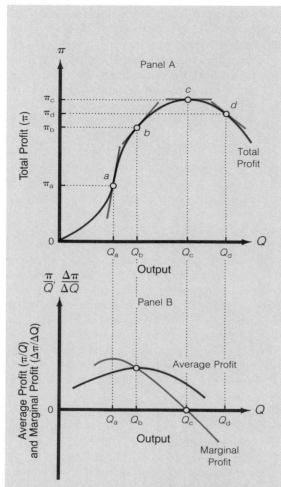

Total profit in Panel A rises as output is expanded until output level Q_c is reached; thereafter, it declines. Maximum average profit occurs in Panel B at output level Q_b, the point at which marginal and average profit are equal. At outputs below Q_b, marginal profit exceeds average profit, "pulling" average profit up. Beyond Q_b, marginal profit is less than average profit, pulling average profit down. When total profit is at its maximum (Panel A), marginal profit is zero and it is negative as output is expanded beyond Q_c in Panel B.

call that slope is defined as rise/run. For short segments of curved lines, on the average, slope equals:

$$\frac{(change\ in\ rise)}{(change\ in\ run)}.$$

Thus, dividing the change in the variable on the y axis by the corresponding small change in the variable of the x axis yields the slope of a function at a particular point. This slope is the ratio of the marginal units of these variables.

As we increase output along the x axis in Panel A of Figure 13 from Q_a to Q_b to Q_c to Q_d, profit (on the y axis) grows from π_a to π_b to π_c, and then falls to π_d. The *marginal profit* as this firm produces slightly larger amounts of output equals the slope of this profit curve at these points, and is graphed in Panel B. Notice that average profit per unit rises whenever it is less than the extra profit made on extra units of output, and falls when the marginal profit is below the average profit.

Firms seek maximum profits, which in this case occur at output level Q_c. Notice that the slope of the profit function is zero where the profit function is at its *maximum*. Similarly, if the marginal cost of output starts below the average cost per unit of output and then rises, average costs are minimized where the marginal cost equals the average cost, as at point z in Figure 14. This is the *minimum* point of this average cost curve.

The Law of Equal Marginal Advantage

The goal of economic efficiency is attained only if equivalent goods or similar resources are allocated in equally advantageous ways **at the margin.** This idea is known as the **law of equal marginal advantage.** For example, if the last dollar you spend on gasoline fails to yield the added pleasure you would receive if it were spent on an extra milk shake, you will gain by spending less on gasoline and more on milk shakes.

People generally change their patterns of consumption or production whenever resources (in this example, the command over resources represented by your last few dollars) are inefficiently allocated. Thus, you would gain by drinking an extra milk shake and burning a bit less gasoline, and undoubtedly make these sorts of adjustments with very little conscious thought. You settle into a stable consumption pattern only when the last cent you spend on any single good yields satisfaction equal to that gained from the last cent spent on any other good.

Similar *marginal adjustments* span the realm of economic decision making. Here is an example

FIGURE 14 Average and Marginal Costs

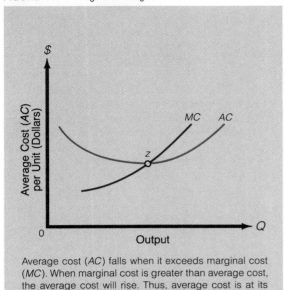

Average cost (AC) falls when it exceeds marginal cost (MC). When marginal cost is greater than average cost, the average cost will rise. Thus, average cost is at its minimum at point z, where AC = MC.

drawn from choices about work. Suppose that you and your identical twin are equally strong, experienced, and intelligent. If your twin works an 8-hour day and produces $64 worth of mowed lawns while you generate $48 worth of cleaned windows with similar effort, something is wrong. You will (and should) shift into mowing lawns so that your labor resources are allocated equally advantageously—at $8-per-hour instead of the $6-per-hour you have been earning.

Whenever equivalent resources are not used to equal advantage, there is economic inefficiency.

Other applications of the dictate that efficiency requires similar resources to be allocated in equally advantageous ways at the margin include the notions that:

1. People's time must be divided between work and leisure so that the gain from the last hour an individual works (the individual's wage) just equals the subjective value of the last hour of leisure enjoyed.
2. The last dollar a firm pays for labor must generate the same amount of extra production (and profit) as the last dollar spent on capital, or land, or energy inputs.
3. The dollar value to a consumer of the right to consume a particular good must equal the value of other production that society sacrifices in making that marginal unit of the good available to that consumer.

Do not worry if these applications of the law of equal marginal advantage seem a bit murky at this juncture. As you continue through this book, you will constantly encounter its corollaries and will see that competitive processes tend to drive a market system so that this requirement for economic efficiency is met.

This chapter has described two tools that you will use extensively in the coming chapters: elasticity and thinking on the margin are vital for understanding the decisions of consumers and suppliers. If you feel befuddled at times when you encounter an application of elasticity, or when you are in the midst of reading about such things as marginal utility, average physical product, or total, average, and marginal costs, don't give up in despair. Refer back to this material to help you with terminology and then keep plugging forward. We promise that many people far less intelligent than you are have mastered these concepts by diligent study and a bit of reflection.

CHAPTER REVIEW: KEY POINTS

1. The *price-elasticity of demand* is a measure of the responsiveness of the amount demanded to small price changes and is defined as:

$$e_p = \frac{\text{relative change in quantity demanded}}{\text{relative change in price}}$$
$$\cong \%\Delta Q \div \%\Delta P.$$

2. Problems result when calculating elasticity if initial prices and quantities are used as bases. As a result, economists typically use *midpoint bases*. The price-elasticity of demand is negative but, for convenience, we use absolute values to avoid the negative sign.

3. If price-elasticity is less than one, then demand is relatively unresponsive to changes in price and is said to be *inelastic*. If elasticity is greater than one, the demand is very responsive to price changes and is *elastic*. Demand is *unitarily elastic* if the elasticity coefficient equals one.

4. Elasticity, price changes, and total revenues (expenditures) are related in the following manner: If demand is inelastic *(elastic)* and price increases *(falls)*, total revenue will rise. If demand is elastic *(inelastic)* and price rises *(falls)*, total revenue (expenditures) will fall. If demand is unitarily elastic ($e_p = 1$), total revenue will be unaffected by price changes.

5. Along any negatively sloped linear demand curve, parts of the curve will be elastic, unitarily elastic, and inelastic. The price-elasticity of demand rises as the price rises.

6. *Income-elasticity of demand* is the proportional change in the amount of a good demanded divided by a given proportionate change in income. Normal goods have income-elasticities above zero, while inferior goods have negative income-elasticities.

7. *Cross-elasticity of demand* measures the respon-

siveness of the quantity demanded of one good to price changes in a related good. That is, price cross-elasticity is the proportional change in the quantity of good *X* (Chevrolets) divided by a given proportional change in the price of good *Y* (Fords). If the cross-elasticity of demand is positive *(negative)*, the goods are *substitutes (complements)*.

8. The *price-elasticity of supply* measures the responsiveness of suppliers to changes in prices, and is defined to parallel that for the price-elasticity of demand: the proportional change in the amount supplied divided by a given proportional change in price. The price-elasticity of supply is typically positive, reflecting the positive slope of the supply curve.

9. The individual who actually loses purchasing power because of a tax is said to bear the tax's *economic incidence (tax burden)*. This may be quite different from the individual who is legally responsible for the tax, who bears its *legal incidence*. When these individuals differ, the tax has been shifted. A tax can be *forward-shifted* (to consumers) or *backward-shifted* (to labor or other resource owners).

10. If demand is perfectly inelastic or supply is perfectly elastic, a tax will be completely forward-shifted. If supply is perfectly inelastic or demand is perfectly elastic, the tax will be completely backward-shifted.

11. *Incremental* or *marginal* changes direct rational decision making. If a marginal unit of something is positive *(negative)*, its total will rise *(fall)*. If the marginal unit is zero, the total is unaffected. If the marginal exceeds *(is less than)* an average, the average rises *(falls)*. The average is unchanged if marginal equals average.

12. The *law of equal marginal advantage* dictates that similar resources be used in equally valuable ways to achieve efficiency.

QUESTIONS FOR THOUGHT AND DISCUSSION

1. Compute the elasticities in the following situations.
   a. The Jukes family buys 360 lollipops annually at a price of $0.20 each but would consume 480 per year if the price dropped to $0.16. Their price-elasticity of demand is ⌊1.285⌋.

   b. The U.S. Air Force purchased 170 ashtrays for their latest jets when the price was $875 each, but ordered only 130 when the defense contractor raised the price to $1,125. The Air Force's price-elasticity of demand for ashtrays is ⌊1.06⌋.

c. If American drivers burned 185 million gallons of gasoline on average when the price was $1.15 per gallon, but cut back to 155 million gallons weekly when the pump price rose to $1.35 per gallon, the price-elasticity of the market demand for gasoline equals __1.10__.

d. If a $5.98 sale on regular $8.99 cassettes raises a store's sales from 600 to 6,000 per week, the price-elasticity of the demand faced by the store is roughly __4.07__

e. If a boom raises national income from $4.0 trillion to $4.4 trillion and macadamia nut sales jump from 3 to 5 million pounds annually, the income-elasticity of demand for the nuts is __5.25__

f. If each 1 percent hike in the price of mousetraps causes a 2 percent decline in the quantity of cheese sold, the price cross-elasticity of demand for these complementary goods is roughly __2.0__.

g. When the Kallikak family can sell Shar-Pei puppies for $1,800 each, they offer 60 to the market annually, but when the price falls to $600 apiece, they are willing to sell only 12 each year. The price-elasticity of their supply is __1.33__.

h. When the temperature drops from 34° F to 18° F, average attendance at Cincinnatti Bengal football games dips from 56,000 fans down to 28,000 die-hards. During cold spells, the temperature elasticity of the demand for Bengal tickets is __1.083__.

i. When 200,000 gallons of water are applied per acre, 4 tons of jelly beans are harvested from each acre annually, but cutting back to 140,000 gallons causes the crop per acre to fall to 2 tons annually. The water elasticity of jelly bean production is __1.889__

j. If doubling your consumption of pasta to 6 pounds per week causes you to blossom from a svelte 125 to a rotund 175 pounder, your pasta elasticity of blubber is __.5__.

2. Some sports fans support the home team regardless of how well the team does; others only buy tickets if the team is a winner. Demand grows as a team's record improves. Would you expect the price-elasticity of demand to rise or fall as a result of a winning season? That is, would you expect season ticket prices to rise more than proportionally relative to the prices of other tickets as a team's record improved, or less than proportionally? Is the elasticity of supply of tickets to sporting events zero, or is it positive over the long run? Why?

3. Revenues from oil exported by members of the Organization of Petroleum Exporting Countries (OPEC) rose each year until 1981 after the price of oil began to rise in the early 1970s. What does this sug-

gest about the short-run price-elasticity of the inter-national demand for oil? Even though oil prices rose, worldwide consumption of oil also rose. What does this suggest about the income-elasticity of the demand for oil?

4. What would happen to the elasticity of demand for oil from the perspective of OPEC countries if all countries that import oil decided to impose sliding tariffs just equal to any future increases in OPEC's oil prices?

5. Suppose you calculate that the price-elasticity of demand for your firm's product is 0.7. Your firm's policies should be changed immediately to increase profits. What policies should be changed? How do you know this? _raise price_

6. Suppose you are the State Tax Commissioner, and your state legislature decides to raise $120 million in annual tax revenues by imposing a $1 tax per case of beer. They have looked at the figures, and 10 million cases of beer are sold monthly at $3 per case in your state. If you were called to testify before the Legislative Tax Committee, what would you have to say about their prospects for $120 million in new revenues? Suppose that you estimate that the price-elasticity of the demand for beer equals one. How high would the tax need to be to yield the desired revenues?

7. Prices for small, gas-efficient imported cars rose even faster than the prices of American gas hogs during the 1970s, but these imports cornered a growing share of the American market. Rising gas prices were a key to this puzzle. What does this suggest about how demands for gasoline, imported cars, and full-sized Detroit products are related? Analyze pairs as complements or substitutes for all possible pairs.

8. The concepts of average and marginal occur in many areas other than economics. Describe the effects on averages of the following marginal events:
   a. What happens to your average for this class if your score on the next (marginal) test is above your current average? Suppose that you do not do quite as well on the final exam as on the next test. How is it possible for your average to rise even though the marginal test score is falling?
   b. Manute Bol, a 7'7" center for the Washington Bullets basketball team, walks into your class. What happens to the average height of people in your classroom? To average income?
   c. Fill in the following table to show what happens to the average temperature in Denver in February if, as the month progresses, the following high temperatures are recorded. (A hand calculator will help.)

long run — bends out
SR straight up
_S_SR / LR_

Date	Temperature	Average	Date	Temperature	Average
Feb. 1	16°	_____	Feb. 15	31°	_____
2	18°	_____	16	16°	_____
3	23°	_____	17	15°	_____
4	23°	_____	18	23°	_____
5	20°	_____	19	42°	_____
6	26°	_____	20	34°	_____
7	29°	_____	21	14°	_____
8	37°	_____	22	24°	_____
9	24°	_____	23	24°	_____
10	14°	_____	24	48°	_____
11	12°	_____	25	50°	_____
12	22°	_____	26	39°	_____
13	35°	_____	27	40°	_____
14	30°	_____	28	55°	_____

Is there a consistent relationship between changes in the marginal (observed) temperature for sequential days and the average? (NO!) What is the simple relation between the marginal (observed) temperature and the average for the month?

d. Explain how an increase in the rate of inflation might still reduce the average rate of inflation over a decade.

e. Can you specify a simple mathematical law governing the relations between marginals and averages, and identify five situations outside of economics where this law is important?

CHAPTER 21 The Foundations of Consumer Choice

goods and bads	marginal utility	consumer surplus
commodities and services	law of diminishing marginal utility	diamond-water paradox
substitution effect	principle of equal marginal utilities per dollar	rational ignorance
income effect		caveat emptor vs.
utilitarianism		caveat venditor

The microeconomic tools introduced in the preceding chapter may have seemed a bit mechanical, but in this chapter you will see that marginal analysis provides a logical view of consumer decision making, which often seems dominated by fads and whims. You will discover that economics relies on some concepts of human behavior that are closely akin to psychology in explaining the choices consumers make as they try to maximize their satisfactions, either individually or as family units. The consumer behavior studied in this chapter is vital information for business decision making, which you will study in the next few chapters.

This chapter begins by categorizing things that satisfy or displease people and how people react to price changes. Its focus then turns to utility analysis, which offers a psychological interpretation of consumer behavior. The issue of consumer sovereignty versus consumer regulation is then discussed. Optional material on indifference analysis concludes this chapter. All these concepts should provide many insights into your own behavior and the behavior of others in their everyday living and consuming.

Goods and Bads

A **good** is anything that adds to human happiness; **bads** detract from the enjoyment of life. *Consumption goods* directly add to our happiness and include most ordinary objects of everyday use: food, clothing, cars, and so on. *Capital goods* include the machines and other resources that add to our happiness less directly, through the consumer goods they generate. Distinguishing between these types of goods may require looking at use. For example, identical cars are consumer goods when used by households, but capital goods when used by business. And oversupplies may convert some goods into bads: many home gardeners are inundated with more zucchini than they or their neighbors can eat, and much of it winds up in the trash.

Commodities are produced goods that can be owned—television sets, cans of tuna, and garden hoses are examples. We can purchase and enjoy **services** without necessarily buying the items or agents that produce them: tuition gives you access to classes, but you own neither your chair nor your instructor. Other services include haircuts, television broadcasts, police protection, and medical care.

It is important to note, however, that all goods are reducible to services through their physical and chemical effects. For example, at a biological level, different foods service different parts of our bodies. Houses protect us from foul weather and clothes warm us and adorn us. Machines transform the commodities that are enjoyed when they generate services. In fact, virtually every economic activity has value only to the extent that it generates useful services. Capital goods, land, and commodities simply embody streams of services.

Market societies permit private ownership of most service-producing goods. Americans cannot own slaves, however, regardless of how much anyone wants one. Curiously, you do not even legally own yourself. But both services and things that can be owned universally have prices, and these prices fluctuate to signal changes in costs or in our desires for goods or the resources that produce them. How consumers adjust when prices change is the next topic on our agenda.

Effects of Price Changes

How purchasing patterns respond when the prices of goods change can be decomposed into substitution effects and income effects.

Substitution Effects

You will buy less of any good that rises in price, substituting for it goods that decline in relative price. Substitution is the primary cause of negative slopes along demand curves, and the **substitution effect** is that portion of the change in quantity demanded due *solely* to a change in relative prices.[1] Most goods have numerous possible uses. When the price of a good is reduced, it will be advantageous to devote the good to more of these uses.

For example, buses now provide low-priced transportation for many of us. Rides would be economical for far more people if fares were $0, and derelicts might sleep on warm buses instead of in cold alleys or under bridges. A $15 bus fare would induce most of us to walk, drive cars, or hire taxis. When ballpoint pens were introduced in the 1940s, they were refillable, cost about $25 each, and were a status symbol for business executives. They currently cost about a quarter, are used by almost everyone, and are discarded when the ink runs dry. Expensive ink pens are a rarity, and pencils are less commonly used than they would be if ballpoints still cost $25.

These examples suggest that we substitute some uses of some goods for similar uses of related goods as relative prices change. The critical point is that it is always advantageous to substitute away from goods that become relatively more expensive and to expand the uses of goods that become cheaper. The substitution effect is the major underpinning for the law of demand: *quantity demanded falls as price increases, and vice versa.*

The substitution effect is the change in purchasing patterns caused by changes in relative prices alone, artificially assuming that total purchasing power is constant. But price changes do alter the purchasing power of your income. We need to deal separately with how such changes in real income alter purchasing patterns.

Income Effects

If prices rise, the purchasing power of your dollars fall; if prices fall, a dollar will purchase more consumer goods. **Income effects** are the adjustments people make because the purchasing power of a given income is altered when prices change.[2]

---

1. Mathematically, the substitution effect of a change in the price of a good is always negative. This means that an increase in the price ($\Delta P > 0$) of some good (coffee, for example) will result in a substitution effect (toward tea?) that decreases the amount of coffee consumed ($\Delta Q < 0$). Thus, $\Delta Q/\Delta P$ is negative. Conversely, the substitution effect means that a decrease ($\Delta P < 0$) in the relative price of a good (say, ham) will cause increases ($\Delta Q > 0$) in the quantity consumed (and substitution away from beef). Again, $\Delta Q/\Delta P$ is negative.

2. The income effect may be either negative, positive, or zero. All else being equal, when the price of a good rises, your purchasing power falls. For most goods, the income effect (Y) is positive. For example, a decrease in the price of gasoline (G) increases the purchasing power of your income ($\Delta Y > 0$). This alone results in higher levels of gas purchases ($\Delta G > 0$). Thus $\Delta G/\Delta Y$ is positive. However, the income effect is negative for inferior goods such as lard, potatoes, lye soap, or black-eyed peas. For example, if a large part of your diet consists of potatoes because you are poor and they are cheap, your purchasing power increases if the price of potatoes falls ($\Delta Y > 0$) and you can afford to buy tastier foods to secure your daily caloric needs. Even though you may buy more potatoes because of the substitution effect, the independent effect of your higher real income is to reduce potato consumption. ΔPotato < 0 so ΔPotatoes$/\Delta Y$ is negative.

Suppose that tuition were $400 per semester hour and absorbed so much of your paltry budget that at first you could afford to take classes only part-time. If you were then awarded a 90 percent reduction in tuition because of your stellar performance, you could afford everything you had been buying previously and might simply pocket the $360 per semester hour covered by your scholarship. Instead, you would probably enroll for more courses, in part because of the substitution effect of this change in the relative cost of your education, but also because of the now greater purchasing power of your income. This income effect would enable you to enroll in even more courses, or you might buy more books, a better calculator, a few new clothes, tastier food, or more frequent concert tickets.

A slightly different type of income effect (ignored until recently by most economists) occurs when your monetary income is affected by changes in prices. If growth of demand causes prices to rise, some sellers' incomes must increase. Suppose that you are the resident manager of an apartment building you also own. If rental rates in your area rise, there is an increase in the opportunity cost of living in your own apartment instead of renting it out, but you have experienced increased wealth and income because of the higher rent you can charge for your other apartments. You might move into a smaller apartment because of the substitution effect, but if you are typical, you will opt for more luxurious accommodations. This explains why some Arab sheiks drive more and bigger gas guzzlers longer distances when oil prices rise.

Utility

Digging deeper into the theory of consumer behavior leads us into a bit of history. Nineteenth-century economists were fascinated by **utilitarianism,** a school of thought founded by an eccentric English philosopher named Jeremy Bentham. This philosophy sprang from the idea that the pain or pleasure yielded by any activity respectively adds or detracts from a person's *utility,* or satisfaction. Its advocates proposed a variety of social reforms in hopes of achieving their central goal, *the greatest happiness for the greatest number.* Utilitarians assumed that individual pleasure can be measured and then summed, each person being weighted equally, to calculate aggregate social welfare.

Imagine that everyone came equipped with forehead gauges that recorded satisfaction in *utils,* an imaginary measurement, much as your electric meter measures kilowatts. Over lunch your head registers: 1 cheeseburger = 73 utils; 17 french fries = 31 utils; a small cola = 24 utils; fried cherry pie = 38 utils; heartburn = −18 utils; Bromo-Seltzer = 9 utils . . . net gain from lunch = 157 utils. Measuring the subjective value of national income would be a snap; government could simply sum everyone's gains in total utility. A utilitarian goal would boil economic policy down to doing whatever was necessary to maximize the total utility score.

The appealing notion of achieving the "greatest happiness for the greatest number" is even now the basis for policies advocated by many politicians and economists, but raises some profound normative issues. The Russian author Dostoyevski confounded moral-minded utilitarians with his anguished question: "What if eternal happiness for the rest of humanity could be bought with the horrible death by torture of an innocent babe?" Policies that *unambiguously* maximize social utility in an ethical manner could not be formulated even if "utilometers" existed.

Modern economics rejects direct measurement of utility because: (*a*) most of us cannot specify our preferences more precisely than by a rank order (first, second, third, and so on) of possible bundles of goods, and (*b*) satisfaction is not scientifically comparable between individuals. People differ in the intensity of their preferences and there is really no way to ascertain exactly how much anyone likes candy (or anything else) relative to someone else's enjoyment of candy. This has led economists to develop *indifference analysis,* a more scientific technique explored at the end of this chapter. Even so, utility analysis offers some rich insights into human behavior.

Marginal Utility

Constructing any aggregate measure of utility remains a futile dream, but marginal utility analysis does offer insights into how people use resources to maximize their individual satisfaction. **Marginal utility (*MU*)** is the gain in satisfaction derived through the consumption of some small additional amount of a good. Your marginal utilities from different goods reflect your subjective preferences. Al-

Jeremy Bentham (1748–1832)

Jeremy Bentham—lawyer, philosopher, and social reformer—can hardly be called an economist, although his influence on subsequent economic thought was immense. He admired the ideas of Adam Smith but rejected Smith's view that people's interests are smoothly and automatically reconciled through the *invisible hand* of the competitive marketplace. Bentham focused on conflicts between private and public interests, especially as manifested in illegal activities. He agreed that Smith's "harmony of interests" would be desirable but did not see it as a natural consequence of human behavior. Thus, Bentham devoted his long life to designing institutions that would bring about the harmony of interests Smith took for granted.

Bentham tried to integrate law, economics, politics, and education into a unified science of behavior. His theory identified pleasure and pain as the forces controlling human actions. The goal of Bentham's hedonistic philosophy was the attainment of "the greatest good", or *maximum utility*.

Bentham's most conspicuous successes were in the area of English law and judicial procedure. He applied the principles of utility and "felicific calculation" to crime and punishment, suggesting that the evil of a crime is proportionate to the number of people hurt by it. It follows, therefore, that punishment for crimes should not be based on mere motive, but on the amount of social pain caused by a felony. Properly speaking, Bentham viewed law and law enforcement from the economic perspective of incentives. He theorized that stiffer punishments would raise the "cost" of crime, compelling self-interested individuals to commit fewer misdeeds, in turn serving the public interest.

It is an understatement to say that Bentham was eccentric. His pet pig roamed freely through his mansion, and he once petitioned the London City Council for permission to line his driveway with mummified human cadavers, which he thought "far more aesthetic than flowers." At the age of 32, Bentham immodestly "dreamt the other night that I was a founder of a sect; of course a personage of great sanctity and importance. It was the sect of the utilitarians."

In spite of his personal eccentricities, Bentham's dream proved prophetic. His ideas attracted a loyal group of disciples, including the philosophers James Mill and his son John Stuart, and his proposals for social reforms were widely translated into action. Benthamite principles were among the intellectual wellsprings of many nineteenth-century social reforms. Possibly the secret of Bentham's success is that he instilled in his disciples not only specific ideals but provided concrete plans to achieve them.

Bentham also dreamed of immortality. His sizable estate was left to the University of London on the condition that his body be embalmed in a certain way, stuffed and dressed in his own suit of clothes, and that it attend all meetings of the University's trustees. In this way, Bentham hoped to be "present" whenever utilitarian principles were discussed at "his" university. Bentham's wishes were carried out. (Minutes of all trustees' meetings record him as "present but not voting.") Over 150 years later, the dauntless utilitarian still resides in his glass closet in a corridor at University College, the University of London.

though the subjective gains from a dollar's worth of goods may vary substantially among individuals, the following section shows how we can approximate the relative satisfactions from various goods to a given individual by looking at marginal utility in monetary terms.

The Law of Diminishing Marginal Utility

Suppose that you enjoy quenching your thirst on hot days with fresh lemonade; frozen or artificial will not do. If we measure utility in dollar terms, then MU_L is roughly the amount you would willingly pay for an extra lemonade. After three sets of tennis on a 90-degree afternoon, you stroll into your town's only air-conditioned lemonade stand where the server, an old friend, informs you that icy, fresh lemonade is now $1 per glass. Your throat parched, you decide that one glass is barely worth $1. As you finish it and rise to leave, the ade-tender offers you a break: a second lemonade for only $0.85. "All right," you say, "just one more." After gulping it down, you are already off your stool when the ade-tender asks,

"How about another for $0.60?" Sitting back down, you put money on the counter. After your third lemonade, she asks, "How about a fourth at the old price of $0.50?" Somewhat befuddled, you nod your head. The four lemonades have cost you $2.95 ($1.00 + $0.85 + $0.60 + $0.50), as shown in Panel A of Figure 1. At the old price of $0.50, you would have paid a total of only $2.00.

After the fourth lemonade you are ready to face the heat outside but the ade-tender offers you still

FIGURE 1 *Total and Marginal Utility of Lemonade*

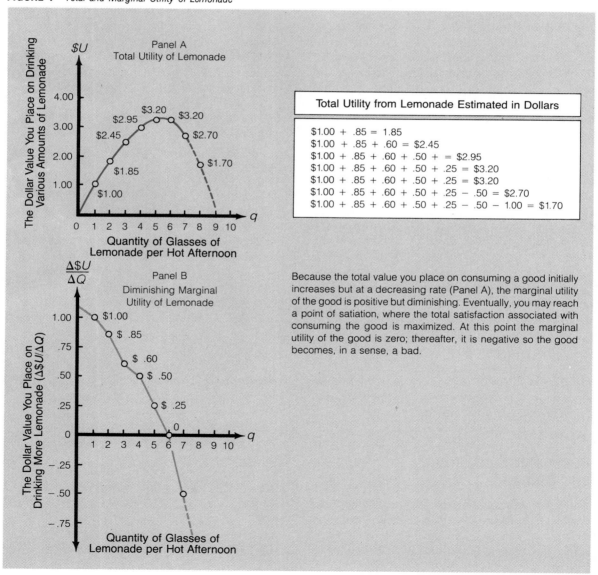

Total Utility from Lemonade Estimated in Dollars

$1.00 + .85 = 1.85
$1.00 + .85 + .60 = $2.45
$1.00 + .85 + .60 + .50 + = $2.95
$1.00 + .85 + .60 + .50 + .25 = $3.20
$1.00 + .85 + .60 + .50 + .25 = $3.20
$1.00 + .85 + .60 + .50 + .25 − .50 = $2.70
$1.00 + .85 + .60 + .50 + .25 − .50 − 1.00 = $1.70

Because the total value you place on consuming a good initially increases but at a decreasing rate (Panel A), the marginal utility of the good is positive but diminishing. Eventually, you may reach a point of satiation, where the total satisfaction associated with consuming the good is maximized. At this point the marginal utility of the good is zero; thereafter, it is negative so the good becomes, in a sense, a bad.

another, and for only $0.25. You cannot pass up the bargain. Then she says, "A good customer like you deserves a sixth lemonade on the house." It is 90 degrees in the shade, so you assent. Feeling a bit water-logged, you turn down the offer of a seventh even though it is free. "Tell you what," she says, "will you drink it if I pay you $0.50?" Being an impoverished student, you agree. You also drink an eighth, for which you are paid $1. Ultimately, however, you approach your capacity. You offer to drink the ninth for the $3 she offers, but only if you can wait a half hour. Since "It's now or never," you decide to pass. (You would drink the ninth for $25, but she will not offer that much.)

Panel B of Figure 1 shows how the marginal utilities in dollars are related to your total satisfaction from lemonade (Panel A). The points on both curves are connected as if the server had offered these deals by sips rather than glassfuls. Study the relationship between total utility and marginal utility. The accumulated area under the marginal utility curve (note the expanded vertical axis) equals the height of the total utility curve.

The declining marginal utility from lemonade as you drink more and more during a given time interval occurs with virtually all goods and all people. Observing that similar reactions were common, classical economists generalized this behavior into

✗ The **law of diminishing marginal utility:** *The marginal utility associated with consuming equal successive units of a good will eventually decline as the amount consumed increases.*

The word *eventually* is important. Beer fanciers might enjoy their first beer of the evening immensely, and their second beer even more. However, they almost certainly will not enjoy their eleventh beer of the evening as much as their third. Benjamin Franklin's observation in *Poor Richard's Almanac,* "Fish and visitors stink in three days," says far more about the diminishing marginal utility of visitors than about the deterioration of fish.

Consumer Equilibrium and Demand

You may have noticed that the marginal utility curve in Panel B of Figure 1 contains all the information required of a demand curve for lemonade. This is correct because consumers will buy an *extra* unit of a good only if its marginal utility is at least as great as its price. Thus, according to this demand curve, you would buy only one lemonade if the price were $1, two at $0.85, three at $0.60, four at $0.50, five at $0.25, and would drink six lemonades only if they were free. This example illustrates why early economists explained the negative slopes of all demand curves by the law of diminishing marginal utility.

✓ ### Equating Marginal Utilities per Dollar

We have asserted that satisfaction can be approximated by looking at utility in terms of money. While we cannot compare different people's utilities from consuming goods, we may be fairly sure that their individual marginal utilities from particular goods are roughly proportional to the prices of the goods. The reason for this is that people will change their spending patterns whenever relative prices and marginal utilities are not in balance. The following example shows why. For convenience, this example assumes that $1 buys 1 util at the margin in the initial equilibrium.

Suppose that you love ice cream and buy an average of six $1 cones per week: 3 rocky roads (r) and 3 chocolates (c). Each extra cone initially yields 1 util of satisfaction ($MU_r = MU_c = 1$). This occurs at point x in each panel of Figure 2. If you begin to tire of rocky road and increasingly like plain chocolate, the marginal utility of chocolate cones relative to rocky road rises. Say, $MU_r = 0.75$, while $MU_c = 1.25$, a movement from points x to y in each panel. MU_c/P_c is simply the marginal utility (in utils) you get from the last cent you spend on chocolate ice cream; MU_r/P_r is the marginal utility derived from the last cent spent on rocky road. At point y in both panels, MU_c/P_c exceeds MU_r/P_r, given your current snacking habits. You will start buying more chocolate cones and less rocky road weekly, initially gaining 1.25 utils for each extra $1 spent on chocolate while losing only 0.75 utils for each rocky road cone sacrificed.

However, the law of diminishing marginal utility comes into play and the marginal utility of chocolate will fall while the marginal utility of rocky road rises. This movement is from point y to z in each panel. All cones cost $1, so your purchases stabilize when:

$$MU_c/P_c = MU_r/P_r = 1/\$1 = 1.$$

Similar adjustments occur whenever an individual's marginal utilities for all goods purchased are not

FIGURE 2 Realigning Marginal Utilities Through Changes in Consumption Patterns

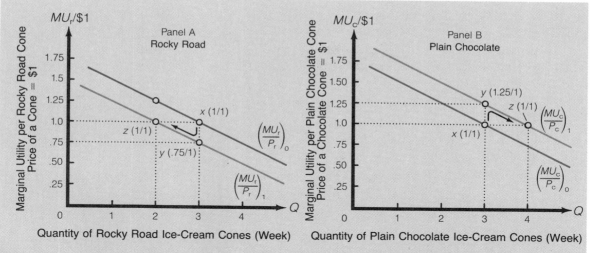

A decline in the marginal utility of rocky road ice cream results in lower consumption, while a rise in the marginal utility of plain chocolate ice cream causes greater purchases. In equilibrium, $MU_r/P_r = MU_c/P_c$.

proportional to their market prices; you will be in equilibrium only when:

$$MU_a/P_a = MU_b/P_b = \ldots = MU_z/P_z,$$

where $a, b, \ldots, z$ are the various goods you buy. This equation can be interpreted to mean that *the last cent spent on each good will yield the same satisfaction as the last cent spent on any other good.*

Identical resources will be equally advantageously allocated at the margin, so that each dollar is allocated in equally advantageous ways to a consumer. This application of the law of equal advantage to consumer behavior is known as the **principle of equal marginal utilities per dollar.** *Dollar* is used as an arbitrary small denomination of money. In a complete equilibrium, the last *cent* spent on ice cream yields the same satisfaction as the last *cent* spent on lemonade, clothes, books, or housing. A little reflection should suggest that this is roughly true of your own spending pattern.

Let's use this format to describe how quantities demanded change as relative prices change. Figure 3 supposes that your family's purchases of apples (*a*) and bananas (*b*) is initially in equilibrium when you consume 6 pounds of apples and 4 pounds of bananas monthly if they cost the same amount per

pound. Pounds of the fruit originally exchange one-for-one, and at point *x* in Panels A and B, $MU_a/P_a = MU_b/P_b$. If the price of apples rises relative to the price of bananas so that a pound of apples now costs as much as 1.25 pounds of bananas, then a pound of bananas costs only as much as 0.8 pounds of apples and MU_a/P_a is less than MU_b/P_b; you will adapt by buying more bananas and fewer apples (point *y* in each panel.) As you consume fewer apples the MU_a will rise, while the MU_b falls as you eat more bananas.

Experimenting with other changes in relative prices and the resulting adjustments in your consumption pattern trace out demand curves for apples and bananas. Thus, in equilibrium, the higher-priced goods you purchase uniformly generate more marginal utility than lower-priced goods you buy: The more you pay for a good, the more it is worth to you at the margin. Ultimately, the last dollar you spend on any good, including your holdings of cash, yields the same satisfaction as the last dollar spent on any other good.

Market prices and the subjective demand prices discussed in Chapter 3 are different ways of viewing opportunity costs. Demand prices can be thought of as the ratios of the marginal utilities of various goods.

FIGURE 3   *Price Adjustments and Marginal Utility*

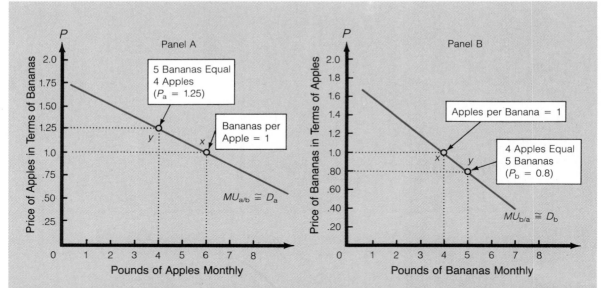

If the price of apples is the same as that of bananas, in equilibrium the two will yield the same marginal utility, which occurs at point *x* in each panel. A hike in the price of apples relative to bananas (so that 5 bananas are needed to "buy" 4 apples) causes lower consumption and higher marginal utility of apples. As a result, each apple is subjectively more valuable. At the same time, rising consumption of bananas reduces their marginal utility. These changes occur as your family moves from point *x* to point *y* in each panel.

Only if market prices and demand prices are in accord will you buy. In equilibrium, your subjective price ratios will be equal to the relative market prices of all the goods you choose to purchase. That is, $MU_a/MU_b = P_a/P_b$ for any two goods we choose to label *a* and *b*, respectively.[3]

Consumer Surplus

We can look at an individual's demand curve for some good from two different perspectives:

1. Most of the time we see demand curves as answers to the question, "How much will be bought at each possible price?" The quantity demanded depends on the price.

2. Alternatively, we might view demand curves as graphing answers to the question, "If people have certain amounts of good *X*, what is the most that they would be willing to pay for an extra unit of good *X*?"

Here, price is viewed as depending on quantity. Both approaches yield the same demand curves.

The view that the marginal value of a good depends on the amount available to us provides a key to specifying in monetary terms the satisfaction gained from being able to buy at a single market price. Using our original lemonade example (see Figure 4), you paid a total of $2.95 for the first four glasses of lemonade, but only $0.50 for the fourth (last) glass. But if lemonade sold for a flat price of $0.50 per glass, you would spend $2 to drink four lemonades, thereby gaining $0.95 worth of utility. This gain represents consumer surplus.

Consumer surplus is the difference between the amounts people would willingly pay for various amounts of specific goods and the amounts they do pay at market prices; this is roughly the area below

3. The reason this equation is compatible with the principle of equal marginal utilities per dollar is that in equilibrium, MU_a/P_a equals MU_b/P_b; if we multiply each side of the equation by P_a/MU_b and then simplify, we obtain the result that MU_a/MU_b equals P_a/P_b.

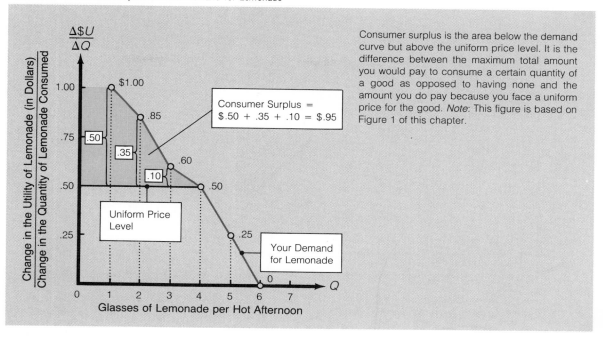

FIGURE 4 *Consumer Surplus and the Demand for Lemonade*

Consumer surplus is the area below the demand curve but above the uniform price level. It is the difference between the maximum total amount you would pay to consume a certain quantity of a good as opposed to having none and the amount you do pay because you face a uniform price for the good. *Note:* This figure is based on Figure 1 of this chapter.

the demand curve but above the price line. Even though consumer surplus cannot be measured quantitatively, among its various applications is that consumer surplus permits qualitative assessments of the efficiency of a number of government policies, a topic addressed in a later chapter.

The Diamond-Water Paradox

Two hundred years ago, economists were stumped by an apparent paradox. Why are absolute necessities such as water valued (priced) so cheaply, while frivolities like diamonds are highly valued and command outrageous prices? Questions about the **diamond-water paradox** were used to stump Ph.D. candidates in economics for generations. The diamond-water paradox arises from difficulties in distinguishing between total utility and marginal utility.

Suppose that Panel A in Figure 5 depicts your family's demand for water. If you are typical, the price of water is so low that you treat drinking water as if it were free: You drink water until an extra glass would actually detract from your well-being—the marginal utility is zero. However, because you know that your water bill (which averages $20 monthly) reflects total use, you are probably somewhat careful about water-

ing your lawn, washing your car, running bath water, and so on.

How much would you be willing to pay if you were offered the choice of 100 gallons of water for $500 monthly or no water at all? If you could afford it, you would willingly pay at least $500 per month for water, and you would limit your use of water to drinking, preparing food, and sponge baths. Your lawn and plants would die, your car would go dirty, and you would forget about washing machines and flush toilets. (Do you think this might explain why Bedouin camels stink?) If you had to, you would pay considerably more for the 10,000 gallons of water you use each month than the $20 you do pay, so water yields an enormous consumer surplus.

The total utility of water is substantially higher than its marginal utility and price, while the total utility of diamonds is close to their marginal utility and price. We have shaded the areas representing consumer surpluses in Figure 5. This analysis should help you understand why diamonds, which are not nearly as necessary to life as water, are valued and priced much higher than water. Most of us have few, if any, diamonds, so the total utility, marginal utility, and price are nearly identical.

FIGURE 5   *The Diamond-Water Paradox*

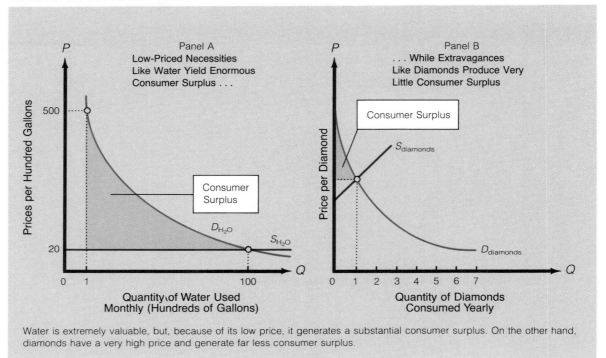

Panel A
Low-Priced Necessities
Like Water Yield Enormous
Consumer Surplus . . .

Consumer Surplus

D_{H_2O}

S_{H_2O}

Prices per Hundred Gallons

500

20

0   1   100

Quantity of Water Used
Monthly (Hundreds of Gallons)

Panel B
. . . While Extravagances
Like Diamonds Produce Very
Little Consumer Surplus

Consumer Surplus

$S_{diamonds}$

$D_{diamonds}$

Price per Diamond

0   1   2   3   4   5   6   7

Quantity of Diamonds
Consumed Yearly

Water is extremely valuable, but, because of its low price, it generates a substantial consumer surplus. On the other hand, diamonds have a very high price and generate far less consumer surplus.

Goods as Bundles of Attributes   The theory of consumption has been expanded recently to consider each individual good as embodying a variety of utility-relevant characteristics or *attributes*. Cigarettes provide oral gratification and give smokers "something to do with my hands"; they are also carcinogenic, generate hostility from nonsmokers, and waste time. Similarly, Sugar Smacks have a certain texture and taste and loads of calories. Rice and potatoes have very similar attributes and are thus substitutes; each is also quite complementary with steak.

The Problem of Rational Choice

Many observers are dubious that people are as rational as economic theory presumes. If you asked typical shoppers in a grocery store if their buying patterns caused their marginal utilities for various goods to be in fixed proportions to the prices of these goods, they would think you were off your rocker. Suppose instead that you asked them why they do not buy more or less of particular goods than they

do, or why they reject other items. They would probably begin talking about some things being "good buys," while refering to others as "too high," or "not worth it to me."

Most people seem to behave as economic models of demand suggest, even if they find incomprehensible the economic jargon used to describe their behavior. There is, however, far from unanimity that people really act in very rational or calculating ways. Take a moment to read the biographical sketch of Thorstein Veblen, a founder of the view known as institutionalism, which largely rejects the kind of reasoning we have described.

√ ***Uncertainty and Imperfect Information***   We make decisions in an imperfect world rife with uncertainty. You can never be 100 percent certain of the attributes of a specific unit of any good, no matter how familiar. You may buy a moldy loaf of your favorite bread or be injured by an exploding bottle of cola. There is even less certainty about unfamiliar goods that are bought only once or twice in a lifetime. No one who undergoes surgery can ever be certain in

Thorstein B. Veblen (1857–1929)

The economic characterization of human behavior as the rational calculation of benefits and costs seemed ludicrous to Thorstein Veblen, one of the great iconoclasts and tragicomic figures of economics. Veblen was trained in philosophy but concentrated on economics because of what he perceived as deficiencies in economic analysis. A first-generation American of Norwegian stock, Veblen viewed capitalism and the American scene as if he were a newcomer to the planet. He found the institutions and behavior of Americans more than a bit strange—exotic and bizarre are probably more appropriate terms. His intellectual work consists primarily of "cultural analysis," the high-water mark of which is pungent criticism. A good example of his satire is contained in this attack on the marginal utility principle:

The hedonistic conception of man is that of a lightning calculator of pleasures and pains, who oscillates like a homogeneous globule of desire . . . under the impulse of stimuli that shift him about the area but leave

him intact. . . . He is an isolated, definitive human datum, in stable equilibrium except for the buffets of the impinging forces that displace him in one direction or another. . . . When the force of the impact is spent, he comes to rest, a self-contained globule of desire as before.

Veblen believed that human behavior is best analyzed as interactions of instincts and habits and that many social processes can be interpreted as results of cultural lags. In his doctrine of *conspicuous consumption* (status competition), Veblen explained how the desire to "keep up with the Joneses" motivates people to buy goods in a way that is culturally determined, not price determined. In a more general sense, Veblen insisted on studying the origin and nature of economic institutions. He was especially critical of the *leisure class* and businessmen, whom he viewed as parasites. He argued that conventional economics fails to consider social and economic institutions, artificially reducing human nature to a matter of rational calculation.

As eccentric as Bentham, Veblen washed his dishes in a rain barrel and seldom bathed. Though grubby and quite homely, he was a "lady killer" and lost several academic positions because he had a bad habit of seducing the wives of colleagues and administrators. He was still an assistant professor when he died at age 72.

Veblen's criticisms of economic theory were largely based on antirationalist premises and were certainly not the first of their kind. However, Veblen's savage humor and great erudition made him a formidable critic of the business system. He originated a distinctively American line of inquiry into economics, *institutionalism,* which continues to find proponents to this day.

advance about the precise outcome of an operation. Nor, for that matter, can any surgeon. Uncertainty exists because we have only imperfect information about the present and no crystal ball to predict the future.

Information is costly. Acquiring full information might be incredibly expensive. Hence, rational consumers will search for information only as long as the expected benefit exceeds the expected cost and

may choose to be **rationally ignorant** of much information. For example, most standard items people buy are available at a wide range of prices, and most people pay more than the lowest price at which a good is available at a given point in time. Searching until you were sure that you were paying the least possible amount for a good, however, would probably absorb more time and effort than any resulting monetary saving was worth. Similarly, you might spend a lifetime trying to identify the perfect spouse for you from the population of single people of the opposite sex. The costliness of the search, however, probably accounts for findings that geographical closeness is a major determinant of whom one marries. But broadening the options available in any decision making situation can be costly and pose unforeseen problems.

Bewildering Arrays of Choices

Each year, thousands of products fade into oblivion, but even more thousands are launched in the marketplace. Ever widening ranges of choice become available as firms attempt to attract customer bases sufficient to make their product lines profitable. This is often held up as a major advantage of the market system: even eccentric tastes and preferences may be accommodated when almost innumerable different goods are available. Typical grocery stores now carry over 15,000 different items; together, the stores in a large shopping mall often offer five times as many.

One result of having many choices and constant flux in markets is that the additional information required for wise consumer decisions is costly.[4] One example of this occurs when firms modify products slightly in hopes of getting noncustomers to sample their goods: "Try our new, improved _____ ." You might become somewhat agitated if you searched high and low for a familiar red box of your favorite cereal, concluded that the store was out, and then, on a later shopping expedition, discovered that the maker had switched to a blue box.

More serious levels of confusion arise when choices are wider. A gourmet may agonize over a lengthy menu at a posh restaurant. Some people spend days trying to find the perfect gift for a friend or the perfect suit for a job interview. Selecting goods would be a much simpler process if fewer options were available. You may know people who would have little problem in finding a TV program to watch if fewer channels were available, but who can't stop pushing the channel changer when a cable system offers 50 or 60 choices.

---

4. Product differentiation may also drive up production costs, and hence, prices—a process we describe later in this book.

Shortly after he emigrated from the Soviet Union to the United States, the economist Aaron Katzenelenbogen remarked that among the biggest culture shocks was learning to feel comfortable while choosing from the millions of options offered in our society. He suggested that some people who are unaccustomed to making decisions may feel less pressured in more regimented societies. For example, the arranged marriages common in traditional societies might reduce the anxiety many people experience when less rigid mating rituals prevail. Career choices might be far less traumatic for some people if everyone were simply assigned a job. There are, however, institutions in market economies that reduce requirements for people to choose. Children can be enrolled in schools that require uniforms, eliminating any quandary about what to wear. A military career limits the scope of individual choice. At the extreme, prison eliminates the most choices for inmates. Indeed, some convicts become so "institutionalized" that they cannot bear life outside prison walls.

Most of us, however, enjoy the wide range of options in a market system, and many view the cars, houses, or clothes we purchase as expressions of our individuality. We are accustomed to the inconvenience and confusion encountered when sorting out the things we want to buy or the activities we want to do. These are parts of the transactions costs and uncertainty that cause the total price paid by a consumer to exceed the revenue received by a seller. An even greater problem is that *rational ignorance* may yield decisions that seem wrong in retrospect. This partially explains the high U.S. divorce rate, and why some people suffering a serious illness may be stuck with incompetent quacks and die for lack of information about skilled specialists who might have cured their disease.

Caveat Emptor, Caveat Venditor, and Government Edict

Can consumers make appropriate choices for themselves? ***Caveat emptor*** ("let the buyer beware") is an ancient legal doctrine that buyers are the best judges of whether or not they receive full value and so should bear the consequences of their own decisions. But the doctrine of ***caveat venditor*** ("let the seller beware") also has a long history, reflected in prohibitions against fraud and in imposing on sellers legal liabilities for damages if unknown dangers lurk within a product. Society is making firms increasingly responsible for the safety and reliability of their products. Naturally, these regulatory costs are passed forward as higher prices, forcing us to buy "built-in" insurance policies on some goods we purchase.

However, the strongest trend is toward outright government edict, either to prohibit or mandate certain transactions. A century ago, there were no legal restrictions on the purchase of drugs. Today, many drugs are absolutely banned (LSD and heroin are examples); others are available to consumers only with a doctor's prescription. It is no longer legal to produce automobiles without a "laundry list" of safety equipment (never mind that around 90 percent of car passengers do not buckle up).

Cyclamates (an artificial sweetener) were withdrawn from the market in the late 1960s. This may have caused some folks to die of "fat attacks" until NutraSweet appeared in 1983. During this interval, the incidence of heart disease may have been artificially high because heavy people could not choose to trade the risk of heart attack from obesity for the risk of cancer associated with certain diet foods. This list could be extended substantially.

We know that it is impossible to pigeonhole people's ideas precisely. However, those who favor con-

trol by the marketplace over government regulation generally have faith in the ability of people to choose for themselves. They reason that if the consumer's problem is a lack of information, government can either provide the information or leave it to organizations such as the Consumers Union. On the other side of the fence sit those who distrust the market system and have little faith in the ability of the "average guy" to choose.

The positions you take on such issues depend on whether you view individuals themselves or government experts to be better judges of a person's well-being. Should using a seat belt be mandatory? Should AIDS patients be denied access to potentially beneficial drugs until the Food and Drug Administration has approved them? Should hang gliding be prohibited? If you know that you will die of cancer if you drink a case of artificially sweetened cola every day for 127 years and you want to do it anyway, should the government let you? These and similar questions about the role of government regulation are addressed in a later chapter.

Some consumer issues and the basis of demand theory have been our focus in this chapter; in the next, you will study the nature of a firm's production and costs. These foundations of demand and supply will be blended in the next part of this book to explain the pricing and output decisions of firms under a variety of market situations.

CHAPTER REVIEW: KEY POINTS

1. *Substitution effects* are the changes in consumer purchasing patterns that emerge if relative prices change, artificially assuming that the purchasing power of income is constant.

2. *Income effects* are the changes in buying patterns that occur solely because the purchasing power of one's income changes when the prices of individual goods rise or fall.

3. *Utilitarianism* proposes that the best society is the one that provides the greatest happiness for the greatest number of people.

4. The *law of diminishing marginal utility* states: The marginal utility of any good eventually declines as the amount consumed increases.

5. Measured in dollars, the declining portion of a marginal utility curve translates into a demand curve.

6. Maximum consumer satisfaction requires that the last cent spent on any good yield the same gain in satisfaction as the last cent spent on any other good: $MU_a/P_a = MU_b/P_b = \ldots = MU_z/P_z$. This is known as the *principle of equal marginal utilities per dollar*.

7. *Consumer surplus* is the area above the price line and below the demand curve. It is a consumer's gain from buying at a uniform price instead of paying prices equal to the marginal utility of each unit.

8. We are seldom certain about the *attributes* of any single unit of a good. Information is costly. Hence, our effective consumer demands may not maximize our satisfaction.

9. There is an increasing tendency toward government edict as a means of overcoming transactions costs or solving the problems of rational ignorance and uncertainty. Do government experts know better than you do what things are good for you and what things will harm you?

QUESTIONS FOR THOUGHT AND DISCUSSION

1. The following problems illustrate some of the ethical questions that pose difficulties for a utilitarian approach. What are your thoughts on these issues?
   a. A hospital has just enough medicine to cure ten 20-year-old college students or one 70-year-old derelict. Failure to administer the medicine to a patient will result in the patient's immediate death. Who should get the medicine? Would your answer change if the 70-year-old owned the medicine?
   b. Allowing a corporation to build a shopping center will create traffic congestion and reduce property values in a middle-class suburb. Should the shopping center be built? Would your answer change if you knew that the corporation would donate all profit to build houses for homeless people?
   c. A convicted murderer is scheduled to be executed next Tuesday. She is the only inmate in a prison scheduled for demolition next month. An enormous fire breaks out. Should $100,000 of taxpayer's money be spent to rescue this prisoner?

2. In what sense is the law of diminishing marginal utility an aspect of the general law of diminishing returns (described briefly in Chapter 2)? Can you think of at least four different meanings of the word *utility*?

3. Explain why marginal utilities diminish more rapidly as consumption of a particular good is increased when we consider very short periods (a day) as opposed to longer periods (a year).

4. Is there any utility derived from utility analysis? Critique the suggestion that "Utility analysis is useless because utility cannot be measured precisely, nor are utilities interpersonally comparable."

5. What problems do you see in implementing social policies that have as their goals achieving "the greatest happiness for the greatest number"?

6. Some companies state that their policy is "Satisfaction guaranteed or your money will be cheerfully refunded." Are there some goods for which such guarantees by retailers do not alleviate a need for government regulation? If so, what are they?

7. What are some of the attributes that distinguish goods whose regulation we can leave to the marketplace from those for which government regulation of consumer purchases seems appropriate? What criteria might be appropriate to differentiate between people who should be allowed to make their own choices from people who "need to be looked after"? Society does allow some people to make some choices that are denied others. Can you name some instances?

OPTIONAL MATERIAL: INDIFFERENCE CURVE ANALYSIS

The impossibility of measuring utility by a more objective unit than in mythical "utils" vexed economists until early in this century, when a new approach, indifference analysis, finally allowed them to sidestep this difficulty. This modern approach to consumer choice begins with a look at individual budget constraints.

Budget Lines

Human society cannot maintain consumption beyond a production-possibility frontier constructed for the world. Recall that the production-possibility frontier is concave (bowed out) from the origin because significant changes in patterns of production cause diminishing returns to be encountered. Each individual family is similarly constrained by its income in choosing among consumption alternatives. However, because the purchasing pattern a family chooses generally will not affect market prices, the consumer's budget line is straight. **Budget lines** depict the choices available to consumers who face constant prices and who have given levels of income. Figure 6 shows budget lines for two levels of income using the assumption that asparagus (A) and a proxy for all other goods, called shmoo, (B) each costs $1 per pound. Any point in the AB space represents a specific combination of asparagus and shmoos—and would require a certain level of income.

We can write the family's budget constraint as equal to:

$$Y = P_aA + P_bB. \qquad \text{(Equation 1)}$$

All family income (Y) is spent on either asparagus (A) or shmoos (B). Since income is limited, asparagus can be traded for shmoos as long as the family stays within its income constraint (Equation 1). Subtracting P_aA from each side yields:

$$P_bB = Y - P_aA. \qquad \text{(Equation 2)}$$

Finally, we can solve for the amounts of B, given certain purchases of A, if we divide Equation 2 by P_b:

$$B = Y/P_b - P_aA/P_b. \qquad \text{(Equation 3)}$$

Equation 3 defines the budget constraints for the family in Figure 6.

Because both asparagus and shmoos cost $1 per

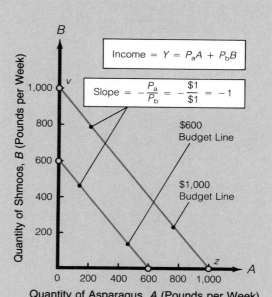

FIGURE 6 Typical Budget Lines for Two Levels of Income

$$\text{Income} = Y = P_aA + P_bB$$

$$\text{Slope} = -\frac{P_a}{P_b} = -\frac{\$1}{\$1} = -1$$

Budget lines depict the maximum possible combinations of goods available to consumers with given incomes and faced with specific prices. The slopes of budget lines reflect the relative prices of goods and higher incomes yield higher budget lines. The budget line facing a consumer is analagous to the production-possibilities frontier facing society.

pound $(P_a = P_b)$, point y represents the situation where the family has $1,000 per week, all of which is spent on shmoos. Note that $Y/P_b = \$1,000/\$1 = 1,000$ pounds of shmoos. Point z represents just the opposite: all income is spent on asparagus, nothing is spent on shmoos.

The slope of the budget line equals $-(P_a/P_b)$ and is equal to -1 since the prices of shmoos and asparagus are the same. Thus, as income changes, the family's budget line moves in or out, but as long as the ratio of the two prices remains the same, the slope of the budget constraint will not change.

Suppose that the price of asparagus doubles to $2 a pound. The budget line would pivot; a consumer with a $600 weekly income would now be able to buy a maximum of only 300 pounds of asparagus but

FIGURE 7 *Budget Lines for $600 Income with Various Prices for Good A*

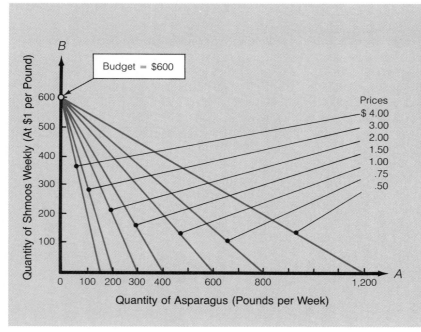

Prices
$ 4.00
3.00
2.00
1.50
1.00
.75
.50

All else being equal, as the price of asparagus falls, the budget line expands and becomes less and less steep. This reflects the declining price of asparagus relative to its alternatives. Alternatively, as the price of asparagus declines, more and more can be purchased if the entire budget is spent on asparagus.

could still buy as much as 600 pounds of shmoo. Alternatively, if the price of asparagus fell to $0.50 a pound, up to 1,200 pounds of asparagus might be purchased from a $600 income. Budget lines reflecting various possible prices for asparagus, with the price of shmoos still at $1 a pound and with a $600 weekly budget, are shown in Figure 7.

The Nature of Indifference Curves

Suppose that we picked two arbitrary combinations of shmoos and asparagus, bundle *x* and bundle *y* shown in Figure 8. Indifference analysis assumes that you always prefer more of each good to less, and that you either: (*a*) prefer bundle *x* to *y*, (*b*) prefer *y* to *x*, or (*c*) are indifferent (don't care) between bundle *x* or bundle *y*.[5] Suppose that you prefer *x* to *y*. Now let

us create a new bundle *z* by adding small amounts of asparagus or shmoos or both to combination *y* until you are indifferent between *x* and the new bundle *z*.

Indifference curves reflect a consumer's preferences and connect all bundles of goods between which the consumer is indifferent. In Figure 8 we have connected the points representing the combinations where you are indifferent between *x, z,* and similarly desirable bundles. This is an **indifference curve.** Indifference curves have the following properties:

1. Every possible combination of goods is on some indifference curve.

2. Indifference curves are negatively sloped since you will have to get more of one good in order to maintain your level of satisfaction when you give up some of the other good.

3. Indifference curves that are further from the origin are preferable because they represent larger bundles of goods.

4. Indifference curves never intersect.

---

5. Steven Plant argues that the assumptions of indifference analysis are so unrestrictive that his cat, because it is capable of choosing between bundles (tuna, milk, dry food) in an orderly way and suffers from diminishing marginal utility, is a rational consumer. See his "Illustrating the Rationality Assumption" in *Great Ideas for Teaching Economics,* 3/e, edited by R. T. Byrns and G. W. Stone, Jr. (Scott, Foresman and Company, 1987).

FIGURE 8   Typical Indifference Curves

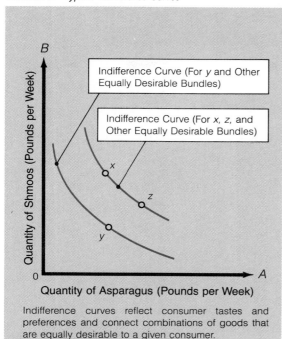

Indifference curves reflect consumer tastes and preferences and connect combinations of goods that are equally desirable to a given consumer.

5. The slope of an indifference curve reflects the relative subjective prices (marginal utilities) of the goods, $-MU_a/MU_b$.

6. Indifference curves are convex (bowed in toward the origin).

The first five of these properties should be fairly obvious. The sixth is predicated on the law of diminishing marginal utility. In this context, this means that consumers prefer variety to sameness. The following example asks you to use your intuition to show why.

Suppose that steak is your favorite meat and that you do not especially like chicken. What would happen if your meat intake were restricted to steak for a solid year? We would bet that you would sacrifice a few steaks for a box of fried chicken. The more you have of a single thing, the more you are willing to give it up in order to have a given larger amount of something else. This causes indifference curves to be bowed toward the origin (convex). You should try to prove this to yourself, using a graph, before proceeding.

Consumer Equilibrium

Figure 9 shows a $600 weekly budget line when the prices of shmoos and asparagus are both equal to $1 a pound, as well as various indifference curves for one consumer. Indifference curve I_2 represents the highest level of satisfaction this consumer can attain, given her level of income. Any other indifference curve that is on or below the budget line (for instance, I_0 or I_1) represents a lower level of satisfaction than I_2. Indifference curves such as I_3 would be preferable to I_2, but are not feasible since they lie beyond the consumer's budgetary constraint.

Indifference curve I_2 is tangent to the budget line at point z. The amounts of asparagus and shmoos associated with point z (A_0 and B_0) represent this consumer's best choices for consumption, given current prices and income. Notice that at point z the slopes of the budget line and I_2 are equal. This means that relative market prices (the slope of the budget line) equal relative marginal utilities (the slope of the indifference curve).

FIGURE 9   A Consumer's Equilibrium

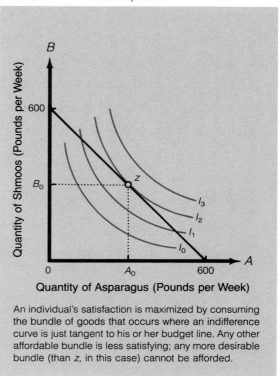

An individual's satisfaction is maximized by consuming the bundle of goods that occurs where an indifference curve is just tangent to his or her budget line. Any other affordable bundle is less satisfying; any more desirable bundle (than z, in this case) cannot be afforded.

FIGURE 10   *Consumer Equilibria and the Price Consumption Curve*

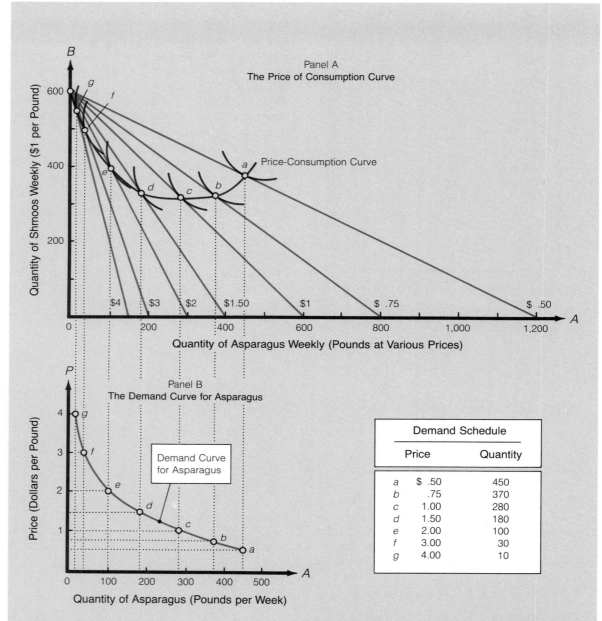

Panel A
The Price of Consumption Curve

B

Quantity of Shmoos Weekly ($1 per Pound)

600

400

200

g

f

e

d   *c*   *b*

a   Price-Consumption Curve

$4 $3 $2 $1.50 $1 $ .75 $ .50

0   200   400   600   800   1,000   1,200   A

Quantity of Asparagus Weekly (Pounds at Various Prices)

P

Panel B
The Demand Curve for Asparagus

Price (Dollars per Pound)

4   *g*

3   *f*

2   *e*

   d

1   *c*

   b   *a*

Demand Curve
for Asparagus

0   100   200   300   400   500   A

Quantity of Asparagus (Pounds per Week)

Demand Schedule		
	Price	Quantity
a	$ .50	450
b	.75	370
c	1.00	280
d	1.50	180
e	2.00	100
f	3.00	30
g	4.00	10

The price-consumption curve is traced out by the successive tangencies between indifference curves and the budget lines representing alternative prices for asparagus. In Panel A, points *a* through *g* show declining consumption of asparagus as its price rises. Points *a* through *g* from the price-consumption curve in Panel A translate into points *a* through *g* on the demand curve in Panel B.

Thus the slope of indifference curve I_2 at point z is $-MU_a/MU_b$ and the slope of the budget line at point z is $-P_a/P_b$. Since both are equal at point z, then

$$\frac{-MU_a}{MU_b} = \frac{-P_a}{P_b} \qquad \text{(Equation 4)}$$

or, in equilibrium,

$$\frac{MU_a}{P_a} = \frac{MU_b}{P_b}. \qquad \text{(Equation 5)}$$

Notice that indifference curve analysis yields the same condition for consumer equilibrium as the principle of equal marginal utilities per dollar, but we do not have to assume that consumers have "utilometers" and accurately measure utility for each product.

Deriving the Individual's Demand Curve

We will keep this person's income at $600 weekly and look at changes in the consumer's equilibrium as the prices of asparagus vary. This permits us to extract the information necessary to graph a demand curve for asparagus.

Panel A of Figure 10 superimposes a set of indifference curves on the budget lines from Figure 7 for a person with $600 weekly income who faces various possible monetary prices for asparagus. We have connected the equilibria for these different prices of asparagus with a **price-consumption curve.** Each point on this curve represents a different price for asparagus on its corresponding $600 budget line. At these points of tangency, indifference curves reflect consumer preferences and budget lines reflect income constraints. Each tangency point represents maximum satisfaction given the constraints of this consumer's income and the relative market prices of the two goods. We can find the quantity of asparagus associated with each price by dropping a line from the price-consumption line to the horizontal (asparagus) axis. Voila! We have the information needed to build a demand schedule and draw a demand curve, as in Panel B of Figure 10. Points a through g in the two panels correspond.

CHAPTER 22 Foundations of Producer Decision Making

inputs and outputs

short run vs. long run

explicit and implicit costs

economic vs. accounting profits and losses

production functions and the total product curve

average and marginal physical products of labor

law of diminishing marginal returns

fixed and variable costs

ATC = AFC + AVC

marginal cost (MC)

equal marginal productivities per dollar and least cost production

economies and diseconomies of scale

Underpinnings for consumer demands were discussed in the previous chapter, but the notion of supply has been addressed only intuitively. In this chapter, we explore production relationships: How the links between inputs and outputs determine costs and influence managerial decisions about how much to produce and which technology to use. Then, in the next few chapters, we investigate how different levels of competition for consumers' dollars interact with production costs to determine prices, output, and consumer purchases. First, however, we need to examine production and costs in some detail.

Inputs and Outputs

Production occurs when goods are transformed to make them more valuable in *form, place, possession,* or *time,* and normally involves applying knowledge and energy to materials. By "more valuable," we

mean that the goods ultimately generate greater consumer utility.

Altering *form* entails reshaping the physical or chemical structure of materials; crude oil is less valuable than gasoline. Augmenting *place* utilities requires transportation; fresh lobster is far more valuable in a restaurant's glass tank than in the ocean. *Possession* utilities are generated when ownership rights to goods are transferred from people who value the goods less to those who value them more; realtors match home buyers who are moving into an area with sellers who are moving out. *Time* utilities are created when goods are made more accessible when they are wanted most; speculators buy wheat when it is harvested and then store it for sale in periods when wheat production is nil. Businesses survive and prosper only by making goods more convenient in form, place, or time, or by moving them into the possession of people who value them more highly.

Those things that enter a production process are known as **inputs;** the transformed materials are **outputs.** Inputs include machine or labor hours, physical space (such as acres used yearly), raw materials, and partially processed (intermediate) products bought from other firms. A firm's output may be purchased by consumers, by other firms, or by government. Note that inputs and outputs are both *flow* concepts—they are measured per unit of time.

The Short Run and the Long Run

People often talk about the short-run versus the long-run consequences of some event. For example, in the short run, winning a pie-eating contest may give you a bellyache. If you repeatedly win pie-eating tournaments, in the long run you'll be able to get a job in a sideshow as Fatty _____ (fill in your last name). Short and long runs in economics (and pie-eating contests) refer to the completeness of adjustment rather than to time periods per se.

In production theory, the **short run** is a period during which the amount of at least one resource is fixed and firms can neither enter nor exit a market. Fewer options are available in the short run than in the **long run,** during which a firm can completely adjust the amounts of all resources and can either enter or leave industries.

The specific time intervals required for different firms to achieve long-run adjustment differ markedly. Some firms could liquidate all their assets within days; others may take years. (How long would it take to duplicate General Motor's worldwide physical plant? To liquidate GM's assets?) We will focus on short-run managerial decisions before considering longer planning horizons.

Economic Costs of Production (Read all)

You have learned that economists view the value of the best alternative forgone as the economic cost of anything from peanuts to romantic trysts. One way to break down the opportunity costs of production is to view them as either explicit or implicit costs.

Explicit Costs and Implicit Costs   Explicit costs require outlays of money. For example, wages paid employees, rent payments, and utility bills all involve explicit outlays of funds. **Implicit costs** are the opportunity costs of resources the firm's owner makes available for production with no direct cash outlays. Examples include the interest that could be earned were the owner's assets not partially tied up in the business and the value of the entrepreneur's labor. Both implicit and explicit costs bear heavily on rational business decision making.

Bookkeeping, a fairly mechanical exercise, focuses only on explicit costs and is aimed primarily at tracking flows of funds and maintaining records for computing taxes. Accounting requires analytical evaluation for decision making—purposes not served by many common bookkeeping practices. Fortunately, accounting standards increasingly conform to the economic view of cost. Let us look at some problems that may emerge if implicit costs are overlooked.

Economic and accounting definitions of profit seem identical: *Profit* is a firm's total revenue minus its total costs. Economists, however, include explicit and implicit costs when they think of *total* (opportunity) *cost,* while bookkeepers often fail to include in total cost many implicit costs incurred by a business.

Here is an example of how **economic profits** and **accounting profits** differ. Imagine that 2 years after receiving your college degree your annual salary as a stockbroker is $23,000, you own a building that rents for $10,000 yearly, and your financial assets generate $3,000 per year in interest. On New Year's Day, after deciding to be your own boss, you quit your job, evict your tenants, and use your financial assets to establish a health food restaurant and pogo-stick shop.

At the end of the year, your books tell the following story:

Sales of food	$ 18,000	
Sales of pogo sticks	112,000	
TOTAL SALES REVENUE		**$130,000**
Cost of food	$ 23,000	
Cost of pogo sticks	62,000	
Employees' wages	20,000	
Utilities	5,000	
Taxes	5,000	
Advertising expenses	10,000	
TOTAL (Explicit) COSTS (subtract from revenue)		**$−125,000**

"Congratulations," your bookkeeper pipes up, "you made a
NET (accounting) PROFIT of . . . . **$ 5,000!"**

"Hold it just a moment," you say, "I have studied economics. You forgot to subtract my *implicit costs*. Being in this business caused me to lose as income:

Salary	$ −23,000
Rent	−10,000
Interest	−3,000
TOTAL IMPLICIT COSTS	**$ −36,000.**"

"Therefore, I've had an economic profit that's negative, a

LOSS of . . . . **$ −31,000.**"

"You must be a dolt not to recognize that I've lost my shirt in this harebrained business!"

However, if you enjoy operating the restaurant and pogo-stick shop more than you did your best alternative (being a stockbroker), your increased job satisfaction is called psychic income. *Psychic income* refers to any nonmonetary satisfaction gained from an activity and, as in this case, is an implicit revenue. Bookkeeping profit overstates economic profit unless psychic income exceeds an entrepreneur's implicit costs, an exceedingly rare event.

The explicit cost data required to compute accounting profit for tax purposes are more accessible than the additional implicit cost data needed to estimate economic profits or losses. Thus, taxes and national income accounts are based on accounting data, but rational business decisions tend to be based on economic costs and profits.

Good accountants recognize the inadequacy of conventional bookkeeping concepts of costs and profits so that, after calculating taxable profits, they subtract implicit costs from bookkeeping profit in order to provide management with a better picture of a firm's track record. Too many businesses have experienced positive accounting profits but economic losses; they failed even though they were "profitable" concerns according to bookkeepers.

Normal Profits as Production Costs   One lesson in this example is that the profit viewed as "normal" by financial analysts should be thought of as a production cost. If a firm's accounting profit is below the profit normally received by companies with similar risks and levels of investment, in the long run the owners will move their resources into activities where at least normal profits are expected. Why? Because the opportunity costs borne by the firm are too high for it to continue operating in an area that yields subnormal accounting profits. Firms ultimately either adapt or dissolve if normal accounting profits are not made.

Economic profit occurs only when a firm generates revenue that more than covers *all* production costs. **Economic loss** is a parallel concept that occurs when revenue fails to cover the opportunity costs of production. The two concepts differ only by sign. In a competitive market, economic profits and losses will be zero in the long run because profits attract new sellers like picnics attract ants; persistent economic losses (negative profits) cause firms to exit the market or perish. Economic profits or losses persist only when barriers limit entry into or exit from an industry. Profits stimulate competition and bigger supplies, while losses are signals that society wants resources shifted elsewhere.

Production in the Short Run

Production functions express relationships between various given combinations of inputs and the maximum outputs that each combination can produce. *Output* = f (*inputs*) is an example, and is read as "output is a function *f* of inputs." The function *f* specifies the amounts of output (*Q*) that can be produced from various combinations of inputs and summarizes the current state of technology. In this context, technology encompasses current knowledge about production techniques, as well as such things as government regulations, weather, and the laws of physics and chemistry.

Production functions are commonly written $Q = f(K,L)$ where K equals capital services, and L equals labor services used per production period. (We will ignore land and entrepreneurship for now.) Suppose that our production engineers indicate that 1,000 swimsuits could be produced daily using 600 machine hours (75 machines in continuous use on an 8-hour shift) and 800 labor hours (100 workers during the 8-hour shift). The function f summarizes a given production relationship of this type. A technological advance raising productivity by 50 percent would require us to switch from the f production function to, say, g. Now, $Q = g(K,L)$, and 600 machine hours plus 800 labor hours yield 1,500 swimsuits.

Imagine that 5 years after you finish your degree you are in the sand and gravel business. Most firms can vary labor more easily than any other basic resource. Thus, to keep things simple for now, we will assume that your nonlabor resources are all fixed in the short run because you have long-term leases on fixed amounts of capital equipment (trucks and bulldozers) and land, but that you control the amount of labor you hire.

Obviously, if no one works in your business, production and revenue will both be zero. Working alone, you might be able to excavate and sell 10 tons of earth material daily. Suppose that you hire an assistant and find that production increases to 22 tons daily. Because you have more than doubled production while labor inputs only doubled, are we to conclude that you are not very good at your job? Not at all.

Working alone, you must run the truck, handle all marketing, operate the bulldozer at the excavation site, keep the books—the list goes on and on. The cliché "Chief Cook and Bottlewasher" fits too closely for comfort. After hiring an assistant, you can drive the truck while your helper excavates, keep the books while your employee runs the bulldozer, and so on. You are able to produce much more as a team

than as separate individuals because of the gains from *specialization of labor*. As you hire even more workers, you might find that specialization enables production to continue to rise more than proportionally for the first few extra workers. Eventually, however, the advantages of specialization will be overwhelmed as the law of diminishing marginal returns comes into play, and each extra worker adds less than the preceding worker did to total production.

Marginal and Average Physical Products of Labor

Suppose that you have hired several employees and your work force is so specialized that you spend all your time pushing a pencil; you now decide to do some analysis using economic concepts you learned in college. Consider Table 1. If you know what total output is for each level of labor hired (columns 1 and 2), calculating output per worker is simple. Just divide total output (Q) by labor (L). Output per worker (Q/L) is called the **average physical product of labor,** or **APP_L.** These figures are entered in column 3 of the table.

TABLE 1 *Total Output and the Average and Marginal Physical Products of Labor (Sand and Gravel Operation)*

(1) Workers per 8-hr. Shift (L)	(2) Tons of Sand and Gravel Removed Daily (Q)	(3) Average Physical Product of Labor (Q/L)	(4) Marginal Physical Product of Labor ($\Delta Q/\Delta L$)
0	0	0	0
1	10	10.00	10
2	22	11.00	12
3	36	12.00	14
4	52	13.00	16
5	70	14.00	18
6	86	14.33	16
7	100	14.28	14
8	112	14.00	12
9	122	13.55	10
10	130	13.00	8
11	137	12.45	7
12	143	11.92	6
13	148	11.38	5
14	152	10.85	4
15	155	10.33	3
16	157	9.81	2
17	158	9.29	1
18	158	8.78	0
19	157	8.26	−1

FIGURE 1 *The Total Product Curve, Marginal and Average Physical Products of Labor (Sand and Gravel Example)*

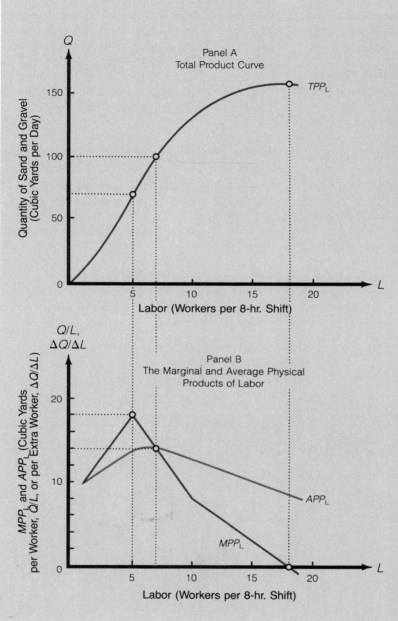

As more and more labor is employed, total output (Panel A) initially increases at an increasing rate because of the advantages of labor specialization. In this range, the marginal and average physical products of labor both grow (Panel B). As congestion begins to emerge, total output continues to grow, but at a falling rate. In this range, average physical product continues to climb, but marginal productivity diminishes. Once marginal physical product falls below average physical product, average physical product begins to fall. However, the total product continues to rise until the marginal physical product is zero. This occurs when congestion or other problems are so severe that further labor inputs cause declines in output.

You will also be interested in how much each additional worker adds to total output, a concept known as the **marginal physical product of labor,** or **MPP_L.** Labor's marginal physical product is vital to the decision about how many workers to hire.

Profit-maximizing firms like yours will not hire extra workers if the extra revenue from their marginal physical products would be less than the extra costs incurred in hiring them. Only workers who generate at least as much revenue as it costs to hire them will be employed, a decision we explore in detail in a coming chapter. Under most circumstances, the productivity of each worker (the MPP_L) will be higher as the amounts of other resources employed increase—you can certainly produce more sand and gravel per day using a bulldozer on an acre of open field then you can using a shovel on a city lot.

The MPP_L is calculated by looking at small differences in the amounts of labor used and the resulting changes in production. With large numbers of workers (as at automobile assembly plants), we would divide a given change in the amount of labor (ΔL) into the resulting change in output (ΔQ) to approximate the MPP_L. With a small firm like your sand and gravel operation, ΔL equals one worker. The marginal physical products of labor ($\Delta Q/\Delta L$) for your firm are reported in column 4 of Table 1.

The **total product curve** for your sand and gravel operation, as graphed in Panel A of Figure 1, relates production and various levels of labor inputs, holding other resources constant.[1] Panel B shows the corresponding marginal and average physical products of labor.

The Short-Run Law of Diminishing Marginal Returns

A problem of congestion emerges as your organization grows. The passenger compartments of your dump trucks become crowded and more time is wasted at the excavation site waiting to load trucks that arrived earlier. A second challenge emerges from coordinating increased work effort: making sure that the left hand knows what the right hand is doing, keeping coffee breaks from expanding to 30 minutes, and so on. Table 1 indicates that the problems of congestion and loss of coordination eventually become so severe that the seventeenth worker adds only one cubic yard of material per day, the eighteenth's contribution is nil, and hiring the nineteenth worker actually yields a loss of output.

You may think that the decline in extra output as extra workers are employed is a consequence of hiring better workers first and then hiring mediocre or inferior workers. This is unnecessary to explain di-

minishing marginal returns. In fact, we might assume that the workers were interchangeable clones from a robot factory. Every worker then becomes the last or marginal worker because if you fired any one of them, you would have one less employee. Declining amounts of capital, land, and supervision per worker cause marginal physical products to diminish as the number of workers grows, and this occurs regardless of the qualities of the individual workers.

> The **law of diminishing marginal returns:** *When successive equal increases of variable resources (for example, labor) are added to some fixed factor influencing production (such as capital or land), although productivity may rise initially, marginal physical products must eventually decline.*

In the short run, the law of diminishing marginal returns is encountered because of the impossibility of increasing all resources proportionally; capital and land per worker fall as more workers are hired, inevitably leading to diminishing additions of output as extra labor is employed. No exception to this basic economic law has ever been discovered. Were it not for diminishing returns, enough food might be grown in a flower pot to feed the world.

Table 1 and Figure 1 reflect the output that might be produced by various numbers of workers who put in 8-hour days. The advantages of specialization enable each of the first five workers to add more than the preceding worker to total output, but the forces that compel marginal productivity to diminish overwhelm any gains from further specialization for the sixth and subsequent workers.

There are tight relationships between production and the costs that influence business decision making. Now that we have delved into production, we turn to the process that translates the total, average, and marginal physical products of labor into production costs.

Short-Run Production Costs

We have divided production costs into explicit and implicit costs. A different grouping is into components called fixed costs and variable costs. All production costs fall within these two categories, so total costs (TC) equal total fixed costs (TFC) plus total variable costs (TVC), or

$$TC = TFC + TVC.$$

---

1. Note that total product curves and production functions are not the same things. A production function allows all inputs to vary, while the total product curve assumes that only one input changes. We are using labor as the variable input, but had we held labor constant and varied capital (or land), the analysis would be quite similar, although the specific curves would differ.

Business people commonly refer to fixed costs as *overhead*, while variable costs are often called *direct costs* or *operating costs*.

Fixed Costs

Every firm has at least one resource that is fixed in the short run, which implies that its short-run cost cannot be varied; this is a **fixed cost.** Most implicit costs are fixed costs. Since they must have been incurred at some previous time, fixed costs are also known as *historical* or *sunk costs.* For your sand and gravel operation, fixed costs would include such things as business licenses, the value of your time, rent you are obligated to pay because of a lease, principal and interest payments on leases for trucks and other equipment; franchise payments, and utility hookup charges. Even though you may be required to make such payments during each time interval, your fixed costs will not be affected by your firm's output.

Fixed Costs and Decision Making

History is bunk.   *Sunk costs are sunk.*
    —Henry Ford   —Anonymous

Suppose that you bought an expensive imported bicycle and were dismayed when the price was slashed 2 weeks later. Then you broke your leg and decided to sell the bike to cover the unexpected medical bills. Which of the following is *least* relevant to the price you should charge: (*a*) the price you paid, (*b*) the current sales price, (*c*) storage costs, (*d*) expected enjoyment from riding after you get out of your cast, or (*e*) the current prices of similar used bikes?

If you chose answer (*a*) to this question, you may intuitively understand the irrelevancy of fixed cost for rational decision making, a point illustrated in Focus 1. Many people are astounded when told that fixed costs have no bearing on rational decisions about how much to produce, how much to charge for your output, and so on.

FIGURE 2   *Fixed, Variable, and Total Costs when Operating Expenses Are Proportional to Output*

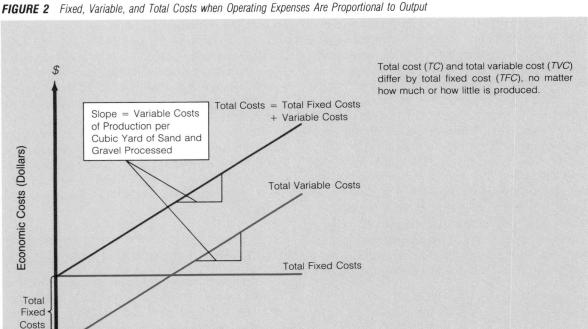

Total cost (*TC*) and total variable cost (*TVC*) differ by total fixed cost (*TFC*), no matter how much or how little is produced.

Fixed costs are meaningful only to the extent that, like history or archaeology, we can learn from them. Since they are fixed, there is a sense that no alternative exists and that the opportunity costs of fixed resources are zero, at least in the short run. Therefore, the only costs that should affect production decisions are those that vary with output because there are alternatives to incurring these costs.

Variable Costs

Such expenses as labor costs, gasoline, truck maintenance, and office supplies will be positively related to the amount of business your sand and gravel operation does. Any costs incurred only when a firm produces are **variable costs.** If variable costs were exactly proportional to the number of tons of earth processed, the relationships between output and fixed, variable, and total costs would be as depicted in Figure 2.

Total fixed costs (*TFC*) are unaffected by production. In the figure, total variable costs (*TVC*) are assumed to be exactly proportional to output. Thus, the constant slope of the total variable cost curve equals the variable cost incurred per cubic yard pro-

cessed. The total cost (*TC*) curve is the vertical summation of the fixed plus variable cost curves. After you understand this simple linear model, we can consider more realistic cost situations, as represented in Table 2 and Figure 3 by the data for your sand and gravel business.

Labor is assumed to be the only variable resource in the short run and the supply of workers is perfectly elastic at $50 per 8-hour shift. You may hire as many workers as you wish from this horizontal labor supply curve. All other resources and costs are assumed constant, and total fixed cost is assumed to be $100 per day.

The total physical product curve (*TPP*) in Figure 1 shows the amounts of labor (*L*) required to produce varying levels of output. When we multiply the horizontal (labor) axis of Figure 1 by the wage rate (*w*), it becomes the total wage bill ($w \times L$) incurred for each level of labor you might hire. (Multiplying any function by a constant does not change the fundamental relationship.) Since wages are the only variable costs of production, this wage bill equals total variable cost (*TVC*). Thus, we have the relationship between the quantity of output and total variable costs—the *TVC* curve shown in Figure 3.

TABLE 2 *Total Output, Total Costs, and Fixed and Variable Costs (Sand and Gravel Example)*

(1) Workers per 8-hr. Shift (L)	(2) Tons of Sand & Gravel Removed Daily (Q)	(3) Wages per Worker (8 hrs. Daily) (w)	(4) Total Variable Cost (w × L) (TVC)	(5) Total Fixed Cost (TFC)	(6) Total Costs (TVC + TFC = TC)
0	0	$50	0	$100	$ 100
1	10	50	$ 50	100	150
2	22	50	100	100	200
3	36	50	150	100	250
4	52	50	200	100	300
5	70	50	250	100	350
6	86	50	300	100	400
7	100	50	350	100	450
8	112	50	400	100	500
9	122	50	450	100	550
10	130	50	500	100	600
11	137	50	550	100	650
12	143	50	600	100	700
13	148	50	650	100	750
14	152	50	700	100	800
15	155	50	750	100	850
16	157	50	800	100	900
17	158	50	850	100	950
18	158	50	900	100	1,000
19	157	50	950	100	1,050

FIGURE 3 *Total Costs, Total Fixed Costs, and Total Variable Costs (Sand and Gravel Example)*

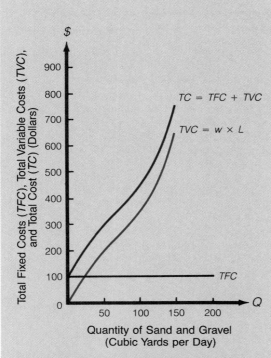

The total cost (*TC*) and total variable cost (*TVC*) curves are "parallel" because the difference between them is total fixed cost (*TFC*), which is constant. Both first increase at a decreasing rate, because total product (from Figure 1) initially increases at an increasing rate. Then, as total product continues to rise, but at a decreasing rate, *TC* and *TVC* rise at increasing rates.

When total fixed costs (*TFC*) are added vertically to the *TVC* (wage bill) curve, we have a picture of how your total costs (*TC*) vary with output; this is a crucial consideration for production decisions. We need to explore your costs a bit more, however, before we launch into decision making. Notice that if you turn Figure 3 sideways, it "mirrors" Panel A in Figure 1. This occurs because variable costs reflect wages and labor inputs and labor inputs determine the amount of output, so there is natural, close relationship between total cost, production, and the amount of labor employed. Now we will explore how other costs, too, are closely related to the average and marginal products of labor.

Average Costs

Some definitions will enable us to examine costs more completely. **Average total cost (*ATC*)** is the total cost incurred per unit of output, and is sometimes termed *unit cost,* or simplified to *average cost.* **Average fixed cost (*AFC*)** is the fixed cost per unit of output. **Average variable cost (*AVC*)** is the variable cost per unit of output. Table 3 lists these costs for your sand and gravel operation.

You have now analyzed the total costs of excavating various amounts of earth, so arriving at average costs only requires dividing these totals by the level of output. We know that total costs are comprised of fixed and variable costs. Average total cost (*ATC*) equals average fixed cost (*AFC*) plus average variable cost (*AVC*). Proof? Total cost = total fixed cost + total variable cost, so

$$\frac{\text{total cost}}{\text{quantity}} = \frac{\text{total fixed cost}}{\text{quantity}}$$
$$+ \frac{\text{total variable cost}}{\text{quantity}}$$

and

$$ATC = AFC + AVC.$$

Graphs of these averages will show you how they are typically related to production.

Average Fixed Costs Just because total fixed costs do not vary with output does not mean that the *AFC* curve is horizontal. *AFC* = *TFC/Q*, where *TFC* is constant. Figure 4 shows how the *AFC* is related to the output of your excavation operation, calculated in column 6 of Table 3. Total fixed costs are a constant amount so that, as output increases, fixed costs per unit of output decline. Because of this, a business person might talk about spreading overhead through high volume.[2]

Developing graphs for *ATC* and *AVC* will be easier if we first introduce marginal cost, which is the most important cost concept for decision making.

---

2. Notice that if we arbitrarily select any two points on the *AFC* curve (say, *a* and *b*), the rectangles formed by dropping horizontal and vertical lines to the axes have identical areas ($100). (Since *AFC* = *TFC/Q*, multiplication of *AFC* by *Q* yields *TFC*: *TFC/Q* × *Q* = *TFC*, which is constant.) Thus, the *AFC* curve is a rectangular hyperbola. Recall that unitary elastic demand curves are rectangular hyperbolas.

TABLE 3 *Average Total Costs, Average Fixed Costs, Average Variable Costs, and Marginal Cost*

(1) Workers per 8-hr. Shift (L)	(2) Tons of Sand and Gravel Removed Daily (Q)	(3) Total Variable Cost (w × L) (TVC)	(4) Total Fixed Cost (TFC)	(5) Average Variable Cost (3)/(2) (AVC)	(6) Average Fixed Cost (4)/(2) (AFC)	(7) Average Total Cost (5) + (6) (ATC)	(8) Marginal Cost (Δ3)/(Δ2) (MC)
0	0	0	$100	—	—	—	—
1	10	$ 50	100	$5.00	$10.00	$15.00	$ 5.00
2	22	100	100	4.54	4.55	9.09	4.17
3	36	150	100	4.17	2.78	6.95	3.57
4	52	200	100	3.85	1.92	5.77	3.13
5	70	250	100	3.57	1.43	5.00	2.78
6	86	300	100	3.49	1.16	4.65	3.13
7	100	350	100	3.50	1.00	4.50	3.57
8	112	400	100	3.57	0.89	4.46	4.17
9	122	450	100	3.69	0.82	4.51	5.00
10	130	500	100	3.85	0.77	4.62	6.25
11	137	550	100	4.01	0.73	4.74	7.14
12	143	600	100	4.20	0.70	4.90	8.33
13	148	650	100	4.39	0.68	5.07	10.00
14	152	700	100	4.60	0.66	5.26	12.50
15	155	750	100	4.84	0.65	5.49	16.67
16	157	800	100	5.10	0.64	5.74	25.00
17	158	850	100	5.38	0.63	6.01	50.00
18	158	900	100	5.69	0.63	6.32	—
19	157	950	100	6.05	0.64	6.69	—

FIGURE 4 *Average Fixed Costs*

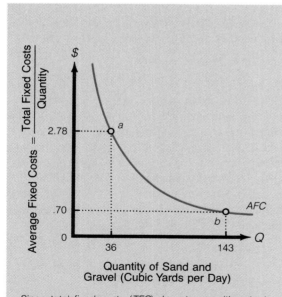

Since total fixed costs (*TFC*) do not vary with output (*Q*), increases in output cause average fixed costs (*AFC* = *TFC/Q*) to decline. Business people refer to this as "spreading their overhead."

Marginal Cost   **Marginal cost (*MC*)** is the change in total cost associated with producing an additional unit of output. Since *TC = TFC + TVC,* any change in total cost necessarily emerges from changes in either fixed or variable costs:

$$\Delta TC = \Delta TFC + \Delta TVC.$$

Dividing this equation by a small change in output (ΔQ) reveals that

$$MC = \frac{\Delta TC}{\Delta Q} = \frac{\Delta TFC}{\Delta Q} + \frac{\Delta TVC}{\Delta Q}.$$

Output does not affect fixed costs, so $\Delta TFC/\Delta Q = 0$ and $MC = \Delta TC/\Delta Q = \Delta TVC/\Delta Q$. Thus, marginal cost equals the changes in either the total cost or the total variable cost incurred in producing an additional unit of output; changes in fixed cost are definitionally zero. Marginal cost for your sand and gravel firm is listed in column 8 of Table 3.

Figure 5 shows how average variable cost (*AVC*) and marginal cost (*MC*) change as you processed various amounts of earth. Why are these cost curves U-shaped? Recall that the marginal physical product of labor (MPP_L) initially rose as you hired more work-

FIGURE 5 *Marginal Cost and Average Variable Cost*

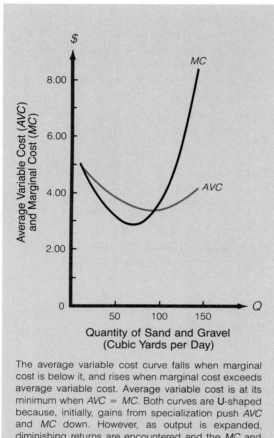

The average variable cost curve falls when marginal cost is below it, and rises when marginal cost exceeds average variable cost. Average variable cost is at its minimum when $AVC = MC$. Both curves are U-shaped because, initially, gains from specialization push AVC and MC down. However, as output is expanded, diminishing returns are encountered and the MC and AVC rise.

average variable cost (AVC) curves. Summing the amounts of AVC and AFC associated with each level of output yields the average total cost (ATC) curve depicted. Graphically, the AFC and AVC are summed vertically to arrive at ATC. Notice that as output increases, differences between the AVC and ATC curves diminish. This convergence of the ATC and AVC curves occurs because their vertical differences equal AFC, which declines as output increases. We now take a quick look at how costs relate to production.

Relating Costs to Production

Comparing Figures 1 and 3 allows you to see one way that total costs are related to total physical product. Before we use graphs to show the connections between average physical product and average costs and between marginal physical product and marginal cost, we will outline the relationships with a little algebra.

Recall the simplifying assumption for your sand and gravel firm that all nonlabor resources were fixed. Therefore, total variable cost (TVC) equals the wage bill ($w \times L$), and average variable costs ($AVC = TVC/Q$) equal wL/Q. Since the average physical product of labor (APP_L) is Q/L, if we invert APP_L (it is then $1/(Q/L) = L/Q$) and multiply by the wage (a constant, w), we have calculated the average variable costs of production [$w/(Q/L) = w/APP_L$]. Algebraically,

$$AVC = TVC/Q = wL/Q$$
$$= w(L/Q) = w(1/APP_L) = w/APP_L.)$$

Because only labor costs change as you process more tons of earth, marginal costs ($MC = \Delta TC/\Delta Q$) are simply the changes in the total wage bill associated with higher production: $MC = \Delta(wL)/\Delta Q$. The wage rate is constant, so $MC = \Delta(wL)/\Delta Q = w\Delta L/\Delta Q$. Since the marginal physical product of labor (MPP_L) equals $\Delta Q/\Delta L$, we can invert the MPP_L, multiply by w, and arrive at the marginal cost of production. Again the algebraic sequence is:

$$MC = \Delta TVC/\Delta Q$$
$$= \Delta(wL)/\Delta Q = w\Delta L/\Delta Q = w(\Delta L/\Delta Q)$$
$$= w(1/MPP_L) = w/MPP_L.$$

Table 4 replicates the total, average, and marginal physical products of labor for your sand and gravel firm from Table 1. Using this data, you can now calculate average variable costs and marginal costs, re-

ers but then fell when diminishing marginal returns were encountered. This means that the labor costs of additional output (its *MC*, in this case) initially decline, but diminishing returns ultimately cause marginal costs to rise as more workers produce higher outputs. Similarly, the average physical product of labor (APP_L) initially rose, but eventually declined as more workers were employed. This causes the **U** shape of average variable cost curves. In a moment we will detail these relationships between production levels and costs.

Graphically Summing Average Costs
In Figure 6 we tack an average fixed cost (AFC) curve onto a graph with typical **U**-shaped marginal cost (MC) and

FIGURE 6 Short-Run Costs of Production

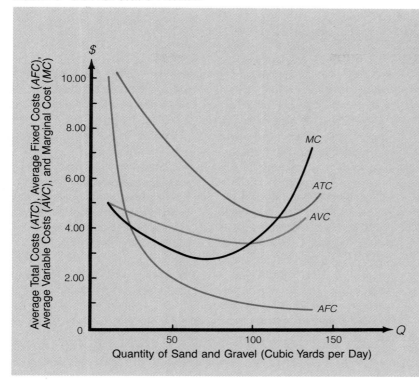

As long as marginal cost (MC) is below average total cost (ATC) or average variable cost (AVC), then ATC and AVC, respectively, will fall when output is increased. When MC exceeds AVC or ATC, then AVC and ATC will rise as output is expanded. The ATC and AVC curves are generally **U**-shaped. Gains from specialization eventually are overcome by diminishing returns, so the ATC, AVC, and MC curves are all **U**-shaped. Higher levels of output spread a firm's overhead, so the AFC curve declines continuously. Notice that the MC curve intersects the AVC and ATC curves at their minimum values.

TABLE 4 Relating Production and Costs (Sand and Gravel Example)

(1) L	(2) Q	(3) (Q/L) APP	(4) (ΔQ/ΔL) MPP	(5) w	(6) (w/APP) AVC	(7) (w/MPP) MC	(8) AFC	(9) ATC
0	0	—	—	$50	—	—	—	—
1	10	10.00	10	50	$5.00	$ 5.00	$10.00	$15.00
2	22	11.00	12	50	4.54	4.17	4.55	9.09
3	36	12.00	14	50	4.17	3.57	2.78	6.95
4	52	13.00	16	50	3.85	3.13	1.92	5.77
5	70	14.00	18	50	3.57	2.78	1.43	5.00
6	86	14.33	16	50	3.49	3.13	1.16	4.65
7	100	14.28	14	50	3.50	3.57	1.00	4.50
8	112	14.00	12	50	3.57	4.17	0.89	4.46
9	122	13.55	10	50	3.69	5.00	0.82	4.51
10	130	13.00	8	50	3.85	6.25	0.77	4.62
11	137	12.45	7	50	4.01	7.14	0.73	4.74
12	143	11.92	6	50	4.20	8.33	0.70	4.90
13	148	11.38	5	50	4.39	10.00	0.68	5.07
14	152	10.85	4	50	4.60	12.50	0.66	5.26
15	155	10.33	3	50	4.84	16.67	0.65	5.49
16	157	9.81	2	50	5.10	25.00	0.64	5.74
17	158	9.29	1	50	5.38	50.00	0.63	6.01

FOCUS 1

Sunk Costs in Stud Poker

In the following example, intended to help you see why fixed costs are irrelevant, all you need to know about stud poker is that a hand with four similar cards (four 7s) beats any hand with three identical cards (three queens and two 10s, for example).

Suppose that a notoriously poor player is dealing five-card stud, dealing four players plus himself one card each in the hole (face down) then one card each face up. Both you and the player to your left have aces showing. With **? A,** she bets $10,000 (we might as well fantasize a bit). You peek at your hole card and discover that you have a sec-

ond ace—**A A**—so you call. The dealer, showing **? 3** is the only other player who calls. (We told you he was a bad player.) The dealer rolls the player on your left a seven—**? A 7,** you another ace—**A A A,** and himself another three—**? 3 3.** Having three aces yourself, you hope the dealer has three 3s and you bet $25,000. The dealer calls, but the other player folds her hand. You are then dealt a king—**A A A K,** and the dealer rolls a third three for himself—**? 3 3 3.** Afraid that the dealer (a wild man) has four 3s, you reluctantly call his $50,000 bet. Now the dealer deals you a second king. You

have **A A A K K**: a full house with aces up! He blithely rolls another 3, so he is sitting with **? 3 3 3 3.** (The lunatic probably has something like a 6 in the hole.) He bets a dime. *The big question:* Should you call the bet? *The answer:* If you are rational, absolutely NOT. No matter what the dealer has in the hole, you lose, because a hand with four of a kind beats a full house. Why should you lose another dime? The $85,000 you put in the pot is no longer yours. It is a sunk cost and, so, is irrelevant to your rational decision.

---

ported in columns 6 and 7, respectively. You then calculate average fixed costs (column 8) by dividing fixed costs by the various possible output levels. Adding the *AFC* to the *AVC* then yields figures for the *ATC* of production (column 9).

Average Product and Average Variable Cost   Figure 7 shows that when six workers are on the job (points *b*), average product is at its maximum (14.33 tons) and average variable cost is at its minimum value ($3.49). Because workers receive a constant wage, we can calculate the amount spent on labor when *AVC* (which is wL/Q) is at its lowest value. Symmetrically, from this wage bill, you can infer the amount of labor hired when average variable cost is minimized. This result can also be seen in Table 4.

Let us get away from technical descriptions for a moment and look at the intuitive result of this analysis. If the average amount produced per worker (APP_L) is at its highest value (point *b* in Panel A), then the average amount spent on labor per unit of output (AVC) logically must be at its lowest value (point *b* in Panel B).

Marginal Product and Marginal Cost   The marginal physical product of labor for your sand and gravel firm is drawn in Panel A of Figure 7, and the corresponding marginal cost curve is shown in Panel B. These curves parallel the data in Table 4 and, thus, are reflections of each other. Marginal product is at its maximum (18 tons daily) and marginal cost is at its minimum ($2.78) if five workers are hired. Clearly, if the last worker hired produced the most (maximum MPP_L at point *a* in Panel A), then the last few tons of gravel processed cost the least (minimum *MC* at point *a* in Panel B). The exercises in Focus 2 will help you understand the tight relationship between various aspects of production and costs.

The relationship between production and costs is critical when we look at the supply decisions of firms. Of course, production costs are only one dimension of a firm's decision matrix. The other side is demand. In the next few chapters, demand-originated constraints on firms facing various degrees of competition will be dealt with at length.

To simplify our analysis of short-run production and costs, only labor has been allowed to vary. How-

FIGURE 7 *The Relationships Between* APP$_L$, MPP$_L$, AVC, *and* MC

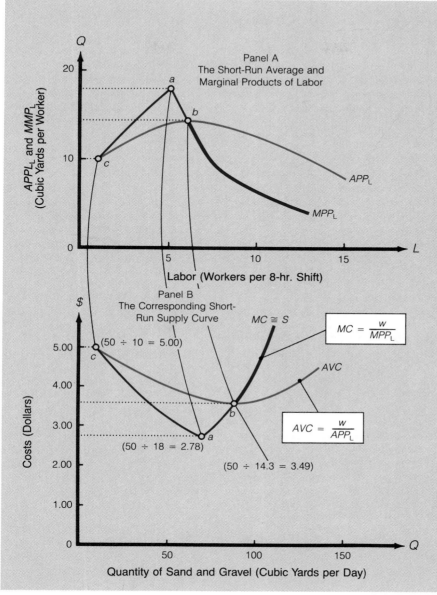

For simplicity, we assume that only labor (L) can be varied in the short run. Thus, all marginal costs and variable costs are associated with the wage bill (wL). When the marginal physical product of labor (MPP$_L$) is at its maximum (point a in Panel A), the last worker hired added the most to production, and so the marginal cost (MC) of the last unit produced is at its minimum (point a in Panel B). Similarly, when the average physical product of labor (APP$_L$) is at its maximum point (point b in Panel A), the average amount of labor used (and hence, the average amount of wage cost) per unit of output is at a minimum, so average variable cost (AVC) is also at its minimum (point b in Panel B).

Panel A
The Short-Run Average and Marginal Products of Labor

Panel B
The Corresponding Short-Run Supply Curve

$MC \cong S$

$$MC = \frac{w}{MPP_L}$$

$$AVC = \frac{w}{APP_L}$$

(50 ÷ 10 = 5.00)

(50 ÷ 18 = 2.78)

(50 ÷ 14.3 = 3.49)

Quantity of Sand and Gravel (Cubic Yards per Day)

ever, the results would be substantially the same if we allowed all resources but one to vary. Long-run production costs must be approached in a slightly different way because all of a firm's resources are variable. Technology is assumed constant in the long run, however, in part because resources may be var-

ied more quickly than technology is likely to change, and in part because the effects of technological changes tend to be somewhat unpredictable. We will deal with technological change later in this chapter when we discuss potential super long-run adjustments.

Costs in the Long Run

The long run is a period sufficient for a firm to use its discretion to completely vary all resources and costs. No resource is fixed in the long run, so there are no long-run fixed costs. Just when do fixed costs become variable? In the long run, you might sell previously fixed resources to other firms and rid yourself of obligations to meet fixed payments, but the original obligation is still a sunk cost—you cannot change history. Alternatively, you might obligate your firm to pay for more machinery, another short-run fixed cost. Until your name is on the dotted line for a new building or machine or to renew a franchise or lease, these are variable costs. Then they become fixed costs, but only for the short run.

In the long run, a firm may enter or leave an industry and either expand or contract the scope of any operation. More land, buildings, or new machinery can be acquired. Or it can sell land or allow leases to lapse: old equipment can either be sold or depreciated and scrapped.

FIGURE 8   *Total Product, Marginal Product, and Average Product of Labor with Different Amounts of Land and Capital*

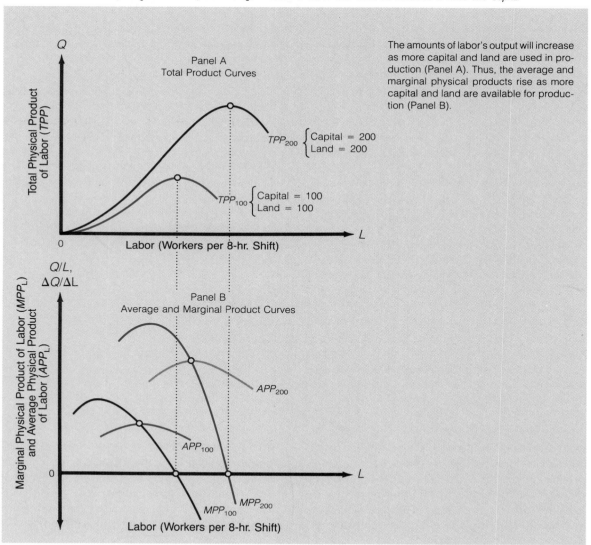

The amounts of labor's output will increase as more capital and land are used in production (Panel A). Thus, the average and marginal physical products rise as more capital and land are available for production (Panel B).

Least Cost Production We allowed only labor to vary when we analyzed the short run, but all resources are variable in the long run. This allows managers who seek maximum profit to achieve technical efficiency in production by altering the resource mix so that the production cost for any given amount of output is minimized. Equivalently, they try to maximize the output produced for a given total cost.

Efficiency requires conformity with the law of equal advantage, which, applied to consumer behavior, yields the principle of equal marginal utilities per dollar we described in the preceding chapter. In a parallel way, the **principle of equal marginal productivities per dollar** applies the law of equal advantage to production: the marginal physical products of resources must be proportional to the prices of the resources. This means that

$$\frac{MPP_L}{w} = \frac{MPP_K}{i} = \frac{MPP_N}{r} = \ldots,$$

where MPP_K equals the marginal physical product of capital, MPP_N equals the marginal physical product of land, i equals the interest rate, and r equals the rent rate for land. To see why this equation works, suppose that the last $1 you paid in wages generated 1 ton of sand while the last $1 you spent on capital yielded 2 tons of sand. You would gain an extra ton of sand to sell if you shifted $1 away from labor towards capital.

Similar gains of output (or reductions in cost) are possible for a firm any time the marginal productivities of its resources are not proportional to resource prices. Thus, **least cost production** in the long run entails adjustments until this principle of equal marginal productivities per dollar is met. This principle suggests that relatively higher wages will induce a firm to *substitute* capital for labor. This has occurred in the auto industry in recent years as high labor costs have caused an army of industrial robots to invade the assembly line. Symmetrically, higher capital costs induce substitution towards labor. This should not give you the impression, however, that resources are only substitutes for one another. Resources may also be complements in production.

Labor productivity, for example, tends to be positively related to the capital and land with which labor has to work. Increases in nonlabor resources tend to raise labor's total, average, and marginal physical product curves, as shown in Figure 8. The

close short-run relationships between production and costs (total, average, and marginal products and costs) suggest that in the long run, average and marginal costs will be influenced by all the resources used.

Possible changes in the short-run marginal costs and average total costs of a garment manufacturer with (*a*) 100, (*b*) 200, or (*c*) 300 sewing machines are highlighted in Figure 9. Other average cost curves associated with other plant sizes are also graphed. Under these short-run cost curves, we have placed an *envelope curve,* which reflects the plant sizes associated with the minimum average costs of producing each level of output. This envelope is the long-run average cost (*LRAC*) curve for the firm. Only the plant in which 200 machines are used to produce 4,000 garments per day yields the absolute minimum long-run average cost of production.

Economies and Diseconomies of Scale Notice that the long-run average cost (*LRAC*) curve falls as output rises and then increases as output rises further. **Economies of scale** exist when long-run average costs decline as output rises, and larger firms will be more efficient than smaller firms. **Diseconomies of scale** occur in the range where average costs rise with increases in output. That is, in this range, reducing the scale of operations is efficient because it allows production at lower average costs.

It might seem that if all resources were expanded by some fixed proportion, output would necessarily expand by that same proportion. However, the advantages of specialization may cause output to expand more than proportionally as the scale of operation initially grows from some small level. These advantages give rise to economies of scale, causing average production costs to fall.

On the other end of the spectrum, diseconomies of scale emerge because of the application for the long run of the law of diminishing returns. The firm can decide how much capital, land, or labor to use, but diminishing returns remain pervasive, even in the long run, because it is impossible for a firm to vary all technological influences on production proportionally and simultaneously.

Even in the long run, powerful firms cannot precisely tailor laws or regulations that influence production costs to suit themselves. Moreover, such influences on production as weather and gravity and the laws of physics and chemistry are totally beyond

FIGURE 9 The Long-Run Average Cost Curve

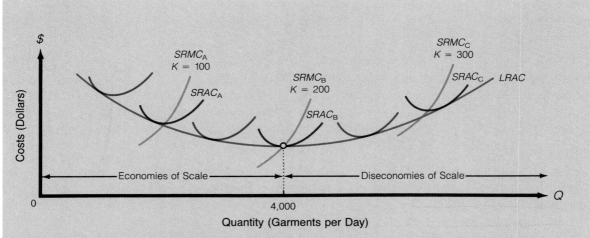

Short-run costs depend on the fixed amounts of capital and land used in concert with labor, which, for convenience, we have assumed is the only variable factor of production in the short run. The long-run average cost (*LRAC*) curve is an envelope of short-run average cost (*SRAC*) curves. There are economies of scale if expanding land and capital result in declining average costs. Diseconomies of scale are present when average costs rise as capacity grows.

on test

✱ long run vs. super long run
(fixed technology)   (variable technology)

our control, and technology is assumed constant except in the super long run. Kenneth Boulding has been credited with a variant of the following example of diseconomies of scale that should drive the problem of long-run diminishing returns home to you.

Imagine that we could shrink the White House to a size at which a champion high-jumping flea could hop over it. Now, increase the heights of both the flea and the White House proportionally until the White House has attained its normal size. The flea will be the size and weight of an elephant. Is there any way it could manage the leap now? Can you imagine what strength would be required for it to make this jump? Move over, Clark Kent.

One reason why giant firms encounter diseconomies of scale is that managerial control deteriorates as more and more layers are added to any hierarchical organization. The mass of information that must be digested and then acted on grows, so that coordinating the activities of ever larger numbers of people becomes an ever more formidable task. Another difficulty is that huge organizations require decision making at many different levels, and not all these decision makers will single-mindedly focus on doing

everything with maximum efficiency so that maximum profits are realized. Like dinosaurs, organizations may become so large and clumsy that they perish.

Measuring Long-Run Average Costs   Any firm that fails to exploit economies of scale will have higher average costs than those of competing firms who do; firms that are too small for efficient operation must either grow or fail. Many people think that production by bigger firms is almost always less costly on average than for smaller firms. While it is true that a firm must be large enough to exploit the economies of scale that are available, bigger plants may encounter diseconomies of scale and be forced to reduce the scope of their operations or sink.

Some studies of the decline of Portugal as a world power during 1400–1600 indicate that Portuguese shipbuilders made wooden sailing ships that were too large, given the technology of the time. The high output (cargo) levels of the Portuguese shipping industry were more than offset when bad weather sank a large part of their fleet. And cost disadvantages suffered by the U.K./French *Concorde* resulted in financial nosedives by the government sponsors of

⟨not on test⟩

The following exercises will show you how closely production is related to costs.* Note how these curves' inflection points, maximums, and minimums are related and you'll attain a deeper understanding of this chapter's material.

1. If labor is the only variable input in the short run, and the wage rate *(w)* is fixed, then the total product curve can be converted into a *TVC* curve by multiplying the labor *(L)* axis by *w*. Draw a total product curve on a

*These exercises were suggested by J. M. Swint in "Transitions from Production to Costs," in *Great Ideas for Teaching Economics,* 3/e, edited by Ralph T. Byrns and Gerald W. Stone, Jr. (Glenview, Illinois: Scott, Foresman and Company, 1987).

clean sheet of paper (see Figure A), then turn the page over and rotate it 90° clockwise. Hold it up to the light and you will see a *TVC,* assuming that $w = \$1$. Adding a constant amount equal to fixed cost to the bottom of the vertical axis results in a mapping of total cost, with quantity *(Q)* on the horizontal axis.

2. When labor is the only variable resource, short-run marginal cost equals w/MPP_L and average variable cost equals w/APP_L. Draw typical marginal physical product (MPP_L) and average physical product (APP_L) curves on a clean sheet of paper, as shown in Figure B. When you turn the paper upside down and back-

wards against a light, you can see that the relationship between MPP_L and APP_L is mirrored in what appear to be marginal cost *(MC)* and average variable cost *(AVC)* curves. This impression is basically correct. However, *MC* and *AVC* curves are mapped with quantity *(Q)* on the horizontal axis, while the MPP_L and APP_L curves have labor *(L)* on the horizontal axis. Since labor input *(L)* and output *(Q)* are positively related throughout the relevant range of production, this "mirrored" relation is only slightly warped—the maximum MPP_L and minimum *MC* correspond precisely, as does the maximum APP_L with the minimum *AVC*.

FIGURE A

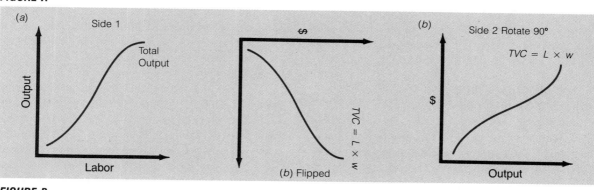

FIGURE B

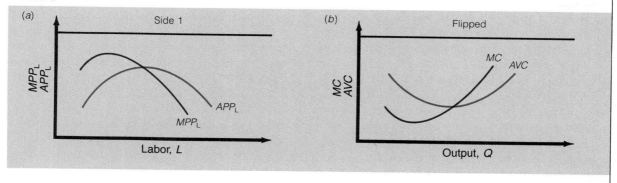

these attempts to push airline flights on bigger and faster planes. How large do you think the optimal convenience store or gas station should be? How about oil refineries? Atomic power plants? In the 1930s, the largest automobile assembly plant in the world was Ford's River Rouge plant. It was never fully utilized, and today much of it has been torn down. It was simply too large to be efficient.

The ranges where economies or diseconomies of scale are actually encountered vary substantially among industries. Engineering estimates and the few statistical studies of cost functions that are available indicate that there are typically substantial ranges of output for which average costs are roughly constant, as depicted in the middle of the *LRAC* curve in Figure 10.

An idea known as the *survival principle* suggests that clustering within an industry of firms or plants of a particular size is good evidence of efficient scales of operations. Some economists have tried to apply this principle to specific industries. Detractors, however, argue that survival depends on a multitude of factors (luck, monopoly power, business acumen, growth or decline of an industry, and so on) and therefore that some firms may survive even if their operations are inefficient. Although measuring long-run costs is unavoidably imprecise, the concept is still quite useful in analyzing industry adjustments to changes in demands, resource prices, or other events.

Technological Change and the Super Long Run

Long-run adjustments allow a firm to enter an industry and grow infinitely or to shrink its capacity to zero and leave an industry; a firm can perfectly adjust its purchases of resources but, by assumption, we hold technology constant. Firms and industries grow in response to profit opportunities or wither when persistent economic losses seem unavoidable. Large profit-making opportunities, however, may induce investments in research and development so that technology changes, generating new products or driving down costs.

In many cases, major technological breakthroughs come in waves and influence a wide variety of industries or forms of production. Predicting the direction of such sweeping technological advances is impossible. In a few instances, however, profit incen-

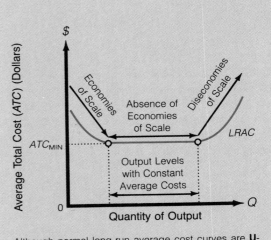

FIGURE 10 *Typical "Real World" Average Cost Curves*

Although normal long-run average cost curves are **U**-shaped, there is typically a large range of production where average costs are constant and there are neither economies nor diseconomies of scale.

tives within a specific industry cause the direction of technological change to be reasonably predictable. The **super long run** is a period sufficiently long for firms to not only perfectly vary the amounts of resources they command but, possibly, to alter technology as well.

Consider, for example, technological adjustments to offset rising energy costs. Prior to the 1970s, many industries were accustomed to low-cost and abundant sources of energy. Their technologies required vast amounts of energy. Firms frantically began searching for more energy-efficient technologies when energy prices quadrupled in 1974–75 alone. New types of insulation were developed, as were production processes that required less heat or permitted heat to be recycled. The cries of car buyers for more miles per gallon were echoed in many industries by pleas for machines that used energy more efficiently.

We cannot say whether technological advances cause super long-run average cost curves to display greater economies of scale or a greater prevalence of diseconomies of scale when compared to normal long-run average cost curves. We can be sure, however, that technological advances make options available that reduce average production costs. Because the precise effects of technological changes are so difficult to predict, we consider only normal long-run adjustments as we examine the responses of firms to changing circumstances in the next few chapters. This means that firms can grow or shrink by acquiring more or fewer resources as their prospects for profit change.

This chapter concludes this part of the book. You have used marginal concepts to explore both utility analysis (a foundation for demand) and production and costs (the foundations of supply). You will find all these concepts, and elasticity analysis as well, linked in the coming chapters as we examine business decisions about what prices to charge for output and how much to produce.

CHAPTER REVIEW: KEY POINTS

1. A *production function* expresses the relationship between *outputs* and *inputs*. Production transforms goods to make them more valuable in form, place, time, or possession. A *total (physical) product curve* shows how output is affected as the amount of only one input changes.

2. The *short run* is a period in which at least one resource and one cost are fixed. In the *long run* all resources can be varied, but technology is assumed constant. In the *super long run,* technology may advance in response to profit opportunities within an industry. These periods, therefore, are not defined by time, but rather by the nature of the adjustment process.

3. Economic costs include both explicit and implicit costs. *Explicit costs* involve outlays of money for goods or resources. *Implicit costs* are opportunity costs associated with resources provided by the owner and used in the business. Payments for rent, electricity, and wages are explicit costs, whereas the values of the owner's labor and capital are implicit costs.

4. Bookkeeping rarely considers implicit costs, while both implicit and explicit costs are included in economic costs. Consequently, *accounting profits* often overstate the economic profitability of an enterprise because the opportunity costs of owner-provided resources are ignored.

5. The *average physical product of labor* (APP_L) is equal to Q/L. The *marginal physical product of labor* (MPP_L) equals $\Delta Q/\Delta L$ and is the output generated by an additional unit of labor.

6. When increases in a variable resource are applied to a fixed resource, although the marginal physical product of the variable factor may initially rise, at some point marginal product inevitably falls according to the *law of diminishing marginal returns.*

7. The firm's total costs can be separated into *fixed costs* (or *overhead*) and *variable* (or *operating*) *costs.* Fixed costs do not vary with output, but variable costs do. Short-run fixed costs are sunk and do not enter into rational decision making. Leases, utility hookup charges, the opportunity costs of the owner's resources, and other overhead expenses are fixed costs. Wages paid employees, bills for raw materials, and other costs that change when output is changed are variable costs.

8. When total fixed costs and total variable costs are each divided by output, *average fixed costs* (*AFC*) and *average variable costs* (*AVC*) are obtained, respectively. Summing the two yields *average total cost* (*ATC*). *Marginal cost* (*MC*) is defined as the additional cost of producing one more unit of a good and is equal to $\Delta TC/\Delta Q$.

9. Firms can enter or leave an industry in the long run because all resources are variable. The *long-run average cost curve* (*LRAC*) is found by examining numerous short-run average cost curves (different sizes of plants) and constructing an *envelope curve* showing the minimum long-run average costs for each level of output. Long-run average cost curves typically have *economies of scale* (*LRAC* falling) over some portion of the curve, but eventually exhibit *diseconomies of scale* (*LRAC* rising).

10. Measuring long-run costs is a complex and difficult problem. One method is to examine the size (and the cost structure) of firms that have been successful and have "survived" in an industry over a long period of time, but reasons other than efficiency may explain why one firm survives while another fails.

QUESTIONS FOR THOUGHT AND DISCUSSION

1. Suppose that you offered to buy pizza and cold drinks to bribe your friends to help you move into a new apartment and were deluged with offers of help. What problems would you encounter if too few actually showed up? How would this affect your "average cost" per box or stick of furniture moved? What are some possible "fixed factors" that would decrease the efficiency of your move and drive up its cost if too many people volunteered to help? How would this raise the cost of your move? How many big strong friends do you think would be the ideal number to accomplish this task?

2. Why does marginal cost decline if output increases at an increasing rate when additional workers are hired? Why does average variable cost decline as long as the marginal physical product of labor is greater than the average physical product of labor?

3. The average productivity of labor rises as long as labor's marginal productivity exceeds the average. We call this range of production Zone 1. Do you think firms would knowingly choose to operate in Zone 1, where hiring additional workers raises average productivity? Why, or why not? Would a firm ever operate in Zone 2, the range of output where the marginal returns from labor were positive but diminishing? Would they operate in Zone 3, where the marginal physical productivity of labor is negative? In what zone will firms operate? (A colleague of the authors, in an observation about another professor, described the individual as a "Zone 3 personality." What do you suppose was meant by this remark? Have you ever worked with such a person?) Draw a typical total product curve and include average and marginal physical products. Identify these production zones. *Note:* Firms always try to operate in one of these zones, but most firms will close down rather than operate in the other.

4. Describe the forces that, as more and more labor is hired, cause output to rise at an increasing rate and then at a decreasing rate and that may ultimately cause output to fall as more labor is employed. How do these forces affect marginal and average costs in a similarly systematic fashion? Why? Can you think of any production processes that would not operate in accord with these general principles? What are they?

5. What are the similarities and differences between the ways the general law of diminishing returns (described in Chapter 2) applies to consumption and to production?

6. Can you construct a total product curve for "knowledge of economics," with your study time as the variable (labor) input? How might this curve shift with variations in time with tutors, reference books, reading the *Wall Street Journal,* studying only when you are too tired to party, and so on? (*Hint:* Review Figure 8.) At what point would the law of diminishing marginal returns come into play? Should you cease studying at the onset of diminishing returns? You may have heard people suggest that "when you reach the point of diminishing returns, it's time to quit." Are they using this term correctly?

OPTIONAL MATERIAL: THE GEOMETRY OF TOTAL, AVERAGE, AND MARGINAL PRODUCTS

You have previously encountered the *rise/run* formula for calculating slope. We can use this formula to show geometrically just how total, average, and marginal physical products are related.

Pick any point on the total product curve (TPP_L) in Panel A of Figure 11. Now, using a straightedge (you can make one by folding a piece of paper), connect that point with the origin. The slope of this line is Q/L, so if you construct bar graphs of all slopes of rays from the origin to all points on the total product curve, you would get a graph of the average physical product of labor. Since no ray from the origin to the total product curve is steeper than the one that is just tangent (touches) at point b, the amount of labor associated with b (on the horizontal axis) has the maximum value of the average product of labor

FIGURE 11   The Total, Marginal, and Average Physical Products of Labor

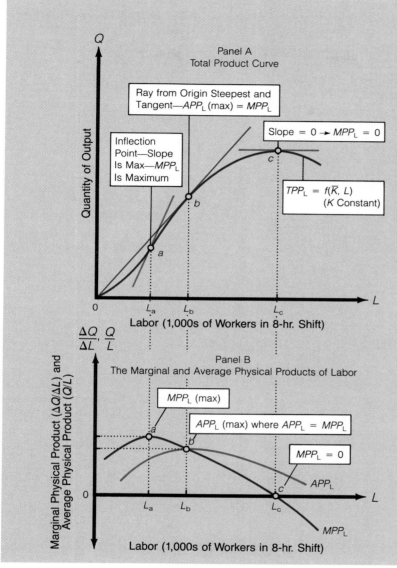

As more and more labor is employed, total output (Panel A) initially increases at an increasing rate because of the advantages of labor specialization. In this range, the marginal and average physical products of labor both grow (Panel B). As congestion begins to emerge, total output continues to grow, but at a falling rate. In this range (point *a* to point *b*), average physical product continues to climb, but marginal productivity diminishes. Once marginal physical product falls below average physical product (beyond point *b*), average physical product begins to fall. However, the total product continues to rise until the marginal physical product is zero at point *c*. This occurs when congestion or other problems are so severe that further labor inputs cause declines in output.

(measured on the vertical axis of Panel B). Every point other than *b* on the total product curve lies on a ray with less slope than the one to point *b*. Therefore, the APP_L curve increases up to L_b, and declines thereafter.

We can use similar analyses of slope to derive geometrically the MPP_L curve. Let us start with an easy point, that at which the total product curve achieves its maximum value. A tangent to the total product curve at *c* has a slope of zero. The marginal physical product of labor is zero at *c*. A little more or less labor will not influence output appreciably. Do you see the connection? Tangents to the total product curve have a slope equal to $\Delta Q/\Delta L$, which is the MPP_L. The MPP_L at L_c is zero. Let us look at some other points. At point *b* (labor = L_b), we know that the APP_L is at its maximum. Moreover, the ray from the origin to point *b* is just tangent to the total product curve. Can you see the implication? The APP_L is just equal to the MPP_L where the APP_L is maximized. If you now take your straightedge and place it tangent to the total product curve just below point b, you will see that it is steeper than the ray from the origin to point b. Implication? The MPP_L is greater than the APP_L at lower levels of labor usage than L_b. Now move the straightedge to a tangent point just to the right of point b. It will be less steep than the ray from the origin at point b. Thus, the MPP_L is below the APP_L if more than L_b labor is employed.

If you now move your straightedge so that it is tangent to the total product curve and then keep it tangent to the TPP curve as we add more labor (move to the right), you will see that the straightedge lies below the TPP curve and that the slope (MPP_L) increases up to point a. Thereafter, the straightedge tangent lies above the TPP curve, but its slope (the MPP_L) decreases. Conclusion? The MPP_L has its max-

imum value at point a (labor = L_a). Point a is known as an **inflection point.** Below point a, the TPP curve is increasing at an increasing rate; above point a, the TPP continues to increase, but at a decreasing rate.

Let us summarize our findings about the MPP_L and APP_L:

1. The MPP_L equals zero when the TPP curve is at its highest value (point c).

2. The MPP_L equals the APP_L when the APP_L is maximized (point b).

3. The MPP_L is above the APP_L as we consider levels of labor where the APP_L is increasing (points left of b); the MPP_L is below the APP_L where the APP_L is falling (points to the right of b).

4. The MPP_L is maximized at the TPP curve's inflection point, which occurs at a level of labor below that where the APP_L is maximized (point a).

OPTIONAL MATERIAL: ISOQUANTS AND PRODUCTION

How the resource mix is varied in the long run to maximize a firm's profit was touched on in our discussion of the principle of equal marginal productivities per dollar. Now we will address these long-run adjustments using slightly more sophisticated tools.

Isoquants

Producing any given amount of output can be accomplished with numerous combinations of inputs. For example, suppose you own a firm that packages and

sells "Birdhouse" gourd seeds to home gardeners who grow houses for their feathered friends. You estimate that you can wholesale 10,000 cases of packaged seeds at $2 per case over the course of a season. Five of the many different possible combinations of capital (machines) and labor (workers) that will accomplish the job are listed in Table 5. These combinations run the gamut from a few machines with many workers hand-counting and stuffing the packages to production processes using numerous automated machines and very few workers to load seeds

TABLE 5 *The Various Combinations of Labor and Capital that Will Package 10,000 Cases of "Birdhouse" Gourd Seeds*

Point	Units of Capital (K)	Units of Labor (L)	Output: Cases of Gourd Seeds (Q)	Total Cost if w = $1,000, r = $1,000 (TC)
a	1	9	10,000	$10,000
b	2	5	10,000	7,000
c	3	3	10,000	6,000
d	5	2	10,000	7,000
e	9	1	10,000	10,000

FIGURE 12 *Equal Output Curve (Isoquant) for Bird Seed*

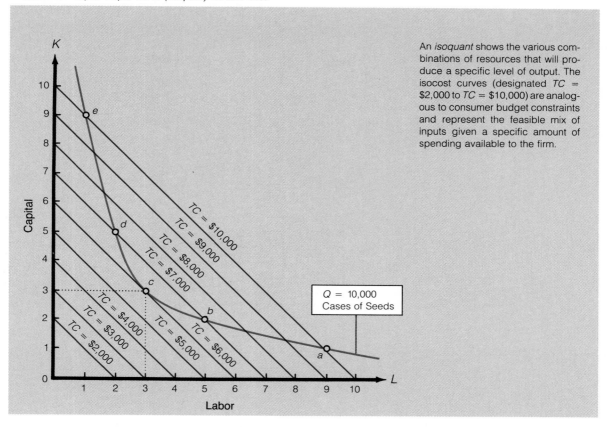

An *isoquant* shows the various combinations of resources that will produce a specific level of output. The isocost curves (designated $TC = \$2,000$ to $TC = \$10,000$) are analogous to consumer budget constraints and represent the feasible mix of inputs given a specific amount of spending available to the firm.

and watch the machines work. As you might expect, the process you would eventually gravitate to will be the one with the lowest cost. The last column of Table 5 depicts the total costs of packaging 10,000 cases of seeds if labor and capital each cost $1,000 per unit. To minimize the costs of producing 10,000 packages, you would employ three machines and three workers. The information in Table 5 is graphed in Figure 12; a smoothly curved line connects the five combinations from Table 5. This curve represents all possible mixtures of labor and capital that can produce 10,000 cases, and is referred to as an **isoquant.**

Isoquants are similar to the consumer indifference curves discussed in the optional material at the end of the preceding chapter, but with one major difference. Isoquants show constant levels of output, which is measurable; indifference curves show constant levels of satisfaction, which cannot be measured with precision. Just as the slope of an indifference curve reflects the relative subjective desirability of the two goods considered ($-MU_a/MU_b$), isoquants reflect the relative marginal productivities of the two resources ($-MPP_L/MPP_K$). We will develop this point more in a moment.

Isocost Curves

Superimposed on the isoquant for 10,000 cases of seeds in Figure 12 is a set of isocost curves. **Isocosts** represent different levels of expenditures by your firm for various combinations of labor and capital when the price of labor is $1,000 per unit and the price of capital is $1,000 per unit. These isocosts are

FIGURE 13 *Diminishing Returns and Isoquants*

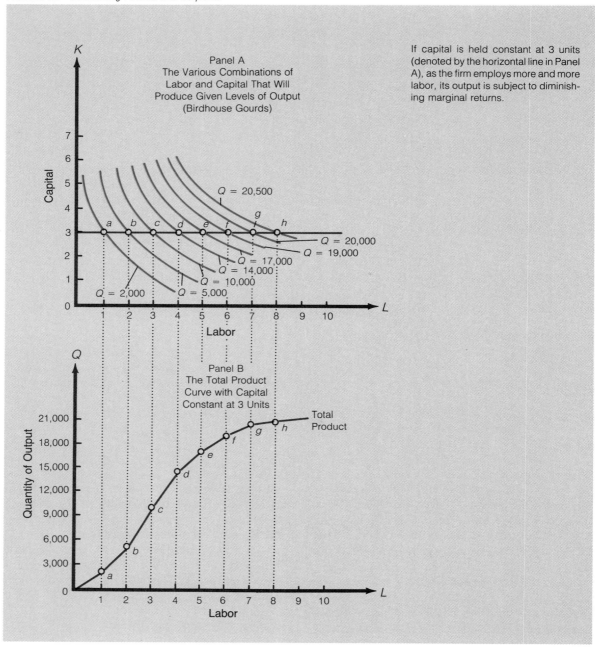

Panel A
The Various Combinations of
Labor and Capital That Will
Produce Given Levels of Output
(Birdhouse Gourds)

If capital is held constant at 3 units (denoted by the horizontal line in Panel A), as the firm employs more and more labor, its output is subject to diminishing marginal returns.

$Q = 20,500$
$Q = 20,000$
$Q = 19,000$
$Q = 17,000$
$Q = 14,000$
$Q = 10,000$
$Q = 5,000$
$Q = 2,000$

Panel B
The Total Product
Curve with Capital
Constant at 3 Units

Total Product

close relatives of the consumer budget lines described in the optional material in the previous chapter. Just as the slope of the budget line reflects the prices of the two goods considered ($-P_a/P_b$), the slopes of isocosts reflect the prices of the resources

considered ($-w/r$, where w is the wage rate and r is the unit cost of capital). Notice that production process a ($L = 9, K = 1$) results in total costs of $10,000, which lies on the $TC = \$10,000$ isocost curve. As Figure 12 illustrates, 10,000 cases of seeds can be packaged at a minimum cost of $6,000 using three workers and three machines (point c). Graphically, costs are minimized for a given level of output where the isocost curve is just tangent to the isoquant, representing an output level of 10,000 packages. At this point, $MPP_L/MPP_K = w/r$. This is similar to the tangency between consumer indifference curves and budget lines in which maximum satisfaction is attained for a given budget. Recall (from the preceding chapter) that this point conformed to the principle of equal marginal utilities per dollar: $MU_a/MU_b = P_a/P_b$. Thus, in accord with the principle of equal marginal productivities per dollar, our result that $MPP_L/MPP_K = w/r$ means that maximizing profit requires the marginal payments to resource owners to be in accord with the resource's contribution to production.

One final note: Just as there are numerous isocost curves that represent different levels of cost, there are also numerous isoquants for production levels other than 10,000 packages. We have simplified the analysis by assuming that you expected 10,000 packages of seeds per season to be the most profitable level of output.

Diminishing Marginal Product

The analysis in this chapter assumes that the typical production process eventually is subject to diminishing returns to the variable input. The same principle applies to production analysis using isoquants. Figure 13 illustrates the diminishing marginal physical product of labor when the amounts of other resources are held constant. In Panel A of Figure 13, capital is held constant at 3 units. Points a through b

represent the amounts of labor needed to produce output levels ranging from 2,000 to 20,500 units. In Panel B, the total product curve is derived from Panel A when capital is fixed at 3 units, and shows diminishing returns to labor. As we add more and more labor to a fixed stock of capital, the increased output from hiring additional labor eventually falls.

Substituting One Resource for Another

Let us take a moment to examine what happens to the marginal products of labor and capital relative to each other when we substitute labor for capital or vice versa. When we change from production process c to production process b (move from point c to point b in Figure 12), we "give up" one unit of capital; to keep production constant, we must hire two units of labor, which suggests that the third machine does the work of two workers. When we move from point b to point a (giving up another machine), how many workers must be hired to keep production constant? The answer is four, suggesting that the productivity of four workers is required to replace that lost from the second machine. As we substitute more and more labor for capital (move down and to the right on the isoquant in Figure 12), ever increasing amounts of labor are necessary to keep production constant. Alternatively, the marginal product of labor declines relative to that of capital. The opposite is true when capital is substituted for labor (movements to the left on the isoquant). Thus, the law of diminishing marginal productivity is reflected in the shapes of isoquants, which are convex (bowed in) from the origin.

PART 7

The Structure of Product Markets

Highly Concentrated Markets

Monopoly

1. One-firm industry
2. No close substitutes for products
3. Substantial and effective barriers to entry

Oligopoly

1. Few firms
2. Decision making mutually interdependent
3. Major barriers to entry

Monopolistic Competition

1. Numerous potential firms and buyers
2. Differentiated products
3. No entry or exit barriers

Pure Competition

1. Numerous potential firms and buyers
2. Similar porducts
3. No entry or exit barriers.

Competitive Markets with Low Concentration

Vigorous competition is the norm for most landscapers, retailers, and home builders. Other firms only broadly compete for customers; your local phone company may vie with book stores or travel agents for shares of your budget. Some firms specialize in such standard goods as lumber, while others focus on unique products like art or organ transplants. A small town may support only one gas station, while high capital costs create monopolies in bigger markets: one giant firm, COMSAT, operates most communications satellites.

The figure at the left illustrates the continuum of market structures. We analyze pure competition in Chapter 23. Then, in Chapter 24, problems caused by monopolies are contrasted with the results of pure competition. Having discussed these extremes, we then survey monopolistic competition and oligopoly in Chapter 25. Part Seven concludes with discussions of antitrust policies (Chapter 26) and the regulation of business (Chapter 27). Government antitrust actions and regulations are attempts to direct market allocations of resources and incomes in ways thought to be more economically efficient or socially preferable.

We need to discuss the power to set prices, or lack of it, before we investigate different output market structures. As the figure shows, purely competitive buyers and sellers have no choice but to accept the going price; their only real choices lie in the quantities they buy or sell. These buyers and sellers are called *price takers*, or *quantity adjusters*. For example, you are a quantity adjuster when buying food. You can buy as much or as little as you like, but you have very little leverage with which to dicker over the price.

The weakness of competition in some markets enables sellers to set prices, at least within some range. Because the demand curves that face them slope down, these *price makers* can manipulate prices only by simultaneously limiting the quantities produced and sold. For example, the international OPEC oil cartel was able to boost oil prices substantially during the 1970s, but only by restricting output by setting maximum production quotas for each member country.

Any price-making firm is said to possess *monopoly power*. A firm need not be a monopoly per se to possess monopoly power. All it requires is some power as a price maker. Before dealing with price makers, we will examine the world of pure competition and price takers.

CHAPTER 23 The Competitive Ideal

> price takers
> entry and exit
> profit maximization
> total revenue minus total cost (TR − TC)
>
> marginal cost equals marginal revenue (MC = MR)
> shutdown point
> firm and industry short-run supply curves
>
> zero economic profits
> increasing-cost and decreasing-cost industries
> marginal social cost equals marginal social benefit (MSC = MSB)

Economic models of competition focus on the results of competitive market structures rather than on rivalry between firms. These structures, as we shall see, imply a business environment that is so competitive that firms have no discretion about pricing and are forced to be efficient merely to survive.

In this chapter we first cover the conditions necessary for a competitive market structure. Short-run pricing and output decisions are then examined, followed by a look at long-run results of entry and exit. Long-run competitive results are evaluated and provide a benchmark for efficiency when evaluating other market structures.

The World of Pure Competition

Competitive industries meet certain well-defined structural conditions. When a market has these characteristics, we can predict how prices and output will be determined, or how they will change if circumstances change. A market is *purely competitive* if:

1. There are large numbers of both potential buyers and potential sellers.
2. Firms in the industry produce a homogeneous (standardized) product.
3. Each buyer or firm is so small relative to the industry that any decision by any one of them to increase its purchases or output will not appreciably affect either the total demand or supply of the product or its price.
4. There are no significant barriers to entry or exit. This means that new firms can easily enter the industry if doing so appears profitable. Conversely, existing firms can leave the industry if they expect to experience losses.

Standard size staples, pencils, paper clips, rubber bands, many agricultural products, computer floppy disks, and other relatively homogeneous products are examples of products produced in competitive markets. Each buyer or seller is too small to significantly affect the total demand or supply of the product single-handedly, leaving buyers and sellers in competitive markets as quantity adjusting **price takers;** they have no choice but to accept the price determined in the market. This means that individual competitive buyers view the supply curves facing them as perfectly elastic (horizontal) at the going market price. Similarly, competitive sellers perceive the demand curves they confront as horizontal at the current market price.

Competition Versus Competing

In general usage, competition connotes struggle or rivalry between individuals or groups. We all grow up competing for grades, merit badges, positions on a team, and dates. Consider a farmer in Illinois. Farmers compete with other farmers. How do farmers set the prices for their corn, wheat, pigs, or soybeans? Do they argue that their products are superior and so should command a higher price? Do they offer coupons or "instant winner bingo" to buyers? They obviously do not.

Purely competitive price setting occurs for many farm products and other raw materials (coal or crude oil) or primary products (steel or lumber) on more than 240 business days each year at commodity exchanges in major cities throughout the world. The Chicago Board of Trade is the most important commodity exchange in the world. The prices that farmers are paid are determined on these commodity exchanges by the interactions of market supplies and demands for each of numerous categories of farm products. These market prices are set in an auction environment by the bids and offers of buyers and sellers or their broker representatives.

Commodity exchanges seem chaotic to casual visitors. Much of the trading is by "public outcry." In a large hall (the trading floor), hundreds of wild-eyed traders scream bids and offers, holding their hands at various angles above their heads with different numbers of extended fingers. The noise level dwarfs that of many sporting events. No single buyer or seller is of much consequence in setting prices as bids and offers are accepted or rejected. From one minute to the next, a trader may swing from trying to buy soybeans for a customer in Japan to trying to sell corn from a silo in Nebraska, although most traders specialize in only a few commodities. Once the price is determined, individual farmers can sell their entire harvests to commodity traders at the going market price.

Markets for precious metals are also extremely competitive. If you decided that your sand and gravel operation was boring (it was the pits, anyway) and that gold mining might be more romantic and remunerative, you could buy a mine and sell all the gold you extracted at the price fixed on the commodity market. This is illustrated in Figure 1. The demand curve facing the competitive firm is a horizontal line (**d**) at the market price (P_e). Competitive firms decide the quantities of particular goods to produce and sell at current prices. Even firms mining hundreds of claims and using millions of dollars worth of equipment can sell gold only at the going price. This is why competitive firms are price takers. Competitive firms compete in one dimension—efficient production.

This form of competition, which emphasizes decisions about quantities, contrasts sharply with competition among automakers, for example. It is extremely difficult and costly for a new auto producer to enter the market. The collapse of DeLorean Motor Company, after much desperate action by its founder to keep it afloat, is illustrative. Cars are not standardized, and the pricing and output decisions of any of the big three American automakers or their foreign counterparts clearly affect the sales of other producers. These firms compete through advertising, styling, and aggressive marketing, as well as through pricing strategies. Although these firms are competing, they do not compete solely on the basis of efficient production of output at a market determined price, as do firms in purely competitive markets.

Freedom of **entry and exit** may be the most important ingredient in maintaining a competitive market over time.[1] In the early 1970s, farming became immensely profitable. Existing farmers expanded their operations, and new farms entered the market. Supplies of farm commodities increased, causing market prices to fall and reducing the incentives for further entry. In fact, during 1982–86 many farmers were driven out of business or to the verge of bankruptcy.

Few industries conform precisely to the assumptions of the purely competitive model. (Remember, however, that a model need be no more complex

---

1. A recent hypothesis called *contestable markets theory* contends that a potent threat of entry alone is sufficient to yield the same results as pure competition even if there are only one or two firms in an industry at present. We deal more with this theory in the next three chapters.

FIGURE 1 *Demand Curves for a Competitive Firm and a Competitive Industry*

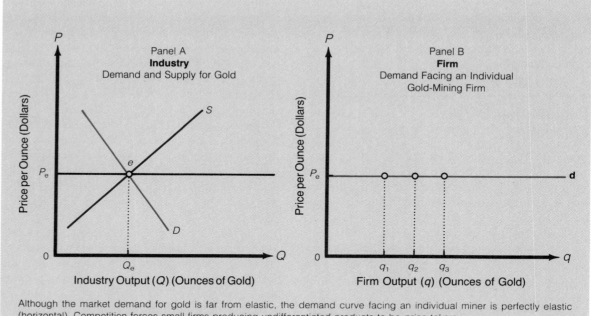

Panel A
Industry
Demand and Supply for Gold

Panel B
Firm
Demand Facing an Individual
Gold-Mining Firm

Although the market demand for gold is far from elastic, the demand curve facing an individual miner is perfectly elastic (horizontal). Competition forces small firms producing undifferentiated products to be *price takers*.

than is required for the purposes at hand. Models are judged not by the realism of their assumptions, but rather by the accuracy of their predictions.) Although rare in practice, you will learn that purely competitive markets tend to be efficient, yielding economic solutions that seem more equitable than those of other market structures. For these reasons, pure competition has become the normative yardstick by which other market structures are judged.

More importantly, many results from simple competitive models apply to markets that deviate substantially from pure competition. For example, the competitive model underpins supply-and-demand analysis, which enables us to predict with reasonable accuracy the effects of certain events on prices and outputs. Qualitatively similar movements of prices and outputs occur even when market structures are far from purely competitive. Understanding how competitive markets react to changes in circumstances allows us to use supply-and-demand analysis to explain the changes in the prices and outputs that take place every day in our economy. Not surprisingly, the ranges of potential supply adjustments differ markedly when we consider different time frames.

Supply Responses and Time

An industry's response to changes in demand depends in part on the time available for firms to adjust. Alfred Marshall, an eminent British economist, designed a way for economists to treat time systematically. Adjustments are typically classified as occurring in the **market** (immediate) **period,** the **short run (SR),** or the **long run (LR).** In general, the impact on quantities will be greater and the effect on prices less the longer an industry has to accommodate changes in demands. To put this another way, the longer an industry has to respond, the greater its market elasticity of supply. In the market period, we assume, for simplicity, that supply is perfectly inelastic. Supplies are somewhat elastic in the short run and much more elastic in the long run.

This relationship can be seen in Figure 2. Suppose that the original demand for gold is D_0, price is $600, and equilibrium quantity sold is Q_0. If demand rises to D_1, during the market period prices for existing stocks of gold would rise to $850 per ounce, reflecting the temporary inability of the industry to produce

Alfred Marshall (1842–1924)

Economics is such a broad field that most economists become specialists, advancing knowledge in at most a few areas. However, a few master economists have broadly expanded the frontiers of economic reasoning. You will encounter their names and ideas throughout this book. Adam Smith, David Ricardo, John Maynard Keynes, Karl Marx, and, in our own time, Paul Samuelson have covered the gamut of economic theory. Alfred Marshall belongs in this elite group.

Born of middle-class parents in the London suburb of Clapham, Marshall was destined for the ministry, according to his stern, evangelical father. An independent sort, Marshall refused a classics scholarship at Oxford and instead studied mathematics at Cambridge. His exposure to philosophy led to Marshall's lifelong concern with the social problems of industrial England. The realization that poverty was at the root of many social problems led him into economics, in which he excelled. Marshall's most famous student, John Maynard Keynes, referred to Marshall as the greatest economist of the nineteenth century.

Marshall was an extremely careful and thorough writer who tried to avoid controversy. Many of the ideas that

eventually appeared in his *Principles of Economics* (1890) were developed much earlier, but Marshall's patience and diligence paid huge dividends. The influence of this book has been both significant and lasting. Despite the many changes that have occurred in economics since his death, a large portion of economic theory remains distinctively Marshallian. A partial list of Marshall's major contributions includes the concepts of *competitive equilibrium* (in the long run and in the short run), *price elasticity of demand, internal and external economies of scale, increasing and decreasing cost industries, quasi-rent,* and *consumer surplus.*

Perhaps Marshall's greatest contribution was the way he worked time into his entire method of economic analysis, bequeathing to subsequent generations of economists not only a number of analytical tools, but also guidelines for their effective use. Marshall handled the problem of continuous change in economics through the judicious use of conditional clauses that he grouped under the heading *ceteris paribus. Ceteris paribus* ignores the disturbing effects of certain tendencies for a time, which permits the issue to be studied narrowly and makes it more capable of precise

handling. The firm handling of a narrow issue in this fashion helps to treat broader issues that contain the narrow one; as understanding is gained at each step, more and more restrictions can be relaxed.

This method is illustrated in Marshall's treatment of demand, in which the number of consumers, their tastes, expectations, money incomes, and the prices of other goods are assumed constant when discussing the determination of the equilibrium price and quantity. As things change over time, however, each of these restrictive assumptions may be relaxed one at a time so that the analysis proceeds to a different equilibrium point. Marshall applied this same method, with very fruitful results, to the theories of value and production. In so doing, he developed a method of analysis that economists use to this day.

more to accommodate the higher demand. If this increase in demand persists, mining firms might increase production by using overtime labor, hiring new workers, or employing any of several other short-run devices. This results in an increase in the

quantity supplied by existing firms in the industry, yielding a short-run price of $725, which is somewhat less than the $850 price per ounce that prevailed in the market period immediately after demand rose to D_1. Finally, prospectors will discover

FIGURE 2 *Industry Supply Response and the Market Period*

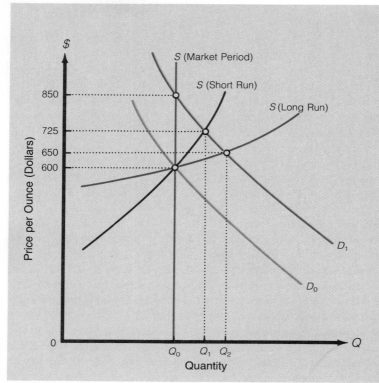

In the market period (*MP*), production is fixed and supply is nearly perfectly inelastic. (For convenience, we ignore possible variations in inventories.) In the short run, existing firms can vary their outputs so the industry supply curve is more elastic. In the long run, supply is much more elastic because firms can either enter or leave the industry in response to profit signals.

new lodes of ore; as new mine operators respond to the increased profitability of the industry, supplies will increase further and the long-run equilibrium price will be less ($650). In the long run, quantity changes will always be greater and price changes will be less for a given change in demand than in the market period or the short run. This occurs because the production options open to firms in an industry expand as the time available for adjustment increases.

Firms cannot modify their production during a single market period to take advantage of profit opportunities or to minimize their losses when demands change. Firms can adjust somewhat in the short run but not completely, because at least one factor of production is fixed. Only in the long run are all resources variable so that firms are free to enter or leave a market as their owners choose. And in the super long run, it is even possible for technology to

change as miners seek newer ways to take advantage of the higher market demand and price of gold. As the time period for decisions grows longer, competitive firms have greater flexibility. We will now discuss the short-run decisions of competitive firms and then examine the long run.

Short-Run Competitive Pricing and Output

All firms are assumed to maximize their profits, but how do they do so? Are the short-run adjustments of competitive firms different from those in the long run? Profit-maximizing behavior can be described in a number of ways. We begin with the short-run **total revenue minus total cost (*TR* − *TC*)** approach, which is the simplest.

Total Revenue Minus Total Cost Approach

The competitive firm is a price taker (the price is set by the market), leaving the choice of how much to produce (quantity adjustment) as its major decision.[2] How much should a competitive firm produce? Should it produce and sell as much as possible to maximize profits? The example described in Table 1 leads us to the answer. Suppose you can choose weekly gold output levels ranging from nothing to twelve ounces and that the market dictates a price of $600 per ounce. Whether you sell one ounce or twelve this week, each ounce of gold is sold for $600. The total revenue curve in Panel A of Figure 3 shows how revenue changes as output rises; its slope is constant at $600 per ounce of gold. If fixed costs are $570 weekly, the production costs associated with each level of output are shown in column 4 of Table 1 and graphed in Panel A as *TC*.

Subtracting total costs from total sales revenue is one reasonably straightforward approach used to estimate the amount of gold that maximizes your profit. Once this is done, you can mine gold to produce the output where this difference—profit (π)—is the largest. Looking at column 5 in Table 1, we see that producing seven ounces of gold yields $1,200, the maximum profit. In Panel A of Figure 3, profit is maximized where the vertical distance between total revenue and total costs is the greatest; in Panel B, profit is maximized where the vertical distance between the profit curve and the horizontal axis is the greatest. In this example, the profit-maximizing level of output occurs at seven ounces.

The chief lesson here is that there are at least two sides to any profit-maximizing production decision, regardless of market structure. First you must consider the demand side (total revenue and price), then the supply side (production costs). Each must be taken into account to arrive at the appropriate output and/or pricing decisions.

Notice also that there are two break-even levels of output, illustrated in both Table 1 and Panel A of Figure 3. **Break-even points** occur where total revenue equals total cost and economic profits are zero. You may have learned in other business classes that knowing break-even points is very useful to management. If a production activity appears to be risky, you would naturally like the production process to break even at a low level of output and sales.

The total revenue minus total cost approach is easily understood. A more fruitful approach for operational decision rules, however, is the **marginal**

---

2. There are choices regarding what technology to use, what kind and how much labor to employ, and numerous other day-to-day business decisions. For simplicity, we lump all these as parts of the output decision for the moment, postponing our discussion of resource markets until later chapters.

TABLE 1 *Hypothetical Cost Data for a Competitive Gold Miner*

(1) Weekly Output in Ounces (*q*)	(2) Price per Ounce (*P*)	(3) Weekly Total Revenue (*TR*)	(4) Weekly Total Cost (*TC*)	(5) π Weekly Profit (3) − (4)
0	$600	0	$ 570	$ −570
1	600	$ 600	810	−210
2	600	1,200	1,000	200
3	600	1,800	1,240	560
4	600	2,400	1,530	870
5	600	3,000	1,920	1,080
6	600	3,600	2,410	1,190
7	600	4,200	3,000	1,200
8	600	4,800	3,690	1,110
9	600	5,400	4,480	920
10	600	6,000	5,370	630
11	600	6,600	6,360	240
12	600	7,200	7,450	−450

cost equals marginal revenue (MC = MR) approach. The total revenue minus total cost (*TR − TC*) and the marginal revenue equals marginal cost (*MR = MC*) approaches yield mathematically equivalent results but arrive at profit maximization by different routes and provide different insights.

know this

Marginal Revenue Equals Marginal Cost Approach

In the preceding chapter, we spent considerable time analyzing marginal cost. Now we need to understand marginal revenue before turning to a discus-

FIGURE 3 TR − TC *Approach to Finding Maximum Profits*

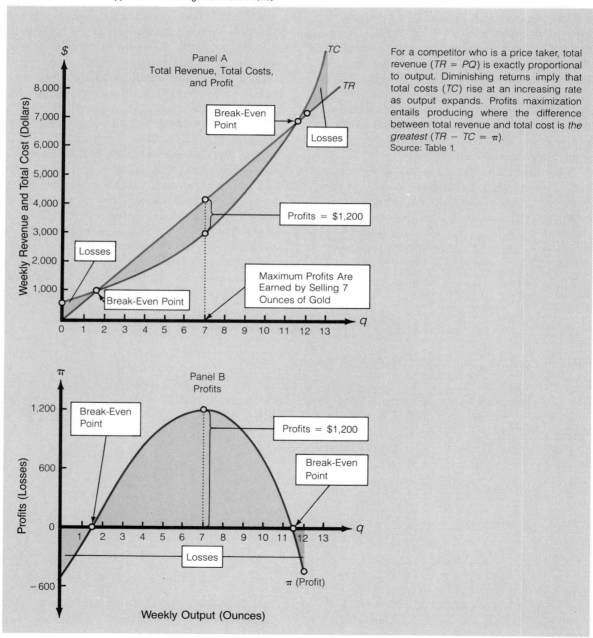

For a competitor who is a price taker, total revenue (*TR = PQ*) is exactly proportional to output. Diminishing returns imply that total costs (*TC*) rise at an increasing rate as output expands. Profits maximization entails producing where the difference between total revenue and total cost is *the greatest* (*TR − TC = π*).
Source: Table 1.

sion of how profit-maximizing firms combine these concepts to determine the most profitable output levels.

Marginal Revenue

Marginal cost is the addition to total cost associated with the production of one more unit. Analogously, **marginal revenue** is defined as the increase in total revenue associated with the sale of one more unit of output.

Let us return to your gold mine. The price of gold is set in the international commodity market for precious metals centered in New York, London, and Zurich, so individual mining firms are price takers. What is the marginal revenue from selling one more ounce if the going rate for gold is $600 per ounce? Miners get $600 for each ounce sold, regardless of how many ounces they sell as individuals. Keep in mind that each firm (gold mine) is too small to significantly affect the total market price or output.

Return for a moment to Figure 2. Individual mine operators perceive the demand curves that face them as horizontal at the $600 price. This perception of their individual demand curves as perfectly elastic means that each mine operator expects total revenues to be exactly proportional to output because price is fixed and total revenue equals price times quantity $(P \times Q)$. Thus, because market price is constant regardless of the amount sold, each ounce of gold is expected to generate marginal revenue equal to $600.

Look again at the data presented in Table 1. The market price is assumed to be $600 per ounce, as column 2 indicates. Marginal revenue is defined as the change in total revenue associated with the sale of one more unit, so as we go from five ounces to six ounces of gold sold, total revenue jumps from $3,000 to $3,600 weekly for a net change of $600. *Marginal revenue equals the price (*MR = P*) of the commodity in competitive markets.* Our next order of business is ascertaining how competitive firms use price and cost information to maximize profits.

Profit Maximization

Suppose you have information about the marginal cost and the sales price of each unit of production. How much should be produced and sold? One rule of thumb might be: Do anything that brings in at least as much money as it takes away. This rule translates into economic jargon: Produce and sell anything for which marginal revenue is at least as great as marginal cost.

The revenue associated with selling one more unit of gold (from Table 2) is graphed in Figure 4 as the demand curve **d** $(P = MR = \$600)$. Marginal cost from your cost data (from column 7 in Table 2) is graphed as the curve labeled *MC* in Figure 4. Consider what happens when you produce and sell the seventh ounce of gold. The extra revenue your firm receives is $600, but the seventh ounce of gold only costs $590 to produce. Thus, extra profit from the sale of this seventh unit is $10. In fact, you will increase total profit by the shaded triangle below the demand curve as you increase output from six to seven ounces.

What would happen to total profit if you decided to produce and sell more than seven ounces? If your output is eight ounces, you receive only $600 for the eighth ounce, but it costs $690 to produce. You will lose $90 on the eighth ounce if you decide to produce and sell it. In fact, since marginal cost exceeds marginal revenue for production beyond seven ounces, your profits will fall by the area of the shaded triangle above the demand curve as output rises from seven to eight ounces. Conclusion? Produce and sell until $MR = MC$, which, in this example, occurs at seven ounces.

This analysis leads to the following rule: Profit-maximizing firms will undertake production and sales until marginal cost just equals the marginal revenue derived from the sale of the product. Price and marginal revenue are equal in a competitive industry, so the profit-maximizing competitive firm produces until marginal cost is equal to price. In pure competition, $P = MR = MC$ for maximum profits.

Marginal revenue and marginal cost data for your gold mine (from Table 2) are graphed in Figure 5 on page 464, along with average total cost. Using the marginal revenue equals marginal cost approach, the profit-maximizing output is still seven ounces (point *e*). The $TR - TC$ approach provides one way to compute total profit. Total revenue equals price times quantity; for seven ounces of gold at $600 per ounce, this is $4,200. Geometrically, this is the area *0dec* in Figure 5. But how much is total cost? Since average total cost for seven ounces is $428.58 for each ounce (point *a*), the total cost for all seven ounces is $3,000 ($428.58 \times 7 = \$3,000$). The area *0bac* geometrically represents total cost (average cost times quantity). Thus, total weekly profit is $1,200 ($4,200 - \$3,000$), which is the shaded area *bdea* in Figure 5. An alternative way to calculate total profit is to multiply aver-

FIGURE 4 MR = MC *Approach to Finding Maximum Profits*

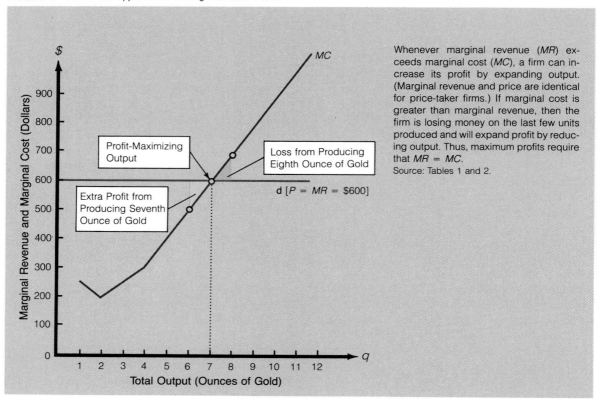

Whenever marginal revenue (*MR*) exceeds marginal cost (*MC*), a firm can increase its profit by expanding output. (Marginal revenue and price are identical for price-taker firms.) If marginal cost is greater than marginal revenue, then the firm is losing money on the last few units produced and will expand profit by reducing output. Thus, maximum profits require that *MR* = *MC*.
Source: Tables 1 and 2.

age profit per unit times output. Price minus average total cost ($P - ATC$) equals average profit per unit, so average profit per unit when seven ounces are produced is the distance *ae* in Figure 5, which is $171.42 ($600 − $428.58). Thus, total weekly profit is still $1,200 ($171.42 × 7—the shaded area *bdea*, which also equals $TR - TC$). We cannot overemphasize that whether we look at maximizing total revenue minus total cost or use the marginal revenue equals marginal cost approach, the solution is the same for the firm's profit-maximizing decision.

Figure 5 also shows what happens if the price of gold falls to roughly $385 per ounce. At this price, marginal revenue equals marginal cost at point *f*, or an output level of roughly five ounces. Average total cost, however, is in the $380 range, so the firm barely breaks even at a $385 price per ounce of gold. The break-even price in a competitive industry occurs when the demand curve facing each individual firm

(the price line) is tangent to the minimum point of the average total cost curve. Typical firms will neither incur economic losses nor enjoy economic profits at such a price, so there will be no net tendencies for the industry to shrink or grow because of entry and exit. In a moment you will see that this break-even situation characterizes firms in competitive industries in long-run equilibrium.

Measuring profits graphically is useful, but decisions must be made even when we do not know the exact changes in profits because of a given action. What is important is the direction of change—will profits rise or fall if the firm makes a given decision? Expected marginal benefits (revenues) and costs are crucial for rational decisions of many different kinds. For example, whenever public policy decisions are made (for tax structures, incentive systems, or various rules or regulations), the same kinds of questions arise: If a particular policy were altered, in what

TABLE 2 Cost Data for Your Competitive Gold Mine

(1) Weekly Output in Ounces (q)	(2) Total Fixed Cost (TFC)	(3) Total Variable Cost (TVC)	(4) Total Cost (TFC + TVC) (TC)	(5) Average Variable Cost (TVC/Q) (AVC)	(6) Average Total Cost (TC/Q) (ATC)	(7) Marginal Cost (ΔTC/ΔQ) (MC)	(8) Price Equals Marginal Revenue (P = MR)	(9) Total Revenue (TR = PQ)	(10) Profit (π)
0	$570	0	$ 570	0	—	—	$600	0	$ −570
1	570	240	810	$240.00	$810.00	$ 240	600	600	−210
2	570	430	1,000	215.00	500.00	190	600	1,200	200
3	570	670	1,240	223.33	413.33	240	600	1,800	560
4	570	960	1,530	240.00	382.50	290	600	2,400	870
5	570	1,350	1,920	270.00	380.00	390	600	3,000	1,080
6	570	1,840	2,410	306.67	401.67	490	600	3,600	1,190
7	570	2,430	3,000	347.14	428.58	590	600	4,200	1,200
8	570	3,120	3,690	390.00	461.25	690	600	4,800	1,110
9	570	3,910	4,480	434.44	497.78	790	600	5,400	920
10	570	4,800	5,370	480.00	537.00	890	600	6,000	630
11	570	5,790	6,360	526.33	578.19	990	600	6,600	240
12	570	6,880	7,450	573.33	620.83	1,090	600	7,200	−450

price − marginal revenue

direction would social welfare, net consumer satisfaction, or business profits change? If decision makers know this, they can gradually adjust policies until they reach an optimal solution.

on test

Loss Minimization and Plant Shutdown   Business, unfortunately, is not always profitable. One of two choices must be made when sales revenues cannot cover costs. The firm will experience losses if it elects to produce and sell output. If the firm shuts the plant down, however, it will incur losses equal to fixed costs. Which decision will yield the smallest loss?

Assume that the demand for gold collapses and the price falls to $300 per ounce, as shown in Figure 6. Just how much output, if any, should your mine produce and sell? If we return to our rule that the firm maximizes profit (or minimizes losses) by

equating marginal revenue and marginal cost, optimal weekly output for the firm in this instance will be four ounces (point *a*). At this level of output, total revenue will be $1,200, but total costs of $1,530 impose a loss of $330 weekly. The same result is obtained if we analyze this situation using an average revenue minus average cost approach. In Figure 6, average revenue (price) is $300 and average cost is $382.50. Thus, the average loss per unit of output of $82.50 times four ounces results in a total loss of $330 (the colored area *efca* in Figure 6). If the firm had decided to close its plant rather than sell the product below average total cost, losses would equal fixed costs, of $570 in our example. Remember that fixed costs are those that the firm incurs whether any output is produced or not. These include such expenses as rental payments, utility charges (for minimum service), administrative overhead, and insurance. Fixed (sunk) costs are not opportunity costs

FIGURE 5 *Measuring Short-Run Profits*

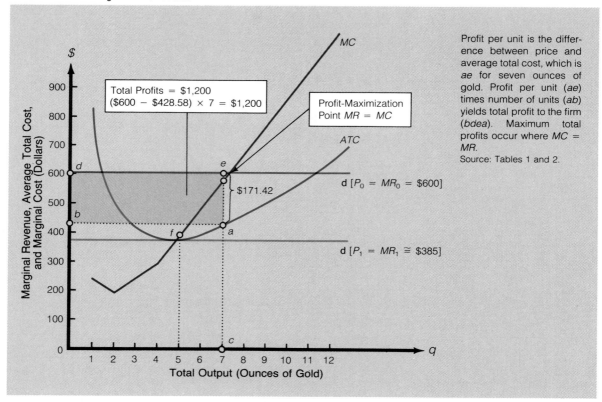

Total Profits = $1,200
($600 − $428.58) × 7 = $1,200

Profit-Maximization Point MR = MC

d [$P_0 = MR_0 = \$600$]

$171.42

d [$P_1 = MR_1 \cong \$385$]

Marginal Revenue, Average Total Cost, and Marginal Cost (Dollars)

Total Output (Ounces of Gold)

Profit per unit is the difference between price and average total cost, which is *ae* for seven ounces of gold. Profit per unit (*ae*) times number of units (*ab*) yields total profit to the firm (*bdea*). Maximum total profits occur where MC = MR.

Source: Tables 1 and 2.

in the short run because there is no alternative to incurring these costs.

Variable costs are the opportunity costs the firm pays for its production. Average variable costs of $240 (point *b* in Figure 6) are incurred in wages, materials, and other variable expenses when four ounces of gold are mined. Consequently, average variable costs will be covered as long as the mine can sell the gold for more than $240 per ounce. As the mine operator, you could allocate the difference between price ($300) and average variable costs ($240) to a fund to cover fixed costs. Even if all your fixed costs are not covered, at least some can be. Suffering a loss of $330 is better than suffering a loss equal to the fixed cost of $570. Notice that the critical costs to cover are variable costs, not fixed costs. As the saying goes, sunk costs are *sunk*.

When will it pay the firm to shut down the plant? The answer is fairly simple. When the price the firm receives for the product is insufficient to cover average variable costs, the firm would do as well or better to close its doors. This is illustrated in Figure 7. When the price falls below $215 per ounce of gold, which is the minimum value of the average variable cost curve, you should close the mine. At a price of $215, the business just recoups its variable costs from the sale of two ounces of gold weekly since variable costs are $215 per unit for labor, materials, and so forth. Consequently, total losses are $570 whether or not two ounces of gold are produced and then sold for $215; nothing is contributed to fixed costs from the production and sale of these units.

What happens if the price of the product falls below $215—say, to $200 per ounce? If the firm continues to produce two ounces of gold, in addition to $570 in fixed costs, the firm will lose at least $15 more per ounce, resulting in total losses of $600 [$570 + ($15 x 2)]. Producing at all would be a bad

FIGURE 6 *Loss Minimization in the Short Run*

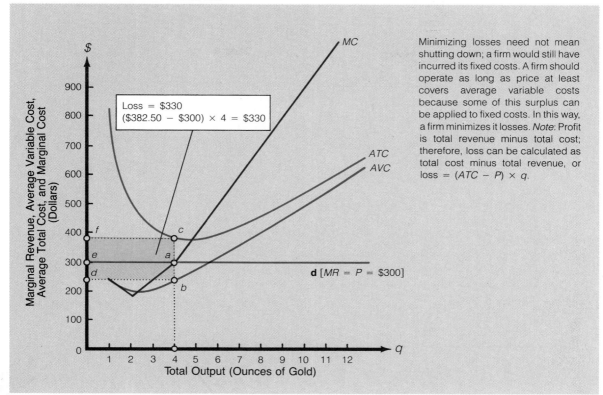

Loss = $330
($382.50 − $300) × 4 = $330

d [*MR* = *P* = $300]

Minimizing losses need not mean shutting down; a firm would still have incurred its fixed costs. A firm should operate as long as price at least covers average variable costs because some of this surplus can be applied to fixed costs. In this way, a firm minimizes it losses. *Note:* Profit is total revenue minus total cost; therefore, loss can be calculated as total cost minus total revenue, or loss = (*ATC* − *P*) × *q*.

decision if you were trying to minimize losses. The best decision when prices fall below $215 would be to abandon the mine, at least temporarily. Thus, a $215 price corresponds to the **shutdown point** for the mine in this example. It is the lowest price that will induce you to operate the mine; you'll never attempt to mine less than two ounces of gold.

Short-Run Supply Curves of Purely Competitive Firms

You may have figured out that *the short-run supply curve of the competitive firm is its marginal cost curve as long as price exceeds the minimum point of the average variable cost curve.* These points on the marginal cost curve reflect the profit-maximizing outputs that correspond to various market prices of the product. If price falls below minimum average variable costs (*AVC*), marginal costs and marginal

revenue become irrelevant; the firm's best move is to close the plant and suffer losses equal to fixed costs. However, any time the price exceeds the shutdown point (the minimum value of *AVC*), the firm will minimize its losses or maximize its profits by supplying that quantity of output where *P* = *MR* = *MC*.

This is a firm's short-run supply response. The conclusion is that the purely competitive **firm's short-run supply curve** is that portion of its marginal cost curve that lies above the average variable cost curve, as illustrated in Figure 8. When price and marginal revenue equal P_0, the firm will supply only q_0. As the price rises, the firm will increase the quantity it supplies to maximize profits (or minimize losses) by equating that price with marginal costs, so as price increases to P_1 and P_2, the firm will supply q_1 and q_2, respectively. Now let us see how individual supply curves are combined to form the industry supply curve.

FIGURE 7 *Short-Run Shutdown Point*

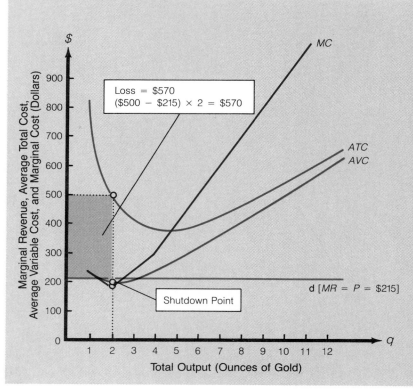

The short-run shutdown point is at a price of $215 per ounce and an output of two ounces per week. At any price below $215, the firm's losses would be larger if it continued to produce. At prices below $215, variable costs of production will not be covered. Thus, at prices below $215, the firm will close its doors to minimize losses.

Source: Tables 1 and 2.

(Graph labels: MC, ATC, AVC, Loss = $570, ($500 − $215) × 2 = $570, Shutdown Point, d [MR = P = $215]. Vertical axis: Marginal Revenue, Average Total Cost, Average Variable Cost, and Marginal Cost (Dollars). Horizontal axis: Total Output (Ounces of Gold).)

FIGURE 8 *The Firm's Short-Run Supply Curve*

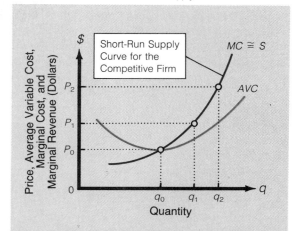

A competitive firm's short-run supply curve is its marginal cost curve, as long as the point where the price equals marginal cost ($P = MC$) occurs above the minimum of the average variable cost curve. If price cannot cover average variable cost, the firm will shut down.

Read for test

The Short-Run Industry Supply Curve

A purely competitive industry is comprised of a large number of firms, so there is a predictably tight relationship between the industry supply curve and firm supply curves. Consider, for simplicity, an industry comprised of two firms. In Panel A of Figure 9, the individual supply curves of both firms are presented. When the market price is $1, the first firm is willing to supply 10 units and the second firm is willing to supply 30 units. Together, they supply 40 units at the $1 price, as plotted in Panel B. You should remember from Chapter 3 that this process is called *horizontal summation.* We simply add the quantities produced by each firm at each possible price to arrive at the **industry short-run supply curve.** You can verify this graphically by adding together the quantities that each firm will turn out at various prices, and you will see that these total quantities supplied conform to those plotted in Panel B.

We have now related individual and market supplies. The output decisions of individual firms sum to determine the industry supply schedule. This industry supply, in conjunction with consumer demands for the product, determines the market-clearing price. The industry is in equilibrium when firms supply all they are willing to at the going price and consumers are able to buy all they desire at that price.

Firms maximize profits by producing a level of output where $MR = MC$. If price falls below AVC, firms will minimize losses by closing their doors. Will the market remain in a short-run equilibrium? What role will profits play in the longer run? What happens if new firms enter the industry? What happens if technological breakthroughs are introduced that substantially reduce production costs? These and other issues are examined in the following section as we step from short-run to long-run adjustments in purely competitive industries.

Know this well

Long-Run Adjustments in Competitive Industries

The number of firms in an industry is fixed in the short run. We turn now to scrutiny of perhaps the most important characteristic of the competitive industry—freedom of entry and exit over the long run. The number of firms in an industry may rise with entry, or fall as existing firms fail or move into different product lines. The ability to enter or leave an industry is fundamental to the smooth operation of the competitive market system. Economic profits are signals that attract new firms to an industry, while economic losses tell owners to liquidate existing firms or to look for new product lines.

Economic Profits as Market Signals

Recall (from the preceding chapter) that economic profits are a surplus after all implicit and explicit costs of production are subtracted from total revenues. Thus, average total costs include allowances for the opportunity costs of capital and the entrepreneurial talents used by the firm, among other things. Normal accounting rates of return to these resources must be earned. A firm's owners will move their resources into other activities if they suffer economic losses. On the other hand, if revenues exceed all production costs, the firm may try to expand over the long run in an attempt to capture as much economic profit as possible. Any such profits ultimately will attract new competitors into the industry, however, erasing economic profits.

FIGURE 9 *The Industry Supply Curve*

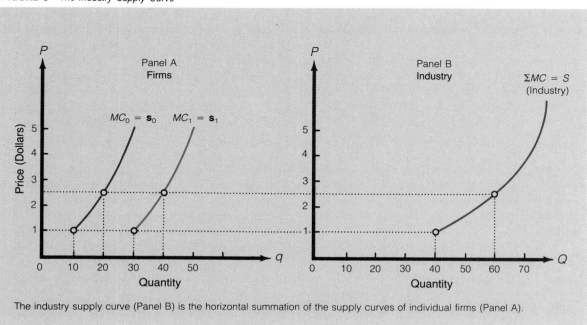

The industry supply curve (Panel B) is the horizontal summation of the supply curves of individual firms (Panel A).

Suppose that the markets for statues and for potted houseplants are both in equilibrium and that both are homogeneous products. Neither economic profits nor losses are experienced by the firms in either industry. Then the demand for indoor plants plummets as interior decorators unite to convince people that plants are passé and that no corner in any room in any building in the country is complete without an imitation early Greek statue. Statue makers are deluged with new orders, while florists and garden shops throughout the country watch their sales fall. Specials and discounts become the order of the day in the houseplant industry, and short-run economic losses occur as prices, outputs, and total revenues decline. On the other hand, the prices and outputs of statuaries soar and economic profits are widespread in the short run.

In the long run, resources move away from the houseplant industry. New investment falls, and florists train for other work as flower shops fold. Investment gravitates into statuary making equipment as new firms flock to the industry in search of profits, and more workers become statue makers. Thus, over the long run, competition eliminates both economic losses in the plant industry and economic profits in statuaries; plant prices recover from their depressed state, and statue prices fall from their short-run peaks.

With this example in mind, let us turn to a more detailed discussion of the adjustment process. Remember, the long run is a period sufficiently long to allow all resources (including capital) to move into or out of an industry. New firms move into growing industries, while existing firms wither or die in declining industries. Thus, we expect resources to flow from less profitable industries into more profitable industries. Entry and exit from competitive industries can be accomplished with ease. Many entrepreneurs seem to specialize in "hit-and-run" competition, jumping into markets where economic profits are being realized and leaving as soon as other markets appear more profitable. This hit-and-run pattern is socially beneficial because it ensures that even erratic consumer demands are accommodated quickly.

The Process of Competition

If firms in a particular industry make **zero economic profits** on average, then (all else equal) there will be no long-run changes in the number of firms in the industry, the amount of product supplied, or the price of the product.[3] If economic profits are experienced by most firms in an industry, however, competitive pressures tend to eliminate these profits over time because either prices will fall or costs will increase. Conversely, economic losses tend to cause prices to climb or costs to decline, or both.

Price Changes Eliminate Economic Profits or Losses

If firms in an industry begin to earn positive economic profits, there are incentives for existing firms to expand their capacities and production to try to capture greater profits for themselves. There are also incentives for entrepreneurs outside the industry to enter this market. Both of these long-run adjustments increase the industry's output. This drives down prices because consumers will buy more than they are buying only if prices decline.

On the other hand, if most firms in an industry experience economic losses, then some will cut their production and, in the long run, the firms with the highest opportunity costs (best alternative uses of their resources) will leave the industry. Thus, the long-run effects of economic losses are that the industry's supply will decline and prices will rise.

How Profits or Losses Affect Costs   Competition will grow for the resources used by a profitable industry. If the supplies of all resources used are perfectly elastic for the industry as a whole, there will be expansions of production with no increase in average costs of production. Resource costs will rise as production in an industry rises, however, to the extent that some resources are especially suited for some industries and not others. For example, what do you think happens to the costs of acquiring oil drilling rights as the price of oil balloons? What happens to the prices of agricultural land when food prices soar? Costs rise to reduce profits in both cases.

Here is another example of how rising costs eliminate profits. Suppose that one of your competitors experienced extremely high profits because the firm hired an exceptionally efficient management team.

---

3. Recall that normal returns to capital owners and entrepreneurial talent are economic costs; zero economic profits mean that all costs are covered. In other words, the firm's resources cannot be used more advantageously elsewhere.

Might you or some other competitor try to hire members of this team? What would happen to their salaries?

The market forces that cause costs to rise in an industry in which most firms make economic profits also cause declines in costs in instances where most firms incur losses. Both average costs and marginal costs rise in profitable industries and shrink when economic losses are the norm. To simplify the analysis in the following discussion, we focus only on price (not cost) adjustments. Remember, however, that changes in either prices or costs will eliminate economic profits or losses in competitive markets in the long run. Moreover, we assume in the following discussion that prices adjust smoothly towards long-run equilibrium. You should recognize that some firms may overreact in unison to economic profits or losses, so that prices may swing somewhat before ultimately converging on their equilibrium values.

Long-Run Equilibrium in a Competitive Industry

Firms run close to capacity when an industry is profitable, but they produce far less than capacity when business conditions are sour. Consider the industry illustrated in Figure 10. This industry is in the short-run equilibrium described in Panel A before the entry of new firms. Industry demand and supply are D_0 and S_0, respectively, with industry output equal to Q_0; each firm produces an output of q_0 where $P = MR = MC$. Typical firms in this competitive industry are making short-run economic profits equal to the darkened area, causing firms to willingly incur higher than minimal costs as they produce extra output to exploit profit opportunities.

Entry occurs easily in competition, so this is a short-run situation because entrepreneurs outside the industry will seek shares of these profit opportunities. After new firms enter, industry supply increases to S_1, with a correspondingly higher output of Q_1 and a lower equilibrium price, P_1. But observe what has happened to the individual firms. As prices decline, each firm adjusts to a new profit-maximization output (q_1), which is lower than the original level (q_0). Consequently, our industry is now composed of more firms, but the absense of economic profit means that each produces less than before. What has happened to profit? Each firm previously in the industry was earning positive economic profit. After entry occurs, the lower prices and lower outputs that result have driven economic profits back to "normal" levels; that is, zero economic profits are realized. Product price has fallen to the minimum of long-run average costs ($LRAC$). Remember that the opportunity costs of the firm's owners are included in average costs. Accounting profits are not zero in the industry, they are simply at normal levels—being just high enough so the owners earn as much in this industry as in their next best option.

You might question whether symmetric exit adjustments occur in unprofitable situations. Such adjustments are illustrated in Panel B of Figure 10, which shows individual firms initially encountering short-run losses. Price is originally at P_0, which is below average total cost (ATC) but above average variable costs (not shown in the figure) since firms are continuing to operate. Losses are equal to the darkened area. The least efficient firms incur the largest losses and will fold or move into a different activity. Industry supply will shrink as these firms leave the industry, so the price will rise and losses will be eliminated. Profits might temporarily reappear if enough firms leave, curtailing the exodus of firms. Ultimately, however, price rises to P_1 and profits return to "normal" levels. Notice that this is just the opposite of the adjustment process described in the profitable situation above. Industry output falls, but individual firm outputs grow as the price recovers to normal levels when some firms exit the industry.

At the ends of periods with economic losses or profits, why do we settle into a situation where profits are at "normal" levels (zero economic profits)? A moment's reflection should provide the answer. Competitive theory presumes that entry and exit are virtually costless, so the logical stopping point occurs when each firm in the industry earns only normal profits. Only then will there be no net incentives for firms to enter or leave the industry. Freedom of entry and exit are vital for a competitive economy, but as Focus 1 on page 472 indicates, government increasingly puts a damper on the ability of firms to enter or leave an industry.

Another important result of long-run competitive adjustments is that all firms in the industry are forced to adopt the most efficient technology available. This is shown in Figure 11. Long-run pressures will force the price of the product to P_{LR} because competition forces each firm onto the lowest portion of the $LRAC$ curve. Any firm not adopting the technologies and amounts of capital that yield the lowest minimum short-run average cost curve (*SRAC*) will earn less than normal accounting profits and will founder in the long run. No firm stays in any industry if it suffers sustained economic losses. Since $P = MC = ATC$ in the long run, the long-run equilibrium point is the lowest point on the *LRAC* curve and it must be the

FIGURE 10   *Entry and Exit and Long-Run Price, Output, and Profit*

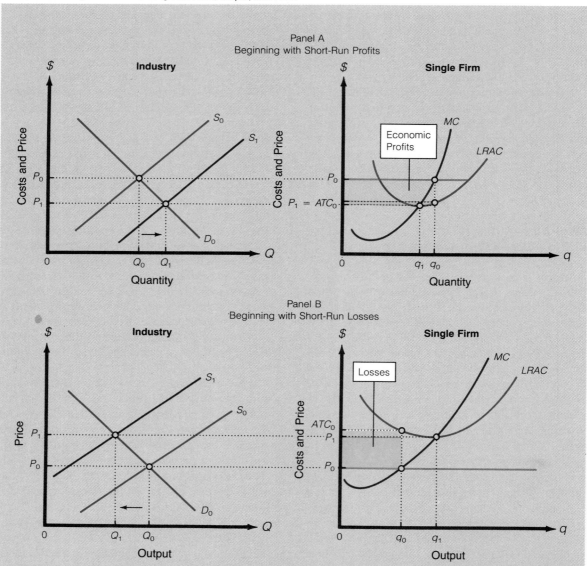

Firms in industries where economic profits are realized will produce where $P = MC$ and output is greater than that associated with minimum average cost. However, the entry of new competitors will cause industry supply to grow and price to fall. As this occurs, existing firms reduce output until $P = MC = LRAC$. *LRAC* is at its minimum and there are no economic profits when competitive firms are in long-run equilibrium.

If most firms in an industry are suffering economic losses, they will restrict production below the minimum point of their *LRAC* curves. As some firms leave the industry, the market supply falls and price increases. As the price rises, existing firms will expand their production to the level of output where long-run average cost is minimized. At this point, $P = MC = LRAC$, and neither economic profits nor economic losses are experienced.

FIGURE 11 Long-Run Equilibrium for the Competitive Firm

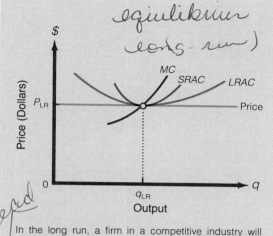

equilibrium
(long-run)

Read

In the long run, a firm in a competitive industry will produce where $P = MR = MC = SRAC = LRAC$, and the size of the plant will minimize the average costs of production. Neither economic profits nor economic losses will be realized; the firm's total revenues will just cover all its costs, including normal accounting profits to compensate owners for the resources they provide.

FIGURE 12 Long-Run Supply (Constant-Cost Industry)

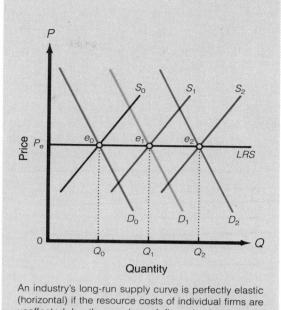

An industry's long-run supply curve is perfectly elastic (horizontal) if the resource costs of individual firms are unaffected by the number of firms in the industry. Industries that use only small percentages of highly specialized resources in an economy will operate under constant costs.

Read

lowest point on the relevant *SRAC* curve as well. This means that outputs in competitive markets will be produced at the lowest possible long-run average cost. Hence, competition yields economic efficiency. As you will see in a later section, this result has profound implications for maintaining competition in a free-market economy.

Long-Run Industry Supply Curves

Now that you have some ideas about competitive adjustment processes, we can examine the long-run supply curve for the competitive industry as a whole. The horizontal summation of existing firms' short-run supply curves yields the short-run industry supply curve. The **long-run industry supply curve** reflects the effects on output as entry and exit occur in response to changes in demand. The industry is in long-run equilibrium only after all desired entries and exits have occurred so that active firms realize only normal profits.

Because new products and technologies are constantly introduced, many industries are in constant motion. The economy continually gropes towards

equilibrium, even though full long-run equilibrium may never be attained in even most industries. However, the concept of long-run equilibrium is still valuable because of both its analytical convenience and its powers of prediction. Without the notions of short-run and long-run equilibrium, we have analytical mush—no reference points from which to compare other points in time, nor to predict the eventual trends of outputs and prices.

The long-run industry supply curve can take three general forms: (*a*) constant costs, (*b*) increasing costs, and (*c*) decreasing costs. We will examine each of these.

Constant-Cost Industries Figure 12 illustrates the long-run supply curve (*LRS*) of a constant-cost industry. As demand grows from D_0 to D_1 to D_2, the long-run responses are increases in short-run supplies from S_0 to S_1 and S_2, respectively, as the number of firms in the industry grows proportionally with demand. As entry occurs, long-run average costs are the same for the new entrants as for the established

FOCUS 1

Competition in Jeopardy: Entry and Exit Restrictions

The hallmark of competition, freedom to enter or exit an industry, is increasingly under attack. Government licenses, taxes, and regulations have always restricted entry somewhat, but until recently, exit has been virtually free of government intervention. There is now mounting pressure for national legislation to govern how speedily a firm can close a plant or leave an industry.

Several states, notably Maine, Massachusetts, South Carolina, and Wisconsin, along with the cities of Philadelphia and

Vacavill, California, have recently passed laws restricting how fast and under what conditions a firm can close a plant in their areas. These laws typically require 90-day notices before plant closings, and in some instances specify exit penalties or mandatory severance pay for each worker displaced. Workers laid off by Atari in 1983 filed a class action lawsuit on the grounds that they received no prior warning of layoffs. Many unions are now negotiating contracts with "no plant closing" provisions.

Proponents of this legislation argue that restrictions on plant closings would reduce local economic disruptions. Prenotification would give employees time to locate alternative work, and communities time to attract new firms. Opponents worry that such restrictions may make it more difficult for competitive industries and firms to react to changing market conditions. If this occurs, they argue, the social benefits of vigorous competition will be seriously eroded.

---

firms. All cost curves for individual firms are identical; the number of firms in the industry adjusts proportionally as demand changes. Thus, the long-run supply curve for a constant-cost industry is perfectly elastic.

Increasing-Cost Industries   Industries deviate from the constant-cost model for a variety of reasons. For an industry to expand with equilibrium price and costs remaining constant, the total amounts of resources used by firms in the industry must not affect the prices of these inputs.[4]

The requirement that input prices not rise as an industry's output rises may be difficult for large industries because supplies of specialized resources are limited and can be made available only at ever higher costs. In **increasing-cost industries,** average production costs rise as the number of firms in the industry grows. As new firms enter the market, they add to the demands for existing resources. As

these demands increase, so do the equilibrium prices for these specialized inputs. The average total cost and marginal cost curves for each company in the industry rise because all firms experience these resource price increases. Thus, growth in market demand results in an upward shifting of the long-run break-even points for each firm as minimal long-run average costs rise. This is illustrated in Figure 13.

If industry demand increases from D_0 to D_1, the industry expands as new firms enter; the competition for resources drives the short-run supply curve to S_1, resulting in an equilibrium price of P_1. These rising equilibrium costs and prices result in a long-run supply (*LRS*) curve that is positively sloped. For the industry to supply greater quantities to the market, higher prices must be paid to cover higher resource costs. Moreover, these higher costs will cause fewer firms to enter the industry than would enter constant-cost industries experiencing similar growth of demand.

Most industries are characterized by increasing costs in the long run. Even though it does not perfectly conform to our competitive ideal, our domestic petroleum industry faces increasing costs as it

---

4. Note that if all industries were constant-cost industries, the production-possibilities frontier would be a straight line. You may want to review the material in Chapter 2 if you are not sure why this is true.

attempts to increase the production of domestic crude oil. Most of the readily accessible oil has been depleted. Higher oil prices mean landowners will charge more for drilling rights. Future oil supplies will be drawn from more expensive off-shore drilling or from deeper wells, where production costs are considerably higher. Alternatively, Americans might look to other energy sources, most of which are substantially more expensive than petroleum.

Decreasing-Cost Industries The expansion of an industry may induce efficiencies in complementary industries. For example, expansion of the automobile industry early in this century permitted a flock of support industries to flourish. As these complementary industries expanded, firms implemented new technologies and moved down their long-run average cost curves, resulting in lower prices for the intermediate products to the auto industry. These lower prices for intermediate products (tires, batteries, and the like) resulted in reductions in the prices of automobiles. Today, similar events are taking shape with microchips and other numerous high-tech products. Thus, in a **decreasing-cost industry,** expanding demand is met with industry growth

that leads to lower average costs and equilibrium price. Such an industry is illustrated in Figure 14.

While decreasing costs might characterize a few industries at a few points in time, most industries fall into constant- or increasing-cost categories. As a result, increasing demands in the long run mean that prices will rise. The possibility that technological advances may be spurred by the search for profits, however, means that some industries may experience decreasing costs in the super long run. This seems to be true of many high-tech products today.

Evaluating Competitive Markets

Some important conclusions in this chapter are useful in evaluating competition:

1. Competitive industries are characterized by freedom of entry and exit by firms that are *price takers* and *quantity adjusters.*
2. Each firm maximizes profits (or minimize losses) by producing the output that equates price with marginal costs ($P = MR = MC$).

FIGURE 13 *Long-Run Supply for an Increasing-Cost Industry*

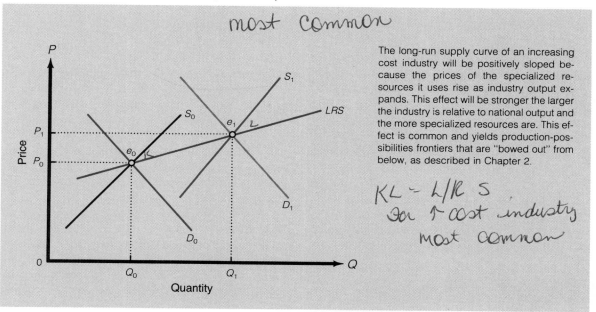

most common

The long-run supply curve of an increasing cost industry will be positively sloped because the prices of the specialized resources it uses rise as industry output expands. This effect will be stronger the larger the industry is relative to national output and the more specialized resources are. This effect is common and yields production-possibilities frontiers that are "bowed out" from below, as described in Chapter 2.

KL ~ L/R S,
for ↑ cost industry
most common

FIGURE 14 *Long-Run Supply for a Decreasing-Cost Industry*

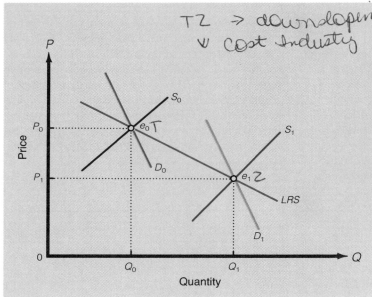

TZ → downslopings
↓ cost industry

Decreasing-cost industries generate negatively sloped long-run supply curves, and are extremely uncommon because such decreasing costs rely on either substantial economies of scale or positive externalities within the industry or in the support industries that supply them with intermediate goods. In fact, many economists argue that this is only a theoretical possibility, never encountered in the actual world of production.

The concepts of constant, increasing, or decreasing costs apply *only* for the long run. Decreasing-cost industries do not seem so implausible, however, if we consider the possibility of super-long-run technological advances.

3. In the long run, competitive firms are forced to adopt the most efficient technologies, and *LRMC* = *P*.[5] This will also be the minimum point on the *LRAC* curve because the long-run dynamics of entry and exit will drive economic profits to zero regardless of whether the industry is characterized by constant, increasing, or decreasing costs. Accounting profits will be at "normal" levels. Thus, in the long run, $P = MR = SRMC = SRAC = LRMC = LRAC$.

Read

Economic Efficiency

when does it occur + what does it mean

In a purely competitive market, producers employ resources until the marginal cost to them of producing the last unit of a good just equals its price. In the absence of external costs (e.g., pollution) or external benefits (e.g., education, inoculations), the opportunity cost to society of using these resources equals the marginal cost of the resources to producers. If there are no externalities (discussed in depth in a later chapter), these resource costs equal *marginal social cost* (*MSC*). Competition through freedom of

entry and exit ensures the lowest possible average cost of production and ensures that there is no waste in production. A competitive economy is an efficient economy because one aspect of economic efficiency is that all goods must be produced at their lowest possible opportunity cost.

Social Welfare

Does competition also serve society well? Efficiency may seem a cold and austere concept when people's welfare is at stake. You will see in the coming chapters covering other output market structures and resource markets that competition yields greater equality in income distribution than other market structures do. While more equal, the distribution of income that might be generated even if the economy were perfectly competitive may still be viewed by many as unfair.

Economic analysis is not directly concerned with the fairest way to divide the pie. If we assume, however, that the proper distribution of income is a normative problem best settled in the political arena and that the resulting political outcome is viewed as acceptable, then the competitive market system not only is efficient, it also maximizes social welfare. Here is why.

---

5. There are technical differences between short-run marginal costs (*SRMC*) and long-run marginal costs (*LRMC*) that we do not consider in this book. These differences are dealt with in texts designed for courses in intermediate microeconomics.

→ occurs when P=MC, then we have Res. allocation efficiency
mfg.. needs are being met

Your demand curve for a given product is based on the marginal benefits (utility) that you would receive from consuming various possible amounts of the product, as we discussed in a previous chapter. Our assumptions imply that the marginal utility you receive from consuming is also the marginal benefit society receives. That is, your gain is also society's gain because you are a member of society. When we sum all consumer demands, we derive the market demand curve for an industry's product, which is also the *marginal social benefit* (*MSB*) to all of society from having a bit more of the good.

With consumer benefits and producer costs in mind, we can refer to the industry supply and demand curves, respectively, as the marginal social cost (*MSC*) and marginal social benefit (*MSB*) curves. When a competitive industry is in long-run equilibrium, **marginal social cost equals marginal social benefit (*MSC* = *MSB*):** the industry is producing where the marginal social benefit from the last unit produced is just equal to the marginal social cost of the resources needed to produce that unit of product. This concept is illustrated in Figure 15.

The $MSB = MSC$ condition is optimal from society's point of view. Since the opportunity costs of resources represent alternatives for all of society, we want our resources to be used as efficiently as possible. If production is at an inefficient level, then it is possible for some people to gain without imposing losses on others.

Consider an output level of Q_0 in Figure 15. The benefit to society from producing a bit more output than Q_0 is P_0, which is considerably greater than the cost (P_1) of the resources required to produce a little more of the good. This suggests that society as a whole could gain if more resources were employed in the production of this commodity. And in a competitive industry they will be. If Q_0 were initially produced and sold at a price of P_0, the firms in a competitive industry would receive economic profits. This would cause the industry to expand until equilibrium output Q_e is reached at a price and (average and marginal) production cost of P_e. The adjustment process is just reversed if industry output exceeds Q_e. Competitive markets tend to squeeze the last bit of gain possible from the resources available.

FIGURE 15 *Economic Efficiency and Competition*

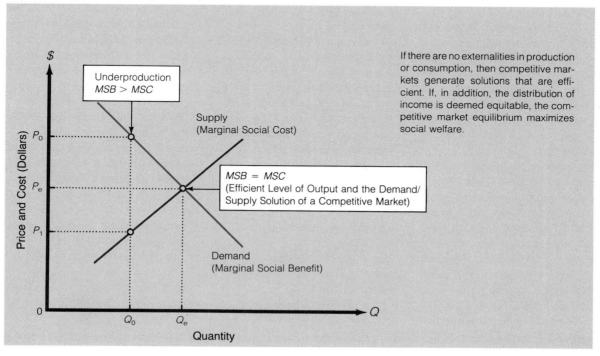

Underproduction
$MSB > MSC$

Supply
(Marginal Social Cost)

$MSB = MSC$
(Efficient Level of Output and the Demand/
Supply Solution of a Competitive Market)

Demand
(Marginal Social Benefit)

Price and Cost (Dollars)

P_0

P_e

P_1

Q_0 Q_e

Quantity

If there are no externalities in production or consumption, then competitive markets generate solutions that are efficient. If, in addition, the distribution of income is deemed equitable, the competitive market equilibrium maximizes social welfare.

Leon Walras (1834–1910) and Vilfredo Pareto (1848–1923)

Leon Walras has been described as an architect rather than a builder of economics, meaning that he designed a general system of analytical principles rather than laid in the bricks and mortar of economic theory. Walras tackled the complex problem of the interdependence of all sectors of the economy and represented this complexity in a system of simultaneous equations.

This great architect of economics was descended from a Dutch journeyman tailor who migrated to the south of France in 1749. His father was a classmate of Cournot (discussed in the next chapter) in Paris and, like Cournot, was an administrator in the French educational system. The young Walras learned from Cournot the meaning of functional relations between variables. However, concerns about the limits of Cournot's demand curve for a single good led Walras to seek a wider framework within which to express the demand for a good as a function not only of its own price, but of a host of prices of related goods. This was the point of departure for his *general equilibrium model* of an economy.

Most economic writers before Walras followed the lead of Alfred Marshall and employed a convention in dealing with particular markets called *partial equilibrium analysis.* This still common and useful convention calls for ignoring some determinants of demand and supply in order to concentrate on the more direct causes of equilibrium price and quantity. Walras departed from this practice by insisting on recognizing the interdependencies that exist between markets because the process of price determination necessarily occurs in all markets simultaneously. To isolate one market for study without regard to the others was no more appropriate, in Walras's view, than studying the position of the earth in the solar system without regard to other planets. His *architectonics* consequently was an elaborate but highly abstract system of mathematical equations that painstakingly detailed the economic conditions for simultaneous equilibrium in every economic market. Walras's general equilibrium approach to economics did not win favor with the reigning academic hierarchy in France, forcing him to take a teaching position in Switzerland at the University of Lausanne, where he labored until he was replaced in 1893 by Vilfredo Pareto.

Pareto, born of a Genoese father and French mother, was trained as an engineer. At 45, he accepted the chair at Lausanne. Pareto's system of thought and his vision of social processes differed from Walras's, but Pareto cast his pure theory of economics in much the same mold, extending and refining Walras's general equilibrium system. Moreover, Pareto did what Walras had not been able to do: he founded a full-blown school of thought. His disciples cooperated in theoretical research, cultivated personal contacts, and defended one another in controversy. The school, reflecting Pareto's own heritage, was primarily Italian.

Two of Pareto's contributions to economics are especially noteworthy.

First, he identified a situation of maximum efficiency for a society as one in which it is impossible to increase the happiness of one individual without decreasing that of someone else. Today all the conditions specifying economic efficiency are referred to as "Pareto optimal." Second, Pareto proved that a state of maximum efficiency and social welfare are identical with equilibrium under perfect competition. This led him to conclude that the problems in reaching a position of maximum efficiency, as well as their solutions, were the same for a collectivist economy as for an economy founded on private property.

Pareto's work spilled over into the field of sociology. His chief objective was to develop general equilibrium models covering the whole spectrum of social phenomena. Both he and Walras were aware that their equations could not be solved due to the lack of data and the large number of variables involved. Nevertheless, theirs was a great achievement from the standpoint of logical clarity, and the impact of their thoughts on modern economic theory ranks them both among the dozen most influential economists of all time.

Decentralized Decision Making and Freedom

The ideas of Adam Smith and other early advocates of capitalism were forged during a period of revolt against the dictatorial decision making of monarchs. Isaac Newton and other scientists had observed the movements of the earth, moon, and stars and concluded that the interactions of natural forces led to a stable and orderly universe. Smith perceived that the invisible hand of the marketplace had a similarly beneficial influence on economic activity and that the iron fist of a central government was exercised far too often. Following in the century-old footsteps of Smith, Leon Walras spelled out with mathematical precision how economic behavior is coordinated in a competitive market system. Then Vilfredo Pareto developed a modern theory of economic welfare that still dominates economic thinking today. Most importantly, Pareto proved that maximum efficiency and the equilibrium of a competitive economy are identical, and that any equilibrium not in accord with that of competition fails to maximize social welfare.

Most modern advocates of the market system point to the economic efficiency of competition as one of its major virtues but prize even more the absence of any need for a central authority to make economic decisions. In a truly competitive market system, each household and firm makes decisions that, in large measure, affect only themselves. This diffusion of market power means that as individuals, we do not control each other. According to the proponents of relying on the marketplace rather than government, this diffusion of coercive power allows the maximum possible personal freedom for every individual.

Efficiency, equity, and the absence of centralized coercion are all reasons why a competitive market structure is the standard against which we measure the performance of all other market structures. From society's point of view, it might seem desirable for all industries to be competitive so that Adam Smith's invisible hand would bring about the results we have described. As you will see in the next chapter, however, competition and access to markets may be very limited if technology dictates that large firms, relative to the size of the market, will be most efficient.

Some Shortcomings of Market Economies

Many industries are far from competitive—in some, competition is impractical. We examine the behavior of firms that have varying degrees of monopoly power in the next two chapters. In some cases, this power emerges naturally because of technology; in others, it is a consequence of illegal collusion or government policies to protect other goals (patents, licensing, to protect the public health, and so on). In the last two chapters of this part of the book, we scrutinize government attempts to regulate business and to reduce monopolistic practices through antitrust actions.

Even if the economy were quite competitive, there might still be problems of fraud, inequity in the distributions of income and wealth, or externalities that the market would not resolve in ways society deems appropriate. Moreover, certain goods will not be provided optimally by a private market system. Atomic bombs, police services, and legal decisions are examples of items no society would want to see sold only to the highest bidder.

Some economists also argue that research and development require bigness; such efforts might be less than optimal if left to small competitive firms. Finally, there are questions about what social restrictions, if any, should be imposed on trade between people in different countries. The tools you have learned to use in the last few chapters will prove valuable in the remainder of this book as we examine the outcome of private market behavior and assess corrective government policies for these problems.

CHAPTER REVIEW: KEY POINTS

1. Freedom of *entry and exit* is the hallmark of competition. A purely competitive market is comprised of numerous potential buyers and sellers of a homogeneous product, none of whom controls its price. All buyers and sellers are sufficiently small relative to the market so that none is a *price maker*.

2. A competitive buyer faces a perfectly elastic supply curve, while competitive sellers face perfectly elastic demand curves. In competition, all are *price takers,* or *quantity adjusters*.

3. We assume that no firm can adjust output in the *market period,* so total supply is perfectly inelastic. In the *short run (SR)*, existing firms in an industry can vary output, but at least one productive factor is fixed and entry and exit cannot occur. Total supply is at least somewhat elastic. Supply is much more elastic in the *long run (LR)* because all factors of production are variable and firms may enter or leave the industry.

4. The competitive firm maximizes profits by producing output up to the point where *total revenues minus total costs (TR − TC)* is maximized, or *marginal revenue equals marginal cost (MR = MC)*. Price must be greater than the minimum of the average variable cost curve, however, which is the *shutdown point*. Because competitive firms face perfectly elastic demands, price and marginal revenue are identical. *Break-even points* are the quantities at which total revenue and total cost are equal.

5. The competitive *firm's short-run supply curve* is its marginal cost curve above the minimum of the average variable cost curve. Horizontally summing the marginal cost curves of existing firms yields the *short-run industry supply curve*.

6. In the long run, competition eliminates *economic profits* through entry of new firms, and economic losses are eradicated by exit from the industry. Thus, competitive firms receive exactly enough revenue over the long run to pay the opportunity costs of resources used, and realize only *zero economic profit*.

7. Short-run economic profits are ultimately eliminated because either output will be expanded by both existing and new firms in a competitive industry or increased competition for profitable inputs will drive up resource costs. The long-run adjustments that eliminate short-run losses follow precisely reversed patterns.

8. In the long run, firms are forced by competitive pressures to adopt the most efficient (least costly) plant size and technologies. They operate at output levels where

$$P = MR = SRAC = SRMC = LRAC = LRMC.$$

For *constant-cost industries,* the minimum *LRAC* for firms is the same no matter how many firms are in the industry. Costs increase for each firm as firms enter *increasing-cost industries,* and decrease for decreasing-cost industries. Thus, the *long-run industry supply curve* is positively sloped for *increasing-cost industries,* horizontal for *constant-cost industries,* and negatively sloped for *decreasing-cost industries*.

9. A competitive market is efficient in the sense that goods are produced at the lowest possible opportunity cost. Every feasible bit of net gain is squeezed from the resources available, and *marginal social benefits* and *marginal social costs* are equated by the forces of supply and demand in a competitive market (*MSB = MSC*), assuming the absence of externalities. This will be socially optimal and maximize social welfare if the distribution of income is deemed appropriate. A market system does not require that decision-making power be vested in a central authority. This permits substantial personal freedom and the absence of coercion.

QUESTIONS FOR THOUGHT AND DISCUSSION

1. The stock market is sometimes viewed by critics of the market system as the epitome of monopolistic capitalism. Are most people who buy or sell stock price makers or price takers? Do you think stock and commodity markets basically meet the requirements for competitive markets? Why or why not?

2. Would you expect someone who selected a portfolio of stocks by throwing darts at stock market reports in the *Wall Street Journal* to experience systematically different economic profits than someone who spent years securing expertise in financial analysis and who then spent hours every day studying the stock mar-

FIGURE 16 The Market for Eye Tattoos

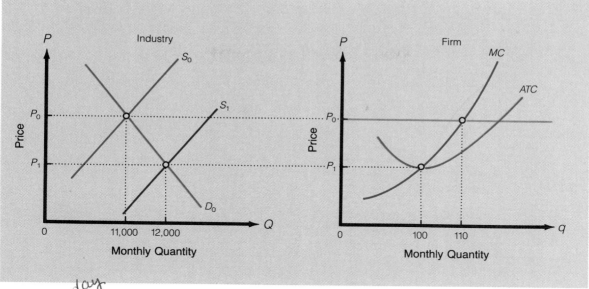

Industry — Firm

Due Thursday

ket? If not, what might explain systematically different rates of return reported by their bookkeepers?

3. Cost and output data for a competitive firm are provided in the table below. Assume that fixed costs are equal to $40 and that the market price facing the firm is $30 per unit.

Quantity	1	2	3	4	5	6	7	8
TVC	30	55	75	90	110	135	165	200

What is the profit-maximizing rate of output? What does maximum profit equal? At what price will the firm close its doors? What output would this firm produce in the long run if the price remains constant?

4. Is the economy of a big city more competitive than that in a small town or given neighborhood? How? Do you think your local grocer has monopoly power? How much? Can you cite examples of both entry and exit from the marketplace among firms located within 5 miles of your home? What industries have been involved? Do you know of any giant firms that have emerged, almost from oblivion, in the past 5 years?

Any that have failed? Would you conclude from your answers that our economy is basically competitive or noncompetitive?

5. The *Wall Street Journal* notes, "As everyone knows, competition is vital to the preservation of a healthy, efficient market economy. But competition sometimes seems to have few friends." What do you think the *Wall Street Journal* meant?

6. In 1978–79, the Hunt brothers (Texas billionaires) *rose dramatica* allegedly attempted to corner the silver market and make it monopolistic. What happened to the price of silver during this period? Was their effort successful? *temporail* What obstacles are faced by anyone who tries to *resource control* monopolize a previously competitive industry?

7. Some women are now using tattoos to give the effect of permanent cosmetic eye shadow. The industry demand and supply and representative individual firm demand and cost curves for "eye tattoos" are illustrated in Figure 16. How many firms comprise the industry in the short run? What will happen to the price of eye tattoos in the long run? How many firms will be in the industry in the long run?

CHAPTER 24   Monopoly

Monopoly means different things to different people. In many of us, monopoly brings up fond memories of a game involving Boardwalk, Park Place and the B & O Railroad, in which the winner winds up owning all the property and money. When we get away from this popular board game, monopoly is a term loaded with sinister overtones. Some politicians and parts of the media equate monopoly with concentrations of economic power and control and blame monopoly power for such evils as inflation and poverty. Business owners and managers sometimes strive to eliminate their competition so that they will enjoy a monopoly position, a situation they view as ideal. Marxists perceive widespread monopoly capitalism as a natural consequence of a competitive market system and as the final stage before capitalism succumbs to a communist revolution.

Monopolies raise the specters of concentrated power, inequitable income distributions, and economic inefficiency. But what exactly is a monopoly? A firm has a **monopoly** in a market if it is the single producer of a product for which there are no close substitutes. Every product and every producer confronts some competition. Even your local electric

power company faces competition from solar cells and gasoline- or diesel-based electric generating systems. But are these substitutes for electric services sufficiently close that they pose threats to the abilities of power companies to retain their customers? It's doubtful. Public utilities are probably the purest forms of monopoly that exist in the United States today.

This chapter focuses on the theory of pure, unregulated monopoly, even though very few pure monopolies exist and there are even fewer that are not regulated by some government agency. This theory provides a rationale for regulation. Moreover, comparisons of monopoly and competitive models point out the differences between the pricing and output decisions of firms having considerable market power as compared to those without such power.

The first systematic analysis of monopoly was pursued more than a century ago by a French economist, Antoine Augustin Cournot. One central concern of Cournot and of economists today is the inefficiency that may result from monopoly. Why might monopolies be economically inefficient? These and related questions are the focus of this chapter.

Antoine Augustin Cournot (1801–77)

The life of Antoine Augustin Cournot was testimony to Andrew Carnegie's assertion, "It does not pay to pioneer." The value of Cournot's work was recognized only after his death. His life was characterized by anonymity and tragedy. This genius of economics and philosophy was born into a family of French farmers who had tilled the same lands for almost 300 years. He spent most of his life as a school superintendent, and even that job was secured only through the influence of his friend Poisson, the famous French physicist and statistician. Cournot is remembered best in his homeland as a philosopher; in the English-speaking world he is hailed as a brilliant pioneer in economics.

Cournot's first and most influential work in economics remains the only one that has been translated into English. It fairly bristles with originality, for it was Cournot who formally introduced demand and supply curves into economics; who derived, mathematically, the marginal revenue equals marginal cost rule for profit maximization; and who specified the equilibrium conditions for firms operating as monopolies, interdependent oligopoly firms, and firms operating under perfect competition.

The kernel of Cournot's theory of the firm is contained in his analysis of profit maximization by a monopolist. As an illustration, Cournot considered a monopoly proprietor who could *costlessly* supply water from a mineral spring containing unique healthful qualities. Sale of a single liter of water might bring an extremely high price, but Cournot demonstrated that a monopoly will not charge the highest price it can get. Rather, it will adjust its price to maximize total receipts; since costs are zero, this is equivalent to maximizing profit.

Cournot demonstrated that this is accomplished when marginal revenue (derived from the demand curve) equals marginal cost ($MR = MC$). Cournot's procedure seems commonplace today, but before 1838 there simply was no formal theory of profit maximization. Practically every fundamental axiom in the economic theory of the firm stems from Cournot's trailblazing analysis.

Cournot's demeanor was solitary and melancholy, traits that seem to intrude on his writing. His books are austere, crowded with facts and rigorous mathematical proofs. He confessed to a fellow French economist that he was very unpopular with his publishers because none of his books sold enough to be profitable until years after their first appearance.

Cournot's work was hampered by other economists' discomfort with mathematics and because his most productive years were absorbed by his duties as a school administrator. In addition, the gradual deterioration of his eyesight impaired the accuracy of his mathematical notations. For their part, the prejudice and shortsightedness of his contemporaries blinded them to his advances in economic theory, advances that were not widely recognized until more than two decades after his death.

Monopoly Markets

The definition of monopoly opens the door for numerous questions. How does a firm become a monopoly? A monopoly in some products may enrich the firm's owners at the expense of the rest of society, but does a monopoly position guarantee riches? How does a monopoly prevent entry by other firms into an industry? How narrowly are the terms *product* and *close substitutes* defined?

You can probably think of many products for which there is only one producer or seller. Does this mean that these sellers are monopolists? Not necessarily. For example, Scott, Foresman and Company has the exclusive right to publish this text. Does this make Scott, Foresman a monopolist? Clearly not, because there are a number of close, albeit imperfect, substitutes for this text. Not only is a monopolist the only seller of a given product, but the product itself must also be without close substitutes. This means that a monopolist's control of a market must encompass any reasonably close substitutes for the product, a task easier said than done.

Consider the market for cameras producing instant snapshots. Today Polaroid is the only producer of cameras that provide finished pictures in 60 seconds or less. Are regular cameras really close substitutes for instant picture cameras? Should the appropriate market for ascertaining whether or not Polaroid has a monopoly be the market for the "instant picture" camera rather than for cameras as a whole? When you consider the closeness of substitutes, a publisher's monopoly on a particular book is clearly inferior to Polaroid's monopoly for instant cameras.

Monopoly Pricing and Output

A purely competitive firm can sell all it chooses to produce at whatever price prevails in the marketplace. Therefore, in competitive markets marginal revenue (the added revenue derived from selling an additional unit of output) equals the market price. That is, each unit sold adds the market price to total revenue regardless of how many units are produced and sold. A competitive firm faces a horizontal demand curve.

The demand curve facing a monopolist is the entire market demand curve because a monopolist is the sole source of a particular product without close substitutes. Unlike competitive firms, which can sell all they individually produce without affecting the prevailing market price, the monopolist completely controls the supply side of the market and must select the **monopoly price and output** combination at which its product will be sold. Monopoly firms are price makers, while competitive firms are price takers and can only select the *quantities* they will produce and sell. This consideration plays an important role in the monopolist's decision making process and clearly distinguishes monopolistic pricing behavior from that of competitive firms. Should the monopolist charge an amount equal to that

which the most desperate buyer will pay? What price should the monopolist charge? What price maximizes monopoly profits?

Monopoly Power and Demand

The law of demand implies that the demand curve facing a monopolist will be downward sloping: price will be inversely related to quantity demanded. If a firm with monopoly power can only charge one price for its output, then the price must be lowered for it to produce and sell more. The differences between the marginal revenues for competitive firms and for firms with monopoly power are illustrated in Figure 1.

Whenever monopoly power occurs, any extra units produced cannot be sold at the previous market price because consumers are unwilling to purchase additional units at that price. When the price is lowered to sell extra units, a monopolist must lower its price for all units sold. For example, if Polaroid wanted to sell more cameras next year, it could not just lower the price for the few extra customers who required discounts to buy over the next year; Polaroid would be forced to lower the price of the camera in question to virtually all customers. Thus, marginal revenue will equal the price a monopolist receives from selling an extra unit minus the revenue lost because prices must be reduced on all other units sold.

The demand curve for the monopolist in Panel B of Figure 1 is D and is based on the data beside the figure. Note that this demand curve is the industry's demand curve since by definition the monopolist is the only firm in the industry. Total revenue (TR) equals the price per unit (P) times the number of units sold—quantity (Q)—and is listed in column 3 of the data. If the firm sets its price at $9, it could sell 3 million units and total revenue yearly would be $27 million. If the firm then lowered its price from $9 to $8, it would sell 4 million annually; total revenue would increase from $27 million to $32 million for a total of an extra $5 million. Why would total revenue fail to rise by $8 million, the full price of the million units sold? The answer is straightforward. The firm received $8 for each of the additional 1 million units sold, but it lost $1 per unit on the first 3 million units sold, resulting in an average increase in total revenue of only $5 for each of the last million units sold ($8 − 3 = 5$).

FIGURE 1 *Marginal Revenue for Competition and Monopoly*

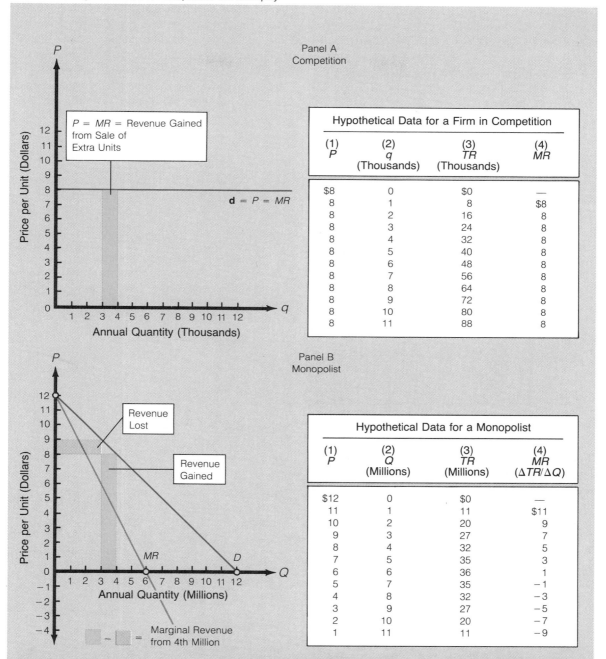

Panel A
Competition

Hypothetical Data for a Firm in Competition			
(1) P	(2) q (Thousands)	(3) TR (Thousands)	(4) MR
$8	0	$0	—
8	1	8	$8
8	2	16	8
8	3	24	8
8	4	32	8
8	5	40	8
8	6	48	8
8	7	56	8
8	8	64	8
8	9	72	8
8	10	80	8
8	11	88	8

Panel B
Monopolist

Hypothetical Data for a Monopolist			
(1) P	(2) Q (Millions)	(3) TR (Millions)	(4) MR ($\Delta TR/\Delta Q$)
$12	0	$0	—
11	1	11	$11
10	2	20	9
9	3	27	7
8	4	32	5
7	5	35	3
6	6	36	1
5	7	35	−1
4	8	32	−3
3	9	27	−5
2	10	20	−7
1	11	11	−9

The revenue gained by a perfectly competitive firm when it sells an additional unit of output equals the price of the output (*MR = P*) because demand for the firm's product is perfectly elastic (Panel A). A firm with monopoly power must reduce price in order to sell extra output, so marginal revenue is always less than price (*P > MR*). In Panel B, a monopolist can sell 3 million units at $9 each ($27 million) or 4 million units at $8 ($32 million). Thus, the fourth million only adds $5 per unit, on the average, in revenue ($32 million − $27 million = $5 million).

The numerical values of marginal revenue are listed in column 4 of the data beside the figure. Marginal revenue is equal to $\Delta TR/\Delta Q$ and is labeled MR in the figure. Notice that when quantity sold exceeds 6 million units and price is reduced below $6, marginal revenue is actually negative. This means that total revenue actually falls when extra units are sold and the price is lowered.

Total Revenue, Marginal Revenue, and Elasticity

Recall (from the chapter on elasticity) that there is a close relationship between elasticity, price, and total revenue. For example, if expanding output requires such large price reductions that total revenue falls, the demand curve is price inelastic and marginal revenue is negative. The relationships between demand, marginal revenue, price, total revenue, and price

FIGURE 2 *Relationship Between Demand, Marginal Revenue, Total Revenue, and Elasticity (ε)*

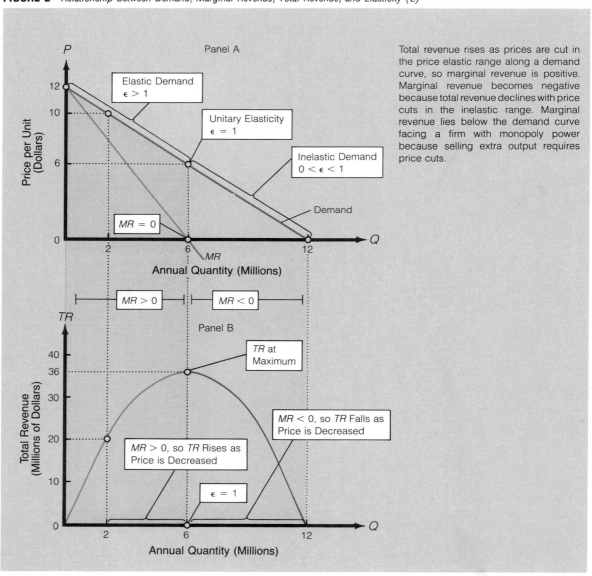

Total revenue rises as prices are cut in the price elastic range along a demand curve, so marginal revenue is positive. Marginal revenue becomes negative because total revenue declines with price cuts in the inelastic range. Marginal revenue lies below the demand curve facing a firm with monopoly power because selling extra output requires price cuts.

elasticity are graphed in Figure 2, which is based on the data used to develop Panel B of Figure 1.

When quantity is less than 6 million units and the price is above $6, the demand is price elastic. The price cuts associated with increasing output are proportionately smaller than are the increases in output. Thus, when output is raised and prices are lowered, total revenue rises slightly. Another way to view this is that marginal revenue is positive when the price is above $6. Whenever marginal revenue is positive, demand is elastic. Conversely, total revenues fall as the price is reduced below $6: demand is inelastic. Just the opposite happens to total revenue when price is raised for all prices below $6. Thus, when marginal revenue is negative, we are in the inelastic range of the demand curve. If price is changed slightly and total revenue does not change, marginal revenue is zero and demand is in the unitary elastic range. Let us now examine how the monopolist sets prices and output to maximize profits in the short run. As you will see shortly, the concept of marginal revenue is vital to this decision.

Profit-Maximizing Price and Output

Profit maximization is probably the dominant goal of all firms, including monopolies; in the parlance of accounting, "The bottom line is what counts." Keep in mind that you need information about both revenues (demand) and costs (supply) to determine the profit-maximizing price and output. Like any firm, the monopolist will continue to produce and sell additional units of output as long as the additional units add to total revenue at least as much as they cost. This is just another way of saying that the firm will continue to produce and sell as long as marginal revenue is greater than or equal to marginal cost ($MR \geq MC$).

In Figure 3 we have added data for costs of production to the revenue data in our previous example. The firm will produce and sell 4 million units at a price of $8 each, receiving total revenues of $32 million. Average total costs are $6 per unit, so $24 million is absorbed in total costs, leaving a total profit of $8 million. Looking at Panel A of the figure, total profit is the shaded rectangle (*bcde*) and equals price ($8) minus average total cost ($6) times the number of units sold (4 million), for total profits of $8 million.

Why does the firm sell 4 million units? Why not 3 million or 5 million? Maximizing profits requires the firm to produce and sell an extra unit any time the money brought in from an extra sale (*MR*) at least covers its cost of production (*MC*). If only 3 million units were sold, this monopoly firm would be forgoing profits equal to the shaded triangle to the left of point *a* in Panel A, where $MR = MC$. Whenever marginal costs exceed marginal revenues, a firm will lose by producing the extra units of output. If 5 million units were sold, the last million would add costs that exceed revenues by the amount of the shaded triangle to the right of point *a* (where $MR = MC$).

The rule for profit maximization is that the firm should produce output up to the point where $MR = MC$. A mathematically equivalent alternative rule is that the firm should maximize profits by producing where the difference between total revenue and total costs is greatest, as shown in Panel B. The data from our example are shown as "Total Revenues" and "Total Costs" in Panel B of Figure 3.

Loss-Minimizing Price and Output

One common myth is that monopolists always make profits. Monopolists can control the prices they charge for their products, so it seems natural that they will earn economic profits. Figure 4 depicts an instance where a monopolist would actually suffer losses if the good or service were produced. There are literally thousands of patented products for which demand is insufficient to justify production. The cost structures associated with these products are so high that there never is a price and output combination where the monopolist can make a profit. For example, you could probably not make a profit if you had a monopoly on machines that rewove the "runs" in pantyhose or resharpened disposable razor blades. Demands would be trivial relative to the costs of providing such services.

Even if a monopolized product initially passes the market test, rising costs or diminishing demand may cause a monopoly to fail. In the short run, if P_e is above average variable costs, the firm would continue to produce despite its losses. But what about the long run? The monopolist has two options: leave the industry and put its capital to more profitable use, or try to bolster demand sufficiently to bring its operations into the black, perhaps through aggressive marketing. Operating monopolists rarely lose

FIGURE 3 *Profit Maximization and the Monopolist*

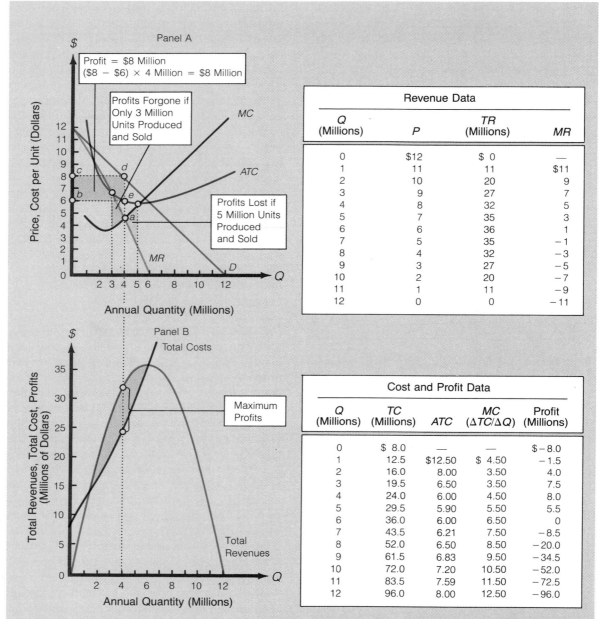

Revenue Data			
Q (Millions)	P	TR (Millions)	MR
0	$12	$ 0	—
1	11	11	$11
2	10	20	9
3	9	27	7
4	8	32	5
5	7	35	3
6	6	36	1
7	5	35	−1
8	4	32	−3
9	3	27	−5
10	2	20	−7
11	1	11	−9
12	0	0	−11

Cost and Profit Data				
Q (Millions)	TC (Millions)	ATC	MC (ΔTC/ΔQ)	Profit (Millions)
0	$ 8.0	—	—	$−8.0
1	12.5	$12.50	$ 4.50	−1.5
2	16.0	8.00	3.50	4.0
3	19.5	6.50	3.50	7.5
4	24.0	6.00	4.50	8.0
5	29.5	5.90	5.50	5.5
6	36.0	6.00	6.50	0
7	43.5	6.21	7.50	−8.5
8	52.0	6.50	8.50	−20.0
9	61.5	6.83	9.50	−34.5
10	72.0	7.20	10.50	−52.0
11	83.5	7.59	11.50	−72.5
12	96.0	8.00	12.50	−96.0

Profit can be shown as quantity sold times price minus average total cost [π = Q(P − ATC)], as in Panel A, or as the vertical difference between total revenue and total cost (π = PQ − TC), as in Panel B. Maximum profits are realized only if marginal revenue equals marginal cost (MR = MC).

FIGURE 4 Loss-Minimizing Output for a Monopolist

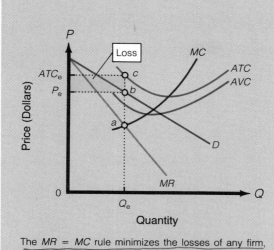

The *MR = MC* rule minimizes the losses of any firm, including a monopoly, as long as variable costs are covered by revenues. Can you alter the relationship between demand and average variable cost so that the monopoly depicted here would shut down? Does the monopoly firm have a single, specific shutdown point? Why not?

a patent is issued for 17 yrs.

money. Losses will not persist in the long run because the firm will move its capital into a more lucrative business.

Is There a Long Run for Monopolists?

In competitive markets, short-run economic profits are signals for other firms to enter the industry and try to share in any profits, driving economic profits to zero in the long run. Will this be the case in an industry controlled by one firm? It depends on how difficult it is to prevent new firms from entering the market and exploiting potential profit opportunities.

If new competitors can somehow be prevented from entering the industry, the monopolist may adjust its productive capacity along its long-run average cost curve to most profitably accommodate long-term variations in demand, as shown in Panel A of Figure 5. Alternatively, the owners or managers of a monopoly that is protected from the discipline of competition may decide to follow the path of least resistance and allow the company to operate very inefficiently. Why not hire your lazy relatives and friends at high salaries if a monopoly position ensures that you will have a high income anyway? Why

bother to work hard or try to control costs? And why worry about quality and consumer satisfaction? Any customers who are going to buy the monopolized product must buy from your company.

If those who control a monopolized company choose "the good life," inefficiency may drive up fixed costs, absorbing much of potential monopoly profits. This sort of adjustment is shown in Panel B of Figure 5. Of course, in the long run an inefficiently run monopoly is a natural target for takeover by profit seekers (corporate raiders) who will manage the firm efficiently, so the inefficient previous owners can retire to the beach or mountains. These two earning prospects—long-term economic profits or leading a comfortable and easy life with a high income—are both good reasons for a monopolist to fear market entry by new competitors.

Maintaining Monopoly Power: Barriers to Entry

Maintaining a monopoly position requires keeping other firms out of the industry. This is accomplished through barriers to entry. A **barrier to entry** is any obstacle that makes it unprofitable or impossible for new firms to enter an industry. Entry can be thwarted in several ways. Some barriers to entry are technological or "natural"; others are artificial. **Artificial barriers to entry** *(made)* are either legally permissible (e.g., annual style changes, excessive national advertising) or established by law (e.g., patents). Some are illegal, and some may even be beyond the control of the monopolist (e.g., certain government regulations). Monopolists are ingenious in their attempts to keep competitors out of a market. Where key natural resources are involved, one firm may attempt to corner the market, precluding other firms from entering the industry.

Artificial Barriers to Entry The most obvious legal barrier is outright government prohibition of competition. The U.S. Postal Service maintains its monopoly position by statutes that prohibit most competition for profitable first-class mail carrying. For example, its competitors cannot deliver to mailboxes. Without these constraints, we would expect competition for delivery of first-class mail similar to that for parcel-post deliveries from United Parcel Service and other package handlers. In fact, a few firms have entered the first-class mail business by putting

FIGURE 5 *Long-Run Adjustments by Monopoly Firms*

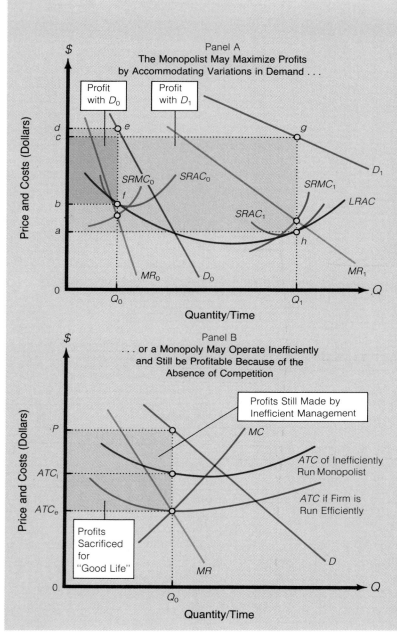

Panel A
The Monopolist May Maximize Profits by Accommodating Variations in Demand . . .

Profit with D_0

Profit with D_1

Price and Costs (Dollars)

$SRMC_0$ $SRAC_0$ $SRMC_1$ $LRAC$ $SRAC_1$

MR_0 D_0 D_1 MR_1

Quantity/Time

Panel B
. . . or a Monopoly May Operate Inefficiently and Still be Profitable Because of the Absence of Competition

Price and Costs (Dollars)

Profits Still Made by Inefficient Management

MC

ATC of Inefficiently Run Monopolist

ATC if Firm is Run Efficiently

P

ATC_i

ATC_e

Profits Sacrificed for "Good Life"

MR D

Quantity/Time

If demand were D_0 in Panel A, a profit-maximizing monopoly firm would have a small plant, charge a high price, and earn profits equal to area *bdef*. If demand grew to D_1, the monopolist would expand its production facilities and realize greater profits equal to area *acgh*. Thus, in the long run, a monopolist may accommodate variations in demand through growth or contraction. However, a monopoly whose management was not threatened by competition might make the long-run adjustment of operating inefficiently, as long as it realized satisfactory profits. Panel B assumes that such sloppy management is a fixed cost. (Of course, in the long run, even sloppy managers die.)

the mail into plastic bags and hanging these packages on the doorknobs of recipients. There are other companies like Emery or Federal Express that now offer one-day hand delivery service between many major cities.

Other important legal barriers to entry include patents and copyrights. Patent and copyright monopolies may be justifiable as incentives for research and development leading to technological advances or the enrichment of our culture. The granting of a pat-

Patents, Trademarks, Copyrights, and Counterfeit Goods

Patents, trademarks, and copyrights all impart monopoly rights on inventions, business identities, and intellectual property. Obtaining these rights is a costly endeavor.

Inventions like the telephone and the electric light have revolutionized our lives and have brought riches to their inventors. Today immense expenditures are being poured into genetic research, research on faster microchips that can access larger computer memories, and research into more attractive consumer products. Both public and private research and development expenditures in 1985 were over $100 billion, and over a million scientists and engineers were employed.

Trademarks are another device conveying monopoly power to firms. Several million dollars were spent developing the EXXON name. Hundreds of countries were checked to ensure that the name was not previously trademarked and would not connote anything offensive to consumers. Then hundreds of millions of dollars were spent helping the public remember the new trademark. Firms

like Gucci, Cartier, and Chanel invest heavily in their trade names. Chanel, for example, spends over $1 million a year on trade-name security alone.

Copyrights protect intellectual property in a number of areas including books, records, video tapes, and computer software, as well as product designs (e.g., Cabbage Patch Kids). Software developers have formed an organization to fight unauthorized duplication, and record producers use ASCAP and BMI to pressure businesses to license music for commercial purposes. ASCAP and BMI send people into businesses to see if they play background music to entertain customers. If, for example, a radio is playing, they will ask the owner to purchase a license to play the radio in the store. If the owner refuses, the agent for ASCAP or BMI will immediately retain an attorney and file a lawsuit. The law is clear—playing music for commercial purposes without a license is unlawful unless you own the copyright to the music itself. ASCAP and BMI then prorate their proceeds to the copyright holders of the music being played.

Today, counterfeit goods are threatening all these forms of monopoly power. Numerous products are counterfeited. The imitations are typically of inferior quality. Replicas of aircraft parts and bogus "high-strength" fasteners are showing up in civilian and military aircraft. The U.S. Department of Commerce estimates that over three-quarters of a million jobs are lost to imported product "knock-offs", the industry's term for counterfeited goods.

Interestingly, secrecy is the order of the day on both sides of this problem. For those counterfeiting products, the reason is clear. However, businesses are hesitant to admit that their product line has been reproduced. Many fear that publicity may encourage further copying or that their customers will become wary of their brand names. In any event, counterfeiting substantially weakens the monopoly power associated with many patents, trademarks, and copyrights.

---

ent monopoly provides expectations of monopoly profit to inventors, potentially allowing them to earn a handsome return on their inventive effort. However, patents and copyrights are licenses for monopoly; patents bar competitive production for a period of 17 years, and they may be renewed. Patents were the principal barrier to entry protecting the Polaroid Company for years, giving the firm a monopoly in the market for "instant picture" cameras. At times, however, unethical firms "pirate" patented or copyrighted products, as discussed in Focus 1.

Licensing and bonding restrictions, ostensibly used to protect consumers from shoddy or fraudulent practices, may really be disguised barriers to entry. Detailed government regulations that require extensive reporting and adherence to elaborate rules may pose barriers that limit the ability of smaller firms to compete effectively. For example, there is evidence that the Food and Drug Administration's stringent regulation of the pharmaceutical industry reduced research and development efforts by big drug companies and drove most small drug companies completely out of the market. While many government regulations may serve worthwhile purposes, barriers preventing competition by smaller firms are a cost that society pays for regulation.

Natural Barriers to Entry

Not all barriers to entry result from the efforts of existing firms. Barriers to entry may also be consequences of either the nature of a product or the cost structures inherent in some kinds of production. Natural gas is one product that leads to a single firm in any service area because of **natural barriers to entry.** Imagine the nuisance and inconvenience if 20 gas companies serviced your neighborhood and consumers did not collude to give their business to one company. How often would the streets be torn up to install new gas pipelines? How many pipes would run down every alley? How many companies might you need to contact before digging to plant a tree or excavate a drainage ditch? Installing a new storm sewer system would entail incredible expense.

Figure 6 illustrates a situation of *natural monopoly* arising from a production process. An unregulated monopoly will charge P_3 for Q_2 amount of output, reaping profits equal to the shaded area. This production process is characterized by high fixed costs and relatively low variable costs. Economies of scale are tremendous because average costs decline when overhead costs are spread across large amounts of output. A monopoly emerges naturally whenever economies of scale are substantial relative to the market demand for the product. Here is why. Suppose that four firms were initially in the market, each breaking even while producing Q_0 at a price of P_3, where $Q_0 = Q_2/4$. Each firm would try to expand its output because if it can wrest customers from its competitors, the marginal costs of production would be far below the marginal revenues it would receive. As industry output expands, however, price falls much faster than average total costs fall. Suppose, for example, that each firm doubles output. Since the industry output will be Q_3, price will be P_0. However, if all firms are the same size (Q_1), average cost will be P_2, and these firms all will be losing $P_2 - P_0$ on each unit produced. Eventually, three of the firms will leave the market, leaving the fourth to collect the full monopoly profits (the shaded area in Figure 6).

Such natural monopolies as utility companies are regulated in our society in attempts to ensure that customers receive the benefits of economies of scale. Without this regulation, natural monopolies could generate monstrous profits that, as you will see in a moment, might be very inefficient from society's vantage point. In later chapters we will consider some of the illegal barriers to competition when there are artificial attempts to monopolize. We will also investigate the potential benefits of regulation when technology makes monopoly a natural outcome of the marketplace.

Contestable Markets

No firm can exercise monopoly power to reap sustained economic profits unless it can prevent competitors from entering the market. According to a recent hypothesis called **contestable markets theory,** easy entry into a market can force even firms that are the sole sellers of products with no close substitutes to produce the same levels of output and set the same prices as would firms in a purely competitive environment.[1] The doctrine of contestable markets pivots on the idea that the level of competition in a market is *less* related to the number of firms currently in an industry than to the *ease of market access* by other firms if prospects of economic profits exist.

Conventional analyses of industries have assumed that the number of firms in an industry determines the extent of monopoly and, consequently, the prices charged for output. Contestable markets theory turns this assumption on its head, presuming that the prices consumers are willing to pay for given amounts of products determine the numbers of firms in an industry if outsiders can always freely enter the market. One conclusion is that even when a single firm currently supplies all the output in a given market, the firm is forced to behave as if it were in competition if that market is "contestable." This theory has important ramifications for the antitrust policies we consider two chapters hence.

---

1. A summary of the doctrine of contestable markets is contained in *Contestable Markets and the Theory of Industry Structure,* by W. Baumol, J. Panzar, and R. Willig (New York: Harcourt Brace Jovanovich, Inc., 1982).

FIGURE 6 A Natural Monopoly Market

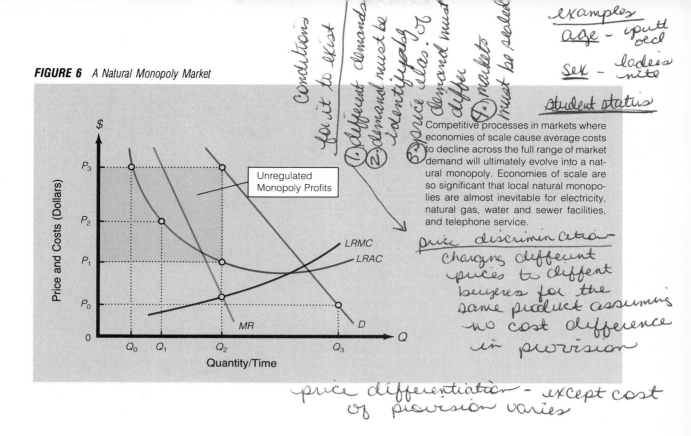

Competitive processes in markets where economies of scale cause average costs to decline across the full range of market demand will ultimately evolve into a natural monopoly. Economies of scale are so significant that local natural monopolies are almost inevitable for electricity, natural gas, water and sewer facilities, and telephone service.

Price Discrimination

Monopoly power implies some control over price. We have shown how a monopoly erects barriers to entry and how a monopoly maximizes profit assuming that it charges only one price for its product. In an earlier chapter, we discussed consumer surplus and noted that it was the difference between the amounts people would willingly pay for various amounts of specific goods and the amounts they do pay at market prices. But if the monopolist is able to isolate consumers into separate submarkets and has control over price, different groups of customers can be charged different prices and the monopolist can appropriate the consumer surplus.

Price discrimination occurs when a good or service is sold at different prices that do not reflect differences in production costs. This is the conversion of consumer surplus from the consumer to the producer. People who think "discrimination" in general is outlawed may be surprised at the widespread occurrence of price discrimination.

Have you walked into a local theater to see a first-run movie and paid a different price than the person sitting next to you did? Theaters often have different prices for children, students, adults, and senior citizens. Does it cost the theater more to seat a 22-year-old at a given show than it does a senior citizen? Clearly not. Doctors and dentists commonly argue that they are providing special benefits to the poor when they charge their richer patients more than their poorer patients for the same service. (Do you suppose they charge whatever the market will bear?) The airlines have different ticket prices for roughly the same service (depending on early reservations and special promotions). These are all examples of price discrimination.

Why do firms charge different customers different prices? Is such discrimination beneficial to society or harmful? And what conditions make price discrimination possible?

Requirements for Price Discrimination

Any firm *must* have some monopoly power to practice price discrimination. This is not to say that the firm must be a monopolist. Monopoly power is possessed whenever a seller individually is a price maker rather than a price taker. That is, the enterprise has some control over prices, which occurs whenever the demand curve facing a firm has negative slope. In this sense, your neighborhood store has monopoly power even though it is not a monopolist.[2]

A second condition required for price discrimination is that customers be separable into submarkets with different demand elasticities. These different elasticities may be due to different incomes, tastes and preferences, locations, and so on. Once the firm has separated its consumers into two or more groups, the firm must be able to prevent arbitrage. *Arbitrage* occurs if customers who pay the preferential (low) price can turn around and sell to customers charged the higher price. Medical treatment is one area where price discrimination abounds because arbitrage is impossible. One patient cannot sell another a gall bladder operation or an inoculation against polio or measles. Another interesting example of arbitrage is described in Focus 2. Price-discrimination schemes by firms that cannot prevent arbitrage will be short-lived.

In summary, the firm must have some monopoly power and must be able to separate the market into different groups with different elasticities of demand. Once this is accomplished, the firm must also be able to prevent the lower-price users from selling to higher-price users. We will now look at the effects of two types of price discrimination on monopoly profits.

Profit Maximization and Price Discrimination

A monopolist will not charge different customers different prices unless it is profitable to do so. Let us first consider the case of perfect price discrimination. A firm practicing perfect price discrimination is able to extract from all consumers their *demand prices* for each unit of the good—the highest outlays the individual would be willing to pay rather than do without.

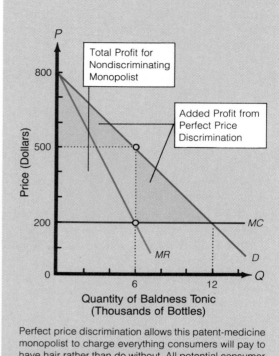

FIGURE 7 *Monopoly Profits and* Perfect Price Discrimination

Perfect price discrimination allows this patent-medicine monopolist to charge everything consumers will pay to have hair rather than do without. All potential consumer surpluses are converted into revenues for the perfectly price-discriminating firm.

This case is illustrated in Figure 7, where we consider a hypothetical monopolist who markets a tonic that actually cures baldness. In this figure, to keep the graphical presentation simple, we have assumed that marginal costs are constant at $200 per unit.[3] If the monopoly firm simply charged a single profit-maximizing price, it would charge $500 per bottle of tonic and sell 6,000 units. Total profit would be $1,800,000 [($500 − $200) × 6,000 = $1,800,000]. Through price discrimination, a monopolist can do better. For the firm to fully extract its customers' consumer surpluses, it must sell the first unit for $799, the next several hundred for $798, then the next several hundred for $797, and so on, until the last few units are sold for only a few cents over $200.

---

2. Perfectly competitive firms would find it difficult to charge different prices for a homogeneous product because the demand curves they confront are horizontal. If one firm in competition raised its price to a given class of consumers, these buyers would simply go elsewhere and their business would be lost to the company. A competitive firm could (if it were altruistic) sell its product below the prevailing market price to a given group but would lose some of its normal profits in the process.

---

3. Note that whenever marginal costs are constant, they are also equal to average variable costs. Take a few moments to make sure you know why.

Arbitrage and Price Discrimination

George Stocking and Myron Watkins reported a classic case of arbitrage in their book, *Cartels in Action:*

Rohm & Haas of Philadelphia and Dupont [were] the only American producers of methyl-methacrylate plastics. They marketed methyl-methacrylate in the form of molding powders, for a variety of industrial uses, at $0.85 a pound. To licensed dental laboratories they supplied, at more than $22 a pound, prepared mixtures consisting of methyl-methacrylate powder (polymer) and liquid (monomer), both essential to the manufacture of dentures. At the same time they refused to sell the monomer in any other form to any other buyer. In this way they apparently planned to force the dental trade to rely exclusively upon them for supplies. The enormous price spread attracted "bootleggers" who found that they could "crack" the commercial powders back to the liquid, and sell the polymer and monomer together at a profit to the dental trade. To combat this practice, at the suggestion of a licensee, Rohm & Haas considered adulterating the cheap commercial powders so that, for use in dentures, they would come under the ban of the Pure [sic] Food and Drug Administration. The licensee suggested that:*

A millionth of one percent of arsenic or lead might cause them to confiscate every bootleg unit in the country. There ought to be a trace of something that would make them rear up.

Although Rohm & Haas thought this was a "very fine" suggestion, there is no evidence that they put it into effect.

Source: G. W. Stocking and M. W. Watkins, Cartels in Action (New York: Twentieth Century Fund, 1946), pp. 402–4.

Perfect price discrimination allows this producer to appropriate all of the consumer surplus that exists above a price of $200. In Figure 7, price discrimination allows the firm to increase its profits from the rectangular area associated with normal monopoly pricing to the entire shaded area. The effect of perfect price discrimination is to raise profits from $1,800,000 (the rectangular area) to $3,600,000 (the area of the entire triangle above marginal costs). Clearly, perfect price discrimination pays; it enables the monopolist to charge everything the market will bear.

Most firms are unable to determine the maximum that each individual is willing to pay for each unit of a given product. At best, a firm may be able to break up the general buying public into a few distinct groups for whom arbitrage is impossible and whose elasticities of demand differ. How can this be profitable? The answer is depicted in Figure 8. The demands of two groups of consumers are illustrated.

Fixed costs are zero and marginal cost equals $2 per unit. In Market A, the firm charges $5 per unit and makes a total profit of $18,000; in Market B, the price will be less ($3.75) and profit will equal $12,250, for a total profit of $30,250. If the firm simply charged the monopoly price, it would sell 13,000 units at $4.25 and make a total profit of $29,250. Price discrimination allows this firm to make $1,000 more per month than regular monopoly profits by segregating customers into two groups and charging them different prices.

This form of price discrimination is fairly common. Examples include discount coupons for groceries, special airline fares for select groups, senior citizens' discounts, and student rates for movie tickets or bus rides. Other forms of price discrimination are more subtle. Private party phones cost less than business phones, and long-distance rates historically were set to generate much larger profits than local services. These gaps were far greater than the cost

FIGURE 8 Group Price Discrimination and Firm Profitability

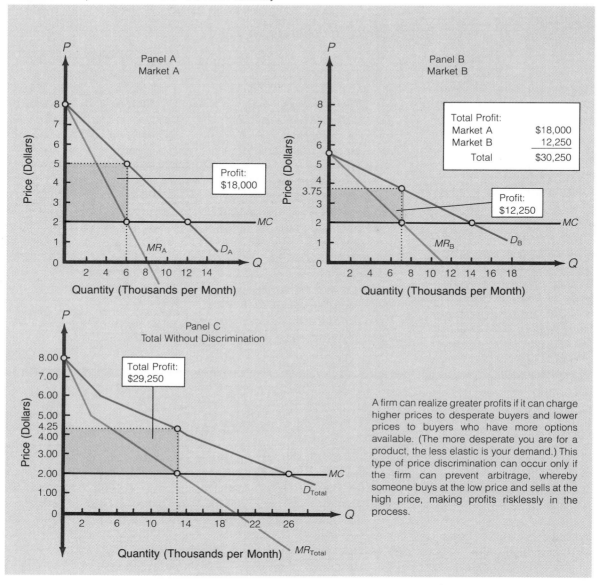

A firm can realize greater profits if it can charge higher prices to desperate buyers and lower prices to buyers who have more options available. (The more desperate you are for a product, the less elastic is your demand.) This type of price discrimination can occur only if the firm can prevent arbitrage, whereby someone buys at the low price and sells at the high price, making profits risklessly in the process.

differentials. (Reorganization of the Bell system in January 1983 changed this situation somewhat.) Another example is magazines, which commonly grant preferential rates to new subscribers relative to the rates offered renewals.

Before we challenge you to think of other examples of price discrimination, we need to describe some activities that are not price discrimination. When downtown parking lots charge monthly rates that are lower than weekly rates, weekly that are lower than daily, and daily that are lower than hourly, they might appear to be price discriminating. However, their wage costs for parking attendants or ticket collectors fall as the bulk of their trade becomes long-term instead of short-term parking. Similarly, quantity discounts granted major purchasers of goods commonly reflect reductions in transaction cost. Lower rates for weekend parking or off-peak long-distance telephone calls also reflect lower opportunity costs, not strictly differences in the desperation of buyers. Weekend parking spaces or off-hour phone calls are not the same goods as spaces or calls during business hours. Price discrimination is not present whenever differences in opportunity costs are reflected in prices of similar goods.

on test

Comparing Competitive and Monopoly Markets

In the previous chapter, we indicated that the prices and outputs of competitive markets result in economic efficiency. Since monopoly pricing and outputs differ from those of competitive markets, should you conclude that unregulated monopolies that do not price discriminate are less than economically efficient? In general, the answer is yes. Moreover, such monopolies produce less and charge higher

prices than competitive industries, and also cause what many people perceive as inequity in the distribution of income.

Differences in Prices and Outputs

Equilibrium in the competitive market shown in Panel A of Figure 9 will be at point *a,* with industry output equal to Q_c and price equal to P_c. The competitive industry's supply curve is the sum of all marginal cost curves (above $AVCs$) of the firms in the industry. Contrast the results of the competitive model with those for an unregulated but nondiscriminating monopolist, described in Panel B of the figure. Industry demand for the product is the same, and the marginal cost curve for the monopolist is assumed to be the same as that which collectively characterizes firms in the competitive industry. Equilibrium price and output will be P_m and Q_m, respectively. Not only is the monopoly price higher, but the monopoly output is lower than for a competitive industry.

pure monopoly – charges a higher price than a competitive firm produces less " " " "

FIGURE 9 *Competition Versus Nondiscriminating Monopoly*

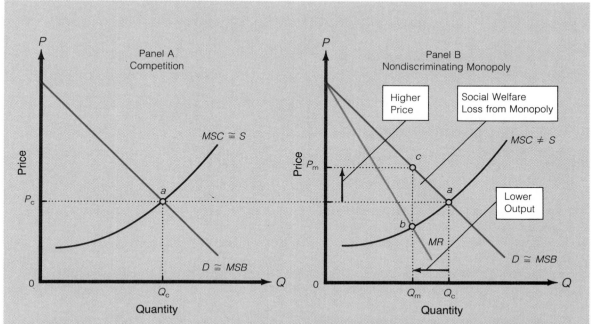

Efficiency requires that marginal social benefit equal marginal social cost (MSB = MSC). This condition is met in competitive markets where supply equals demand (Panel A). Because price is greater than marginal cost in equilibrium for a nondiscriminating monopoly (Panel B), some could gain without losses to anyone if output were increased, as long as the monopolist's additional costs were covered.

Take special note of the fact that in Panel B the marginal cost curve for the monopolist is not the supply curve for the industry. Price is not a given for firms with monopoly power. Since the monopolist is able to select the price that maximizes profit, the marginal cost curve is not the supply curve. We have denoted this as $MSC \neq S$. In fact, the quantities supplied by a firm with monopoly power cannot be ascertained from price alone; the monopolist wants to know how desperate buyers are (How elastic are their demand curves?) before making decisions about both price and production. There is no supply curve per se.

The Inefficiency of Monopoly

In the preceding chapter, you learned that the demand curve for any industry's product represents society's marginal benefit curve for that product. The market price (P) approximates marginal social benefit (MSB). Since competition forces each manufacturer to use the least costly methods of production feasible, the marginal social costs of production are reflected in competitive supplies; this is shown in the competitive panel of Figure 9 with the notation that marginal social cost approximates supply ($MSC \cong S$). Equilibrium in the competitive market at point a equates society's marginal (opportunity) cost of producing this good with the marginal benefits that society receives from the product ($P = MSC \cong MSB$). The maximum total net benefits from available resources are realized only if the price equals the cost for the last unit produced and sold ($P = MC$). This is the reason competitive markets set standards for efficiency by which all other market structures are judged.

At the equilibrium for a nondiscriminating monopoly, price (marginal social benefit) exceeds marginal social cost; society would benefit more from additional units of the product than it would cost to produce them. That is, $P > MSC$. At first glance, this might seem desirable; society seems to get more from the marginal unit than it sacrifices. Actually, this situation is not desirable. Society would like more of its resources devoted to the production of any product for which marginal benefits exceed marginal costs. Resources are not allocated efficiently because the monopolist produces too little and charges too much. The potential gains to consumers from extra

production exceed the extra production costs, so **monopolistic inefficiency** causes losses of social welfare equal to area abc in Panel B.[4] Although price discrimination might sound as nasty as other forms of discrimination, it may remedy some of the inefficiency associated with monopoly power.

Price Discrimination and Efficiency

Surprisingly, price discrimination may overcome some of the inefficiency associated with unregulated monopoly power. In Figure 10, a nondiscriminating monopolist will charge a unit price of P_m for output equal to Q_m, yielding profits of $Q_m \times (P_m - P_c)$—area P_cP_mba.

---

4. This is known as a welfare loss triangle.

FIGURE 10 *Efficiency Gains of Monopoly Price Discrimination*

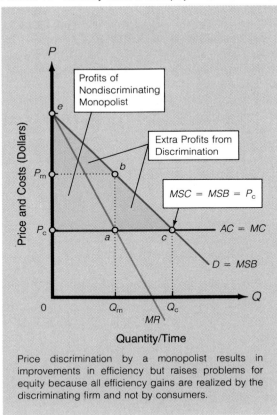

Price discrimination by a monopolist results in improvements in efficiency but raises problems for equity because all efficiency gains are realized by the discriminating firm and not by consumers.

If this monopolist gained the ability to price discriminate perfectly, profits would expand to the entire shaded area in Figure 10 (area P_cec). Note that the price charged for the last unit sold, Q_c, will be P_c, which is identical to the constant unit price that would emerge from the operation of a competitive market. In addition, the marginal social costs and marginal social benefit will both equal the price of that last unit. Thus, price discrimination can lead to the economic efficiency we associate with pure competition. However, under pure competition, the bulk of the net social benefits of the marketplace represent consumer surplus, while these benefits are generally appropriated by the owners of a monopoly firm if it can price discriminate. This solution may be efficient, but many people think it unfair.

Monopoly and Inequity

That monopoly firms are able to charge prices far in excess of opportunity costs is a source of delight for monopolists. Most of us, however, view monopoly pricing as a means of gouging the public to provide high incomes for a few people. Their outsized earnings are achieved at the expense of the general public, both because the inefficiency associated with nondiscriminating monopoly behavior causes real national income to fall below its potential and because the purchasing power of nonmonopoly incomes is depleted. The total value of the national pie is reduced so that nondiscriminating monopolists can have more pie. When a monopolist is able to price discriminate, some of the problems of inefficiency may be overcome but the distribution of income will tend to be made even less equal and, perhaps, even less equitable.

In summary, the unregulated exercise of monopoly power causes economic inefficiency ($P > MC$), which implies that national income will be below its potential. The lack of competitive pressure may permit some monopolists to operate in a slack and wasteful fashion, worsening the problem. Moreover, monopoly power may pose problems of inequity in the distribution of income, a problem we address in more detail in a later chapter.

Ideally, all industries would be competitive. Unfortunately, this is impossible because certain production technologies embody enormous economies of scale and lead to natural monopolies, or certain firms are able to erect significant barriers to entry. Even if one firm is the sole supplier in a market, if that market is "contestable", the firm may not enjoy monopoly profits.

Natural monopolies are typically regulated in an attempt to ensure optimal and efficient operation. The government uses antitrust laws to try to make other industries behave as if they were competitive, or it may split some industries into smaller firms to ensure competition. In the next chapter we examine monopolistic competition and oligopoly—the spectrum between monopoly and competition. After we discuss these market structures, the next chapters consider regulation of industry and antitrust policy, which represent government attempts to reach the competitive ideal.

CHAPTER REVIEW: KEY POINTS

1. An unregulated *monopoly* controls the output and price of a product for which there are no close substitutes.

2. There are very few *pure* monopolies in the United States today. Because a large number of firms do have significant monopoly power, models of pure monopoly do provide insights into their behavior. All firms with the ability to control prices have *monopoly power;* some firms possess it in greater degree than others.

3. Monopoly power is maintained through *barriers to entry.* These may take the form of *artificial barriers to entry* (such as government prohibitions, patents, licenses, excessive model changes, and so on). Other barriers to entry may be *"natural"*—the result of large economies of scale, where average costs decline over an extremely large range of output. If market demand falls within such ranges, there is a natural monopoly.

4. The nondiscriminating monopolist's *marginal revenue* is less than its price. Marginal revenue is equal to the price the monopolist receives from the sale of the additional unit minus the revenue lost because prices must be reduced on all other units sold. Monopoly power causes the marginal revenue curve to lie below the demand curve.

5. The demand for the good is elastic when output is below the quantity where marginal revenue is zero. Demand is unitarily elastic at the point where marginal revenue is zero. Demand is inelastic for outputs above the point where marginal revenue is zero.

6. The monopolist will maximize profits (or minimize losses) by selling that output where marginal revenue and marginal costs are equal. The price charged will correspond to the maximum price from the demand curve at this $MR = MC$ level of output.

7. Monopolists' profit-maximizing (or loss-minimizing) levels of output do not normally occur at the minimum points on average cost curves. This level of output can either be less or more than the minimum average cost output.

8. If the monopolist is able to maintain its monopoly position in the long run, then pricing and output decisions as well as economic profits will reflect variations in demand. The monopolist may also choose to follow inefficient, but comfortable, policies.

9. *Price discrimination* entails sales of essentially the same good at different prices when the differences are not related to variations in costs. Price discrimination occurs in airline fares, theater ticket prices, charges for medical and dental services, and in many other areas.

10. For a firm to price discriminate effectively, it must have some monopoly power plus the ability to separate the individual customers into groups with different price elasticities of demand for the good. Further, it must prevent *arbitrage*—the selling of the good to high-price customers by low-price customers.

11. By using price discrimination, a firm can increase its total profits. *Perfect* price discrimination has the effect of appropriating for the firm all the consumer surplus associated with the product.

12. From society's point of view, the nondiscriminating monopoly is less economically efficient than are competitive industries. The monopolist typically produces less than the competitive industry and sells at a higher price. Price discrimination may reduce the problem of inefficiency but raises even more serious questions about equity in the distribution of income.

QUESTIONS FOR THOUGHT AND DISCUSSION

1. The following table lists the demand schedule and total variable costs for a monopolist. Assume that fixed costs are equal to 30. Graph the demand, marginal revenue, average total cost, and marginal cost curves. What is the profit-maximizing rate of output for the nondiscriminating monopolist? What will be the profit-maximizing rate of output if the monopolist can perfectly price discriminate? What is the profit differential between the nondiscriminating and discriminating monopolists?

Output	1	2	3	4	5	6	7	8	9	10
Price	100	90	80	75	70	65	60	50	40	30
TVC	100	175	225	265	300	330	365	410	475	575

2. Price discrimination occurs when a firm charges different prices for a given good and the price differentials do not reflect differences in cost. Suppose that there are substantial differences in costs in serving different customers but a uniform price is charged. In what sense is this also price discrimination?

3. Some observers of the American business scene think that monopoly power is so common that most giant firms do not maximize profits; they seek only satisfactory profits. Once these have been secured, management tries to maximize sales or growth, or to ensure comfortable, plush personal lives for management personnel. Pursuing the soft life is easy to understand, but how would modern corporate managers gain by maximizing growth or total sales? Do you think these commentators are right?

4. College students in some areas have access to only one institution. In other locations, numerous private or public colleges and universities are available. Since higher education is generally nonprofit, how do these institutions exercise their differing levels of monopoly power? Would you expect treatment of students to differ between private and tax-supported schools? If so, how? Do you think schools behave differently when demand is growing, as in the 1960s, than when it is falling, as in the 1980s? How?

5. Government has a legal monopoly on violence. National defense, police services, prisons, and the like are all inherently violent. Do you think violence is lower because of government's monopoly power? Would a society without government be less violent, as anarchist philosophers suggest? Can you apply the analysis of this chapter to this question?

6. Suppose you are the owner-operator of three of the four downhill ski slopes in Aspen, Colorado. Your competitor suggests that you join together and offer a four-mountain, 6- or 7-day coupon booklet for tourists. The specially priced booklets would be sold through local travel and tour guides and would permit visitors to ski any mountain on any day of their visit. The proceeds of the booklets would be distributed based on a survey of where the skiers actually used the lift tickets included in the booklet.

   a. Who stands to benefit from such a proposal?

   b. For what reasons might you not want to accept such a proposal?

   c. Does your control of three of the four mountains in Aspen constitute a monopoly? Is it significant monopoly power?

   d. If you decided to offer a three-mountain, 6- or 7-day special coupon booklet yourself, do you think it would sell? What would that do to your competitor? What could your competitor do to combat this threat?

   e. Would it be *economically efficient* to force you to agree to the four-mountain, 6- or 7-day package? Would it be *fair*?

pure comp.

Chamberlain
Robinson
1. *monopolistic comp.*
2. *oligopoly - Duopoly*

pure monopoly

CHAPTER 25 Imperfect Competition: Oligopoly and Monopolistic Competition

Monopolistic Competition
1. *many firms - most retail businesses*
2. *produce a differenciated product or service*
3. *relatively easy entry into the market*
4. *a lot of non-price competition*
   (competing anyway other than price)
   - - - advertising - - -

Differentiation
Real ?
Imagined ?

Advertising - "Goods + Bads"
promote sexism   *Creates artificial wants*
is self cancelling   *diverts resources*
diseconomies of scale many jobs are created
causes visual blight   lead to economies of scale
encourages undesirable activities encourages to save rather than consume

oligopolies	concentration ratios	kinked demand curve model
monopolistic competition	pure oligopolies	limit-pricing models
product differentiation	impure oligopolies	cartel
conscious interdependence	merger	joint-profit maximization

The top 200 American firms control roughly 60 percent of all manufacturing assets in the U.S. and are responsible for the bulk of our production. These firms are in industries that lie between the extremes of pure competition and pure monopoly. None is a price taker; all have some monopoly power.

Many of our major industries are dominated by a few giant corporations. These firms individually do not have the freedom of action enjoyed by unregulated monopolists because they must consider the reactions of other companies as they make decisions about prices, production, and marketing strategy. Industries in which the decisions of firms are inextricably and consciously linked are called **oligopolies.** Although the theories of perfect competition and monopoly each provide some insights into the behavior of oligopolists, neither purely competitive firms nor monopolists base their decisions on the expected reactions of other firms. Hence, theories of oligopoly are not just blends of competitive and monopoly models.

Oligopoly models must qualitatively account for interdependence in decision making. Different theories of oligopoly abound because the dynamics of interdependence differ markedly from one industry to another. Just as proper play in a poker game depends not only on the cards you are dealt but also on the characteristics of your opponents, oligopolists' strategies differ depending on their individual positions relative to those of both their current competitors and potential rivals now outside the industry. Consequently, economists are frustrated by the absence of a unique model that is sufficiently general to cover all oligopoly markets. In this chapter, we present some representative models that attempt to explain oligopolistic pricing and output.

Oligopoly models are more closely related to monopoly than to pure competition. In a slightly more competitive mode are models of **monopolistic competition.** Many firms have "monopolies" over their brand name products but face vigorous competition from numerous producers of close substitutes for their brands. These firms do not base business decisions on the anticipated individual reactions of their many competitors, so they are not mutually interdependent in the way oligopolists are. They are not pure competitors, however, because they do have some power to set prices.

The continuum running from pure competition to monopolistic competition through oligopoly to pure monopoly is not especially smooth. Deciding where a particular industry fits is often difficult, and the most accurate classification may change over time. For example, 25 years ago auto making was clearly an oligopoly; General Motors, Ford, and Chrysler sold roughly 95 percent of all cars in the United States. Studebaker, DeLorean, and Packard have died, but competition from Toyota, Nissan, BMW, Subaru, Mazda, Isuzu, Volkswagen, Saab, Volvo, American Motors, Mercedes-Benz, Fiat, and others seems to have moved automaking toward the monopolistically competitive category.

Although it may seem obvious that most firms are neither pure competitors nor pure monopolists, models of firm behavior in this vast middle ground were few and far between before the 1930s. The models that did exist seem incredibly naive in the light of the works of E. H. Chamberlin and Joan Robinson (see their Biography). Indeed, many economists would still argue that this area of economic theory is inadequate and that we need more general models of how firms that have less than complete monopoly power make decisions about output and prices.

Although it may be difficult to determine exactly which model of oligopoly or monopolistic competition best explains the behavior of a particular industry, several models are useful in analyzing the specific policies of some of our major companies. Economists have never claimed that all decisions could be explained by one or two simple economic models. As you study this chapter, however, you should gain insights into how the business world operates between the polar extremes of pure competition and unregulated monopoly.

Product Differentiation

The model of pure competition assumes that firms produce identical products. While this assumption may fit farmers and firms in a few other industries, most firms sell products that differ from those of their rivals. Differentiated products may be normal when our tastes and preferences are still in flux and may be a sign of competition in process. Homogeneity, on the other hand, may occur as a consequence of orders from some central authority. For example, covered wagons in typical Western movies are quite similar because the film industry has created an image and had them built to order. Most pioneers did not load their belongings into picturesque prairie schooners during the real migration to the Old West. They rode, instead, in a motley assortment of whatever wagons were available; two men from St. Louis reportedly moved their gear to Denver in a wheelbarrow in 1867. Nevertheless, companies use **product differentiation** to try to make us take special notice of their products or to value these products differently than those of rival firms.

Some people might argue that gasoline is gasoline, but the oil companies clearly feel that customers can be made to perceive differences through promotion and advertising. Another example is soap. Are there truly meaningful differences between All, Tide, and Dash laundry detergent? Soap makers spend millions each year to persuade us that there are. Ford, American Motors, GM, Chrysler, and numerous foreign producers, all sell automobiles that provide the same basic transportation services. Despite the fact that automobiles are similar in many ways, most of us have preferences for certain cars based on advertising, styling, the reputed frequency of repair, or our past experience.

Product differences can be real or illusory. Differentiation only requires that consumers perceive differences. An example of a differentiated product that is physically homogeneous is aspirin, which at one time was sold under the brand name Aspirin. All five-grain aspirins are pharmaceutically identical, but today many people buy nationally advertised brands of the drug rather than cheaper generic substitutes. Why? While physically identical, different brands of aspirin are not homogeneous in the eyes of all consumers because marketing programs create imagi-

E. H. Chamberlin (1899–1967) and Joan Robinson (1903–83)

Until Edward Hastings Chamberlin blended the theories of monopoly and competition, the case of many sellers offering differentiated products had been overlooked. Earlier mainstream economists concentrated on the theory of pure competition, which assumes many sellers of homogeneous products. Chamberlin instead saw close competitors in nearly every market attempting to gain monopoly power by differentiating their products. For example, a firm might allege the superiority of its product over "Brand X."

Born in La Conner, Washington, Chamberlin revised his Ph.D. dissertation from Harvard and published *The Theory of Monopolistic Competition* in 1933. This was one of the rare cases when a dissertation had a profound impact on economic theory. The central feature of Chamberlin's analysis is that it portrays the demand curves facing most firms as being negatively sloped due to product differentiation. Firms that successfully differentiate their products can raise prices without losing all their customers, although they do sell less output. This fact introduces elements of monopoly. In the long run, however, competition tends to lower this negatively sloped demand curve to a point of tangency with the firm's long run average cost curve so that no monopoly profits are realized. Chamberlin's theory combined with the ideas of the British economist Joan Robinson to spark numerous studies of industrial markets in the 1940s and 1950s.

"I don't know much math, so I have to think."

—*Joan Robinson*

An avowed radical and Marxist, the iconoclastic Joan Robinson was a combatant in virtually every major controversy in economic theory and policy from the 1930s through the 1970s. However, her friends and foes united in admiring her innovative ideas and research. She married the prominent economist E. A. G. Robinson shortly after completing her formal education and was among the small group of Cambridge University economists who aided John Maynard Keynes in launching the Keynesian Revolution.

At almost exactly the same time that Chamberlin issued his theory of monopolistic competition from Cambridge, Massachusetts, Joan Robinson launched a parallel theory from Cambridge, England in her *The Economics of Imperfect Competition*. However, Robinson's treatment of *imperfect competition* emphasizes oligopolistic interdependence and views competition and monopoly as mutually exclusive, while Chamberlin identified "monopolistic competition" in modern business as a fusion of the two. Robinson refined the theory of price discrimination, introduced the concept of *monopsony power* (that is, the ability of powerful buyers to control prices), and separated average revenue (demand) from marginal revenue curves.

Robinson's writings blended the insights of Keynes, Marx, and neoclassical reasoning in a manner uniquely her own. Her work bridged capital theory, the theories of value and distribution, macroeconomics, and the economics of policymaking, but her contributions in the area of imperfect competition were her most noteworthy. In Robinson's phrase, she and Chamberlin introduced a "box of tools" sharper and more generally applicable than those that preceded their analyses.

nary differences. Meaningless differences also can be found in many headache remedies or pain relievers that advertisements tell us contain "the ingredient that doctors recommend most." What we are not told is that the secret ingredient is aspirin; some folks seem convinced that "the more you pay, the more it's worth." Of course, product differentiation may also be real. Real differences in cars, for example, may be related to durability, styling, or service.

The value to firms of marketing programs and advertising that differentiate products is obvious. Purely competitive firms are price takers that sell identical products. Firms use product differentiation in attempts to increase the demands for their products and reduce their price elasticities. This provides these firms with some degree of monopoly power; they become price makers. A successful campaign to differentiate its product enables a firm to sell more product even if it raises the price.

In Figure 1, we show that product differentiation gives firms some control over price. Without this control, firms can only adjust output levels to maximize profits because the demand curve facing a purely competitive firm is perfectly elastic. Successful product differentiation expands the demand curve and makes it less elastic. One important result is that the marginal revenue curve now lies below the demand curve, much like that of the monopolist described in the previous chapter. Another result is that the prices charged vary among the firms in an industry in which differentiation is rampant.

The demands facing oligopolists or monopolistically competitive firms are more elastic than the industry (monopoly) demand since there are substitutes for these firms' products. Still, these firms can increase prices and not lose all their customers. Some of us will continue to eat Wheaties even if the price is raised a bit, but if General Mills boosts the price too much relative to the prices of other cereals, our loyalty fades and we feed our faces a bit differently.

Monopolistic Competition

Monopolistically competitive industries have three major characteristics:

1. A large number of potential suppliers.
2. Each firm's product is slightly different from others in the industry.
3. Entry or exit is relatively easy.

Thus, monopolistic competition is similar to pure competition in having easy entry or exit among many competitors, but differs in that each firm produces a differentiated product. Once a monopolistically com-

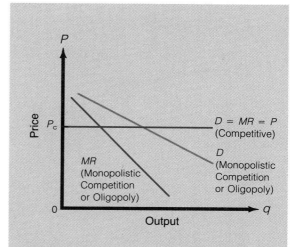

FIGURE 1 Product Differentiation and Firm Demand

There are numerous perfect substitutes for the output of competitive firms, so demand is perfectly elastic. The absence of perfect substitutes makes the demand for the output of a monopolistically competitive firm less than perfectly elastic. Because of this small amount of monopoly power, the marginal revenue curve for a monopolistically competitive firm is always below the price of the output. The fewness of competitors similarly causes oligopolists to possess monopoly power so that the demand curve exceeds the marginal revenue curve.

petitive firm differentiates its product to increase the magnitude and decrease the elasticity of the demand curve it confronts, it can act a little like a monopoly because it has acquired some monopoly power.

Short-Run Pricing and Output

The short-run price and output combination that maximizes profits is illustrated in Figure 2. Regardless of market structure, all firms maximize profits by selling that output where marginal revenue and marginal costs are equal. For the successful monopolistically competitive firm depicted in Figure 2, this is point a; output of q_0 is sold at a price of P_0. In the short run, this firm earns an economic profit equal to the shaded area. A monopolistically competitive firm might suffer losses in the short run; if the firm's average cost curve was everywhere greater than the

FIGURE 2 *Short-Run Profitable Equilibrium: Monopolistic Competition*

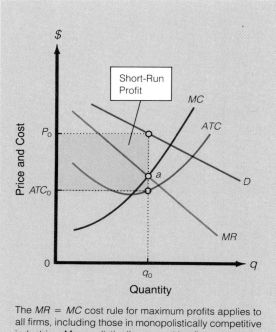

The *MR* = *MC* cost rule for maximum profits applies to all firms, including those in monopolistically competitive industries. Monopolistically competitive firms can make economic profits in the short run.

prevented, so the industry adjusts much like a purely competitive industry. As new firms enter and try to share in economic profits, prices are driven down and costs may rise, causing any profits to disappear. Prices must fall when new competitors expand their offerings and try to take customers from existing firms. This shrinks demands for successful firms' products, ultimately leaving them in an equilibrium of the sort illustrated in Figure 3. Marginal revenue and marginal cost are equal at point *a,* and the long-run average total cost curve (*LRAC*) is just tangent to the demand curve at point *b*. This tangency allows the firm to sell its product at a price just equal to average cost ($P_e = ATC_e$), resulting in only normal profits in the long run. However, price is above marginal cost ($P_e = ATC_e > MC$). The prices set by different firms in a monopolistically competitive industry vary because of product differentiation, but only within a fairly narrow range.

Notice how this long-run equilibrium compares with a purely competitive equilibrium. If this firm were in a purely competitive industry, equilibrium would be at point *c* and the firm would be producing more and selling its product at a lower price ($P_c = \min LRAC = MC$). Does this mean that society sustains economic losses due to inefficiency associated with monopolistic competition? The answer is MAYBE.

demand curve, profits would be impossible. However, like all firms, a monopolistic competitor would minimize losses by selling that output that equates marginal revenue and marginal cost, assuming that the price it could set (average revenue) exceeds average variable costs.

Long-Run Adjustments

Attempts by monopolistically competitive firms to differentiate their products are motivated not only by short-run profit opportunities but also by hopes of sustaining these profits in the long run. Unfortunately for them, typical monopolistically competitive firms earn only normal profits in the long run. A quick look at these industries' characteristics will tell you why.

Any economic profits could be preserved in the long run only if other firms could be barred from the economically profitable industry, but entry cannot be

Resource Allocation and Efficiency

Pure competitors and monopolistically competitive firms each earn only normal profits in the long run, so what are the possible sources of inefficiency in a monopolistically competitive market? The answer lies in the costs and benefits of product differentiation to consumers.

The price paid by consumers exceeds the marginal cost of production for the monopolistically competitive firm. Our analyses in the two preceding chapters suggested that pure competition is efficient because marginal social benefit equals marginal social cost ($P = MSC$) in a purely competitive equilibrium, but that a nondiscriminating unregulated firm with monopoly power is inefficient because in equilibrium the marginal social benefit exceeds the marginal social cost ($P > MSC$) of production. Because the price (marginal social benefit) charged by any monopolistically competitive firm exceeds its mar-

FIGURE 3 *Monopolistic Competition: Long-Run Equilibrium and Efficiency*

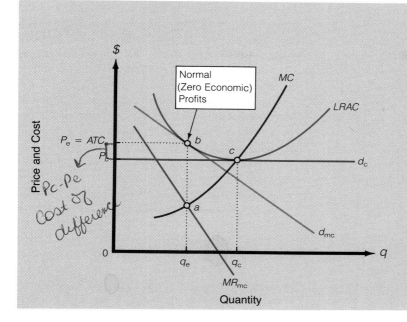

In the long run, entry and exit from the industry will prevent the monopolistically competitive firm from experiencing either economic profits or losses. Economic profits would be possible if the demand curve exceeded average costs over any range of output; economic losses would be unavoidable if the average cost was above demand at all output levels. Thus, competition yields an equilibrium where demand is just tangent to the average cost curve, and price equals average cost ($P = AC$). For the competitive firm in the long run, $P = MR = MC = ATC$, so there is economic efficiency. The long-run equilibrium for the monopolistically competitive firm is such that $P > MR$ and $MR = MC$. Even though $P = AC$, $P > MC$ suggests that there is economic inefficiency.

ginal cost, it appears that monopolistically competitive solutions are economically inefficient.

Some economists rebut this conclusion with the argument that any minor inefficiencies are the prices we pay for a greater range of choices. Suppose you do not value this diversity of substitutes and are unwilling to suffer losses from this type of economic inefficiency. One solution is to buy only generic or unbranded products. Alternatively, government could set specifications for various products and forbid firms to deviate from government formulas. You would be able to buy any Model T Ford you wanted—as long as it was black.

The other side of the coin is that some costs of product differentiation have nothing to do with styling, unique features, or other real differences. The economic inefficiency apparent whenever price exceeds marginal cost may arise, in the case of monopolistic competition, from wasteful advertising and promotion. For example, some social commentators believe that marketing campaigns may persuade buyers to purchase useless items or mislead consumers into thinking they need a particular brand product when in reality there are several close substitutes. Can you remember the worst advertisement you

have ever seen or heard? If so, the advertiser partially accomplished its goal by making an unforgettable impression.[1]

Most economists would argue that informative advertising or marketing provides consumers with extra services and more accurate information so that better economic choices can be made. *Informative advertising* conserves on resources because transaction costs are reduced. *Persuasive advertising* is clearly wasteful, however, as indicated in Figure 3. A purely competitive market determines a market price of P_c and each firm produces q_c units in the long run. Contrast this situation with the long-run output for monopolistic competition in this figure, in which we assume that advertising and promotion incorrectly persuade consumers that physically identical products differ in desirability and that consumers develop "brand loyalty." The price of the product is higher (P_e) and the quantity sold by each firm is less, q_e.

---

1. This point is made by Robert M. Kenney, "Emphasizing the Effect of Advertising on Consumer Choice," in *Great Ideas for Teaching Economics*, 2e, edited by R. T. Byrns and G. W. Stone (Scott, Foresman and Company, 1981).

Note that the monopolistically competitive firm has a higher equilibrium value for the average total cost curve than does the competitive firm. At the minimum point, the competitive firm could produce for P_c per unit; the comparable value for the monopolistically competitive firm is P_e. Advertising expenses and the costs of artificial differentiation account for this higher cost structure. The major resource allocation problem associated with the monopolistically competitive industry is that costs, and therefore prices, are higher and the output sold by each firm is less. This is similar to the results of unregulated monopoly, but the extent of any resource misallocation is less.

Is product differentiation desirable because consumers benefit from a greater range of choice, or is most product differentiation artificial and imaginary, a consequence of misleading promotion by monopolistically competitive firms? Your answer to this question indicates whether or not you think monopolistically competitive markets are economically efficient. It may be that your answer will vary from one industry to the next.

Oligopoly

Less competitive than monopolistically competitive industries, oligopolies lie towards the monopoly end of the spectrum of market structures. In an oligopoly market, a small number of producers control much of the industry's output. Because a few firms are dominant in an oligopoly, rivals are cognizant of each other's pricing and output policies. Thus, their behavior is based on **conscious interdependence.**

Few Firms Comprise the Industry

Oligopolistic markets are characterized by a small number of sellers of given products. What exactly is meant by the phrase *small number?* Certainly more than one firm, but would 10 or 20 sellers still be considered few? The answer is not clear-cut. What is critical is whether or not a handful of *interdependent* large companies consciously dominate an industry. If so, it is oligopolistic.

Concentration ratios are the percentages of sales by the largest four (or eight) companies in an industry. A quick glance at Figure 4 provides some examples of relatively concentrated industries. Industries are **pure oligopolies** if firms produce homogeneous outputs. Examples include the steel and aluminum industries. Industries are **impure oligopolies** if the products of the various firms are slightly differentiated. Tire makers and tobacco firms are impure oligopolists.

The term *concentration* is often used to identify oligopolistic industries. Figure 4 indicates that industries such as those that produce automobiles, tires, aircraft, and cigarettes are highly concentrated. In the aircraft industry, for example, the four largest firms generate 66 percent of the industry's total sales; the eight top firms account for 86 percent of the industry. Note, however, that you should be wary of relying too much on concentration ratios as indicators of monopoly power. First, these ratios only consider concentration by American firms over goods sold in the United States and there may be substantial competition from imports. Second, markets may be contestable if entry into an industry composed of very few firms is relatively easy. The industries toward the right in Figure 4, however, may be among the more oligopolistic industries in the United States.

Why Oligopoly Exists

There are three major causes of oligopoly: (*a*) economies of scale, (*b*) merger, and (*c*) substantial barriers to entry.

Economies of Scale   Technical efficiency for some products requires enormous plants and massive equipment. The industry gravitates into a natural monopoly when economies of scale are such that only a single firm of considerable size relative to the market is able to produce at a low cost. An industry tends toward the oligopoly mold if economies of scale are less formidable.

In a pioneering study of economies of scale and market structure, Joe Bain estimated that industries such as those producing copper, typewriters, and tractors require plants that can each supply more than 10 percent of the total market to be efficient. These industries, therefore, might be expected to be composed of ten or fewer firms. While Bain's study focused on manufacturing economies of scale, in some industries (automobiles, for example) there may be economies of scale in distribution that determine the optimal size of the efficient firm. Bain con-

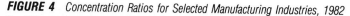

FIGURE 4 *Concentration Ratios for Selected Manufacturing Industries, 1982*

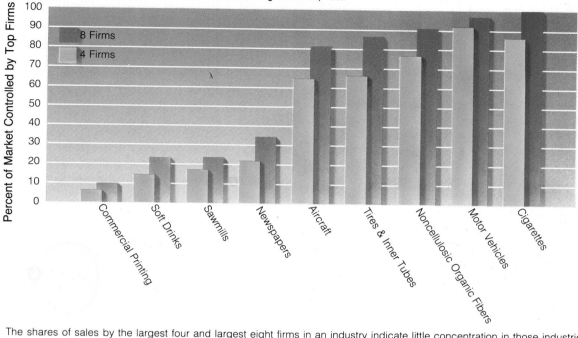

The shares of sales by the largest four and largest eight firms in an industry indicate little concentration in those industries toward the left side of this figure (e.g., commercial printing, soft drinks) but substantial concentration in those toward the right side (motor vehicles, cigarettes). These numbers must be taken with a grain of salt, however, because only the sales of domestic firms are considered. For example, inclusion of imports would cause a much lower concentration ratio for the automobile industry.

Source: U.S. Department of Commerce, Bureau of the Census, *1982 Census of Manufactures, Concentration Ratios in Manufacturing,* April 1986.

cluded, however, that the overall concentration of American industry was far greater than could be justified by economies of scale of any sort.

Although studies of efficient plant sizes are important, technology may change so rapidly that some industry studies are obsolete shortly after they are written. One of the offshoots of technological changes in the nineteenth century (e.g., steel, railroads) was pressure for ever larger plant sizes. Substantial barriers to entry exist if new techniques of production (e.g., robotics) are significant and require a large scale of operation. Experienced managers of existing firms may be able to adapt to new technologies rapidly, producing enough to meet market demands and making it virtually impossible for new firms to get a toehold in an industry. In the past two or three decades, technological advances in manufacturing (e.g., electronics) have probably been relatively less favorable to huge companies than to

small ones. However, some disadvantages of large firms may have been offset by improvements in communications and computerization of operations.

Artificial Barriers to Entry A second way that oligopolies prevent their markets from being contestable is by erecting artificial barriers to entry. For example, it is not unusual for existing firms to introduce model changes or to undertake excessive promotion campaigns. Annual model changes and expensive marketing programs may be beyond the financial capacities of potential entrants. Alternatively, existing firms may introduce numerous combinations of the basic product (such as differentiated cereals, cigarettes, or over-the-counter drugs), leaving little shelf space in retail outlets for potential competitors. Another strategy to bar entry occurs when lobbyists for mature (senile?) industries and their unions exert political pressures to erect import quotas and tariff walls to limit foreign competition. Textiles, automobiles, and steel are all industries that have received protection from foreign competition.

Merger Oligopolies are also created through **merger**—the absorption of one firm by another. A company may prefer to expand by merger rather than through the rockier path of using retained earnings, sales of new stock, or borrowing. Merger is often an easier route and may have the additional benefit of eliminating a competitor. Absorbing a direct competitor is called *horizontal merger*.

Recent *takeover* attempts by *corporate raiders* highlight the two sides of corporate mergers. Raiders argue that they inject new vigor into inefficiently managed firms. Predictably, the existing managers of takeover targets often fear for their own economic security, the jobs of employees, and the financial interests of stockholders. Communities become embroiled in these battles when a target company represents the town's economic lifeblood. Focus 1 examines some issues surrounding the recent increase in corporate raiding.

Mutual Interdependence

When there are only a few firms in the industry and entry is restricted, each firm recognizes that any successful strategy will be countered by others. For example, when Chrysler introduced big rebates in the late 1970s, General Motors and Ford met the challenge quickly with similar rebates, denying Chrysler its hoped-for advantage. When CBS aired the nighttime soap, "Dallas", NBC and CBS countered with "Knot's Landing", "Falcon Crest", "Dynasty", "Hotel" and other soap operas. Any successful competitive technique used by one oligopolist will be matched quickly by others as they attempt to maintain their respective market shares.

This mutual interdependence and assessment of rivals' expected reactions to changing policies results primarily from the paucity of firms dominating the industry. Successful decision making in oligopolistic industries depends on predicting competing firms' responses to any changes in prices or quality. If an oligopolistic company fails to analyze its rivals' reactions carefully and accurately, the bad news is ultimately reflected in the bottom line of its annual reports. The importance of predictability leads to pressures for cooperation among oligopolistic firms. You will see in a moment that this cooperation is neither in the interests of individual consumers nor society as a whole.

Oligopolistic Decision Making

The complexity of oligopolistic interdependence poses considerable problems for any analysis. Business rivals react to each other in many ways. An obvious strategy is for oligopolists to band together and act as a monopolistic unit, sharing both the market and monopoly profits. This is known as forming a cartel. Another tactic is to allow one firm to set prices for the entire industry. Price leadership models leave pricing decisions to the largest firm or to the one with the lowest cost structure.

There are many other assumptions that may describe cooperation and competition among the few, but models of oligopolistic scheming are generally either *collusive* or *noncollusive*. In the remainder of this chapter, we investigate only three of the many oligopoly models that have been proposed. The kinked demand curve and most limit-pricing models are noncollusive, while cartel models depend on collusion. Other, more complex oligopoly models are the topics of more advanced courses in economics.

Noncollusive oligopoly pricing may be natural if only a few firms comprise an industry. Each firm may realize that others will offset any strategy intended to increase market shares and profits. Alternatively, the industry may be dominated by a single firm that sets price policies for other companies to follow. Without overt agreements among the firms, prices are raised and lowered in unison.

For a long time it was thought that prices in highly concentrated industries were unresponsive to changes in costs or demands. The famous kinked demand curve model of oligopoly pricing sought to explain this "stickiness" of prices in oligopolistic industries as the natural result of noncollusive behavior.[2]

---

2. In his Nobel Prize acceptance address, George Stigler discouraged the use of kinked demand curves because of insufficient empirical support for sticky prices predicted by the model. Nevertheless, the kinked demand curve model is the *best* model to illustrate oligopolistic interdependencies.

FIGURE 5 *Price Stability and Cost Changes under Oligopoly (Kinked Demand Curve Model)*

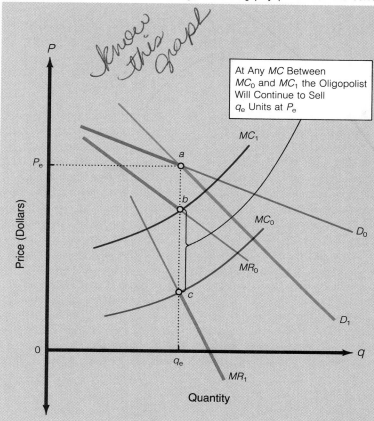

> At Any *MC* Between MC_0 and MC_1 the Oligopolist Will Continue to Sell q_e Units at P_e

If an oligopolist's competitors are likely to match any price reductions but ignore price increases, then the demand facing each firm is comparatively inelastic with respect to price cuts but is highly elastic in response to price hikes. Only the thicker portions of the demand and marginal revenue curves shown are relevant for such firms. Prices are "sticky" if oligopolistic firms face kinked demand curves. Even if costs change substantially, such firms will not alter their prices because they fear that none of their competitors will follow price hikes, but all will match price cuts.

The Kinked Demand Curve

The two basic assumptions behind the **kinked demand curve model** of oligopoly pricing behavior are:

1. Other firms maintain their current pricing policies if any firm raises its prices.
2. All firms match any price reductions by any single firm.

To see the importance of these assumptions, look at Figure 5. At point *a*, the price is currently P_e and q_e units of the product are sold by each firm in this pure oligopoly. Demand curve D_0 represents the highly elastic demand curve facing the firm if no other firms follow its price changes. If a firm is alone in lowering its price, it will gain appreciably in sales (a move-

ment along D_0 to the right of q_e). However, if the firm raises its price and the others do not follow, it will lose a considerable portion of its sales (movement along D_0 to the left of q_e). When one firm raises its prices and others do not, the competitors' products become better substitutes from the vantage point of consumers.

If rivals match all price changes, however, demand curve D_1 represents the firm's less elastic options. If the firm lowers its prices and all other firms do the same, the firm's sales increase very little. The firm's sales decrease very little if the firm raises its prices and so do its rivals. Along D_1 little is lost by any one firm to the others because their relative prices are constant. All that happens is that firms share in gains or losses of sales based on the elasticity of the total demand for the industry's product. The

Lollipops, Poison Pills, and Corporate Raiders

Competition stimulates managers to respond to rapidly evolving technologies . . . requires that firms adapt to changing market demands and calls upon them to adjust to fluctuating capital market conditions . . . breaks down entrenched market positions, unsettles comfortable managerial lives, and provides incentives for innovative forms of business organization and finance.

—Council of Economic Advisors (1985)

The first half of the 1980s witnessed a remarkable upsurge in huge corporate mergers. During 1981–83, five industries—oil and gas, banking and finance, insurance, mining and minerals, and food processing—accounted for over half of all mergers. Figure 6 illustrates this current merger and acquisition trend. Although the number of mergers and acquisitions has been relatively stable since the mid 1970s, there has been a sharp upward trend in the sizes of the companies merged. Thus, fewer deals have generated a larger dollar volume of merger and acquisition activity.

Many of these mergers were *hostile takeovers*—they were opposed by the existing management. This explosion of aggressive takeover activity has injected a colorful new vocabulary into the previously staid world of corporate finance: words like *greenmail, poison pills, lollipops, junk bonds, white knights,* and *cash cows* now pepper conversations along Wall Street.

Corporate raiding (*leveraged takeovers*) uses creative financing to acquire a controlling interest in an undervalued corporation. A new firm is typically incorporated from which to launch the takeover. Investment bankers then put together a package of *junk bonds* (risky bonds with low credit ratings) to be issued by the paper corporation once it gains control through a *tender offer* (an offer to purchase a given percent of existing stock of the target company for a premium price). The investment bankers obtain commitments from pension funds and other institutional investors to buy the junk bonds after the tender offer is accepted.

FIGURE 6 *Trends in Merger and Acquisition Activity*

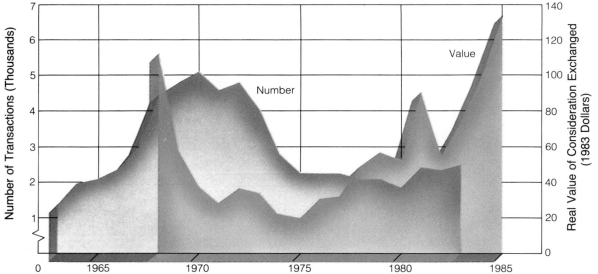

Source: From *Economic Report of the President,* 1985. Reprinted by permission of W. T. Grimm and Company. Data measure only publicly announced transactions and include transfers of ownership of 10 percent or more of a company's assets or equity, provided the value of the transaction is at least $500,000.00.

Once in control, raiders raise cash by selling off pieces of the acquired company. As one takeover expert says, "We take a minnow, identify a whale, then look to its assets to finance the transaction." Thus, small but aggressive firms can absorb much larger corporations. The most attractive candidates for acquisition, called *cash cows,* are firms that generate massive cash flows but whose stocks are undervalued by the market.

Managers of targeted firms wield many defensive weapons, including

1. Greenmail—buying the raider's stock back at a premium.
2. Poison pills—requirements that any acquirer of a target company sell stock in the merged entity at half price to current shareholders.
3. Lollipops—using notes to buy large blocks of its own stock at a huge premium, but excluding the raider from the offer.
4. White Knights—finding a buyer that the company prefers to the raider.

Figure 7 summarizes a study of 429 tender offers which concluded that hostility towards a takeover was greater when the incumbent management owned less stock. As managers' stockholdings rise, the average potential wealth gain to management increases and is reflected in a greater likelihood of a friendly response.

Public Policy

Public policy toward corporate raiding should depend on whether takeovers are socially beneficial. Proponents of a laissez-faire approach to mergers argue that raiding is simply a part of the process of vigorous competition described by Joseph Schumpeter as "creative destruction." They contend that takeovers facilitate (*a*) production and distribution economies in related industries, (*b*) technology transfers, (*c*) lower per unit costs, (*d*) shifting of assets to higher valued uses, and (*e*) improved management.

Opponents of hostile corporate takeovers charge that raiding increases concentration, encourages managers to focus on short-term performance at the expense of long-term growth, and imposes severe economic losses on our society. They also argue that corporate managers are responsible not only to stockholders, but to other *stakeholders* including employees, customers, suppliers, and the communities in which they operate. These opponents would widen the "social responsibilities" of American corporations.

The latest wave of mergers may already have crested. Congress considered stricter regulation of corporate takeovers, but backed off when the stock market boomed in 1985–86. The incentives for takeovers melted away as the market values of previously underpriced stocks soared. If the dip in merger activity in 1985–86 proves to be only temporary, we may see a renewal of interest in regulation of takeovers.

Source: "The Market for Corporate Control," Economic Report of the President, *1985, Chapter 6.*

FIGURE 7   Target Management Responses to and Outcomes of Takeover Attempts, 1978–83

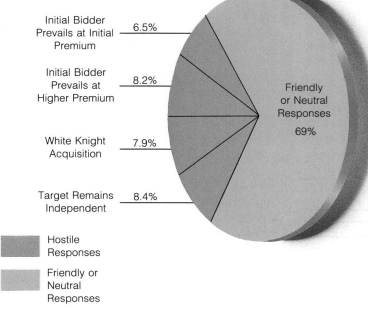

Initial Bidder Prevails at Initial Premium — 6.5%

Initial Bidder Prevails at Higher Premium — 8.2%

White Knight Acquisition — 7.9%

Target Remains Independent — 8.4%

Friendly or Neutral Responses 69%

Hostile Responses

Friendly or Neutral Responses

Source: From Economic Report of the President, 1985. Reprinted by permission of W. T. Grimm and Company.

respective marginal revenue curves for D_0 and D_1 are labeled MR_0 and MR_1.

The assumptions that underlie this model imply that only a portion of each curve is relevant; price decreases will be duplicated by rivals, but price increases will not. The appropriate demand curve for its product from the firm's point of view is the thicker portion of the D_0 curve for outputs less than q_e, and the thicker portion of D_1 for outputs above q_e. The corresponding portions of the marginal revenue curves are emphasized similarly. Note that the relevant marginal revenue curve has a discontinuity (gap) at output q_e between points b and c, which corresponds to the "kink" in the firm's demand curve; hence, the name kinked demand curve.

The importance of the kink in the demand curve and the discontinuity in the marginal revenue curve is illustrated in Figure 5. Profit-maximizing behavior requires producing where marginal revenue equals marginal cost, so q_e output is sold at a price of P_e as long as the marginal cost curve stays between MC_0 and MC_1. Thus, this model explains why prices might be relatively sticky in oligopolistic industries even if costs of production change. Marginal cost can rise from point c to point b without necessitating any change in price.

Although this kinked demand curve theory seems to be based on reasonable assumptions about rivalry in oligopolistic markets, critics of the model have pointed out some serious problems. First, price rigidity does not seem to be more the norm in oligopolistic industries than in other industries.[3] Firms in concentrated industries appear to quickly pass cost increases along as they occur. After all, competing on the basis of advertising, product quality, and new product development may increase costs without significantly expanding demand. If profits are squeezed for one firm only, there is little that one firm can do but hold to the current price. However, if profits of all oligopolists within an industry are under pressure, all firms might follow the one that raises price and form a new kink at the higher price level.

Second, kinked demand curve models do not explain why entry fails to occur, nor how oligopoly emerges. A third deficiency is that the kinked demand curve model provides no insight as to how

equilibrium price, P_e, is established. Finally, these models offer little insight into how prices change. These problems have caused the model to be used only sparingly by researchers. The major advantage of the kinked demand curve model is its simplicity in conveying the flavor of strategic business behavior when few firms compete in a market.

Limit Pricing to Deter Entry

Kinked demand curve models do not explain how oligopolistic industries arrive at equilibrium prices or how prices change, nor do they explain how oligopolies are maintained over the long run. If an industry is earning economic profits, presumably other firms will desire to share in these profits. Entry would swell industry supplies over time and create excess capacities at existing market prices, forcing prices down. This ultimately will eliminate or reduce profitability in the industry.

Limit-pricing models attempt to rectify these failings of kinked demand curve models; limit-pricing strategies by oligopolists depend on high fixed costs that yield substantial economies of scale, so that small firms suffer significant cost disadvantages relative to large ones. By setting a price below the short-run profit-maximizing price, existing firms make it unprofitable for new firms to enter the industry. Existing firms earn lower profits in the short run, but there is no way for a new firm to enter the business profitably. By setting lower prices and producing more, existing firms can deter entry by new firms and ensure long-run economic profits.

Will established oligopolists pursue a limit-pricing strategy, or will they collude to set the monopoly price in the near term, knowing that high prices and profits will encourage entry and thereby reduce profits in the long run? The answer depends on how low the limit price must be to deter entry and on comparisons of the profitability associated with taking monopoly profits now versus barring entry. If companies are more concerned with profits today and discount future profits heavily, higher short-run prices that attract more competition will result. The answer may depend on the size of the individual firms. Larger firms may be more worried than smaller firms about long-run profits since the smaller firms may view short-run profits as sources for potential growth.

---

3. This was the finding of George Stigler, reported in "The Kinky Oligopoly Demand Curve and Rigid Prices," *Journal of Political Economy*, October 1947, pp. 432–49.

Maintaining the entry-deterring price may require illegal collusion by the existing firms. Whether or not collusion will be required is related closely to the number of firms that dominate an industry. The more firms there are, the more likely that collusion will be required for successful limit pricing. The sparseness of evidence of collusion in the United States today has proven a stumbling block to widespread acceptance of collusive limit-pricing models.

Cartels

A **cartel** is an organization of firms that jointly make decisions regarding prices and production for the entire group. For most Americans, OPEC (Organization of Petroleum Exporting Countries) has made the term *cartel* a household word. Most Americans would not have recognized the word before 1973–74, when OPEC became a common topic of conversation.

Cartels generally require outright collusion among member firms. However, if the industry is sufficiently concentrated (two or three firms), tacit collusion is possible. Collusive price-fixing agreements for most manufactured products are illegal in the United States but are quite legal in many international markets. Consequently, all well-known cartels operate in international markets.

Numerous cartels exist today, primarily in markets for natural resources. International cartels control most of the sales in markets for such basic resources as copper, tin, bauxite (used to produce aluminum), diamonds, chrome, phosphate, petroleum, coffee, and bananas. Many of these cartels are coordinated by the governments of the major producing countries. In the past, the markets for many other commodities were cartelized, including sugar, rubber, nitrates, steel, radium, magnesium, and electric lights. Why do cartels seem to come and go? What characteristics are required to form and maintain a cartel? How do cartels set prices and production?

Cartel Requirements   The first and most important requirement for the formation and effective maintenance of any cartel over time is that its members have control over the bulk of production. Cartels have trouble maintaining high prices if numerous fringe competitors are not members. In addition, this control must be concentrated in a few hands. A small group will be more likely than a large group to agree about pricing and output strategies because the members of any group will have different goals and objectives. The product also must be rather homogeneous; there cannot be close substitutes for successfully cartelized products. Cartelization might occur in a highly diverse market, but agreement would be needed for an array of prices. Once the cartel price is established, sales territories or production quotas must be set. Doing this for multiple goods and prices would be extremely difficult.

Cartelization will be facilitated the less elastic the total demand for the product. A cartel's ability to raise both price and total revenue requires an inelastic market demand for its product. Less elastic demand also makes excess capacity less of a problem as the price is increased. Finally, some method is needed to monitor member compliance and prevent cheating.

Cartel Pricing Policies   Once a cartel is formed, its members must decide what price to charge and how much to sell. Most cartels try to price like a monopolist and sell the monopoly output. This approach is called **joint-profit maximization** and is diagrammed in Panel A of Figure 8. The cartel sets price at P_0 and restricts the combined output of its members to Q_0. The monopoly profit (shaded) is the largest profit obtainable for the industry, but a central problem remains: sharing the output and profit among the members of the cartel.

Allocating production is done in numerous ways, depending on the nature of the product and the market. In some instances, exclusive market territories are assigned; each firm agrees to sell only in its own territory. Where this approach is unworkable, production (*output*) quotas are established for each firm. This is the present approach of the OPEC cartel. Each member country agrees to limit its sales to the quota of crude oil specified by the OPEC cartel leadership.

Cheating   There are many incentives to cheat in a cartel. Assume for a moment that you are one of ten members of the cartel described in Panel A of Figure 8 and are currently selling your equal share ($q_0 = Q_0/10$) of the total output Q_0 at the cartel set price P_0. Your firm's marginal cost curve is shown in Panel B of Figure 8. At q_0 output, your profits equal $C_0 P_0 xy$ in Panel B, which is the equivalent of $C_0 P_0 xy$ in Panel A, once we adjust for differences in scale between Panels A and B.

FIGURE 8 *Cartels and the Incentive to Cheat*

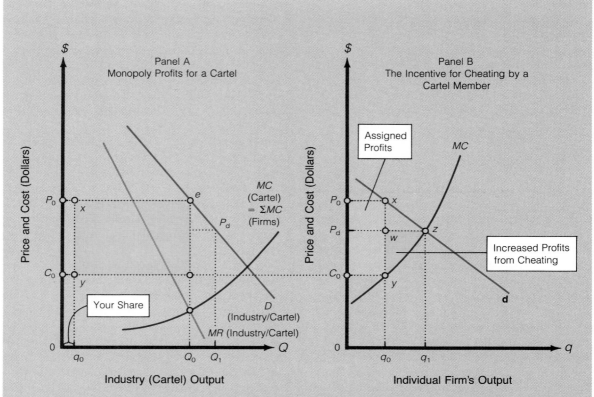

A cartel is intended to permit firms in an industry to share monopoly profits (Panel A). However, each firm can increase its own profits by offering secret price concessions to other firms' customers, or by servicing unmet demand (Panel B). Thus, there is a powerful incentive for cartel members to cheat, and cartels tend to be unstable. However, when governments help in establishing or perpetuating cartels, any cheating is easier to control, so moderately stable cartels may result.

If you can persuade all your competitors to maintain the cartel price (P_0) and then secretly offer a discounted price P_d to selected customers, you will increase your profits by: (*a*) taking away some of their customers and (*b*) servicing some of the demand that is unmet because of this higher cartel price. The marginal revenue to you from cheating exceeds your marginal cost. Your profits will increase because (*a*) you are not giving price cuts to your assigned customers (*b*) your competitors do not give price cuts to the customers they retain and (*c*) you can sell to more buyers—the customers who will not buy at a cartel price of P_0, but who are willing to pay P_d for $Q_1 - Q_0$ amounts of product. Your profits will rise by the area *ywz* in Panel B, which is the

difference between your marginal cost of producing extra output $q_1 - q_0$ and the price P_d you receive for each extra unit of production.

Instability Cheating on a cartel agreement can be profitable, but only if the cheater is undetected. If widespread cheating is uncovered, cartel agreements collapse and the members may all cut prices and behave in a fairly competitive fashion, with the result that the profits that originally motivated formation of the cartel vanish. The fact that undetected cheating offers the prospect of great profits is one of the greatest threats to the stability of a cartel.

Is cheating likely to go unnoticed? Nobel Prize-winning economist George Stigler has noted that:

The detection of secret price-cutting will of course be as difficult as interested people can make it. The price cutter will certainly protest his innocence, or, if this would tax credulity beyond its taxable capacity, blame a disobedient subordinate. The price cut will often take the indirect form of modifying some non-price dimension of the transaction. The customer may, and often will, divulge price reductions, in order to have them matched by others, but he will learn from experience if each disclosure is followed by the withdrawal of the lower price offer. Indeed the buyer will frequently fabricate wholly fictitious price offers to test the rivals. Policing the collusion sounds very much like the subtle and complex problem presented in a good detective story.[4]

In addition to the profitability associated with cheating, there are other hazards to the stability of cartels. Where individual sales to customers are large and relatively infrequent, there will be incentives to give customers price concessions to ensure that you keep them as customers. Where the production process is characterized by large economies of scale or the industry has high fixed costs, there will be a tendency for price cutting during periods of reduced demand so that overhead costs can be spread across larger output and sales. For example, cracks in the effectiveness of OPEC appeared during the international recession of 1981–83: worldwide consumption shrank, and an oil glut emerged because OPEC members routinely cheated and exceeded their quotas, offering crude oil at averages of from $3 to $8 below the $34-per-barrel official price.

Perhaps the most dangerous of all threats to a cartel is that high prices and profits will induce potential competitors to enter the industry or to develop substitutes for the cartel's products. For example, there was increasing emphasis on developing alternatives to petroleum as an energy source after the OPEC cartel became effective and increased the price of oil by around 1,000 percent during 1974–81. A second example is Brazilian coffee. From World War II into the 1970s, the Brazilian government cut back export permits to bolster the price of coffee. Result? Brazilian coffee declined as a percentage of the world market as new coffee producers were attracted by high prices.

Profits would increase in most industries if competitive firms were free to collude about prices, enforce output quotas or territories, and prevent the

entry of new competitors. Consequently, history is rich with instances of attempted cartelization. OPEC and cartels in diamonds, coffee, and bananas are evidence that such combinations may be successful, at least in the short run. These organizations are seen as blueprints for success by the producers of many raw materials and primary products throughout the world. Most have ultimately failed because of cheating, inability to deter entry, or government prosecution. Focus 2 indicates that the breakdown of OPEC took quite a while. All long-term successful cartels have depended on government regulation and intergovernmental cooperation to prevent cheating and deter entry; rarely do cartels survive without government support.

Most cartels violate U.S. antitrust legislation, the subject of our next chapter, but even in the United States, laws against cartelization largely exempt agricultural cooperatives, athletic organizations, labor unions, such professional bodies as the American Medical Association, and certain types of exporters. Farmer organizations, the AFL-CIO, the AMA, and similar associations all act as loose cartels to restrict output and hold prices up, primarily by limiting the entry of new suppliers. Similarly, the National Collegiate Athletic Association (NCAA) is a legal "buyers' cartel," which has rules against paying their workers (college athletes) more than room, board, and tuition. Unfortunately, every year another coach or school is sanctioned by the NCAA for cartel violations. Some schools have even withdrawn from NCAA athletics as a result of cheating scandals. Such organizations act as cartels in the United States.

Evaluating Oligopoly

What can we say about oligopolistic industries compared to purely competitive or monopolistically competitive industries? Firms in oligopolistic industries have considerable monopoly power, yielding economic inefficiency similar to that described for monopoly. In equilibrium, the marginal social benefit (price) of their products exceeds the marginal social cost. Compared with competitive or monopolistically competitive industries, output will tend to be less and prices to consumers will be higher.

If oligopoly is a result of economies of scale, however, the possibility exists that consumers could end up paying lower prices than would be true in a com-

---

4. George J. Stigler, *The Organization of Industry* (Homewood, IL: Richard D. Irwin, Inc., 1968), p. 44.

FOCUS 2

The Rise and Fall of OPEC

Crude oil prices ranged between $1.80 and $4.00 per barrel from World War II until the 1970s, while gasoline ranged from $0.22 to $0.35 per gallon, including taxes. The Organization of Petroleum Exporting Countries (OPEC), formed late in the 1960s, was a sleeping giant that exercised little economic clout until 1974–75. Figure 9 shows that when this giant cartel finally awoke, it did so with a vengeance.

During 1974–75 alone, OPEC raised the price of crude oil from $4 to $10 per barrel. Output quotas were assigned to OPEC members and, with only limited cheating, these production limits were honored for a brief period. Price hikes continued, with a barrel of oil hitting the $20 mark by 1977, $30 in 1980, and finally peaking at an official price of $34 per barrel in 1982–83. By 1986, however, the spot price of oil had fallen to less than $15 per barrel, and gasoline had fallen from its high of

$1.45 in 1981 to around $0.70 per gallon. After adjusting for inflation, the real prices of petroleum products were close to pre-OPEC levels. What happened?

Part of the answer is the demand side. The long-term growth of world oil consumption dropped sharply throughout this era. Most industrialized nations are oil importers and skyrocketing oil prices slowed the rate of economic growth and precipitated high unemployment and substantial inflation in much of the world from 1974–83. Growth in the demand for oil also shriveled because its high price stimulated energy conservation: more insulation was put into private residences, office buildings, and manufacturing facilities; cars and planes were modified to achieve greater fuel efficiency; and industry adopted less energy-intensive technology.

The other key to the collapse of OPEC's high prices came from the supply side. The late 1970s were an era of

feverish exploration for new sources of energy. Vast pools of oil were developed in such areas as Mexico, Alaska, and the North Sea. Coupled with the decline in world energy demand, these swelling supplies of non-Opec oil put pressure on individual OPEC members to boost their output because they relied heavily on oil exports for their national income.

Cheating by OPEC members who exceeded their assigned quotas was relatively minor in the 1970s, but so many members were violating the OPEC agreements that by 1984 the spot price of oil was $4 to $8 below the official $34 price. Oil flooded the world market, and the price plummeted. Although OPEC had enjoyed substantial success for almost a decade, the growth of external supplies and cheating had seriously undermined the OPEC cartel by 1986. Whether these forces have been fatal to the long-term effectiveness of the OPEC cartel remains to be seen.

FIGURE 9   *Oil and Gas Prices on a Roller Coaster*

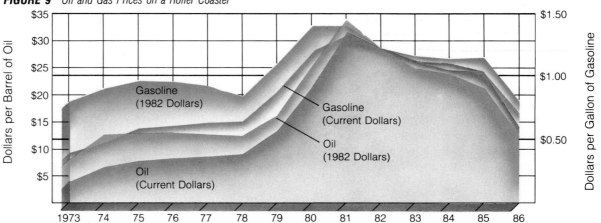

OPEC drove up the prices of oil and gasoline substantially during 1974–81. By 1986, however, conservation, the development of non-OPEC sources of energy, and the growth of cheating on limits to production by OPEC members appeared to have doomed the success of this oil cartel.

Source: U.S. Department of Commerce, Bureau of the Census, *Statistical Abstract of the United States,* 1986, and *Economic Report of the President,* 1986.

petitive market. Furthermore, if research and development (R&D) leading to technological change requires massive outlays, small competitive firms may be unable to finance adequate innovation. Some economists suggest that society benefits over the long run when expenditures for these purposes by large oligopolistic firms are made possible only by short-term monopoly profits.

Evidence on the effects of oligopolies is mixed. In some instances, economies of scale prevail in an industry and are responsible for its oligopolistic nature. In other instances, satisfactory economies of scale can be realized by smaller firms, and oligopoly is sustained only because of artificial barriers to entry. Finally, the evidence does not support the idea that large firms are especially responsible for new inventions and technological advances in our economy. If anything, it appears that the desire for increased monopoly power has been the driving force behind the creation of most oligopolies.

CHAPTER REVIEW: KEY POINTS

1. Most markets in the United States fit neither the competitive nor the monopoly molds. The bulk of industries are either monopolistically competitive or oligopolistic.

2. *Product differentiation* refers to differences that consumers perceive in products that are close substitutes. These differences can be real or imagined. They are created by such things as advertising and promotion and/or by differences in the actual goods. Product differentiation is intended to expand the demand for the firm's output and make demand less elastic.

3. *Monopolistic competition* occurs when entry into an industry is easy and there are large numbers of suppliers of slightly differentiated products. Product differentiation allows some firms to acquire monopoly power. Demands for a competitive firm's products are perfectly elastic (horizontal at the market price), but the monopolistically competitive firm's demand curve is negatively sloped, though still highly elastic.

4. Monopolistically competitive firms produce and sell levels of output that equate marginal revenue and marginal cost. The price is then determined by demand. This is similar to pure monopoly, but the level of short-run monopoly profits will generally be smaller, given that numerous other firms sell closely substitutable products.

5. Entry is relatively easy in monopolistically competitive markets, so accounting profits are reduced to normal levels (zero economic profits) in the long run. However, equilibrium output will be less and prices will be higher under monopolistic competition than in purely competitive markets. These higher prices and lower levels of production are the price consumers pay for product differentiation.

6. Oligopolies emerge for several reasons. Some products require substantial investment in plant and equipment so that efficient production requires servicing a considerable portion of the total industry demand. *Mergers* also facilitate the creation of oligopolies by joining competitors into single firms. Finally, oligopolies may exist because of legal or other artificial barriers to entry that deter new firms from entering the industry.

7. An *oligopoly* is an industry comprised of a few sellers who recognize their mutual interdependence. Competitive strategies by one firm in the industry will normally be countered by the other sellers.

8. There are hundreds of oligopoly pricing models, but they break down into two major categories: *collusive* and *noncollusive*. The *kinked demand curve model* assumes that if one firm raises its prices, other firms will ignore the increase, while if the firm lowers its price, other firms in the industry will match the price cut. The result is a demand curve for the firm that is kinked at the current equilibrium price. This irregularity leads to a discontinuity (gap) in the marginal revenue curve. Consequently, changes in costs may not lead to changes in prices. This theory leads to forecasts of "sticky" prices in oligopolistic industries, but they have not been borne out empirically. Kinked demand curve models also fail to explain how the original equilibrium price is established, or how prices change.

9. *Limit pricing* is another model of how oligopolists maintain their market power by deterring entry. Oligopolists may establish a low price, making it unprofitable for new firms to enter the industry. Existing firms then accept lower short-run profits to preserve economic profits over the long run.

10. A *cartel* is an effort by firms in an industry to collude, setting prices and limiting output for all of its members. Cartels must be concentrated in the hands of a few firms that control significant proportions of an industry's output. The product needs to

be reasonably homogeneous, since agreements regarding heterogeneous products would be complicated and difficult to enforce.

11. Cartels try to *maximize joint profits* (act like monopolists) and then allocate territories or industry output quotas by agreement among their members. The stability of any cartel is threatened by the profitability associated with undetected price cuts, or "cheating"; by potential new entrants who seek to share in profits; and by adverse legal action. Collusion is illegal in most markets in the United States.

12. Industry output will be less and prices will be higher under oligopoly than in competitive or monopolistically competitive markets. Arguments have been advanced that suggest that monopoly profits for large firms are necessary to finance extensive research and development activities and facilitate technological advance. The evidence does not confirm this hypothesis.

QUESTIONS FOR THOUGHT AND DISCUSSION

1. Are the following examples of persuasive or informative advertising?
   a. Newspaper want ads. I
   b. "Coke's the one." P
   c. "Merrill Lynch is 'bullish' on America." P
   d. "Del Monte now offers more than twenty Mexican food products." (TV ad.) I
   e. "Symphony Homes—spacious mountainview living for as little as $59,950." I
   f. "Allstate—the 'good hands' people." P
   g. Coupons for new products in grocery store advertisements. I
   h. "You could drive from here to the moon and back before the gas you'd save with a Toyota would be worth more than the money you'd save buying a Pontiac." I
   i. "Buy a new Dodge before March 30 and get a $500 rebate from Chrysler." I
   j. "Use _____, the cough medicine more doctors recommend." P

2. What factors enabled the OPEC cartel to raise prices so dramatically during the 1970s? What factors contributed to the difficulties experienced by OPEC in the 1980s?

3. The term *invention* covers the research and development of a product or technique. *Innovation* means implementing an invention into production. Can you cite three major inventions made by organizations that were small at the time? Three major innovations by firms with oligopoly power?

4. In the 1950s and 1960s, IBM had a stranglehold in the computer industry, Xerox had a near-monopoly in copying equipment, and Polaroid was the only producer of "instant picture" cameras. What has happened in these markets since then? *more competition*

5. One unusual model of oligopoly suggests that firms will attempt to capture as large a share of the market as possible by locating in the center of the markets. This model suggests that people will not be served if they want substantially different products than the majority of people. According to the developer of this model, Harold Hotelling, this accounts for such things as parallel programming by television networks, the middle-of-the-road images sought by politicians, the homogeneity of apple cider, the similarities between Protestant churches, and the phenomenon of four gas stations at the corners of busy intersections, among other things. How do you think his view that there is too little product differentiation stacks up against the view that monopolistic competition causes too much artificial product differentiation?

6. What is the essential difference between a price taker and a price maker? Is the difference between IBM and the corner grocery store one of quantitative dimensions rather than qualitative? If not, what are the qualitative differences between the two firms? At what percent of the market does monopoly power become significant?

7. What evidence might you look for if you wished to discover whether or not some concentrated industry was contestable and thus vulnerable to competition?

8. Standard economic models predict that whenever firms wield monopoly power, price will exceed marginal cost and, hence, there will be inefficiency in equilibrium. These models assume that there is only a single price for a given good, but the reality is that quantity discounts, coupons, and other marketing promotions commonly create tremendous disparities in prices at any point in time. Does the pervasiveness of price discrimination counter much of the argument that monopolistically competitive or oligopolistic markets are inherently inefficient? Why or why not?

CHAPTER 26 Antitrust Policy: Reducing Monopoly Power

Lerner index of
  monopoly power
  (LMP)
concentration ratio
Herfindahl-Hirschman
  index (HHI)
promotional profits

Sherman Antitrust Act
Clayton Act
Federal Trade
  Commission (FTC)
  Act
Robinson-Patman Act

Celler-Kefauver
  Antimerger Act
rule of reason
per se doctrine
conscious parallelism
  of action

The game of Monopoly (the one with "Boardwalk" and "Park Place") ends when one player acquires enough property (preferably with hotels) to bankrupt the remaining players when they land on any of it. A similar fate (but with a twist) was predicted for capitalism by Karl Marx. He believed that the bankrupt and exploited masses eventually would overthrow monopolists and create a new economic structure.

Marx suggested that an ever smaller group of capitalists would own all capital in the system, driving wages to the bare minimum necessary for human maintenance (just above starvation levels). Workers (the *proletariat*) eventually would tire of this exploitation and would unite to overcome oppressive capitalists and create the ultimate social order that Marx envisioned. The evidence suggests that this prediction is inaccurate for the United States and other developed countries because all communist revolutions to date have occurred in largely agricultural

countries. Moreover, these revolutions seem to have centered on political issues rather than economic issues per se.

Does this imply that capitalists are not greedy or will not attempt to control and exploit markets? Clearly not. Adam Smith recognized that business owners will collude to acquire monopoly profits when he noted that, "People of the same trade seldom meet together, even for merriment and diversion, but the conversation ends in a conspiracy against the public, or in some contrivance to raise prices." Smith also felt that business commonly entered into collusive agreements to "sink the wages of labor."[1] Smith and other classical economists viewed monopolies and conspiracies to monopolize with disdain.

---

1. Adam Smith, *An Inquiry Into the Nature and Causes of the Wealth of Nations*, 1776, Book I.

The history of trusts and monopolies over the past two centuries suggests that capitalists can be greedy and have attempted to gain monopoly positions in numerous industries. Farmer uprisings of a century ago, spurred by the farmers' feelings that they were exploited by early railroads, are one example of groups in revolt against what they considered exorbitant prices.

The preceding three chapters focused on the unfettered consequences of the four main market structures. Pure competition yields the greatest economic efficiency and unregulated monopoly the least. Many people also believe monopoly power causes inequity in the division of income. This chapter centers on how government might prevent monopolistic abuses in a market economy and concludes with an evaluation of the effectiveness of these methods. Before we consider them, we will take a quick look at industry's current structure and discuss the inferences for the economic performance of the hundreds of thousands of firms in our economy.

In the absence of easy entry, as the average size of the largest firms in an industry grows relative to the entire market, the industry approaches a monopolistic structure. There is a tendency for people to think that *bigness* and *monopoly power* are synonymous. However, if an industry is huge, it may contain many large firms, none of which has significant monopoly power. There can be competition among giants. In many instances, big corporations are the result of technology, economies of scale, or the nature of the product.

Measuring Market Power

How can we tell if monopoly power is increasing or decreasing in a particular market? We might rely on hunches, but more scientific approaches have attempted to develop quantitative estimates of the market power concentrated in the hands of a few firms in a given industry.

The Lerner Index of Monopoly Power

The theory presented in the last three chapters suggests that, as monopoly power increases, the gap between marginal cost and price widens. This led

Abba P. Lerner to propose the **Lerner index of monopoly power (*LMP*)**, which is defined as:

$$LMP = \frac{price - marginal\ cost}{price}.$$

The Lerner index will equal zero for a purely competitive industry because price and marginal cost will be equal. The use of monopoly power causes *LMP* to grow because the equilibrium gap between price and marginal cost rises. The major problem in measuring market power with the Lerner index is that estimating marginal cost with accounting data is difficult. This led some researchers to calculate Lerner indices using average cost rather than marginal cost data. Such estimates have a major drawback: purely competitive industries that temporarily enjoyed economic profits would be interpreted as monopolistic. Moreover, existing firms may reduce prices to inhibit entry (limit pricing), and *LMP* would interpret such reductions in price relative to marginal or average costs as diminished market power.

Market Concentration Ratios

Another method of estimating market power relies on market concentration ratios of the type discussed in the previous chapter. A market **concentration ratio** can be calculated as the percentage of total industry sales, employment, assets, value-added, or output accounted for by the largest four or eight firms, although any number of firms could be used. Table 1 presents some recent concentration ratios for sales in the commercial printing and aircraft industries.

TABLE 1 Concentration Ratios: Commercial Printing and Aircraft, 1982

	Percent of Industry Shipments (Sales)	
Number of Firms	**Commercial Printing**	**Aircraft**
Largest 4	6	64
Largest 8	10	81
Largest 20	17	98
Largest 50	24	99+

Source: U.S. Department of Commerce, Bureau of the Census, MC 82–5–7, 1982 Census of Manufactures (Washington, D.C.: U.S. Government Printing Office, April 1986.)

TABLE 2 Concentration Ratios for Selected Industries, 1967–82

Industry	Percent of Shipments					
	Four Largest Firms		Eight Largest Firms		Total Number of Firms	
	1967	1982	1967	1982	1967	1982
Motor vehicles and car bodies	92	92	98	97	107	284
Cigarettes	81	(D)	100	(D)	8	8
Telephone, telegraph apparatus	92	76	96	83	82	259
Organic fibers, noncellulosic	84	77	94	91	22	44
Tires and inner tubes	70	66	89	86	119	108
Aircraft	69	64	89	81	91	139
Photographic equipment	69	74	81	86	505	723
Soap and other detergents	70	60	78	73	599	642
Motor vehicle parts and accessories	60	61	68	69	1,424	2,000
Blast furnaces and steel mills	48	42	66	64	200	211
Electronic computing equipment	66	40	83	57	134	685
Farm machinery and equipment	44	53	56	62	1,526	1,787
Petroleum refining	33	28	57	48	276	282
Construction machinery	41	42	53	52	578	817
Pharmaceutical preparations	24	26	40	42	791	584
Paper mills	26	22	43	40	203	135
Bread, cake, and related products	26	34	38	47	3,445	1,869
Periodicals	24	20	37	31	2,430	3,143
Radio & TV communications equipment	22	22	37	35	1,111	2,083
Newspapers	16	22	25	34	7,589	7,520
Sawmills and planing mills	11	17	15	23	10,016	5,810
Bottled and canned soft drinks	13	14	20	23	3,057	1,236
Commercial printing, letterpress	14	14	21	19	11,955	10,211
Commercial printing, lithographic	5	6	8	10	6,718	17,332

Source: U.S. Department of Commerce, Bureau of the Census, MC 82–5–7, 1982 Census of Manufactures, April 1986.
Note: (D): Withheld to avoid disclosure.

The largest four and the largest eight commercial printers are all about the same size and control 6 and 10 percent, respectively, of total printing sales; the aircraft industry is much more concentrated. Alone, these data are inconclusive. However, coupled with other data, this information might be useful in explaining differences in pricing and output behavior between the two industries.

Table 2 presents the four-firm and eight-firm concentration ratios (*CR*s) for 24 industries in the United States. As you move down from the top of the table, concentration (*CR*8 for 1977) declines. Changing industry concentration can be interpreted from data for changes in concentration ratios and for the number of firms in the industry. For example, market power among firms producing electronic computing equipment appears to have become significantly less. Not only has its concentration ratio declined, but the computer industry had nearly seven times as many firms in 1977 as in 1967. This undoubtedly reflects technological advances that are still taking place in that industry.

In general, however, concentration ratios for most industries did not change significantly between 1967 and 1977. Although the number of firms in many industries increased, the largest firms normally retained their shares of industry sales. Relative stability of our industrial structure is supported by the data in Table 2. However, conglomerate mergers have aided the largest 100 American firms in acquiring a slowly

FIGURE 1 *Proportion of Manufacturing Assets Held by the 100 and 200 Largest Corporations, 1950–84*

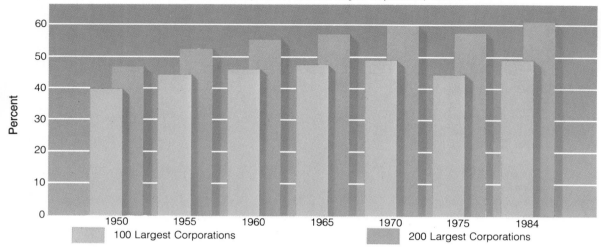

The share of manufacturing assets held by the 100 and 200 largest firms has been growing since the Great Depression. These figures suggest a trend toward greater concentration in the ownership of manufacturing assets in our economy.

Source: *Statistical Abstract of the United States,* 1986.

growing share of all manufacturing assets over the past half century. As Figure 1 illustrates, the top 200 firms (0.1 percent of all manufacturing corporations) control nearly 70 percent of all manufacturing assets, and this percentage has risen slowly over the last half century. Huge corporate takeovers and mergers have recently accelerated this trend. Virtually all these huge organizations operate in a number of industries, and nearly all operate across national boundaries. Thus, although concentration within specific industries has basically stabilized, giant multinationals are increasingly important players on the international economic scene. In addition to their huge shares of manufacturing assets (capital), these corporations also account for growing proportions of employment, sales, and profits.

When we consider conglomerates, there is considerable controversy over whether bigness and badness are closely related. Enormous conglomerates may not have as much monopoly power as huge firms that operate only in a single industry, but they do have substantial economic clout and may exercise their power in the political arena. Multinational firms are of special concern because of their interest in international politics, but even giants are not immune to the pressures of the marketplace. Although many of the 100 or 200 largest companies seem

firmly entrenched at the top of the heap, there has been some turnover of these huge organizations.

A common argument defending concentration is that it is necessary because of economies of scale and capital requirements in a particular industry. High capital costs naturally impose substantial barriers to the entry of new competition if profits are less than certain. Table 3 shows the real values of capital per employee for various industries from 1950 through 1980. The three most major capital-intensive industries in the United States are public utilities, petroleum, and communications. The remaining industries employ significantly less capital. Sales per employee roughly parallel the pattern of capital per employee. High capital requirements do pose considerable barriers to entry, although wildcat oil operations are evidence that the prospect of profits can sometimes overcome high capital costs.

Firms with heavy capital requirements incur large fixed costs. Where there are substantial economies of scale, average costs fall across a wide range of output. In the short run, average variable costs may reach their minimum (the shutdown point) at very low prices. These economies of scale foster cutthroat competition during periods of slack demand. Price wars commonly cause the numbers of firms in an industry to shrink as losers go bankrupt. In addition,

TABLE 3 *Capital Stock per Hour Worked, 1950–80 (Reflects Capital/Labor Ratios, in 1972 Dollars)*

Industry	1950	1980	Percentage Change 1950–80
Public utilities	$69.49	$170.20	144.9
Petroleum	34.25	73.11	113.5
Communications	21.14	69.81	230.2
Transportation	34.56	36.09	4.4
Primary metals	13.99	31.04	121.8
Mining	21.02	23.89	13.7
Tobacco	17.21	37.51	117.9
Chemicals	15.10	31.19	106.6
Paper	14.07	22.41	59.3
Transportation equipment	6.84	15.62	128.4
Nonelectric machinery	6.78	12.23	80.4
Food	8.95	19.29	115.5
Services	5.80	9.13	57.4
Finance and insurance	5.15	10.61	106.0
Textiles	3.64	9.63	164.6
Printing and publishing	6.01	7.11	18.3
Construction	1.98	3.40	71.7
Furniture	4.24	5.11	20.5
Apparel	1.88	3.01	60.1

Source: The Conference Board, New York, N.Y., *Economic Road Maps.*

price wars generate pressures for collusive price-fixing agreements, or to cries from the industry for government "bail outs" and protective regulations and controls.

One of the greatest deficiencies of concentration ratios lies in identifying industry categories properly. Firms must be classified into industry groups whose products are easily substituted by consumers. Drawing demarcation lines between close and distant substitutes is difficult. One solution might be to examine the cross-elasticities of demand between products. Unfortunately, the data required to estimate cross-elasticities are rarely available to researchers.

Alone, even information on substitutability by consumers might be inadequate to define an industry; production substitutability must be considered as well. Markets are *contestable* if a number of firms use roughly the same types of plant and equipment to manufacture different products, and if switching from one product line to another is easy. Firms that can easily cross industry boundaries should be grouped as potential competitors.

Although Standard Industry Classification (SIC) codes attempt to classify industries, major difficulties occur where SIC codes are overly inclusive, especially on the demand side. Many patented products with no close substitutes are lumped with other products of only a roughly similar nature. For example, a decade ago photocopying machines were not separated from other copying equipment. Xerox dominated photocopying equipment at that time. Are mimeographs, ditto machines, and printing presses really close substitutes for Xerox equipment? Even recognizing such difficulties, however, concentration ratios provide crude snapshots of concentrations of market power.

The Herfindahl-Hirschman Index

Traditional economic theory suggests that economic profits are more likely to be earned in concentrated industries, using concentration ratios as the measuring rod for economic concentration and monopoly power. However, a Federal Trade Commission study discovered that a single company's market share quite often is the best predictor of economic profits, regardless of whether or not it is in a concentrated industry.[2] The study concluded that, on the average, a 10 percent increase in market share results in a 2 percent increase in profitability.

This evidence recently caused the Antitrust Division of the Justice Department to begin to rely on the Herfindahl-Hirschman index. The **Herfindahl-Hirschman index (HHI),** which estimates industry concentration by emphasizing the firms with the largest market shares, is measured by the following formula:

$$HHI = \sum_{i=1}^{n} S_i^2,$$

where S_i is the market share of the ith firm. When the industry is a pure monopoly ($S_i = 100 = 100\%$), then $HHI = 10,000$. The value of the HHI declines as the number of firms in the industry increases or the firms become more uniform in size. The index places the greatest weight on the largest firms by squaring market shares.

Consider one market where four firms have 20 percent each and 20 firms have one percent each, and a second market where one firm has 77 percent and the remaining 33 firms each have 1 percent. In both markets the four-firm concentration ratio would be 80 percent, but the HHI would be quite different: 1,620 and 5,962, respectively. The differences in concentration hidden by four-firm concentration ratios are captured by the HHI.

Operationally, the HHI and price-elasticity measures are being used by the Antitrust Division to screen proposed mergers. Beginning in 1982, the Antitrust Division has used merger guidelines that consider both the postmerger concentration (as measured by the HHI) and the increase in concentration resulting from the merger. The Justice Department ignores mergers where the resulting HHI (after merger) would remain below 1,800. If the resulting value of the index after merger is above 1,800, the Justice Department carefully reviews the merger—and might be inclined to disapprove.

READ EXAMPLES

2. "Attacking the Test that Curbs so Many Mergers," _Business Week;_ November 16, 1981, p. 151.

Overall, the Reagan Administration has virtually "immunized" mergers in relatively unconcentrated industries from challenge. Recent mergers such as General Electric/RCA, Chevron/Gulf, and Texaco/Getty Oil (in which a $12 billion judgment may end up costing Texaco the farm) typify the current policy. This represents a radical shift from earlier administrations, which rejected almost all major merger proposals. (See the discussion of the Von's Grocery court decision in Focus 1 later in this chapter for a sample of previous policies.)

Mergers and Monopoly Power_____

If major competing firms merge, industry concentration must increase, whether measured by concentration ratios or the Herfindahl-Hirschman index. If the industry is already concentrated and the firms are among its leaders, the market power gained through merger may be both substantial and socially undesirable. On the other hand, merger of small firms into one viable competitor in an industry with relatively high concentration can be beneficial to society if the merged firm is better able to compete with existing giants. The tough task, of course, is to develop a coherent public policy that prohibits all harmful mergers, but only them.

The Urge to Merge

There are numerous possible motives for a company's wanting to merge. An obvious reason is to eliminate a competitor and increase a firm's market power. Alternatively, firms may desire merger to exploit cost savings if there are economies of scale in information, marketing, advertising, production, or financial aspects of the business, or to pool complementary technologies or patents.

For example, when several firms recently merged to form Hal Roach Studios, the new management moved into a position to exploit a revolutionary technique that adds color to old black and white films. The merged firms included one holding the rights to a "classics" library, another with independent television stations across the nation, and a third that held movie and television distribution agreements worldwide. The earnings potential for the integrated corporation vastly exceeded that of the sum of the individual firms.

Promotional profits are the rewards received by those who engineer mergers that are beneficial to the final merged company. If a merger enhances the expected future profitability of the surviving firm, for example, the price of the stock of the surviving firm will rise, making its value greater than that of the total stock in the previous firms. A higher price for a company's stock is how the stock market reflects any increased monopoly power or cost savings and expected higher profits. Potential promotional profits to holders of large blocks of stock (often the promoters of merger) provide substantial incentives to merge competing firms.

Major Merger Movements

There have been three important merger movements in the United States in the last century. A fourth may be developing. Each of these major waves of mergers, depicted in Figure 2, has arisen from the economic conditions and legal restrictions of the times.

One Co. merges w/ another Co. in same industry

Horizontal Acquisition: The First Wave
The first merger wave was in the late nineteenth and early twentieth centuries. Many early mergers were associated with the names of some of the tycoons of that era: John D. Rockefeller, Andrew Carnegie, Cornelius Vanderbilt, Jay Gould, Jim Fisk, and J. P. Morgan.

buyers competitor a

FIGURE 2 Major Merger Movements (Number of Manufacturing and Mining Firms Acquired, 1895–1984)

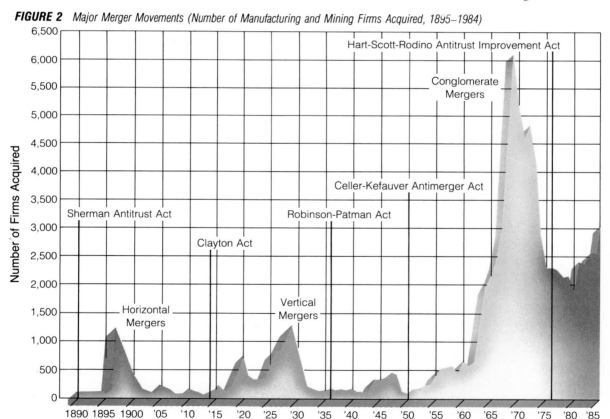

Sources: Data for 1895–1968 from F. M. Scherer, *Industrial Market Structure and Economic Performance* (Chicago: Rand McNally & Company, 1980), p. 120. Scherer cites the following sources for the data: Ralph L. Nelson, *Merger Movements in American Industry, 1895–1956* (Princeton: Princeton University Press, 1959), p. 37; U.S. House of Representatives, Select Committee on Small Business, Staff Report, *Mergers and Superconcentration* (Washington, D.C., 1962), pp. 10, 266; and U.S. Federal Trade Commission, *Current Trends in Merger Activity*, 1968 (Washington, D.C., March 1969). Data for 1963–1984 from *Economic Report of the President*, 1985.

They and other "robber barons" aggressively consolidated their control over oil, steel, sugar, railroads, banking, and other industries. Corporate holding companies known as **trusts** permitted these men to gain control of vast amounts of capital. History is filled with colorful stories about the chicanery they used to acquire the assets of their competitors. John D. Rockefeller, for one, was accused of using cutthroat predatory pricing to eliminate smaller rivals. Reformers claimed his Standard Oil trust reduced oil and gas prices in one area below cost and, when rivals were bankrupted, it then purchased their assets at distress prices. Once Standard Oil's competitors were vanquished, Rockefeller allegedly would raise prices to compensate for past losses, thereby reaping monopoly profits. The evidence is mixed, however, that this sequence of events ever occurred.

The vast majority of the mergers and acquisitions during this period were **horizontal mergers,** which are relatively quick ways to obtain market dominance. Such giants as U.S. Steel, General Electric, and Standard Oil were formed during this period. Once market dominance was established, monopolistic excesses appeared to be commonplace. Perceived abuses by these major companies fomented a general outcry for restrictions on trusts, leading to the passage of the Sherman Antitrust Act in 1890, which attempted to forbid horizontal mergers. Ironically, horizontal mergers mushroomed until loopholes were tightened by the Clayton Act in 1914.

Vertical Acquisition: The Second Wave
A second irony is that the second merger wave immediately followed passage of the Clayton Act, only ending with the onset of the Great Depression. The majority of mergers during this period were vertical. **Vertical mergers** entail gaining control over various stages of production ranging from raw materials to finished manufacturing. Because the Sherman and Clayton Antitrust Acts squelched most horizontal mergers through specific prohibitions on "monopolization or attempts to monopolize," firms desiring to grow via merger were routed towards vertical mergers. Some horizontal mergers did occur, but only trivially compared with the monopolization that occurred during the first great merger wave.

Conglomerates: The Third Wave
The Great Depression took the wind out of the sails of the merger movement. The collapse of the stock market in 1929 made realization of promotional profits nearly impossible, and slack demands for output curtailed mergers based on economies of scale. Figure 2 shows that the merger rate fell drastically and remained low throughout the Depression. Some merger agreements were reached following World War II, but the third big wave did not appear until late in the 1950s, again, ironically, on the heels of major antitrust legislation—the Celler-Kefauver Act of 1950. This third wave lasted into the early 1970s.

The vast majority of the mergers during this period were of the conglomerate form. A **conglomerate merger** combines two or more firms from unrelated industries. For example, Dupont's (a chemical company) 1982 acquisition of Conoco Oil was a conglomerate merger. One of the most famous conglomerates is International Telephone and Telegraph (ITT), which mushroomed in 1960. ITT's assets grew from roughly $900 million in 1960 to over $6 billion in 1970. About two-thirds of this 700 percent growth occurred through mergers with companies in unrelated industries.

The Urge to Purge

Mergers and acquisitions do not always produce happy and successful marriages. Successful mergers tend to share certain features: (*a*) they involve companies in closely related businesses (horizontal mergers), (*b*) the price paid by the acquiring firms is not excessive, (*c*) the acquisition is financed with stock swaps or cash rather than debt (bond financing), and (*d*) the management of the acquired firm continues to run the company.[3]

A common problem with mergers is that good executive skills in one business are not easily adapted to another. Conflicting corporate "cultures" can make an acquisition worthless, as Exxon discovered when, in 1975, it attempted to garner a share of the office automation business. Over the next decade, Exxon poured over $2 billion into its office products division. Exxon executives, accustomed to

---

3. "Do Mergers Really Work?", *Business Week,* June 3, 1985, p. 88–100.

3–5 year planning horizons in the oil business, could not make decisions quickly enough to keep pace with the rapidly changing technology associated with office automation. In 1985, Exxon finally sold its office products division at a loss.

The 1980s have seen both mergers and its flip side, "voluntary restructuring", the jettisoning of bad acquisitions. Many companies are scaling back to "do what they do best." For example, ITT disposed of nearly 100 subsidiaries in the first half of the 1980s. Relaxed merger rules of the Reagan Administration (discussed below) have allowed firms to more freely swap assets.

Moreover, *corporate raiding* has pressured management to see if undervalued plums can be disposed of at prices higher than those reflected in the price of the company's stock. Assets in the hands of firms unable to milk them for the highest possible return are prime targets for corporate raiders and other disposal experts. When this corporate streamlining trend will end is uncertain, but it has been encouraged by the Reagan Administration.

Public Policy Toward Business

Government policies about industrial structure have been directed along two broad lines. The first, regulation, has existed since the adoption of the U.S. Constitution: Article I, Section 8 gives Congress the power "To regulate Commerce with foreign Nations, and among the several States. . . ." While any law passed by Congress could be considered regulation, in the next chapter we focus on instances where some government body sets comprehensive rules for a specific market about prices, outputs, or operating and managerial procedures. In such situations, government substitutes regulation for the forces of competition.

The second general approach to dealing with industry structure has been through enforcement of various antitrust laws. Several additional laws have amended the Sherman Antitrust Act of 1890. In general, the antitrust approach is to make industrial structure conform as much as possible to the assumptions of pure or monopolistic competition. Where this is not possible, law and regulation ideally force the industry's performance to mimic the competitive ideal. The remainder of this chapter is devoted to examining antitrust policies.

Antitrust Policy

The previous three chapters set the stage for antitrust policy. The rationale for vigorous antitrust actions is fairly simple. In pure competition, sellers adjust output until the last unit produced provides benefits just equal to production costs. That is, marginal social benefits equal marginal social costs ($MSB = MSC$), so that the market operates in an economically efficient manner. When firms exercise monopoly power, the price of the last unit sold tends to exceed both its cost and the competitive price. Because the price (marginal social benefit) charged by a firm exceeds marginal social cost, there is economic inefficiency. Therefore, competitive markets are more allocatively efficient than those controlled by firms with monopoly power. Moreover, consistent monopoly profit may result in concentrations of wealth and economic power that are not compatible with most social and political ideas of equity.

While this analysis may seem fairly straightforward, there is considerable disagreement as to whether large corporations that have considerable monopoly power are really bad. One legal point of view is that monopoly is bad per se. The idea of a benevolent monopoly is discarded in favor of the argument that monopoly power is only acquired if abuse is intended. A natural policy conclusion from this point of view is to eliminate all monopoly power through forced *divestiture,* the breaking up of large corporations into numerous independent small companies. For example, AT&T was recently forced to divest itself of all its local operating companies.

The Argument for Bigness

(for) ① required innovation

Defenders of modern corporate giantism argue that large corporations are made necessary by capital-intensive and highly complex modern technology. Many also contend that large enterprises are necessary to comply with the maze of federal, state, and local regulations governing modern business practice. Small firms have difficulty acquiring the capital needed to sustain these endeavors.

Different presidential administrations have interpreted antitrust laws quite differently, but public policy has generally presumed that monopoly power is socially undesirable and should be curtailed. This presumption is based primarily on the economic the-

② too to cope w/ govt regulation
③ complex +

ory you have learned in the last few chapters. The stated goals of antitrust policy are to outlaw monopolization of markets and to prohibit specific misconduct associated with monopoly power. We need a brief overview of our major antitrust laws before evaluating the success of antitrust in the United States.

The Antitrust Laws

Five major antitrust laws have been enacted. The thrust of each is to limit monopoly power or to prohibit undesirable business practices. All were passed in response to public perceptions of business abuses—allegations against Standard Oil, the railroads, and others. At one point in our history, there was strong political support for a constitutional amendment to outlaw monopolies. Against this background, the Sherman Antitrust Act was enacted in 1890.

know names, dates, + provisions for test

The Sherman Act   The two major provisions of the **Sherman Antitrust Act** are:

Section 1: Every contract, combination in the form of trust or otherwise, or conspiracy, in restraint of trade or commerce among the several States, or with foreign nations, is hereby declared to be illegal.

Section 2: Every person who shall monopolize, or attempt to monopolize, or combine or conspire with any other person or persons, to monopolize any part of the trade or commerce among several States, or with foreign nations, shall be deemed guilty of a felony. . . .

Both sections then go on to spell out the penalties for violation of the law. They are fines of up to $1 million for a corporation, or $100,000 for an individual, or imprisonment not exceeding 3 years, or both, at the discretion of the court.[4]

Enforcement of Section 2 has proved especially challenging. Proving "monopolization" calls for determining the relevant market. This requires scrutiny of both the nature of the market (geographic charac-

teristics) and the nature of the product itself (substitutability from the vantage point of both consumers and other potential producers). Once these questions are settled, the court must determine what constitutes a monopoly in terms of percentage of the market. Must the firm control 100 percent of a market to be guilty of monopolization? Should a 90 percent market share be illegal? 80 percent? 70 percent? Section 2 also prohibits "attempts to monopolize." What conduct is intended to produce a monopoly? It seems ironic from today's perspective, but early court cases often focused on union strike activities as violations of the Sherman Act. These cases and other ambiguities in the Sherman Act led to passage of more specific antitrust laws.

The Clayton Act   The Sherman Act was amended by the **Clayton Act** in 1914, which spelled out particular offenses more precisely and introduced into law the phrase "where the effect [of various practices] may be to substantially lessen competition or tend to create a monopoly." Specifically:

Section 2: It shall be unlawful for any person engaged in commerce . . . to discriminate in price between different purchasers of commodities of like grade and quality. . . .

Section 3: It shall be unlawful for any person engaged in commerce . . . to lease or make a sale or contract for sale of goods, wares, merchandise, machinery, supplies or other commodities . . . or fix a price charged therefor, or discount from or rebate upon, such price, on the condition, agreement or understanding that the lessee or purchaser thereof shall not use or deal in the goods . . . , or other commodities of a competitor or competitors of the lessor or seller. . . .

Section 4: [This section is quite technically written and prohibits mergers where the effect is to substantially lessen competition or tend to create a monopoly.]

Section 8: [This section focuses on interlocking directorates, prohibiting any individual from being a director of two or more competing corporations if any of the companies has capital in excess of $1 million.]

Many qualifications and specific standards have been enumerated by the courts in enforcing the price discrimination section (Section 2). For exam-

---

4. The Sherman Antitrust Act was originally passed in 1890. The fine for violations of the act was increased from $5,000 to $50,000 in 1955 and increased to $100,000 for individuals and $1,000,000 for corporations in 1976. The 1976 amendments also made Sherman Act violations felonies and raised the maximum prison term from 1 year to 3 years.

ple, price discrimination is permitted if a defendant can show that it does not reduce competition. (For example, discount for senior citizens to movies and supersaver fares on airlines.) Moreover, price discrimination is permitted for intangible properties or services, or where differences in costs account for different prices.

Business has taxed the courts' ingenuity in dealing with various schemes such as tie-in sales and restrictive agreements under Section 3. (IBM used to lease its computers and would not permit its equipment to be attached to equipment of other manufacturers. A. B. Dick tied sales of ink to its mimeograph machines.) Business continually devises new schemes to get around Section 3, which are subsequently attacked under the Clayton Act by the government.

The Federal Trade Commission Act

The **Federal Trade Commission (FTC) Act** of 1914 created a commission, the FTC, to investigate and challenge any "unfair methods of competition . . . , and unfair or deceptive acts or practices in or affecting commerce." The act did not define "unfair practices", but instead left the interpretation of the statute and the determination of what practices are unfair or deceptive up to the FTC, subject to review by the courts. Court reviews have been very restrictive and limited the effectiveness of the FTC for decades. Today, the FTC focuses largely on false and misleading advertising. These efforts, together with other investigations of fraud and unfair or deceptive business tactics, help to protect consumers. More recently, the FTC has turned its attention to restrictive state and local regulations and to licensing practices that provide little benefit to consumers. The FTC's vigor in challenging perceived unfair business practices ebbs and flows with the political tides of the various presidential administrations, but in large measure the FTC remains the consumer's watchdog.

The Robinson-Patman Act

Section 2 of the Clayton Act was amended by the **Robinson-Patman Act** in 1936. This act was designed to limit price discrimination in the form of special promotional allowances. Discounts were permitted only where justified by differences in costs or when introduced as "good faith" efforts to meet competition. Because quantity discounts have been attacked under the Robinson-Patman Act, many economists have criticized the law as a protector of small firms from competition rather

than a guarantor of competition. There are enormous differences between protecting competitors from failure and promoting competition.

The Celler-Kefauver Antimerger Act

The Clayton Act prohibited the acquisition of stock in one company by a competitor. The Supreme Court, however, distinguished between acquisition of stock and acquisition of assets (plant, equipment, and so on). If one firm acquired the assets of another, even through illegal acquisition of voting stock, the merger was allowed. This was the path to numerous mergers during the 1930s and 1940s. In 1950, the Celler-Kefauver Antimerger Act attempted to close this loophole in the law.

The **Celler-Kefauver Antimerger Act** made it illegal to acquire either the stock or assets of a competitor. Additionally, the act erected special hurdles for mergers if there was a trend toward concentration in an industry. If two relatively small firms tried to merge to improve their competitive position, the Celler-Kefauver Antimerger Act (as interpreted) would prohibit such a merger, even if this might improve competition (see the Von's Grocery case in Focus 1). Until recently, this act virtually eliminated horizontal and vertical mergers among major corporations. The five major acts and their general contents are summarized in Table 4.

Exemptions from Antitrust Laws

The language of the Sherman Antitrust Act states that every combination in restraint of trade is in violation of the law. As this act was interpreted by the courts, political pressures and economic realities arose, causing various groups to be exempted.

Agricultural Cooperatives

The Clayton Act exempted agricultural associations so that nonprofit cooperatives could be formed without violating the antitrust laws, although some constraints try to prevent cooperatives from setting their prices "unduly" high.

Labor Unions

National policy favors the right of workers to unionize and bargain collectively. The Sherman Antitrust Act, however, originally was used to stifle union activity. Sections 6 and 20 of the Clayton Act exempted collective bargaining by workers from antitrust actions.

FOCUS 1

Von's Grocery—The Numbers, Ma'am, Just the Numbers!

The belief that a competitive industry structure was required for competitive performance was once a hallmark of antitrust policy. Nowhere was this more evident than in the *United States* v. *Von's Grocery Company* (1966) case. Von's Grocery Company of Los Angeles had acquired a direct competitor, Shopping Bag Food Stores. The merger combined the third and sixth largest local grocery chains for a combined market share of 7.5 percent. The number of owner-operated single grocery stores had declined from 5,365 in 1950 to 3,590 in 1963. Over the same period, the number of chains nearly doubled.

In finding that the merger violated the Clayton Act, the court noted: "It is enough for us that Congress feared that a market marked at the same time by both a continuous decline in the number of small businesses and a large number of mergers would slowly but inevitably gravitate from a market of many small competitors to one dominated by one or a few giants, and competition would thereby be destroyed. Congress passed the Celler-Kefauver Act to prevent such a destruction of competition."

The Court simply counted heads and totally ignored the competitive changes that were taking effect. The dissent argued that "local competition is vigorous

to a fault, not only among chain stores themselves but also between chain stores and single-store operators." Over three-quarters of the acquisitions between 1961 and 1964 (including Von's) were "market extensions, involving neither the elimination of direct competitors in the Los Angeles market nor increased concentration of the market."

A vigorous dissent, however, noted that the majority's opinion "is nothing more than a requiem for the so-called 'Mom and Pop' grocery stores—the bakery and butcher shops, the vegetable and fish markets—that are now economically and technologically obsolete in many parts of the country."

Sports Organizations Curiously, the courts have almost totally exempted professional baseball and have provided specialized exemptions for other amateur and professional sports organizations from antitrust actions on the strange doctrine that they are not in interstate commerce because sports activities are "entertainment, not business." Thus, the NFL, NBA, NCAA, AAU, and a variety of other associations in our multibillion-dollar sports industry are reasonably free to collude against their employees, potentially competitive organizations, or each other.

Export Industries The Webb-Pomerene Act of 1918 largely exempts from antitrust actions those associations whose express purpose is export trade. Many countries historically have encouraged the formation of cartels for purposes of international trade. The Webb-Pomerene Act enables American companies to engage in joint ventures when competing with foreign cartels. Export trade associations may legally act

somewhat like cartels for American firms, but only in their international operations.

Regulated Industries The next chapter discusses how detailed regulation replaces market processes in some industries. Normally, the tighter public regulation is, the greater the chance for exemption from antitrust laws. Because regulatory agencies presumably express the public interest, exemption from antitrust prosecution seems sensible so that any gains from cooperation between regulated firms may be realized by the public.

The Antitrust Laws in Practice

The complexity of modern business raises numerous issues for public policy. The major focus of current antitrust enforcement is through the Sherman Act, as amended. However, Sections 1 and 2 are rather broadly written. What do the words *monopolize* and *attempts to monopolize* mean? How will individual firms know what behavior is prohibited? And how will oligopolists be treated? Which practices will be permitted and which prohibited? Finally, how will firms know if they can merge without the threat of legal action from the federal government? All these questions raise important issues for antitrust enforcement.

Monopolization and Monopoly Power

If Section 1 of the Sherman Act were interpreted literally, almost every major transaction in the country restricts trade in some way. The Sherman Act was not explicit about what was legal and what was illegal, leaving that decision to the courts. Nor does Section 2 clearly specify what constitutes a monopoly. To make matters worse, the courts historically have been a bit schizophrenic in interpreting the Sherman Act.

The Rule of Reason In two early cases, the Supreme Court decided that trusts (monopolies) could either be "good" or "bad" and that the Sherman Act only outlaws "bad" or unreasonable, restraints on trade. These landmark cases involved Standard Oil and the American Tobacco Company and established what has been called the **rule of reason,** which developed standards to distinguish good and bad trusts. Both Standard Oil and American Tobacco were judged "bad" trusts and were subjected to divestiture; they were subsequently split into several companies.

Where a firm could show that its conduct was based on sound business practice and was a logical consequence of its general practice, some obviously anticompetitive practices (refusals to deal and tie-in sales) were permitted. Such factors as percentage of the market affected, expected duration of the practice, relative strengths of the parties involved, and the size and nature of the relevant market determined if the courts would allow certain "reasonable" conduct.

The Per Se Doctrine In the 1945 case of *U.S. v. Aluminum Co. of America (Alcoa),* the Supreme Court hinted at a new antitrust approach to monopolization, known as the **per se doctrine.** The Court reasoned that the Sherman Act does not condone "good" trusts and forbid "bad" trusts; it prohibits all monopolization and restraints on trade. Whether or not a firm abused its power or obtained its monopoly by reasonable methods was irrelevant. The fact of monopoly was sufficient. In this instance, Alcoa was

TABLE 4 *Summary of Antitrust Laws*

Statute and Year of Enactment	Major Provisions
Sherman Antitrust Act (1890)	Prohibits contracts, combinations, and conspiracies in restraint of trade and forbids monopolization or attempts to monopolize.
Clayton Act (1914)	Prohibits certain forms of price discrimination, contracts that prevent buyers from dealing with sellers' competitors, acquisition of one corporation's shares by another if the effect will be to substantially lessen competition, and interlocking directorates between competing corporations.
Federal Trade Commission Act (1914)	Established the FTC to investigate unfair and deceptive business practices.
Robinson-Patman Act (1936)	Amended the Clayton Act (Section 2) to prohibit discounts and other special price concessions. Price discrimination is permissible only where it is: 1. based on differences in cost. 2. a good faith effort to meet competition. 3. based on differences in marketability of product.
Celler-Kefauver Antimerger Act (1950)	Amended Section 7 of the Clayton Act to plug the loopholes that permitted merger via acquisition of assets. In addition, the law prohibited mergers where there was a trend toward concentration.

forced to sell some assets to other companies to enhance competition in the industry.

Under the per se doctrine, certain contracts, combinations, or conspiracies seem inherently so contrary to competition that they are held to be illegal per se. The government needs only to show that the parties have entered into such agreements; whether or not competition has been harmed is immaterial. Among the per se violations are: (*a*) price-fixing agreements that in any way stabilize prices for a particular good, (*b*) allocation schemes that divide customers or markets into territories, (*c*) agreements between competitors to refuse to deal with certain suppliers or customers, and (*d*) "tie-in sales," where a dominant seller forces a buyer to purchase peripheral products in order to purchase the desired good.

Once this per se approach was adopted, the critical question became: Just what constitutes a monopoly? The courts have looked at such factors as the number, size and strength of the firms in the market, the nature of technology, and any economies of scale to determine whether or not monopoly exists.

Antitrust Policy in Oligopoly Markets

Oligopolies, like monopolies, do not yield allocative efficiency. However, the Sherman Antitrust Act outlaws "monopolies" and "attempts to monopolize." The previous chapter suggested that stability in pricing might be one hallmark of oligopoly. When oligopolistic prices change, we would predict that all prices in the industry will change simultaneously and by roughly similar amounts due to the close relationship among the firms in the industry.

Conscious Parallelism of Action   Noncollusive oligopolistic interaction may cause identical behavior that is as effective in restraining trade as an overt cartel agreement among firms, but there are no witnesses or documents to prove conspiracy. The dilemma is clear—parallel oligopolistic actions lead to socially undesirable economic effects, but the parallel action results from oligopolistic interdependence; the Sherman Antitrust Act requires formal proof of active conspiracy.

The FTC developed the doctrine of **conscious parallelism of action** to deal with this problem.

In several landmark cases, the Supreme Court inferred conspiracy from parallel action by competitors. This approach lasted for several decades but was eventually overturned. The courts now must examine the totality of conduct rather than look only at parallel action; identical behavior is not illegal by itself. The courts recognize that parallel business policies may be either the result of independent judgment, a symptom of competition, or the result predicted by our models of noncompetitive markets. Today, findings of monopolization require clear evidence of conspiracy.

Shared Monopoly   A different antitrust approach to oligopoly was introduced during the Carter Administration in an action by the FTC against the four leading producers of breakfast cereals: Kellogg, General Mills, General Foods, and Quaker Oats. The FTC and Justice Department charged that the breakfast cereal market is effectively a **shared monopoly** because these four firms allegedly used their market power to exclude their competitors and earn monopoly profits.

This particular antitrust action was rather controversial because of the novel approach used by the FTC and the Justice Department. Both charged the cereal industry with excessive brand proliferation as the major barrier to entry. Each time new firms attempted to enter the industry, these four companies responded by introducing their own nationally advertised versions of the challenger's product. The result, according to the FTC, was monopolization of supermarket shelf space by the "big four," throttling potential competition.

In effect, the FTC accused these cereal makers of following the joint-profit maximization approach discussed in the previous chapter. The four manufacturers argued that they were being harassed for being too successful and for taking advantage of economies of scale in advertising, marketing, and management. The FTC charged that the firms had a tacit agreement not to cut price to compete but, rather, to use nonprice competition (games, puzzles, or prizes) to maintain a stable pricing structure.

This particular antitrust approach, not yet accepted by any court, may never develop beyond an embryonic stage because cases against cereal makers and tobacco firms were abandoned by the Reagan

CHAPTER REVIEW: KEY POINTS

1. *Monopoly power* exists whenever a firm can set the price of its output. (*Monopoly power* and *monopoly* are not synonymous.) As monopoly power increases, the gap between price (P) and marginal cost (MC) widens. The *Lerner index of monopoly power* (*LMP*) uses this fact to measure monopoly power as $(P - MC)/P$. However, estimating MC with accounting data is difficult, and using average costs as a proxy for MC may overstate monopoly power.

2. Market concentration ratios provide some evidence of monopolization or oligopolistic power. Market *concentration ratios* are the percentages of total sales, output, or employment in an industry controlled by a small number of the largest firms in the industry. Concentration ratios for the Big 4, Big 8, Big 20, and Big 50 are computed for many industries.

3. Major difficulties are encountered in defining an industry. The existence of *close consumption substitutes* is one consideration; the ease with which potential competitors might enter an industry (*contestability*) is another. The Department of Commerce lumps firms into Standard Industrial Classifications (SICs) to try to solve this problem, but with only mixed success.

4. The *Herfindahl-Hirschman index* (*HHI*) is the sum of squared market shares (ΣS_i^2). Squaring places more emphasis on big firms. The Justice Department now uses the *HHI* as a guide to the permissibility of mergers.

5. *Concentration* varies substantially between industries. Nearly 100 percent of all cigarettes produced and sold in the United States are produced by fewer than eight companies, and the eight largest printing companies produce about one-tenth of all printing. However, roughly 70 percent of all manufacturing assets are controlled by the 200 largest American corporations. The numbers on industrial concentration grew dramatically from 1890 to 1929, but have only crept up slowly since.

6. Big firms might be justified by enormous capital requirements or substantial economies of scale. In those instances, proper public policy may take the form of regulation (dealt with in the next chapter). The major thrust of public policy where no such justifications for bigness exist has been to encourage competition through *antitrust actions*. The current level of concentration is testimony to the apparent failure of this policy.

7. One reason for merger is to increase the scope of a firm's operations so that economies of scale in information, marketing, advertising, production, or financial management may be exploited. A second reason, which is far more important for public policy, is that merger may eliminate business rivals and facilitate increases in economic concentration and monopoly power. Increases in monopoly power that result from merger may be reflected rapidly in higher prices for the merged companies' stock. This creates *promotional profit* for current stockholders.

8. The first major wave of mergers in the United States lasted roughly from 1890 until 1914, and saw companies buying out their competitors through *horizontal mergers.*

9. Most horizontal mergers were outlawed with the passage of the *Clayton Antitrust Act,* so a wave of *vertical mergers,* lasting from 1914 until the 1929 Stock Market Crash resulted in further economic concentration. Vertical mergers unite suppliers of raw materials or intermediate goods with processors or other firms further along the production chain.

10. Merger activity died during the Great Depression, but revived in the mid-1950s. Since most vertical mergers were prohibited by the Celler-Kefauver Antimerger Act, companies that were very dissimilar were merged into *conglomerates.* Merger activities slowed down during the early 1970s but had re-emerged during the 1980s.

11. The *big five antitrust laws* are summarized in Table 4.

12. Agricultural cooperatives, athletic organizations, labor unions, export trade associations, and regulated industries are largely exempt from antitrust actions.

13. In applying the *Sherman Antitrust Act,* the Court has historically taken two different approaches. The *rule of reason* approach prohibits bad monopolies and permits reasonable restraints on trade, while the *per se doctrine* forbids all monopolies regardless of conduct.

14. Merger policy today is based on various factors, but if the postmerger *HHI* exceeds 1,800, the Department of Justice is likely to challenge the merger.

QUESTIONS FOR THOUGHT AND DISCUSSION

1. It has been argued that the emergence of large firms that wield sizable monopoly power represents an inevitable outcome of an unencumbered competitive process. Do you agree or disagree? Explain why.

2. When the Oakland Raiders moved to Los Angeles in 1982, they touched a vital nerve of the National Football League. This move, which was subsequently upheld by the courts, weakened the NFL's influence over the movement of franchises and threatened to undercut the pooling of network television revenues (60 percent of NFL income). Today, the NFL is pressuring Congress for a blanket antitrust exemption. Do you think professional sports should be exempt from antitrust laws? Should owners of professional teams be permitted to move their teams at their discretion? Critics of the NFL argue that the league "is more interested in limiting the number of teams and ensuring profits for the existing 28 owners." Do you agree?

3. The Antitrust Division of the U.S. Department of Justice and the Federal Trade Commission are responsible for ensuring that industrial performance closely approximates the performance of the competitive ideal. Would it be feasible or even beneficial for these federal watchdogs to use the antitrust laws to impose competitive structures on all industries that are highly concentrated? Why?

4. In some concentrated industries, most notably cigarettes and breakfast cereals, the largest firms introduce new brands so rapidly that entry into the industry by smaller firms may be virtually impossible. Should these barriers to entry be permitted? Would consumers lose if existing firms were required to reduce the numbers of brands they market? Explain.

5. A decade ago, the computer industry was dominated by a few companies. Today, competition is fierce. What accounts for the change—government antitrust action? Is the same thing likely to occur in steel, aluminum, and other basic industries? Why?

6. In 1982, the Justice Department proposed to attack a horizontal merger if, after defining the relevant product market for the merged firm, a hypothesized price increase of 5 percent could be expected to be sustained for over a year. Is this a reasonable measure of increased concentration from a merger? Why?

7. Government antitrust actions have been notoriously large and expensive (the recent IBM and AT&T cases are examples). The typical *private* antitrust case involves about $50,000 in legal fees for each side, about 30 hours of top executives' time, and is usually completed within 2 years. Because private antitrust actions are relatively inexpensive, some have argued that the law should be liberalized to permit more private antitrust suits and curtail the federal government's role. Do you think this is a workable solution to the mounting costs of federal antitrust litigation? What problems might this pose?

Aspen Skiing Company v. Aspen Highlands Skiing Corporation (1985)

Firms with monopoly power are convenient targets for private antitrust suits from smaller rivals. Is a company with considerable monopoly power under an obligation to cooperate with its smaller business competitors or to enter into a joint operating agreement? Or must it refuse to deal with competitors? This recent Supreme Court decision examines these issues.

Aspen is a destination ski resort with a reputation for "super powder," "a wide range of runs," and an "active night life," including "some of the best restaurants in North America."

Between 1958 and 1964, three independent companies operated the Ajax, Highlands, and Buttermilk mountains. A fourth mountain, Snowmass, opened in 1967. In the early years, each company offered its own day or half-day tickets for use of its mountain. In 1962, however, the three competitors also introduced an interchangeable ticket. The 6-day, all-Aspen ticket provided convenience to the vast majority of skiers who visited the resort for weekly periods, but preferred to remain flexible about what mountain they might ski each day during the visit. It also emphasized the unusual variety of ski mountains available in Aspen.

As initially designed, the all-Aspen ticket program consisted of booklets containing six coupons, each redeemable for a daily lift ticket at Ajax, Highlands, or Buttermilk. The price of the booklet was often discounted from the price of six daily tickets, but all six

coupons had to be used within a limited period of time—seven days, for example. The revenues from the sale of the 3-area coupon books were distributed in accordance with the number of coupons collected at each mountain.

In 1964, Buttermilk was purchased by Aspen Skiing Co. (Ski Co.), and, in 1967, Ski Co. opened Snowmass. In the 1971–1972 season, the coupon booklets were discontinued and an "around the neck" all-Aspen ticket was developed. This refinement on the interchangeable ticket was advantageous to the skier, who no longer found it necessary to visit the ticket window every morning before gaining access to the slopes.

Ski Co. and Highlands used random sample surveys to allocate the revenues from the 4-area, 6-day ticket. Highlands' share of the revenues from the ticket was 17.5% in 1973–74, 18.5% in 1974–75, 16.8% in 1975–76, and 13.2% in 1976–77. During these four seasons, Ski Co. did not offer its own 3-area, multi-day ticket in competition with the all-Aspen ticket. By 1977, multi-area tickets accounted for nearly 35% of the total market.

In the 1970's the management of Ski Co. increasingly expressed their dislike for the all-Aspen ticket. They complained that a coupon method of monitoring usage was administratively cumbersome. They doubted the accuracy of the survey and decried the "appearance, deportment, [and] attitude" of the college students who were conducting it. In addition, Ski Co.'s president had expressed the view that the

4-area ticket was siphoning off revenues that could be recaptured by Ski Co. if the ticket was discontinued. In 1978, Ski Co. offered Highlands a 4-area ticket provided that Highlands would agree to receive a 12.5% fixed percentage of the revenue. Highlands rejected the offer of the fixed percentage.

In its place, Ski Co. offered the 3-area, 6-day ticket featuring only its mountains. In an effort to promote this ticket, Ski Co. embarked on a national advertising campaign that strongly implied to people who were unfamiliar with Aspen that Ajax, Buttermilk, and Snowmass were the only ski mountains in the area.

Highlands finally developed an "Adventure Pack," which consisted of a 3-day pass at Highlands and three vouchers, each equal to the price of a daily lift ticket at a Ski Co. mountain. The vouchers were guaranteed by funds on deposit in an Aspen bank, and were redeemed by Aspen merchants at full value. Ski Co., however, refused to accept them. Later, Highlands redesigned the Adventure Pack to contain American Express Traveler's Checks instead of vouchers. Ski Co. accepted these in exchange for daily lift tickets.

Without a convenient all-Aspen ticket, Highlands basically "becomes a day ski area in a destination resort." Highlands' share of the market declined steadily.

In 1979, Highlands filed a complaint alleging that Ski Co. had monopolized the market for downhill skiing services at Aspen in violation of Section 2 of the Sherman Act.

Although Ski Co.'s pattern of conduct may not have been "bold, relentless, and predatory", the record in this case comfortably supports an inference that the monopolist made a deliberate effort to discourage its customers from doing business with its smaller rival. The sale of its 3-area, 6-day ticket, particularly when it was discounted below the daily ticket price, deterred the ticket holders from skiing at Highlands. The refusal to accept the Adventure Pack coupons in exchange for daily tickets was apparently motivated entirely by a decision to avoid providing any benefit to Highland—even though accepting the coupons would have entailed no cost to Ski Co. itself, would have provided it with immediate benefits, and would have satisfied its potential customers. Thus the evidence supports an inference that Ski Co. was not motivated by efficiency concerns and that it was willing to sacrifice short-run benefits and consumer good will in exchange for a perceived long-run impact on its smaller rival.

QUESTIONS

1. This case seems to stand for the rule that if a firm has monopoly power and no valid business reason to refuse to deal with a competitor, it must do so or face treble damages under the Sherman Antitrust Act. Do you agree with this rule?

2. Suppose the four mountains in Aspen were owned by four separate firms, but one mountain was vastly superior to the other for skiing. Assume further that the firm owning the superior mountain refused to enter into a 4-mountain, 6-day package with the other firms. Do you think this case would require cooperation or joint marketing of the four mountains?

3. Suppose that Aspen Skiing Company and Aspen Highlands Skiing Corporation decided to merge. What would happen to the Herfindahl-Hirschman index? Do you think the Justice Department would permit the merger? How are this case, Von's Grocery, and the current merger guidelines related? Is there a significant difference between the joint marketing arrangement required in this case and merger of the two firms?

4. Do these two firms have incentives to enter into price competition? In effect, has the court ordered and immunized joint-profit maximization under the guise of protecting consumer convenience?

5. Should the court have only considered the Aspen ski market as the relevant market? Is there competition from other ski resorts in Colorado and the West?

6. Is the effect of this case to eliminate "making a higher profit and making life harder for your competitors" as valid business reasons? Is the Court correct when it states that Ski Co.'s acceptance of Adventure Pack coupons entailed no cost to Ski Co. itself?

CHAPTER 27 The Role of Government Regulation

public interest theory of regulation	*natural monopoly*	*occupational licensing*
	block pricing	*consumer protection*
industry interest theory of regulation	*rate base*	*caveat emptor*
	rate structures	*caveat venditor*

It is trite to say that life is growing increasingly complex. The important point about this for our purposes is that complex societies are also regulated societies. There was a time when you could count on your fingers the regulations governing most American industries. Today, you would need the appendages in a bushel basket of centipedes. Government regulation of business is a massive task for regulators, for the firms they oversee, and for hordes of lawyers and consultants from both sides. Concerns about pollution and the environment; consumer and occupational safety and health; discrimination against women and minority groups; and a host of other social, economic, and political problems have all contributed to the rising tide of business regulation. However, businesses are not alone in being regulated.

A vast body of law governs our private behavior. Consumers are controlled through consumer protection statutes and regulations. While the burdens of consumer protection legislation are most apparent in their effects on firms, the range of consumer choice generally is reduced by regulation as well. There are laws that mandate school attendance until your midteens, prohibit self-prescription of penicillin or heroin, require you to drive on the right-hand side of the road and below 55 miles an hour, forbid you to walk your dog without a leash and a shovel, deny you access to cyclamates (an artificial sweetener). . . . Even the lowly hamburger does not escape (see Focus 1).

Many observers of American business charge that the private economy has been abandoned to the wolves of an intervening government. Instead of providing a chicken for every pot, the government has its finger in every pie. The opponents of extensive modern regulation charge that many legal restraints (especially price controls on specific commodities) reduce supplies and drive up production costs. They argue that bureaucratic red tape and silly rules stifle our productivity and account for the recent malaise in our economy.

Have it Their Way

Your Hamburger: 41,000 Regulations

PICTOGRAM ®

The hamburger, staple of the quick, inexpensive meal, is the subject of 41,000 federal and state regulations, many of those stemming from 200 laws and 111,000 precedent-setting court cases.

These rules, cited in a three-volume study by Colorado State University, touch on everything involved in meat production—grazing practices of cattle, conditions in slaughterhouses and methods used to process meat for sale to supermarkets, restaurants and fast-food outlets. Together, they add an estimated 8 to 11 cents per pound to the cost of hamburger.

The chart on this page gives just a sampling of the rules and regulations governing the burger you buy at the corner sandwich stand.

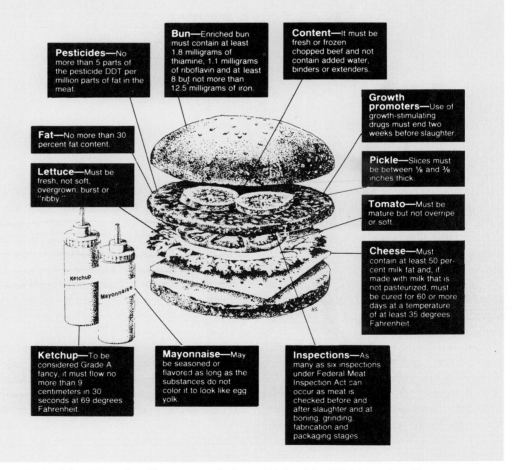

Bun—Enriched bun must contain at least 1.8 milligrams of thiamine, 1.1 milligrams of riboflavin and at least 8 but not more than 12.5 milligrams of iron.

Pesticides—No more than 5 parts of the pesticide DDT per million parts of fat in the meat.

Content—It must be fresh or frozen chopped beef and not contain added water, binders or extenders.

Fat—No more than 30 percent fat content.

Lettuce—Must be fresh, not soft, overgrown, burst or "ribby."

Growth promoters—Use of growth-stimulating drugs must end two weeks before slaughter.

Pickle—Slices must be between ⅛ and ⅜ inches thick.

Tomato—Must be mature but not overripe or soft.

Cheese—Must contain at least 50 percent milk fat and, if made with milk that is not pasteurized, must be cured for 60 or more days at a temperature of at least 35 degrees Fahrenheit.

Ketchup

Mayonnaise

Ketchup—To be considered Grade A fancy, it must flow no more than 9 centimeters in 30 seconds at 69 degrees Fahrenheit.

Mayonnaise—May be seasoned or flavored as long as the substances do not color it to look like egg yolk.

Inspections—As many as six inspections under Federal Meat Inspection Act can occur as meat is checked before and after slaughter and at boning, grinding, fabrication and packaging stages.

Source: Reprinted from U.S.News & World Report *issue of Feb. 11, 1980. Copyright, 1980, U.S.News & World Report.*

Economic models of market structure were developed earlier in this book: As an industry becomes less competitive, markets may fail to promote social welfare. For this and other reasons (e.g., externalities), government intervenes in markets, hoping to achieve competitive output and pricing. In this chapter, we will examine (*a*) the nature and extent of regulation, (*b*) economic reasons for regulation, (*c*) cases for and against consumer protection, and (*d*) some practical problems of regulation.

Government Intervention

The initial reaction of many people after they have made some deal where they got less than they paid for is, "There ought to be a law . . . (to prevent people from being "cheated" this way)." The result has been a proliferation of regulations. Today, hundreds of government bureaus and agencies regulate business without any central referee to coordinate what may be conflicting or unreasonable policies. Many politicians find a responsive voting public when they campaign against regulations and red tape, which they contend serve no useful or valid purposes.

The Rise of Government Regulation

Figure 1 surveys the growth of American regulatory agencies. Except for a few muckrakers and social reformers, most people once favored moderate laissez-faire capitalism. The Great Depression dislodged widespread belief in the free market system like a blow from a sledgehammer. By the end of the 1930s, government's role in the economy had expanded substantially and, perhaps, irreversibly.

Much of the regulation introduced in the 1930s was designed to buffer against violent swings in the business cycle. New regulations included tighter reins over banking, an Agricultural Adjustment Act designed to prop up the family farmer, various mortgage loan programs, more controls in the electric power generating business, a bigger voice in securities transactions and labor relations, and an ex-

FIGURE 1 *Number of New Federal Regulatory Agencies Created, by Decade*

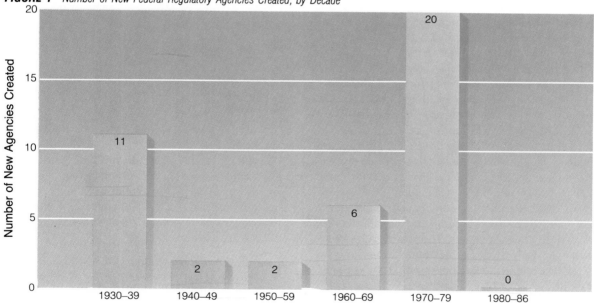

The power of the federal government to regulate commerce is established in the Constitution. This power was exercised little before the 1930s, but the 1960s and 1970s were an "Age of Regulation."

Source: *Business Week*, 3 September 1979, p. 39. Data from the Center for the Study of American Business. Updated by authors.

panded welfare system. The shock of the Great Depression quite clearly altered the role most Americans perceived for their government.

The 1940s and 1950s, on the other hand, were almost barren of new regulatory agencies. Then, in the 1960s and 1970s, a new wave of sentiment for regulation erupted. As Figure 1 illustrates, regulatory agencies more than doubled from 1960 to 1980, with the 1970s alone accounting for over half of all regulatory agencies. This round of regulatory creation was not the consequence of a strong economic upheaval; paradoxically, it occurred during a period where real disposable personal income rose by over 40 percent—one of the more prosperous periods in our history. The election of Ronald Reagan in 1980 signaled an abrupt halt to the creation of new regulatory agencies.

Economist Robert Heilbroner has suggested three phases in government's relationship with industry. Its first role is as *promoter;* its second, as *regulator;* and, finally, it acts as a *guarantor.* He cites the railroad industry as an example. During the last half of the nineteenth century, government actively promoted rail transport with right-of-way land grants and other subsidies. This was followed by close regulation of the industry during the first half of this century. Finally, government now guarantees the railroads' existence. Much of the rail system was effectively nationalized into Amtrak and Conrail in the 1960s and 1970s. Similar scenarios have been played out in the nuclear, petroleum, and automobile industries. (Remember the Chrysler loans?) Whether it is possible to reverse this process is the subject of debate.

So many groups now have vested interests in particular regulations that proposals to eliminate rules often generate tremendous political pressures to retain them. When the Reagan administration proposed complete deregulation of the alcoholic beverage industry, consumer groups and the industry both vigorously fought the idea. The simple rules of the past apparently have become outmoded as our economy has become more sophisticated. Today's regulatory maze may also be found wanting as our society evolves further. One explanation for regulatory growth is the complexity of today's products. Kenneth Boulding has suggested that just as an astronaut in a space capsule must follow a far stricter regimen than a cowboy on the prairie, so too must a space-age economy be on tighter rules than the simpler economy of an earlier era.

The Extent of Government Regulation

Some people may wonder if the government will run out of three-letter acronyms to identify federal agencies. They need not worry. There are 26^3, or 17,576, possible three-letter combinations. The alphabet soup of regulatory bodies includes such well-known agencies as the IRS, FAA, FTC, FDA, EPA, ICC, OSHA, and the SEC. Focus 2 lists some major federal regulatory agencies and describes their functions. Estimates are that at least 5 to 10 percent of our national resources are devoted to regulating or complying with regulation, so regulation permeates almost all aspects of the economy. Numerous charges of overregulation have been leveled at our vast governmental bureaucracies.

Direct Costs of Regulation

A frequent charge against government is that the costs of bureaucratic rules governing business escalate every year. Critics argue that rules, regulations, and red tape increase the costs of doing business and the cost of living. A 1981 study of federal regulation of economic activity provides some insight into the cost of government regulation.[1] Two types of costs are considered:

1. *Administrative costs.* These include the salaries of government workers, inspectors, office supplies, and other "overhead" expenses.
2. *Compliance costs.* These are costs incurred primarily by the private sector, but also by state and local governments, in the process of complying with federal regulations.

The authors of the study, Murray Weidenbaum and Robert DeFina, found that compliance costs in total are almost 20 times the administrative costs. Based on their analysis, nearly $200 billion per year is required to meet federal regulatory requirements today, which is equivalent to:

1. roughly 4 percent of the Gross National Product.
2. nearly $1,000 per person per year living in the United States.
3. 18 percent of the federal budget.

---

1. Murray L. Weidenbaum and Robert DeFina, *The Rising Cost of Government Regulation* (St. Louis, Mo: Center for the Study of American Business, 31 January 1981).

FOCUS 2

Major Federal Regulatory Agencies

The federal government consists of virtually hundreds of departments, agencies, divisions, commissions, boards and bureaus to regulate commerce. The following is a partial list of the most important federal regulators.

Agency	Major Function(s)
	Product Markets
Antitrust Division of the Justice Dept.	Promotes and maintains competitive markets by enforcing federal antitrust laws.
Federal Communications Commission	Regulates broadcasting, telephone, and other communication services.
Federal Maritime Commission	Regulates foreign and domestic ocean commerce.
Federal Trade Commission	Protects consumers from unfair trade practices, false advertising, and overly restrictive licensing to maintain competition.
Interstate Commerce Commission	Regulates interstate surface transportation, including trucking, railroads, and water carriers.
	Labor Markets
Equal Employment Opportunity Commission	Investigates complaints of discrimination based on race, religion, sex, or age in hiring, promotion, firing, wages, testing, and all other conditions of employment.
National Labor Relations Board	Regulates and enforces collective bargaining agreements between companies and unions, and certifies elections of bargaining representatives.
	Financial Markets
Commodity Futures Trading Commission	Regulates futures trading on eleven U.S. futures exchanges.
Comptroller of the Currency	Supervises operations of over 4,700 national banks.
Federal Deposit Insurance Corporation	Examines, insures, and regulates banks that are members of the Federal Reserve System.
Federal Home Loan Bank Board	Supervises and regulates savings institutions which specialize in financing of residential real estate.
Federal Reserve Board	Regulates banks and all financial institutions that offer draftable (checking) accounts.
Securities & Exchange Commission	Regulates all public securities markets to promote full disclosure.
	Energy and Environment
Corps of Engineers	Oversees construction along rivers, harbors, and waterways.
Environmental Protection Agency	Develops and enforces environmental standards for air, water, toxic waste, and noise.
Department of Energy	Oversees national energy policy.
Nuclear Regulatory Commission	Licenses and regulates civilian nuclear power facilities to protect public health and safety and the environment.
	Health and Safety
Consumer Product Safety Commission	Requires reporting of product defects and redesign and labeling to reduce unreasonable risks of injury from consumer products.
Federal Aviation Admin.	Regulates aviation industry.
Food & Drug Admin.	Protects against impure and unsafe foods, drugs and cosmetics, and other potential hazards.
Occupational Safety & Health Admin.	Regulates workplace safety and health conditions.
National Highway Traffic Safety Admin.	Regulates motor vehicle safety through safety standards, uniform national speed limit, and protects consumers from vehicles with reset odometers.

Source: U.S. Office of the Federal Register, *The United States Government Manual 1984/1985*, 1984.

4. roughly twice the amount that the federal government spends on health.

5. two-thirds of the amount devoted to national defense.

6. over one-third of private investment in new plant and equipment.

The total of $200 billion probably underestimates true costs, because nearly 20 regulatory agencies (Department of Energy, Consumer Product Safety Commission, and others) were not included in the study due to lack of data at that time.

The estimate *is* considerable, but it only gives us half of the true picture because the study made no attempt to measure the value of the *benefits* we derive from regulation. One could infer from the study that regulatory activities represent as much as 10 percent of our national income each year. While a complete evaluation would require an estimate of the benefits of government regulation, these figures should be useful to Congress when it evaluates proposals for deregulation or more regulation.

Indirect Costs of Regulation

Governmental budget outlays have swollen as public demands for various regulatory programs have grown. The costs of government go far beyond the national budget, however, because many programs with laudable objectives often generate indirect costs through their effects on workers, consumers, and other participants on the economic stage.

Consider the effects of a program like unemployment compensation. Many workers receive what is effectively a paid vacation if they are laid off. Unemployment compensation is largely untaxed and is often as much as 80 percent of a worker's take-home wage. Thus, the cost of the security of knowing that your income will not totally collapse if you are laid off is that this program creates incentives for some people to quit their jobs at the public's expense.

Similarly, government farm programs, intended to bolster the incomes of family farmers, actually line the pockets of large corporate farms and create incredible surpluses of some farm goods. One recent estimate is that every man, woman, and child in America would need to eat a box of cornflakes every day for a year to eliminate the corn now stored at government expense.

Still another example is the infamous "three martini" business lunch. Firms offer a variety of tax-free fringe benefits to their employees because, were these benefits paid in cash, the employees' income taxes would rise. The result is that some employee benefits are disguised as legitimate business expenses. Thus, many employees drive company cars that are newer and grander than they would select themselves, join country clubs that they could not join if the company were not paying their dues, and indulge in more elaborate lunches than they would eat if they were paying the tab themselves.

Finally, business executives are always looking over their shoulders at what government might say about a strategic business decision, and may not do what is necessary to improve economic efficiency, innovate new products, or provide the best service possible for consumers. We have estimates of the direct costs of regulatory compliance, but how about the indirect costs of having talented people who look for loopholes around taxes or regulations instead of improving a firm's products?

These indirect costs of government regulation are incurred whenever people adjust to government policies in ways not intended by policymakers. It may be that the complexity of laws and regulations is made necessary because many people find ways to avoid very simple rules. Thus, the complicated lives we lead as we try to adhere to a maze of bureaucratic rules are among the indirect costs of government. But costs are only one side of the equation. We will now examine some benefits from regulation.

Why Is Business Regulated?

At first glance, this must seem like a simpleminded question. Most of us perceive many shortcomings in the marketplace. In previous chapters, you saw how monopoly power causes economic inefficiency and apparent inequity. Misrepresentations of products by sleazy firms, unsafe working conditions, and many other maladies seem common in our market economy. The reasons for business regulation seem obvious.

The idea that people need protection from such business abuses is known as the **public interest theory of regulation.** By *public interest,* we mean that it seems to be in the public's interest for certain business activities to be regulated. This rationale has been widely accepted for years. When regulation has not operated in the public interest, the standard interpretation has been that these imperfections are simply consequences of imperfect people doing their jobs as regulators in imperfect ways. Only recently has this explanation for regulatory peccadilloes been questioned.

After decades of studying the American economy, Nobel Prize winner George Stigler identified numerous instances where regulation failed to guard public interests. He asked an obvious question: If the public interests are not being served, whose are? According to Stigler, one answer is that regulation often serves the interests of regulated industries rather than those of the general public. This view is known as the **industry interest theory of regulation.** A third alternative, the *public choice* view, emphasizes that the interests of regulatory bureaucrats are served by larger budgets and more complex regulations. A detailed discussion of this view is left for a later chapter. In this chapter, we will examine the traditional rationale for regulation—the public interest theory—before reviewing Stigler's alternative interpretation.

[handwritten: a lot of govt. reg. maximize]

The Public Interest Theory of Regulation

The public interest theory of regulation centers on some possible failures of the market system: externalities, monopoly power, and imperfect information. Problems of monopoly power and externalities are the foundations for much of business regulation. The idea that imperfect information adversely affects market solutions is used most to rationalize regulation of labor markets and consumer protection.

Regulating Monopoly Power

Antitrust policy is one tool aimed at reducing monopoly power. Antitrust actions, however, may cause economic inefficiency if there are substantial economies of scale in production. If, at most, a few firms can achieve the lowest possible production costs and accommodate demand in an industry, then requiring a multiplicity of small competitive firms to operate causes costs to be inefficiently high. A **natural monopoly** is one possibility. Straightforward examples include railroads, electricity generation, and highways.

Government provides highways, but most natural monopolies are privately owned. These industries are characterized by high fixed costs and huge economies of scale. Limiting the sizes of firms to promote competition would be inefficient and a mistake; costs would be excessive and the public could not enjoy the benefits of the lower prices attainable through economies of scale. Public policymakers, however, are faced with a dilemma. If a monopoly develops, how can it be prevented from restricting output and raising prices to earn monopoly profits?

The dilemma posed by a natural monopoly is diagrammed in Figure 2, which depicts a market where economies of scale are such that only one firm can operate efficiently. If there were two firms in the industry, each producing Q_m, average total costs for each firm would be AC_m. Since $2Q_m = Q_0$, the prices (P_0) these two firms could charge would fall far below AC_m because of limited demand. Consumers would ultimately gain little by having two firms competing with each other, however, because each business would lose money continuously until one went bankrupt. If more than two firms entered the industry, average total costs would be even higher. Unfortunately, if consumers were confronted with an unregulated monopoly, output would be restricted to Q_m and sold at a price of P_m, possibly exceeding the price associated with some competition. Price exceeds marginal cost in this monopoly solution, so there is economic inefficiency.

The public interest can clearly be better served if there is only one firm in order to exploit the benefits of economies of scale. If the regulated unit price is restricted to P_r, the firm could realize normal profits and consumers would enjoy a price lower than the unregulated price P_m. However, price equals marginal cost is the point where the socially optimal price is charged and the socially optimal quantity is sold. This reflects the desirable resource allocation characteristics associated with the model of competition. Is there any way for the regulator to require that the last unit Q_0 be sold at a price of P_0 so that efficiency is realized? If a price of P_0 is charged for every unit of output, the firm will receive revenue equal to area OP_0aQ_0, which is inadequate to cover total costs equal to area OP_1bQ_0. No firm would be willing to stay in business if regulations forced such constant losses.

Block pricing is a technique that can efficiently generate sufficient revenues to cover all costs, in-

PROBLEMS W/ AC PRICING

① what should go into the rate base? what should be included in the AC of production

FIGURE 2 *The Dilemma of the Natural Monopolist*

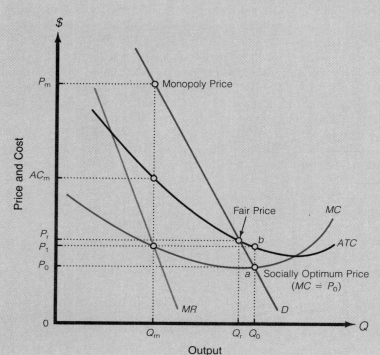

An unregulated monopolist will charge P_m, which is far above marginal cost (MC) and results in severe problems for the goals of efficiency and equity. The "fair price" P_r will just cover costs, but still exceeds MC and so results in inefficiency. A uniform socially optimal price, P_0, would be efficient but would not cover average total cost (P_1). No firm would be willing to suffer losses consistently, which poses a dilemma for society. How can we secure efficiency and still ensure that investors in firms of this type receive fair rates of return?

1. mc pricing
P = mc econ efficiency occurs
problem - firm will go under
2. use
Ⓐ Average Cost pricing
Ⓑ Full
Ⓒ cost of service pricing where D = ATC.

cluding a normal rate of return. There is an initial minimum fee charged all users, but the more you use of the regulated monopolist's product, the lower the price for extra units. For example, block pricing is used to set rates for electric companies. You pay a hookup fee and then a minimum monthly charge. As you use more and more electricity, your total bill rises but the rate per extra kilowatt hour declines. Figure 3 replicates the cost and demand data in Figure 2 but shows that with block pricing, revenues (the entire shaded area) can cover costs (the entire crosshatched area). Because the price of the last unit equals its production cost in this example, marginal social benefit equals marginal social cost and this market operates efficiently. Notice that block pricing uses price discrimination to yield efficiency. Block pricing is commonly used for public utilities (natural gas, electric, and telephone services), for railroads and other forms of regulated transportation, and for pipelines.

All this may seem relatively simple when it is just part of a diagram. However, implementing regula-

tion is complex and time-consuming, absorbing the efforts of thousands of people. In practice, *rate making* (setting utility prices) requires that the agency select a period of time over which calculations will be made (usually the preceding year). The agency then adds up all the company's operating costs, including depreciation and taxes. A reasonable accounting profit, derived from multiplying the rate base by the percentage rate of profit allowed, is added to operating costs. (The **rate base** is the value of the firm's capital to which the profit rate applies.) The regulatory body then adjusts **rate structures** so that total revenue will cover these operating costs, including an allowance for normal profit.

Invariably, there are disagreements over such things as: (*a*) items to be included in the rate base and their appropriate values, (*b*) a fair rate of return, (*c*) allowable costs, and (*d*) how rates should be structured. If all "costs" are allowed, the utility would have few incentives to be efficient. Executive limousines, private jets, resort homes, and similar luxuries would all become "costs." On the other hand, rates

FIGURE 3 How Block Pricing Permits Revenues to Cover Costs and Facilitates Efficiency (MSB = MSC)

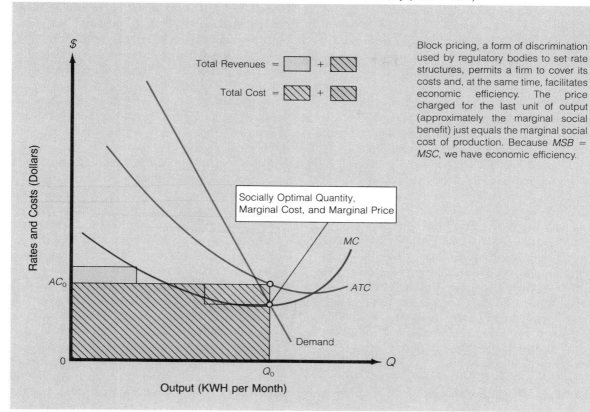

Total Revenues = ▢ + ▨

Total Cost = ▨ + ▨

Socially Optimal Quantity, Marginal Cost, and Marginal Price

Block pricing, a form of discrimination used by regulatory bodies to set rate structures, permits a firm to cover its costs and, at the same time, facilitates economic efficiency. The price charged for the last unit of output (approximately the marginal social benefit) just equals the marginal social cost of production. Because *MSB = MSC*, we have economic efficiency.

must be high enough to protect the financial health of the company or it will be unable to attract investors. Finally, the regulatory commission must continually monitor the quality of service.

Control over pricing is generally the regulatory approach to caging monopoly power. There are other regulatory tools to control potential abuses of monopoly power, but we do not have the space to deal with them here. Externalities are another problem of the marketplace that have been used to justify regulation. However, direct regulation generally has been used rather than the price system.

Externalities and Direct Regulation

Externalities exist whenever some production or consumption activity confers benefits or costs on a party not directly engaged in the activity. Pollution is one example of negative externalities that harm groups who do not consume the product.

Some forms of passenger protection in autos carry externalities. Others do not. If particular pieces of safety equipment, like seat belts and air bags, protect only a car's occupants, these can be sold to individuals just like air scoops, AM-FM radios, and so on. Drivers and their passengers are the primary beneficiaries of this equipment. This safety equipment directly saves the individual buying them from harm, and the externalities are negligible.[2] However, shock absorbing bumpers are an example of safety equipment that carries externalities. The buyer gains, but other drivers do also. Damage to both cars is reduced when one car with a shock absorbing bumper collides with another car. External benefits are conferred upon nonpurchasers of the shock ab-

2. This argument ignores the effect on insurance rates of added injuries to occupants who do not wear protective restraints, and also assumes that the harm to the passenger consists only of medical costs.

sorbing bumpers, but payments for such external benefits are almost impossible to collect. Thus, private purchases of shock absorbing bumper systems will be less than is socially optimal. Consequently, the "public interest" now requires that manufacturers provide such mechanisms on cars. This is an example of a positive externality in which government regulation requires the provision of a particular good. Inoculations against communicable diseases and education requirements are also examples of activities embodying positive externalities.

Not all externalities are positive. Pollution of all kinds represents a negative externality. Such an externality imposes costs on individuals outside the transaction in question. When one firm discharges noxious waste into a stream, people who use the stream for recreation pay part of the costs, whether they consume the product that generates the pollution or not. No single firm will voluntarily control its waste adequately if cleaning up imposes costs not borne by its competitors. Competitors will undercut the prices required to cover the costs of nonpolluting firms. Government intervention may be necessary to compensate for these third-party costs. Generally, this regulation is direct, limiting some forms of pollution quantitatively and absolutely forbidding other, more dangerous pollutants. We leave a detailed discussion of externalities and alternative environmental policies to a later chapter.

Imperfect Information

The market operates properly when relatively good information is shared by both buyers and sellers. Sellers in many cases, however, can reasonably be assumed to have better information than consumers. For example, consumers do not have staffs of safety engineers to assess automobiles or other high-technology equipment. A knowledgeable seller would have incentives to disguise a lack of automotive safety if a problem were discovered after production was under way. The Ford Pinto case is a notorious example.[3] Firms also commonly have better information than workers about on-the-job safety.

One possible solution is for the government to provide information to the public. Alternatively, various private organizations evaluate products. For example, *Consumer Report, Road and Track,* and *Motor Trend* are all sources of information about automobile performance and safety. Even if information is readily available, however, some people argue that the public lacks the expertise to assess it. As a result, the government often uses its own experts and then specifies whether a given product can be sold or a given work practice can continue.

Many people believe that imperfect information justifies government regulation to monitor product safety, fraudulent sales practices, contents of foods and drugs, toy safety, and occupational safety and health, among other areas. Product characteristics other than imperfect information, externalities, or declining costs that tend to encourage regulation include (*a*) goods considered vital to consumers, (*b*) goods for which supplies or demands fluctuate significantly, (*c*) products that are hooked directly to the consumer's property by such things as wires or pipes, and (*d*) products that are reasonably homogeneous. Each of these areas either arouses public concern or makes regulation easy to implement. Focus 3 illustrates how the imperfect information and the potential for fraud, coupled with instability of demands and supplies, may warrant government regulation in securities markets.

All the preceding public interest rationales represent conventional reasons for economic regulation. However, George Stigler recently introduced a fundamental change in the way many economists view much of economic regulation.

An Alternative View of Regulation

The state—the machinery and power of the state—is a potential resource or threat to every industry in the society. With its power to prohibit or compel, to take or give money, the state can and does selectively help or hurt a vast number of industries.

—George J. Stigler (1971)[4]

---

3. Ford was acquitted of criminal charges that it knew that the placement of the gas tanks in its Pinto was dangerous. Nevertheless, the company lost millions of dollars in civil suits brought by people maimed when rear-ended Pintos exploded into fiery coffins.

4. George J. Stigler, "The Theory of Economic Regulation," *The Bell Journal of Economic & Management Science,* Spring 1971.

Options, Rules, and Efficiency

Recent changes in the securities market have been nothing short of revolutionary. The range of choices available to investors, hedgers, and speculators has grown immensely. Nowhere is this more evident than in the options market. An option is the right to buy or sell a specific stock (the underlying stock) at a certain price for a limited period of time. A *call option* gives the owner the right to buy the stock, while a *put option* gives the owner the right to sell the stock. The price at which the stock may be bought or sold is known as the *exercise* (or *striking*) price. Options typically exist for only 3, 6, or 9 months, and so carry an *expiration date*.

On April 26, 1973, the Chicago Board of Trade's Options Exchange (CBOE) initiated standardized trading in options. Options previously had been traded in over-the-counter markets that required brokers to match buyers and sellers, with different option prices and expiration dates spread all over the calendar. The CBOE made options trading more efficient by: (*a*) creating a clearing house to execute options contracts,

(*b*) establishing a market to standardize prices, and (*c*) specifying that expiration dates could fall on only certain days of the month. These reforms made it easier to calculate the values of options and keep track of them. Before 1973, less than 500 thousand options traded annually; over 200 million are now traded on the CBOE.

Option prices are influenced by such factors as the: (*a*) price and volatility of the underlying stock, (*b*) striking price, (*c*) time remaining to expiration, (*d*) interest rate, and (*e*) dividend rate of the underlying stock. The price of the underlying stock is probably most important. A call option is *in the money* if the stock price is above the striking price. The prices of in-the-money options tend to vary dollar-for-dollar with changes in prices of the underlying stock.

Options allow leveraged speculation, but can also be used to hedge and reduce risk. For example, suppose you owned 100 shares of Apple Computer. Assume the market price is $20 and the 6-month call option with a striking price of $23 is selling for $4. You

could sell a "covered call" (your call is covered by the 100 shares you own) and get $400 now. You are, in effect, selling your stock for $24 per share if the stock's price rises above $23, and you receive $400 to offset losses if the stock price falls. You have thus reduced your "downside" risk by selling the option. However, you have also limited your "upside" reward potential as a trade-off to the reduced risk. As you might expect, option trading is far more sophisticated than our simple transaction suggests. The important point is that as financial instruments, options can be used to balance risk in an investment portfolio.

The market was limited before the CBOE introduced standardized options; even large financial institutions steered clear of puts and calls. The financial regulations established by the CBOE converted what had been a relatively exotic financial instrument into a popular asset in many portfolios. Rules and regulations can, as this example illustrates, enhance efficiency in some markets.

The public interest view of regulation prevailed until the early 1970s. If the public interest approach is accepted, however, we would expect to find regulation primarily in highly concentrated industries (to regulate monopoly power), in industries with significant economies of scale, or in those exhibiting substantial externalities. Many regulations in such areas as taxi service, air transportation, trucking, and some professional licensing arrangements (barbering, for example) find little support in the public interest rationale.

Does Business Benefit from Regulation?

The Constitution gives Congress the power "to regulate commerce among the several states." The government can tax, forcibly alter the allocation of resources, or change the economic decisions of households and firms without their consent. The state can use these great powers to increase or decrease profitability in any industry through four major mechanisms:

1. direct subsidies to the industry, special tax breaks or punitive taxes, or advantageous or harmful operating regulations.
2. restrictions or encouragement of entry or exit.
3. subsidies, taxes, or regulatory limitations on complementary or substitute products.
4. direct price-fixing policies (price floors or ceilings).

All four mechanisms have been used to alter the profitability of various industries. The merchant marine is heavily subsidized, as is the education industry. Entry restrictions were effective in the airline industry, where the Civil Aeronautics Board (CAB) did not license a single new trunk line during the 40 years following its establishment in 1938. Another example is the trucking industry, which is regulated by the Interstate Commerce Commission (ICC). From the late 1930s into the early 1980s, the number of licensed carriers in operation dwindled, while the number of new applications for certificates steadily grew. In the 1960s and 1970s, there were typically over 5,000 new applications annually, while the number of companies in operation continually shrank.[5] Law and medicine, too, are professions that have benefited greatly from restrictions on entry.

Government policies have also been directed at an industry's substitutes and complements. Laws prohibiting margarine sales or barring the use of yellow food dyes that allowed margarine to mimic butter's appearance were enacted in the 1950s when the dairy industry fought to hold its market for butter. The trucking industry vigorously supported development of the interstate highway system. Naturally, railroads opposed its development. Today many building trade unions block laborsaving technology in the construction industry through opposition to changes in local building codes. The consequence is that many building codes require outdated, labor intensive construction techniques that drive costs up but provide employment for union workers. Direct price fixing is found in milk and cheese price supports and in many farm and tobacco subsidy programs.

Most of these regulations can hardly be considered in the public interest. Some students of this subject hold to the notion that regulatory agencies were created to promote the public welfare but are misdirected or incompetently managed so that the original purposes of regulation are not achieved. Other economists argue that agencies, once formed, have been captured by the industry they were created to monitor. Regulators need expertise to regulate, and what better sources are there for this expertise than from within the industry itself? The industry's experts know the problems and may know how to solve them. Furthermore, since agencies are constantly confronted by the industry's experts in hearings and other forums, regulators frequently become persuaded by industry arguments. This partially explains why regulations often favor the industry rather than the public, leading to great dissatisfaction on the part of many observers and advocates of regulation.

An Economic Model of Regulation

George Stigler concludes that public interest theories fail to explain numerous regulatory situations because these explanations assume that regulation is forced upon industry. But what if we assume, instead, that firms or industries seek regulation because it serves their private interests? As you might expect, the implications are vastly different from those based on public interest theories.

Stigler's *industry interest theory of regulation* suggests that government is the supplier of regulatory services to firms in an industry. The costs of these services are paid through lobbying for such services, campaign contributions, or other compensation to policymakers who favor the regulations that the industries want.

Probably the most important benefit to an industry from regulation is entry restriction. All firms prefer monopoly power to "cutthroat" competition; many heads of industries invariably try to mold their firms into cartels. Free market cartels are difficult to hold together, however, given the incentives for members to cheat. One way to stabilize a cartel is through state regulation of entry and prices. One contradiction of American law is that cartelization is outlawed in some instances and implemented

---

5. Ibid.

through law in others. Thus, the railroads supported the enactment of the Interstate Commerce Act, airlines supported the introduction of the Civil Aeronautics Board in 1938, and so on. Virtually all regulated industries mount major legal offensives when deregulation of their markets is proposed. The conviction of Teamsters Union officials in late 1982 for conspiring to bribe a member of Congress to oppose trucking deregulation clearly makes this point.

Occupational licensing is an obvious use of the political process to improve the economic conditions of particular groups. The license is a barrier to entry into the profession. Thus, licenses are required for barbers, doctors, dog groomers, lawyers, plumbers, realtors, and travel agents. You can be jailed or fined if you attempt to operate without a license. The call for licensing is often clothed in public interest rhetoric so the public will not object to its pockets being picked. As the supply of new potential entrants into the profession mushrooms to take advantage of higher earnings, entry restrictions evolve that require ever higher qualifications for new applicants. It is not unusual to exclude through higher standards newer members of a profession whose credentials far surpass those held by "grandfathered" long-term practitioners. Of course, all this is done in the name of increasing professional quality for the public.

Stigler's theory may explain much of regulation. The voice of business is not the only input into the regulatory process, however, and, in many cases, firms in different industries have conflicting interests. Real concerns about social well-being permeate the political process, and genuine public interest considerations may prevail.

In summary, rationales for government intervention in business activities emerge from several sources. No single explanation covers all government regulation in America. Some regulation is due to externalities associated with the products of a given industry. Other controls are based on economies of scale in production, information problems, or the nature of the product itself. Finally, some regulation is the result of an industry's ability to promote its self-interest through regulation (and some serves the interests of bureaucratic regulators). Each of these explanations seems appropriate to some specific cases. But the overseeing of business is only part of the regulatory landscape. The activities of consumers are also shaped by governmental regulation.

Consumer Protection

Consumption is the sole end and purpose of all production; and the interest of the producer ought to be attended to only so far as it may be necessary for promoting that of the consumer. The maxim is so perfectly self-evident that it would be absurd to attempt to prove it.

—Adam Smith (1776)[6]

Consumer protection is considered separately from business regulation because, even though firms are normally the entities directly regulated, consumers ultimately bear the brunt or gain the fruits of these rules. Who is really regulated becomes a foggy issue. Is the lawn mower industry regulated because it can sell only lawn mowers equipped with elaborate protective devices, or are consumers regulated because they are denied the opportunity to purchase a mower (presumably at lower cost) without elaborate safety mechanisms?

If, as Adam Smith suggested, business exists for the sole purpose of serving consumers' needs, then consumer protection legislation may be a wasted effort. Firms not serving consumers properly will invariably fail. Unfortunately, as in so many areas of economics, there is no simple approach to this complex area. Business does exist to provide for the needs of its consumer constituency, but it does not always follow that consumer protection will be wasted or redundant. Consider some arguments for and against consumer protection legislation.

The Arguments Favoring Consumer Protection

Consumers are presumed to be sovereign in capitalistic economies, using their money to "vote" for the goods they want. We generally assume that consumers are capable of making reasonable choices to maximize their own welfare. In an economy dominated by numerous buyers and sellers, this assumption has considerable merit; competition often works very well. Consequently, the prevailing approach in this country for many years was characterized by the doctrine of ***caveat emptor:*** "Let the buyer beware." Under this doctrine, consumers alone bear the consequences for the use, misuse, safety, and overall

---

6. Adam Smith, *The Wealth of Nations.*

quality of their purchases. Buyers bear the burden of proof when suing sellers for fraud or deception; the seller is presumed not liable unless proven guilty of fraud or some similar violation of law.

A landmark case early in this century overturned the basic assumption of *caveat emptor*. In *MacPherson* v. *Buick Motor Company* (1916), the automaker was held liable for the personal injuries of MacPherson, who was injured when a wheel collapsed because it was made of defective wood. The court concluded that manufacturers could be held liable if their products were negligently manufactured. The field of product liability law grew from this case, and the concept of *caveat emptor* faded into the sunset. Today, writers in the field often refer to the doctrine of ***caveat venditor:*** "Let the seller beware." Product liability has evolved into a complex legal field, but generally the pendulum has swung far in the direction of protecting consumers. With this legal coat of armor protecting the consumer, further consumer protection regulation might seem unnecessary.

However, there are other reasons to protect consumers. As we noted earlier, whenever externalities are associated with the consumption of a product, the private market may not "internalize" these benefits or costs properly. The result is that too little is produced if externalities are positive, too much if externalities are negative. If lawn mowers without guards cause damage to third parties (via noise or damage to property), these costs will be borne by society and not just by lawn mower owners. There will be more than an optimal number of hazardous and noisy lawn mowers.

The concept of *caveat emptor* implicitly assumes that both consumers and producers have a similar level of knowledge regarding the safety and effectiveness of any given product. This parity in knowledge may have been reasonably true when we were a nation of small farmers and shopkeepers and technology was simple, but it can hardly be the case with today's complex array of products. This "progress" is the reason for laws requiring manufacturers to show the contents of products on their labels, for "truth-in-lending" legislation, and so on. Even with government requirements that producers reveal certain information, many products are so complicated that typical consumers may find it nearly impossible to detect basic flaws. The time required for all consumers to become technically knowledgeable about such things as automobiles, major appliances, televisions, and other electronic equipment would obviously be prohibitive. Consumers are not in a position to make "expert" evaluations of the usefulness, safety, and performance characteristics of many highly complex products.

Under either *caveat emptor* or *caveat venditor* doctrines, people are allowed to buy or sell goods, subject to legal recourse. The government, however, flatly prohibits production, sales, or purchase of certain kinds of goods. Prohibited narcotics, cyclamates, and flammable children's clothing are examples. In these cases, consumers are considered unable to properly assess the information that is available. Curiously, some goods only suspected of being harmful, such as food colorings, are prohibited, while substances known to be harmful, like tobacco or alcohol, are permitted.

Modern corporations often use sophisticated advertising to entice consumers to buy their wares. Consumers have few ways to verify most advertising claims short of purchase and consumption. Where the price of a good is high, the loss to any one consumer could be a disaster. Producers generally possess information on rates of product failure and are often accused of building obsolescence into the designs of some products. How can consumers protect themselves? Reasonable certainty regarding quality and safety is provided by regulation. This certainty can be shared costlessly by consumers. This public good aspect of consumer certainty is another strong argument for government intervention. For example, if medicine is uniformly of high quality because of regulation, your sense of security when taking a drug does not reduce my sense of security in taking the same medicine.

The Arguments Against Consumer Protection

Opponents of consumer protection regulation point to the abridgment of economic freedom associated with reducing the range of products available to consumers. Competition alone, they argue, will force business to respond to consumer needs. Most are quick to recognize, however, that the market system does not operate perfectly. The characteristics of a product may either exceed or fall short of expectations. No manufacturer is able to make any good totally risk free or perfect. Modern production techniques may limit defects, but imperfections always remain.

Consumers desiring safer products might be able to obtain them by paying the higher prices necessary to cover the higher costs. Individuals differ in their willingness to incur risk, which should be reflected in the types of products they consume. Consumer protection rules tend to make products quite similar, destroying diversity, one of the principal benefits of the market system.

Opponents of consumer protection legislation also argue that the poor are hurt most by this form of government interference in the market. Since the poor have severe budget limits, they may have to purchase goods of inferior quality if they are to consume at all. If regulation eliminates lower quality products from the market, the poor may be effectively prohibited from consuming some kinds of goods. Wealthier groups are able to afford the added costs and generally buy higher quality goods in any event. For example, compulsory auto safety equipment drives up the relative prices of economy cars far more than those of luxury cars, which often have safety equipment as standard features—and even then, few people wear seat belts. As a result, the rich are relatively less affected by consumer product safety legislation, while lower income groups bear its brunt.

Finally, opponents argue that safer products may not reduce accidents to the extent predicted. Some recent studies of the effects of auto safety devices and their impact on the overall accident and injury rate have produced startling results. Sam Peltzman concludes in one such study that the enhanced safety of the vehicle leads to changes in the behavior of drivers.[7] He argues that, housed in safer vehicles, some drivers become more reckless, causing more accidents, higher insurance rates, less safe highways, and increased pedestrian deaths. The evidence is incomplete, however, and considerable research remains before conclusive results can be obtained.

Consumer protection may be warranted when product externalities exist, when products are so technologically sophisticated that sellers have superior information about product quality, or when the price of the product is so high and purchases are so infrequent that a single loss to a consumer would spell disaster. Alternatively, consumer protection reduces freedom, may inhibit competition from re-

sponding to consumer needs, reduces product choice, and may not accomplish the desired goal of safer products. These and other regulatory problems make the practical aspects of regulation challenging.

Some Practical Problems of Regulation

Some of the thorny problems confronting regulators who try to protect the public are the topic of this section. We also take a quick look at some areas of consumer protection. Finally, we provide an overall evaluation of public regulation.

Public Utility Regulation

Utility companies must be able to attract funds from sales of stocks and bonds, so when public utility commissions set rate structures, they normally target rates of return in the 8–12 percent range. Short-run changes in fuel costs, demand, or efficiency can cause a firm to earn more or less than the target rate. If a firm repeatedly experiences losses or earns in excess of the target return, the regulatory commission usually adjusts rates so that the firm's profit rate returns to normal. Regulation in practice is a complex process. When people are not especially concerned about their utility bills, these regulated monopolies may be able to operate inefficiently and still squeeze favorable rate structures from regulators. When higher costs focus the public eye on utility bills, as has occurred recently, however, popular outcry may prevent utility companies from charging rates that are high enough to cover their costs.

Some economists perceive little evidence that consumers have gained from regulation and argue that regulation of utilities especially has failed to perform the tasks identified by theory. The process of overseeing tends to become rigid and unresponsive to changing conditions over time. In fact, many of these economists suggest that unregulated monopolies might outperform their regulated cousins (see Focus 4). The debate over the quality of public utility regulation persists, and rate setting agencies are looking for ways to improve their performance. While reform is often suggested, it seems improbable that any major changes will be implemented in the near future.

---

7. Sam Peltzman, "The Effects of Automobile Safety Regulation," *Journal of Political Economy,* 1975, p. 677.

FOCUS 4

Paying for Power Plant Failures

Power plant failures, abandonments, and cost overruns have become commonplace during the past decade. Some public utility commissions have recently decided not to consider some cost overruns and the costs of abandoned plants as parts of the rate base.

Pressure from consumer groups has created a "heads you win, tails I lose" situation for utility stockholders. Some states even have statutes that require that, "no part of the costs of either abandoned plants or the excess capacity of plants coming into service can or should be borne by consumers." Curi-

ously, these same groups demand rate reductions when the utility makes extraordinarily successful investments.

This approach to public utility regulation has two pitfalls: (*1*) utilities are forced to bring uneconomical power plants into service to get the costs into the rate base; and (*2*) where abandoned plant costs are excluded, stockholder value may be expropriated. Public utility commissions can burn stockholders once, but the market will get its revenge when the company tries to raise capital in the future.

Because of these problems, today's most successful utilities are those that took steps in the 1970s to minimize their future power plant needs. Encouraging energy conservation and cogeneration were among the programs used to avoid building more plant capacity. Modern utilities are looking at these and other alternatives as substitutes for new capacity. The result is that in many ways utility power has become capacity-capped. What the future holds, according to some observers, is "brownouts" in the 1990s and exploding rates if OPEC is ever able to strike again.

Other Regulations in Practice

Consumer regulations are diverse and varied, but they can be separated into a few categories. First, the earliest consumer protection statutes dealt with protecting the consumer from harm from food, drugs, or cosmetics that were mislabeled, misbranded, or adulterated. A second group of laws protects consumers from unfair competition and false or misleading advertising. A third category deals with product safety. This category took on special importance when the Consumer Product Safety Commission was established in 1972. In the labor market, several agencies protect workers from hazardous working conditions, discrimination based on sex or race, and abuses by management or unions of their fundamental rights to collective representation. Another broad category of regulation hems in the financial and banking industry.

Evaluation of Public Regulation

In recent years, numerous politicians have pledged to reduce the level of government intervention in the private sector. The news media have carried dozens

of horror stories of overregulation. Deregulation of airline fares in 1978 caused airline ticket prices to fall dramatically and led to a boom in air travel. The case of airline ticket prices became a shining example of the benefits consumers gain once government price fixing is removed. In 1980, banking and other financial institutions began a phase-in of deregulation. In addition, congressional proposals for further deregulation in trucking, railroads, and several other industries are currently on the drawing board.

There seems to be general agreement that some regulation is necessary. But when has regulation gone too far? The president of Dow Chemical Company contends that fully one-third of the millions Dow spends on environmental, transportation, health and safety, and other forms of regulation is wasted. He cited a case where Dow spent $60,000 per plant to lower all railings from 42 inches to roughly 32 inches to meet Occupational Safety and Health Administration (OSHA) requirements. This was done even though Dow's in-house studies had concluded that the 42-inch railings were considerably safer.[8]

---

8. *Business Week*, April 4, 1977, p. 50

FOCUS 5

The Marlin Toy Case

The Marlin Toy Products Company of Horicon, Wisconsin provided jobs for 85 of the town's 1,400 residents. Its most important products, accounting for about 40 percent of its output, were two children's toys. One was a transparent plastic sphere containing artificial birds and tiny, brightly colored plastic pellets, and the other was a similar sphere containing pellets and plastic butterflies. In November 1972, the Food and Drug Administration (FDA) notified the Marlin Toy Company that both toys were unsafe, reasoning that if a sphere broke, a child might be tempted to eat the pellets. However, since Marlin first marketed the toys in 1962, no customer had complained to Marlin of harm caused by the spheres. The toys had already passed three safety tests: Marlin's, an insurance company's, and a department store's. Nevertheless, Marlin recalled the spheres to remove the pellets. Within a month, the FDA said it was satisfied and promised to delete the toys from the next published list of banned products. Because the list of banned products is released only once every 6 weeks, Marlin lost most of its Christmas 1972 toy sales, in addition to its loss through recall of the banned toys.

Marlin proceeded to manufacture thousands of the toys, hoping to recover during the 1973 Christmas holiday sales the losses it had sustained from the 1972 recalls. But in September 1973, the newly formed Consumer Product Safety Commission published a special holiday list of dangerous toys whose sale was prohibited—including the toys Marlin had redesigned months before to the satisfaction of the FDA. Unfortunately for Marlin, a clerical error caused the company's products to be included on the commission's new list. By the time the error was acknowledged, it was too late. Stores all over the country had canceled toy orders from the company for the 1973 Christmas season. By January 1974, the company faced bankruptcy, having lost at least $1.2 million is sales, which does not include what had been lost in good will.

Adapted from Martin C. Schnitzer, Contemporary Government and Business Relations, (Chicago: Rand McNally Publishing Company, 1978), pp. 389–90.

Amid the complaints of overregulation stands the case of Marlin Toy Products Company, described in Focus 5. As that case and the study by Murray Weidenbaum and Robert DeFina suggest, regulation is not free. In the neighborhood of $200–$400 billion is devoted to regulatory activity. Big government may create problems just as enormous as those posed by big business or big labor.

Deregulation in the Eighties

Ronald Reagan's election in 1980 resulted in the enactment of several federal deregulation proposals formulated during the Carter Administration, most notably the deregulation of the trucking and airline industries. The economic pressures generated from airline deregulations led to many changes in the industry, including Continental's use of the federal bankruptcy statute to void its union contracts and two-tier wage agreements where new and old employees were subject to different wage ladders.

Regulation often involves a complex combination of price and entry restrictions that can lead to higher prices and less service. Moreover, the competition among regulated firms tends to be especially based on advertising, product quality, or new product development ignoring price competition. Regulation is often a compromise among conflicting public interest, industry interest, and bureaucratic objectives, which makes the results of deregulation somewhat unpredictable. Deregulation of American Telephone and Telegraph Company taught us that deregulating the provision of a good or service often involves submarkets that may be quite different from each other. The deregulatory policy that works well in one submarket may fail in another. An example of this failure occurred when Seattle recently deregulated taxis.[9]

---

9. Richard O. Zerbe, Jr., "Seattle Taxis: Deregulation Hits a Pothole," *Regulation,* November/December, 1983, pp. 43–48.

In the past, local transit unions viewed taxis as threats to their negotiated wages. Cities often view taxis as threats to municipally owned transit systems and respond favorably to union pleas for taxi regulation. The predictable results have been higher fares, lower taxi usage, slower response time, and significant medallion (or license) values. Today, taxi cabs are popular local targets for deregulation.

The Seattle taxi market consists of two distinct submarkets: radio-dispatched cabs (roughly 60 percent of the market) and cabs waiting in line for customers at airports, railroad stations, or hotels. By 1980, Seattle adopted rules permitting free and open entry of taxis and permitted cabs to alter fares as often as every 3 months by filing a simple rate change. Deregulation was expected to undo all the negative effects full-scale regulation had been charged with.

In the radio-dispatched submarket, deregulation apparently lived up to expectations. Average fares declined and response time improved. In the other submarket, however, deregulation produced a unique set of problems. First, long lines of independent taxis developed into a logistics problem. Some drivers left their cabs to hustle customers, others blocked driveways, and still others were violent in their quest for customers.

At the airport, waiting cabs were confined to a holding area and called up to the terminal as needed. This system restricted price competition since many passengers were visitors and did not know the going price for a cab, were on expense accounts, or were intimidated by having only one cab available. The result was a significant disparity in taxi rates going to

and from the airport ($25 to downtown versus $16 from downtown to the airport). The quality of cabs and cabbies also deteriorated and taxis often refused short hauls. These problems caused Seattle to reexamine the issue and eventually adopt a maximum fare scheme based on the median rate for all taxis. As you might expect, the maximum rate has tended to become the rate charged.

Deregulation of taxis in Seattle, after minor modifications, has probably been favorable, but the experience illustrates the complexities that can result and the care with which significant economic changes to particular markets must be approached. Deregulation may not be as simple as its proponents claim. No one expects to see regulation eliminated, but perhaps its efficiency will improve. This reappraisal will probably focus on ways to bring business into the process in a responsible manner. Some regulations that work against the public interest may be eliminated. The government's supervisory role may continue to grow, but reports of extensive overregulation may force such controls to be either more effective or to fade in importance.

Every attempt at deregulation appears to be more than offset as new regulations are added to the books. For example, regulation increasingly governs public smoking, consumer protection laws for consumer software purchases, and the use of "junk bonds" in corporate finance. The future might bring under the regulatory umbrella such wide ranging issues as biogenetic research, euthanasia, no-drive days to reduce pollution, sexually transmitted diseases, and liquor promotions such as happy-hours and two-fers.

CHAPTER REVIEW: KEY POINTS

1. The *public interest theory of regulation* focuses on some possible failures of the price system. These possibilities include poor information, fraud, externalities, and monopoly power. Since laissez-faire markets will not provide the socially optimal quantity of a product with externalities, direct regulation is commonly used in an attempt to protect the public interest.

2. A *natural monopoly* involves substantial economies of scale, rendering direct competition impractical. Society has turned to regulation to prevent natural monopolies from reaping enormous profits and to move them towards socially efficient levels of output. The public interest may be served by requiring the firm to use *block pricing*. Block pricing uses price discrimination both to achieve efficiency and to equate total revenues from sales of the service with total costs of production, including a normal accounting profit.

3. The *industry interest view of regulation* expressed by George Stigler suggests that industries can gain from regulation, and therefore "demand" regulation from the government. As Stigler has noted, the state can, and often does, change the profitability of an industry through four main mechanisms:
   a. direct taxes or subsidies,
   b. restrictions on entry,
   c. impacts on an industry's complementary or substitute products, and
   d. direct price-fixing policies.

4. Stigler views the government as the supplier of regulatory services to various industries. The costs to the industries of obtaining favorable regulation include campaign contributions and lobbying expenses.

5. The bulk of regulatory agencies in this country were created during three decades. The first great surge occurred during the 1930s, when policymakers attempted to buffer the impact that the violent swings in the business cycle had on our economic system. Well over half of all regulatory agencies, however, came into existence in the 1960s and 1970s. It is not obvious why regulation increased so dramatically during a period of relative prosperity and high economic growth.

6. The law of product liability has evolved from an approach of *caveat emptor*, which means "Let the buyer beware", to one of *caveat venditor*, which means "Let the seller beware." Direct mandates or prohibition of some transactions are also becoming increasingly common. For example, new cars are required to have specific safety equipment and some new drugs are banned. *Caveat emptor* is most appropriate when both producers and consumers have roughly equal access to knowledge about the product. Today, however, producers commonly have considerably more information about complex products than do consumers. It would be prohibitively costly for consumers to detect design and manufacturing flaws in most goods. In addition, modern corporations may use their massive financial and market power to manipulate consumers. Advertising claims are difficult for consumers to verify. Thus, government regulation is seen by many as the only practical solution to the problem of misrepresentation.

7. Opponents of *consumer protection* regulations argue that unregulated competition will force producers to respond to consumer needs, even though this response may be imperfect. Those individuals who want safer products will pay for them, and those willing to incur more risk will not. Furthermore, opponents argue that the poor are hurt most by consumer protection, which removes inferior but cheaper products from the market. For many of the poor, consumption opportunities are limited already, and removing the inferior (usually cheaper) products from the market may force them out of the market entirely.

8. Regulating public utilities is considerably more difficult than simple theory would suggest. Major problems arise in determining the *rate base,* a "fair" rate of return, and allowable costs. Regulatory agencies face an extremely difficult task in their efforts to balance the interests of consumers and utility investors.

9. Regulation is increasingly attacked as misguided and "nit-picky." Various deregulation schemes have been implemented in the 1980s. The next decade will probably bring continued reappraisal of the government's role as regulator, but whether this will translate into further reductions in regulation is highly speculative.

QUESTIONS FOR THOUGHT AND DISCUSSION

1. The Occupational Safety and Health Act (OSHA) requires that workplaces be made as safe as possible (or more so, according to some critics), with little or no regard for costs. How would you expect OSHA regulations to affect the prices of goods previously produced under hazardous conditions relative to the prices of those that have always been produced in safe work environments? What would you expect to happen to wages in previously hazardous industries? In previously safe industries? What will happen to real wages economywide? To health insurance rates? Should it matter for the purposes of OSHA regulation if the risks of particular occupations are well-known? If so, why?

2. Under what circumstances should specific goods (for example, flammable clothing, saccharine, heroin, or marijuana) be prohibited? Under what circumstances should producers be liable for harmful or defective products? When, if ever, should the government provide information about consumer products instead of levying regulatory actions limiting or requiring access to goods (such as prescription drugs or automotive safety equipment, respectively)? When should consumers bear the consequences of faulty goods?

3. Suppose you were a Food and Drug Administration (FDA) official charged with licensing new drugs. There are two types of errors to which you might fall prey: (a) you might license a harmful drug, or (b) you might keep a very beneficial drug off the market. What do you think is the nature of the trade-off between these types of errors? Which of these two types of errors would you wish to minimize if your goal is: (a) to maximize your prospects for job security or promotion, (b) to maximize the public welfare? Are there natural checks in the marketplace if you make the first type of error? If you make the second type of error? What are the probable effects on research and development activities of pharmaceutical companies if you minimize the licensing of harmful drugs? If you minimize keeping good drugs off the market? In which direction do you think you would lean if you were a typical FDA official?

FIGURE 4 *A Natural Monopoly*

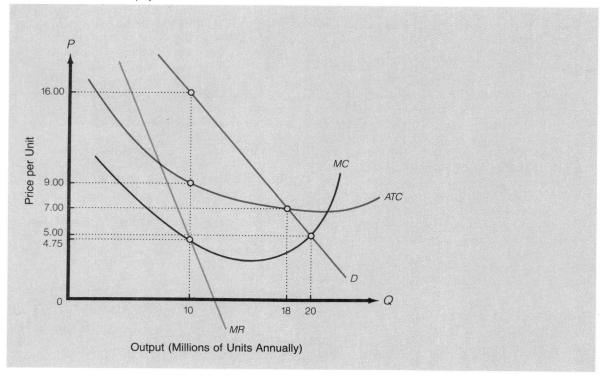

Output (Millions of Units Annually)

4. Some economists have developed proposals that they suggest will eliminate the need for public utility regulation, infuse an element of competition into situations of natural monopoly, ensure economic efficiency, and eliminate the problems of income distribution posed by monopoly power. The proposals take two forms. First, government licenses to provide such services as electricity, gas, or telephones could be sold to the highest dollar bidder. The proceeds from this license auction could then be rebated to the utility's customers. Alternatively, these monopoly licenses could be awarded to the firm that bids the lowest rate structure. Do you think these proposals provide economic efficiency? Equity? What problems could arise with implementation of these schemes?

5. Assume the demand and costs curves depicted in Figure 4 accurately portray a natural monopoly. What would be the total annual profits earned by this monopolist? At what price and output level would society's welfare be maximized? What would be the regulatory price? At this price, what would be the monopolist's annual profit?

6. Two surveys in 1986 revealed that, "a 2-to-1 majority of Americans believe the breakup of American Telephone and Telegraph was a bad idea, and few think telephone service has improved since the breakup. . . ." Twenty percent of those surveyed indicated they had considered canceling telephone service because of increased costs. Do you agree that things are worse since the breakup? Is this another case of the government "fixing something that wasn't broken"? What did the government hope to gain by splitting AT&T into eight separate companies? Are the current problems simply short-term corrections for a long history of monopoly?

7. In 1981, the Reagan Administration proposed almost total deregulation of the alcoholic beverage industry. Not only were consumer groups appalled by the proposal, but, paradoxically, the industry was appalled as well. The industry, it seemed, did not want "government off of its back." The industry went so far as to argue that the Federal Bureau of Alcohol, Tobacco, and Firearms is "a very lean, highly efficient organization . . . [providing] a very high return for its tax dollar. . . ." Why would the industry oppose deregulation? Are the tangled vines of federal regulation better than 50 sets of state regulations? Would consumers gain by deregulation of the alcoholic beverage industry?

PART 8   Markets for Productive Resources

We investigated markets for consumer goods in the previous part of this book, focusing on how household demands interact with production costs to determine prices and outputs. Most production costs are ultimately payments to the suppliers of labor, land, capital, or entrepreneurial talent: demands and supplies of these resources meet in markets that share many of the characteristics of markets for consumer goods. And just as markets for consumer goods range from purely competitive to monopolistic, resource markets range from situations of diffused power (competitive big city markets for secretaries) to single sellers (Bruce Springsteen) or buyers (the U.S. Marine Corps).

In Chapter 28, we develop a competitive approach to resource markets called *marginal productivity theory.* As the chapter unfolds, this foundation for resource demands is blended with a theory of factor supplies to explain resource prices and allocations in competitive markets. We focus on competitive labor markets, but the forces of marginal productivity are exerted in competitive markets for all resources.

The uses of economic power to alter wage structures and employment by large firms and such organizations as unions and employer associations are the subject of Chapter 29. Naturally, unions try to use their economic clout to raise wages, while firms try to maximize their profits by holding wages and other production costs in check.

Discussions of how markets for land, capital, and entrepreneurship determine rates of rent, interest, and economic profit await you in Chapter 30, which concludes with an overview of how marginal productivity operates to distribute total income among the owners of different resources.

CHAPTER 28

Wages and Employment in Competitive Labor Markets

marginal productivity theory	marginal factor cost (MFC)	labor force participation rates
derived demand	wage rate (w)	human capital
marginal revenue product (MRP)	elasticity of demand for labor	minimum-wage laws
value of the marginal product (VMP)	supply of labor	comparable worth

I Decision to Hire or Fire workers
A) Comp. Market
i. Resource market - pay all workers the same
ii. Product Mkt - sell all units at the same price

Derived demand - Derivation
a resource because a D exists
for the final good or service

Resource demands and supplies meet in markets that, on the surface, seem quite similar to markets for consumer goods. There are, however, some basic differences that we need to explore. Most resources satisfy human wants only indirectly; producing the things people want requires combining labor, capital, land, and entrepreneurial talent. Thus, people's direct demands for consumer goods create **derived demands** for resources. These derived demands are based on the productive contributions of the resources to final consumer goods. In a sense, the supplies of most resources are also derived in that resource owners seek income so that they can demand goods and services.

In this chapter, we investigate some forces at work in all resource markets but focus on competitive labor markets. First, we explore firms' demands for labor when both labor markets and output markets are competitive. The choices people make about employment is our second area of concern: these choices underpin labor supplies. We then look at *human capital theory,* which provides insights into how people acquire specialized skills to enhance their individual employment opportunities. The resulting differences in workers influence both the demand side and the supply side of labor markets. Our final topics in this chapter are the effects in competitive labor markets of such government policies as minimum-wage laws and the application of a comparable worth doctrine. In the next chapter, we will examine how limits to competition in labor markets may justify some government actions.

Derived Demands for Resources

Demands for resources are *derived* because they depend on consumer demands for the goods the resources ultimately produce. This is why job opportunities for computer programmers, electronics engineers, and technicians have mushroomed as industrial technology has advanced. Conversely, the demand for teachers collapsed when the post-World War II baby boom went bust and school enrollments dropped in the 1970s. In the 1980s, a resurgence of demand for teachers is accompanying the enrollment of the offspring of 1950s baby boomers.

The demand for final goods is one dimension of the demand for labor: the other is labor productivity, which depends on technology and the prices and availability of other resources. But how do profit seeking firms translate these influences into a hiring decision? Recall that firms maximize profit by expanding output until marginal revenue equals marginal cost ($MR = MC$). A parallel condition specifies how firms maximize profits in labor markets: they hire additional labor and thus produce and sell more output until the last unit of labor adds as much to revenue as it adds to costs.

Marginal revenue product (*MRP*) is the extra sales revenue from the output generated by an extra unit of some resource. The extra cost of hiring an additional unit of a resource is its **marginal factor cost (*MFC*).** The profit-maximizing rule for output

decisions leads to the idea that more resources will be hired as long as the extra funds brought in by the resource (its *MRP*) are at least as great as the money taken away (its *MFC*). Thus, hire more of any input whenever $MRP \geq MFC$. This principle is the cornerstone for resource acquisitions in all competitive resource markets.

The Demand for Labor

Assume again that you own and operate a gold mine in Colorado and that labor is the only variable input: other influences on production are fixed. The law of diminishing marginal returns means that beyond some point, extra workers add less and less to total production. For simplicity, the possibility that specialization might initially yield increasing returns is ignored in the operating data listed in Table 1. The mine yields 3 ounces of gold per week if you hire only one miner. Employing a second miner raises total output to 5 ounces per week, for a gain of 2 ounces per week. This is labor's marginal physical product (*MPP*$_L$); it is listed in column 3 for up to 10 workers.

Computing the marginal revenue product requires calculating the extra revenue from the gold each additional miner produces. The price of gold (P) is set in a highly competitive international market. The value of the gold produced by the marginal

[handwritten: assumes mfc = $600] *[handwritten: MP change]* *[handwritten: $MPP = \dfrac{\Delta Q}{\Delta L}$]*

TABLE 1 Data for Western Gold Mine

(1) Number of Workers L	(2) Total Oz. of Gold Produced per Week q	(3) Marginal Physical Product of Labor MPP	(4) Price of Gold per Oz. P = MR	(5) Value of the Marginal Product of Labor VMP = MRP
1	3.0	3.0	$500	$1,500
2	5.0	2.0	500	1,000
3	6.8	1.8	500	900
4	8.4	1.6	500	800
5	9.8	1.4	500	700
6	11.0	1.2	500	600
7	12.0	1.0	500	500
8	12.8	.8	500	400
9	13.4	.6	500	300
10	13.8	.4	500	200

Note: This table assumes that other factors are fixed and that gold is sold in a competitive market.

[handwritten: $MRP = (MPA)(MR_x)$]

[handwritten right margin: resource D curve = VMP or MRP]

[handwritten: $VMP (MPA)(Px)$ where A = resource Prod]

FIGURE 1 *The Competitive Firm's Demand for Labor (Data for Western Gold Mine)*

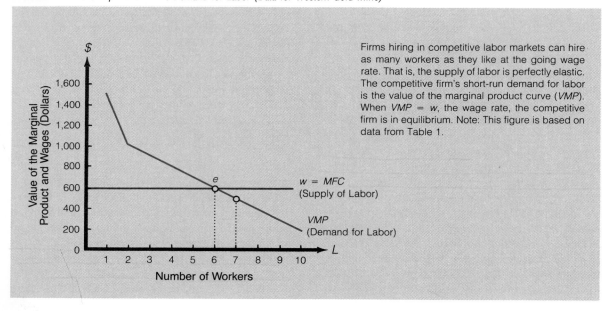

Firms hiring in competitive labor markets can hire as many workers as they like at the going wage rate. That is, the supply of labor is perfectly elastic. The competitive firm's short-run demand for labor is the value of the marginal product curve (*VMP*). When *VMP* = *w*, the wage rate, the competitive firm is in equilibrium. Note: This figure is based on data from Table 1.

worker is $P \times MPP_L$, and is known as the **value of the marginal product (VMP).** In purely competitive markets, $P = MR$, so the marginal revenue product ($MRP = MR \times MPP_L$) and value of the marginal product are identical ($VMP = MRP$). We have assumed the going price of gold to be $500 per ounce (column 4). The value of the marginal product (*VMP*) listed in column 5 is computed by multiplying columns 3 and 4.

The competitive firm's demand for labor is based on the value of the marginal product of labor. Note that *VMP* is influenced by both the productivity of labor (MPP_L) and the demand for the product (*P*). Labor's *VMP* curve for your gold mine is illustrated in Figure 1: this is the short-run demand curve for labor at your mine.

The number of miners you will hire to maximize profits depends on what you have to pay them. Mining gold requires back breaking work in remote areas, so assume that you must pay $600 per week to each worker. The wage rate is unaffected by your hiring if you recruit from a purely competitive labor market; as many miners as you might want to hire are available for $600 per week. At this weekly wage rate, you employ six miners (point *e*) because the value of the marginal product of the sixth worker is also $600.

Would you hire a seventh? No, because the extra $500 in revenue to you is less than the $600 cost of hiring the seventh miner. You would hire a seventh miner only if weekly wages were $500, an eighth miner at $400 weekly, and so on. And if wages rose to $700 weekly, the sixth miner, who generates only $600 in marginal revenue product, would be laid off.

Thus, profit-maximizing firms will hire as long as *MRP* is at least as great as *MFC*. This leads to the rule that purely competitive firms operating in competitive labor markets hire until the *VMP* of the last worker signed on equals that worker's marginal factor cost. In competitive labor markets, marginal factor cost equals the **wage rate (*w*),** so profit maximization requires that *VMP* = *w*.

The conclusion of this analysis is that, all else equal, the value of the marginal product curve is the competitive firm's demand curve for labor. Just as changes in commodity prices cause movements along demand curves for goods, changes in wages cause movements along demand curves for labor. And, by way of summary, the *VMP* curve is underpinned by the demand for the product as reflected in its price (*P*) and by the production technology used (MPP_L).

FIGURE 2 Shifts in the Demand for Labor

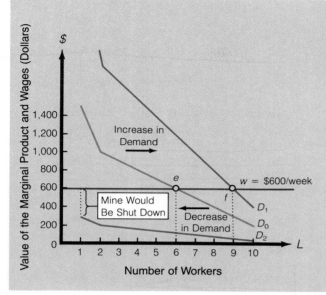

The value of the marginal product of labor equals the output price times the marginal physical product of labor ($VMP = P \times MPP$). Thus, changes in the price of output will shift the VMP curve, which is the competitive firm's short-run demand for labor.

		Demand for Labor Data		
		D_0	D_1	D_2
L	MPP_L	$(P = 500)$	$(P = 1,000)$	$(P = 100)$
1	3.0	1,500	3,000	300
2	2.0	1,000	2,000	200
3	1.8	900	1,800	180
4	1.6	800	1,600	160
5	1.4	700	1,400	140
6	1.2	600	1,200	120
7	1.0	500	1,000	100
8	0.8	400	800	80
9	0.6	300	600	60
10	0.4	200	400	40

recognize changes in graphs (increase or decrease)

Shifts in Demands for Labor

The demand curve for labor ($VMP = P \times MPP_L$) may shift if there are changes in the: (*a*) prices of output, (*b*) prices of other resources, (*c*) production technology, or (*d*) inherent productivity of workers.

Output Prices Many people view gold as a very secure asset. If political turmoil and economic uncertainty became widespread, the worldwide demand for gold might skyrocket. If gold rose to $1,000 per ounce, the demand for miners' labor (VMP) would increase from D_0 to D_1 in Figure 2. Although the amount of gold each miner produces is unaffected, each level of output has doubled in value because the price of gold has doubled, so VMP rises; profit-maximizing employment rises from six to nine miners (point *f*) at the $600 weekly wage.

If the gold market then collapsed and gold fell to $100 per ounce, your demand for miners would decline to D_2. You would close the mine since the VMP of a worker never exceeds $300 per week but each miner's wage is $600. Not only must you pay the fixed costs of owning the mine, but you would lose an additional $300 per week even if you retained only one employee. You are clearly better off to shut down and lose only your fixed costs any time the price of gold falls below $200 per ounce.

Prices of Other Resources Changes in the prices of other resources, and, consequently, in their employment, can also shift demands for labor. Resources are frequently complementary. For example, the miners' productivity will tend to rise if lower capital costs induce you to invest in new capital equipment. Replacing dull or broken picks and shovels with newer tools allows miners to process and recover more gold. Rising marginal physical products of labor would raise their VMPs and your demand for labor. Similarly, higher capital costs and reductions in capital per worker might decrease your demand for miners' services. In addition to their complementarity, however, resources are also substitutes for one another. For example, declines in capital costs or huge wage hikes could cause miners to be replaced by machinery.

Technological Change Technological changes may boost the demand for labor in a very direct way. If newly invented machinery increased every miner's productivity, you would hire more miners. But technological changes do not universally increase the demand for labor. Sophisticated new excavation equipment might enable machinery to replace some miners. The process of replacing human labor with machinery is known as **automation.** During the 1960s, some social analysts feared that growing automation would structurally disemploy a growing pool of workers. These fears have proven groundless because producing, repairing, and operating automatic machinery requires labor. Some forecasters predict that industrial robots will increasingly take over routine assembly line work, and that employment will shift primarily towards service industries.

Automation may cause temporary but traumatic dislocations of workers, even if falling demands for labor in some markets are offset by growing demands in other occupations. Many auto workers lost their assembly line jobs when "robots" were introduced in the early 1980s, compounding the high unemployment in Detroit and other "motor cities" caused by slack sales worldwide during 1979–83. In the long run, however, this automation may have saved more jobs than it destroyed. Without domestic automation, the growing comparative advantages of foreign automakers threatened the survival of the entire American auto industry and all its jobs.

The Quality of Labor
Demands for labor rise when people work harder or acquire more productive skills. Education or on-the-job training can enhance labor productivity. Conversely, if, on average, miners quit working as diligently, their *VMP*s and your demand for their labor would fall.

Elasticity of Demand for Labor

We have seen that the demand for labor is a derived demand and that employment varies inversely with the wage rate. But how much do wage changes affect employment? The responsiveness of the amount of labor demanded (ΔL) to a change in wages (Δw) is measured by the **elasticity of demand for labor,** which is roughly:[1]

$$e_L = \%\Delta L \div \%\Delta w.$$

The elasticity of demand for labor is directly related to: (*a*) the elasticity of demand for output, (*b*) labor's share of total costs, (*c*) the ease of sub-

stitution between labor and other resources, and (*d*) the time allowed for adjustments to changes in wages.

The Elasticity of Demand for the Final Product
The more elastic the demand for a final output, the more difficult it is for the firm to raise prices to cover increases in labor costs. A wage hike will reduce the quantity of labor demanded considerably when higher wages cannot be easily passed forward to consumers because the demand for the good is very elastic. Alternatively, if falling wages cause production costs and prices to drop, sales and employment will rise; the greater the elasticity of demand for the product, the more sales and employment rise. Thus, the more elastic (*inelastic*) the demand for the product, the more elastic (*inelastic*) the demand for labor.

Labor's Share of Total Costs
The effect of a given change in wages on the quantity of labor employed is positively related to labor costs as a proportion of total costs. For example, if labor costs are only 10 percent of total cost, a 20 percent wage hike raises total costs (and price) by roughly 2 percent. On the other hand, if labor absorbs 80 percent of total costs, a 20 percent wage hike exerts pressure for a 16 percent rise in price. For the same rise in wages, employment will be less affected in the first instance because output prices need to rise so little to cover the higher wage costs. Thus, the demand for labor is more elastic the greater labor's share of total cost.

The Ease of Factor Substitution
The easier it is to substitute one resource for another, the greater the elasticities of demand for both resources. For example, if it is easy to switch from coal to oil or natural gas in generating electricity, then small changes in the relative prices of these fuels yield huge changes in the primary fuel used, and utility companies' demands for each fuel will be very elastic. Similarly, the demand for labor is very elastic if workers are easily replaced by machines, and vice versa, but the demand for labor tends to be more inelastic the more difficult it is to substitute other resources for labor.

Time
Longer time periods to adjust to changing wages enable firms to more easily substitute among resources. Technological change also becomes more feasible. For example, from the 1940s into the 1960s,

---

1. Precise computation of e_L would require using midpoint-based formulas paralleling those described in our chapter on elasticity.

soaring wage rates for coal miners stimulated automation and the development of more efficient excavating techniques. Thus, the elasticity of demand for labor tends to grow as the time horizon expands to allow greater substitution among both technologies and resources.

You should now have some ideas about ways that output prices and productivity shape the demands for resources and about some determinants of the elasticities of resource demands. To this point, we have assumed that a firm could hire all the labor it desires at a fixed market wage, but demand is only one dimension of any resource market. Understanding labor markets requires us to examine supply as well.

The Supply of Labor

The **supply of labor** depicts the amount people are willing to work per time period at alternative wage rates. The supplies of labor for individual markets and the economy as a whole are determined by the:

1. population size and labor force participation rates.
2. hours individuals are willing to work.
3. rates and structures of wages.
4. education, the training, and the skills of potential workers.

All these influences on labor supplies are considered below, although our discussion of education and training is lengthy and so we postpone it until after we consider labor market equilibrium.

Population and Labor Force Participation

Almost 60 percent of our population now participates in the labor force. However, **labor force participation rates** (members of the work force as percentages of specific groups) change across time and vary by age, sex, and other characteristics. Labor force participation rates for 1985, by age and gender, are shown in Figure 3. The highest rates predictably occur for people aged 20 to 54. Some participation

FIGURE 3 *Labor Force Participation Rate by Age and Gender, 1985*

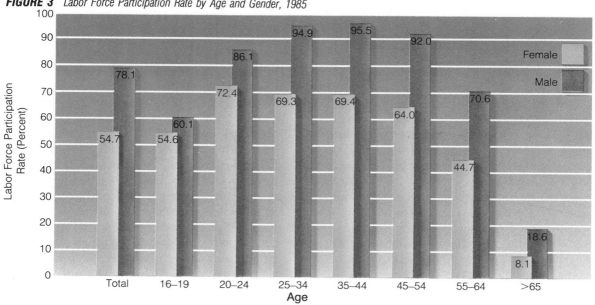

Gender and age are only two of the many variables that influence participation in the labor force. Others include education, spouse's income or other family income, race, and number and age of children in the family.

Source: *Statistical Abstract of the United States*, 1986; *Economic Report of the President*, 1986.

rates have changed sharply in the recent past. In the early 1950s, only 37 percent of women over 20 were in the work force. Today, over half of all women work outside their homes. The rate for men has fallen over this same period, dropping from 86 percent to roughly 75 percent. Explaining variations in labor force participation requires us to examine some influences on individual labor supply decisions.

✓Individual Supplies of Labor

Suppose you were offered a job at $10 per hour and could set your own work schedule. Even if you are a full-time student, you might reduce your course load a bit to take advantage of such an offer. Assume that you decide to work 20 hours a week. If the offer were raised to $25 per hour, you might drop out of school altogether and work 40 or 50 hours per week. This means that your labor supply curve is positively sloped between wages of $10 and $25, as shown by curve *ab* Figure 4.

Let's really get outrageous. If you were offered $100 per hour, would you work more than 50 hours weekly? Unlikely. At a very high wage, you might feel that you were making plenty of money with only 20 hours of work weekly. Two thousand dollars is a tidy sum, and if you work long hours, you might not have time to enjoy the fruits of your labor. Thus, in Figure 4 we show a *backward-bending* supply of labor for all wages above $25 per hour.

Why are individual labor supplies often negatively sloped at high wage rates? Recall the income and substitution effects that we explored as separate aspects of people's responses to price changes for a good. Changes in wage rates alter the price of *leisure,* which can be viewed as a good that is negatively related to the amount of labor supplied. You have less leisure time the more you work. The *substitution effect* of a higher wage is to reduce your consumption of leisure activities relative to work. As your wage rises, you tend to work more and consume less leisure time because the opportunity cost of free time has risen.

The substitution effect occurs because the higher your wage, the more income you surrender when you take off from work. There is, however, an offsetting *income effect:* The demand for leisure, as for any

FIGURE 4 *The Individual's Supply of Labor*

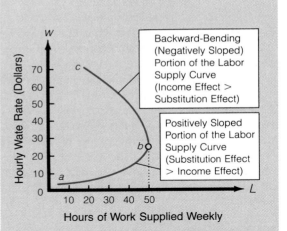

As the wage rate rises, it becomes increasingly costly not to work; therefore, the *substitution effect* induces people to increase the hours they work and reduce leisure. On the other hand, higher wages make greater incomes possible, and this *income effect* will cause people to want more leisure time to enjoy their income. If the substitution effect is more powerful than the income effect, the supply of labor is positively sloped. This tends to be the case when wages are low. However, at high wage rates, the income effect may overpower the substitution effect, in which case the supply of labor is backward bending.

normal good, rises with income. Thus, your higher income causes you to want to "buy" more leisure by working less.

The income and substitution effects operate in opposite directions when the wage rate changes. At low wages, the substitution effect is generally more powerful than the income effect because total income is so low. Thus, a higher wage rate leads to the provision of more work because people tend to substitute work (and the potential for greater consumption) for leisure. When the substitution effect is greater than the income effect, the labor supply curve is positively sloped. When your wages and total income are very high, however, the income effect tends to dominate the substitution effect in your labor decision. This results in a backward-bending supply curve for your labor similar to the curve *bc* in Figure 4.

A rise in the wages of any member of a household may affect the labor supply decisions of other members. A wage increase for the primary breadwinner, for example, may induce other members to cut back their work effort as the family unit consumes more "household services" from other family members. If market wages rise for members of households other than primary breadwinners, families may substitute in the other direction. For example, if a primary worker's earnings failed to keep pace with inflation, other members of a family might enter the labor market to maintain its standard of living. Social roles, customs, and numerous other nonfinancial considerations also influence labor decisions. For example, the birth of a child may temporarily take its mother out of the work force. Desires for education or training also affect the timing and duration of individual participation in the labor force.

Supplies of Labor to Firms or Industries

Even if all individual supplies of labor were backward bending, the supply of labor facing any firm or industry would still be either perfectly elastic or positively sloped. The explanation for this seeming paradox is actually very simple.

Suppose that the Ace Corporation, a major accounting firm in a large city, raises its wage offers slightly. No matter how content accountants happen to be, some will overcome job change inertia and leave their current jobs to take Ace's offer. More pay for the same work sounds pretty good, and the more Ace is willing to pay, the greater will be the number of accountants available to meet Ace's labor requirements. Ace, an individual firm, is clearly faced with a positively sloped supply curve of accountants, even if the total labor supply of current accountants is backward bending. But how about the supply of workers facing the accounting industry? If wages for all accountants doubled, might backward-bending supplies of labor for all current accountants mean that less accounting gets done? NO!

One reason is that some workers with accounting skills who are not presently using them would respond to higher pay by moving back into this line of work. Many young people seeking a remunerative career might also view accounting more favorably. These young people, plus established workers in areas with skills closely related to accounting (such as bookkeepers or financial planners), would view the doubling of accountants' wages as a strong incentive to acquire more training in that field. This occurred throughout the 1970s, and business colleges were flooded with accounting majors. The amount of accountants' services available gradually rose in response to higher wages. The same happens in virtually any industry with growing needs for any type of labor. Higher wages are magnets that attract extra labor services in the long run, even if individual workers may have backward-bending labor supply curves.

In summary, individual supplies of labor are normally positively sloped, but may bend backwards at relatively high wage rates. Even if individual labor supply curves are negatively sloped, however, the supplies of labor facing firms or industries will be positively related to wage rates. The demand for labor depends on labor productivity, technology, the demand for the final product, and the levels of other productive factors employed. We are now in a position to merge labor market supplies and demands to see how equilibrium wages and employment are determined.

Labor Market Equilibrium

Horatio Alger stories were very popular earlier in this century. A standard plot of these yarns: Horatio Alger, a poor young country bumpkin, comes to the sinful "Big City." Through righteous thoughts and modest exertion, he wins fame, fortune, and the hand of a fair damsel. Unfortunately, righteousness, wishful thinking, or modest exertion seldom secure a high income. The Horatio Alger legend may occasionally come true, but marginal productivity theory probably more accurately reflects how labor markets will affect your future well-being.

Wages and Employment

Figure 5 depicts the interaction of labor supplies and demands for both an individual firm and all firms hiring from a given labor market. The market demand for labor, D_L, is only roughly the sum of indi-

read carefully

FIGURE 5 *Equilibrium in the Competitive Labor Market*

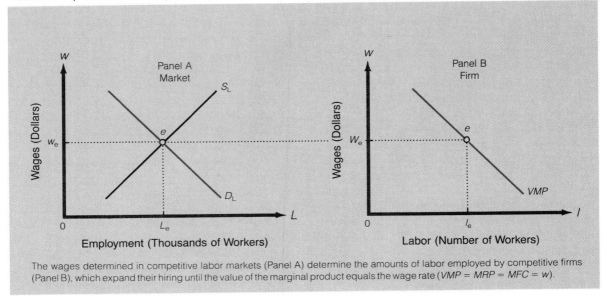

The wages determined in competitive labor markets (Panel A) determine the amounts of labor employed by competitive firms (Panel B), which expand their hiring until the value of the marginal product equals the wage rate ($VMP = MRP = MFC = w$).

vidual firms' demands.[2] The market supply of labor is precisely the sum of individual labor supplies and is denoted S_L. The interactions of labor supply and demand determine the equilibrium wage (w_e) and employment (L_e).

Equilibrium processes resemble those in purely competitive markets for goods. Wages that are above equilibrium create labor surpluses and unemployment. The unemployed will ultimately bid wages down as they try to secure jobs, but this can be a painful and time-consuming process. A depression may result if this situation is common.

If current wages are below equilibrium, shortages of labor create a tight job market, and employers will bid wages up in attempts to fill vacancies. During 1974–84, wages rose sharply for anyone with exper-

tise in petroleum or computers. "Head hunters" from employment agencies contacted some people every week or so to see if they were interested in changing jobs. Eventually, however, wages move towards equilibrium. Each firm faces a labor supply curve that is horizontal at the existing market wage (w_e), and can hire as much labor as it wishes at that wage.

Purely competitive firms hire only until the value of the marginal product of labor ($VMP = MRP$) equals marginal factor cost, which is the wage rate ($MFC = w$). In Figure 5, L_e workers are hired at a wage of w_e (point e). Thus, the market clears when $VMP = MRP = MFC = w_e$, and anyone qualified and willing to work at the prevailing wage will be employed; at the same wage, firms hire exactly as much labor as they wish. Purely competitive markets for capital, land, or entrepreneurial skills, which are explored two chapters hence, operate in a similar fashion.

Labor Market Efficiency

Adam Smith's "invisible hand" receives high marks for efficiency in competitive product markets. The demand curve for any good reflects society's marginal benefits, and its supply curve reflects society's

---

2. In deriving the market demand curves for consumer goods, we horizontally sum individual demands. In competitive factor markets, such summations of *VMP* curves are only a first approximation. Assume wages fell. Each firm in the industry would demand more labor and produce more output, but this added output could be sold only at lower prices. When the price of the product declined, each firm's *VMP* would shift to the left and less labor would be demanded, as you saw in the gold mine example. This effect reduces the market elasticity of the demand for labor, partially offsetting the employment effect of lower wages. Simple summation does not allow for the effects of changes in factor costs on product prices. We leave an expanded discussion of this point to advanced classes.

marginal opportunity costs. Resources are efficiently allocated where the demands and supplies for goods meet, and these allocations reflect societal wants given the prevailing income distribution.

A similar efficiency occurs in competitive resource markets. The demand for labor reflects society's demands for the goods that labor produces and is roughly equivalent to society's *marginal benefit* curve from employment. The labor supply curve facing an industry reflects the *marginal costs* to society of employing labor in that industry, because that labor might also be at leisure or employed in other industries. This is diagrammed in Figure 6.

Society receives what it pays for when competitive labor markets are in equilibrium (point *e*) because the marginal benefits and marginal costs of employment are equal. Suppose employment were only at L_0. The marginal social benefits from additional employment and production equal w_1 (point *a*), while marginal costs are only w_0 (point *b*). A net social gain equal to distance *ab* can be realized by shifting another unit of labor into this industry. Thus, em-

ployment level L_0 is below the socially optimal level of employment in this industry. On the other hand, if employment were L_1, the net loss to society from employment of the last worker would be distance *cd*.

Society's resources are allocated efficiently only when marginal benefits and costs are equal, a result achieved in competitive labor markets because marginal benefits and costs are reflected, respectively, in the demand and supply for labor. J. B. Clark, the first internationally prominent American economist, was the developer of the $VMP = w$ rule for efficiency in labor markets. As our Biography of him indicates, his ideas still dominate analyses of resource markets.

Supply and demand analysis normally assumes that each unit of the item considered is identical. Human labor, however, is far more variegated than long-stemmed roses, bulldozers, or parcels of land. Some variations among people are innate and some are accidental, but many are cultivated to amplify differences in human productivity.

Human Capital

People are not born with the same potential intelligence or strength, but inherited differences are magnified or offset by acquired skills that make us more productive. Acquiring or sharpening our productive skills is called *investment* in **human capital.** Most of us spend years in school or in on-the-job training (*OJT*) preparing ourselves to be better and more productive workers. Self-improvement fanatics may spend most of their lives acquiring human capital. We bring to our training or education certain natural aptitudes and strengths. Our abilities to perform certain tasks are honed as we invest in human capital.

Investment in Education

Education is a lifelong process.

—*Anonymous*

Investment in new machinery or other physical capital requires sacrifices of potential current consumption so that higher levels of future income and consumption can be realized. Acquiring new skills through education requires similar sacrifices. The time and money you are sacrificing to go to college are examples.

FIGURE 6 *Efficiency in Competitive Labor Markets*

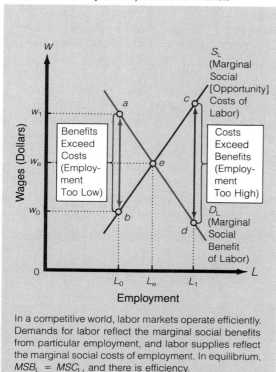

In a competitive world, labor markets operate efficiently. Demands for labor reflect the marginal social benefits from particular employment, and labor supplies reflect the marginal social costs of employment. In equilibrium, $MSB_L = MSC_L$, and there is efficiency.

J. B. Clark (1847–1938)

John Bates Clark was the leading American economic theorist at the turn of the century. His position in American economics was similar to that of Alfred Marshall in British economics. Although Clark did not have the advantage of the vigorous intellectual stimulation Marshall received at Cambridge, he was still an important innovator in economic theory.

Clark's complete writings were intended to restructure the classical theories of value and distribution, but his most enduring contribution to economics is found in *The Distribution of Wealth* (1899), which set forth the *marginal productivity theory of income distribution*. Clark sought to prove that every unit of labor and capital is paid precisely the value it adds to total product—its marginal productivity. His model hinges on resource mobility, pure competition, and the law of diminishing returns.

Labor and capital are each interchangeable, according to Clark, so that each worker or piece of capital is, in a sense, the last one. He reasoned that, although tasks within a firm differ in importance, if a worker engaged in an important task were removed, the remaining work would be reassigned so that all essential tasks would be done, leaving the least important tasks undone. This means that no single unit of labor is more important than any other.

Firms operate in a region of their production functions where diminishing marginal returns cause each worker added to a work force to increase total product by an amount smaller than did the previous worker. Competition provides an incentive for the employer to add workers as long as the last one hired contributes at least as much to total revenue as the cost of employing that worker. Because every worker is the marginal worker, and because the *last* worker hired adds to the employer's gross income the same amount as the wage rate in a competitive labor market, all workers are paid the values of their marginal products.

Properly understood, Clark's marginal productivity theory is a rebuttal to Marx's charge that competitive capitalism systematically robs labor because workers contribute more to total product than the wages they receive. Clark maintained, on the contrary, that the payment to capital is also determined by its marginal productivity and that there is no "surplus value" expropriated from labor as alleged by Marx. Whatever amount of labor is employed, capital so shapes itself that each unit of equivalent labor is working with the same amount of capital. Thus, the product of every unit of capital is also equivalent to every other; when every unit is paid the value of its contribution to total product, there is no surplus to be expropriated. In short, each factor receives a payment determined by the product of its own final increment, and the reward to capital, no less than the reward to labor, is a necessary payment for its productivity.

Early economists were even more prone to take positions on normative issues than economists today, many of whom pride themselves on their scientific objectivity (if such a thing is possible). Clark tried to use his positive findings to "prove" that payments of income according to contribution (marginal productivity) are inherently equitable. The fact that his idea is as controversial today as when he first pronounced and published his "proof" is testimony that normative issues cannot be resolved scientifically.

College is partially a consumption experience for many students, offering football games, parties, and other social opportunities. Most students, however, perceive earning a degree as one step towards a higher income stream and access to "the good life."

If you view your education primarily as an investment that should increase your future income, it is important to select your major carefully since some majors may prepare you to be a scholarly short-order cook.

Decisions about investing in human capital involve balancing higher lifetime earnings against the costs of acquiring more valuable skills. As a college student, you must pay for tuition, books, and other out-of-pocket expenses, and you have less time for employment during your student years. Moreover, your first job as a new college graduate may not yield the wage you might have earned had you gone directly from high school into the labor market and had 4 years of work experience. After a few years on the job, however, your income will probably exceed that of most high-school graduates who went directly into the labor market.

Figure 7 graphs typical out-of-pocket costs and income forgone against lifetime earnings from a college degree. The solid line in the figure is a typical earnings profile for college graduates over their working lives, while the dashed line traces average earnings for high-school graduates who do not go to college. Area A represents out-of-pocket expenses, B is forgone earnings, and C is the gross returns to average college graduates. As long as your area C is sufficiently larger than $A + B$ to cover a normal rate of return, you can benefit by investing in your education. (We detail this type of calculation two chapters hence.) Naturally, the higher the returns from your education, the greater are your personal benefits.

Society as a whole, however, shares in both the costs (through taxes) and benefits of much training and education. Education tends to make life more predictable and pleasant for everyone. For example, we all benefit from widespread literacy. Can you imagine the traffic snarls if most drivers could not read traffic signs? We also benefit by having well-educated voters. Moreover, well-educated people tend to eventually receive higher incomes, pay more taxes, and commit proportionally fewer crimes. Finally, more productive workers expand average standards of living by the extra output their higher productivity provides.

These are only a few of the benefits shared by educated people with society as a whole. These collective benefits may justify some sharing of education costs through taxes. However, the share of gains going to others declines as we progress through the education system. Things we learn in grade school make us semicivilized. High school civilizes us even more, on average if not in every case. But benefits derived from our college educations will be received

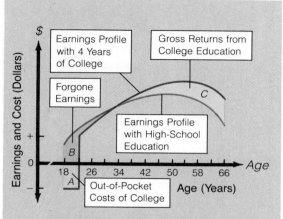

FIGURE 7 The Individual's Investment in Education

High-school graduates who immediately enter the work force will not incur the costs of education borne by their college bound peers (A) and will initially have higher incomes (B). However, typical college educated people eventually surpass the incomes of those who do not extend their formal education (C).

primarily by each of us individually, either in the form of consumption now or higher wages later.

Marginal productivity theory suggests that you will receive more income to the extent that a degree makes you more productive. The onset of diminishing returns, however, implies that more education eventually yields successively smaller additions to your lifetime income. These reflections are supported by the private rate of return estimates developed by numerous economists over the last few years. A summary of estimates for incremental additions to education is presented in Figure 8. For example, the personal rate of return from completing the last year of high school (9–11 to 12 years) is 16 percent. These studies suggest that private rates of return decline as individuals become more educated, with the expected returns from graduate programs being especially low except for medical school.

One cautionary note: The returns shown in this figure reflect only private earnings and do not include the social benefits and personal gratification derived from extended education. For example, the public benefits from the works of Einstein, Keynes, or most Nobel Prize winners probably could not have been produced by people with only high-school educations.

FIGURE 8 *Private Rates of Return to Selected Additional Years of Schooling*

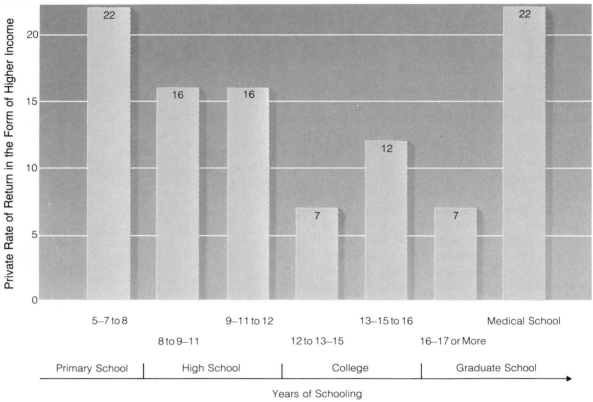

Investment in education seems subject to the law of diminishing returns. Although the monetary rate of return diminishes as people extend their educations, the social and cultural amenities of advanced training obviously cause many to think continued education is worthwhile. Moreover, external benefits may cause the social rate of return to education to be higher than the figures shown here.

Source: J. T. Addison and W. S. Siebert, *The Market for Labor: An Analytical Treatment* (Glenview; Ill: Scott, Foresman and Company, 1978), p. 158.

Formal education is one way to acquire human capital, but, as Focus 1 indicates, some critics believe formal education to be vastly overrated as a predictor of individual productivity. Proficiency in some occupations is enhanced little by schooling, but grows immensely with experience and on-the-job training.

Training and Work Experience

Economists distinguish between general and specific training. **General training** increases a worker's marginal productivity equally for many firms. For example, general training on a computer raises a worker's potential productivity with many firms, and acting lessons may open up many roles to an actor. **Specific training,** on the other hand, only increases the productivity of the worker where currently employed. For example, convicts learning to make license plates primarily increase their productivity for prison work, or actors rehearsing specific lines only perform better in certain roles.

A firm will invest in a worker's human capital only if it expects the employee to stay on the job long enough for the firm to recoup at least a normal return on its investment. How can a company that invests large sums to train electronics technicians

Credentialism

Some critics of modern employment practices think that college degrees are artificial barriers to entry into many occupations. They believe that incompetent practitioners of many professions are protected from competition by people who might be extremely able but who lack the formal education required, either legally or by standard practice, to secure a job. IBM would hire neither Steve Jobs nor Steve Wozniak (the founders of Apple Computers) as computer engineers: neither had a college degree. Today, GE would not hire its founder, Thomas Edison, as a scientist; he lacked even a grade-school education. Abe Lincoln could not practice law in most states today; he apprenticed as an attorney but never attended college. Socrates, Aristotle, Plato, and most of your professors lack the credentials now required to teach high-school courses in the United States.

According to these critics, there are many people who could successfully do jobs not currently open to them because they lack the necessary degrees. Moreover, acquiring the degrees would waste their time, because degree programs allegedly fail to teach virtually anything required by many jobs. Do you think a management trainee in a department store should be compelled to have a degree? Many chain stores have such requirements. Degrees are no guarantee of competence, nor does the lack of formal education mean that someone is incompetent. Think about this issue when you next encounter an incompetent jerk with an advanced degree.

ensure that they will not quit before the firm recovers its investment? Other firms are willing to pay the going wage for trained electronic technicians. Firms will not provide much general training unless the trainees bear the costs, typically by accepting wages lower than the values of their marginal products. Apprenticeship programs are prime examples: apprentices pay for their general training by accepting wages far below those paid to fully trained workers.

The military uses a different approach. It guarantees substantial general training but requires recruits to legally commit to several years of service. This partially explains why the military harshly penalizes AWOL personnel or deserters. (Private employers cannot mimic the military's example because slavery is illegal.)

While much of a technician's training is general, some portion normally represents specific training. The expertise gained when a technician works only on one company's product often cannot be transferred to other firms; that training is specific to that employer. Firms can ignore competition for such services because these job-specific skills have no value to other firms.

Firms consequently absorb the costs of specific training and share in the returns. Military weapons training and knowledge about a particular cost accounting system within a given firm or about a specific delivery route are examples. A firm tries to pay specifically trained workers more than its competitors would but less than the values of their marginal products. These slight wage premiums reduce worker turnover and ensure that, on the average, firms secure returns on their investments in specific training.

Turnover and quit rates among a firm's employees are related to the levels of specific training and wage premiums it pays its workers. Firms have strong incentives to retain employees who have substantial specific training. Higher wages are one way to reduce quit rates, but firms employ many non-wage incentives as well. Seniority rules and pension plans that tie benefits to longevity with a firm are designed to reduce worker turnover and enable firms to recoup their human capital investments. Unfortunately, their shorter remaining work lives may automatically exclude some older workers from job openings that require substantial specific training.

TABLE 2 *Major Labor Laws and Regulations*

Labor Law or Regulation	Purpose	Administrative Agency
Wages & Hours of Work Fair Labor Standards Act, 1938 (both state and federal)	Controls such matters as: a. child labor b. hours of work, particularly for minors c. minimum wages	Department of Labor
Equal Pay Act, 1963	Prohibits employers from discriminating on the basis of race or sex in paying wages for equal work performed (equal pay for equal work)	Department of Labor
Workers' Compensation Acts (state statutes) Similar federal statutes are: Federal Employees' Liability Act (railway workers) Jones Act (maritime workers) Longshoremen's and Harbor Workers' Compensation Act (dock workers)	Provides a system to pay workers or their families in the event the worker is killed, injured, or incurs an occupational disease while employed	State workers' compensation agencies (usually entitled "Industrial Commission")
Occupational Safety and Health Act, 1970	Requires each employer to furnish each employee a place of work free from recognized hazards likely to cause injury or death	Department of Labor (Occupational Safety and Health Administration)
Unemployment Compensation (state statutes and the Social Secutiy Act of 1935)	Provides for payments for temporary periods to workers unemployed through no fault of their own	State Unemployment Compensation Boards
Equal Employment Opportunity (Civil Rights Act of 1964 and Equal Employment Opportunity Act of 1972)	Designed to eliminate job discrimination against employees, applicants, or union members based on race, color, religion, sex, or national origin	Equal Employment Opportunity Commission (files civil actions in Federal District Court) Office of Federal Contract Compliance
Social Security Act of 1935	Provides income at retirement (age 62–65), disability and death benefits, hospital and medical insurance (Medicare) to people over 65	
Pension Reform Act, 1974	Regulates funding requirements, coverage, termination insurance coverage, and management of trust	Internal Revenue Service, Department of Labor, and Pension Benefit Guaranty Corporation
Collective Bargaining National Labor Relations Act, 1935 (Wagner Act, amended by Taft-Hartley Act in 1947)	Complex act regulating all phases of collective bargaining. Act defines various unfair union and management labor practices, provides for elections of representatives, provides for right to strike, gives states the opportunity to enact state "right-to-work laws," etc.	National Labor Relations Board (NLRB)
Labor-Management Reporting and Disclosure Act, 1959 (Landrum-Griffin Act)	Provides for an elaborate system of regulation of union internal activities. Mandates such things as (a) a "Bill of Rights" for union members, (b) elaborate information reporting by union bylaws, etc., (c) yearly financial reports, and (d) democratic election of officers	Department of Labor

This is one example of ways that market outcomes sometimes seem inequitable and, occasionally, even cruel. These cases often result in attempts to legislate more socially acceptable employment policies. The remainder of this chapter points to the likelihood that such policies will fail if markets are competitive. In the next chapter, we deal with lack of competition in labor markets—situations where policies have greater chances for success.

Government Regulation of Labor Markets

Many labor markets are far from competitive. Some imperfections originate in the private sector (unions or employment discrimination) but some also emerge from government policies. Labor markets are governed by many legal restrictions, ranging from limits on the employment of youngsters to health and safety regulations to minimum-wage laws. Table 2 summarizes the thrust of major U.S. labor laws. Many economists believe that some laws create inefficiency and inequity and are inconsistent with their stated objectives. Minimum-wage laws, for example, may hurt far more workers than they help, with young workers and members of minorities being especially harmed.

Minimum Wages and Unemployment

When Tom Edison was in the midst of a long string of experiments to develop a practical light bulb, he was asked whether he was making any progress. He replied, "Why certainly. I've learned a thousand ways you can't make a light bulb."[3] Similarly, our society has tried numerous remedies for teenage unemployment, but teenage unemployment rates, especially among minorities, continue to rise. Edison eventually developed a good light bulb, but he kept track of things that did not work. Teenage unemployment continues to grow, perhaps in part because the problem may be aggravated by misguided policies.

Minimum-wage laws are presumably intended to alleviate poverty by ensuring workers a living wage. But these laws will accomplish their objectives only if inexperienced and unskilled workers get jobs. Figure 9 shows the effect of imposing a minimum wage of $3.35 an hour in a competitive labor market for unskilled workers where the equilibrium hourly wage is $2.50 and equilibrium employment is 7 million workers. When a legal floor on wages is imposed at $3.35 hourly, 2 million unskilled workers are laid off. Another million enter the job market at this higher wage, so 3 million out of 8 million are now unemployed, and the unemployment rate among the unskilled rises from 0 to 37.5 percent. This model illustrates that legal wage floors create surpluses of workers and unemployment just as surely as price floors for goods cause surpluses of goods.

Minimum-wage laws may be linked to growing teenage unemployment. In the 8 years before 1955, when minimum wages first crept over $1.00 per hour, the teenage unemployment rate hovered around 10 percent; in the 12 years after 1974, when the minimum wage rose above the $2.00 mark, teenage unemployment averaged over 18 percent. (Inflation in this era would have decreased the disemployment effect, but this was roughly offset by the growing proportion of the labor force covered by minimum-wage laws, which increases the disemployment effect.)

One less-than-obvious side effect of legal wage floors is that these laws may foster discrimination. In the words of one specialist in this area, Walter B. Williams:

> Aside from causing unemployment for some, the minimum wage law encourages racial discrimination. If an employer must pay a minimum of $2.90 an hour no matter whom he hires, he may as well hire someone whose color he likes. Economists would explain this by saying that the minimum wage law prevents the worker from offering a "compensating difference" for less preferred characteristics. The same principle applies to groceries. Less preferred chuck steak can compete with more preferred filet mignon only by offering a compensating difference—a lower price. If we had a minimum price law for steak of, say, $4.00 per pound, sales of chuck would fall relative to sales of filet. Because uniform minimum price laws encourage people to discriminate against goods and services they perceive as less valuable, chuck steak would be "unemployed."[4]

---

3. This anecdote is related by Steven P. Zell in "The Problem of Rising Teenage Unemployment: A Reappraisal," *Economic Review,* March 1978, Federal Reserve of Kansas City, March 1978.

4. Walter B. Williams, "Minimum Wage, Maximum Folly," *The Smith-Kline Forum for a Healthier America,* No. 6 (September 1979).

FIGURE 9 *Minimum Wages and Unemployment*

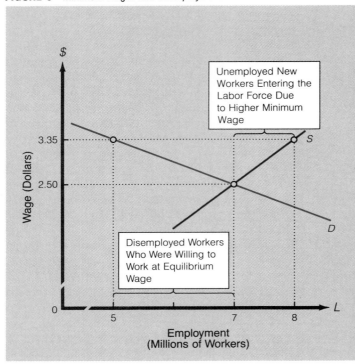

Unemployed New Workers Entering the Labor Force Due to Higher Minimum Wage

Disemployed Workers Who Were Willing to Work at Equilibrium Wage

Wage (Dollars)

3.35

2.50

0   5   7   8   L

Employment
(Millions of Workers)

Minimum-wage laws may cause the involuntary unemployment of many impoverished people who have few marketable skills. This result may prove especially harmful for young people who are denied work experiences that would enhance their future employability.

Indeed, Panel A of Figure 10 shows that between 1948 and 1955, black teenagers had lower average rates of unemployment than whites; since 1956, black teenagers have lost steadily and now suffer double the unemployment rate experienced by white teenagers. Panel B suggests that many black teenagers may be so discouraged that decreasing numbers participate in the labor market, while participation rates among white teenagers have grown slightly over time. Small wonder that Milton Friedman, a Nobel Prize winner in economics, has called minimum-wage laws "the most anti-Negro legislation ever passed."

Sex Discrimination and Comparable Worth

The slogan "equal pay for equal work" has become law. History is replete with cases where women and members of minority groups were denied equal access to jobs or paid less than some Caucasian males received for the same work. Some women workers would like to extend the law to raise wages in the occupations into which most women were once channeled—nursing, teaching, and clerical work. They argue that holders of these jobs are systematically underpaid. For example, nurses are typically far more educated and bear more responsibility than hospital janitors. Advocates of the **comparable worth** doctrine are aghast that janitors are commonly more highly paid. Such apparent discrepancies in pay relative to the value of a job must be the results of sex discrimination, according to their reasoning. Remedies to compel "equal pay for *comparable* work" are now being sought in the courts, state legislatures, and the Congress.

Until recently, unequal access to remunerative employment did push many women into occupations that pay relatively little, but the question remains of whether a law requiring "equal pay for comparable work" will achieve the goals of its advocates. The first problem with implementing this approach is ascertaining how much particular jobs should pay. The markets to which this doctrine

FIGURE 10 *Teenagers and the Minimum Wage*

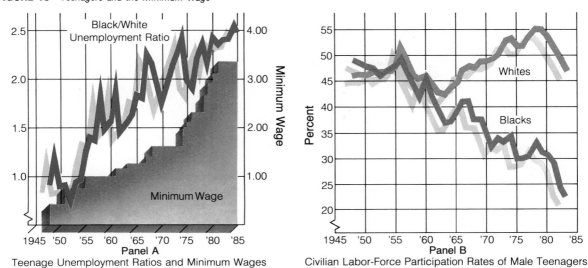

Panel A
Teenage Unemployment Ratios and Minimum Wages

Panel B
Civilian Labor-Force Participation Rates of Male Teenagers
Age 16–19, by Race, 1948–83

As minimum legal wages have risen (Panel A), black male teenagers apparently have lost jobs to white male teenagers. As a result, many black teenagers have dropped out of the labor market (Panel B).

Source: U.S. Department of Labor, Bureau of Labor Statistics, *Handbook of Labor Statistics,* June 1985, and *Economic Report of the President,* 1986.

would apply tend to be quite competitive, but we presumably cannot rely on market wage solutions. This means that officials from some government agency will need to consider the qualities of each job: skill requirements, how pleasant the work environment is, and the relative risks to workers are only a few of the many factors that would need to be considered. Weighing education and classroom teaching duties against hot, sweaty, and dangerous work on a construction crew, for example, is unavoidably subjective. The slow and costly process of unraveling such complex issues would be unlikely to satisfy many people.

Suppose that all these problems were resolved. The basic problem remains that the supplies of nurses, teachers, and clerical workers have been relatively large in the competitive markets for these skills, depressing the equilibrium wages for these jobs. New legal requirements raising wages to above the equilibrium pay for holders of jobs that have historically been "women's work" will, unfortunately, have effects similar to those of a legal minimum wage. Many women currently employed in these occupations would lose their jobs, and there would be surpluses of secretaries, teachers, and nurses.

These surpluses would be translated into unemployment.

One reason that excessive unemployment in these occupations would arise is because employers would have strong incentives to find substitutes as higher salaries were legally mandated. For example, office work would become even more automated. Receptionist slots would be pared to the bone. Electronic filing systems would be simplified to reduce requirements for some clerical work. Business correspondence would become more standardized to minimize the need for individualized letters, and firms would rely even more heavily on negotiations by telephone. Nurses would find more of their tasks taken over by orderlies or technicians. Schools would be pressured to raise student/teacher ratios in attempts to contain costs.

Thus, the comparable worth approach might be like some of the policies we described in Chapter 4: many members of the groups targeted for help may be harmed in unforeseen ways. Fortunately, this problem may cure itself as time elapses and women increasingly shun traditional "women's careers" to become doctors, lawyers, pilots, architects, or engineers.

Our discussions of minimum-wage laws and comparable worth have assumed that the labor markets for unskilled workers and traditional "women's work" are highly competitive. The past few chapters have emphasized that competitive markets for either consumer goods or productive resources tend to be efficient, and that government policy is likely to be counterproductive. In the next chapter, we will investigate the effects of inadequate competition in the workplace. You will see that lack of competition tends to cause inefficiency and, perhaps, inequity. These flaws of the market system may be remediable through appropriate government action. The trick, of course, is to design and implement efficient and equitable policies. Wishful thinking or good intentions are not enough.

CHAPTER REVIEW: KEY POINTS

1. The demand for any resource is related to the: (*a*) amounts of other factors employed, (*b*) production technology used, and (*c*) demand for the product. Because the demand for labor (or any input) hinges on the demand for final products, it is a *derived demand.*

2. *Marginal revenue product* (*MRP*) is the firm's revenues generated by hiring the marginal unit of some input. In pure competition, this is the same as *VMP.* Labor (or any factor) will be employed up to the point where the additional revenue competitive firms receive (*value of the marginal product,* or *VMP*) just equals the cost of an additional unit of the resource (*marginal factor cost,* or *MFC*). In competitive labor markets, the marginal factor cost (*MFC*) equals the *wage rate (w),* so pure competition in all markets means that

$$VMP = MRP = MFC = w.$$

3. Increases (*decreases*) in the demand for the product, in labor productivity, or in the amounts of other resources used will normally increase (*decrease*) the *VMP* and demand for labor. Technological changes may either increase or decrease labor demands. *Automation* is the replacement of workers by new technologies.

4. The *elasticity of demand for labor* is directly related to the: (*a*) *elasticity of demand for the final product,* (*b*) *labor's share of total costs* represented by the wage bill, (*c*) ease of factor *substitution,* and (*d*) time.

5. The supply of labor depends on: (*a*) wage rates and structures, (*b*) labor force participation, (*c*) the number of hours people are willing to work, and (*d*) the education, training, and skills of workers.

6. Workers experience both *income* and *substitution*

effects when wage rates change. Increased wages cause labor to substitute work for leisure because work expands consumption opportunities and leisure is more costly. However, higher wages mean that for a given amount of labor effort, workers will earn more income, and, if leisure is a normal good, they will want to consume more leisure and work less. If the substitution effect is larger than the income effect, supplies are positively sloped. Backward-bending labor supplies result when income effects dominate substitution effects.

7. While the individual's labor supply curve may be backward bending, the supply of labor to any industry will always be positively sloped. Industry supplies and demands for labor establish the *equilibrium wage* as each firm hires additional units of labor until the value of the marginal product equals the market wage rate.

8. Demand curves for labor represent the marginal benefits society receives from additional employment, and supply curves reflect the marginal cost to society of using those resources. Employing labor to the point where $D_L = S_L$ is efficient because society's benefits equal society's costs from additional employment. More or less employment than where $D_L = S_L$ yields inefficient resource allocations since society gets more (*or less*) than it desires in an opportunity cost sense.

9. Labor quality improves through investments in *human capital* that include formal education and on-the-job training. Education benefits both the individual and society at large. Training is classified as either general or specific: *General training* enhances a worker's productivity equally for many firms, while *specific training* only increases the worker's productivity for the current employer.

10. Turnover and quit rates are negatively related to the levels of specific training workers have received and to the wage premiums paid them. Firms that invest heavily in their employees have strong incentives to retain them and do so: (*a*) by paying higher wages than other firms will offer, and (*b*) through special rules based on seniority or pension provisions that reward longevity with the firm.

11. *Minimum-wage laws* have intensified the unemployment of unskilled workers (especially teenagers) and may foster discrimination. Widespread implementation of a *comparable worth* doctrine would require bureaucratic comparisons of jobs to determine wages, and might stimulate disemployment of many workers in the occupations into which women have historically been channeled.

QUESTIONS FOR THOUGHT AND DISCUSSION

1. Marginal productivity theory suggests that people are paid according to the productive contributions of their resources, including labor. But such things as seniority rules clearly create situations where some people who are paid less are more productive than some people who are paid more. Do you think that the forces of marginal productivity generate a strong tendency for payment to be roughly proportional to contribution? Why or why not?

2. Some very successful and affluent people like to brag about having started with nothing. They commonly assert that they owe "nothing to nobody." Marginal productivity theory suggests that technology and the amount of capital and the number of people we work with are powerful influences on our productivity and income. How are the "rugged individualists" who believe they have "done it on their own" both supported and rebutted by marginal productivity theory?

3. A theory developed by some 1930s radicals held that pay should be determined by how vital a job is to society. For example, people who maintain traffic lights or collect trash would be more highly paid than Hollywood stars or the promoters of such fads as *Trivial Pursuit*. Do you think this argument has merit? Why, or why not?

4. Some highly skilled, intelligent, well-educated people work very hard and receive little in return. Is someone who earns a Ph.D. in music and who practices constantly and becomes the world's 211th best oboe player entitled to be paid more than a gas station attendant? Is consummate artistry or esoteric knowledge undervalued in a capitalist economy? If so, how should we determine appropriate incomes for people whom the market system spurns?

5. Distinguishing between labor and human capital can be extremely difficult. Are there any tasks that can be accomplished by raw labor untempered by some education or experience? If so, what are they?

6. In his book *Inequality,* Christopher Jencks argues that subsidized public education may lead to a meritocracy in which incomes differ greatly not because of inheritances of wealth but because of genetic differences. Does income often depend more on who you are than what you can do? Do you think public education facilitates social stability by providing nonviolent avenues for poor children to channel their energies toward becoming rich and powerful adults? Is a meritocracy fairer than an aristocracy based on birth?

7. Firms cannot predict precisely how productive or honest any prospective employee will be once hired and on the job. What are shortcomings of each of the following devices some employers use to try to screen job applicants? (*a*) School grades, diplomas, or degrees. (*b*) Letters of recommendation. (*c*) On-the-job training or work experience with other employers. (*d*) Impressions from interviews. (*e*) Tests of aptitudes, skills, or personality. (*f*) Lie detector examinations. Which devices do you think are most effective? Which do you think are given too much weight by many employers? Which other mechanisms are (or should be) used to screen job applicants? What are their advantages? Shortcomings?

8. Several studies, after adjusting for other individual characteristics, suggest that short men are paid less than tall men, and that short men are less likely to be promoted. Other studies suggest that attractive people tend to receive higher pay and quicker promotions than those who are considered either plain or beautiful. Are these results consistent with marginal productivity theory? Do you think these studies are correct? If so, what do you think accounts for these and similar findings?

CHAPTER 29 Labor Markets: Monopoly Power, Monopsony Power, and Labor Unions

value of the marginal product

marginal revenue product

marginal factor cost (MFC)

monopsony power

exploitation

labor unions

craft unions (AFL) vs. industrial unions (CIO)

strikes

closed shop

open shop

union shop

union-nonunion wage differential

Product markets range from the purely competitive to the monopolistic. Resource markets run a similar gamut. The preceding chapter focused on competitive labor markets. In this chapter, we examine problems posed by inadequate competition in resource markets. Concentrated economic power causes three basic problems in resource markets: (*a*) firms with monopoly power restrict output and, thus, have less demand for resources than if product markets were purely competitive; (*b*) resource buyers with clout may reduce quantities demanded to hold resource prices down; and (*c*) resource sellers possessing monopoly power may reduce the quantity available in order to boost the resource price.

Labor markets are especially plagued by noncompetitive influences: distortive regulations abound, and powerful unions restrict supplies to drive wages up, while powerful employers flex their economic muscle to depress wages. In this chapter, our first theme is the effects of deviations from competition in labor markets. We will address problems posed from the demand side when employers exercise substantial power, either as sellers of goods or as buyers of labor. Then we'll look at problems of concentrated power from the supply side, among sellers of labor—primarily, labor unions. Finally, we survey the history and current status of American unionism.

Monopolies' Diminished Demands for Labor

You already know that firms with monopoly power raise prices and restrict output to maximize profit. The result for resource markets is that fewer resources are employed than if these markets were competitive.

Return once more to the gold mine example of earlier chapters. Suppose that gold production began to trickle off, but one day you stumbled upon an enormous vein of tantalite ore. Tantalum is used to line tanks that hold liquids, in specialized chemical processes, as an alloy in tungsten-carbide cutting tools, and in electronics. It is crucial for certain industrial applications. Tantalum is quite rare, so assume that you gain substantial monopoly power.

Relevant portions of the demand for tantalum and your production function are listed in Table 1. Tantalum output for various numbers of miners parallels that for gold production, but the demand curve for tantalum slopes downward, reflecting your monopoly power. For example (from columns 2 and 3 of Table 1), if you sell 50 pounds per week, you can charge $90 per pound. Raising output to 110 pounds, however, requires a price cut to $50 per pound.

Recall that monopoly power causes marginal revenue to be below price because added output is salable only if prices are reduced for all units produced. You must now decide: (a) what price to charge and how much to produce to maximize profits, and (b) how many workers to hire to get the job done. Naturally, the answer to question (a) automatically answers question (b), because it takes a specific number of workers to produce the most profitable level of output.

Any firm maximizes its profit by employing more labor until the revenue generated by the last worker hired (MRP) just equals the wage outlays associated with hiring the last worker (MFC). If all markets are purely competitive, this translates into the rule that the value of the marginal product ($VMP = P \times MPP = MRP$) equals the wage rate ($MFC = w$), so $VMP = MRP = MFC = w$.

The rule that maximum profits are obtained when $VMP = w$ works only for a purely competitive firm operating in a competitive labor market. The more general rule for profit maximization is that $MRP = MFC$. Monopoly power causes the value of the marginal product to exceed the marginal revenue product and reduces the amount of labor hired.

Let's see how this applies to your tantalum mine. Column 3 of Table 1 shows that hiring more workers boosts tantalum output but lowers its price. The marginal revenue from each extra pound of tantalum mined by any extra workers (column 5) is below its price. Thus, each additional miner adds $MR \times MPP$ to your dollar sales volume (column 7—the marginal revenue product, MRP, of labor), and this is less than the value of the marginal product (column 8), which is $P \times MPP$. For example, the third miner raises out-

TABLE 1 Data for Tantalum Production

Production Function		(3)	(4)	(5)	(6)	Demand for Labor	
(1)	(2)				Marginal Physical Product of Labor MPP $(\Delta Q/\Delta L)$	(7)	(8)
Number of Workers L	Pounds of Tantalum Produced per Week Q	Price of Tantalum per Pound P	Total Revenue TR $(P \times Q)$	Marginal Revenue MR $(\Delta TR/\Delta Q)$		Marginal Revenue Product of Labor MRP $(MR \times MPP)$	Value of the Marginal Product of Labor VMP $(P \times MPP)$
1	30	$100	$3,000	$100.00	30	$3,000	$3,000
2	50	90	4,500	75.00	20	1,500	1,800
3	68	80	5,440	55.22	18	940	1,440
4	84	70	5,880	27.50	16	440	1,120
5	98	60	5,880	0	14	0	840
6	110	50	5,500	−31.67	12	−380	600
7	120	40	4,800	−70.00	10	−700	400

FIGURE 1   Equilibrium Level of Employment for the Tantalum Monopolist

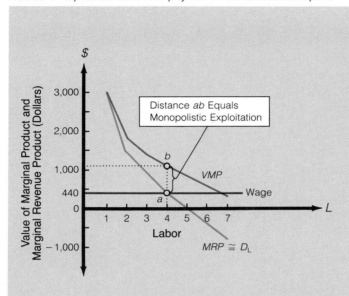

The value of the marginal product ($VMP = P \times MPP$) is the amount of revenue a competitive firm gains when it hires its last worker. The revenue gained from hiring the marginal worker is lower for a firm with monopoly power, because $P > MR$. Hence, the marginal revenue product ($MR \times MPP$) is less than the value of the marginal product. Note: The VMP and MRP shown are drawn from Table 1.

put by 18 pounds of tantalum (from 50 to 68 pounds per week), but its price falls from $90 to $80 per pound. The $10 price cut on the first 50 pounds of tantalum causes your revenue from hiring the third miner to be only $940 (column 7) instead of the $1,440 (18 × $80) realized from selling the tantalum produced by the third miner (column 8).

Thus, because monopoly power causes the price of output to exceed its marginal revenue, labor's **value of the marginal product ($VMP = P \times MPP$)** is greater than its **marginal revenue product ($MRP = MR \times MPP$)**. The maximum profit rule requires that the marginal revenue product equals the **marginal factor cost** ($MRP = MFC$). Profit is maximized for your tantalum mine when

$$VMP > MRP = MFC = w.$$

The revenue the last worker adds (MRP) equals the cost of hiring (MFC), which in this case is the competitive wage rate w, but this wage rate is below the value of the marginal product. Your monopoly power allows you to pay workers less than the marginal social value of their output. Let us now look at this graphically.

Your monopoly power forces us to distinguish between the VMPs and MRPs of additional workers. Because $MRP = MR \times MPP$, marginal revenue prod-

uct also equals the change in total revenue realized by hiring one more unit of labor ($MRP = \Delta TR/\Delta L$). Both MRP and VMP (columns 7 and 8 from Table 1) are diagrammed in Figure 1. Suppose that you now hire labor from a competitive market at $11 per hour, or $440 weekly. To equate the MRP with the $440 wage, you would hire four workers (point a). Note that at point a, $MRP = MFC$ ($MRP = $440 = MFC$). The fifth worker adds nothing to total revenue ($MRP = 0$) but would cost $440 per week—clearly a losing proposition.

Whenever resource suppliers are paid less than the values of their marginal products, they are said to be *exploited*.[1] Because you are a monopolist, the VMP of the fourth worker is $1,120 (point b), which is considerably more than the fourth worker's MRP and wage of $440. The difference between the VMP and w (line ab, or $680) is called the rate of **monopolistic exploitation** of labor. Another source of exploitation arises if firms exert economic clout as resource buyers.

---

1. *Exploitation* sounds like a very judgmental term, but it is the standard language of this analysis. The early work in this area was done by Marxist economists. This does not invalidate their analysis, but it does explain the use of such explosive terminology.

Monopsony in a Labor Market

No single firm's hiring of labor significantly affects the wage rate in a purely competitive labor market. For example, in large cities the prevailing wages of secretaries, paralegals, sales clerks, and delivery people are unaffected by any one firm's hiring. Contrast such markets with situations where a textile mill or copper mine dominates employment in a small town. Sole buyers of any good or resource are referred to as **monopsonists.** A buyer possesses **monopsony power** if restricting the purchases of a good or resource reduces the price the buyer must pay.

A labor monopsonist is the sole employer in a specific labor market and faces the entire labor supply. Thus, its hiring decision determines the wage rate. A labor market in which a monopsonist pays all workers equally is outlined in Table 2. Hiring three workers requires the monopsonist to pay a wage rate of only $380 per week to this community's three most eager beavers. To simplify this analysis, we will assume that wage discrimination is impossible. Thus, employing four local workers forces the monopsonist to raise its wage offer to $485 to attract the fourth, slightly less eager beaver to work, and necessitates a raise of $105 each to the preceding three workers.

The important conclusion is that monopsony power boosts marginal factor cost (*MFC*) above the wage rate. When the firm hires three workers at $380 per week, its labor costs are $1,140; weekly labor costs rise to $1,940 if the firm employs four workers at $485. Hiring the fourth worker without practicing wage discrimination requires that the three workers originally hired at $380 receive raises to $485 per week, which increases total labor costs by $800, not $485. Such wage hikes cause the *MFC* to exceed the wage rate for each level of employment. The marginal factor cost shown in column 4 of Table 2 is the change in total labor costs from hiring one extra worker. How does the excess of this monopsonist's *MFC* over the wage rate affect its hiring? Figure 2 shows the labor supply and its *MFC* to this monopsonist.

A monopsonist's marginal factor cost curve is above the labor supply curve, just as a marginal revenue curve is below the product demand curve facing a monopoly. The value of the marginal product from our gold mine of previous chapters is also shown, so Figure 2 depicts a monopsony selling a competitive output and *VMP = MRP*. This firm maximizes profit by hiring labor until the *MRP = MFC* at $800 (point *a* in Figure 2), but only pays $485 each to the four workers willing to work for that weekly wage (point *b*).

A labor monopsonist hires fewer workers and pays lower wages than a firm hiring in a competitive labor market. If this firm faced a $600 wage from a competitive labor market, it would hire six workers (point *c*). Thus, the monopsonist pays workers less than a competitive employer would. Absent its monopsony power, this firm would hire four workers at a competitive wage of $800 (point *a*). Monopsony power enables it to hire four workers for a $485 wage, far below the values of their marginal product (*VMP* = $800). The difference ($315) is termed **monopsonistic exploitation** of labor.

TABLE 2 *Supply of Labor Data for a Firm with Monopsony Power*

(1) Labor *L*	(2) Weekly Wage *W*	(3) Total Labor Cost *TC*$_L$ (*W* × *L*)	(4) Marginal Factor (Labor) Cost *MFC* (Δ*TC*$_L$/Δ*L*)
1	$250	$ 250	$ 250
2	300	600	350
3	380	1,140	540
4	485	1,940	800
5	550	2,750	810
6	600	3,600	850
7	700	4,900	1,300
8	800	6,400	1,500

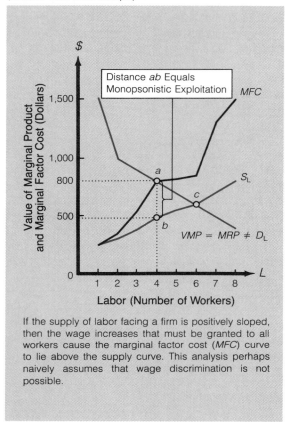

FIGURE 2 *Equilibrium Wage and Employment for a Monopsonist Who Is a Competitor in the Product Market (Western Gold Mine Example)*

Distance *ab* Equals Monopsonistic Exploitation

$VMP = MRP \neq D_L$

If the supply of labor facing a firm is positively sloped, then the wage increases that must be granted to all workers cause the marginal factor cost (*MFC*) curve to lie above the supply curve. This analysis perhaps naively assumes that wage discrimination is not possible.

Are there any pure monopsonists around today? Generally no, although some big firms located in small communities may dominate local labor markets and exercise substantial monopsony power. A more common type of monopsonistic exploitation occurs when firms control individual employees sufficiently to wage discriminate.

Wage Discrimination

Have you ever worked for a company that discouraged workers from sharing information about wages or salaries? Many firms that do not have standard pay scales treat salary information as confidential. This is a common practice when a firm practices **wage discrimination,** which occurs when different workers receive pay that is inconsistent with their individual marginal productivities. This is possible only if a firm

has some monopsony power, just as price discrimination for goods requires a firm to possess monopoly power. This type of monopsony power may be exercised whenever any employee views a particular firm as offering special advantages such as location, job security, or opportunities for promotion.

In an earlier chapter, our discussion showed that price discrimination may remedy some of the economic inefficiency that occurs when firms exercise monopoly power. Wage discrimination may similarly cure some of the economic inefficiency caused by monopsony power. For example, if the monopsonist shown in Table 2 and Figure 2 could perfectly wage discriminate, it would hire six workers (exactly the same as by a competitive firm) rather than the four it hires as a nondiscriminating monopsonist. However, it would respectively pay the first through sixth workers weekly wages of only $250, $300, $380, $485, $550, and $600—the total weekly wage bill would be only $2,565, instead of the $3,600 that would be paid weekly by a purely competitive employer. The $1,035 difference represents monopsonistic exploitation. Although this wage discrimination does facilitate efficiency, it is widely viewed as inequitable.

Women may suffer especially from wage discrimination because many employers traditionally view women's work decisions as secondary to their husbands' career moves. Reasonable job security for women has been bait to facilitate wage discrimination. The resulting potential for exploitation is a powerful argument for "equal pay for equal work" laws, which may promote equity without hindering efficiency. A problem with extending this reasoning to the doctrine of comparable worth (discussed in the previous chapter) is that most employers in the highly competitive labor markets that would be covered by "comparable worth" have little monopsony power.

Employers who treat salary information as confidential argue that publicizing wage differentials just leads to interminable bickering about which employee deserves what. Under this system, employees have little incentive to reveal their own pay, but seek information about the pay of others. If you learned that someone made relatively less than you did, you would probably be silent if their work was comparable to yours. If, however, someone with a comparable job made more than you did, you might use the information to negotiate a raise from your employer. If you think about this for a moment, you will understand why many workers join employers in a conspiracy of silence when salary information is confidential. Although secrecy may reduce quibbling about salaries when pay scales are not standardized, the major advantage for employers is that confidentiality facilitates wage discrimination and monopsonistic exploitation.

Minimum-Wage Laws and Monopsony Power

The effects of minimum-wage laws in competitive labor markets are summarized in Panel A of Figure 3. The prevailing wage is $3.25 before the minimum wage is introduced into the competitive market, and 70 units of labor are employed (point *a*). When a $4.00 minimum-wage law is imposed, employment falls to 58 (point *b*), and unemployment increases to 40 units of labor (98 minus 58); more people want to work at the higher wage (point *c*).

The effect of a minimum wage may be quite different if firms exert monopsony power in labor mar-

kets. Before enactment of a minimum wage in Panel B, fewer workers are employed (50) at a lower wage ($2.75) by the monopsonist (point *g*) than by a comparable competitive firm (point *a*). Introducing the minimum wage alters the monopsonist's *MFC* by forcing the firm to pay at least $4.00 per hour, at which it can hire up to 98 workers. Average wages must rise to attract more than 98 workers, so the monopsonist's *MFC* curve becomes *bcdf,* and the profit-maximizing employment level is 58 workers at $4.00 per hour.

The result that minimum-wage hikes may yield both higher wages and higher employment in monopsonistic markets is often cited as a possible benefit of minimum-wage legislation. Critics of these laws rebut this analysis by citing studies showing that minimum-wage laws have their biggest impact in competitive labor markets for unskilled workers and teenagers. Disemployment follows higher minimum-wage laws in competitive labor markets. Disemployment is also likely if firms practiced systematic wage discrimination before a minimum wage was enacted.

FIGURE 3 *Effects of Minimum-Wage Laws in Competitive and Monopsony Markets*

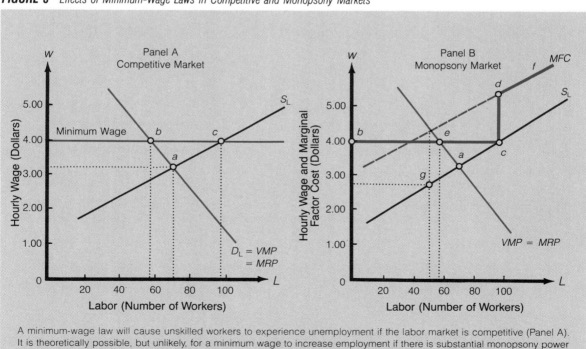

A minimum-wage law will cause unskilled workers to experience unemployment if the labor market is competitive (Panel A). It is theoretically possible, but unlikely, for a minimum wage to increase employment if there is substantial monopsony power in the labor market (Panel B).

FIGURE 4 *Summary of Wage and Employment Equilibria*

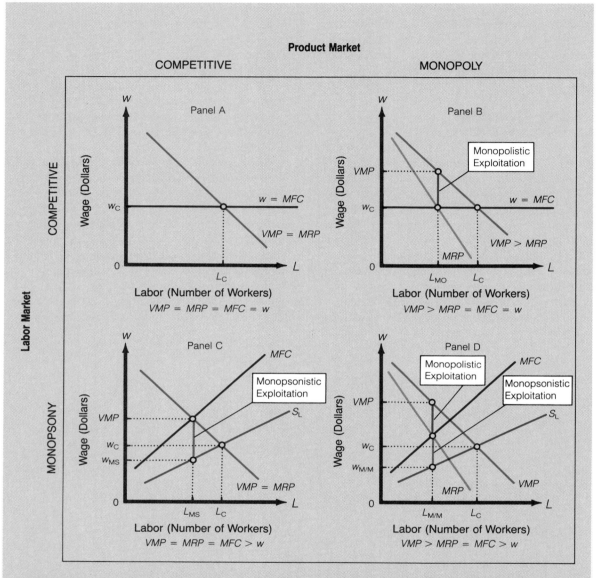

The marginal value of labor to society is the *VMP* curve; the marginal social cost of labor is the competitively determined wage (*w*). In a competitive world (Panel A), there is no exploitation of labor, and economic efficiency exists because the marginal benefit to society of a specific employment just equals marginal social cost (*VMP* = *w*, so *MSB* = *MSC*). Monopolistic exploitation (Panel B) is accompanied by inefficiency because *VMP* > *MRP* implies that the marginal social benefit exceeds the monopolist's marginal private benefit from hiring extra workers (*MSB* > *MPB*), so *MSB* > *MSC*. Monopsonistic exploitation (Panel C) is a situation where the monopsonists' marginal private costs are greater than the marginal social costs of employment (*MFC* > *MSC* = *w*), so again there is inefficiency. Panel D illustrates the case where the factors leading to inefficiency because of monopoly and monopsony power are combined.

(We just showed how wage discrimination increases employment by monopsonistic firms. Minimum-wage laws may eliminate this effect.) Thus, Panel A

probably correctly suggests that minimum wages foster unemployment. Several European countries have reduced teenage unemployment with lower minimum wages for teenagers than for adults, but President Reagan's 1983 proposal to drop the minimum wage for teenagers to $1.67 (half of the adult minimum) was defeated.

A Summary of Imperfect Competition by Employers

The precise translation of the $MRP = MFC$ rule into equilibrium wage and employment levels depends on a firm's product and labor markets, as summarized in Figure 4. When product and labor markets are both competitive (Panel A), the firm hires until $VMP = w$, which is an efficient solution. Panel B shows that when a monopolistic seller hires workers from a competitive labor market, workers are paid less than the values of their marginal products and fewer workers are hired than under purely competitive conditions. A monopsony labor market combined with a competitive product market is depicted in Panel C. Firms with monopsony power also hire fewer workers at lower wages than would pure competitors. Finally, Panel D illustrates equilibrium wages and employment when the firm is both a monopsonist in the labor market and a monopolist in the product market. Not surprisingly, the monopsonist/monopolist tends to hire fewer workers at lower wages than in any other market structure and is the most exploitative—the difference $VMP - w$ is greatest.

You have seen how imperfect competition by employers may distort labor markets. We will now examine the supply side and labor unions.

Unions and Collective Bargaining

The managers of most large corporations represent the interests of the many shareholders who own these firms. In the same way, **labor unions** represent the interests of many workers and negotiate work contracts for their members. Major labor contracts cover thousands of workers. The relationships between firm managers and union leaders are often mixtures of public hostility and private symbiosis. Just as oligopolists act strategically because they are interdependent in setting prices and output, negotiations by labor unions and management at times resemble a card tournament—or war. There are several models that have been developed to characterize this process.

Bilateral Monopoly

One early model of collective bargaining is that of **bilateral monopoly,** which assumes that a union is the sole agent for a firm's labor (a monopoly on the labor [supply] side), while the firm is the sole employer of union labor (a monopsony on the hiring [demand] side). The monopsonist employer depicted in Figure 5 would prefer to hire L_e units of labor at a wage rate of w_e. The union, on the other hand, would want the L_e units of labor to be paid at least w_u. Given the marginal revenue product (MRP) curve shown, wage rate w_u is the maximum that the firm would be willing to pay for L_e units of labor.

The wage limits for bargaining range from w_u to w_e, but this model fails to predict exactly what the wage settlement will be. Moreover, we assumed that the union seeks the highest wage consistent with full employment of its L_e members. Union leaders may have other goals, such as maximum wages for workers with seniority or job security for union officials.

FIGURE 5 Bilateral Monopoly in Labor Markets

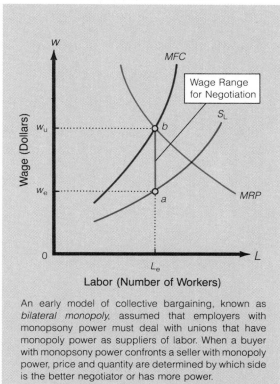

An early model of collective bargaining, known as bilateral monopoly, assumed that employers with monopsony power must deal with unions that have monopoly power as suppliers of labor. When a buyer with monopsony power confronts a seller with monopoly power, price and quantity are determined by which side is the better negotiator or has more power.

For these reasons, the bilateral monopoly model does little to explain the bargaining process and is useful only in specifying some general limits to bargaining. About all we can say at this point is that the negotiated wage tends to be closer to the wage desired by the party (union or management) with the greater power or bargaining savvy.

Union Strategies to Raise Wages

Demands for labor are downward sloping so that wage hikes reduce the quantity of labor demanded and, thus, normally eliminate some jobs. This is one trade-off that union negotiators must weigh; disemployment may be an especially heavy threat if an industry is largely nonunion. Giant national unions try to protect their members by organizing entire industries. In cases of purely local labor markets (construction, for example), only local workers must be unionized to protect union jobs from nonunion competition. A union can choose from several strategies to raise wages once an industry is organized. Consider Figure 6. Without unionization, firms' demands for labor would be D_{L0} and the supply of labor, S_{L0}, with resulting employment of L_e workers at a wage of w_e (point a).

A first union strategy might be to try to shrink labor to this industry by shifting the labor supply curve leftward to S_{L1}, raising the union wage to w_u (point b). The union movement predictably has supported policies such as child labor laws, restrictive immigration policies, compulsory retirement plans, laws to "protect" women from hard or hazardous work, and shorter work weeks. Craft unions commonly require lengthy apprenticeship programs to restrict competition from other workers. Some unions charge high initiation fees or simply limit new union membership. All these tactics shift the supply of union labor to the left.

Second, where unions control the entire work force for an industry, they may simply set the wage at w_u through bargaining. This creates a huge labor surplus and substantial unemployment or underemployment. The union then uses a *hiring hall* to spread the work available to its members. Rules to allocate jobs range from "first come, first served" to strict "seniority."

Finally, if the union can negotiate a wage of w_u and then shift the demand for their members' labor to D_{L1}, union members will suffer only minor unemployment at point c. Examples of this approach include using political clout to obtain local building

FIGURE 6 *Various Union Strategies to Raise Wages*

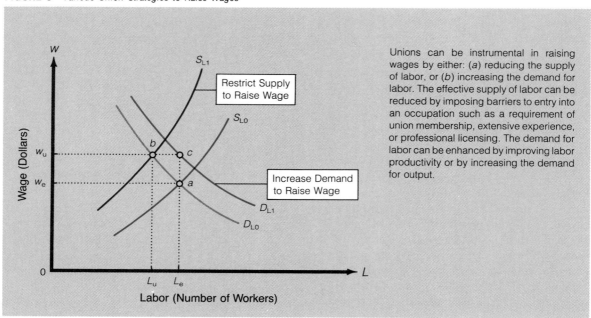

Unions can be instrumental in raising wages by either: (*a*) reducing the supply of labor, or (*b*) increasing the demand for labor. The effective supply of labor can be reduced by imposing barriers to entry into an occupation such as a requirement of union membership, extensive experience, or professional licensing. The demand for labor can be enhanced by improving labor productivity or by increasing the demand for output.

codes that require labor-intensive construction technologies or lobbying for quotas to limit foreign competition for union members' services. Unions may also work with management to increase worker productivity.

Featherbedding refers to work rules that artificially boost the number of workers required for certain tasks. It has been a union strategy to maintain or expand demands for labor in several industries—rail transportation, printing, and shipping (dock workers). For example, long after coal engines were replaced by diesel, railroad unions insisted that trains carry firemen who rode along even though there were no coal fires to tend.[2] For years, New York musicians had a union contract requiring standby orchestras for every event at which out-of-state musicians played.

Wage Setting and the Duration of Strikes

Bilateral monopoly models identify a range of wages within which union and management will agree but fail to predict precisely what the final wage will be. Moreover, these models ignore **strikes.** Sir John Hicks, a Nobel Prize winner, developed a more versatile model of collective bargaining, adapted in Figure 7.[3] The employer willingly offers a wage of w_0 without a strike, but the union insists on a wage of w_1, a difference so great that a strike begins at time zero (0).

The strike is a financial and emotional roller coaster for the workers involved. After the euphoria of a brief vacation, reality begins to knock at the worker's doors. Backlogs of do-it-yourself projects around their houses are finished, and boredom sets in as the strike drags on. As unemployment checks and union benefits run out, strikers begin to exhaust their past savings and worry about paying their bills. The hardships of long-term idleness cause union wage demands to trickle down along the union resistance curve graphed in Figure 7.

Over the same period, management grows more willing to pay the higher wages traced out as the employer's concession curve. Strikes are seldom sur-

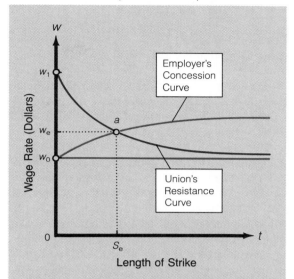

FIGURE 7 Hicks' Theory of Industrial Disputes

The onset of a strike (time 0) is a signal that union workers demand much higher wages than management is willing to pay. As time elapses, workers become willing to settle for less as their financial reserves evaporate, and management is increasingly willing to raise its wage offers as its inventories decline and stockholders and customers apply pressure to settle. Declining wage demands and rising wage offers intersect to signal the end of this particular strike at time S_e.

prises, so most firms are able to meet easily foreseen customer orders out of stockpiled inventories. Managers often form skeletal work crews during a strike, but eventually inventories shrink and managers become exhausted; the operation grinds towards a halt, raising the willingness to pay higher wages. The intersection of the employer's concession curve and the union resistance curve marks the end of this strike. The final wage settlement is at w_e, and the expected duration of this strike is S_e. As you can see, this simple model offers considerable insight into labor negotiations.

We have now examined some aspects of imperfect labor markets from both the demand side—monopsony and monopoly—and the supply side—labor unions. This provides a background for a broader look at labor market institutions that shape economic activity in the United States, including a brief history of the American labor union movement and some effects of unionism.

---

2. Some states had laws requiring firemen on each train. Such a requirement was a part of the Arizona State Constitution until 1964.

3. J. R. Hicks, *The Theory of Wages* (London: The Macmillan Company, 1932), Chapter VII.

Labor Unions

Unions traditionally have been organized around a particular craft or industry. Plumbers, machinists, air-traffic controllers, and other workers organized on the basis of particular skills rely on *craft unions* to bargain with management. *Industrial unions,* on the other hand, organize all the workers in such industries as mining, steel, autos, and rubber. Some of today's largest unions are indicated in Table 3.

Until their merger, the **American Federation of Labor (AFL)** consisted only of craft unions and competed with the **Congress of Industrial Organization (CIO),** which covered only industrial unions. **Jurisdictional strikes** often erupted when both attempted to organize the same workers. For example, conflicts in chemical plants sometimes became violent between the CIO's Oil, Chemical, and Atomic Workers Union (OCAW) and AFL craft unions representing electricians or machinists. A treaty between AFL and CIO unions was finally consummated with their 1955 merger into the AFL-CIO.

Today, jurisdictional fights exist primarily between AFL-CIO unions and such independents as the Longshoremen or the Teamsters. These disputes focus on which union will represent given workers and what goals to pursue. Job security and higher wages involve trade-offs. For example, the United Mine Workers Union traditionally sought rapid wage hikes despite the resulting mass substitution of capital for labor and consequent disemployment of many union members. Other unions prize job security and so temper their demands for higher wages.

Union Security

Unions try to ensure job security for their members in part because union leaders seek security themselves. Special clauses in many union contracts are designed to strengthen the hands of union leaders as sole bargaining agents for their members. The strongest protection a union can have, a **closed shop** agreement with management, requires union membership as a prerequisite for employment. The Taft-Hartley Act of 1947 outlawed this form of union security.

Open shops are at the opposite pole from closed shops. Unions legally must negotiate for all workers in an organized firm, but dues or membership are at the option of each worker. Thus, the open shop may permit nonunion free riders. Unions cannot control nonmembers, so firms can thwart strikes with nonunion workers (called **scabs** by union members), yet these nonunion workers receive all benefits accorded union workers.

The **union shop** is similar to a closed shop. Employers may hire either union or nonunion labor, but new employees must join the union within a specified period to keep their jobs. Under a union shop arrangement, workers can be expelled from union membership only for nonpayment of dues. This protects workers from being expelled (with loss of their jobs) for infractions such as disagreeing with the union leadership or violating union policies.

Besides eliminating the closed shop, the Taft-Hartley Act allowed states to pass *right-to-work laws* outlawing the union shop. Nineteen states, primarily in the South and Midwest, have adopted such laws. Unions responded with **agency shop** agreements that require nonunion employees to pay union dues as a condition of their employment. This arrangement has been defended on the grounds that it prevents nonunion workers from free riding; all workers are represented by the union and so should share the costs of collective bargaining.

Unions are able to exert some control over workers through the use of **check-off provisions** in contracts, which require employers to deduct dues from employees' paychecks. These provisions make it easier for unions to collect dues and retain members. The Taft-Hartley Act prohibits firms from deducting union dues unless authorized by a majority of workers, but roughly 80 percent of union contracts now have check-off provisions.

Unions did not develop overnight. The path to modern collective bargaining was paved with strife between union organizers and business managers. Business owners and managers do not want to share power with labor. The next section briefly examines the history of union development in this country.

The American Union Movement

A forerunner of modern unions was the Carpenters' Society of Philadelphia, established in 1724, which both bargained for wage increases and organized charity work. Interestingly, it fined its members if

TABLE 3 *Some of Our Union Giants*

Union	1983 Membership
AFL-CIO (TOTAL)	13,758,000
Food and Commercial Workers	1,007,000
United Steelworkers	707,000
State and County Employees	959,000
Electrical Workers	820,000
United Autoworkers	1,010,000
Independent	
Teamsters	2,000,000

Source: *Statistical Abstract of the United States,* 1986.

they disclosed their wages to nonmembers.[4] The first true union was the Federal Society of Cordwainers (shoemakers), formed in 1794. Its sole purpose was to negotiate higher wages. During the early 1800s, numerous unions emerged and then faded away, but within a century, unions had become fixtures on the national scene.

Until the Great Depression, business firms commonly fought union organizers with discharges, violence, and **yellow-dog contracts,** by which workers agreed not to join any union. Employers also circulated **blacklists** of union sympathizers and other "troublemakers." Finally, unions faced considerable legal adversity. Judges sympathetic to business owners issued **injunctions** (or restraining orders) against numerous union acts, including strikes or boycotts. If a union violated an injunction, its leaders could be held in contempt of court and jailed.

In the Danbury Hatters' case in 1908, the Supreme Court declared unions to be combinations in restraint of trade, violating the Sherman Antitrust Act of 1890.[5] The United Hatters of North America had tried to organize the Loewe Hat Company of Danbury, Connecticut. After a series of strikes failed, the union organized a nationwide boycott of Loewe's products. The court found that this boycott had caused Loewe a loss of $80,000 and applied the triple damage clause of the Sherman Act to the union. This case, more than

any other, forced unions into the political arena. The Clayton Act (1914) reflected a strong union lobbying effort and largely exempted union activity from the provisions of the Sherman Act. Today, union weapons such as strikes and boycotts are legal.

Union growth during the 1920s was hampered by aggressive tactics that firms used to prevent the organization of their workers. Unions were labeled un-American, and yellow-dog contracts were standard operating procedure. Several violent strikes, notably the Boston Police strike of 1919, caused antiunion sentiment to grow. Demands for the services of skilled workers from craft unions fell as mass production techniques spread. The prosperity of the 1920s aggravated declines in union membership because industrial workers saw little reason to unionize in an era of booming wages and secure jobs.

The Great Depression softened the mood of the country toward unionism. Believing they were on the brink of disaster, many workers collectively acted to buffer the chaos of the business cycle, and total union membership tripled between 1933 and 1940. Organizing drives were aided by passage of the Wagner Act in 1935. This prolabor legislation guaranteed the right to organize unions and made it an unfair labor practice for a firm to refuse to negotiate with a union supported by a majority of its workers.

The percentage of trade union membership within the labor force continued to grow through the 1940s, but the Wagner Act was widely viewed as too one-sided in favor of unions. Dissatisfaction with what were felt to be labor abuses during organizing campaigns resulted in passage of the Taft-Hartley Act

---

4. William Miernyk, *The Economics of Labor and Collective Bargaining* (Lexington, MA: Heath, 1965), p. 14.

5. *Loewe* v. *Lawlor*, 208 U.S. 274 (1908).

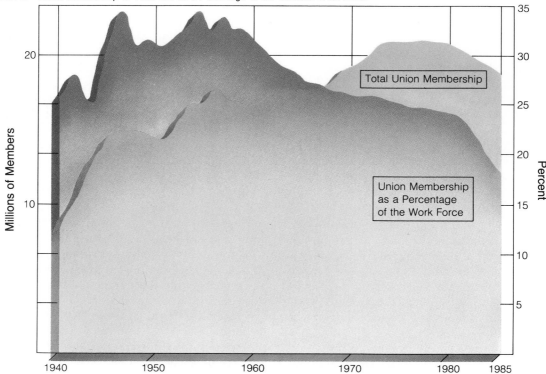

FIGURE 8 *Union Membership in Total and as a Percentage of the Nonfarm Work Force*

Total union membership has been falling in recent years, but, because the labor force has grown substantially, union membership as a percentage of the work force has been declining even faster.
Source: Bureau of Labor Statistics.

(1947), which outlawed secondary boycotts (refusals by union members of one firm to handle any intermediate products produced by other firms that were being struck) and jurisdictional strikes (where the only issue was which union would represent workers), and which also permitted states to pass right-to-work laws forbidding union shops.

Although many people fear that unions are growing increasingly powerful, their influence is probably waning. Union membership faltered in the 1950s, and again in the early 1980s, as shown in Figure 8. A major problem facing union organizers is the growing importance of white-collar workers, who tend to be antiunion. Some of the chronology of the union movement is detailed in Table 4 on pages 596 and 597. With this brief history in mind, we now turn our attention to effects of unions that extend beyond the unionized sectors of the economy.

Economic Effects of Labor Unions

In addition to concerns about the political power of large unions, opponents of unions worry about three possible economic effects of unions: (*a*) distorted wage structures, (*b*) inflationary pressures, and (*c*) disruptions caused by strikes.

Union-Nonunion Wage Differentials Most people believe that unions can raise their members' wages substantially over nonunion wages. Figure 9 illustrates how a **union-nonunion wage differential** can develop. Assume that markets for union (*U*) and nonunion (*NU*) workers are initially identical, with 20 million workers employed in each sector at a wage of w_e. Total employment equals 40 million. The markets for union and nonunion workers are illustrated in Panels A and B, respectively.

If negotiation raised union members' wages to w_1, 5 million (20 million − 15 million) union workers would be disemployed. After all, one cost of higher wages is less employment. As these workers abandon the job market or seek nonunion jobs, the supply of union labor falls to S_1. Nonunion wages drop to allow the absorption of some of the 5 million disemployed union workers. The nonunion wage would shrink to w_2 as the nonunion labor supply swells to S_2, amplifying the wage differential. Note that total employment falls a bit because some people disemployed from the union sector will be unwilling to work at this depressed nonunion wage rate.

Two surveys by H. Gregg Lewis (1963 and 1986, respectively), summarized more than 200 studies of the relative wage effects of unions during the period 1920–79. Lewis placed the average wage gap in the 15–20 percent range, varying from a Depression-era high of almost 50 percent to a low of 2 percent following World War II.[6] Lewis's work suggests that

wage gaps are greatest during economic downturns and least during periods of economic prosperity. He estimated that during 1967–79, the average wage gap was 15 percent. The sharp decline in unionization during the 1980s, however, may mean that union-nonunion wage gaps have been falling. Lewis noted that this wage gap varies substantially, however, and appears to be affected by geographic region, the type of job, and such characteristics of typical workers as marital status, race, health, and age. This gap widens as an industry becomes relatively more unionized and narrows when unemployment in an industry grows, or if most firms in an industry are larger, or when typical workers are relatively more educated.

Many people think that unions have boosted the wages of most workers. If this were true, then unionism would increase labor's share of national income. Numerous studies indicate that this has not occurred historically, nor is labor relatively better paid in countries that are more unionized when compared with countries where unions are less important. You should remember, also, that union wage differentials are created in part by depressing the wages of workers in nonunionized sectors of the economy.

---

6. H. G. Lewis, *Unionism and Relative Wages in the United States: An Empirical Inquiry,* 1963, and *Union Relative Wage Effects: A Survey,* 1986, (both from Chicago: The University of Chicago Press).

FIGURE 9 *Union and Nonunion Wage Differentials*

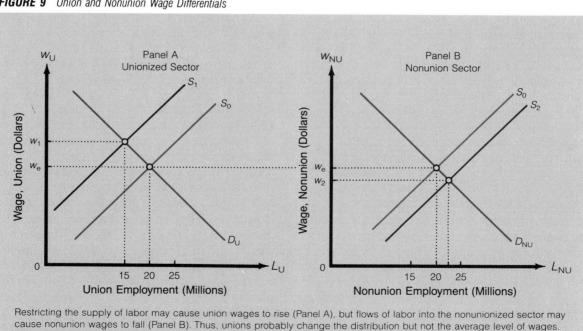

Restricting the supply of labor may cause union wages to rise (Panel A), but flows of labor into the nonunionized sector may cause nonunion wages to fall (Panel B). Thus, unions probably change the distribution but not the average level of wages.

TABLE 4 *American Labor History: Important Events*

1778—	Journeymen printers of New York City united to demand higher wages, but they disbanded after the increase was granted.
1786—	Philadelphia printers gained a minimum wage of $6.00 a week in the nation's earliest authenticated strike.

1806—	The Philadelphia Journeymen Cordwainers went bankrupt after members were found guilty of criminal conspiracy following a strike for higher wages.
1834—	The National Trades Union formed as the first national labor federation, but failed to survive the financial panic of 1837.
1842—	In *Commonwealth* v. *Hunt,* the Massachusetts Court held labor unions to be legal. Massachusetts and Connecticut laws prohibited children from working more than 10 hours a day.
1862—	The "Molly Maguires," a secret society of Irish coal miners, were charged with acts of terrorism against mine bosses; 24 of their leaders were convicted and 10 were executed.
1869—	The Knights of Labor organized, gaining 700,000 followers by winning railroad strikes and advocating the 8-hour day. It collapsed after the emergence of the AFL.
1884—	A Bureau of Labor was formed in the Department of Interior, growing into the Department of Labor in 1913.
1886—	One policeman was killed and several were wounded in the Chicago Haymarket riot, arousing public opinion against union "radicalism" and retarding the drive for the 8-hour day.
	The American Federation of Labor (AFL) was founded.
1890—	The United Mine Workers first organized in Columbus, Ohio.
1894—	The American Railway Union struck the Pullman Co., but was defeated by injunctions and federal troops. Eugene V. Debs and several other leaders were imprisoned.

Unions and Inflation   Some opponents of unions rant and rave that curing inflation requires controlling "those *#@&$%&! unions." Inflation is blamed on unions on the theory that, through collective bargaining or strikes, they artificially boost wages. Firms then pass these higher costs forward by charging higher prices, stimulating unions to demand higher wages to offset their members' losses from inflation, and so on. This high-wage/higher-price/higher-wage spiral is thought by many to be the principal cause of inflation in the United States.

Critics of this analysis point out that unions represent under 20 percent of all workers and argue that increases in union wages can only raise prices modestly. If union labor absorbs 20 percent of all production costs and unions negotiate 10 percent wage hikes, output prices need only rise by 2 percent on the average. Pointing to Figure 9, they might argue that union wage hikes are largely offset by the resulting reductions in nonunion wages. They feel that blaming rapid inflation on unions is ludicrous.

One rebuttal is that this analysis ignores the strength of unions in key industries that manufacture crucial inputs such as steel, automobiles, and chemicals for other sectors of the economy. Higher wage costs and prices for major intermediate products rip-

ple through the economy as upward price pressures on all outputs. Union wages are often standards for many nonunion firms that match collective bargaining agreements to avoid unionization. Finally, if higher wages create massive unemployment and the federal government responds with expansionary macroeconomic policies, there is a classic supply-side inflation cycle. The debate surrounding the impact of union wage increases on inflation will probably continue for as long as unions exist.

Losses from Strikes   Unions are blamed for innumerable economic woes. One question that arises is: If unions represent only one worker in five, how can they cause rapid inflation, economic chaos from strikes, and other social ills? Economists have not reached unanimity about unions, but most believe their impact to be much exaggerated. Strikes and the closed-door collective bargaining process make juicy material for the media. Publicity often makes union organizing and bargaining look like bloody battles. Collective bargaining is a frustrating process, but it works most of the time. Only about 2–4 percent of all negotiations result in strikes, and most of these last less than two weeks, as Figure 10 illustrates.

Most strikes occur because the bargaining parties

1908— The United Hatters' boycott of D. E. Loewe and Co. was held to be in restraint of trade under the Sherman Antitrust Act.

1912— Massachusetts passed a minimum wage for women and minors.

1914— The Clayton Act limited the use of injunctions in labor disputes and legalized picketing and other union activities.

1917— A strike by copper miners from the Industrial Workers of the World (IWW) was ended when the Bisbee, Arizona sheriff deported 1,200 "wobbly" strikers. Union efforts to organize workers signing "yellow-dog" contracts were held to be unlawful (*Hitchman Coal & Coke Co.* v. *Mitchell*).

1921— The Supreme Court held that nothing in the Clayton Act legalized secondary boycotts (*Duplex* v. *Deering*).

1933— Frances Perkins became Secretary of Labor, the first woman named to the Cabinet.

1935— The National Labor Relations (Wagner) Act established nationally the right of workers to organize unions. The Congress of Industrial Organizations (CIO) was formed to foster industrial unionism.

1937— General Motors agreed to recognize the United Automobile Workers and U.S. Steel recognized the Steel Workers Organizing Committee as the bargaining agent for its members.

1947— The Taft-Hartley Act forbade closed shops and secondary boycotts, and permitted states to pass "right-to-work" laws eliminating union shops.

1949— An amendment to the Fair Labor Standards Act (1938) directly limited child labor for the first time.

1953— The Supreme Court upheld the right of the International Typographical Union (AFL) to compel a newspaper to pay for the setting of type not used, and of the American Federation of Musicians (AFL) to demand that a local "standby" orchestra be employed when a traveling orchestra was hired. The Court said that neither practice violated the "featherbedding" ban in the Taft-Hartley Act.

1955— Merger of the American Federation of Labor and Congress of Industrial Organizations (AFL-CIO) brought under one roof unions representing approximately 16 million workers—over 85 percent of all union members in the United States.

1959— The Labor-Management Reporting and Disclosure (Landrum-Griffin) Act specified as illegal certain improper activities by labor or management.

1962— Federal employees' unions were granted the right to bargain collectively with government agencies.

1963— The Equal Pay Act of 1963 revised the Fair Labor Standards Act to prohibit wage differentials based on gender.

1964— The Civil Rights Act of 1964 barred employment discrimination on the basis of race, color, religion, sex, or national origin.

1968— The Age Discrimination in Employment Act made it illegal for employers to discriminate against persons aged 40 to 65.

1970— The first mass work stoppage in the 195-year history of the Post Office virtually paralyzed mail service. The Occupational Safety and Health Act established safety and health standards in the nation's workplaces.

1975— The Trade Act was designed to help workers displaced by imports with up to 52 weeks of pay and assistance in retraining, placement, and relocation. Interns and residents backed by the American Medical Association struck 22 New York City hospitals.

1981— Air traffic controllers represented by PATCO illegally struck and many of these federal employees were fired.

cannot reach agreement over wage issues. The other major causes of strikes are union organization and security; administration of such things as work rules, overtime questions, or safety; interunion and intraunion matters (union rivalry, assignment of work between competing unions, sympathy strikes); and job security disputes.

Strikes may have significant costs beyond the income lost by the strikers. When Teamsters stage a nationwide shutdown, businesses incur higher costs in getting their products to customers. Some sales may be lost because of inability to meet delivery deadlines. After a strike is settled, most firms recoup through increased shipments, and all that is suffered is delay. But this is not always the case. Strikes by farm workers may leave crops rotting on the ground. Strikes by fire fighters offer graphic examples of losses when products go up in smoke. Strikes that reduce supplies cause consumers to bear the costs as higher prices and lower consumption.

FIGURE 10 *Number of Major Strikes and the Percentage of the Labor Time Lost, 1947–83.*

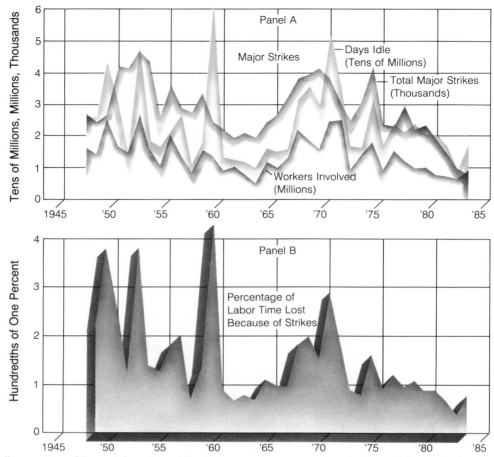

Only a small percentage of the work force is on strike during any given year, and most of these strikes last only a short period. Although some of the numbers in Panel A seem large, Panel B indicates that well under 1 percent of labor time is lost because of strikes.

Source: U.S. Department of Labor, *Handbook of Labor Statistics,* June 1985, p. 409.

Collective bargaining between union and management is now an accepted way to set wage rates and working conditions. Strikes and economic disruption are the prices we pay for this social institution, which has recently expanded to the government sector.

Public Employee Unions

The Wagner (National Labor Relations) Act gave private sector employees the right to organize and compels management to bargain in good faith with the workers' elected representatives, but it originally exempted government workers. Public sector unions were almost nonexistent until 1962, when President Kennedy issued an executive order granting federal Civil Service employees the right to organize—public employee unions spread across the land. Strikes and wage negotiations were prohibited, but unions now bargain about federal policies governing such issues as promotions, discharges, transfers, or leaves of absence. However, unless state or local legislation recognizes their public employee unions, the rules of the game are often remnants left over from the nineteenth century.

The public has traditionally opposed strikes by public employees, especially teachers, nurses, fire fighters, and police officers. Statutes generally forbid strikes by public employees and substitute binding arbitration as a means of resolving conflicts. Nonetheless, strikes do occur. Figure 11 indicates that public sector unions and strike activity have grown markedly since 1960.

Public employees mix collective bargaining with old-fashioned politics to pressure elected officials into meeting their demands. Authority often is split between executive and legislative branches, posing major problems for public sector negotiations. One organization may have authority to negotiate, while another must approve pay hikes via government budgets. Public employees often exert pressures to raise wages (or their shares of the budget) by having officials discontinue some other service.

Public sector bargaining may continue to grow as taxpayers demand ever more from government and, therefore, more from government employees. A case where public union militance backfired was the air traffic controllers union (PATCO), which violated court orders not to strike in 1981. Strikers lost their

jobs, and their union was abolished. The conflict between taxpayer demands for lower taxes and increased services on the one hand and public employee demands expressed through their unions on the other will remain troublesome for government at all levels over the next few years.

This chapter has explored the effects on wages and employment when substantial amounts of economic power are wielded in labor markets by resource buyers (monopoly power and monopsony) or resource sellers—primarily, unions. The markets for land, entrepreneurship, and capital examined in the next chapter tend to be far more competitive, but you may find a few cases where some of the analysis of this chapter seems to apply. More normally, markets for nonlabor resources tend to operate according to the marginal productivity theory introduced in the previous chapter, but each does so in its own unique way.

FIGURE 11 *Public Sector Work Stoppages (Strikes)*

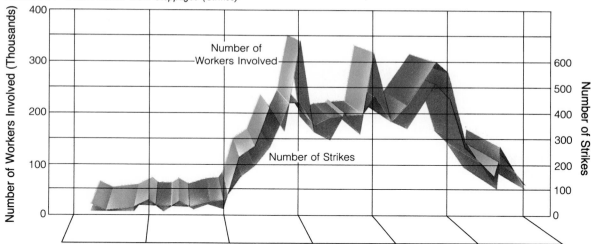

Public sector unionism was negligible until the middle of the 1960s, but since then, strikes by firefighters, police officers, and teachers have all become increasingly common.

Source: U.S. Department of Labor, *Handbooks of Labor Statistics,* 1982, 1985.

CHAPTER REVIEW: KEY POINTS

1. The *marginal revenue product curve* (*MRP*) for a firm selling in an imperfectly competitive product market will be below the *value of the marginal product of labor* (*VMP*) curve. All firms will hire labor until the marginal revenue product equals the *marginal factor cost* (*MFC*) of labor. Because *MRP* < *VMP* for employees of firms with monopoly power, they are paid less than the values of their marginal products. This difference is called *monopolistic exploitation*.

2. A *monopsonist* is the sole buyer of a particular resource or good. Labor monopsonists face an entire market supply of labor and, if all workers are paid equally, their marginal factor cost curve will lie above the labor supply curve. Relative to pure competitors, labor monopsonists pay lower wages and hire fewer workers. In addition, labor will be paid less than the value of its marginal product, a difference referred to as *monopsonistic exploitation*.

3. When competitive conditions prevail in both resource and product markets, the firm hires labor until *VMP* = *MRP* = *MFC* = *w*. When monopoly prevails in the product market but the monopoly firm hires labor under competitive conditions, labor is hired until *VMP* > *MRP* = *MFC* = *w*. Given a competitive product market and monopsony power in the labor market, a firm will maximize profits by hiring labor until *VMP* = *MRP* = *MFC* > *w*. Finally, when a firm has both monopoly and monopsony power, labor is hired up to the point where *VMP* > *MRP* = *MFC* > *w*. Any difference between *VMP* and *w* represents *exploitation*, a term borrowed from Marxist jargon.

4. A minimum wage legally set above the equilibrium wage in competitive labor markets will raise unemployment. It is possible, but unlikely, that minimum wages might increase employment and wages simultaneously, but only where there is substantial monopsonistic exploitation of unskilled workers and wage discrimination is not practiced, an unlikely combination. A union wage hike might have the same effect. However, the markets where minimum-wage hikes raise existing wages are typically rather competitive. Thus, increased unemployment is the normal result when minimum wages are increased.

5. *Bilateral monopoly,* a very early model of collective bargaining, describes the limits to the wage bargaining process but provides little predictive power. Sir John Hicks's bargaining model predicts both final wage settlements and the duration of strikes.

6. *Labor unions* have typically employed three methods to increase the wages of their members: (*a*) reductions of the supply of workers to an industry; (*b*) establishing higher wages and then parceling the available work to members; and (*c*) policies designed to increase demands for union labor.

7. Unions have traditionally organized into craft or industrial unions. Craft unions were the bulwark of the *American Federation of Labor* (*AFL*); industrial unions comprised the *Congress of Industrial Organizations* (*CIO*). Frequent jurisdictional disputes over which organization would represent particular workers caused the two to merge into the AFL-CIO in 1955.

8. Unions and their leaders use several kinds of agreements with organized firms to protect their prerogatives as sole bargaining agents for workers. *Closed shops* require workers to be union members as a precondition for employment. At the other end of the spectrum, *open shops* permit union and nonunion members to work side by side. This arrangement is quite unsatisfactory to unions since nonmembers receive the benefits of collective bargaining but need not pay union dues. *Union shops* are compromises between closed and open shops. The employer can hire union or nonunion workers, but an employee must join the union within some specified period (usually 30 days) to retain the job. The Taft-Hartley Act of 1947 outlawed the closed shop and permitted individual states to pass right-to-work laws forbidding union shops. In many of these states, *agency shops* have been created to protect unions from free riders. Workers may choose not to belong to the union but must pay dues.

9. Unionism developed in a hostile environment. The Great Depression shifted public policy in favor of collective bargaining. As trade unionism grew, many felt that unions became corrupt and too powerful, and tighter organizing and financial reporting constraints were imposed on labor organizations. The union movement was relatively stable from roughly 1950 until 1980, but has declined as a percentage of the total labor force in the 1980s. The labor force increasingly consists of white-collar workers who are reluctant to join unions.

10. *Wage differentials* between union and nonunion workers average roughly 15 percent, but vary substantially by region and between industries. Some people blame inflation on excessive union wage demands. Large wage hikes in key industries may set the pattern for other industries. Higher wages

may raise unemployment and induce public officials to pursue expansionary macroeconomic policies, further intensifying inflationary pressures. Since organized labor represents less than one-fifth of the work force, it is unlikely that unionism explains much inflation.

11. A small percentage of collective bargaining negotiations end in *strikes,* and most are short. Strikes often impose costs on individuals and firms that are not direct parties to labor negotiations. Strikes may cause shortages, shipping delays, or losses of perishable products.

12. Public sector unions have been growing in recent years. Public employee unions frequently mix politics and collective bargaining to win their demands. The public officials who negotiate contracts are seldom responsible for developing government budgets; thus, they may have only weak incentives to resist union wage demands.

QUESTIONS FOR THOUGHT AND DISCUSSION

1. Some economists insist that there are so many "greedy capitalists" that exploitation and wage discrimination are impossible. How might competitive drives for profits ensure that everyone is paid "what they're worth"? Then how do we account for wage differentials between sexes and races if vigorous competition leads to payment of the value of the marginal product?

2. Many firms view salary information as confidential. Can you cite reasons for this practice other than wage discrimination? Do you believe these other reasons are valid?

3. If most firms in certain highly competitive industries (e.g., textiles) monopsonistically exploit their employees and wage discriminate, what would happen to employment if they were forced to quit these practices? Would their current workers be better off? Why or why not?

4. Some people argue that wage structures are compressed relative to individual workers' productivities. In other words, people who make the top incomes tend to be underpaid relative to their productivity, while workers at the bottom of the pay scale are overpaid relative to their productive contribution. Do you think these critics are correct? If so, what does this suggest about the vigor of competition in labor markets? If you think that reality is the opposite of this idea, what features of the labor market cause overpayment of people with relatively high salaries and underpayment of people who have relatively low incomes?

5. The standard model of monopsony leads to substantial underemployment relative to competition and opens up the possibility that minimum-wage laws may expand employment. Can you use logic paralleling the discussion of price discrimination from our chapter on monopoly to show that perfect wage discrimination will cause a monopsonist to hire the same amount of labor as would be employed in a purely competitive labor market? What are the implications of this analysis for economic efficiency? Equity? Do you think that firms having monopsony power also typically have the ability to wage discriminate? Which do you think more common, monopsony power or the ability to wage discriminate by paying workers in inverse proportion to their desperation for employment?

6. Some economists argue that by permitting collective bargaining, we are condoning monopolies despite the fact that the Sherman Antitrust Act outlaws monopolies. Is there anything inherently more palatable about labor monopolies than about product monopolies? By encouraging unions to expand through various laws protecting collective bargaining, are we creating what John Kenneth Galbraith has called "countervailing power", where big unions bargaining for workers offset the effects of concentrated industry? Is there any reason to suspect that the two forces, big labor and big business, will not combine like OPEC to gouge the little consumer? What forces, if any, keep this from happening?

7. Between 1980 and 1986, union membership had declined to less than 18 percent of the labor force. What do you think accounts for the reduction in union membership during this period? Do you foresee labor unions recovering from this decline, or will it continue? Why do you think so?

8. Right-to-work laws presently exist in 19 states. Since they outlaw the union shop, how can unions in these states protect themselves from free riders? What arguments can you make in favor of right-to-work laws? Against? More than one student of labor relations has commented that the name *right-to-work* was a stroke of genius; that without it few people would vote for the legislation. Are right-to-work laws appropriately named? Why or why not?

9. The Taft-Hartley Act outlaws the closed shop, yet in some industries or occupations it is virtually impossible to find employment unless you belong to a union. Are these unions doing something illegal? How do you explain this apparent contradiction between the law and reality? Why would employers agree to hire only union members if they did not have to?

10. Some economists argue that the most effective union to date is the American Medical Association. Do you agree? Does the AMA operate like a labor union? In what ways? Name some other professional societies that perform the same functions as unions for their members. Should these associations be subjected to the same democratic standards and financial reporting standards that are applied to unions? How do you think medical doctors would feel if the AMA changed its name to United Medical Doctors of America, Amalgamated Brotherhood of Medical Doctors, or some similar moniker?

CHAPTER 30 Rent, Interest, Profits, and Capitalization

economic rent	monopoly profit	capitalization
nominal interest rates	risk	rates of return
real interest rates	uncertainty	present values
pure economic profit	innovation	perpetuity

Market forces shape land rents, interest on capital, and the profits of entrepreneurs much as they determine workers' wages. The derived demands for all these resources are based on the prices of output and each resource's marginal contribution in producing the goods consumers want. Producing the goods people want most requires altering materials so that they become more valuable in form, space, time, or possession. Market prices direct these transformations.

Resources are also altered to make them more valuable. For example, acquiring human capital is a way to make an individual's labor more valuable. Most workers try to learn skills that will increase their wage incomes. Similarly, the drive to increase their incomes cause the owners of nonlabor resources to mold their assets to accomplish economic tasks. Investment in capital, for example, can take innumerable forms; whether new capital will be new punch presses, buildings, measuring instruments, bulldozers, hand tools, or industrial robots depends on the form of capital its owners predict will be most remunerative. Entrepreneurs try to develop special expertise in forms of production that they expect to become most profitable, and land owners plant or sculpt their acreage or build shopping malls on it so that their land is most valuably used.

You may be surprised to learn that the markets for capital, land, and entrepreneurial talents tend to be even more competitive than markets for labor. Mobility is a key. Workers tend to be bounded geographically and by habit, but investors compete in international markets—rapidly channeling financial capital between investments when even slight differentials arise in rates of return; economic capital follows soon thereafter. Entrepreneurs also respond quickly to the slightest whiff of a profit opportunity. Although land cannot move geographically, flows of other resources when higher resource payments beckon make land mobile between uses if not spaces.

As you proceed through this chapter, keep in mind that markets for capital, entrepreneurship, and land are all relatively competitive and tend to conform to the principles of marginal productivity theory discussed earlier.

Resource Ratios and Productivity

We indicated earlier that the amounts of other resources used in a production process are major determinants of labor productivity. For example, even unskilled workers in the United States work with much more capital and consequently produce far more than their counterparts in, say, India. Thus, American trash collectors each process more garbage than Indian trash collectors because Americans use more trucks, crushers, and other equipment. The relatively high amount of capital per worker in industrialized countries is a major reason that workers in advanced nations typically enjoy higher wages than those paid to most workers in less developed economies.

The flip side of this is that capital productivity rises as the number of workers per machine grows. Large amounts of capital per worker in the United States mean that the amount of labor per unit of capital is low relative to less developed countries such as India. Thus, while output per worker is high in the United States relative to India, output per unit of capital is probably higher in India. In the United States, hand shovels are often idle on big construction projects; in India, a shovel typically is more productive and might be used for three shifts every day.

Figure 1 indicates that as capital per worker (K/L) grows, the average physical product of labor (Q/L, or output per worker) grows, but the average physical product of capital (Q/K, or output per unit of capital) falls. Similar relationships hold for marginal physical products ($MPPs$) and factor payments. The upshot of this is that labor productivity and wages tend to be higher the greater the capital-to-labor ratio, while interest payments and the productivity of capital tend to be higher the larger the labor-to-capital ratio.

The concept described here holds for virtually all resource ratios: (*a*) capital is more productive and highly paid the greater the amounts of labor, entrepreneurial talent, or land working with capital; (*b*) entrepreneurs will be more productive and highly remunerated the fewer the entrepreneurs attempt-

FIGURE 1 *Outputs per Unit of Input Depend on Capital-to-Labor Ratios*

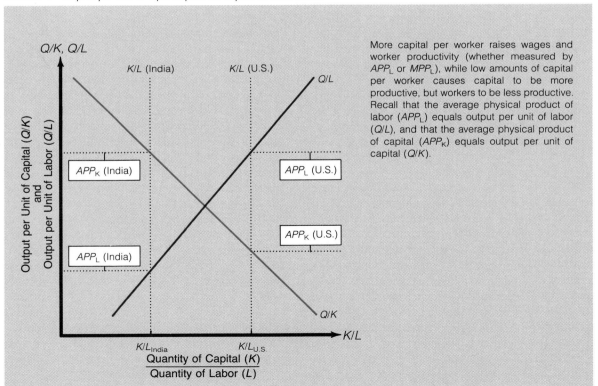

More capital per worker raises wages and worker productivity (whether measured by APP_L or MPP_L), while low amounts of capital per worker causes capital to be more productive, but workers to be less productive. Recall that the average physical product of labor (APP_L) equals output per unit of labor (Q/L), and that the average physical product of capital (APP_K) equals output per unit of capital (Q/K).

ing to use other given resources; and (c) land will be more productive and draw higher rents the more capital and labor are used to work the land. For example, relative to vast desolate ranches on which a few cowhands try to keep track of a few scattered cattle, small flower farms covered with greenhouses and automatic watering equipment and using large amounts of hand gardening produce much more valuable output per acre.

Although the general principles of marginal productivity govern markets for labor, land, capital, and entrepreneurial talent, each market has some unique characteristics. You have already explored labor markets, so we will now examine these other markets.

Economic Rents

When you hear the word rent, you probably think of monthly payments to landlords, the price you pay for the temporary use of a videotape, or a truck or trailer at the local "Rent-All." As seems too often true, economists have taken a perfectly good word, rent, and attached their own special meaning to it. **Economic rent** is realized whenever the owner of any resource is paid more than the minimum amount necessary to elicit the quantity supplied of that productive resource. Thus, economic rent is a very broad concept that may apply to parts of many payments to resource owners.

Economic rents may have little to do with apartment leases or similar "rental" values. For example, many rock musicians often spend years "paying their dues"—working for peanuts in smoke-filled bars and generally hustling just to get by. If they hit it big and begin to pull down seven-figure annual incomes, there is an enormous difference between their superstar incomes and the small amounts for which they were once willing to play music. Economists view such differences as economic rents. Land is about the only resource, however, that generates "pure" economic rents.

Pure Land Rents

Land has the unique characteristic that its supply is absolutely fixed. The amount of land available to society cannot change even if payments to landowners ranged from zero to infinity; its supply is perfectly inelastic at Q_s in Figure 2. If demand is D_0, rent per

FIGURE 2 Economic Rent for Raw Land

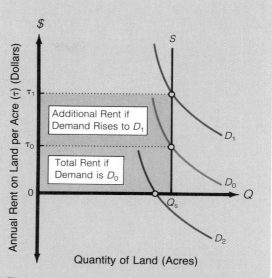

The annual rental value of any factor that is fixed in supply is determined strictly by demand. Pure economic rents are realized only if supply is absolutely fixed, as is the case with locations or the physical characteristics of land. Can you think of anything else that has a perfectly inelastic supply?

acre will be τ_0 and total rent is the lightly shaded area. If the output price rose or a technological advance enhanced land's physical productivity, raising the derived demand for land to D_1, rent per acre would rise to τ_1, yielding total rent equal to the entire shaded area. What will the rent for raw land be if demand is D_2? Zero, and some land will be idle. All payments received for the fixed supply of land are pure rents determined solely by the strength of demand.

The clearest examples of pure economic rents are payments for the use of unimproved land. Note that when people construct dikes, drain swamps, or clear forests, they create capital, not new land. (Recall that any improvement that increases the productivity of natural resources is classified as capital.) Consequently, the supply of land is perfectly inelastic. Changes in demand will result in proportional changes in the economic rents for land. The demand and rental rates for different parcels of land differ according to their location and their physical characteristics.

FIGURE 3 *Value of an Acre of Land, Depending upon Location*

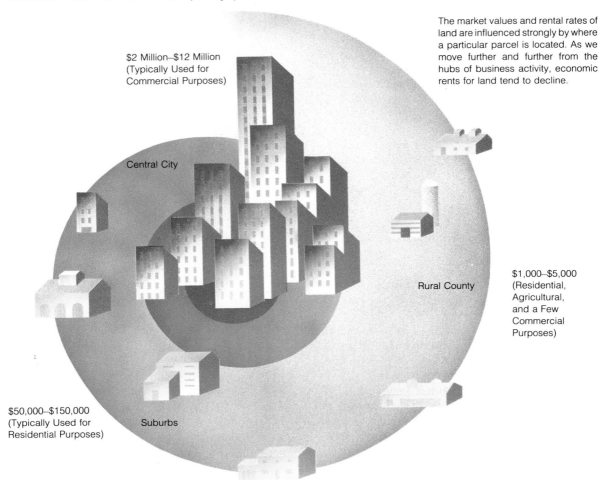

$2 Million–$12 Million
(Typically Used for
Commercial Purposes)

Central City

Rural County

The market values and rental rates of
land are influenced strongly by where
a particular parcel is located. As we
move further and further from the
hubs of business activity, economic
rents for land tend to decline.

$1,000–$5,000
(Residential,
Agricultural,
and a Few
Commercial
Purposes)

$50,000–$150,000
(Typically Used for
Residential Purposes)

Suburbs

Location Rents   Why is a vacant square block in Manhattan priced higher than an acre of prime Kansas wheat land? Transportation costs are a major reason. From this perspective, the customer populations differ, causing different values. One facet of **location rents** is that if a seller can locate so that customers bear lower transportation costs than are incurred in buying from a competitor, the advantageously located seller can charge more for a product.

Suppose that you owned an isolated Kansas farm and replicated a chunk of downtown Manhattan on the north forty, including a hamburger stand. If you cut the price charged at the New York hamburger stand by half and put on an advertising campaign worthy of Ronald McDonald, your sales would fall far short of those by your New York rival. The reason is

that for the average hamburger buyer, the total cost of a hamburger (including transportation costs) would be far less at the New York stand than at yours. New Yorkers would become regular customers only if you charged such a low price for hamburgers that transportation costs were overcome. Fat chance!

Another facet of location rents is that a firm is able to pay lower prices for its inputs if it locates so that its input suppliers (workers, for example) gain from lower transportation costs than would be incurred from selling to a competing firm. When being in business at a particular location gives a firm the ability to charge more or to pay less, the owner of the location will become aware of these advantages and charge rents sufficiently high that only normal profits are received by the firm.

For example, suppose you leased a building in a run-down area of Chicago and established a fancy French restaurant. Then suppose that a huge luxury hotel unexpectedly located in the next block—business would boom and you might profit substantially in the short run. When your lease was up, however, your landlord would raise your rent to exploit the increased profitability of the location. Economic rents of this type are known as *location* or *site rents* and are illustrated in Figure 3.

Rents Due to Physical Characteristics   Marginal productivities and the rental rates of parcels of land reflect differences in fertility or the values of minerals they bear. Some land is not used at all. Windswept deserts and arctic tundra are examples of land so barren and remote that its marginal productivity is effectively zero.

David Ricardo, who originated the theory of pure rent, observed that marginal (barely useful) land commands zero rent whenever equally productive parcels are vacant. For example, you could always live "rent free" at an oasis in the Sahara if at least one comparable oasis were vacant. If the owner tried to charge any positive rent, you would move to a vacant oasis. The production cost saved by using more productive land versus marginal land equals the rental value per period of the more productive land.

Competition for the cost reducing qualities of particular land permits a landowner to charge rents that reflect the productivity differences between the superior land and the marginal (zero rent) land. Ricardo viewed land rent as an **unearned surplus** because the fixed supply of land would still be available even at a zero price. Henry George became famous by arguing that this unearned surplus to landowners could be taxed without creating economic inefficiency.

Rents to Other Resources

The concept of economic rent originated with David Ricardo's analysis of corn and land used to produce it. Economic rents are received, however, whenever any resource owner is paid more than the minimum amount necessary to induce that owner to supply a given quantity of the resource. Thus, many owners of scarce resources or talents earn economic rents.

The economic rents received whenever resource supply curves are imperfectly elastic are illustrated in Figure 4, which portrays a normal, positively sloped

labor supply curve for professional wrestlers. Market equilibrium occurs at point *e* when 450 wrestlers work for annual incomes averaging $80,000. Notice that only the most reluctant wrestlers (those making up the labor supply very near the equilibrium point) are paid the bare minimums necessary for their services. All other wrestlers would work for less and so receive economic rents as surpluses above their minimum acceptance wages. Total rents received by wrestlers equal the darkened area above the supply curve but below the wage rate.

Rents and Efficiency

Economic rent is the surplus received by a resource owner whenever income exceeds the opportunity cost of providing the resource to society as a whole. Economic rents are fairly common because most productive resources are at least partially fixed; their

FIGURE 4 *Economic Rent and Professional Wrestlers*

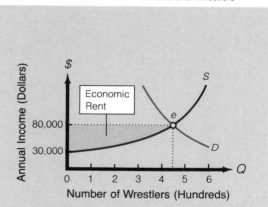

Economic rents are realized whenever the supplier of a productive factor receives more than the minimum necessary to make the factor available to the market. Thus, the area above the supply curve but below the price line represents economic rents. This is sometimes called the *supplier's surplus*. In markets for output, such areas represent *producer surplus*, which is the flip side of consumer surplus. Recall that consumer surplus is the area below a demand curve but above the price line. It is the difference between what a buyer would willingly pay for a specific quantity of a good and the amount actually paid because goods can be bought at a uniform price.

BIOGRAPHY

Henry George (1839–97)

FIGURE 5 *Effect of a Tax on Land: Landowners Bear the Burden*

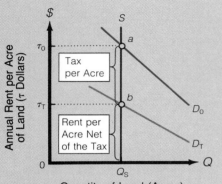

Landowners alone bear the full burdens of land taxes because the total amount competitive renters will pay for the use of land is determined strictly by its productivity. If landlords attempt to shift a land tax forward in the form of higher rental rates, there will be surplus land available and pressures for reductions in rents. The rental rate for land is always "all the market will bear."

H igh birth rates and the arrival of millions of immigrants caused rapid growth of the nineteenth-century American economy. Fertile frontier lands were homesteaded and urban land values boomed. Henry George and his followers believed landowners unjustly reaped major benefits from economic growth, which George perceived as rightfully belonging to society in general. In *Progress and Poverty* (1879), George proposed a **single tax** on land equal to the surplus that landowners were receiving and thought these revenues could finance all government spending. His reasoning is illustrated in Figure 5.

Equilibrium economic rent per acre before the land tax is τ_0 (point *a*). A tax equal to half of annual rent would cut the net rent per acre to landowners to τ_T. Landowners cannot change the supply of land to drive its rental rate up. Attempts to raise rents would fail because surpluses of vacant land would develop. The rent that can be charged land users is strictly demand determined, so landowners cannot avoid the full burden of a pure land tax.

How would a land tax affect allocation? If untaxed land were used optimally, the most profitable uses would remain so after imposing the tax. (If you're able to keep half of all rent, 50 percent of the *highest* possible economic rent is the best you can do.) Thus, land taxes seem allocatively neutral.

The central thrust of George's economics is that land rent can be taxed heavily without distorting production incentives. George felt that "nothing short of making land common property can permanently relieve poverty and check the tendency of wages to the starvation point." He proposed to do this not by directly nationalizing land, but by the roundabout method of taking away the unearned income that proprietors enjoyed from land rents.

Land nationalization schemes were quite common in George's day, but he generally opposed government intervention and proposed leaving land titles in individual ownership, merely taxing all land at 100 percent of its rental value. This levy should be, according to George, a single tax to replace all other taxes. *Progress and Poverty* became the best-selling work on economics of the period and the bible of the single-tax movement.

A single tax on land sounds appealing, but it suffers from several flaws: (*a*) potential revenue would probably not cover today's total government spending; (*b*) administering the tax would be complex because distinguishing the values of land from its improvements—clearing, irrigation, buildings—is quite difficult; (*c*) rent does provide resource owners with incentives to find users who most highly value the resources; and (*d*) land is not the only resource that generates economic rents. A single tax on land rent would impose the full burden of paying for government on landowners. This seems unfair from the vantage point of current landowners.

George's single-tax movement reached its apex in his 1886 race for mayor of New York City. Running as the candidate of the United Labor Party, George finished second but there was wide speculation that he might have won an honest ballot count. Henry George died during another run at the mayor's office in 1897, but nevertheless left his imprint on economic reform movements at home and abroad.

supplies are not perfectly elastic for the entire economy. It is this "fixity" that generates economic rents.

The displeasure of people who view the income distribution as unfair is generally aimed at high incomes received from interest, profit, or rent. Upon hearing about multimillion-dollar-a-year sports figures or movie stars, they may express sentiments such as "No one is worth more than $ _____ ($100,000?) annually." Do economic rents serve any purpose beyond the enrichment of the owners of land or specialized talents? If not, these surpluses can be completely taxed by government with no net loss to society. But both the short- and long-run consequences of taxing economic rents might actually cause inefficient allocations of resources.

Short-Run Allocation

Even in the short run, the drive to maximize economic rent creates incentives for resource owners to use their productive resources in the most valuable ways possible and to maintain them properly. Suppose that you own a city block that will potentially rent for $1 million annually. If this rent were taxed 100 percent, would you have any incentive to seek the highest bidder so that the land would be put to its most valuable use? Absolutely not!

Henry George argued that land would be used efficiently even if a 50 percent site tax on land were imposed because "half of something is better than half of nothing." But what if the tax were 99.99 percent? The $100 received if you found the $1 million bidder for the use of your land would be unlikely to overcome transaction costs. You might simply let your land lie idle. But what if the site tax were only 80 percent? Or 30 percent? Any tax rate, however low, reduces the incentive to put the land to its most valuable use.

Some movie stars, opera singers, novelists, and athletes realize incomes that seem outrageous. Much of such income is economic rent, so why not impose 100 percent taxes on annual incomes over $100,000? This question is partially answered if you ponder how you would react were you in this position. For example, you might immigrate to avoid confiscatory taxes. High income tax rates explain why many English actors and rock stars have become Swiss or American citizens.

If immigration seems unattractive, why bother to be worth more than $100,000 annually? Established actors might study their lines less diligently or do fewer films. Might opera singers begin to smoke, or fail to avoid colds or laryngitis? Would successful authors write as much? Would sports superstars play as hard or often? Would they willingly play in industrial towns, or might most gravitate to sunny resort areas? Some might still strive to excel out of personal pride, but, after a certain point, we suspect that cold, hard cash motivates most people whose specialized skills earn large economic rents.

In summary, rents are important even in the short run because they are incentives to maintain rent generating resources and because they are important in ensuring that those who most highly value scarce resources are able to use them.

Long-Run Allocation

Many resources that draw economic rents because they are semifixed for the economy as a whole in the short run are far from fixed over the long haul. Prospects of high income motivate people to invest in assets that subsequently command economic rent. Today's opportunity costs become tomorrow's fixed costs as resources jell into fixed assets. For example, medical students undergo years of expensive training in hopes of high economic rents once their M.D. degrees are in hand. Investors in buildings or capital equipment draw economic rents over the useful lives of these assets.

Would tomorrow's superstar athletes have as much incentive to polish their skills if the economic rents enjoyed by basketball's Pat Ewing, tennis's Martina Navratilova, or football's Dan Marino were taxed away? NO! Would the lawyers of the next generation be as skilled as F. Lee Bailey or Richard "Racehorse" Haynes if the incomes of top attorneys were limited because they are economic rents? From whence would come future Luciano Pavarottis, Robert Ludlums, or Eddie Murphys? The long-run effects of taxing all economic rent would be disastrous because there would be few incentives to invest in oneself or in capital equipment; the entire economy would stagnate.

It should come as no surprise that the annual rental value of any resource is tied closely to its selling price, which is the wealth associated with owning a resource or other asset. Before we discuss capitalization, which is the process of translating rents or other flows of income into wealth, you need an understanding of interest and profits, which also may be capitalized through the process described near the end of this chapter.

Interest

You may have deposits in a bank account that draw interest. Why does the bank pay you interest? The answer seems obvious: because the bank can make loans at higher interest rates than it pays depositors. Most loans, however, are made to business investors who buy economic capital—machines, buildings, and other enhancements to the productivity of natural resources. Thus, interest is ultimately a payment to providers of economic capital. Interest payments are somewhat roundabout in advanced economies, being spread among those who own capital directly and others whose saving and financial investment make it possible for society to accumulate economic capital. To keep our analysis simple, we will focus on interest payments to holders of financial capital. Similar reasoning applies to direct owners of economic capital.

Interest Rates

Nominal interest rates are the percentage monetary premiums paid per time period for the use of money. The ultimate lenders are those who save by spending less than their income. If you pay a dime annually for each dollar you owe on a car loan, the annual interest rate is 10 percent. (The people you truly owe are depositors in the lending institution.)

There are many nominal interest rates at any point in time because of differences in borrowers and debt instruments—car loans, mortgages, government or corporate bonds, and so on. These "IOUs" are a large component of the financial capital in this country. Interest rates vary among these financial instruments because of:

1. *Risk.* Different borrowers have different probabilities of defaulting on their loans. Naturally, higher "risk premiums" in the interest rate are charged the greater the risk of default.

2. *Maturity.* The time until a loan is repaid also varies. Interest rates are generally higher the longer it will take to retire a loan.

3. *Liquidity.* Better developed markets for specific debt instruments drive interest rates down because the transaction costs incurred in buying or selling such IOUs will be lower. Competition among lenders to grant certain types of loans facilitates liquidity.

Interest rates in the U.S. commonly range from a government-subsidized 5 percent annually to a loan shark's 5 percent weekly. References to "the" rate of interest normally mean the nominal interest rate charged annually on long-term (20–30-year) risk free loans. Interest rates on negotiable long-term government bonds or those charged to "prime" borrowers are good approximations of this concept.

The **real interest rate** is the percentage of purchasing power annually paid by borrowers to lenders. It differs from the nominal interest rate if the price level changes. Real interest is crucial for the decisions of both borrowers and lenders, and can be computed by subtracting the percentage annual rate of inflation from nominal interest rates. For example, 14 percent nominal interest yields only 6 percent real interest when annual inflation is 8 percent.

Interest income is a payment to providers of economic capital. In Chapter 2, you learned that saving makes new capital available; thus, the ultimate capital suppliers in our economy are savers. Just what factors determine the interest rate? After adjusting for inflation, the real interest rate depends on:

1. *The premiums savers require to delay gratification.* Most of us want goods now rather than later, unless we are rewarded for waiting. If 10 percent more goods are required to get us to wait a year to consume some income, the real interest rate tends towards 10 percent.

2. *The premiums for sacrificing liquidity.* Less liquid assets generate higher rates of return, or we would all hold cash.

3. *The productivity of new capital,* which produces extra goods for future use. If new capital reproduces 12 percent of its value in new goods each year, the interest rate tends toward 12 percent.

Over the long run, these three factors are reflected in the demands and supplies of loanable funds.

Markets for Financial Capital

We need to review certain aspects of capital markets before we consider the market for loanable funds. Firms construct buildings, buy machinery, or purposely increase inventories only if they expect to profit by doing so. Firms can finance these investments with funds from: (*a*) retained earnings; (*b*) sales of the company's stock; (*c*) sales of bonds, or (*d*) loans from financial institutions. Naturally, the depositors (savers) are the real lenders. The third approach is called **debt capital.** For simplicity, we will focus on debt capital in the remainder of this section. The thrust of our analysis would not change if we separately considered each form of financial capital. Keep in mind that financial capital is merely a tool used to secure economic (physical) capital.

Demands for Loanable Funds

Investors demand funds for a variety of investments, each of which is expected to yield profits to the business borrower. Just as the demand for labor depends on labor's marginal productivity, the demand for capital depends on its marginal productivity. Capital's marginal productivity (its *MRP*) as a percentage of expenditures on capital is known as the **rate of return on investment (r).** Like the demands for other resources, the demand for capital is a derived demand.

The demand for capital goods generates demand for **loanable funds** to finance new investment. In Figure 6, this demand for loanable funds is expressed in terms of rates of return and real interest rates. One explanation for the negative slope of demand curves for capital and loanable funds is that greater investment causes more and more capital to be used with fixed amounts of land and labor. The *law of diminishing marginal returns* then causes successive doses of capital to be decreasingly productive.

An alternative approach is to recognize that firms rank potential investment projects from the highest expected rate of return to the lowest. Assuming that funds from retained earnings or new stock offerings are insufficient, these projects underpin the demand for loanable funds shown in Figure 6. Only a few projects will yield a 20 percent rate of return or greater ($1 billion worth in Figure 6). As the rate of return requirement falls, firms find that more projects are advantageous. If interest costs fall to 10 percent, $4 billion worth of projects are profitable (point *b*); $8 billion in new investments generate rates of return of at least 5 percent (point *c*).

Investors do most of the borrowing in this country, but consumers and all levels of government also borrow substantially. Consumer purchases of homes and automobiles fall sharply when interest rates rise, as we saw during the economic slump of the early 1980s. Although the federal government's borrowing seems unaffected by interest rates, state and local governments borrow more to finance schools, parks, and roads when their interest costs are less. Thus,

FIGURE 6 The Demand Curve for Debt Capital (Loanable Funds)

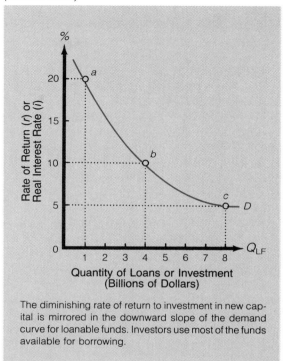

The diminishing rate of return to investment in new capital is mirrored in the downward slope of the demand curve for loanable funds. Investors use most of the funds available for borrowing.

when consumer, investor, and government demands for loanable funds are combined, the market demand curve slopes downward. As with all other markets, however, demand is only half of the story.

Supplies of Loanable Funds

The costs of new buildings or machinery are obviously important in determining the level of business investment. Because the supply curves for capital goods are positively sloped, the costs and prices of investment goods tend to rise during prosperity as demand for investment goods increases, choking off short-term surges in investment. Conversely, declines in the costs of investment goods during economic downturns slow the fall of investment spending.

The major cost of investment, however, is the interest rate. Investors' opportunity costs climb when interest rates rise. Those who have money may make loans instead of buying investment goods. If they must borrow to invest, then a hike in the interest rate makes investment less attractive. Refer back to Figure 6. If the interest rate is 5 percent, then $8 billion in investments have expected rates of return of more than 5 percent and would be profitable; less than a 5 percent rate of return implies that investment is not profitable. As the rate of interest rises, the quantity of loanable funds demanded falls because fewer projects appear profitable.

The supply of loanable funds is positively related to the price received. The ultimate lenders (savers who supply loanable funds) receive interest for the use of their funds. The major alternative for saver/lenders is to use the funds for current consumption, but a few, who value liquidity highly or who expect interest rates to rise, may hoard their savings. High interest rates confront individuals with higher opportunity costs of current consumption (or hoarding), and many save (providing funds to the capital market) and use their future wealth (amount saved plus interest) for consumption at a later time.

Equilibrium Interest Rates   Equilibrium in the financial capital market is illustrated in Figure 7. The initial demand for funds D_0 reflects the rates of return expected by business (plus consumer or government borrowing). It is negatively sloped because investments become less profitable as interest rates rise. The initial supply curve S_0 is positively sloped because household saving grows as interest rates paid savers rise—the opportunity costs of current consumption rise.

The rate of return on new investment equals the interest rate in equilibrium, which occurs at the intersection of the demand (D_0) and supply (S_0) curves in Figure 7. The initial equilibrium rate of return and interest rate will be 8% and the quantity of investment loans will equal Q_0. Suppose that expected returns on new capital investments rise so that the demand for loanable funds increases to D_1. Equilibrium interest and investment loans would rise to 10 percent and Q_1, respectively. Trace the effects of the following changes on interest rates and the amounts of investment loans:

1. households decide to delay consumption and save more.
2. investors become more optimistic.
3. families decide that times are sufficiently secure that they can reduce their holdings of currency or other highly liquid assets.

When families increase the rate at which they postpone consumption, the loanable funds available for investment rise and interest rates fall. When investors grow more optimistic, expected rates of return, interest rates, and financial investments all rise. If households feel more secure, they reduce the liquidity of their assets by increasing their financial investments in stocks and bonds, and interest rates fall.

Economic Profit

Most people misunderstand the role of profit in a market system and substantially overestimate the shares of profit out of sales dollars, national income, and as a return on invested capital. Earlier, you learned that accounting profit is the difference between a firm's total revenues and its *explicit costs,* which are payments for the use of resources not owned by the firm. Only after subtracting *implicit costs* (the opportunity costs of resources that the owners provide for a firm's operations) from accounting profit do we have **pure economic profit,**

FIGURE 7   *The Market for Loans*

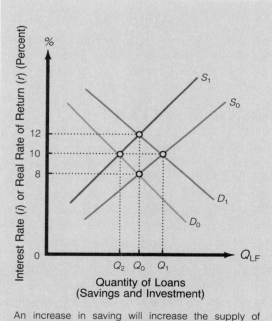

An increase in saving will increase the supply of loanable funds and decrease the interest rate. Reduced anxiety about the future tends to expand both the demand for and the supply of loanable funds.

which is a surplus over opportunity cost and so is a form of pure rent to the firm's owners.

In a purely competitive but unchanging economy in which the future was certain and transaction costs were zero, economic profit would always be zero and the implicit payments necessary to maintain owner-provided resources would absorb all accounting profits. In reality, transaction costs are significant, and continuous changes make the future uncertain. Many of these changes are wrought by entrepreneurial quests for profits. Moreover, monopoly power is commonplace. This leads to the major sources of pure economic profits: (*a*) monopoly power, (*b*) innovation, and (*c*) uncertainty.

Monopoly Profit

Monopoly power enables some firms to generate total revenue far in excess of the opportunity costs of the resources they use. But can a monopolist continually enjoy economic profit? Transaction costs, uncertainty, and barriers to entry create short-run profit opportunities. **Monopoly profit** may persist into the long run if barriers prevent entry by competitors; but profits will stimulate resource flows that eliminate monopoly profit if markets are contestable. If so, profit will have served its function by signalling where society desired greater production. If barriers preclude entry in the long run, however, monopoly profit encourages least-cost production, but economywide efficiency will not occur.

The capitalization process we will describe in a moment suggests that predictable monopoly profits are realized only by people who own a firm when it secures its monopoly position. These monopoly profits will be capitalized in the long run into a higher market value for ownership of the firm and thus a higher opportunity cost, so that subsequent buyers of ownership shares can expect only normal profits.

Rewards for Innovation

Another explanation for profit is **innovation,** or the development and implementation of a new product or production process. If your firm is among the first to introduce a successful product or try a more efficient technology, you will reap economic profits. Economic profits are eroded by competition as imitators follow in the footsteps of successful innovators.

Thomas Edison, for example, became rich when he established General Electric as the outlet for his genius, but General Electric now faces hordes of competitors and realizes only normal profits. More recently, the invention and development of the Polaroid camera by Edwin Land resulted in immense profits for him and his family.

The innovation theory of profits was first expressed by Joseph Schumpeter as an explanation for the business cycle. When a significant innovation was made, many entrepreneurs would attempt to capitalize on the profit opportunities, and their collective investments would fuel an economic boom. Once the advantages from the innovation were fully absorbed, investment would decline, pushing the economy into a downturn to await another major innovation.

Risk Bearing and Uncertainty

Crystal balls or computer programs that precisely forecast the future have not been invented, but we can estimate the probability of many future occurrences and try to exploit potential gains while guarding against possible misfortune. If the likelihood of some potential future event is fairly predictable, many people will adjust in similar ways so that only normal rates of return can be expected. Buying insurance policies is one adjustment against life's possible hazards, or you might *self-insure* by taking your chances. Some aspects of the future, however, seem totally unpredictable. A windfall of unexpected profit for bearing the risk of just being in a particular business may be your reward if fortune smiles, or you may get clobbered if disaster unexpectedly strikes your industry.

The eminent economist Frank Knight first distinguished risk from uncertainty.[1] **Risk** exists when the probability of a given event can be estimated. For example, if a firm can reliably predict that, on average, a production process will yield 3 defective units out of 100, it can adjust for these risks by considering "losses due to defects" as a normal cost of doing business. Similarly, the probabilities of fire, certain accidents, or the death of a key executive can be predicted fairly reliably, and insurance is available.

---

1. Frank H. Knight, *Risk, Uncertainty, and Profit* (Boston: Houghton-Mifflin Co., 1921).

Again, these risks will be reflected in production costs and output prices.

Uncertainty, on the other hand, occurs when a potential occurrence is so unpredictable that forecasts are unavoidably pure guesswork. It forces entrepreneurs to weigh imperfect information and base their decisions on subjective judgments. Profits, to Frank Knight, are rewards for bearing uncertainty. Entrepreneurs undertake investments with the expectation of generating sufficient revenues to cover all costs, including allowances for all risks, but the unfolding of time may yield events beyond any entrepreneur's wildest expectations or fears. Uncertainty, in Knight's view, makes it impossible to anticipate pure economic profits or losses.

The Economic Role of Profits

Uncertainty, innovation, and monopoly power are the major sources of economic profit. But what function do profits perform? Economic profits are powerful signals that prices exceed average production costs and indicate that social welfare will be improved if resources are shifted from unprofitable to profitable sectors of the economy. Conversely, industrywide economic losses are signals that too many resources are devoted to production of a particular good and could beneficially be shifted elsewhere.

Profits are also a stimulus for efficiency. Entrepreneurs' desires for profits will cause costs to be cut wherever possible, freeing resources for other uses. Competition forces profits down to normal levels as imitators mimic the activities of successful firms, whether success is derived from being in a certain product line or using a more efficient technology. Competition also punishes those who fail to produce efficiently by inflicting economic losses on relatively high-cost firms.

Profits also reward the entrepreneurs who innovate new products and technologies in an uncertain business environment. The drive for entrepreneurial profit propels society along the path to economic growth and progress. Focus 1 discusses entrepreneurship.

Flows of predictable rents, interest, or profits are translated into wealth through the process of capitalization whenever the resources that generate the income flows can be sold. In the next section, we examine the mechanics of how competition for income streams determines the market values of income-generating assets.

Capitalizing Income Streams

Suppose that you manage a rock group called "Nuclear Winter," currently being booked as a warm-up act for more popular bands. The group's third album suddenly goes platinum and phones begin to ring. Promoters want "Winter" to headline upcoming concerts, but it is solidly booked for the next 6 months at $5,000 per appearance.

Who will benefit from the group's popularity during the next 6 months? Promoters who contracted with your band prior to its hit album will realize economic profits by selling out their concert dates even if they increase ticket prices. How long will these economic profits (which could also be considered rents) continue to be received by individual concert promoters?

Being a smart promoter yourself, you will quit booking "Winter" as an opening act and will raise its fee when you negotiate future contracts so that individual concert promoters earn only normal profits. This **capitalizes** the rents from the group's special skills. The fee now reflects the higher ticket prices and attendance for each performance. If you held exclusive rights to book the group, you could sell the contract for a fat profit.

A similar capitalization process occurs in farming. If grain prices soar because, say, the Soviet Union suffers a drought and makes huge purchases in world markets, farmers temporarily enjoy economic profits. What happens to the price of farmland when this happens? It rises because the expected profits are capitalized into higher land values. Even farmers who own their land find the opportunity cost of holding it rising, squeezing out the economic profit derived from farming. Their higher wealth naturally would keep them from mourning their fates too loudly.

Investors prefer more income to less, and they want it sooner rather than later. Thus, the capitalized value of an income stream will be larger (*a*) the greater the income stream, and (*b*) the more quickly income is realized. Truly understanding these relationships requires knowing how to calculate present values and rates of return.

So You Want to Be an Entrepreneur. . . ?

Work provides many people with the primary meaning for their lives. Surveys indicate that most college students want interesting, secure, and remunerative careers. Many also express desires for jobs that reward hard work with rapid advancement or that contribute to social well-being. Finding "the right job" may entail a little job hopping, but most people eventually spend most of their lives employed by one large company. With luck, it will have a good pension plan.

Several studies suggest that successful entrepreneurs typically march to the beat of their own drummer. Many seemed misfits early in their careers, losing a series of jobs because they refused to be the team players favored by many employers. Most equated compromise with losing and would do almost anything to get their own way.

People afflicted with personalities that make it difficult for them to get along in large organizations often express desires to "be my own boss," but few who go off on their own ever enjoy much success. Indeed, most who eventually succeed do so only after a series of failures. It is hard to overstate how devastating bankruptcy can be, especially to entrepreneurs who have staked their dreams on the success or failure of an enterprise.

What separates highly successful entrepreneurs from most small proprietors or heads of giant corporations? Several characteristics are commonly shared by successful entrepreneurs:

1. *Vision and timing.* Entrepreneurs need the ability to see opportunities where others see only problems. This often requires being in the right place at the right time. Different people interpret the same complex of facts differently. Successful entrepreneurship seems to involve organizing information so that solutions to problems become obvious. The solution may involve reducing production cost, improving the quality of an existing good, or innovating a totally new good.
2. *Conviction and action.* Once entrepreneurs find a key to solving a problem, they act on their convictions. Some people may see solutions to problems, but want security and the conventional "good life" and so lack the faith to pursue their idea to its conclusion. Highly successful entrepreneurs have a very different goal; they want to leave their mark on the world.
3. *Bearing of risk and uncertainty.* Successful entrepreneurs typically

have such faith in their business plans that they will risk vast capital and time to accomplish their goals. This often requires rejecting the financial security that most people seek.
4. *Workaholism.* Most people want high income from a job that allows leisure time every evening and on weekends and regular vacations. A 40-hour, 9-to-5 job is not a goal of most successful entrepreneurs, some of whom put in over 100 hours per week for decades.

G. L. S. Shackle, a prominent economist, describes enterprise as "action in pursuit of the imagined, deemed possible."* Entrepreneurs imagine alternative uses of resources, and by organizing resources to correspond to their individual visions, they alter the course of history. If this brief discussion has not squelched any desire you might have had to be an entrepreneur because of a wish to shape human history, then you need to watch for opportunities to provide things that people want, be willing to absorb some risk, and work extraordinarily hard. Then pray for luck.

*G. L. S. Shackle, "Forward" in The Entrepreneur, by Robert F. Herbert and Albert N. Link (New York: Praeger Publishers, 1982).

Present Values

Economic investment generates additional salable output over the future, yielding an income stream to the investor. The income stream per time period as a percentage of the dollar outlay for a capital good is called the **rate of return.** Determining whether an investment will be profitable requires calculating its **present value,** which is the value today of all expected future receipts of income.

Suppose that you were offered a guaranteed right to $100 payable one year from today and that your savings account earned 6 percent interest annually. What is the most you would be willing to pay for this IOU? Certainly less than $100. You can calculate the amount at which you will do equally well with your money in either the savings account or this IOU by answering the following question: How much money would I have to put in the bank at a 6 percent interest rate per year so that when the interest earned in one year is added to the original amount, the total equals $100? This problem boils down to $1.06(PV) = \$100$, where PV stands for present value. If you divide both sides of this equation by 1.06 and then solve for $PV = \$100/1.06$, you have the answer. Similar questions can be answered for any interest rate, any time period, or any amount of money using the following formula:

Present Value

$$PV = \frac{Y_1}{(1 + i)^1} + \frac{Y_2}{(1 + i)^2}$$ Equation 1

$$+ \ldots + \frac{Y_n}{(1 + i)^n}$$

$$= \sum_{t=1}^{n} \frac{Y_t}{(1 + i)^t}$$

where:

Y_t = payment expected at time t.
i = annual interest rate or discount rate.
t = time period.
n = number of time periods over which payments are to be made.
Σ = an arithmetic operator meaning "sum across."

A numerical example should help you see how the formula works. If you use a 6 percent interest rate to discount $100 payable one year from today, the PV = $100/1.06, which equals $94.34. This amount in a savings account paying 6 percent interest would yield $94.34 × (.06) = $5.66; at the end of the year your principal plus interest would total to $94.34 + $5.66, which is $100. If you had to wait two years for the $100, what is the most you would pay, assuming the interest rate is 6 percent? The answer is $89, because $100/[1 + .06]^2 = $89. Naturally, an IOU paying $100 next year plus $100 two years hence would be worth $94.34 + $89.00 = $183.34.

The present value formula in Equation 1 may appear formidable, but there is a shortcut in calculating present values if the annual income expected

from an asset is fixed into the indefinite future at a constant, Y_t. Such assets, known as **perpetuities** are computed with the following equation:

Present Value for Perpetuities

$$PV = \frac{Y_t}{i}$$ Equation 2

Thus, if a parcel of land is expected to generate annual rent of $10,000 forever and the interest rate is 10 percent (.10), the present value of this land is $100,000. If a government bond promises to pay $1,000 annually forever to its owner and the interest rate is 8 percent, the bond is worth $12,500. Bonds of this type, called *consols,* are issued by the Bank of England.

Rates of Return

While present value calculations are very important to financial analysts, investors are more often interested in rate of return analysis. If you are majoring in accounting or finance or are just interested in investment analysis, you should pay special attention to both present value and rate of return formulas—you will undoubtedly see them again.

Investors usually have some idea as to the income stream they might expect from an investment. We can determine the rate of return (r) by solving the following formula:

Rate-of-Return Calculation

$$P = \sum_{t=0}^{n} \frac{Y_t}{(1 + r)^t}$$ Equation 3

where P equals the price of the investment good, r equals the annual rate of return, and all other variables are as defined above. Since we know price (P) and expected income in each time period (Y_t), the only unknown is r, the rate of return. For example, if an asset selling for $100 today will pay $110 a year from today, the rate of return is 10 percent. A $112 payment yields a rate of return of 12 percent. Thus, the larger the expected income in each time period, the greater the rate of return for a given price.

Comparing Present Values and Rates of Return

How are present value and rate of return calculations related to each other and to the capitalization process? If the present value is at least as great as the price ($PV \geq P$), then the expected rate of return is at least as great as the interest rate ($r \geq i$), and you will invest because the asset appears profitable. You will not invest if the price of an asset exceeds your estimate of present value because the expected rate of return will be less than the market rate of interest.

Generally, we know the price (P), the going interest rate (i), and the income expected each year (Y_t) from an investment when we evaluate it.

Break-Even Investments

$$PV = \sum_{t=0}^{n} \frac{Y_t}{(1 + r)^t} \qquad \text{Equation 4}$$

When Equation 4 holds, the investment is a *break-even* proposition. For example, if an investor could reasonably expect $224 a year hence and the interest rate were 12 percent, a current price of $200 would make an investment strictly a break-even proposition. However, your assessment of the present value of an asset may be either higher or lower than the price asked. Similarly, you may estimate the rate of return either above or below the market interest rate.

Present value calculations solve for the current worth of an income stream by discounting expected future income with the market rate of interest, both of which we know. Rate of return analysis also assumes that we know how much income to expect in the future and when it will be received, but solves for an unknown *implicit* interest rate (r), while using the known current price to arrive at a solution.

Capitalization and Competition

There is tremendous competition for profits. If you are an astute investor, there will probably be several other astute people who would assess a given investment much as you do. If present value appears to exceed price substantially, there may be bidding wars that rapidly drive the price toward present value. Even if you do manage to pick up what you view as a bargain, you certainly would not then sell it for less than its present value to you.

Thus, the equilibrium price of any asset is its present value. Moreover, after adjusting for risk, competition causes the rate of return expected from any asset to equal the market rate of interest. The process that discounts expected future income by the interest rate to arrive at present value and price is *capitalization.*

How might you use your knowledge of the capitalization process? Assume you own 1,000 shares of a "wildcat" oil company earning $1 per share per year. If market conditions required a 10 percent rate of return, shares of the stock would sell for $10. Now assume that the company hit a gusher expected to triple its annual earnings. The market will quickly raise shares to roughly $30 after the gusher is announced. What rate of return can be expected by people who buy the stock after this discovery? Roughly 10 percent, just as before. Similar capitalization processes determine most resource prices.

Thus, capitalization makes enormous profits possible for the people who set up sports franchises and watch them succeed, while people who subsequently buy a piece of paper called a "franchise" for millions of dollars can expect to make only normal returns.

One possible road to riches requires finding assets for which the current owners have underestimated future earning power. You can then purchase these assets relatively cheaply. When the true earning capacity of the assets becomes known, you can become rich by selling the assets for considerably more. One roadblock that makes this a difficult avenue to wealth, however, is vigorous competition from many other bright people who are also looking for bargains.

The Marginal Productivity Theory of Income Distribution

In our chapter on production and costs, we showed that least-cost production by profit-maximizing firms forces them to use combinations of resources so that the marginal products of particular resources are proportional to resource prices. This concept translates into the principle of equal marginal productivities per dollar:

$$\frac{MPP_L}{w} = \frac{MPP_K}{r} = \ldots$$

This is one way that the law of equal marginal advantage applies to production. Multiplying all *MPP*s by the price (P) of the output produced reveals that competitive firms must operate so that the values of the marginal products of all resources are proportional to their prices:

$$\frac{VMP_L}{w} = \frac{VMP_K}{r} = \ldots$$

But resource prices are equal to marginal factor costs if resource markets are competitive, and the market compels competitive firms to pay resource owners incomes equal to the resources' *VMP*s, so:

$$\frac{VMP_L}{MFC_L} = \frac{VMP_K}{MFC_K} = \ldots = 1.$$

This suggests that, in equilibrium, a competitive market system will divide income according to the contribution towards production of an individual's resources. Of course, neither product nor resource markets are perfectly competitive, but this brief review does point out some central tendencies for market distributions of income.

The marginal productivity theory of income distribution that we have developed in this part of the book cannot even hint, however, at the most equitable income distribution. We address this normative question late in the next part of this book.

We have now discussed markets for goods and resources, touching upon certain government policies along the way. The next part of the book explores in greater detail the microeconomic role of government in a market system. We will address various types of inefficiency and inequity whose causes range from inherent problems with market solutions to failures inherent in government decision making.

CHAPTER REVIEW: KEY POINTS

1. *Economic rent* exists whenever resource owners receive more than the minimum required for them to supply given amounts of the resource.
2. Land has a unique economic characteristic—it is fixed in supply. Thus, its supply curve is perfectly inelastic, and all payments for the use of land are pure rent. Land rents vary by location and particular physical characteristics.
3. Land is not the only resource that generates economic rents. Other factors that are supplied at prices above the minimum amounts required to elicit their availability also generate economic rents.
4. "Single taxers" inspired by Henry George propose a 100 percent tax on land rent as a single tax to finance all government spending. They argue that taxing this unearned surplus would not distort the allocation of land, and thus would not hinder economic efficiency. The *single-tax proposal* suffers from: (*a*) inability to finance the entire public sector, (*b*) administrative problems in distinguishing land values arising out of improvements made by owners from rent as an unearned surplus, and (*c*) reduced incentives for landowners to put their land to the best possible uses if rent is taxed away.
5. Economic rent promotes economic efficiency by providing resource owners with incentives to put their assets to the most valuable uses.
6. *Nominal interest* rates are the percentage annual monetary premiums paid for the use of borrowed funds. Interest rates on financial instruments vary according to: (*a*) risk, (*b*) maturity, and (*c*) liquidity.

"The" interest rate normally means the rate on a long-term risk free bond.

7. In the long run, *real* (purchasing power) *interest rates* depend on: (*a*) premiums required to induce savers to delay consumption, (*b*) desires for liquidity, and (*c*) the productivity of capital investments. These factors determine interest rates through the supply and demand for *loanable funds*. Government macroeconomic policies also influence loanable funds markets.
8. *Pure economic profits* are the residual remaining after adjusting accounting profits for the opportunity cost of the resources provided by a firm's owners. Profit may arise from *monopoly power,* from bearing business *uncertainty,* or from *innovation.*
9. Profits channel resources to their most productive uses in a market economy and stimulate economic progress as entrepreneurs endure business uncertainty while innovating to secure profits. Profits provide incentives for efficiency; economic losses will be imposed on competitive firms that do not produce at the lowest possible cost.
10. *Present values* are the sums of the discounted values of future income that may be expected from owning an asset. The present value of an asset and its price will be identical in equilibrium. If the present value exceeds price, then the asset is a profitable investment, because the expected rate of return exceeds the interest rate. *Capitalization* is the process whereby prices gravitate toward present values of assets.

QUESTIONS FOR THOUGHT AND DISCUSSION

1. Land taxes may not cause gross misallocations of land, but property taxes are widely perceived as dissuading owners from improving land in an optimal fashion. High property taxes are also blamed for the deterioration of the urban cores of large cities. How elastic is the supply of improvements to land vis-à-vis the supply elasticity of land per se? How might land values be distinguished from improvements if land taxes replaced property taxes?

2. Economic rents and economic profits are both "surpluses" in excess of opportunity costs from the vantage point of society as a whole. They are unnecessary to secure resources socially. Rent on the land used by any firm is a true opportunity cost to that firm, however, while economic profits are not. It is true that rents are often opportunity costs to the individual user, but not to the entire society?

3. The Soviet Union, following Marx's theory that interest is a mechanism capitalists use to exploit workers, rejects using an interest rate to discount the future benefits from investment projects. Explain how ignoring interest rates might cause saving to flow into less than socially optimal investments.

4. Accounting profits generally exceed economic profits because accountants may fail to consider implicit costs. Can you think of activities that might generate "implicit revenues" so that economic profits would exceed accounting profits? Might this be how firms in some competitive lines of business continually generate accounting losses but continue to operate?

5. Some people who start a successful enterprise encounter major difficulties in managing their companies once the firm is on its feet. For example, Steve Wozniak and Steven Jobs built Apple Computers from a tiny operation housed in a garage into a billion-dollar concern between 1976 and 1981, but professional managers and stockholders had banded together and ousted both from leadership of the company by 1985. What are the differences in the personalities required to be innovative entrepreneurs and professional managers? Is it likely that one person can embody both sets of attributes? Can you cite other cases in which people who were strong "starters" were weak "finishers?" Where a strong starter established a series of successful companies, but was never able to maintain control once success was enjoyed? Where strong starters proved quite capable of effective management once an enterprise was successful?

6. Big cash winners on TV game shows or in magazine subscription contests commonly are paid in installments over a period of years. Suppose you were a contestant on "Name That Tune" and won $100,000, receiving $20,000 today and $20,000 at the end of each of the next four years. If the interest rate is 10 percent, what is the present value of your winnings? Are there other reasons to believe that the values of prizes are overstated? What would you guess is the average percentage of overstatement?

PART 9

The Microeconomics of Government Policy

Microeconomic theory provides an array of tools that aid our analyses of problems that confront policymakers at all levels of government. We have used such tools as elasticity, marginalism, diminishing returns, and the law of equal marginal advantage to investigate problems that arise for public policy in such areas as regulation, antitrust, and labor relations. But this barely scratches the surface of the kinds of government policymaking into which microeconomic reasoning can offer valuable insights. Other areas include: (a) agriculture, (b) crime and punishment, (c) defense, (d) education, (e) energy, (f) health, (g) science and technology, and (h) urban problems. Looking at all possible problem areas would require a book twice as long as this one and a course twice as long as the one in which you are enrolled—exhausting your pocketbooks and the patience of your professors and our publishers. You will have opportunities to study many of these topics if you take further courses in economics.

This part of the book begins with a framework for examining policies. First, in Chapter 31, we develop a normative theory of the public sector by investigating areas in which the market may fail to allocate resources acceptably. *Market failures* identify economic functions that government may be better suited to fulfill. Then, we survey the structure of American taxes, measuring both current taxes and proposed tax reforms against principles of efficiency and equity. In Chapter 32, we focus on *public choice*, an approach that views political behavior from an economic perspective. This area of study provides clues about *government failure*—just as the market may fail at times, public policies are frequently less than ideal. In Chapter 33, we examine questions of resource management and environmental quality. Finally, in Chapter 34, we address the problem of poverty and issues surrounding the redistribution of income. Applying microeconomic tools to these areas should familiarize you with how to use economic reasoning when you want to investigate any of a multitude of problems.

CHAPTER 31 Market Failures and Public Microeconomics

market failures	ability-to-pay principle of taxation	total burden of a tax
public goods	horizontal equity	value-added taxes (VATs)
merit goods and bads	excess burden of a tax	flat rate taxes
benefit principle of taxation		consumption taxes

This chapter addresses economic functions that may be appropriate for government in a market economy. Private markets operate under rules set by government, but public policy is typically more invasive when the marketplace is perceived to fail. We will look at different types of *market failure* and certain government corrections. Some normative principles of taxation are also a concern: Who should pay for government, and how? Then we survey the strengths and weaknesses of several taxes to assess how well our current system conforms to normative principles of taxation. This chapter concludes with a review of some proposed tax reforms. In the next chapter, we use economic analysis to explore political decision making and *government failure*. There, you will find answers to many questions you may develop about why public policy so often deviates from the ideals we describe in this chapter.

A Normative Framework for Government

Economic problems are ideally resolved equitably and efficiently. Recall that **market failures** identify economic functions that government may be better suited to fulfill. They can be categorized as problems of (*a*) *distribution,* (*b*) *stabilization,* or (*c*) *allocation.* People exert political pressure for redistributions of income or wealth when they perceive inequity; inefficiency is a problem when unemployment is excessive, the price level is volatile, or when resources are misallocated.

Richard Musgrave, a specialist in public finance (the study of the economics of government), has argued that muddled thinking and misguided policies arise from attempts to resolve different problem areas simultaneously.[1] He proposed a three-part budget framework to clarify and resolve economic issues by first classifying them as problems of allocation, distribution, or stabilization. Each area would be dealt with separately by using the best tools available, with any side effects then being treated by the best cures for them. Thus, the allocation branch would try to cure inefficient resource allocations while assuming that any resulting inequity or instability will be remedied by the distribution or stabilization branches of government. Suppose, for example, that prisons would be largely self-supporting and more efficient if more inmates worked in prison industries, but that this might cause a loss of jobs in the private firms currently producing competing goods. The allocation branch would ignore this potential disemployment because full employment is the responsibility of the stabilization branch. We will briefly consider Musgrave's proposed distribution and stabilization branches of government before looking at problems with market allocations.

The Distribution Branch

The **distribution** branch of government would concentrate on achieving equity—an unavoidably normative issue—and would rely on taxes and transfer payments. Only taxes collected from people whom policymakers deem to have "too much" could be given as transfers to those perceived to have "too little." The distribution budget would balance at all times. Musgrave assumes that poor people are adequate money managers so that no direct allocations of goods are required; poverty would be cured with cash grants, and there would be no food stamps, public housing, or Medicaid. We will deal later with some normative and practical problems encountered in redistributing income.

The Stabilization Branch

Market systems may be unstable; cyclical swings in employment and the price level can impose widespread hardships. Musgrave's **stabilization** branch of government would concentrate on achieving full employment, price-level stability, and economic growth. Since the Great Depression of the 1930s, our federal government has used a mix of macroeconomic policies to try to achieve these goals.

The budget of the stabilization branch would be the only part of the total budget ever out of balance, and it would rely solely on positive or negative taxes.[2] When rising prices posed a problem, the stabilization branch would run a budget surplus by imposing positive taxes to siphon away some private purchasing power. The resulting dip in demand would dampen inflationary pressures. If the economy suffered from recession, negative stabilization taxes (driving the budget into deficit) would increase the purchasing power of consumers and investors. Increases in disposable income would stimulate demand, bolstering output and employment. The stabilization budget would balance during stable and prosperous periods.

Stabilization is a macroeconomic concern, and redistribution is treated later in this book. Consequently, we will ignore these topics for now and will concentrate on government allocations of goods and services.

The Allocation Branch

The **allocation** branch of government would provide goods that would be provided inefficiently, if at all, if left to private decision making. The allocation branch should divert resources from the private to the public sector as long as the marginal benefits exceed the benefits society would receive were the resources used to produce private goods. The values of the private goods foregone are the opportunity costs of the governmentally provided goods.

For example, spending on national defense has been a major issue of the 1980s. In an efficient economy, more spending for national defense involves a trade-off because resources must be bid away from competing uses. One possible way to acquire more resources for defense is to cut funding for social programs. For example, when President Reagan sought more defense spending (his "Star Wars" proposal),

---

1. Richard A. Musgrave, *The Theory of Public Finance* (New York: McGraw-Hill, 1959), especially Chapters 1–3.

2. Note that Musgrave's stabilization budget conducts a Keynesian style of fiscal policy but relies on variations in taxes alone, eschewing changes in government spending as a stabilization tool.

he proposed to reduce government spending in agriculture, transportation, education, housing, welfare, and other areas. Alternatively, national defense might grow at the expense of private consumption or investment.

This allocation process can be seen in Figure 1, which depicts marginal social benefits and costs assumed for Star Wars satellites. For any fewer than 89 satellites, society gains on balance by producing more. What about the ninetieth? Society's marginal benefit in deterring war is less than the marginal cost of the ninetieth satellite, so putting it in orbit would be inefficient.

There are, however, numerous difficulties with this approach. If contractors compete vigorously for government contracts, market prices will reflect the marginal social costs of resources, but, as you may have heard, outrageous billings by defense contractors seem common. Another problem arises if policymakers' decisions fail to mirror voters' preferences and benefits. (These problems are treated in the next chapter.) Moreover, forecasting marginal social benefits is often a guessing game, especially for projects expected to yield benefits over a long time horizon

or that embody significant externalities. In spite of such difficulties, however, modern *cost/benefit* techniques can provide reasonable estimates of marginal social benefits and costs in many cases.

Ideally, only Musgrave's allocation branch of government would directly alter resource allocations. The stabilization and distribution branches would affect allocation indirectly and only by their influence on the size or distribution of national income. Taxes collected from the beneficiaries of governmentally provided goods would exactly pay for such goods, and the allocation branch would run a balanced budget.[3]

Musgrave's proposed division of budgeting into three branches—allocation, distribution, and stabilization—aids clear thinking, but in actual budget making, special interests may oppose straightforward solutions to certain issues because of their side effects. For example, a sales tax might be efficient, but groups concerned about equity may oppose it because of its alleged regressivity. As a result, policymakers are often forced to choose one goal at the cost of another. Before looking at such trade-offs, however, we need to consider the kinds of market misallocations that cause most people to look to government for a cure.

Market Failure: Allocation

Competitive markets allocate production and consumption for most goods so that marginal social benefits equal marginal social costs. When marginal social benefits and costs diverge, the market is said to have "failed" allocatively. In such cases, government may be used to provide the socially optimal quantities of some goods and to limit economic bads. (Some critics view greater efficiency as a futile hope because they perceive that costly inefficiency plagues government bureaucracies.)

Musgrave's budget format suggests that government should directly allocate resources only when private suppliers fail to provide certain goods in accord with consumer preferences. Why might the private sector inadequately service consumers? After

FIGURE 1 *The Socially Optimal Quantity of Star Wars Satellites*

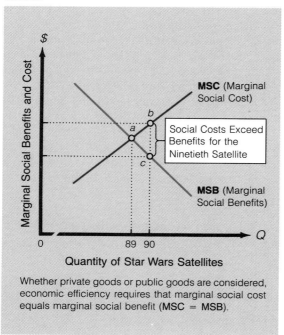

Whether private goods or public goods are considered, economic efficiency requires that marginal social cost equals marginal social benefit (MSC = MSB).

---

3. People would not be faced with separate tax bills from the allocation, distribution, and stabilization branches of government. These budgets would be consolidated so that each taxpayer would pay only the net taxes due or receive a net transfer payment.

all, if consumers strongly desire a particular good, won't they willingly pay a price high enough to buy it? Unfortunately, the market system is destined to provide too much or too little of some goods in some very predictable areas. Inadequate competition, externalities, and public goods (e.g., national defense or a system of justice) are the three main reasons why the private sector fails to achieve efficiency because, in unchecked market equilibria, marginal social benefits (*MSB*) will tend to diverge from marginal social costs (*MSC*).

Lack of Competition

Firms that exercise monopoly power charge higher prices and produce less than the socially preferred output (that produced were markets purely competitive). Long-run average cost curves that decline over a wide range of output relative to the market may make competition inefficient and create pressures for natural monopoly. As we showed in previous chapters, antitrust actions may curb monopoly power and promote competition, or regulation can steer the behavior of natural monopolists into a more efficient mode.

Externalities

Exchanges occur only when all parties *directly* involved in transactions expect to gain. The marketplace works best when only these parties are affected. Competition maximizes individual welfare and the general interests of society through specialization and exchange; the marginal social benefits of transactions are equated with their marginal social costs, given the current income distribution. But certain technical characteristics may cause inefficient market solutions for some goods. For example, pollution and obnoxious billboards might be even more prevalent if the market operated unchecked. Riding in a car would be even more dangerous if every driver had to negotiate with every other driver for the right-of-way, and big city traffic might suffer terminal gridlock. Lack of regulations requiring immunization might allow epidemics of deadly diseases to sweep through the population. (You may have heard of "Typhoid Mary", a restaurant worker who infected thousands of people in her day.)

Such market failures arise because people not directly engaged in certain transactions are affected.

Market prices and quantities tend not to reflect the preferences of these third parties, so maximum social welfare may not be achieved through market solutions. **Externalities** occur when private calculations of benefits or costs differ from the benefits or costs to society because third parties gain or lose from a transaction. This important topic is the focus of a coming chapter. It is time to examine the market failure that seems to require the most of government—the public goods problem.

Public Goods

You can solve the problem of wanting additional pairs of shoes with a trip to a shoe store. But suppose that you feel an urgent need for more public parks or a stronger national defense. You can be sure that if you voluntarily send a big check to the National Park Service or the Department of Defense, these agencies will spend your money. Even if they spent it wisely, however, you would not have appreciably better access to parks or be noticeably better defended. The problem is that these are examples of *public goods.*

The absence of any identifiable effect causes people to limit their voluntary contributions for such goods. Voluntary funding, if any, tends to fall far short of that needed for optimal provision of a public good. Recall (from Chapter 5) that a public good is one whose every unit can be enjoyed by numerous individuals at the same time. This is known as *nonrivalry*—the marginal cost of providing the good to extra consumers is zero. Once a public good is available, denying access to a consumer is prohibitively expensive, a characteristic called *nonexclusion.*

Rivalry and Nonrivalry   Consumption by any individual exhausts a **rival good** so that no one else can consume the same unit of it. You cannot eat a peanut butter sandwich if I eat it first; if you are going to eat peanut butter, it must be in a different sandwich. I cannot use your raincoat if you are wearing it. Peanut butter sandwiches and raincoats are each examples of rival goods. However, we can enjoy the same TV programs without rivalry. When your television receives signals, it does not affect the signals received by my set. A police patrol can simultaneously protect both you and your neighbor from burglary. Police protection and television broadcasts are examples of **nonrival goods.**

TABLE 1 *Rivalness and Exclusion*

	Rival	**Nonrival**

Exclusive	*Pure private goods* will be efficiently provided by the marketplace:
	  Beer
	  Candy bars
	  Automobiles
	  Records
		Excess capacity situations. The private market will provide, but government regulation may be used to attain efficiency if economies of scale are significant:
		  Movies
		  Airline flights
		  Rapid transit trips
		  Cable TV

Nonexclusive	Pollution. Regulation is normally used to resolve:
	  Air, water, or noise pollution
	  Litter
	Assignment of property rights is sometimes used.
		Pure public goods. There will be less than efficient amounts provided unless government steps in:
		  National defense
		  Flood-control projects
		  Weather forecasts

Exclusion and Nonexclusion A theater can exclude you from seeing a film; you must buy an admission ticket. Restaurants do not have to serve you unless you wear a shirt and shoes. Movies and meals are **exclusive goods.** Contrarily, if a Star Wars satellite protects you from attacks by foreign enemies, your neighbor is also automatically protected. And fencing a national park might be both expensive and in conflict with the purpose of the park. These are **nonexclusive goods.** Nonexclusion occurs whenever it is prohibitively expensive to prevent people from enjoying a good.

Product Characteristics and Market Failure

Goods and services come in several combinations of rival/nonrival and exclusive/nonexclusive relationships. Table 1 summarizes these possibilities, but each type of combination is somewhat unique.

Pure Private Goods Goods that are both rival and exclusive are **pure private goods** and tend to be efficiently provided by the marketplace. Most goods, from abalone to zithers, are pure private goods.

Excess Capacity A combination of nonrivalry and exclusiveness generally entails excess capacity. Theaters with empty seats or unsold tickets for airline flights offer examples of nonrival goods, but you can be excluded from flying or enjoying movies. Unless

economies of scale are the cause of excess capacity and are so significant that monopoly power is a problem, competitive markets normally provide these goods efficiently.

Rival/Nonexclusion The market fails whenever the costs of excluding a person who does not pay for a good are prohibitive relative to the value of that good. A nonexclusive but rival good is typically overused, if it is provided at all. If I enjoy scenery but also value the roadside as a garbage site, I may toss beer cans out my window as I drive down the highway. The resultant eyesore and the costs of cleaning up my litter are borne by taxpayers at large; my personal costs are trivial. (Most antilitter laws are only weakly enforced.)

Pollution and the despoliation of scenery become rampant when both nonexclusion and rivalry for the use of a resource are present. In England, everyone once had access to certain property that was held in common, but the "commons" were often treated as though no one owned them. Individuals had little incentive to maintain common property, and it was typically abused and run down.

Pure Public Goods A **pure public good** is both nonexclusive and nonrival. Weather forecasts on television may simultaneously benefit both you and me in making plans for picnics; preventing weather information from spreading is prohibitively difficult. If a private meteorologist tried to sell forecasts and you subscribed for this information, the meteorologist could do little to prevent you from passing along the information. Hence, the U.S. Weather Service is the major source of basic weather forecasting.

Merit Goods and Bads

Some goods are deemed either so socially desirable or undesirable that government intervenes even though the marketplace would resolve consumer wants efficiently. This occurs when a democratic majority, some elite group, or a petty dictator decides that certain things are desirable and that other things are undesirable, regardless of consumer preferences. For example, welfare programs often provide goods rather than cash because of a sense that the preferences of the poor are inappropriate (i.e., they might spend it on booze). The Surgeon General requires warnings on cigarette packages because some smoker somewhere may not have heard about tobacco's dangers. Similarly, primary education is compulsory because "ignorant" parents may not value it adequately for their children. Compulsory education, low-income housing, and food stamps are examples of **merit goods.** Bans against certain drugs or X-rated movies are examples of sanctions against **merit bads.**

Possible rationales for intellectually or morally elite groups to overrule individual preferences include arguments that:

1. ignorance, uncertainty, or the "evil" inherent in the human soul may cause people to act improperly.
2. consumers are gullible and easily misled by advertising.
3. market information is asymmetric—suppliers know more about their products than their customers do, and tend to keep negative information secret.
4. income redistribution is most effective when the poor are provided the things they need instead of money.

This last point is especially elitist in that welfare givers perceive welfare recipients as inherently incompetent. (Are the poor in dire straits because they lack income or because they are stupid?) We will not deal with merit goods further in this chapter, leaving it to you to ascertain whether consumer sovereignty or elitist judgments should dominate in situations where people's choices significantly affect only themselves.

Providing for Public Goods

Pure public goods are both nonexclusive and nonrival, and so differ markedly from private goods. As a result, the construction of their market demands differs as well.

Private Demands Versus Public Demands

Recall that market demands for private goods are the *horizontal* summations of all individual demand curves—we add together the quantities demanded at each price. This is shown for lobsters, a *private good,* in Panel A of Figure 2. The total demand curve for a **public good**, however, is the **vertical summation** of all the individual demand curves, as illustrated in Panel B. We all gain by having an extra police patrol car cruising our neighborhood at night, so our demand for this additional surveillance reflects the dollar amount we would pay *collectively* for this protection. The total demand curve for a public good is constructed by adding the dollar amounts we each would willingly pay to have each possible level of the good.

Optimal Public Goods

Once we have calculated total demands for public goods, how do we determine how much of each to provide? And how much should individuals be required to pay? One possible answer is the **benefit principle of taxation:** each person is taxed in proportion to the marginal benefits each derives from a governmentally provided good.

Panel B of Figure 2 illustrates this principle by showing Alan's (A) and Beth's (B) individual demands for police patrols together with their total demand curve. The total demand is the vertical summation of Alan's and Beth's demands. We assume that the costs of patrolling are $6 per patrol. However, Alan and Beth differ in their benefits from each patrol. If 3 patrols are provided each night, Alan values each patrol at $2, while Beth values each at $4. The $6 cost per patrol will be covered if each pays in proportion to their gains [($2 × 3) + ($4 × 3)].

Contrast this with the optimal provision of private goods as depicted in Panel A; each individual pays the same price per unit, but each consumes a different quantity of lobsters. Alan consumes 35 pounds of

FIGURE 2 *Market Demands for Private and Public Goods*

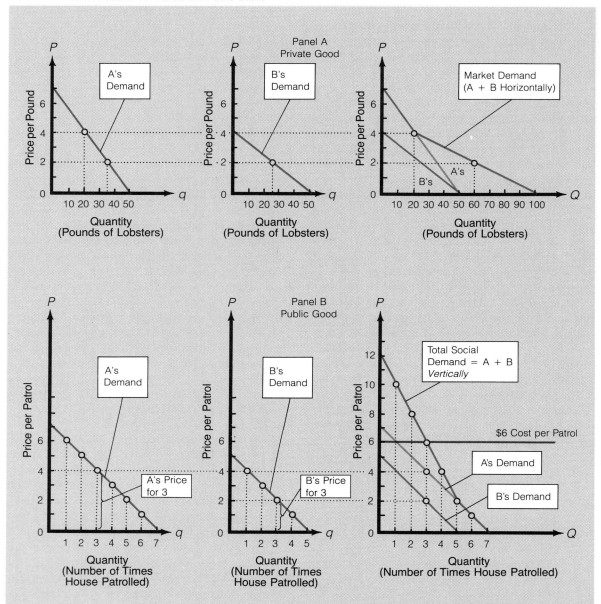

We all face the same prices for private goods but buy different quantities, so the market demand is the *horizontal* summation of our individual demands (Panel A). We all consume the same amounts of pure public goods but value them differently, so the total demand for public goods is derived by *vertically* summing our individual demands (Panel B). Sufficient revenue to pay for the socially optimal amount of a public good can be generated if each individual contributes his or her marginal benefit (in dollar terms) times the amount provided. In this case, three patrols nightly at $6 per patrol could be secured if B paid $6 ($2 X 3) and A paid $12 ($4 X 3). Unfortunately, neither A nor B will voluntarily reveal a preference because both will try to be "free riders." Thus we use involuntary tax levies to pay for public goods. It will only be by chance that both A and B are taxed in accord with the benefits they receive and that the optimal amount of the public good is provided.

lobsters annually at $2 per pound, while Beth is satisfied with 25 pounds at that price.

The preceding solution to the public goods problem automatically answers the question of who should pay taxes. This benefit approach, however, is not the only way to levy taxes.

The Microeconomics of Taxation

Taxes are the price we pay for civilization.
—Oliver Wendell Holmes, Jr.

We have outlined some areas in which government plays a role in a market economy. Regulation may be important at times, but the provision of government goods and services normally requires the government to spend money. Budget outlays can be funded by borrowing, but most government spending is financed by taxes. Many Americans complain loudly about the taxes we pay. As Table 2 shows, however, most foreigners who are lucky enough to live in advanced economies pay far more.

Efficiency and Equity in Taxation

Even the most rabid anarchist benefits from some government programs. The central questions are:

1. How great are the total benefits from government programs?
2. How are these benefits distributed?
3. How much should individuals pay for publicly provided goods?

The *law of equal marginal utilities per dollar* (discussed earlier) states that consumers are in an efficient equilibrium when the marginal utilities of all goods for each consumer are proportional to their relative prices. Competitive markets for purely private goods achieve this result automatically. In a sense, Musgrave's allocation branch of government would ideally provide the amounts of public goods that people would demand were pure competition possible for these goods. If taxes are viewed as the prices consumers pay for government, then individual satisfactions are universally maximized when each consumer's equilibrium can be described as:

$$\frac{MU_a}{P_a} = \frac{MU_b}{P_b} = \cdots = \frac{MU_n}{P_n} = \frac{MU_G}{(\text{Tax per } G)},$$

TABLE 2 *Taxes as a Percentage of International Output*

Country	1965	1985
Sweden	35.8%	51.8%
France	35.0	45.2
Austria	34.7	42.1
Italy	27.2	41.0
England	30.6	39.4
Canada	25.9	35.9
Portugal	18.5	34.9
Greece	20.6	32.4
Australia	24.7	32.0
Switzerland	20.7	31.9
United States	26.2	30.3
Japan	18.4	28.1
Spain	14.7	26.1

Source: Reprinted with permission from U. S. News & World Report issue of August 27, 1984. Copyright © 1984 by U. S. News & World Report, Inc.

where letters *a, b, . . . , n* stand for private goods and *G* stands for any publicly provided good. This equation simply adds public goods explicitly to the equilibrium that maximizes an individual's satisfaction. The budget of Musgrave's allocation branch of government would always be balanced, with beneficiaries paying taxes that would exactly pay for all public goods.

The Benefit Principle

The *benefit principle of taxation* is an ancient normative doctrine that taxes should be in proportion to the benefits people receive from government. This principle conforms to the gut feeling most of us have that you should pay for what you get. In the police patrol example, tax revenues just adequate for optimal amounts of this public good can be secured by levying taxes so that citizens share costs in proportion to the marginal benefits they receive.

Taxation strictly according to marginal benefits is, unfortunately, impractical for most pure public goods. The public sector provides an incredible array of goods, and the costs of collecting and processing the information required for appropriately different taxes is prohibitive. Individuals cannot be excluded from enjoying the benefits whether they paid taxes or not. These characteristics of public goods lead to the *free rider* problem.

Benefit Taxes and Free Riders   Most people would be reluctant to reveal their preferences for public goods if they would be taxed accordingly. This is especially true for huge projects (e.g., national defense) that benefit masses of people, most of whom are not known to the individual taxpayer.

Suppose that taxes were based strictly on your reported benefits from a public good. Some people might assert that they want little or none of the public good in question. Extremely crafty types might even say that the good harms them, so that they would receive tax credits. Once other people agree to buy some of a public good, free riders can enjoy it cost-lessly. If many people attempt to free ride, the public good may not be available at all. Generally, a public good that is privately marketed will be available in less than optimal quantities because of the free rider problem.

User Charges   General tax revenues are used to pay for most goods provided through the public sector, but the benefit approach to allocating public goods has been the basis for user charges that relate taxes to expected benefits. When a governmentally provided good has the exclusion characteristics of a private good, benefits can be approximated and users can be charged accordingly. Examples include bus fares and entry fees for public museums, zoos, parks, or toll roads. Gasoline taxes are also roughly proportional to benefits; owners of heavy trucks or drivers of huge gas hogs pay more gas taxes than drivers of fuel-efficient compact cars, but they also put more wear and tear on the highways that gasoline taxes support.

Although the benefit principle of taxation is often inapplicable because individuals' preferences for many public goods are concealed, general tax revenues are used to fund numerous activities where user charges could be easily applied. For example, should vegetarians pay for meat inspections? User charges imposed on meat packers would be shifted forward to meat buyers. Similarly, federal tests of new medicines could be billed to the pharmaceutical companies that want to market them. If airports, air traffic controllers, and airplane safety inspectors were paid for by airlines and private plane owners, these tax burdens would not be borne by people who benefit little from air transport. President Rea-

gan's proposed 1986–87 budget advocated funding numerous federal programs with user charges, but most of these programs remain a drain on general revenues.

Political and practical difficulties, however, are only two of the drawbacks of benefit taxes. Benefit taxation may conflict with principles of taxation that are based on concerns about equity.

The Ability-to-Pay Principle

An alternative to the benefit principle of taxation is the idea that taxes should be proportional to one's ability to pay. Broadly, this **ability-to-pay principle** suggests that the "fairest" tax is one based on your financial ability to support government activities. The benefit and ability-to-pay principles may be somewhat more compatible than surface appearances might suggest. Rich people may benefit more than poor people from such public goods as national defense or police and fire protection because rich people may stand to lose more from disasters. Thus, both principles may support the idea that the rich should pay more taxes than the poor.

Richard Musgrave labels as **vertical equity** the idea that a rich individual should pay more taxes than a poor one for each to bear the same burden in supporting government. He has also offered horizontal equity as an additional desirable property of any tax. Simply stated, the doctrine of **horizontal equity** is an argument that fairness demands that "equals be treated equally."

More specifically, people in equivalent circumstances (equal income?) should pay identical taxes. Thus, horizontal equity dictates that equals should pay equal taxes; vertical equity, that "unequals" should be treated unequally. Wealth and income are normally viewed as appropriate measures of one's ability to pay taxes. Progressive taxation is not necessary for vertical equity, however; even regressive tax systems might satisfy this equity principle as long as the rich paid absolutely more than the poor.

Funding for the balanced budget of Musgrave's distribution branch would be provided from ability-to-pay taxation. The rich would pay positive taxes, and welfare payments would probably be based on a negative-income tax system of the type we discuss later in this part of the book.

Excess Burdens and Neutrality

The **total burden of a tax** can be measured by the amount of money that would have to be paid the individual on whom the burden falls to make that person just as well off with the tax as without it. The **excess burden of a tax** is the difference between the total burden and the tax revenue collected by government. Thus:

**total burden of a tax =
government revenues + excess burdens.**

Economists commonly share the concerns of people who are irritated by apparent inequity in the tax system, but most economists focus on areas where greater precision is possible. Specialists in public finance are especially disturbed by excess burdens, most of which are caused by the non-neutral effects of taxation.

In his *Wealth of Nations,* Adam Smith suggested that efficiency in taxation requires taxes to be certain (unavoidable), convenient, and that collection costs should be minimized relative to the tax yield. In addition to administration costs and taxpayer compliance costs, taxes impose excess burdens if they distort the prices faced by consumers, workers, savers, investors, or business decision makers. For example, if the government imposes a tax that ultimately collects $100 from you but warps your decisions, the tax may burden you by more than $100. This distortion does not help the government, and collecting the tax imposes an excess burden on you.

Supply-and-demand analysis can allow us to examine excess burdens more closely. In Figure 3, S_0 and D_0 represent the nontaxed supply and demand for quarts of bourbon. For simplicity, we assume constant production costs at P_0 per quart.

Suppose that a tax of t per quart is now imposed on bourbon. This "tax wedge" shifts the supply curve to S_t from the buyer's perspective. As buyers and sellers adjust to this tax, consumers watch the price of a quart of bourbon rise from P_0 to P_t, while the amount sold falls from Q_0 to Q_t. At Q_t quarts of bourbon monthly, the difference between the price paid by the buyer (P_t) and the price received by the seller (P_0) is exactly equal to the tax t. Prior to the tax, consumers paid OP_0cQ_0 for Q_0 quarts of bourbon, but would have been willing to pay $OdcQ_0$. Thus, they enjoyed a consumer surplus of P_0dc. The increase in

FIGURE 3 *The Excess Burden of a Tax*

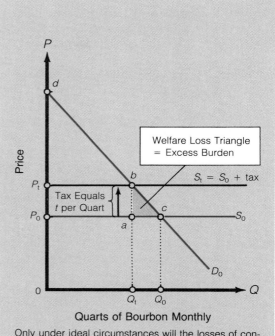

Only under ideal circumstances will the losses of consumer surplus and economic rent (or producer surplus) due to a tax be fully offset by tax revenues. In the case shown here, the full burden of the tax is borne by consumers, who lose surplus P_0P_tbc while government gains revenue of P_0P_tba. There is a "deadweight" welfare loss of abc.

the consumers' price to P_t causes a loss of consumer surplus of the area that is below the consumer demand curve but above the original price (P_0) and below the new price (P_t). This area of consumer surplus lost equals the trapezoid P_0P_tbc.

Government, however, gains monthly tax revenues of t per bottle for Q_t quarts of bourbon, a total of area $P_0P_tba,$ which it can use to meet taxpayers' wants. Therefore, the total loss of consumer surplus minus the gains to government equals the area abc (which is $P_0P_tbc - P_0P_tba$). The shaded triangle abc (sometimes called the *welfare-loss triangle*) represents a *deadweight loss* to society from this tax; it is the excess burden of the tax. These losses, however, may be more than offset by gains in consumer surplus from the goods government buys with the tax revenues. Of course, if government spending is inefficient, the "welfare-loss triangle" may understate the total loss to consumers. Government ideally minimizes the welfare-loss triangles incurred in securing any given total of tax revenues.

Neutrality The neutrality principle combines and extends Adam Smith's certainty, convenience, and economy principles. Ideally, the costs of transferring purchasing power from private hands into the public purse are minimized. A neutral tax distorts neither consumer buying patterns nor the production methods used by firms. Its total burden just equals the tax revenue collected, meaning that there are no excess burdens. The crucial idea behind **tax neutrality** is that the tax directly causes only income effects, not substitution effects.[4] That is, a neutral tax does not induce changes in behavior to avoid the tax; behavior changes only because of lost purchasing power. This requires that taxes be unavoidable.

No action by taxpayers (perhaps at the behest of their lawyers) should enable them to avoid the burden of payment, and the only impact on taxpayers should be declines in their purchasing power. For example, tax structures should not encourage fringe benefits in work contracts instead of direct wage payments or financial investment in tax-free municipal bonds rather than in capital equipment. Nor should it encourage consumption of housing instead of groceries or automobiles. (Our income tax system has done all these things.) Taxes that directly alter the relative benefits and costs facing consumers or business decision makers are nonneutral and inefficient. A neutral tax will be more certain, convenient, and economical than a nonneutral tax.

All taxes, unfortunately, are non-neutral. Most taxes cause substitution effects by directly altering relative prices, thereby changing the behavior of consumers and firms. As a result, taxes are often evaluated by their relative neutrality. Because all taxes are somewhat flawed, economists normally try to specify which are the most nearly neutral (those with the smallest excess burdens) and least inequitable in generating governmental revenues.

---

4. You may want to review the discussion of income and substitution effects from the chapter on consumer choice.

Evaluating the Current Tax System

The best taxes are old taxes.
—A Legislator's Proverb

Just how efficient and equitable are the important taxes now used by our federal, state, and local governments? Current sources of taxes are indicated in Figure 4.

Personal Income Taxes

One flaw of our progressive **personal income tax** is that rising marginal tax rates may discourage investment, work effort, and other attempts to make income. Another is that our income tax system historically has been ambiguous and rife with loopholes. These factors erode the tax base and cause legislators to raise tax rates. For example, if erosion of the base causes a tax rate of 40 percent to be applied to only half of potential nontaxed income, then the rate could be dropped to 20 percent if all potential income were taxed.

And what is income, anyway? Many advocates of tax reform favor a comprehensive definition of income; your taxable income would be your total annual consumption spending plus the change in your net wealth over the period. That is,

$$Y_t = C_t + \Delta W_t,$$

where Y refers to income, C refers to consumption, ΔW refers to the change in your wealth, and t identifies the time period considered. For example, if you spent $8,000 during the year on consumer goods and if the value of your house increased by $5,000 but you lost $2,000 in the stock market, your total income would be $11,000 ($8,000 + $5,000 − $2,000 = $11,000). An income tax structure without loopholes, but at much lower than present rates, could be applied.

Under our current system, some income is not counted at all: the bulk of gifts, grants or awards, and most fringe benefits are nontaxed. Other income has received preferential treatment when compared with income from wages or salaries; lower taxes on capital gains from investments are an example. Special exemptions, deductions, and credits have been rampant. Pension plans such as Individual Retirement

FIGURE 4   *Source of Revenues: Federal, State, and Local (1985)*

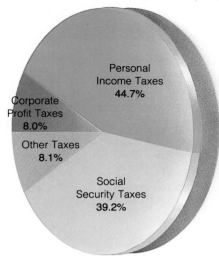

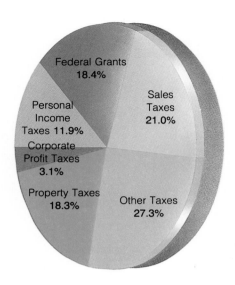

Federal Government Revenues (1985)
$785.7 Billion
Source: *Economic Report of the President,* 1986, pp. 251–52.

State and Local Governments (1985)
$542.8 Billion

Accounts (IRAs) as well as energy and child day-care tax credits are examples. Only after these were subtracted from gross income did you finally arrive at your true taxable income.

The tax rates for married couples filing joint returns in the United States for 1985 are shown in Table 3, which indicates that the income tax is moderately progressive and also debunks the myth that you might lose money by moving into a higher tax bracket. The *marginal tax rate* is the percentage of *extra* income you pay in taxes—it would have exceeded 100 percent for this bit of folklore to be true. You could not lose money by making a higher income because the marginal tax rate in the United States did not exceed 50 percent.[5] Table 3 also shows that marginal tax rates in Great Britain have been much higher than in the United States. This has led many to suggest that England's weak economic performance in the last few decades can be traced directly to the powerful disincentive effects of high marginal tax rates at relatively low incomes.

For all the flaws of our income tax system, there seems to be widespread support for income taxation with some degree of progressivity. Few Americans favor abolishing the Sixteenth Amendment, which authorized income taxes. The major bone of contention has been how our income tax system should be reformed.

Taxes are a powerful force in shaping economic behavior. The Internal Revenue Code has been extremely complex, creating opportunities for individuals and entrepreneurs to use tax loopholes to legally avoid tax liabilities. Tax *avoidance* is legal, but high marginal rates have provided huge incentives for tax *evasion,* which means illegal nonpayment of taxes. These possibilities violate all of Adam Smith's principles of certainty, convenience, and economy.

At first glance, our progressive income tax system might seem a good example of an ability-to-pay tax, but many loopholes have crept in over the years. A family with a wage and salary income of $18,000 may

---

5. Naturally, we ignore the implicit marginal tax rates of more than 100 percent that emerge from some regulations governing welfare payments. This problem is treated later in this part of the book.

TABLE 3 U.S. and British Personal Income Tax Schedules

United States—Federal, 1985 (Married Couples Filing Joint Returns)			Great Britain—1984 (All Persons)		
Taxable Income Bracket	Base Tax[a]	Marginal Tax Rate[b]	Taxable Income Bracket[c]	Base Tax[d]	Marginal Tax[b]
$ 0– 3,540	$ 0 + 0		$ 0– 9,090	. . .	32%
3,540– 5,720	. . .	11%	9,090–11,340	$ 2,910 +	38%
5,720– 7,910	239.80 + 12%		11,340–13,750	3,760 +	43%
7,910– 12,390	502.60 + 14%		13,750–15,330	4,800 +	48%
12,390– 16,650	1,129.80 + 16%		15,330–17,890	5,560 +	53%
16,650– 21,020	1,811.40 + 18%		17,890–22,570	6,920 +	58%
21,020– 25,600	2,598.00 + 22%		22,570–25,410	9,630 +	63%
25,600– 31,120	3,605.60 + 25%		25,410–29,850	11,420 +	68%
31,120– 36,630	4,985.60 + 28%		29,850–39,340	14,440 +	73%
36,630– 47,670	6,528.40 + 33%		over 39,340	21,370 +	81%
47,670– 62,450	10,171.60 + 38%				
62,450– 89,090	15,788.00 + 42%				
89,090–113,860	26,976.80 + 45%				
113,860–169,020	38,123.30 + 49%				
169,020– . . .	65,151.70 + 50%				

Source: Internal Revenue Service Form 1040, 1986; Inland Revenue, 1985.

[a]Beginning in 1985, U.S. income taxes were adjusted for inflation.
[b]The marginal tax rate is the tax on the excess over the bottom of the income bracket.
[c]These dollar brackets are based on an exchange rate of $1.50 per British pound.
[d]There is an additional investment tax surcharge on the excess of investment income over $3,690 as follows: 10% on the first $1,760; 15% on the remainder.

have paid twice as much in taxes as a similar family with investment income of $30,000. The principles of vertical and horizontal equity have often not been met by the income tax system. A number of studies indicate, however, that even after allowing for the heavier exploitation of loopholes by high-income families than by low-income families, the incidence of our income tax system has generally been, on average, mildly progressive.[6] Not all loopholes are designed only for the rich. Moreover, the idea that loopholes offer huge advantages for those who use them is quite exaggerated, as Focus 1 indicates.

The income tax structure has also been far from neutral. Exemptions, deductions, tax credits, oil and mineral depletion allowances, and other tax loopholes have abounded, and people changed their behavior in order to take advantage of these special treatments. Competition for tax loopholes causes overinvestment in tax-sheltered areas. For example, much of the 1970's explosion in housing prices resulted from surges in demands as middle-class tax-

payers bought homes to take advantage of the deductibility of interest payments and the reporting exclusion of increases in the values of their homes.

You know how complicated computing your federal tax liability can be if you have ever filed a Form 1040 (the long form). State income tax computations are sometimes even more complex. Most economists favor eliminating almost all exemptions, credits, and deductions except for necessary business expenses. Then tax rates could be lowered substantially and still yield the same tax revenues. This eliminates much of the vertical and horizontal inequity in income taxes and substantially reduces the economic inefficiency caused by preferential tax treatments for some sources of income.

Payroll Taxes

You may be surprised to learn that the **Social Security tax** will soon be the single largest source of federal revenues. Social Security taxes, unemployment compensation, and workmen's disability taxes are **payroll taxes.** That is, they are based primarily on the payrolls that firms pay.

6. Joseph A. Pechman, Who Paid the Taxes, 1966–1985? (Washington, D.C.: Brookings Institution, 1985).

Tax Loopholes: Private Benefits and Public Costs

Most people perceive tax loopholes as mechanisms that allow rich people to escape their fair shares of the national tax burden. But do the rich really gain much from loopholes? Contrary to the implications of tidbits that frequently appear in the media (for example, columns reporting that "Daddy Warbucks only paid $314.83 in taxes last year on his billion dollar income"), few people gain very much by using tax loopholes. Here is an example to show why.

Assume that most investors were in a 50 percent tax bracket, and that all investment markets were initially in equilibrium and could be expected to yield after-tax rates of return equal to 10 percent. Now suppose that the Turkey Farmers Association persuaded Congress to declare that frozen turkeys were vital to the national defense and that income from turkey farming should be exempted from all federal taxes.

This raises the after-tax rate of return from turkeys to 20 percent, and many investors could be expected to try to take advantage of this loophole. As money flowed into turkey farms, however, the resulting sharp drop in turkey prices would be paralleled by a decline in the rate of return from turkey farm-

ing. Simultaneously, other investment areas would decline because of outflows of resources towards turkey farming. In these unfavorable areas, the prices of goods would rise, and this would be paralleled by increases in rates of return for them. The law of equal advantage implies that the final equilibrium would entail equal after-tax rates of return from all investments, including turkey farming.

Those who used this loophole would gain very little from it. Such loopholes ultimately only shift resources towards tax-sheltered areas, which means that fewer resources are employed in less favored industries than market forces alone indicate are optimal. Overall, tax loopholes reduce government revenues, but loophole users' gains are trivial. And the distorted structure of national output reflects loopholes instead of consumer preferences.

If loopholes ultimately provide so little gain to those who use them, then why have proposals to plug loopholes aroused such outrage? The answer is that closing a loophole can impose huge losses on people who currently use them. For example, many people have bought expensive houses because interest on mortgages is deductible from

taxable income. This deductibility has artificially raised the demand for houses and pushed up real estate prices. Were this deduction eliminated, current home owners would lose, not only because of higher taxes, but because housing prices might plummet as well.

Who gains from loopholes? In large measure, the gainers are those who acquire specialized resources before favorable tax laws are enacted. They can become wealthy when the values of tax-sheltered areas are capitalized. Another group that gains are the tax attorneys, CPAs, and "financial planners" who advise people who want to avoid taxes. But even this group gains very little because most are competent people who would have been successful in other areas had tax loopholes never existed.

Tax reform historically has meant providing relief to groups that seem overburdened because of loopholes enjoyed by too many other groups. This caused incredible complexity in the tax codes as loopholes piled on top of loopholes over time. In 1986, to the surprise and delight of most experts, meaningful tax reform did result in major simplification and the elimination of some major loopholes.

Try this multiple-choice question. Which of the following groups bears the burden of the Social Security tax: (*a*) workers, (*b*) employers, (*c*) consumers, (*d*) a 50/50 split between workers and employers, or (*e*) a 50/50 split between workers and consumers.

One of the most pervasive myths of taxation is the idea that the Social Security tax is split 50/50 by employers and employees. This is the legal incidence of the tax, which in 1986 required employers and employees each to pay 7.15 percent of the first $42,000 in wage income. Table 4 shows how this tax

TABLE 4 *Social Security Tax Hikes*

Year	Maximum Covered Base ($)	Tax Rate[a] (Percentage)	Maximum Amount of Tax[a]
1934	2,000	2.0	$ 40
1970	7,800	9.6	748
1975	14,100	11.7	1,650
1980	25,900	12.3	3,176
1985	39,600	14.1	5,584
1990	b	15.3	b

Source: *Statistical Abstract of the United States*, 1986.
[a]Half of these rates and amounts are legally levied on employers; the other half is legally borne by employees.
[b]The maximum amounts taxed will be determined by revenue needs and the rates at which average wage incomes rise.

has changed over the years. (Of course, firms cannot pay taxes; only people can. To make this myth consistent, the firm's share is presumably forward-shifted in higher prices to customers.) The simple fact is that the full tax is borne almost solely by workers. Here is an example to show why.

Suppose you are a department manager for ABC Corporation and your marginal revenue product is $2,500 monthly. If there are no other employment expenses such as taxes to consider, competition will force ABC to pay you $2,500 monthly. Now suppose you insist, as a condition of your employment, that ABC send $150 monthly to your Aunt Mary. The company, however, will not retain your services unless you agree to allow them to deduct it from your check; if the law dictates that they send checks for $150 to the widowed aunts of all employees, they will reduce wages correspondingly. It makes no sense to keep an employee who is worth only $2,500 if total employment costs exceed $2,500. So if money also must be sent to Uncle Sam because you are employed, you will bear this full burden: Your gross salary will be reduced by the amount of the tax.

Another difficulty with payroll taxes is that they fall only on labor income. If you earn a $30,000 salary and your neighbors receive $40,000 in profits from the sale of stock, you pay the tax but they do not. Hence, the tax is neither horizontally nor vertically equitable. Moreover, it is regressive. People who receive their incomes strictly from nonwage sources typically have higher incomes than wage earners, but they do not pay payroll taxes.

Some critics of Social Security describe it as a welfare system of payments made by the poor to the rich,

although it was sold politically as a pension program based on a trust fund. Under the original social security concept, tax contributions were to be held in a trust fund that would be used to provide future benefits so that the program would be self-sufficient. This insurance/actuarial principle was adhered to in the early years of the system and surpluses were accumulated.

Since 1955, however, the Social Security system has been a "pay-as-you-go" program. This means that current workers are taxed to meet current Social Security payments to retirees. Even the recent influx of baby boomers into the labor market has not remedied the growing Social Security burden as the ranks of older Americans have swollen. The burdens on workers born between 1960 and the year 2000 may become horrendous when baby boomers begin to reach age 62 in 2008. Many critics question any system that allows one generation to systematically extract transfer payments from another, or which permits a 65-year-old retiree who draws $100,000 in investment income to receive welfare payments from 18-year-old dishwashers who work for minimum wages. Under our current Social Security system, precisely these sorts of thing occur.

Among the many proposals for reform are (*a*) raising the minimum age for retirement benefits, (*b*) cutting all benefits, (*c*) eliminating benefits to the wealthy, (*d*) eliminating the payroll tax format so that all revenues would come from general revenues, and (*e*) replacing the Social Security system with a "negative income tax" plan. Pressure will mount to modify the system as the population of older people continues to grow, raising the burden of payroll taxes.

Sales and Excise Taxes

Sales taxes are percentage taxes that are broadly levied on dollar sales volumes; **excise taxes** are per unit taxes levied on specific commodities or services. Most sales taxes are collected by state and local governments. If sales taxes cover all goods and services, they are reasonably neutral and efficient. Sales taxes are not neutral, however, to the extent that they exempt items such as food, housing, or labor services. They distort relative prices and economic behavior.

Excise taxes are selective, being commonly applied to items like telephone calls, electric service, gasoline, and tires. Some excise taxes, called *sin taxes* (e.g., on cigarettes and liquor), are especially popular ways to raise revenues. Again, price distortions create economic inefficiency.

Sales and excise taxes are widely attacked as regressive under the reasoning that the percentages of income devoted to purchases of taxed goods is higher for the poor than for the rich. Those who attack the regressivity of sales taxes commonly advocate soaking "rich" corporations. This strategy may be a mistake, as the following analysis indicates.

Corporate Income Taxes

Corporate accounting profits are taxed at rates that rapidly rise to 46 percent. (Proposed 1986 reforms reduce this to 33 percent.) There is an unsettled controversy as to whether any changes in the tax rate are immediately forward-shifted to consumers in the form of price increases, or whether the burden of the tax falls on stockholders in the short run. It appears, however, that in the long run consumers bear the bulk of the burden of this tax. The reason? **Corporate income taxes** apply to accounting profits, which are largely normal profits, not economic profits. The corporate income tax raises costs, and ultimately prices, because normal accounting profits are a long-run cost of production. Moreover, even a tax on pure profits is ultimately borne in part by consumers because overall investment in our economy is dampened; the reduced capital stock drives up prices.

The tax is distortional to the extent that it is forward-shifted; that is, the prices of goods manufactured primarily by corporations are increased relative to the prices of goods most often produced by unincorporated firms. A sad bit of irony is that if, relative to rich people, poor people devote larger percentages of their incomes to the mass-produced goods supplied by corporations, it may be that the burden of the tax is regressive. People who think that corporate income taxes "soak the rich" are probably wrong.

If the tax is backward-shifted, then people will be reluctant to invest in corporations. (Remember that firms cannot truly pay taxes; only people can—in this case, stockholders.) The size of the corporate sector will be reduced relative to noncorporate firms until after-tax rates of return are equalized. There is also the issue of "double taxation of dividends." After the corporate income tax has been paid, dividends to stockholders are taxed at their individual income tax rates.

The inefficiency and inequity of the corporate income tax combine to make it among the worst of all current taxes from the viewpoints of many economists. One proposed reform that makes some sense is to eliminate corporate income taxes and allocate corporate profits to stockholders, who would then pay normal personal income taxes on their shares of corporate profits. Economists from across the political spectrum differ very little in their dislike of the corporate income tax, but politicians almost universally favor it because their constituents often see the tax as a way for the "little guy" to get even with Big Business.[7]

Property Taxes

The supply of land is perfectly inelastic. Hence, **land taxes** are relatively neutral—a tax on pure land rents has almost no effect on the price of land relative to other resources or goods. People often mistakenly apply this reasoning to property taxes. However, property taxes are among the least popular levies of all.

A **property tax** is based on the value of landholdings *plus* capital improvements. While the supply of land is perfectly inelastic, the supply of improve-

---

7. President Reagan casually proposed eliminating corporate income taxation in 1983, but adverse reactions from other politicians and the media quickly squelched the idea.

Self-Assessment of Property Taxes

Some property owners pay less than 10 percent of the average share of property taxes, while others pay more than 600 percent over the average. These 6,000 percent differences are a major reason why the property tax is extremely unpopular. Discrepancies occur because: (*a*) assessment techniques are not standardized, (*b*) occasional dishonest assessors take bribes for low evaluations, and (*c*) time elapses between assessments. Rising property values can cause identical homes to be on the tax rolls at very different figures if one was assessed yesterday while the other was assessed years ago.

Hiring more assessors to make all assessments current would raise public spending and would not standardize assessment techniques or cure dishonesty.

An alternative approach relies more on market forces to determine property values. First, all assessors on the public payroll could be discharged, cutting needs for tax revenues. Then, postcards could be made available, much as income tax forms are now distributed, on which property owners would annually write deed numbers and the values of their properties *to them*. All *self-assessments* would be matters of public record. Once each year the tax clerk could total all property values in the tax district, compute the millage *(tax rate)* necessary to cover public spending, and mail out tax bills.

You might object that people would systematically understate their property values under this self-assessment system. The simple way to eliminate almost any cheating is to allow property to be pur-

chasable by buyers willing to pay, say, 20 percent more than the amounts the owners stated that their property was worth *to them*.

This system would ensure that every parcel of property would be assessed at close to its market value so that owners would pay taxes in proportion to the values of their holdings. People whose property is currently assessed at more than the average percent of market value would enjoy a tax reduction, while those not currently paying their fair share of taxes would experience tax hikes. This self-enforcing plan for property assessment by the owners might yield small discrepancies in evaluations, but the 6,000 percent differences common under the present system would be eliminated.

---

ments is very elastic in the long run. Suppose you own prime land in an area where property taxes are high. If you put a new building on it, you will pay higher taxes. Thus, the property tax is a disincentive to development. Similarly, if you are a slum landlord with tenants whose poverty severely limits the rents you can charge, will you repair or modernize your buildings if your tax bill jumps substantially as a consequence? NO! Many students of the urban scene attribute the decay of many central cities partly to high property taxes.

Another major problem with property taxes is assessment. Property must be valued in order to levy a tax. Critics charge that property assessment is unequal, discriminates against more recent purchasers, and occasionally stimulates graft and corruption. Focus 2 discusses an alternative assessment scheme.

Inheritance and Gift Taxes

The federal tax schedule for **inheritance taxes** is presented in Table 5. Again, there is an impression of substantial progressivity. You might think that inheritance taxes could be avoided if you just gave your heirs the money. There is, however, a federal **gift tax** that largely plugs that loophole. Very wealthy individuals avoid the inheritance tax in other ways. For one thing, they can establish trusts that delay disbursements of estates until long after a person's death. For example, if you had assets of $200 million, you might leave the money to your grandchildren with funds being paid out only when they reached age 35, allowing your children to live on the interest in the interim. This is only one of the many loopholes that make the inheritance tax an "optional tax" in the words of some experts.

One proposed reform of the income/inheritance tax systems is to merge them. That is, any inheritances or gifts would simply be treated as taxable income. (Notice the similarity between the income tax schedule in Table 3 and the inheritance tax schedule in Table 5.) Do you think this would simplify things? Can you think of any drawbacks to this proposal?

Tax Reform Proposals

Rankings of the fairness of various taxes yield similar responses from the general public and tax experts. Virtually no taxes are thought fair. Our review of major taxes suggests that badly flawed taxes have historically far outweighed equitable and efficient taxes. Contrary to the legislator's proverb, most old taxes are *not* good taxes. Widespread dissatisfaction has led to some widely discussed proposals for tax reforms to bring our tax system into closer harmony with sound principles of taxation.

Value-Added Taxes (VATs)

Our tax system has distorted incentives, stifled economic performance, and been loaded with loopholes. Social Security and corporate income taxes are among possible targets for abolition. But what might be used to replace revenues generated by these taxes? A favorite contender of many reformers is the value-added tax (VAT).

Value-added taxes (VATs) are quite similar to retail sales taxes, but apply only to the difference between a firm's sales and its purchases from other firms. Thus, a VAT is a fixed percentage of a firm's payments for its use of land, labor, or capital, and is not applied to any intermediate goods the firm purchases from other firms. The result is a tax that is equivalent to a sales tax. And like sales taxes, VATs tend to be forward-shifted.

One major virtue of the VAT is that it is reasonably neutral. Another is that it is extremely difficult to evade the tax, which partially accounts for its use throughout much of Europe. One drawback is that VATs are largely hidden; final customers may be unaware of the amount of VAT embodied in the price of a product. A normative objection is that, like retail sales taxes, VATs may be somewhat regressive. Finally, VATs require more cumbersome accounting than retail sales taxes since VATs must be paid at several levels of production. Nonetheless, value-added taxes are probably more efficient and less inequitable than corporate income taxes, Social Security taxes, or a number of other levies in the government's tool box.

Flat-Rate Taxes

Many critics claim that attempts to make income taxes highly progressive are self-defeating. They argue, first, that high marginal tax rates at the upper end of the income spectrum discourage investment and so, in the long run, actually hold down the incomes of most "working stiffs"—those whose productivity would be enhanced were they working with more capital. The obsolescence of British manufacturing and the comparatively slow growth of British wages are cited as examples of this problem. A second difficulty is that high marginal tax rates increase the payoff from lobbying for new loopholes. These loopholes reduce the true progressivity of our tax system to a mere shadow of the nominal rates. Few high income individuals fail to exploit loopholes. In the words of Barry Bracewell-Milnes, "An economy breathes through its tax loopholes" when high marginal tax rates prevail. Progressivity has been combined with complex loopholes so that even tax

TABLE 5 *Marginal Tax Rates for Federal Estate and Gift Taxes (Effective January 1, 1988)*

Taxable Net Estate or Gift ($ Thousands)	Marginal Tax Rates
$ 0– 10	18%
10– 20	20%
20– 40	22%
40– 60	24%
60– 80	26%
80– 100	28%
100– 150	30%
150– 250	32%
250– 500	34%
500– 750	37%
750–1,000	39%
1,000–1,250	41%
1,250–1,500	43%
1,500–2,000	45%
2,000–2,500	49%
over 2,500	50%

Source: Internal Revenue Service, Publication 448 (September 1984).

Surprise! The Tax Reform of 1986

President Reagan made tax reform a top priority during his 1984 reelection bid, but most observers were skeptical—they had heard similar campaign promises for decades. Their cynicism seemed justified during the first part of Reagan's second term. The President's lean and muscular tax proposal began to sprout flab when many special interest groups successfully lobbied for favorable tax loopholes. Reform legislation meandered aimlessly through Congress, and Washington insiders speculated that reform might flatten tax rates a bit, but that any new tax law would not be much improvement over the old.

Then in the summer of 1986, the Senate's Tax Committee met privately. Few senators wanted their names on the monstrosity they saw emerging, so they drafted a much simpler tax bill almost from scratch. This bill astounded the cynics and was widely praised as far superior to the old law. It was intended to be *revenue neutral,* which means that as much tax revenue was expected in the new plan as under the old system. Major loopholes were closed, which allowed both individual and corporate tax rates to be cut sharply. A tremendous momentum developed to keep its major features intact, and it passed the Senate overwhelmingly in June 1986.

Individual Income Taxes

Income taxes were eliminated for most low-income families, and the bill replaced the 11 tax brackets under the old system (ranging from 12 to 50 percent) with two brackets—15 percent and 27 percent. This did not mean that most people would pay lower taxes. The bill was not intended as a general tax cut. The major direct advantages of the bill to individuals were its consistency and simplicity.

Consistency (loophole closure) was expected to rebuild public confidence that people in similar circumstances pay similar taxes (horizontal equity), and that people with high incomes pay their "fair share" (vertical equity). *Simplicity* makes it less necessary to keep detailed breakdowns of personal finances. (Some studies indicate that such accounting absorbs resources equal to 1–2 percent of personal income.)

Regardless of source, most income would be taxed more uniformly under the Senate bill. Capital gains from investments in stock or real estate, for example, historically had been taxed at around half the investor's normal marginal rate. This preferential treatment would be dropped. In addition, deductions would be eliminated for most (*a*) medical expenses, (*b*) state and local sales taxes, (*c*) casualty losses, (*d*) interest on consumer loans, and (*e*) deposits into most Individual Retirement Accounts. Tax credits and income averaging were also largely abandoned. The senate bill did, however, largely retain the deductability of real estate interest and property taxes, the two major "middle-class" loopholes. Pressure from state and local governments also caused interest income from state and municipal bonds to remain tax exempt. Nevertheless, most public finance experts perceived the Senate bill as a giant step in the direction of greater efficiency and equity.

Business Taxes

The old 46 percent corporate tax rate had been softened over time by much lower tax rates for capital gains, accelerated depreciation allowances for investments, and generous investment tax credits. The new bill slashed the corporate tax rate to 33 percent, but capital gains were treated as normal income, investment tax credits were curtailed, and the rates at which real estate investments could be depreciated were reduced sharply.

Prospects

At the time of this writing, a joint committee of the Senate and the House (which had passed a more modest reform bill) was meeting. The reforms in the Senate bill, with minor changes (retention of IRAs?), were expected to pass and would (*a*) allow consumer preferences to replace tax planning as a basis for many economic decisions, and (*b*) be evidence that loud dissatisfaction among voters can severely limit the influence of special interest groups in making national policies—a topic we tackle in more depth in the next chapter.

experts have often been uncertain as to how much they owed at the end of a year. A third problem is that high marginal tax rates are incentives for illegal tax evasion.

One proposed answer for all these problems is the **flat rate tax.** Some analysts have suggested that a flat income tax of roughly 20 percent without any exemptions or deductions would (*a*) generate more revenue than the progressive tax system that existed through 1985, (*b*) eliminate most tax evasion, (*c*) reduce the amount of unnecessary paperwork required from firms and households, and (*d*) cure the ulcers and headaches common around April 15 of each year. Critics of this proposal, however, fear that a flat income tax system would be an inequitable retreat from society's fight against poverty.

Even the most optimistic advocates of a flat rate system were surprised by the flattening of our income tax structure in 1986. As Focus 3 suggests, tax reform legislation reduced the nominal progressivity of our tax structure and plugged some major loopholes, substantially simplifying the entire income tax system.

Consumption Taxes

Other critics argue that the major flaw in our income tax system is that, in a shortsighted quest for greater equality, income taxes kill the goose that lays the golden eggs. These critics view disparities in consumption levels, not income, as the root of social inequity. They argue that resource use *(consumption)* is more appropriate as a measure of ability to pay than are potential claims to resources *(income)*. Another drawback to taxing income is that it is a severe disincentive to save and invest. The critics' solution is to allow all saving as a deduction from taxes, effectively replacing income taxes with a tax on consumption alone.

A **consumption tax** could be at least as progressive as any income tax system, so problems of regressivity are not necessarily raised. Moreover, according to the advocates of this approach, the resulting increase in saving and investing would greatly enhance labor productivity, and technological breakthroughs would allow substantial economic growth.

We have looked at the types of government activities that can be rationalized as proper cures for market failures, and have examined various tax structures. Questions about why government spending and taxes so frequently depart from the ideal have been addressed only peripherally, however. Many of these questions are answered when we look at political dimensions of policymaking. The next chapter examines political behavior from an economic perspective.

CHAPTER REVIEW: KEY POINTS

1. Some market solutions may be inefficient; others are inequitable in the minds of many people. It has become conventional to categorize *market failures* as problems of either *allocation, distribution,* or *stabilization.* Attacking problems individually according to this division would permit the use of the best policy tool to solve any problem. Any side effects then may be addressed with appropriate measures. This three-branch distinction is useful for planning, but is tempered by politics in actual budgetary situations.

2. Musgrave's *distribution* branch would secure funding by taxing those who have "too much", and would provide higher incomes for the needy via a negative income tax of some sort. This budget would be continuously balanced.

3. The *stabilization* branch would run deficits through tax cuts to buffer recessions, and surpluses to dampen inflationary pressures. This would be the only part of the government budget ever out of balance.

4. The *allocation* branch would provide public goods that the market will not provide efficiently because of extreme economies of scale in production or because of nonrivalry and nonexclusion in consumption. *Nonrivalry* means that a good is not used up when an individual consumes it; a beautiful sunset is an example. *Nonexclusion* means that it is

prohibitively expensive to deny access to a good. Note, however, that public provision does not require public production. Private firms often produce goods that government then distributes.

5. A good that is both nonrival and nonexclusive is a *pure public good*. Public goods will be less than optimally provided by the market system, if provided at all, because of attempts to *free ride*. A rival but nonexclusive good embodies *externalities* that often hinder the efficiency of market solutions. Pollution may be the problem if externalities are negative (costly); underproduction may result if externalities are positive (beneficial).

6. *Merit goods and bads* may be mandated or prohibited by an elite group, regardless of consumer preferences. Compulsory education and bans on X-rated movies, respectively, are examples.

7. The *benefit principle of taxation* suggests that people should pay taxes in proportion to the marginal benefits they receive from a governmentally provided good. Ideally, Musgrave's allocation branch would run a balanced budget based on the benefit principle.

8. The total demand for a pure public good is the *vertical summation* of individual demand curves since all can enjoy the good simultaneously, while demands for private goods are summed horizontally. Adequate revenue for optimal quantities of public goods is generated if people pay taxes equal to their marginal benefits multiplied by the amount of public good provided.

9. The *ability-to-pay principle of taxation* would require people to pay taxes in proportion to their income, wealth, or possibly, their consumption. This principle is a close relative of the idea that government policies should move the distribution of income closer to equality than the market distribution of income.

10. The principle of *horizontal equity* suggests that equals should pay equal taxes; *vertical equity* requires higher taxes on the wealthy than on the poor.

11. If the loss to a taxpayer exceeds the government revenue gained, there is an *excess burden* of taxation. *Neutral taxes* impose only income, not substitution, effects and impose no excess burdens.

12. The *personal income tax* system is nominally progressive, but exemptions, deductions, and various tax loopholes historically marred it so that it has been both inefficient and inequitable.

13. *Social Security taxes* are the second largest and fastest growing source of federal revenues. They and other *payroll taxes* are borne primarily by workers. Moreover, they are regressive, typically declining proportionately as personal income rises.

14. *Sales taxes* are reasonably efficient but, like income taxes, are marred by numerous exemptions. Many *excise taxes* apply to "sin" or "wasteful luxuries." Unless they are based on a benefit principle of taxation (for example, public zoo ticket fees or gasoline taxes), they tend to cause inefficiency and tend to be regressive. (Poor people smoke and drink as much, by volume, as rich people.)

15. The *corporate income tax* discriminates against the corporate form of business and against the goods produced primarily by corporations. In the long run, the bulk of this tax is probably forward-shifted to consumers. Thus, in the minds of most experts, this tax tends to be both inefficient and inequitable.

16. *Property taxes* provide disincentives for improvement and are blamed by some for the deterioration of central cities.

17. *Inheritance* and *gift taxes* have high and progressive rates, but can be avoided because these tax laws are riddled with loopholes.

18. A *value-added tax (VAT)* is similar to a sales tax in that it is forward-shifted. VATs only apply to the value added by each firm. VATs, *flat rate taxes,* and progressive *consumption taxes* (not income) have been proposed as replacements for corporate income taxes or Social Security taxes.

QUESTIONS FOR THOUGHT AND DISCUSSION

1. Richard A. Musgrave classifies all market failures as problems of either allocation, distribution, or stabilization, and he suggests that government can remedy each through appropriate policy. Are there any economic problems that fall outside these categories? If so, what are they? Do you think that Musgrave is correct in arguing that each problem should be addressed with the tool that is best for alleviating it alone, and that undesirable side effects should be treated by separate policies? Why or why not?

2. Some casual surveys conducted by the authors revealed that a substantial majority of students favor

reducing the size and scope of government and taxation. Then we presented students with a list of current and proposed areas of government action and asked whether specific programs should be: (*a*) eliminated, (*b*) reduced somewhat, (*c*) maintained at about current levels, or (*d*) expanded. The overall response to this detailed survey led inescapably to the conclusion that students want more government, not less. When asked how to reconcile these responses, the most common argument from students is that they want more services to be more efficiently provided so that taxes can be reduced. A cynical colleague commented that trying to make government more efficient is a bit like trying to teach pigs to sing—it just frustrates you and annoys the pigs. Other than the call for greater efficiency in government, can you reconcile favoring less government but, overall, wanting more extensive public services?

3. Prohibitions against prostitution, homosexual behavior, and certain drugs are widespread. Education is compulsory for American youngsters. Local politicians repeatedly try to outlaw things they view as pornographic, but consistently lose cases when the constitutionality of such laws is challenged in court. Many people defend all of these types of social regulation on the grounds that, although they personally do not need restrictions (to, e.g., avoid becoming heroin addicts), the "average person" does. What types of regulation over merit goods or bads do you think are warranted? Why? Which "merit" regulations do you think unnecessarily limit private choices? Why?

4. Consider such shared social institutions as public officials, our justice system and the rule of law; also consider regulations such as traffic laws. In what senses are these public goods? Does government regulation that attempts to ensure the qualities or safety of certain products provide some security to consumers? If so, is this security a public good? Why or why not?

5. Many people quietly support the sentiments of "tax resisters" who defiantly refuse to pay income taxes. If tax resistance becomes even more widespread, what will happen to the tax burdens of those who conscientiously pay every bit of their legal tax liabilities each year? What are the effects (psychological and otherwise) on someone who pays taxes honestly when someone else admits to cheating and then says that "everybody does it?" Do honest taxpayers subsidize tax cheats?

6. What problems might arise if value-added taxes (VATs) were used to replace the revenues lost from reducing or eliminating Social Security or corporation income taxes? What benefits would result from implementing value-added taxes? Would it matter whether the VAT applied only to consumer goods and services or to both consumption and investment goods?

7. An increasingly popular proposal is to entirely replace the current tax system with a single, flat rate income tax. What are the virtues of this proposal? The drawbacks? The advocates of this approach have managed to tilt recent tax legislation in their favor. How much have recent changes in income tax rates reduced the nominal progressivity of our tax structure? Have some loopholes been eliminated recently so that the actual progressivity of taxes has been affected less? If so, what loopholes have been plugged? (Answering this question may require some library research.)

8. Discuss the proposition that inheritance taxes should be eliminated, and that inheritance should be treated just like regular income for purposes of income taxation.

9. Can you use indifference curves to show that general percentage taxes are more efficient than taxes that apply only to a few commodities? (This is difficult.)

CHAPTER 32 Public Choice

public choice	point voting	pork barrel legislation
rational ignorance	median voter	rent-seeking
majority rule	special interest groups	bureaucracy
unanimity	logrolling	empire-building

The previous chapter outlined some causes of market failure and described ideal corrections for these failures. Some people assume that government can infallibly cure market flaws, an idea known as the *nirvana fallacy.* Government policies are frequently marred by inefficiency and inequity, however, causing many students to wonder, "Why does policy seem so inconsistent with economic analysis?" The answer is that no allocative mechanism works well in every situation. There are shortcomings with markets, queuing, brute force, chance, merit, tradition, and government. The trick is to use the best mechanism for the task at hand. This involves trade-offs. Choosing government to remedy perceived market failures, for example, may mean that the flexibility of response found in markets is lost. Government policymaking cannot be divorced from such realities as lobbying by special interest groups, the desires of incumbents to be reelected, or bureaucratic inertia.

An emerging area of study called **public choice** examines political behavior from an economic perspective. Its practitioners believe that the motives underlying people's behavior in the political arena differ little from those behind their performance in the private sector. Economists suspect that equal proportions of saints and greedy sinners will be found among workers, voters, union leaders, bureaucrats, professors, business tycoons, or politicians.

In this chapter, we first investigate some political behavior typical among private citizens: Why do so few people vote, and why do so many seem oblivious to political issues? Then we peruse some alternative voting systems: Is majority rule superior to unanimity or point voting in reflecting voters' preferences? Our next broad topic is political competition—government as a mechanism through which politicians and special interest groups compete to use scarce resources. Finally, we look at government bureaucracy, focusing on ways that individuals may serve their private interests when they lack profit incentives as motives for efficiency.

Private Citizens and Politics

Consumers vote their dollars for the things they want in private transactions, but consumers have different numbers of dollar votes. In modern democracies, adult citizens (except convicted felons) have equal rights to vote, so their opinions theoretically carry equal weight. Then why do so many people seem indifferent about politics?

Why People Don't Bother to Vote

An election year cliché is that "every vote counts." If people were always rational and if the outcome of every election hung on every vote and was crucial for everyone, then all eligible citizens would vote. We would not hear TV commentators lamenting voter apathy after every election. Fewer than 10 percent of adult citizens even bother to go to the polls in most local elections. Even in hotly contested national elections, a 60 percent turnout is unusually high. Many people evidently conclude that the personal benefits of voting are outweighed by the personal costs. The following is one explanation for why many people judge that voting is not worth the effort.

Suppose that opinion polls indicate that 70 million people plan to vote in the 1992 presidential election and that voters are split 50/50 between the Republican and Democratic candidates. This split maximizes the probability that your vote would matter if presidents were elected by popular vote. What is the probability that a single vote would change the outcome of this election? The probability of an exact 50/50 split of the vote is identical with the probability of flipping a coin 70 million times and obtaining exactly 35 million heads and 35 million tails—infinitesimal. Even if only 100 people voted, the probability that you might be the tie-breaker if you were the 101st voter is less than 4 percent. The probability that any single voter will be the tie breaker is, of course, much lower the larger the number of votes.

The transaction costs of voting are not trivial when you consider the time and resources used to register, walk or drive to the polls, wait in line, learn about candidates and issues, and so on. This raises the question of why so many people do vote. Although the costs of voting are low, the probability of one vote swinging any important election is nearly zero. Some people argue that, "If you don't vote, you have no right to complain", but there is no law or religious commandment to that effect. Some people may vote because political campaigns share some of the qualities of spectator sports: although the stakes are generally higher, voting is a bit like cheering for your favorite football team or buying a ticket to a game. The most likely motive for voters is that they derive

pleasure from thinking of themselves as good citizens, or that failing to vote makes them feel guilty. Apathetic nonvoters who contend that individual votes "don't matter" are statistically correct.

Rational Political Ignorance

Better the devil you know than the devil you don't know.

—Unknown

Can you remember the names of even five people who were on the ballot during the last election? How much did you know about the candidates' positions on tax reform? Automobile pollution standards? Trade with the Soviet Union? Support for agriculture? If you are typical, your answers to these and similar questions are, "Not much."

Information is costly. The future is uncertain. Therefore, consumers and producers operate with only imperfect information about markets. They are, to some degree, **rationally ignorant.** Similarly, voters rely on information that is far short of perfect. The personal payoff from having in-depth knowledge about all the candidates and issues decided in any important election is trivial, and generally far less than the benefits of information about market choices. For example, textile import quotas now cost consumers billions of dollars annually. If your share is only $5 to $10 and the probability of influencing an election with your vote is negligible, then the time and effort required to learn about candidates' positions on import quotas so that you can vote wisely may be much greater than the personal benefits from a more informed vote. There are, however, significant personal benefits in knowing about the qualities and prices of clothing you buy.

Election results share many attributes of public goods—your president is my president, we share the same sets of laws, and so on. Thus, we should not be surprised that many voters select candidates on the basis of charisma, a flashing smile and a shock of wavy hair, or an impression that a certain candidate is sober, dependable, or reflective. Small wonder that every major political campaign abounds with public relations flacks. Most of the time, the procedure followed when decisions are made by votes is that the majority rules. This is not, however, the only possibility.

Systems of Voting

Feudal kings or queens once dictated most government policies. Even today, only a minority of people have any say about how they are governed; over half of the world's 5 billion people live in countries controlled by dictators. Even though single votes have little direct influence on elections, those of us fortunate enough to live in democracies can vote to collectively determine who will make policies for us. This raises the question of how accurately different voting systems reflect voters' preferences.

Majority Rule

Any group of a dozen or more people will find it difficult to agree on anything—even if they are not economists. Group decisions tend to be middle-of-the-road compromises that are inconsistent with any individual's preferences. Whenever we vote and use a simple **majority rule,** we can be almost certain of losses by members on the minority side of the vote. Majority voting may even result in economic inefficiency, since the minority's losses may outweigh all gains to the side able to swing a majority of votes.

Potential Inefficiencies Some outcomes of majority voting are efficient, but the example in Table 1 should open your eyes to the possibility of inefficient results as well. In this case, Proposal X is defeated even though the benefits outweigh the costs by $300, but Proposal Y is adopted even though its costs ($2,000) exceed the benefits ($1,700) by $300.

Notice that if potential gainers from Proposal X shared their gains with the potential losers, all could gain from its passage; if potential losers from Proposal Y compensated the potential gainers, all could gain from its defeat. Thus, passage of Proposal X and defeat of Proposal Y would both be efficient moves. Majority rule voting yields inefficient results for both proposals, however, because it is illegal to pay money for people's votes. (This is one reason for secret ballots.) Markets for votes might shrink the inefficiency inherent in many voting situations, but a market approach to voting is widely viewed as unethical or inequitable.

The basic problem is that intensities of preference can be registered easily in the marketplace but not under majority rule voting. You can buy more or fewer anchovy pizzas, but even if you passionately care who is elected dog catcher, your vote counts no more than that of someone who simply likes the sound of a candidate's name and casts a vote that offsets yours.

Potential Inconsistencies Another problem is that majority rule voting may yield inconsistent results, especially if sequential elections (party primaries, for example) are used to narrow choices. It is, for example, common for analysts to claim that Republican Smith could beat any Democrat in an election for president, but that he does not have a chance because loyal Republicans will nominate Republican Jones, who cannot beat any Democratic nominee. An easy illustration of this point considers a three-party system, as reflected in Table 2. Assume that the voters are roughly divided into thirds between the Tory,

TABLE 1 *Inefficient Outcomes under a Simple Majority Rule*

A Beneficial Proposal (X) is Defeated					An Excessively Costly Proposal (Y) is Adopted				
			Votes					**Votes**	
Individual	**Benefits**	**Tax Cost**	**Aye**	**Nay**	**Individual**	**Benefits**	**Tax Cost**	**Aye**	**Nay**
A	$ 700	$ 400	X		A	$ 425	$ 400	X	
B	600	400	X		B	575	400	X	
C	350	400		X	C	450	400	X	
D	375	400		X	D	150	400		X
E	275	400		X	E	100	400		X
Total	$2,300	$2,000	2	3	Total	$1,700	$2,000	3	2

TABLE 2 *Potential Inconsistencies in Voting*

	Tory Versus Whig	Whig Versus Populist	Populist Versus Tory
	Parties in Runoff		
Tory voter preferences	Tory	Whig	Tory
Whig voter preferences	Whig	Whig	Populist
Populist voter preferences	Tory	Populist	Populist.
Winner	Tory	Whig	Populist

Whig, and Populist parties, and that the ultimate winner must receive over 50 percent of the vote. If no one receives a clear majority of the vote, then there is a runoff election between the top two candidates.

Suppose that Tory voters despise Populists and will vote for Whigs if there are no Tories in a runoff election. Whig voters, however, vote for Populist Party candidates over Tory candidates in runoff elections. To complete this circle, Populist voters will support Tory over Whig candidates. Table 2 shows the potential results if no candidate receives a clear majority in an initial election. Tory candidates win against Whigs in runoff elections, who would win against Populists, who, in turn, would beat the Tories.

Some analysts believe that the possible inconsistencies apparent in these results of majority rule voting may also foment instability, with parties taking turns being in power. The resulting flip-flops in economic policies create chaos for long-range planning by private decision makers—consumers, workers, or investors. Unstable policies would not be a problem if changes required unanimous votes.

Unanimity

Some decisions are deemed so important that society requires more than a simple majority vote; minority opinions are weighed more heavily in determining critical social policies. A constitutional amendment requires either a constitutional convention called by three-fourths of all state legislatures or their ratification of an amendment approved by two-thirds of the members of both the U.S. Senate and the House of

Representatives. Similar congressional votes are required to override a presidential veto. A jury trying a criminal case must reach a unanimous verdict in most states, or the case may be retried. In such situations, requiring **unanimity** or near unanimity limits exploitation of a minority. Moreover, any changes in social regulation under pure unanimity rules presumably would benefit everyone or the changes would never be adopted. Thus, any changes would clearly be moves toward economic efficiency.

One difficulty with requiring unanimity is that individuals who, on balance, are relatively unaffected by some proposal could withhold their votes to "blackmail" the people who would gain much from the proposed change. In a sense, requiring unanimity gives everyone the power to say, "It's my ball, so we play by my rules or we don't play." However, although some people might negotiate disproportional gains for themselves simply because of their political leverage, no voter would ever expect to lose from any unanimous vote.

A far more serious problem is that a unanimity rule is heavily biased in favor of the existing situation. Unanimity might operate well if an overwhelming majority of people view the current situation as equitable, but it totally blocks political remedies for inequity, leaving only informal negotiation, violence, or the market as avenues open for people to pursue what they perceive as justice. For example, a unanimity requirement precludes any redistribution of income or wealth other than one that is strictly voluntary. A final flaw is that even though a unanimity rule protects the existing rights of minorities, it also provides only crude indications of the intensity of people's preferences.

Point Voting

One proposal to reflect the intensities of preferences better than any "one person, one vote" rule is the use of **point voting**—the assignment of equal numbers of points to all voters, which they can allocate among various issues as they see fit. Voters ideally would allocate their points in proportion to their intensities of preference: that is, in proportion to their net expected gains or losses from given proposals. Thus, if individuals A, B, C, D, and E each have 100 points to allocate between the proposals we considered in Table 1, they would ideally vote as in Table 3. Proposal X passes and Proposal Y fails; these results are the opposite of the inefficient results under simple majority rule voting. Since Proposal X yields net benefits while Proposal Y's costs exceed its benefits, these ideal "point voting" results are preferable to the results of a simple majority rule.

The major drawback to point voting is that people might skew their voting points towards issues that they expected to be close, figuring that others would ensure the passage or failure of issues not expected to be close. Suppose, for example, that you favored more spending for both national defense and medical research. If you expected a landslide vote on a national defense proposal but a close vote on medical research, you would probably place all your votes on the medical research proposal. Point voting systems are flawed to the extent that people try to forecast the outcomes of elections and then use their votes strategically, instead of voting their true preferences. Election results would conform neither to the majority's will nor to reasonable benefit/cost decision making.

Regardless of which voting system is used, most people view government as failing if election results do not reflect voters' interests and preferences. Elections are critical for candidates and for private interests who want to shape government policies. We will now consider some forces that shape political campaigns and the policies of those who manage to get themselves elected.

Politicians and Parties

Politics is the art of compromise.

—Unknown

Some people seek political office to mold policy to their ideals, hoping to make this a better world. Others want prestige and revel in the exercise of power. The first step on the path to election is to project an image that voters will support when they mark their ballots. One obstacle is that no one can be all things to all people. To the extent that politicians establish positions on the issues, they can be sure of offending some voters in some ways.

"Lumpiness" in Voting

I voted for the lesser of two evils.

—Unknown

When consumers operate in the marketplace, their purchases can be fine-tuned to closely match their tastes and preferences. Even with such "lumpy" pur-

---

TABLE 3 *The Results from Table 1 if Determined by Ideal Point Voting**

	Proposal X					Proposal Y			
			Votes					**Votes**	
Individual	Benefits	Tax Cost	Aye	Nay	Individual	Benefits	Tax Cost	Aye	Nay
A	$ 700	$ 400	92		A	$ 425	$ 400	8	
B	600	400	53		B	575	400	47	
C	350	400		50	C	450	400	50	
D	375	400		9	D	150	400		91
E	325	400		20	E	100	400		80
Total	$2,300	$2,000	145	79	Total	$1,700	$2,000	105	171

*Ideal point voting would mean that all voters would apportion their votes based on net benefits (benefits − costs). For example, Individual A's net benefits from proposal X are $300 ($700 − $400); net benefits for proposal Y are $25 ($425 − $400). Thus, Individual A's voting pattern would be 92 votes ($\frac{\$300}{\$325} \times 100$) for proposal X and 8 votes ($\frac{\$25}{\$325} \times 100$) for proposal Y.

chases as automobiles, you can buy a slightly bigger or smaller car, more or fewer options, keep it longer than your neighbor typically does, or trade it in sooner. Such fine gradations are not available in the political arena.

Even if you understand two candidates' campaign platforms, you may favor Madison's stands on education and welfare spending, but prefer Monroe's views on international relations. Voting is a *lumpy decision,* somewhat akin to tie-in sales contracts that require you to buy some things you do not want in order to get the things you desire. Casting your political vote involves trade-offs because you cannot vote for a set of positions different from those taken by one of the candidates.

This is one reason that most public figures either state their positions on controversial issues in inoffensive terms or they waffle—smoothly avoiding direct answers to barbed questions aimed at them by reporters or their political opponents. Rational ignorance among voters and the complexity of most issues are two other reasons that politicians frequently side-step taking a stand. A fourth is that most serious political candidates strive for a moderate image.

The Median Voter Model

The differences between candidates for an office are often more form than substance. It seems that all favor a strong national defense, adequate welfare for the "truly" needy, a balanced budget, and low taxes—positions become as predictable as calls to support "motherhood, apple pie, and the flag." Why do party platforms and political speeches so often seem like xerox copies of one another?

The **median voter** model partially explains similarities of this sort. In Figure 1, we assume that the preferences and voting patterns of individuals can be ranked very simply and are normally distributed along a continuum from the extreme left (revolutionary communism, perhaps) to the extreme right (fascism?). Point M is in the precise center of this spectrum and identifies the median voter—exactly half of all voters lie to the left, with the other half being to the right of this position.

Suppose that there are two candidates for some office. The median voter can tip the scales in the election, providing the margin of victory if the winner must receive 50 percent plus 1 vote. Thus, whichever

FIGURE 1 How Voter Distributions Push Candidates and Parties Toward the Middle

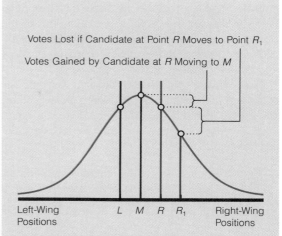

The "bell-shaped" curve is based on the assumption that voters are normally distributed from left-wing to right-wing political positions. A right-wing candidate at point R gains by moving toward the political center at point M, but is likely to lose substantial support from a move from R to the more extreme R_1. These losses of votes will be maximized if this candidate's opponent moves to a position just to the left of the candidate's position. The respective potential losses and gains pressure right-wing candidates and parties to move toward middle-of-the-road positions. Naturally, similar pressures would cause a serious left-wing candidate to shift toward the political center at point M.

candidate adopts positions on the issues that are closest to point M will capture the median vote and win the election. Regardless of their initial positions (say, L and R, respectively), both candidates find that shifting their positions slightly toward point M boosts their standings in public opinion polls. Figure 1 also uses a slightly right-wing candidate to illustrate how movements toward the extremes lose votes, while shifts to the center gain votes. The same would be true of a left-wing candidate. As the candidates each try to maximize their expected votes, each creeps toward point M. Ultimately, their positions may be almost indistinguishable.

You might think that a new, third candidate could win this race by entering at, say, point L in Panel A, leaving the original candidates to split the votes from halfway between points L and M all the way to the extreme right. But this third candidate would also find that moving towards point M increases support by voters. This suggests that, ultimately, virtually all serious candidates for election gravitate towards point *M*. Similar forces are at work in elections ranging from that for president of your local PTA to the U.S. presidency, pressuring not only political candidates, but political parties as well, to gradually adopt middle-of-the-road policies.

The dynamic world of politics is enormously oversimplified in this median voter model; otherwise, there would be no differences between candidates or party platforms. Among other reasons, differences exist because:

1. Voters' opinions on the numerous issues in any election cannot be simply described from left to right, and their opinions are only loosely correlated. For example, there may be no predictable connections between people's opinions on welfare, the environment, international trade, and law and order issues.
2. Voter distributions change according to circumstances so that it is impossible for politicians to know exactly where the median voter is on any controversial issue at any point in time.
3. Some politicians do have strong personal beliefs about some issues.

In spite of these qualifications, the median voter model explains the middle-of-the-road clustering of politicians and parties, which ignores the preferences of vast numbers of less moderate voters. It also hints at reasons for the dominance of the two-party system.

Two-Party Systems

Shifts in the distribution of voters' preferences over time help explain why political control tends to cycle between two parties in most democratic countries. Normally, one party locates slightly to the left of center, with the other being slightly right of center. Each then advertises itself as "the party of the future" and hopes that circumstances will move more voters in its direction.

The two parties, being reasonably comfortable with each other, then compete through expensive campaigns. A typical congressional campaign now requires a war chest of over $1 million; Louis Lehrman, a 1984 U.S. Senate candidate from New York, allegedly spent $14 million campaigning for a job that pays less than $100,000 annually–*and lost*. Campaign spending on television spots alone now ex-

ceeds $100 million in presidential election years. Such barriers frustrate third-party challenges to either dominant party. Another technique to bar entry is to make it difficult for a third party to get on the ballot. For example, the dominant parties may support laws requiring that petitions be signed by huge numbers of voters before the third party can be on the ballot if it did not receive more than 5 percent of the votes in a prior election.

Third parties tend to be launched from the extremes of the political spectrum and to be based on single issues. If a third party began to attract more voters than either dominant party expected, the closest major party normally adopts the third-party position on that issue. If leaders of a third party seriously want political power, it tends to become more moderate and is eventually absorbed by the closest major party. Thus, mature democracies tend to operate under the control of two major parties. Third parties rarely displace major parties, and then only when a major party fails to respond to changes in voter preferences.

Political Allocation

Two things you never want to see made are hotdogs and the law.

—*Unknown*

Rational political ignorance, low voter turnouts, lumpiness in voting for a candidate, and the tendency for parties and politicians to cluster around middle-of-the-road positions are among the reasons that government policies only weakly mirror voter preferences. Lobbying and protracted negotiations among elected representatives are among the mechanisms that result in budgets and laws intended to balance the desires of **special interest groups,** including those of voters. These mechanisms sometimes provide pressures for policies to more closely conform to voter preferences, but at other times exacerbate problems inherent in political decision making.

Logrolling

Economists generally favor trading because both sides expect to gain or no trade occurs. Legislators commonly trade votes to obtain passage of proposals they favor, a process known as **logrolling.** For example, one legislator might want more funding to clean up the environment, while another seeks higher agricultural price supports. Trading votes may enable both to get what they want. Logrolling may also be beneficial by allowing legislators to register the intensities of their preferences. Votes about matters upon which a legislator is reasonably indifferent are traded for votes on proposed legislation about which the lawmaker has strong feelings. This process can aid in the attainment of efficiency by allowing strongly held minority views to overcome weak opposition by the majority.

Economists recognize, however, that some exchanges may not be socially beneficial. An extreme case would be an agreement wherein you trade part of your loot from a bank robbery for my services as a lookout and getaway driver. Society's problem is that we are not the only people affected by this transaction—the losses of our victims must be considered. Less dramatic but similarly damaging trades can take place through logrolling. This is especially a problem with **pork barrel legislation,** which occurs when federal spending is used for projects that generate benefits that are primarily local.

For example, Arizonans make up about 1 percent of our population and pay about 1 percent of federal taxes. Even if the cost of a canal system to convey water into the dry parts of Arizona would cost $2 billion but generate benefits of only $1 billion, Arizona's senators and representatives would be pressured by their constituents to favor federal funds to build it. Only 1 percent of the costs would be paid by Arizonans, but they would receive most of the benefits—a good deal for Arizonans, but a crummy deal for other voters.

Most pork barrel legislation is packaged with other pieces of pork and then tied to major laws that are national in scope. Presidents cannot selectively veto parts of a law, and so must either accept or veto the entire package. Logrolling by lawmakers who are sympathetic to the goals of special interests is only one mechanism that interest groups use to secure policies they favor.

Special Interests

Majority rule voting tends to slight minority interests, but vigorous political action can enable determined minorities to impose policies that are weakly opposed by the majority of voters. For example, opin-ion polls consistently indicate that most Americans favor more restrictions on private firearms. Yet, for decades, the National Rifle Association has led a successful movement to prevent national gun registration and other curbs. Why? Typical voters care relatively little about gun control and are rationally ignorant of most candidates' positions on this issue. Thus, gun fanciers whose votes and campaign contributions may be based on this issue alone make most politicians leary of pushing gun control. The Equal Rights Amendment also had wide (but weak) popular support, and lost because of opposition by a large and vocal minority. Similarly, people with strong feelings about abortion, prayer in schools, or protecting our steel industry from foreign competition may have disproportionately strong voices in determining certain social policies.

Voting is not the only way for special interests to accomplish their political goals. Money talks, and big money talks loudly. A well financed minority may contribute sufficient campaign funds to affect who gets elected and to shade some politicians' positions on certain issues. Alternatively, campaign volunteers can beat the bushes to get other voters to support specific candidates. Money and bodies also may be turned out to propagandize for important minority issues. And then logrolling comes into play when politicians try to pass legislation favored by the interest groups that back them, including pork barrel projects for the folks in their home districts.

As we indicated earlier, one way that a democracy reflects intense preferences is for a minority to exert vigorous pressure and attain the policies it favors. Much legislation enacted to benefit interest groups, however, may bear inefficiently high levels of social cost.

Rent-Seeking

People are self-interested and will try to manipulate allocative mechanisms to enrich themselves. In competitive markets, this normally entails trying to produce goods better or at lower costs than the goods made by competitors. This increases a society's total production and potential consumption. Government can be similarly beneficial when it specifies rules that correct market failures, but economic legislation and regulation often seem tailored for special interest groups. One problem with special interest legislation is that the gains to interest groups are often less than the costs imposed on the general public. Indeed, inefficiency in collective decision making arises primarily because costs are spread across a relatively anonymous, heterogeneous, and poorly informed public, while the benefits accrue to small cohesive groups.

Rent-seeking is the term applied to attempts by interest groups to manipulate public policy where the interest group's gains would be overshadowed by losses to the larger public. (Recall that economic rent is any income received in excess of the minimum required to secure the resources that people make available.) Figure 2 uses overly restrictive licensing of taxicabs to show why rent-seeking behavior is economically inefficient and reduces social well-being.

Suppose that the taxi market is initially in a competitive equilibrium, with supply S_0 being perfectly elastic at price P_0, and that demand is D_0. Consumer surplus equals triangle P_0ad, and cab companies cover all their costs, including a normal return on their investment. If major taxi operators thought that regulators could be persuaded to restrict competition, they could follow a rent-seeking strategy. They might cite horror stories to prove that some unwary tourists were gouged by unethical drivers as evidence of the evils of "cutthroat" competition. Suppose that taxi licenses were restricted to Q_1 and granted only to solid, reputable companies. Cab fares would rise to P_1, shrinking consumer surplus to P_1ab. The loss of consumer surplus equals the trapezoid P_0P_1bd. You might think that the "deadweight loss" to society would equal triangle cbd and that taxi companies would reap economic rent equal to P_0P_1bc.

Rent-seeking, however, also absorbs resources directly. Interest groups incur costs when seeking favorable laws or regulations, and they devote resources to mold public policies as long as the expected marginal gains exceed their expected marginal costs. Consultants, lawyers, and professional lobbyists might be hired by the parties on all sides of an issue; time and money may be absorbed by hearings in front of regulatory boards or legislative committees. In some cases, unethical lawmakers or regulators who recognize the potential gains may demand bribes for favorable policies. None of these costs are incurred productively. The net result of

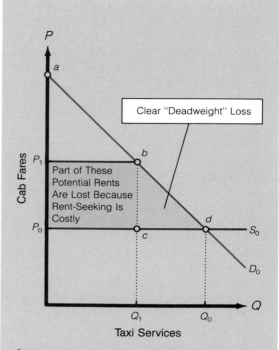

FIGURE 2   *Why Gains to Rent-Seekers are Often Far Less than the Resulting Social Losses*

Suppose that rent-seeking cab companies persuade taxi regulators to follow overly restrictive licensing policies. If taxi services fall from Q_0 to Q_1, cab fares will rise from P_0 to P_1 and consumer surplus will shrink from P_0ad to P_1ab. There is a clear "deadweight" loss equal to cbd. Moreover, those who retain their cab licenses will not gain rents (profits) equal to P_0P_1bc. Some of the potential rents will be dissipated because of costs incurred in securing these political restrictions on market entry.

rent-seeking behavior is a continuing social loss for as long as inefficient policies are in place, plus losses equal to the costs incurred by interest groups to secure favorable laws or regulations or to oppose unfavorable ones.

We have now discussed voting procedures, political campaigning, and the legislative process from a public choice perspective. Once laws are made, they must be administered. This brings us to the topic of government bureaucracy, which falls under the executive branch of government.

Bureaucracy

A government could print a good edition of Shakespeare's works, but it could not get them written.
—*Alfred Marshall*

The word **bureaucracy** commonly refers to any large task-oriented organization. Whether private or public, large organizations must develop extensive sets of formal operating rules or the coordination of tasks becomes impossible. The resulting mountain of red tape causes many people to view *bureaucracy* as almost synonymous with mindless inefficiency and getting the runaround.

The federal government is by far our largest employer. State and local governments also hire their share of workers, as shown in Table 4. Most government employees work in the agencies, or *bureaus*, that implement the laws passed by legislatures. Relatively few government employees are elected to office or appointed by elected officials; most are either civil servants or military personnel.

Many government bureaucrats work hard because they deeply believe that the mission of their agency is important and worthwhile. Economic theory suggests, however, that the best starting point for analysis of behavior is the assumption of self-interest. Anyone who has worked in a large organization knows that opportunities for raises and promotions are closely tied to the organization's fortunes; prosperity and growth yield larger personnel budgets in both public and private bureaucracies. Thus, we can expect career employees of any large organization to push for growth and to fight budget cuts.

Government bureaucracies tend to have even worse reputations than business bureaucracies. Major differences between public and private bureaucracies emerge because their incentive structures differ. Most divisions of private firms serve as profit centers, and their growth tends to depend on serving more customers better and at lower cost. There are few direct ways to measure the efficiency of most government bureaus, which rely on tax revenues to cover their costs. Legislators tend to consider whether a public service is provided adequately. If not, the standard solution is to boost funding. Thus, paradoxically, less efficiency may cause growth of a bureau's budget. The opposite trend occurs in the private sector.

Have you noticed that it is often easier to buy auto insurance than to get a license for a new car? That the time absorbed in buying $100 worth of groceries is often less than the time spent waiting in line at the Post Office to buy a roll of stamps? Rewards for efficiency are few in government bureaucracies and may cause relative inefficiency, with two results: (*a*) services may be supplied to the public at the convenience of government employees rather than vice versa, and (*b*) government tends to pay relatively high prices for the things it buys. You may have read about the Department of Defense paying outrageous prices for hammers, coffee pots, or similar items. Focus 1 details some reasons for the occurrence of such apparent waste. The basic problem, however, probably originates with the warped incentive structures common in many government bureaus. The tendency for *empire-building* is only one of many types of bureaucratic behavior that emerge from inefficient incentive structures.

Empire-Building

In large organizations, a manager's status and salary tend to be positively related to the numbers and levels of employees supervised and the amounts of money for which the manager is responsible. This provides managers at all levels with incentives to acquire as many employees as possible. This is known as **empire building.** In business, this usually requires showing that your division has extraordinary profit potential. In government bureaus, however, it normally requires emphasizing to legislators the enormity of the problem that your agency

TABLE 4 Government Employment

	Millions of Government Employees		
	1970	1975	1984
Federal			
Military	3.1	2.1	2.1
Civilian		2.7	2.8
State		3.2	3.7
Local		8.8	9.5

Source: Bureau of Labor Statistics, "Monthly Employment and Earnings," 1986.

Government Contracts

Most government contracts are awarded to the lowest bidder, but recent military contracts for new weapons systems have uniformly been plagued by mammoth "cost overruns," which means that taxpayers have ended up paying much more than the original contract specified. Why? Many people think that recent media reports hint at an answer: in 1985, the Department of Defense (DOD) paid $400 for $17 hammers, $56 for $0.08 Allen wrenches, and $27 for screws that hardware stores sell for less than a dime. The prices of custom-built items for aircraft were even more startling: $600 armrests and toilet covers, $400 ashtrays, and $17,000 coffee pots. The U.S. Army finally abandoned the Sergeant York battle tank after sinking almost $8 billion into the project; it just would not do the job for which it was intended.

Critics cite examples of this sort to indict defense contractors for price-gouging and the military bureaucrats who administered these contracts for flagrant incompetence. If the basic problems were this simple, the solution would be incredibly straightforward: prosecute dishonest contractors and

deny them future contracts, and hire more competent people to administer military procurement. Although this might help, the ultimate solution (if there is one) is not this simple. Nor are such problems unique to the military. Government office buildings, flood control projects, highways, and nuclear power plants also often entail sloppy work and huge cost overruns. Some defense contracts require delivery of weapons systems years into the future, and inflation may drive up costs. Contract specifications are often vague because designs are still on the drawing board. Bids on such projects cannot be ironclad. Still other problems lurk in bureaucratic behavior.

C. Northcote Parkinson, an English writer, developed some "laws" of bureaucracy, one of which is "work expands to absorb the time available." As a project unfolds, specifications tend to grow excessively complex, which can be extremely costly. This occurs because many bureaucrats try to stay (or look) busy. One easy way to stay busy is to constantly write directives that detail the work of people you supervise. The 1985 DOD recipe for fruitcake is an unintentionally comic example—it took 18

pages. The recipe for a modern aircraft carrier runs hundreds of thousands of pages. If the ratio of overspecification for fruitcake holds for U.S. Navy ships, the excess costs from this problem alone sums to billions of dollars.

Another problem is that contractors and contact administrators may share interests that violate the public interest. For example, many retired generals and admirals ultimately go to work for defense contractors. If you were about to retire as a high-ranking military officer, might you be "understanding" about exorbitant costs incurred by a contractor in accommodating your design changes—especially if that firm was a major employer of someone with your expertise?

We can only touch on some problems of government procurement; a detailed discussion would take volumes. DOD contract foibles have been on display recently, but many government contracts seem executed at much higher costs than private contracts would be. The ultimate problem is inadequate incentives for efficiency. The costs of the resulting inefficiencies are borne by taxpayers.

---

is supposed to cure. Thus, law enforcement officials predictably talk about the increasing harm from anarchy in the streets and organized crime, educators discuss teacher shortages and the growing demands placed on our schools, admirals and generals talk about unrest in the Middle East and the aggressiveness of communist revolutionaries, agriculture officials talk about the plight of the family farm—the ways that bureaucrats try to build the demands for their services seem endless.

The Growth of Government

Part of the problem is that few experts ever conclude that their area will be of less concern in the foreseeable future. Thus, there are few credible witnesses to dispute claims that society needs to devote more resources in any number of directions. The result is that legislators, who may want to slash taxes, are inundated with well-documented requests for more funding for a variety of programs.

Pressing social problems seem to beget new programs that acquire lives of their own, even if the original problem fades away. Trying to identify areas to cut is often an exercise in frustration. Interest groups (including bureaucrats) become accustomed to programs that benefit them and always want more rather than less. Attempts to cut any spending category provoke intense lobbying about the budget. One common strategy used by bureau chiefs to combat proposed budget cuts is to assert that any cuts threaten a bureau's most popular services. This strategy usually arouses loud support from the bureau's clients. This was one tactic used by some opponents of President Reagan's attempts to cut social spending in the early 1980s. His supporters viewed cutting the *growth* of spending as a victory. The final result of the political processes described in this chapter? Government grows and grows, with no end in sight.

Self-Corrections in Politics and Markets

We have discussed how the market operates and how it may fail. This part of the book focuses on the tasks of government in a market economy and why the government may fail to accomplish these tasks appropriately. Most economic issues can be placed on a continuum that stretches from, on one end, problems efficiently resolved in markets to, at the other extreme, issues that seem to require collective action. Whether a particular issue is best resolved in markets or through government is sometimes murky in the broad middle of this continuum. The answer may depend largely on the relative speed and precision with which these allocative mechanisms correct errors or adjust to changing circumstances.

On average, markets tend to respond quickly and efficiently to changes in consumer wants or mistakes made by business decision makers. For example, if markets fail to synchronize the plans of the buyers and sellers of a pure private good (thermal underwear or beef tacos, for example), price adjustments tend to cure the resulting shortages or surpluses rather quickly. On the other hand, markets may never adequately provide such public goods as national defense, so these goods are provided through government.

Political adjustments are inherently slow in a democracy, however. When an elected official becomes extremely unpopular, voters must normally wait for the next election to "throw the rascal out"; coups or assassinations are undemocratic. If a legislature enacts a disastrous policy, it may take years to accomplish the required legal change. Once on the books, laws, regulations, and spending programs are hard to remove. Even though political solutions may be slow and inexact, government policy may be superior to private decision making when markets fail because of concentrated economic power, nonrivalry, nonexclusion, or inequity. Table 5 summarizes some failings of both the marketplace and government as allocative mechanisms. In the next two chapters, we examine public policies to control externalities and to redress what many people perceive as inequity in the distribution of income that results from market forces.

TABLE 5 *Market Failures Versus Political Failures*

Market Failure	Political Failure
1. Uncertainty about the future.	1. Uncertainty about the future.
2. Rational ignorance about consuming and investing.	2. Rational political ignorance.
3. Free riders for public goods.	3. Nonvoting because of public good aspects of voting.
4. Externalities and pollution.	4. "Tie-in sales" aspects of voting and inability to "fine-tune" spending patterns to voter preferences. All voting systems fail to reflect intensities of preference.
5. Monopoly power.	5. Disproportionate political power for special interests.
6. Inequity in the distributions of income and wealth.	6. Majorities may inefficiently or inequitably vote against interests of minorities.
7. Greediness and unhealthy forms of competitiveness are fostered.	7. Fosters bureaucracy and empire-building.

CHAPTER REVIEW: KEY POINTS

1. No allocative mechanism works ideally under all circumstances. Just as the market fails in some instances, there are, unfortunately, forces within all political systems that prevent government from smoothly reflecting the preferences of the people that it governs. The application of economic analysis to political behavior is known as *public choice.*

2. The probability that one vote will swing a major election is close to infinitesimal. Because the personal payoffs from voting are small, many people do not vote, nor do most find it personally worthwhile to inform themselves on a broad range of social issues. This is known as *rational political ignorance,* and tends to be more prevalent than the lack of information confronted when people make market decisions.

3. All voting systems are flawed in that economic efficiency may be lost through political decision making. *Majority rule* voting tends to impose losses on those taking minority positions; this is inefficient if their losses exceed the majority's gains. Majority rule may also lead to inconsistent or unstable political choices.

4. A *unanimity* rule ensures that all changes in laws are efficient because everyone must expect to gain before he or she will acquiesce to a change. People who are reasonably indifferent about a policy change, however, might require excessive compensation for agreeing to the change from those who stand to gain much from that change. This give-and-take process would make changes in policies a very cumbersome and time-consuming process. Moreover, a unanimity rule assumes that the initial situation is equitable, which may be untrue in some cases.

5. *Point voting* would allow voters to indicate their preferences by allocating votes in proportion to how strongly they felt about some issues relative to others. This system is flawed, however, by the potential for strategic behavior; people might not vote their preferences per se, tending instead to weigh their votes according to how they expected others to vote.

6. Voting is a *lumpy* process; we cannot pick and choose among the political stances taken by the candidates for an office. The market permits us to fine-tune our decisions, but we generally can choose only a single candidate or platform when we vote.

7. Attempts to maximize their chances for election cause candidates and political parties to try to attract the *median voter,* whose vote tends to determine the outcomes of elections. Rational ignorance among voters causes many candidates to avoid taking stands on issues while attempting to project a moderate image. Political competition for the support of the median voter causes candidates and parties to cluster around *middle-of-the-road* positions, and creates pressures for the existence of a *two-party system.*

8. *Logrolling* occurs when lawmakers trade votes. This process allows legislators to register the intensities of their preferences because they trade votes for things about which they care relatively little for votes about things which they have relatively strong feelings for. Logrolling can, however, result in inefficient amounts of *pork barrel legislation.* This type of legislation occurs when projects that have primarily local benefits are paid for by a broader taxpaying public.

9. *Special interest groups* may be overrepresented because of low voter turnouts, widespread rational political ignorance, and intense lobbying. However, intensities of preference may be better reflected in political decisions because of this overrepresentation.

10. *Rent-seeking* involves attempts by special interest groups to manipulate government policies for private gain even though the social costs of special laws or regulations would exceed the expected benefits to the interest group that seeks economic rents.

11. The efficiency of most government *bureaucracies* is hard to measure, and the absence of a profit motive reduces incentives for efficiency in the public sector. Managerial salaries and "perqs" are often tied to the numbers of employees supervised and the size of the agency budget. This combination leads to *empire-building* and further growth of government.

QUESTIONS FOR THOUGHT AND DISCUSSION

1. The market system and government are both allocative mechanisms. What are some of the advantages and disadvantages of each? In what areas now dominated by market forces should government assume a greater role, if any? In what areas should government allow market forces greater latitude? Why?

2. Since World War II, government transfer payments as percentages of national income have grown sharply, and federal spending on goods and services have fallen relative to state and local spending. What might be some explanations for these changes in patterns of government outlays?

3. Voting is optional in the United States, but it is illegal not to vote in some countries. Do you think making voting compulsory would reduce political apathy? How would compulsory voting affect the behavior of politicians? Would government policies be more or less in accord with voter preferences? Why?

4. Medical doctors are sometimes accused of building the demands for their services by exaggerating minor health problems and heightening the concerns of their patients. How might high-level government bureaucrats enhance the sizes and powers of their agencies through similar processes? What political institutions would they need to manipulate? Can you cite any cases where this type of thing seems to have occurred?

5. One proposal to alter the current federal budgeting system is to allow taxpayers to specify the percentages of their income taxes to be allocated to each government budget category. Proponents of this unequal "point voting" system argue that this would eliminate lobbying by special interests for government programs requiring expenditures of tax revenues and would result in budgets more closely attuned to taxpayers' desires. Do you think these arguments have merit? Can you mount other arguments for this proposal? Should the preferences of those who pay a lot of taxes be given more weight than the preferences of those who pay fewer taxes or no taxes? What would you expect the effects to be on income redistribution programs were this proposal adopted? How might strategic behavior cause the budget to fail to truly reflect even taxpayers' preferences?

6. Which of the following voting systems best preserves the rights of minorities? (*a*) plurality, (*b*) majority, or (*c*) unanimity. Why?

7. Votes generally fail to reflect the intensity of people's preferences about issues. What mechanisms in the U.S. political system enable people to sway policies about which they feel strongly? Do you think these mechanisms improve the efficiency of policymaking?

8. It is illegal to buy votes in the United States. Can you explain why this ban on the sale of votes is economically inefficient? Would it be desirable to make it legal for people to sell their votes? Why or why not?

9. At times, several positions are filled through a single election. For example, the top three (or five, or seven) vote getters might be elected to a school board or as county commissioners. Why do some voters cast their ballots for fewer than the number of candidates who will gain office, even if they have preferences among those for whom they don't vote?

10. To what extent do you think that private bureaucrats are insulated from pressures for efficiency? Is this a serious problem?

CHAPTER 33 Externalities and Environmental Economics

externalities	property rights	bubble concept
optimal pollution	pollution rights	offset policy
pollution abatement	effluent charges	internalization
moral suasion		

"Three Billion Years Plus a Few Minutes"

ooze
cohesion, opulence
twinges, space, undulations
slithering, boring, hatching, germination
increase, complexity, blooming, coordination, cooperation
predation, parasitism, migration, competition, adaptation, selection
crowding, starvation, disease, populations, diversity, camouflage, mimicry
specialization, reduction, exclusion, conversion, blight, drought
pressure, defeat, decline, smoke, decimation
explosion, abuse, ignorance, teeming
contamination, residual, choking
silence, stillness
ooze

—William T. Barry

"Three Billion Years Plus a Few Minutes" by William T. Barry in *Reflection*.
Reprinted by permission of the author.

William Barry eloquently reminds us of the fragility of our existence. Roughly 5 billion people now rely on the earth as a life-support system, and, at present population growth rates (1.7 percent annually), 75 million more are added each year. World population should approach 6 billion by the year 2000. Our environment's capacity to sustain current population is already strained at the seams in places. As we try to stretch this capacity through extensive use of the earth's resources and technological advances, environmental destruction and resource depletion rear their ugly heads. Problems like acid rain, nuclear waste, and pollution encircle the globe.

Developed economies in Western Europe, North America, Japan, and the Soviet Union contain less than one-third of the world population but use roughly four-fifths of all resources. Critics characterize most developed nations as "throwaway" economies: fresh raw materials enter the maw of a production-consumption system but ultimately decompose to heat and waste. The transformation to a sounder ecology may be quite painful. Some scarce resources seem about to vanish, so attaining a uniformly high quality of life may require substantial recycling. The only other hope may be technological advances based on resources that are now unusable. Environmental quality is costly. Cleaning up reduces production, raises costs and prices, lowers national income, and foments social and economic disruption.

A continuing debate rages about how much purity to seek and what techniques to use. At one extreme, some critics view economic analysis as irrelevant and "greedy capitalism" as the root cause of environmental decay. Their position tends to be, "Forbid all pollution." At the opposite pole are those who believe that fully specified property rights harmonize economic activity so that a market economy naturally achieves a healthy ecological equilibrium. We will examine both extreme views and some intermediate positions as well; but first, let us readdress externalities—the origin of many environmental problems. It is important to begin by recognizing that externalities may be either beneficial or harmful.

Externalities

When only the parties *directly* involved in transactions are affected, competition tends to maximize both individual welfare and the public interest; marginal social benefits tend to equal marginal social costs. But if people external to transactions are harmed or helped, market prices and quantities generally fail to account for their preferences and social welfare may not be efficiently served. **Externalities** occur when private calculations of benefits or costs differ from the benefits or costs to society—they are present whenever third parties gain or lose from an activity. Externalities may emerge from either consumption or production.

External Benefits

Some *external benefits* originate in production. For example, a utility company might dam a river to generate electricity, and nearby residents may gain a recreation area in the process. Or construction of a large manufacturing plant in a community may induce other firms to locate nearby to profit from a resulting economic boom. Or a pharmaceutical company might develop knowledge to prevent or cure some deadly disease. Legal monopolies on knowledge are prohibited, however, so it would be unable to prevent a competitor from using the new knowledge. (Only specific techniques that are uniquely embedded in some commodity or piece of equipment are patentable.)

External benefits occur not only in production, as the previous examples show, but in consumption as well. If you landscape your yard, your neighbors may benefit without sharing in your expenses. Their property values rise, and they gain through more attractive scenery, sweet-smelling flowers, and the like. If you and your family are innoculated against a contagious disease, your neighbors benefit because their chances of contracting the disease decline. If you study economics and political science in your spare time, you may enjoy a happier and more productive life. But if, at the same time, you become a more informed voter and better citizen, these gains are shared with the rest of the people in this country. These are just a few of the possible external benefits from some forms of consumption.

Without compensation for those who generate external benefits, activities that embody positive externalities may be at less than optimal levels. For example, applied research may be profitable for a private firm because specific applications are patentable, but basic research is seldom pursued privately because the broad benefits from new knowledge cannot be marketed by the researchers. Similarly, education yields gains to children, but others also gain if better educated people tend to be better informed voters and more productive citizens. If education were strictly private, it might be overpriced and far fewer people would extend their schooling. People would quit buying education as soon as another unit of learning cost more than it was worth to them. They would not consider any gains to their neighbors when deciding how far to pursue their educations.

From the consumption side, suppose that planting flowering trees in your yard boosts both your personal satisfaction and the value of your property. Your demand for flowering trees is shown in Figure 1 as demand curve D_p. You can purchase all the trees that you desire for P_0 and will plant Q_0 trees. But your

FIGURE 1 *Positive Consumption Externalities*

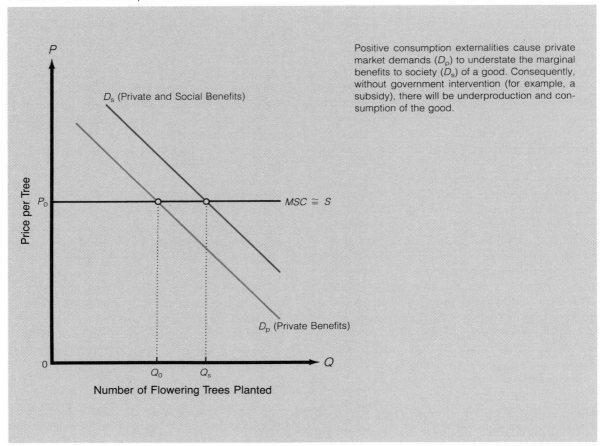

Positive consumption externalities cause private market demands (D_p) to understate the marginal benefits to society (D_s) of a good. Consequently, without government intervention (for example, a subsidy), there will be underproduction and consumption of the good.

Price per Tree

Number of Flowering Trees Planted

neighbors may enjoy the trees nearly as much as you do, as reflected in demand curve D_s, which incorporates your private demand plus the social benefits to your neighbors from your flowering trees. The marginal social benefits of your actions are the sum of any private benefits to you plus any external benefits enjoyed by other people.

Maximum social welfare occurs when marginal social benefits and costs are equal, so the optimal quantity of planted trees would be Q_s. The problem is that you may not plant Q_s trees unless you are compensated for your investment beyond Q_0. Without compensation covering the external benefits to your neighbors, you all will miss an opportunity to gain, with no one losing. The reason is that in your private decision making, you tend to weigh external benefits much less heavily than your private costs and benefits.

One cure for potential underproduction is communal arrangements, which may be either implicit or explicit. Implicit agreements occur when neighbors encourage each other to improve their properties through such things as informal and friendly competition—who has the nicest house, the prettiest lawn, and so on. Implicit agreements tend to work best when only a few people are involved.

Explicit agreements (community covenants or zoning) are more common when larger numbers must cooperate—all residents of some subdivisions may be required to have so many square feet of living space, or they are restricted from painting their homes other than approved colors, or each agrees to spend a certain amount on landscaping, and so on. In general, as the number of people affected by an externality grows, restrictions on behavior tend to become more formal and inflexible.

External Costs

Pollution is the common term for a wide range of negative externalities and can arise from either consumption or production. Water pollution flows primarily from production processes; air and noise pollution result about equally from both. For example, both industrial wastes and the residues from washing dishes flow into our sewer systems and then into our water supplies. Automobiles, smokestack industries, and coal-fired electric generation all contribute to the smog that engulfs many major cities and results in corrosive acid rain that falls on even the most remote regions of our world. External costs are generated in many forms of production. Examples include noise pollution near airports, unsightly billboards and junkyards, or factories that belch noxious smoke.

Negative production externalities are illustrated by the 1879 case of *Sturges* v. *Bridgman*.[1] Sturges, a

---

1. U.S. Supreme Court Case 11 Ch. D. 852 (1879). For a detailed analysis of this case, see Ronald Coase, "The Problem of Social Costs," *Journal of Law and Economics* (Chicago: University of Chicago Press, October 1960).

doctor whose office was next to that of Bridgman, a confectioner, added an examination room next to the confectioner's kitchen. Noisy equipment kept the doctor from examining patients with a stethoscope in the new room, so the doctor sued to prevent the confectioner from operating the equipment. An injunction was granted on the grounds that the machinery imposed external costs on the doctor. (After a bit of reflection, you might conclude that the doctor imposed external costs on the candy maker.)

Suppose that farmers use inorganic sprays on their artichoke crops and then irrigate their fields, washing some of the pesticide onto adjacent properties and into nearby lakes or streams. If this pesticide works its way up the ecological chain—harming both your fishing and health—then you, who may hate artichokes, partially bear the cost of artichoke production. Assume all farmers exude external costs of $2 per pound of artichokes when using chemical sprays. In Figure 2, the supply curve S_0 is based only on farmers' costs, but the marginal social cost is **MSC,** which is $2 higher.

Suppose that farmers (and ultimately, their customers) are now taxed $2 per pound of artichokes if harmful pesticides are used; this covers the full social

FIGURE 2 *Internalizing Pollution Costs: Market Equilibrium with External Costs (Diseconomics) in Production*

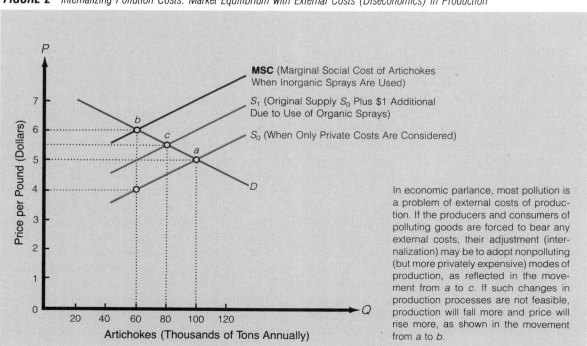

In economic parlance, most pollution is a problem of external costs of production. If the producers and consumers of polluting goods are forced to bear any external costs, their adjustment (internalization) may be to adopt nonpolluting (but more privately expensive) modes of production, as reflected in the movement from *a* to *c*. If such changes in production processes are not feasible, production will fall more and price will rise more, as shown in the movement from *a* to *b*.

costs of production. The price initially rises from $5 to $6 per pound, and quantity produced falls to 60,000 tons annually. The reason the price rises and the quantity falls is straightforward. When farmers' private costs rise by $2 per pound, there is a $2 vertical shift of supply from S_0 to **MSC.** Farmers previously grew 100,000 tons for private costs of $5 per pound. Now private costs are $2 per pound more than before for each level of output as long as harmful sprays are used.

Unfortunately for artichoke growers, consumers would not continue to buy 100,000 tons if the price were to climb to $7 per pound. The higher production costs will cause marginal farmers to fail, and consumers will reduce their artichoke consumption to 60,000 tons annually as the price rises to $6 per pound. Equilibrium moves from point a to point b in the short run, but farmers will look for ways to avoid this $2 pollution charge. Suppose that in the long run they discover nonpolluting organic sprays costing $1 more than inorganic sprays. When they use the inorganic sprays to avoid the $2 tax, the supply of artichokes will rise from **MSC** to S_1.

What is the final socially optimal output in Figure 2? The answer is 80,000 tons of artichokes at a price of $5.50 per pound (point c). At this price, consumers buy and farmers sell what they want, and society's resources are used efficiently. A competitive market system fails to achieve such results if large numbers of people are harmed or large numbers of people pollute.

What can we conclude from this analysis? First, external costs cause the private market to provide too much of a product because the full costs are not borne by customers. That is, the social costs of production (which equal total private costs plus any external costs) are not charged to consumers. If the full costs are paid by consumers, less is produced and consumed. When a pollution charge is imposed, producers will search for ways to clean up their acts while reducing total costs, which now include any external costs.

Could any lone individual reduce pesticide pollution? You might pay farmers to stop or sue for damages. Either solution is possible, but the latter often involves transaction costs (attorney fees, etc.) that exceed the damage done. For example, the costs to an individual of suing all air polluters in Los Angeles would be very high relative to the potential personal recompense for the harm done. People may seek legal remedies, however, when damages are extreme. The key is to force each firm to **internalize** (fully consider) the costs of any pollution imposed on innocent third parties. If each purchaser of a good pays full marginal social production costs, including environmental damages, externalities are internalized, which yields optimal amounts of production and consumption.

Consider such problems as neighbors who party loudly until dawn, drunk and reckless drivers, violent criminals, litterbugs, and people who live like or keep pigs in urban areas. In one sense, these are market failures because consumption-based external costs are imposed on other people. Similar annoyances and dangers might be even more common if society followed a strict laissez-faire approach. Many analysts, however, view these events as examples of government failure because a fundamental task of government in a market economy is to protect broadly defined legal rights to property, which may include rights to peaceful and tidy neighborhoods and safe streets. Society has generally tried to control natural tendencies towards overproduction of irritating or dangerous external "bads" through zoning, social regulation, or other legal sanctions.

The case of garbage removal from the Slob family's property is shown in Figure 3. Suppose that this family is immune to informal social pressures to maintain their property. When the Slobs decide how frequently to have trash hauled away, they ignore the diseases their neighbors might contract, declines in the values of adjacent property, or obnoxious odors from their trash. Unless the Slobs are compelled to consider these external costs, they will choose point a, leaving Q_0 garbage around their houses at a private cost of P_0 per unit. Society might just legally require them to have all their trash hauled off. However, this attitude ignores the benefits that the Slobs (or even ourselves) derive from being able to let the garbage pile up temporarily instead of bundling it and having it removed at all points in time. After all, the Slobs are members of society. What we would like to do is make sure that they consider the effects on their neighbors from leaving trash lying around.

The demand curve D reflects the Slob family's gain from littering its own property, cleaning up only occasionally rather than being fastidious at all times. The curve labeled **MSC** in Figure 3 reflects the losses from litter suffered by both the Slobs and their neighbors, with the **MC** curve reflecting the Slobs'

FIGURE 3 *The Costs and Benefits of the Slob Family's Garbage*

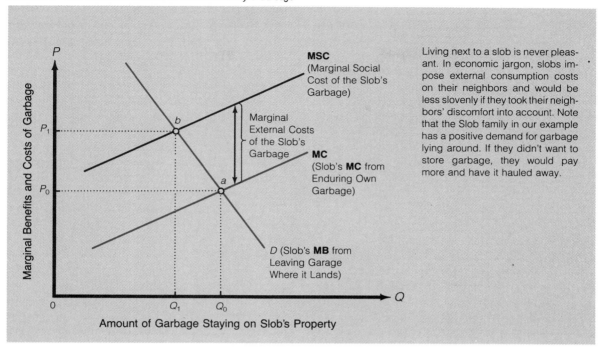

MSC
(Marginal Social Cost of the Slob's Garbage)

Marginal External Costs of the Slob's Garbage

MC
(Slob's **MC** from Enduring Own Garbage)

D (Slob's **MB** from Leaving Garage Where it Lands)

Living next to a slob is never pleasant. In economic jargon, slobs impose external consumption costs on their neighbors and would be less slovenly if they took their neighbors' discomfort into account. Note that the Slob family in our example has a positive demand for garbage lying around. If they didn't want to store garbage, they would pay more and have it hauled away.

marginal private cost. Suppose that the Slobs have the legal right to accumulate trash. In this case, the vertical distance between the two cost curves represents the amount neighbors would be willing to pay the Slobs to reduce the accumulation of trash to a level of Q_1, the socially optimal level. If neighbors could legally limit the Slob's debris, this vertical distance is the price the neighbors would charge to allow the Slobs to accumulate garbage. Note that the optimal amount of trash is not zero. After all, we all have a little garbage on hand at all times, don't we? No one's home is constantly immaculate, even on the days when garbage is collected.

Summary: External Benefits and Costs   Unrestricted private markets produce too much (*too little*) of a good when external costs (*benefits*) are present. Externalities are a common market failure because people tend to weigh their private costs and benefits far more heavily than the costs borne or benefits received by outsiders. People who try to maximize their own welfare equate the marginal private benefit (**MB**) from an action with its marginal private costs (**MC**). This is normally quite rational because trying

to identify and negotiate with all third parties may be prohibitively costly. Thus, market demands mirror marginal private benefits while market supplies reflect marginal private costs.

Society tries to compel decision makers to internalize externalities by assigning certain legal rights to specific groups, through tax incentives or subsidies, or via outright mandates or prohibition. Pollutants are the most notable examples of negative externalities. Ideally, firms will internalize any pollution costs so that consumers ultimately pay full production costs—private plus external (social) costs. Growing amounts of pollution have created a variety of public policies to deal with this problem.

Pollution as a Public Bad; Abatement as a Public Good

A public good, once produced, benefits a large group of people, none of whom can be excluded from enjoying its use. Pollution control, or **abatement,** generally fits this definition. If auto emissions are controlled in your town, everyone can breathe cleaner air and no one can be excluded once the air is cleaner. Thus, environmental quality is a public good. Both the public good and externality aspects of pollution and its control suggest that government might steer production and consumption toward optimal levels. Optimal output levels require marginal social benefits and costs to be equated. This occurs when all pollution costs are internalized; if they are borne by the consumers and producers of goods whose production or use generates pollution, users and makers will weigh these costs and their decisions will be both personally and socially efficient.

Is Optimal Pollution Zero?

Could we eliminate pollution? Zero pollution sounds nice, but your first question should be: How much would it cost? If perfect purity were costless, all of us would demand the immediate abolition of pollution—but the costs of 100 percent purity are prohibitive. This may sound familiar. There are trade-offs between environmental quality on the one hand and, on the other, many goods that seem necessary for even moderate standards of living. What is the **optimal pollution** level? Figure 4 provides an answer using cost-benefit analysis, which does exactly what its name suggests. It compares the costs and benefits of some activity—in this case, pollution abatement.

Panel A of Figure 4 depicts the total benefits and costs from pollution abatement. The total benefit curve reflects the fact that an increasingly clean environment yields less and less in additional benefits as we approach 100 percent abatement. This is reflected in a downward sloping marginal social benefit (**MSB**) curve in Panel B. The marginal benefit to society represents the sum of all benefits to individuals from each reduction in pollution. Our "output" from pollution abatement translates into a given percentage reduction in pollution. Hence, as we move out along the horizontal axis, more abatement is achieved and the environment becomes cleaner.

The total cost of pollution abatement in Panel A rises as we expand efforts to reduce pollution. In Panel B, the positively sloped marginal social cost (**MSC**) of reducing pollution reflects diminishing marginal returns and increasing marginal costs. More ambitious attempts to reduce pollution entail ever greater sacrifices of resources. Maximizing social welfare requires achieving **MSB = MSC** (in this

example, at points e and f). To extend abatement beyond the optimal level of pollution (Of) would waste resources because further reductions in pollution cost more than they are worth. This analysis contradicts the widely held notion that society should completely eliminate pollution regardless of costs. To push pollution control until the total benefits equaled the total costs (point b in Panel A) would mean that the last bit of cleanup effort would cost society ac (in Panel B), while yielding additional benefits of only ad. Society, by cleaning up beyond the optimal level of Of percent to Oa percent receives additional benefits of $feda$ but uses additional resources worth $feca$ to complete the job. The result is a waste of resources equal in value to the shaded area dec.

Alternative Solutions to Environmental Pollution

Nearly everyone recognizes that something must be done to control environmental decay. That is where agreement ends. Extreme conservationists argue for nearly total elimination of environmental degradation and feel that the social benefits from reducing pollution are overwhelming. To them, only technological limits should be allowed to constrain abatement; economic analysis is irrelevant. Others argue for looser environmental standards and oppose many current regulations and standards as too stringent and costly.

Various methods are available to reduce pollution. These methods can be classified according to their degree of intervention in the market process. The least interventionist is *moral suasion,* followed by various market techniques, then tax and subsidy incentives, and finally, outright government regulation and prohibition. We will examine each of these approaches.

Moral Suasion

Moral suasion carries no legal authority—its goals are to persuade offenders to voluntarily reduce their offending practices and to sensitize people to a problem. For example, "Don't Be a Litterbug" campaigns have reduced the trash on public highways. Moral suasion, in the form of adverse publicity or consumer boycotts of a polluter's products, might per-

FIGURE 4 *Determining the Optimal Level of Pollution*

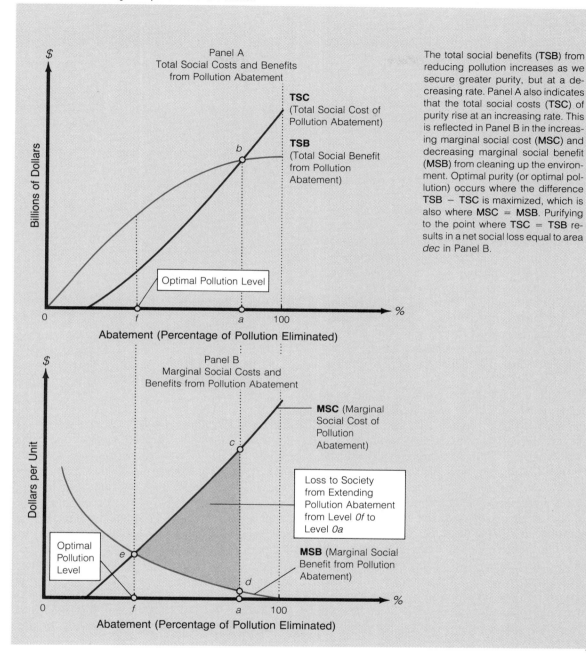

Panel A
Total Social Costs and Benefits
from Pollution Abatement

TSC
(Total Social Cost of
Pollution Abatement)

TSB
(Total Social Benefit
from Pollution
Abatement)

Optimal Pollution Level

Abatement (Percentage of Pollution Eliminated)

Panel B
Marginal Social Costs and
Benefits from Pollution Abatement

MSC (Marginal
Social Cost of
Pollution
Abatement)

Loss to Society
from Extending
Pollution Abatement
from Level *0f* to
Level *0a*

MSB (Marginal Social
Benefit from Pollution
Abatement)

Optimal
Pollution
Level

Abatement (Percentage of Pollution Eliminated)

The total social benefits (**TSB**) from reducing pollution increases as we secure greater purity, but at a decreasing rate. Panel A also indicates that the total social costs (**TSC**) of purity rise at an increasing rate. This is reflected in Panel B in the increasing marginal social cost (**MSC**) and decreasing marginal social benefit (**MSB**) from cleaning up the environment. Optimal purity (or optimal pollution) occurs where the difference **TSB** − **TSC** is maximized, which is also where **MSC** = **MSB**. Purifying to the point where **TSC** = **TSB** results in a net social loss equal to area *dec* in Panel B.

suade the polluter to desist. This approach is not very powerful, however, because many products are marketed nationwide, public relations campaigns are very expensive, and voluntary boycotts ask people to act against their own pecuniary interests. In the early years of the environmental movement, adverse publicity and threats of boycotts were the only methods available.

Market Solutions

Numerous economists argue that the environmental problem could be easily solved if appropriate property rights were assigned to various individuals or groups. Much private property is owned only in a limited way. For example, you may own a car, but there are numerous restrictions on how it can be used. Similar limits apply to ownership of land and buildings, guns, or ham radio equipment.

Lawsuits for Damages

An extensive body of common law has developed to resolve conflicts between property owners. If **property rights** were assigned to protect you from being damaged by pollution, then you could sue harmful polluters. Lawsuits may work fairly well when the pollution can be traced directly to a given polluter and the damage can be shown to be caused by that party's effluent. (The Atlas Chemical Company case at the end of this chapter shows how the courts can resolve problems caused by pollution.) But suppose that a firm were given the right to pollute. Your only remedy might be to pay the firm to reduce pollution—if it were worth it to you.

Using the courts to enforce rights to pollute or to be protected from pollution has several disadvantages. First, legal procedures are slow and costly. (Cases tried in federal courts in 1985 had been initiated an average of 25 months earlier.) Furthermore, such solutions may not be available if the damaged individual lacks the resources to bring a suit. These solutions alone may leave society saddled with excessive waste. A slightly different problem is that where there are numerous polluters and "pollutees," it may be difficult to determine who harmed whom and to what degree. Lawsuits would face almost unsurmountable difficulties in solving problems of fouled air in crowded industrial areas. Legal remedies seem to work best where the number of polluters is small and their victims are few and easily identified. However, residents near the Love Canal in New York State and in Times Beach, Missouri, experienced at first hand the nightmare that pollution can produce. Fearful for their own health and that of their children, outraged by plummeting property values and mountains of red tape encountered in seeking restitution, the victims of these famous incidents learned how difficult it can be to correct the harm done by even easily identified polluters.

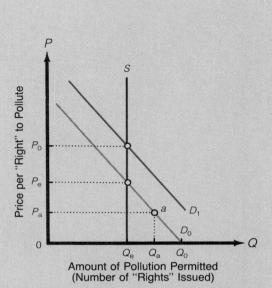

FIGURE 5 *A Market for Pollution "Rights"*

When the right to pollute is strictly limited but for sale on the open market, the demand D_0 for pollution rights depends on the marginal productivity of the environment as a receptacle for industrial waste. Such a market will operate in much the same fashion as markets for other factors of production.

Assigning Pollution "Rights"

A second approach that makes use of the marketplace is for the public sector to sell individuals licenses to discharge wastes. Ronald Coase, a prominent economist, has shown that efficiency will be the same (the pollution level will be optimal) no matter who is assigned the rights, polluter or harmed party, as long as those affected are easily identified, have roughly the same bargaining power (income), and can bargain without cost.[2] This process is diagrammed in Figure 5. The demand for **pollution rights,** labeled D_0, is downward sloping like most demand curves. Pollution would be Q_0 if it were unrestricted and costless. This is the quantity of pollution when the environment can be used freely as a garbage dump.

Assume that the community decides to permit only Q_e pollution. Pollution quotas might be auctioned. Business demands to pollute reflect the contribution of pollution to the revenues and profits of

2. Coase, R. H., "The Problems of Social Cost," *The Journal of Law and Economics,* Vol. III (Chicago: University of Chicago Press, 1960).

the firm. In this sense, the environment is just another resource input to the firm. A firm willing to pay only P_a for each right to pollute (point a) undoubtedly can clean up its act for P_a or less per unit of effluent. Business would be willing to pay P_e each for Q_e pollution rights. If purity lovers would be hurt more than P_e by each unit of pollution, they could buy and retain the pollution rights. In this way, the initial sale of these rights would generate revenue for the community. If an auction were held and Q_e rights were sold, then excessive pollution $(Q_0 - Q_e)$ would be eliminated.

Assume that the Q_e pollution rights are sold to a group of manufacturers on a lake. What happens if other firms want to locate polluting plants on the lake? A new firm can buy rights from the owners of existing pollution rights. This might require buying an especially polluting plant, shutting it down, and transferring the pollution rights to a new facility. Alternatively, the new firm could pay existing firms to install more antipollution equipment. Both techniques reflect a shift in the demand for the right to contaminate from D_0 to D_1 in Figure 5. The value of pollution rights rises, but the level of waste does not. Consumers of the goods entailing pollution pay the full cost of production as the higher cost of polluting is shifted forward.

This approach has several advantages. First, polluters have strong incentives to clean up their effluents. Also, this plan requires very little administratively except monitoring. Plus, if the government decides later to reduce pollution, it can enter the market and buy existing rights. Or it might sell even more rights as a source of revenue. This may be a cheap and attractive alternative to direct regulation. Unfortunately, this approach will only work in a relatively enclosed environment, like a lake or river under the control of local authorities. As spillovers become more pervasive, this method becomes more difficult to administer. Another major shortcoming is that some voters and politicians seem to equate pollution with sin and are outraged at the idea of allowing economic reasoning to dominate what is, for them, a moral issue.

Price Mechanisms for Abatement

We have seen that markets can be structured so that external pollution costs will be internalized. However, the costliness of organizing markets and assigning pollution rights has caused many economists to suggest using tax penalties or **effluent charges** to curb environmental decay. This is a modified use of market forces to achieve optimal resource allocations when externalities are present. In this instance, the government sets the fee (charge) on pollution or the reward for reducing pollution, and polluters are allowed to adjust without overt coercion.

Effluent Charges   The effluent charge approach is illustrated in Panel A of Figure 6. Again, suppose that a group of polluting manufacturers is located on a public lake that could also be used for recreation and fishing. Water pollution reduces the enjoyment derived from boating, skiing, fishing, and picnics.

Assume also that the community leaders estimate that the external cost per unit of effluent is \$0.50 when only optimal pollution occurs. To attain the optimal level of discharge into the lake, the community charges the firms \$0.50 per unit of discharge. Because the **MC** curve in Panel A shows that the costs to the firms of reducing their pollution are less than the effluent charge, pollution will fall by 300 units. The firms will not remove more since the costs of removal exceed the charge; this is the cost to society of putting up with extra pollution.

Output Taxes   In a similar vein, the community could tax the outputs of polluting firms. Suppose that each unit of output of a product is associated with three units of effluent. Only if it is impossible to change the ratio of outputs to effluents will output taxes and effluent charges yield the same results. An output tax of \$1.50 per unit would reduce pollutants to the socially optimal level, as diagrammed in Panel B of Figure 6. The demand for the industry's product is labeled D_0, and the private costs of production (excluding the social costs of pollution) are labeled S_0. When an output tax of \$1.50 is imposed, industry supply shifts to S_1, a constant vertical distance of \$1.50. Equilibrium output falls from 400 units to 300 as the external costs from pollution are internalized through the tax.

Both approaches can be tied together in the following way. Without either an effluent charge or output tax, total output for the industry is 400 units of the product, which generates 1,200 units of effluent. If the cost to society of the effluent is \$0.50 per unit, then total external cost to society is \$600. When a charge of \$0.50 per effluent unit is imposed, the industry cleans up or reduces its pollution by 300 units, leaving 900 and paying total effluent taxes of

FIGURE 6 *Effluent Charges and Output Taxes*

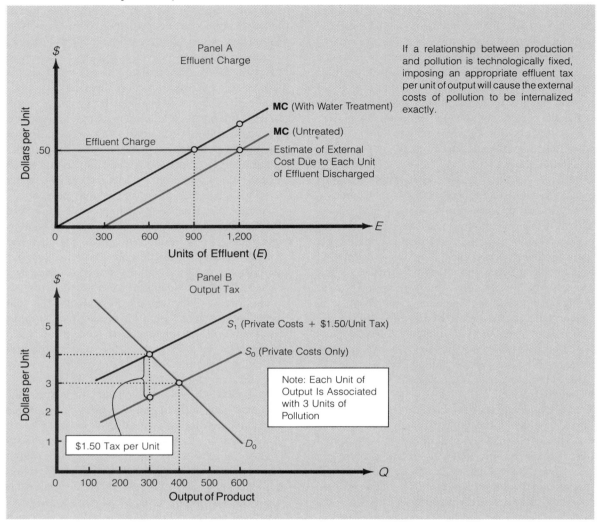

Panel A
Effluent Charge

MC (With Water Treatment)

MC (Untreated)

Effluent Charge

.50

Estimate of External
Cost Due to Each Unit
of Effluent Discharged

Dollars per Unit

0   300   600   900   1,200

Units of Effluent (*E*)

If a relationship between production
and pollution is technologically fixed,
imposing an appropriate effluent tax
per unit of output will cause the external
costs of pollution to be internalized
exactly.

Panel B
Output Tax

S_1 (Private Costs + $1.50/Unit Tax)

S_0 (Private Costs Only)

5

4

3

2

1

$1.50 Tax per Unit

D_0

Note: Each Unit of
Output Is Associated
with 3 Units of
Pollution

Dollars per Unit

0   100   200   300   400   500   600

Output of Product

$450. In a similar way, if effluents are inextricably linked to output, the $1.50 output tax reduces production (and therefore pollution) to 300 units of product. Total pollution taxes again equal $450, and 900 units of effluent are emitted when 300 units of output are produced.

Pollution charges and output taxes face several problems. For these devices to be useful in moving towards an optimal level of environmental protection, the specific damages and appropriate charges must be determined. In the real world, pollution is pervasive, and the exact damages associated with a given pollutant are quite difficult to determine. But it is equally necessary to know about damages in order to prescribe optimal regulations. Continually monitoring and administering effluent charges can be especially difficult and costly, so output taxes might seem to be preferable on efficiency grounds. Unfortunately, output taxes provide no incentives for firms to clean up their manufacturing processes so that more outputs would be available with less pollution. Pollution and output are reduced proportionally. Since the tax is paid regardless of the individual firm's pollution, output taxes provide no incentives for the firm to adopt environmentally advantageous technologies.

Subsidizing Abatement The government might use subsidies (the opposite of taxes) to encourage pollution abatement. Federal grants to pay for pollution control equipment have been used extensively to subsidize cleanups of state or local government sewage facilities. However, urban sewage systems are now required to charge for sewer services as a condition for maintaining access to these federal funds.

Subsidies to private firms that reduce pollution ultimately are subsidies to these firms' customers, but they are unlikely to be effective unless the subsidies make purification more profitable than pollution. Subsidies to encourage private pollution abatement could take such forms as grants to pay for equipment, tax credits, or rapid depreciation allowances. There has been, however, substantial political opposition to subsidizing pollution abatement by private firms, so few such subsidies have been available.

Effective pollution control programs force firms to internalize any external social costs so that waste-spilling companies or their customers pay full (private plus social) costs. Direct regulation is often used, but tends to be a sledgehammer approach.

Regulations and Prohibition

One politically popular method for reducing environmental damage is direct regulation. Regulations requiring complete prohibition may be desirable in the case of extremely dangerous materials. For example, total bans on discharge are standard procedure for some radioactive wastes. When totally eliminating some form of pollution is too costly relative to the benefits, the government has often tried to limit noxious wastes through regulations and standards.

Regulation is costly to administer and provides firms no incentives to reduce pollution once a standard is met. Every stringent rule provokes imaginative attempts to discover loopholes around it. This typically results in an incredibly complex patchwork of directives to prevent cheating or avoidance. In some instances, there are no obvious or acceptable alternatives to direct regulation. We need to recognize, however, that the quality of life depends at least as much on production and economic growth as it does on purity, and that there are trade-offs between these goals.

Are Any Abatement Policies Optimal?

Each policy discussed so far has its particular advantages and disadvantages, summarized in Table 1. None is the "best" for all situations. As in other areas of government policy, "best" depends upon specific social goals and the nature of particular problems.

Where pollution occurs in a closed environment (a lake or stream) and few people are involved, market approaches tend to be viable. Polluters and pollutees might simply be allowed to bargain with each other until they reach a solution. Effluent charges or subsidy schemes may also work efficiently. Where the problem includes aspects of public goods, these approaches begin to break down. Standards and regulations may be appropriate if a problem is widespread and diverse. With extremely hazardous substances, complete prohibition may make the most sense. Different policies are inevitably needed to solve different problems.

The question of environmental protection is complex, but this section has provided some guidelines for analysis. Securing adequate energy supplies and bolstering our economic growth are increasingly balanced against environmental protection and the quality of life as we move towards the twenty-first century. The history of environmental protection in the United States suggests that the Environmental Protection Agency increasingly relies on market solutions to environmental deterioration, although regulation remains a major weapon.

Environmental Policy in the United States

We have examined various techniques to reduce pollution. As we noted earlier, political lags and other difficulties mean that sound economic policies are embraced only slowly, if at all, and that transitions are often quite rough. Environmental protection in accord with modern economic analysis generally faces substantial obstacles, both technical and political.

The History of Pollution Control

One view of pollution suggests that the fundamental problem is the absence of clearly defined property rights. There are generally four stages in the development of property rights: (*a*) common access/non-scarcity, (*b*) common access-scarcity/tragedy of the commons, (*c*) agency restrictions, and (*d*) fee-simple property rights. The evolution of environmental quality in the United States is a textbook case of the development of property rights to a scarce resource and of government intervention in this activity.

Common access resources are available on a first-come, first-served basis. Problems are few until the particular resources become scarce and overutilization occurs. They are then quickly depleted, or they become congested or polluted. Examples are such things as litter or the massacre of bison and extinction of passenger pigeons. General environmental use is now beyond this stage. At some point, the greater productivity derived by private use of the resource causes common use policies to be abandoned. The enclosure movement in England and range wars between cattle ranchers and sheep herders in the old American West are examples of conflicts during the transition from common use to limited use. Sometimes, though not always, we move on to the phase where fee-simple property rights are specified.

A fee-simple property right is one where the owner has the right to use the property in any fashion so long as the physical property of others is unaffected. There are two aspects of this definition: (*a*) fee-simple property rights allow for all uses, including sale and destruction; (*b*) only physical

TABLE 1 *Summary and Evaluation of the Various Environmental Policy Options*

Policy Option	Advantages	Disadvantages
Moral suasion	Least disruptive to market processes. Educates and sensitizes people to nature of environmental problems. Permits individual choice.	Ineffective in reducing pollution levels.
Market solutions (lawsuits and pollution "rights")	Requires little government intervention. Reduces pollution to a given level depending upon the policy established. Relatively easy to administer. Private lawsuits enable individuals harmed to recover.	Sometimes hard to develop "good" estimates of external costs for particular pollutants and polluters. "License" to pollute is politically unpopular. It may be difficult to prove in a lawsuit who damaged whom. Lawsuits can be costly and expensive. Typically require a "closed" environment to administer effectively.
Tax penalties and subsidies (effluent charges, output taxes, and subsidies)	Relatively easy to administer. Largest polluters have greatest incentives to reduce pollution. Generates revenue to further clean up environment.	Sometimes difficult to estimate appropriate charge or tax. Monitoring compliance can be expensive, especially when large numbers of polluters are involved. Output taxes provide few incentives to clean up pollution or adopt cleaner technology.
Direct regulation	Can be used to keep extremely harmful pollution below dangerous levels. Standards can preserve horizontal equity of the program. Politically most popular.	Once standard is set, polluter has no incentive to reduce pollution below standard (important if standard is less than socially optimal level). Administrative regulation often quite complex and cumbersome. Most interventionist in scope. Large bureaucracy is created to administer program. Does not generate its own revenue. Can become captive agency of particular special-interest groups.

characteristics are legally protected, not valued. Fee-simple property rights are a basic ingredient for the attainment of economic efficiency in a competitive market economy.

Fee-simple property rights are seldom used to allocate scarce resources when the public sector is involved. There are many reasons for this. The two basic ones are: (*a*) fee-simple property rights are often very costly to define and enforce; and (*b*) property rights exchanges may reduce the value of property owned by others. The cost of property rights definition and enforcement can be a major impediment to the use of fee-simple property rights. Stop lights, nontransferable hunting licenses, pro rata shares of common pool oil leases, and technological restrictions on oceanic fishing are all cases where the costs of defining and enforcing fee-simple property rights are so huge that alternatives have been developed.

Political intervention is common when one person's actions reduce the values of other people's property. If your job pays $10 an hour and I offer to do the same job for $5 an hour, the value of your labor is reduced. Thus, we restrict access to some labor markets. Our immigration policies are one example. If you sell fresh milk for $1 a gallon and I offer to sell it for $0.50 a gallon, the value of your milk is reduced. Thus, transactions in many commodity markets are controlled. The world is fraught with almost countless examples of government restrictions on the sale of goods that might impair the *value* (but not the physical characteristics) of the property rights of others.

Pollution Control in the United States

By the late 1960s, it was increasingly obvious that the United States had moved into the second phase of property rights: the tragedy of the commons. Environmental degradation was widespread, no longer affecting only isolated cities like Gary, Indiana, or Pittsburgh (which, incidentally, made great strides toward improved air quality). With the passage of environmental quality control legislation for both water and air, Congress more formally delineated our rights to use the environment.

Longstanding arguments about environmental regulation are often rancorous. Environmentalists of-ten react to any environmental deterioration with moral indignation and are accused of largely ignoring the costs of purity. Cost-benefit calculations are shunned in favor of hard-and-fast regulations requiring greater purity. On the other hand, environmentalists commonly complain that bureaucrats fail to aggressively combat pollution. For example, turmoil at the EPA in 1983 reflected outrage that regulators were "selling out" to polluting industries. This rhetoric has been counterbalanced: many firms confronted with the costs of cleaning up have been very vocal opponents of Environmental Protection Agency (EPA) regulation, criticizing what they see as the ineptitude of environmental managers and politicians. In spite of this furor, there appears to be a smooth and predictable development of environmental policy.

The first step in the movement away from common, unrestricted use of the environment required identifying exactly what created problems such as air pollution. Smog was first noticed in the 1940s as a haze against the foothills behind Pasadena, California, slightly east of Los Angeles. Although smog was first thought to be a passing thing, pressure gradually mounted to clean the persistent brown cloud. The initial impetus for controlling the impure air came from the banking community, which feared default of Los Angeles municipal bonds. The problem was that no one could identify the nature of smog—where it came from or what its effects might be.

When the EPA was first charged with responsibility for improving national environmental quality, the only practical solution it perceived was simply to mandate cleanup by all polluters. Pollution abatement was originally treated on a case by case basis, but uniform mandates quickly seemed necessary on two grounds. First, the EPA set mandatory guidelines because such an approach to policy was thought to be easy to monitor. Second, uniform standards constitute equal legal treatment of the affected parties and are nondiscriminatory constitutionally, even though they may dictate unequal burdens of pollution control.

During this period of uniform pollution control, society learned more about pollution and how to measure it, paving the way for pollution rights to emerge as a marketable good. At the same time, political obstacles shaped mandatory rules and standards. Special interest groups lobbied to have rules written to benefit them. Surprisingly, special interest groups have, as often as not, pressed for increased environmental purity. In other words, it is a mistake to think that regulations harm all firms. Some are harmed and some are not. Big steel makers like rules that drive their smaller competitors out of business. The demise of small firms promotes environmental quality. Firms in polluted regions want pollution control requirements to be as burdensome on firms in cleaner areas. This also enhances environmental protection. In most cases, however, special interest pressures have caused inefficiencies in regulation.

In spite of special interest groups, there has been a steady movement toward more convenient and transferable environmental property rights. In the late 1970s, the EPA began allowing the bubble concept to be implemented in many situations. The "bubble" is a performance standard imposed for the area surrounding a plant or a group of adjacent plants, as opposed to the standards originally imposed on each specific source within a plant. The **bubble concept** allows firms to transfer pollution rights between individual sources within a plant while at the same time maintaining some standard overall level of environmental quality. There is a continuing evolution from the bubble concept to pollution rights that are marketable between plants. The gains from exchange that exist within a plant are also available between plants.

Marketable permits to pollute now exist in a rudimentary form. The EPA now allows an **offset policy** for air quality. A new firm wishing to enter an overpolluted area can do so if it induces other businesses to reduce their emissions. Air quality must show a net improvement, and the new firm must meet the individual standards imposed on the others. What this means is that a new entrant can bargain with existing firms, either paying them to shut down or to employ more pollution control measures. Such offsets are now advertised for sale in the *Wall Street Journal*.

Although recognition of market solutions has crept into the regulatory postures of agencies like the EPA, there are still many inefficiencies that exist only to enhance the wealth of special interests. For instance, the bubble concept applies only to old "grandfathered" plants, not new ones. The new-versus-old disparity in environmental quality controls is a recurrent theme. Another example of special interest effects is that the net improvement in the environment necessary to qualify an offset as legal is a political football that is often kicked from one end of the field to the other. Firms with offsets for sale commonly try to influence regulators to require great improvements in environmental quality before allowing a new firm to enter a blighted area; this succeeds in driving up the value of existing rights to pollute.

The Future of Environmental Protection

To outline from whence we have come is history; science means prediction. Thus, the preceding theory of evolution in environmental quality leads to some inferences about future events. The most obvious prediction is that we will increasingly enjoy improved environmental quality. As the EPA and the other regulatory agencies become more adept at their jobs, pollution control will cost less and society will demand more purity.

Markets for pollution permits will probably never be as unregulated as those for cars or land. Certain restrictions will be maintained in order to enhance the wealth of special interest groups. Even the market for land is not completely unfettered. Zoning laws and other legal requirements exist to protect the value of certain locations vis-à-vis others. It should not be surprising to find this same effect in air pollution rights. Finally, it seems unlikely that pollution taxes will ever be a widespread method of allocating the environment for the disposal of waste. In contrast, both uniform standards and marketable pollution permits endow the regulated firms with this value. It is unlikely that the political process will take this value from them.

To summarize the economics of environmental quality, first we must recognize that the environment is a scarce resource that has competing uses. Second, the political process weighs the cost of property rights definition and enforcement—and the profitability to special interest groups from property rights restrictions—against the inherent efficiency of private property ownership. Our experience in the environmental arena chronicles the changing equilibrium of these forces. As property rights become more completely defined and easily enforced, society is increasingly likely to use private property assignments to allocate the use of our environment.

CHAPTER REVIEW: KEY POINTS

1. Positive *externalities* occur when an activity confers benefits on external third parties. Too few of such activities are undertaken because decision makers tend to ignore the external benefits.

2. Pollution situations in which damaged third parties are uncompensated, and hence unconsidered, are examples of negative externalities. Negative externalities impose costs on third parties. Too many activities generating negative externalities are undertaken because decision makers weigh the costs imposed on others too lightly.

3. Environmental quality is a public good, and controlling environmental pollution is costly. There are trade-offs between protecting the environment and producing goods that generate pollution, so the *optimal pollution* level generally is not zero.

4. *Pollution abatement* may occur through negotiation, *moral suasion* (jawboning and bad publicity), lawsuits initiated by damaged parties, controls (government ceilings on pollution levels), the use of *effluent charges,* or government subsidies for pollution control. No single solution applies to all situations of negative externalities; they must generally be resolved on a case by case basis.

5. The four stages in the development of property rights are (*a*) common access/nonscarcity, (*b*) common access-scarcity/tragedy of the commons, (*c*) agency restrictions, and (*d*) fee-simple property rights. The term *fee-simple property rights* means that you can do anything you want with your property so long as you do no physical damage to the property of others.

6. *Pollution rights* might be auctioned and then made transferable. The EPA initially relied heavily on direct regulation through pollution ceilings, but is increasingly using *property rights* solutions to control environmental deterioration.

7. The *bubble concept* sets a pollution performance standard for a plant. A firm can transfer rights to pollute within or between plants inside the "bubble" as long as the standard is met.

8. The *offset policy* allows new firms that wish to produce in a polluted area to operate if they can induce existing firms to reduce air pollutants to "offset" the newcomer's emissions.

QUESTIONS FOR THOUGHT AND DISCUSSION

1. Some analysts insist that external costs are so inherently bilateral that it is hard to determine who is the polluter and who is the pollutee. If a polluter is the one who imposes costs on others, then, when regulation secures greater purity, the people who benefit are the polluters because they impose "cleanup" costs on the factory and its customers. In this view, whether the factory should pay for pollution abatement or whether those who desire purity should "bribe" the firm to install pollution abatement equipment is entirely arbitrary. Moreover, the government need not interfere because, in this view, the parties will privately bargain until an optimal solution is reached. What problems do you see with this approach to environmental quality?

2. What motivates some business firms to argue for stringent uniform standards of allowable pollution nationwide? Do you think it is efficient to require the same standards of firms in metropolitan areas as in isolated areas? If not, which firms should be forced to meet higher standards? Why?

3. Suppose that you are deeply concerned about the welfare of poor people in this country. If you have access to a "magic button" that, when activated, will eliminate all pollution in the United States, should you push the button? Curiously, the answer may be NO! You will need to draw upon material from the last few chapters to explain why you might not. Now suppose that a second "magic button" will eliminate all urban street crime. Should you push this button? Why or why not?

4. Technological optimists believe that research and development will advance with sufficient speed so that pollution, the energy crisis, and the rapid rate of use of depletable resources will be overcome through normal operations of the marketplace. Technological pessimists fear that the advance of technology will only hasten environmental decay and the depletion of our resources. To them, only stringent government regulation will forestall stripping the planet of resources and irremediably poisoning our environment. Into which camp do you fall? Why?

5. If your property or person is harmed by pollution, you can sue for damages. What are some of the shortcomings of using the civil courts to resolve the dangers posed by pollutants?

Atlas Chemical Industries, Inc. v. M. P. Anderson (1974)

Industrial pollution has become commonplace. Newspapers regularly report situations where the EPA has ordered a firm or industry to stop polluting or to reduce its pollution to "acceptable standards." The following case illustrates yet another approach to solving some of our environmental problems. It involves a lawsuit by a private individual for damages to his property arising from industrial discharge of harmful matter.

In 1922, Atlas Chemical Industries, Inc., (Atlas), constructed an activated-carbon processing plant at Marshall, Texas. This plant has been in continuous operation since its establishment and converts lignite into activated carbon by a process using acids and large quantities of water to wash the lignite. Since 1922, the wash water containing lignite, carbon, and other waste elements has been continuously discharged into Darco Creek. Because of the lignite, carbon, and other constituents, the wash water has an inky black color and tends to leave a black deposit when the solids settle out. Until 1974, when acid-neutralization facilities were installed at the plant, the wash water had an acid content.

Over the years since the establishment of the Atlas plant, the creek waters on M. P. Anderson's land have been black, and a black sediment has built up in the creek bottom and creek waters and regularly deposited on 60 acres of M. P. Anderson's land as a result of frequent flooding. Due to the Atlas effluent, the creek waters have been rendered useless, and grass and vegetation in the area of the stream have been destroyed.

In common law actions for damages resulting from this intentional discharge of pollutants, the doctrine of strict liability, as in the classic law of nuisance and trespass, shall apply. In order to prove a *prima facie* case [a case supported by sufficient evidence to warrant submission to a jury] in such pollution litigation, the plaintiff will be required to prove by a preponderance of the evidence the following:

a. That plaintiff has property rights and/ or privileges in respect to the use or enjoyment of water, air, land, or other property or interests invaded or interfered with by defendant; and
b. That the defendant has committed an act or acts of commission or omission which
   1. endangers or destroys the life of a living thing or being; or
   2. gives offense to persons of ordinary sensibilities; or
   3. obstructs reasonable and comfortable use of the property; or
   4. is a substantial invasion of the public or private use and enjoyment of property; or
   5. creates an unreasonable risk or danger to a person, land, or other personal property; or
   6. constitutes the alteration of the physical, thermal, chemical, or biological quality of, or the contamination of, any water in this state that renders the water harmful, detrimental, or injurious to humans, animal life, vegetation, or property; or to public health, safety, or welfare; or impairs the usefulness of enjoyment of water for any lawful or reasonable purpose; and
c. That the conduct of the defendant or his act or acts of omission or commission are or were the legal or producing cause of the invasion, injuries, or damages; and
d. That the invasion, or the commission of the acts or the omission of the act or acts is or was intentional. The intentional act, omission, or invasion may be one in which the defendant perpetrates the invasion or interference; or is substantially certain to result from his conduct; and
e. The amount of plaintiff damages.

We believe the public policy of this state to be that however laudable an industry may be, its owners or managers are still subject to the rule that its property cannot be used to inflict injury to the property of its neighbors. To allow industry to inflict injury to the property of its neighbors without just compensation amounts to adverse condemnation, which is not permitted under our law. We know of no acceptable rule of jurisprudence which permits those engaged in important and desirable enterprises to injure with impunity those who are engaged in enterprises of lesser significance. The costs of injuries resulting from pollution must be internalized by the industry as a cost of production and borne by consumers or shareholders or both and not by the injured individual.

During the Industrial Revolution in this country, the law shifted to accommodate economic growth and those who invested therein and was changed to the detriment of isolated individuals who have collectively come to bear the cost of such growth. In recent years, however, the U.S. Congress and the state legislature have recognized that we literally cannot live with the pollution caused by industrial waste and have passed various statutes, rules, and regulations controlling the disposal and emission of pollutants. It is as if we have allowed a monster (pollution) to be created which will either devour or destroy us all. "[P]ollution is waste. We can't get rid of waste by moving it from here to there. We already are at the stage where 'there' is getting so full that it's backing up to 'here'." No longer can we permit industrial development and pollution at the expense of individuals. The social utility of allowing uncontrollable pollution without compensation for the injury caused thereby is no longer tolerable. Neither the benefit of pollution-causing activity to the community nor the comparative investments of plaintiff or defendant will be factors considered in determining whether there is a compensable injury. Citizens who are injured should be allowed to maintain an action for an interference which is unreasonable and offensive to persons of ordinary sensibilities. During this century, the course of law has been to incorporate economic growth and the protection of important production, which quickly became the paramount value in the resolution of conflicting interests in pollution litigation. "But in this age of environmental concern it is clear that this value warrants no greater emphasis than others. Thus, it is time for the reassessment of the law to the end of redressing its imbalance, a time for reflection on where responses to legitimate needs in another time carry the law."

Judgment for M. P. Anderson in the sum of $61,375.

QUESTIONS

1. Will this decision enhance the allocation of resources in Texas?
2. What did the court mean by the phrase "the costs of injuries resulting from pollution must be internalized by the industry"? Do you agree with that statement? Why or why not?
3. What are some of the costs of such a decision?
4. Do you expect there to be a large number of private suits for pollution damage in Texas? Do you agree with the requirements for a *prima facie* case?
5. Texas has a Water Quality Board to supervise and regulate the quality of water in the state. If Atlas met the standards required by the Texas Water Quality Board, would you have decided for Atlas instead of Anderson? Why?
6. The award to Anderson in this lawsuit was for past damage to his land. If Atlas Chemical Industries, Inc. continues to discharge effluents that harm Anderson's land, should he be permitted to sue again? What limits would you set on recoverable damages?
7. How could Atlas avoid damages in the future? Do any of these approaches internalize the harm to the firm?

CHAPTER 34 Redistribution of Income and Wealth

the contribution
  standard
the needs standard
the equality standard
Lorenz curves

employment
  discrimination
occupational
  discrimination
human capital
  discrimination
welfare: $B_i/B_0 > T_i/T_0$

disincentives
Aid to Families with
  Dependent Children
  (AFDC)
family allowance plans
  (FAPs)
negative income taxes
  (NITs)

Most of us wake up each morning knowing that we will have full bellies and roofs to sleep under that night. But haunting images of starving children regularly appear on television. About half of the world's people suffer from malnutrition and live in squalor. Not surprisingly, poor people tend to be less healthy and die younger than those who command more resources. In the United States, slum dwellers and derelicts consume far less than do prosperous suburbanites, and the incomes of migrant farm workers fall far below the national average. Overseas, the opulence enjoyed by some wealthy people contrasts even more starkly with the lives of the impoverished.

Why is the relative prosperity that most Americans, Japanese, and Western Europeans enjoy so rare elsewhere? Why are some people poor, while others consume conspicuously and extravagantly? Do prosperous people have a duty to share with the less fortunate? If voluntary sharing seems inadequate, should government redistribute income and wealth? These are among the questions addressed in this chapter.

We will first discuss whether "money can buy happiness." One requirement for *redistribution* to be a potential cure for poor people's misery is that money can buy happiness. We then present some alternative ethical criteria that address redistributing income and wealth. Finally, we identify influences on present distribution patterns, describe current American welfare programs, and look at proposed reforms for what some people call "the welfare mess."

Prosperity and Happiness

Would most of us like more wealth than we have? Almost certainly. Jeremy Bentham, the utilitarian philosopher, offered two important propositions about wealth and utility. The first is reasonably well accepted: All else equal, more income or wealth makes people happier. Bentham's second proposition is more controversial: On the average, additional income means more to the poor than to the rich. That is, income itself may be subject to the law of diminishing marginal utility. We will deal with these issues in turn.

Does Money Buy Happiness?

We do not mean this question literally, of course, but rather, are the rich happier than the poor? Many religious people reject this idea, believing that the only path to true happiness is grounded in their particular faith. Soap operas, pulp magazines, and bad novels often suggest that the price of being rich is a life of pain and suffering. (Most of us would gladly risk such misery.)

Several studies indicate that, on average, health and longevity are positively related to income and wealth. Prosperous people also tend to rate themselves happier than people who are not, as the study reported in Figure 1 shows. In such a survey, people were asked how happy they were. The responses shown in Panel A were assigned weights of +2 for "very happy," +1 for "pretty happy," and zero for "not too happy," leading to the *utility score* in Panel B. Utility scores climb as income rises, supporting Bentham's idea that higher income yields greater happiness, although there is a possibility of reverse causation—cheerful people may get better jobs and do better financially.

Do Extra Dollars Mean More to the Poor than to the Rich?

A positive answer to this question suggests that *if* we ignore the effects on production and investment, society might gain through redistributions of income and wealth from the rich to the poor. This is a big "if." Small wonder that it is among the most controversial propositions in economics.

This issue cannot be settled objectively because there is no scientific way to compare utility between people. People who favor greater equality of income might argue that extra dollars are most valuable to the poor because necessities surely generate more *utils* than do such luxuries as the mink coats or golf clubs purchased by the rich. Defenders of current distributions could respond that income must mean more to the well-to-do because most work hard for their high incomes. Advocates of redistribution might then assert that (*a*) the poor lack the resources possessed by people with high incomes, (*b*) discrimination denies equal opportunities to many poor people, or even (*c*) the disutility associated with work is relatively higher for the poor because they lack access to pleasant and remunerative jobs. Defenders of the status quo might then argue that wealthy people save and invest much larger proportions of their high incomes and that without these investments the lot of the poor would be even worse. This battle spins in circles, but it is impossible to scientifically ascertain the best income distribution. This does not mean, however, that it is a waste of effort to try to understand these normative issues.

Ethical Criteria for Distribution

When wealth is centralized, the people are dispersed. When wealth is distributed, the people are brought together.
　　　—THE ANALECTS OF CONFUCIUS, Book 14

Controversies over who should have what predate the written word. Distribution has been thought unfair by most "have nots" in all societies, and by many conscience stricken "haves" as well. At least three schools of thought offer competing answers about how to distribute income fairly.

One view is that income should be based on contribution; a second, that income should be distributed according to need; and a third, that income should be distributed equally. Distributions in all modern economies are based on a blend of these criteria. Those whose contributions are valued more tend to receive higher incomes so that they will have incentives to contribute. Many people with special needs receive tailored attention from private or public charities. Finally, progressive income taxes and welfare payments are two of the mechanisms intended to make incomes more equal. The ethical bases of these criteria differ markedly.

The Contribution Standard

. . . he that will not work shall not eat.
　　　—John Smith
　　　THE GENERAL HISTORIE OF VIRGINIA, 1624

As we've already discussed, markets determine income payments to resource suppliers. Competition distributes income in proportion to the values of the

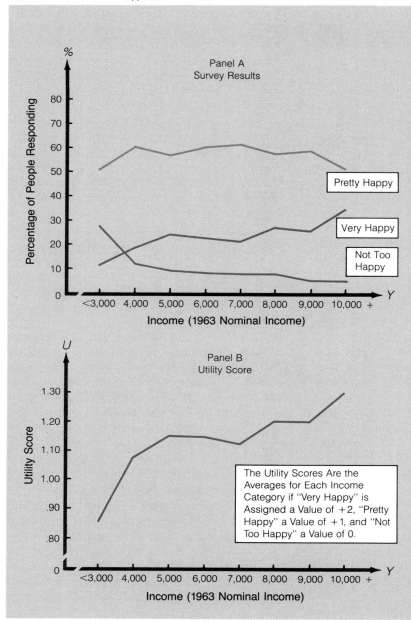

FIGURE 1 Income and Happiness

Panel A
Survey Results

Pretty Happy

Very Happy

Not Too
Happy

Income (1963 Nominal Income)

In Panel A, the percentage of people who rate themselves "pretty happy" seems unaffected by income. However, the response "very happy" is far more common for people with higher incomes, and relatively few of them are "not too happy." Many low-income people consider themselves "not too happy," while few are "very happy." This suggests that general satisfaction with life is positively related to income, as shown in Panel B. Source: Drawn from a survey of Illinois residents, reported in N. M. Bradburn and D. Caplovitz, *Report on Happiness* (Chicago: Aldine, 1965).

Panel B
Utility Score

The Utility Scores Are the Averages for Each Income Category if "Very Happy" is Assigned a Value of +2, "Pretty Happy" a Value of +1, and "Not Too Happy" a Value of 0.

Income (1963 Nominal Income)

marginal products and amounts of resources people supply. Marginal productivity theory provides roots for the **contribution standard,** whose advocates believe that rewarding contribution ranks high in economic efficiency because it encourages work effort, investment, and attempts to profit by serving other people's demands. An implicit assumption is that markets accurately gauge productivity. Thus, who gets how much is fairly determined by an impersonal market system, without the arbitrariness and favoritism inherent in centralized decision making.

Income differences generated by a contribution standard are not a disadvantage, according to its champions, in part because people with high incomes save proportionally more, facilitating investment and economic growth. This yields gains to both the rich and the poor. (One cliché is that "A rising tide lifts all boats.") Moreover, inequality is equitable if it results from smarter or harder work, longer hours, or saving and investing. For example, should a cab driver who works a 60-hour week subsidize one who works 40 hours? Should a factory worker who draws interest from savings squeezed from a slim paycheck share the interest with others who spend everything they make? Advocates of the contribution standard answer NO to such questions, asserting that it is compatible with capitalism, sets efficient incentives for production and economic growth, and maximizes individual freedom. Moreover, a contribution standard uses "carrots" (*income*) to reward productivity instead of the "sticks" (*punishment for sloth*) common under other systems.

Opponents of the contribution standard, however, wonder how well markets measure productivity. They argue further that the very young, the very old, and the handicapped among us must share in our income if our society is to be fair and humane.

The Needs Standard

From each according to ability, to each according to needs.

—Louis Blanc

Some people lack the skills or the physical or mental attributes to be very productive. Others inherit land and capital and, by ownership alone, claim to be productive. Citing these and other perceived inequalities, many opponents of the contribution standard favor distributing "to each according to needs."[1] This famous Marxist slogan is difficult to implement, how-

---

1. An interesting historical note is that Marx viewed distribution according to need as an objective to be implemented only after a "dictatorship of the proletariat" gave way to "pure communism." According to Marx, the most glaring inequity of capitalism is that workers are paid less than the values of their *average* products because exploitative capitalists steal any production in excess of subsistence wages. Thus, Marx was an advocate of a productivity standard, were productivity defined by averages rather than marginal products. After Marx's death, John Bates Clark developed marginal productivity theory and the argument that payments to owners of their resources' marginal products would absorb all production. It would be interesting, were it possible, to know what Marx's own reaction would have been to Clark's rebuttal of the exploitation doctrine.

ever, and poses severe problems for production incentives. How do you determine a person's needs? Distributing primarily according to a **needs standard** requires a bureaucratic assessment of people's needs. Why would anyone bother to work if distribution were strictly by need? Is it proper to replace economic incentives with the coercive force of government?

These and other problems with distributing according to needs were discussed in more depth in Chapter 2. Trade-offs between efficiency and equity, however, can be heart wrenching. Most people agree that at least the basic needs of those who cannot provide for themselves must be accommodated because we should not allow orphans, the aged, the severely handicapped, or society's misfits to starve.

The Equality Standard

Dividing income equally avoids the great disparities in income that occur under the contribution standard and dispenses with the immense bureaucracy required for a need standard. All that an **equality standard** requires is accurate national income accounting and a census of population: divide national income by population, then mail each family a check for its share. Moreover, there is an economic rationale that an equal distribution of income generates the maximum economic welfare possible in a society, under certain conditions.

Suppose you were the utilitarian ruler of a country and were intent on maximizing social happiness. You have the right to divide a given national income to accomplish this goal. You suspect that some of your subjects would be reasonably happy with very little, while others would gain great happiness from higher monetary incomes. You, unfortunately, cannot measure any individual's gain in happiness from a higher money income, nor can you objectively compare happiness between individuals. If you try to find out who would gain the most from more than an equal share, most people will exaggerate their needs and some may lie to you. If you are convinced that each person gains from higher income but that, on average, the poor gain more than the rich, then the expected happiness of the community will be maximized if you simply divide all income equally.

Like distribution according to needs, however, equal sharing of income erodes personal incentives for productivity. One ideal of socialism is to replace the selfish individuals assumed in most economic theory with people filled with desire to work for the betterment of all humanity. Attempts to educate masses of people into altruistic modes of behavior have uniformly failed, however, and enforced production quotas have often replaced income incentives for production in such countries as the Soviet Union and China.

Inequality and Inequity

Life is unfair.
—*John F. Kennedy (1960)*

If differences are perceived as inequitable, then evidence that Kennedy was right abounds. People differ in their natural abilities, inheritances, opportunities, in the times and places they were born, in age, race, sex, or religion. Most of all, they differ in luck. Some face discrimination, some are maimed or die in car wrecks or wars, and some are homely, demented, or physically or mentally impaired. Others are attractive, healthy, bright, buy winning lottery tickets, or are born with silver spoons in their mouths.

Some inequities might be correctable through government policies or social reforms. For example, the inequity of slavery was ended by the Civil War, and legal changes have reduced discrimination by race and sex in education, employment, and housing. Other apparent inequities may never be overcome. It is impossible, for example, for a genius to transfer IQ points to someone less intellectually gifted, or for a world-class sprinter to give speed to us slowpokes.

No society has ever achieved a consensus that everyone was treated fairly because equity is unavoidably subjective. Suppose that everyone agreed with the idea of *horizontal equity:* equals should be treated equally. Even this would do little to resolve equity in a world where every person is somewhat unique. Advocates of the contribution standard argue that inequality of income or wealth is frequently justified by differences in the productivity of individuals' resources. Yet difficulties in specifying equity when people and circumstances differ have caused critics of a contribution standard to focus on inequality as evidence of inequity.

Just how unequal is income distribution in the United States? Table 1 shows pretax and pretransfer distributions of income since 1935. Although changes proceed only at a snail's pace, notice that the share of the middle 60 percent of recipients is now over half of all income. Moreover, because taxes are mildly progressive while transfers tend to be regressive, Table 1 understates the share of net income received by people at the bottom and overstates the share of people at the top. Before we explore how much tax and transfer policies reduce inequality, we need to introduce a device for comparing distributions of income or wealth.

Lorenz Curves

It is hard to see changes in the income distribution and the extent of inequality from Table 1. **Lorenz curves,** developed by a German statistician, allow visual comparisons between distributions across

TABLE 1 *The Distribution of Income Before Taxes and Transfers, 1935–84*

Family Group	Percent of Total Income					
	1935	1950	1960	1970	1980	1984
Lowest 20 percent	4.1	4.5	4.8	5.4	5.3	4.7
Second 20 percent	9.1	12.0	12.2	12.2	11.6	11.0
Middle 20 percent	14.1	17.4	17.8	17.6	17.5	17.0
Fourth 20 percent	20.9	23.4	24.0	23.8	24.0	24.4
Highest 20 percent	51.7	42.7	41.3	40.9	41.6	42.9
Total	100.0	100.0	100.0	100.0	100.0	100.0

Source: *Statistical Abstract of the United States,* 1986.
Note: Numbers may not add up to 100 due to rounding.

FIGURE 2 *Lorenz Curve (Income Before Taxes and Transfers)*

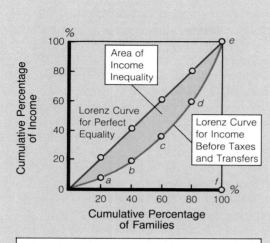

Approximate Income Distribution		Cumulative Income Distribution		
Group	% of Total Income	Group	% of Total Income	Point in Figure Above
Lowest 20%	5	First 20%	5	a
Second 20%	12	First 40%	17	b
Middle 20%	18	First 60%	35	c
Fourth 20%	24	First 80%	59	d
Highest 20%	41	Total	100	e

Lorenz curves illustrate unequal distribution. In this figure, the cumulative shares of pretax income are shown (on the vertical axis) for ever larger proportions of the population, beginning at the bottom of the income ladder. The area between the Lorenz curve and the 45° reference line indicates the extent of inequality.

time and between countries. On the axes of the Lorenz curve in Figure 2 are the cumulative percentages of families and family incomes before taxes and transfers. The data (from Table 1) are sequentially summed to form the cumulative distribution listed below the figure. For example, if the lowest 20 percent and the second lowest 20 percent of the population, respectively, receive 5 percent and 12 percent of all income, then the lowest 40 percent of the population receives 17 percent of total income. And if the middle 20 percent gets 18 percent of total income, then the lowest 60 percent of the population receives 35 percent (5 + 12 + 18 = 35). And so on.

If the Lorenz curve were a diagonal like the straight line *0*, then income would be distributed evenly—each fifth of the population would receive one-fifth of income. If one family had all income while the rest of us had nothing, the Lorenz curve would be identical to the bottom and right-hand axes—line *0fe*. The Lorenz curve for the United States is the curved line. The shaded area reflects inequality; the larger this area, the more unequal the income distribution.

You should note that income will probably never by equally distributed, if only because of lifetime earnings patterns. Younger families typically earn less than more established families, primarily because of differences in work experience and past saving. Even if every family had identical lifetime incomes, inequality would exist at every point in time because of typical age/earnings profiles.

The Changing Distribution of Income

How much has income inequality been reduced in the United States? Table 1 suggests that the pretax distribution of income has changed little since 1950. However, high income families pay more taxes and receive fewer transfer payments, on average, than those with less income. Figure 3 shows pretax income distributions for 1929 and 1984, along with a dashed Lorenz curve for 1972 (the only year for which data are available) reflecting the greater equality of net income that results after taxes and transfer payments.

The state of economic development is a powerful influence on the relative distribution of income, with more advanced countries tending to have greater income equality regardless of the economic system. For example, several studies indicate that distribution is more equal in such capitalist countries as United States, Japan, and West Germany than in such avowedly socialist countries as Cuba, Iraq, Ethiopia, or Nicaragua. The shift towards greater equality in the United States shown by the pretax Lorenz curves for 1929 and 1984 largely reflects the growing prosperity of the middle class over the past 50 years. Most transfer and tax policies designed to reduce inequality are of more recent vintage, having been distilled during the social ferment of the 1960s.

Income inequality has generated many hotly debated proposals for redistribution. But redistributing

FIGURE 3 Lorenz Curve Depiction of Income Distribution in the United States (Before Taxes and After Adjustment for Taxes and Transfers)

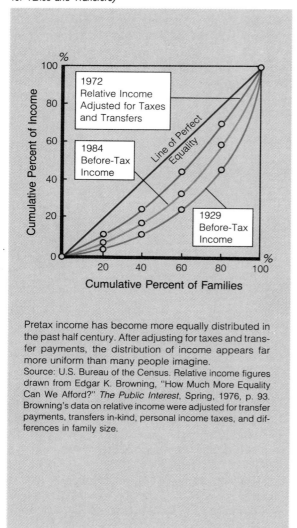

Pretax income has become more equally distributed in the past half century. After adjusting for taxes and transfer payments, the distribution of income appears far more uniform than many people imagine.
Source: U.S. Bureau of the Census. Relative income figures drawn from Edgar K. Browning, "How Much More Equality Can We Afford?" *The Public Interest*, Spring, 1976, p. 93. Browning's data on relative income were adjusted for transfer payments, transfers in-kind, personal income taxes, and differences in family size.

income raises such questions as: Should society provide welfare to a rich person who suffers severe but temporary business losses? Should a welfare recipient who wins $10,000 in a lottery be cut from the welfare rolls for a year or two? Such paradoxes for income redistribution schemes have given rise to other controversial proposals that concentrate on redistributing wealth because, as the preceding questions show, income and prosperity are only roughly correlated.

The Distribution of Wealth

Wealth is the sum of assets—financial and economic capital plus property—minus liabilities. Do poor people occasionally have high incomes? Do wealthy people sometimes experience low incomes? The surprising answer to both questions is YES. Wealth is cumulative unspent income and is a stock variable, while income is a flow variable.[2] Wealth tends to generate income, but some high-income people don't save and never achieve wealth; you may have read about high rolling financiers or big lottery winners declaring bankruptcy. On the other hand, some wealthy people occasionally have low-income years. This is common for retirees, among others. Most welfare programs are intended for people plagued by both little wealth and low income.

If you thought the income distribution was skewed towards the top, look at the wealth distribution in Figure 4. A 1986 Bureau of the Census study indicates that the lowest fifth of households had under 0.5 percent of assets, while the top 12 percent held 38 percent of wealth.[3] White families average 12 times as much wealth as blacks, and 8 times as much as hispanics. Only 2 percent of minority families were classified as wealthy, while 14 percent of whites were in the richest bracket. The wealthy tend to be professional or self-employed and in stable homes. The poor tend to be uneducated and in broken homes. The major determinant of wealth, however, seems to be age. Typical heads of wealthy families are older than 55, while young families are often poor. Time allows you to acquire wealth—another good reason for preferring growing older to its alternative.

Determinants of Distribution

Now that you have seen snapshots of the distributions of income and wealth, we need to explore why some people are rich and some are poor. Some rich people inherited fortunes. (Parent selection may be

---

2. *Stock variables* are timeless, while *flow variables* lack meaning without a time period. A millionaire's assets exceed debts by at least $1 million, and time is irrelevant. It matters greatly, however, whether you make $100 hourly or weekly.

3. All studies of wealth, including this one, ignore human capital. In equilibrium, wealth and income are proportional if human capital is included in wealth.

FIGURE 4 Lorenz Curves for Income and Wealth

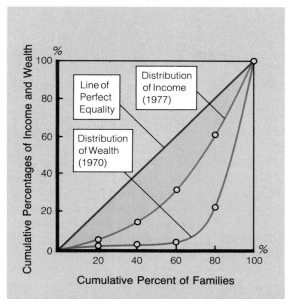

Measured wealth is much less equally distributed than income. However, critics of these statistics argue that this difference only considers nonhuman wealth. Because human capital is much more evenly distributed across the population, its inclusion would presumably cause the distributions of income and wealth to be virtually identical. Can you use arguments developed in our earlier discussion of capitalization processes to argue that the distributions of income and wealth must be identical in equilibrium?

the most useful skill anyone can have.) Productive assets generate income with no labor efforts by their owners, so heirs and heiresses to fortunes generally land in high income brackets. Even though rent, interest, and corporate profit account for only about one-fifth of all income, the bulk flows to the top 2 percent of the populace.

A second reason for income differentials is that, contrary to slogans and wishful thinking, we are not all created equal. Some of us are born with talents that especially suit us for remunerative careers. This is most obvious in entertainment or professional sports. Frustration will be your only reward if you cannot carry a tune but try to sing professionally or stand less than 6'8" tall and pursue a career as a cen-

ter in the National Basketball Association. Levels of energy, motivation, amiability, and insight also separate individuals. Some people make choices that seem to destine them to poverty. Perpetual students in esoteric disciplines, most artists, actors, and musicians, and some ministers select occupations for psychic income, not material rewards. Discrimination based on race, sex, age, ethnic background, height, or general appearance also causes differences in the options available to otherwise equally gifted individuals.

Occupational restrictions may also keep qualified people out of some jobs. For example, doctors are the highest paid professionals, on average, but medical practice requires specialized education, and the slots available in medical schools are limited. Some people step into management of a family business, while others bounce from job to job for years before settling into one that suits them. Finally, luck may play a major role in who gets a high paying job and who doesn't—although some people seem to manufacture their own luck.

Poverty in America

Many people view the presence of poor people in this country as evidence of the inequity of capitalism. In their minds, any economy generating over $4 trillion in output should not allow the squalor and deprivation seen in our urban ghettos and many rural communities. Critics of this position note that the poor in the United States are not nearly as destitute as the down and out in India, North Africa, or other less developed regions. Defenders of our current distributions also point out that the "poor" in this country often have televisions, refrigerators, and numerous other items that are considered luxuries in most other countries. Focus 1 points out that poverty is far from an absolute concept; our views of poverty depend on average standards of living in a society.

What Does Poor Mean?

Identifying the poor requires a definition of poverty. The 20 percent of our population with the lowest income is sometimes viewed as impoverished, but such an approach makes poverty incurable. Other

Poverty: A Relative Concept

Friend: *How's your spouse?*
Economist: *Relative to what?*
—An Unknown Pundit

This quip reflects a tendency among economists to measure almost everything relative to some alternative. *Poverty,* which is a "lack of wealth or material comfort", is no exception. People might agree that anyone without the physical means to sustain normal life is absolutely impoverished, but beyond that definition, poverty seems a relative concept that is determined by time and place. For example, many Americans below our official "poverty line" have amenities enjoyed only by the wealthy in less developed countries and seem prosperous relative to beggars and slum dwellers in some countries. And consider how standards of living have changed over the centuries.

The average life span of Europeans who survived childhood 1,000 years ago was less than 45 years. People in developed economies now typically live into their 70s because of advances in nutri-tion and medicine. Polio, cholera, small pox, diptheria, and leprosy are now extinct or quite rare in developed economies. Canning and refrigeration make it possible to store food for long periods, and the growth of commerce has enriched diets throughout the world. Even the nobility of medieval times did not have access to things that many Americans who are classified as poverty-stricken take for granted: aspirin, fast food restaurants, telephones, running water, automobiles, electric lighting, indoor plumbing, garbage collection, paved roads, public education and transportation, antibiotics, grocery stores, "painless" dentistry, television, and heating systems for their homes—this list could be extended for several pages.

Some Americans at society's bottom rungs—bag ladies and derelicts—do lead miserable lives, but food stamps and transfer payments make "life on the dole" at least physically tolerable in most advanced economies. Suppose that you had to choose between (*a*) the physical comforts of a typical U.S. family relying on welfare for all its income in 1988, and (*b*) the standard of living enjoyed by noble members of King Arthur's court. If you ignore the trappings of power enjoyed by feudal nobility, we suspect that you would be reluctant to trade the range of choices available to most poor Americans for life in a damp and drafty castle.

This does not mean that poor Americans have a soft life. There is no doubt that the most destitute people in our society are often homeless, cold, and hungry. Our point, instead, is that poverty is determined by cultural norms, of which material comforts are only one dimension. Wealth and income ultimately provide their holders with freedom, power, and deference from others. Poor people have relatively less power and fewer choices over their lives. And, to paraphrase Rodney Dangerfield, they "don't get no respect."

definitions rely on estimates of the costs for families of various sizes and compositions of a "minimum" diet needed for life—soybeans, liver, lard, and other basic products. Such bland menus contain adequate nutrients, but would quickly bore anyone.

You may have heard of the *poverty line,* an index estimating the costs of securing the minimal requirements for food, shelter, fuel, clothing, and transportation. This index is adjusted for family size, sex and age of the family head, number of minor children, and whether residence is rural or urban. Poverty thresholds in 1986 for various families are presented in Table 2. The poverty threshold for an average family of four now exceeds $10,000 in annual income.

Although historically one family in eight has been impoverished on average, there is tremendous turnover among the poor. During a typical decade, more than 90 percent of the poor population changes; some people fall into poverty, replacing others who move above the poverty line. In spite of policies designed to reduce inequality, roughly 1–2 percent of all people remain destitute year after year.

TABLE 2 *Poverty Cutoff Levels by Size of Family and Sex of Head of Household, 1986*

Size of Family	Poverty Threshold
1 person	$ 5,345
Under 65 years	5,440
Over 65 years	5,050
2 persons	6,870
Head under 65 years	7,080
Head over 65 years	6,370
3 persons	8,400
4 persons	10,700
5 persons	12,720
6 persons	14,360
7 or more persons	17,760

Source: U.S. Bureau of the Census, *Current Population Reports,* Series P–23, No. 28 and P–60, Nos. 81, 115, and 116, updated by authors.

Private charity alleviates some poverty, but many people see government aid as the only real remedy for the misery of poor people. Figure 5 indicates that a drop in the percentage of families below the poverty line followed the launching of several welfare programs with the declaration of a "War on Poverty" in 1964, although rapid economic growth may have provided the biggest boost to their standards of living. The attack on poverty has been two-pronged, stressing job opportunities where practical and income maintenance programs for those who cannot or will not work. Federal funding for most of these programs grew continuously for over two decades, but roughly 30 million people remained below the poverty line in 1986, and the poverty rates of black families were almost five times greater than for white families.

Reductions in the growth of social spending during the early 1980s, combined with a sharp jump in

FIGURE 5 *Percentage of U.S. Families Who Are Poor, 1960–1983*

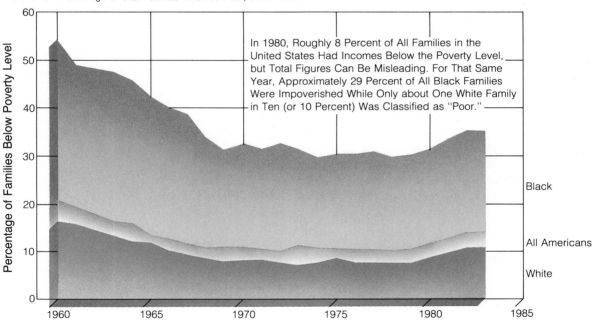

In 1980, Roughly 8 Percent of All Families in the United States Had Incomes Below the Poverty Level, but Total Figures Can Be Misleading. For That Same Year, Approximately 29 Percent of All Black Families Were Impoverished While Only about One White Family in Ten (or 10 Percent) Was Classified as "Poor."

Black

All Americans

White

Social programs developed in the 1960s probably account for much of the gradual reduction in measured poverty that has occurred. However, the economic slumps of 1974–75, 1980, and 1982–83 were periods when the percentage of those living below the poverty line increased. The number of people living in poverty is substantially less when you include in-kind government transfers as income. Finally, the data in this figure indicates that black families on average are more than three times as likely to be poor as are their white counterparts.

Source: U.S. Department of Commerce, Bureau of the Census, *Current Population Report, Consumer Income,* "Characteristics of the Population Below the Poverty Level: 1983," Series P–60, No. 147, February 1985.

unemployment rates, may have worsened the plight of many people at the bottom of the income scale. This precipitated pressures for more federal funding from many who are concerned about poverty, but these pressures were offset somewhat by opponents of welfare spending. Some opposition may emerge from prosperous taxpayers who are unwilling to share, but a growing chorus of critics are skeptical that poverty can be cured by "throwing money at it." Their view, elaborated in Focus 2, is that current welfare programs yield limited gains to some poor people, but reduce work incentives among both taxpayers and welfare recipients and foster among many recipients an unhealthy dependence on government.

Some analysts divide the impoverished into *involuntary* and *voluntary* categories. Involuntary poverty occurs among people who cannot provide for themselves; those who voluntarily choose to be impoverished could earn adequate income, but prefer to rely on welfare programs. One recent study suggests that by 1983, welfare programs were so generous that each additional $4,000 spent on welfare caused one additional family to voluntarily fall into poverty.[4] How might higher welfare spending cause people to accept lower total income? Do you know workers who hate their jobs and would cheerfully quit working if society freely gave them half their current income? Similar choices may explain why increasing numbers of people choose to be poor.

Continuing debates between the advocates and opponents of welfare programs are mirrored in swings in social policies. Knowledge of some characteristics of typical poor families should help you understand why there are people who live on the ragged edge throughout their lives.

Profiles of Poverty

F. Scott Fitzgerald once said "The rich are different from you and me." Ernest Hemingway replied, "Yes, they are different. They have more money." This exchange can be turned upside down. Are the poor inherently different from the rich, or do they simply lack money?

Numerous studies indicate that certain personal characteristics are closely related to poverty. Some of these characteristics are not matters of choice: blacks, hispanics, American Indians, and new immigrants tend to be poverty stricken more often than other population groups. The poor have relatively less education and labor participation, greater rates of illness and physical or mental disability, and relatively more children and heads of household who are female or very young or very old, as reflected in Figure 6.

Perhaps the most important determinant of income is the relationship of the family (or individual) to the labor market. Numerous studies suggest that income-earning opportunities are crucial for remedies to poverty. If jobs are the key, then government policies to maintain full employment might reduce poverty by providing job opportunities for the less fortunate. But high employment alone will not solve the problem of poverty. Unless discrimination is a barrier, job openings are generally won by those who are most willing and qualified to work. Many poor people lack the experience, training, and education a good job requires. Moreover, there are regional "pockets" of unemployment and poverty caused by the decline of some industries: Appalachian coal mining from the 1920s into the 1970s is an example. Centers for such "smokestack" industries as steel and autos experienced similar problems in the early 1980s.

Alternative Views of Poverty

Some critics of welfare programs cite evidence that the poor tend to commit more crimes and are less able, less motivated, less mobile, more reproductive, and less educated than the general population. To these critics, the high incidence of poverty among certain racial or ethnic groups reflects failings of the cultural norms common among these groups. There are, after all, prosperous members of every group. The success stories of many recent immigrants, especially from Vietnam and Cuba, are cited as evidence that protracted welfare is unnecessary. To these critics, the basic problem is failure to conform to the work ethic that has enabled other members of these

4. "The New Structural Poverty: A Quantitative Analysis," by L. Gallaway, R. Vedder, and T. Foster, in *War on Poverty—Victory or Defeat?*, Hearings before the Joint Economic Committee, June 20, 1985, U.S. Government Printing Office, 1986.

FIGURE 6 *Family Characteristics by Income Level, 1983*

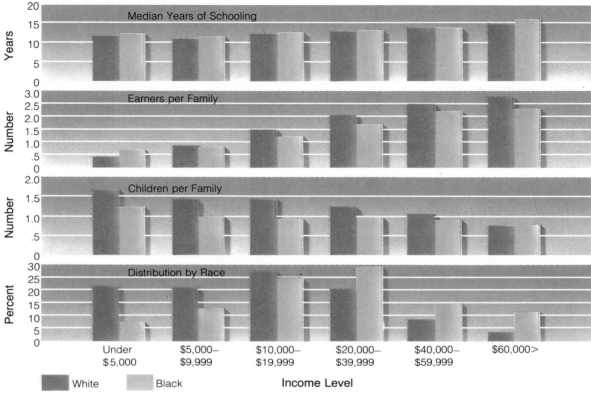

Caucasian families with few children and more than one highly educated worker bringing home the bacon tend to have the highest incomes. Black families with numerous children, few workers, and low levels of education are commonly caught in the trap of poverty.

Source: U.S. Department of Commerce, Bureau of the Census, *Current Population Report,* "Money Income of Households, Families and Persons in the United States: 1983," Series P–60, No. 146, April 1985.

same groups to succeed. These critics argue that many poor people are responsible for much of their own misery and that welfare payments are largely wastes of taxpayers' money because they reenforce the bad choices made by most of those who wind up poor.

A counterargument is that blaming the poor for their problems is misguided: that poor youngsters are obvious victims of poverty, and that lack of education, immobility, or low labor force participation rates often reflect lack of opportunity or outright discrimination. Moreover, many of the aged poor have been poor all their lives, many large families were poor before they became large, and so on. If members of certain groups are denied equal chances to

participate in the economy, those who lack skills or suffer from discrimination will remain poor. Studies suggest that racial discrimination may have accounted for as much as 40 percent of poverty in the 1960s, but more recent studies yield substantially lower estimates, an indication that discrimination may be abating.[5]

5. See J. Haworth, J. Gwartney, and C. Haworth, "Earnings, Productivity, and Changes in Employment Discrimination During the 1960s," *American Economic Review,* March 1975, pp. 158–168, and J. Long, "Earnings, Productivity, and Changes in Employment Discrimination During the 1960s: Additional Evidence," *American Economic Review,* March 1977, pp. 225–227. Thomas Sowell in *Ethnic America* (Basic Books, 1981) provides estimates that discrimination accounted for only about 10 percent of black/white wage differentials by the late 1970s.

FOCUS 2

Progress and Poverty Programs

Annual spending on social programs grew from $29.5 billion to $484.5 billion between 1960 and 1985, but the number of people living below the poverty line actually grew over this period. Architects of the "War on Poverty," begun in 1964, often assigned responsibility to the broad society for poor people's woes and saw welfare programs as compensation for social injustice. Many people maintain similar attitudes today and advocate further expansion of these programs to remedy poverty. Some recent critics of our welfare system paradoxically blame much of current poverty on attitudes and programs instituted during the 1960s. Prominent among these critics are Thomas Sowell, an economist, and Charles Murray, a political scientist.

In his 1984 book *Losing Ground,* Murray cites evidence of deterioration in the quality of life among many groups that seem stuck at the bottom. Between 1960 and 1965, black students' academic aptitude test scores rose from 68 percent to 79 percent of the average scores of whites; 1965 was the peak year for both groups. The av-

erage scores of black students on these tests had fallen to less than half of white norms by 1980. Annual rates of violent crime rose from 161 to 581 per 100,000 population between 1960 and 1980. One black child in 5 was born to an unmarried mother in the 1950s; roughly half of all black infants today are illegitimate, and rates of white illegitimacy rose from less than 1 in 50 to over 1 in 10. Six out of 7 white families include a married couple; the rate for black families has fallen sharply, to only 3 out of 5.

The basic problem, according to these recent critics, is that the rhetoric supporting many welfare programs implies that the poor bear no responsibility for alleviating their own poverty and that no stigma should be attached to being on welfare. This point of view means that the poor should not be expected to do anything for themselves; it is society's responsibility to lift people out of poverty.

These critics contend that such attitudes cause many poor people to feel like victims who cannot deal with their own problems, and who psychically

cannot claim responsibility for their accomplishments. They become trapped in a culture of poverty. Few avenues of escape are open through which to gain any sense of personal pride. The result is that some welfare families may remain on welfare for generations—suspended in a childish state of dependence on a system that is encouraged by social workers.

What solutions are available? Few critics of the current welfare system favor abandonment of all welfare programs. Cutting all public assistance to zero would flood the nation's streets with many more millions of destitute and desperate people. Instead, most of these critics propose that programs be restructured to provide more incentives for poor people to work, to keep their families together, and to diligently pursue their education and on-the-job training. Most of all, welfare programs should seek to instill in poor people a sense that they control their own destinies. In the words of Murray, "The lesson is not that we can do no good at all, but that we must pick our shots."

Economic Discrimination

Economic discrimination occurs when equivalent resources (*labor*) receive different payments (*wages*) even though their potential productive contributions are identical. There are many reasons for discrimination in labor markets. **Personal discrimination,** or **bigotry,** may play a major role, whether it is an employer's bigotry or the fear of bigotry from potential customers or other workers. This may par-

tially account for the lower average wages of women and members of some minority groups. On the other hand, managers' friends and relatives and some Caucasian males may receive preferential treatment.

Economic discrimination in labor markets takes several forms. Members of certain groups may suffer because:

1. **Wage discrimination** causes them to be paid less than members of other groups for equal work.

2. **Employment discrimination** excludes them from certain jobs.

3. **Occupational discrimination** bars them from certain occupations.

4. **Human capital discrimination** denies equal access to education or on-the-job training.

5. Outright **bigotry** fosters inequitable housing conditions, higher prices, and reduced medical care, for example.

Although bigotry stimulates the other four types of discrimination, it is not necessarily their only cause. For example, low prospective wages yield reduced incentives for investment in human capital, ultimately widening income differences.

Most of us agree that it is undesirable to discriminate on the bases of sex, race, or other characteristics irrelevant to economic contribution or personal worth. The battle against discrimination predates the American Revolution. From the time of President Lincoln's Emancipation Proclamation through the present, we have slowly marched toward an era in which government enforces a variety of civil rights legislation ensuring equal access to such things as education, housing, and employment opportunities.

Legal controversy has been a hallmark of policies intended to achieve equal opportunity: busing children to integrate our schools or imposing *affirmative action* plans to overcome past occupational, wage, and employment discrimination. Although the path to equal opportunity has been rocky, there has been major progress on the civil rights front in the past few decades. Disagreements continue, however, about the extent to which discrimination accounts for income differentials between groups, what kinds of discrimination are involved, and what policies will best remedy its effects.[6] One approach emphasizes welfare programs to compensate the victims of such earlier social policies as segregation or slavery, although extensive welfare programs are also advocated on other grounds.

---

6. Thomas Sowell, for one (in his *Ethnic America, ibid.*), has argued that affirmative action has been more hindrance than help to members of minority groups. For example, he suggests that other people who encounter minorities in professional positions or high-level jobs commonly assume that these individuals gained their status not from competency, but to "fill some quota." A prospective employer may, thus, discount the previous experience of minority applicants who might otherwise be perfect for particular jobs and who would get these jobs were it not for the presumption that their previous experience was based solely on affirmative action requirements.

Public Policies to Eliminate Poverty

Just who is "on welfare"? Who should receive welfare? How much? Such questions are meaningless without a definition of welfare: **welfare** is received by anyone for whom the ratio of the personal benefits received (B) from government programs relative to the taxes paid (T) are greater than for average taxpayers. Thus, a person is on welfare if $B_i/T_i > B_0/T_0$, where B_i and T_i are the individual's benefits and taxes and B_0 and T_0 are the total benefits and taxes in the community or society. This can also be written as $\boldsymbol{B_i/B_0 > T_i/T_0}$. For example, people are on welfare if they receive 2 percent of the total benefits from government programs ($B_i/B_0 = 0.02$) but only pay 1 percent of the taxes used to support government ($T_i/T_0 = 0.01$).

Our welfare system is an amalgam of many programs. In fact, people who are quite wealthy may be "on welfare." For example, some wealthy recipients contributed far less to Social Security than they received after they reached retirement age. Most welfare recipients are, however, in low income groups. One major welfare program provides aid for dependent children.

Aid to Families with Dependent Children

Aid to Families with Dependent Children (AFDC) is federally mandated but administered by state and local governments. Explosive growth in AFDC rolls over the past two decades has been attributed to (*a*) relaxed requirements that increased the number of eligible families, (*b*) reductions in the social stigma from being on welfare, (*c*) work **disincentives** and pressures to dissolve families inherent in AFDC payment structures, and (*d*) payment differentials that cause the poor to flock into areas where welfare benefits are the most generous. The rapid growth in enrollment has created widespread concern that the AFDC system is out of control.

Panel A in Figure 7 illustrates the work disincentive effects of the original AFDC programs. Assume that if a given family has no earnings, the AFDC grant is $3,000 annually (point *a* in Panel A). If the family earns up to an additional $3,000, the basic grant remains the same (point *b*). When the family's earn-

FIGURE 7 *Work Disincentives and Welfare Programs*

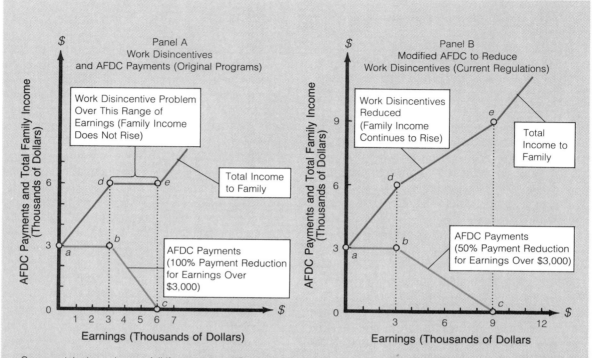

Can your take-home income fall if you earn more? When welfare programs are disjointedly tied to family income, the answer is yes. This incentive not to work is gradually being remedied, but Panel A reflects that this was a severe problem in the early 1970s. Under current regulations, the poor may face a marginal tax rate of 50 percent or more on additional income from employment, as shown in Panel B. While this still acts as a disincentive to work, it is much less severe than in the early 1970s when the adjusted marginal tax rate was often more than 100 percent for the working poor.

ings exceed $3,000, however, AFDC grants are reduced dollar-for-dollar, so this poor family gains nothing by earning between $3,000 and $6,000 yearly (points *d* to *e*). Even worse, extra income is taxed and there may be losses of *in-kind* subsidies (Medicaid, food stamps, or public housing subsidies). This opens up the possibility that a welfare family's spendable income could fall faster than its earnings grew.

Poor families were often penalized for working, so many followed the path of least resistance. AFDC benefits are especially skimpy if families include an able-bodied male, which has pressured many males to abandon their wives and kids. Panel A shows that a 100 percent payment reduction on earned income over $3,000 is equivalent to a 100 percent marginal tax rate on earned income. Families do not gain from

higher earnings if the entire increase goes to the government. These disincentives in AFDC and similar programs have contributed to the "welfare mess," as it has been labeled by the media.

In the late 1970s, modest reforms of AFDC rules were aimed at cutting the 100+ percent implicit tax rate faced by many poor families, but further changes during 1981–83 reversed some of these reforms. Average "marginal tax rates" on AFDC benefits are now estimated at around 50 percent. Today's regulations are less distortive than earlier programs in this respect. Panel B of Figure 7 shows how lower implicit tax rates allow greater work incentives. As earnings exceed $3,000, benefits fall at a rate of only $.50 per $1, not dollar-for-dollar. Labor earnings now raise welfare families' spendable income; this was a rarity under the early system.

AFDC, unemployment compensation, and Social Security are among the many welfare programs that dispense cash grants. Other systems attempt to aid the poor through in-kind subsidies, including public housing, food stamps, Medicare and Medicaid, and various education, training, and rehabilitation programs. In-kind subsidies generally entail relatively high administrative costs and implicitly assume that recipients are incompetent to manage money were it given directly to them. Most economists are skeptical of this reasoning, and view in-kind payments as inefficient. For example, it costs taxpayers roughly $1.12 to give a poor family a food stamp with a face value of $1. The $1 food coupon is worth less than $1 to most recipients because it cannot be used for purchases other than food. Cash grant programs will typically provide benefits to poor people that are closer to their costs to taxpayers. Thus, in-kind transfers are relatively inefficient forms of welfare.

Another problem area is that many government transfer programs are based on criteria other than poverty. If farmers, the elderly, families headed by single women, the members of certain minority groups, or the disabled tend to be poor, it does not follow that separate programs are required for each group. Programs to aid the blind, the infirm, the aged, or members of minority groups do not exclude the wealthy blind, the wealthy handicapped, the wealthy aged, or wealthy minorities. Similarly, there are affluent farmers, bankers, and TV station owners who are welfare recipients by our definition of welfare. They benefit from special subsidies or regulations bearing no relation to the taxes they pay.

Welfare Reform

Transfer payments of various types have been the fastest growing component of federal, state, and local government spending in the United States since World War II. A number of reforms have been proposed. Some are intended to cut the growth of transfer payments; other reforms would redistribute more income to the poor.

Workfare

The hardships of unemployment during the Great Depression resulted in a national system of **unemployment compensation** administered by the various states. Unfortunately, the side effects of this program may be as undesirable as the broken families and idleness generated by AFDC. Sporadic employment patterns are encouraged, some income goes unreported, and some people who are not truly interested in work during some periods claim to be looking for jobs—causing unemployment statistics to be overstated and misdirecting macroeconomic policymaking. Some who believe that the welfare system as a whole encourages idleness advocate *workfare* to replace welfare. Workfare would require able-bodied people who sought unemployment compensation or other public assistance to do jobs for the local government units that dole out such benefits.

Consolidation

The current welfare system is mired in paperwork caused by excessive regulations, and income maintenance programs are fragmented among unemployment compensation, AFDC, food stamps, Medicaid, public housing, Social Security, and private charity. Ridding welfare programs of the work disincentives embedded in current policies is one major task of welfare reform; another is placing the welfare system under a single administrative umbrella, reducing duplication and costs. Some major programs are not based on income and, thus, benefit people who are not poor. There may be substantial gains from consolidation—both for taxpayers and for impoverished recipients. For these reasons, many economists favor a negative income tax approach to replace existing programs. Overall, we want to get more money into the hands of the truly poor, but where possible, we wish to preserve incentives for them to earn income on their own.

Family Allowance Plans

Many European nations and most British Commonwealth countries now have **family allowance plans (FAPs).** Transfer payments are based on the minor children in a family and are generally adequate to feed and clothe each child. Family allowance plans provide basic income floors, but the incomes from these plans are then taxed as normal income and the progressivity of income taxes shrinks the FAP subsidy as a family's income rises.

Poverty seems especially unfair and harmful to children, so variants of family allowance plans were proposed by the Nixon, Ford, and Carter Administrations. A family allowance plan would be much easier and cheaper to administer than the current welfare system. It would provide greater incentives for work than the many current welfare programs that confront the poor with very high marginal tax rates; poor people's net incomes would always rise if they worked.

Finally, it would eliminate the current situation where some poor people are technically ineligible for welfare but pay taxes to provide welfare to people who are better off. (For example, an impoverished family headed by a low-wage working male may pay taxes to provide AFDC for a family without a working head of household. The AFDC payments can exceed the family income of the working male.) Insufficient income for a given family unit, including children, would be the sole criterion for net (after-tax) receipts of welfare.

Negative Income Taxes

Negative income taxes (NITs) are variants of family allowance plans. These plans attempt to balance the goals of equity and efficiency, beginning with an income floor. The level of assistance is reduced as additional income is earned by the family, but less than dollar for dollar. A typical NIT plan is diagrammed in Figure 8. The basic NIT floor on family income in this example is $6,000 and, as the family earns an additional dollar in income, NIT benefits are reduced by $0.40. Thus, the negative income tax rate is 40 percent. When the family earns $15,000 on its own, NIT benefits are zero [$6,000 − ($15,000 × $0.40) = $0]. Beyond $15,000, the family pays positive taxes like everyone else. Most economists envi-

FIGURE 8 Negative Income Taxes

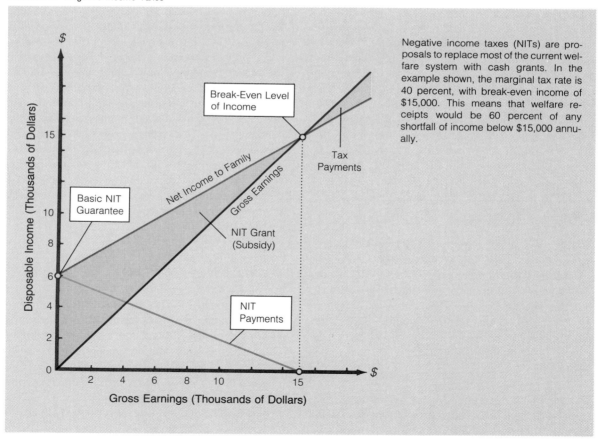

Negative income taxes (NITs) are proposals to replace most of the current welfare system with cash grants. In the example shown, the marginal tax rate is 40 percent, with break-even income of $15,000. This means that welfare receipts would be 60 percent of any shortfall of income below $15,000 annually.

sion these plans replacing all other income assistance plans. They would be administered through the Internal Revenue Service.

Conflicts Within NITs Negative income taxes would be simple to administer and would eliminate the need to dovetail numerous programs but, like any form of income assistance, NITs must balance equity and efficiency. This entails setting support levels that preserve work incentives, provide equitable income floors, and minimize administrative costs. Equity considerations might dictate high support floors while efficient work incentives require low negative marginal tax rates. The cost of a program escalates when these attributes are combined. For example, in Figure 8, if poverty levels for average families were considered to be $6,000, then the plan as diagrammed would subsidize both the poor and some nonpoor; families with earnings between $6,000 and $15,000 continue to receive subsidies.

High basic floors, low negative income tax rates, and low break-even income levels cannot coexist because, mathematically:

$$\frac{\text{break-even}}{\text{level of income}} = \frac{\text{basic income floor}}{\text{negative income tax rate}}$$

Thus, as the income floor rises or as the negative income tax rate falls, the break-even level of income rises. Tax revenues fall and the total cost of the program rises. Reduced disincentives for work may, however, cut costs by making many of the poor less reliant on the public dole. Moreover, if an NIT plan replaced the current hodgepodge of welfare programs, administrative costs should fall—allowing increases in the income floor and/or reductions in taxes.

There are other criticisms of NIT proposals, however. Some argue that NIT plans are too inflexible to solve many specific problems facing the poor. For example, older people may not be able to respond to work incentives, while youngsters need special care and assistance that parents may not provide. Others argue that in-kind services should supplement income assistance because many families may not wisely use the funds provided under an NIT plan. Proponents argue that an NIT package could provide both sufficient work incentives and an adequate income floor while replacing a bureaucratic, erratic, and expensive system with a consistent program.

In this chapter, we have looked at ethical criteria for the distribution of income and have shown that economic analysis can offer insights into solutions for issues that have a high normative content. For example, economic analysis can address such questions as whether reasonable welfare payments will lift more people out of poverty than are induced to become impoverished. Statistical studies of such issues are still relatively primitive, however. As we conclude this part of the book, we hope that you can see how microeconomic analysis can facilitate clear thinking about an enormous variety of public policies.

CHAPTER REVIEW: KEY POINTS

1. *Lorenz curves* are one method to measure inequality. Lorenz curves for income are graphical representations of the cumulative percentages of income received by given cumulative percentages of families. If the Lorenz curve is a straight-line diagonal, the income distribution is perfectly equal. Deviations from this diagonal reflect inequality in distribution.

2. Tracing the pretax and pretransfer *income distribution* since 1935 gives the appearance of little change, although the share of middle class families has grown. When taxes and transfers are considered, the U.S. income distribution has become markedly more equal since the early 1930s.

3. The Social Security Administration has developed income indices that define poverty lines for various family sizes, ages, and locations.

4. The causes of *poverty* are many and varied. Relative to middle- or upper-class families, the poor tend to have less education, few earners, and more children. These characteristics of the poor are not necessarily the causes of poverty. *Discrimination* may be an important factor. Persistent discrimination reduces incentives to invest in education and to acquire marketable skills. Discrimination is often cited as the primary reason that a relatively large proportion of black families are in the lower income categories.

5. The government's principal program to fight poverty is *Aid to Families with Dependent Children (AFDC)*. A

floor on family income is established, but as the family earns additional income, reductions of benefits from AFDC often pose extreme *disincentives* for work. Given the large number of different programs designed to help the poor, $1 increases in earned income sometimes result in more than $1 of lost benefits.

6. *Negative income tax plans (NITs)* have been suggested as solutions to the "welfare mess." Negative income tax proposals provide a floor on income; as additional income is earned, benefits are reduced but by less than the additional income earned. NIT proposals contain two essential elements: a basic floor income and a negative income tax rate. In-

creases in the floor or reductions in the negative tax rate increase the costs of the program. Equity considerations indicate needs for higher floors, while efficiency considerations point to needs for lower negative tax rates. Both goals cannot be satisfied with any one negative income tax plan.

7. Opponents of NIT proposals argue that guaranteed income floors will not solve all the problems of the poor. Proponents argue that providing sufficient income will solve the major problems. In general, NIT plans consolidate numerous programs under one administrative roof and might allow either reduced costs or increased benefits.

QUESTIONS FOR THOUGHT AND DISCUSSION

1. Should society extend welfare to the less fortunate? Should the circumstances causing their poverty be considered? If so, how? Should cash grants be emphasized, or should society directly provide: (*a*) housing? (*b*) medical care? (*c*) food stamps? Why?

2. Should we seek equality of opportunity or equality of result?

3. In what sense are income and wealth exactly proportional in equilibrium? (You may need to review the capitalization process discussed in a previous chapter to answer this question.)

4. Society devotes increasing amounts of resources to medical care for critical and sometimes incurable diseases or injuries. It is not unusual, for example, for the medical expenses of a very premature infant to exceed $1 million, and even if it survives, the long-term consequences for the child are often tragic. Many parents cannot afford such outlays, and hospitals often simply treat these costs as overhead costs to be borne by other patients. Is this use of society's resources appropriate? What are some possible opportunity costs? Is this equitable? Why or why not?

5. Family assistance plans and negative income taxes presume that the poor lack money but not the skills to manage it. Administrative costs of these programs would be relatively low. Food stamp programs, Medicaid, and the provision of social workers seem predicated on the idea that poor people would not spend money properly if it were given to them. These programs bear high administrative costs. Do you think the poor are better off if their spending is closely supervised? If so, up to what proportion of government outlays for welfare could be spent for adminis-

trators and red tape before it would be better just to give money to the poor?

6. In John Rawls's *A Theory of Justice* (Harvard, 1971), he proposes the following mental exercise as an approach for deciding how society might be made fairer. Suppose you were given a computer with a data bank containing every economic mechanism ever tried and every theory ever proposed to answer the questions of What? How? For Whom? and When? You also have the advice of any social philosopher, living or dead. Your task is to design a just society, and you must address many issues, including distributing wealth and income. Your final overall plan will be instituted worldwide. The hook is that your position in the world will then be decided randomly— providing a powerful incentive for you to consider the final positions of all people. What are some changes you would make to current social institutions?

7. In *Anarchy, State, and Utopia* (New York: Basic Books, 1974), Rawls's colleague, Robert Nozick, argues that over time, individuals acquire inalienable rights. His *entitlement theory of justice* is an ethical argument for the adage that "Possession is nine-tenths of the law." In Nozick's view, you are entitled to your property unless it can be proven that you, or the people who transferred it to you, unethically acquired it. He concludes that government redistributions of wealth or income are ethically wrong because they violate people's basic rights to choose how their property will be used. In his words, "There is no justified sacrifice of some of us for others." Do you think that historical events ethically justify the degree of inequality that now exists? Why or why not?

GLOBAL ECONOMICS

PART 10

The International Economy

International trade is becoming progressively more important to the United States. Until now, this book has focused on a *closed* economy. In this section, we open the economy up and consider how international trade and finance affect standards of living everywhere in the world.

People in many countries sing the protectionist's song—"restrict imports of 'cheap' foreign goods." Yet almost everyone ultimately gains from international trade, and it is generally foolish to severely restrict trade. These are among the major topics we address in Chapter 35.

The last vestiges of an international gold standard collapsed in the early 1970s. Many who are concerned with the problem of international payments continue to cry nostalgically for its return. The advantages and disadvantages of the different means available to pay for imports and to be paid for exports are at the heart of our discussion in Chapter 36.

Finally, the last chapter of this book examines some of the various philosophies that underlie alternative economic systems and how these philosophies have been put into practice. In our modern world, everyone should know something about how other economies operate and what their advantages and disadvantages are.

CHAPTER 35 | # International Trade

There are enormous advantages to specialized production and exchange. The gains to Hawaiians and Texans from trading sugar and pineapples for gasoline and cotton are fairly obvious examples. Similar advantages are derived from transactions whether the people with whom we deal are American or foreigners. The exchange of goods and services across national boundaries is called **international trade.** Trade is generally a positive sum game; both sides expect to gain or they do not trade. International trade involves more complications than domestic transactions, however, because of differences in currencies and national policies.

In this chapter, we discuss the nature of international trade and some of the advantages and possible disadvantages of commerce among nations. Who gains? Who loses? How large are these gains and losses? We will also evaluate some arguments against free trade.

The Size and Scope of Trade

International trade subtly affects the daily lives of American consumers in ways most of us don't even notice. We drink coffee from South America, cocoa from Ghana, or tea from India; wear Swiss watches and clothes made in China or Korea; watch televisions made in Japan; and burn gasoline refined from Arab oil in Volkswagens, Fiats, or Toyotas. And most of our shoes, the graphite in our pencils, and even the elastic in our underwear comes from abroad.

Year after year, international trade grows in importance throughout the world. Among industrialized nations, international trade as a percentage of GNP ranges from 6 to 10 percent in the United States to roughly 30 percent in Great Britain. In absolute terms, the sheer size of the United States makes it the single most important international trader; our ex-

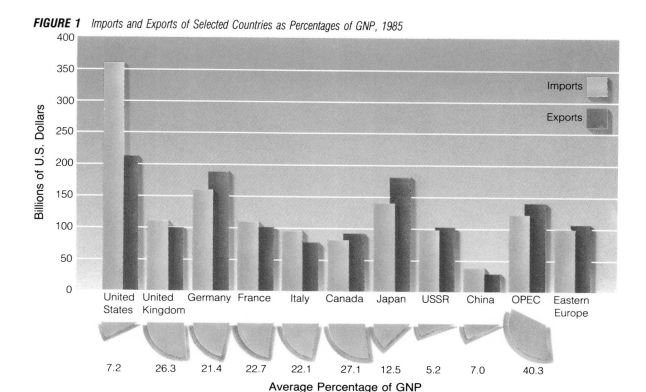

FIGURE 1 *Imports and Exports of Selected Countries as Percentages of GNP, 1985*

Although the United States is a major trader, trade is less important to us as a percentage of GNP than it is to any other developed nation. Curiously, Japan is not as heavily dependent on trade as some might think. Highly specialized countries, such as OPEC member nations, are heavily dependent on trade. The major communist powers are not major traders.

Source: *Economic Report of the President,* 1986.

ports and imports each exceed $200 billion annually. Statistics that indicate the importance of international trade in some of the world's major trading nations are displayed in Figure 1. Generally, however, international trade is even more crucial to small countries than to large ones.

Foreign countries are markets for the goods we produce. Imports add to our Aggregate Supply; they are sources of consumption and investment goods. At the same time, however, they detract from Aggregate Demand, making marketing more difficult for the producers of the domestic goods with which they compete. Consequently, macroeconomic policymakers throughout the world must contend with the impact of international trade on domestic inflation, unemployment, economic growth, and the level of GNP.

Why Do Nations Trade?

The United States contains vast amounts of fertile land, immense supplies of raw materials, an unmatched stock of capital equipment, and a highly skilled work force. Our GNP is more than twice that of our nearest competitor, but exports and imports each average 6–10 percent of our GNP. Why do we bother to trade with the rest of the world?

One reason for foreign trade is that certain natural or technological resources are inadequate to provide for domestic consumption and investment. This is why we import Bolivian tin and export airplanes, farm equipment, and computers to Bolivia. Even when self-sufficiency is possible, foreign trade is often advantageous. Figure 2 indicates the composi-

FIGURE 2 *The Percentage Composition of U.S. Exports and Imports, 1985*

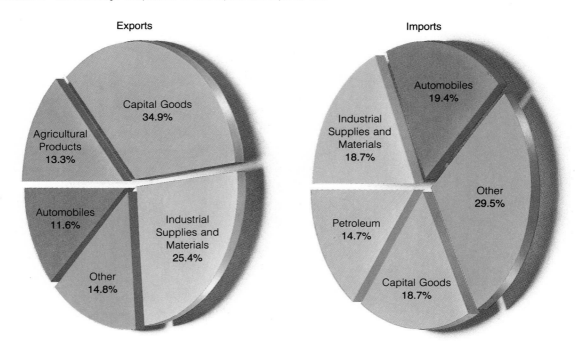

The composition of our exports appears roughly balanced, except for net imports of fuels and minerals and net exports of machinery and agricultural products. However, each of these broad categories disguises a rich diversity of imports and exports.

Source: *Economic Report of the President,* 1986.

tion of U.S. foreign trade and Figure 3 reveals which regions are our principal trading partners.

For any economic system to operate efficiently, it needs every form of production to be done at the lowest possible opportunity cost. If the opportunity costs of producing everything everywhere are minimized, the total value of global production is maximized. This requires international trade—a way for consumers to get goods at lower costs without having to travel to where they are produced, and for resource owners (e.g., labor) to receive higher income without having to relocate to wherever their products are most advantageously consumed.

The Incomplete "Principle" of Absolute Advantage

The concept of **absolute advantage** emerges from the fact that some individuals (or nations) can produce more of a good from given resources than

can others. For example, one Arabian worker can get more oil out of 10 acres of Arab land than could one Georgian working the same size plot in Georgia. However, the Georgian might be able to raise more peanuts per acre than could the Arab. In this case, the Arab has an absolute advantage in oil production, while the Georgian has an absolute advantage in peanut growing. Obviously, each could gain from specialized production and trade. This notion led early economists (for example, Adam Smith) to offer the **principle of absolute advantage:** Nations gain by producing goods that they can make at lower resource cost and exchanging their surpluses for goods that others can produce at lower resource costs.

The major problem with the absolute advantage explanation of trade is that it does not explain how trade can be beneficial when one of the trading parties has an absolute advantage in producing almost all goods (or, in a simple model, each of two goods).

FIGURE 3 *Major U.S. Trading Partners, 1985*

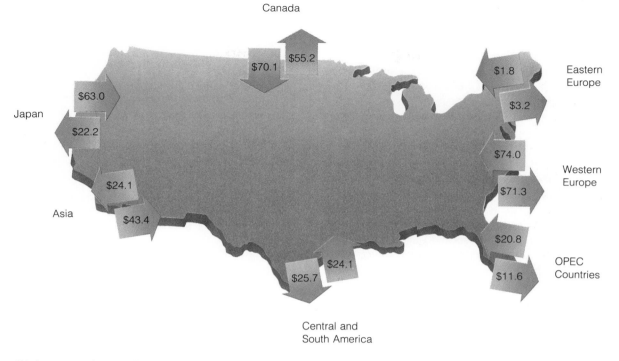

Canada

Japan

Asia

Eastern Europe

Western Europe

OPEC Countries

$70.1 $55.2 $1.8 $3.2 $63.0 $22.2 $74.0 $71.3 $24.1 $43.4 $20.8 $24.1 $25.7 $11.6

Central and South America

We have recently run deficits with most of our major trading partners, especially Japan and the OPEC countries.
Note: All figures presented here are in billions of U.S. dollars.
Source: *Economic Report of the President,* 1986.

 ## The Law of <u>Comparative Advantage</u>

Suppose that typical American workers can produce either four handwoven wicker baskets or eight electric typewriters annually, while Chinese workers can average only two wicker baskets or one typewriter. The absolute advantage approach offers no reason why Americans might gain through trade. The law of comparative advantage was developed by David Ricardo (1772–1823) and shows how trade can enrich people in both countries, even though American workers have absolute advantages in both goods.

Table 1 helps to illustrate this key concept in international trade. Without trade, two typewriters must be sacrificed to produce each wicker basket in the United States, while in China, each basket costs only half of a typewriter. Imagine that you could costlessly move between the United States and China and that you initially had one basket. You could begin by trading it for two typewriters in the United States and

then trade the typewriters for four baskets in China, for which you would receive eight typewriters in the United States, and so on. Successively trading American typewriters for Chinese blankets, and vice versa, would enable you to grow rich.

China increasingly would specialize in basketry and the U.S. in typewriter production. As long as the costs of baskets relative to typewriters did not change (price ratios of 2:1 in the U.S. and 1:2 in China), no one in either country would lose and you would gain. This specialization and exchange is an example of how trade can increase economic efficiency; you have gained and no one has lost.

Our example is a bit misleading since we assumed that the prices of typewriters relative to baskets did not change in either the United States or China. Moreover, you had no competition as a trader. Since merchants who deal internationally face substantial competition, it is unlikely that you can get rich as an arbitrager.

Arbitrage and Trade We encountered *arbitrage* in Chapter 4—the process of buying at a lower price in one market and selling at a higher price in another market; both prices must be known to the arbitrager and the price differential must exceed transaction costs. Whenever differentials in relative prices between markets exceed the transaction costs associated with intermarket transfers of goods, arbitragers profit without risk by buying at the lower price and selling at the higher price.

This process increases demand in the market with the lower price, driving the price up, and increases supply in the market with the higher price, sending the price down. Hence, arbitrage pressures relative prices toward equality in all markets. In our example, the relative price of typewriters to baskets might go from 2:1 in the United States and 1:2 in China to, say, 1:1 in both countries. Americans import "cheap" baskets from China while the Chinese import "cheap" typewriters from the United States.

Because competition between arbitragers tends to keep the economic profits of traders near zero, the gains you might have experienced in our example actually would have been split between Americans and Chinese. American typewriter makers and basket consumers would gain as the price of typewriters relative to baskets rose. (The price of baskets in the United States falls.) Similarly, Chinese basket makers and typewriter consumers would gain as the prices of baskets relative to typewriters rose. However, American producers and Chinese consumers of baskets might lose, and so might American consumers and Chinese producers of typewriters. In a moment we will prove that the gains generally exceed the losses.

Using similar examples, David Ricardo (in 1817) came up with the following law:

The **law of comparative advantage:** *Mutually beneficial trade can always take place between two countries whose pretrade relative opportunity costs and price structures differ.*

Ricardo's Biography has more information.

The Terms of Trade The law of comparative advantage suggests that mutually beneficial trade can take place whenever the relative costs of production differ between nations. The phrase *terms of trade* refers to the prices of exported goods relative to imported goods after trade is in full swing:

$$\text{terms of trade} = \frac{\textbf{prices of exports}}{\textbf{prices of imports}}.$$

In our example using typewriters and baskets, typewriters initially cost only half a basket in the United States but two baskets in China, while baskets cost two typewriters in the United States but only half a typewriter in China; trade yielded a 1:1 price ratio for these goods in both countries. Intuitively, the terms of trade should settle somewhere between the relative prices of the goods in the two countries before trade occurs.

Gains from Trade

You gained from being an arbitrager in our example. We know, however, that competition among arbitragers would distribute the bulk of these gains from trade between Chinese and American households. There are several different ways that people in different nations gain from trade.

Uniqueness Gains First, there are **uniqueness gains** derived because, without trade, some goods simply might not be available in certain regions. For

TABLE 1 Outputs per Worker and Their Costs

| Country | Typewriters per Worker | Baskets per Worker | Pretrade Costs | | Free Trade Costs |
			Typewriters per Basket	Baskets per Typewriter	
United States	8	4	2	1/2	1:1
China	1	2	1/2	2	1:1

David Ricardo (1772–1823)

David Ricardo's genius was illustrated in the practical world of affairs as well as in the realm of ideas. Disinherited by his wealthy Jewish father for marrying a Quakeress at the age of twenty-one, Ricardo and his bride joined the Unitarian church, which at the time was viewed as a radical sect.

Ricardo successfully pursued a business career as stockjobber and then as loan contractor. When he was forty-two, his accumulated wealth permitted him to retire from business. Bored with the idle life, he turned his attention to politics and intellectual pursuits. After a hesitant beginning as a writer on economic subjects, Ricardo etched his name on the pages of history by publishing a treatise, *On the Principles of Political Economy and Taxation*. He was not an accomplished writer, having a heavy-handed, obscure, and abstract style. Nevertheless, the force of his logic almost immediately attracted a close-knit band of gifted, if dogmatic, disciples.

Ricardo's appeal was based on his ability to cast a wide assortment of serious problems into simple analytical models. These simple models considered only a few strategic variables but yielded sweeping conclusions of a very practical nature. One example of Ricardo's penetrating insight concerns the doctrine of comparative costs. Earlier economists had taught that it pays a country to concentrate on the production of those goods it can produce more cheaply than any other country and to import those goods it can obtain at less cost than it could produce them at home. Ricardo developed the following not-so-obvious implication of this doctrine: Under free trade, not all goods are necessarily produced in countries where their absolute cost of production is lowest. He demonstrated that it could benefit a country to import something, even though it could produce the same product with fewer resources at home. Ricardo's demonstration rests on the idea of relative efficiency, or comparative costs.

Ricardo's principle is developed in greater detail in the present chapter, but it is important to note that the core of all free trade arguments harks back to this Ricardian principle. Ricardo's discussion of land rent and his analysis of taxation were also trailblazing works that place modern economists forever in his debt.

---

example, diamonds, chromium, tin, petroleum, and many other minerals are not distributed smoothly across the earth's surface. Goods that must be produced with these natural resources would not be available at all to many of the world's people without international trade. This is also true of certain food, fiber, and animal products, such as various spices, bananas, coffee, cocoa, tobacco, and frozen fish.

Short-Run Specialization Gains

People gain from imports even if they could produce the same goods because, through specialization, there are increases in the purchasing power of their incomes. Access to export markets increase the values of what many people produce. Even those who do not work directly on exported goods ultimately have higher incomes because of competition in resource markets. Moreover, they are able to buy goods at lower prices and opportunity costs than if they had to rely solely on domestic production. These are the **short-run specialization gains** from international trade. Some people who compete with imports may suffer disruptions to their incomes and temporarily lose because of expanded trade, but in a moment we will prove that even alone, these short-run gains from trade generally outweigh any losses.

Long-Run Dynamic Gains There are longer run **dynamic gains** from trade that occur because trade speeds the process of economic growth and development. These include gains from the spread of new technologies, which would be unknown in some regions if the people of each country worked in isolation from their neighbors. Technological advances tend to feed on each other—one researcher has an idea that is improved upon by another, who stimulates a third, *ad infinitum*. Can you imagine how primitive our world would be if every national group had to rediscover for itself the wheel, electricity, and the advantages of indoor plumbing? Another aspect of the dynamic gains from trade is that the higher levels of national production and incomes generated through trade make it easier for people to save and invest, also facilitating economic growth and development.

International Political Stability Finally, there are gains in the form of **political spin-offs** from the economic advantages of international trade. To the extent that trade raises our standards of living, it also makes us more dependent upon the people of other nations, and they on us. This raises the potential losses from war and other hostilities, and reduces the likelihood of conflict; we all have more incentives to be friendly if we are interdependent.

Net Gains from Specialization

Some of these gains from trade are fairly obvious. We turn now to demonstrating those gains that are the least clear in the minds of many people. Exchange confers *net* gains to the participants; even in the short run, the gains from specialization and trade generally exceed any losses. Comparative advantage is the key concept we use to investigate the gains (and losses?) from trade.

In our example in which Chinese baskets were traded for American-made typewriters, you, as the merchant, realized gains by buying where prices were relatively low and selling where they were higher. The benefits were not shared between Americans and Chinese.

Here is a simple short-run model to illustrate that there are generally net gains from trade and to suggest who shares in them. Although we consider only two countries, the logic does not change if we con-

sider any country vis-à-vis the rest of the world, or a host of products instead of only two. In fact, dealing with larger numbers of countries and goods increases the net gains that are realized. We will begin with the following assumptions:

1. Production-possibilities curves for both China and the United States are characterized by constant opportunity costs.
2. Resources can move freely among industries, but are immobile between countries.
3. Only two goods (typewriters and woven baskets) are produced and traded.
4. There are technological differences between production in the United States and in China.
5. Goods may be transported freely between countries.
6. All prices are perfectly flexible.

These assumptions may not be very realistic, but they are used only to illustrate a point; relaxation of these assumptions does not change the basic conclusions of this analysis.

Let us begin by assuming that the aggregate production relationships for the United States and China are similar to those suggested earlier in Table 1. We will assume that workers in the United States can annually produce 400 million baskets, 800 million typewriters, or any combination in between. These production options yield constant opportunity costs of two baskets per typewriter. Similarly, Chinese workers are able to produce 400 million typewriters or 800 million baskets annually. (We assume that China's labor force is four times as large as ours.)

Constant opportunity costs of production yield linear production-possibilities frontiers (*PPFs*) like those shown as solid lines in Figure 4. (Note that Figure 4 is a graphical reflection of Table 2.) These production-possibilities frontiers can also be thought of as **consumption-possibilities frontiers (*CPFs*)** since, without trade, neither country could sustain consumption beyond these boundaries. Suppose that both countries are originally producing and consuming at points *a* in Panels A and B. Finally, assume that the final trading ratio is 1:1—one typewriter trades for one basket.

The United States will specialize in the good with lowest production costs, typewriters, with an annual production of 800 million units. Each typewriter may now be traded for a basket so that a total of up to 800 million typewriters plus baskets might be consumed. The American *CPF* expands as shown in Panel A of

FIGURE 4 How Trade Expands Consumption Possibilities

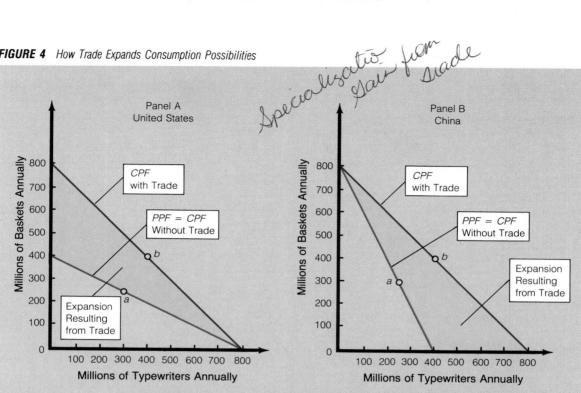

Panel A
United States

Panel B
China

CPF
with Trade

PPF = CPF
Without Trade

Expansion
Resulting
from Trade

CPF
with Trade

PPF = CPF
Without Trade

Expansion
Resulting
from Trade

Millions of Baskets Annually

Millions of Typewriters Annually

Prior to trade, a country's sustainable consumption possibilities are limited by its production-possibilities frontier. When trade commences, both trading partners experience net gains from trade because, by specializing in those goods they produce at lowest relative cost and by importing those things that they find costly to make themselves, they can each consume more of *all* goods. Thus, their consumption possibilities expand beyond their production possibilities, just as we gain individually by trading with others instead of relying strictly on what we personally produce.

TABLE 2 Specialization Gains from Trade

Country Commodity	(1) Output and Consumption Before Trade (Millions)	(2) Production After Trade Commences (Millions)	(3) Exports (−) Imports (+) (Millions) Terms of Trade Are 1:1	(4) Consumption After Trade (Millions) (2) + (3)	(5) Gains from Trade (Millions) (4) − (1)
United States					
Typewriters	300	800	−400	400	100
Baskets	250	0	+400	400	150
China					
Typewriters	250	0	+400	400	150
Baskets	300	800	−400	400	100

Figure 4. Symmetrically, China will specialize in basket production (800 million annually) and, by trading baskets for typewriters, will be able to expand its consumption to any combination of baskets and typewriters along the *CPF* curve in Panel B.

For simplicity, we have assumed that after trade has commenced, each country consumes at point *b* in both panels. Table 2 outlines the specific gains from trade to each country. In the United States, annual consumption of typewriters rises by 100 million units and annual consumption of baskets rises by 150 million units. Similar gains are realized by China.

Notice that people in both countries are able to consume more of both commodities. This is a very real possibility with any specialization and exchange, whether within national boundaries or internationally. At a local level, an example is the home builder whose family has a much nicer house than if the family had to produce its own food, clothing, and all of the other amenities of life, in addition to its own home.

Even in the short run, moving toward free trade is, in a sense, like economic growth fostered by tremendous technological advances. We can consume more even though we have not increased the resources available. The results of this analysis are unambiguous; even in the short run, the gains from free trade to both countries will typically outweigh any losses. Trade is normally a positive sum game.

In our example, the final terms of trade were 1:1, or the exact midpoint of the no-trade prices. There is no reason to expect an exact midpoint solution—the prices of all goods, including those traded internationally, are also influenced by the forces of demand. The production-possibilities frontiers we have used here only affect supplies. We have focused on the supply side, but explicitly considering the demand side would not substantively change our conclusion that trade confers net gains to the trading parties.

Short-Run Gainers and Losers from Trade

You lose anytime the price of the thing you sell falls relative to the prices of the things you buy. Thus, economists talk about an "adverse change in the terms of trade" whenever the prices of exported goods fall relative to the prices of imported goods. For example, an adverse change in the terms of trade affected the United States in the early 1970s: the price of imported oil skyrocketed, while the increasing competition we faced in export markets precluded similar hikes in the prices of merchandise we sold abroad.

When trade is first initiated, the changes in the relative prices of imports and exports benefit some people and harm others. On balance, though, the gains exceed any losses. In a sense, some individuals may suffer adverse changes in their individual "terms of trade" if free trade exposes their products to competition from foreigners whose production costs are lower. We will examine a simple demand and supply model of the international woven basket market so that you can see why free trade is not universally popular.

For simplicity, we will assume that the dollar is the common currency throughout the world; the complications associated with a multicurrency world are the subject of international finance. We will also abandon the confines of our "constant cost" model.

Figure 5 depicts market demands and supplies for baskets in the United States (Panel A) and in China (Panel C). Without trade, the price of baskets in the United States would be $800 (or 2 typewriters). At every price below $800, there is an excess demand (XD) for baskets in the United States. Domestic producers are willing to supply fewer baskets than American buyers would want to purchase. This excess demand, or shortage (the horizontal distance between the supply and demand curves), is graphed as XD_a in the center panel of Figure 5 and indicates how many baskets would be imported at various prices.

In China, baskets would cost only $400 each (or half a typewriter) without the American export market. At prices exceeding $400, Chinese wicker weavers are willing to sell more baskets than Chinese consumers are willing and able to buy. This excess supply (XS), or surplus (the horizontal distance between the supply and demand curves), is graphed as XS_c in the center panel of Figure 5 and indicates how many Chinese baskets would be available for export at various prices greater than $400.

Equilibrium between our willingness to import and China's willingness to export occurs when our excess demand is equal to their excess supply. With free trade, baskets will sell for $600 in both the United States and China; annual Chinese production will increase to 11 million baskets, but American production will drop by 1 million baskets annually. Moreover, Chinese purchases of baskets decline by 1 million, while American basket buying rises by 2 million annually.

Individual Gainers and Losers Who gains and who loses? Chinese basket makers gain—they sell more baskets at higher prices. American basket buyers gain—the price of a new basket in the United States

FIGURE 5 *International Excess Demands and Supplies*

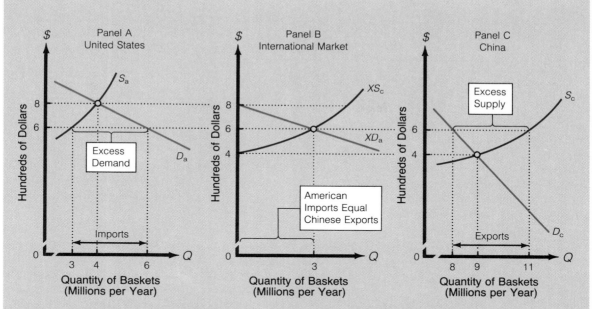

Panel A shows that at basket prices below $800, the United States has excess demands. Panel C indicates that China has excess supplies of baskets at prices above $400. When American excess demands confront China's excess supplies in international markets (Panel B), imports and exports must be equal, and a price is determined that will prevail in both markets. (Excess supplies are the horizontal distances from demand to supply curves; excess demands are the horizontal distances from supply curves to demand curves.)

has declined (from $800 down to $600) and purchases have increased. Now, for those who lose, at least in the short run. American basket makers lose because the price falls to $600 (from $800). Chinese basket buyers lose as the price rises to $600. New basket ownership in China may decline and basket production in the United States falls. Note, however, that the total world production of baskets has risen by 1 million units.

Because (in this example) Americans are buying $1.8 billion worth of baskets from China ($600 × 3 million), we will have "balanced trade" if we annually export $1.8 billion worth of typewriters to the Chinese. We could build figures for the typewriter market similar to Figure 5 and would conclude that trade causes typewriter prices to fall in China, while the prices of typewriters rise in the United States. In addition, employment and output of the Chinese typewriter industry declines, but less than the American typewriter industry grows. There will be more

of both typewriters and baskets after trade commences.

Table 3 summarizes the gainers and short-term losers from trading typewriters for baskets, and vice versa. You should keep in mind, however, that this analysis only looks at short-run *specialization* gains and losses from trade in only two goods. When the analysis is broadened to consider the much wider array of goods that are actually traded internationally, and when the uniqueness, dynamic, and political spin-off gains are considered as well, it is hard to imagine that anyone loses from free trade in the long run.

Can we be fairly certain that if we consider only the short-term gains and losses that the gains to the four groups of winners more than offset the costs imposed on the four groups of losers? We can. The previous section suggests that each country will enjoy net gains from free trade in most cases. The total value of production and consumption rises in both

TABLE 3 *Gainers from Specialization and Short-Run Losers from Trade*

Country	Gainers	Losers
United States	Typewriter sellers Basket buyers	Typewriter buyers Basket sellers
China	Typewriter buyers Basket sellers	Typewriter sellers Basket buyers

countries. Worldwide production of each good rises as trade is initiated. Because the consumption-possibilities frontier expands for both countries, the gainers in each country could (but seldom do) compensate the losers from trade so that every man, woman, and child in both countries gains. (If I gain $50 from a transaction that causes you to lose $20, we will both be ahead if I share my gain by giving you $25.)

Trade Adjustment Assistance

Most of the successful movements to restrict trade have been launched by groups who lose because they suffer comparative disadvantages when forced to compete with foreign producers. They are effective politically because they are strongly opposed to the importation of particular products. Suppose that 100,000 people would lose $10,000 apiece annually if restrictions on textiles imports were eliminated (a total of $1 billion). At the same time, 200 million other Americans will shell out an average of an extra $10 a year for clothing (a total of $2 billion) if textile imports continue to be restricted. In other words, you have 100,000 people who will vote for or against politicians based largely on their platforms on textile quotas and 200 million people who are, for the most part, oblivious to their personal losses and of politicians' positions on trade. It is fairly easy to see why trade is so restricted, isn't it?

Let us see why trade restrictions are inefficient and what might be done to ensure that everyone gains from free trade. In our example, if the 200 million consumers each contributed $6 annually to a relief fund for the 100,000 textile workers, each textile worker could receive $12,000 annually. If we set up the relief fund only with the precondition that textiles be freely imported, textile workers would

gain ($2,000 each) and so would textile consumers ($4 each annually). Clearly, this would be a move in the direction of economic efficiency; everyone gains and no one loses.

Examples like this caused the inclusion in recent trade acts of *adjustment assistance* provisions, intended to provide retraining and financial assistance for workers displaced because of liberalized international trade. It is, unfortunately, very difficult to identify the losers from lowering barriers to trade. The Congress has failed to provide much funding for this program, viewing it as a welfare program for the middle class. Trade adjustment assistance was among the first programs on the chopping block when President Reagan sought to reduce government spending. The net result is that the 1980s have been a period of rising sentiment for trade restrictions. Support for higher trade barriers is voiced by many unions and managers of declining industries threatened by foreign competition.

Arguments Against Free Trade

Free trade generally enhances economic efficiency. Goods tend to be produced at minimum opportunity cost and then traded by their producers for other goods that are subjectively more valuable. This leads to maximization of the value of the world's production. Then why is free trade the exception instead of the general practice? The answer lies in arguments *against* free trade and *for* import barriers against foreign goods. Some arguments are partially valid, but others verge on the irrational. All too commonly, irrational arguments prove persuasive, or partially valid charges against free trade are applied incorrectly. We will begin by examining the least defensible of these and then work up the ladder to the most telling thrusts against free trade.

The Exploitation Doctrine

Some people perceive trade as a zero sum game. They reason that if one trading party gains, the other party must lose. Thus, if we gain, we must be exploiting our trading partner. This sort of reasoning may hold for poker or roulette, but the clear-cut gains from trade we have described indicate that people on both sides of an exchange gain. Transactions do not occur without expectations of gain. The belief that people in less developed countries lose absolutely and so are exploited when they trade with people in developed countries is clearly erroneous.

A slightly more sophisticated argument is that trade results in "relative oppression" of the less powerful trading party. That is, the gains from trade to the more powerful party far outweigh any benefits to the less powerful trader. This argument is normally wrong because the gains from trade are generally largest to small countries: the less your trade affects the terms of trade offered by your trading partners, the greater is your ability to take advantage of differences in the relative opportunity costs of production.

Perhaps it is easiest to see this point with some concrete examples. Monaco, a very small country, relies very heavily on trade and would be far less prosperous if it did not operate in the world market. The United States and Germany, on the other hand, have wide markets internally as well as a diversity of resources. These two giants rely less on international trade than do countries like Monaco or even Switzerland. Can you imagine how destitute the tiny Arab emirate of Kuwait might be without trade? Its natural resources consist largely of sand, camels, oil, and more sand. Through trade, the Kuwaiti per capita income now exceeds that of most Americans.

Retaliation

Many countries restrict imports from the United States, so why shouldn't we retaliate with barriers against their exports? This argument is often directed at Japan, which severely restricts imports of American machinery and agricultural products. The problem with this line of reasoning is that it ignores the harmful effects on American citizens of retaliatory policies. When we restrict imports, we reduce the amounts of goods and services available to Americans, and domestic prices rise. Although foreign governments' restrictive policies may hurt us, we can only com-

pound the damage through retaliatory policies. We may harm foreign producers, but we harm ourselves as well. In fact, some analysts argue that the worldwide depression of the 1930s was substantially worsened because of escalating retaliation by many major trading nations, and they fear that a major trade war could cause another global depression.

Antidumping

The accusation that foreign producers compete unfairly by "dumping" is raised almost anytime an American producer is undersold. **Dumping** occurs when a country exports goods at lower prices than those charged domestically for identical goods. Dumping might result from international price discrimination, which is a policy of charging desperate (domestic) buyers more than less desperate (foreign) buyers are charged. In such a case, customers in the country "dumped on" are the beneficiaries of the discriminatory policy. Alternatively, a foreign government might attempt to create jobs by subsidizing exports. (Japan is commonly accused of such policies.) Finally, there may be "predatory" dumping, which means that a country follows a strategy of driving competitors out of the market in order to establish a worldwide monopoly. Presumably, prices could then be raised to yield monopoly profits. However, there is scant evidence of dumping, and it is dubious that dumping actually occurs. And even if it does occur, the customers who buy at lower prices benefit from dumping. Should our government protect Americans from low prices?

Infant Industries

Although loud clamoring for protection is now heard from **senile industries,** a slightly more valid but still misleading argument for trade restrictions is the protection of **infant industries.** Shortly after the American Revolution, Alexander Hamilton argued that British industrial superiority only reflected a head start over American economic development. He felt that protection of American infant industries from low-cost British competition was necessary for this country's industrialization.

Figure 6 shows what happens if production costs decline as industrialization proceeds. If the world price is P_w for some commodity and average production costs follow the path of AC_0 over time, eventually declining to P_w, then in the long run a protected

FIGURE 6 *The Error in Infant Industry Arguments*

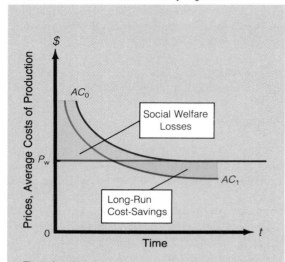

The infant industry argument suggests that protection should be used so that immature industries can become competitive in the world market. However, tariffs or quotas designed to buffer infant industries from foreign competition will cause losses of social welfare (the blue area) unless they are offset by extraordinarily low costs (the red area) in the long run. Of course, if such cost savings are possible, there is no need for protection because profit-seekers will invest in this industry anyway.

infant industry will mature, be competitive in the world market, and not require a protective tariff. Notice, however, that if consumers buy constant quantities of the protected good in each period, they lose an amount equal to the red area below AC_0 and above P_w. This loss is inefficient because these burdens are not offset by lower costs after the industry is established.

A path like AC_1 is necessary for the efficient establishment of a new industry. The discounted value of the long-run lower costs (gray) must exceed the initial losses (red). Of course, if entrepreneurs perceive that in the long run they will achieve average production costs that are below world prices, they will build the new industry without protection. And even if the infant industry argument is sometimes partially valid, it would be better to subsidize the industry than to protect it with trade barriers.

Even though it contains the barest kernel of logic and is largely invalid, the infant industry argument has been used by many less developed countries to justify protectionist policies. The almost uniform result is inefficient production and little or no increase over time in per capita income.

For example, protection of a government-subsidized Indian automobile plant was rationalized by an infant industry argument in the 1970s. Directed by Sanjay Ghandi, the former prime minister's son, the factory ultimately produced only a few vehicles that were about as large and reliable as Fiats—at an average cost of around $60,000 each (in 1986 dollars). The high price tag is an example of how ignoring comparative advantages can lead to financial disaster. Indians would have been far better off if their government had focused on production that used labor (its abundant factor) more intensively and capital (its scarce resource) less.

Trade Deficits and Imbalances of International Payments

Concerns about deficits in balances of trade or payments are, in part, throwbacks to a discredited theory called *mercantilism*. Mercantilists argued that a country grows stronger by exporting more than it imports and drawing the balances in gold. Adam Smith shot this theory down by pointing out that, not money, but the real goods and resources available are the true economic strength and wealth of a nation. Nevertheless, there may be times when trade or payment imbalances are legitimate concerns for policymakers.

Some people advocate tariffs or quotas to reduce trade or balance of payment deficits. The resource misallocations that result are seldom worth any improvement in the balance of payments. If we are running a trade deficit and there are net outflows of funds that "weaken the dollar," it is usually better to allow natural market adjustments or macroeconomic policies to rectify the imbalance.

Moreover, there is the very real threat that other countries will retaliate if we impose trade barriers to solve imbalances of trade or payments. Finally, shouldn't we be happy that foreigners are willing to sell us more than we sell them—if they are willing to take dirty green paper for the difference? Just as decapitation will cure the common cold, trade barriers may cure deficits in the balances of trade or payments, but better remedies are available.

Job Destruction

The unending argument that imports reduce domestic employment is based on some simpleminded logic: If we do not import some good, then we will produce it ourselves. One fallacy in this thinking is obvious: If imports reduce employment, exports expand employment. In fact, one recent study suggests that almost 50 percent more jobs are created in export industries than are lost because of imports. Another problem is that import restrictions are likely to invite retaliation and cause job destruction in export industries.

When imports threaten the survival of an industry, the marketplace is signaling that the industry is relatively inefficient and may be senile. Resources will be allocated more efficiently and ultimately be better paid if they are moved into areas in which they have comparative advantages. Import restrictions keep comparatively inefficient industries operating and retard the growth of efficient ones. We can trade good jobs for bad jobs through tariffs or quotas, but we do not operate efficiently when we do so.

Harmful Income Redistribution

When trade occurs, those who own relatively scarce resources gain more than the losses imposed on those whose resources are relatively abundant worldwide. To use a very simple model, the U.S. is comparatively abundant in capital (capital is relatively scarce worldwide) and has relatively few labor resources, which are plentiful globally. With trade, U.S. capital owners have greater access to customers, while American workers face competition from low wage foreign labor. This simple model suggests that wages fall while returns to capital rise; the net gains from trade are received exclusively by capital owners. Although capital owners could more than compensate workers for the income reductions caused by trade, our institutions are not geared to accomplish such transfers (e.g., federal failure to fund trade adjustment assistance). Hence, working class people suffer while the rich get richer.

This simple model may explain some of the American labor movement's support for tariffs and quotas. If we are truly concerned about inequality in income distribution, however, we should not ignore the gains to poor foreign workers when their products are exported, nor should we forget the uniqueness, dynamic, and political spin-off benefits of trade.

This argument also fails to consider some of the major sources of our comparative advantages. A partial rebuttal is that, more than any other form of resource, the United States has relative abundances of rich farmland and highly skilled, technology oriented labor. These productive factors are relatively scarce in the rest of the world, so American agricultural incomes and the incomes of highly skilled workers are enhanced by international trade. The post-World War II industrialization of Western Europe and Japan has shifted this country's gains from trade away from capitalists toward highly skilled workers and farmers. Less developed countries have also benefited enormously from increased competition among modern industrial powers for raw materials.

Exploiting Monopoly/Monopsony Power

When a country is a major importer or exporter of some good, it can flex its economic muscles through trade restrictions to drive prices up or down. For example, a country having monopoly power might be able to impose an export tariff that would be borne in part by "foreign devils." If so, it is conceivable that the citizens of the exporting country would gain.

The monopolistic or monopsonistic unit may gain tremendously by manipulating its levels of output or purchases and, hence, prices—but only by imposing even greater losses on its customers or suppliers. For example, the Organization of Petroleum Exporting Countries (OPEC) jacked up oil prices by over 1,000 percent during the 1970s by agreeing to raise prices and restrict the outputs of member countries. They prospered for a period—but at the cost of worldwide economic recession, which was especially hard on less developed countries. Brazil and Colombia, somewhat less successfully, are among the countries that have combined to raise coffee prices, but only at considerable cost to coffee drinkers.

Diversity

Changes in world demands or supplies can be devastating if a country specializes in the production of only a few major goods. Colombia's reliance on coffee is one example. Droughts, floods, or coffee blight can easily wipe out a year's income, or large harvests in Brazil might severely depress world prices. Diversification is one way of spreading the risk, just as farmers rotate their crops to "rest the soil" and spread their risks.

Protection of developing industries may encourage diversity, but at some cost in efficiency. These efficiency losses might be thought of as insurance premiums. This argument, which on rare occasions may be valid for narrowly specialized countries, would not apply to the United States or other highly diversified economies. And even in small countries, drives for diversification have been so frequently misdirected that opportunities for development were lost.

National Defense

Certain products are crucial for our national defense. Hence, we might want to protect such industries as aircraft or weaponry from foreign competition to ensure domestic supplies in the event of national emergency. This argument is often misused and results in perverse policies. For example, the suggestion that we would not want to be dependent on foreign oil has been used for the past century to justify "Drain America First" policies that have actually increased our long-run dependence on foreign oil suppliers.

To this point, we have only discussed barriers to importing goods. The flip side of this is export restriction. National defense certainly provides some reasons for bans on exports of critical products and materials. Sales of scrap metals to Japan prior to World War II clearly proved to be bad business. Would we want Libya, Iran, Palestinian terrorists, or the Mafia to be able to buy atomic weapons on a free market basis? We think the answer is obvious, and trust that you will as well.

One final note: One of the immeasurable gains from trade is that it causes specialization and mutual interdependence. This raises the price of conflict and provides incentives to avoid war. The benefits of trade may promote peace and international harmony

FIGURE 7 *The Effects of Quotas and Tariffs*

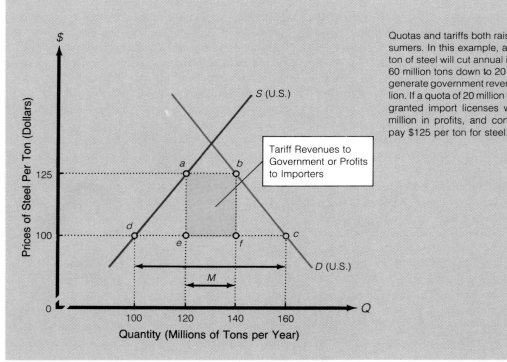

Quotas and tariffs both raise prices to consumers. In this example, a tariff of $25 per ton of steel will cut annual imports (*M*) from 60 million tons down to 20 million tons and generate government revenues of $500 million. If a quota of 20 million tons is set, those granted import licenses will realize $500 million in profits, and consumers will still pay $125 per ton for steel.

and reduce the need for national defense as a political spin-off.

Tariffs and Quotas

A number of mechanisms can be used as barriers to free trade, but the most important are tariffs and quotas. Each can be imposed on either imports or exports, but restrictions on imports are far more common than export barriers. In the United States, tariffs on exports are forbidden by the Constitution.

A **tariff** is a special tax that applies only to goods traded internationally. **Quotas** limit the quantities of goods that may be imported or exported over a given time interval. Both quotas and tariffs raise the prices of imported goods and tend to be inefficient in that potential gains from trade are not fully realized. However, quotas cause side effects that make them especially harmful. Let us investigate the reason for this.

Suppose that we have a tariff on imported steel of $25 per ton, that the internationally traded price is $100 a ton, and that U.S. demands and supplies of steel are as depicted in Figure 7. Without a tariff, the United States will import 60 million tons of steel annually, and domestic production will be 100 million tons. The $25 per ton tariff allows American steel makers to increase production profitably to 120 million tons but cuts domestic steel usage by 20 million tons (to 140 million). Imports fall 40 million tons. Government collects revenues from the tariff equal to the shaded area *eabf,* or $500 million ($25 × 20 million).

Replacing this $25 tariff by an import quota of 20 million tons annually leaves the domestic price at $125 per ton, but government would collect no revenues. Importers who are fortunate in securing import licenses would collectively pick off profits of $500 million—20 million tons of steel costing $100 per ton could be sold for $125 a ton. These potential profits make import licenses very valuable and provide substantial inducements for bribery and corruption.

Another problem with quotas is that they tend to be rigid and fail to accommodate changes in demand. Growth in demand can be met by imports under a tariff system, but not under import quotas. Finally, quotas retard the incentives of foreign producers to do research and innovate more so than do tariffs. Conclusion: From the perspective of the citizen/taxpayer, tariffs are preferable to quotas; however, either mechanism causes economic inefficiency.

International trade is a major source of economic development. At the same time, consumer demands grow and broaden as their incomes grow, so trade tends to expand as the world economy grows. In this chapter, we have explored the gains from trade and exposed the fallacies behind most arguments against free trade. We hope you will remember these discussions when people debate trade policies.

CHAPTER REVIEW: KEY POINTS

1. International trade is important to people throughout the world. The smaller and less diversified an economy, the greater the importance of its international trade.
2. The *law of comparative advantage* suggests that there will be net gains to all trading parties whenever their pretrade relative opportunity costs and price structures differ between goods.
3. A country's *consumption-possibilities frontier (CPF)* expands beyond its *production-possibilities frontier (PPF)* with the onset of trade or with the removal of trade restrictions.

4. The *terms of trade* are the prices of exports relative to the costs of imports. An *adverse change in the terms of trade* lowers the country's *CPF.* Conversely, a favorable change in the terms of trade expands a country's *CPF.*
5. Domestic producers of an imported good may suffer short-term losses from trade, as might domestic consumers of exported goods. However, their losses are overshadowed by the specialization gains to the consumers of imports and the producers of exports. The gainers could always use parts of their gains to compensate the losers so that, on balance, no one loses

from trade. Moreover, *uniqueness, dynamic,* and *political spin-off* gains from trade make it unlikely that anyone loses from trade in the long run.

6. Even the most valid of the arguments against free trade are substantially overworked. The arguments that are partially valid include the ideas that: (*a*) the income redistributions from trade are undesirable; (*b*) desirable diversity within a narrow economy is hampered by free trade; (*c*) national defense requires restrictions to avoid dependence on foreign sources and (more validly) export restrictions to keep certain technologies out of the hands of potential enemies; and (*d*) major exporters of a commodity can exercise monopolistic power by restricting exports, while important consuming nations can exercise monopsonistic power through import restrictions.

7. Any exercise of international monopoly/monopsony power causes worldwide economic inefficiency. Those who lose because of trade restrictions will lose far more than is gained by the "winners" in the same situation.

8. If trade is to be restricted, tariffs are preferable to quotas because of greater flexibility, the increase in tax revenues, and the smaller incentives for bribery and corruption.

9. *Trade adjustment assistance* is one vehicle through which the gainers from trade might compensate the losers so that all would gain. However, the difficulty of identifying the losers and the failure to fund this program adequately have resulted in mounting pressures for trade restrictions.

QUESTIONS FOR THOUGHT AND DISCUSSION

1. Restrictions on oil imports on the grounds of national security undoubtedly led to greater domestic exploitation. Because petroleum is a depletable resource, this may account for our current increased, rather than decreased, dependence on "unreliable foreign sources." What alternatives to import restrictions would assure the availability of oil in the event of national emergency? Would these mechanisms work as well to assure availability for goods other than nonrenewable resources?

2. Should American consumers pay higher prices because of trade barriers to protect the jobs of workers in senile industries? Do such policies in effect "protect consumers from lower prices"? What limits do you think there should be on international free trade? Are there valid reasons for protectionist policies?

3. The American steel, auto, and television receiver industries were all in bad shape—even before the economy began to slump in the early 1980s. Plant closings in these industries led to calls for tariffs and quotas on steel, autos, and televisions. Do restrictions on trade make more sense in a slumping economy than in one that is prosperous? What are some disadvantages to using trade restrictions to bolster declining industries or a stagnant economy?

4. More advanced models of international trade "prove" that international transactions tend to "equalize" factor payments (e.g., the purchasing power of wages and rates of return to capital). More rapid growth in labor incomes in Japan and Western Europe than in the United States seems to support this theory. Can you use the ideas from this chapter to explain how resource payments tend to equalize?

5. How do a nation's endowments of labor, natural resources, and capital shape the kinds of outputs in which it has comparative advantages? What influence might weather have? Can you think of other determinants of a country's areas of comparative advantage?

6. Most models of international trade assume that goods move across international borders but that people and capital do not. Can you use the principles you have learned in this chapter to explain immigration patterns and international capital flows?

CHAPTER 36

International Finance

exchange rates	fixed exchange rates	surpluses and deficits
appreciation and	gold standard	exchange controls
depreciation	flexible (floating)	macroadjustments
revaluation and	exchange rates	currency flows
devaluation	balances of payments	
foreign exchange	and trade	

The previous chapter addressed some issues of international trade but left unanswered questions about **international finance**—how transactions are funded when some traders are based in countries that use francs or pesos while their trading partners are accustomed to dealing in yen or dollars. Our first concern in this chapter is how prices are established when traders use different currencies. You may have heard about deficits or surpluses in balances of payments, which are accounts that summarize international flows of money. Our second topic discusses the consequences of imbalances of international payments and how they are resolved. Finally, we will look at influences on the international value of the dollar over the past few years.

Exchange Rates

Most international transactions require the currency of the buyer to be exchangeable for the currency of the seller. For example, Americans generally want

dollars when they sell to foreign customers. This requires foreigners who buy from Americans to acquire U.S. dollars to consummate these transactions.[1] They express their demands for dollars by supplying their own currencies. Similarly, we demand foreign goods, make loans to foreigners, or invest abroad by supplying dollars—all of which translates into demands for foreign currencies. The relative demands and supplies of various currencies determine their relative prices, which are called exchange rates.

Suppose that you buy a pound of Brazilian coffee. Your grocer will cheerfully accept U.S. dollars to pay the coffee wholesaler, and the wholesaler probably

---

1. The U.S. dollar is so strong internationally that foreigners often require dollar payments when they sell to other foreigners. OPEC, for example, has stated its oil prices in dollars. Thus, if Kuwaitis sell oil to the Czechs, they may be reluctant to accept Czechoslovakian korunas, requiring dollars instead. This creates an *international transaction demand* for dollars; few other currencies are used internationally as mediums of exchange, and none as commonly as the dollar. More about this in a moment.

pays dollars to the importer. But most Brazilian coffee growers do not ultimately want dollars from the importer; they want Brazilian cruzeiros to pay their workers and suppliers. This means that dollars must be exchanged for cruzeiros. Thus, your coffee purchase is ultimately translated into a demand for cruzeiros in international money markets and, simultaneously, into a supply of dollars. The price of one currency (cruzeiros) in terms of another (dollars) is called the **exchange rate.** If $1 can be exchanged for 500 cruzeiros, then the cruzeiro is priced at $.002—one-fifth of a cent—and the Brazilian exchange rate is 500. It takes 500 cruzeiros for a Brazilian to buy a dollar's worth of U.S. merchandise. Note that these exchange rates are reciprocals of each other: if $1 = 500 cruzeiros, then a cruzeiro = 1/500th of a dollar.

Currency Appreciation and Depreciation

Exchange rates are like other prices in that changes in supplies and demands cause exchange rates to fluctuate unless governments control them. Table 1 shows exchange rates for a specific day in 1986 of a number of currencies for the U.S. dollar. There is **appreciation** of a nation's currency if market forces cause foreign currencies to become cheaper. For example, if the cruzeiro's price fell from $.002 to $.001, a dollar would buy twice as many cruzeiros and, thus, has appreciated. **Depreciation** of the dollar, on the other hand, means that foreign currencies have increased in value. A depreciated dollar buys fewer cruzeiros (and less coffee) than previously.

Revaluation and Devaluation

Supply and demand have largely determined exchange rates since 1973. Before then, treaties were widely used to set exchange rates. At times, however, these international agreements were undone by powerful market forces. When **fixed exchange rates** are renegotiated, the currency that appreciates is said to be **revalued,** and the depreciating currency is said to be **devalued.** In an earlier era, many currencies were based on a **gold standard** by which a fixed amount of money exchanged for a certain

amount of gold. Gold standards automatically yield fixed international exchange rates.

Even today, some exchange rates are fixed and occasionally must be altered. For example, exchange rates among European Common Market currencies are fixed, and tend to "float" in unison vis-à-vis other currencies. When the French economy suffered from high inflation and a flight of capital during 1983, however, the French franc was *devalued* relative to the German deutsche mark, the British pound, the Dutch guilder, and all other Common Market currencies. The franc also *depreciated* relative to major currencies external to the Common Market. Realizing how market forces affect exchange rates is fundamental to understanding how the international economy operates.

Demands and Supplies of Currencies

Foreign money is known collectively as **foreign exchange.** Demands for foreign exchange resemble domestic demands for money. Although most demands for foreign exchange are based on international transactions, some key currencies (primarily the dollar) are demanded for precautionary reasons or because they are viewed as stable assets. (The transaction, precautionary, and asset demands for money were discussed previously.) For the moment, however, we will focus on the transaction demand for foreign exchange.

For simplicity, assume that the only two currencies in the world are American dollars ($) and German deutsche marks (DMs). Our demand for deutsche marks is mirrored in our willingness to supply dollars. To see this, consider point *a* in both panels of Figure 1. Each point *a* shows that if the exchange rate is one-for-one, we are willing to supply one billion dollars for one billion deutsche marks. When we can get DM2 for $1 (point *b* in Panel A), we are willing to supply $2 billion dollars to get DM4 billion (each DM costs $0.50 at point *b* in Panel B). And so on. Comparing the matched points between Panels A and B will confirm that any information in one is duplicated in the other.

Changes in exchange rates cause movements along international supply and demand curves for a

TABLE 1 *Exchange Rates of Various Currencies in U.S. Dollars as of June 17, 1986**

Country	U.S. $ Value June 16	Foreign Units per U.S. $ June 16
England (pound)	1.5250	.6557
Canada (dollar)	.7227	1.3837
Argentina (peso)	1.1494	.870
Australia (dollar)	.6955	1.4378
Austria (schilling)	.064756	15.4425
Belgium (franc)	.022267	44.91
Brazil (cruzeiro)	.072622	13.770
Denmark (krone)	.1228	8.1450
Finland (mark)	.1953	5.1195
France (franc)	.1428	7.0015
W. Germany (mark)	.4551	2.1975
Greece (drachma)	.007225	13.840
Holland (guilder)	.4037	2.4770
India (rupe)	.0820	12.1951
Ireland (R) (pound)	1.3825	.7233
Israel (shekel)	.6698	1.4930
Italy (lire)	.000662	1509.5
Japan (yen)	.006050	165.30
Mexico (peso) f	.001587	630.00
Norway (krone)	.1330	7.5200
Portugal (escudo)	.006757	148.00
Saudi Arabia (riyal)	.2666	3.7505
So. Africa (rand)	.3925	2.5478
Spain (peseta)	.007110	140.65
Sweden (krona)	.1403	7.1300
Switzerland (franc)	.5525	1.8100
f—floating rate		

*Exchange rates are quoted in the daily editions of most major newspapers.

currency, paralleling the way that price changes cause changes in quantities demanded or supplied along supply and demand curves for goods. And, just as we assume certain influences are constant when we construct standard demand curves, isolating the effects of exchange rates on the quantity of dollars demanded to build the German demand curve for dollars requires holding similar influences constant. These influences are: (*a*) the prices of substitutes (foreign goods are the relevant substitutes); (*b*) foreign incomes; (*c*) foreign tastes and preferences; (*d*) expectations about exchange rate changes and rela-tive inflation rates in both countries; and (*e*) the dol-lar prices of U.S. goods. Symmetrically, we hold American incomes, prices, preferences, expectations, and foreign prices in DMs constant when drawing the U.S. supply curve of dollars. Changes in any of these variables cause the demand or supply of dol-lars to shift.

Although we hold the dollar prices of American goods constant in the United States and the DM prices of German goods constant in Germany, the dollar prices of imports from Germany and the DM prices of our exports will change proportionally if

FIGURE 1 *The U.S. Supply of Dollars and Its Mirror Image: The Demand for Foreign Exchange*

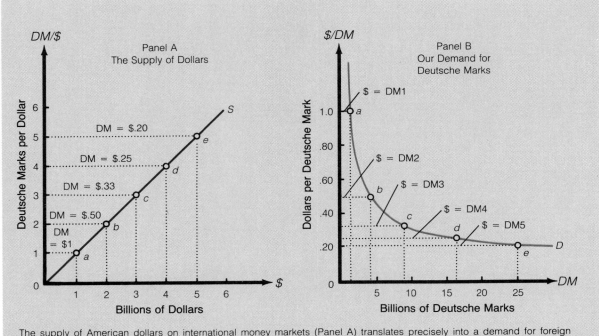

The supply of American dollars on international money markets (Panel A) translates precisely into a demand for foreign currencies (Panel B).

exchange rates fluctuate. This is the key to why the demand and supply curves of dollars (or DMs) slope down and up, respectively.[2]

The Supply of Currencies

The supply of dollars, shown in Panel A of Figure 1, is based on offers by Americans to buy foreign currencies, which we then use to buy foreign goods and services or to invest abroad. This supply curve slopes upward because if foreign currency becomes more expensive, it costs more dollars to buy foreign goods and services. Many previous American buyers of imports may drop out of the market or shift to substitutes (movements such as $e \rightarrow d \rightarrow c \rightarrow b \rightarrow a$).

Conversely, if our exchange rate rises and we can buy more DMs per dollar, we will be willing to supply greater quantities of dollars. This supply curve will shift if there are changes in American incomes or tastes, or changes in the prices of the foreign goods we import.

The Demand for Currencies

Our transaction demand for deutsche marks in Panel B of Figure 1 is really a demand by Americans to buy German consumer goods and to invest overseas. We measure the price of the DM in terms of dollars. Like most demand curves, this demand curve slopes down from left to right. If DMs become more expensive in terms of dollars, the dollar prices of German goods and investments rise and Americans will buy fewer German goods and invest less abroad. Instead, Americans will buy more American goods and invest

---

2. Technically, this requires that international demands and supplies of goods be elastic, conditions that we assume are met throughout our exposition in this chapter.

FIGURE 2 *The Relationships Between Our Supply of Dollars and Demands for Foreign Exchange and Foreign Demands for Dollars and Supplies of Foreign Exchange*

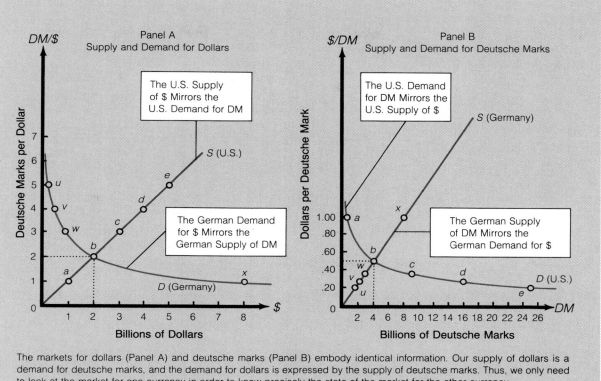

The markets for dollars (Panel A) and deutsche marks (Panel B) embody identical information. Our supply of dollars is a demand for deutsche marks, and the demand for dollars is expressed by the supply of deutsche marks. Thus, we only need to look at the market for one currency in order to know precisely the state of the market for the other currency.

more domestically. This means that they will demand fewer DMs. When DMs are cheaper, Americans will buy more of them because imports from Germany will be cheaper, as will dollar investments in Germany.

Equilibrium Exchange Rates

The supply curve of dollars is actually a "flipped over" demand curve for foreign currencies, as shown in Panel B of Figure 1. (Remember that exchange rates are the reciprocals of each other.) We offer (supply) dollars in order to buy foreign exchange and, ultimately, foreign goods. The demand curve for dollars is similarly a "flipped over" supply curve of the foreign currency.

This means that we can look at the same market with either set of curves. That is, our demand for foreign currency (Panel B) mirrors our supply of dollars (Panel A); foreign demands for dollars (Panel A) are the supplies of foreign currencies (Panel B). We only need to look at one market in order to know precisely what is happening in the other. Henceforth, we will only look at the dollar market; no additional information is gained by looking at the market for DMs (which was, you'll remember, used here to represent all foreign currencies).

Interactions between these supply-and-demand curves determine equilibrium exchange rates and quantities of dollars and foreign currencies. In Figure 2, the equilibrium price of German DMs is $0.50. This is the same as saying that the equilibrium price of the dollar is DM2. If the exchange rates of the dollar and deutsche mark are in equilibrium, does this necessarily mean that the values of international transactions are offsetting so that there are no net flows of foreign exchange between countries? Answering this question requires that we first investigate **balances of payments,** which are the accounts that record international transactions.

Balances of Payments and Trade

Most Americans just shrug with a "What? Me worry?" reaction when Dan Rather, Tom Brokaw, or Ted Koppel announce the latest deficit in our balance of payments. The U.S. has run a balance of payments deficit in all but two years since 1951. Persistent deficits seem to have little effect on our lives. And anyway, what does a deficit in our balance of payments mean?

The U.S. balance of payments account records flows of payments between the United States and the countries with which Americans transact. In the simplest terms a **deficit** occurs in our balance of payments whenever money outflows from the United States exceed the country's monetary inflows. We experience a balance of payments **surplus** in the rare periods when our money inflows exceed outflows.

These movements of funds are controlled by the forces of supply and demand operating through international money markets. All transactions that increase international supplies of a country's currency (which are the same as increased demands in that country for foreign currencies) are *debits* in its balance of payments accounts. Transactions appear as *credits* if they generate increased supplies of foreign currencies (and demands for the country's domestic currency).

There is no special reason for inflows of dollars from sales of U.S. exports to match the outflows of dollars for our purchases of imports. If the dollar value of imports exceeds the dollar value of exports, then the U.S. experiences a **balance of trade deficit.** But if the dollar value of our exports exceeds the dollar value of imports, there is a **balance of trade surplus.** Table 2 summarizes the U.S. balance of payments account. As you can see, international sales

of merchandise are only one source of the demands and supplies of dollars in international money markets.

Foreign Demands for Dollars

Among the reasons that the United States has been able to run huge and persistent deficits in its balances of payments are our size, importance in world trade, and history of political and economic stability. This has created transactions, precautionary, and asset demands for the dollar as a unique international money so that it is used for many international transactions even if no Americans are involved.

Transaction Demands Foreigners have transactions demands for dollars not only so that they can buy U.S. goods or invest in the United States, but also to facilitate transactions with each other. For example, if Saudi Arabia exports oil to Brazil, it is unlikely that Brazilians will be able to pay for the oil with Saudi rials, and the Saudis may be unwilling to accept Brazilian cruzeiros. The dollar provides a solution to this dilemma—Saudis will take dollars in exchange for their oil. The international acceptability of dollars causes Brazilians, Saudis, and other foreigners to seek dollars even if they have no intention of buying from U.S. companies.

Precautionary and Asset Demands Rich and prominent foreigners who fear revolutions or personal chaos in their own countries may want to acquire dollars for precautionary reasons. This was evident when Ferdinand Marcos fled the Philippines. He and his entourage carried suitcases filled with dollars and were reputed to have had vast dollar accounts in Swiss banks. Foreign economic instability may also be a source of asset demands for dollars. For example, Israelis or South Americans may use dollar-denominated securities to hedge against rapid inflations in their own countries.

The point is that persistent deficits in the U.S. balance of payments may not be a sign of disequilibrium. Foreigners may want dollars more than they want the U.S. goods that the dollars would buy. We have become the world's banker, which means that we supply dollars the way other countries supply cars or cameras. In a sense, dollars may be the major

TABLE 2 *U.S. Balance of Payments, 1985 (Billions of Dollars)*[a]

Debits		Credits		Balances	
Current Account		**Current Account**			
Merchandise Imports	$338.3	Merchandise Exports	$214.0	Balance of Trade	−$100.9
Service Imports	124.3	Service Exports	145.7	Balance on Current Account	−117.7[b]
Capital Account		**Capital Account**			
U.S. Overseas Investment	$ 19.1	U.S. Investment by Foreigners	$ 16.3		
Private Loans to Foreigners	7.9	Private Loans from Foreigners	71.6		
U.S. Loans to Foreign Governments	−1.9	Foreign Government Loans to United States	6.4		
		Net Balance of Payments	−48.5	Net Effect on Monetary base	3.2

Source: *Federal Reserve Bulletin* and *International Economic Conditions,* April 1986, Federal Reserve Board of St. Louis.
[a]Totals may not add because of rounding error and the deletion of minor accounts for simplicity.
[b]The balance of trade was −$100.9 billion in 1985, but after pension payments and U.S. government grants to foreigners, the balance on current account grew to −$117.7 billion.

U.S. export, and Americans gain substantially by the payments deficit. The production cost of dollars is trivial, and the U.S. economy gains tremendous *seignorage* (differences between money's face value and its production cost) in the process of supplying international money.

There are occasions, however, when imbalances of payments are symptoms of disequilibrium. We need to examine the ways that foreign exchange markets can bring international supplies and demands of a currency into balance.

Curing Exchange Rate Disequilibria

Suppose that the exchange rate of the dollar for the DM is artificially held below equilibrium at, say, $0.25 per DM (DM4 per dollar) as shown in Figure 3. Relative to equilibrium, German DMs are too cheap and dollars are too expensive. Situations like this offer one explanation for imbalances of international payments. In this example, there is a *surplus* of dollars on international markets, and the United States will experience a *deficit* of payments. Germany runs a compensating balance of payments *surplus*. If we constructed a graph depicting the DM market, it would show a shortage of DMs internationally. Be sure that you understand how surpluses of a currency imply that the issuing country experiences a balance of payments deficit, while a currency shortage implies a surplus in a country's balance of payments. This jargon is sometimes confusing.

Regardless of the cause of deficits or surpluses in a country's balance of payments, there are four basic ways of dealing with these imbalances. We can (*a*) allow change in the exchange rate, (*b*) adopt controls to ration foreign exchange, (*c*) follow macroeconomic policies to shift the supply or demand curves for foreign exchange, or (*d*) allow flows of money from deficit to surplus countries.

Each of these mechanisms has been widely used in some regions during some periods. Most payments, whether domestic or international, were made in currencies denominated in gold until World

FIGURE 3 *U.S. Balance of Payments Deficit Caused by Exchange Rates that Do Not Yield Equilibrium*

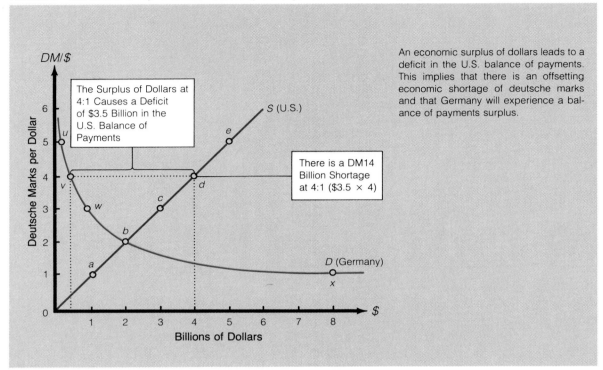

An economic surplus of dollars leads to a deficit in the U.S. balance of payments. This implies that there is an offsetting economic shortage of deutsche marks and that Germany will experience a balance of payments surplus.

War I. Under the ideal *gold standard,* there is little or no trouble in exchanging one currency for any other because all their values in terms of gold are fixed. For instance, an ounce of gold exchanges for an ounce of gold. But the supply of gold did not keep pace with the volume of transactions in rapidly growing economies, so countries everywhere in the world abandoned the gold standard and turned to *fiat* (paper) money.

The worldwide abandonment of gold-denominated money and movement to fiat currencies raise the question: What are the appropriate exchange rates between currencies? One answer to this question is given if governments intervene through fixed exchange rate agreements (price controls) or through other regulations intended to stabilize exchange rates. Alternatively, it can be left to supply and demand. Since 1973, although some countries have "tied" their exchange rates to those of other countries (e.g., currencies in the European Common Market are linked), exchange rates have generally been flexible—governed largely by the forces of the marketplace.

Flexible (Floating) Exchange Rates

In Figure 4, there would be no deficits or surpluses if the DM rose to $0.50, which means $1 is only worth DM2 instead of DM4. As the price of the dollar fell and the price of foreign exchange rose, we would export more and import less, restoring equilibrium. This solution is called **flexible** (or **floating**) **exchange rates** and has been more or less the dominant system used over the past decade. That is, supply and demand have largely determined exchange rates.

One major objection to flexible exchange rates is that they may allow too much uncertainty to enter the sphere of international transactions because of **ex-**

change risk. Uncertainty is encountered because buyers and sellers in international trade would each like the value of future payments stated in their own currencies; otherwise they might suffer losses.

Suppose, for example, that you were an importer of German cameras, and you contracted to buy 1,000 cameras to be delivered and paid for 120 days from today. If the contract specified payment in DMs and the DM appreciated in the next four months, you would wind up paying more dollars for the deutsche marks due than you had expected. On the other hand, if dollar payments were specified and the DM appreciated, the exporter would receive fewer DMs than expected. This exchange risk is a potent argument against flexible exchange rates. Defenders of flexibility counter this objection by pointing out that importers and exporters can insure against exchange risk by dealing in **forward markets** that match future inflows against future outflows of dollars. This insurance, however, involves transaction costs that are absent if exchange rates are absolutely fixed. Critics also charge that flexible exchange rates encour-

age destabilizing speculation but, as we discussed in Chapter 4, it is unlikely that speculation is destabilizing in the long run.

Although flexible exchange rates automatically adjust for surpluses and deficits and have many of the desirable characteristics associated with market solutions, many governments reject flexible exchange rates and try to resolve problems with international payments in other ways.

Macroeconomic Corrections

A balance of payments deficit will evaporate if the supply-and-demand curves shown in Figure 5 shift to intersect at an equilibrium exchange rate (price) of DM4 instead of DM2. One way to accomplish this is to have the deficit country follow contractionary fiscal policies. This will shrink domestic Aggregate Demand, including the demand for imported goods. Another possibility is to reduce the money supply when a balance of payments deficit (a foreign exchange shortage) poses a problem. The resulting recessionary fall in output and/or deflation of domestic prices will cause us to import less. Either contractionary monetary or fiscal policies reduce the international supply of dollars, as shown in Figure 5.

Contractionary macroeconomic policies also induce lower prices for American exports and encourage foreigners to buy more from us. The supply of foreign currency (DMs) grows along with foreigners' demands for dollars in Figure 5. (Remember that the supply curve of DMs mirrors the demand for dollars.) The original deficit in payments (distance *ab*) is eliminated as the economy moves from disequilibrium in the balance of payments (point *d*) to equilibrium (point *c*).

Some experts argue that deficits pose few problems. After all, deficit countries actually export money, which has a very low production cost, and receive goods and services embodying much higher production costs. These analysts recommend that surpluses in the balance of payments in some countries be cured with expansionary macroeconomic policies, causing domestic prices to rise in surplus countries and the prices of their imports to fall. Their surpluses of receipts from international trade would therefore be eliminated.

FIGURE 4 *Flexible Exchange Rates: A Market Solution to Balance of Payments Deficits*

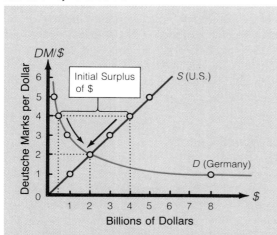

If exchange rates are flexible, an economic surplus of dollars will cause the dollar to depreciate until the quantity of dollars demanded equals the amount supplied. Symmetrically, the deutsche mark will appreciate until equilibrium is reached. American balance of payments deficits and German balance of payments surpluses will be reduced or eliminated.

FIGURE 5 *Using Macroeconomic Adjustments to Eliminate Deficits*

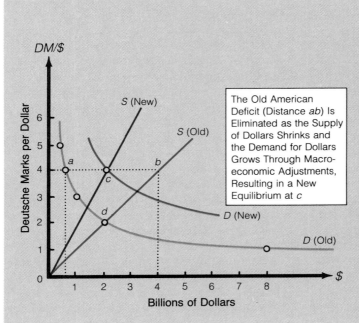

The Old American Deficit (Distance *ab*) Is Eliminated as the Supply of Dollars Shrinks and the Demand for Dollars Grows Through Macroeconomic Adjustments, Resulting in a New Equilibrium at *c*

Flows of funds from imbalances of payments will cause Aggregate Demand to grow in surplus countries. If all countries are close to full employment, the prices of domestic goods in surplus countries will rise, making imports better buys. The resulting growth in imports will be reflected in rising demands for the currencies of deficit countries. At the same time, monetary outflows will dampen Aggregate Demand in deficit countries. There will be decreases in the prices of domestic goods relative to imports, and the international supplies of deficit countries' currencies will decline as imports fall. Thus, the exchange rate remains stable, with all adjustments coming in the form of higher prices in countries that initially experienced surpluses and lower prices in deficit countries. This solution poses no special problem if prices are perfectly flexible. However, if prices are rigid downward, macroeconomic adjustments may impose severe hardships.

These sorts of **macroadjustments** are automatic under a gold standard—the policy of most developed countries in the half century preceding World War I. Payments deficits reduced a country's supply of gold money; surpluses increased it. But because corrections brought about through macropolicy require deflation and stimulate unemployment in countries experiencing a deficit, they tend to be unpopular with the people who live in those countries. Nor do most leaders of countries having excessive surpluses in their balances of payments welcome the suggestion that expansionary or inflationary macroeconomic policies are in order.

Several foreign finance ministers, for example, urged the American government to follow contractionary policies in the 1960s and 1970s to cure our chronic balance of payments deficits. We rejected their suggestions with counterproposals that their governments should pursue expansionary policies to cure their chronic surpluses, and they predictably ignored us. An interesting about-face occurred when contractionary U.S. monetary policies in the early 1980s dampened U.S. inflation and bolstered the international value of the dollar—foreign governments urged the Reagan Administration to follow more expansionary policies to fight the worldwide recession that was at least partially attributable to our counterinflationary policies. A foreign diplomat compared dealing with the United States to ". . . sharing a bed with an elephant; you must be careful when you nudge the beast to get it to roll over."

Exchange Controls

We might ration foreign exchange to eliminate deficits. At $0.25 per DM, only DM2 billion (at point *a* in Figure 6, worth $500 million) are available to Americans, but they would like to buy DM16 billion ($4 billion at point *b*) worth of German goods. The U.S. government could allocate the available DM2 billion among would-be importers through licenses, or it could restrict certain imports by using quotas or tariffs. Many Americans wanting to tour Germany or buy German cameras or VWs would have to do without.

Such techniques are called **exchange controls** and are used in most underdeveloped countries today. Exchange controls are extremely inefficient and embody many difficulties associated with quotas (described in the preceding chapter). Controls must be exercised through some government agency, and they create almost irresistible incentives for smuggling, bribery, graft, black marketeering, and general corruption.

Fixed Exchange Rates

Our earlier discussions of price controls indicated that if prices are fixed above their equilibrium values, there will be surpluses; while if the price of a good is held below its equilibrium value, there will be a shortage of that good. The same results hold for international currency markets.

If we have accumulated reserves of foreign exchange, or if we can beg, borrow, or steal reserves of foreign currencies from our friends and allies, we can rely on international **currency flows** or debt as the fourth and final solution to a balance of payments deficit. In Figure 6, $0.5 billion dollars (DM2 billion) of our annual foreign exchange needs are met by regular inflows of foreign currency. How can we accommodate our remaining $3.5 billion (DM14 billion) outflow of funds?

The U.S. Treasury used some of the gold it had acquired over the previous century to pay parts of chronic deficits experienced from 1951 to 1973. Most of these deficits, however, were absorbed by foreign central banks when our trading partners bought the surplus dollars. In our example, the German government can supply DMs or other currencies "on loan" to the United States and take the excess dollars off the market. This enables the two countries to maintain

FIGURE 6 *Using Exchange Controls to Prevent Deficits or Currency Flows When Deficits Occur*

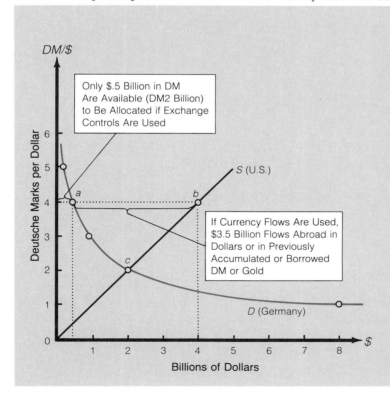

Only $.5 Billion in DM Are Available (DM2 Billion) to Be Allocated if Exchange Controls Are Used

If Currency Flows Are Used, $3.5 Billion Flows Abroad in Dollars or in Previously Accumulated or Borrowed DM or Gold

Exchange controls can be used to artificially maintain the price of a currency above the equilibrium exchange rate, but this requires government rationing of the limited foreign exchange that is available. Alternatively, persistent balance of payments deficits may permit an exchange rate to be above equilibrium if the deficit country can borrow from surplus countries or draw down its stocks of gold or previously acquired foreign currencies.

fixed exchange rates. Persistent U.S. deficits will cause ever greater piles of American dollars to accumulate in German banks. The widespread acceptability of the dollar may enable Germans to use U.S. currency to pay for their imports. But then these dollars wind up consuming space in other foreign central banks. There is a limit to the amount of dollars foreign governments willingly absorb.

Figure 7 shows how foreign governments (e.g., Germany) can guarantee that our currency will never fall below certain values if they buy the dollars sent out as our balance of payments deficits. Similarly, we can set floors for the values of their currencies (e.g., DMs) if we buy their money when they run deficits. This system requires an international agreement to "fix" exchange rates.

In 1944, the Bretton Woods Agreement was struck, establishing the International Monetary Fund and a system of fixed exchange rates. The Interna-

tional Monetary Fund lingers on, but the fixed exchange rate died of natural causes in 1973. Under the Bretton Woods Agreement, most nations "pegged" the value of their currency to the dollar, which the United States was willing to redeem for gold at $35 per ounce. Because the values of all major currencies were pegged to the dollar (and thus, to gold), these currencies were "fixed" relative to each other as well.

Fixed exchange rates pose no special problems as long as exchange rates reflect the relative supplies and demands of currencies. In other words, fixed exchange rates do not cause any special problem as long as their values are the same as flexible exchange rates would be. Even if fixed exchange rates are initially in equilibrium, however, differences in macroeconomic policies or rates of economic growth between countries, or changes in tastes or technologies will cause the relative supplies and demands of

FIGURE 7 *Fixing Exchange Rates Through International Agreement*

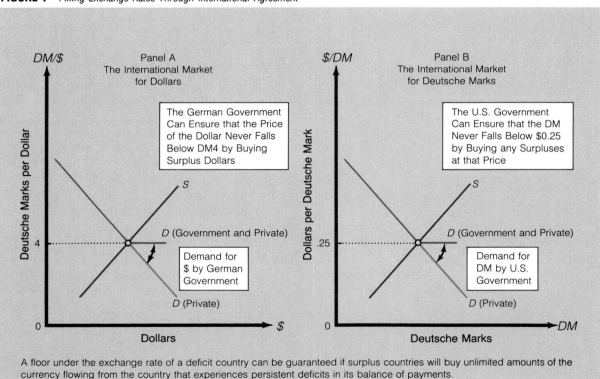

A floor under the exchange rate of a deficit country can be guaranteed if surplus countries will buy unlimited amounts of the currency flowing from the country that experiences persistent deficits in its balance of payments.

currencies to change. Shortages and surpluses emerge. Persistent disequilibria in balances of payments may appear whenever fixed exchange rates fail to reflect currencies' true demands and supplies.

In summary, there are only four basic ways to deal with surpluses or deficits in balances of payments: (*a*) change the price (float), (*b*) ration (control), (*c*) shift the curves (macroadjustments), or (*d*) allow currency flows. Similar solutions apply equally to surpluses or shortages of wheat, gasoline, schoolteachers, or skateboards. You can add frills and elaborations, but this simple supply-and-demand analysis is what the complex world of international finance is really all about.

The Dirty Float: 1973 to ?

Most exchange rates have been flexible since 1973, but with some government intervention. In most markets for goods and services, surpluses or shortages are cured by price changes, a process detailed in Chapter 3. Floating systems allow exchange rates to vary, so it would seem that U.S. balance of payments deficits (surpluses of dollars) should be cured automatically if they are signs of disequilibrium. But if imbalances of payments should vanish automatically, then why have U.S. payments deficits been so persistent? As we suggested earlier, one part of the answer is that foreigners have often wanted American dollars even more than they have wanted American goods. This suggests that our consistent deficits in international payments may be signs of economic and political health. Parts of U.S. deficits may be true symptoms of international imbalances, however, because governments everywhere have constantly intervened in foreign exchange markets.

Explaining Persistent U.S. Payments Deficits

If a country runs large and persistent deficits, foreign banks will accumulate substantial amounts of that country's currency because foreign suppliers will exchange the payments they receive for their own money. Why have foreign private and central banks permitted the United States to persistently run balance of payments deficits since 1951?

The answer to this question is multifaceted. First, between the end of World War II and 1971, the dollar was the only major currency redeemable for gold, at least for purposes of international payments. Foreign central banks could present $35 to the U.S. Treasury and demand one ounce of gold. It was illegal for Americans who were not jewelers, coin collectors, or dentists to own gold bullion, bars, or coins during this period. Any American gold not used industrially or in teeth or jewelry was used to back the dollar for international transactions.

The end of World War II saw the United States as the only major country with its manufacturing capacity intact. We supplied much of the world's needs and generally demanded payment in gold because most other currencies were either unstable or worthless. Hence, as we entered the 1950s, the United States had substantial gold on hand. The dollar was a nearly perfect substitute for gold for purposes of international payments because it was redeemable for gold.

This meant that our money was often viewed as being at least as valuable as the American goods that might be bought with it by, say, the Italians; people in other countries would cheerfully accept dollars when they would not accept lire in payment for Italian purchases. In a sense, the convertibility of United States dollars into gold (under a "partial reserve system" much like that used by commercial banks) enabled the United States to create "international money."

International trade in the post-World War II period grew far more rapidly than the quantity of gold available for international payments. The acceptability of the U.S. dollar as an international *key currency* made it possible for the U.S. Treasury and the FED to accommodate increasing world demands for an international medium of exchange by simply printing money. Americans gained through seignorage from this ability to print international money because we were able to export less than the total value of the goods we imported. In a sense, we consumed more than we produced. The difference was made up by the dollars we printed that circulated among foreign countries, never being redeemed for American output or resources. The international acceptability of the dollar has been the major reason that the United States was able to run persistent and large deficits between 1951 and the present.

The relative prices of most currencies in international exchange markets presumably have been set by supply and demand since 1973. We may still run deficits under a floating exchange rate system, however, if foreigners commonly demand our dollars instead of American goods and services. Even so, foreign demand for dollars as insurance or as an internationally accepted means of payment do not completely explain the magnitudes of the U.S. balance of payments deficits throughout the 1970s.

The central banks and treasuries of a number of countries accumulated dollars during the 1970s to prevent the exchange rate of the dollar from falling even further or more rapidly than it did; the "float" has been a dirty float. Why would foreign governments (for example, Japan) wish to maintain high prices for imports from the United States and concomitant low prices for Japanese products exported to Americans? Part of the answer is that employment and growth in the Japanese and some other economies are heavily dependent on their export industries. In addition, the Japanese farmers and manufacturers who compete with imports from the United States are very powerful politically.

When the Japanese central bank buys and holds the dollars paid for Japanese exports, the effect is the same as a tariff on their imports and a subsidy on their exports. This Japanese policy of acquiring growing amounts of dollars has resulted in subsidies to American consumers by Japanese consumers. Until Japanese taxpayers and voters catch on, we may continue to gain at their expense.[3] Curiously, our government opposes Japanese trade barriers against American imports, and from 1969 to the present, it has pressured the Japanese government to adopt policies to eliminate the U.S. trade deficit with Japan. Can you figure out why?

In sum, the United States has been able to run balance of payments deficits fairly consistently for over three decades because:

1. Until the early 1970s, the international monetary system, under the Bretton Woods Agreement, used fixed exchange rates that were adjusted only in the event of "fundamental disequilibrium." It was advantageous to many of our trading partners to maintain the primacy of the dollar until inflationary pressures from the Vietnam era and the emergence of other sound national currencies led to the downfall of the fixed exchange rate system, which had required the soundness of the dollar as a foundation.

2. There has been a strong demand for the dollar for use as an international medium of exchange.

3. Dollar holdings have been viewed as "insurance" in politically or economically unstable countries.

4. Such countries as Japan and West Germany have supported the dollar at artificially high exchange rates in order to boost American demand for their exports. These policies have increased employment and economic growth in these countries.[4]

The Dance of the Dollar

The dollar was indisputably the world's key currency from the end of World War II until the mid-1960s. Then the exchange value of the dollar declined relative to most major currencies during the 1970s, hitting its low in 1978. The dollar then recovered steadily until late 1985, as Figure 8 demonstrates. But why did the dollar fall during the 1970s? Why was it so strong in the early 1980s? And why did it weaken somewhat after 1985? There are a number of explanations, all of them at least partially correct.

We know that the price of anything will fall if supply grows relative to demand, and vice versa. Some explanations for the fall of the dollar during the 1970s focus on reduced desires by foreigners to hold dollars; others focus on increased supplies of dollars in international markets. Although growing supplies and falling demands for the dollar (or vice versa) are interrelated, we will deal first with factors that alter international demands for dollars.

Inflation and Exchange Rates

There was substantial inflation during the 1970s—not only in the United States, but throughout the world. When our inflation abated in the early 1980s,

---

3. This support for the dollar can be viewed as a hidden subsidy that Japan, and more especially, Germany, uses to induce the United States to provide defense services. Tens of thousands of American soldiers are stationed in Germany.

4. Throughout the 1970s, our government urged foreign governments to run budget deficits, increase their money supplies, and reduce trade barriers against American products, among other measures.

FIGURE 8 *The Dance of the U.S. Dollar*

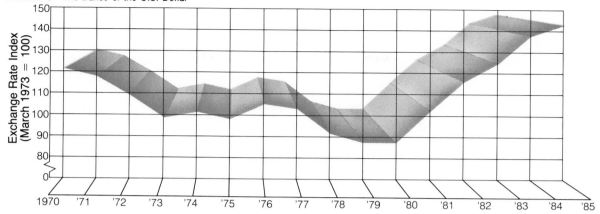

The overall depreciation of the dollar relative to the average of other major currencies during the 1970s reflected the maturation of other currencies, the declining prestige of the United States, problems with inflation, the deterioration of our terms of trade as the prices of imports grew faster than the prices of our exports (for example, oil imports versus machinery exports), rising concern about the future of the dollar and of the American economy, and a host of other problems. The dollar's strong recovery as the 1980s began signaled a reversal of this downward spiral.

Source: *Economic Report of the President*, 1986.

the dollar surged upward in international exchange markets.

Relative Inflation   When prices increase faster in the United States than elsewhere, we buy more imports and supply more dollars internationally, but the demands for our exports and dollars fall. This line of reasoning leads to a classical explanation for falling exchange rates—inflation in the United States during the 1970s reduced foreign demands for dollars. Coupled with an increased supply of dollars, we have one part of the explanation for declining exchange rates. Then, as American inflation abated in the early 1980s, the recovery of the dollar became stronger. Thus, relative inflation causes depreciation of a currency, while less than the average international rate of inflation causes exchange rate appreciation.

Expectations   There was a growing perception internationally during the 1970s that more than any other major industrialized country, the United States was committed to expansionary and, consequently, inflationary policies. Increased income, whether real or inflated, causes higher demands for imports. If other countries are not expected to follow similarly expansionary policies, there are growing pressures for balance of payments deficits.[5]

U.S. inflation throughout the 1970s probably generated international expectations of continued inflationary policies and relative inflation in this country. Such expectations led foreigners to treat dollars as hot potatoes; their dollar holdings fell dramatically at times between 1974 and 1980.

Whenever international money managers have expected the United States to experience both continued relative inflation and substantial balance of trade deficits, there has been downward pressure on the dollar. When U.S. monetary growth began to slow in 1979, the dollar began its recovery. An American recession during 1981–83 spread to the rest of the world as it choked off our demands for imports and constricted the international supply of dollars. High U.S. interest rates also attracted short-term financial investments by foreigners, further strengthening the

---

5. This action reduces the exchange rate of the dollar, and by increasing the prices of our imports and decreasing the prices of U.S. exports, eliminates the deficits.

dollar. It seems ironic that recessions bolster the dollar, but they do.

By 1985, the exchange rate of the dollar was so high that foreign finance ministers and American policymakers were alarmed. They agreed to follow policies to depreciate the dollar. Accordingly, foreign central banks sold dollars on international markets, increasing the supply to private financiers. Fear that the United States might begin following more expansionary macroeconomic policies caused many private financial institutions to be leery of holding many dollars. Coupled with record deficits in the U.S. balances of payments and trade that caused the international supply of dollars to swell, the dollar drifted downward during 1985–86. There were many analysts, however, who believed that this engineered weakening of the dollar was doomed to fail.

Portfolio Adjustments

For some time after World War II, the U.S. dollar and gold were viewed as the only stable international mediums of exchange. The world's supply of gold grew more slowly than the volume of international transactions. Consequently, institutions like central banks and international corporations were happy to use the dollars made available by our balance of payments deficits to meet their transaction demands for money and desires for liquid assets.

Economic instability in the United States beginning during the Vietnam conflict led to diminished confidence in the dollar. During the same period, numerous industrialized economies throughout the world matured or reached full recovery from World War II; their currencies became attractive parts of the liquid portfolios of many countries' central banks, competing with the dollar as a reserve asset. The growing availability of suitable substitutes for dollars led financial institutions around the world to diversify, holding smaller proportions of their assets in dollars.

When the dollar began to depreciate a little during the mid-1970s, it fell off the pedestal that had caused so many countries to hold dollars. The huge proportion of international reserves held by foreign central banks in U.S. currency caused the "dollar overhang" to collapse. For example, in 1977 alone almost 60 percent of the dollars held by OPEC countries were exchanged for other currencies, intensifying pressure for the dollar to fall.

In the late 1970s, a number of countries attempted to price their exports (e.g., OPEC oil) not in terms of dollars alone but based on an index of such strong foreign currencies as the Swiss franc and the German deutsche mark. These experiments temporarily weakened the dollar because it was demanded less for international transactions. Ultimately, however, these experiments failed, forcing renewed reliance on the dollar as the world's key currency and further bolstering the dollar's recovery in the early 1980s.

Oil and the Balance of Trade

During the 1970s, our cumulative payments deficit was roughly $90 billion. This added almost 30 percent to the total amount of dollars held abroad. Substantial parts of payment deficits over this period are attributable to imports of oil. The international price of oil grew sharply for roughly 8 years after OPEC began exercising its muscles in 1973. Because American production technology is extremely energy intensive, higher oil prices only slowly reduced our oil imports. The dollar value of oil imports grew dramatically during the 1970s, worsening our balance of payments deficit. This—and our own increasing preferences for Japanese electronics, cameras, and cars—pushed down the exchange rate of the dollar. But by the early 1980s, our imports of crude oil were declining and the dollar began showing considerable strength in international financial markets.

The Monetarist Explanation

All the factors we have offered provide bits and pieces of a solution to the temporary decline of the dollar. Predictably, some monetarists attribute the slide of the dollar to too rapid growth in the U.S. money supply (and declining rates of monetary growth were credited with its recovery). We will use the deutsche mark (DM) to explain the monetarist mechanism. The reasoning goes that if the supply of dollars relative to the demand for dollars grows faster than the supply of DMs grows relative to the demand for them, then the dollar will depreciate relative to the deutsche mark.

The problem with this approach is that while it is unquestionably true, it has little explanatory value. In fact, during the 1970s, the U.S. money supply grew less rapidly than the money supplies of virtually any other major country, yet the dollar danced downward relative to almost every major currency. Monetarists were unable to explain the declining demand for the dollar, other than by vague references to inflation; then the dollar's recovery was attributed to diminishing inflation.

In summary, among the possible explanations for the decline of the dollar during the 1970s were:

1. relative inflation of the dollar.
2. expectations that inflation in the U.S. would remain higher than elsewhere.

3. expected continuation of trade deficits.
4. adjustments of international portfolios against the dollar.
5. modest depreciation caused the dollar to lose its "halo."
6. larger trade deficits caused by high and rising oil prices.
7. too rapid monetary growth in the U.S.

The recovery of the dollar in the 1980s apparently occurred because of reversals in a number of these factors. Each explanation seems logically plausible, yet none alone is a satisfactory explanation for the swings in the exchange rate of the dollar, and some are even contrary to the evidence.

CHAPTER REVIEW: KEY POINTS

1. Since we have no world currency, we must establish the value of each national currency in terms of all others. The *exchange rate* is the value of one currency in terms of another.
2. The U.S. *balance of payments* account records the flow of money into and out of the country and provides information about our trade relationships with other countries.
3. *Flexible,* or *floating, exchange rates* permit the value of currencies to be set by market forces. If a country experiences a balance of payments *surplus* (*deficit*) under such a system, it is an indication that the country's citizens or government (*foreigners*) desire foreign (*domestic*) currencies.

4. A *fixed exchange rate system* imposes price ceilings and price floors on currencies. This system often results in persistent disequilibria in balances of payments.
5. Explanations for the decline of the dollar range from relative inflation to expectations of continued inflation and payments deficits to the emergence of other strong international currencies to the cartelization of oil to too rapid monetary growth. Opposite trends then strengthened the dollar. Each of these explanations bears the germ of truth, but none alone is adequate to explain the dance of the dollar.

QUESTIONS FOR THOUGHT AND DISCUSSION

1. One popular myth is that surpluses in the balances of trade and payments are necessarily good omens, while deficits are symptoms that a country may be suffering from economic anemia. Yet persistent U.S. balance of payments deficits during the past three decades may have been unavoidable simply because of the relative vigor of the American economy. How is this so? How have Americans gained from the trade deficit? From the payments deficits? How have they lost from these deficits? On balance, have the gains outweighed the losses?
2. Conventional theories of international finance suggest that imbalances of payments are signs of disequilibrium. However, a recent theory called "global monetarism" hypothesizes (among other things) that surpluses can be expected when people

in some countries have a greater desire for more money than they do for more goods, while people in other countries have "too much" money and are willing to trade some of their money for imports. How might persistent surpluses or deficits occur in equilibrium?

3. Global monetarists also favor fixed exchange rates, arguing that flexible exchange rates make no more sense than reducing the price of the quarter relative to the penny if there are surpluses of quarters and shortages of pennies. What are the major differences, if any, between these situations? Do these economists have a point? What mechanisms are available to accommodate deficits or surpluses under fixed exchange rates? What are the implications of fixed exchange rates for the independence of macroeconomic policies?

4. After the dollar declined in the 1970s, foreign tourists found the United States an excellent place to shop for bargains. The United States was not such a haven for foreign shoppers after the dollar began recovering in the 1980s. The Mexican peso depreciated severely in 1982–83, and many Americans scurried to Mexico for bargains. Why do such bargains for foreigners sometimes emerge when a currency depreciates or is devalued? What does the existence of such bargains suggest about whether these currencies are temporarily overvalued or undervalued? What does your answer suggest about the way balances of payments might change for these countries in the very near future?

5. Under what circumstances might depreciation or devaluation of a currency cause deficits in a country's balance of payments to worsen? How is your answer related to elasticities of demands and supplies for exports and imports? Why is any worsening of payments deficits likely to be strictly a short-term problem?

CHAPTER 37 Capitalism and Its Alternatives

libertarianism
anarcho-syndicalism
utopian socialism
Fabian socialism

Christian socialism
communism (Marxism)
dialectical materialism
class warfare

central planning
indicative planning
welfare state
small is beautiful

Much of this book describes how markets function, but there are many alternative mechanisms that allocate resources and distribute goods. Other economic systems' operations and some criticisms of capitalism are addressed in this chapter. We begin with an overview of capitalism and its strongest defenders, the libertarians. Our second topic, anarcho-syndicalism, shares with libertarianism a distaste for government, but is much less enamored of capitalism. Then we survey several types of socialism, in which government dominates economic activity. Next, a bird's-eye view of how different social philosophies, including Marxism, are expressed in contemporary economies. The chapter concludes with discussions of possible limits to economic growth and "Buddhist economics"—the idea that the ultimate solution to economic want is spiritual rather than physical. When you've finished this chapter, you should have a sense of how capitalism fits into the spectrum of mechanisms that people use to deal with scarcity.

Perspectives on Capitalism

Markets play very limited roles in the lives of two-thirds of the world's population. Many market activities are illegal in countries whose leaders oppose capitalism. In other nations, the primitive state of economic development limits market transactions. Although the higgling and haggling of the marketplace predate written history, the structure of capitalism was not stated systematically until the publication of Adam Smith's *Wealth of Nations* (1776). This book, which was the first comprehensive survey of economics, spawned countless studies of market economies.

The virtues of capitalism require intense competition in a free market environment. But its critics claim that only greed and other base motives are nurtured by competition, which permeates everything from schools to athletics to the business arena. They also point to the growing power of corporations as an inevitable consequence of capitalistic competition. Giant multinational corporations flourish, dominating world trade. The arguments for the superior efficiency of capitalism assume vigorous competition among many small firms, a situation that actually exists in only a few sectors of most modern market economies.

Modern capitalism, according to its critics, is corrupt, unstable, inefficient, exploitative, dehumanizing, and outmoded. These critics view capitalism as pitting a wealthy, autocratic elite against starving, miserable masses, and they predict that it will soon "be swept into the dustbin of history." Advocates of capitalism naturally believe that the critics are wrong and cite numerous virtues of the price system. The two most important virtues are freedom and efficiency.

Libertarianism

Power corrupts, and absolute power tends to corrupt absolutely.
—*Lord Acton*

Libertarians, the modern champions of laissez-faire capitalism, join anarchists in a dislike of bureaucracy and government. Anarchists see giant corporations and big government as twin threats to freedom and as exploiters of labor. **Libertarians** focus more narrowly on problems posed by government. In their view, corporate abuses would evaporate if government did not suppress competitive behavior and foster concentrations of economic power.

Libertarians prize individual freedom as the single most important social value and see other goals as almost meaningless without it. They constantly look for areas where government coercion can be eliminated. Among the many government activities that libertarians believe could and should be eliminated or left to private choice are:

1. the military draft.
2. laws controlling prescription drugs, narcotics, consensual sex between private individuals, and pornography.
3. laws giving parents controls over teenagers.
4. regulation of utility companies.
5. discretionary monetary and fiscal policies.
6. public parks, roads, and highways.
7. mandatory automotive safety equipment.
8. wage and price controls.
9. usury laws.
10. social security.
11. education.
12. welfare.
13. the postal service.
14. radio and television broadcasting.
15. professional licensing.

Libertarians view most government actions as unnecessary hindrances to freedom and advocate free market solutions as ideal cures for almost every human problem. They would restrict government to protecting private property rights and enforcing contracts. The fact that government has never been so limited explains why some libertarians call laissez-faire capitalism "the unknown ideal." But libertarians cannot claim a monopoly in their opposition to government.

Anarcho-Syndicalism

There's no government like no government.
—*An Anarchist Slogan*

One group of capitalism's foes perceive modern corporate giants and government as parasites that exploit the powerless working class. This group consists of anarchists, who would retain private property rights, and syndicalists, who desire collective worker-ownership of nonhuman resources. Aversion to government is the glue that binds anarchism to syndicalism. Both groups are convinced that government is always the servant of a ruling elite. In a system of industrial capitalism, capitalists and professional managers control government; under centrally planned socialism, government is in the grip of an enormous bureaucracy. Anarchists and syndicalists believe that governments monopolize and institutionalize violence through imperialistic wars and police brutality. Hence, both groups would do away with the twin evils of corporate capitalism and the state.

Anarchism

Anarchists are popularly stereotyped as wild-eyed bomb throwers, but a little research reveals that their philosophy derives from the view that the absence of government would reduce worldwide violence and exploitation. Philosophical anarchists count on cooperation among people to ensure social harmony in the absence of law.

Anarchists are not necessarily opposed to the market system, but they view modern capitalism as a system in which professional corporate managers and government officials are in cahoots to exploit workers. Corporations exist only because of government recognition. In an idealized anarchy, individuals' rights to what they produce could not be "stolen" by capitalists who rely on government to legitimize their exploitation of workers. Most anarchists would recognize private property rights and disavow social ownership of anything. In this position, anarchism is closer to libertarianism than to socialism.

But how might governments be eradicated? Answers to this question range from pacifism to bloody revolution. William Godfrey, an English clergyman, and the Russian Prince Kropotkin thought that if we all just ignored government, it would dry up and blow away. The image of anarchists as bomb throwers originated a century ago with the teachings of Mikhail Bakunin, who convinced his followers that random violence could precipitate the collapse of governments and capitalism. Instead, when Bakunin's followers began throwing bombs, the resultant widespread fear of violence brought anarchism a lasting disrepute.

Syndicalism

Many of the socialist reformers described in the next section have faith that their goals can be achieved democratically through the ballot box. Syndicalists disagree, viewing the state as an oppressive vehicle manipulated by power hungry plutocrats. Syndicalism was the brainchild of the French philosopher Georges Sorel (1847–1922). Sorel, like many Frenchmen, was profoundly critical of government, viewing stupid wars, corruption, and gross mismanagement as its consequences.

Syndicalism echoes anarchism in demanding the abolition of both the state and corporate capitalism. The economy would be reorganized into *syndicates,* which are, effectively, industrywide trade unions. Thus, there would be an auto syndicate, an iron and steel syndicate, an electronics syndicate, and so on. Syndicalism resembles socialism in that private ownership of nonhuman resources would be abolished; each industry would be owned by its workers and run by elected worker committees. Syndicates would replace government and control the workplace, but would leave individuals alone in all other matters.

Syndicalism arrived in the United States in 1905 with the founding of the Industrial Workers of the World (IWW) by Daniel Deleon, Eugene V. Debs, and "Big Bill" Haywood, all of whom are legends in the history of American radicalism. Debs collected over a million votes as the Socialist candidate for president during World War I, even though he had been jailed for sedition by President Woodrow Wilson.

IWW members, known as *wobblies,* grew to more than 100,000 before World War I. They intended to overthrow capitalism by locking out managers and seizing factories. The IWW was especially powerful among Western miners, railroad workers, and merchant seamen, who participated in more than 150 violent strikes before succumbing to internal strife arising from the lack of a coherent vision of what to do "after the revolution."

Today, syndicalist ideas find watered-down expression in Western Europe and North America in "profit sharing" plans and in union demands for voices in managerial decisions. In Eastern Europe, the trend towards decentralized socialism is somewhat syndicalist, Yugoslavia being especially distinguished by "worker management." *Solidarity,* the worker organization led by Lech Walesa that gave fits to the Polish government in the early 1980s, had syndicalist goals.

Evolutionary Socialism

The unifying theme of socialism is the call for social ownership of the nonhuman factors of production—capital and natural resources. This does not necessarily mean that under socialism you would not own your own toothbrush. Ideally, it does mean that land, factories, and all major capital equipment would be held in trust by government so that everyone could share equitably in national income.

There may be more species of birds than of socialists, but not many. Within the socialist camp, there are schisms about the best path to socialism, how far social ownership should extend, and which groups should make social and economic decisions. Some socialists believe that socialism will evolve democratically through the ballot box. Others insist that capitalists control political processes, leaving violent revolution as the only way to institute socialist goals. The most conspicuous of these are *communists,* who have tried to adapt the ideas of Karl Marx to the more complex circumstances of the twentieth century. Much of the world's population now finds itself governed by Marxists of one breed or another. Before we explore Marxism, we will briefly outline other forms of socialism.

Utopian Socialism

The names of dreamers who have sought to improve our imperfect world are scattered throughout history books. Sir Thomas More (1478–1535), a saint and martyr of the Catholic Church who served as a statesman in the court of England's Henry VIII, was one such dreamer. More's famous book, *Utopia,* borrowed a Greek word meaning "no place." Today, *utopian* commonly refers to unrealistic ideals. More blamed poverty, waste, and avarice on private property, and proposed the creation of Utopia, where everyone would share everything. Greed would vanish, social decisions would be democratic, and opportunities for cultural enrichment would abound. People would work for the common good in jobs of their choice. Prices would be unnecessary because there would be as much joy from giving as from receiving; differences in satisfaction between supplying and demanding would disappear.

More's ideas were largely ignored until early in the nineteenth century, when social ferment and the prospect of revolution swept Europe. **Utopian socialism** blossomed. Prominent utopians of this period included the French philosopher Charles Fourier (1772–1837) and the philanthropist Robert Owen (1771–1858). Owen, though born into poverty, became wealthy as a Scottish cotton mill owner while still in his twenties. Infatuated with the utopian vision, he financed several self-contained, communally owned villages in Scotland and the United States. Neat rows of houses, free education, better working conditions, and wages in proportion to hours worked attracted thousands of people to this grand experiment. But all utopian communities of this period were (predictably?) poorly managed and uniformly failed.

It seems ironic that many of Owen's dreams have been integrated into public policies in most mixed economies in Western Europe and North America. Free public education, socialized medicine in much of Europe and medical insurance in the United States, healthier working conditions, and substantial parts of our current welfare system are the offspring of the ideas of the utopian socialists.

Fabian Socialism

Founded in England in 1884, the **Fabian Society** abandoned the ideal of small communities, urging instead municipal ownership of public utilities and nationalization of heavy industry. Otherwise, their agenda echoed reforms proposed by utopian socialists: Outlawing child labor, limiting working hours for women, providing free education and medical care, redistributing income and wealth, extending the right to vote, and ensuring cleaner and safer work environments.

The early Fabians included several young intellectuals who later gained prominence: author and playwright George Bernard Shaw, science fiction writer H. G. Wells, economist and historian G. D. H. Cole, and Sidney and Beatrice Webb, a married team of economists. This small band grew and, as it collected members who were active in the British union movement, evolved into the present British Labour party.

Christian Socialism

It is easier for a camel to pass through a needle's eye than for a rich man to enter the Kingdom of Heaven.
—The Gospel of Matthew

Many conservative theologians interpret Christianity as supporting the status quo. The sanctity of private property and the idea that kings rule by "divine right" are among the gospels preached by some orthodox clerics. These clerics cite the scripture to "render unto Caesar that which is Caesar's and unto God that which is God's" to justify existing distributions of wealth, status, and power. In this view, social struggle is a diversion from spiritual development.

Even so, the "social gospel" movement was launched a century ago by a group of French Catholic priests who had borrowed many of the ideas of Thomas More. Charity, good works, and social reforms are at the core of **Christian socialism.** Repudiating the violence advocated by revolutionary socialists, the "social gospel" stresses the dignity of work and favors labor unions. It resembles Fabian socialism in its goals, even though most Fabians were atheists or agnostics.

Pope Leo XIII and Pope Pius XI affirmed the support of the Catholic Church for Christian socialism. Pope John Paul II followed in this tradition when he denounced violent revolution, but he also urged labor reforms and supported the Polish *Solidarity* movement. Protestant theologians who were attracted to Christian socialism included Paul Tillich and Reinhold Niebuhr. The ''social gospel'' remains a powerful force within the World Council of Churches, as a mainspring of the ecumenical movement, and in numerous church-related social reform programs. An offshoot of this movement is the ''liberation theology'' espoused by radical South American priests who advocate violent revolution to overthrow repressive governments. This philosophy blends Christian socialism with elements of Marxism.

Marxism: Revolutionary Socialism

The history of . . . society is the history of class struggles.

—*Karl Marx*

Few people have left footprints on history comparable to those of Karl Marx. In the century following his death, more than one-third of humanity has come to be governed by professed Marxists.

History as Economic Dialectics

Marx extended economic analysis far beyond the realms studied by most economists. Marxists believe that all of history can be interpreted as resolutions to *contradictions* emerging from the competing interests of people in different economic classes. This interpretation is rooted in **dialectical** analysis, a method originated by the German idealist philosopher, Georg Hegel.

According to Hegelian dialectics, every concept, or **thesis,** has meaning only when pitted against its opposite, or **antithesis.** Thus, the idea of *long* means nothing unless contrasted with its antithesis, the idea of *short; rich* means nothing without *poor.* Interactions between a thesis and its antithesis yield a

synthesis, which advances our understanding of an ever-changing reality. Thus, the notions of long and short synthesize into the concept of *distance,* and rich and poor yield the concepts of *income* and *wealth.* These syntheses advance our understanding of the world and of relations between people. Hegel believed that historical changes were dominated by dialectical changes in ideas, resulting in more accurate perception.

Marx rejected as irrelevant the Hegelian focus on ideas, instead insisting that history unfolds through dialectical processes among economic interests—the material world holds the keys to historical change. This is why Marxism is sometimes called **dialectical materialism;** if cause and effect relationships embedded in the dialectical process never change, then precise explanations of the past permit perfect predictions about the future.

Marx believed he had discovered the fundamental laws of history in the perception that all social and cultural changes are determined by juxtaposing thesis and antithesis in the ways we produce, exchange, distribute, and consume goods. These ''contradictions'' (from the Marxist jargon) are rooted in conflicts between different socioeconomic groups or *classes.*

For example, the Marxist view of the Industrial Revolution is that it pitted an aggressive new class of manufacturers against vested agricultural interests throughout Europe, but especially in England. The ascendance of industrialization led to entirely new government policies, including a resurgence of British imperialism. Laws were adopted that evicted most peasants from their land and forced them to work in factories. Exploited workers were then pitted against industrial magnates, whom they would eventually displace during a short but bloody revolution.

Marx viewed this sequence as inevitable. In dialectical terms, thesis (feudal agricultural interests) met antithesis (industrial entrepreneurs—the *bourgeoisie*), leading to synthesis (the triumph of industrialization) within which there was a contradiction (wretchedness of the working masses). This synthesis became the new thesis (industrial capitalism), which, in confronting its antithesis (workers, known as *proletarians,* resent exploitation), leads to a new synthesis (the *dictatorship of the proletariat*).

In Marxist analysis, each stage of economic development is necessary and collapses only when it

Karl Marx (1818–83)

Marx was a genius . . . the rest of us were talented at best.

—Friedrich Engels

During the twentieth century, the ideas of Karl Marx have had a larger impact on human history than the thoughts of nearly any other social philosopher. Marx's thoughts have left indelible marks in a number of academic disciplines including philosophy, education, psychology, history, and economics. Nevertheless, his major work, *Das Kapital,* must be seen for what he meant it to be: a critical analysis of capitalism as an economic system. Although Marx's was clearly the dominant contribution, virtually all his work was done in collaboration with his friend, Friedrich Engels. Curiously, Engels lived comfortably on his income from owning and managing a factory.

Scholars disagree on the extent to which events in Marx's life colored his thoughts on society, but two characteristics of Marx's personality and experience are prominent. One is that adversity often came his way. For example, although Marx received a Ph.D. in philosophy from the University of Jena, no university would hire him to teach. His inflammatory rhetoric and close association with political radicals deprived him of a stable income and led to his expulsion from Germany. Exile was to play an important role in his life. Later, Marx was also forced by the governments of Belgium and France to leave those countries.

He finally settled his family in England, which was far too tolerant of individual freedoms to expel him. He sporadically tried to eke out a living as a journalist, serving for a time as a foreign correspondent to the *New York Herald-Tribune.* (Would the course of history have been different if the newspaper had ever given Marx a raise?) Had it not been for occasional doles from Engels, the entire Marx household might have starved. As it was, they were destitute.

Another factor in Marx's experience was ambivalence. Some have attributed this trait to his parents' conversion to Christianity from Judaism, done more for social convenience than from conviction. During adulthood, Marx was constantly torn by his dual commitment to scholarly understanding and political action. He knew that his passion for reading and studying interfered with his political activism. At the same time, his political zeal crept into his scholarship so that his writings seethe with partisan outbursts and scathing condemnations of class interests.

Despite these characteristics, or perhaps because of them, Marx left a lasting mark on the world. His originality as a social thinker lies in an ambitious attempt to synthesize all social knowledge since the time of Aristotle. Through a better understanding of the conditions of human development, Marx hoped to accelerate the process by which humanity moves to the highest stage of development. His vision of this ultimate society, dimly sketched, was that of a communist system based on rational planning, cooperative production, and equality of distribution. Above all, it was to be a society liberated from all political and bureaucratic hierarchies.

Today's professed Marxist societies score very poorly on this last point, but for Marx the "withering away of the state" was critical. Perhaps the tendency of his followers to compromise on this matter was what led Marx to declare on his deathbed, "I am not a Marxist."

reaches maximum efficiency—paralleling the larvae–pupae–cocoon–adult maturation process of a butterfly. Thus, Marxists declare that "capitalism contains the seeds of its own destruction." But why should the chain of events leading to the overthrow of capitalism be inevitable? Answering this question requires digging a bit deeper into Marxist doctrine.

Wages and Value

What makes something valuable? Most contemporary economists use supply-and-demand analysis to explain relative prices. Marxists view this approach as superficial and argue that the value of a good is proportional to the labor time socially necessary for its production. For example, if ballpoint pens require twice the labor needed to produce wooden pencils, then pens are worth twice as much as pencils. This *labor theory of value* was the standard explanation of prices from the time of John Locke until late in the nineteenth century.

But what is "socially necessary labor"? And what about the roles capital and land play in production? Marx defined *socially necessary labor* to include not only direct labor time, but also the labor used to construct factories and to produce the capital equipment used in production. Marxists view all commodities and capital as *embodied* labor. Thus, production that uses up capital actually transforms the labor embodied in capital into a different form of congealed labor.

Interestingly, Marxists perceive only "hands-on" working time as labor. Service workers and pencil pushers are not regarded as providing true labor. (Adam Smith had similar reservations about managers and service workers.) Moreover, not all hands-on work is socially necessary. For example, if you make mud pies that no one wants, your output could not be sold and your labor is not socially necessary. The labor theory of value is basically a supply approach, but by specifying that only socially necessary labor counts, Marxists bring demand in through the back door.

If prices are proportional to the amounts of direct and embodied labor in products, what determines wages? Karl Marx relied on the *subsistence theory of wages* developed by earlier thinkers to answer this question. This theory holds that wages will barely be adequate for biological needs, with minor adjustments to meet the social and customary needs of workers. Unlike most classical economists, Marx believed that unemployment, not population pressures, forces wages toward subsistence levels. When workers produce more than is required to meet a payroll, capitalists are able to exploit workers by paying them less than the value of their production. These differences are termed *surplus values* in the Marxist idiom. Marxists view all payments of interest, rent, and profits as surplus value.

Surplus Value and Capital Accumulation

According to Marxist dogma, people in mature industrial societies are divided into two classes: *capitalists* and *workers*. Workers, also known as the *proletariat,* own nothing but their own labor. Capitalists control working conditions and hours. A "reserve army of the unemployed" will take the jobs of workers unwilling to accept the working conditions laid down by capitalists. Competition from this surplus labor compels workers to accept subsistence wages. By setting longer working hours than those necessary to cover the subsistence wage, capitalists "appropriate" surplus values from workers. For example, if a worker can produce the subsistence wage in 5 hours but is forced to work 10 hours, a capitalist employer can appropriate surplus value equal to 5 hours of labor time.

Workers are unable to save because they only receive subsistence wages. Antithetically, capitalists receive more than is necessary for their subsistence and convert most of this "stolen" surplus value into the embodied labor known as capital. This exploitation enables capitalists to accumulate capital, to protect their privileged positions, and to avoid exploitation themselves. (Big fish eat little fish.) Because capital accumulation facilitates economic growth, capitalism is viewed as a necessary stage of development. Once society has accumulated sufficient capital, however, the capitalist "robber barons" are dinosaurs on their way to extinction.

Class Warfare

The proletarians have nothing to lose but their chains. They have a world to win. Workingmen of all countries unite!

—Karl Marx and Friedrich Engels
THE COMMUNIST MANIFESTO (1848)

Marxists view ever greater accumulations of capital as an inevitable result of competition among capitalists for surplus values. Marx believed that capitalism is plagued by a number of contradictions. Ever greater capital accumulation creates one such contradiction. Who will buy the goods produced by growing stocks of congealed labor? Workers can afford little from their subsistence wages, while capitalists spend far less than the surplus values they appropriate as their incomes. This leads to "underconsumption" and declining rates of profit. In Marxist theory, this contradiction foments business cycles in capitalist economies.

Marxists believe that capitalism is dynamically unstable. This means that each cyclical decline will be worse than the previous one, while successive economic booms accelerate at unsustainable rates. This occurs, according to Marx, because some capitalists will be wiped out during each depression and will be forced to join the proletariat. Thus, capital will be controlled by a shrinking pool of entrepreneurs. The final stage predicted by Marxists, *monopolistic finance capital,* involves an incredible concentration of economic power held by financial trusts. During this stage, imperialist wars rage among capitalist nations. Finally, massive unemployment will trigger short but violent revolutions, during which workers will seize control over the means of production that were stolen from them over many generations.

Marxist Predictions

The works of Marx and his collaborator, Engels, were written over a century ago. At that time, the evils of the factory system seemed blatant, and the aroma of revolution wafted throughout Europe. Marx and Engels were far from alone in predicting revolutions to overthrow the existing order. However, their *dialectical materialism* generated several predictions about the road to revolution:

1. ever greater unemployment and misery of workers.
2. declining rates of profit.
3. explosive business cycles.
4. rising concentrations of economic power.
5. increasingly aggressive imperialistic policies.
6. bloody revolutions (**class warfare**) as capitalistic economies reach maturity.

Mature capitalistic economies would fall to communism like rotten fruit. Class struggles would end when the proletariat overthrew capitalists and their middle-class lackeys, the *petit bourgeoisie.* A short "dictatorship of the proletariat" would follow, during which workers would share the full values of production (subsistence wages plus surplus values). Then, government would wither away, as unnecessary as an appendix. **Communism** would evolve as the final synthesis, characterized by a classless society in which people would live and work under the condition "from each according to ability, to each according to needs." And everyone would live happily ever after. In the end, the communist ideal resembles More's *Utopia.*

Most Marxist predictions seem way off target. Unemployment rates vary over the business cycle, but there is no discernible upward trend over the past century, even though growing percentages of the world's people have moved into the industrial labor force. The purchasing power of wages has risen rapidly over time. Are industrial workers increasingly miserable when most have color televisions and paid vacations? As Joan Robinson, a modern Marxist, noted, " 'You have nothing to lose but the prospect of a suburban home and a motor car' would not have been much of a slogan for a revolutionary movement."

Average rates of profit have varied widely over the past century, but there are no discernible long-run trends. Sporadic booms and busts have plagued capitalism, but with decreasing severity during the past half century. Marx was, however, almost alone in correctly predicting greater industrial concentration. Economic power did become more concentrated from 1850 to 1930, but recent evidence of accelerating industrial concentration is hard to glean from the data.

Increased roles for government, including the development of the modern welfare state, apparently have placed a safety net under the living standards of the poor, dampened business cycles, and diminished the growth of concentration. Most of the evils of capitalism identified by Marxists have been at least partially cured by the growing role of government in the market system. Marx's assertion that "the state is nothing but the organized collective power of the ruling classes" is almost certainly wrong.

Perhaps the most telling rebuttal of Marxist predictions is that communist revolutions have bypassed most industrialized capitalist nations, occurring instead in feudal agricultural economies. The Soviet Union, China, Cuba, Vietnam, Campuchea, Nicaragua, and other underdeveloped countries have "gone communist." Czechoslovakia and East Germany were industrialized before falling to Marxism, but were conquered or destabilized by wars. Imperialistic wars started by capitalist nations largely ended around the turn of the last century.

FIGURE 1 *Per Capita GNP for Selected Countries (in Billions of 1985 U.S. Dollars)*

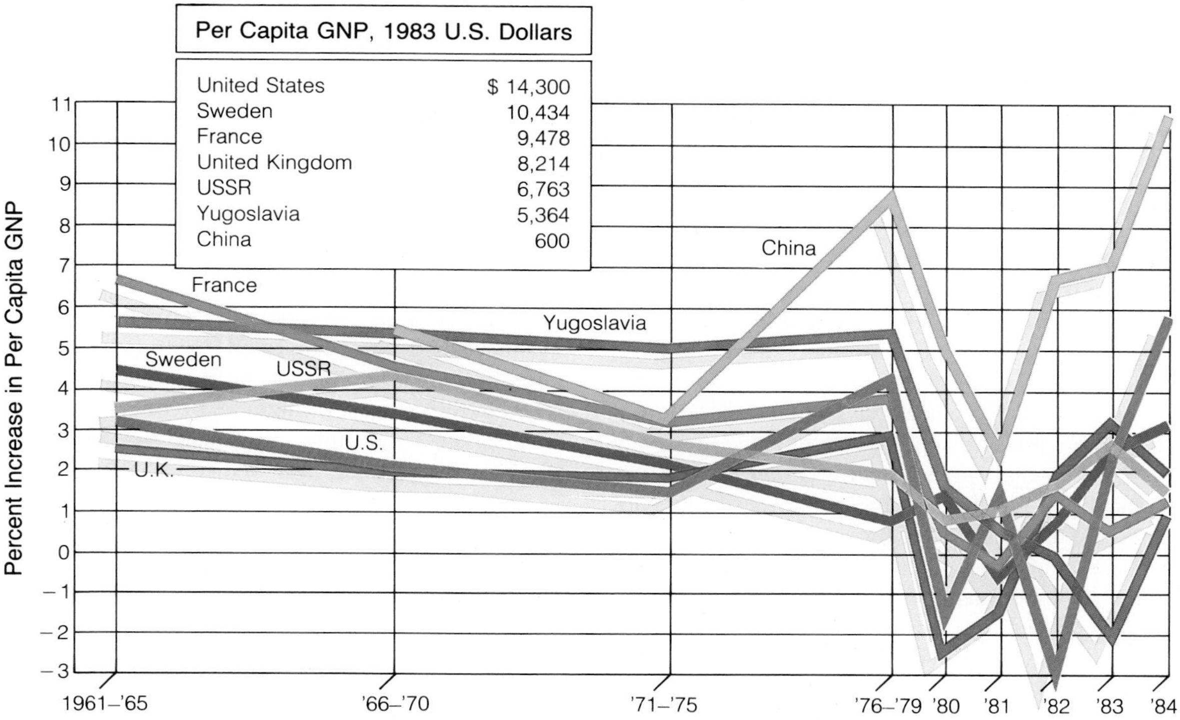

Per Capita GNP, 1983 U.S. Dollars	
United States	$ 14,300
Sweden	10,434
France	9,478
United Kingdom	8,214
USSR	6,763
Yugoslavia	5,364
China	600

Source: CIA, *Handbook of Economic Statistics*, 1985.

Today, significant imperialism originates mainly from the Soviet Union (the USSR's recent offensive in Afghanistan is one example) and Cuba (the Angolan and Ethiopian revolutions were executed in part by Cuban troops). Marxists have pointed to the Vietnam War as evidence of American imperialism, but economic motives for our involvement are hard to find. Marx, referring to Czarist Russia in 1867, asserted: "The policy of Russia is changeless. . . . Its methods . . . may change, but the polar star of its policy—world domination—is a fixed star." It is ironic that one of the few correct Marxist prophecies concerns the first country to follow the Marxist path.

One famous Marxist slogan is: "Religion is the opiate of the masses." Paul Samuelson, a Nobel Prize winner, has rephrased this: "Marxism is the opiate of the Marxists." No matter how brutal some socialist regimes are (for example, the Soviet Union under Stalin or Cambodia under Pol Pot) or how poorly Marxian predictions conform to the world, many Marxists persist in believing that humanity would be better off if it were dominated by worldwide communism.

Have ideal societies been implemented when Marxists have gained control? Unfortunately, Marx and Engels wrote thousands of pages on capitalism and its ultimate collapse, but less than a hundred pages hint at the economic order that was to succeed capitalism. When communist revolutions succeeded in feudal rather than industrialized countries, the new leaders were on their own. Markets could no longer answer the What? How? and Who? questions; alternatives had to be invented.

The next section examines the economies of six countries with varying combinations of central planning and market decision making: the USSR, China, France, Sweden, Yugoslavia, and Great Britain. Figure 1 indicates the levels of development of these six relative to the United States and compares their respective growth since 1960.

Alternative Economic Systems_____

The conditions under which men produce and exchange vary from country to country, and within each country again from generation to generation. Political economy, therefore, cannot be the same for all countries and all historical epochs.

        —*Friedrich Engels*

Ownership of resources under socialism and capitalism alike implies the right to receive the income generated by the resources and to decide how the resources are to be used. In socialist economies ownership is collective, with government acting as trustee over capital and land. Conversely, both ownership of and decision making about all resources are largely private in capitalist economies.

Even if ownership is primarily private, the government allocates most resources in all wartime economies and under Fascist regimes (Hitler, Mussolini, et al.). Alternatively, ownership may be collective but controlled at industry or local levels, where small groups effectively act as entrepreneurs, in keeping with syndicalism or decentralized socialism. All these alternative systems have been tried in some fashion.

Central Planning

The idea of central planning elicits outrage from most of American business. Ironically, **central planning** resembles planning within many corporate giants, and central planning bureaucracies are similar to corporate hierarchies. But if a government directly controls resources and rejects use of the marketplace, how does it determine what, how, when, and for whom to produce? The major alternative to a market system is central planning. In large, diversified economies, it is overwhelmingly difficult to coordinate production and distribution. This has not prevented the use of central planning by the USSR, China, and some of their satellites.

The Soviet Experience   The October Revolution of 1917 was led by Vladimir Ilyich Ulyanov (more widely known by his alias, Lenin). Under Bolshevik communism, the Soviet economy floundered until the inception of the first *Five Year Plan* in 1929 under Iosif Djugashvili (known as Stalin). The Soviet economy averaged annual growth estimated at 4–6 percent between 1929 and 1970, a remarkable accomplishment, especially when you consider the destruction of industry that occurred during World War II. Although Soviet economic growth has faltered in recent years, the economic distortions common under central planning make this earlier feat of growth even more impressive.

Central planning requires establishing detailed production targets for every sector of the economy. After production quotas are set, the Soviet central planning agency, *Gosplan,* must channel the outputs of some industries to others. For example, sufficient coal and iron ore are required for the steel industry to meet its quota. Glitches are common. Coordination problems were almost insurmountable prior to the development of computers. Even today, production processes sit idle more often than not while waiting for necessary intermediate goods.

Once the central plan is set, responsibility for meeting the quotas is left to "enterprise managers." Much of their income now depends on how well they meet their quotas. Production quotas are set in *success indicators*—specific terms such as product mix, weight, number of units, value, and so on. Each indicator unfortunately leads to a different type of distortion.

Suppose, for example, that you were in charge of the nail industry, and your quota was set in tons of nails. What would be the easiest way for you to beat your quota? By weight, heavy spikes are easier to produce than small nails. Naturally, if your quota were set in numbers of nails, you would produce lots of tacks. Length? Long skinny nails. Value? Only high-priced steel would become nails. When sewing machine quotas have been set in terms of value, the output is inoperable sewing machines, ornately decorated with gold filigree. Similarly, quotas for square feet of housing generate warped floors and cracked walls; required units of clothing invite sloppy sewing on shoddy material. Former Premier Kruschev cited a case where the chandelier quota was expressed in tons. You can imagine what happened. The consequence is that consumers' needs are poorly met, and most intermediate goods are of inferior quality. In fact, many failures of central planning occupy warehouse space for years and finally become landfill.

Why are similar problems rare in market economies? The answer is fairly simple. Managers of capitalist enterprises know that profits require production to be cost efficient and to consist of goods that consumers demand. Otherwise, firms will go bankrupt. Why do the Soviets continue to rely on central planning? Part of the answer lies in Marxist ideology. Because the market system is intolerable, central planning is viewed by many Marxists as necessary. Another part of the answer is that the leaders of the bureaucracies engaged in planning are unwilling to surrender their political power. But the strongest explanation is that the Soviet Union has grown in spite of the inefficiencies that emerge from planning.

Why has growth defied the hindrances of central planning? Wages and prices in the Soviet Union are established within Gosplan. Setting high prices for consumer goods and holding wages down has enabled planners to divert substantial production to the military and into investment in heavy industry. Even high prices and low wages, however, have not prevented the long lines for consumer goods in which most adult Soviet citizens spend roughly 10 percent of their time.

It seems paradoxical that the surplus values extracted from workers have probably been larger under central planning than in most capitalist economies. During earlier Five Year Plans, massive investment depressed the living standards of most Soviet citizens. Today, because of these earlier sacrifices, Soviet consumers are getting slightly larger pieces of a much larger pie. But there are invariably shortages of many products and surpluses of others because the forces of supply and demand are ignored. Moreover, the real costs of most goods far exceed their prices in rubles because of the time people must spend acquiring information about availability, and then waiting in queues to get them.

The **convergence hypothesis,** first stated in the 1960s by a Soviet economist named Lieberman, suggests that capitalist economies will become increasingly socialistic, while centralized socialism increasingly will rely on market forces. Today, most meats and vegetables in the Soviet Union are traded through private enterprise *kolkhoz* markets (which planners would like to eliminate, but can't if they want people to have food). Growing regulation in the United States is also cited as evidence of the convergence hypothesis.

Contrary to Lieberman's hypothesis, there is also evidence of divergence. The Reagan Administration's attempts to deregulate business have been paralleled in the USSR by a crackdown on "economic crime": the illegal buying and selling by some private Rus-

sians of everything from blue jeans to cars to heavy industrial machinery. Without the grease of underground capitalism, the Soviet economy might grind to a halt. Our underground economy is probably tiny compared with the Soviet underground markets, which have allowed a large number of ruble millionaires to buy their ways into the privileged lifestyles of their country's ruling class.

Marx's dream of a "withering away of the state" has turned into the nightmare of a rigid bureaucracy controlled by a small clique. When Mikhail Gorbachev assumed power in 1985, he tried to institute sweeping reforms but had to settle for cosmetic changes. Roberto Michels, an early sociologist, may have explained why with an idea he termed "The Iron Law of Oligarchy." Michels observed that British and Italian union leaders jealously guarded their power, that their attempts to retain power commonly involved use of a vertical hierarchy of underlings, and that leaders' successors were just like themselves. He theorized that virtually all organizations from local PTAs to the United Nations follow this pattern. Certainly the Soviet leadership has followed this pattern, with one generation of high-living bureaucrats being succeeded by another.

The Chinese Experience   When Mao Tse-tung led the Communists to victory in 1949, he imposed an oppressive but stable government on China, which had known little except political turmoil, oppression, and famine for centuries. China's new leaders initially viewed the Soviets as parent figures and imported a host of Soviet policies, including central planning. Even after an ideological schism in the 1950s evolved into border skirmishes and general hostility between the two countries, the Peoples' Republic of China remained a strong command economy. In many ways, there was less economic freedom in China than in the USSR. For example, Soviet workers typically had more choices about their employment than the Chinese had.

Mao was determined to reshape his people and insisted that "the new man in the new China" dutifully and selflessly work for the common good rather than personal advancement. He abhorred the use of material incentives to encourage work effort and, with his radical followers, was hostile toward technical experts and professional managers. Consequently, communal leaders and factory managers were frequently chosen because of adherence to

Maoist principles instead of ability to do the job. According to Mao, all work is equally valuable, and the "new Chinese man" should be able to perform every type of work. Thus, China often compounded the inefficiency of central planning with failures to benefit from a specialized work force.

In spite of these problems, the People's Republic compiled an enviable record of economic growth, although there were severe downturns when Mao instituted "The Great Leap Forward" from 1958 to 1960 and "The Great Proletarian Cultural Revolution" from 1966 to 1969. During these periods, many of the experts who had managed to get the economy going were purged. These disruptions caused great losses of Chinese production and income, as was indicated in Figure 1.

China has averaged 4–7 percent annual growth since the death of Mao and the ouster of his cohorts. A major reason is that experts and skilled professional managers eventually regained power after each purge. In the 1980s, Deng Xiaoping, a practical leader determined to modernize China, began opening up the Chinese economy to market determination of prices and outputs. Central planning is gradually giving way to a decentralized form of socialism.

Although the People's Republic of China still officially follows egalitarian policies, entrenched party leaders obviously live far more comfortably than the masses of Chinese. Elaborate parties to entertain visiting foreign dignitaries hint at this luxury. Even so, the distribution of income and wealth may be a bit more equal in China than in capitalist economies or in the Soviet Union.

Many evils have been virtually eradicated under Chinese communism, including illiteracy, child prostitution, begging, and starvation. Medical care is widely available where once it was unknown. Unlike many other underdeveloped countries, China is quite sanitary. The Chinese are not litterbugs. The Chinese Revolution extracted significant costs in human life over a 25-year period, however, and restrictions on individual freedom are only slowly being phased out.

After Marco Polo visited the court of Kublai Khan, he described China to fifteenth-century Europeans as cruel and mysterious. China remains a mystery to Western economists because Chinese statistics are even more misleading and less available than Soviet statistics. As the nation becomes more modernized

and open to the West, we will undoubtedly get better information about the Chinese economy.

Decentralized Socialism, Indicative Planning, and Welfare States

Modified capitalism and centrally planned socialism, as practiced respectively in the United States and the Soviet Union, delineate a range of economic systems that leaves a vast middle ground. Private ownership of productive resources may be blended with substantial planning and extensive welfare systems, or social ownership of resources may be combined with market determinations of what is produced and how production occurs. There is actually more economic planning in France, a nominally capitalistic country, than in such avowedly Marxist countries as Yugoslavia or Rumania.

France and Indicative Planning   Although the French economy is primarily capitalistic, it uses planning far more than other modern Western economies. The leaders of government, industry, and labor unions meet regularly to exchange information and to negotiate targets for industrial production. Through this process, the French attempt to coordinate their activities so that specific shortages, surpluses, and production bottlenecks can be avoided. For example, if the housing industry expects a boom, the lumber and brick industries are alerted and construction unions are notified to step up their apprenticeship programs. A bumper crop of superior French wines might cue government officials to negotiate for reduced foreign tariffs on French exports. The French government has also tightly controlled investment planning. By setting up plans to coordinate economic activities, it normally secures voluntary compliance to the overall plan. However, when specific unions or industries fail to comply, the government has shown little reluctance about using sanctions and price controls. Government is very significant in the French economy, collecting 2 francs in taxes out of every 5 francs of GNP.

Planning expanded under the administration of François Mitterand, elected in 1981. Mitterand nationalized banking as well as some heavy industry. Although the French economy performed very well for a period after the inception of **indicative planning**, with fairly consistent growth and negligible unemployment from the mid-1950s until the mid-

1970s, it faltered even more than most others in the early 1980s. This resulted in France's redirection to a somewhat greater reliance on markets in the mid-1980s.

Sweden's Welfare State

Sweden is typical of Scandinavian **welfare states.** Productive resources are largely privately owned, but high taxes and a massive welfare system mean that income from these resources is distributed across the society. Extreme poverty has been eliminated because the welfare system covers every Swede from the cradle to the grave. Thus, the Swedish economy has been called "welfare capitalism."

Worker productivity in Sweden is unsurpassed anywhere, and per capita income now rivals that in the United States, in spite of the diminished incentives that many people consider vital to hard work. Only about 5 percent of all Swedish enterprises are government operated. More than 90 percent of all businesses are private; roughly 5 percent are operated as producer or consumer cooperatives.

Many Americans view themselves as very heavily taxed, with 30 percent of gross domestic product absorbed in taxes. In Sweden, taxes absorb roughly half of the country's GNP, the highest tax take of any industrialized capitalist economy. The tax system is surprisingly simple, relying heavily on a very progressive income tax structure to foot the bill for most social programs.

Swedish prosperity is unquestionably aided by the fact that the nation has not been heavily involved in a major war for more than a century and that it allocates few resources to national defense. A long history of industrialization has fostered a well-developed work ethic. Although collective bargaining is widespread, negotiations between unions and management have generally been peaceful.

Worker Management in Yugoslavia

Like many Eastern European countries, Yugoslavia emerged from World War II as a Soviet satellite. However, Yugoslavia's strong man, Marshall Josip Broz, known as Tito, had an independent streak. Breaking with the Soviet Union in 1950, Yugoslavia abandoned rigid central planning and adopted a system uniquely its own.

This system is very similar to syndicalism. Yugoslavia's economy combines social ownership of productive resources with market determinations of prices and outputs and enterprise management by workers' councils. Planning is of a moderate indicative planning variety, with substantial attempts to coordinate the economy through meetings between workers' councils and government officials.

Yugoslavia has experimented with several mechanisms, including price controls, to achieve stable economic growth. However, a syndicalist-like fear of "state bureaucratism" has limited the role of the central government. In keeping with classical Marxism, Yugoslavs believe that the onset of socialism should precipitate a "withering away of the state." In their minds, this decay of the state cannot begin soon enough. Consequently, most economic activity is conducted by 566 small communes, or self-contained government units.

Most economic policies have been adopted in a pragmatic fashion rather than on the basis of pure Marxist theory. Some policies have worked very well; others have proved disastrous. Consequently, Yugoslavia has experienced economic swings similar to those in many Western economies that have followed stop-go economic policies.

Although still far from a wealthy country, Yugoslavia has developed substantially since World War II, averaging roughly 4 percent annual growth. Whether this syndicalist path will continue will depend on whether the Yugoslavs are able to stay out of the Soviet orbit. Still, the modest success of worker management in Yugoslavia has prompted interest in this concept in such diverse economies as the People's Republic of China and Great Britain.

Has the Sun Set on Britain?

Rudyard Kipling's famous line, "The sun never sets on the British Empire," was true when he wrote it at the turn of the century. However, since World War I, the British Empire's colonies have evolved into only a very loose confederation, and there are now roughly a dozen countries that have surpassed Great Britain as a world power. Mighty civilizations have risen and fallen before, but why did the world's first industrial giant fall by the wayside? Some observers attribute Britain's decline to World War I. Others point to a lack of coherent and consistent economic policy.

Just as the Middle East has spawned many important religions, Great Britain is the birthplace of most of the world's economic systems. Utopian and Fabian socialism, the welfare state, the roots of capitalist ideology, and Keynesian demand management policies all found British soil to be a fertile breeding ground. Marx researched most of the three volumes of *Das Kapital* in the British Museum.

The decline of Britain may have resulted from erratic policies that meandered among the ideas expressed by a multitude of economic prophets. From the time of John Locke's writings about private property until World War I, Britain was among the most capitalistic of countries. Then Fabian socialism gave birth to Labour governments that nationalized much of British industry.

Militant unionism and an unwillingness to promote new investment have rendered British industry obsolete. Britain has been reluctant to allow entrepreneurs to pursue the most profitable investments available; instead, political pressures have channeled investment spending towards senile industries. The extensive and expensive British welfare system appears to have squelched work incentives, while high tax rates and threats of nationalization have dampened new investment and technological innovations. Highly progressive tax rates, especially on investment income, have stymied entrepreneurship and left English workers using antique technology. But wealth is apparent on London streets. This paradox is explained by the fact that wealthy English people choose to squander their money on furs and Rolls-Royces rather than engage in risky investments from which confiscatory taxes prohibit much of a rate of return.

Just as the Roman Empire dissolved and Italy emerged, the British Empire has devolved into England. Italy and England have followed similar paths in terms of economic power and international influence. Whether England's downward spiral is halted may be contingent on how well Prime Minister Thatcher succeeds in her announced plans to resurrect the marketplace.

Is Small Both Beautiful and Necessary?

Scarcity exists when people want more than is available. There are two basic ways of dealing with the problem of scarcity. The first, emphasized in all of the economies we have described and by most economists of both capitalist and socialist persuasions, is to stretch resources as much as possible by maximizing production to try to accommodate human de-

sires. The second approach is to try to reduce human wants to levels consistent with the resources at hand. Those who advocate this second path are opposed to both capitalist and socialist visions of the proper economic system.

One set of critics attack vast material production as an improper goal that leads us away from fulfilling our spiritual needs. These critics focus on inner peace and living in harmony with nature as more appropriate goals. According to them, **small is beautiful.** Religious leaders who preach that materialism pits individual against individual and against the divine will are legion. The teachings of E. F. Schumacher, who developed his *Buddhist economics* from Buddhist and Hindu ideas, are representative of this view.

Other critics of capitalism accept material production as desirable but argue that unchecked capitalism devours depletable resources and will leave nothing for future generations. These critics argue that there are natural *limits to growth* and view environmental despoliation as part of the price we pay for excessive economic development. They fear the onset of a new Dark Age in which human society will have "run out" of everything, and believe that if "small is beautiful," small is also necessary to our survival.

Buddhist Economics

Minimizing human wants is the central thrust of many idealists and religious people who recognize that people have fundamental material needs but who consider color televisions, flashy clothes, and sporty cars as distractions that impede spiritual development. Thus, things that many of us consider necessary for "the good life" are actually perceived as obstacles in the way of the good life favored by these idealists. Such critics believe that most of our material demands are foisted on us by capitalists, who use the demands for their products to cajole people into working 40 hours a week or more.

Under a capitalistic system, income, status, and worth depend on work, so we stimulate work by creating artificial demands. Although many religions require their priests to take vows of poverty, certain aspects of Buddhism contain the most elaborate strictures, which assert that the path to nirvana (enlightenment) requires only minimal material comforts. These critics think that socialists have bought the line, "more means better," although the socialist stress on replacing competition with cooperation is at least partly in keeping with the religious values underlying the Buddhist approach.

In a best-selling book, *Small Is Beautiful: Economics as if People Mattered,* E. F. Schumacher elaborated the economic ideas of Mohandas Gandhi, a Hindu who led India to independence from Britain after World War II.[1] Gandhi emphasized decentralization, local self-sufficiency, and small scale, labor intensive technology; he rejected mass production and the sophisticated technology that characterize modern industrial states. Gandhi recognized that production in isolated villages is inevitably lower than in densely populated cities in which crowds of people work on assembly lines in loud, noxious factories. However, he felt the benefits of the simple life were well worth the costs of the foregone production. Gandhi's philosophy is akin to Buddhism in that it emphasizes the spiritual enrichment to human life available, in this case, by avoiding industrialization.

Limits to Growth

Some critics argue that strong controls are needed to contain economic growth. They cite the energy crisis of the 1970s, widespread concern over pollution, and computer forecasts as evidence that excessive desires for consumer "goodies" will soon deplete the natural resources of "Spaceship Earth." These critics, including such prominent economists as Kenneth Boulding, argue that capitalism encourages people in highly developed economies to seek ever higher consumption. In their view, this "cowboy" mentality promotes a disregard for the pollution generated by heavy industry and "Anti-Earth gas guzzlers." It also depletes the minerals, timber, and other resources necessary to sustain future generations.

They point out that known reserves of petroleum, coal, metallic ores, and other finite raw materials are insufficient to supply the world's populations if less developed countries grow to the standards of living enjoyed by people in North America and Western Europe. Moreover, their projections suggest that even without economic growth, if raw materials continue to be depleted at current rates, most will be gone within two or three generations. Their solutions? Get natural, rid ourselves of plastic-oriented mind-sets, and generally scale everything down.

Defenders of capitalism and growth try to rebut these arguments by suggesting that technological advances will permit continued growth, and that automatic changes in relative prices will force us to use natural resources more efficiently as they become scarcer. Moreover, they suggest that as our technology advances, we will learn to use raw materials presently seen as worthless. Those who advocate limits to growth are generally pessimistic that technology will bail us out of the difficulties they foresee.

---

1. E. F. Schumacher, *Small Is Beautiful: Economics as if People Mattered* (New York: Harper and Row, 1973).

CHAPTER REVIEW: KEY POINTS

1. Pure capitalism is based on private property rights and laissez-faire government policies. Government is limited to providing defense, policing crime, and enforcing property rights and contracts.

2. *Libertarianism* is a philosophy that rejects almost all but the simplest government activities. It strongly advocates laissez-faire capitalism.

3. *Anarchy* is the absence of government. *Syndicalism* is a system in which an industry's workers own the means of production, which are controlled by democratically elected worker councils. Syndicates are, effectively, trade unions that own their industries.

4. *Socialism* entails eliminating private ownership of nonhuman productive resources and replacing it with collective ownership.

5. *Marxism* is based on *dialectical materialism,* which suggests that the course of human history is determined by clashes between an economic *thesis* and its *antithesis* that yield a *synthesis,* or progression for human life.

6. Marxism postulates conflicts between economic classes that emerge from the theft by capitalists of *surplus values,* which are the excesses of production over subsistence wages. These surplus values are translated into accumulations of capital.

7. Marx predicted (*a*) growing wretchedness and unemployment of the working class, (*b*) accelerating concentrations of capital, (*c*) declining rates of profit, (*d*) explosive business cycles, (*e*) increasingly aggressive imperialistic policies, and (*f*) bloody revolutions as capitalist economies reached full maturity. In most respects, except for the (now slowing) concentration of capital, these predictions seem totally erroneous.

8. The Soviet Union and the People's Republic of China have used *central planning* extensively, and have managed very high growth rates in their command economies by forcing consumption down in order to raise social saving and investment. These economies have been plagued with inefficiency; great loss of freedom has been just one among the many costs of their rapid economic development. China seems increasingly willing to let market forces operate now that Mao Tse-tung is dead and pragmatic new leaders are at the helm.

9. *Indicative planning* is used in France to coordinate the activities of industries, unions, and government. Although not as bureaucratic as Soviet central planning, government has used strong legal and economic sanctions to ensure compliance with its plans.

10. Northern European nations such as Sweden have extensive welfare programs financed by heavy tax rates. However, industry is largely in private hands, and labor productivity is as high as anywhere in the world.

11. *Worker management* of industry has been used in Yugoslavia, which has rejected Soviet-style central planning in favor of indicative planning. The results of this experiment in syndicalism have been mixed, but have attracted attention.

12. Perhaps the most radical criticisms of capitalism and all economies based on material production assume that the proper solution to scarcity is to curtail our material wants and to simplify economic activity, even if this requires large losses of production. Less radical critics argue that there are *limits to growth,* and that we must all learn to live with less.

QUESTIONS FOR THOUGHT AND DISCUSSION

1. People work not only to receive their wages and salaries, but also to gain the approbation of their peers and the respect of their neighbors. Many business firms confer impressive sounding titles on their employees or recognize long service with the proverbial gold watch. Worker heroes in the Soviet Union are awarded "Stakhanovite" medals if they consistently exceed their production quotas. "Self-criticism" and plaudits dished out in group therapy sessions shaped the personalities and work habits of Mao's "new man in China." These are a few of the many techniques that have been tried in attempts to mold or reduce greed as one type of motivation for work. Do you think human beings are inherently self-interested, or

do you think we are only conditioned to be greedy? If conditioning explains our greed, are the techniques we have described likely to be successful in reducing or channelling this self-interested behavior? Can you think of other techniques that would reduce avaricious behavior? Do you think it would be better if we were all less greedy? Why or why not? How do your answers to these questions relate to which economic system you think operates most efficiently and most compatibly with human welfare?

2. Suppose you were the president of an extremely impoverished country. After reading this chapter, would you choose socialism, capitalism, or some other system as the best path to accomplish economic growth and development? Why?

3. The role of government would be extremely limited if a libertarian became president and if libertarians were elected to majorities in Congress. Assuming that they did not all resign as a means of reducing government, what are some of the institutions or regulations that libertarians would eliminate or modify?

Epilogue

Where do you go from here? A few of you may regret having taken economics; others may feel that the time it took to prepare for the course was well spent, but you have no intention of extending your formal training in economics. Still others may choose to take one or two more courses in this field. We can promise those of you who fit into any of these categories that you will encounter economic analysis over and over again, regardless of the path your life takes.

But this epilogue is really addressed to those few students who find the analytical methods we use to address economic problems so intriguing that you are considering a career in the area. We are grateful that there are so few of you; otherwise, the supply of economists might be so monstrous that those of us who love economic reasoning would not be able to live comfortably doing the work we like best. John Maynard Keynes once issued a challenge that we would like to echo:

> The study of economics does not seem to require any specialized gifts of an unusually high order. Is it not, intellectually regarded, a very easy subject compared with the higher branches of philosophy and pure science? Yet good, or even competent, economists are the rarest of birds. An easy subject, at which very few excel! The paradox finds its explanation, perhaps, in that the master-economist must possess a rare combination of gifts. He must reach a high standard in several different directions and must combine talents not often found together. He must be a mathematician, historian, statesman, philosopher—in some degree. He must understand symbols and speak in words. He must contemplate the particular in terms of the general, and touch abstract and concrete in the same flight of thought. He must study the present in the light of the past for the purposes of the future. No part of man's nature or his institutions must lie entirely outside his regard. He must be purposeful and disinterested in a simultaneous mood; as aloof and incorruptible as an artist, yet sometimes as near the earth as a politician.
>
> —J. M. Keynes (1924)

Everyone who wishes to be an economist would do well to pursue the lofty goals implicit in Keynes's description.

GLOSSARY

NAME INDEX

SUBJECT INDEX

GLOSSARY

Ability-to-Pay Principle The idea that the rich should pay more taxes than the poor in supporting governmentally provided commodities and services. (See also Benefit Principle of Taxation.)

Absolute Advantage The early idea that nations should produce the goods for which fewer resources are absorbed than in other countries and exchange their surpluses for goods produced with fewer resources elsewhere; replaced by the Law of Comparative Advantage.

Absolute Price The monetary price of a good. (See also Relative Price.)

Administration (Implementation) Lag The period that passes before discretionary changes in policy can be instituted; monetary policy can be implemented quickly through the actions of the Federal Reserve Board and the Federal Open Market Committee; fiscal policies encounter substantial implementation lags because discretionary changes in taxes or government expenditures require changing the law.

Administrative Costs of Regulation Include the salaries of government workers, inspectors, office supplies, etc. (See also Compliance Costs of Government Regulation.)

Aggregate Demand Curve The negative relationship that exists between the general price level (P) and the quantity demanded (Q) of total national output.

Aggregate Expenditures The sum of consumption, investment, government purchases, and net exports; $[C + I + G + (X - M)]$.

Aggregate Expenditures Curve The relationship between Aggregate Expenditures and income; positively sloped because income induces spending. Sometimes known as a Keynesian cross diagram.

Aggregate Supply Curve A positive relationship between real national production (Q) and the absolute price level (P).

Aid to Families with Dependent Children (AFDC) One of the major programs designed to alleviate poverty; originally this program was characterized by a payment structure which provided overwhelming incentives for recipients not to work.

Allocative Mechanisms Alternative modes for a society to use in deciding how inputs will be allocated among competing ends and how incomes and production will be distributed.

Anarchism The idea that government should be eliminated, leaving people largely free to do as they please. Anarchists believe that social harmony would evolve naturally through cooperative efforts. Most philosophical anarchists recognize the importance of private property rights and, hence, completely disavow social ownership.

Appreciation of a Currency When the exchange rate (price) of a currency increases as measured by its exchange rates with other currencies.

Arbitrage The risklessly profitable process of buying a good at a lower price in one market and selling the same good at a higher price in another market; forces relative prices of the same good toward equality in all markets.

Artificial Barriers to Entry Significant barriers to entry that are not caused by natural market forces. These barriers are erected by government or by existing firms to exclude competition.

Asset Demand for Money The demand for money that exists because people (a) perceive money as being without risk relative to alternative assets, (b) confront transaction costs in acquiring other assets that exceed their expected rates of return, and (c) expect the prices of alternative assets to fall in the near future.

Automatic (Built-in) Stabilizers Government tax and spending mechanisms that automatically drive the federal budget into deficit when the economy slumps or into a surplus when the economy suffers from inflationary pressures; tend to stabilize economic activity. (See also Nondiscretionary Fiscal Policy.)

Automation Technological advances that result in the replacement of human labor by machinery.

Autonomous Expenditure Spending that is not related to income; this occurs at zero income. Investment, government purchases, net exports, and part of consumer spending are all treated as autonomous in very simple Keynesian models.

Autonomous Spending Multiplier The number which, when multiplied by the sum of the autonomous components of Keynesian Aggregate Demand, yields equilibrium income; in very simple Keynesian models, this multiplier equals the reciprocal of the marginal propensity to save. (See also Multiplier Effect.)

Average Fixed Cost (*AFC*) Total fixed cost (*TFC*) per unit of output (*Q*); *TFC/Q* graphs as a rectangular hyperbola.

Average Physical Product of Labor (*APP*$_L$) Production per worker; equals total output (*Q*) divided by labor (*L*); *Q/L*.

Average Propensity to Consume (apc) The proportion of disposable income consumed; **apc** = C/Y_d.

Average Propensity to Save (aps) The proportion of disposable income saved; **aps** = S/Y_d.

Average Revenue Revenue per unit of output; synonym for price in the absence of price discrimination; equals total revenue (*TR* or *PQ*) divided by output; *TR/Q*.

Average Revenue Product Revenue per unit of an input; is computed by dividing a given total revenue (*TR*) by the amounts of given resources (e.g., workers (*L*)) generating this revenue (e.g., *TR/L*).

Average Total Cost (*ATC*) The total cost incurred per unit of output; often termed *average cost* (*AC*) or *unit cost*; *ATC* = *AVC* + *AFC*.

Average Variable Cost (*AVC*) Variable cost per unit of output; equals *TVC/Q*.

Bad, Economic Anything the consumption of which decreases human happiness.

Balance of Payments A record of the payments between a country and the countries with which it trades. Balance of payments deficits occur when a country's payments of money to foreigners exceed its receipts from foreigners. A balance of payments surplus occurs when a country's receipts from foreigners exceed its payments to foreigners.

Balance of Trade (Deficit, Surplus) The relationship between a country's annual exports and imports. A deficit in the balance of trade exists when the dollar value of a country's imports exceeds the dollar value of its exports. A surplus in the balance of trade exists when the dollar value of a country's exports exceeds the dollar value of its imports. Differs from balance of payments because foreign investment flows and loans, etc., affect payments.

Barrier to Entry A significant obstacle of some sort that either discourages or prevents the entry of firms into an industry.

Barter Trading goods and services for other goods and services rather than money.

Basic Economic Problem Scarcity, which means that fewer goods are freely available than people want to consume.

Basic Economic Questions *What* economic goods will be produced, *when* and *how* will resources be used for which types of production, and *who* will be allowed to use the goods?

Benefit Principle of Taxation The idea that individuals should be taxed in proportion to the marginal benefits that they receive from governmentally provided commodities and services. (See also Ability-to-Pay Principle.)

Bilateral Monopoly Occurs when a monopoly supplier confronts a monopsonistic buyer.

Blacklisting Circulation by employers of lists to bar hiring of union organizers or other "troublemakers."

Black Market Transactions that violate legal price ceilings.

Block Pricing Price discrimination for utility rates.

Board of Governors The governing body of the Federal Reserve System. Six regular board members are appointed to staggered 14-year terms of office; the Chair is appointed to a 4-year term.

Bonds Promises by government or corporations to pay certain amounts of money by specific future dates.

Break-Even Point The rate of output at which total revenue equals total cost.

Bretton Woods Agreement (1946) Established both the International Monetary Fund and a fixed exchange rate system with the dollar as the world's key currency. Other nations agreed to peg their currencies to the dollar.

Budget Deficits or Surpluses Occur, respectively, when government outlays exceed or fall below government revenues.

Budget Line A line showing various combinations of goods which cost the same amount as the consumer's income.

Bureaucracy A large organization with many employees, called *bureaucrats;* tends to be governed by many rules and regulations, called *red tape.*

Business Cycles Alternating periods of expansion and contraction in economic activity.

Business Firms Centers of production; they sell goods in output markets and buy services in resource markets.

Buyers' Market Occurs when the prevailing market price lies above the equilibrium price, resulting in a surplus.

Capital All physical improvements made to natural resources that facilitate production, including buildings and all machinery and equipment.

Capital Deepening When the percentage growth of the capital stock exceeds the rate of growth of the labor force; real per capita output normally increases.

Capitalism An economic system based on private property rights and emphasizing private, as opposed to governmental or collective, decision making. (See also Free Enterprise System, Laissez-Faire, Market System, Socialism.)

Capitalization The process whereby income streams are transformed into wealth, resulting in the elimination of economic profits.

Capital Widening When the labor force and the capital stock experience identical percentage rates of growth.

Cartel An organization of firms that jointly make decisions about prices and production for the entire group, usually attempting to charge monopolistic prices and limit production to monopolistic rates of output. OPEC is an example.

Caveat Emptor An ancient legal doctrine which suggests that buyers are the best judges of whether or not they receive full value from the units of goods they purchase, and that buyers should bear the consequences of their own decisions; it means "let the buyer beware."

Caveat Venditor A legal doctrine reflected in prohibitions against fraud and in sellers' legal liability for damages if unknown dangers lurk in a product; a Latin phrase meaning "let the seller beware."

Celler-Kefauver Antimerger Act (1950) This act made it illegal for major firms to acquire the stock or assets of their competitors.

Central Bank An institution whose function it is to make a nation's financial system operate as smoothly as possible; generally acts as the government's banker.

Central Planning or **Centralized Decision Making** Major economic decisions are made by some central authority, as in the Soviet Union.

Certificates of Deposit (CDs) Very long-term, high-value savings accounts issued by financial institutions.

Christian Socialism Emphasizes the virtues and dignity of work and advocates labor unionization; rejects the violent means to overthrow capitalism advocated by radical socialists and communists.

Circular Flow Model Depicts how households and business firms interact. Households are centers for wealth holding and consumption, and they buy goods from the firms that produce them; firms buy resources from households in order to produce goods and services.

Classical Theory A systematic study of the functioning of a market economy which concluded that, in the long run, the economy would always attain full employment at equilibrium GNP, assuming the validity of Say's Law and flexible wages, prices, and interest rates.

Clayton Act (1914) This act specified particular offenses more precisely than did the Sherman Act (1890); the Clayton Act forbade price discrimination and interlocking directorates, exempted collective bargaining from antitrust actions, and exempted agricultural associations so that nonprofit corporations could be formed without violating antitrust laws.

Closed Shop A firm that has agreed to hire only union members; these agreements are illegal under the Taft-Hartley Act.

Coincident Indicators Data series that tend to reach their high points or low points approximately at the same time as aggregate economic activity reaches its high points and low points.

Collective Bargaining The process by which workers who are members of a labor union negotiate with an employer to set wages, hours, and working conditions.

Command Economy These economic systems resolve the basic economic questions through central planning; allocations of inputs and distributions of goods are coordinated by a bureaucracy.

Commodity Any tangible produced good that may be owned.

Commodity Money Has substantial value independently of what it will buy. Gold and silver coins are examples.

Common Stock Ownership shares in a corporation.

Communism An idealized classless society in which all people would live and work under the condition "from each according to ability, to each according to needs"; under communism, all nonhuman property would be owned collectively.

Comparable Worth The idea that jobs filled by women should generate wages equal to those paid to men with comparable skills.

Comparative Advantage, Law of The idea that mutually beneficial trade can always take place between two countries (or individuals) whose pretrade cost and price structures differ.

Competition A process driving price close to opportunity cost. Pure competition requires: (*a*) numerous potential buyers and sellers; (*b*) homogeneous outputs or inputs, precluding nonprice competition; (*c*) each buyer and seller to be small relative to the market so that no single decision will influence the price of the item or service; and (*d*) an absence of long-run barriers to entry or to exit. (See also Contestable Markets Theory.)

Complementary Goods Goods that are consumed together, such as tennis racquets and tennis balls; a negative cross-price elasticity of demand exists between complementary goods.

Compliance Costs of Government Regulation Costs incurred mainly by the private sector (and also by state and local governments) in the process of complying with regulations. (See also Administrative Costs of Regulation.)

Concentration Ratio The percentage of some aspect of market power (e.g., sales) wielded by the leading 4 or 8 firms in an industry.

Conglomerate A firm that operates in several different industries.

Constant Cost Industry The long-run industry supply curve is horizontal; constant per unit production costs are incurred for every output level because the supplies of all the resources used in the industry are perfectly price elastic.

Consumer Equilibrium (the Cardinal Utility Approach) A consumer maximizes total utility when the last cents spent on each good yield the same number of utils of satisfaction; there is no reallocation of spending by which total utility can be increased.

Consumer Equilibrium (the Indifference Curve Approach) Consumers maximize satisfaction upon reaching tangency between their budget constraint lines and the highest attainable indifference curves.

Consumer Price Index (*CPI*) A statistical comparison, over time, in the prices of many goods purchased by typical urban consumers; the base year equals 100, with subsequent changes in the price level reflecting inflation (over 100) or deflation (under 100).

Consumer Surplus A gain to consumers arising from differences between the amounts of money they would willingly pay to consume goods and the amounts that they must pay in order to consume the good; the area below their demand curves but above the price line.

Consumption Spending by households for goods used to gratify human wants; the major component of Aggregate Demand.

Contestable Markets Theory A recent theory suggesting that all advantages of pure competition as a market structure are realized if freedom of entry and exit exists, and that the number of firms currently in a market is not as important for efficiency as is the threat of potential new entrance. (See also Competition.)

Contraction (Recession) A decline in economic activity; unemployment and inventories rise unexpectedly.

Contribution Standard The idea that income should be distributed according to the productivity of one's resources.

Corporation An organization formed under state law that is considered a legal person distinct and separate from its owners.

Cost-Push Inflation Upward price level movements that originate on the supply side of the economy; most theories of cost-push inflation are institutional in nature; cost-push cycles of inflation generate clockwise adjustment paths of inflation versus real output.

Costs of Unemployment, Economic Include the opportunity costs of the output unemployed workers could have produced were they employed.

Credit A promise to pay at some future date is exchanged for money.

Cross-Elasticity of Demand A measure of the responsiveness of the quantity demanded of one good to changes in the price of another; computed by dividing the percentage change in quantity demanded of a good by the percentage change in price of another good: $\%\Delta Q_x/\%\Delta P_y$; positive for substitute goods, but negative for complementary goods.

Crowding-Out Hypothesis The idea that increases in government spending inevitably cause reductions in some private activity, normally consumption or investment.

Crude Quantity Theory of Money A monetary theory that the price level is exactly proportional to the nominal money supply (M).

Currency Coins and paper money.

Cyclical Deficit The difference between government revenues and outlays that emerges because the macroeconomy is operating below its potential level of output. (See also Structural Deficit.)

Cyclical Unemployment Unemployment that results from a recession.

Decentralized Decision Making When most decisions about what to produce, when and how to produce, and who gets to use output are determined in privately operated markets.

Decentralized Socialism Economic systems characterized by social ownership of resources, but which rely on markets to resolve the economic problem by setting equilibrium prices and quantities.

Decrease in Demand An entire demand curve shifting downward and to the left; occurs only if one or more of the nonprice determinants of demand change. Less will be purchased at each possible price.

Decrease in Supply The entire supply curve shifts to the left; occurs only if one of the nonprice determinants of supply changes so that less will be available at each possible price.

Decreasing-Cost Industry An industry for which the long-run supply curve is negatively sloped, reflecting declines in per unit costs as production in the industry increases.

Deflating The use of a price index to adjust monetary values for changes that occur to the price level over time.

Deflationary Gap See Recessionary Gap.

Demand Purchases of a good that people are actually willing and able to make, given the prices and choices available to them.

Demand Curve A graph of the maximum quantities of a good that people are willing to purchase at various market prices.

Demand Deposits Funds kept in a financial institution that by law must be available upon the depositor's demand; checking accounts.

Demand, Law of The quantity demanded of an economic good varies inversely with its price.

Demand Price The highest price that buyers are willing and able to pay for a specific amount of a good or resource. Also known as *subjective price*. (See also Supply Price.)

Demand Schedule A table reflecting the maximum quantities of a given good or resource that will be purchased at various market prices.

Demand-Side or **Demand-Pull Inflation** Hikes in the general price level that originate on the demand side of the economy; originates from either excessively rapid increases in the rate of growth of the nominal money supply or upward shifts in autonomous real expenditure schedules; demand-pull inflation generates a counterclockwise adjustment path of inflation versus real output.

Depreciation The amount of capital used up during a period. Also known as the capital consumption allowance.

Depreciation of a Currency A decrease in the value of one currency measured in terms of its exchange rates with other currencies.

Depression A sharp and sustained decline in business activity.

Derived Demand The demand for a resource that exists because of its productivity; resource demands are derived from demands for output.

Devaluation of a Currency Occurs when exchange rates are either "pegged" or fixed under a gold standard and some government decides to decrease the gold content of its currency; not synonymous with depreciation of currency.

Development, Economic Qualitative changes in an economic system; economic development occurs when there are improvements in either the quality of life or the quality of goods, or both.

Dialectical Materialism Karl Marx's explanation of historical changes; according to this theory of history, all massive social and cultural changes are determined by contradictions that exist in the ways that societies produce, exchange, distribute, and consume goods; for the most part, these contradictions are embedded in conflicts that exist between the different classes in society.

Diminishing Marginal Returns, Law of When additional equal units of a variable input are applied to fixed inputs, a point is inevitably reached where total output increases at a diminishing rate as additional units of the variable input are applied to the fixed inputs; diminishing marginal returns are pervasive even in the long run because it is virtually impossible to vary all of the influences on production both proportionally and simultaneously.

Diminishing Marginal Utility, Principle of Consumption of successive units of a good eventually causes an additional unit of the good to yield less satisfaction than that from the preceding unit.

Diminishing Returns, Law of The further any activity is extended, the more difficult (and costly) it eventually becomes to extend it further.

Dirty Float Occurs when governments intervene in a "floating" foreign exchange market in order to stabilize exchange rates.

Discount Rate (d) The interest rate that the FED charges member banks when they borrow money from FED "discount windows."

Discretionary Fiscal Policy Deliberate changes in government spending and tax policies for economic stabilization purposes.

Discrimination, Economic Occurs when equivalent units of a resource receive different rates of remuneration even though their potential marginal contributions to total output are the same.

Diseconomies of Scale A firm's average costs rise as output rises.

Disequilibrium When the forces for change in a system are not offsetting.

Disincentives Penalties that discourage an activity; often applied to government policies that discourage productive activities.

Disinflation A significant decrease in the rate of inflation, this normally creates pressures for recessions.

Disposable Personal Income (*DPI*) The after-tax income households receive in a given year; equals consumption plus saving ($C + S$).

Dissaving Negative saving; occurs when desired consumption expenditures exceed income; takes place when families go in debt or draw upon past savings in order to afford their purchases.

Distortion Costs of Inflation Losses from distorted decisions caused when inflation warps relative prices and reduces certainty.

Distribution Branch The arm of government in Musgrave's three-branch framework that would ensure equity in income distribution; this budget branch uses taxes and transfers of money to attain equity.

Divestiture When court orders require large corporations to break down into smaller independent companies.

Double Coincidence of Wants Must occur before trading can take place in a barter economy; refers to the fact that you must locate someone who has what you want and who also wants what you have in order to effect barter transactions.

Dumping Occurs when a country sells an export at lower prices than those prices charged domestically for the same good; might result from international price discrimination, which is a policy of charging desperate domestic buyers more than is charged less desperate foreign buyers; predatory dumping occurs when a country follows a strategy of driving competitors out of a market for a particular good in order to establish a monopoly.

Durable Goods Consumer goods that are useful for more than one year.

Economic Growth The quantitative change experienced by an economic system; economic growth occurs when a society acquires greater productive capacity which can be used for consumption or investment.

Economic Incidence of a Tax The final burden of a tax; that is, who actually pays the tax through lower purchasing power.

Economic (Capital) Investment Purchases of new output that can be used for further production. The four basic types of new capital are: (*a*) new business structures, (*b*) new residential structures, (*c*) new machinery and equipment, and (*d*) inventory accumulation.

Economic Profits The excess of revenues over the opportunity costs of the resources employed; these profits are a reward to an entrepreneur if they exceed the minimum necessary to continue the firm's existence and are a premium for risk bearing and innovating.

Economic Rent Surpluses reaped by owners of a resource if it is paid more than the minimum necessary to elicit the supply of the resource. (See also Rent.)

Economics The study of how individuals and societies allocate their limited resources in attempts to satisfy their unlimited wants.

Economies of Scale When long-run average costs fall as output rises.

Efficiency, Economic Occurs when the opportunity cost of some specific amount of a good is at its lowest possible value, and when maximum production from given resources and costs is achieved; implies that gains to anyone entail losses to someone else.

Efficient Markets Theory The idea that all possible gains that are foreseeable will be exploited by private individuals.

Elasticity The sensitivity of one variable relative to some other variable. (See also Income-Elasticity of Demand, Price-Elasticity of Demand (or Supply).)

Eminent Domain Government's legal right to acquire property without the previous owner agreeing to the price the government pays.

Empire-Building Exaggerating the difficulty of the mission of a bureaucracy so that the budget of the agency will be expanded.

Employment Act of 1946 A basic guide to national economic policy, this act established the Council of Economic Advisors and set priorities of full employment with price level stability, but provided few directives to the executive branch as to just how such goals should be achieved.

Employment Discrimination Occurs when particular groups suffer a higher incidence of unemployment than do other groups.

Entrepreneurship The organizing function which combines the services provided by other resources so that goods are produced.

Entry and Exit into an Industry If there are no barriers to entry and exit, entry into an industry by outside competitors or exit of existing firms will continue until economic profits are zero; positive profits will attract new entrants, while economic losses will cause exit from an industry. Threats of potential entry are crucial for competition and the key to "contestable" markets theory.

Equal Distribution of Income Standard One ethical criterion for distributing income and wealth; assumes that an extra dollar means more to the poor than to the rich, and ignores the disincentives for production that occur when incomes are independent of productivity.

Equal Marginal Advantage, Law of Efficiency requires similar resources to be used in equally advantageous ways. In consumption, this means that the last dollar spent on any good must generate the same satisfaction as the last dollar spent on any other good. In production, the last dollar spent on any factor must yield the same production as the last dollar spent on any other factor.

Equal Marginal Productivities per Dollar, Principle of The last few cents spent on any resource must yield the same additional output as the last few cents spent on any other resource. This is a requirement for least cost production and maximum profit.

Equal Marginal Utilities per Dollar, Principle of The last few cents spent on any good yield identical amounts of satisfaction or utility; algebraically, this requires $MU_1/P_1 = MU_2/P_2 = \ldots = MU_m/P_m$, where the subscripts 1 through m-1 denote commodities and m denotes money.

Equation of Exchange ($MV = PQ$) M denotes the nominal money supply, V denotes the income velocity of money, P denotes an index for the general price level, and Q denotes real output; a tautology, since it is true by definition.

Equilibrium Exists when the pressures that bring about change in the market system are in balance. Macroeconomic equilibrium—when desired demand expenditure equals actual income or output. Microeconomic equilibrium—when the quantities of a good or resource demanded and supplied are equal.

Equilibrium (Market-Clearing) Price The market price that clears the market.

Equilibrium Quantity The quantity of a good which is marketed at the equilibrium price.

Equity Fairness, a normative concept; value judgments are inherent in specifying what is fair.

Escalator Clauses Contractual obligations specifying that future payments of money will be adjusted for price level changes.

Excess Burdens of a Tax The amounts by which the total burden of a tax exceeds government revenue yielded by the tax.

Excess Demand The amount by which the quantity demanded exceeds the quantity supplied when the prevailing market price lies below the market-clearing price; normally associated with shortages.

Excess Reserves (XR) The amounts by which banks' legal (total) reserves exceed their required reserves.

Excess Supply The amount by which the quantity supplied exceeds the quantity demanded when the prevailing market price lies above the market-clearing price; normally associated with surpluses.

Exchange Controls Legal limits on the ability to buy or sell foreign currencies; frequently stimulate black markets for foreign money.

Exchange Rate The value of one currency expressed in terms of another currency or some combination of other currencies.

Excise Tax A per unit tax levied on a specific good.

Exclusive Good A good is exclusive if individuals can be excluded from access to the good at a relatively low cost; if these people do not pay, they may be excluded from consuming the good.

Expansion (Recovery) The phase of the business cycle when economic activity begins to increase; employment rises, inventories fall unexpectedly.

Expected Rate of Inflation The percentage annual rate at which economic transactors expect the general price level to rise.

Expenditure Approach to Estimating GNP GNP equals the sum of personal consumption, investment, government purchases of commodities and services, and net exports:
$$\text{GNP} = C + I + G + (X - M).$$

Explicit Costs Outlays of money to individuals or firms that are external to the producer; some examples are wages paid employees, rent payments, utility bills, and purchases of intermediate goods.

Exploitation Payment of wages that are less than the value of the marginal product of labor. May result from an employer's monopsony power as a hirer of labor or because a firm has monopoly power.

Exports Goods manufactured in this country and purchased abroad by foreigners.

External Supply Shocks These shocks, which originate outside the economy, shift the Aggregate Supply curve to the left; rising production costs create pressures for supply-side (cost-push) inflation and increasing unemployment.

Externalities Market failures that occur whenever some activity affects economic transactors who are not directly involved in the activity. Pollution is an example of a negative externality; education generates positive externalities to the extent that all of society gains from being a part of a more educated populace. External costs and benefits are largely ignored by individual decision makers.

Fabian Socialism This socialist theory advocates nationalizing only heavy industry; all other property would be privately owned, although extensive welfare programs would ensure that people's needs were met.

Family Allowance Plan (FAP) Many European nations and British Commonwealth countries now have family allowance plans that are based on the number of minor children in every family; these payments are usually adequate to feed and to clothe each child in the family and are made regardless of a family's level of income.

Featherbedding The employment of workers who are not in productive jobs; normally a result of union pressure or inefficient government regulation.

Federal Funds Market A privately operated network that enables banks to borrow or lend large amounts of money for very short periods.

Federal Open Market Committee (FOMC) The real policymaking body within the Federal Reserve System, it is comprised of all seven members of the Board of Governors, the President of the New York District Bank, and four other rotating District Bank presidents.

Federal Reserve System (FED) The central bank of the United States; created by Congress in 1913 to buffer financial crises by acting as a bankers' bank and lender of last resort; the most important role of the FED is conducting monetary policy.

Federal Trade Commission (FTC) Act (1914) Created the FTC and empowered it to challenge any "unfair methods of competition . . . , and unfair or deceptive acts or practices in or affecting commerce."

Fiat Money Money that is worthless as a commodity and which has value only because of its use as a medium of exchange.

Final Goods Goods purchased by the consumers or investors who ultimately use them.

Financial Capital Securities; paper claims to goods or resources.

Financial Intermediation The process by which household saving is made available through financial institutions to those desiring to spend in excess of their income (especially investors).

Financial Investment Paper documents representing financial claims on assets, created when purchases of stocks, bonds, and real estate are made.

Fine-Tuning Government attempts to make the economy function as smoothly as possible by frequently changing both monetary and fiscal policies to offset even minor fluctuations in economic activity.

Firm An entity that operates one or more plants and which buys productive resources from households.

Fiscal Drag A tendency to generate budget surpluses in a growing economy, assuming that government spending and tax rates remain unchanged; arising because of our progressive income tax, fiscal drag retards growth of Aggregate Demand.

Fiscal Policy Policies for government spending or setting tax rates or revenues to either stimulate or contract economic activity; intended to offset cyclical fluctuations in economic activity.

Fisher Effect Adjustments of nominal interest rates as borrowers and lenders compensate for expected inflation in order to secure some equilibrium "real" rate of interest.

Fixed Costs The total of all short-run costs not related to the level of production; fixed costs are also known as historical, sunk, or overhead costs, and are irrelevant for rational decision making.

Fixed Exchange Rate System A system of exchange rates in which international agreement is struck to fix the value of all currencies in terms of one another; the exchange rates of currencies are not allowed to respond to changes in the relative supplies and demands for the currencies; balance of payments surpluses and deficits occur in a fixed exchange rate system when equilibrium exchange rates differ from the fixed (pegged) exchange rates and can be eliminated only through adjustments of Aggregate Demands or Aggregate Supplies.

Flexible (Floating) Exchange Rate System The major alternative to a system of fixed exchange rates; under this exchange rate system, the supplies and demands of individual currencies determine the equilibrium and actual exchange rates for all currencies.

Flexible Wages, Prices, and Interest Rates According to classical theory, full employment was guaranteed by the existence of perfectly flexible wages, prices, and interest rates.

Flow Variable An economic variable that is only meaningful if measured over a period of time; income and production are examples.

Foreign Exchange A stock of foreign currencies held as an asset.

Forward (Futures) Markets Markets in which contracts to deliver currencies or products at some future date are bought and sold.

Fractional Reserve Banking System A banking system in which banks are legally required to hold only a fraction of their demand deposit liabilities in the form of reserves.

Free Enterprise System Agreements to trade are made by private buyers and sellers; ownership of resources is private, not social. (See also Capitalism, Laissez-Faire, Market System, Socialism.)

Free Good A good for which the quantity demanded fails to exceed the quantity available at a price of zero.

Free Rider Problem A problem encountered in the consumption of public goods; refers to the lack of incentives for people to reveal their true preferences for public goods once these goods are provided; non-exclusive goods can be consumed at a zero price by those who contribute nothing to cover their production costs.

Frictional Unemployment Unemployment that is a by-product of normal economic activity; it arises because no one possesses perfect knowledge concerning job opportunities nor free mobility between places of employment; lends a certain flexibility to the economy.

Functional Distribution of Income A breakdown of total income into the proportions paid to owners of various types of resources.

Functional Finance The view that balance in the economy is important and that imbalance in the federal budget is not important.

Future Goods Investments (postponed present consumption) which have the effect of increasing productive capacity.

Gains from Specialization of Labor The increased output yielded when workers use different types of specific expertise in performing a particular productive task.

Gains from Trade Improvements in human welfare because trading parties gain by acquiring (*a*) unique goods that they could not produce, (*b*) goods at lower costs than could be yielded by own-production, (*c*) transfers of technology, (*d*) greater income that, through higher saving, stimulates investment, and (*e*) calmer relations with other people because of mutual interdependence.

General Equilibrium Analysis A method of analysis which not only looks at the direct effects of some variables on others, but also at indirect effects and feedbacks among the economic variables.

General Training Training that increases the productivity of a worker equally for numerous possible places of employment.

GNP (Implicit Price) Deflator A price index composed largely of components from the *CPI* and *PPI*; used to adjust nominal GNP for changes in the price level.

GNP Gap The amount by which current GNP is below full employment GNP.

Gold Standard Money may be exchanged at a fixed rate for gold; e.g., until 1933, one ounce of gold could be bought from the U.S. Treasury for $35 or sold to it for $35.

Good, Economic Anything which satisfies a human want and, in so doing, increases human happiness.

Gresham's Law Bad money drives out good.

Gross National Product (GNP) The value of all production that takes place annually.

Herfindahl-Hirschman Index (*HHI*) The sum of the squares of the market shares of the firms in an industry; *HHI*s are now used as a guideline for antitrust actions.

Hoarding Holding money in idle cash balances; money that is hoarded is not spent on consumption or investment; causes velocity to fall.

Horizontal Combination A firm which has numerous plants producing identical or similar products.

Household Income Used for consumption, saving, or taxes.

Households Individual or family units that provide input services, and that are the ultimate storehouses of wealth; they purchase goods in the output markets, and they sell resources in input markets.

Human Capital Improvements made in the labor embodied in human beings; people invest in human capital so that their labor services become both more productive and more highly paid.

Human Capital Discrimination Reduces access by certain groups to schooling, on-the-job training, or to human capital investments.

Humphrey-Hawkins (Full Employment and Balanced Growth) Act (1978) Augments the Employment Act of 1946 by (*a*) identifying specific economic priorities; (*b*) directing the president to establish goals based on those priorities; and (*c*) creating procedures to improve the coordination and development of economic policy between the president, the Congress, and the Federal Reserve System.

Hyperinflation or **Galloping Inflation** Increases in the price level at rates exceeding 50 percent per month.

Idle Cash Balances Money that is hoarded.

Impact Lag The period that passes before newly implemented changes in policy have an impact on economic activity; the impact lag of tax policy is short relative to that of monetary policy.

Implicit Costs The opportunity costs of the physical and financial resources that a firm's owner makes available for production without direct outlays of money; some examples are the values of the entrepreneur's labor and land tied up in the firm.

Imports Goods produced in foreign countries and consumed or invested domestically.

Income Approach to Estimating GNP GNP equals the sum of personal consumption, total saving, and total taxes ($GNP = C + S + T$).

Income Effect Changes in patterns of consumption brought about because price changes also change the purchasing power of our money incomes; the income effect may be positive, negative, or zero.

Income-Elasticity of Demand A measure of the responsiveness of the quantity demanded of a good to changes in real income; computed by dividing the percentage change in the quantity demanded of a good by the percentage change in real income: $\%\Delta Q_{xd}/\%\Delta Y$. (See also Elasticity, Price-Elasticity of Demand (or Supply).)

Incomes Policies Measures intended to curb inflation without reducing Aggregate Demand expenditures; these policies include jawboning, wage and price guidelines, and wage and price controls.

Income Velocity (V) of Money ($V = PQ/M$) The number of times annually that the average unit of money changes hands during the process of purchasing GNP (PQ).

Increase in Demand When the entire demand curve shifts upward and to the right; more will be purchased at every price; occurs only if one of the nonprice determinants of demand changes.

Increase in Supply When the entire supply curve shifts rightwards; buyers will be offered more at every price; occurs only if a nonprice determinant of supply changes; causes equilibrium price to decrease.

Increasing-Cost Industry An industry whose long-run supply curve is an upward sloping line; higher costs per unit are incurred as production in the industry increases.

Index Numbers Numbers used to make relative comparisons of a specific variable between time periods.

Indicative Planning France, whose economy is primarily capitalistic, uses indicative planning which entails trying to coordinate economic activity by setting production targets for major industries.

Indifference Curve A line connecting the various combinations of two goods that yield the same total utility; the consumer is indifferent among the various bundles of goods along an indifference curve.

Indirect Business Taxes Various taxes that are viewed by business firms as costs of production; are not part of National Income since they are not resource payments. Examples are sales and excise taxes.

Induced Expenditures Expenditures that depend on income.

Industrial Policy Government uses subsidies, tax breaks, and protection from foreign competition to support "target industries" that have high productivity, strong "linkages", or future importance.

Industry All firms that compete in some product market.

Industry Interest Theory of Regulation Regulation of industry serves not the public interest, but instead serves the particular interests of the regulated industries.

Infant Industry Argument for Tariffs The notion that emerging industries need to be protected from more efficient, established, foreign competitors.

Inferior Good A good for which the income-elasticity of demand is negative; that is, the demand for this type of economic good varies inversely with real income; more technically, a good for which the income effect of a price change is negative.

Inflation Upward movements of the absolute price level.

Inflationary Gap The amount by which autonomous expenditures exceed those necessary for full employment income or output.

Informative Advertising Accurate information provided to consumers so that good economic choices can be made at lowered transaction costs; not a waste of resources.

In-Kind Transfers Welfare paid, not as cash, but rather as, e.g., food stamps, educational grants, or housing allowances.

Innovation In the 1930s, Joseph Schumpeter argued that progress in capitalist systems is driven by major innovations, including: (*a*) the introduction of a new good, or new quality in a familiar product; (*b*) the introduction of new technology; (*c*) the opening of a new market; (*d*) the discovery of a major source of raw materials; and (*e*) the reorganization of a major industry.

Inputs Things used in the production process, such as labor and raw or semifinished materials.

Interest Payments per time period for capital services.

Intermediate Goods Semiprocessed goods used in the production of other economic goods.

International Trade Exchanges of goods across national boundaries; facilitates efficient uses of the world's scarce resources.

Investment Additions to the economy's real capital stock, i.e., all final purchases of capital equipment (machinery, tools, etc.), all residential or commercial construction, and changes in inventories.

Invisible Hand Automatic market adjustments toward equilibrium.

Involuntary Saving Occurs when government policies decrease consumption in order to stimulate capital accumulation; governments can force individuals to save a portion of their income through taxation, inflationary financing of government expenditures, or by setting low wages and high prices.

Jawboning Oratory used by policymakers to persuade people or institutions to act against their individual interests; especially common as an exhortation to hold prices below equilibrium levels.

Joint-Profit Maximization The goal of a cartel among oligopolistic firms that try to share the profits that a monopoly would make if it controlled the industry.

Key Currency An international medium of exchange; the acceptability of the U.S. dollar as an international medium of exchange was the major reason that the U.S. has been able to run persistently large balance of payments deficits since 1951.

Keynes Effect The initial decreases (*increases*) in both the nominal interest rate and the real interest rate brought about by an increase (*decrease*) in the rate of growth of the nominal money supply.

Keynesian Aggregate Demand Total spending on domestically produced goods during a given year; $C + I + G + (X - M)$.

Keynesian Aggregate Supply The net value of all new goods and services available for purchase in a country during a given year.

Keynesian Fiscal Policy Policies designed to combat the problems associated with inadequate Aggregate Demand which plagued economies throughout the world during the 1930s.

Keynesian Government Growth Ratchet The tendency for government to grow because policymakers cut taxes and expand spending during economic downturns but do not raise taxes or cut spending during inflationary episodes.

Keynesian Investment Schedule The idea that investment demand is insensitive to movements of the interest rate, but that it is very sensitive to changes in expectations.

Keynesian Liquidity Preference The idea that the demand for money is extremely sensitive to interest rate movements and may even become horizontal at very low interest rates.

Keynesian Model A framework used to describe how output responds to changes in Aggregate Demand; generally ignores price level changes.

Keynesian Monetary Transmission Mechanism The idea that changes in the nominal money supply affect consumer spending only indirectly; money $\rightarrow$ interest rate $\rightarrow$ investment $\rightarrow$ income represents the chain of events emanating from a change in the money supply's rate of growth.

Keynesian Theory Specifies that macroeconomic adjustments involve changes in quantities below full employment and that price level changes only become the major adjustment mechanism when Aggregate Demand grows at full employment.

Keynes's Fundamental Psychological Law of Consumption Consumption expenditures increase as income rises, but by a smaller amount.

Kinked Demand Curve Model of Oligopoly An oligopolistic pricing model that explains noncollusive oligopolistic behavior and predicts stickiness or rigidity of prices in oligopolistic industries.

Labor Labor services are typically measured in terms of the total amount of time worked during a given interval.

Labor Force Participation Rate (LFPR) The proportion of a population in the labor force; computed by dividing the labor force by the total population.

Labor Theory of Value The idea that the value of anything is exactly proportional to the labor time socially necessary for its production; this approach was the standard economic explanation of price until late in the 1800s and is still an article of faith among Marxists.

Labor Union A worker organization that negotiates labor contracts with firms' managers to set wages and the conditions of work.

Laffer Curve A figure illustrating the idea that very high tax rates may so discourage productive efforts that fewer tax revenues are collected than if tax rates were substantially lower.

Lagging Indicators Data series that reach their respective high points and low points after the economy has peaked or troughed.

Laissez-Faire This philosophy embraces the notion that a market system operates most efficiently when government minimizes its activity in the economy; according to this philosophy, governments should provide national defense and police protection, specify property rights, and enforce contracts drawn up between economic agents—and little or nothing else. (See also Capitalism, Socialism.)

Land Includes all material resources, such as unimproved land, minerals, water, air, timber, wildlife, and fertility of the soil.

Leading Indicators Data series that reach their respective high points and low points before business cycle peaks and troughs.

Legal Barriers to Entry Governmentally erected barriers to entry into an industry; these barriers maintain monopoly power by legally prohibiting or limiting competition from other firms; barriers include patents, copyrights, and licensing or bonding restrictions.

Legal Incidence of a Tax Falls on the party who legally must pay the tax to government, but the economic burdens may be shifted to others.

Legal Reserves Total bank reserves; the sum of bankers' required reserves and excess reserves.

Lerner Index of Monopoly Power (*LMP*) An estimate of monopoly power using the percent by which price of output exceeds marginal cost; monopoly power is then measured as: $(P - MC)/P$.

Libertarianism A philosophy based on the notion that individual freedom is the most important social goal; libertarianism emphasizes the inherently coercive nature of government and urges reliance on the free market system to resolve nearly every human problem.

Limit Pricing Occurs when firms that possess monopoly power set a profitable price that is low enough to discourage potential entrants.

Liquidity How easy (costless) it is to turn an asset into cash; the transaction cost entailed with the purchase or sale of an asset is directly related to its illiquidity.

Liquidity Preference The total demand for money in a Keynesian model; derived by summing the transactions, precautionary, and asset (speculative) demands for money.

Liquidity Trap The horizontal portion of the Keynesian liquidity preference curve; occurs only when economic transactors choose to hold all increases in the nominal money supply in idle cash balances; it is doubtful if perfect liquidity traps have ever existed.

Logrolling When legislators trade votes.

Long Run (*LR*) A period of sufficient duration for all feasible resource adjustments to any event to be completed.

Long Run Average Cost Curve (*LRAC*) A curve showing the minimum average costs of producing each level of output after adjusting all resource inputs, including the size of the plant.

Long-Wave Theory of Business Cycles A theory of long (50–60-year) waves in economic activity was developed in the 1920s by a Russian economist named Kondratieff.

Lorenz Curve A Lorenz curve shows the degree of inequality that exists in distributions of income or wealth in a particular society.

M1 = currency + demand deposits in commercial banks + all interest-paying checkable accounts.

M2 = *M*1 + time deposits.

M3 = *M*2 + long-term deposits (Certificates of Deposit, or CDs).

Macroeconomic Equilibrium Occurs when Aggregate Supply and Aggregate Demand are equal; when this occurs, the economy is stationary.

Macroeconomics The branch of economics concerned with aggregate variables such as the levels of total economic activity, unemployment, inflation, the balance of payments, economic growth and development, the money supply, and the federal budget.

Majority Rule When the winning side of a vote must capture 50 percent plus one vote.

Malthusian Prognosis Reverend Thomas Malthus, an early nineteenth-century English economist, promulgated the dismal notion that all workers were doomed to live a subsistence existence; in formulating his forecast, Malthus neglected to consider the favorable impact of technological advances on the world's ability to produce food.

Mandatory Wage and Price Controls Price ceilings that carry legal penalties for noncompliance; instituted primarily during wars.

Marginal Cost Equals Marginal Revenue (*MC = MR*) A condition required for maximum profits. Typically, $MR > MC$ for units prior to the $MR = MC$ level of output, so extra output boosts profit or cuts losses. Higher output levels entail $MR < MC$ and would not be produced.

Marginal Cost (*MC*) The change in total cost associated with producing an additional unit of output; computed by dividing the change in total cost (ΔTC) by the change in output (ΔQ): $MC = \Delta TC/\Delta Q = \Delta TVC/\Delta Q$.

Marginal Factor Cost (*MFC*) The additional cost incurred in purchasing the services of an additional unit of a productive input; computed by dividing the change in total cost of production (ΔTC) by the change in input (ΔN): that is, $\Delta TC/\Delta N$; also computed by dividing the change in total variable costs of production (ΔTVC) by the change in input (ΔN): that is, $\Delta TVC/\Delta N$.

Marginalism The idea that decisions are based on the effects of small changes from a current situation.

Marginal Physical Product of Labor (MPP_L) The additional output produced by an additional unit of labor; computed by dividing the change in total output (ΔQ) by the change in labor (ΔL): $\Delta Q/\Delta L$.

Marginal Propensity to Consume (mpc) The change in saving brought about by a small change in disposable income: $\text{mpc} = \Delta C/\Delta Y_d$.

Marginal Propensity to Save (mps) The change in saving brought about by a small change in disposable income: $\text{mps} = \Delta S/\Delta Y_d$.

Marginal Revenue (MR) The additional revenue associated with selling an additional unit of output; computed by dividing the change in total revenue by the change in output: $MR = \Delta TR/\Delta Q$.

Marginal Revenue Product (MRP) The additional total revenue generated by an additional unit of a variable input; computed by dividing the change in total revenue (ΔTR) by the change in input (ΔN): that is $\Delta TR/\Delta N$; or by multiplying marginal revenue by the marginal physical product of a unit of input: that is, $MR \times MPP_n$.

Marginal Social Benefits (MSB) Computed by summing the marginal private benefits and the marginal external benefits, if any, from consuming additional units of commodities or services.

Marginal Social Costs Computed by summing the marginal private costs and the marginal external costs, if any, incurred in producing additional units of commodities and services.

Marginal Utility (MU) The additional utility or satisfaction derived by a consumer from the consumption of an additional unit of a good.

Margin Requirements An FED tool that sets the legal minimum percentage down payments required for purchases of stock.

Market Any mechanism that enables buyers and sellers to strike bargains and to transact.

Market Demand Curve A graphic representation totalling all individual demand curves; it is derived for most goods by horizontally summing all individual demand curves.

Market Economies Systems that rely on market interaction of supplies and demands to resolve the economic problem; the price system is used to coordinate the diverse plans of consumers and producers.

Market Equilibrium When neither shortages nor surpluses exist because, at the prevailing price, the quantities demanded and supplied are equal.

Market Failure When the market resolution of an economic problem is inefficient, inequitable, or unstable.

Market Period An interval too short to allow changes in decisions about amounts of output, so that only prices may be varied.

Market Price The price that is confronted in the market whether we buy or not.

Market Supply Curve A figure derived by horizontally summing all individual supply curves.

Market System See Capitalism, Free Enterprise System, Laissez-Faire, Socialism.

Maximizing Behavior *Homo sapiens* are perceived as human calculators who strive to maximize pleasure and to minimize pain.

Measure of (Net) Economic Welfare (MEW) A welfare measure obtained after deducting from GNP items that do not contribute to economic welfare and adding items that do, but which are not counted in GNP.

Measure of Value and Unit of Account The function performed by money as a common denominator through which the relative prices of goods are stated; reduces the information costs associated with exchange.

Median Voter Model Suggests that the median voter must be captured to achieve a majority of the vote, and attempts to explain why political parties and candidates tend to be so similar, and why two parties tend to dominate electoral processes.

Medium of Exchange The most important service that money provides; refers to standard items used to execute transactions.

Menu (Repricing) Costs of Inflation The costs in time and effort incurred in redesigning rate schedules and repricing goods.

Mercantilism A discredited economic doctrine that fostered imperialism and advocated surpluses in a country's balance of trade.

Merger The joining of two or more firms into a single firm.

Merit Goods or Bads Rival and exclusive goods that some elite deems either so desirable or undesirable that government intervenes, even though markets could satisfy consumer wants efficiently.

Microeconomics The branch of economics that focuses on individual decision making, the allocation of resources, and how prices, production, and the distribution of income are determined.

Middlemen Business firms that convey goods from the ultimate producer to the ultimate user. Middleman operations are only profitable if they reduce transaction costs.

Mixed Economies Societies in which some allocations rely on the market system while others rely on government or some other allocative mechanism.

Model The structure of a theory.

Monetarism The idea that erratic growth in the money supply is the major cause of macroeconomic instability.

Monetarist Monetary Transmission Mechanism The idea that changes in the growth rate of the nominal money supply affect private spending directly; an increase in the money supply yields a proportional rise in nominal GNP: $\Delta MS \to \Delta(C + I) \to \Delta Y$ is the causal chain emanating from a change in the monetary growth rate.

Monetary Base or High-Powered Money (MB) The total of bank reserves plus currency held by the nonbanking public.

Monetary Growth Rule The idea that the economy will be relatively stable if the money supply is set to grow at a low fixed percentage rate regardless of short-run economic conditions.

Money Illusion Decision makers suffer from money illusion if their decisions are based on movements of the monetary values of economic variables rather than on the real values of the variables.

Money Multiplier (m_p, m_a) Potentially equals the reciprocal of the reserve requirement ratio ($m_p = 1/rr$)—the number which, when multiplied by a change in total reserves, yields the potential change in the money supply. Actually, $m_a = MS/MB$ because of currency holdings of the public, excess reserves, and other leakages.

Monopolistic Competition An industry in which many firms sell slightly differentiated goods and there is freedom of entry or exit; monopolistic competition resembles pure competition, but goods are heterogeneous and each firm possesses a bit of monopoly power.

Monopoly The lone seller of a good that has no close substitutes.

Monopoly Power Possessed whenever a seller can force prices up by restricting output.

Monopsonist The sole buyer of a particular good or resource.

Monopsony Power Possessed whenever a buyer can force price down by restricting purchases.

Moral Suasion See Jawboning.

Multiplier Effect The total change in spending that results when new autonomous spending boosts income which, in turn, is spent, creating more income, and so on. (See also Autonomous Spending Multiplier.)

National Banks Banks chartered by the Comptroller of the Currency and that must be members of the Federal Reserve System.

National Debt The value of government bonds in the hands of the public or foreigners.

National Income (NI) A measure of economic activity computed by summing all resource incomes; equals the sum of wages and salaries, rents, interest, and corporate and noncorporate incomes.

Natural Barriers to Entry Significant barriers to entry that result from the nature of the economic good or from the cost structure inherent in its production.

Natural Monopoly A market in which only one seller can most efficiently produce an economic good; the production process is characterized by tremendously large fixed costs and relatively small variable costs; emerges where the market demand is small relative to the economies of scale.

Natural Rate Theory The notion that the economy is inherently stable and that unemployment and real interest will coincide with their natural rates in the long run; according to this theory, traditional Keynesian policy goals are unattainable because attempts to drive down unemployment or real interest rates more than can be reconciled with people's preferences are self-defeating in the long run.

Negative Externality When a market transaction imposes costs on third parties not directly involved in any aspect of the exchange.

Negative Income Taxes (NIT) Negative income tax plans represent attempts to reconcile equity and efficiency considerations in resolving the problems posed by income inequality and poverty; the negative income tax plan maintains incentives for recipients to work to earn additional income.

Net Investment Gross investment minus depreciation; represents net additions to an economy's capital stock or productive capacity.

Net National Product (NNP) The net value of commodities and services produced in the economy after adjusting for the fact that we have used up productive capacity; equals GNP minus depreciation; also equals National Income (NI) plus indirect business taxes.

Neutral Tax Imposition of a neutral tax distorts neither consumer buying patterns nor the methods used by firms in the conduct of their business; in other words, the imposition of a neutral tax does not distort relative prices by inducing substitution effects.

New Classical Macroeconomics Modern theories that extend classical theories of competitive markets, normally resulting in underpinnings for laissez-faire macroeconomic policies.

Nominal Rate of Interest The average annual percentage monetary premium paid for the use of money.

Nominal Values The current dollar values of economic variables.

Nondiscretionary Fiscal Policy Changes in government outlays and tax revenues that occur automatically as economic conditions change. (See also Automatic (Built-in) Stabilizers.)

Nondurable Goods Goods that are used up in less than one year.

Noneconomic Costs of Unemployment Include the psychological trauma of being unemployed and the social unrest unemployment engenders.

Nonexclusive Good A good is nonexclusive if an individual can enjoy it without paying for the right to consume; the result when it is relatively expensive to prevent individuals from consuming a good.

Nonrival Good A good is nonrival if consumption of the good by an individual does not prevent consumption of the same unit of that good by other individuals.

Normal Good A good for which the income-elasticity of demand is positive.

Normal Profits A normal cost of production; income that entrepreneurs must receive to make production worthwhile to them.

Normative Economics Deals with values and addresses what should be rather than what is.

Occam's Razor The "principle of parsimony," which suggests that the simplest workable theories are also the best and most useful.

Occupational Discrimination Exclusion of certain groups from particular occupations.

Oligopoly A market in which several large firms control most of an industry's output. The few firms that comprise the industry must each consider other firms' reactions before setting its policies; mutually interdependent behavior is the unique characteristic of oligopoly; the importance of predictability leads to cooperation between firms. Pure oligopolies produce homogeneous outputs, while impure oligopolies produce slightly differentiated outputs.

Open-Market Operations (*OMO*) When the FED's Open Market Committee buys and sells U.S. bonds; these operations determine the size of the money supply by altering the amounts of reserves in the banking system.

Open Shop A firm that employs workers without considering union membership.

Opportunity Cost The value of the next best opportunity to a good or to some activity.

Opportunity Cost of Money Keynesians view the true price of money as the interest rate, since the closest alternatives to money as an asset are stocks, bonds, and other assets that pay interest. Monetarists argue,

instead, that the true price of money is the reciprocal of the absolute price level—the purchasing power of money—since money is a substitute for all other goods and assets.

Outputs Transformed materials; the results of production.

Paradox of Thrift The possibility suggested by Keynesian analysis that an increase in saving at all income levels (depicted by an upward shift of the saving function) may cause equilibrium income or output to decrease, and could result in less saving rather than more.

Partial Equilibrium Analysis A method of economic analysis which looks at the direct effects of some chosen variables on others, assuming other influences constant.

Partnership An unincorporated firm formed by two or more persons.

Patents Legal barriers to entry that extend to their holders a renewable right to produce an economic good for 17 years and that prohibits the production of the good by other firms; intended to promote research and development of new goods and technologies.

Peak (Boom) The phase of the business cycle when a preponderance of measures of economic activity are at their high points.

Per Capita Income A crude measure of economic well-being computed by dividing National Income by the population.

Perfectly Price Elastic Demand or Supply Curves Horizontal lines at the current market price; perfectly price elastic demand or supply curves have a price elasticity of infinity at every point.

Permanent Income (Wealth) The average income expected over one's lifetime; according to Milton Friedman, permanent income explains a person's patterns of consumption and money holdings.

Perpetuity A bond that will pay a fixed amount of money each year until it is purchased by the government that issued it.

Personal Discrimination Bigotry; generates inequitable housing conditions, higher prices for comparable goods, reduced medical care, and other problems.

Persuasive Advertising Designed to persuade or to mislead consumers rather than to inform them; entails a waste of resources.

Phillips Curve An inverse statistical relationship between the rate of change of the general price level and the rate of unemployment; in 1959, A. W. Phillips, an English economist, reported findings to provide an empirical foundation for the idea that policymakers faced a permanent trade-off between unemployment and inflation; during the 1970s, the Phillips curve proved highly unstable.

Planned Injections Equal to Planned Withdrawals A condition necessary for macroeconomic equilibrium. Injections include all forms of autonomous spending; withdrawals represent such dilutions from spending streams as saving or taxation.

Planned or Intended Investment The amount of investment that business firms desire to make at each income level, assuming that business expectations remain unchanged.

Planned or Intended Saving The amounts of saving desired at each income level, assuming that savers' expectations remain constant.

Plant A production facility with a specific location, it may be involved in processing, fabrication, assembly, wholesale, or retail.

Plurality When the outcome of an election is determined by which side gets the most votes; a majority is unnecessary.

Point Voting When each voter is assigned a certain number of votes and can cast them among various electoral issues depending on the intensity of preferences.

Political Business Cycles Swings in economic activity that occur when macroeconomic policies are manipulated to improve incumbents' chances of reelection. The economy booms before elections and stagnates after them.

Pollution In economic parlance, a negative externality.

Pollution Abatement Programs Techniques used to reduce pollution.

Pork Barrel Legislation that yields benefits that are primarily local, but where funding is by the national government.

Positive Economics Value-free descriptions of and predictions about relationships among economic variables.

Positive Externality Occurs when a market activity bestows benefits on economic transactors who are not direct parties to the activity.

Potential GNP What an economy could produce at high rates of utilization of all resources; full employment GNP approximates potential GNP.

Precautionary Demand for Money The amount of money that economic transactors desire to hold to cover unexpected expenses; is positively related to income or wealth.

Present Value The present value of any asset is the value today of the expected income stream associated with the asset, discounted by the interest rate; the demand price of the asset.

Pretrade Costs The rate of exchange that exists domestically between two goods prior to international trade; also referred to as the domestic terms of trade; given by the slope at each point along the production-possibility frontier.

Price Ceiling A maximum legal price set at the behest of buyers.

Price Discrimination Occurs when essentially the same good is sold at different prices, and price differentials do not reflect different production costs; perfect price discrimination absorbs all potential consumer surplus derived from consuming a good.

Price-Elasticity of Demand (or Supply) Measures of the responsiveness of the quantity demanded (*supplied*) of a good to changes in the price of the good; computed by dividing percentage changes in quantities demanded (*supplied*) of a good by the percentage changes in its price: $\%\Delta Q_{xd}/\%\Delta P_x$ (or $\%\Delta Q_{xs}/\%\Delta P$). (See also Elasticity, Income-Elasticity of Demand.)

Price Floor A minimum legal price set at the behest of sellers.

Price Taker or **Quantity Adjuster** A competitive buyer or seller whose actions do not affect prices; they can choose only among quantities.

Private Debt Debts owed by consumers or business firms.

Private Ownership System Resources are privately owned.

Product Differentiation When consumers perceive differences in competing goods; real differences in similar products may be related to their durability, styling, or other physical characteristics; imaginary differences result from advertising or the imaginations of consumers; firms use product differentiation in attempts both to shift the demands for their products to the right and to decrease the price elasticity of the demands for their goods.

Production Occurs when materials are transformed in ways that make them more valuable.

Production Function The technical relationship that exists between inputs and outputs; allows all inputs to vary as different rates of production are achieved; not synonymous with total product curve.

Production-Possibility Frontier (PPF) A curve showing the various combinations of goods that an economy could produce, assuming a fixed technology and full employment and efficient resource utilization.

Profit The excess of a firm's total revenues over total cost; accounting profits consider only the explicit costs incurred by a firm; economists view total costs in terms of opportunity costs, which include both explicit and implicit costs; is a return to entrepreneurship for bearing uncertainty and innovating.

Progressive Taxes Tax rates which vary directly with income, so that the proportion of income devoted to taxes rises as income rises.

Promotional Profits The increases in the values of stock controlled by individuals who engineer a merger.

Property Rights Legal rights that people possess over property; the broadest of property rights are fee-simple property rights that allow individuals: (*a*) to use goods in any manner so long as other people's property rights are not violated; (*b*) to exchange these property rights for others; and (*c*) to deny the use of their goods to others.

Property Tax A tax based on the value of capital improvements and land.

Proportional Taxes Tax rates that do not vary with income; the same percentage of income is collected in taxes regardless of the income level.

Proprietors Individuals in business for themselves.

Psychic Income The value of nonmonetary satisfaction gained from an activity.

Psychological Theories of the Business Cycle Focus on the herd instincts of human beings coupled with prolonged periods of optimism and pessimism.

Public Choice Economic interpretations of political behavior.

Public Debt Created when the government spends more than it collects in tax revenue; the government increases the public debt when it sells bonds to the public in order to finance a deficit.

Public Finance Microeconomic study of government taxing and spending.

Public Good A public good is a good which can be consumed by more than one individual at a time (nonrivalry) and whose consumption cannot be denied a consumer who desires it (nonexclusion) once the good is provided.

Public Interest Theory of Regulation This theory suggests that government should control unethical business practices and regulate businesses plagued by such market failures as: (*a*) externalities, or (*b*) monopoly power derived from economies of scale.

Public Ownership System A system in which the government owns nonhuman resources and acts as collective trustee for its citizens.

Pure Private Good A pure private good is both rival and exclusive; the marketplace is well suited for providing pure private goods efficiently.

Pure Public Good A pure public good is both nonrival and nonexclusive; the government may need to provide pure public goods to ensure efficiency.

Quantity Demanded The amount of a good purchased at a given price.

Quantity Supplied The amount of a good supplied at a given price.

Quantity Theory of Money The idea that the dominant determinant of the price level is the money supply. An extreme version attributes all inflation to excessive monetary growth.

Queuing Allocating goods or resources on a first come/first served basis. This tends to result in queues (lining up for access).

Quota A quantitative restriction on trade, the imposition of quotas raises the prices of imported goods and causes failure to fully realize potential gains from international trade.

Rate Base The value of a regulated firm's capital stock to which a normal rate of return applies.

Rate of Return The annualized average size of the income stream per time period as a percentage of the dollar outlay for an investment.

Rational Expectations The notion that markets operate so efficiently that policy goals will not be achieved, even in the short run, unless the timing and the effects of demand-management policies come as surprises to the public.

Rational Ignorance The result when individuals decide that the marginal costs of more information exceed its marginal benefits.

Real Rate of Interest The annual percentage premium of purchasing power paid by a borrower to a lender for the use of money; the amount of extra goods, expressed in percentage terms, that can be enjoyed if consumption is delayed; computed by adjusting the nominal interest rate for the rate of general price change.

Real Values The current dollar value of economic variables after adjustment for price level changes.

Recession Modern name for a depression.

Recessionary Gap A deficiency in autonomous expenditure that must be filled to reach full employment output.

Recognition Lag Arises because policymakers' perceptions about current economic conditions are clouded, and time and effort are required to gather. compile, process, and interpret data to gain some feeling for any widespread changes in economic activity; applies equally to both monetary and fiscal policies.

Regressive Taxes Tax rates which vary inversely with income, so that tax payments decline relative to income as income rises.

Regulation Q Empowered the FED to limit the interest rates paid on time deposits in commercial banks; now phased out.

Reindustrialization See Industrial Policy.

Relative Price Price of a good in terms of another good. (See also Absolute Price.)

Rent Payments per time period for the services of land. (See also Economic Rent.)

Rent-Seeking Attempts by special interest groups to shape public policies to their advantage, even though such policies may impose excessive costs on the general public.

Required Reserves (*RR*) The reserves that banks are legally required to hold against their deposits.

Reserve-Requirement Ratio (rr) The fraction of its deposit liabilities that a bank must hold in reserves.

Reserves The amounts of money held in a bank's vault or on deposit at the FED to meet withdrawals of deposits.

Resources Land, labor, capital, and entrepreneurship.

Risk The likelihood of an event for which a probability can reasonably be estimated. (See also Uncertainty.)

Rival Good A good is rival if consumption of a unit of the good by one individual exhausts that particular unit so that another individual cannot consume it.

Robinson-Patman Act (1936) Amended Section 2 of the Clayton Act; this act was designed to limit price discrimination; however, it permitted discounts if they could be justified by differences in costs of production of if they were introduced as "good faith" efforts to meet competition.

Rule of Reason The rule of reason approach to the Sherman Act; permitted certain restrictive business practices of a firm despite their anticompetitive effects if the firm could show that its conduct was based on sound business practice and was secondary to its primary business practices.

Rule of 72 The time required for some variable to double is calculated by dividing its percentage annual growth rate into 72. This approach adjusts for compounding (e.g., interest on interest).

Sales Tax A percentage tax that is typically levied on the sales value of most commodities and/or services.

Saving The change in one's total wealth over some period of time.

Say's Law "Supply creates its own demand"; that is, the very act of producing a product creates an equivalent amount of demand, since people do not work for the sake of work alone; named after the classical economist, Jean Baptiste Say.

Scarce Good A good for which the quantity demanded exceeds the amount available at a zero dollar price.

Scarcity A state that results because resources are limited and cannot accommodate all of our unlimited wants.

Seasonal Unemployment Unemployment that varies with the season.

Seignorage The profits made by governments when they coin or print money.

Sellers' Market When the prevailing market price lies below the equilibrium price, resulting in a shortage.

Services Intangible economic goods.

Sherman Antitrust Act (1890) Our first antitrust law; specifies that "every contract, combination in the form of trust or otherwise, or conspiracy, in restraint of trade or commerce among the several States, or with foreign nations, is hereby declared illegal"; and, according to the second section, "every person who shall monopolize, or attempt to monopolize . . . shall be deemed guilty of a felony."

Shifted Backward A tax is shifted backward when its economic incidence falls on owners of resources supplied to the firm.

Shifted Forward A tax is said to be shifted forward when the economic incidence of the tax falls on the consumer.

Shortage Occurs if some people cannot buy all of an economic good for which they are willing to pay the going price.

Short Run (*SR*) An analytic period of time in which at least one resource is fixed so that firms can neither enter nor leave the marketplace—a firm can shut its plant down, but it cannot leave the industry.

Shutdown Point The price/output combination at which total revenue just equals total variable costs; in the short run, the firm must at least cover the variable costs of production; if it cannot, then it will shut down and minimize its losses by incurring only fixed costs.

Socialism A system characterized by collective ownership of property and government allocation of resources. (See also Capitalism, Free Enterprise System, Laissez-Faire.)

Socially Necessary Labor The Marxist concept that includes not only direct labor time, but also the labor time used to construct factories and to produce capital equipment; Marxists view all commodities and capital as congealed labor.

Special Interest Groups Groups that can gain from public policies that may not be in accord with the interests of other groups or society as a whole.

Specialization When different resources (e.g., people's labor) are used to produce different goods. This is most advantageous when resources are allocated so that every good is produced at the lowest possible opportunity cost.

Specific Training Training that a firm provides a worker that only increases the productivity of the worker for that firm.

Speculative Demand for Money Inversely related to the interest rate; refers to the amount of money that economic transactors desire to hold at alternative interest rates for the purpose of speculating against movements in the prices of stocks or bonds.

Speculators Middlemen who buy a good in the hope of selling it at a higher price at a later point in time. Profitable speculation tends to reduce price volatility and the risks to others of doing business.

Spillovers (Externalities) When benefits or costs are bestowed upon third parties who are not part of a transaction; produce false price signals and lead to nonoptimal decisions.

Stabilization Branch This branch of government in Musgrave's framework would be responsible for achieving full employment, price stability, and economic growth.

Stagflation The simultaneous occurrence of high rates of inflation and high rates of unemployment; stagflation, or inflationary recession, occurs during both demand-induced and supply-induced cycles of inflation when Aggregate Supply declines relative to Aggregate Demand.

Standard Industry Classification (SIC) Codes Categories developed by the Bureau of Census in order to classify industries.

Standard of Deferred Payment Money performs this function by being acceptable in the payment of contractual obligations involving future payments.

State Banks Banks that are chartered by state governments; they have the option of becoming members of the Federal Reserve System.

Statutory (Legal) Incidence of a Tax Falls on the party responsible for paying the tax, but a tax's economic incidence may be shifted.

Stock Variable An economic variable that can be measured holding time constant.

Store of Value Money is a store of value in that, except for inflation, it is a relatively riskless way of holding wealth.

Structural Deficit The budget shortfall that would result because of the design of current government tax and outlay programs, were the economy operating at its capacity. (See also Cyclical Deficit.)

Structural Unemployment Unemployment that arises because workers do not possess the skills required for existing job opportunities.

Subsistence Theory of Wages The theory that classical economists used to explain how wage rates were determined; this theory suggests that wages would be sufficient to meet the biological needs of workers, with only minor adjustments to meet the social and customary needs of workers.

Substitute Goods Goods that are substituted one for another in consumption; positive cross price-elasticities of demand exist between substitute goods.

Substitution Effect The change in the pattern of consumption brought about by a change in the relative price structure; the substitution effect of a price change is always negative, for consumers will always substitute cheaper goods for more expensive goods; the substitution effect is generally so powerful that it serves as the theoretical underpinning for the law of demand.

Superior Good A good for which the income-elasticity of demand is greater than one; that is, the demand for this kind of economic good is very sensitive to real income changes.

Super Long Run A time interval sufficient for firms to alter technology in response to profit opportunities.

Supply The amounts of goods or resources that producers or owners are willing to sell in the market under various conditions.

Supply Curve A graphic representation of the maximum quantities of a good or resources that producers or owners are willing to supply at various market prices.

Supply, Law of The quantity of an economic good supplied varies directly with the price of the economic good.

Supply Price The lowest price at which sellers are willing to make a specific quantity of a good available. (See also Demand Price.)

Supply-Side Economics A reemphasis on the importance of the effects of government policies on Aggregate Supply; this rebuts Keynesian emphasis on Aggregate Expenditures.

Surplus or **Excess Supply** The excess of the quantity supplied over the quantity demanded at a given price.

Surplus Value The difference between the total value of what workers produce and what workers are paid for their labor services; surplus value is expropriated by the capitalists, according to Marxists; surplus value is the sum of rent, interest, and profits.

Survival Principle The idea that the most efficient firms in an industry are those that remain viable over time; the optimal size of firms is indicated by the size of the firm that survives in an industry over time.

Syndicalism A revolutionary sociopolitical theory that advocates the overthrow of government and the reorganization of society into syndicates, which are effectively industrywide trade unions.

Taft-Hartley Act (1947) This legislation amended the Wagner Act and made certain union labor practices unfair, outlawed the closed shop, and permitted individual states to pass "right-to-work" laws that ban union shops.

Tariff A tax on internationally traded goods; the imposition of tariffs raises the prices of imported goods and prevents full realization of potential gains from international trade.

Tax-Based Incomes Policies (TIPs) Recent proposals that tax policies can be used to set incentives so that the decisions taken by business and labor will conform to some socially acceptable level of inflation; the general theory behind these proposals is similar to the analysis of externalities.

Technological Change Occurs when a given stock of productive inputs produces a greater quantity of output, or when a given amount of output can be produced with fewer productive inputs; refers to greater efficiency in market processes, improved knowledge concerning the use of productive inputs in production, the advent of completely new production processes, improvements in the quality of human and nonhuman resources, and new inventions and innovations. The idea of progress is tightly bound up in the process of technological change.

Terms of Trade The prices of exported goods relative to imported goods after international trade has commenced.

Theory A testable hypothesis concerning the way in which observable facts are related.

Tie-In Sales Attempts by monopolistic firms to exploit their market power by using tie-in sales agreements that require customers to buy another product as a condition for buying the monopolized good.

Total Burdens of a Tax The amounts of money that individuals would have to be paid to make them just as well off with the tax as without.

Total Cost All costs to the firm of producing a particular rate of output; computed by multiplying the quantity of a good produced by the per unit cost of producing the good.

Total Product Curve The technical relationship that exists between production and various levels of one input, assuming that other resources are held constant.

Total Revenue The dollar value of a firm's sales; computed by multiplying the quantity of a good sold by its per unit price.

Total Revenue Minus Total Cost ($TR - TC$) Approach The profit-maximizing firm will produce that rate of output at which total revenue exceeds total cost by the greatest amount.

Trade Adjustment Assistance Provides retraining and financial assistance for workers disemployed because of liberalized international trade.

Transaction Costs The costs associated with gathering information about products and transporting goods and people geographically or between markets.

Transactions Demand for Money The amount of money that economic transactors desire to hold in order to execute expected transactions; is positively related to income and wealth.

Transfer Payments Transfers of income from one set of households to another set through such programs as welfare payments, social security, and food stamps.

Trap of Underdevelopment Less developed countries typically remain underdeveloped for the following reasons: (*a*) high rates of population growth that result in low per capita incomes; (*b*) negligible capital accumulation because of low saving rates fostered by low per capita incomes; (*c*) rather primitive products are purchased by consumers; and (*d*) low labor productivity.

Trough (Depression) Phase of the business cycle when most measures of economic activity are at their low point.

Unanimity A requirement that all voters agree before new policies are implemented.

Uncertainty When a reasonable estimate cannot be made of the probability that some event will occur. (See also Risk.)

Unemployment A condition that occurs when an individual wants work but is without a job.

Unintended Inventory Changes Acting as a balancing item for the economy, these changes in inventories resolve any differences between the planned saving and planned investment functions and assure that actual saving and actual investment are equal at all times.

Union Shop A firm that will hire nonunion workers, but joining the union is a requirement for continued employment.

Usury Law A legal ceiling on the interest rates that lenders may charge borrowers.

Util An imaginary unit of measurement of satisfaction.

Utilitarianism A philosophy developed in England during the 1800s by Jeremy Bentham, an eccentric English philosopher and social reformer; this school of thought embraced the notion that satisfactions or utilities of individuals could be measured, and it sought "the greatest happiness for the greatest number."

Utopian Socialism All property would be collectively owned and all decisions would be made democratically.

Value Added The excess of a firm's revenues over the amount it pays to other firms for intermediate goods; used to calculate GNP and, in much of Europe, as a major base for taxes.

Value-Added Approach to Estimating GNP GNP equals the sum of the values added to economic goods at each level of production.

Value of Money The purchasing power of money, which is determined by the interaction of the supply of and demand for money.

Value of the Marginal Product (VMP) The value of the output produced by an additional unit of a variable input; computed by multiplying the price of output (P_x) by the marginal physical product of a unit of input (MPP_N): that is, $VMP = P_x \times MPP_N$.

Variable Costs Costs that vary with the level of production; variable costs are also known as direct costs or prime costs, and are the only costs that rational decision makers consider.

Vertical Combination A firm having different plants producing products at different production levels within an industry.

Voluntary Saving The voluntary decisions of individuals to defer consumption until some future date.

Voluntary Unemployment The frictional unemployment that exists when everyone who wants to work at the prevailing wage rate has a job or can find one rapidly.

Wage Discrimination Occurs when members of a particular group are paid less than are members of other groups for doing equal work.

Wage-Price Controls Legal restrictions most often used to keep prices from coinciding with their equilibrium levels.

Wages Payments per time period for labor services.

Wagner Act (1935) Guaranteed labor the right to organize independent unions and made a company's refusal to negotiate with an elected union an unfair labor practice.

Webb-Pomerene Act (1918) Exempts export trade associations from antitrust litigation.

Yellow-Dog Contracts Contracts that were widely used by business firms during the antiunion years to prevent the formation of labor unions by their employees; as a condition of employment, workers were forced to sign a yellow-dog contract, which was an agreement not to join a labor organization.

Zero Economic Profit The long-run equilibrium state of pure competition. All opportunity costs are covered by revenues, but there will be no net resource movements because no better opportunities exist elsewhere.

NAME INDEX

*fn: Some names recur so frequently in this book (e.g., Adam Smith, John Maynard Keynes, and Milton Friedman) that not all references to them in the text are cited here.

SUBJECT INDEX

Average costs, 434–36
Average fixed cost (*AFC*), 434–35
Average physical product of labor
(*APP*$_L$), 141
  geometry of, 446–48
Average propensity to consume
(**apc**), 167–68
Average propensity to save (**aps**),
167–68
Averages and marginals, 401–2
Average total cost (*ATC*), 434
Average variable cost (*AVC*), 434

Backward-bending supply curve of
labor, 568
Backward shifting of taxes,
398–401
Balanced budget multiplier,
204–5
Balance of payments, 720
  and domestic stabilization policies,
723–24
  and expectations, 729
  and inflation, 728–29
  of United States, 721, 727–28
Balance of trade, 720
Balancing federal budget, 199
  annually, 215
  over the business cycle, 215
  and Gramm-Rudman Act, 217–19
Bank of the United States, 242
Banks, 253
  and the creation and destruction of
money, 231–35, 239
  (See also Money, Federal Reserve
Banks)
Barriers to entry, 452–55, 487–90
Barriers to trade, 712
Barter, 114, 225
Basic economic questions, 26
Benefit principle of taxation, 627–30
Big business, argument for, 527–28
Bilateral monopoly, 589–91
Blacklists, 593
Black markets, 71, 725
Block pricing of utility rates, 545–47
Board of Governors of the Federal
Reserve System, 243
Bond prices and interest rates,
260–61
Bonds, 84
Bottlenecks in labor markets, 330

Bracket creep of income taxation,
118
Break-even rates of output, 459
Bretton Woods Agreement (1946),
726
Britain, economic growth, 745
  tax rates, 634
Brute force, 34
Bubble concept of pollution
abatement, 672
Buddhist economics, 746–47
Budget deficits or surpluses (See
Fiscal policy)
Budget line, 421
Built-in stabilizers, 205–7
Bureaucracy, 653–54
Business cycles, 144
  American, 148–50
  defined, 90
  early theories of, 150–58
  indicators, 146–47
  Kondratieff long waves, 153
  pattern, 144–46
  political, 351
  social aspects of, 146–48
Business firms, 83
  legal forms, 83–85

Capital
  accumulation, 371, 739–40
  economic, 10
  financial, 10
  gains taxes, 640
Capital consumption allowance, 130
Capital deepening, 374
Capital gains taxes, 640
Capital goods (See Capital,
Investment)
Capitalism, 37–38, 376, 733–34
  Marxist interpretation, 153, 737–40
Capitalization, 614–17
Capital to labor ratios, 29, 634
Capital widening, 374
Cartels, 513–15
Cartesian coordinates, 18
Caveat emptor, 418–19, 551
Caveat venditor, 418–19, 552
Ceiling prices, 70
Celler-Kefauver Antimerger Act of
1950, 529
Central banks, 242–43
Centralized decision making, 36

Right-to-work laws, 592
Risk, 610, 613–14
Risk aversion, 253
Risk avoidance and money, 261
Rival good, 90, 625–26
Robinson-Patman Act of 1932, 529
Rule of Reason, 531
Rule of 72, 366
Rules vs. discretion, 357–59

Sales tax, 637
Saving
  and capital information, 370
  in classical theory, 153–58
  defined, 165
  involuntary, 373
  voluntary, 371
  (See also Consumption schedule)
Savings and loan associations, 253
Saving schedule, 163–71
Say's Law, 154
Scarcity, 9
Seasonal unemployment, 105
Securities, defined, 254
Securities markets, 254
Seignorage, 229
  international, 721
Self-insurance, 613
Services, 81, 125, 407–8
Sherman Antitrust Act of 1890, 528
Shifting of taxes (See Incidence)
Shortage, 57
  and price ceilings, 70–71
Short run, 55, 427, 453–58
Short-run period of production, 427,
  431–36
Shutdown point, 463–65
Single tax movement, 608
Slope of a line, 22
"Small is beautiful", 746–47
Social costs of inflation, 117
Social costs of unemployment, 106
Social goods (See Public goods)
Socialism, 38, 376
  Christian, 736–37
  evolutionary, 735–37
  Fabian, 736
  Marxist, 737–41
  utopian, 736
Social Security system, 634–36
Sole proprietorship, 84

Solidarity, Polish union, 735
Soviet Union, 741–42
Special interest groups, 651
Specialization, 14, 141
Specialization gains from exchange
  and trade, 703–8
Specific training, 574–77
Speculative demand for money, 260
Speculator, 66, 69
Spillovers (See Externalities)
Spin-offs, 152
Stabilization branch, 623
Stabilization policies (lags in),
  345–48
Stagflation, 298, 300, 315–17, 320
Standard of deferred payment
  (money), 227
Standard unit of account (money),
  226
Stock, 84
Stock market crash of 1929, 157–58
Store of value (money), 227
Strikes, 591–92, 596–99
Structural deficits, 209–10
Structural unemployment, 104
Subjective prices, 42
Subsistence theory of wages, 739
Substitute goods, 47, 396
Substitution, 43–44
  and demand, 43, 408
Substitution effect, 43, 408, 568, 632
Sunk costs, 432, 438
Sunspot theory of business cycle, 150
Super long run, 444–45
Supply
  Aggregate, 303–9
  changes in, 51, 54, 63
  complements in production, 53
  curve, 50
  defined, 50
  determinants of, 54
  elasticity of, 396–97
  law of, 50
  price, 50
  taxes and subsidies, 54
  time, 54, 456–58
Supply curve, 50
  under competition in long run, 471
    constant-cost industry, 471
    decreasing-cost industry, 473
    increasing-cost industry, 472
  and marginal cost, 465
  market, 51, 471
  and time, 54, 456–58

GNP = C + I + G + X - m   S

People spent more than they earned]

Year	Personal Consumption Expenditures ($ Billions)	Gross Private Domestic Investment ($ Billions)	Government Purchases of Goods and Services ($ Billions)	Net Exports of Goods and Services ($ Billions)	Gross National Product ($ Billions)	National Income ($ Billions)	Personal Income ($ Billions)	Consumer Personal Savings ($ Billions)
1929	77.3	16.7	8.9	1.1	103.9	84.7	84.3	2.6
1930	69.9	10.3	9.2		90.4	75.4	77.0	1.4
1931	60.5	5.6	9.2		75.8	59.7	65.9	0.7
1932	48.6	1.0	8.1		58.0	42.8	50.2	-1.6
1933	45.8	1.6	8.3	0.4	56.0	39.4	46.3	-0.9
1934	51.3	3.3	9.8		65.1	49.5	54.0	0.4
1935	55.7	6.4	10.0		72.2	57.2	60.4	2.1
1936	61.9	8.5	12.0		82.5	65.0	68.6	3.6
1937	66.5	11.8	11.9		90.4	73.6	74.1	3.8
1938	63.9	6.5	13.0		84.7	67.4	68.3	0.7
1939	67.0	9.5	13.6	1.2	91.3	71.2	72.1	1.8
1940	71.0	13.4	14.2	1.8	100.4	79.6	77.6	3.0
1941	80.8	18.3	25.0	1.5	125.5	102.8	95.2	10.0
1942	88.6	10.3	59.9	0.2	159.0	136.2	122.4	27.0
1943	99.5	6.2	88.9	-1.9	192.7	169.7	150.7	32.7
1944	108.2	7.7	97.1	-1.7	211.4	182.6	164.5	36.5
1945	119.6	11.3	83.0	-0.5	213.4	181.6	170.0	28.7
1946	143.9	31.5	29.1	7.8	212.4	180.7	177.6	13.6
1947	161.9	35.0	26.4	11.9	235.2	196.6	190.2	5.2
1948	174.9	47.1	32.6	7.0	261.6	221.5	209.2	11.1
1949	178.3	36.5	39.0	6.5	260.4	215.2	206.4	7.4
1950	192.1	55.1	38.8	2.2	288.3	239.8	228.1	12.6
1951	208.1	60.5	60.4	4.5	333.4	277.3	256.5	16.6
1952	219.1	53.5	75.8	3.2	351.6	291.6	273.8	17.4
1953	232.6	54.9	82.8	1.3	371.6	306.6	290.5	18.4
1954	239.8	54.1	76.0	2.6	372.5	306.3	293.0	16.4
1955	257.9	69.7	75.3	3.0	405.9	336.3	314.2	16.0
1956	270.6	72.7	79.7	5.3	428.2	356.3	337.2	21.3
1957	285.3	71.1	87.3	7.3	451.0	372.8	356.3	22.7
1958	294.6	63.6	95.4	3.3	456.8	375.0	367.1	24.3
1959	316.3	80.2	97.9	1.5	495.8	409.2	390.7	21.8
1960	330.7	78.2	100.6	5.9	515.3	424.9	409.4	20.8
1961	341.1	77.1	108.4	7.2	533.8	439.0	426.0	24.9
1962	361.9	87.6	118.2	6.9	574.6	473.3	453.2	25.9
1963	381.7	93.1	123.8	8.2	606.9	500.3	476.3	24.6
1964	409.3	99.6	130.0	10.9	649.8	537.6	510.2	31.5
1965	440.7	116.2	138.6	9.7	705.1	585.2	552.0	34.3
1966	477.3	128.6	158.6	7.5	772.0	642.0	600.8	36.0
1967	503.6	125.7	179.7	7.4	816.4	677.7	644.5	45.1
1968	552.5	137.0	197.7	5.5	892.7	739.1	707.2	42.5
1969	597.9	153.2	207.3	5.6	963.9	798.1	772.9	42.2
1970	640.0	148.8	218.2	8.5	1,015.5	832.6	831.8	57.7
1971	691.6	172.5	232.4	6.3	1,102.7	898.1	894.0	66.3
1972	757.6	202.0	250.0	3.2	1,212.8	994.1	891.6	61.4
1973	837.2	238.8	266.5	16.8	1,359.3	1,122.7	1,101.7	89.0
1974	916.5	240.8	299.1	16.3	1,472.8	1,203.5	1,210.1	96.7
1975	1,012.8	219.6	335.0	31.1	1,598.4	1,289.1	1,313.4	104.6
1976	1,129.3	277.7	356.9	18.8	1,782.8	1,441.4	1,451.4	95.8
1977	1,257.2	344.1	387.3	1.9	1,990.5	1,617.8	1,607.5	90.7
1978	1,403.5	416.8	425.2	4.1	2,249.7	1,838.2	1,812.4	110.2
1979	1,566.8	454.8	467.8	18.8	2,508.2	2,047.3	2,034.0	118.1
1980	1,732.6	437.0	530.3	32.1	2,732.0	2,203.5	2,258.5	136.9
1981	1,915.1	515.5	588.1	33.9	3,052.6	2,443.5	2,520.9	159.4
1982	2,050.7	447.3	641.7	26.3	3,166.0	2,518.4	2,670.8	153.9
1983	2,229.3	501.9	675.7	-5.3	3,401.6	2,718.3	2,836.4	133.2
1984	2,423.0	674.0	736.8	-59.2	3,774.7	3,039.3	3,111.9	172.5
1985	2,581.9	670.4	814.6	-74.4	3,992.5	3,215.6	3,294.2	129.7
1986	2,710.0	680.0	910.0	-60.0	4,260.0	3,400.0	3,480.0	156.0

Source: Economic Report of the President, 1986.

Note: 1986 data preliminary.